BaseBall america®
PROSPECT
HANDBOOK

2006
Baseball America Inc.
Durham, N.C.

EDITORS
Jim Callis, Will Lingo

ASSOCIATE EDITORS
John Manuel, Allan Simpson

CONTRIBUTING WRITERS
Bill Ballew, Mike Berardino, J.J. Cooper, Matt Eddy, Aaron Fitt,
Kevin Goldstein, Will Kimmey, Chris Kline, Alan Matthews,
Matt Meyers, John Perrotto, Tracy Ringolsby, Phil Rogers

PHOTO EDITOR
Matt Meyers

EDITORIAL ASSISTANT
Mike Groopman

DESIGN & PRODUCTION
Phillip Daquila, Matt Eddy, Linwood Webb

COVER PHOTOS
Jeremy Hermida by Carl Kline (main image) and Robert Gurganus (background)

COVER DESIGN
Linwood Webb

BaseBall america

President/CEO: Catherine Silver
Vice President/Publisher: Lee Folger
Editors in Chief: Will Lingo, John Manuel
Founding Editor: Allan Simpson
Executive Editor: Jim Callis
Design & Production Director: Phillip Daquila

BaseballAmerica.com

TABLE OF CONTENTS

FOREWORD

I n a small to mid-size market like Cleveland, there is one clear parameter for sustainable success: the consistent commitment to young talent. And because our game is fraught with human frailties, we can never have enough prospects.

As we faced the challenge of turning over our roster and rebuilding a championship franchise, we did so with the understanding that the decisions we made to trade our core players would have to be good ones.

We had one chance to infuse talent and speed up the process of rebuilding. And as we continue to build off of our recent success, our market makes it difficult for us to compete in free agency. Therefore we must seek young talent from every source available—internally through drafting and developing and from other teams through trades.

We base our trade decisions on a broad range of information: scouting reports, medical files, character and personality assessments and third-party analysis like what is provided in the Baseball America Prospect Handbook. A wealth of information on players exists in outside publications, but none quite so thorough or full of insight as the Prospect Handbook.

For 25 years, Baseball America has provided baseball enthusiasts with unique and comprehensive viewpoints into the inner workings of the game at every level.

The Prospect Handbook takes that analysis one step further by providing scouting reports on every organization's top prospects, organizational and prospect rankings and draft analysis. So whether you are making pivotal trades to acquire young prospects and build a champion, or you are an avid fan who wants to be informed like an insider, Baseball America's Prospect Handbook is the one source you cannot afford to be without.

Mark Shapiro
General Manager
Cleveland Indians

INTRODUCTION

Every year, just before the Prospect Handbook goes out the door, a feeling comes over me that I like to call Prospect Handbook euphoria. The result of too much caffeine and not enough sleep? Perhaps. The realization that this massive undertaking is finally complete? Certainly. But more than anything else, it's the feeling that this book is the best of its kind—and in my opinion, it's not even close

We know you can find prospect rankings anywhere. We look at them too. But Baseball America's rankings have gained so much respect over the 25 years we've been around because so much work and care go into every list.

The people who wrote up each organization's rankings have talked to scouts, minor league managers, instructors, farm directors, scouting directors, and anyone else they can find with an educated opinion on the players in every farm system. And don't think we don't do statistical analysis, either. There's a reason you see all those numbers beneath each player's scouting report.

After a writer gathers all of his information and ranks his prospects, though, comes his toughest test: vetting his list with Jim Callis. Jim has strong, educated opinions on nearly every prospect you'll read about in this book, and he challenges at least a few rankings on every list.

Jim edits every organization (except the four he writes up himself), and then the writeups have stats and other complementary information added, and the pages are laid out, cut and proofed before they go to the printer. Just determining how many individuals have a hand in getting the Prospect Handbook into your hands each year is almost impossible.

One of the most important and underappreciated roles, though, is that of our production staff, which improves the look of the book every year. Go back through your collection of Prospect Handbooks and check out how much better the book is now than it was back in 2001. That's the result of hours of tweaking the design from year to year, and continual tinkering as the book goes from computer screen to printed page.

And this year the book has gotten on the page earlier than ever before. We hope you're reading the book even before spring training has started, giving you even more time to get ready for the season—and perhaps even for your big fantasy auction. Yes, we know the Prospect Handbook is your secret weapon for fantasy domination, but we promise not to tell anyone else.

Because the book went to press earlier this year, players are listed with the organizations they were with on Dec. 12. We know players like Andre Ethier (and inevitably others) have changed organizations, but you can still find them with their old clubs by using the handy-dandy index in back. You'll also find scouting reports for 2005 draft picks Justin Upton and Mike Pelfrey—who signed too late to be included in their organization writeups—on Page 494. And of course you can always visit BaseballAmerica.com for the most up-to-date prospect information anywhere.

Remember that for the purposes of this book, a prospect is anyone who is still rookie-eligible under Major League Baseball guidelines (no more than 50 innings pitched or 130 at-bats), without regard to service time.

You'll also find grades for each team's drafts from 2001-2004 in each organization section. The grades are based solely on the quality of the players signed, with no consideration given to whom they were traded for or how many first-round picks the club had or lost.

Will Lingo
Editor in Chief
Baseball America

PROFILING **PROSPECTS**

Among all the scouting lingo you'll come across in this book, perhaps no terms are more telling and prevalent than "profile" and "projection."

When scouts evaluate a player, their main objective is to identify—or project—what the player's future role will be in the major leagues. Each organization has its own philosophy when it comes to grading players, so we talked to scouts from several teams to provide general guidelines.

The first thing to know is what scouts are looking for. In short, tools. These refer to the physical skills a player needs to be successful in the major leagues. For a position player, the five basic tools are hitting, hitting for power, fielding, arm strength and speed. For a pitcher, the tools are based on the pitches he throws. Each pitch is graded, as well as a pitcher's control, delivery and durability.

For most teams, the profiling system has gone through massive changes in recent years because of the offensive explosion in baseball. Where arm strength and defense used to be a must in the middle of the diamond, there has been an obvious swing toward finding players who can rake, regardless of their gloves. In the past, players like Jeff Kent and Alfonso Soriano wouldn't have been accepted as second basemen, but now they are the standard for offensive-minded second basemen.

While more emphasis is placed on hitting—which also covers getting on base—fielding and speed are still at a premium up the middle. As teams sacrifice defense at the corner outfield slots, they look for a speedy center fielder to make up ground in the alleys. Most scouts prefer at least a 55 runner (on the 20-80 scouting scale; see chart)

at short and center field, but as power increases at those two positions, running comes down (see Michael Young, Jim Edmonds). Shortstops need range and at least average arm strength, and second basemen need to be quick on the pivot. Teams are more willing to put up with an immobile corner infielder if he can mash.

Arm strength is the one tool moving way down preference lists. For a catcher, it was always the No. 1 tool, but with fewer players stealing and the slide step helping to shut down running games, scouts are looking for more offensive production from the position. Receiving skills, including game-calling, blocking pitches and release times, can make up for the lack of a plus arm.

On the mound, it doesn't just come down to pure stuff. While a true No. 1 starter on a first-division team should have a couple of 70 or 80 pitches in his repertoire, like Josh Beckett and Mark Prior, they also need to produce 250-plus innings, 35 starts and 15-plus wins.

A player's overall future potential is also graded on the 20-80 scale, though some teams use a letter grade. This number is not just the sum of his tools, but rather a profiling system and a scout's ultimate opinion of the player.

70-80 (A): This category is reserved for the elite players in baseball. This player will be a perennial all-star, the best player at his position, one of the top five starters in the game or a frontline closer. Alex Rodriguez, Barry Bonds and Pedro Martinez reside here.

60-69 (B): You'll find all-star-caliber players here: No. 2 starters on a championship club and first-division players. See Andy Pettitte, Miguel Tejada and Eric Chavez.

55-59 (C+) The majority of first-division starters are found in this range, including quality No. 2 and 3 starters, frontline set-up men and second-tier closers.

50-54 (C) Solid-average everyday major leaguers. Most are not first-division regulars. This group also includes No. 4 and 5 starters.

45-49 (D+) Fringe everyday players, backups, some No. 5 starters, middle relievers, pinch-hitters and one-tool players.

40-44 (D) Up-and-down roster fillers, situational relievers and 25th players.

38-39 (O) Organizational players who provide depth for the minor leagues but are not considered future major leaguers.

20-37 (NP) Not a prospect.

THE SCOUTING SCALE

When grading a player's tools, scouts use a standard 20-80 scale. When you read that a pitcher throws an above-average slider, it can be interpreted as a 60 pitch, or a plus pitch. Plus-plus is 70, or well-above-average, and so on. Scouts don't throw 80s around very freely. Here's what each grade means:

80	Outstanding
70	Well-above-average
60	Above-average
50	Major league average
40	Below-average
30	Well-below-average
20	Poor

MINOR LEAGUE DEPTH CHART

AN OVERVIEW

Another feature of the Prospect Handbook is a depth chart of every organization's minor league talent. This shows you at a glance what kind of talent a system has and provides even more prospects beyond the top 30. Each depth chart is accompanied by a quick take on a system's strengths and weaknesses, as well as where it ranks in baseball (see facing page for the complete list). The rankings are based on the quality and quantity of talent in each system, with higher marks to clubs that have more high-ceiling prospects or a deep system. The best systems have both.

Players are usually listed on the depth charts where we think they'll ultimately end up. To help you better understand why players are slotted at particular positions, we show you here what scouts look for in the ideal candidate at each spot, with individual tools ranked in descending order.

LF
Hitting
Power
Fielding
Arm Strength
Speed

CF
Fielding
Hitting
Speed
Power
Arm Strength

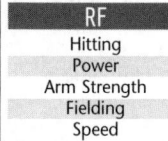

RF
Hitting
Power
Arm Strength
Fielding
Speed

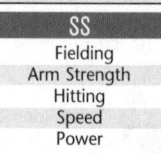

3B
Hitting
Power
Fielding
Arm Strength
Speed

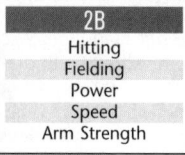

SS
Fielding
Arm Strength
Hitting
Speed
Power

2B
Hitting
Fielding
Power
Speed
Arm Strength

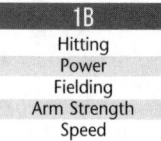

1B
Hitting
Power
Fielding
Arm Strength
Speed

C
Fielding
Arm Strength
Hitting
Power
Speed

STARTING PITCHERS			
No. 1 starter	**No. 2 starter**	**No. 3 starter**	**No. 4-5 starters**
• Two plus pitches	• Two plus pitches	• One plus pitch	• Command of two major league pitches
• Average third pitch	• Average third pitch	• Two average pitches	
• Plus-plus command	• Average command	• Average command	• Average velocity
• Plus makeup	• Average makeup	• Average makeup	• Consistent breaking ball
			• Decent changeup

CLOSER
• One dominant pitch
• Second plus pitch
• Plus command
• Plus-plus makeup

TALENT RANKINGS

	2005	2004	2003	2002	2001
1 Los Angeles Dodgers	2	14	25	28	23
Even without top 2005 draft pick Luke Hochevar, the Dodgers have depth and star power.					
2 Florida Marlins	14	14	8	10	9
Postseason fire sale brought depth, top-tier talent to a system that already had some of both.					
3 Los Angeles Angels	1	3	5	17	25
Elite infielders head impressive group of hitters; pitching hinges on '04 picks Weaver, Adenhart.					
4 Arizona Diamondbacks	13	13	21	23	29
Diamondbacks would move up even higher with unsigned 2005 No. 1 overall pick Justin Upton.					
5 Milwaukee Brewers	3	1	16	26	30
Despite graduating young talent to Milwaukee, Brewers still have plenty left on the farm.					
6 Minnesota Twins	4	5	4	6	15
Healthy return by Jason Kubel would provide boost to organization loaded with young pitching.					
7 Boston Red Sox	21	23	27	28	24
Quantum leap forward for organization that has needed good news in a difficult offseason.					
8 Atlanta Braves	5	4	2	7	5
Lowest ranking in years for Braves only comes after sending 18 rookies to big league club.					
9 Colorado Rockies	6	15	25	24	16
Fruits of three consecutive productive drafts starting to percolate up through the system.					
10 Tampa Bay Devil Rays	9	9	10	15	6
Former scouting director Tim Wilken left behind much-improved pitching depth.					
11 Cleveland Indians	7	6	1	20	26
Depth is the Tribe's biggest strength, and Adam Miller could be a star if he's healthy.					
12 Chicago White Sox	12	20	15	9	1
Championship closer Bobby Jenks heads list with outfield depth to spare.					
13 Baltimore Orioles	25	19	30	29	27
A farm system on the way up could improve even more if Adam Loewen fulfills his potential.					
14 Detroit Tigers	29	22	12	18	18
Biggest mover on the list thanks to pair of elite power arms, Justin Verlander and Joel Zumaya.					
15 Chicago Cubs	10	7	3	1	2
Felix Pie takes up mantle as top prospect in a rapidly thinning organization.					
16 Texas Rangers	16	16	19	8	13
Trio of Double-A pitchers, improved depth give new GM Jon Daniels pieces to deal.					
17 New York Yankees	24	27	17	5	7
Premium talent on hand, but Yankees' top prospects have yet to venture beyond A-ball.					
18 San Francisco Giants	17	24	11	12	22
Bulk of top hitters reach make-or-break Double-A in '06; Matt Cain gives team elite arm.					
19 Pittsburgh Pirates	18	11	18	22	19
Last two first-round picks, Neil Walker and Andrew McCutchen, provide best hope for impact.					
20 Houston Astros	22	29	23	3	10
Farmhands helped big league team to first pennant, yet minor league talent still improved.					
21 St. Louis Cardinals	30	28	28	30	23
Early returns on their bountiful 2005 draft boost stock of previously moribund system.					
22 Philadelphia Phillies	20	21	7	11	12
Jim Thome trade nets pair of lefties who can step in if top prospect Cole Hamels gets hurt again.					
23 Kansas City Royals	28	19	26	21	14
No. 2 overall pick Alex Gordon, Billy Butler provide 1-2 punch for club in need of hope.					
24 Washington Nationals	26	30	29	16	21
Scouting director Dana Brown has done well in tough circumstances to accumulate talent.					
25 Toronto Blue Jays	15	8	6	13	17
System has some depth, particularly on the mound, but few players project as regulars.					
26 Oakland Athletics	8	17	22	19	11
Talent inevitably eroded after A's graduated four impact rookies to big leagues in 2005.					
27 Seattle Mariners	11	12	9	2	4
Utter lack of pitching prospects has roots in run of poor drafts in late 1990s, early 2000s.					
28 San Diego Padres	27	25	20	4	8
At least the best the Padres have to offer are close to helping the big league club . . .					
29 Cincinnati Reds	23	26	24	14	3
While nearly all the Reds' best hopes for the future are in A-ball or below.					
30 New York Mets	19	10	13	27	20
It's Lastings Milledge and a lot of players who wouldn't make other teams' top 10s.					

TOP 50 PROSPECTS

There's at least one thing we agree on: Delmon Young is the best prospect in the game. The Devil Rays outfielder, Baseball America's 2005 Minor League Player of the Year, was the No. 1 prospect across the board in our annual snapshot of how BA's senior editorial employees view the prospect landscape.

Opinions start varying wildly after that, naturally, as personal preferences start to show themselves. From lists like these that go as deep as 150 players or more, we assemble Baseball America's annual Top 100 Prospects list, which comes out just as spring training begins.

Just as a reminder, the rules for these lists are the same for any prospect who appears in this book: Players must meet the rookie standards of no more than 130 at-bats or 50 innings in the major leagues, though we do not consider service time in our eligibility requirements.

Alex Gordon   *Royals*

As with any prospect list, these rankings represent how each person regarded the top minor league talent in the game at a moment in time. Ask us again in a few months how the prospects stack up, and you'll get a different answer—though we suspect Young will still come out on top.

JIM CALLIS

1. Delmon Young, of, Devil Rays
2. Brandon Wood, ss, Angels
3. Jeremy Hermida, of, Marlins
4. Stephen Drew, ss, Diamondbacks
5. Alex Gordon, 3b, Royals
6. Prince Fielder, 1b, Brewers
7. Francisco Liriano, lhp, Twins
8. Lastings Milledge, of, Mets
9. Matt Cain, rhp, Giants
10. Chad Billingsley, rhp, Dodgers
11. Ian Stewart, 3b, Rockies
12. Conor Jackson, 1b, Diamondbacks
13. Andy Marte, 3b, Red Sox
14. Carlos Quentin, of, Diamondbacks
15. Justin Verlander, rhp, Tigers
16. Jon Lester, lhp, Red Sox
17. Andy LaRoche, 3b, Dodgers
18. Howie Kendrick, 2b, Angels
19. Billy Butler, of, Royals
20. Troy Tulowitzki, ss, Rockies
21. Ryan Zimmerman, 3b, Nationals
22. Jonathan Papelbon, rhp, Red Sox
23. Jarrod Saltalamacchia, c, Braves
24. Chris Young, of, White Sox
25. Daric Barton, 1b, Athletics
26. Felix Pie, of, Cubs
27. Nick Markakis, of, Orioles
28. Carlos Gonzales, of, Diamondbacks
29. Joel Guzman, ss/3b, Dodgers
30. Hanley Ramirez, ss, Marlins
31. Jason Kubel, of, Twins
32. Cameron Maybin, of, Tigers
33. Anibal Sanchez, rhp, Marlins
34. Scott Olsen, lhp, Marlins
35. Jeff Clement, c, Mariners
36. Ryan Braun, 3b, Brewers
37. Russell Martin, c, Dodgers
38. Scott Elbert, lhp, Dodgers
39. Dustin McGowan, rhp, Blue Jays
40. Homer Bailey, rhp, Reds
41. Adam Miller, rhp, Indians
42. Anthony Reyes, rhp, Cardinals
43. Bobby Jenks, rhp, White Sox
44. Philip Hughes, rhp, Yankees
45. Erick Aybar, ss, Angels
46. Jered Weaver, rhp, Angels
47. Kendry Morales, 1b, Angels
48. Jason Hirsh, rhp, Astros
49. Troy Patton, lhp, Astros
50. Cole Hamels, lhp, Phillies

WILL LINGO

1. Delmon Young, of, Devil Rays
2. Jeremy Hermida, of, Marlins
3. Brandon Wood, ss, Angels
4. Francisco Liriano, lhp, Twins
5. Ian Stewart, 3b, Rockies
6. Lastings Milledge, of, Mets
7. Chad Billingsley, rhp, Dodgers
8. Ryan Zimmerman, 3b, Nationals
9. Andy LaRoche, 3b, Dodgers
10. Jarrod Saltalamacchia, c, Braves
11. Matt Cain, rhp, Giants
12. Joel Guzman, ss/of, Dodgers
13. Hanley Ramirez, ss, Marlins
14. Howie Kendrick, 2b, Angels
15. Andy Marte, 3b, Red Sox
16. Justin Verlander, rhp, Tigers
17. Nick Markakis, of, Orioles
18. Neil Walker, c, Pirates
19. Stephen Drew, ss, Diamondbacks
20. Alex Gordon, 3b, Royals
21. Prince Fielder, 1b, Brewers
22. Conor Jackson, 1b, Diamondbacks
23. Bobby Jenks, rhp, White Sox
24. Felix Pie, of, Cubs
25. Jason Hirsh, rhp, Astros
26. Anthony Reyes, rhp, Cardinals
27. Edison Volquez, rhp, Rangers
28. Chris Young, of, White Sox
29. Philip Hughes, rhp, Yankees
30. Homer Bailey, rhp, Reds
31. Jon Lester, lhp, Red Sox
32. Billy Butler, of, Royals
33. Erick Aybar, ss, Angels
34. Jeff Clement, c, Mariners
35. Andrew McCutchen, of, Pirates
36. Marcus Sanders, ss, Giants
37. Adam Loewen, lhp, Orioles
38. Joel Zumaya, rhp, Tigers
39. Scott Olsen, lhp, Marlins
40. Jonathan Papelbon, rhp, Red Sox
41. Kenji Johjima, c, Mariners
42. Mark Rogers, rhp, Brewers
43. Adam Miller, rhp, Indians
44. Jeremy Sowers, lhp, Indians
45. Cameron Maybin, of, Tigers
46. Jeff Niemann, rhp, Devil Rays
47. Daric Barton, 1b, Athletics
48. Brian Anderson, of, White Sox
49. Ryan Sweeney, of, White Sox
50. Tom Gorzelanny, lhp, Pirates

ANDREW WOOLLEY

Matt Cain   *Giants*

RICH ABEL

KEN BABBITT

Ryan Zimmerman *Nationals*   **Jon Lester** *Red Sox*

JOHN MANUEL

1. Delmon Young, of, Devil Rays
2. Jeremy Hermida, of, Marlins
3. Brandon Wood, ss, Angels
4. Chad Billingsley, rhp, Dodgers
5. Stephen Drew, ss, Diamondbacks
6. Justin Verlander, rhp, Tigers
7. Francisco Liriano, lhp, Twins
8. Ryan Zimmerman, 3b, Nationals
9. Matt Cain, rhp, Giants
10. Jarrod Saltalamacchia, c, Braves
11. Prince Fielder, 1b, Brewers
12. Ian Stewart, 3b, Rockies
13. Howie Kendrick, 2b, Angels
14. Lastings Milledge, of, Mets
15. Alex Gordon, 3b, Royals
16. Andy LaRoche, 3b, Dodgers
17. Chris Young, of, White Sox
18. Nick Markakis, of, Orioles
19. Jon Lester, lhp, Red Sox
20. Andy Marte, 3b, Red Sox
21. Conor Jackson, 1b, Diamondbacks
22. Carlos Quentin, of, Diamondbacks
23. Bobby Jenks, rhp, White Sox
24. Troy Tulowitzki, ss, Rockies
25. Billy Butler, of/dh, Royals
26. Scott Olsen, lhp, Marlins
27. Russell Martin, c, Dodgers
28. Hanley Ramirez, ss, Marlins
29. Adam Loewen, lhp, Orioles
30. Joel Zumaya, rhp, Tigers
31. Daric Barton, 1b, Athletics
32. Felix Pie, of, Cubs
33. Dustin McGowan, rhp, Blue Jays
34. Anthony Reyes, rhp, Cardinals
35. Jonathan Papelbon, rhp, Red Sox
36. Anibal Sanchez, rhp, Marlins
37. Jeff Clement, c, Mariners
38. Ryan Braun, 3b, Brewers
39. Philip Hughes, Yankees
40. Homer Bailey, rhp, Reds
41. Mark Rogers, rhp, Brewers
42. Adam Miller, rhp, Indians
43. Erick Aybar, ss, Angels
44. Carlos Gonzales, of, Diamondbacks
45. Neil Walker, c, Pirates
46. Jeremy Sowers, lhp, Indians
47. Cameron Maybin, of, Tigers
48. Jonathan Broxton, rhp, Dodgers
49. Brian Anderson, of, White Sox
50. Elvis Andrus, ss, Braves

ALLAN SIMPSON

1. Delmon Young, of, Devil Rays
2. Brandon Wood, ss, Angels
3. Stephen Drew, ss, Diamondbacks
4. Francisco Liriano, lhp, Twins
5. Jeremy Hermida, of, Marlins
6. Lastings Milledge, of, Mets
7. Justin Verlander, rhp, Tigers
8. Alex Gordon, 3b, Royals
9. Howie Kendrick, 2b, Angels
10. Jarrod Saltalamacchia, c, Braves
11. Chad Billingsley, rhp, Dodgers
12. Cameron Maybin, of, Tigers
13. Prince Fielder, 1b, Brewers
14. Andy Marte, 3b, Red Sox
15. Hanley Ramirez, ss, Marlins
16. Andy LaRoche, 3b, Dodgers
17. Conor Jackson, 1b, Diamondbacks
18. Joel Guzman, ss, Dodgers
19. Carlos Gonzales, of, Diamondbacks
20. Ian Stewart, 3b, Rockies
21. Carlos Quentin, of, Diamondbacks
22. Matt Cain, rhp, Giants
23. Homer Bailey, rhp, Reds
24. Ryan Zimmerman, 3b, Nationals
25. Philip Hughes, rhp, Yankees

26. Nick Markakis, of, Orioles
27. Troy Tulowitzki, ss, Rockies
28. Neil Walker, c, Pirates
29. Jon Lester, lhp, Red Sox
30. Anibal Sanchez, rhp, Marlins
31. Bobby Jenks, rhp, White Sox
32. Felix Pie, of, Cubs
33. Jeff Clement, c, Mariners
34. Jonathan Papelbon, rhp, Red Sox
35. Adam Loewen, lhp, Orioles
36. Craig Hansen, rhp, Red Sox
37. Daric Barton, 1b, Athletics
38. Erick Aybar, ss, Angels
39. Andrew McCutchen, of, Pirates
40. Joel Zumaya, rhp, Tigers
41. Elvis Andrus, ss, Braves
42. Chris Young, of, White Sox
43. Javier Herrera, of, Athletics
44. Scott Olsen, lhp, Marlins
45. Jeremy Sowers, lhp, Indians
46. Ryan Braun, 3b, Brewers
47. Brian Anderson, of, White Sox
48. Mark Rogers, rhp, Brewers
49. Jason Hirsh, rhp, Astros
50. Cole Hamels, lhp, Phillies

Howie Kendrick *Angels*

ARIZONA
DIAMONDBACKS

BY **KEVIN GOLDSTEIN**

The Diamondbacks improved by 26 wins in 2005, but after the previous season's 51-111 debacle there was nowhere to go but up.

The team began its offseason housecleaning by dealing Randy Johnson to the Yankees, and then made a splash in the free-agent market by signing righthander Russ Ortiz and third baseman Troy Glaus to big-money contracts that were criticized for both their length and dollar amount. While Glaus performed to expectations, Ortiz and other veteran pitchers struggled.

The Diamondbacks will move forward with a front office that has experienced significant turnover. Franchise founder Jerry Colangelo left in a dispute over the direction of the club in 2004. Former agent Jeff Moorad was approved as a general partner in February 2005. Joe Garagiola Jr., the only GM in franchise history, resigned to become Major League Baseball's senior vice president of baseball operations in August. Red Sox assistant GM Josh Byrnes came aboard in October to replace Garagiola, and he hired Boston director of baseball operations Peter Woodfork to be his assistant GM.

On the diamond, the Diamondbacks are trying to make a transition from veterans to youth. Two of the top hitting prospects in the system, 2003 first-round picks Carlos Quentin and **Conor Jackson**, have nothing left to prove in the minors, yet are blocked. Plans are to give Jackson an opportunity to play first base every day in 2006 despite Tony Clark's renaissance, while Quentin may have to wait out the contracts of outfielders Luis Gonzalez and Shawn Green.

The Diamondbacks system has taken a major step forward over the last three years with the help of scouting director Mike Rizzo. Leading the way is Stephen Drew, as Arizona took advantage of other teams' fear of the shortstop's signability to scoop him up with the 15th overall pick in 2004. The Diamondbacks didn't sign Drew until a week before the 2005 draft, but he performed well enough in his pro debut and in the Arizona Fall League to earn consideration as the major league shortstop as early as 2006.

With the No. 1 overall pick in 2005, Arizona selected shortstop Justin Upton. In their minds, that gave the Diamondbacks the best player in each of the last two drafts. Upton would rank atop this prospect list if he had signed. Negotiations with Upton and advisor Larry Reynolds hadn't been contentious, but the sides remained far apart at the end of 2005.

In a system loaded with hitters but weak on arms, Rizzo spent eight of his next nine selections on college pitchers. Supplemental first-rounder Matt Torra and righthander Micah Owings both made the top 10 list. The progression of this group will be crucial to the Diamondbacks' future, as they look to be more conservative on the free-agent market. If they can outlast or unload the bloated contracts that will be an issue over the next three years, Arizona should contend annually in the weak National League West.

TOP 30 PROSPECTS

1. Stephen Drew, ss
2. Conor Jackson, 1b
3. Carlos Quentin, of
4. Carlos Gonzales, of
5. Dustin Nippert, rhp
6. Miguel Montero, c
7. Garrett Mock, rhp
8. Matt Torra, rhp
9. Micah Owings, rhp
10. Sergio Santos, ss
11. Chris Carter, 1b/of
12. Matt Green, rhp
13. Greg Smith, lhp
14. Tony Pena, rhp
15. Enrique Gonzalez, rhp
16. Jon Zeringue, of
17. Matt Chico, lhp
18. A.J. Shappi, rhp
19. Brian Barden, 3b/2b
20. Brandon Medders, rhp
21. Jamie D'Antona, 3b/1b
22. Cesar Nicolas, 1b
23. Jason Bulger, rhp
24. Josh Kroeger, of
25. Alberto Gonzales, ss
26. Jereme Milons, of
27. Emilio Bonifacio, 2b
28. Kellen Raab, lhp
29. Agustin Murillo, 3b
30. Jason Neighborgall, rhp

LARRY GOREN

ORGANIZATION OVERVIEW

General manager: Josh Byrnes. **Farm director:** A.J. Hinch. **Scouting director:** Mike Rizzo.

2005 PERFORMANCE

Class	Team	League	W	L	Pct.	Finish*	Manager
Majors	Arizona	National	77	85	.465	11th (16)	Bob Melvin
Triple-A	Tucson Sidewinders	Pacific Coast	68	76	.472	t-11th (16)	Chip Hale
Double-A	Tennessee Smokies	Southern	64	76	.457	7th (10)	Tony Perezchica
High A	Lancaster JetHawks	California	75	65	.536	3rd (10)	Bill Plummer
Low A	South Bend Silver Hawks	Midwest	84	56	.600	+1st (14)	Mark Haley
Short-season	Yakima Bears	Northwest	30	46	.395	8th (8)	Jay Gainer
Rookie	Missoula Osprey	Pioneer	34	42	.447	t-6th (8)	Hector De la Cruz
OVERALL 2005 MINOR LEAGUE RECORD			**355**	**361**	**.496**	**18th (30)**	

*Finish in overall standings (No. of teams in league). +League champion.

ORGANIZATION LEADERS

BATTING   *Minimum 250 at-bats
*AVG   Jackson, Conor, Tucson .... .354
   R   Green, Andy, Tucson 125
   H   Green, Andy, Tucson 182
  TB   Green, Andy, Tucson 311
  2B   Green, Andy, Tucson 46
  3B   Green, Andy, Tucson 13
  HR   Carter, Chris, Lancaster/Tennessee 31
 RBI   Carter, Chris, Lancaster/Tennessee 115
  BB   Schindewolf, Erik, Lancaster 87
  SO   Garthwaite, Jay, Lancaster 131
  SB   Bonifacio, Emilio, South Bend 55
*OBP   Jackson, Conor, Tucson .... .457
*SLG   Drew, Stephen, Lancaster/Tennessee .... .596
PITCHING   #Minimum 75 innings
   W   Shappi, A.J., Lancaster/South Bend 16
   L   Kinsey, Chris, Lancaster/South Bend 15
#ERA   Perrault, Josh, South Bend 1.74
   G   Stockman, Phil, Tennessee/Tucson 64
  CG   Michalak, Chris, Tucson 3
  CG   Nippert, Dustin, Tennessee 3
  SV   Elliott, Matt, South Bend 32
  IP   Shappi, A.J., Lancaster/South Bend 181
  BB   Rocha, Angel, South Bend/Yakima 89
  SO   Mock, Garrett, Lancaster 160

BEST TOOLS

Best Hitter for Average .... Conor Jackson
Best Power Hitter .... Chris Carter
Best Strike-Zone Discipline .... Conor Jackson
Fastest Baserunner .... Marland Williams
Best Athlete .... Jereme Milons
Best Fastball .... Dustin Nippert
Best Curveball .... Dustin Nippert
Best Slider .... Micah Owings
Best Changeup .... Kellen Raab
Best Control .... A.J. Shappi
Best Defensive Catcher .... Orlando Mercado
Best Defensive Infielder .... Alberto Gonzales
Best Infield Arm .... Jerry Gil
Best Defensive Outfielder .... Carlos Quentin
Best Outfield Arm .... Carlos Gonzales

PROJECTED 2009 LINEUP

Catcher .... Miguel Montero
First Base .... Conor Jackson
Second Base .... Alex Cintron
Third Base .... Troy Glaus
Shortstop .... Stephen Drew
Left Field .... Chad Tracy
Center Field .... Carlos Quentin
Right Field .... Carlos Gonzales

No. 1 Starter .... Brandon Webb
No. 2 Starter .... Javier Vazquez
No. 3 Starter .... Dustin Nippert
No. 4 Starter .... Garrett Mock
No. 5 Starter .... Matt Torra
Closer .... Jose Valverde

LAST YEAR'S TOP 20 PROSPECTS

 1. Carlos Quentin, of
 2. Conor Jackson, of
 3. Sergio Santos, ss
 4. Jon Zeringue, of
 5. Greg Aquino, rhp
 6. Chris Snyder, c
 7. Josh Kroeger, of
 8. Jamie D'Antona, 3b
 9. Ramon Pena, rhp
10. Matt Chico, lhp
11. Garrett Mock, rhp
12. Koyie Hill, c
13. Brian Bruney, rhp
14. Dustin Nippert, rhp
15. Enrique Gonzalez, rhp
16. Mike Gosling, lhp
17. Jason Bulger, rhp
18. Bill Murphy, lhp
19. Carlos Gonzales, of
20. Ross Ohlendorf, rhp

TOP PROSPECTS OF THE DECADE

Year	Player, Pos.	2005 Org.
1997	Travis Lee, 1b	Devil Rays
1998	Travis Lee, 1b	Devil Rays
1999	Brad Penny, rhp	Dodgers
2000	John Patterson, rhp	Nationals
2001	Alex Cintron, ss	Diamondbacks
2002	Luis Terrero, of	Diamondbacks
2003	Scott Hairston, 2b	Diamondbacks
2004	Scott Hairston, 2b	Diamondbacks
2005	Carlos Quentin, of	Diamondbacks

TOP DRAFT PICKS OF THE DECADE

Year	Player, Pos.	2005 Org.
1996	Nick Bierbrodt, lhp	Out of baseball
1997	Jack Cust, 1b	Athletics
1998	Darryl Conyer, of (3rd round)	Out of baseball
1999	Corey Myers, ss	Diamondbacks
2000	Mike Schultz, rhp (2nd round)	Diamondbacks
2001	Jason Bulger, rhp	Diamondbacks
2002	Sergio Santos, ss	Diamondbacks
2003	Conor Jackson, of	Diamondbacks
2004	Stephen Drew, ss	Diamondbacks
2005	*Justin Upton, ss	None

*Has not signed.

ALL-TIME LARGEST BONUSES

Travis Lee, 1996 .... $10,000,000
John Patterson, 1996 .... $6,075,000
Stephen Drew, 2004 .... $4,000,000
Byung-Hyun Kim, 1999 .... $2,000,000
Corey Myers, 1999 .... $2,000,000
Mike Gosling, 2001 .... $2,000,000

MINOR LEAGUE DEPTH CHART

Arizona Diamondbacks

Rank: 4

STRENGTH: Shortstop. Stephen Drew supplanted Sergio Santos, and could be supplanted himself if Arizona ever signs Justin Upton.

WEAKNESS: Second base. Any of the Diamondbacks' shortstops could wind up here in the future.

*Depth charts prepared by **John Manuel** and **Chris Kline**. Numbers in parentheses indicate prospect rankings.*

LF
Josh Kroeger (24)
Chris Rahl
Brandon Burgess
Alex Frazier
Jay Garthwaite

CF
Jereme Milons (26)
Jarred Ball
Marland Williams
Steve Garrabrants

RF
Carlos Quentin (3)
Carlos Gonzales (4)
Jon Zeringue (16)

3B
Brian Barden (19)
Jamie D'Antona (21)
Agustin Morillo (29)
Mark Reynolds
Ricardo Sosa

SS
Stephen Drew (1)
Sergio Santos (10)
Alberto Gonzales (25)
Danny Richar

2B
Emilio Bonafacio (27)

1B
Conor Jackson (2)
Chris Carter (11)
Cesar Nicolas (22)
Javier Brito

C
Miguel Montero (6)
Koyie Hill
Wilken Castillo
Orlando Mercado Jr.
Phil Avlas
Frank Curreri

RHP

Starters	Relievers
Dustin Nippert (5)	Brandon Medders (20)
Garrett Mock (7)	Jason Bulger (23)
Matt Torra (8)	Jason Neighborgall (30)
Micah Owings (9)	Kyle Bono
Matt Green (12)	Kyler Newby
Tony Pena (14)	Mike Schultz
Enrique Gonalez (15)	Ryan Doherty
A.J. Shappi (18)	Eduardo Baeza
Koley Kolberg	Esmerling Vasquez
Ross Ohlendorf	Maels Rodriguez
Adam Bass	
Cody Evans	

LHP

Starters	Relievers
Greg Smith (13)	Matt Chico (17)
Kellen Raab (28)	Doug Slaten
Mark Romanczuk	Garrett Bauer
Bill Murphy	Vince Davis
Ryan Schreppel	Hipolito Guerrero

DRAFT ANALYSIS

2005

Best Pro Debut: RHP Micah Owings (1) went straight to Lancaster, a launching pad in a high Class A hitter's league, and went 1-1, 2.45 with a 30-4 strikeout-walk ratio in 22 innings. LHP Greg Smith (6) was named Rookie-level Pioneer League pitcher of the year after going 8-5, 4.15 and leading the league in wins, innings (82) and strikeouts (100). A plus curveball is his best pitch.

Best Athlete: No. 1 overall pick Justin Upton (1), who remains unsigned but is expected to eventually come to terms, can do it all. He's a superstar hitter with 80 speed and a 70 arm on the 20-80 scouting scale. Among the players under contract, it's OF Chris Rahl (5). His worst tool is his power, which is average.

Best Pure Hitter: Upton, with Rahl the best among the current signees.

Best Raw Power: Upton has more power than his brother B.J., the second overall pick in the 2002 draft, had at the same stage of his career. Among the players who've signed, it's Rahl, though Owings had excellent power as a two-way player at Tulane.

Fastest Runner: Once again, Upton and Rahl. Rahl is an above-average runner.

Best Defensive Player: Though many clubs said they'd immediately move him to center field to expedite getting his bat to the majors, Arizona insists Upton can stay at short and just needs more repetitions. If he does move to center, Upton still would be the best defender in this group. Rahl and 3B Rusty Ryal (14) stand out most among those who already have signed.

Best Fastball: RHP Jason Neighborgall (3) has had major control difficulties for years, but he can put triple digits on a radar gun and pitch at 96-97 mph. Owings

DAVID SCHOFIELD

Upton

pitched at 94-97 mph working out of the bullpen. RHP Matt Torra (1) has a 92-95 mph heater, while RHP Matt Green (2) has a lively 91-93 mph sinker.

Best Breaking Ball: Arizona grades Owings' mid-80s slider and Torra's 12-to-6 curveball as plus-plus pitches.

Most Intriguing Background: Upton and his brother became the highest-drafted siblings in draft history. Cuban defector Maels Rodriguez (22) was clocked at 100 mph during the 2000 Olympics, but injuries have sapped him of velocity. Smith manages an irregular heartbeat caused by a tiny hole in his heart, but his condition isn't life-threatening. Owings' brother Jon Mark is an outfielder in the Braves system. Unsigned C J.B. Paxson (33) turned down a Purdue football scholarship as a defensive end to play baseball at Walters State (Tenn.) CC.

Closest To The Majors: Owings, though Upton still could beat him to Arizona.

Best Late-Round Pick: Rodriguez, if his arm bounces back.

The One Who Got Away: RHP Brett Jacobson (11) was a first-rounder until his velocity dropped last spring. It didn't bounce back over the summer and he became part of a banner Vanderbilt recruiting class.

Assessment: Most clubs expected Arizona to go cheap after taking Upton to kick off the 2005 draft. Instead, the Diamondbacks grabbed a number of quality college arms.

2004 It took nearly a year to sign him, but getting SS Stephen Drew (1) with the 15th overall pick was a coup. RHP Garrett Mock (3) and 1B/OF Chris Carter (17) have made positive early impressions. *GRADE:* A

2003 1B Conor Jackson (1) and OF Carlos Quentin (1) will bat in the heart of Arizona's order for years to come. Taking Quentin despite his impending Tommy John surgery was a gamble that paid off huge. *GRADE:* A

2002 RHP Dustin Nippert (15) has recovered from Tommy John surgery to become the system's top pitching prospect. C Chris Snyder (2) and RHP Lance Cormier (4) had regular roles with the Diamondbacks last year. *GRADE:* C+

2001 RHP Jason Bulger (1) and $2 million LHP Mike Gosling (2) haven't done much, but IF/OF Chad Tracy (7) broke out in the majors last year. OF Scott Hairston's (3) bat still holds some promise. *GRADE:* B+

*Draft analysis prepared by **Jim Callis**. Numbers in parentheses indicate draft rounds.*

STEPHEN
DREW

SS

LARRY GOREN

Born: March 16, 1983.
Ht.: 6-1. **Wt.:** 195.
Bats: L. **Throws:** R.
Drafted: Florida State, 2004
(1st round).
Signed by: Luke Wrenn.

The talented trio of Drew brothers (Stephen and older siblings J.D. and Tim) have been drafted a total of four times in the first round—and Stephen almost made it five. The top position player available in the 2004 draft, Drew slipped to Arizona at No. 15 because of his bonus demands. Negotiations dragged into the spring of 2005, and he joined Camden in the independent Atlantic League. He finally signed with Arizona on May 30, minutes before a midnight deadline. Drew agreed to a five-year, $5.5 million major league contract that included a $4 million bonus and another $2 million in easily obtained incentives. His indy league time allowed Drew to hit the ground running at high Class A Lancaster, despite missing two weeks with a nagging hamstring injury. He tired at Double-A Tennessee as his layoff took its toll, but rebounded to hit .337 with six homers in the Arizona Fall League.

One scout calls Drew "the perfect combination of baseball tools and baseball skills." He's a middle infielder who's a middle-of-the-order run producer as well. He uses the same set-up and has the same picture-perfect swing as his brother J.D., and Drew already has an advanced knowledge of the strike zone. He has the ability to hit for average with power to all fields. His stroke has natural loft and plenty of backspin in its finish. Because he never played in a college summer league or with Team USA, Drew's ability to hit with wood was a question mark, but that issue was eliminated with his strong pro debut. Defensively, Drew has good reactions and soft hands while flashing above-average arm strength. He's a slightly above-average runner, though the hamstring troubles muted his speed.

Questions about Drew's makeup and desire lingered throughout his amateur career. His seeming unwillingness to play summer ball in college, as well his constant time off with injuries, left some to wonder if Drew's desire matches his obvious abilities. J.D. has had the same tag in the major leagues. Drew's stoic on-field demeanor is also often interpreted as a lack of fire, though he begged his way back into the lineup with the hamstring problems when the Diamondbacks wanted to shut him down. At the plate, Drew can overadjust to cold streaks, becoming either overly contact-oriented or pull-conscious. He's often lazy in the field, waiting on grounders and flipping throws to first base. He doesn't always show the first-step quickness to stay at shortstop, though he has the athleticism to be an above-average second baseman or center fielder.

In just three months, Drew established himself as Arizona's shortstop of the future. However, the anticipated signing of 2005 first-round pick Justin Upton could move Drew to another position in the middle of the diamond. With no obvious candidate at the major league level, he'll get a spring-training opportunity to win the major league starting job unless the Diamondbacks bring in a veteran.

Year	Club (League)	Class	AVG	G	AB	R	H	2B	3B	HR	RBI	BB	SO	SB	OBP	SLG
2005	Camden (Atl)	IND	.427	19	82	17	35	8	3	4	18	8	18	0	.484	.744
	Lancaster (Cal)	A	.389	38	149	33	58	16	3	10	39	26	25	1	.486	.738
	Tennessee (SL)	AA	.218	27	101	11	22	5	0	4	13	12	24	2	.301	.386
MINOR LEAGUE TOTALS			.320	65	250	44	80	21	3	14	52	38	49	3	.414	.596

2 CONOR JACKSON 1B

Born: May 7, 1982. **B-T:** R-R. **Ht.:** 6-2. **Wt.:** 225. **Drafted:** California, 2003 (1st round). **Signed by:** Fred Costello.

Jackson has hit at least .300 at every minor league stop in his brief pro career, and his .354 average at Triple-A Tucson represented a career high when he was called up in late July. He was unable to replicate his success with Arizona due in part to his inconsistent playing time. While Jackson's bat is his only above-average tool, it's exceptional. His simple mechanics and contact-oriented approach allow him to spray line drives into the gaps seemingly at will. His pitch recognition is off the charts, and he's strong enough to hit at least 20 homers annually. Drafted as a third baseman, he now projects to be an average first baseman. Jackson can be too passive at times at the plate, waiting for the perfect pitch instead of hammering one he could drive. Arizona straightened his stance at the end of 2004, but returned to a pronounced wide setup in 2005, sapping him of some power. Despite Tony Clark's 30-homer season, the Diamondbacks want Jackson's bat in their lineup. He should be their everyday first baseman in 2006.

Year	Club (League)	Class	AVG	G	AB	R	H	2B	3B	HR	RBI	BB	SO	SB	OBP	SLG
2003	Yakima (NWL)	A	.319	68	257	44	82	35	1	6	60	36	41	3	.410	.533
2004	Lancaster (Cal)	A	.345	67	258	64	89	19	2	11	54	45	36	4	.438	.562
	El Paso (TL)	AA	.301	60	226	33	68	13	2	6	37	24	36	3	.367	.456
2005	Tucson (PCL)	AAA	.354	93	333	66	118	38	2	8	73	69	32	3	.457	.553
	Arizona (NL)	MLB	.200	40	85	8	17	3	0	2	8	12	11	0	.303	.306
MAJOR LEAGUE TOTALS			.200	40	85	8	17	3	0	2	8	12	11	0	.303	.306
MINOR LEAGUE TOTALS			.332	288	1074	207	357	105	7	31	224	174	145	13	.423	.530

3 CARLOS QUENTIN OF

Born: Aug. 28, 1982. **B-T:** R-R. **Ht.:** 6-1. **Wt.:** 225. **Drafted:** Stanford, 2003 (1st round). **Signed by:** Fred Costello.

Quentin's pro debut was delayed by Tommy John surgery after he was drafted in 2003, but he has made up for lost time. He has batted .316 with 42 homers in two pro seasons. Quentin is a classic corner outfielder with above-average hitting skills, plate discipline and power. Despite his plate-crowding tactics—he leads the minors with 72 hit by pitches in the last two years—he can cheat on inside pitches and crush them as easily as he takes outside pitches to the opposite field. His instincts make him a plus baserunner and have enabled him to get by in center field when he moved there in July. His arm hasn't regained its pre-surgery strength but is solid for right field. Quentin's effort in center field was universally praised, but he just doesn't cover enough ground to play there on a regular basis. His pure speed is average at best. Luis Gonzalez, Shawn Green and Chad Tracy are blocking Quentin on Arizona's outfield corners, but he has nothing left to prove in Triple-A. He could begin his big league career in center and move to right down the road.

Year	Club (League)	Class	AVG	G	AB	R	H	2B	3B	HR	RBI	BB	SO	SB	OBP	SLG
2003	Did not play—Injured															
2004	Lancaster (Cal)	A	.310	65	242	64	75	14	1	15	51	25	33	5	.428	.562
	El Paso (TL)	AA	.357	60	210	39	75	19	0	6	38	18	23	0	.443	.533
2005	Tucson (PCL)	AAA	.301	136	452	98	136	28	4	21	89	72	71	9	.422	.520
MINOR LEAGUE TOTALS			.316	261	904	201	286	61	5	42	178	115	127	14	.428	.534

4 CARLOS GONZALES OF

Born: Oct. 17, 1985. **B-T:** L-L. **Ht.:** 6-1. **Wt.:** 180. **Signed:** Venezuela, 2002. **Signed by:** Miguel Nava.

Gonzales' tools always had excited the Diamondbacks, and he exploded in 2005. He won the MVP award and ranked as the No. 1 prospect in the low Class A Midwest League, where managers rated him the best batting prospect, best defensive outfielder, best outfield arm and most exciting player. Most aspects of the game come easy to Gonzales. He has a quick, fluid swing and strong wrists, projecting as a .300 hitter with 30-plus homer power. He makes adjustments like a veteran and commands the strike zone well. He takes good routes and has a plus arm in right field. Gonzales' speed is currently just average, and it should continue to regress as he fills out. He can get pull-happy and has some holes on the outer half of the plate, but those are easily correctable issues. He doesn't walk as much as he could because he makes contact so easily. Gonzales has the chance to be a special player, but there's no reason to rush him, especially considering Arizona's outfield. He'll begin 2006 in high Class A, where he could put up monster numbers in the friendly confines of Lancaster.

Year	Club (League)	Class	AVG	G	AB	R	H	2B	3B	HR	RBI	BB	SO	SB	OBP	SLG
2003	Diamondbacks (DSL)	R	.283	58	205	38	58	13	2	1	18	19	10	15	.363	.380
2004	South Bend (MWL)	A	.238	100	319	39	76	15	6	2	25	16	44	9	.296	.342
2005	South Bend (MWL)	A	.318	95	352	60	112	21	7	1	42	20	42	12	.359	.426
MINOR LEAGUE TOTALS			.281	253	876	137	246	49	15	4	85	55	96	36	.337	.385

5 DUSTIN NIPPERT — RHP

Born: May 6, 1981. **B-T:** R-R. **Ht.:** 6-7. **Wt.:** 215. **Drafted:** West Virginia, 2002 (15th round). **Signed by:** Greg Lonigro.

Considered the system's best pitching prospect entering 2004, Nippert pitched poorly before requiring Tommy John surgery that June. He surprisingly returned in late May and won the Double-A Southern League ERA title. He picked up his first major league win with five one-hit innings against the Dodgers in late September. In a system loaded with elite offensive prospects, Nippert is one of the few pitchers with impact potential. His fastball sits at 92-94 mph and touches 96, and he can throw his spike curveball for strikes or bury it in the dirt. He has the makings of a decent changeup, and his height and arm action allow him to deliver all of his pitches on a steep downward plane. Nippert struggled with his control in his brief big league stint, as he lost confidence and began to nibble at the plate. His fastball can get straight, but he makes up for it with his command and his downhill plane. Nippert will get the chance to win a rotation job in spring training. A little Triple-A seasoning wouldn't hurt if he doesn't make it.

Year	Club (League)	Class	W	L	ERA	G	GS	CG	SV	IP	H	R	ER	HR	BB	SO	AVG
2002	Missoula (Pio)	R	4	2	1.65	17	11	0	0	55	42	12	10	2	9	77	.208
2003	South Bend (MWL)	A	6	4	2.82	17	17	0	0	96	66	32	30	4	32	96	.191
2004	El Paso (TL)	AA	2	5	3.64	14	14	0	0	72	77	45	29	0	40	73	.273
2005	Tennessee (SL)	AA	8	3	2.38	18	18	3	0	117	95	33	31	4	42	97	.226
	Arizona (NL)	MLB	1	0	5.52	3	3	0	0	15	10	9	9	1	13	11	.185
MAJOR LEAGUE TOTALS			1	0	5.51	3	3	0	0	15	10	9	9	1	13	11	.185
MINOR LEAGUE TOTALS			20	14	2.65	66	60	3	0	339	280	122	100	10	123	343	.224

6 MIGUEL MONTERO — C

Born: July 9, 1983. **B-T:** L-R. **Ht.:** 5-11. **Wt.:** 190. **Signed:** Venezuela, 2001. **Signed by:** Junior Noboa.

Montero was seen as a catcher with some promise, but nobody expected his 2005 breakout campaign. He challenged for the California League triple crown and played in the Futures Game, though he slowed down in Double-A, in part because of a ribcage injury. Under the tutelage of Lancaster manager Bill Plummer and hitting coach Damon Mashore, Montero shortened his swing and began to let his strength work for him at the plate. He focused on just putting good wood on the ball instead of trying to pull everything. He has average arm strength, blocks balls well and calls a good game. Montero's Double-A struggles also were the result of a return to bad habits. He began to overswing, allowing pitchers to expose his holes. His throws sometimes lack accuracy, and he erased a slightly below-average 32 percent of basestealers in 2005. Even the Diamondbacks were surprised by Montero's explosion, and they rewarded him by assigning him to the Arizona Fall League. He'll begin 2006 by trying to show he can handle Double-A.

Year	Club (League)	Class	AVG	G	AB	R	H	2B	3B	HR	RBI	BB	SO	SB	OBP	SLG
2001	Diamondbacks (DSL)	R	.220	43	118	15	26	5	1	1	17	17	19	7	.343	.305
2002	Missoula (Pio)	R	.263	50	152	21	40	10	1	3	14	17	26	2	.343	.401
2003	Missoula (Pio)	R	.301	59	196	24	59	10	2	4	32	9	15	2	.352	.434
2004	South Bend (MWL)	A	.263	115	403	47	106	22	2	11	59	36	74	8	.330	.409
2005	Lancaster (Cal)	A	.349	85	355	73	124	24	1	24	82	26	52	1	.403	.625
	Tennessee (SL)	AA	.250	30	108	13	27	1	2	2	13	7	26	1	.311	.352
MINOR LEAGUE TOTALS			.287	382	1332	193	382	72	9	45	217	112	212	21	.354	.456

7 GARRETT MOCK RHP

Born: April 25, 1983. **B-T:** R-R. **Ht.:** 6-4. **Wt.:** 215. **Drafted:** Houston, 2004 (3rd round). **Signed by:** Trip Couch.

Mock was seen as a first-round talent entering his junior year at Houston, but a broken ankle hurt his performance and he fell to the third round. In his first full season, he gutted through pitching at one of the friendlier hitter's parks in baseball to lead the California League in wins and strikeouts. Mock has a full arsenal, touching 94-95 mph with his four-seam fastball while mixing in an 88-91 cutter with excellent movement. His slider and curveball are both quality offerings, and he commands all of his pitches well. He's a big-bodied power pitcher who maintains his stuff deep into games. Scouts remain concerned about the difference between Mock's stuff and results. He gives up too many hits, leaving too many pitches over the heart of the plate when he clearly has the command to work the corners. His changeup needs more work, but it should be an average pitch in the end. Mock's bulldog approach helped him survive the tough environment of the California League, and with a few refinements, he could take off. He'll start 2006 in Double-A.

Year	Club (League)	Class	W	L	ERA	G	GS	CG	SV	IP	H	R	ER	HR	BB	SO	AVG
2004	Yakima (NWL)	A	2	0	1.54	5	5	0	0	23	18	8	4	1	4	14	.228
	South Bend (MWL)	A	3	2	3.00	8	8	1	0	54	49	21	18	2	12	37	.251
2005	Lancaster (Cal)	A	14	7	4.18	28	28	0	0	174	202	95	81	19	33	160	.284
MINOR LEAGUE TOTALS			19	9	3.68	41	41	1	0	252	269	124	103	22	49	211	.273

8 MATT TORRA RHP

Born: June 29, 1984. **B-T:** R-R. **Ht.:** 6-3. **Wt.:** 225. **Drafted:** Massachusetts, 2005 (1st round). **Signed by:** Matt Merullo.

Torra was seen as just a solid arm with a weak program entering 2005, but he became a supplemental first-round pick who signed for $1.025 million after leading NCAA Division I with a 1.14 ERA for a 16-33 Massachusetts team. After racking up high pitch counts for the Minutemen, he worked just 10 innings in his pro debut before being shut down with biceps tendinitis. Torra made significant improvements to his physical condition prior to the 2005 season, and his stuff took off. He works low in the strike zone with a 92-94 mph fastball that he can dial up to 96. He throws a power curve with true 12-to-6 break that he can begin or end in the strike zone with equal effectiveness. His mechanics are simple and repeatable. Torra has yet to face any sort of advanced competition. His changeup is still a work in progress. His heavy college workload was a concern to some scouts. Torra should be 100 percent for spring training and will begin 2006 at one of Arizona's two Class A affiliates. He could reach Double-A by the end of the year.

Year	Club (League)	Class	W	L	ERA	G	GS	CG	SV	IP	H	R	ER	HR	BB	SO	AVG
2005	Yakima (NWL)	A	0	1	1.80	5	2	0	0	10	11	3	2	1	4	10	.297
MINOR LEAGUE TOTALS			0	1	1.80	5	2	0	0	10	11	3	2	1	4	10	.297

9 MICAH OWINGS RHP

Born: Sept. 28, 1982. **B-T:** R-R. **Ht.:** 6-5. **Wt.:** 220. **Drafted:** Tulane, 2004 (3rd round). **Signed by:** Mike Valarezo.

The Rockies drafted Owings in the second round in 2002 after he made a run at the national high school career home run record. A two-way star at Georgia Tech, he fell to the 19th round (Cubs) in 2004 because of signability concerns. After transferring to Tulane and leading the Green Wave in homers and pitching strikeouts in 2005, he went in the third round and signed for $440,000. Scouts long preferred Owings' power arm to his bat, and he showed why in his pro debut. He saw his fastball jump to 94-97 mph as a reliever. He also made some adjustments with his mid-80s slider, which became a plus pitch with late downward break. He's an aggressive strike-thrower who's not afraid to work inside. Owings' changeup is average at best, and will be his point of emphasis when he returns to the rotation in 2006. He still needs to mature from thrower to pitcher, working harder on setting hitters up instead of challenging them on every pitch. Arizona believes Owings could move quickly as a reliever but offers more value as a starter. He'll most likely open 2006 in the Lancaster rotation.

Year	Club (League)	Class	W	L	ERA	G	GS	CG	SV	IP	H	R	ER	HR	BB	SO	AVG
2005	Lancaster (Cal)	A	1	1	2.45	16	0	0	0	22	17	6	6	0	4	30	.221
MINOR LEAGUE TOTALS			1	1	2.45	16	0	0	0	22	17	6	6	0	4	30	.221

10 SERGIO SANTOS   SS

Born: July 4, 1983. **B-T:** R-R. **Ht.:** 6-2. **Wt.:** 240. **Drafted:** HS—Hacienda Heights, Calif., 2002 (1st round). **Signed by:** Mark Baca.

Arizona continually has pushed Santos since it drafted him in 2002's first round, and he finally hit a wall at Triple-A in 2005. He didn't get his average above .200 until late May, and he hit only one home run after July 1. Santos' pure tools remain impressive despite his poor performance. He has plus bat speed and good power for a shortstop. While he slumped at the plate, he did improve significantly in the field. Santos has soft hands and an above-average arm, and he made great strides in his reads and work on double plays. Santos overreacted to his slow start and fell apart mechanically, leaving him susceptible to inside pitches and completely inept against lefthanders (.148 average). While he has a quick first step at shortstop, his speed limits his range, and he may be better suited for third base. Despite his rough season, most scouts still see significant potential in Santos. Clearly not ready for the majors, he'll return to Triple-A. If Stephen Drew is assigned to Tucson, Santos will move to a different position to accommodate him.

Year	Club (League)	Class	AVG	G	AB	R	H	2B	3B	HR	RBI	BB	SO	SB	OBP	SLG
2002	Missoula (Pio)	R	.272	54	202	38	55	19	2	9	37	29	49	6	.367	.520
2003	Lancaster (Cal)	A	.287	93	341	55	98	13	2	8	49	41	64	5	.368	.408
	El Paso (TL)	AA	.255	37	137	13	35	7	1	2	16	8	25	0	.293	.365
2004	El Paso (TL)	AA	.282	89	347	53	98	19	5	11	52	24	89	3	.332	.461
2005	Tucson (PCL)	AAA	.239	132	490	55	117	21	3	12	68	34	108	2	.288	.367
MINOR LEAGUE TOTALS			.266	405	1517	214	403	79	13	42	222	136	335	16	.328	.418

11 CHRIS CARTER   1B/OF

Born: Sept. 16, 1982. **B-T:** L-L. **Ht.:** 6-0. **Wt.:** 195. **Drafted:** Stanford, 2004 (17th round). **Signed by:** Fred Costello.

The Diamondbacks believe they got a steal in Carter. After a stellar freshman season at Stanford, he was buried on the Cardinal roster for two years because of a shoulder injury and defensive inefficiencies. Since signing as a 17th-round pick in 2004, he has led the short-season Northwest League in slugging and RBIs in his debut, then followed up by topping the system in homers and RBIs in his first full season. Carter's tremendous bat speed and plus-plus power make him a potential middle-of-the-order threat. Built like a fireplug, he's capable of hitting 500-foot bombs. He doesn't need to make perfect contact to hit the ball out, nor does he have to pull the ball. He's a grinder who gives it his all, despite a lack of physical gifts. Carter's power bat is not just his only plus tool, it's his only tool that even grades out as at least average. He's a well-below-average runner and limited defensively to first base, where he's awkward and lacks range. Stuck behind former college rival Conor Jackson on Arizona's depth chart, Carter has seen time in left field but isn't an option there. He struggles with good breaking balls, and some see him as a classic 4-A slugger. He'll return to Double-A to open 2006, with a decision on his position not necessary until his bat forces its way into the lineup.

Year	Club (League)	Class	AVG	G	AB	R	H	2B	3B	HR	RBI	BB	SO	SB	OBP	SLG
2004	Yakima (NWL)	A	.336	70	256	47	86	15	1	15	63	46	34	2	.438	.578
2005	Lancaster (Cal)	A	.296	103	412	71	122	26	2	21	85	46	66	0	.370	.522
	Tennessee (SL)	AA	.297	36	128	21	38	4	0	10	30	19	11	0	.397	.563
MINOR LEAGUE TOTALS			.309	209	796	139	246	45	3	46	178	111	111	2	.397	.546

12 MATT GREEN   RHP

Born: Jan. 5, 1982. **B-T:** R-R. **Ht.:** 6-5. **Wt.:** 195. **Drafted:** Louisiana-Monroe, 2005 (2nd round). **Signed by:** Mike Valarezo.

Green was one of the top high school prospects in Louisiana in 2001, but he decided to stay at home and pitch at Louisiana-Monroe, where his father Jerry once played basketball. Green missed his freshman year after taking a line drive to the head, and went undrafted despite being eligible in 2003 and 2004. He began to generate some buzz after his sophomore year with a strong showing in the summer Jayhawk League, and he took another step forward last spring under the tutelage of Indians alumnus and volunteer assistant coach Chuck Finley, a 200-game winner in the big leagues. Green finished fifth in NCAA Division I with 141 strikeouts as a junior before signing for $500,000 bonus as a second-round pick.

His main weapon is a 91-93 mph fastball that touches 97. His primary breaking pitch is a slider known more for its velocity than break, though it has the makings of a plus pitch. His changeup also shows promise. Green needs to pitch with more confidence, as he's prone to attempting to get batters to chase pitches as opposed to challenging them. The Diamondbacks see Green as a future starter, though some scouts see him as more of a late-inning reliever. He'll begin the year in the rotation at one of Arizona's two Class A affiliates.

Year	Club (League)	Class	W	L	ERA	G	GS	CG	SV	IP	H	R	ER	HR	BB	SO	AVG
2005	Missoula (Pio)	R	4	3	5.55	15	12	0	0	60	77	41	37	6	26	59	.316
MINOR LEAGUE TOTALS			4	3	5.55	15	12	0	0	60	77	41	37	6	26	59	.316

13 GREG SMITH   LHP

Born: Dec. 22, 1983. **B-T:** L-L. **Ht.:** 6-2. **Wt.:** 190. **Drafted:** Louisiana State, 2005 (6th round). **Signed by:** Matt Valarezo.

Smith spent two years as a middle reliever at Louisiana State before taking off as a starter in 2005, when he had a 28⅔-innings scoreless streak and became the first Tigers pitcher to record back-to-back complete-game shutouts since former No. 1 overall pick Ben McDonald in 1989. Smith overmatched batters during his pro debut at Rookie-level Missoula, leading the Pioneer League in wins, innings and strikeouts. He has excellent command of an average fastball with good movement, using it to set up his out pitch, a big-breaking curveball that's effective against both lefties and rightes. His changeup is more than just a show-me pitch, but he rarely throws it. Smith projects as a middle-of-the-rotation starter because of his stuff, though his lack of size leads some scouts to profile him as a reliever. Doctors discovered a tiny hole in his heart when he was a freshman, but it's not life-threatening and doesn't affect his pitching. Coming from a major college program, Smith wasn't tested by Rookie ball. His full-season debut will give Arizona a much better feel for how good he can be, and he may skip two levels and head directly to high Class A.

Year	Club (League)	Class	W	L	ERA	G	GS	CG	SV	IP	H	R	ER	HR	BB	SO	AVG
2005	Missoula (Pio)	R	8	5	4.15	16	14	0	0	82	69	40	38	8	18	100	.231
MINOR LEAGUE TOTALS			8	5	4.15	16	14	0	0	82	69	40	38	8	18	100	.231

14 TONY PENA   RHP

Born: Jan. 9, 1982. **B-T:** R-R. **Ht.:** 6-1. **Wt.:** 220. **Signed:** Dominican Republic, 2002. **Signed by:** Junior Noboa.

Pena's has become the poster child for the Dominican age scandals early in the decade. Once thought to be Adriano Rosario and five years younger, he missed almost all of 2004 while his true identity and the circumstances of his signing were investigated. Given an opportunity to compete for Arizona's fifth starter's job in spring training last year, he developed a strained elbow that bothered him throughout the season. Pena's fastball, once in the upper 90s, sat at 91-93 mph in 2005. His breaking ball and changeup are both average, and he commands all of his pitches well. Without his power fastball, Pena struggled with the intricacies of pitching, failing to set up hitters and grooving too many fastballs. Some scouts think his aggressiveness lends itself better to relief work. The Diamondbacks hope a well-rested Pena will be at 100 percent for 2006. If he shows up firing bullets at spring training, he'll begin the year in Triple-A and should get his first big league look later in the season.

Year	Club (League)	Class	W	L	ERA	G	GS	CG	SV	IP	H	R	ER	HR	BB	SO	AVG
2002	Missoula (Pio)	R	1	2	6.30	4	4	0	0	20	26	15	14	0	3	14	.321
	Diamondbacks (DSL)	R	3	1	2.05	10	10	1	0	57	41	16	13	0	7	57	.193
2003	South Bend (MWL)	A	9	5	2.86	27	27	0	0	160	149	69	51	3	30	119	.247
2004	El Paso (TL)	AA	3	3	5.44	7	7	0	0	43	47	27	26	4	5	36	.280
MINOR LEAGUE TOTALS			16	11	3.34	48	48	1	0	280	263	127	104	7	45	226	.247

15 ENRIQUE GONZALEZ   RHP

Born: July 14, 1982. **B-T:** R-R. **Ht.:** 5-10. **Wt.:** 195. **Signed:** Venezuela, 1998. **Signed by:** Carlos Porte.

Signed out of Venezuela at age 16, Gonzalez didn't reach Double-A until 2005, his seventh year in the system. He led Tennessee in victories and strikeouts, finishing strong with a 2.27 ERA in his final 10 starts. Gonzalez has good command of an above-average fastball that sits at 92-94 mph and touches 96-97 several times a game. He also mixes in a cutter and an average slider. His changeup lacks deception, but he has confidence in the pitch and keeps hitters on their toes with his willingness to use it. His fastball is a little too straight, so when his secondary stuff isn't working, hitters easily can look for his heat. While his move to the rotation in mid-2004 has made him a better pitcher, his future big league role may be as a reliever. He's not big, leading to concerns about his durability over a full major league season. Gonzalez will begin the year in Triple-A.

Year	Club (League)	Class	W	L	ERA	G	GS	CG	SV	IP	H	R	ER	HR	BB	SO	AVG
1999	Diamondbacks (DSL)	R	7	3	1.64	12	11	1	0	71	41	21	13	0	24	82	.169
2000	Diamondbcks (AZL)	R	1	0	1.53	11	0	0	1	18	16	13	3	0	12	17	.239
	Tucson (PCL)	AAA	1	0	0.00	1	0	0	0	4	1	0	0	0	1	1	.091
2001	South Bend (MWL)	A	4	12	4.01	26	26	1	0	146	142	81	65	9	53	92	.257
2002	Lancaster (Cal)	A	1	4	12.27	5	5	0	0	18	34	27	25	3	14	11	.410
	Yakima (NWL)	A	5	2	2.45	11	11	0	0	66	53	27	18	2	23	57	.219
	South Bend (MWL)	A	1	2	3.74	4	4	0	0	22	23	16	9	1	9	20	.271
2003	South Bend (MWL)	A	4	3	2.13	55	0	0	3	72	58	22	17	5	29	63	.218
2004	Lancaster (Cal)	A	13	6	3.22	42	17	0	0	142	128	64	51	13	44	110	.242
2005	Tennessee (SL)	AA	11	8	3.46	27	27	2	0	161	160	76	62	8	52	146	.264
MINOR LEAGUE TOTALS			48	40	3.29	194	101	4	4	720	656	347	263	41	261	599	.244

16 JON ZERINGUE   OF

Born: Aug. 29, 1983. **B-T:** R-R. **Ht.:** 6-2. **Wt.:** 205. **Drafted:** Louisiana State, 2004 (2nd round). **Signed by:** Mike Valarezo.

The Diamondbacks admit they rushed Zeringue in 2005. His assignment to Double-A for his first full season was understandable considering he tore up high Class A in his 2004 pro debut. But Zeringue struggled with his approach, lost his power and was physically spent by the end of the year, batting just .186 in the final month. He still has the tools to project as an everyday player if he can get back on track. He has a quick bat and can drive the ball to all fields, and he's a good right fielder who runs efficient routes and has a plus arm. Zeringue pressed once his struggles began, and began to overswing and expand his strike zone. He's a guess hitter who looks for fastballs he can drive. Once Southern League pitchers figured that out, they threw him nothing but breaking balls outside the zone. His lack of conditioning played a role in his late-season decline, and he participated in Arizona's offseason program to help him cope with the rigors of a full season. Despite his poor showing, the Diamondbacks have faith that Zeringue can bounce back in a return to Tennessee in 2006.

Year	Club (League)	Class	AVG	G	AB	R	H	2B	3B	HR	RBI	BB	SO	SB	OBP	SLG
2004	Lancaster (Cal)	A	.335	56	230	36	77	14	3	10	41	14	53	9	.374	.552
2005	Tennessee (SL)	AA	.241	126	436	46	105	18	4	6	51	19	86	11	.283	.342
MINOR LEAGUE TOTALS			.273	182	666	82	182	32	7	16	92	33	139	20	.314	.414

17 MATT CHICO   LHP

Born: June 10, 1983. **B-T:** L-L. **Ht.:** 5-11. **Wt.:** 190. **Drafted:** Palomar (Calif.) JC, 2003 (3rd round). **Signed by:** Mark Baca.

Chico took a circuitous route into the pros, turning down nearly $700,000 as a Red Sox second-round pick out of high school, then flunking out of Southern California and Palomar (Calif.) Junior College. He was pitching in a San Diego semipro league when the Diamondbacks took him in the third round in 2003. He had no trouble with the lower levels of pro ball but got hit hard in Double-A in both 2004 and 2005. After Chico was demoted to high Class A last year, Lancaster pitching coach Jeff Pico changed his approach and tweaked his mechanics. Chico has the stuff to be a starter in the big leagues, starting with a fastball that sits at 88-91 mph and can touch 94. He has an average curveball and has made nice progress with his changeup, which he throws with good arm action. Chico must learn how to set up batters more effectively. He displays a lot of confidence on the mound, but needs to understand how to pitch as opposed to trying to blow batters away. Chico was one of the youngest starting pitchers in the Southern League last year, and the Diamondbacks hope his experience there will serve as a lesson learned. He'll return there to start 2006.

Year	Club (League)	Class	W	L	ERA	G	GS	CG	SV	IP	H	R	ER	HR	BB	SO	AVG
2003	Yakima (NWL)	A	7	4	3.53	17	13	0	0	71	75	28	28	4	25	71	.274
2004	South Bend (MWL)	A	8	5	2.57	14	14	2	0	88	59	26	25	9	27	89	.190
	El Paso (TL)	AA	3	7	5.78	14	12	0	0	62	82	53	40	7	36	59	.323
2005	Tennessee (SL)	AA	1	7	5.98	10	10	0	0	53	75	44	35	8	15	35	.341
	Lancaster (Cal)	A	7	2	3.76	18	18	0	0	110	101	50	46	13	39	102	.243
MINOR LEAGUE TOTALS			26	25	4.08	73	67	2	0	384	392	201	174	41	142	356	.266

18 A.J. SHAPPI   RHP

Born: Oct. 16, 1982. **B-T:** R-R. **Ht.:** 6-2. **Wt.:** 195. **Drafted:** UC Riverside, 2004 (9th round). **Signed by:** Mark Baca.

Shappi's pro career got off to a blistering start, as he won 16 of his first 18 decisions, including an 11-1 run at low Class A South Bend to start 2005. He got knocked around after a promotion to high Class A, yet still tied Toronto's Zach Jackson for the overall minor league lead in wins with 16. Shappi is a strike-throwing machine, and he has to be fine with his command because he can't get hitters out on pure stuff. His fastball sits in the high 80s, and while his slider is an above-average pitch, it also lacks velocity. He also throws a usable changeup. All of Shappi's pitches are made better by his outstanding command and his ability to hit the corners at will. His low pitch counts allow him to work deep into games, and he finished sixth in the minors in innings pitched. A Rhodes Scholar candidate at UC Riverside, Shappi brings a lot of intelligence to the mound. He understands his limitations as well as batters' weaknesses. His lack of a true out pitch leaves him susceptible to left-handers and eventually may lead him to the bullpen. Despite his struggles in Lancaster, the Diamondbacks believe Shappi is ready for Double-A.

Year	Club (League)	Class	W	L	ERA	G	GS	CG	SV	IP	H	R	ER	HR	BB	SO	AVG
2004	Yakima (NWL)	A	4	1	1.75	12	11	0	0	67	64	17	13	4	8	65	.266
	Lancaster (Cal)	A	1	0	3.00	2	1	0	0	6	6	2	2	1	1	8	.261
2005	South Bend (MWL)	A	11	1	2.86	15	15	2	0	104	98	38	33	7	15	59	.250
	Lancaster (Cal)	A	5	6	5.10	12	12	0	0	78	94	51	44	13	20	56	.297
MINOR LEAGUE TOTALS			21	8	3.26	41	39	2	0	254	262	108	92	25	44	188	.270

BRIAN BARDEN

3B/2B

Born: April 2, 1981. **B-T:** R-R. **Ht.:** 5-11. **Wt.:** 195. **Drafted:** Oregon State, 2002 (6th round). **Signed by:** Ed Gustafson.

Barden consistently has hit for average throughout his minor league career, and he took another step forward in Triple-A last year by establishing career highs in home runs and RBIs. He has a line-drive approach and uses all fields, and he did a better job of recognizing mistakes and punishing them in 2005. Barden never will be a true power hitter, and he racks up too many strikeouts for a player whose primary offensive value revolves around his batting average. He's a free swinger who draws few walks. He's no more than an average runner, though he has good instincts on the basepaths. He's an above-average defender at third base, with good hands, quick reactions and plus arm strength. Blocked by Troy Glaus in Arizona, Barden saw time at second base last year. The Diamondbacks think he could fill in at all four infield positions if needed. He'll get a shot in spring training to earn a reserve role on the big league club.

Year	Club (League)	Class	AVG	G	AB	R	H	2B	3B	HR	RBI	BB	SO	SB	OBP	SLG
2002	Yakima (NWL)	A	.333	4	15	5	5	1	0	0	2	1	0	0	.412	.400
	Lancaster (Cal)	A	.335	64	269	58	90	19	1	8	46	16	63	3	.370	.502
2003	El Paso (TL)	AA	.287	109	383	50	110	24	5	3	57	29	78	10	.348	.399
2004	El Paso (TL)	AA	.303	48	195	33	59	10	6	3	28	10	48	1	.335	.462
	Tucson (PCL)	AAA	.283	89	332	50	94	30	5	8	50	17	83	3	.324	.476
2005	Tucson (PCL)	AAA	.307	135	518	78	159	36	5	15	85	38	111	14	.363	.483
MINOR LEAGUE TOTALS			.302	449	1712	274	517	120	22	37	268	111	384	31	.350	.463

BRANDON MEDDERS

RHP

Born: Jan. 26, 1980. **B-T:** R-R. **Ht.:** 6-2. **Wt.:** 195. **Drafted:** Mississippi State, 2001 (8th round). **Signed by:** Mike Valarezo.

The Diamondbacks had to wait three years for Medders to fulfill the promise of his 2001 pro debut, as he failed in a conversion to the rotation in 2002 and missed most of 2004 after labrum surgery. After he replaced an injured Jason Bulger as Tucson's closer in early 2005, Medders was one of the most reliable relievers in the Arizona bullpen during the second half. He has a low-90s fastball with plenty of sink, and he added a cutter that was a key to his success. He also throws an average slider and an occasional changeup. His awkward delivery hides the ball for a long time, making all of his pitches difficult to pick up. Scouts praise his aggressiveness. To profile as more than a setup man, Medders needs to find an effective pitch against lefties, who hit .339 against him at Tucson and 78 points higher than righties did against him in the majors (.239 versus .161). Medders enters 2006 with a job in the Arizona bullpen all but locked up.

Year	Club (League)	Class	W	L	ERA	G	GS	CG	SV	IP	H	R	ER	HR	BB	SO	AVG
2001	Lancaster (Cal)	A	1	2	1.32	31	0	0	3	41	26	8	6	1	15	53	.182
2002	Lancaster (Cal)	A	4	8	5.38	43	12	0	15	99	111	73	59	9	36	104	.282
2003	El Paso (TL)	AA	5	3	4.41	56	0	0	7	69	65	37	34	3	26	72	.244
2004	Tucson (PCL)	AAA	0	0	4.26	11	0	0	0	13	15	7	6	3	4	17	.273
2005	Tucson (PCL)	AAA	3	2	2.48	36	0	0	8	36	31	11	10	3	18	44	.230
	Arizona (NL)	MLB	4	1	1.78	27	0	0	0	30	21	6	6	2	11	31	.194
MAJOR LEAGUE TOTALS			4	1	1.78	27	0	0	0	30	21	6	6	2	11	31	.194
MINOR LEAGUE TOTALS			13	15	4.01	177	12	0	33	258	248	136	115	19	99	290	.250

21 JAMIE D'ANTONA 3B/1B

Born: May 12, 1982. **B-T:** R-R. **Ht.:** 6-2. **Wt.:** 215. **Drafted:** Wake Forest, 2003 (2nd round). **Signed by:** Howard McCullough.

D'Antona was the system's biggest disappointment in 2005. Wake Forest's career home run leader with 58, D'Antona had been grouped with Conor Jackson and Carlos Quentin as part of the "Three Amigos." Arizona's first three picks in the 2003 draft, they all produced in high Class A and were promoted together to Double-A in mid-2004. While Jackson and Quentin now are pushing for big league jobs, D'Antona has severely regressed. He has tremendous raw power and doesn't strike out much, but his overly long swing and pull-conscious approach left him behind most fastballs and exploitable on the inner half of the plate in 2005. Drafted as a third baseman, he has a plus-plus arm but is slow and clumsy in the field. He moved to first base in the final month of the season. D'Antona needs to makes adjustments in his approach, and will return to Double-A in an attempt to rediscover his power.

Year	Club (League)	Class	AVG	G	AB	R	H	2B	3B	HR	RBI	BB	SO	SB	OBP	SLG
2003	Yakima (NWL)	A	.277	70	271	46	75	18	1	15	57	35	60	0	.356	.517
2004	Lancaster (Cal)	A	.315	68	273	45	86	18	1	13	57	16	36	2	.353	.531
	El Paso (TL)	AA	.211	19	71	2	15	3	1	0	7	2	16	0	.230	.282
2005	Tennessee (SL)	AA	.249	125	410	58	102	25	2	9	49	44	67	5	.322	.385
MINOR LEAGUE TOTALS			.271	282	1025	151	278	64	5	37	170	97	179	7	.333	.452

22 CESAR NICOLAS 1B

Born: April 17, 1982. **B-T:** R-R. **Ht.:** 6-4. **Wt.:** 230. **Drafted:** Vanderbilt, 2004 (3rd round). **Signed by:** Scott Jaster.

Scouting director Mike Rizzo likes to budget for a low-cost college senior in the fifth round of the draft, and he may have found a bargain in Nicolas in 2004. He didn't sign until last spring, then led the Midwest League in on-base and slugging percentage in his pro debut. He also ranked third in homers despite missing six weeks early in the season with a broken right hand. He also hit .424-2-10 in the postseason as the Silver Hawks won the league title. Nicolas is a hulking first baseman. He has an excellent approach at the plate, understands the strike zone and features big-time pull power. His power bat is his only tool, however. He's a lumbering runner who relies on excellent instincts to make up for a lack of athletic gifts at first base. At 23 Nicolas was older than most MWL players, and some observers thought his performance was mainly just a matter of picking on younger pitching. He's exactly the type of player who could put up huge numbers at Lancaster's launching pad, but the Diamondbacks will look to get him to Double-A at some point in 2006.

Year	Club (League)	Class	AVG	G	AB	R	H	2B	3B	HR	RBI	BB	SO	SB	OBP	SLG
2005	South Bend (MWL)	A	.302	91	325	70	98	30	1	21	70	58	60	1	.428	.594
MINOR LEAGUE TOTALS			.302	91	325	70	98	30	1	21	70	58	60	1	.428	.594

23 JASON BULGER RHP

Born: Dec. 6, 1978. **B-T:** R-R. **Ht.:** 6-4. **Wt.:** 210. **Drafted:** Valdosta State (Ga.), 2001 (1st round). **Signed by:** Michael Valarezo.

Bulger was a surprise first-round pick in 2001 out of NCAA Division II Valdosta State (Ga.), where he was primarily an infielder for three years. He doubled as the team's closer as a senior and showed a mid-90s fastball that got scouts excited. Two of his brothers pitched professionally in 2005, Brian in independent ball and Kevin in the Royals system. Jason finally made it to the majors in 2005 after struggling as a starter for two years and having Tommy John surgery in 2003. Shelled by the Phillies in his big league debut, he recovered to deliver scoreless outings in six of his last eight appearances. Big and athletic, he fits the profile of a classic power reliever. His plus-plus fastball features plenty of sink, sits at 93-96 mph and touches 98. His curveball shows promise and he can throw it for strikes. Bulger can struggle with his command and is prone to overthrowing. He'll show too much confidence in his fastball and needs to learn how to mix it up better, particularly against lefthanders. At 27, Bulger isn't going to get much better but his stuff is good enough. He'll report to spring training as a favorite to earn a job in the Arizona bullpen.

Year	Club (League)	Class	W	L	ERA	G	GS	CG	SV	IP	H	R	ER	HR	BB	SO	AVG
2002	South Bend (MWL)	A	4	9	4.94	20	20	1	0	95	111	65	52	5	39	84	.291
	Lancaster (Cal)	A	1	1	5.40	2	2	0	0	10	11	7	6	0	3	12	.289
2003	Lancaster (Cal)	A	2	1	6.75	4	4	0	0	17	23	13	13	3	5	20	.311
2004	Lancaster (Cal)	A	0	1	1.52	21	0	0	11	24	14	4	4	0	10	31	.165
	El Paso (TL)	AA	0	3	3.91	24	0	0	8	25	24	12	11	0	19	26	.240

Year	Club (League)	Class	W	L	ERA	G	CG	SV	IP	H	R	ER	BB	SO	AVG
2005	Tucson (PCL)	AAA	3	6	3.54	56	0	0	4	56	50	28	22	3	27	55	.244
	Arizona (NL)	MLB	1	0	5.40	9	0	0	0	10	14	6	6	1	5	9	.333
MAJOR LEAGUE TOTALS			1	0	5.40	9	0	0	0	10	14	6	6	1	5	9	.333
MINOR LEAGUE TOTALS			10	21	4.28	127	26	1	23	227	233	129	108	11	103	228	.264

24 JOSH KROEGER — OF

Born: Aug. 31, 1982. **B-T:** L-L. **Ht.:** 6-2. **Wt.:** 200. **Drafted:** HS—San Diego, 2000 (4th round). **Signed by:** James Keller.

After Kroeger hit .331-19-87 in 2004 while splitting time between Double-A El Paso and Tucson, some scouts still questioned whether his big numbers were simply the result of playing in friendly-hitter environments. They also wondered if his overly aggressive approach would continue to serve him well. Those concerns were well-founded, as Kroeger struggled through a disappointing 2005. While Kroeger's skills are solid across the board, he lacks the plus tool needed to project as an everyday player. He's a good athlete who turned down a football scholarship from NCAA Division II Truman State (Mo.) as a wide receiver. He has a smooth swing, some power and average speed. His range and arm are solid on an outfield corner. Kroeger improved his conditioning in 2005, and responded with a career high in stolen bases while also proving he can hold his own in center field when needed. Kroeger's lack of plate discipline and slider-speed bat continue to hurt him, and good lefthanders can tie him up inside. He'll return to Triple-A in 2006, and is starting to get buried by the Diamondbacks' outfield depth.

Year	Club (League)	Class	AVG	G	AB	R	H	2B	3B	HR	RBI	BB	SO	SB	OBP	SLG
2000	Diamondbacks (AZL)	R	.297	54	222	40	66	9	3	4	28	21	41	5	.359	.419
2001	South Bend (MWL)	A	.274	79	292	36	80	15	1	3	37	18	49	4	.324	.363
2002	Lancaster (Cal)	A	.235	133	497	63	117	20	7	7	58	23	136	2	.274	.346
2003	Lancaster (Cal)	A	.341	78	305	50	104	30	6	5	55	35	58	6	.409	.528
	El Paso (TL)	AA	.274	54	208	26	57	9	2	3	22	10	54	3	.315	.380
2004	El Paso (TL)	AA	.331	65	245	44	81	28	4	9	46	21	48	2	.393	.588
	Tucson (PCL)	AAA	.332	59	208	30	69	23	0	10	41	15	47	2	.376	.587
	Arizona (NL)	MLB	.167	22	54	5	9	3	0	0	2	1	21	0	.182	.222
2005	Tucson (PCL)	AAA	.261	129	472	73	123	28	3	14	62	36	108	17	.316	.422
MAJOR LEAGUE TOTALS			.167	22	54	5	9	3	0	0	2	1	21	0	.182	.222
MINOR LEAGUE TOTALS			.285	651	2449	362	697	162	26	55	349	179	541	41	.337	.439

25 ALBERTO GONZALES — SS

Born: April 18, 1983. **B-T:** R-R. **Ht.:** 5-11. **Wt.:** 170. **Signed:** Venezuela, 2003. **Signed by:** Miguel Nava.

The Diamondbacks have placed a premium on Latin American prospects under scouting director Mike Rizzo, and Gonzales is their latest Venezuelan find. He was slowed in the first half of 2005 by a series of nagging injuries, but hit at least .300 in every month after April and managers rated him the Midwest League's best defensive shortstop. He's fantastic with the glove, with plus range to both sides. He excels at both starting and turning double plays. His fundamentals are top notch, and he made just 11 errors all year, a remarkably low number for a low Class A shortstop. Gonzales understands his limitations offensively, using a flat, quick stroke to lace line drives all over the field. His ability to make contact is his lone offensive skill, as he offers little in the way of power or plate discipline. He's an average runner. Gonzales could reach the majors on his glove alone and projects as a utilityman. He'll move to high Class A in 2006.

Year	Club (League)	Class	AVG	G	AB	R	H	2B	3B	HR	RBI	BB	SO	SB	OBP	SLG
2003	Diamondbacks (DSL)	R	.283	58	205	38	58	13	2	1	18	19	10	15	.363	.380
2004	South Bend (MWL)	A	.238	100	319	39	76	15	6	2	25	16	44	9	.296	.342
2005	South Bend (MWL)	A	.318	95	352	60	112	21	7	1	42	20	42	12	.359	.426
MINOR LEAGUE TOTALS			.281	253	876	137	246	49	15	4	85	55	96	36	.337	.385

26 JEREME MILONS — OF

Born: Feb. 5, 1983. **B-T:** R-R. **Ht.:** 6-2. **Wt.:** 205. **Drafted:** HS—Starkville, Miss., 2001 (21st round). **Signed by:** Clarence Johns (Dodgers).

The Diamondbacks picked up a pair of supremely athletic outfielders from the Dodgers in a pair of 2004 deals. Swapped straight up for Elmer Dessens, Milons has outperformed Reggie Abercrombie, who was part of the Steve Finley trade. Milons turned down Division I-A football scholarships offers to sign with Los Angeles, and all six of his siblings played college sports, with his brother Freddie making it to the NFL as a wide receiver. Jereme, the MVP of the 2005 Midwest League all-star game, remains extremely raw but his total package reminds some scouts of a young Torii Hunter. Milons has plus speed and power potential, with a fluid swing that gets the bat into the zone quickly. He's a very good center field-er with a strong arm for the position. Milons can show flashes of greatness, and then in the same game show why he's still in Class A. He needs to improve his pitch recognition, and his defensive effort came into question last year. He seemed to go all out to make spectacu-lar catches but dog it on routine plays. He'll likely advance to high Class A in 2006.

Year	Club (League)	Class	AVG	G	AB	R	H	2B	3B	HR	RBI	BB	SO	SB	OBP	SLG
2002	Dodgers (GCL)	R	.243	45	152	28	37	8	1	1	23	10	24	9	.297	.329
2003	Ogden (Pio)	R	.308	51	195	37	60	7	5	1	23	19	47	10	.369	.410
2004	Columbus (SAL)	A	.273	103	436	70	119	14	6	10	53	30	99	25	.321	.401
	Vero Beach (FSL)	A	.205	11	39	5	8	1	0	0	2	3	9	4	.256	.231
	South Bend (MWL)	A	.172	11	29	1	5	0	1	0	1	0	10	1	.200	.241
2005	South Bend (MWL)	A	.265	123	491	81	130	28	8	10	66	32	114	11	.310	.415
MINOR LEAGUE TOTALS			.268	344	1342	222	359	58	21	22	168	94	303	60	.317	.391

27 EMILIO BONIFACIO   2B

Born: April 23, 1985. **B-T:** B-R. **Ht.:** 5-11. **Wt.:** 180. **Signed:** Dominican Republic, 2002. **Signed by:** Junior Noboa.

Bonifacio reached low Class A as a 19-year-old in 2004, and Arizona felt a return there last year wouldn't put him behind schedule. The move paid off as he made improvements across the board. A small, speedy second baseman in the mold of Luis Castillo, Bonifacio never will hit for power but is a capable hitter who uses all fields. His most significant growth came in understanding his role as an igniter atop a lineup, as he more than doubled his walk total while also cutting down his strikeouts. Once on base, Bonifacio has plus-plus speed and knows how to use it, swiping 95 bases in 122 tries over the past two seasons. His quickness helps him defensively as well. He has good range but needs to improve his reads off the bat, and his footwork is sloppy, particularly around the bag. Bonifacio will spend his third straight year with Alberto Gonzales as his double-play partner, as they'll team up in high Class A this season.

Year	Club (League)	Class	AVG	G	AB	R	H	2B	3B	HR	RBI	BB	SO	SB	OBP	SLG
2002	Diamondbacks (DSL)	R	.300	68	227	60	68	9	5	1	15	51	55	51	.428	.396
2003	Missoula (Pio)	R	.199	54	146	20	29	1	1	0	16	18	43	15	.298	.219
2004	South Bend (MWL)	A	.260	120	411	59	107	9	6	1	37	25	122	40	.306	.319
2005	South Bend (MWL)	A	.270	127	522	81	141	14	7	1	44	56	90	55	.341	.330
MINOR LEAGUE TOTALS			.264	369	1306	220	345	33	19	3	112	150	310	161	.342	.325

28 KELLEN RAAB   LHP

Born: Feb 16, 1982. **B-T:** L-L. **Ht.:** 6-6. **Wt.:** 225. **Drafted:** Wisconsin-Parkside, 2003 (25th round). **Signed by:** Mike Daughtry.

Raab sparked some attention from scouts at NCAA Division II Wisconsin-Parkside in 2003, but he fell out of favor when he came down with a tired arm late in the spring and saw his velocity slip from the low 90s to the low 80s. The Diamondbacks drafted him in the 25th round and didn't have him pitch, immediately putting him on their offseason throwing program instead. A tall lefthander with the ability to throw strikes, Raab made continuous improvements throughout 2005 after joining the South Bend rotation in May. His fastball sits at 89-91 mph and peaks at 94, and he does an excellent job of adding and subtracting from it to throw off hitters' timing. His changeup has the makings of a plus pitch. Raab's primary breaking ball is a slider, which is average at best. His past makes his stamina a concern, but he held up in 2005 and can fall back on being a lefthanded spe-cialist if needed. He'll start 2006 in high Class A with a chance to move up at midseason.

Year	Club (League)	Class	W	L	ERA	G	GS	CG	SV	IP	H	R	ER	HR	BB	SO	AVG
2003	Did not play—Injured																
2004	Yakima (NWL)	A	3	3	4.38	19	8	0	0	62	67	33	30	4	19	56	.266
2005	South Bend (MWL)	A	7	6	4.44	27	22	1	0	150	170	83	74	10	36	133	.288
MINOR LEAGUE TOTALS			10	9	4.42	46	30	1	0	212	237	116	104	14	55	189	.281

29 AGUSTIN MURILLO   OF

Born: May 5, 1982. **B-T:** R-R. **Ht.:** 6-3. **Wt.:** 194. **Signed:** Mexico, 2002. **Signed by:** Jack Pierce.

The Diamondbacks scout Mexico heavier than most teams and feel they've found a sleep-er in Murillo. Like fellow infielders Alberto Gonzales and Emilio Bonifacio, Murillo took a step forward in most aspects of his game while repeating low Class A last year. Athletic and strong, he's a good hitter with some pop in his bat. The key to his 2005 success was that he made great strides in his pitch recognition, consistently putting himself in hitter's counts. He can become a little too enamored with his power at times. Murillo is no more than an average runner, and he could lose some speed as he fills out. He's an average defender with enough arm for third base. He's already 23, so the pressure of time is upon him. Murillo will join Gonzales and Bonifacio in high Class A this year.

Year	Club (League)	Class	AVG	G	AB	R	H	2B	3B	HR	RBI	BB	SO	SB	OBP	SLG
2003	Missoula (Pio)	R	.302	74	278	48	84	22	2	5	39	17	34	2	.357	.450
2004	South Bend (MWL)	A	.263	101	357	46	94	16	1	4	38	23	48	10	.316	.347
2005	South Bend (MWL)	A	.296	126	494	94	146	34	3	17	82	53	80	5	.368	.480
MINOR LEAGUE TOTALS			.287	301	1129	188	324	72	6	26	159	93	162	17	.349	.430

30 JASON NEIGHBORGALL   RHP

Born: Dec. 19, 1983. **B-T:** R-R. **Ht.:** 6-5. **Wt.:** 205. **Drafted:** Georgia Tech, 2005 (3rd round). **Signed by:** Howard McCullough.

At the cost of a third-round pick and $500,000, Arizona took Neighborgall, the ultimate high-risk, high-reward player in the 2005 draft. He likely would have been a first-round pick out of high school in 2001, but he sought a Josh Beckett-like big league contract ($7 million). The Red Sox took him in the seventh round and floated a seven-figure offer, but he opted to attend Georgia Tech instead. After struggling with his control as a freshman, the wheels came completely off as a sophomore, as Neighborgall pitched just 6⅔ innings while walking 24. As a junior, he started well before falling apart again, finishing with a 7.13 ERA and 53 walks in as many innings. The numbers from his pro debut were markedly worse. He's one of the most fascinating and frustrating pitching prospects in baseball. He's one of the few pitchers in the game with two pitches (fastball and slider) that earn 70 or better raw grades on the 20-80 scouting scale. But at the same time, his extreme control problems leave most scouts doubting he'll ever make it. He sits in the upper 90s with his heater and consistently hits triple digits. His slider features two-plane break and comes at hitters with velocity (88-91 mph) that's typical of a fastball. He even sells his changeup with excellent arm action, and it can be a third plus pitch at times. Much of Neighborgall's troubles can be traced to his mechanics, which are just plain awful. His shoulder flies open, and his extremely violent landing often leaves him offline from the plate. His problems are also partly mental, as he has little confidence. The Diamondbacks admit there's no magic formula to fix Neighborgall. They started off in instructional league by having him pitch out of the stretch to remove the number of moving parts, and getting his landing to be both softer and more aligned with the plate. While they were happy with his progress, they have no timetable for him. If he pitches well in spring training, he'll begin the year as a starter in low Class A.

Year	Club (League)	Class	W	L	ERA	G	GS	CG	SV	IP	H	R	ER	HR	BB	SO	AVG
2005	Missoula (Pio)	R	1	2	11.12	15	7	0	0	23	21	40	28	1	45	29	.236
MINOR LEAGUE TOTALS			1	2	11.12	15	7	0	0	23	21	40	28	1	45	29	.236

BRAVES

BY **BILL BALLEW**

It's no secret the Braves have relied on their farm system throughout their unprecedented current run of 14 consecutive division championships. In 2005, Atlanta took its dependence on homegrown players further by using 18 rookies, including 12 who made their major league debuts. The Braves fielded a lineup with at least seven position players signed and developed by the organization in more than half their games, and had at least one rookie in the lineup in every game after May 28.

Atlanta didn't plan it that way. At the start of the 2005 season, the likes of outfielder **Jeff Francoeur**, catcher Brian McCann and reliever Blaine Boyer were at Double-A Mississippi and appeared to be at least a year away from the big leagues. Others, including righthander Kyle Davies and outfielders Ryan Langerhans and Kelly Johnson, were looked upon as complementary parts. Injuries and poor performances, however, forced general manager John Schuerholz to consider a different route, beginning on Memorial Day weekend.

In addition to promoting from within, Schuerholz used the Braves system to acquire veterans. The most prominent deal took place right after the 2004 Winter Meetings, when Atlanta got Tim Hudson for prized lefthander Dan Meyer and big leaguers Juan Cruz and Charles Thomas. That was bookended by the Braves using top prospect Andy Marte to bring in shortstop Edgar Renteria from the Red Sox at the 2005 Winter Meetings.

In between the Braves made several other key deals, such as shipping righthanders

Roman Colon and Zach Miner to Detroit for Kyle Farnsworth prior to the trading deadline to bolster the bullpen.

While all the comings and goings forced the Braves to make more than 100 roster moves at Triple-A Richmond alone, additional talent continued to enter the system. The Braves had yet another promising draft under the guidance of scouting director Roy Clark despite signing just two players taken after the 13th round. First-round righthander Joey Devine reached the major leagues in a hurry, and second-round shortstop Yunel Escobar attracted raves for his bat and glove. Lefty Beau Jones (supplemental first round), righty Jeff Lyman (second) and outfielder Jordan Schafer (third) all ranked among the top 20 prospects in the Rookie-level Gulf Coast League. Atlanta also signed six draft-and-follow selections from 2004, and a couple of significant foreign standouts, Venezuelan shortstop Elvis Andrus and Australian lefthander Steve Kent. Kent paid his own way to Atlanta to try out before signing for $280,000.

Even with all the big league promotions, the Braves maintain depth at several positions. They're loaded at catcher, shortstop and third base after they deemed all three spots major weaknesses earlier in the decade. While positions players stand out the most in the system, Atlanta also has quality pitching, its calling card for years.

TOP 30 PROSPECTS

1. Jarrod Saltalamacchia, c	16. Van Pope, 3b
2. Elvis Andrus, ss	17. Martin Prado, 2b
3. Yunel Escobar, ss	18. Jake Stevens, lhp
4. Anthony Lerew, rhp	19. Josh Burrus, of
5. Joey Devine, rhp	20. Maximiliano Ramirez, c
6. Chuck James, lhp	21. Jose Ascanio, rhp
7. Brandon Jones, of	22. Luis Hernandez, ss
8. Eric Campbell, 3b	23. Brady Endl, lhp
9. Beau Jones, lhp	24. James Jurries, 1b
10. Matt Harrison, lhp	25. Clint Sammons, c
11. Scott Thorman, 1b	26. Jairo Cuevas, rhp
12. Blaine Boyer, rhp	27. Jeff Lyman, rhp
13. Macay McBride, lhp	28. J.C. Holt, 2b
14. James Parr, rhp	29. Jon Mark Owings, of
15. Brayan Pena, c	30. Jordan Schafer, of

ORGANIZATION OVERVIEW

General manager: John Schuerholz. **Farm director:** Dayton Moore. **Scouting director:** Roy Clark.

2005 PERFORMANCE

Class	Team	League	W	L	Pct.	Finish*	Manager
Majors	Atlanta	National	90	72	.556	2nd (16)	Bobby Cox
Triple-A	Richmond Braves	International	56	88	.389	14th (14)	Pat Kelly
Double-A	Mississippi Braves	Southern	64	68	.485	6th (10)	Brian Snitker
High A	Myrtle Beach Pelicans	Carolina	61	79	.436	7th (8)	Randy Ingle
Low A	Rome Braves	South Atlantic	72	65	.526	5th (16)	Rocket Wheeler
Rookie	Danville Braves	Appalachian	47	20	.701	2nd (10)	Paul Runge
Rookie	GCL Braves	Gulf Coast	24	28	.462	8th (12)	Luis Ortiz
OVERALL 2005 MINOR LEAGUE RECORD			324	348	.482	24th (30)	

*Finish in overall standings (No. of teams in league).

ORGANIZATION LEADERS

BATTING
*Minimum 250 at-bats
*AVG	Pena, Brayan, Richmond	.326
R	Young, Matt, Rome	85
H	Thorman, Scott, Mississippi/Richmond	164
TB	Thorman, Scott, Mississippi/Richmond	268
2B	Saltalamacchia, Jarrod, Myrtle Beach	35
3B	Blanco, Gregor, Mississippi	12
HR	Jurries, James, Richmond	21
	Thorman, Scott, Mississippi/Richmond	21
RBI	Thorman, Scott, Mississippi/Richmond	92
BB	Blanco, Gregor, Mississippi	73
SO	Esquivel, Matt, Myrtle Beach	140
SB	Snead, Esix, Richmond	46
	Suero, Ovandy, Danville	46
*OBP	Young, Matt, Rome	.412
*SLG	Campbell, Eric, Danville	.634

PITCHING
#Minimum 75 innings
W	James, Chuck, Miss./Myrtle Beach/Richmond	13
	Parr, James, Rome	13
L	Villa, Kelvin, Myrtle Beach/Rome	11
#ERA	James, Chuck, Miss./Myrtle Beach/Rich.	1.79
G	Brooks, Frank, Richmond	54
CG	Harrison, Matt, Rome	2
SV	Childers, Jason, Richmond	16
IP	Harrison, Matt, Rome	167
BB	O'Connor, Brian, Mississippi/Richmond	65
SO	James, Chuck, Miss./Myrtle Beach/Rich.	193

BEST TOOLS

Best Hitter for Average	Jarrod Saltalamacchia
Best Power Hitter	Jarrod Saltalamacchia
Best Strike-Zone Discipline	Wes Timmons
Fastest Baserunner	Ovandy Suero
Best Athlete	Brandon Jones
Best Fastball	Anthony Lerew
Best Curveball	Beau Jones
Best Slider	Joey Devine
Best Changeup	Chuck James
Best Control	Matt Harrison
Best Defensive Catcher	Clint Sammons
Best Defensive Infielder	Luis Hernandez
Best Infield Arm	Luis Hernandez
Best Defensive Outfielder	Gregor Blanco
Best Outfield Arm	Jon Mark Owings

PROJECTED 2009 LINEUP

Catcher	Brian McCann
First Base	Adam LaRoche
Second Base	Marcus Giles
Third Base	Chipper Jones
Shortstop	Edgar Renteria
Left Field	Jarrod Saltalamacchia
Center Field	Andruw Jones
Right Field	Jeff Francoeur
No. 1 Starter	Tim Hudson
No. 2 Starter	Anthony Lerew
No. 3 Starter	Kyle Davies
No. 4 Starter	Jorge Sosa
No. 5 Starter	Chuck James
Closer	Joey Devine

LAST YEAR'S TOP 20 PROSPECTS

1. Jeff Francoeur, of
2. Andy Marte, 3b
3. Brian McCann, c
4. Kyle Davies, rhp
5. Anthony Lerew, rhp
6. Jake Stevens, lhp
7. Luis Hernandez, ss
8. Kelly Johnson, of
9. Jarrod Saltalamacchia, c
10. Blaine Boyer, rhp
11. Jose Ascanio, rhp
12. Scott Thorman, 1b
13. Roman Colon, rhp
14. Ryan Langerhans, of
15. Wilson Betemit, 3b/ss
16. Macay McBride, lhp
17. T.J. Pena, ss
18. Charlie Morton, rhp
19. Gonzalo Lopez, rhp
20. Chuck James, lhp

TOP PROSPECTS OF THE DECADE

Year	Player, Pos.	2005 Org.
1996	Andruw Jones, of	Braves
1997	Andruw Jones, of	Braves
1998	Bruce Chen, lhp	Orioles
1999	Bruce Chen, lhp	Orioles
2000	Rafael Furcal, ss	Braves
2001	Wilson Betemit, ss	Braves
2002	Wilson Betemit, ss	Braves
2003	Adam Wainwright, rhp	Cardinals
2004	Andy Marte, 3b	Braves
2005	Jeff Francoeur, of	Braves

TOP DRAFT PICKS OF THE DECADE

Year	Player, Pos.	2005 Org.
1996	A.J. Zapp, 1b	Reds
1997	Troy Cameron, ss	Padres
1998	Matt Belisle, rhp (2nd round)	Reds
1999	Matt Butler, rhp (2nd round)	Out of baseball
2000	Adam Wainwright, rhp	Cardinals
2001	Macay McBride, lhp	Braves
2002	Jeff Francoeur, of	Braves
2003	Luis Atilano, rhp	Braves
2004	Eric Campbell, 3b (2nd round)	Braves
2005	Joey Devine, rhp	Braves

ALL-TIME LARGEST BONUSES

Jeff Francoeur, 2002	$2,200,000
Matt Belisle, 1998	$1,750,000
Jung Bong, 1997	$1,700,000
Macay McBride, 2001	$1,340,000
Joey Devine, 2005	$1,300,000

MINOR LEAGUE DEPTH CHART

Atlanta Braves

Rank: **8**

STRENGTH: Lefthanded pitching. The Braves have southpaws with upside throughout the system.

WEAKNESS: Righthanded pitching. The Braves are thinner than usual particularly at the upper levels.

Depth charts prepared by **John Manuel** *and* **Chris Kline**. *Numbers in parentheses indicate prospect rankings.*

LF
Josh Burrus (19)
Onil Joseph
Carl Loadenthal
Bill McCarthy
Ardley Jansen

CF
Jordan Schafer (30)
Gregor Blanco
Nate Weidenaar

RF
Brandon Jones (7)
Jon Mark Owings (29)
Jamie Romak
Matt Esquivel
Steve Doetsch
Carlos Duran

3B
Eric Campbell (8)
Van Pope (16)
Wes Timmons

SS
Elvis Andrus (2)
Yunel Escobar (3)
Luis Hernandez (22)
T.J. Pena
Diory Hernandez

2B
Martin Prado (17)
J.C. Holt (28)
Ovandy Suero

1B
Scott Thorman (11)
James Jurries (24)
Manny Rodriguez

C
Jarrod Saltalamacchia (1)
Brayan Pena (15)
Maximiliano Ramirez (20)
Clint Sammons (25)

RHP

Starters	Relievers
Anthony Lerew (4)	Joey Devine (5)
Blaine Boyer (12)	James Parr (14)
Jairo Cuevas (26)	Jose Ascanio (21)
Jeff Lyman (27)	Charlie Morton
Luis Atilano	Kevin Barry
Sean White	Glenn Tucker
Mike Broadway	David Williams
Todd Blackford	
Jared Shaffer	
Nick Tisone	

LHP

Starters	Relievers
Chuck James (6)	Macay McBride (13)
Beau Jones (9)	Matt Coenen
Matt Harrison (10)	Will Startup
Jake Stevens (18)	Brian O'Connor
Brady Endl (23)	
Jonathan Venters	
Jo Jo Reyes	
Kelvin Villa	

DRAFT ANALYSIS

2005

Best Pro Debut: SS Yunel Escobar (2), a Cuban defector, was a fairly unknown commodity when he entered the draft in mid-May. Yet he was able to go to low Class A Rome and hit .313-4-19. RHP Joey Devine (1) went 1-1, 2.77 with six saves and 36 strikeouts in 28 innings with the Braves' three highest affiliates, mostly in Double-A, en route to the majors. RHP David Williams (37) was an all-star in the Rookie-level Gulf Coast League, where he had seven saves and a 0.47 ERA.

Best Athlete: Some teams liked OF Jordan Schafer (3) more as a lefthanded pitcher, but Atlanta will develop him as a center fielder. His tools are at least average across the board.

Best Pure Hitter: Escobar. The Braves had more information on him than most teams because minor league catcher Brayan Pena grew up with him in Cuba.

Best Raw Power: Atlanta signed just six hitters out of the draft, and none is a true masher. Escobar has the bat speed to possibly hit 20 homers per season.

Fastest Runner: OF Quentin Davis (13) has 65 speed on the 20-80 scouting scale, a step ahead of Schafer, who rates a 60.

Best Defensive Player: The Braves say Escobar's hands and arm are as good as they've seen in an amateur shortstop in recent years. He made just six errors in 48 games at Rome.

Best Fastball: Atlanta signed five pitchers who can reach the mid-90s. Devine leads the way with a fastball that tops out at 97, followed by RHP Jeff Lyman (2), who gets up to 96. LHP Beau Jones (1) and RHPs Mike Broadway (4) and Tyler Bullock (6) all can

Bullock

touch 95. Broadway's fastball has the best life among that group.

Best Breaking Ball: Righthanded hitters have a tough time dealing with Devine's slider, which he throws from a low three-quarters angle. Jones has the best curveball.

Most Intriguing Background: Bullock is a converted catcher who didn't become a full-time pitcher until last year. RHP Michael Nix' (11) uncle Paul is a former head baseball coach at Auburn.

Closest To The Majors: Atlanta's need for bullpen help made Devine the first 2005 draftee to reach the majors. Devine became the first player ever to surrender grand slams in both of his first two big league appearances, and he also gave up the season-ending homer to Chris Burke in the National League Division Series. Escobar could start 2006 in Double-A.

Best Late-Round Pick: The Braves like Davis' athleticism and liked what they saw out of RHP Rudy Quinonez (12) and Williams out of the bullpen.

The One Who Got Away: RHP Louis Coleman (28) took his feel for pitching and changing speeds to Louisiana State. RHP Tommy Hanson (22) should be a premium draft-and-follow this spring.

Assessment: When the Braves' first pick came up at No. 26, the top three players on their board were Devine, Jones and Escobar. They never imagined they'd be able to get all three.

2004 The Braves didn't have a first-rounder but their top pick, 3B Eric Campbell (2), led the Appalachian League in several offensive categories last season. RHP James Parr (4), 3B Van Pope (5) and C Clint Sammons (6) are look like keepers. **GRADE:** C+

2003 Jarrod Saltalamacchia (1) has become one of the game's elite catching prospects, while draft-and-follow OF Brandon Jones (24) is a quality athlete. LHP Matt Harrison (3) emerged as this crop's best pitcher in 2005. **GRADE:** B+

2002 Atlanta lured OF Jeff Francoeur (1) away from Clemson football, with spectacular results. He and C Brian McCann (2) were part of Atlanta's rookie resurgence last year. LHP Dan Meyer (1) had a disastrous 2005 after being traded to Oakland. LHP Chuck James (20) continues to dominate in the minors. **GRADE:** A

2001 RHPs Kyle Davies (4) and Anthony Lerew (11) have surpassed a trio of first-rounders: LHP Macay McBride, OF Josh Burrus and 2B Richard Lewis (now with the Cubs). **GRADE:** B

*Draft analysis prepared by **Jim Callis**. Numbers in parentheses indicate draft rounds.*

JARROD
SALTALAMACCHIA

C

MIKE JANES

Born: May 2, 1985.
Ht.: 6-4. **Wt.:** 195.
Bats: Both. **Throws:** Right.
Drafted: HS—West Palm Beach,
Fla., 2003 (1st round supplemental).
Signed by: Alex Morrales.

While Brian McCann was establishing himself as a quality young backstop in the majors, Saltalamacchia made a case for being the best catching prospect in the minors. The 36th overall pick of the 2003 draft, he has made impressive leaps in mental and physical maturity, leading to rapid improvement on the diamond. After working on his strength and conditioning during the offseason, he established personal bests across the board and rated as the No. 1 prospect in the high Class A Carolina League. He also got married on the beach at midseason. Following the regular season, Saltalamacchia posted a solid showing in the Arizona Fall League and served as a catalyst on Team USA in an Olympic pre-qualifying tournament. He went 7-for-8 at the plate in three games, singling in the game-winning run in the bottom of the ninth versus Mexico and swatting a pair of solo home runs against Panama. His brother Justin played briefly in the Braves system in 2003.

Just 20, Saltalamacchia has a professional approach beyond his years and power from both sides of the plate. He has a sweet, textbook swing from the left side, with natural loft that should lead to significant home run totals at higher levels. His swing from the right side has become much smoother than when he initially signed, but remains somewhat mechanical. He'll strike out, though not in excessive amounts. Coming out of high school, Saltalamacchia's footwork behind the plate was considered suspect, but he since has proven to be a solid defender with a plus arm. He has refined his throwing mechanics, though he could use more accuracy after throwing out just 26 percent of basestealers at Myrtle Beach. He has nonstop energy, works well with pitchers and has shown more feel for calling a game. What impresses the Braves most about Saltalamacchia's catching is his tremendous desire to improve and his ability to process instruction and put it to use. He's an above-average athlete for a catcher and his sturdy body should hold up well behind the plate. While he's a below-average runner, he's smart on the bases and quicker than most backstops.

Numerous clubs inquired about Saltalamacchia's availability during the Winter Meetings, but he's as close to untouchable as any player in the organization. He'll continue his steady progress by moving up to Double-A Mississippi this year. Even though the Braves traded Johnny Estrada in December, they still have McCann and Brayan Pena ahead of him in the system. That means Saltalamacchia will have plenty of time to refine his game, though he could push for a promotion to Triple-A Richmond in 2006. He should be ready for the big leagues at some point in 2007.

Year	Club (League)	Class	AVG	G	AB	R	H	2B	3B	HR	RBI	BB	SO	SB	OBP	SLG
2003	Braves (GCL)	R	.239	46	134	23	32	11	2	2	14	28	33	0	.382	.396
2004	Rome (SAL)	A	.272	91	323	42	88	19	2	10	51	34	83	1	.348	.437
2005	Myrtle Beach (Car)	A	.314	129	459	70	144	35	1	19	81	57	99	4	.394	.519
MINOR LEAGUE TOTALS			.288	266	916	135	264	65	5	31	146	119	215	5	.376	.472

2 ELVIS ANDRUS   SS

Born: Aug. 26, 1988. **B-T:** R-R. **Ht.:** 6-0. **Wt.:** 185. **Signed:** Venezuela, 2005.
Signed by: Rolando Petit.

Andrus, whose older brother Erold plays in the Twins system, showed off his tools on a summer showcase tour in 2004 and signed as a 16-year-old in January 2005. The Braves challenged him by sending him to the Rookie-level Gulf Coast League and he had no trouble adapting to pro ball and the United States. He even hit .400 in the Rookie-level Appalachian League championship series. Andrus' maturity far exceeds his age, both on the field and off. At the plate, he uses the entire field and possesses plus power that should increase as his body matures. On defense, his arm, range, footwork and quickness are all exceptional tools. After tiring in August, Andrus needs to add strength to his lithe frame. He tends to try to do too much at times, though experience should help him learn to play within himself. Andrus will compete for a job in the low Class A South Atlantic League in 2006, where he almost certainly would be the youngest player in the league at 17. He's at least three or four years away from Atlanta, but his upside is huge.

Year	Club (League)	Class	AVG	G	AB	R	H	2B	3B	HR	RBI	BB	SO	SB	OBP	SLG
2005	Braves (GCL)	R	.295	46	166	26	49	6	1	3	20	19	28	7	.377	.398
	Danville (Appy)	R	.278	6	18	3	5	1	0	0	1	4	4	1	.409	.333
MINOR LEAGUE TOTALS			.293	52	184	29	54	7	1	3	21	23	32	8	.380	.391

3 YUNEL ESCOBAR   SS

Born: Nov. 2, 1982. **B-T:** R-R. **Ht.:** 6-2. **Wt.:** 200. **Drafted:** Miami (no school),
2005 (2nd round). **Signed by:** Gregg Kilby.

Escobar was the most coveted of five Cuban defectors who entered the 2005 draft, causing teams to scramble when he declared himself eligible in mid-May. Atlanta was able to gain additional insight on him because he was a childhood friend of Braves catcher Brayan Pena. After signing for $475,000 as a second-round pick, Escobar had no problems handling low Class A. Escobar has solid all-around tools, featuring a steady glove, strong arm and a potent bat with budding power. He also has a large athletic frame that allows him to play a physical brand of baseball. He possesses strong hands and wrists as well as above-average arm strength. He made just six errors in 48 games at low Class A Rome. Escobar's range isn't remarkable. He's not as fast as most shortstops, though he has average speed and fluid actions. He's still adjusting to living in the U.S. and away from his family. Escobar could quickly develop into the Braves long-term answer at shortstop, though Elvis Andrus will have something to say about that.

Year	Club (League)	Class	AVG	G	AB	R	H	2B	3B	HR	RBI	BB	SO	SB	OBP	SLG
2005	Danville (Appy)	R	.400	8	30	9	12	2	1	2	8	5	4	0	.472	.733
	Rome (SAL)	A	.313	48	198	30	62	13	3	4	19	14	30	0	.358	.470
MINOR LEAGUE TOTALS			.325	56	228	39	74	15	4	6	27	19	34	0	.375	.504

4 ANTHONY LEREW   RHP

Born: Oct. 28, 1982. **B-T:** L-R. **Ht.:** 6-3. **Wt.:** 220. **Drafted:** HS—Wellsville, Pa.,
2001 (11th round). **Signed by:** J.J. Picollo.

Lerew is a poster boy for the Braves' extensive scouting efforts, as they spotted him though he was more of a football standout in high school. He took off on the mound in 2004 when he added 4-5 mph to his fastball. He pitched in the Futures Game in 2005 and made his major league debut in September. Scouts love Lerew's loose, easy arm action, which produces an explosive plus fastball that sits at 91-94 mph. He's aggressive and shows no fear in going after hitters. His command and the overall quality of his pitches improved in 2005. An outstanding athlete, he has the mindset and ability to start or relieve as needed. On occasion, Lerew loses the feel for his otherwise solid changeup, which has good late action. He's still fine-tuning a slider that's a plus pitch at times. The Braves would like Lerew to get at least another half-season in Triple-A. They believe he could mirror Kyle Davies and step into the Atlanta rotation if needed in mid-2006.

Year	Club (League)	Class	W	L	ERA	G	GS	CG	SV	IP	H	R	ER	HR	BB	SO	AVG
2001	Braves (GCL)	R	1	2	2.92	12	7	0	0	49	43	25	16	3	14	40	.228
2002	Danville (Appy)	R	8	3	1.73	14	14	0	0	83	60	23	16	2	25	75	.205
2003	Rome (SAL)	A	7	6	2.38	25	25	0	0	144	112	45	38	7	43	127	.215
2004	Myrtle Beach (Car)	A	8	9	3.75	27	27	0	0	144	145	75	60	12	46	125	.271
2005	Mississippi (SL)	AA	6	2	3.93	14	14	1	0	76	70	34	33	6	32	64	.246
	Richmond (IL)	AAA	4	4	3.48	13	13	0	0	72	63	34	28	9	23	53	.232
	Atlanta (NL)	MLB	0	0	5.63	7	0	0	0	8	9	5	5	1	5	5	.290
MAJOR LEAGUE TOTALS			0	0	5.63	7	0	0	0	8	9	5	5	1	5	5	.290
MINOR LEAGUE TOTALS			34	26	3.03	105	100	1	0	568	493	236	191	39	183	484	.236

5 JOEY DEVINE — RHP

Born: Sept. 29, 1983. **B-T:** R-R. **Ht.:** 6-0. **Wt.:** 212. **Drafted:** North Carolina State, 2005 (1st round). **Signed by:** Billy Best.

Devine set a North Carolina State career record for saves. After signing for $1.3 million as the 27th overall pick, he became the first member of the 2005 draft class to reach the majors. The first pitcher in big league history to surrender grand slams in each of his first two appearances, Devine also served up the 18th-inning homer to Chris Burke that ended the National League Division Series. An excellent athlete, Devine has a 92-97 mph fastball and a mid-80s Frisbee slider. His pitches are difficult to pick up from his low three-quarters arm slot. The Braves love his makeup and the way he handled adversity in the majors. His low arm slot can leave him susceptible to lefthanders (who hit .312 against him in the minors), so Devine may have to develop a changeup. His control wasn't as sharp at higher levels. Devine probably needs a little more time in the minors. Before too long, he should figure into the back of Atlanta's bullpen.

Year	Club (League)	Class	W	L	ERA	G	GS	CG	SV	IP	H	R	ER	HR	BB	SO	AVG
2005	Myrtle Beach (Car)	A	0	0	0.00	4	0	0	1	5	0	0	0	0	3	7	.000
	Mississippi (SL)	AA	1	1	2.70	18	0	0	5	20	19	13	6	2	12	28	.250
	Richmond (IL)	AAA	0	0	18.00	1	0	0	0	1	3	2	2	0	1	1	.600
	Atlanta (NL)	MLB	0	1	12.60	5	0	0	0	5	6	7	7	2	5	3	.286
MAJOR LEAGUE TOTALS			0	1	12.60	5	0	0	0	5	6	7	7	2	5	3	.286
MINOR LEAGUE TOTALS			1	1	2.77	23	0	0	6	26	22	15	8	2	16	36	.232

6 CHUCK JAMES — LHP

Born: Nov. 9, 1981. **B-T:** L-L. **Ht.:** 6-0. **Wt.:** 170. **Drafted:** Chattahoochee Valley, Ala., CC, 2002 (20th round). **Signed by:** Al Goetz.

The South Atlantic League's most valuable pitcher in 2004, James blazed through three levels in 2005 before his September callup. Along the way, he ranked third in the minors in ERA (2.12) and fourth in strikeouts (193). James' changeup is the best in the system. He has plus command of his 89-91 mph fastball, and he does an excellent job of pitching to both sides of the plate. He keeps hitters off balance by upsetting their timing. James isn't overpowering and his stuff is unlikely to improve. His 0.3 groundball-flyball ratio was the lowest in the minor leagues, and could present problems if he doesn't miss bats in the majors. His slider needs more consistency in order to give him a third pitch as a big league starter. James will compete for a job in Atlanta during spring training, though he most likely will open 2006 with a tuneup in Triple-A. He's capable of developing into a mid-rotation starter.

Year	Club (League)	Class	W	L	ERA	G	GS	CG	SV	IP	H	R	ER	HR	BB	SO	AVG
2003	Danville (Appy)	R	2	1	1.25	11	11	0	0	50	26	9	7	1	19	68	.151
2004	Rome (SAL)	A	10	5	2.25	26	22	1	0	132	92	41	33	6	48	156	.203
2005	Myrtle Beach (Car)	A	3	3	1.08	7	7	0	0	42	20	6	5	1	8	59	.139
	Mississippi (SL)	AA	9	1	2.09	16	16	0	0	86	62	25	20	4	18	104	.199
	Richmond (IL)	AAA	1	3	3.48	6	6	0	0	34	21	13	13	4	10	30	.176
	Atlanta (NL)	MLB	0	0	1.59	2	0	0	0	6	4	1	1	0	3	5	.200
MAJOR LEAGUE TOTALS			0	0	1.59	2	0	0	0	6	4	1	1	0	3	5	.200
MINOR LEAGUE TOTALS			25	13	2.04	66	62	1	0	344	221	94	78	16	103	417	.184

7 BRANDON JONES OF

Born: Dec. 10, 1983. **B-T:** L-R. **Ht.:** 6-2. **Wt.:** 195. **Drafted:** Tallahassee (Fla.) CC, D/F 2003 (24th round). **Signed by:** Al Goetz.

The Royals failed to sign Jones as a 2002 sixth-round pick out of high school, but the Braves took him in the 24th round a year later and landed him in 2004 as a draft-and-follow. He broke his left hand on a slide in late April 2005, costing him two months, and made steady progress once he returned. Jones has impressive tools and athleticism, with natural strength, raw power and a quick swing that should enable him to hit for average at higher levels. His above-average speed and strong arm allow him to play any outfield spot. Some scouts wonder if Jones will develop enough power to be a corner outfielder. He moves well but he has yet to grasp the nuances of baserunning. He also needs to take better angles on balls hit to the outfield. Jones displayed more polish than expected at high Class A. With just 440 at-bats under his belt, he needs a complete season in 2006. He could reach Double-A at some point during the year.

Year	Club (League)	Class	AVG	G	AB	R	H	2B	3B	HR	RBI	BB	SO	SB	OBP	SLG
2004	Danville (Appy)	R	.297	57	209	35	62	6	5	3	33	23	33	4	.366	.416
2005	Braves (GCL)	R	.125	2	8	0	1	0	0	0	2	0	2	0	.125	.125
	Danville (Appy)	R	.286	2	7	0	2	0	0	0	1	1	0	0	.375	.286
	Rome (SAL)	A	.308	43	156	37	48	12	3	8	27	29	29	4	.423	.577
	Myrtle Beach (Car)	A	.350	17	60	7	21	4	0	0	5	9	9	0	.437	.417
MINOR LEAGUE TOTALS			.305	121	440	79	134	22	8	11	68	62	73	8	.393	.466

8 ERIC CAMPBELL 3B

Born: Aug. 6, 1985. **B-T:** R-R. **Ht.:** 6-0. **Wt.:** 190. **Drafted:** HS—Owensville, Ind., 2004 (2nd round). **Signed by:** Sherard Clinkscales.

After a modest pro debut, Campbell showed why he was Atlanta's top 2004 draft pick. He earned co-MVP honors with Danville teammate Max Ramirez in the Appy League, which Campbell led in runs, doubles, homers, RBIs, extra-base hits and slugging percentage. Campbell has excellent vision that allows him to recognize pitches he can drive to all fields with his plus power. His defense is better than advertised and he made a seamless move from shortstop to third base, displaying above-average athleticism, range and arm strength. He has drawn comparisons to former NL home run champ and Gold Glover Matt Williams. Campbell's speed and overall baserunning skills surprised many scouts. Campbell's swing can get a little long from his open upright stance, and he tends to chase breaking balls, which has led to high strikeout totals. While his aggressiveness at the plate is an advantage, he needs to improve his pitch selection and overall bat control. With Chipper Jones and Wilson Betemit at the hot corner, the Braves feel little need to rush Campbell. He's slated to spend most of the 2006 campaign in low Class A.

Year	Club (League)	Class	AVG	G	AB	R	H	2B	3B	HR	RBI	BB	SO	SB	OBP	SLG
2004	Braves (GCL)	R	.251	56	211	30	53	7	0	7	29	15	47	3	.306	.384
	Rome (SAL)	A	.136	7	22	0	3	0	0	0	1	2	7	0	.240	.136
2005	Danville (Appy)	R	.313	66	262	77	82	26	2	18	64	28	64	15	.383	.634
MINOR LEAGUE TOTALS			.279	129	495	107	138	33	2	25	94	45	118	18	.344	.505

9 BEAU JONES LHP

Born: Aug. 25, 1986. **B-T:** L-L. **Ht.:** 6-1. **Wt.:** 205. **Drafted:** HS—Destrehan, La., 2005 (1st round supplemental). **Signed by:** Don Thomas.

Louisiana produced one of its best crops of pitchers ever in 2005, and Jones, who threw a no-hitter in the state playoffs, was the first to go in the draft at No. 41 overall. If Devine had been gone at No. 27, the Braves would have made Jones their first-round pick. He signed for $825,000 and had a solid debut. Jones has a live arm that produces 88-95 mph fastballs with good movement. His curveball is an out pitch in the making, featuring hard downward movement and high-70s velocity. He has a clean delivery and arm action, and he creates excellent deception with all of his pitches. The Braves also love his gritty, determined approach that reminds them of Kyle Davies'. Jones needs to become more consistent with his curve and his command. He also must add more depth and fade to his changeup. At 6-foot-1 and 205 pounds, he's not very projectable, but he already has good stuff and a high ceiling. The Braves will be patient in their development of Jones. He should pitch in the low Class A rotation in 2006.

Year	Club (League)	Class	W	L	ERA	G	GS	CG	SV	IP	H	R	ER	HR	BB	SO	AVG
2005	Braves (GCL)	R	3	2	3.86	8	7	0	0	35	25	15	15	0	16	41	.212
Minor League Totals			3	2	3.86	8	7	0	0	35	25	15	15	0	16	41	.212

10 MATT HARRISON LHP

Born: Aug. 16, 1985. **B-T:** L-L. **Ht.:** 6-5. **Wt.:** 205. **Drafted:** HS—Stem, N.C., 2003 (3rd round). **Signed by:** Billy Best.

Harrison is coming off the biggest breakthrough season of any starting pitcher in the system. After two years in short-season ball, he focused on keeping his fastball down in the strike zone and limiting the number of pitches he threw instead of trying to blow away every hitter. The results were impressive, as one scout said Harrison had the highest ceiling of any pitcher in the South Atlantic League. Harrison's fastball sits in the upper 80s and tops out at 93 mph. He mixes it well with an average changeup and a quality curveball he refined over the course of the season. It's his pinpoint command that sets him apart and impresses scouts. He displays a great feel for pitching, and no Braves farmhand can match his command. At 6-foot-5 and 220 pounds, Harrison possesses great size for a 20-year-old lefty, and that and his free and easy delivery give him workhorse potential. While he commands three pitches, Harrison needs to improve the overall quality of all three offerings. He'll work on that in high Class A this year under the guidance of organizational pitching guru Bruce Dal Canton.

Year	Club (League)	Class	W	L	ERA	G	GS	CG	SV	IP	H	R	ER	HR	BB	SO	AVG
2003	Braves (GCL)	R	3	1	3.69	11	6	0	1	39	40	18	16	2	9	33	.263
2004	Danville (Appy)	R	4	4	4.09	13	12	1	0	66	72	36	30	3	10	49	.278
2005	Rome (SAL)	A	12	7	3.23	27	27	2	0	167	151	65	60	17	30	118	.239
MINOR LEAGUE TOTALS			19	12	3.51	51	45	3	1	272	263	119	106	22	49	200	.252

11 SCOTT THORMAN 1B

Born: Jan. 6, 1982. **B-T:** L-R. **Ht.:** 6-3. **Wt.:** 200. **Drafted:** HS—Cambridge, Ont., 2000 (1st round). **Signed by:** John Steward/Jim Kane.

Already six years into his pro career, Thorman returned to Double-A to begin 2005. He earned a midseason promotion to Triple-A and finished the year leading the system in homers and RBIs. He has impressive raw power and a knack for driving in runs. He has improved his ability to make consistent contact by shortening his swing. He has made significant strides with his glove and footwork, so much so that managers rated him the best defensive first baseman in the Double-A Southern League. He moves well and has a strong throwing arm, having played as a third baseman and switching positions following shoulder surgery in 2001. Thorman still becomes pull-happy at times and was overanxious at the plate following his promotion. He tends to beat himself up when he fails, though he has improved his mental approach. The Braves see similarities between Ryan Klesko and Thorman, who got some outfield time in Triple-A. He's likely headed back there this year, though his power could carry him to the big leagues soon.

Year	Club (League)	Class	AVG	G	AB	R	H	2B	3B	HR	RBI	BB	SO	SB	OBP	SLG
2000	Braves (GCL)	R	.227	29	97	15	22	7	1	1	19	12	23	0	.330	.351
2001	Injured—Did not play															
2002	Macon (SAL)	A	.294	127	470	57	138	38	3	16	82	51	83	2	.367	.489
2003	Myrtle Beach (Car)	A	.243	124	445	44	108	26	2	12	56	42	79	0	.311	.391
2004	Myrtle Beach (Car)	A	.299	43	154	20	46	11	1	4	29	12	19	1	.358	.461
	Greenville (SL)	AA	.252	94	345	31	87	14	3	11	51	39	73	5	.326	.406
2005	Mississippi (SL)	AA	.305	90	348	49	106	21	2	15	65	28	76	2	.360	.506
	Richmond (IL)	AAA	.276	52	210	23	58	10	3	6	27	9	42	0	.313	.438
MINOR LEAGUE TOTALS			.273	559	2069	239	565	127	15	65	329	193	395	10	.339	.443

12 BLAINE BOYER RHP

Born: July 11, 1981. **B-T:** R-R. **Ht.:** 6-3. **Wt.:** 190. **Drafted:** HS—Marietta, Ga., 2000 (3rd round). **Signed by:** Rob English.

Yet another rookie who contributed to Atlanta's NL East title in 2005, Boyer didn't seem big league-ready when he struggled with inconsistency during his first two months in Double-A. Once he straightened himself out, he quickly became a mainstay in the Braves bullpen, which missed him in the postseason when shoulder soreness sidelined him. A starter throughout most of his pro career, Boyer made steady albeit slow progress prior to last season. His most impressive pitch always has been his heavy low-90s fastball that produces groundouts. He also can strike out hitters with his plus curveball. His changeup improved last summer but lacks the depth and fade to be a reliable pitch at this point. Boyer showed more maturity upon reaching Atlanta after wearing his emotions on his sleeve earlier in his career. Provided he can pick up where he left off before having shoulder problems, he should remain a fixture in Atlanta.

Year	Club (League)	Class	W	L	ERA	G	GS	CG	SV	IP	H	R	ER	HR	BB	SO	AVG
2000	Braves (GCL)	R	1	3	2.51	11	5	0	1	32	24	16	9	0	19	27	.200
2001	Danville (Appy)	R	4	5	4.32	13	12	0	0	50	48	35	24	4	19	57	.250
2002	Macon (SAL)	A	5	9	3.07	43	0	0	1	70	52	30	24	0	39	73	.207
2003	Rome (SAL)	A	12	8	3.69	30	26	1	0	137	146	70	56	5	58	115	.271
2004	Myrtle Beach (Car)	A	10	10	2.98	28	28	0	0	154	138	63	51	4	49	95	.250
2005	Mississippi (SL)	AA	2	4	5.03	14	8	0	0	48	62	28	27	4	18	40	.321
	Atlanta (NL)	MLB	4	2	3.11	43	0	0	0	38	32	13	13	1	17	33	.234
MAJOR LEAGUE TOTALS			4	2	3.10	43	0	0	0	38	32	13	13	1	17	33	.234
MINOR LEAGUE TOTALS			34	39	3.50	139	79	1	2	492	470	242	191	17	202	407	.254

13 MACAY McBRIDE
LHP

Born: Oct. 24, 1982. **B-T:** L-L. **Ht.:** 5-11. **Wt.:** 180. **Drafted:** HS—Sylvania, Ga., 2001 (1st round). **Signed by:** Rob English.

Compared to Billy Wagner when he was an overpowering lefthander—he was the South Atlantic League pitcher of the year in 2001 and led the Carolina League in strikeouts the following year—McBride isn't going to fulfill those expectations. But he has emerged as a strong lefthanded reliever. He initially moved to the bullpen after struggling in Double-A during 2004, and found a permanent home there when he was promoted to Triple-A last May. McBride is a fastball/slider pitcher who became more aggressive with his low 90s heater in Triple-A. He also made progress with his slider. At the lower levels, McBride threw an excellent changeup, but he has all but abandoned the pitch after it regressed and he moved to the bullpen. Regaining his quality changeup might make the difference between him becoming a set-up man or a situational lefty. After getting his feet wet in the big leagues last year, McBride will compete for a relief job in Atlanta in 2006.

Year	Club (League)	Class	W	L	ERA	G	GS	CG	SV	IP	H	R	ER	HR	BB	SO	AVG
2001	Braves (GCL)	R	4	4	3.76	13	11	0	0	55	51	30	23	0	23	67	.248
2002	Macon (SAL)	A	12	8	2.12	25	25	2	0	157	119	49	37	6	48	138	.209
2003	Myrtle Beach (Car)	A	9	8	2.95	27	27	1	0	165	164	63	54	5	49	139	.262
2004	Greenville (SL)	AA	1	7	4.44	38	12	0	0	103	113	59	51	9	46	102	.277
2005	Mississippi (SL)	AA	3	1	3.65	6	3	0	0	25	21	11	10	2	12	16	.233
	Richmond (IL)	AAA	1	5	4.33	25	1	0	2	44	49	27	21	5	22	47	.290
	Atlanta (NL)	MLB	1	0	5.79	23	0	0	1	14	18	11	9	0	7	22	.305
MAJOR LEAGUE TOTALS			1	0	5.79	23	0	0	1	14	18	11	9	0	7	22	.305
MINOR LEAGUE TOTALS			30	33	3.22	134	79	3	2	549	517	239	196	27	200	509	.250

14 JAMES PARR
RHP

Born: Feb. 27, 1986. **B-T:** R-R. **Ht.:** 6-1. **Wt.:** 185. **Drafted:** HS—Albuquerque, 2004 (4th round). **Signed by:** Danny Bates.

A two-way standout at Albuquerque's La Cueva High, where his teams won 58 straight games and consecutive New Mexico 5-A state titles, Parr committed to the University of Hawaii before signing with the Braves. The day before Atlanta made him a fourth-round pick in 2004, he won the home run derby at a high school all-America showcase, where his competition included slugging Braves farmhands Eric Campbell and Jon Mark Owings. The Braves liked him better on the mound, however, and he didn't disappoint them by tying Chuck James for the system lead in victories and ranking fourth in ERA in 2005, his first full season. Parr alternated between starting and relieving through mid-July before responding to a full-time job in the rotation by winning six straight starts. After sitting in the high 80s during his pro debut, Parr's fastball spiked back into the low 90s and topped out at 94 mph last year. His fluctuating velocity has been an issue since high school. His heater features excellent movement and bores in on righthanders. Parr complements his fastball with a plus curveball that has tight spin and a good break. He has good command and mixes his pitches well. Parr needs to improve the quality of his changeup in order to remain a starter. He also must work down in the strike zone more consistently. His next stop will be high Class A.

Year	Club (League)	Class	W	L	ERA	G	GS	CG	SV	IP	H	R	ER	HR	BB	SO	AVG
2004	Braves (GCL)	R	3	2	4.24	10	10	0	0	40	39	19	19	2	12	40	.252
2005	Rome (SAL)	A	13	4	3.41	26	18	0	3	127	134	54	48	13	24	98	.269
MINOR LEAGUE TOTALS			16	6	3.61	36	28	0	3	167	173	73	67	15	36	138	.265

15 BRAYAN PENA

C

Born: Jan. 7, 1982. **B-T:** B-R. **Ht.:** 5-11. **Wt.:** 210. **Signed:** Cuba, 2000. **Signed by:** Julian Perez/Rene Francisco.

On the heels of a solid yet unspectacular 2004 season in Double-A, Pena seemed to mature while playing in the Dominican Winter League. He finished fifth in the batting race with a .323 average, then surpassed that mark last year in Triple-A around four callups to Atlanta. A switch-hitter, Pena's ability to put the ball in play earned him the nickname "The Cuban Ichiro." He consistently centers the ball on the bat. The stocky Pena doesn't run well but has done a good job of getting his body in better condition after some scouts worried about his frame early in his career. His defensive work, especially with blocking balls in the dirt and working with pitchers, has made steady improvement over the past few years. He has above-average arm strength and his throws have become more accurate. Pena is blocked by Brian McCann in Atlanta and has Jarrod Saltalamacchia coming up behind him, so he may need a trade to get much big league playing time.

Year	Club (League)	Class	AVG	G	AB	R	H	2B	3B	HR	RBI	BB	SO	SB	OBP	SLG
2001	Danville (Appy)	R	.370	64	235	39	87	16	2	1	33	31	30	3	.440	.468
2002	Myrtle Beach (Car)	A	.211	6	19	3	4	1	0	0	1	3	4	0	.318	.263
	Macon (SAL)	A	.229	81	271	26	62	10	0	3	25	22	37	0	.290	.299
2003	Myrtle Beach (Car)	A	.294	82	286	24	84	14	1	2	27	11	28	2	.320	.371
2004	Greenville (SL)	AA	.314	77	277	30	87	10	4	2	30	15	29	3	.349	.401
2005	Richmond (IL)	AAA	.326	81	282	27	92	21	2	0	25	28	19	3	.383	.415
	Atlanta (NL)	MLB	.179	18	39	2	7	2	0	0	4	1	7	0	.200	.231
MAJOR LEAGUE TOTALS			.179	18	39	2	7	2	0	0	4	1	7	0	.200	.231
MINOR LEAGUE TOTALS			.304	391	1370	149	416	72	9	8	141	110	147	11	.355	.387

16 VAN POPE

3B

Born: Feb. 26, 1984. **B-T:** R-R. **Ht.:** 6-0. **Wt.:** 200. **Drafted:** Meridian (Miss.) JC, 2004 (5th round). **Signed by:** Don Thomas.

Selected in the 28th round by the White Sox as a potential draft-and-follow in 2003, Pope was named the top prospect in the Central Illinois Collegiate League that summer. He returned to Meridian (Miss.) JC and starred as a two-way player before turning down Chicago. Though he had a 90-92 mph fastball, it was his power potential and athleticism that led the Braves to take him in 2004's fifth round. Pope has the look of a classic third baseman. He possesses impressive physical skills with above-average strength and power and line-drive carry to all fields. He has an aggressive approach at the plate and has shown a penchant for jumping on fastballs early in the count. Conversely, Pope can be fooled by off-speed pitches and breaking balls, though he has developed a more consistent eye and improved his pitch recognition during his short time in pro ball. He has the potential to hit 20 or more homers per year once he learns which pitches to lift and drive. Pope runs well and is an above-average defender with the agility, range and arm strength to handle third base. With his impressive body control, he's equally adept at making backhand plays deep behind the bag as he is charging slow rollers. Yet another prospect at one of the deepest positions in the system, Pope is on the verge of a breakout in high Class A this year.

Year	Club (League)	Class	AVG	G	AB	R	H	2B	3B	HR	RBI	BB	SO	SB	OBP	SLG
2004	Danville (Appy)	R	.270	60	233	39	63	18	2	5	39	11	44	5	.333	.429
2005	Rome (SAL)	A	.277	100	386	48	107	24	7	6	60	42	70	0	.347	.422
	Myrtle Beach (Car)	A	.167	25	84	7	14	1	0	1	5	9	21	0	.253	.214
MINOR LEAGUE TOTALS			.262	185	703	94	184	43	9	12	104	62	135	5	.331	.400

17 MARTIN PRADO

2B

Born: Oct. 27, 1983. **B-T:** R-R. **Ht.:** 6-1. **Wt.:** 170. **Signed:** Venezuela, 2001. **Signed by:** Rolando Petit/Julian Perez.

Prado emerged as a prospect in 2004 after spending three seasons in Rookie ball. He has moved rapidly ever since, making the jump to Double-A in mid-2005 while continuing to show he might be Atlanta's second baseman of the future. He made the South Atlantic League all-star team in 2004, and managers rated him the Carolina League's best defender at second base last year. The Braves believe Prado has the makings of becoming a quintessential, gritty middle infielder. He's tough, fearless and extremely competitive with good body control and athletic ability. A confident defender, he has above-average range and a strong, accurate arm. Prado also handles the bat well and has average speed, but his power is minimal. He needs to polish his overall game while becoming more patient in order to increase his walks and on-base percentage. He's likely to open this season back in Double-A, with a midseason promotion to Triple-A a possibility.

Year	Club (League)	Class	AVG	G	AB	R	H	2B	3B	HR	RBI	BB	SO	SB	OBP	SLG
2001	Braves 2 (DSL)	R	.299	61	187	25	56	4	2	0	21	25	33	19	.388	.342
2002	Braves 2 (DSL)	R	.320	59	222	35	71	18	3	1	26	17	16	13	.373	.441
2003	Braves (GCL)	R	.286	59	220	28	63	2	6	0	23	24	30	9	.358	.350
2004	Rome (SAL)	A	.315	107	429	68	135	25	6	3	38	30	47	14	.363	.422
2005	Myrtle Beach (Car)	A	.306	75	297	44	91	13	3	4	34	24	48	9	.353	.411
	Mississippi (SL)	AA	.280	39	143	17	40	7	1	1	11	17	17	3	.354	.364
MINOR LEAGUE TOTALS			.304	400	1498	217	456	69	21	9	153	137	191	67	.364	.364

18 JAKE STEVENS
LHP

Born: March 15,1985. **B-T:** L-L. **Ht.:** 6-3. **Wt.:** 210. **Drafted:** HS—Cape Coral, Fla., 2003 (3rd round). **Signed by:** Alex Morrales.

The system's top lefty entering 2005, Stevens endured a difficult season that the Braves believe will benefit him in the long term. The projectable southpaw battled inconsistency and adversity for the first time, forcing him to try to get by on nights when he didn't have his best stuff. Before last year, Stevens had plus command of three pitches, including a solid-average fastball that peaked at 94. He lost his ability to locate his stuff with precision in 2005, and he also dropped 2-3 mph off his fastball. He also throws an overhand curveball that could become a power pitch, along with a developing changeup. Extremely competitive, Stevens continues to learn how to control his emotions on the mound. Experience and added maturity should take care of that. With a projectable body and good athleticism, Stevens has the potential to rebound this year. A return to low Class A is likely, with a mid-season promotion to Double-A a possibility.

Year	Club (League)	Class	W	L	ERA	G	GS	CG	SV	IP	H	R	ER	HR	BB	SO	AVG
2003	Braves (GCL)	R	3	4	2.87	14	6	0	0	47	49	23	15	2	16	47	.262
2004	Rome (SAL)	A	9	5	2.27	27	19	0	2	135	100	41	34	7	39	140	.204
2005	Myrtle Beach (Car)	A	10	9	4.93	28	28	0	0	148	167	90	81	13	62	102	.288
MINOR LEAGUE TOTALS			22	18	3.55	69	53	0	2	330	316	154	130	22	117	289	.251

19 JOSH BURRUS
OF

Born: Aug. 20, 1983. **B-T:** R-R. **Ht.:** 5-11. **Wt.:** 190. **Drafted:** HS—Marietta, Ga., 2001 (1st round). **Signed by:** Rob English.

Three years into Burrus' pro career, he was hitting .225 and struggling to get out of Rookie ball. The Braves' patience with young prospects may have paid off again, as he showed encouraging signs of development in 2004 before breaking through last season in high Class A. Frequently distracted in the past with his status as a former supplemental first-round pick, he displayed a new focus and confidence in 2005. A cousin of former all-star Jeffrey Hammonds, Burrus boasts impressive tools across the board. Rated the fastest baserunner in the Carolina League last year, he has the best hands for hitting among Braves farmhands. He possesses significant pop thanks to his quick wrists, and his all-around athleticism should enable him to make many of the necessary adjustments at the game's highest levels. Drafted as a shortstop before moving to third base and left field, he's still learning how to make better reads and take better routes on fly balls. His arm strength is just average for left field, and his strike-zone judgment may prove to be his final stumbling block. Still, Burrus has made major strides and should open 2006 back in Double-A.

Year	Club (League)	Class	AVG	G	AB	R	H	2B	3B	HR	RBI	BB	SO	SB	OBP	SLG
2001	Braves (GCL)	R	.193	52	197	24	38	8	2	3	19	14	40	10	.271	.299
2002	Danville (Appy)	R	.236	68	263	34	62	13	1	0	23	35	60	16	.338	.293
2003	Rome (SAL)	A	.178	16	45	4	8	2	0	1	2	1	12	2	.245	.289
	Danville (Appy)	R	.254	53	189	25	48	11	1	1	16	15	48	10	.318	.339
2004	Rome (SAL)	A	.272	126	503	82	137	30	3	11	46	33	123	30	.330	.410
2005	Myrtle Beach (Car)	A	.284	76	299	54	85	20	0	11	53	28	75	25	.349	.462
	Mississippi (SL)	AA	.221	46	172	21	38	6	2	5	21	22	53	9	.311	.366
	Richmond (IL)	AAA	.316	5	19	1	6	2	0	0	0	2	5	2	.409	.421
MINOR LEAGUE TOTALS			.250	442	1687	245	422	92	9	32	180	150	416	104	.323	.372

20 MAXIMILIANO RAMIREZ
C

Born: Oct. 11, 1984. **B-T:** R-R. **Ht.:** 6-0. **Wt.:** 165. **Signed:** Venezuela, 2002. **Signed by:** Rolando Petit.

Three seasons after signing as a 17-year-old third baseman out of Venezuela, Ramirez shared Appalachian League co-player-of-the-year honors with teammate Eric Campbell in 2005. Better yet, Ramirez has made a nice transition to catcher, which began the year before. He threw out 38 percent of basestealers though he lacks plus raw arm strength. His footwork improved over the course of the season, but he looked stiff behind the plate much of the time. Even so, the Braves like Ramirez' overall athleticism and how he handled the Danville pitching staff, traits that should lead to him becoming an above-average receiver down the road. Ramirez is more polished at the plate. He has an excellent eye, plus strength and good bat control, all of which enabled him to tie for the Appy League in hits. He'll be the starting catcher this year at Rome, where he'll work with some of the organization's most promising young pitchers.

Year	Club (League)	Class	AVG	G	AB	R	H	2B	3B	HR	RBI	BB	SO	SB	OBP	SLG
2003	Braves 2 (DSL)	R	.305	52	177	27	54	16	1	5	43	20	27	5	.386	.492
2004	Braves (GCL)	R	.275	57	204	20	56	16	1	8	35	19	50	1	.339	.480
2005	Danville (Appy)	R	.347	63	239	45	83	19	0	8	47	31	41	1	.424	.527
MINOR LEAGUE TOTALS			.311	172	620	92	193	51	2	21	125	70	118	7	.386	.502

21 JOSE ASCANIO   RHP

Born: May 2, 1985. **B-T:** R-R. **Ht.:** 6-0. **Wt.:** 150. **Signed:** Venezuela, 2001. **Signed by:** Rolando Petit/Julian Perez.

The Braves had high expectations for Ascanio heading into 2005, but he took the mound just five times before a fracture in his lower back ended his season. The prognosis is that he'll be ready for the 2006 season, though the Braves have concerns because of the severity of the injury. Ascanio has a slight build but possesses an electric arm that produces overpowering fastballs up to 97 mph. His breaking ball and changeup have lagged behind, but he showed signs of developing a better feel for both offerings before being sidelined. Ascanio's command wasn't as consistent last year as in the past, but much of that has been attributed to his back injury. The Braves have been careful with him during his first four pro seasons by limiting his appearances and pitch counts. If he can stay healthy, Ascanio has the potential to be one of the organization's top pitching prospects.

Year	Club (League)	Class	W	L	ERA	G	GS	CG	SV	IP	H	R	ER	HR	BB	SO	AVG
2002	Braves 2 (DSL)	R	1	4	3.38	12	9	0	0	43	38	21	16	1	21	35	.253
2003	Braves (GCL)	R	4	0	1.37	8	0	0	0	26	26	4	4	0	5	17	.271
2004	Rome (SAL)	A	3	3	3.84	34	0	0	9	66	58	39	28	6	15	64	.227
2005	Myrtle Beach (Car)	A	3	1	6.10	5	3	0	0	21	26	17	14	5	9	12	.310
MINOR LEAGUE TOTALS			11	8	3.59	59	12	0	9	155	148	81	62	12	50	128	.253

22 LUIS HERNANDEZ   SS

Born: June 26, 1984. **B-T:** B-R. **Ht.:** 5-10. **Wt.:** 140. **Signed:** Venezuela, 2000. **Signed by:** Rolando Petit/Julian Perez.

At first glance, it would appear that Hernandez had one of the more disappointing seasons among Braves prospects in 2005. After his stock skyrocketed in high Class A the year before, he struggled as one of the youngest players in the Southern League. The increased speed of the game at the Double-A level overwhelmed him early on, and he didn't lift his average above the Mendoza Line for good until the last day of May. He also was tentative with the glove. Nevertheless, Hernandez proved resilient and should be a better player for having cleared the challenges he faced. He showed improved consistency at the plate during the second half while showing a better grasp of the strike zone. He projects as a light-hitting, slick-fielding shortstop whose defense alone could carry him to the big leagues. He utilizes soft, quick hands, a strong arm and the ability to pick it up the middle and deep in the hole. Hernandez will repeat Double-A this season, but he'll still be just 21.

Year	Club (League)	Class	AVG	G	AB	R	H	2B	3B	HR	RBI	BB	SO	SB	OBP	SLG
2001	Braves 2 (DSL)	R	.209	68	253	39	53	8	4	1	18	23	33	24	.287	.285
2002	Braves (GCL)	R	.254	53	201	34	51	8	4	0	20	19	29	11	.330	.333
2003	Rome (SAL)	A	.231	111	337	27	78	4	1	2	25	24	42	7	.287	.267
2004	Myrtle Beach (Car)	A	.271	117	402	49	109	23	4	6	45	16	70	8	.306	.393
2005	Braves (GCL)	R	.250	1	4	1	1	0	0	1	1	0	2	0	.250	1.000
	Mississippi (SL)	AA	.243	122	415	47	101	12	5	2	32	41	56	5	.315	.311
MINOR LEAGUE TOTALS			.244	472	1612	197	393	55	18	12	141	123	232	55	.304	.323

23 BRADY ENDL   LHP

Born: April 14, 1982. **B-T:** R-L. **Ht.:** 6-5. **Wt.:** 235. **Drafted:** Wisconsin-Whitewater, 2004 (10th round). **Signed by:** Stu Cann.

Endl went 10-2, 2.34 and hit .411-18-63 as a senior at NCAA Division III Wisconsin-Whitewater to earn a spot on Baseball America's Small College All-America Team in 2004. The lefthander, who also earned academic all-America honors and is a substitute teacher in the offseason, has risen rapidly as a pro thanks to his knowledge of pitching and ability to use both sides of the plate. He was leading the Carolina League in ERA before undergoing season-ending surgery on his non-throwing shoulder in early August. Endl is expected to be back at full strength in spring training, throwing his 88-92 mph fastball along with his slider, curve and a changeup he just began incorporating into his arsenal last season. He does a good job of moving his pitches around in the strike zone, but needs to gain more consistency with his overall pitch quality and location. The Braves rave about Endl's poise. He's slated for Double-A in 2006.

Year	Club (League)	Class	W	L	ERA	G	GS	CG	SV	IP	H	R	ER	HR	BB	SO	AVG
2004	Danville (Appy)	R	2	3	2.79	16	0	0	1	29	24	10	9	1	9	36	.216
2005	Myrtle Beach (Car)	A	6	7	3.39	20	20	0	0	109	87	55	41	8	61	101	.219
MINOR LEAGUE TOTALS			8	10	3.26	36	20	0	1	138	111	65	50	9	70	137	.219

24 JAMES JURRIES   1B/OF

Born: April 13, 1979. **B-T:** R-R. **Ht.:** 6-0. **Wt.:** 190. **Drafted:** Tulane, 2002 (6th round). **Signed by:** Don Thomas.

For the second straight season Jurries topped the organization in home runs, tying Scott Thorman with 21 after clubbing a career-best 25 in 2004. He got off to a tough start in April when he was suspended for 15 days for violating the minor league ban on performance-enhancing substances. Jurries admitted his mistake, saying he took a foreign substance over the winter while playing in Venezuela. He had a quiet month upon his return, connecting for just one homer in May before drilling 15 over the final three months. In addition to having power, Jurries hits to all fields and has solid plate discipline, though he's prone to swinging and missing. A former third baseman who moved to first base after turning pro, Jurries spent most of the last two months of last season playing right field. He showed an adequate arm and good mobility despite being a below-average runner. The Braves hope his defensive versatility will enable him to make the final step to the big leagues, and they'll let him compete for a job in spring training.

Year	Club (League)	Class	AVG	G	AB	R	H	2B	3B	HR	RBI	BB	SO	SB	OBP	SLG
2002	Danville (Appy)	R	.333	4	15	4	5	1	0	1	4	2	2	0	.412	.600
	Myrtle Beach (Car)	A	.290	48	176	23	51	9	3	5	30	17	26	2	.352	.460
2003	Greenville (SL)	AA	.284	129	465	73	132	35	4	9	54	48	108	4	.354	.434
2004	Greenville (SL)	AA	.306	18	72	15	22	4	0	7	14	5	15	1	.359	.653
	Richmond (IL)	AAA	.267	102	318	46	85	16	0	18	56	32	96	0	.336	.487
2005	Richmond (IL)	AAA	.284	106	363	53	103	23	3	21	72	41	107	1	.357	.537
MINOR LEAGUE TOTALS			.282	407	1409	214	398	88	10	61	230	145	354	8	.352	.489

25 CLINT SAMMONS   C

Born: May 15, 1983. **B-T:** R-R. **Ht.:** 6-0. **Wt.:** 195. **Drafted:** Georgia, 2004 (6th round). **Signed by:** Al Goetz.

With his ability to take charge of a pitching staff, Sammons makes teams better. He was the leader of a Georgia team that surged to a surprising third-place finish at the College World Series in 2004, and the Bulldogs didn't even make the NCAA playoffs despite returning most of their players last year. As a pro, Sammons has guided young pitching staffs to the Appalachian League playoffs (at Danville in 2004) and to the fifth-best overall record in the South Atlantic League (at Rome in 2005). He has excellent awareness on the field. He receives the ball well and possesses above-average throwing mechanics, allowing him to erase 40 percent of basestealers last year. Offensively, he has solid knowledge of the strike zone and displays gap power. His greatest improvement has come in learning how to call a game in the pro ranks as compared to college, especially with the Braves' desire for pitchers to work off their fastballs. Sammons profiles as a valuable reserve backstop and he adds to Atlanta's deep corps of catching prospects. He'll make the jump to high Class A in 2006.

Year	Club (League)	Class	AVG	G	AB	R	H	2B	3B	HR	RBI	BB	SO	SB	OBP	SLG
2004	Danville (Appy)	R	.288	40	132	19	38	7	2	0	17	18	26	5	.368	.371
2005	Rome (SAL)	A	.286	121	427	60	122	29	0	4	62	55	66	4	.368	.382
MINOR LEAGUE TOTALS			.286	161	559	79	160	36	2	4	79	73	92	9	.368	.379

26 JAIRO CUEVAS   RHP

Born: Jan. 24, 1984. **B-T:** R-R. **Ht.:** 6-3. **Wt.:** 210. **Signed:** Dominican Republic, 2003. **Signed by:** Roberto Aquino/Julian Perez.

A converted third baseman, Cuevas was the Appalachian League's 2005 pitcher of the year. He throws three pitches for strikes, including a lively 91-93 mph fastball, a developing curveball and a changeup that has a chance to be a plus pitch. His control is stellar and he coaxes a lot of swings and misses. He has good command of his fastball and can be overpowering when he's in a groove. If his changeup continues to develop, he could move quickly into the higher levels. He also exhibits leadership skills and is fluent in both English and Spanish. Cuevas still has to learn the finer points of setting up hitters and which pitch-es to throw in which situations. Still, he has impressed the Braves with his recent progress and should be part of a formidable Rome rotation in 2006.

Year	Club (League)	Class	W	L	ERA	G	GS	CG	SV	IP	H	R	ER	HR	BB	SO	AVG
2003	Braves 2 (DSL)	R	2	4	3.21	12	4	0	1	28	21	20	10	0	21	27	.210
2004	Braves (GCL)	R	2	3	3.09	9	7	0	1	35	29	13	12	1	7	39	.218
	Danville (Appy)	R	0	0	0.00	1	1	0	0	4	1	0	0	0	4	3	.077
2005	Danville (Appy)	R	6	1	1.95	12	10	0	0	55	35	20	12	3	22	69	.179
MINOR LEAGUE TOTALS			10	8	2.50	34	22	0	2	122	86	53	34	4	54	138	.195

27 JEFF LYMAN   RHP

Born: Jan. 4, 1987. **B-T:** R-R. **Ht.:** 6-3. **Wt.:** 215. **Drafted:** HS—Alamo, Calif., 2005 (2nd round). **Signed by:** Nick Hostetler.

The Braves drafted Lyman in the second round last June and signed him away from Arizona State with a $460,000 bonus. His bulldog mentality eased his transition into pro ball. His main pitches are a fastball that sits at 93-94 mph and a sharp curveball. His two-seam fastball features nice run, and he uses a splitter as a changeup. He has good control but will have to do a better job of locating his pitches at higher level. Some scouts worry about his delivery. Though he throws strikes and creates deception, his mechanics are inconsis-tent. Having ironed out a few flaws during instructional league, Lyman should be part of Rome's rotation this year.

Year	Club (League)	Class	W	L	ERA	G	GS	CG	SV	IP	H	R	ER	HR	BB	SO	AVG
2005	Braves (GCL)	R	0	3	4.24	8	7	0	0	34	41	27	16	2	7	28	.295
MINOR LEAGUE TOTALS			0	3	4.24	8	7	0	0	34	41	27	16	2	7	28	.295

28 J.C. HOLT   2B

Born: Dec. 8, 1982. **B-T:** L-R. **Ht.:** 5-10. **Wt.:** 172. **Drafted:** Louisiana State, 2004 (3rd round). **Signed by:** Don Thomas.

Holt displayed impressive resiliency last season after getting off to a rough start in low Class A. He struggled initially while the Braves worked with him to close the wide-open stance he had used to star at Louisiana State and win the 2003 Cape Cod League batting title with a .388 average. Hitting just .212 in early July, he batted .348 the rest of the way to fin-ish at .268. He needs to tighten his strike zone to take better advantage of his speed. A Louisiana high school sprint champion, he can get down the first-base line in 4.0 seconds from the left side. In addition to his changes at the plate, Holt has had some difficulty with the move from center field to second base, a position he played in college as a freshman. Though he has made strides with the pivot, he needs to get better at reading groundballs off the bat. His footwork also needs an upgrade, but his arm strength and accuracy are suffi-cient. Thanks to his solid second half, he'll advance to high Class A this season.

Year	Club (League)	Class	AVG	G	AB	R	H	2B	3B	HR	RBI	BB	SO	SB	OBP	SLG
2004	Danville (Appy)	R	.321	51	209	38	67	15	0	1	21	18	34	17	.377	.407
2005	Rome (SAL)	A	.268	123	441	60	118	23	3	5	50	37	89	12	.324	.367
MINOR LEAGUE TOTALS			.285	174	650	98	185	38	3	6	71	55	123	29	.341	.380

29 JON MARK OWINGS   OF

Born: April 4, 1985. **B-T:** R-R. **Ht.:** 6-4. **Wt.:** 192. **Drafted:** HS—Gainesville, Ga., 2004 (17th round). **Signed by:** Al Goetz.

Owings was considered a tough sign in 2004 because he was committed to Clemson. But the Braves don't let many players escape from their own backyard, and they took the Gainesville, Ga., product in the 17th round and landed him with top-five-rounds money. His older brother Micah signed with the Diamondbacks as a third-rounder last year. Jon Mark's tools have drawn some comparisons to a poor man's Jeff Francoeur. He has above-average power potential and plays a wide-open, aggressive game that can serve as both a strength and weakness. Like Francoeur, Owings is never going to be among the league lead-ers in walks. Yet what he lacks in patience he makes up for with his ability to put solid wood on the ball. His pitch recognition needs some refinement, as does his strike-zone judgment as he faces better pitchers. Defensively, Owings does a good job of tracking the ball and cov-ers a lot of ground. His arm strength is above-average and the accuracy of his throws is improving. He'll start the 2006 season in low Class A.

Year	Club (League)	Class	AVG	G	AB	R	H	2B	3B	HR	RBI	BB	SO	SB	OBP	SLG
2004	Braves (GCL)	R	.226	44	124	14	28	1	3	3	7	13	38	5	.304	.355
2005	Danville (Appy)	R	.293	33	116	27	34	8	2	12	31	6	31	1	.354	.707
	Rome (SAL)	A	.286	2	7	2	2	1	0	0	1	1	0	0	.375	.429
MINOR LEAGUE TOTALS			.259	79	247	43	64	10	5	15	39	20	69	6	.330	.522

30 JORDAN SCHAFER OF

Born: Sept. 4, 1986. **B-T:** L-L. **Ht.:** 6-1. **Wt.:** 190. **Drafted:** HS—Winter Haven, Fla., 2005 (3rd round). **Signed by:** Gregg Kilby.

Baseball America rated Schafer as the nation's top 13-year-old player in 2000, when he played first base for his high school team as a seventh-grader and also starred during the summer. He was more highly regarded as a pitcher back then, and some clubs still liked him more on the mound when it came to the 2005 draft. The consensus is that he has a brighter future as a position player, and the Braves made him a full-time center fielder after signing him for $320,000 in June. Schafer's tools are at least average across the board. Though he didn't put up gaudy numbers in his pro debut, he has a good approach at the plate. He slumped late in the summer when he became too aggressive. He has average speed, good instincts and a plus arm in the outfield. If everything works out for him, he could become another Mark Kotsay. Schafer will bid for a starting job in low Class A during spring training.

Year	Club (League)	Class	AVG	G	AB	R	H	2B	3B	HR	RBI	BB	SO	SB	OBP	SLG
2005	Braves (GCL)	R	.203	49	182	18	37	12	3	3	19	13	49	13	.256	.352
MINOR LEAGUE TOTALS			.203	49	182	18	37	12	3	3	19	13	49	13	.256	.352

BALTIMORE
ORIOLES

BY **WILL LINGO**

Are the Orioles the team that was 14 games better than .500 on June 21, or the team that collapsed in the second half of the season and finished with four fewer victories than in 2004?

Are they the team that featured promising young pitchers like **Erik Bedard** and Daniel Cabrera and an improving farm system, or  the team that ran has-beens like Rafael Palmeiro and Sammy Sosa onto the field? Are they a step or two from being a legitimate contender, or would they be better off unloading their veterans and building with young players? In short, where are the Orioles going and how do they intend to get there?

The 2005 season, their first with new neighbors the Nationals just down Interstate 95, started with great promise as Baltimore spent 62 straight days in first place in the first half. While that was better than fans should have expected, the rest of the season was much worse. There were injuries, with Brian Roberts' breakout season ending in August with a torn ligament in his elbow. There were veteran busts, and plenty of scandal and dissension. Palmeiro created the biggest distraction, getting suspended for a positive steroid test in August, soon after his 3,000th hit. Sidney Ponson got arrested for the third time in nine months—his second alcohol-related offense—after which the Orioles terminated his contract.

The combination cost manager Lee Mazzilli his job in August. He was replaced by Sam Perlozzo on an interim basis, and Perlozzo eventually got the full-time job. Co-general manager Jim Beattie was forced

out after the season, leaving the job to Mike Flanagan. Flanagan hired former Mets GM Jim Duquette as his new right-hand man.

After the season, as free agents spurned Baltimore's offers, shortstop Miguel Tejada expressed his frustration with the franchise's direction and Baltimore looked into trade possibilities. While trading one of the game's best players might seem like the last thing the Orioles need, it might make sense if they got formidable young talent in return. The first half of 2005 notwithstanding, the team is more than a player or two away from the playoffs. At least its once-barren farm system has improved considerably.

Baltimore has several intriguing pitchers who already have reached the big leagues. The big league lineup has fewer young impact players, but the system should contribute several outfielders over the next couple of years, led by top prospect Nick Markakis. The 2005 draft provided an infusion of talent, with four players from that crop figuring into the top 10. Past Orioles drafts had been damaged by severe budget limitations and/or meddling from owner Peter Angelos, but scouting director Joe Jordan said he had no financial restrictions or interference with his first draft. He even got extra money to sign two late-round picks, righthander David Hernandez (16th round) and outfielder Danny Figueroa (43rd round), who showed promise.

TOP 30 PROSPECTS

1. Nick Markakis, of
2. Adam Loewen, lhp
3. Hayden Penn, rhp
4. Nolan Reimold, of
5. Chris Ray, rhp
6. Garrett Olson, lhp
7. Brandon Snyder, c
8. J.J. Johnson, rhp
9. Brandon Erbe, rhp
10. Val Majewski, of
11. Jeff Fiorentino, of
12. Radhames Liz, rhp
13. Sendy Rleal, rhp
14. Brian Finch, rhp
15. Dave Haehnel, lhp
16. John Maine, rhp
17. Nate Spears, 2b
18. Kieron Pope, of
19. Chris Britton, rhp
20. Ryan Keefer, rhp
21. Walter Young, 1b/dh
22. Aaron Rakers, rhp
23. Brandon Fahey, ss
24. Chorye Spoone, rhp
25. Marino Salas, rhp
26. Paco Figueroa, 2b/of
27. Eli Whiteside, c
28. Arturo Rivas, of
29. Mark Fleisher, 1b
30. Tripper Johnson, 3b

ORGANIZATION OVERVIEW

General manager: Mike Flanagan. **Farm director:** David Stockstill. **Scouting director:** Joe Jordan.

2005 PERFORMANCE

Class	Team	League	W	L	Pct.	Finish*	Manager(s)
Majors	Baltimore	American	74	88	.457	10th (14)	L. Mazzilli/S. Perlozzo
Triple-A	Ottawa Lynx	International	69	75	.479	t-9th (14)	Dave Trembley
Double-A	Bowie Baysox	Eastern	74	68	.521	4th (12)	Don Werner
High A	Frederick Keys	Carolina	79	61	.564	+1st (8)	Bien Figueroa
Low A	Delmarva Shorebirds	South Atlantic	72	67	.518	9th (16)	Gary Kendall
Short-season	Aberdeen IronBirds	New York-Penn	27	48	.360	14th (14)	Andy Etchebarren
Rookie	Bluefield Orioles	Appalachian	31	36	.463	5th (10)	Jesus Alfaro
OVERALL 2005 MINOR LEAGUE RECORD			352	355	.498	16th (30)	

*Finish in overall standings (No. of teams in league). +League champion.

ORGANIZATION LEADERS

BATTING *Minimum 250 at-bats
*AVG	Florence, Branden, Aberdeen/Frederick	.325
R	Castro, Bernie, Ottawa	81
H	Castro, Bernie, Ottawa	158
TB	Delgado, Mario, Frederick	240
2B	Markakis, Nick, Bowie/Frederick	41
3B	Rivas, Arturo, Delmarva	8
HR	Delgado, Mario, Frederick	26
RBI	Fransz, Jason, Delmarva	111
BB	Markakis, Nick, Bowie/Frederick	61
	Rivas, Arturo, Delmarva	61
SO	Bass, Bryan, Frederick	135
SB	Castro, Bernie, Ottawa	41
*OBP	Markakis, Nick, Bowie/Frederick	.390
*SLG	Florence, Branden, Aberdeen/Frederick	.572

PITCHING #Minimum 75 innings
W	Johnson, J.J., Bowie/Frederick	12
L	Four tied at	11
#ERA	Britton, Chris, Frederick	1.38
G	Rakers, Aaron, Ottawa	57
	Rice, Scott, Bowie	57
CG	J.J. Johnson, Bowie/Frederick	2
SV	Haehnel, David, Delmarva/Frederick	18
	Ray, Chris, Bowie	18
IP	Borkowski, Dave, Ottawa	183
BB	Loewen, Adam, Frederick	86
SO	Johnson, J.J., Bowie/Frederick	174

BEST TOOLS

Best Hitter for Average	Nick Markakis
Best Power Hitter	Nolan Reimold
Best Strike-Zone Discipline	Val Majewski
Fastest Baserunner	Jarod Rine
Best Athlete	Nolan Reimold
Best Fastball	Chris Ray
Best Curveball	Garrett Olson
Best Slider	Ryan Keefer
Best Changeup	Sendy Rleal
Best Control	Chris Britton
Best Defensive Catcher	Eli Whiteside
Best Defensive Infielder	Brandon Fahey
Best Infield Arm	Bryan Bass
Best Defensive Outfielder	Nick Markakis
Best Outfield Arm	Arturo Rivas

PROJECTED 2009 LINEUP

Catcher	Ramon Hernandez
First Base	Melvin Mora
Second Base	Brian Roberts
Third Base	Brandon Snyder
Shortstop	Miguel Tejada
Left Field	Val Majewski
Center Field	Nolan Reimold

Right Field	Nick Markakis
Designated Hitter	Jay Gibbons
No. 1 Starter	Adam Loewen
No. 2 Starter	Erik Bedard
No. 3 Starter	Hayden Penn
No. 4 Starter	Daniel Cabrera
No. 5 Starter	Garrett Olson
Closer	Chris Ray

LAST YEAR'S TOP 20 PROSPECTS

1. Nick Markakis, of
2. Hayden Penn, rhp
3. Adam Loewen, lhp
4. Val Majewski, of
5. Jeff Fiorentino, of
6. John Maine, rhp
7. Chris Ray, rhp
8. Tripper Johnson, 3b
9. Eli Whiteside, c
10. Nate Spears, 2b/ss
11. Walter Young, dh/1b
12. Dave Haehnel, lhp
13. Bob McCrory, rhp
14. Jacobo Sequea, rhp
15. Dennis Robinson, rhp
16. Eddy Rodriguez, rhp
17. Fredy Deza, rhp
18. J.J. Johnson, rhp
19. Aaron Rakers, rhp
20. Brian Finch, rhp

TOP PROSPECTS OF THE DECADE

Year	Player, Pos.	2005 Org.
1996	Rocky Coppinger, rhp	Out of baseball
1997	Nerio Rodriguez, rhp	Cardinals
1998	Ryan Minor, 3b	Lancaster (Atlantic)
1999	Matt Riley, lhp	Rangers
2000	Matt Riley, lhp	Rangers
2001	Keith Reed, of	Orioles
2002	Richard Stahl, lhp	Orioles
2003	Erik Bedard, lhp	Orioles
2004	Adam Loewen, lhp	Orioles
2005	Nick Markakis, of	Orioles

TOP DRAFT PICKS OF THE DECADE

Year	Player, Pos.	2005 Org.
1996	Brian Falkenborg, rhp (2nd round)	Cardinals
1997	Jayson Werth, c	Dodgers
1998	Rick Elder, of	Out of baseball
1999	Mike Paradis, rhp	Out of baseball
2000	Beau Hale, rhp	Orioles
2001	Chris Smith, lhp	Orioles
2002	Adam Loewen, lhp	Orioles
2003	Nick Markakis, of	Orioles
2004	*Wade Townsend, rhp	Devil Rays
2005	Brandon Snyder, c	Orioles

*Did not sign.

ALL-TIME LARGEST BONUSES

Adam Loewen, 2002	$3,200,000
Beau Hale, 2000	$2,250,000
Chris Smith, 2001	$2,175,000
Darnell McDonald, 1997	$1,900,000
Nick Markakis, 2003	$1,850,000

MINOR LEAGUE DEPTH CHART

Baltimore Orioles

Rank: 13

STRENGTH: Outfield. Conceivably, the O's entire outfield could be homegrown in 2007, with Nolan Reimold on the horizon.

WEAKNESS: Infielders. Not much offensive punch at any spot, particularly at the hot corner.

*Depth charts prepared by **John Manuel** and **Chris Kline**. Numbers in parentheses indicate prospect rankings.*

LF
Val Majewski (10)
Keiron Pope (18)

CF
Jeff Fiorentino (11)
Arturo Rivas (28)
Danny Figueroa
Bobby Andrews

RF
Nick Markakis (1)
Nolan Reimold (4)
Jake Duncan

3B
Tripper Johnson (30)
Rob Marconi

SS
Brendan Fahey (23)
Stuart Musselwhite

2B
Nate Spears (17)
Paco Figueroa (26)
Jonathan Tucker

1B
Walter Young (21)
Mark Fleisher (29)
Dustin Yount
Paul Chmiel
Jason Fransz
C.J. Smith

C
Brandon Snyder (7)
Eli Whiteside (27)
Ryan Hubele

RHP

Starters	Relievers
Hayden Penn (3)	Chris Ray (5)
J.J. Johnson (8)	Sendy Rleal (13)
Brandon Erbe (9)	Chris Britton (19)
Radhames Liz (12)	Ryan Keefer (20)
Brian Finch (14)	Aaron Rakers (22)
John Maine (16)	Marino Salas (25)
Chorye Spoone (24)	Blake Owen
David Hernandez	James Hoey
Kevin Hart	
Luis Ramirez	
Cory Morris	
Ryan Stadanlick	

LHP

Starters	Relievers
Adam Loewen (2)	Dave Haehnel (15)
Garrett Olson (6)	Richard Salazar
Carlos Perez	Richard Stahl
	Kurt Birkins

DRAFT ANALYSIS

2005

Best Pro Debut: The Orioles' top four picks all enjoyed strong debuts. C Brandon Snyder (1) was the No. 1 prospect in the Rookie-level Appalachian League, where he hit .271-8-35. OF Nolan Reimold (2) earned the same distinction in the short-season New York-Penn League, where he batted .294-9-30. Reimold added six more homers at high Class A Frederick, where he and LHP Garrett Olson (1) helped the Keys win the Carolina League title. Olson went 2-1, 1.99 with 59 strikeouts in 54 innings between the NY-P and CL. RHP Brandon Erbe (3) was the most spectacular, striking out 48 of the 78 batters he faced in the Appy League, where he was the top pitching prospect.

Best Athlete: Reimold may have five plus tools. Snyder, who also was a prep shortstop, is more athletic than most catchers.

Best Pure Hitter: Snyder has a line-drive stroke with an advanced approach and the ability to pull pitches for power.

Best Raw Power: Reimold, who led NCAA Division I with a .770 slugging percentage at Bowling Green State during the spring, has more present power than OF Kieron Pope (4), who already has a big league body. Pope isn't as refined at the plate as Reimold but could catch up to him.

Fastest Runner: OF Danny Figueroa (43) barely played the last two seasons at Miami because of Tommy John and shoulder surgeries, but he's a well-above-average runner.

Best Defensive Player: Figueroa has excellent instincts in center field. 2B Paco Figueroa (9), his twin, is also a savvy, versatile defender.

Best Fastball: Though Erbe, a Baltimore high school product, had a mediocre spring, area scout Dean Albany stayed on him and

Pope

determined he was signable despite a commitment to Miami. Erbe's velocity rose once the weather heated up, and he was throwing 94-98 mph in pro ball. RHP Chorye Spoone (8), another homestate pitcher, was still throwing 94-96 mph in instructional league.

Best Breaking Ball: Olson's out pitch is his 12-to-6 curveball. It breaks away from lefthanders while his 88-92 mph fastball runs in on them.

Most Intriguing Background: With the Figueroas, Baltimore was the only team to take two brothers in the 2005 draft. Snyder's father Brian pitched in the majors.

Closest To The Majors: As a lefty with three pitches, Olson is the prime candidate.

Best Late-Round Pick: Baltimore planned on tracking RHP David Hernandez (16) as a draft-and-follow. But area scout James Keller determined he was signable, so the Orioles came away with a pitcher who shows a 90-93 mph fastball and a plus slider at times. 1B Mark Fleisher (14) is one of the few corner infield prospects in the system with a chance to hit for power.

The One Who Got Away: The Orioles hoped OF Brandon Kendricks (15) would attend a junior college, but they lost his rights when he went to Prairie View A&M.

Assessment: First-year scouting director Joe Jordan made finding athletes a priority and was successful. On the pitching front, Olson and Erbe already are two of Baltimore's top mound prospects.

2004 Negotiations with RHP Wade Townsend (1) were a fiasco, but the Orioles may be better off after Townsend blew out his elbow in 2005. OF Jeff Fiorentino (3) already has played in the majors. **GRADE: D**

2003 Most clubs thought Nick Markakis (1) would star as a pitcher, but he quickly became Baltimore's top prospect as an outfielder. RHP Chris Ray (3) could be the Orioles' closer this year. **GRADE: A**

2002 LHP Adam Loewen (1) continues to make progress, while RHP Hayden Penn (5) rushed to the majors at age 20. OF Val Majewski (3) has had injury problems but remains one of the system's best bats. **GRADE: B**

2001 LHP Chris Smith was a classic first-round bust as the No. 7 overall pick, while 2B Mike Fontenot (1) and 3B Bryan Bass (1) have been little better. RHP J.J. Johnson (5) pitched in the 2005 Futures Game. **GRADE: D**

Draft analysis prepared by Jim Callis. Numbers in parentheses indicate draft rounds.

MARKAKIS

OF

Born: Nov. 17, 1983.
Ht.: 6-1. **Wt.:** 175.
Bats: L. **Throws:** L.
Drafted: Young Harris (Ga.) JC, 2003 (1st round).
Signed by: Dave Jennings.

TOM PRIDDY

The debate regarding Markakis being a hitter or pitcher is officially a footnote to history now, after he put up gaudy offensive numbers in his first complete minor league season. Managers rated him the top hitting and power prospect in the Class A Carolina League in a midseason survey, and he won the home run derby as well as MVP honors in the California-Carolina League all-star game. His numbers improved after a promotion to Double-A Bowie. Markakis was Baseball America's Junior College Player of the Year in both 2002 and 2003, and he turned down the Reds in the draft twice, declining a $1.5 million draft-and-follow offer shortly before the 2003 draft. Most teams preferred him as a lefthander, but the Orioles liked his potential with the bat more and signed him for $1.85 million The debate flared again briefly in 2004 when Markakis pitched as well as hit for the Greek team in the Athens Olympics. But his aptitude as a hitter and rapid development leave no doubt that he'll reach the major leagues as an outfielder, and he should be an all-star once he gets there.

Markakis has adapted to professional baseball faster than even the Orioles expected. He has all the physical tools for success—the ability to hit to all fields with power, and the speed, instincts and arm to play anywhere in the outfield. His aptitude for the game is what makes him a premium prospect. "His intangibles are every bit as good as his ability," one scout said. He has shown the ability to make adjustments to better pitching as he has moved up through the minors, and shows outstanding bat control in the zone. He has established a firm foundation at the plate, where before he would slide through the ball rather than turning on it, and it has allowed him to wait on pitches and read them better. Most scouts think he could play center field in the big leagues, but the Orioles regard him as a prototype right fielder because of his arm and instincts.

Though Markakis' power started to emerge in 2004, it still has a ways to go. At the beginning of his pro career, he tried to yank everything out, but now he's willing to hit the ball the other way. Eventually he should be able to hit those pitches over the fence consistently and should start to pull the ball out again. Markakis is fast enough to steal 20-25 bases a year, but he hasn't worked on it much. If he can improve his baserunning and basestealing, it would add another dimension to a well-rounded game.

In a perfect world, Markakis would get another season to put the finishing touches on his game before he moves up to the big leagues. But there should be plenty of job opportunities in the Baltimore outfield during spring training, so he'll get a long look in big league camp. If he doesn't set the world on fire, he could open at either Double-A or Triple-A Ottawa, with a likely promotion to Baltimore by the second half.

Year	Club (League)	Class	AVG	G	AB	R	H	2B	3B	HR	RBI	BB	SO	SB	OBP	SLG
2003	Aberdeen (NY-P)	A	.283	59	205	22	58	14	3	1	28	30	33	13	.372	.395
2004	Delmarva (SAL)	A	.299	96	355	57	106	22	3	11	64	42	66	12	.371	.470
2005	Frederick (Car)	A	.300	91	350	59	105	25	1	12	62	43	65	2	.379	.480
	Bowie (EL)	AA	.339	33	124	19	42	16	2	3	30	18	30	0	.420	.573
MINOR LEAGUE TOTALS			.301	279	1034	157	311	77	9	27	184	133	194	27	.380	.471

ADAM LOEWEN

LHP

Born: April 9,1984. **B-T:** L-L. **Ht.:** 6-5. **Wt.:** 215. **Drafted:** Chipola (Fla.) JC, D/F 2002 (1st round). **Signed by:** John Gillette/David Jennings.

Loewen's $3.2 million bonus and $4.02 million big league contract were the biggest deals ever given to an amateur by the Orioles. He was ineffective in 2004 and came down with a small tear in his labrum, which he rehabilitated without surgery. He was inconsistent in 2005 but came on strong late in the summer and led the Arizona Fall League with a 1.67 ERA. Loewen has the stuff to pitch at the front of a big league rotation, with a 92-93 mph fastball that touches 94 with life and finish deep in the zone. His curveball is also a plus pitch. He was dominant at times late in the season as his pitches and command came together. Mechanical problems have caused Loewen to struggle with his control, but he made improvements with high Class A Frederick pitching coach Scott McGregor. His changeup is still a step down from his fastball and curveball, and his curve is inconsistent. Loewen got better by working harder and improving his concentration. His contract means he has to stick in the big leagues by 2007, which is realistic if he continues the progress he made late last season. He'll open 2006 in Double-A.

Year	Club (League)	Class	W	L	ERA	G	GS	CG	SV	IP	H	R	ER	HR	BB	SO	AVG
2003	Aberdeen (NY-P)	A	0	2	2.70	7	7	0	0	23	13	7	7	0	9	25	.167
2004	Delmarva (SAL)	A	4	5	4.11	20	19	1	0	85	77	47	39	3	58	82	.250
	Frederick (Car)	A	0	2	6.75	2	2	1	0	8	7	6	6	2	9	3	.259
2005	Frederick (Car)	A	10	8	4.12	28	27	1	0	142	130	77	65	8	86	146	.245
MINOR LEAGUE TOTALS			14	17	4.07	57	55	3	0	259	227	137	117	13	162	256	.241

HAYDEN PENN

RHP

Born: Oct. 13, 1984. **B-T:** R-R. **Ht.:** 6-3. **Wt.:** 195. **Drafted:** HS—Santee, Calif., 2002 (5th round). **Signed by:** Ray Krawczyk.

Penn had made fast progress but wasn't ready for the big leagues when he got an emergency callup at the end of May. Injuries to the Baltimore staff kept him there for almost six weeks. Because of his struggles and mention in midseason trade rumors, he lost focus when he first returned to Double-A, but recaptured his form in August. Three plus pitches that he throws for strikes give Penn a strong foundation, and he complements his stuff with strong aptitude and the attitude that he always can beat the hitter. His fastball sits in the low 90s and touches 96, and his changeup is his second-best pitch. Polishing his curveball filled the missing piece in his repertoire. As big league hitters showed him, Penn needs to improve his fastball command. He tends to leave too much of the ball in the hitting zone. He tried to overthrow when he was in Baltimore. Like Nick Markakis, Penn could use more seasoning but may be the best solution to filling a big league hole. Even if he doesn't break camp with the team, he'll be in Baltimore sometime in 2006.

Year	Club (League)	Class	W	L	ERA	G	GS	CG	SV	IP	H	R	ER	HR	BB	SO	AVG
2003	Orioles (GCL)	R	0	0	2.73	1	1	0	0	3	3	1	1	0	1	4	.273
	Bluefield (Appy)	R	1	4	4.30	12	11	0	0	52	58	27	25	4	19	38	.283
2004	Delmarva (SAL)	A	4	1	3.33	13	6	0	1	43	30	18	16	4	19	41	.201
	Frederick (Car)	A	6	5	3.81	13	13	0	0	73	59	33	31	7	20	61	.224
	Bowie (EL)	AA	3	0	4.88	4	4	0	0	20	22	12	11	0	9	20	.278
2005	Bowie (EL)	AA	7	6	3.83	20	19	1	0	110	101	51	47	11	37	120	.248
	Baltimore (AL)	MLB	3	2	6.34	8	8	0	0	38	46	30	27	6	21	18	.295
MAJOR LEAGUE TOTALS			3	2	6.34	8	8	0	0	38	46	30	27	6	21	18	.295
MINOR LEAGUE TOTALS			21	16	3.89	63	54	1	1	303	273	142	131	26	105	284	.245

NOLAN REIMOLD

OF

Born: Oct. 12, 1983. **B-T:** R-R. **Ht.:** 6-4. **Wt.:** 207. **Drafted:** Bowling Green State, 2005 (2nd round). **Signed by:** Marc Ziegler.

Though he was the Mid-American Conference player of the year and led NCAA Division I with a .770 slugging percentage, Reimold had an up-and-down spring that had scouts split on his value. Orioles scouts saw him early and loved him, and he sealed the deal in a predraft workout at Camden Yards. He rated as the top prospect in the short-season New York-Penn League. Reimold instantly became the Orioles' best power prospect, but he showed a surprisingly well-rounded game. He's an above-average hitter who can drive good fastballs, and he runs well enough to play anywhere in the outfield. His plus arm and offensive profile fit best in right field. Reimold just needs experience. He has huge holes in his strike zone, at times taking too many pitches and other times getting impatient and hacking. He also needs to adjust to offspeed pitches. He fits the prototype for the hitters new scouting director Joe Jordan wants to bring in—athletes with size, speed and a passion for baseball. He'll open the season back in high Class A.

Year	Club (League)	Class	AVG	G	AB	R	H	2B	3B	HR	RBI	BB	SO	SB	OBP	SLG
2005	Aberdeen (NY-P)	A	.294	50	180	33	53	15	2	9	30	29	44	2	.392	.550
	Frederick (Car)	A	.265	23	83	17	22	6	0	6	11	12	27	3	.371	.554
MINOR LEAGUE TOTALS			.285	73	263	50	75	21	2	15	41	41	71	5	.385	.551

5 CHRIS RAY
RHP

MIKE JANES

Born: Jan. 12, 1982. **B-T:** R-R. **Ht.:** 6-3. **Wt.:** 200. **Drafted:** William & Mary, 2003 (3rd round). **Signed by:** Marc Tramuta.

A starter in his first season and a half as a pro, Ray moved to the bullpen in 2005—the role that always seemed to be his destiny—and rocketed to the big leagues. He dominated in Double-A before making his debut in June and holding his own in middle relief. Ray has the stuff and attitude to be a closer. His heavy fastball sits in the mid-90s and touches 96-97 with good movement. He complements it with a hard slider, and he has a plus splitter that he occasionally throws as well. He likes the ball at the end of the game and goes after hitters. Most of Ray's weaknesses were eliminated when he moved to the bullpen and no longer needed a changeup. He needs to refine his command, and he can't throw the splitter more often because it puts too much torque on his elbow. In Double-A at the outset of 2005, Ray could enter spring training as the Orioles' top closer candidate after they declined to match Toronto's huge contract offer to B.J. Ryan. Ray probably will compete with LaTroy Hawkins, with the loser setting up the winner.

Year	Club (League)	Class	W	L	ERA	G	GS	CG	SV	IP	H	R	ER	HR	BB	SO	AVG
2003	Aberdeen (NY-P)	A	2	0	2.82	9	8	0	0	38	32	15	12	0	10	44	.225
2004	Delmarva (SAL)	A	2	3	3.42	10	9	0	0	50	43	21	19	3	17	46	.240
	Frederick (Car)	A	6	3	3.81	14	14	1	0	73	82	31	31	6	20	74	.296
2005	Bowie (EL)	AA	1	2	0.97	31	0	0	18	37	17	5	4	3	7	40	.140
	Baltimore (AL)	MLB	1	3	2.65	41	0	0	0	41	34	15	12	5	18	43	.222
MAJOR LEAGUE TOTALS			1	3	2.65	41	0	0	0	41	34	15	12	5	18	43	.222
MINOR LEAGUE TOTALS			11	8	2.98	64	31	1	18	199	174	72	66	12	54	204	.242

6 GARRETT OLSON
LHP

RODGER WOOD

Born: Oct. 18, 1983. **B-T:** R-L. **Ht.:** 6-1. **Wt.:** 200. **Drafted:** Cal Poly, 2005 (1st round supplemental). **Signed by:** Gil Kubski.

Olson was the top prospect in the Alaska League in 2004, and followed that with a good spring at Cal Poly. He jumped all the way to high Class A in his first summer and emerged as Frederick's best pitcher in the playoffs. Olson showed three good pitches with plus command at Cal Poly, and his stuff was better at Frederick than any of the Orioles scouts had seen in college. He pitched in the low 90s more consistently and also showed a power curveball that runs away from lefthanders. All of his pitches have so much life that it's hard for hitters to square the ball. Olson still needs to refine his changeup. Counting the playoffs, he logged 200 innings between college and pro ball. That workload might raise eyebrows, but Baltimore kept a close eye on his pitch counts, usually limiting him to 50 per outing. He worked so efficiently that he was able to get a lot of innings out of his pitches. The Orioles admit they got a better pitcher than they expected in Olson. He'll probably open 2006 back in high Class A.

Year	Club (League)	Class	W	L	ERA	G	GS	CG	SV	IP	H	R	ER	HR	BB	SO	AVG
2005	Aberdeen (NY-P)	A	2	1	1.58	11	6	0	1	40	22	7	7	1	13	40	.164
	Frederick (Car)	A	0	0	3.15	3	3	0	0	14	10	5	5	0	7	19	.192
MINOR LEAGUE TOTALS			2	1	1.99	14	9	0	1	54	32	12	12	1	20	59	.172

7 BRANDON SNYDER
C

RODGER WOOD

Born: Nov. 23, 1986. **B-T:** R-R. **Ht.:** 6-2. **Wt.:** 205. **Drafted:** HS—Centreville, Va., 2005 (1st round). **Signed by:** Ty Brown.

Snyder is the son of former big league pitcher Brian and a baseball rat who has played with strong competition most of his life, including the standout Midland Redskins summer team. He was the 13th overall pick in June, signed for $1.7 million and finished the summer rated as the top prospect in the Rookie-level Appalachian League. Snyder is a polished offensive player who uses the whole field and already shows power. He has an efficient swing and takes the barrel straight to the ball with a consistent approach. He's not afraid to take pitches and work counts. While he has the tools to be a good defensive catcher, Snyder hasn't played there much. He played all over the field in high school before settling behind the plate late in his senior season. He has a plus arm but will need time learning the nuances of the position. Short-season Aberdeen manager Andy Etchebarren, a longtime big league catcher, jump-started Snyder's progress at the position. His bat should play even if he has to move to third. He'll open the season at low Class A Delmarva.

Year	Club (League)	Class	AVG	G	AB	R	H	2B	3B	HR	RBI	BB	SO	SB	OBP	SLG
2005	Bluefield (Appy)	R	.271	44	144	26	39	8	0	8	35	28	36	7	.380	.493
	Aberdeen (NY-P)	A	.393	8	28	4	11	2	0	0	6	2	7	0	.419	.464
MINOR LEAGUE TOTALS			.291	52	172	30	50	10	0	8	41	30	43	7	.386	.488

8 J.J. JOHNSON
RHP

RICH ABEL

Born: June 27, 1983. **B-T:** R-R. **Ht.:** 6-5. **Wt.:** 232. **Drafted:** HS—Endicott, N.Y., 2001 (5th round). **Signed by:** Jim Howard.

The Orioles were very patient with Johnson, not exposing him to full-season ball until his fourth pro season and even then holding him back in extended spring as he recovered from mononucleosis. He broke out in 2005, winning Carolina League pitcher-of-the-year honors, leading the league in strikeouts and pitching in the Futures Game. While Johnson doesn't have one dominant pitch, he has three solid pitches with good command and a body that should allow him to be a workhorse. His fastball ranges from 90-93 mph, and his curveball is also a plus pitch. His changeup is a good third pitch. He's not afraid to work inside and led the CL with 19 hit batters. Because he can't overpower them with his stuff, Johnson needs to refine his command as he faces more advanced hitters. He also is learning to use his curveball and changeup more often. While Johnson has just burst onto the prospect scene, he should move more quickly from here. He'll open the season in Double-A and could be in the big leagues by 2007.

Year	Club (League)	Class	W	L	ERA	G	GS	CG	SV	IP	H	R	ER	HR	BB	SO	AVG
2001	Orioles (GCL)	R	0	1	3.85	7	4	0	0	19	17	10	8	3	7	19	.239
2002	Bluefield (Appy)	R	4	2	4.36	11	9	0	0	56	52	36	27	5	16	36	.250
2003	Bluefield (Appy)	R	3	2	3.68	11	11	0	0	51	62	24	21	2	18	46	.291
2004	Delmarva (SAL)	A	8	7	3.29	20	17	0	0	107	97	44	39	9	30	93	.246
2005	Bowie (EL)	AA	0	0	0.00	1	1	0	0	7	3	0	0	0	2	6	.136
	Frederick (Car)	A	12	9	3.49	28	27	2	1	160	139	77	62	11	64	168	.231
MINOR LEAGUE TOTALS			27	21	3.54	78	69	2	1	399	370	191	157	30	137	368	.245

9 BRANDON ERBE
RHP

MIKE JANES

Born: Dec. 25, 1987. **B-T:** R-R. **Ht.:** 6-4. **Wt.:** 180. **Drafted:** HS—Baltimore, 2005 (3rd round). **Signed by:** Ty Brown.

Because of his commitment to Miami and an inconsistent senior season, most teams weren't sure where to draft Erbe. The Orioles had a good feel for him because he played for a summer travel team coached by area scout Dean Albany, so they took him in the third round and signed him for $415,000. He emerged as the best pitching prospect in the Appalachian League. After seeing Erbe pitch last summer, the Orioles feel like he might have the best pure stuff in the 2005 high school draft class. He threw his fastball from 94-98 mph most of the summer, and the ball explodes out of his hand. He has the long, lanky pitcher's body that scouts love, and a funky delivery that makes him deceptive to hitters. Erbe's secondary pitches need work. His breaking ball is above-average at times and is usually in the zone, but it's inconsistent. He shows a feel for a changeup but never has had to use it much. Erbe has an incredible amount of ability, and the next couple of seasons will show his ability to harness it. He'll open the season in low Class A and will play all of 2006 at age 18.

Year	Club (League)	Class	W	L	ERA	G	GS	CG	SV	IP	H	R	ER	HR	BB	SO	AVG
2005	Bluefield (Appy)	R	1	1	3.09	11	3	0	1	23	8	10	8	1	10	48	.103
	Aberdeen (NY-P)	A	1	1	7.71	3	1	0	0	7	6	6	6	0	4	9	.261
MINOR LEAGUE TOTALS			2	2	4.15	14	4	0	1	30	14	16	14	1	14	57	.139

10 VAL MAJEWSKI

OF

Born: June 19, 1981. **B-T:** L-L. **Ht.:** 6-2. **Wt.:** 200. **Drafted:** Rutgers, 2002 (3rd round). **Signed by:** Jim Howard.

In a season with plenty of big league opportunity, Majewski couldn't take advantage because a labrum tear in his throwing shoulder kept him out all season. He had surgery in spring training after rest and rehab didn't work, and he didn't return until instructional league. He went to the Arizona Fall League and headed to the Dominican League to continue to make up at-bats. Majewski is a professional hitter who makes hard, consistent contact when he's healthy. He has a strong approach at the plate and should hit for power and average. His makeup is off the charts, so there was no doubt he would work hard to rehabilitate his injury. The shoulder injury is Majewski's only remaining question mark. His swing looked slow early in the fall but came around by the end of the AFL season. Previously seen as an ideal right fielder, he could move to left if he doesn't recover his arm strength. Majewski worked hard this offseason to make up for lost time, and he'll start 2006 in Triple-A to get more at-bats and get his arm back in shape. If he's healthy, he could be called up quickly.

Year	Club (League)	Class	AVG	G	AB	R	H	2B	3B	HR	RBI	BB	SO	SB	OBP	SLG
2002	Aberdeen (NY-P)	A	.300	31	110	22	33	7	4	1	15	13	14	8	.376	.464
	Delmarva (SAL)	A	.118	7	17	2	2	0	0	1	3	1	1	0	.158	.294
2003	Delmarva (SAL)	A	.303	56	208	38	63	15	8	7	48	28	20	10	.383	.553
	Orioles (GCL)	R	.333	1	3	0	1	0	0	0	0	0	0	0	.500	.333
	Aberdeen (NY-P)	A	.375	4	16	2	6	2	2	0	3	1	2	1	.412	.750
	Frederick (Car)	A	.289	41	159	15	46	18	1	5	20	7	23	0	.321	.509
2004	Bowie (EL)	AA	.307	112	433	71	133	24	5	15	80	33	68	14	.359	.490
	Baltimore (AL)	MLB	.154	9	13	3	2	1	0	0	1	0	1	0	.154	.231
2005	Did not play—Injured															
MAJOR LEAGUE TOTALS			.154	9	13	3	2	1	0	0	1	0	1	0	.154	.231
MINOR LEAGUE TOTALS			.300	252	946	150	284	66	20	29	169	84	128	33	.358	.504

11 JEFF FIORENTINO

OF

Born: April 14, 1983. **B-T:** L-R. **Ht.:** 6-1. **Wt.:** 185. **Drafted:** Florida Atlantic, 2004 (3rd round). **Signed by:** Nick Presto.

Fiorentino's promising pro debut in 2004 had Orioles officials expecting him to move quickly, but not this quickly. He jumped from Class A to the big leagues in May when injuries hit in Baltimore, as the club looked for someone who could play defense and hold his own at the plate. Fiorentino, not surprisingly, quickly showed he wasn't ready to hold his own against big league pitching, and he remained in a funk even after getting sent back to Frederick. He finally came around in August, batting .347-12-33 for the month. Fiorentino has a stiff setup at the plate, but he uses his quick hands to get the bat through the hitting zone. He's athletic enough to play anywhere in the outfield, and some in the organization think he'd profile best as a center fielder. Former scouting director Tony DeMacio and his staff drafted Fiorentino with the idea of giving him a chance at catcher, where he played some in college, but he hasn't gone behind the plate as a pro. It's not clear he'll have enough power for an outfield corner, though there are some club officials who say he has the potential to have more power than Nick Markakis or Val Majewski. Fiorentino must cut down on his strikeouts, and he also needs more repetitions in the outfield to refine his routes. Fiorentino's overall package of solid tools is good enough to reach the majors, but he'll need to develop his power or prove he can play center field to be a starter.

Year	Club (League)	Class	AVG	G	AB	R	H	2B	3B	HR	RBI	BB	SO	SB	OBP	SLG
2004	Aberdeen (NY-P)	A	.348	14	46	9	16	7	1	2	12	9	4	3	.474	.674
	Delmarva (SAL)	A	.302	49	179	40	54	15	2	10	36	20	50	2	.379	.575
2005	Baltimore (AL)	MLB	.250	13	44	7	11	2	0	1	5	2	10	1	.277	.364
	Frederick (Car)	A	.286	103	413	70	118	18	4	22	66	34	90	12	.346	.508
MAJOR LEAGUE TOTALS			.250	13	44	7	11	2	0	1	5	2	10	1	.283	.364
MINOR LEAGUE TOTALS			.295	166	638	119	188	40	7	34	114	63	144	17	.366	.539

12 RADHAMES LIZ

RHP

Born: Oct. 6, 1983. **B-T:** R-R. **Ht.:** 6-2. **Wt.:** 170. **Signed:** Dominican Republic, 2003. **Signed by:** Carlos Bernhardt.

Liz made a strong impression in his first season in the United States. He was the story of Orioles' extended spring training camp, dominating hitters with an electric fastball that usually ranges from 94-96 mph and touches 98. Baltimore instructors tried to get him to work on his curveball and changeup, but Liz was reluctant to because no one could touch his heat. So the organization sent him to low Class A, where he got knocked around a bit. Demoted to Aberdeen when the New York-Penn League season opened in June, he earned his way back to Delmarva in August. He would have finished second in the NY-P in ERA if he had enough innings to qualify and ranked fourth in strikeouts despite making just 10 starts, including a 15-whiff outing. Liz has long arms and gets a good downward plane on the ball, and his big hands make it harder for hitters to pick up the ball. His motion reminds some of Hall of Famer Bob Gibson's with the way he falls off toward first base, right foot crossing over his left. The Orioles are trying to make his delivery more fluid so he doesn't put too much stress on his arm. He learned a lot about pitching during his first stint in Delmarva, getting behind in the count and looking overwhelmed at times. His curveball and changeup made progress, though they still need work, as does his command. The Orioles say Liz has the size, strength and athletic ability to be a big league starter, but he could relieve if his secondary pitches don't develop. He'll probably go back to low Class A to open the season.

Year	Club (League)	Class	W	L	ERA	G	GS	CG	SV	IP	H	R	ER	HR	BB	SO	AVG
2003	Orioles (DSL)	R	2	2	3.18	9	7	1	0	45	40	16	16	1	12	43	.233
2004	Orioles (DSL)	R	8	4	2.62	15	14	2	0	82	53	32	24	2	28	109	.177
2005	Aberdeen (NY-P)	A	5	4	1.77	11	11	0	0	56	36	14	11	1	19	82	.188
	Delmarva (SAL)	A	2	3	4.46	10	10	0	0	38	33	23	19	2	23	55	.231
MINOR LEAGUE TOTALS			17	13	2.84	45	42	3	0	222	162	85	70	6	82	289	.201

13 SENDY RLEAL — RHP

Born: June 21, 1980. **B-T:** R-R. **Ht.:** 6-1. **Wt.:** 165. **Signed:** Dominican Republic, 1999. **Signed by:** Carlos Bernhardt.

Rleal has moved exceedingly slow through the system, thanks to his slight frame and nagging injuries earlier in his career. He had a breakthrough season in Double-A last year, however, establishing himself as one of the best relief prospects in the organization and getting added to the 40-man roster. He began the season setting up Chris Ray, and he didn't miss a beat after taking over Bowie's closer role when Ray jumped to Baltimore. He shows three plus pitches at times, and his changeup is the best in the organization. It's his out pitch against lefthanders. His fastball sits at 93-95 mph and touches 96-97, with good movement and sink. He also throws a hard, late-breaking slider as an occasional third pitch. Rleal has good control and should be in line for a big league job soon. He'll compete for a spot in the Baltimore bullpen in spring training but is expected to open the season in Triple-A. It shouldn't be long before he's setting up Ray again, however.

Year	Club (League)	Class	W	L	ERA	G	GS	CG	SV	IP	H	R	ER	HR	BB	SO	AVG
1999	Baltimore (DSL)	R	4	3	3.47	9	9	0	0	47	43	24	18	3	20	43	.243
2000	Bluefield (Appy)	R	6	2	3.39	13	12	0	0	61	61	26	23	5	25	55	.268
	Delmarva (SAL)	A	0	1	10.91	1	1	0	0	3	3	5	4	0	3	4	.214
2001	Delmarva (SAL)	A	3	6	3.57	20	20	1	0	103	79	50	41	9	27	83	.207
2002	Delmarva (SAL)	A	1	0	6.10	28	1	0	1	41	53	28	28	4	15	34	.317
2003	Frederick (Car)	A	3	5	3.16	44	0	0	11	57	35	20	20	8	23	59	.177
2004	Bowie (EL)	AA	4	0	2.66	39	0	0	3	47	41	16	14	7	12	60	.227
2005	Bowie (EL)	AA	4	4	2.04	56	0	0	16	71	46	19	16	4	18	75	.187
MINOR LEAGUE TOTALS			25	21	3.43	210	43	1	31	431	361	188	164	40	143	413	.227

14 BRIAN FINCH — RHP

Born: Sept. 27, 1981. **B-T:** R-R. **Ht.:** 6-4. **Wt.:** 195. **Drafted:** Texas A&M, 2003 (2nd round). **Signed by:** Joe Almaraz.

Finch was one of the more notable failures of the psychological testing favored by former director of baseball-information system Dave Ritterpusch, who was fired after the 2005 season along with his assistant, Ed Coblentz. Ritterpusch was a huge proponent of psychological profiles, and based on Finch's, the Orioles decided he could handle a jump to Double-A in 2004, 11 months after he signed. Finch got pounded and couldn't recover, even after taking a step back to high Class A. He had to go back to Frederick again in 2005 to get himself straightened out. He did just that, earning Carolina League pitcher-of-the-week honors early in the season and then MVP honors in the league championship series. He wasn't overpowering but gutted out a win in a decisive Game Five against Kinston with five shutout innings. He showed better poise and command all season and looked much more like the pitcher who was a second-round pick in 2003. Finch has the arsenal of a middle-of-the-rotation big league starter, with a 90-93 mph fastball, a good slider and an improving changeup. He must keep his fastball down to be successful, and he's still inconsistent with his slider. He also hasn't found a changeup grip he's completely comfortable with, so there's still work to do. His control also can improve. The Orioles did him a huge favor by keeping him in one place all season and allowing him to have success. He should move into the Double-A rotation this year and could pitch in the big leagues in 2007 if he continues making progress.

Year	Club (League)	Class	W	L	ERA	G	GS	CG	SV	IP	H	R	ER	HR	BB	SO	AVG
2003	Aberdeen (NY-P)	A	1	3	1.93	8	5	0	0	28	19	9	6	0	5	29	.183
2004	Delmarva (SAL)	A	2	2	1.44	5	5	0	0	25	23	11	4	0	2	14	.228
	Bowie (EL)	AA	2	6	8.68	11	10	0	0	48	73	46	46	5	16	32	.354
	Frederick (Car)	A	1	4	7.96	9	9	0	0	37	59	35	33	5	15	22	.364
2005	Frederick (Car)	A	10	10	3.38	27	27	1	0	154	157	72	58	13	60	124	.265
MINOR LEAGUE TOTALS			16	25	4.53	60	56	1	0	292	331	173	147	23	98	221	.284

15 DAVE HAEHNEL   LHP

Born: July 21, 1982. **B-T:** L-L. **Ht.:** 6-4. **Wt.:** 185. **Drafted:** Illinois-Chicago, 2004 (8th round).
Signed by: Troy Hoerner.

Teams always have been tempted to use Haehnel as a starter, but he always has been successful as a reliever so he usually has pitched out of the bullpen. He was the top prospect in the Jayhawk League in 2003, the summer before his draft year, when Illinois-Chicago actually did use him in the rotation and he finished third in the Horizon League in ERA. Baltimore never has put Haehnel in a rotation. He opened 2005 as the closer in low Class A, then became a setup man after a midseason promotion to high Class A. That's the role he seems best suited for. The velocity on his fastball is average or even a tick below, sitting in the high 80s and occasionally touching the low 90s, but Haehnel gets good sink on it. He also has a deceptive delivery that throws hitters off, and his makeup adds to the package. He trusts his stuff and goes right after hitters. His secondary stuff still needs work, however. He throws a slider and changeup but hasn't used them enough to make them effective against more advanced hitters, so the Orioles are considering using him in long relief or possibly as a starter this year so he can get more innings to improve those pitches. He'll probably open the season back in high Class A, with another midseason promotion in the offing if he performs well.

Year	Club (League)	Class	W	L	ERA	G	GS	CG	SV	IP	H	R	ER	HR	BB	SO	AVG
2004	Aberdeen (NY-P)	A	3	1	1.69	28	0	0	16	37	23	8	7	1	11	61	.170
2005	Delmarva (SAL)	A	1	1	0.79	28	0	0	16	34	20	3	3	1	10	34	.171
	Frederick (Car)	A	3	1	3.41	23	0	0	2	34	27	15	13	1	10	37	.218
MINOR LEAGUE TOTALS			7	3	1.96	79	0	0	34	106	70	26	23	3	31	132	.186

16 JOHN MAINE   RHP

Born: May 8, 1981. **B-T:** R-R. **Ht.:** 6-4. **Wt.:** 190. **Drafted:** UNC Charlotte, 2002 (6th round).
Signed by: Marc Tramuta.

Maine moved quickly through the organization in his first couple of years after being drafted, but he has stalled in his effort to break through from Triple-A to Baltimore. He made his big league debut in July 2004 and made it back last August, winning his first start with five shutout innings against Toronto and spending the rest of the season with the Orioles. Maine succeeds with plus fastball command, throwing at 90-91 mph with natural deception. He also uses a slider and changeup, occasionally mixing in a curveball as well. None of the pitches overmatches hitters, so Maine has to rely on location. He starts to struggle when he tries to get too fine with his pitches and catches too much of the plate. He also had trouble getting big league hitters to respect his complementary pitches. The Orioles tried to add veterans to their rotation in the offseason but had little success, so Maine will be in the big league mix during spring training. If he doesn't win a job in the rotation, he could pitch in long relief or go back to the Triple-A rotation.

Year	Club (League)	Class	W	L	ERA	G	GS	CG	SV	IP	H	R	ER	HR	BB	SO	AVG
2002	Aberdeen (NY-P)	A	1	1	1.75	4	2	0	0	10	6	2	2	0	3	21	.154
	Delmarva (SAL)	A	1	1	1.36	6	5	0	0	33	21	8	5	0	4	39	.178
2003	Delmarva (SAL)	A	7	3	1.53	14	14	1	0	76	43	16	13	1	18	108	.165
	Frederick (Car)	A	6	1	3.07	12	12	1	0	70	48	27	24	5	20	77	.190
2004	Bowie (EL)	AA	4	0	2.25	5	5	0	0	28	16	8	7	1	7	34	.160
	Baltimore (AL)	MLB	0	1	9.73	1	1	0	0	4	7	4	4	1	3	1	.438
	Ottawa (IL)	AAA	5	7	3.91	22	22	0	0	120	123	59	52	12	52	105	.281
2005	Ottawa (IL)	AAA	6	11	4.56	23	23	1	0	128	128	72	65	13	42	111	.257
	Baltimore (AL)	MLB	2	3	6.30	10	8	0	0	40	39	30	28	8	24	24	.248
MAJOR LEAGUE TOTALS			2	4	6.30	11	9	0	0	44	46	34	32	9	27	25	.266
MINOR LEAGUE TOTALS			30	24	3.24	86	83	3	0	466	385	192	168	32	146	495	.226

17 NATE SPEARS
2B

Born: May 3, 1985. **B-T:** L-R. **Ht.:** 5-11. **Wt.:** 165. **Drafted:** HS—Port Charlotte, Fla., 2003 (5th round). **Signed by:** Nick Presto.

With a solid season in high Class A, Spears continued to make steady progress through the system. He batted first or second for Frederick all season as the Keys won their first Carolina League title since 1990. He has no outstanding tool but is a complete baseball player, a slap hitter who moves runners over and does the little things to make a team better. He centers the ball on the bat well but isn't expected to produce much power. Spears has good speed and baserunning instincts, plus he's an average defender. He played most of the season at second base but can fill in at shortstop. There aren't a lot of glaring weaknesses to Spears' game, but at age 20 he already is what he is. He strikes out too much and doesn't walk enough to be a leadoff man, and unless he can add some power he'll probably end up as a utility player. He'll take the next step to Double-A in 2006.

Year	Club (League)	Class	AVG	G	AB	R	H	2B	3B	HR	RBI	BB	SO	SB	OBP	SLG
2003	Orioles (GCL)	R	.289	56	180	38	52	7	5	1	19	40	32	18	.427	.400
2004	Delmarva (SAL)	A	.275	97	371	50	102	12	11	5	37	47	63	7	.358	.407
2005	Frederick (Car)	A	.294	112	445	63	131	30	6	6	41	36	82	8	.349	.429
MINOR LEAGUE TOTALS			.286	265	996	151	285	49	22	12	97	123	177	33	.368	.416

18 KIERON POPE
OF

Born: Oct. 3, 1986. **B-T:** R-R. **Ht.:** 6-1. **Wt.:** 195. **Drafted:** HS—Gay, Ga., 2005 (4th round). **Signed by:** Dave Jennings.

The 2005 draft could go a long way toward boosting a Baltimore system that's already making progress. Pope is the least polished of any of the team's 2005 picks on this list, but if he reaches his ceiling, he could be one of the best. A fourth-rounder signed for $257,500 he has the body of a major leaguer right now, plus great makeup that means he'll work hard to refine his game. He's athletic, with a potent speed/power combination and the chance to have true top-of-the-scale power. He profiles as a corner outfielder, with an arm better suited to left field, and just needs at-bats. He got tired and lost his swing at Rookie-level Bluefield, and he didn't know enough yet about his approach to stop the bleeding. He has good hands, but he swings and misses too much and will need time to develop better baseball instincts. The Orioles say they'll have a better read on his true potential after a season or two of minor league at-bats. Pope likely will stay in extended spring training before joining Aberdeen or Bluefield in June.

Year	Club (League)	Class	AVG	G	AB	R	H	2B	3B	HR	RBI	BB	SO	SB	OBP	SLG
2005	Bluefield (Appy)	R	.228	41	149	23	34	3	1	5	22	8	62	5	.297	.362
MINOR LEAGUE TOTALS			.228	41	149	23	34	3	1	5	22	8	62	5	.297	.362

19 CHRIS BRITTON
RHP

Born: Dec. 16, 1982. **B-T:** R-R. **Ht.:** 6-3. **Wt.:** 250. **Drafted:** HS—Plantation, Fla., 2001 (8th round). **Signed by:** Nick Presto.

Britton made as big a leap as anyone in the system in 2005, coming back from two major injuries to establish himself as a strong bullpen prospect. His career first went off track at the end of 2002, when a comebacker hit him in the face. He had surgery and a metal plate was put in to stabilize the area. Then he had bone chips removed from his elbow in 2003 and missed the entire season. He spent much of 2004 in extended spring as he continued to recover from his injuries, and the Orioles put him in long relief in high Class A to open 2005 so he could work back into shape. Britton took to the role, though, and had a dominant season. He finished 10th in the Carolina League in strikeouts even though he never started a game. He doesn't have dominant stuff but goes after hitters with strike after strike. He has a 90-93 mph fastball and a tight curveball, and he's working on a changeup after getting through last season essentially with two pitches. Baltimore doesn't want to mess with success and plans to keep him in a bullpen role, so the only thing Britton really needs to work on is conditioning. He has a body that can get big if he isn't vigilant. He pitched in Venezuela over the winter after getting added to the 40-man roster, and could move quickly after opening the season in Double-A.

Year	Club (League)	Class	W	L	ERA	G	GS	CG	SV	IP	H	R	ER	HR	BB	SO	AVG
2001	Orioles (GCL)	R	2	3	2.75	12	3	0	0	33	35	20	10	3	12	20	.265
2002	Bluefield (Appy)	R	3	0	4.54	9	8	0	0	36	30	21	18	5	10	27	.227
2003	Did not play—Injured																
2004	Delmarva (SAL)	A	9	4	3.75	27	8	1	1	84	76	38	35	11	31	80	.239
2005	Frederick (Car)	A	6	0	1.60	46	0	0	6	79	47	15	14	5	23	110	.172
MINOR LEAGUE TOTALS			20	7	3.00	94	19	1	7	231	188	94	77	24	76	237	.220

20 RYAN KEEFER

RHP

Born: Aug. 10, 1981. **B-T:** L-R. **Ht.:** 6-3. **Wt.:** 202. **Drafted:** HS—Catawissa, Pa., 2000 (13th round). **Signed by:** Jim Howard.

Keefer looks like the prototype for a big league pitcher but didn't perform like one until 2005. He struggled to find his niche, working as a closer in 2001 and struggling as a starter in 2002-03. He moved into a middle-relief role in 2004 and looked better, then took a huge step forward last year because his stuff was much improved. His fastball went from the high 80s to the low 90s, occasionally touching 95 mph. His slider also got better, as he added depth to it. He showed good control and was effective against both lefthanders and righthanders. Keefer has a tremendous work ethic and always has strived to get better, even when his future didn't look very bright. He went to Venezuela to get in more innings this winter and was shut down early so he'd be fresh for spring training. Keefer no longer is flying under the organization's radar and will compete for a big league bullpen job in spring training. He'll head to Triple-A if he doesn't make the Orioles.

Year	Club (League)	Class	W	L	ERA	G	GS	CG	SV	IP	H	R	ER	HR	BB	SO	AVG
2000	Orioles (GCL)	R	1	2	4.44	13	1	0	0	22	26	13	11	0	6	21	.283
2001	Bluefield (Appy)	R	1	0	0.59	29	0	0	15	31	20	4	2	1	8	46	.179
2002	Aberdeen (NY-P)	A	3	7	3.91	13	13	0	0	69	77	38	30	4	18	64	.280
	Delmarva (SAL)	A	2	3	3.43	22	1	0	6	37	36	15	14	3	11	29	.257
2003	Delmarva (SAL)	A	7	12	4.36	26	26	1	0	149	162	88	72	11	34	94	.277
2004	Frederick (Car)	A	4	4	3.09	63	0	0	4	87	89	32	30	10	26	73	.255
2005	Bowie (EL)	AA	7	3	3.20	54	1	0	1	84	64	33	30	7	32	92	.211
MINOR LEAGUE TOTALS			25	31	3.55	220	42	1	26	479	474	223	189	36	135	419	.256

21 WALTER YOUNG

1B/DH

Born: Feb. 18, 1980. **B-T:** L-R. **Ht.:** 6-5. **Wt.:** 298. **Drafted:** HS—Purvis, Miss., 1999 (31st round). **Signed by:** Russell Bowen (Pirates).

Acquired off waivers from the Pirates in November 2003, Young is one of the most intriguing players in the minors, if only because of his amazing size. His listed weight is always just an estimate, and fluctuates depending on how serious he's about conditioning. He let himself go a little bit in 2005 and hit just 13 home runs in Triple-A. And while he made his major league debut, he didn't show enough to get a long look in Baltimore despite plenty of job openings. Young went to Venezuela for the winter to get himself in better shape and hone his swing, which produces top-end power when he's in a groove. For his size, he's a good athlete who moves well around the first-base bag. He cut down on his strikeouts last year, but his production slipped as well. His size always will be an issue and probably limits him to part-time duty at first, so he'll have to hit enough to prove he can be a DH. Last year was his first Triple-A experience and he has an option remaining, so the Orioles will send him back to Ottawa to get more at-bats before giving him another big league opportunity.

Year	Club (League)	Class	AVG	G	AB	R	H	2B	3B	HR	RBI	BB	SO	SB	OBP	SLG
1999	Pirates (GCL)	R	.231	37	130	9	30	6	2	0	15	4	34	2	.270	.308
2000	Pirates (GCL)	R	.296	45	162	32	48	11	1	10	34	8	29	3	.357	.562
	Williamsport (NY-P)	A	.185	24	92	5	17	4	0	2	12	1	26	0	.200	.293
2001	Williamsport (NY-P)	A	.289	66	232	40	67	10	1	13	47	19	43	1	.353	.509
2002	Hickory (SAL)	A	.333	132	492	84	164	34	2	25	103	36	102	2	.390	.563
2003	Lynchburg (Car)	A	.278	117	431	76	120	15	2	20	87	35	88	2	.348	.462
2004	Bowie (EL)	AA	.274	133	486	88	133	28	1	33	98	47	145	2	.343	.539
2005	Ottawa (IL)	AAA	.288	123	466	48	134	29	1	13	81	30	91	1	.334	.438
	Baltimore (AL)	MLB	.303	14	33	2	10	1	0	1	3	4	7	0	.378	.424
MAJOR LEAGUE TOTALS			.303	14	33	2	10	1	0	1	3	4	7	0	.378	.424
MINOR LEAGUE TOTALS			.286	677	2491	382	713	137	10	116	477	180	558	13	.345	.489

22 AARON RAKERS

RHP

Born: Jan. 22, 1977. **B-T:** R-R. **Ht.:** 6-3. **Wt.:** 205. **Drafted:** Southern Illinois-Edwardsville, 1999 (23rd round). **Signed by:** Earl Winn.

Rakers may run for mayor of Ottawa at this rate. After spending about half the 2003 season there, he pitched effectively and led the Lynx in appearances in 2004 and made his big league debut that September. He returned to Ottawa last year and again led the team in appearances. He's the third Southern Illinois-Edwardsville player to reach the majors, joining Champ Summers and Dennis Werth. Rakers has an average fastball, sitting at 90 mph and occasionally touching 92, and uses a splitter as his out pitch. He has good command and is effective as long as he keeps the ball down. He'll open the season at 29, so there's no reason for him to continue taking up a spot on the 40-man if he's not in the majors. The Orioles gave him a 14-inning look in 2005, and with nothing left to prove in the minors,

Rakers should break camp with the big league club this spring.

Year	Club (League)	Class	W	L	ERA	G	GS	CG	SV	IP	H	R	ER	HR	BB	SO	AVG
1999	Bluefield (Appy)	R	0	0	2.57	3	0	0	0	7	5	2	2	1	3	12	.200
	Delmarva (SAL)	A	4	1	1.42	18	0	0	8	25	9	6	4	0	13	38	.108
2000	Frederick (Car)	A	1	1	1.55	26	0	0	8	41	23	8	7	2	12	57	.163
	Bowie (EL)	AA	3	2	2.79	24	0	0	8	29	20	11	9	5	10	21	.194
2001	Bowie (EL)	AA	4	4	2.39	51	0	0	14	60	53	21	16	8	20	74	.227
2002	Bowie (EL)	AA	5	1	2.06	36	0	0	10	48	39	12	11	3	12	45	.232
2003	Bowie (EL)	AA	5	0	2.75	31	0	0	8	39	27	12	12	7	19	42	.196
	Ottawa (IL)	AAA	2	4	5.13	21	0	0	1	26	19	18	15	1	11	26	.202
2004	Ottawa (IL)	AAA	4	5	2.74	54	1	0	1	79	65	27	24	8	25	80	.218
	Baltimore (AL)	MLB	0	0	4.19	3	0	0	0	4	5	2	2	0	1	3	.278
2005	Ottawa (IL)	AAA	6	5	2.57	57	0	0	7	77	69	26	22	9	21	92	.235
	Baltimore (AL)	MLB	1	0	3.28	10	0	0	0	14	11	5	5	3	3	11	.220
MAJOR LEAGUE TOTALS			1	0	3.50	13	0	0	0	18	16	7	7	3	4	14	.235
MINOR LEAGUE TOTALS			34	23	2.54	321	1	0	65	432	329	143	122	44	146	487	.209

23 BRANDON FAHEY   SS

Born: Jan. 18, 1981. **B-T:** L-R. **Ht.:** 6-2. **Wt.:** 160. **Drafted:** Texas, 2002 (12th round). **Signed by:** Joe Almaraz.

The Orioles long had their eye on Fahey, taking him in the 32nd round of the 2000 draft out of Grayson County (Texas) Community College, but he decided to attend Texas instead. He batted .303 for the 2002 College World Series champions before Baltimore took him again, this time in the 12th round. His father Bill spent 11 seasons in the majors as a backup catcher after going No. 1 overall to the Washington Senators in the secondary phase of the January 1970 draft. Brandon is a rock-solid defensive player with great hands who makes all the plays at shortstop. His offensive production improved in 2005 after he focused on getting stronger so he could hold up better over the course of the season. However, he's still not a very physical player and projects as a bottom-of-the-order hitter with little pop. He has average speed and good instincts on the bases. The Orioles sent Fahey to the Arizona Fall League to get some work at second base, and they see his long-term role as a utilityman. He's familiar with the role already, having played at third base and the outfield in college. Fahey is a hard worker and the kind of player managers like to have in the dugout. He'll move up to Triple-A to open 2005, spending most of his time at shortstop but also getting some work at second base.

Year	Club (League)	Class	AVG	G	AB	R	H	2B	3B	HR	RBI	BB	SO	SB	OBP	SLG
2002	Aberdeen (NY-P)	A	.281	63	253	31	71	10	6	0	15	20	34	5	.333	.368
2003	Frederick (Car)	A	.233	107	365	41	85	11	3	1	22	22	56	4	.279	.288
2004	Frederick (Car)	A	.271	62	181	20	49	7	0	3	19	22	20	3	.354	.359
	Bowie (EL)	AA	.236	63	208	20	49	7	1	1	15	17	27	3	.293	.293
2005	Bowie (EL)	AA	.291	139	502	63	146	21	4	3	47	44	71	17	.349	.367
MINOR LEAGUE TOTALS			.265	434	1509	175	400	56	14	8	118	125	208	32	.323	.337

24 CHORYE SPOONE   RHP

Born: Sept. 16, 1985. **B-T:** R-R. **Ht.:** 6-1. **Wt.:** 215. **Drafted:** Catonsville (Md.) CC, 2005 (8th round). **Signed by:** Ty Brown.

The Padres took Spoone as a draft-and-follow in the 36th round of the 2004 draft but weren't able to sign him last spring. He didn't pitch much until April because he was suspended twice for disciplinary reasons, but he showed enough for the Orioles to take the Baltimore product in the eighth round and sign him for $75,000. Spoone didn't show much in Rookie ball but was one of the organization's best pitchers in instructional league. He has an impressive fastball, generally throwing 93-95 mph and touching 96, and a promising curveball, but he's raw and the inconsistency with his control was evident early. He also has done little work with a changeup, though he showed an interest for learning the nuances of pitching during instructional league. Spoone will compete for a spot in low Class A during spring training.

Year	Club (League)	Class	W	L	ERA	G	GS	CG	SV	IP	H	R	ER	HR	BB	SO	AVG
2005	Bluefield (Appy)	R	2	5	8.03	15	3	0	0	25	27	25	22	3	13	27	.273
MINOR LEAGUE TOTALS			2	5	8.03	15	3	0	0	25	27	25	22	3	13	27	.273

25 MARINO SALAS   RHP

Born: Feb. 2, 1981. **B-T:** R-R. **Ht.:** 6-0. **Wt.:** 175. **Signed:** Dominican Republic, 1998. **Signed by:** Carlos Bernhardt.

Salas has been in the organization so long that he had to re-sign with Baltimore as a minor league free agent before he made it out of low Class A. After his 2005 performance, he finally was added to the 40-man roster. The Orioles call him a late bloomer—an understatement, considering he spent six years in short-season leagues and still hasn't pitched above high Class A. Salas has taken to the closer role, saving 29 games over the last two years. He has improved both his fastball, now pitching at 92-94 mph, and his slider, gaining trust in his No. 2 pitch. He needs to hone his slider further and improve his command of both pitches. Because he lacks an offspeed offering, he had trouble getting lefthanders out in 2005. They batted .299 against him, compared to .185 for righthanders. Salas will go as far as his fastball takes him, and his next destination is Double-A.

Year	Club (League)	Class	W	L	ERA	G	GS	CG	SV	IP	H	R	ER	HR	BB	SO	AVG
1998	Orioles (DSL)	R	3	3	4.16	21	0	0	3	43	47	26	20	4	28	25	.280
1999	Orioles (DSL)	R	8	2	2.87	23	0	0	2	47	46	23	15	5	24	43	.249
2000	Orioles (DSL)	R	3	3	4.30	23	0	0	6	38	39	25	18	8	18	31	.264
2001	Orioles (GCL)	R	1	5	4.81	15	0	0	6	19	21	12	10	0	13	10	.288
2002	Bluefield (Appy)	R	3	0	5.40	27	0	0	0	37	44	31	22	6	21	34	.291
2003	Bluefield (Appy)	R	1	2	4.89	23	0	0	0	35	36	22	19	1	9	27	.271
2004	Delmarva (SAL)	A	2	4	2.15	40	0	0	13	50	51	15	12	5	17	46	.252
2005	Frederick (Car)	A	4	2	3.63	50	0	0	16	62	54	32	25	7	28	63	.233
MINOR LEAGUE TOTALS			25	21	3.84	222	0	0	46	331	338	186	141	36	158	279	.262

26 PACO FIGUEROA   2B/OF

Born: Feb. 19, 1983. **B-T:** R-R. **Ht.:** 5-11. **Wt.:** 182. **Drafted:** Miami, 2005 (9th round). **Signed by:** Nick Presto.

Baltimore was the lone team to draft a pair of brothers in 2005, taking Paco in the ninth round and injury-plagued Danny Figueroa, an outfielder, in the 43rd. A senior, Paco signed for $25,000. The Orioles don't expect him to be an all-star, but they do expect him to reach the big leagues. Figueroa stepped right into the Delmarva lineup and was one of its leading hitters, batting leadoff and playing second base as well as left and center field. He has the versatility to play all over the diamond and profiles as a big league utilityman. He's a savvy, instinctive player. Figueroa has a line-drive swing and knows what kind of player he is, putting the ball in play and showing good plate discipline so he can utiltze his plus speed on the bases. As a four-year college player, he's already pretty refined and will be expected to move quickly. He'll open his first full season in high Class A.

Year	Club (League)	Class	AVG	G	AB	R	H	2B	3B	HR	RBI	BB	SO	SB	OBP	SLG
2005	Delmarva (SAL)	A	.307	40	150	30	46	7	2	0	12	24	25	6	.419	.380
MINOR LEAGUE TOTALS			.307	40	150	30	46	7	2	0	12	24	25	6	.419	.380

27 ELI WHITESIDE   C

Born: Oct. 22, 1979. **B-T:** R-R. **Ht.:** 6-2. **Wt.:** 213. **Drafted:** Delta State (Miss.), 2001 (6th round). **Signed by:** Mike Tullier.

Whiteside made his major league debut in 2005, but he took a major step back offensively in his first exposure to Triple-A. He always has shown the defensive skills to be at least a major league backup, but the question has been whether he'll hit enough. The Orioles haven't given up on him, as they kept him on the 40-man roster. After hitting a career-high 18 homers in 2004, he lost his approach and plate discipline last year. He never will hit for average because he's stiff and has a long swing, and the best Baltimore can hope for is some occasional pop. Whiteside's defense remains strong, as he has an above-average arm and good footwork that allowed him to throw out 40 percent of basestealers in Triple-A. He has the body and strength to handle the rigors of catching every day if he can hit enough to earn such a role. He'll go back to Triple-A to open the season, trying to prove he can be more than a backup.

Year	Club (League)	Class	AVG	G	AB	R	H	2B	3B	HR	RBI	BB	SO	SB	OBP	SLG
2001	Delmarva (SAL)	A	.250	61	212	30	53	11	0	7	28	9	45	1	.300	.401
2002	Frederick (Car)	A	.259	80	313	34	81	19	0	8	42	14	57	0	.296	.396
	Bowie (EL)	AA	.263	27	99	11	26	5	0	2	11	4	18	0	.311	.374
2003	Orioles (GCL)	R	.333	1	3	0	1	1	0	0	1	1	1	0	.500	.667
	Aberdeen (NY-P)	A	.700	2	10	0	7	3	0	0	4	0	1	1	.700	1.000
	Bowie (EL)	AA	.204	81	265	21	54	13	1	1	23	5	44	0	.230	.272
2004	Bowie (EL)	AA	.253	90	297	41	75	18	0	18	60	25	65	2	.310	.495
2005	Ottawa (IL)	AAA	.233	95	317	28	74	22	1	4	27	21	65	1	.283	.347
	Baltimore (AL)	MLB	.250	9	12	1	3	0	0	0	1	0	2	0	.250	.250
MAJOR LEAGUE TOTALS			.250	9	12	1	3	0	0	0	1	0	2	0	.250	.250
MINOR LEAGUE TOTALS			.245	437	1516	165	371	92	2	40	195	79	296	5	.289	.387

28 ARTURO RIVAS   OF

Born: Feb. 2, 1984. **B-T:** R-R. **Ht.:** 6-0. **Wt.:** 189. **Signed:** Venezuela, 2000. **Signed by:** Chu Halabi.

Rivas' performance never has matched up to his tools, but at least he showed signs of making progress in 2005. He spent the entire year in a full-season league and was named to the low Class A South Atlantic League's midseason all-star game. His production wasn't overwhelming but was relatively consistent for a notoriously streaky player. Most important, he got 434 at-bats, nearly matching his total from his first four seasons, when he constantly battled nagging injuries. Rivas is an exciting player if you see him on the right day, showing all five tools and playing a smooth center field with a plus arm. He has a nice swing with a little pop, but he too often tries to hit for power rather than putting the ball in play. He did show the willingness to take a walk last season, but he'll need to cut down on his strikeouts to hit at the top of the order. He batted in every slot except ninth at Delmarva, so he's still feeling his way. His cocky attitude also has turned off some members of the organization. Rivas' performance in high Class A this year will determine whether he moves up this list or off it.

Year	Club (League)	Class	AVG	G	AB	R	H	2B	3B	HR	RBI	BB	SO	SB	OBP	SLG
2001	Bluefield (Appy)	R	.147	11	34	4	5	0	0	0	2	5	13	4	.286	.147
	Orioles (GCL)	R	.308	8	26	6	8	1	0	0	2	4	5	2	.412	.346
2002	Bluefield (Appy)	R	.272	55	213	45	58	11	1	8	34	19	47	11	.342	.446
2003	Bluefield (Appy)	R	.344	9	32	7	11	4	0	0	7	3	6	3	.389	.469
	Delmarva (SAL)	A	.190	44	163	16	31	11	1	1	11	16	42	2	.271	.288
2004	Aberdeen (NY-P)	A	.261	55	184	18	48	8	0	3	22	15	51	4	.315	.353
2005	Delmarva (SAL)	A	.251	125	434	78	109	29	8	9	62	61	94	11	.355	.417
MINOR LEAGUE TOTALS			.249	307	1086	174	270	64	10	21	140	123	258	37	.334	.384

29 MARK FLEISHER 1B

Born: Sept. 18, 1983. **B-T:** R-R. **Ht.:** 6-4. **Wt.:** 235. **Drafted:** Radford, 2005 (14th round). **Signed by:** Ty Brown.

In an organization short on power bats, particularly at the infield corners, Fleisher provides the latest hope. He was one of several seniors with strong makeup drafted by the Orioles later in the 2005 draft, a group that also included Miami infielder/outfielder Paco Figueroa (ninth round) and Texas Christian shortstop Stuart Musslewhite (24th). Fleisher was overshadowed by Coastal Carolina's Mike Constanzo (a second-round pick of the Phillies) in the Big South Conference last spring, but he was the league's second-leading hitter at .375 and hit 11 homers for a 15-40 Radford team. In addition to batting cleanup for the Highlanders, Fleisher was also a starting pitcher. His body draws comparisons to Mark McGwire's, and the Orioles think he could hit a lot of homers as he gets stronger. Fleisher has good balance at the plate and the bat speed and control to hit for both power and average. He also has a good idea of the strike zone and shows the willingness to take a walk. He'll be a solid defender at first base. Fleisher will advance to low Class A in 2006.

Year	Club (League)	Class	AVG	G	AB	R	H	2B	3B	HR	RBI	BB	SO	SB	OBP	SLG
2005	Aberdeen (NY-P)	A	.277	61	231	34	64	12	0	7	32	25	55	0	.356	.420
MINOR LEAGUE TOTALS			.277	61	231	34	64	12	0	7	32	25	55	0	.356	.420

30 TRIPPER JOHNSON 3B

Born: April 28, 1982. **B-T:** R-R. **Ht.:** 6-1. **Wt.:** 200. **Drafted:** HS—Bellevue, Wash., 2000 (1st round supplemental). **Signed by:** John Gillette.

Johnson has moved slowly through the system since signing as a supplemental first-round pick in 2002. He has performed just well enough to tantalize the Orioles and even earned Carolina League all-star honors in 2004. But he followed that up with a disappointing stint in Double-A last year, and time may be running out on him. Defense was once the big question mark about Johnson's game, but that actually has become his strength. He has an average arm and moves well laterally. But Johnson hasn't been able to answer concerns about his bat, particularly regarding his power. Double-A pitchers exploited his long swing and his homer output dropped to 11 from 21 the year before, though he did produce 29 doubles. He performed a little bit better in the Arizona Fall League, batting .333 with two homers in 51 at-bats in a league tilted heavily toward offense, but he struggled against righthanders just as he did during the regular season. Johnson will go back to Double-A to try to prove himself again, and it may be his last chance.

Year	Club (League)	Class	AVG	G	AB	R	H	2B	3B	HR	RBI	BB	SO	SB	OBP	SLG
2000	Orioles (GCL)	R	.306	48	180	22	55	5	3	2	33	13	38	7	.355	.400
2001	Bluefield (Appy)	R	.261	43	157	24	41	6	1	2	26	11	37	4	.312	.350
2002	Delmarva (SAL)	A	.260	136	493	73	128	32	6	11	71	62	88	19	.349	.416
2003	Frederick (Car)	A	.273	123	417	43	114	25	3	5	50	46	92	7	.359	.384
2004	Frederick (Car)	A	.269	129	465	62	125	19	2	21	74	51	93	14	.343	.454
2005	Bowie (EL)	AA	.249	134	507	62	126	29	4	11	59	41	108	7	.309	.387
MINOR LEAGUE TOTALS			.265	613	2219	286	589	116	19	52	313	224	456	58	.339	.405

BOSTON
RED SOX

BY **JIM CALLIS**

Perhaps the Red Sox' New Year's resolution should be to achieve resolution. As 2005 drew to a close, outfielder Manny Ramirez, who demanded a trade Oct. 29 and threatened to not report to spring training otherwise, remained Boston property.

But the burning question in Red Sox Nation is whether former general manager Theo Epstein will be in the club's employ in 2006. Talks on a contact extension with team president Larry Lucchino broke down after they agreed on a three-year, $4.5 million deal, and Epstein stepped down on Oct. 31 without detailing the reasons behind his decision.

Yet rumors that Epstein, the architect of the 2004 championship team and the first three-year streak of postseason appearances in Boston history, will return in some capacity have persisted since he left. When the Red Sox officially replaced him with former Epstein lieutenants Ben Cherington and Jed Hoyer on Dec. 12, Lucchino said at the press conference that Epstein was welcome to come back.

Cherington, 31, joined the Red Sox in 1999 as an area scout and was promoted to farm director in December 2002. Hoyer, 32, was hired by Cherington in 2002 and was an assistant to Epstein for the last two years.

Even if Epstein stays away, the in-house promotions mean that Boston will keep a good chunk of its braintrust. Assistant GM Josh Byrnes took the Diamondbacks' GM job before Epstein resigned, and Byrnes brought director of baseball operations Peter Woodfork with him. But Cherington and Hoyer are obviously sticking around, as is scouting director Jason McLeod. The Red Sox also would like to retain special assistants Bill Lajoie and Craig Shipley, though Lajoie, 71, has health issues, and Shipley may join Byrnes and Woodfork in Arizona.

All the front-office machinations and the sudden loss of Johnny Damon have helped obscure the fact that the Red Sox system is percolating with its most talent in years. **Jonathan Papelbon** came up at midseason and quickly asserted himself as the top set-up man in a beleaguered bullpen. Second baseman Dustin Pedroia, catcher Kelly Shoppach, righty relievers Craig Hansen and Manny Delcarmen and lefty starter Jon Lester may be counted on for key contributions in 2006. The Red Sox had the prospect depth to not have to think twice about including shortstop Hanley Ramirez, righthander Anibal Sanchez and two power arms in a November blockbuster that landed them Josh Beckett, Mike Lowell and Guillermo Mota from the Marlins.

Boston also added plenty of talent in 2005. In his first draft as scouting director, McLeod had five picks before the second round. All five of his choices—outfielder Jacoby Ellsbury, Hansen, righthanders Clay Buchholz and Michael Bowden, infielder Jed Lowrie—had very promising debuts. At the Winter Meetings, the Red Sox traded for a blue-chip prospect, getting third baseman Andy Marte from the Braves for Edgar Renteria.

TOP 30 PROSPECTS

1. Andy Marte, 3b	16. David Pauley, rhp
2. Jon Lester, lhp	17. Ian Bladergroen, 1b
3. Jonathan Papelbon, rhp	18. Christian Lara, ss
4. Craig Hansen, rhp	19. Jeff Corsaletti, of
5. Dustin Pedroia, 2b/ss	20. Cla Meredith, rhp
6. Jacoby Ellsbury, of	21. Jermaine Van Buren, rhp
7. Kelly Shoppach, c	22. Jose Vaquedano, rhp
8. Manny Delcarmen, rhp	23. Lenny DiNardo, lhp
9. Jed Lowrie, ss	24. Mike Rozier, lhp
10. Clay Buchholz, rhp	25. Adam Stern, of
11. Michael Bowden, rhp	26. Abe Alvarez, lhp
12. David Murphy, of	27. Jon Egan, c
13. Luis Soto, of	28. Gary Galvez, rhp
14. Brandon Moss, of	29. Mickey Hall, of
15. Edgar Martinez, rhp	30. Andrew Pinckney, 3b

ORGANIZATION OVERVIEW

General Managers: Ben Cherington/Jed Hoyer. **Farm director:** Vacant. **Scouting director:** Jason McLeod.

2005 PERFORMANCE

Class	Team	League	W	L	Pct.	Finish*	Manager
Majors	Boston	American	95	67	.586	t-2nd (14)	Terry Francona
Triple-A	Pawtucket Red Sox	International	75	69	.521	t-6th (14)	Ron Johnson
Double-A	Portland Sea Dogs	Eastern	76	66	.535	t-2nd (12)	Todd Claus
High A	Wilmington Blue Rocks	Carolina	60	80	.429	8th (8)	Dann Bilardello
Low A	Greenville Bombers	South Atlantic	72	66	.522	t-6th (16)	Chad Epperson
Short-season	Lowell Spinners	New York-Penn	42	33	.560	5th (14)	Luis Alicea
Rookie	GCL Red Sox	Gulf Coast	30	24	.556	3rd (12)	Ralph Treuel
OVERALL 2005 MINOR LEAGUE RECORD			355	338	.512	10th (30)	

*Finish in overall standings (No. of teams in league).

ORGANIZATION LEADERS

BATTING   *Minimum 250 at-bats
*AVG	Otness, John, Greenville	.331
R	Pinckney, Andrew, Greenville	91
H	Pinckney, Andrew, Greenville	158
TB	Pinckney, Andrew, Greenville	272
2B	Pinckney, Andrew, Greenville	33
3B	Youngbauer, Scott, Portland/Wilmington	10
HR	Shoppach, Kelly, Pawtucket	26
RBI	Pinckney, Andrew, Greenville	98
BB	Lombard, George, Pawtucket	67
SO	Lombard, George, Pawtucket	159
SB	Ramirez, Hanley, Portland	26
*OBP	Petagine, Roberto, Pawtucket	.452
*SLG	Petagine, Roberto, Pawtucket	.635

PITCHING   #Minimum 75 innings
W	Three tied at	11
L	Hottovy, Tommy, Wilmington	12
#ERA	Lester, Jon, Portland	2.19
G	Beam, Randy, Portland/Wilmington	53
	Meredith, Cla, Pawtucket/Portland/Wilmington	53
CG	Lester, Jon, Portland	3
SV	Meredith, Cla, Pawtucket/Portland/Wilmington	19
IP	Kester, Tim, Pawtucket	165
BB	Gabbard, Kason, Portland	65
SO	Lester, Jon, Portland	163

BEST TOOLS

Best Hitter for Average	Dustin Pedroia
Best Power Hitter	Andy Marte
Best Strike-Zone Discipline	Dustin Pedroia
Fastest Baserunner	Jacoby Ellsbury
Best Athlete	Jacoby Ellsbury
Best Fastball	Craig Hansen
Best Curveball	Manny Delcarmen
Best Slider	Craig Hansen
Best Changeup	Randy Beam
Best Control	Abe Alvarez
Best Defensive Catcher	Kelly Shoppach
Best Defensive Infielder	Dustin Pedroia
Best Infield Arm	Andrew Pinckney
Best Defensive Outfielder	Jacoby Ellsbury
Best Outfield Arm	Willy Mota

PROJECTED 2009 LINEUP

Catcher	Kelly Shoppach
First Base	Jason Varitek
Second Base	Dustin Pedroia
Third Base	Andy Marte
Shortstop	Jed Lowrie
Left Field	Manny Ramirez
Center Field	Jacoby Ellsbury
Right Field	Trot Nixon

Designated Hitter	David Ortiz
No. 1 Starter	Josh Beckett
No. 2 Starter	Jon Lester
No. 3 Starter	Jonathan Papelbon
No. 4 Starter	Matt Clement
No. 5 Starter	Bronson Arroyo
Closer	Craig Hansen

LAST YEAR'S TOP 20 PROSPECTS

1. Hanley Ramirez, ss
2. Brandon Moss, of
3. Jonathan Papelbon, rhp
4. Jon Lester, lhp
5. Anibal Sanchez, rhp
6. Dustin Pedroia, ss
7. Luis Soto, ss
8. Kelly Shoppach, c
9. Ian Bladergroen, 1b
10. Abe Alvarez, lhp
11. Manny Delcarmen, rhp
12. Christian Lara, ss
13. Mike Rozier, lhp
14. Mickey Hall, of
15. David Murphy, of
16. Chad Spann, 3b
17. Juan Cedeno, lhp
18. Tommy Hottovy, lhp
19. Andrew Dobies, lhp
20. Jimmy James, rhp

TOP PROSPECTS OF THE DECADE

Year	Player, Pos.	2005 Org.
1996	Donnie Sadler, ss	Out of baseball
1997	Nomar Garciaparra, ss	Cubs
1998	Brian Rose, rhp	Reds
1999	Dernell Stenson, of	Deceased
2000	Steve Lomasney, c	Reds
2001	Dernell Stenson, of/1b	Deceased
2002	Seung Song, rhp	Giants
2003	Hanley Ramirez, ss	Red Sox
2004	Hanley Ramirez, ss	Red Sox
2005	Hanley Ramirez, ss	Red Sox

TOP DRAFT PICKS OF THE DECADE

Year	Player, Pos.	2005 Org.
1996	Josh Garrett, rhp	Out of baseball
1997	John Curtice, lhp	Out of baseball
1998	Adam Everett, ss	Astros
1999	Rick Asadoorian, of	Reds
2000	Phil Dumatrait, lhp	Reds
2001	Kelly Shoppach, c (2nd round)	Red Sox
2002	Jon Lester, lhp (2nd round)	Red Sox
2003	David Murphy, of	Red Sox
2004	Dustin Pedroia, ss (2nd round)	Red Sox
2005	Jacoby Ellsbury, of	Red Sox

ALL-TIME LARGEST BONUSES

Risk Asadoorian, 1999	$1,725,500
Adam Everett, 1998	$1,725,000
Mike Rozier, 2004	$1,575,000
David Murphy, 2003	$1,525,000
Jacoby Ellsbury, 2005	$1,400,000

MINOR LEAGUE DEPTH CHART

Boston Red Sox

Rank: 7

STRENGTH: Balance. Aside from shortstop, the Sox have depth and/or impact talent at every spot.

WEAKNESS: First base. While the big league team had opportunity here, no Sox farmhand was in position to seize it.

Depth charts prepared by John Manuel and Chris Kline. Numbers in parentheses indicate prospect rankings.

LF
Jeff Corsaletti (19)
Carlos Fernandez
Justin Sherrod
Yahmed Yema

CF
Jacoby Ellsbury (6)
David Murphy (12)
Adam Stern (25)
Chris Durbin
Willy Mota
Reid Engel

RF
Luis Soto (13)
Brandon Moss (14)
Mickey Hall (29)
Chris Turner
Claudio Arias
Moises Santa

3B
Andy Marte (1)
Andrew Pinckney (30)
Chad Spann

SS
Christian Lara (18)
Alejandro Machado

2B
Dustin Pedroia (5)
Jed Lowrie (9)
Jeff Natale
Tony Granadillo

1B
Ian Bladergroen (17)
Jeremy West
John Otness
Michael Jones

C
Kelly Shoppach (7)
Jon Egan (27)
Dusty Brown

RHP

Starters	Relievers
Jonathan Papelbon (3)	Craig Hansen (4)
Clay Buchholz (10)	Manny Delcarmen (8)
Michael Bowden (11)	Edgar Martinez (15)
David Pauley (16)	Cla Meredith (20)
Jose Vaquedano (22)	Jermaine Van Buren (21)
Gary Galvez (28)	Jamie Vermilyea
Charlie Zink	Tim Bausher
	Chris Jones
	Kyle Jackson

LHP

Starters	Relievers
Jon Lester (2)	Lenny DiNardo (23)
Mike Rozier (24)	Randy Beam
Abe Alvarez (26)	Tommy Hottovy
Ryan Phillips	Hunter Jones
Andrew Dobies	
Adam Blackley	
Tim Cox	
Felix Doubront	

DRAFT ANALYSIS

2005

Best Pro Debut: SS/2B Jed Lowrie (1) hit .328-4-32 and led the short-season New York-Penn League with a .429 on-base percentage. RHP Craig Hansen (1) used 10 scoreless minor league appearances, including eight in Double-A, as a springboard to Fenway Park. OF Jeff Corsaletti (6) and 2B Jeff Natale (32) both excelled at low Class A Greenville. Corsaletti hit .357-4-26, while Natale batted .338-2-35 with a .463 on-base percentage.

Best Athlete: OF Jacoby Ellsbury (1) did nothing to dispel Johnny Damon comparisons before a hamstring injury sidelined him in the NY-P. OF Reid Engel (5) isn't as refined but has similar speed and more power. RHP Clay Buchholz (1) was drafted for his electric arm, but he was a two-way star at Angelina (Texas) JC who offered left-handed power and speed as an outfielder.

Best Pure Hitter: Lowrie, a switch-hitter, who shortened his stroke from the right side after joining short-season Lowell.

Best Raw Power: C Jon Egan (2), though he was a tentative hitter in his pro debut and was more of a pleasant surprise with his catching ability. Egan's status took a hit during the offseason, when he was arrested for driving while intoxicated and police also found traces of cocaine in his wallet.

Fastest Runner: When the Lowell staff was timing players in the 40-yard dash, Buchholz (1) asked if he could participate and ran a 4.25 and a 4.27. Ellsbury's speed rates a 70 on the 20-80 scouting scale, while Engel merits a 65.

Best Defensive Player: Ellsbury has excellent range and instincts in center field.

Best Fastball: Hansen has a wicked 93-95 mph sinker that can reach 97. RHP Michael

Bowden

Bowden (1) also has heavy life on a consistent 92-93 mph fastball. Buchholz pitched at 93-94 mph in junior college but worked more at 88-92 during the summer.

Best Breaking Ball: Hansen's slider is a swing-and-miss pitch but wasn't at its best in his first pro summer. Bowden has a legitimate power curveball, while Buchholz throws both a hard slider and a good curve.

Most Intriguing Background: Natale was also a hockey forward at Trinity (Conn.) Unsigned RHP Kirby Yates' (26) brother Tyler pitched for the Mets in 2004.

Closest To The Majors: Hansen made three appearances for the Red Sox in September and should factor into their bullpen in 2006. Ellsbury, Buchholz and Corsaletti are also on the fast track.

Best Late-Round Pick: Natale has uncanny hand-eye coordination. RHP Chris Jones (29), who has the chance to have a plus fastball and curve, is healthy again after shoulder and heel injuries ruined his last two years at Indiana State.

The One Who Got Away: SS Pedro Alvarez (14), one of the best hitter to come out of New York City since Manny Ramirez, couldn't be lured away from Vanderbilt. The Red Sox signed all 16 picks before him.

Assessment: In his first draft as scouting director, Jason McLeod had five choices before the second round and made good use of them.

2004 2B Dustin Pedroia (2), Boston's top pick, continues to overachieve like he did in college. RHP Cla Meredith (6) became the second player from the 2004 draft to reach the majors, after Oakland's Huston Street. *GRADE:* C+

2003 The Red Sox wouldn't have made the playoffs in 2005 without RHP Jonathan Papelbon (4). OF Matt Murton (1) was traded to the Cubs, while fellow first-round OF David Murphy started to turn a corner. *GRADE:* B+

2002 Boston didn't have a first-round pick, but top choice Jon Lester (2) has become one of the game's top lefty prospects. OF Brandon Moss (8) and LHP Tyler Pelland (9, now with the Reds) also show some promise. *GRADE:* B

2001 Another year without a first-rounder saw the Red Sox land another solid player with their top selection: C Kelly Shoppach (2). 3B Kevin Youkilis (8) looks ready to start in the majors. *GRADE:* B

Draft analysis prepared by Jim Callis. Numbers in parentheses indicate draft rounds.

ANDY
MARTE

Born: Oct. 21, 1983.
Ht.: 6-1. **Wt.:** 195.
Bats: R. **Throws:** R.
Signed: Dominican Republic, 2000.
Signed by: Rene Francisco/
Julian Perez (Braves).

After losing free agent Rafael Furcal to the Dodgers, the Braves wanted Edgar Renteria as a replacement, and the Red Sox were happy to oblige. The teams talked to the Devil Rays about a three-team deal that would have sent Marte (Atlanta's No. 1 prospect) to Tampa Bay and Julio Lugo to Boston. But when the Rays asked for an extra prospect, the Red Sox traded Renteria straight up for Marte. Signed for $600,000 out of the Dominican Republic, he has ranked among the game's top third-base prospects since his first full U.S. season in 2002. Once compared to Miguel Cabrera, he hasn't developed quite as fast but still is just 22. Marte's biggest problem in Atlanta was that Chipper Jones is entrenched at the hot corner and doesn't want to return to the outfield. He got his first big league opportunity in June after Jones strained a ligament in his left foot, but Marte hit just .200 with three RBIs in 12 games before returning to the minors.

Marte has everything teams want in a third baseman, starting with tape-measure power. His stroke has a natural uppercut that generates plenty of loft, and the ball jumps off his bat to all fields. He's an aggressive hitter who punishes mistakes, and he has the bat speed and aptitude to hit for a solid average. His walk rate has increased in each of the last three seasons. Marte also provides quality glovework at the hot corner. Managers rated him the best defensive third baseman in the Triple-A International League—the fourth consecutive year he earned that honor in his league. He moves well to both sides and has a strong, accurate arm. His 15 errors and .950 fielding percentage in 2005 were career bests. The Braves gave him high marks for his maturity and approach.

As with most power hitters, Marte will pile up some strikeouts to go with his homers. His swing can get long at times, and he occasionally gets overanxious and chases breaking balls out of the strike zone. His speed is slightly below average, and he'll get slower as he continues to fill out. However, he's a smart runner who's not a liability on the bases. Marte's elbow bothered him slightly during the season but it wasn't considered a serious problem. There were reports that the Devil Rays backed out of the three-way trade over concerns that Marte had a torn ligament. But the Red Sox found his medical records to be clean, and he played without problems in the Dominican League this offseason.

While he has the tools to become a star, his immediate future remains uncertain. Marte's best chance of cracking Boston's lineup is to wrest the first-base job from Kevin Youkilis. But Marte never has played first base. He doesn't have anything left to prove in Triple-A, but may have to open the season in Pawtucket. It's also possible that the Red Sox will spin him in another trade to address needs at first base, shortstop or center field.

Year	Club (League)	Class	AVG	G	AB	R	H	2B	3B	HR	RBI	BB	SO	SB	OBP	SLG
2001	Danville (Appy)	R	.200	37	125	12	25	6	0	1	12	20	45	3	.306	.272
2002	Macon (SAL)	A	.281	126	488	69	137	32	4	21	105	41	114	2	.339	.492
2003	Myrtle Beach (Car)	A	.285	130	463	69	132	35	1	16	63	67	109	5	.372	.469
2004	Braves (GCL)	R	.467	3	15	4	7	4	0	1	6	2	2	0	.529	.933
	Greenville (SL)	AA	.269	107	387	52	104	28	1	23	68	58	105	1	.364	.525
2005	Richmond (IL)	AAA	.275	109	389	51	107	26	2	20	74	64	83	0	.372	.506
	Atlanta (NL)	MLB	.140	24	57	3	8	2	1	0	4	7	13	0	.227	.211
MAJOR LEAGUE TOTALS			.140	24	57	3	8	2	1	0	4	7	13	0	.234	.211
MINOR LEAGUE TOTALS			.274	512	1867	257	512	131	8	82	328	252	458	11	.359	.485

2 JON LESTER LHP

Born: Jan. 7, 1984. **B-T:** L-L. **Ht.:** 6-4. **Wt.:** 210. **Drafted:** HS—Puyallup, Wash., 2002 (2nd round). **Signed by:** Gary Rajsich.

Lester's long-awaited breakout finally came in 2005, when he was Boston's minor league pitcher of the year. He won the same award in the Double-A Eastern League, which he led in ERA, complete games and strikeouts. He was part of the failed Alex Rodriguez trade talks in 2003, but the Red Sox refused to part with him in the Josh Beckett deal. Lester is a big, physical lefthander with a chance for three plus pitches. His fastball has late life and has risen from 87-88 mph in 2003 to 90-91 in 2004 to 92-93 last year, when he topped out at 95. He has turned his cut fastball into a true slider that's now his No. 2 pitch. He can get both swings and misses and called strikes with his changeup. Once Lester gets a little more consistent with his secondary pitches and his command, he'll be ready for the big leagues. He'll keep batters off balance by throwing an occasional curveball, but it lags behind his other offerings. Boston doesn't have an opening in its rotation, so Lester will head to Triple-A. He should be ready if needed by the second half, and he has the stuff to become a frontline starter.

Year	Club (League)	Class	W	L	ERA	G	GS	CG	SV	IP	H	R	ER	HR	BB	SO	AVG
2002	Red Sox (GCL)	R	0	1	12.86	1	1	0	0	1	5	6	1	0	1	1	.714
2003	Augusta (SAL)	A	6	9	3.65	24	21	0	0	106	102	54	43	7	44	71	.262
2004	Red Sox (GCL)	R	0	0	0.00	1	1	0	0	1	0	0	0	0	2	1	.000
	Sarasota (FSL)	A	7	6	4.29	21	20	0	0	90	82	46	43	2	37	97	.245
2005	Portland (EL)	AA	11	6	2.61	26	26	3	0	148	114	52	43	10	57	163	.215
MINOR LEAGUE TOTALS			24	22	3.38	73	69	3	0	346	303	158	130	19	141	333	.240

3 JONATHAN PAPELBON RHP

Born: Nov. 23, 1980. **B-T:** R-R. **Ht.:** 6-4. **Wt.:** 230. **Drafted:** Mississippi State, 2003 (4th round). **Signed by:** Joe Mason.

The Red Sox wouldn't have made the playoffs last year without Papelbon. Boston won all three of his starts after his July promotion, and in September, he became its primary set-up man. Papelbon's best pitch is a 92-93 mph fastball that sits at 95 when he works in relief, and his heater's late life makes it seem quicker. He can locate it to both sides of the plate and blow it by hitters upstairs. Papelbon honed his fosh changeup into a nasty splitter. His slider rates as a 55 on the 20-80 scouting scale at times. He showed no fear as a rookie thrust into a pennant race. Papelbon rarely had three pitches working for him at the same time in the majors. His splitter and slider still can be refined. He throws a curveball as a starter, but it's a distant fourth pitch. The Red Sox have greater need for relievers than starters, so Papelbon should open 2006 in the bullpen. In the long term, he should front Boston's rotation along with Josh Beckett and Jon Lester.

Year	Club (League)	Class	W	L	ERA	G	GS	CG	SV	IP	H	R	ER	HR	BB	SO	AVG
2003	Lowell (NY-P)	A	1	2	6.33	13	6	0	0	33	43	23	23	2	9	36	.312
2004	Sarasota (FSL)	A	12	7	2.64	24	24	2	0	130	97	43	38	6	43	153	.210
2005	Portland (EL)	AA	5	2	2.48	14	14	0	0	87	59	28	24	9	23	83	.193
	Pawtucket (IL)	AAA	1	2	2.92	7	4	0	1	28	21	9	9	2	3	27	.208
	Boston (AL)	MLB	3	1	2.65	17	3	0	0	34	33	11	10	4	17	34	.260
MAJOR LEAGUE TOTALS			3	1	2.65	17	3	0	0	34	33	11	10	4	17	34	.260
MINOR LEAGUE TOTALS			19	13	3.05	58	48	2	1	277	220	103	94	19	78	299	.219

4 CRAIG HANSEN RHP

Born: Nov. 15, 1983. **B-T:** R-R. **Ht.:** 6-6. **Wt.:** 210. **Drafted:** St. John's, 2005 (1st round). **Signed by:** Ray Fagnant.

Hansen made the Diamondbacks' short list to be drafted No. 1 overall but ultimately fell to the Red Sox at No. 26 because of signability concerns. He landed a four-year, $4.4 million big league contract with a $1.325 million bonus in July, and overcame a tired arm to pitch for Boston in September. Hansen has two dominant pitches and the makeup to be a big league closer. He usually pitches at 93-95 mph with plus sink on his fastball, and he's capable of reaching 97. His slider was the best breaking ball in the 2005 draft, a nasty mid-80s pitch that seems allergic to bats. Hansen's tired arm was simply the result of a two-month layoff after his college season ended, and his stuff wasn't as explosive as usual. When he dropped his arm angle trying to add some bite on his slider, he lost some command with his fastball. Hansen held his own in the majors despite not being at his best. He could use more time in the minors but also could make the Red Sox out of spring training. He's their closer of the (near) future.

Year	Club (League)	Class	W	L	ERA	G	GS	CG	SV	IP	H	R	ER	HR	BB	SO	AVG
2005	Red Sox (GCL)	R	1	0	0.00	2	1	0	0	3	2	0	0	0	0	4	.182
	Portland (EL)	AA	0	0	0.00	8	0	0	1	10	9	0	0	0	1	10	.243
	Boston (AL)	MLB	0	0	6.00	4	0	0	0	3	6	2	2	1	1	3	.429
MAJOR LEAGUE TOTALS			0	0	6.00	4	0	0	0	3	6	2	2	1	1	3	.429
MINOR LEAGUE TOTALS			1	0	0.00	10	1	0	1	13	11	0	0	0	1	14	.229

5 DUSTIN PEDROIA   2B/SS

Born: Aug. 17, 1983. **B-T:** R-R. **Ht.:** 5-9. **Wt.:** 180. **Drafted:** Arizona State, 2004 (2nd round). **Signed by:** Dan Madsen.

Boston's top pick in 2004, Pedroia was the organization's minor league offensive player of the year in 2005. A wrist injury shortly after a promotion to Triple-A kept him from getting called up to Boston. He has extraordinary hand-eye coordination. He's able to swing from his heels yet make consistent contact with gap power. Managers rated his strike-zone discipline and second-base defense the best in the Eastern League last year. His instincts and makeup are excellent. Pedroia's arm and range weren't quite up to par at shortstop, though Boston would have kept him there if he hadn't teamed with Hanley Ramirez last year. Pedroia's speed is a step below-average, but he runs the bases well. He needs to get stronger to hold up over a full season. The Red Sox wouldn't mind giving Pedroia more time in Triple-A. A trade for Mark Loretta and Tony Graffanino's acceptance of arbitration probably ended Pedroia's chances of winning the second-base job this spring, but there's also a hole at shortstop he might fill.

Year	Club (League)	Class	AVG	G	AB	R	H	2B	3B	HR	RBI	BB	SO	SB	OBP	SLG
2004	Augusta (SAL)	A	.400	12	50	11	20	5	0	1	5	6	3	2	.474	.560
	Sarasota (FSL)	A	.336	30	107	23	36	8	3	2	14	13	4	0	.417	.523
2005	Portland (EL)	AA	.324	66	256	39	83	19	2	8	40	34	26	7	.409	.508
	Pawtucket (IL)	AAA	.255	51	204	39	52	9	1	5	24	24	17	1	.356	.382
MINOR LEAGUE TOTALS			.310	159	617	112	191	41	6	16	83	77	50	10	.398	.473

6 JACOBY ELLSBURY   OF

Born: Sept. 11, 1983. **B-T:** L-L. **Ht.:** 6-1. **Wt.:** 190. **Drafted:** Oregon State, 2005 (1st round). **Signed by:** John Booher.

Ellsbury led Oregon State to its first College World Series since 1952, and the Red Sox were elated that he slipped to them as the No. 23 overall pick in the 2005 draft. Signed for $1.4 million, he finished second in the short-season New York-Penn League in steals despite getting a late start and missing two weeks with a hamstring injury. Ellsbury draws Johnny Damon comparisons because he's a lefthanded-hitting center fielder who can run and defend. He has the bat-handling ability, on-base skills and speed to hit atop the order. He's intelligent and has a solid work ethic. Ellsbury's arm is below-average but playable in center field, and he plays shallow to compensate. He doesn't have much home run power, though he had no problem reaching the right-field bullpen during a Fenway Park workout after big league hitting coach Ron Jackson tinkered with his setup to get his swing started quicker. There's no reason Ellsbury shouldn't move quickly through the minors. He'll begin his first full season at high Class A Wilmington and could be pushing for a big league job by 2008.

Year	Club (League)	Class	AVG	G	AB	R	H	2B	3B	HR	RBI	BB	SO	SB	OBP	SLG
2005	Lowell (NY-P)	A	.317	35	139	28	44	3	5	1	19	24	20	23	.418	.432
MINOR LEAGUE TOTALS			.317	35	139	28	44	3	5	1	19	24	20	23	.418	.432

7 KELLY SHOPPACH   C

Born: April 29, 1980. **B-T:** R-R. **Ht.:** 6-1. **Wt.:** 210. **Drafted:** Baylor, 2001 (2nd round). **Signed by:** Jim Robinson.

When the Red Sox re-signed free agents Jason Varitek and Doug Mirabelli after the 2004 season, they sentenced Shoppach to repeating Triple-A. He was named the International League's all-star catcher for the second straight year and led the league in homers per at-bat. Shoppach has some similarities to Varitek in that he has above-average power and strong leadership skills. Shoppach doesn't hit for average but draws enough walks to post respectable on-base percentages. A strong arm and quick release allowed him to throw out 44 percent of IL basestealers. His receiving and game-calling skills are solid. He's pull-conscious and sells out for power, so Shoppach strikes out a lot. Pitchers had their way with him in his first brief taste of the majors last year, so he'll have to make some adjustments. He's a slow runner. By trading Mirabelli to the Padres, the Red Sox have cleared the way for Shoppach to become Varitek's backup with a good spring.

Year	Club (League)	Class	AVG	G	AB	R	H	2B	3B	HR	RBI	BB	SO	SB	OBP	SLG
2002	Sarasota (FSL)	A	.271	116	414	54	112	35	1	10	66	59	112	2	.369	.432
2003	Portland (EL)	AA	.282	92	340	45	96	30	2	12	60	35	83	0	.353	.488
2004	Pawtucket (IL)	AAA	.233	113	399	62	93	25	0	22	64	46	138	0	.320	.461
2005	Pawtucket (IL)	AAA	.253	102	371	60	94	16	0	26	75	46	116	0	.352	.507
	Boston (AL)	MLB	.000	9	15	1	0	0	0	0	0	0	7	0	.063	.000
MAJOR LEAGUE TOTALS			.000	9	15	1	0	0	0	0	0	0	7	0	.000	.000
MINOR LEAGUE TOTALS			.259	423	1524	221	395	106	3	70	265	186	449	2	.349	.470

8 MANNY DELCARMEN   RHP

Born: Feb. 16, 1982. **B-T:** R-R. **Ht.:** 6-2. **Wt.:** 190. **Drafted:** HS—West Roxbury, Mass., 2000 (2nd round). **Signed by:** Ray Fagnant.

Delcarmen was one of the system's top starting pitching prospects before requiring Tommy John surgery in May 2003. He remained in the rotation when he came back in 2004, but switched to the bullpen in the Arizona Fall League after the season. He rocketed to Boston in his new role last year, though he was used sparingly in his seven weeks in the majors. Delcarmen regularly throws 94-95 mph and tops out at 97 as a reliever. His fastball explodes through the zone, and he also can strike hitters out with his hammer curveball. He has the demeanor and the resilient arm to handle relief. His delivery gets out of whack too easily, leading to problems with his command and the consistency of his pitches. He rarely had his standout curve in the majors, forcing him to rely on his decent changeup as his second pitch. Delcarmen profiles as a set-up man, a commodity the Red Sox desperately needed in 2005. Their offseason moves, however, increased the chances Delcarmen will open 2006 in Triple-A.

Year	Club (League)	Class	W	L	ERA	G	GS	CG	SV	IP	H	R	ER	HR	BB	SO	AVG
2001	Red Sox (GCL)	R	4	2	2.54	11	8	0	1	46	35	16	13	0	19	62	.211
2002	Augusta (SAL)	A	7	8	4.10	26	24	0	0	136	124	77	62	15	56	136	.242
2003	Sarasota (FSL)	A	1	1	3.13	4	3	0	0	23	16	9	8	1	7	16	.200
2004	Sarasota (FSL)	A	3	6	4.68	19	18	0	0	73	84	43	38	10	20	76	.301
2005	Portland (EL)	AA	4	4	3.23	31	0	0	3	39	31	23	14	3	20	49	.212
	Pawtucket (IL)	AAA	3	1	1.29	15	0	0	2	21	17	3	3	0	13	23	.218
	Boston (AL)	MLB	0	0	3.00	10	0	0	0	9	8	3	3	0	7	9	.242
MAJOR LEAGUE TOTALS			0	0	3.00	10	0	0	0	9	8	3	3	0	7	9	.242
MINOR LEAGUE TOTALS			22	22	3.67	106	53	0	6	338	307	171	138	29	135	362	.243

9 JED LOWRIE   SS

Born: April 17, 1984. **B-T:** B-R. **Ht.:** 6-0. **Wt.:** 180. **Drafted:** Stanford, 2005 (1st round supplemental). **Signed by:** Nakia Hill.

Lowrie won the Pacific-10 Conference triple crown as a sophomore in 2004 but slipped as a junior, allowing the Red Sox to get him with the 45th overall pick. Lowrie led the New York-Penn League in on-base percentage and played a solid shortstop after manning second base at Stanford. After previous struggles in the Alaska League and with Team USA, he eased doubts about his ability to hit with wood during his pro debut. A switch-hitter, he shortened and smoothed out his swing from the right side. He has good loft power from the left side and knows the strike zone. The Red Sox think he has enough arm strength and athleticism to remain at shortstop for a while. He has average speed. Lowrie's ability to stick at shortstop hinges on his range. His footwork and lateral movement are the question marks, though he was better than expected in both areas. He's not used to making plays from deep in the hole, which give him trouble. Lowrie will skip a level and go to high Class A for his first full season. With Dustin Pedroia playing second base and Hanley Ramirez traded, Lowrie is now the system's top shortstop prospect.

Year	Club (League)	Class	AVG	G	AB	R	H	2B	3B	HR	RBI	BB	SO	SB	OBP	SLG
2005	Lowell (NY-P)	A	.328	53	201	36	66	12	0	4	32	34	30	7	.429	.448
MINOR LEAGUE TOTALS			.328	53	201	36	66	12	0	4	32	34	30	7	.429	.448

10   CLAY BUCHHOLZ   RHP

Born: Aug. 14, 1984. **B-T:** L-R. **Ht.:** 6-3. **Wt.:** 190. **Drafted:** Angelina (Texas) JC, 2005 (1st round supplemental). **Signed by:** Jim Robinson.

After getting just 18 at-bats as a freshman infielder at McNeese State in 2004, Buchholz transferred to Angelina (Texas) Junior College to get more playing time. The move paid off, as he starred as a two-way player and went 42nd overall in the 2005 draft, signing for $800,000. Despite his inexperience on the mound, Buchholz has a fair amount of polish, outstanding athleticism and tremendous potential. While he pitched mostly at 88-92 mph while working on strict pitch limits at short-season Lowell, he often picked up velocity and sat at 93-94 in the late innings at Angelina. His changeup is his second-best pitch right now, and he also has the makings of an above-average slider and curveball. Some teams avoided him in the draft because he was arrested in April 2004 and charged with stealing laptop computers from a middle school and selling them. Boston officials say they aren't concerned about further problems. His secondary pitches come and go. Buchholz will open 2006 at low Class A Greenville. A potential No. 3 starter, he'll move as quickly as he refines his breaking pitches and changeup.

Year	Club (League)	Class	W	L	ERA	G	GS	CG	SV	IP	H	R	ER	HR	BB	SO	AVG
2005	Lowell (NY-P)	A	0	1	2.62	15	15	0	0	41	34	15	12	2	9	45	.219
MINOR LEAGUE TOTALS			0	1	2.62	15	15	0	0	41	34	15	12	2	9	45	.219

11   MICHAEL BOWDEN   RHP

Born: Sept. 9, 1986. **B-T:** R-R. **Ht.:** 6-3. **Wt.:** 215. **Drafted:** HS—Aurora, Ill., 2005 (1st round supplemental). **Signed by:** Danny Haas.

Area scouts who followed Bowden as an Illinois high schooler last spring loved him. His highlight was a 19-strikeout perfect game that Red Sox scouting director Jason McLeod called the best prep pitching performance he had ever seen. But when a slew of directors and crosscheckers showed up for his next start, he pitched in the mid-80s. He was just worn out from spending hours the previous day patching holes in the family driveway, an example of his strong makeup and work ethic. Boston took Bowden with the 47th overall pick in June and signed him for $730,000. Outside of that outing, he consistently showed a heavy 92-93 mph fastball. His curveball, one of the best in the 2005 high school ranks, may be an even better pitch. He started to work on a changeup in instructional league, and the Red Sox were encouraged by his progress. He throws strikes but like most young pitchers, he'll have to refine his location. The one red flag some teams had with Bowden was his unorthodox delivery. But after doing extensive video study, Boston concluded that his mechanics work fine for him, he repeats them well and isn't at any risk. He's a quality athlete—one scouting director clocked him in an above-average 4.2 seconds from the right side of the plate to first base—and his strong frame should make him a workhorse. Bowden took it slow in his debut, working just six innings, but could make the jump to low Class A in 2006.

Year	Club (League)	Class	W	L	ERA	G	GS	CG	SV	IP	H	R	ER	HR	BB	SO	AVG
2005	Red Sox (GCL)	R	1	0	0.00	4	2	0	0	6	4	0	0	0	4	10	.190
MINOR LEAGUE TOTALS			1	0	0.00	4	2	0	0	6	4	0	0	0	4	10	.190

12   DAVID MURPHY   OF

Born: Oct. 18, 1981. **B-T:** R-R. **Ht.:** 6-4. **Wt.:** 192. **Drafted:** Baylor, 2003 (1st round). **Signed by:** Jim Robinson.

The Red Sox deliberated between taking Murphy or Conor Jackson with the 17th overall pick in the 2003 draft. Boston ultimately went for Murphy, while Jackson since has established himself as one of the game's best hitting prospects. Murphy, meanwhile, has encountered more than his share of adversity after signing for $1.525 million. He pulled the muscle off the bone in his left foot in a freak baserunning accident in 2004, ruining his first full season. When he was hitting .230 with one homer through mid-June last year, it looked like his bat might never come around. But Murphy made adjustments and hit .301 with 16 doubles and 13 homers in the final 2½ months. He has plus raw power that's starting to come out, and he should hit more homers if he can add strength to his lanky, athletic frame. The key for Murphy was refining his ability to manage counts, getting ahead so pitchers had to feed him pitches he can drive. He also improved his timing and worked with Portland batting coach Russ Morman to keep his bat in the zone longer. Even when he wasn't hitting, he never stopped working and didn't let his struggles affect his baserunning or defense. One of the reasons the Red Sox took him over Jackson was that they projected Murphy as a center fielder even though he played right field at Baylor. Murphy's conversion has gone well, and he earned the organization's first-ever minor league defensive player of the year award in 2005. Murphy has average speed but covers more than enough ground in center because he plays hard, positions himself well and has good instincts. He goes back well on balls and his arm is above-average for a center fielder. Murphy could push for the Boston center-field job toward the end of 2006.

Year	Club (League)	Class	AVG	G	AB	R	H	2B	3B	HR	RBI	BB	SO	SB	OBP	SLG
2003	Lowell (NY-P)	A	.346	21	78	13	27	4	0	0	13	16	9	4	.453	.397
	Sarasota (FSL)	A	.242	45	153	18	37	5	1	1	18	20	33	6	.329	.307
2004	Red Sox (GCL)	R	.278	5	18	3	5	1	0	0	1	1	2	1	.316	.333
	Sarasota (FSL)	A	.261	73	272	35	71	11	0	4	38	25	46	3	.323	.346
2005	Portland (EL)	AA	.275	135	484	71	133	25	4	14	75	46	83	13	.337	.430
MINOR LEAGUE TOTALS			.272	279	1005	140	273	46	5	19	145	108	173	27	.342	.384

13 LUIS SOTO · OF

Born: Dec. 7, 1985. **B-T:** B-R. **Ht.:** 6-1. **Wt.:** 180. **Signed:** Dominican Republic, 2003. **Signed by:** Louie Eljaua.

After signing for $500,000 in November 2003, Soto began his career in the United States. All went well in the complex-based Rookie-level Gulf Coast League in 2004, but Soto had a harder time making cultural adjustments when he began last season in Greenville. He struggled on the field, looked out of shape and didn't take responsibility for his slow start. After a month, the Red Sox demoted him to extended spring training before eventually turning him loose in the New York-Penn League, where he prospered. A switch-hitter, Soto generates excellent bat speed from both sides of the plate and his power potential is among the best in the system. He still has a lot to figure out at the plate, because he swings at too many first pitches and chases offspeed stuff, but his upside is huge. He's a natural athlete, but Boston moved him off shortstop last year because they wanted to expedite the development of his bat and figured he'd eventually outgrow the position. Soto became a right fielder in spring training. While his routes can be rough, he did show improvement and has the strong arm needed to play in right. He'll give low Class A another try this year.

Year	Club (League)	Class	AVG	G	AB	R	H	2B	3B	HR	RBI	BB	SO	SB	OBP	SLG
2004	Red Sox (GCL)	R	.261	36	134	22	35	9	2	5	16	5	22	4	.289	.470
2005	Greenville (SAL)	A	.212	23	85	6	18	4	0	0	10	4	19	1	.247	.259
	Lowell (NY-P)	A	.293	65	246	39	72	11	1	7	48	27	46	2	.377	.431
MINOR LEAGUE TOTALS			.269	124	465	67	125	24	3	12	74	36	87	7	.330	.411

14 BRANDON MOSS · OF

Born: Sept.16, 1983. **B-T:** L-R. **Ht.:** 6-0. **Wt.:** 195. **Drafted:** HS—Monroe, Ga., 2002 (8th round). **Signed by:** Rob English.

Moss ranked No. 2 on this list a year ago, following a breakout 2004 when he won the batting title and MVP award in the low Class A South Atlantic League before hitting .422 in high Class A. He didn't handle Double-A pitching as well in 2005, however. He still has the same bat speed and nice stroke, and he has more raw power than Portland outfield mate David Murphy. But while Murphy has made adjustments, Moss still needs to refine his approach. Rather than toning down his swing to catch up to good fastballs, he cheats on them. He often swings from his heels, which leads to strikeouts. Adding more patience and strength is the path he needs to take. Moss' bat is his ticket to the majors, as he's a below-average runner and a decent defender with a solid arm in right field. He may not have enough pop to fit the right-field profile, and he continued to struggle in an Arizona Fall League stint. He'd probably be best off if he heads back to Double-A to open the season.

Year	Club (League)	Class	AVG	G	AB	R	H	2B	3B	HR	RBI	BB	SO	SB	OBP	SLG
2002	Red Sox (GCL)	R	.204	42	113	10	23	6	2	0	6	13	40	1	.295	.292
2003	Lowell (NY-P)	A	.237	65	228	29	54	15	4	7	34	15	53	7	.290	.430
2004	Augusta (SAL)	A	.339	109	433	66	147	25	6	13	101	46	75	19	.402	.515
	Sarasota (FSL)	A	.422	23	83	16	35	2	1	2	10	7	15	2	.462	.542
2005	Portland (EL)	AA	.268	135	503	87	135	31	4	16	61	53	129	6	.337	.441
MINOR LEAGUE TOTALS			.290	374	1360	208	394	79	17	38	212	134	312	35	.354	.457

15 EDGAR MARTINEZ · RHP

Born: Oct. 23, 1981. **B-T:** R-R. **Ht.:** 6-0. **Wt.:** 222. **Signed:** Venezuela, 1998. **Signed by:** Levy Ochoa.

Originally signed as a catcher, Martinez spent six years behind the plate and hit .223 before the Red Sox decided a career change was in order in mid-2004. Less than a year after becoming a pitcher, he reached Double-A, and he could work his way into the Boston bullpen in

2006. Martinez always showed a good arm as a catcher, and both that and his knowledge of how to set up hitters have translated well to the mound. He has a lively 93-94 mph fastball that tops out at 96. Though he's just 6 feet tall, he delivers his heat on a good downward angle. His command is solid considering his background, but it will have to get better for him to succeed in the majors. So will his secondary pitches, as he has thrown his slider and changeup for little more than a year. An intelligent pitcher, Martinez has proven to be a quick study and could begin 2006 in Triple-A with just 62 innings of experience.

Year	Club (League)	Class	W	L	ERA	G	GS	CG	SV	IP	H	R	ER	HR	BB	SO	AVG
2004	Augusta (SAL)	A	0	0	0.90	9	0	0	0	10	8	1	1	0	4	5	.211
2005	Wilmington (Car)	A	1	1	2.10	28	0	0	7	34	20	10	8	3	12	46	.167
	Portland (EL)	AA	0	0	1.50	15	0	0	1	18	12	3	3	0	8	13	.190
MINOR LEAGUE TOTALS			1	1	1.73	52	0	0	8	62	40	14	12	3	24	64	.181

16 DAVID PAULEY RHP

Born: June 17, 1983. **B-T:** R-R. **Ht.:** 6-2. **Wt.:** 180. **Drafted:** HS—Longmont, Colo., 2001 (8th round). **Signed by:** Darryl Milne (Padres).

When the Red Sox traded playoffs hero Dave Roberts to San Diego in December 2004, they received three players. Jay Payton sulked over playing time and Ramon Vazquez was a disappointment, and Boston dealt both of them by July. That leaves Pauley, who was added to the 40-man roster. He was originally signed by Padres area scout Darryl Milne, who like Pauley has migrated to the Red Sox. Pauley isn't overpowering on the mound, but he's athletic and has three average pitches. He throws his 88-92 mph fastball on a good downward angle. His curveball is consistent and he has good action on his changeup. He has no problem throwing strikes, and he probably throws too many. Pauley has average life on his fastball but doesn't miss a lot of bats. Even when he's ahead in the count, hitters know he's going to be around the zone. If he can change his approach and entice hitters to chase pitches off the plate, Pauley could become a No. 4 or 5 starter. He's ready for Triple-A.

Year	Club (League)	Class	W	L	ERA	G	GS	CG	SV	IP	H	R	ER	HR	BB	SO	AVG
2001	Idaho Falls (Pio)	R	4	9	6.03	15	15	0	0	69	88	57	46	8	24	53	.308
2002	Eugene (NWL)	A	6	1	2.81	15	15	0	0	80	81	32	25	6	18	62	.266
2003	Fort Wayne (Mid)	A	7	7	3.29	22	21	0	1	118	109	51	43	9	38	117	.245
2004	Lake Elsinore (Cal)	A	7	12	4.17	27	26	0	0	153	155	89	71	8	60	128	.268
2005	Portland (EL)	AA	9	7	3.81	27	27	1	0	156	169	86	66	18	34	104	.274
MINOR LEAGUE TOTALS			33	36	3.92	106	104	1	1	576	602	315	251	49	174	464	.270

17 IAN BLADERGROEN 1B

Born: Feb. 23, 1983. **B-T:** L-L. **Ht.:** 6-4. **Wt.:** 220. **Drafted:** Lamar (Colo.) CC, D/F 2002 (44th round). **Signed by:** Marlon Jones (Mets).

The Red Sox had high hopes for Bladergroen when they acquired him from the Mets for Doug Mientkiewicz in January 2005. The national junior college home run champ with 32 in 2003, he made a run at the South Atlantic League triple crown in 2004 until tearing a ligament in his left wrist in July. Despite having surgery, Bladergroen wasn't nearly at 100 percent in his first season in the Boston system. He had a stress reaction in the wrist, which caused him to be shut down for two months starting in May. When he returned, he still didn't have his usual power. Trying to compensate, he messed up his swing and endured a miserable season. When he's going well, Bladergroen works counts, keeps the bat in the hitting zone well and uses the entire field. Before he got hurt, however, some scouts questioned his bat speed, which isn't exceptional. He's a below-average runner and had problems with his glove in 2005, leading high Class A Carolina League first basemen with nine errors while playing just 64 games in the field. Bladergroen started to get back on track in instructional league and is looking forward to a fully healthy season back in high Class A.

Year	Club (League)	Class	AVG	G	AB	R	H	2B	3B	HR	RBI	BB	SO	SB	OBP	SLG
2003	Brooklyn (NY-P)	A	.285	74	274	33	78	12	3	6	36	21	51	0	.354	.416
2004	Capital City (SAL)	A	.342	72	269	39	92	23	3	13	74	25	55	1	.397	.595
2005	Red Sox (GCL)	R	.444	5	18	4	8	1	1	1	6	3	3	0	.524	.778
	Wilmington (Car)	A	.240	75	263	25	63	6	3	4	31	30	77	0	.337	.331
MINOR LEAGUE TOTALS			.292	226	824	101	241	42	10	24	147	79	186	1	.366	.455

18 CHRISTIAN LARA SS

Born: April 11, 1985. **B-T:** B-R. **Ht.:** 5-11. **Wt.:** 150. **Signed:** Venezuela, 2002. **Signed by:** Miguel Garcia.

Coming into 2005, shortstop was the strongest position in the system. But since then, Hanley Ramirez has gone to the Marlins in the Josh Beckett trade; Dustin Pedroia shifted over to second base and Luis Soto has gone to right field. Unless Pedroia moves back, that leaves Lara as the organization's undisputed top shortstop prospect. He has a chance to be a plus defender, with slightly above-average range and arm strength and instincts that make him even better than his tools. He's steady too, leading South Atlantic League shortstops with a .951 fielding percentage in 2005. The question with Lara is his bat. He hit .330 in his U.S. debut in 2004 but dropped 98 points when he moved up to low Class A last year. He's a switch-hitter with bat-handling skills, but he's going to have to get much stronger. He'll never be a power threat, but he faded badly in his first full season, hitting .181 with five extra-base hits in the final two months. While Lara has some speed, realistically he's going to hit near the bottom of a big league lineup. He's intelligent, works hard and understands what he needs to do. He'll begin 2006 back in low Class A in an effort to get his bat going.

Year	Club (League)	Class	AVG	G	AB	R	H	2B	3B	HR	RBI	BB	SO	SB	OBP	SLG
2003	Red Sox East (DSL)	R	.273	65	256	52	70	7	1	0	22	35	53	24	.365	.309
2004	Red Sox (GCL)	R	.433	15	60	14	26	8	2	0	9	7	10	8	.493	.633
	Lowell (NY-P)	A	.277	32	119	21	33	3	2	0	10	24	23	10	.404	.336
2005	Greenville (SAL)	A	.232	112	384	64	89	14	3	2	31	37	90	6	.304	.299
MINOR LEAGUE TOTALS			.266	224	819	151	218	32	8	2	72	103	176	48	.353	.332

19 JEFF CORSALETTI   OF

Born: Feb. 2, 1983. **B-T:** L-R. **Ht.:** 6-0. **Wt.:** 190. **Drafted:** Florida, 2005 (6th round). **Signed by:** Jon Lukens.

Corsaletti went 0-for-8 in Florida's two-game College World Series championship series sweep at the hands of Texas, but his slump didn't extend into pro ball. After signing in June for $50,000 as a sixth-round pick, he went straight to low Class A and hit safely in his first 15 games. He finished his pro debut with a .357 average, the highest among Boston farmhands with full-season teams. Corsaletti has an effective game plan at the plate. He has a sound swing, knows the strike zone and centers the ball on the bat well. With an open stance and his bat cocked over his shoulder, he reminds some scouts of Luis Gonzalez. Corsaletti doesn't have Gonzalez' power, but he can drive the ball to the gaps and uses the whole field. His speed rates a 55 on the 20-80 scouting scale, he gets out of the batter's box well and he owns good instincts on the bases. Staying in center field would enhance Corsaletti's value, because he profiles as no more than a backup on the corners. He needs more work in center, but he won't get much if he plays alongside 2005 first-rounder Jacoby Ellsbury in high Class A. Corsaletti's arm is well-below-average.

Year	Club (League)	Class	AVG	G	AB	R	H	2B	3B	HR	RBI	BB	SO	SB	OBP	SLG
2005	Greenville (SAL)	A	.357	59	249	49	89	17	2	4	26	32	38	9	.429	.490
MINOR LEAGUE TOTALS			.357	59	249	49	89	17	2	4	26	32	38	9	.429	.490

20 CLA MEREDITH   RHP

Born: June 4, 1983. **B-T:** R-R. **Ht.:** 6-0. **Wt.:** 180. **Drafted:** Virginia Commonwealth, 2004 (6th round). **Signed by:** Jeff Zona.

Meredith followed Huston Street to become the second player from the 2004 draft to reach the majors, getting the call to join a decimated Boston bullpen in early May. He tightened up after the promotion and his arm lacked its usual whip. He surrendered a grand slam to Richie Sexson in his first game, then gave up four runs in two more appearances before returning to Triple-A. He wasn't the same pitcher afterward, posting a 5.59 ERA for the remainder of the season. He started nibbling and trying to trick hitters, rather than going after them with a sinker and no fear as he had before. Meredith is tough to pick up for hitters, especially righthanders, because he uses a crossfire delivery from a low three-quarters angle. His funky motion gives him plus-plus sink on an 87-90 mph fastball, making him a groundball machine. His slider is a fringe-average second pitch, though it floats dangerously high in the strike zone when he doesn't stay on top of it. He throws strikes with ease. Though lefties hit .359 against him in Triple-A, his exceptional movement has been enough to keep them at bay in the past. Once Meredith realizes he doesn't need to reinvent himself, he'll be fine. Ticketed for Triple-A, he could resurface with the Red Sox later in 2006.

Year	Club (League)	Class	W	L	ERA	G	GS	CG	SV	IP	H	R	ER	HR	BB	SO	AVG
2004	Augusta (SAL)	A	1	0	0.00	13	0	0	6	15	8	0	0	0	3	18	.148
	Sarasota (FSL)	A	0	2	2.21	16	0	0	12	16	15	4	4	0	3	16	.234
2005	Portland (EL)	AA	1	0	0.00	12	0	0	9	15	5	0	0	0	3	12	.106
	Boston (AL)	MLB	0	0	27.00	3	0	0	0	2	6	7	7	1	4	0	.462
	Wilmington (Car)	A	0	0	0.00	1	0	0	0	1	1	0	0	0	0	2	.250
	Pawtucket (IL)	AAA	2	5	5.59	40	0	0	10	48	63	30	30	6	12	42	.312
MAJOR LEAGUE TOTALS			0	0	27.00	3	0	0	0	2	6	7	7	1	4	0	.462
MINOR LEAGUE TOTALS			4	7	3.19	82	0	0	37	96	92	34	34	6	21	90	.248

21 JERMAINE VAN BUREN

RHP

Born: July 2, 1980. **B-T:** R-R. **Ht.:** 6-1. **Wt.:** 220. **Drafted:** HS—Hattiesburg, Miss., 1998 (2nd round). **Signed by:** Damon Iannelli (Rockies).

When the Cubs found themselves needing to clear a spot on their 40-man roster in December, they traded Van Buren to the Red Sox for fringe outfield prospect Matt Ciaramella. Van Buren made his big league debut in August, completing a circuitous trek that began when the Rockies drafted him in the second round out of high school seven years earlier. He led the Rookie-level Arizona League in ERA and strikeouts in his 1998 pro debut, but he couldn't get past low Class A before the Rockies released him in March 2003. He spent that season in the independent Central League before hooking up with Chicago. He led the Cubs system in saves in both 2004 and 2005. His slider is his best pitch, and he locates his 90-92 mph fastball well. He also has a changeup and the confidence to throw any pitch in any count. There is some effort to Van Buren's delivery, which can affect his command, and he wasn't aggressive enough during his brief time in the majors. After posting the second-worst bullpen ERA (5.15) in the majors last year, Boston is reworking its relief corps. Van Buren will get a look in spring training but likely will open 2006 in Triple-A.

Year	Club (League)	Class	W	L	ERA	G	GS	CG	SV	IP	H	R	ER	HR	BB	SO	AVG
1998	Rockies (AZL)	R	7	2	2.22	12	11	1	0	65	42	20	16	2	22	92	.182
	Portland (NWL)	A	0	0	3.60	2	2	0	0	10	7	4	4	0	7	9	.212
1999	Asheville (SAL)	A	7	10	4.91	28	28	0	0	143	143	87	78	16	70	133	.266
2000	Portland (NWL)	A	4	5	2.61	13	13	0	0	69	54	27	20	1	30	41	.214
2001	Casper (Pio)	R	3	0	5.32	6	3	1	0	24	25	15	14	2	10	25	.275
	Tri-City (NWL)	A	1	0	7.20	1	1	0	0	5	7	4	4	0	3	2	.304
2002	Asheville (SAL)	A	6	9	4.96	30	17	0	0	107	115	71	59	13	44	88	.276
2003	Fort Worth (Cen)	IND	9	4	3.07	18	18	1	0	111	107	45	38	4	37	113	.255
2004	Lansing (Mid)	A	0	1	1.80	3	0	0	0	5	6	1	1	0	5	7	.300
	West Tenn (SL)	AA	3	2	1.87	51	0	0	21	53	23	11	11	2	24	64	.128
	Iowa (PCL)	AAA	0	0	2.09	3	0	0	1	4	3	1	1	1	0	5	.188
2005	Iowa (PCL)	AAA	2	3	1.97	52	0	0	25	55	33	13	12	5	22	65	.181
	Chicago (NL)	MLB	0	2	3.00	6	0	0	0	6	2	2	2	0	9	3	.118
MAJOR LEAGUE TOTALS			0	2	3.00	6	0	0	0	6	2	2	2	0	9	3	.118
MINOR LEAGUE TOTALS			33	32	3.67	201	75	2	47	540	458	254	220	42	237	531	.231

22 JOSE VAQUEDANO

RHP

Born: July 9, 1981. **B-T:** R-R. **Ht.:** 6-4. **Wt.:** 185. **Drafted:** Vernon (Texas) CC, 2002 (35th round). **Signed by:** Jim Robinson.

Vaquedano made another successful step in his quest to become the first Honduran-born player to reach the majors. He advanced to high Class A and was the hardest starter to hit in the Carolina League, surrendering just a .219 average when he worked out of the rotation. Vaquedano misses bats more because of his ability to locate his pitches than sheer stuff. He throws an 88-91 mph fastball on a tough downward plane, setting hitters up for his deceptive changeup. His slider currently rates as below average, and his ability to refine it may be the difference between projecting him as a back-of-the-rotation starter versus a long reliever. Though Vaquedano has a skinny frame, he has been durable. He's a tough competitor who isn't afraid to challenge hitters with less-than-overpowering stuff. While the Red Sox didn't protect him on their 40-man roster this offseason, they respect what he's accomplished and he's an organization favorite. Vaquedano will have to keep proving himself, with Double-A his next test.

Year	Club (League)	Class	W	L	ERA	G	GS	CG	SV	IP	H	R	ER	HR	BB	SO	AVG
2002	Lowell (NY-P)	A	1	3	4.35	22	0	0	0	39	46	33	19	4	18	35	.293
2003	Lowell (NY-P)	A	7	4	3.30	14	10	0	0	74	67	30	27	4	15	70	.241
2004	Augusta (SAL)	A	4	2	1.88	11	11	0	0	67	59	22	14	5	12	66	.235
	Sarasota (FSL)	A	5	1	3.95	14	8	0	0	68	65	34	30	4	21	60	.265
2005	Wilmington (Car)	A	8	7	3.75	28	23	0	1	146	120	66	61	12	50	117	.224
MINOR LEAGUE TOTALS			25	17	3.44	89	52	0	1	395	357	185	151	29	116	348	.244

23 LENNY DiNARDO

LHP

Born: Sept. 19, 1979. **B-T:** L-L. **Ht.:** 6-4. **Wt.:** 195. **Drafted:** Stetson, 2001 (3rd round). **Signed by:** Joe DelliCarri (Mets).

DiNardo's career has ridden a roller coaster, and it may be about to stop in Boston. As a sophomore in 2000, he went 21-1 between Stetson and Team USA, establishing himself as a possible first-round pick for the following draft. But his fastball dropped from the high 80s to the mid-80s in 2001, and he fell to the Mets in the third round. The Red Sox took him in the major league Rule 5 draft after the 2003 season and retained him by keeping him on the big league roster throughout 2004 (thanks in part to some creative disabled-list time with a shoulder strain and blister). DiNardo's fastball has remained at 84-86 mph but he has advanced because he can't throw it straight. It has natural cutting action, and he can turn over his fastball to achieve some sink. Though he can't light up radar guns, he doesn't hesitate to pitch inside. He also isn't afraid to throw strikes, either. DiNardo has a changeup that he uses to keep righthanders honest, and he can vary the speed of his curveball. He spent most of 2005 as a starter in Triple-A, where his 3.15 ERA would have ranked second in the International League if he hadn't just missed qualifying. DiNardo is 26 and he's far from a sexy prospect, but he has pitched creditably in the majors over the last two seasons, and the Red Sox don't have a better lefty option for their bullpen.

Year	Club (League)	Class	W	L	ERA	G	GS	CG	SV	IP	H	R	ER	HR	BB	SO	AVG
2001	Brooklyn (NY-P)	A	1	2	2.00	9	5	0	0	36	26	10	8	0	17	40	.200
2002	Capital City (SAL)	A	5	5	4.35	24	19	0	1	101	106	60	49	3	56	103	.274
2003	Binghamton (EL)	AA	1	3	3.60	7	7	1	0	40	35	19	16	3	13	36	.236
	St. Lucie (FSL)	A	3	8	2.01	19	13	1	1	85	64	27	19	1	14	93	.211
2004	Sarasota (FSL)	A	0	0	0.00	1	1	0	0	3	2	0	0	0	0	2	.182
	Pawtucket (IL)	AAA	0	0	0.00	1	1	0	0	3	3	0	0	0	0	4	.250
	Boston (AL)	MLB	0	0	4.22	22	0	0	0	28	34	17	13	1	12	21	.298
	Red Sox (GCL)	R	0	0	0.00	2	1	0	0	3	3	0	0	0	0	5	.273
	Portland (EL)	AA	1	0	9.47	3	0	0	0	6	8	6	6	1	1	4	.320
2005	Pawtucket (IL)	AAA	6	3	3.15	23	22	0	0	109	109	51	38	7	35	93	.265
	Boston (AL)	MLB	0	1	1.84	8	0	0	0	15	13	6	3	1	5	15	.236
MAJOR LEAGUE TOTALS			0	1	3.40	30	1	0	0	42	47	23	16	2	17	36	.278
MINOR LEAGUE TOTALS			17	21	3.17	89	69	2	2	386	356	173	136	15	136	380	.247

24 MIKE ROZIER
LHP

Born: July 4, 1985. **B-T:** L-L. **Ht.:** 6-5. **Wt.:** 210. **Drafted:** HS—Stockbridge, Ga., 2004 (12th round). **Signed by:** Rob English.

The Red Sox forfeited their first-round pick in the 2004 draft by signing free agent Keith Foulke, but they gave first-round money to Rozier after taking him in the 12th round. Rozier's $1.575 million bonus is a record for a player taken after the third round (not counting draft-and-follows). Most teams viewed him as a third- to fifth-round talent, and he dropped as far as he did because of signability. He was a three-sport star in high school and had a football scholarship to play quarterback at North Carolina. He looked sharp in instructional league after signing, reminding Boston special assistant Bill Lajoie of Mark Mulder. When Rozier took the mound in his 2005 pro debut, he wasn't the same pitcher, however. His fastball, which sat at 88-92 mph and topped out at 95 in 2004, rarely rose above the high 80s. His curveball, which had been sharp, became sloppy and loopy. He didn't look as athletic and threw with more effort to his delivery. Rozier wasn't in shape to deal with the rigors of pro ball. He has to work out more diligently and learn to eat better. He's still just 19, and he'll have to mature both emotionally and physically. The Red Sox give Rozier credit for competing with mediocre stuff, especially considering he was a teenager in a full-season league. He did improve his changeup, which he didn't need in high school but was his best pitch at the end of the year. He's still young and projectable, and Boston hopes he can apply the lessons he learned the hard way when he repeats low Class A in 2006.

Year	Club (League)	Class	W	L	ERA	G	GS	CG	SV	IP	H	R	ER	HR	BB	SO	AVG
2005	Greenville (SAL)	A	6	5	3.90	21	20	0	0	92	94	50	40	8	49	52	.268
MINOR LEAGUE TOTALS			6	5	3.90	21	20	0	0	92	94	50	40	8	49	52	.268

25 ADAM STERN
OF

Born: Feb. 12, 1980. **B-T:** L-R. **Ht.:** 5-11. **Wt.:** 180. **Drafted:** Nebraska, 2001 (3rd round). **Signed by:** Tyrone Brooks (Braves).

The Red Sox still need to do some more roster juggling before they officially own the rights to Stern, a major league Rule 5 draft pick from the Braves in 2004. Because he spent so much time on the disabled list and rehab assignments after breaking his right thumb in spring training, he came up 18 days short of the minimum 90 he had to spend on active big league duty. He got just 96 at-bats last year, so it was a wasted year of development at age 25. The Red Sox still like his potential to eventually contribute as a line-drive-hitting center fielder who can offer speed and defense. Stern had a breakthrough season in 2004—when he also played center field on Canada's fourth-place Olympic team—after he accepted the fact that power isn't his game. He shortened his stroke and focused on putting the ball in play, the better to take advantage of his plus speed. Drawing more walks also would help in that regard. A very capable center fielder, he has an above-average arm for his position. After Stern logs his required major league time in April, he'll probably go to Triple-A. David

Murphy is scheduled to play center field in Pawtucket, so Stern may have to play on a corner.

Year	Club (League)	Class	AVG	G	AB	R	H	2B	3B	HR	RBI	BB	SO	SB	OBP	SLG
2001	Jamestown (NY-P)	A	.307	21	75	20	23	4	2	0	11	15	11	9	.413	.413
2002	Myrtle Beach (Car)	A	.253	119	462	65	117	22	10	3	47	27	89	40	.298	.364
2003	Braves (GCL)	R	.345	7	29	6	10	1	0	1	6	6	3	2	.457	.483
	Myrtle Beach (Car)	A	.194	28	103	11	20	2	0	0	6	13	21	7	.282	.214
2004	Greenville (SL)	AA	.322	102	394	64	127	26	6	8	47	35	58	27	.378	.480
2005	Pawtucket (IL)	AAA	.321	20	81	16	26	8	0	2	14	8	10	3	.385	.494
	Boston (AL)	MLB	.133	36	15	4	2	0	0	1	2	0	4	1	.188	.333
MAJOR LEAGUE TOTALS			.133	36	15	4	2	0	0	1	2	0	4	1	.188	.333
MINOR LEAGUE TOTALS			.282	297	1144	182	323	63	18	14	131	104	192	88	.343	.406

26 ABE ALVAREZ
LHP

Born: Oct. 17, 1982. **B-T:** L-L. **Ht.:** 6-2. **Wt.:** 190. **Drafted:** Long Beach State, 2003 (2nd round). **Signed by:** Jim Woodward.

The Red Sox thought Alvarez' exceptional command and feel would overcome his fringy stuff when they made him a second-round pick in 2003, but it's time to temper expectations. Part of the Long Beach State pitching factory that also has churned out first- and second-round picks Cesar Ramos, Jason Vargas, Jered Weaver in the last two drafts, Alvarez made an emergency big league start in July 2004, 13 months after turning pro. While he has the best control and one of top changeups in the system, the rest of his pitches are fringy. His 85-88 mph fastball and his curveball are most notable for his ability to throw them for strikes. He has added a cut fastball to help him get inside on righthanders, but it's nothing special either. Alvarez repeats his delivery and competes well. While he has held his own in the upper minors, scouts fear big leaguers will just wait him out and pound him when he comes over the plate with his very hittable stuff. His ceiling is at best as a No. 5 starter, but more realistically, he'll be a middle reliever or lefty specialist.

Year	Club (League)	Class	W	L	ERA	G	GS	CG	SV	IP	H	R	ER	HR	BB	SO	AVG
2003	Lowell (NY-P)	A	0	0	0.00	9	9	0	0	19	9	2	0	0	2	19	.138
2004	Boston (AL)	MLB	0	1	9.00	1	1	0	0	5	8	5	5	2	5	2	.400
	Portland (EL)	AA	10	9	3.66	26	26	0	0	135	133	65	55	13	32	108	.257
2005	Boston (AL)	MLB	0	0	15.65	2	0	0	0	2	6	4	4	1	0	1	.462
	Pawtucket (IL)	AAA	11	6	4.85	26	26	0	0	145	143	84	78	17	31	109	.255
MAJOR LEAGUE TOTALS			0	1	11.05	3	1	0	0	7	14	9	9	3	5	3	.424
MINOR LEAGUE TOTALS			21	15	4.00	61	61	0	0	299	285	151	133	30	65	236	.249

27 JON EGAN
C

Born: Oct. 12, 1986. **B-T:** R-R. **Ht.:** 6-4. **Wt.:** 210. **Drafted:** HS—Hephzibah, Ga., 2005 (2nd round). **Signed by:** Rob English.

Egan's first year as a pro didn't go as expected, on several fronts. A second-round pick in June who signed for $625,000, he had a reputation as a slugger who might not be able to stay behind the plate in the long term. Yet in his debut, his defense outshone his offense. Though he has a big frame, Egan showed surprising agility and good receiving skills. He also threw better than Boston expected, erasing 39 percent of basestealers. Meanwhile, his bat wilted in the heat of the Gulf Coast League. His raw power didn't come out in games and his swing looked sluggish. He was too tentative at the plate. While Egan drew walks, he didn't pull the trigger on pitches he could crush and took too many called strikes. The most alarming part of his year came after the season ended. Egan was arrested for driving while intoxicated and police also found traces of cocaine in his wallet. The Red Sox believe it was a one-time incident and supported him as he dealt with the aftermath, including placing him in a counseling program. He apologized to his teammates after reporting late to instructional league, a significant step for a kid known for his quiet demeanor. He could move up to low Class A this year, but Boston may take it slow and start him in extended spring training before sending him to Lowell in June.

Year	Club (League)	Class	AVG	G	AB	R	H	2B	3B	HR	RBI	BB	SO	SB	OBP	SLG
2005	Red Sox (GCL)	R	.222	35	126	19	28	6	0	1	15	21	29	0	.340	.294
MINOR LEAGUE TOTALS			.222	35	126	19	28	6	0	1	15	21	29	0	.340	.294

28 GARY GALVEZ
RHP

Born: March 24, 1984. **B-T:** R-R **Ht.:** 6-2. **Wt.:** 200. **Signed:** Dominican Republic, 2003. **Signed by:** Louie Eljaua.

The Red Sox never have landed a high-profile Cuban defector, but they did prevail in the spirited bidding for Galvez in February 2003. They beat out the Dodgers, Mariners, Phillies and Yankees with a $450,000 bonus amid reports he turned down a $500,000 offer from another club. He chose Boston because he had developed a relationship with Sox director of international operations Louis Eljaua (who since has joined the Pirates). Visa issues forced Galvez to make his debut in the Rookie-level Dominican Summer League, and he has spent the last two years in low Class A. The Red Sox were pleased with the improvement he showed from 2004 to 2005. He used his 90-91 mph fastball more often last year rather than trying to fool hitters with his offspeed stuff. He also improved his conditioning and looked more confident on the mound. Galvez' curveball, slider and changeup are all average pitches, but he lacks a putaway option. As a result, he must be fine with his location, especially with his fastball, which features little movement. His ceiling isn't high but he's headed in the right direction. He'll pitch in high Class A this year.

Year	Club (League)	Class	W	L	ERA	G	GS	CG	SV	IP	H	R	ER	HR	BB	SO	AVG
2003	Red Sox East (DSL)	R	6	3	1.64	14	11	0	2	71	66	26	13	0	10	65	.234
2004	Augusta (SAL)	A	7	10	5.14	30	22	1	0	140	153	86	80	16	36	102	.281
2005	Greenville (SAL)	A	10	4	3.35	31	18	0	0	126	118	64	47	12	40	87	.242
MINOR LEAGUE TOTALS			23	17	3.73	75	51	1	2	338	337	176	140	28	86	254	.256

29 MICKEY HALL   OF

Born: May 20, 1985. **B-T:** L-L. **Ht.:** 6-0. **Wt.:** 198. **Drafted:** HS—Marietta, Ga., 2003 (2nd round). **Signed by:** Rob English.

In the 2003 draft, Theo Epstein's first as Red Sox general manager, the club took only one high schooler in the first 16 rounds: Hall. A second-rounder who signed for $800,000, he consistently has been one of the youngest players in his leagues. Being the youngest regular in the Carolina League and playing in Wilmington's pitcher-friendly Frawley Stadium caught up to him in 2005. He struggled with pitch recognition against more advanced competition, and his lone hot streak came to an abrupt end when he was hit by a pitch and broke his left index finger in May. He missed the next two months and finished the season in a 14-for-96 (.146) slump. Hall has a good swing and should grow into at least solid power, but he needs to alter his approach to make more contact. A good athlete, he has slightly above-average speed and arm strength, yet spent most of his time in left field last year. He'll probably shift to right field in 2006, when he repeats high Class A with Jacoby Ellsbury and Jeff Corsaletti also slated for Wilmington.

Year	Club (League)	Class	AVG	G	AB	R	H	2B	3B	HR	RBI	BB	SO	SB	OBP	SLG
2003	Red Sox (GCL)	R	.227	21	66	7	15	6	0	0	9	19	24	1	.400	.318
2004	Augusta (SAL)	A	.246	118	403	67	99	24	5	13	63	58	134	13	.342	.427
2005	Wilmington (Car)	A	.216	71	250	31	54	16	4	6	25	32	98	5	.304	.384
	Red Sox (GCL)	R	.259	9	27	4	7	1	0	0	1	5	10	0	.394	.296
MINOR LEAGUE TOTALS			.235	219	746	109	175	47	9	19	98	114	266	19	.337	.398

30 ANDREW PINCKNEY   3B

Born: April 7, 1982. **B-T:** L-R. **Ht.:** 6-1. **Wt.:** 195. **Drafted:** Emory (Ga.), 2004 (34th round). **Signed by:** Rob English.

Pinckney began his college career at Baylor before transferring to NCAA Division III Emory (Ga.), where he became the program's best player since it was reinstituted in 1991. In 2003, he led Division III with 85 hits and carried the Eagles to the D-III College World Series, where he earned all-tournament honors by batting .615. He followed up in 2004 by becoming the first Emory position player to become a first-team all-American and finishing with school records for career batting average (.433) and slugging percentage (.726). A South Atlantic League all-star last year, Pinckney quickly has become an organization favorite because of his all-out, all-the-time style. He has a quick, sound stroke that allows him to hit for average and power against lefthanders and righthanders alike. He made much better contact in 2005 than he did in his pro debut, though he still needs to walk more. Pinckney is a solid athlete with average speed and good instincts. He has the strongest infield arm in the system and the versatility to play all four infield positions. He profiles best at third base, where he spent most of last year, and there has been some talk of trying him as a catcher. The biggest knock on Pinckney at this point is that he has been very old for his levels, playing in low Class A at age 23. Some club officials would like to see him jump to Double-A this year, but he probably won't skip high Class A. If he eventually makes it all the way to Boston, Pinckney will join Parson Perryman as the only big leaguers from Emory.

Year	Club (League)	Class	AVG	G	AB	R	H	2B	3B	HR	RBI	BB	SO	SB	OBP	SLG
2004	Lowell (NY-P)	A	.273	64	242	23	66	9	1	3	25	22	74	2	.338	.355
2005	Greenville (SAL)	A	.311	128	508	91	158	33	9	21	98	36	78	6	.362	.535
MINOR LEAGUE TOTALS			.299	192	750	114	224	42	10	24	123	58	152	8	.354	.477

CHICAGO
CUBS

BY **JIM CALLIS**

On Oct. 14, 2003, the Cubs got within five outs of their first World Series appearance since World War II. Then Luis Castillo lofted a fly ball down the left-field line at Wrigley Field, fate intervened and Chicago hasn't been the same since.

Even after the Marlins roared back to win the National League Championship Series  and ultimately the World Series, the Cubs consoled themselves with thoughts of a bright future built around a young pitching staff and a promising farm system.

That bright future hasn't materialized, as Chicago has underachieved at the major and minor league levels the last two years. The Cubs did post their first consecutive winning seasons since 1971-72 with 89 victories in 2004, but they blew the NL wild-card lead in the final week of the season. Expected to contend again in 2005, they finished with the 10th-best record in the NL at 79-83.

Pitching injuries have hurt terribly. Neither Mark Prior nor Kerry Wood totaled as many wins in 2004-05 as he did in 2003, and Wood's future as a starter is now in doubt. Angel Guzman, then Chicago's top prospect, tore his labrum in July 2003 and has worked just 66 innings since. Chadd Blasko, Luke Hagerty and Billy Petrick also have gone under the knife, while Bobby Brownlie's stuff has regressed and Andy Sisco was lost in the major league Rule 5 draft. Only Carlos Zambrano has lived up to expectations in the last two seasons.

Chicago has had worse luck developing position players. Their only homegrown regular last year was Corey Patterson, once envisioned as a future cornerstone. But Patterson is a stubborn hitter who's either unwilling or unable to make adjustments, and the team turned the page on him in December by trading for Juan Pierre. The only other proven big league regular signed by Chicago since 1998 is Eric Hinske, who was traded before he appeared in a game for the Cubs.

There may be new blood in the 2006 lineup, however. Left fielder **Matt Murton**, acquired from the Red Sox in the 2004 Nomar Garciaparra trade, and shortstop Ronny Cedeno may have played well enough to win over manager Dusty Baker, who never met a veteran he didn't like. The best prospect in the system is center fielder Felix Pie, who could have supplanted Patterson had he not injured his ankle in mid-June. The acquisition of Pierre will allow him more development time.

The Cubs system isn't nearly as strong as it used to be. Injuries, trades and attrition have taken their toll since Baseball America rated the organization's minor league talent no worse than third in baseball each year from 2001-03. The organization also lost John Stockstill, one of the game's better scouting directors, who left in December to become the Orioles' director of professional scouting. The Cubs found a more than capable replacement in Tim Wilken, a longtime scouting director with the Blue Jays and most recently with the Devil Rays.

TOP 30 PROSPECTS

1. Felix Pie, of	16. Geovany Soto, c
2. Mark Pawelek, lhp	17. Grant Johnson, rhp
3. Ronny Cedeno, ss	18. Billy Petrick, rhp
4. Angel Guzman, rhp	19. Mark Reed, c
5. Rich Hill, lhp	20. Michael Phelps, rhp
6. Sean Marshall, lhp	21. Justin Berg, rhp
7. Ryan Harvey, of	22. Bobby Brownlie, rhp
8. Brian Dopirak, 1b	23. Mike Billek, rhp
9. Eric Patterson, 2b	24. Ryan Theriot, ss/2b
10. Carlos Marmol, rhp	25. Buck Coats, of/ss
11. Donald Veal, lhp	26. Mark Holliman, rhp
12. Sean Gallagher, rhp	27. Dylan Johnston, ss
13. Scott Moore, 3b	28. Tim Layden, lhp
14. Jae-Kuk Ryu, rhp	29. Mike Fontenot, 2b/3b
15. Brandon Sing, 1b/of	30. Luis Montanez, of

ORGANIZATION OVERVIEW

General manager: Jim Hendry. **Farm director:** Oneri Fleita. **Scouting director:** Tim Wilken.

2005 PERFORMANCE

Class	Team	League	W	L	Pct.	Finish*	Manager
Majors	Chicago	National	79	83	.488	10th (16)	Dusty Baker
Triple-A	Iowa Cubs	Pacific Coast	64	75	.460	13th (16)	Mike Quade
Double-A	West Tenn Diamond Jaxx	Southern	83	56	.597	1st (10)	Bobby Dickerson
High A	Daytona Cubs	Florida State	69	66	.511	5th (12)	Richie Zisk
Low A	Peoria Chiefs	Midwest	68	72	.486	9th (14)	Julio Garcia
Short-season	Boise Hawks	Northwest	34	42	.447	t-6th (8)	Trey Forkerway
Rookie	AZL Cubs	Arizona	19	37	.339	9th (9)	Steve McFarland
OVERALL 2005 MINOR LEAGUE RECORD			337	348	.492	20th (30)	

*Finish in overall standings (No. of teams in league).

ORGANIZATION LEADERS

BATTING
*Minimum 250 at-bats
*AVG	Murton, Matt, Iowa/West Tenn	.343
R	Walker, Chris, Daytona	97
H	Walker, Chris, Daytona	152
TB	McClain, Scott, Iowa	244
2B	Montanez, Luis, Peoria/West Tenn	37
3B	Walker, Chris, Daytona	14
HR	McClain, Scott, Iowa	30
RBI	Harvey, Ryan, Peoria	100
BB	Sing, Brandon, West Tenn	91
SO	Harvey, Ryan, Peoria	137
SB	Walker, Chris, Daytona	60
*OBP	Murton, Matt, Iowa/West Tenn	.405
*SLG	McClain, Scott, Iowa	.577

PITCHING
#Minimum 75 innings
W	Gallagher, Sean, Daytona/Peoria	14
	Nolasco, Ricky, West Tenn	14
L	Estrada, Jesse, Peoria	12
	Tavares, Anderson, Daytona/Iowa/West Tenn..	12
#ERA	Gwaltney, Lee, Daytona/Peoria/West Tenn ..	2.07
G	Searles, Jonathan, West Tenn	59
	Shipman, Andy, West Tenn	59
CG	12 tied at	1
SV	Van Buren, Jermaine, Iowa	25
IP	Ryu, Jae-Kuk, West Tenn	170
BB	Pinto, Renyel, Iowa/West Tenn	82
SO	Hill, Rich, Iowa/Peoria/West Tenn	194

BEST TOOLS

Best Hitter for Average	Felix Pie
Best Power Hitter	Ryan Harvey
Best Strike-Zone Discipline	Sam Fuld
Fastest Baserunner	Dwaine Bacon
Best Athlete	Felix Pie
Best Fastball	Mark Pawelek
Best Curveball	Rich Hill
Best Slider	Grant Johnson
Best Changeup	John Koronka
Best Control	Jae-Kuk Ryu
Best Defensive Catcher	Geovany Soto
Best Defensive Infielder	Ronny Cedeno
Best Infield Arm	Ronny Cedeno
Best Defensive Outfielder	Felix Pie
Best Outfield Arm	Ryan Harvey

PROJECTED 2009 LINEUP

Catcher	Michael Barrett
First Base	Derrek Lee
Second Base	Eric Patterson
Third Base	Aramis Ramirez
Shortstop	Ronny Cedeno
Left Field	Matt Murton
Center Field	Juan Pierre
Right Field	Felix Pie
No. 1 Starter	Mark Prior
No. 2 Starter	Carlos Zambrano
No. 3 Starter	Mark Pawelek
No. 4 Starter	Angel Guzman
No. 5 Starter	Rich Hill
Closer	Kerry Wood

LAST YEAR'S TOP 20 PROSPECTS

1. Brian Dopirak, 1b
2. Felix Pie, of
3. Ryan Harvey, of
4. Angel Guzman, rhp
5. Billy Petrick, rhp
6. Renyel Pinto, lhp
7. Sean Marshall, lhp
8. Jon Leicester, rhp
9. Grant Johnson, rhp
10. Jason Dubois, of/1b
11. Matt Murton, of
12. Richard Lewis, 2b
13. Bobby Brownlie, rhp
14. Geovany Soto, c
15. Brandon Sing, 1b
16. Ronny Cedeno, ss
17. Will Ohman, lhp
18. Mike Wuertz, rhp
19. Ricky Nolasco, rhp
20. Carlos Marmol, rhp

TOP PROSPECTS OF THE DECADE

Year	Player, Pos.	2005 Org.
1996	Brooks Kieschnick, of	Astros
1997	Kerry Wood, rhp	Cubs
1998	Kerry Wood, rhp	Cubs
1999	Corey Patterson, of	Cubs
2000	Corey Patterson, of	Cubs
2001	Corey Patterson, of	Cubs
2002	Mark Prior, rhp	Cubs
2003	Hee Seop Choi, 1b	Dodgers
2004	Angel Guzman, rhp	Cubs
2005	Brian Dopirak, 1b	Cubs

TOP DRAFT PICKS OF THE DECADE

Year	Player, Pos.	2005 Org.
1996	Todd Noel, rhp	Out of baseball
1997	Jon Garland, rhp	White Sox
1998	Corey Patterson, of	Cubs
1999	Ben Christensen, rhp	Out of baseball
2000	Luis Montanez, ss	Cubs
2001	Mark Prior, rhp	Cubs
2002	Bobby Brownlie, rhp	Cubs
2003	Ryan Harvey, of	Cubs
2004	Grant Johnson, rhp (2nd round)	Cubs
2005	Mark Pawelek, lhp	Cubs

ALL-TIME LARGEST BONUSES

Mark Prior, 2001	$4,000,000
Corey Patterson, 1998	$3,700,000
Luis Montanez, 2000	$2,750,000
Bobby Brownlie, 2002	$2,500,000
Ryan Harvey, 2003	$2,400,000

MINOR LEAGUE DEPTH CHART

Chicago Cubs

Rank: **15**

STRENGTH: Lefthanded pitching. 2005 additions boost an already solid group.

WEAKNESS: Power. The Cubs' top slugging prospects, led by Brian Dopirak, regressed for the most part last season.

*Depth charts prepared by **John Manuel** and **Chris Kline**. Numbers in parentheses indicate prospect rankings.*

LF
Bo Flowers

CF
Felix Pie (1)
Buck Coats (25)
Adam Greenberg
Dwaine Bacon
Chris Walker
Sam Fuld

RF
Ryan Harvey (7)
Luis Montanez (30)
Johnny Defendis

3B
Scott Moore (13)
Casey McGehee

SS
Ronny Cedeno (3)
Ryan Theriot (24)
Dylan Johnston (27)
Carlos Rojas
Sammy Baez

2B
Eric Patterson (9)
Mike Fontenot (29)
Richard Lewis

1B
Brian Dopirak (8)
Brandon Sing (15)
Matt Craig
Kevin Collins

C
Geovany Soto (16)
Mark Reed (19)
Yusuf Carter
Jose Reyes
Jake Fox

RHP	
Starters	**Relievers**
Angel Guzman (4)	Bobby Brownlie (22)
Carlos Marmol (10)	Mike Billek (23)
Sean Gallagher (12)	David Aardsma
Jae-Kuk Ryu (14)	Randy Wells
Grant Johnson (17)	
Billy Petrick (18)	
Michael Phelps (20)	
Justin Berg (21)	
Mark Holliman (26)	
Chadd Blasko	
Todd Blackford	

LHP	
Starters	**Relievers**
Mark Pawelek (2)	Tim Layden (28)
Rich Hill (5)	John Koronka
Sean Marshall (6)	Russ Rohlicek
Donald Veal (11)	Clay Rapada
Darin Downs	Carlos Jan
Carmen Pignatiello	
Jayson Ruhlman	

DRAFT ANALYSIS

2005

Best Pro Debut: LHP Mark Pawelek (1) didn't win a game because he was on tight pitch counts, but he was rated the top prospect in the Rookie-level Arizona League, where he had a 2.72 ERA and 56 whiffs in 43 innings. OF Davy Gregg (27) hit .280-1-19 and led the short-season Northwest League with 36 steals.

Best Athlete: SS Dylan Johnston (4) has the tools to excel both offensively and defensively but needs to add some polish. C/OF Yusuf Carter (12) has the athleticism one might expect from the nephew of five-time all-star Joe Carter.

Best Pure Hitter: Johnston. OF Johnny Defendis (29), who batted .327-2-20 in the NWL, doesn't have a standout tool but makes consistent line-drive contact.

Best Raw Power: Carter has a strong 6-foot-2, 205-pound frame. His 13 homers last spring set an El Paso (Texas) CC record.

Fastest Runner: Gregg has plus-plus speed. His 36 steals were six more than he totaled in three seasons at South Carolina.

Best Defensive Player: C Jake Muyco (8) has outstanding catch-and-throw skills. His defense is well ahead of his offense.

Best Fastball: The ball comes out of Pawelek's hand easy, yet he's able to pitch at 94-95 mph and touch 97. RHP Scott Taylor (5) can hit 93-94 mph, and LHP Donald Veal (2) and RHP Mike Billek (3) did the same during the spring.

Best Breaking Ball: Billek, Pawelek and RHP Mark Holliman (3) all have good curveballs.

Most Intriguing Background: The Cubs selected Carter 24 years after making his uncle the No. 2 overall pick in the June 1981 draft. Unsigned C Michael Brenly's

Veal

(43) father Bob was an all-star catcher and a manager in the majors, and he currently serves as a Cubs television broadcaster. INF Kyle Reynolds' (6) dad Craig is another former all-star. Pawelek's brother Dennis was a White Sox draft pick in 2002 and a backup kicker on Utah's undefeated football team in 2004.

Closest To The Majors: Billek or Holliman, the latter of whom signed late and has yet to make his debut. Because he has a special left arm, Pawelek could pass them both.

Best Late-Round Pick: RHP Michael Phelps (11) and LHP Jayson Ruhlman (23) are potential steals. A sophomore-eligible who sustained a fractured skull when his catcher hit him in the head with a throw in Central Missouri State's season opener, Phelps could have been an early pick had he re-entered the 2006 draft. Ruhlman has deceptive offspeed stuff and showed a 90-93 mph fastball in the Cape Cod League in 2004.

The One Who Got Away: After the Cubs selected speedy Oregon State OF Tyler Graham (14), he learned he could take an injury redshirt season for 2003, allowing him to re-enter the 2006 draft as a redshirt junior. The Cubs signed 28 of their first 30 picks.

Assessment: The Cubs grabbed two of the draft's most dynamic lefthanders in Pawelek and Veal. They took pitchers with their first four picks, while most of the hitters they selected will need time to make adjustments.

2004 The Cubs didn't have a first-round pick but gave first-round money ($1.26 million) to RHP Grant Johnson (2), who had a so-so pro debut last year. 2B Eric Patterson (8) and RHP Sean Gallagher (12) have played like steals so far. **GRADE:** C+

2003 OF Ryan Harvey (1) is a boom-or-bust player, and as he goes, this draft will follow. LHP Sean Marshall (6) could be something if he can stay healthy. **GRADE:** C

2002 Chicago loaded up on arms with four first-round choices, only to see Bobby Brownlie's stuff drop off and Luke Hagerty, Chadd Blasko and Matt Clanton fall prey to injuries. Slugging 1B Brian Dopirak (2) followed a stunning 2004 with a horrid 2005. **GRADE:** C

2001 RHP Mark Prior (1) is still a Cy Young Award winner waiting to happen. RHP Ricky Nolasco (4), 2B/3B Brendan Harris and RHP Sergio Mitre (7) were useful trade bait. **GRADE:** A

Draft analysis prepared by Jim Callis. Numbers in parentheses indicate draft rounds.

FELIX
PIE

OF

ROBERT GURGNAUS

Born: Feb. 8, 1985.
Ht.: 6-2. **Wt.:** 175.
Bats: L. **Throws:** L.
Signed: Dominican Republic, 2001.
Signed by: Jose Serra.

Pie, then 14, had played only street baseball when he stopped by a tryout in his hometown of La Romana in the Domincian Republic in 1999. Jose Serra asked Pie to show what he could do, and his skills impressed the Cubs scout enough that he got Pie involved in more structured baseball and signed him once he turned 16. Pie came to the United States at 17 and since has blazed a trail of success throughout the minors. He won championships with each of the four teams he played with in his first three seasons, and he played in the Futures Game in 2003-04. Both of those streaks ended in 2005 after he injured his right ankle when he slid late into a base in mid-June. A bone bruise initially wasn't expected to sideline him for more than a few weeks, but he never returned, forcing him to bow out of the Futures Game and leaving him unable to contribute to Double-A West Tenn's playoff run, which ended with a loss in the Southern League finals. If he hadn't been hurt, the Cubs say they would have called Pie up when they shipped Corey Patterson to the minors in early July.

Pie has been the best athlete in the system since he made his pro debut in 2002, and his tools are similar to those of Carlos Beltran. Despite being one of the youngest players in his league each year, he consistently has hit for average. He has an uncanny ability to make hard contact even when he chases pitches out of the strike zone. After hitting just 16 homers in his first 287 pro games, Pie started to deliver on his power potential with 11 in 59 games in 2005. He improved his setup, used his legs more in his swing and started to pull pitches more often. His speed is his best tool, making him a basestealing threat and giving him the range to cover the gaps in center field. He also has a strong arm that would fit in right field if needed.

Pie is still raw in many phases of the game. Though it has yet to catch up to him, his plate discipline has slipped as he has risen through the minors. He rarely walks because he lacks patience and is able to put balls out of the zone in play. Intrigued by his newfound power, he fell into ruts where he became too focused on trying to hit homers. Despite his well above-average speed, he's still figuring out how to steal bases and was caught nine times in 22 attempts in 2005. Defensively, he can improve his routes, especially when he comes in on balls. Losing three months of the season cost him valuable development time, though he did return to play with Licey in the Dominican Winter League.

Patterson has fallen short of his considerable potential in part because the Cubs rushed him through the minors without forcing him to address his shortcomings. They contemplated doing the same with Pie but ultimately decided to trade for Juan Pierre in December. That move should give Pie time to add polish to his game at Triple-A Iowa. If Pierre stays in Chicago for the long term, Pie will slide over to right field for the Cubs.

Year	Club (League)	Class	AVG	G	AB	R	H	2B	3B	HR	RBI	BB	SO	SB	OBP	SLG
2002	Cubs (AZL)	R	.321	55	218	42	70	16	13	4	37	21	47	17	.385	.569
	Boise (NWL)	A	.125	2	8	1	1	1	0	0	1	1	1	0	.222	.250
2003	Lansing (Mid)	A	.285	124	505	72	144	22	9	4	47	41	98	19	.346	.388
2004	Daytona (FSL)	A	.301	106	415	79	125	17	10	8	47	39	113	32	.364	.448
2005	West Tenn (SL)	AA	.304	59	240	41	73	17	5	11	25	16	53	13	.349	.554
MINOR LEAGUE TOTALS			.298	346	1386	235	413	73	37	27	157	118	312	81	.357	.462

MARK PAWELEK
LHP

Born: Aug. 18, 1986. **B-T:** L-L. **Ht.:** 6-2. **Wt.:** 180. **Drafted:** HS—Springville, Utah, 2005 (1st round). **Signed by:** John Bartsch.

When he went 20th overall in June, Pawelek became the highest-drafted Utah high schooler ever, surpassing Bruce Hurst, the No. 22 pick in 1976. Pawelek became the first 2005 first-rounder to sign, agreeing to a $1.75 million bonus. He rated as the No. 1 prospect in the Rookie-level Arizona League. Pawelek is a rare lefthander with a chance to have three plus pitches. He has a quick arm that already delivers lively 92-95 mph fastballs, and he could add more velocity as he fills out. Both his curveball and changeup have their moments. His secondary pitches are inconsistent, and the Cubs had Pawelek scrap his slider and splitter because they wanted him to focus on improving three pitches rather than five. His mechanics are sound, though he sometimes rushes and loses balance and command. He'll throw more, better strikes once he repeats his delivery better. The Cubs kept Pawelek on tight pitch counts last summer and will continue to exercise caution because he's still a teenager. He'll move up to low Class A Peoria in 2006.

Year	Club (League)	Class	W	L	ERA	G	GS	CG	SV	IP	H	R	ER	HR	BB	SO	AVG
2005	Cubs (AZL)	R	0	3	2.72	14	13	0	0	43	25	18	13	0	21	56	.170
	Boise (NWL)	A	0	0	0.00	1	1	0	0	3	6	1	0	0	1	4	.462
MINOR LEAGUE TOTALS			0	3	2.54	15	14	0	0	46	31	19	13	0	22	60	.194

RONNY CEDENO
SS

Born: Feb. 2, 1983. **B-T:** R-R. **Ht.:** 6-0. **Wt.:** 180. **Signed:** Venezuela, 1999. **Signed by:** Alberto Rondon.

Cedeno won the Arizona League batting title with a .350 average in his U.S. debut in 2001, then hit just .212 the next two seasons as the Cubs rushed him through Class A. His bat has bounced back, and he spent three months in the majors in 2005, mostly on the bench. He was just starting to get regular playing time in September when a Brad Hennessey pitch broke his left hand. Cedeno has the best actions and arm strength among Chicago's infield prospects, and he has proven that he can be more than just a glove man. His strong hands and wrists give him good bat speed that should allow him to hit for average and maybe 15 homers per year. His speed is slightly above average. To fit near the top of the lineup, Cedeno will need to show more patience and basestealing savvy. He can get homer-happy, but that happens less than it did in the past. Though the Cubs re-signed Neifi Perez, they say he'll be a backup. Cedeno will get the opportunity to start at second base or shortstop, depending on further moves the club makes this offseason.

Year	Club (League)	Class	AVG	G	AB	R	H	2B	3B	HR	RBI	BB	SO	SB	OBP	SLG
2000	La Pradera (VSL)	R	.287	51	167	35	48	8	3	3	14	19	37	13	.370	.425
2001	Cubs (AZL)	R	.350	52	206	36	72	13	4	1	17	13	32	17	.398	.466
	Lansing (Mid)	A	.196	17	56	9	11	4	1	1	2	2	18	0	.237	.357
2002	Lansing (Mid)	A	.213	98	376	44	80	17	4	2	31	22	74	14	.269	.295
	Boise (NWL)	A	.218	29	110	17	24	5	2	0	6	9	25	8	.275	.300
2003	Daytona (FSL)	A	.211	107	380	43	80	18	1	4	36	21	82	19	.257	.295
2004	West Tenn (SL)	AA	.279	116	384	39	107	19	5	6	48	24	74	10	.328	.401
2005	Iowa (PCL)	AAA	.355	65	245	42	87	14	1	8	36	20	31	11	.403	.518
	Chicago (NL)	MLB	.300	41	80	13	24	3	0	1	6	5	11	1	.356	.375
MAJOR LEAGUE TOTALS			.300	41	80	13	24	3	0	1	6	5	11	1	.341	.375
MINOR LEAGUE TOTALS			.265	535	1924	265	509	98	21	25	190	130	373	92	.318	.376

ANGEL GUZMAN
RHP

Born: Dec. 14, 1981. **B-T:** R-R. **Ht.:** 6-3. **Wt.:** 190. **Signed:** Venezuela, 1999. **Signed by:** Hector Ortega.

Guzman was on a roll in Double-A and bucking for a big league callup in mid-2003 when he was diagnosed with a slight tear in his labrum. Though he required only arthroscopic surgery, he has pitched just 66 innings since. The Cubs were enthused by reports he was throwing 93-96 mph in the Arizona Fall League. Before he got hurt, Guzman had arguably the best fastball, curveball and changeup in the system. The velocity and hard sink have returned with his fastball. He always has excelled at throwing strikes, and that hasn't changed. Guzman needs to trust his stuff and his health. He missed most of 2005 with forearm stiffness. He hasn't used his curveball much since his return, and his changeup isn't the plus pitch it once was. He must command both pitches better in the strike zone. It's impossible to count on Guzman or to even know what to expect from him, but he still has one of the highest ceilings in the system. If all goes well in spring training, he could start 2006 in Double-A and make his big league debut later in the year.

Year	Club (League)	Class	W	L	ERA	G	GS	CG	SV	IP	H	R	ER	HR	BB	SO	AVG
2000	La Pradera (VSL)	R	1	1	1.93	7	6	0	0	33	24	13	7	0	5	25	.197
2001	Boise (NWL)	A	9	1	2.23	14	14	0	0	77	68	27	19	2	19	63	.233
2002	Lansing (Mid)	A	5	2	1.89	9	9	1	0	62	42	18	13	3	16	49	.186
	Daytona (FSL)	A	6	2	2.39	16	15	1	0	94	99	34	25	2	33	74	.268
2003	West Tenn (SL)	AA	3	3	2.81	15	15	0	0	90	83	30	28	8	26	87	.249
2004	Daytona (FSL)	A	3	1	4.20	7	7	0	0	30	27	15	14	2	0	40	.235
	West Tenn (SL)	AA	0	3	5.59	4	4	0	0	18	20	11	11	2	4	13	.299
2005	Cubs (AZL)	R	0	0	1.50	4	4	0	0	12	10	3	2	0	1	17	.217
	Peoria (Mid)	A	0	1	4.29	2	2	0	0	6	10	5	3	1	0	7	.345
MINOR LEAGUE TOTALS			27	14	2.61	78	76	2	0	421	383	156	122	20	104	375	.240

5 RICH HILL
LHP

RODGER WOOD

Born: March 11, 1980. **B-T:** L-L. **Ht.:** 6-5. **Wt.:** 205. **Drafted:** Michigan, 2002 (4th round). **Signed by:** Scott May.

Hill always had a knockout curveball, but his inability to throw strikes (6.3 walks per nine innings) held him back in his first three seasons as a pro. The light turned on in 2005, which he credits to improved mental focus. Hill led the minors with 13.4 strikeouts per nine innings and made his major league debut. Hill's 12-to-6 curveball is often unhittable, and batters can't sit on it now that he can locate his 90-91 mph fastball. His changeup shows promise and would give him the third pitch he requires to remain a starter. He has cleaned up his delivery, which also improved his control. For all his progress, Hill didn't throw strikes when he joined the Cubs and big league hitters took advantage. He needs to trust and use his changeup more often. Hill will get a chance to crack Chicago's rotation in spring training, and he has the stuff to be a No. 2 starter. His curve is so good that he should at least become a dynamic lefty specialist.

Year	Club (League)	Class	W	L	ERA	G	GS	CG	SV	IP	H	R	ER	HR	BB	SO	AVG
2002	Boise (NWL)	A	0	2	8.36	6	5	0	0	14	15	19	13	0	14	12	.268
2003	Lansing (Mid)	A	0	1	2.76	15	4	0	0	29	14	12	9	0	36	50	.141
	Boise (NWL)	A	1	6	4.35	14	14	0	0	68	57	40	33	5	32	99	.233
2004	Daytona (FSL)	A	7	6	4.03	28	19	0	0	109	88	64	49	9	72	136	.221
2005	West Tenn (SL)	AA	4	3	3.28	10	10	0	0	58	42	22	21	9	21	90	.200
	Peoria (Mid)	A	1	0	1.13	1	1	0	0	8	5	2	1	0	0	12	.179
	Iowa (PCL)	AAA	6	1	3.60	11	10	1	0	65	53	28	26	11	14	92	.218
	Chicago (NL)	MLB	0	2	9.13	10	4	0	0	24	25	24	24	3	17	21	.260
MAJOR LEAGUE TOTALS			0	2	9.13	10	4	0	0	24	25	24	24	3	17	21	.260
MINOR LEAGUE TOTALS			19	19	3.89	85	63	1	0	352	274	187	152	34	189	491	.214

6 SEAN MARSHALL
LHP

STEVE MOORE

Born: Aug. 30, 1982. **B-T:** L-L. **Ht.:** 6-6. **Wt.:** 195. **Drafted:** Virginia Commonwealth, 2003 (6th round). **Signed by:** Billy Swoope.

Marshall and his twin brother Brian were part of a Virginia Commonwealth staff that led NCAA Division I with a 2.54 ERA in 2003, when the Red Sox took Brian in the fifth round and the Cubs selected Sean in the sixth. Sean has a 2.64 ERA in pro ball, but missed time in 2004 with a ruptured tendon in his left middle finger and again in 2005 with shoulder soreness. Marshall picks up plenty of groundballs and strikeouts thanks to an 88-92 mph sinker that can reach 95. He keeps batters off balance with his curveball, a sharp downer he can change speeds with. He commands both pitches well. The tendon injury was a fluke and his shoulder problems were probably related to compensating for the finger, but Marshall still hasn't proven he can hold up over a full season. He'll have to improve his changeup to remain a starter, and he's working on a slider. The Cubs believe Marshall is on the verge of a breakthrough season in 2006. He'll probably open the year in Double-A but isn't too far from the majors if he can stay healthy.

Year	Club (League)	Class	W	L	ERA	G	GS	CG	SV	IP	H	R	ER	HR	BB	SO	AVG
2003	Boise (NWL)	A	5	6	2.56	14	14	0	0	74	66	31	21	1	23	88	.237
	Lansing (Mid)	A	1	0	0.00	1	1	0	0	7	5	1	0	0	0	11	.192
2004	Lansing (Mid)	A	2	0	1.11	7	7	1	0	49	29	7	6	1	4	51	.172

Year	Club (League)	Class	W	L	ERA	G	GS	CG	SV	IP	H	R	ER	HR	BB	SO	AVG
	West Tenn (SL)	AA	2	2	5.90	6	6	0	0	29	36	20	19	2	12	23	.319
2005	Daytona (FSL)	A	4	4	2.74	12	12	1	0	69	63	24	21	7	26	61	.246
	West Tenn (SL)	AA	0	1	2.52	4	4	0	0	25	16	7	7	1	5	24	.180
MINOR LEAGUE TOTALS			14	13	2.64	44	44	2	0	252	215	90	74	12	70	258	.231

7 RYAN HARVEY — OF

Born: Aug. 30, 1984. **B-T:** R-R. **Ht.:** 6-5. **Wt.:** 225. **Drafted:** HS—Dunedin, Fla., 2003 (1st round). **Signed by:** Rolando Pino.

Though he blew out his right knee at a high school showcase the previous fall, Harvey recovered in time to go sixth overall in the 2003 draft and sign for $2.4 million. He made his full-season debut in 2005 and was a low Class A Midwest League all-star, leading the league in homers and losing the RBI title on the last day of the season. Harvey has massive power potential and is an incredible athlete for a 6-foot-5, 225-pounder. He looks like the blueprint scouts would draw up for a right fielder. He has plus speed and a plus-plus arm that unleashed 90-93 mph fastballs when he pitched in high school. Harvey has a huge ceiling but will have to make several adjustments at the plate to reach it. He's a free swinger with a long stroke who struggles against inside fastballs and chases wayward breaking balls. His two-strike approach is poor. It remains to be seen how well Harvey will do against more advanced pitching, and he'll probably never hit for a high average. But his tools excite the Cubs, and they'll see how he fares at high Class A Daytona in 2006.

Year	Club (League)	Class	AVG	G	AB	R	H	2B	3B	HR	RBI	BB	SO	SB	OBP	SLG
2003	Cubs (AZL)	R	.235	14	51	9	12	3	2	1	7	6	21	0	.339	.431
2004	Cubs (AZL)	R	.400	2	10	1	4	3	0	0	5	0	4	0	.400	.700
	Boise (NWL)	A	.264	58	231	42	61	8	0	14	43	20	78	4	.327	.481
2005	Peoria (Mid)	A	.257	117	467	71	120	30	2	24	100	24	137	8	.302	.484
MINOR LEAGUE TOTALS			.260	191	759	123	197	44	4	39	155	50	240	10	.314	.482

8 BRIAN DOPIRAK — 1B

Born: Dec. 20, 1983. **B-T:** R-R. **Ht.:** 6-4. **Wt.:** 235. **Drafted:** HS—Dunedin, Fla., 2002 (2nd round). **Signed by:** Tom Shafer.

Dopirak ranked No. 1 on this list a year ago, when he was coming off a 39-homer season and an MVP award in the Midwest League. The wheels came off in high Class A in 2005, however, as his average dropped 72 points while he dipped to 16 homers. He's a product of Dunedin (Fla.) High, as are three other prominent Cubs: general manager Jim Hendry, new scouting director Tim Wilken and Ryan Harvey. Dopirak has power comparable to Harvey's, and who has more is a popular debate among Cubs officials. Dopirak can hit the ball out of any part of any park and doesn't need a long swing to do it. He has worked hard to improve defensively. He typically has needed time to adjust to a new level, but Dopirak seemed to panic in 2005. After he started slowly again, he lengthened his stroke and tried to pull everything in an attempt to pump up his homer totals. He has below-average speed and will never be more than adequate at first base. With Derrek Lee in the majors, Chicago can be patient with Dopirak. They'll move him up a level to Double-A in 2006 and hope he can bounce back.

Year	Club (League)	Class	AVG	G	AB	R	H	2B	3B	HR	RBI	BB	SO	SB	OBP	SLG
2002	Cubs (AZL)	R	.253	21	79	10	20	4	0	0	6	6	23	0	.306	.304
2003	Boise (NWL)	A	.240	52	192	25	46	4	0	13	37	24	58	0	.330	.464
	Lansing (Mid)	A	.269	19	78	8	21	3	0	2	10	2	22	0	.305	.385
2004	Lansing (Mid)	A	.307	137	541	94	166	38	0	39	120	48	123	4	.363	.593
2005	Daytona (FSL)	A	.235	132	507	53	119	26	0	16	76	37	107	1	.289	.381
MINOR LEAGUE TOTALS			.266	361	1397	190	372	75	0	70	249	117	333	5	.326	.470

9 ERIC PATTERSON — 2B

Born: April 8, 1983. **B-T:** L-R. **Ht.:** 5-11. **Wt.:** 170. **Drafted:** Georgia Tech, 2004 (8th round). **Signed by:** Sam Hughes.

Patterson may seize the Cubs' leadoff job that his brother Corey has failed to fill. An eighth-round pick who signed for fourth-round money ($300,000), Patterson won the Midwest League batting title and the Cubs' minor league player of the year award in his pro debut. Patterson isn't as strong or as fast as his brother Corey, but he still stands out in both areas. He has 65 speed on the 20-80 scouting scale and surprising pop for his size. Unlike Corey, Eric isn't allergic to walks. He should become an average defender at second base. Patterson can have too much power for his own good, as he sometimes worries too much about homers at the expense of getting on base. He'd be better off shortening his stroke. He's still rough at second base, where he can look stiff and needs to continue to clean up his double-play pivot. Patterson will return to Double-A, where he spent the last week of his first pro season. He has passed Mike Fontenot and Richard Lewis on the organization depth chart and could be starting for the Cubs at some point in 2007.

Year	Club (League)	Class	AVG	G	AB	R	H	2B	3B	HR	RBI	BB	SO	SB	OBP	SLG
2005	Peoria (Mid)	A	.333	110	432	90	144	26	11	13	71	53	94	40	.405	.535
	West Tenn (SL)	AA	.200	9	30	5	6	2	0	0	2	6	7	3	.324	.267
MINOR LEAGUE TOTALS			.325	119	462	95	150	28	11	13	73	59	101	43	.400	.517

10 CARLOS MARMOL   RHP

MICHAEL WALBY

Born: Oct. 14, 1982. **B-T:** R-R. **Ht.:** 6-2. **Wt.:** 190. **Signed:** Dominican Republic, 1999. **Signed by:** Jose Serra.

Marmol spent the first three years of his pro career as a catcher/out-fielder, and unlike many former hitters who convert to the mound, he wasn't totally lost at the plate. He batted .273 while showing gap power and speed, but his powerful right arm was too hard to ignore. The Cubs made him a full-time pitcher in 2003, and he responded by leading the Rookie-level Arizona League in strikeouts. He followed up by tying for the low Class A Midwest League lead in wins in 2004, and a solid year in high Class A earned him a spot on the 40-man roster following the 2005 season. While he still has to develop more feel for pitching, particularly with his command, he's ahead of the game considering his inexperience. His fastball jumped a couple of ticks to 92-94 mph last year, and he also made some progress with his hard breaking ball, which is closer to a slider or a cutter than a curveball. Marmol also is doing well learning a changeup. If everything comes together, he could have three plus pitches. If not, he's an intriguing power arm for the back of the bullpen. He'll return to Double-A this year.

Year	Club (League)	Class	AVG	G	AB	R	H	2B	3B	HR	RBI	BB	SO	SB	OBP	SLG
2000	Cubs (DSL)	R	.314	41	140	32	44	7	2	0	22	11	27	3	.365	.393
2001	Cubs (AZL)	R	.295	40	129	15	38	11	0	0	12	9	30	4	.355	.380
2002	Lansing (Mid)	A	.149	15	47	2	7	0	1	0	4	1	7	0	.167	.191
	Cubs (AZL)	R	.258	47	186	22	48	6	3	1	16	3	35	10	.271	.339
MINOR LEAGUE TOTALS			.273	143	502	71	137	24	6	1	54	24	99	17	.311	.351

Year	Club (League)	Class	W	L	ERA	G	GS	CG	SV	IP	H	R	ER	HR	BB	SO	AVG
2002	Cubs (AZL)	R	0	0	0.00	1	0	0	0	1	1	0	0	0	1	1	.250
2003	Cubs (AZL)	R	3	5	4.19	14	9	0	0	62	54	38	29	5	37	74	.225
2004	Lansing (Mid)	A	14	8	3.20	26	24	0	0	155	131	64	55	15	53	154	.237
2005	Daytona (FSL)	A	6	2	2.99	13	13	0	0	72	60	30	24	7	37	71	.227
	West Tenn (SL)	AA	3	4	3.65	14	14	0	0	81	70	33	33	10	40	70	.239
MINOR LEAGUE TOTALS			26	19	3.41	68	60	0	0	372	316	165	141	37	168	370	.233

11 DONALD VEAL   LHP

Born: Sept. 18, 1984. **B-T:** L-L. **Ht.:** 6-3. **Wt.:** 215. **Drafted:** Pima (Ariz.) CC, 2005 (2nd round). **Signed by:** Steve McFarland.

Scouts have been comparing Veal to former Cubs draft pick Dontrelle Willis since he was an Arizona high school star. He declined reported $500,000 bonuses from the Brewers and Yankees, and ultimately turned down the White Sox after slipping in the 12th round, deciding instead to attend the University of Arizona. A cousin of former NBA star (and former Athletics draft pick) Kevin Johnson, Veal had shoulder problems during fall practice, the result of a torn labrum that didn't require surgery but forced him to redshirt as a freshman while the Wildcats reached the College World Series. He transferred to Pima (Ariz.) CC for the 2005 season, then signed for $530,000 as a second-round pick. Though the Cubs kept Veal on short pitch counts in his pro debut, his talent still was obvious and he rated as the No. 2 prospect in the short-season Northwest League. He pitched mainly at 86-91 mph during the summer but sat at 93-94 mph when he was fresh during the spring. He keeps his fastball down, achieves nice run with it and works it to both sides of the plate. He shows the making of a plus curveball, though his changeup will need significant work. His delivery isn't as extreme as Willis', but Veal has some funk to his motion and his long arms make his pitches difficult to pick up. He's something of a project, as he has a ways to go with his secondary pitches and command, but the payoff could be huge. If Chicago continues to take it slow with Veal, he'll open the season in low Class A.

Year	Club (League)	Class	W	L	ERA	G	GS	CG	SV	IP	H	R	ER	HR	BB	SO	AVG
2005	Cubs (AZL)	R	0	1	5.05	4	3	0	0	11	8	6	6	2	5	14	.205
	Boise (NWL)	A	1	2	2.48	7	6	0	0	29	18	11	8	2	15	34	.180
MINOR LEAGUE TOTALS			1	3	3.18	11	9	0	0	40	26	17	14	4	20	48	.187

12 SEAN GALLAGHER   RHP

Born: Dec. 30, 1985. **B-T:** R-R. **Ht.:** 6-1. **Wt.:** 210. **Drafted:** HS—Fort Lauderdale, Fla., 2004 (12th round). **Signed by:** Rolando Pino.

Gallagher has far exceeded expectations since signing as a 12th-round pick in 2004, but scouts wonder if he's already near his ceiling. The Cubs planned on sending him to extended spring training before shipping him out to short-season Boise last year, but injuries created an opening for Gallagher in the Peoria rotation. He seized the opportunity by not allowing an earned run in his first six starts (which included a combined no-hitter), en route to tying for the Midwest League lead in victories and winning Chicago's minor league pitcher of the year award. However, he leveled off after his hot start and may not have a plus pitch. Gallagher's best offering is his curveball, which managers rated the best in the MWL. But while some see his curve as an above-average pitch, others say it's loopy and slurvy and stands out mainly because he locates it well. His 88-90 mph fastball and changeup are fringe average, and he's not projectable at 6-foot-1 and 210 pounds. Gallagher's command, savvy and presence are all advanced for his age, and he figures to develop into a back-of-the-rotation starter. He'll open 2006 in high Class A, where he made a cameo last September, and could jump to Double-A quickly if he has another torrid streak to open the season.

Year	Club (League)	Class	W	L	ERA	G	GS	CG	SV	IP	H	R	ER	HR	BB	SO	AVG
2004	Cubs (AZL)	R	1	2	3.11	10	9	0	0	35	38	19	12	0	11	44	.275
2005	Peoria (Mid)	A	14	5	2.71	26	26	0	0	146	107	53	44	10	55	139	.206
	Daytona (FSL)	A	0	0	1.80	1	1	0	0	5	6	1	1	1	0	7	.286
MINOR LEAGUE TOTALS			15	7	2.76	37	36	0	0	186	151	73	57	11	66	190	.223

13 SCOTT MOORE   3B

Born: Nov. 17, 1983. **B-T:** L-R. **Ht.:** 6-2. **Wt.:** 180. **Drafted:** HS—Long Beach, 2002 (1st round). **Signed by:** Rob Wilfong (Tigers).

Moore's career was going nowhere when the Cubs picked him up from the Tigers in a three-prospect package for Kyle Farnsworth last February. The eighth overall pick and the recipient of a $2.3 million bonus in 2002, Moore batted .240 with 24 homers and 266 strikeouts over 265 pro games in his first three pro seasons. Faced with repeating high Class A, Moore made adjustments to his approach. He got more selective at the plate, stopped trying to pull everything and didn't get down on himself when he struggled. His swing is still long and he always will pile up strikeouts, but if he generates the plus lefthanded power he showed in 2005, that's fine. He improved so dramatically that he represented Chicago at the Futures Game—in Detroit—and earned a spot on the 40-man roster. Moore has average speed and range at third base, and a plus throwing arm. His mechanics and footwork are rough, however, and he has led Florida State League third basemen in errors for two years running. The Cubs are anxious to see if his breakthrough is for real and should learn more from his Double-A performance in 2006.

Year	Club (League)	Class	AVG	G	AB	R	H	2B	3B	HR	RBI	BB	SO	SB	OBP	SLG
2002	Tigers (GCL)	R	.293	40	133	18	39	6	2	4	25	10	31	1	.349	.459
2003	West Michigan (Mid)	A	.239	107	372	40	89	16	6	6	45	41	110	2	.325	.363
2004	Lakeland (FSL)	A	.223	118	391	52	87	13	4	14	56	49	125	2	.322	.384
2005	Daytona (FSL)	A	.281	128	466	77	131	31	2	20	82	55	134	22	.358	.485
MINOR LEAGUE TOTALS			.254	393	1362	187	346	66	14	44	208	155	400	27	.338	.420

14 JAE-KUK RYU   RHP

Born: May 30, 1983. **B-T:** R-R. **Ht.:** 6-3. **Wt.:** 210. **Signed:** Korea, 2001. **Signed by:** Leon Lee.

When the Cubs signed Ryu out of Korea for $1.6 million in 2001, they figured he'd be contributing at the major league level by now. But when it seemed he might never be remembered for anything beyond killing an osprey by throwing a baseball that knocked it from its perch at Daytona's Jackie Robinson Ballpark in 2003, Ryu turned his career around last year. Hammered in Double-A in 2003 and hampered by elbow tendinitis in 2004, he came back to lead the Southern League in innings and prompted Chicago to protect him on its 40-man roster. Ryu has the best command in the system. He doesn't have a plus pitch, but he can locate all four of his offerings: a fastball that sits at 88-89 mph and maxes out at 91, slider, curveball and changeup. He mixes his pitches well and shows the ability to speed hitters' bats up or slow them down as needed. Ryu used to pitch in the low 90s but still was effective with reduced velocity in 2005. He also seemed to mature after the osprey incident and problems with teammates in the past. Some club officials still wish he were more competitive and took pitching more seriously. If he can build on his development in Triple-A, Ryu likely will make his big league debut this year.

Year	Club (League)	Class	W	L	ERA	G	GS	CG	SV	IP	H	R	ER	HR	BB	SO	AVG
2001	Cubs (AZL)	R	1	0	0.61	4	3	0	0	15	11	2	1	0	5	20	.196
2002	Boise (NWL)	A	6	1	3.57	10	10	0	0	53	45	28	21	1	25	56	.223
	Lansing (Mid)	A	1	2	7.11	5	4	0	0	19	26	16	15	1	8	21	.333
2003	Daytona (FSL)	A	0	1	3.04	4	4	0	0	21	14	14	7	1	11	22	.187
	Lansing (Mid)	A	6	1	1.75	11	11	0	0	72	59	19	14	2	19	57	.225
	West Tenn (SL)	AA	2	5	5.43	11	11	1	0	58	63	37	35	3	25	45	.280
2004	Cubs (AZL)	R	0	0	4.50	2	2	0	0	4	4	2	2	1	0	5	.250
	Boise (NWL)	A	0	2	2.57	5	0	0	0	7	7	3	2	0	5	7	.250
	West Tenn (SL)	AA	1	0	2.95	14	0	0	0	18	22	8	6	0	10	19	.286
	Iowa (PCL)	AAA	0	0	38.57	1	0	0	0	1	2	4	3	1	1	0	.500
2005	West Tenn (SL)	AA	11	8	3.34	27	27	1	0	170	154	67	63	12	49	133	.246
MINOR LEAGUE TOTALS			28	20	3.48	94	72	2	0	437	407	200	169	22	158	385	.247

15 BRANDON SING   1B/OF

Born: March 13, 1981. **B-T:** R-R. **Ht.:** 6-5. **Wt.:** 210. **Drafted:** HS—Joliet, Ill., 1999 (20th round). **Signed by:** Scott May.

It took Sing three tries to succeed in high Class A, but when he finally did he was the Florida State League's MVP and home run champion in 2004. He earned another homer crown after moving up to the Southern League in 2005, and he set franchise home run records both years. Sing's trademark tool, obviously, is his power. His swing can get long at times, but he has a selective eye and a knack for drawing walks. Where he fits on the diamond and in Chicago's lineup is a question. Sing signed as a third baseman and got a shot at second base in instructional league years ago, but his lack of speed and range limited him to first base or an outfield corner. He does have some arm strength and has committed himself to improving defensively, but he probably won't ever be more than adequate. Blocked at first base by Derrek Lee and in left field by Matt Murton, Sing's best hope of starting for the Cubs is in right field. But they didn't protect him on their 40-man roster, meaning he'll have to continue to prove himself this year in Triple-A.

Year	Club (League)	Class	AVG	G	AB	R	H	2B	3B	HR	RBI	BB	SO	SB	OBP	SLG
1999	Cubs (AZL)	R	.265	17	68	4	18	4	1	2	12	5	16	1	.311	.441
2000	Eugene (NWL)	A	.229	61	218	29	50	11	1	9	28	35	75	4	.339	.413
2001	Lansing (Mid)	A	.245	121	417	54	102	27	2	16	50	46	109	3	.328	.434
2002	Daytona (FSL)	A	.248	125	440	65	109	18	5	18	64	64	96	5	.348	.434
2003	West Tenn (SL)	AA	.209	42	139	15	29	7	0	5	23	10	39	2	.256	.367
	Daytona (FSL)	A	.235	39	136	20	32	6	0	4	23	17	29	0	.318	.368
2004	Daytona (FSL)	A	.270	122	408	86	110	27	0	32	94	84	101	1	.399	.571
2005	West Tenn (SL)	AA	.276	127	409	74	113	29	0	26	71	91	110	2	.404	.538
MINOR LEAGUE TOTALS			.252	654	2235	347	563	129	9	112	365	352	575	18	.356	.468

16 GEOVANY SOTO   C

Born: Jan. 20, 1983. **B-T:** R-R. **Ht.:** 6-1. **Wt.:** 230. **Drafted:** HS—Rio Piedras, P.R., 2001 (11th round). **Signed by:** Jose Trujillo.

Since drafting Joe Girardi and Rick Wilkins in 1986, the Cubs haven't had much luck developing catchers. Soto is their best hope to end that drought, playing in Triple-A at age 22 last year and making his major league debut in September. A cousin of former Cubs infielder Ramon Martinez, Soto doesn't have a standout tool but he doesn't have any glaring weaknesses either. While he was inconsistent at the plate against older Pacific Coast League pitchers, Soto showed good patience. He handles the bat well enough to hit for a decent average, and he has enough strength and loft in his swing to reach double digits in homers on an annual basis. He doesn't run well, like most catchers, but he's agile and blocks balls well. Soto's arm strength is probably his best tool. He's still learning how to handle veteran pitches and to call a game, but that's to be expected. He has spent just three years as a full-time catcher after dabbling at the infield corners in his first two pro seasons. He'll repeat Triple-A in 2006 to soak up some more experience.

Year	Club (League)	Class	AVG	G	AB	R	H	2B	3B	HR	RBI	BB	SO	SB	OBP	SLG
2001	Cubs (AZL)	R	.260	41	150	18	39	16	0	1	20	15	33	1	.339	.387
2002	Cubs (AZL)	R	.269	44	156	24	42	10	2	3	24	13	35	0	.333	.417
	Boise (NWL)	A	.400	1	5	1	2	0	0	0	0	0	1	0	.400	.400
2003	Daytona (FSL)	A	.242	89	297	26	72	12	2	2	38	31	58	0	.313	.316

2004	West Tenn (SL)	AA	.271	104	332	47	90	16	0	9	48	40	71	1	.355	.401
2005	Iowa (PCL)	AAA	.253	91	292	30	74	14	0	4	39	48	77	0	.357	.342
	Chicago (NL)	MLB	.000	1	1	0	0	0	0	0	0	0	0	0	.000	.000
MAJOR LEAGUE TOTALS		MLB	.000	1	1	0	0	0	0	0	0	0	0	0	.000	.000
MINOR LEAGUE TOTALS			.259	370	1232	146	319	68	4	19	169	147	275	2	.341	.367

17 GRANT JOHNSON RHP

Born: May 26, 1983. **B-T:** R-R. **Ht.:** 6-6. **Wt.:** 215. **Drafted:** Notre Dame, 2004 (2nd round). **Signed by:** Stan Zielinski.

The Cubs still haven't seen Johnson at his best since making him their top pick (second round) in 2004 and signing him for $1.26 million. He missed all of the 2003 season after surgery to repair a torn labrum, and he was getting back to 100 percent when he turned pro. He signed too late to make his pro debut in 2004, and skipped instructional league to work toward his marketing degree at Notre Dame. In 2005, a pulled quad muscle kept him in extended spring training for the first two months of last season. When Johnson finally got on the mound in June, his stuff was just OK. He showed heavy life on his fastball, but pitched anywhere from 87-93 mph after working consistently at 92-94 while in college. His slider, his money pitch before he hurt his shoulder with the Fighting Irish, was mediocre because he had trouble staying on top of it. His changeup and command didn't stand out either. Chicago hopes Johnson will be healthy and regain his old stuff this year in high Class A. His slider looked better in instructional league.

Year	Club (League)	Class	W	L	ERA	G	GS	CG	SV	IP	H	R	ER	HR	BB	SO	AVG
2005	Peoria (Mid)	A	3	8	3.82	14	14	1	0	73	65	45	31	7	26	52	.242
MINOR LEAGUE TOTALS			3	8	3.82	14	14	1	0	73	65	45	31	7	26	52	.242

18 BILLY PETRICK RHP

Born: April 29, 1984. **B-T:** B-R. **Ht.:** 6-6. **Wt.:** 240. **Drafted:** HS—Morris, Ill., 2002 (3rd round). **Signed by:** Bob Hale.

Signed away from a Washington State football scholarship in 2002—he was recruited as a long snapper—Petrick had developed into one of the system's best righthanders before last year was a total loss. His shoulder had bothered him for the last couple of years, and doctors found fraying in his labrum that had to be fixed with arthroscopic surgery. The problem was discovered before he did major damage. Before he got hurt, Petrick threw a heavy sinker at 90-93 mph. The pitch was difficult to lift, and he has surrendered just seven homers in 280 pro innings. He made strides with his breaking ball in 2004, replacing a loopy curveball with a slider, and had improved his changeup. He still needs to improve his location and do a better job of throwing his changeup with fastball arm speed. Petrick may not be ready to pitch at the beginning of spring training, in which case he'd probably start the season in extended spring. He's still just 21, so the Cubs can afford to take it slow with him.

Year	Club (League)	Class	W	L	ERA	G	GS	CG	SV	IP	H	R	ER	HR	BB	SO	AVG
2002	Cubs (AZL)	R	2	1	1.70	6	6	0	0	32	21	8	6	0	6	35	.189
2003	Boise (NWL)	A	2	5	4.76	14	14	0	0	64	60	49	34	4	27	64	.241
2004	Lansing (Mid)	A	13	7	3.50	26	24	0	0	147	149	66	57	3	43	113	.276
2005	Daytona (FSL)	A	1	4	5.59	9	9	0	0	37	39	23	23	0	19	25	.275
MINOR LEAGUE TOTALS			18	17	3.86	55	53	0	0	280	269	146	120	7	95	237	.258

19 MARK REED C

Born: April 13, 1986. **B-T:** L-R. **Ht.:** 5-11. **Wt.:** 175. **Drafted:** HS—La Verne, Calif., 2004 (2nd round). **Signed by:** Jim Crawford.

Last season was difficult for the Reed brothers. In his first season as a big league regular, Jeremy hit a soft .254 for the Mariners. The Cubs gambled that Mark could handle the jump to low Class A after playing just 10 games in Rookie ball in his 2004 pro debut, and they were wrong. He hit .135 before getting sent to extended spring training, and he never got going during the summer at short-season Boise. Reed's bat is still his best tool. He has good bat speed and uses the whole field, though he must realize that he's not going to hit a lot of homers and is better off focusing at driving balls into the gaps. When he gears up for power, he swings through hittable pitches. Though there's some question as to whether Reed has the arm strength to stay at catcher for the long term, he performed better defensively than offensively in 2005. He threw out 39 percent of basestealers in the Northwest League and showed good blocking skills. He reminds one club official of a young Gregg Zaun. Reed runs the bases well and is more athletic than most catchers, and if he hits as expected he should be able to fit at a variety of positions if he can't remain behind the plate. He's better prepared for his second chance in the Midwest League than he was for his first.

Year	Club (League)	Class	AVG	G	AB	R	H	2B	3B	HR	RBI	BB	SO	SB	OBP	SLG
2004	Cubs (AZL)	R	.351	10	37	5	13	5	1	1	7	4	8	0	.429	.622
2005	Peoria (Mid)	A	.135	14	52	2	7	1	1	0	6	1	12	0	.167	.192
	Boise (NWL)	A	.250	55	184	32	46	10	0	4	18	15	53	7	.310	.370
MINOR LEAGUE TOTALS			.242	79	273	39	66	16	2	5	31	20	73	7	.301	.370

20 MICHAEL PHELPS   RHP

Born: May 26, 1984. **B-T:** R-R. **Ht.:** 6-4. **Wt.:** 195. **Drafted:** Central Missouri State, 2005 (11th round). **Signed by:** Tom Shafer.

Phelps lasted until the 11th round of the 2005 draft only because of major signability questions. Projected to be the ace on a loaded staff at Central Missouri State, a perennial NCAA Division II power, he got hit in the head by a throw from his catcher in the season opener. Phelps missed five weeks with a fractured skull and couldn't crack the Mules rotation when he returned. A draft-eligible sophomore, he figured to be an early-round pick in 2006 if he returned and had a healthy season. Credit area scout Tom Shafer for correctly gauging Phelps' willingness to turn pro and landing him for $55,000. Chicago eased him into pro ball by pitching him out of the bullpen, but challenged him with a pair of promotions, the second to high Class A. Phelps has the stuff to stay in the rotation, as his fastball, curveball and changeup all have the potential to be plus pitches. His fastball sits in the low 90s and tops out at 94, and his changeup may be his best current offering because he locates it so well. The Cubs still haven't determined whether they want to keep Phelps in the bullpen, which would expedite his development, or put him in the rotation this year. He has a chance to reach Double-A by the end of 2006.

Year	Club (League)	Class	W	L	ERA	G	GS	CG	SV	IP	H	R	ER	HR	BB	SO	AVG
2005	Cubs (AZL)	R	0	0	0.00	1	0	0	0	1	0	0	0	0	0	2	.000
	Peoria (Mid)	A	0	1	1.59	12	0	0	1	17	12	5	3	0	3	17	.197
	Daytona (FSL)	A	1	0	4.74	4	0	0	1	6	2	3	3	0	4	8	.100
MINOR LEAGUE TOTALS			1	1	2.31	17	0	0	2	23	14	8	6	0	7	27	.169

21 JUSTIN BERG   RHP

Born: June 7, 1984. **B-T:** R-R. **Ht.:** 6-3. **Wt.:** 190. **Drafted:** Triton (Ill.) JC, D/F 2003 (43rd round). **Signed by:** Steve Lemke (Yankees).

When the Cubs realized they weren't going to make the playoffs, they salvaged three prospects in a pair of late-August trades for veteran outfielders who weren't part of their long-term future. They sent Matt Lawton to the Yankees for Berg, and Todd Hollandsworth to the Braves for righthanders Angelo Burrows and Todd Blackford. All three of the acquisitions throw in the low 90s, with Berg the best prospect of that group. New York drafted him out of Indian Hills (Iowa) CC after he helped the Falcons reach the 2003 Junior College World Series, and signed him as a draft-and-follow after he spent 2004 at Triton (Ill.) JC. He gets good sink on his fastball from a low three-quarters arm slot. He also could add some more velocity as he fills out his lanky 6-foot-3, 190-pound frame. His slider has some promise, though it's not always easy to stay on top of the pitch with his arm angle. His changeup and control still need a lot of work, but his upside is intriguing. A good athlete, he starred in hockey as well as in baseball in high school. Berg probably will pitch in low Class A this year.

Year	Club (League)	Class	W	L	ERA	G	GS	CG	SV	IP	H	R	ER	HR	BB	SO	AVG
2004	Yankees (GCL)	R	3	2	5.87	15	1	0	1	31	40	22	20	3	15	29	.317
2005	Staten Island (NY-P)	A	6	2	3.53	15	9	0	0	59	48	26	23	3	20	52	.226
	Peoria (Mid)	A	0	0	9.45	2	1	0	0	7	9	7	7	0	6	3	.360
MINOR LEAGUE TOTALS			9	4	4.69	32	11	0	1	96	97	55	50	6	41	84	.267

22 BOBBY BROWNLIE   RHP

Born: Oct. 5, 1980. **B-T:** R-R. **Ht.:** 6-0. **Wt.:** 210. **Drafted:** Rutgers, 2002 (1st round). **Signed by:** Billy Blitzer.

The Bobby Brownlie who dominated college hitters and starred for Team USA in 2000-01 has yet to show up in pro ball, and it's increasingly unlikely that he will. Brownlie was an early favorite to go No. 1 overall in the 2002 draft, but he came down with biceps tendinitis that spring and slid to the Cubs at No. 21. He didn't sign until the following March, and after agreeing to a $2.5 million bonus he came down with a sore shoulder midway through his pro debut. Brownlie hasn't had any more health issues since, but his stuff is a far cry from what it once was. He operated with a 92-94 mph fastball and a plus-plus curveball before the biceps tendinitis, but he opened 2005 working at 86-87 mph. He got hammered as a starter and moved to the bullpen, where his fastball rose to 88-89 mph and topped out at 91 mph. When Brownlie returned to the Triple-A Iowa rotation in August, he got shellacked again, so his future appears to be in relief. His curveball is still good though not what it once was, and his changeup may now be his best pitch. He has survived as a pro by improving his command, though he tended to nibble and fall behind in counts as a Triple-A starter. He's destined for another year in Iowa.

Year	Club (League)	Class	W	L	ERA	G	GS	CG	SV	IP	H	R	ER	HR	BB	SO	AVG
2003	Daytona (FSL)	A	5	4	3.00	13	13	1	0	66	48	26	22	2	24	59	.201
2004	West Tenn (SL)	AA	9	9	3.36	26	26	2	0	147	127	62	62	11	36	114	.241
2005	Iowa (PCL)	AAA	6	7	4.75	27	14	0	0	104	98	56	55	11	42	73	.253
MINOR LEAGUE TOTALS			20	20	3.74	66	53	3	0	318	273	144	132	28	102	246	.237

23 MIKE BILLEK
RHP

Born: March 4, 1984. **B-T:** R-R. **Ht.:** 6-4. **Wt.:** 235. **Drafted:** Central Florida, 2005 (3rd round). **Signed by:** Keith Stohr.

The Cubs believe the best is yet to come for Billek, who won six games in three seasons at Central Florida before signing last June for $315,000 as a third-round pick. He didn't get in shape as a sophomore and then was suspended for violating team rules, and his junior season was marred by a nagging hip injury. Billek drew a lot of interest by hitting 95 mph on the Golden Knights' scout day in the fall of 2004, but pitched mostly at 88-90 mph while battling his hip during the spring. Big and strong at 6-foot-4 and 235 pounds, he may profile best as a reliever. In that role he could pitch at 92-94 mph, and he also has shown a harder, tighter curveball when he has come out of the bullpen. Billek pitched as a starter in his pro debut, acquitting himself well in low Class A, and will stay in that role for now. If he comes up with a reliable changeup and shows more consistency with his fastball and curve, he could remain a long-term starter. Billek may open his first full season in high Class A.

Year	Club (League)	Class	W	L	ERA	G	GS	CG	SV	IP	H	R	ER	HR	BB	SO	AVG
2005	Boise (NWL)	A	0	1	2.65	5	5	0	0	17	16	10	5	0	6	20	.239
	Peoria (Mid)	A	2	0	4.06	8	8	0	0	38	33	18	17	6	10	25	.234
MINOR LEAGUE TOTALS			2	1	3.62	13	13	0	0	55	49	28	22	6	16	45	.236

24 RYAN THERIOT
SS/2B

Born: Dec. 7, 1979. **B-T:** R-R. **Ht.:** 5-11. **Wt.:** 170. **Drafted:** Louisiana State, 2001 (3rd round). **Signed by:** Jim Crawford.

A catalyst on Louisiana State's 2000 College World Series champions—Theriot led off the final game's bottom of the ninth with a single and came around to score the title-winning run—he was sent straight to high Class A after signing in 2001 because 2000 first-rounder Luis Montanez was in low Class A. Theriot batted just .204, prompting Chicago to ask him to switch-hit, an experiment that didn't help him over the next three seasons. He reverted to batting solely righthanded in 2005, had the best year of his career and made his big league debut in September after Cedeno broke his hand. Theriot never is going to be an offensive force, but he can handle the bat well. He can bunt, hit-and-run and use the entire field, and he rarely strikes out. He doesn't have much pop, so he needs to hit more balls on the ground to take advantage of his slightly above-average speed. He also can get pull-conscious at times, which doesn't play to his strengths. Though he played mostly second base in Double-A last year to accommodate Buck Coats, Theriot is a legitimate shortstop. His arm, range and instincts are all plus tools, and he impressed the big league staff with his glove and his intensity. He probably will open the year in Triple-A and doesn't project as a regular, but he could have a big league career as a utilityman.

Year	Club (League)	Class	AVG	G	AB	R	H	2B	3B	HR	RBI	BB	SO	SB	OBP	SLG
2001	Daytona (FSL)	A	.204	30	103	20	21	5	0	0	9	21	17	2	.341	.252
2002	Lansing (Mid)	A	.252	130	489	75	123	19	4	1	37	59	77	32	.335	.313
2003	Lansing (Mid)	A	.259	58	220	29	57	8	1	1	17	31	34	21	.353	.318
	West Tenn (SL)	AA	.236	53	178	20	42	3	0	1	9	29	21	9	.351	.270
2004	Daytona (FSL)	A	.273	103	330	47	90	14	3	1	34	48	43	13	.367	.342
2005	West Tenn (SL)	AA	.304	120	448	52	136	28	4	1	53	45	38	24	.365	.391
	Chicago (NL)	MLB	.154	9	13	3	2	1	0	0	0	1	2	0	.214	.231
MAJOR LEAGUE TOTALS			.154	9	13	3	2	1	0	0	0	1	2	0	.214	.231
MINOR LEAGUE TOTALS			.265	494	1768	243	469	77	12	5	159	233	230	101	.353	.331

25 BUCK COATS
OF/SS

Born: June 9, 1982. **B-T:** L-R. **Ht.:** 6-3. **Wt.:** 190. **Drafted:** HS—Valdosta, Ga., 2000 (18th round). **Signed by:** Sam Hughes.

After nearly three years of trying to become a shortstop, Coats started playing center field regularly again last July. He spent most of his first three pro seasons as an outfielder, and he looked so good upon his return that some Cubs officials say he's a better center-field defender than Felix Pie. Coats also has a strong arm for that position and looks more comfortable there than he does at short, where he has made 114 errors in 303 games. He's a good athlete who runs well, and now he needs to get his bat going. The Cubs had envisioned Coats becoming an offensive middle infielder, but he has been ordinary at the plate. He has a sound swing, makes reasonable contact and has a little gap power. Realistically, he fits at the bottom of a big league batting order and looks more like a utilityman who can play almost anywhere on the diamond (he has played seven positions as a pro) than a regular. Coats still played a little shortstop in August and in the Arizona Fall League, and he'll probably see action at a variety of positions in Triple-A this year.

Year	Club (League)	Class	AVG	G	AB	R	H	2B	3B	HR	RBI	BB	SO	SB	OBP	SLG
2000	Cubs (AZL)	R	.296	30	98	20	29	6	3	0	14	12	24	7	.395	.418
2001	Cubs (AZL)	R	.260	33	123	11	32	3	3	1	18	4	19	3	.292	.358
2002	Lansing (Mid)	A	.257	133	501	65	129	21	4	4	47	31	67	14	.303	.339
2003	Lansing (Mid)	A	.277	132	488	64	135	25	7	1	59	64	93	32	.364	.363
2004	Daytona (FSL)	A	.290	112	414	64	120	22	4	8	55	32	90	28	.340	.420
2005	West Tenn (SL)	AA	.282	127	439	47	124	32	6	1	49	38	80	17	.340	.390
MINOR LEAGUE TOTALS			.276	567	2063	271	569	109	27	15	242	181	373	101	.337	.377

26 MARK HOLLIMAN   RHP

Born: Sept. 19, 1983. **B-T:** R-R. **Ht.:** 6-1. **Wt.:** 187. **Drafted:** Mississippi, 2005 (3rd round). **Signed by:** Bob Rossi.

Holliman left some unfinished business at Mississippi in 2005. He and the Rebels lost to Texas in a thrilling super-regional, and he finished his junior season with 281 career strikeouts, one shy of the school record held by former big leaguer Jeff Calhoun. But after deliberating for most of the summer, Holliman signed as a third-round pick for $385,000. He joined the Cubs for instructional league and made a good initial impression. He throws a 90-92 mph fastball that topped out at 94 in college, though at 6-foot-1 he doesn't always do a good job of leveraging it down in the strike zone. He needs to locate it better because it's very hittable when he leaves it up. Both his curveball and slider are plus pitches at times, and he also throws a changeup. His ability to deliver strikes and his strong body allow him to work deep into games. Though he missed what would have been his first pro summer, the Cubs think he's advanced enough to still advance quickly. He'll make his debut at one of their Class A affiliates.

Year	Club (League)	Class	W	L	ERA	G	GS	CG	SV	IP	H	R	ER	HR	BB	SO	AVG
2005	Did not play—Signed 2006 contract																

27 DYLAN JOHNSTON   SS

Born: March 25, 1987. **B-T:** L-R. **Ht.:** 6-0. **Wt.:** 180. **Drafted:** HS—Chandler, Ariz., 2005 (4th round). **Signed by:** Steve McFarland

Johnston led Hamilton High (Chandler, Ariz.) to state 5-A titles in 2003 and 2004 and a runner-up finish in 2005. He hit better as a junior and stood out more with his glove as a senior, but his flashes of all-around brilliance got him drafted in the fourth round last June. Signed for $270,000, Johnston will be a long-term project with the possibility of an exciting payoff at the end. He needs polish in all phases of the game, and the Cubs began tweaking his stance after he went hitless in five of his first six pro games. They've widened his setup and raised his hands. Johnston has plus bat speed and power potential. He's an average runner with OK range at shortstop. He has good hands, well above-average arm strength and a quick release, but he needs to raise his low three-quarters arm slot. As he fills out, it's possible that Johnston will have to move to third base. He'll play shortstop in 2006, when he figures to open the season in extended spring training rather than with a full-season club.

Year	Club (League)	Class	AVG	G	AB	R	H	2B	3B	HR	RBI	BB	SO	SB	OBP	SLG
2005	Cubs (AZL)	R	.182	13	44	4	8	2	0	0	5	6	24	0	.280	.227
MINOR LEAGUE TOTALS			.182	13	44	4	8	2	0	0	5	6	24	0	.280	.227

28 TIM LAYDEN   LHP

Born: Dec. 22, 1982. **B-T:** L-L. **Ht.:** 6-2. **Wt.:** 180. **Drafted:** Duke, 2004 (6th round). **Signed by:** Billy Swoope.

After pulling double duty as a starting pitcher and first baseman at Duke, Layden is finding out that less can be more. The Cubs made him a full-time reliever in 2005, and that may be his ticket to the majors. He's a lefty who throws from a deceptive low angle, and all of his pitches seem to dance. Layden's two primary pitches are a low-90s fastball and a hard slider. He also employs a changeup to keep righthanders honest. He does a tremendous job of keeping the ball down in the zone, as evidenced by his 3.3-1 groundball/flyball ratio last year. To keep climbing the ladder, Layden mainly needs to throw more strikes. The effort in his delivery and the movement on his pitches make that a challenge at times. He'll probably begin this year in high Class A, and he could move quickly if he develops better control.

Year	Club (League)	Class	W	L	ERA	G	GS	CG	SV	IP	H	R	ER	HR	BB	SO	AVG
2004	Cubs (AZL)	R	1	1	2.62	12	9	0	0	45	42	19	13	0	26	28	.251
2005	Peoria (Mid)	A	4	4	4.62	38	0	0	4	51	43	30	26	2	22	53	.223
	Daytona (FSL)	A	1	0	1.35	3	0	0	0	7	5	1	1	1	1	4	.227
MINOR LEAGUE TOTALS			6	5	3.53	53	9	0	4	102	90	50	40	3	49	85	.236

29 MIKE FONTENOT   2B/3B

Born: June 9, 1980. **B-T:** L-R. **Ht.:** 5-8. **Wt.:** 160. **Drafted:** Louisiana State, 2001 (1st round). **Signed by:** Mike Tullier (Orioles).

Ryan Theriot's double-play partner on Louisiana State's 2000 national championship team, Fontenot went 19th overall in the draft to the Orioles a year later. Part of the Sammy Sosa trade with Baltimore before the 2005 season, Fontenot spent his second straight year in Triple-A and also got his first two big league at-bats. If Fontenot is to get more playing time in the majors, it probably will come as a utilityman. Despite the uncertainty surrounding Chicago's middle-infield situation, his name never came up as a possible solution, and he's probably headed for a third season in Triple-A. Fontenot has slightly above-average speed and good pop for his size, but he tries to hit for power too much and isn't a big base-stealing threat. He doesn't cover as much ground defensively as his speed would suggest, and his arm is below average. Exclusively a second baseman in the Orioles system, he also saw extensive time at third base and got brief looks at shortstop and in the outfield last year. He doesn't profile as a good defender at any position.

Year	Club (League)	Class	AVG	G	AB	R	H	2B	3B	HR	RBI	BB	SO	SB	OBP	SLG
2002	Frederick (Car)	A	.264	122	481	61	127	16	4	8	53	42	117	13	.333	.364
2003	Bowie (EL)	AA	.325	126	449	63	146	24	5	12	66	50	89	16	.399	.481
2004	Ottawa (IL)	AAA	.279	136	524	73	146	30	10	8	49	48	111	14	.346	.420
2005	Chicago (NL)	MLB	.000	7	2	4	0	0	0	0	0	2	0	0	.600	.000
	Iowa (PCL)	AAA	.272	111	379	60	103	22	10	6	39	59	77	3	.377	.430
MAJOR LEAGUE TOTALS			.000	7	2	4	0	0	0	0	0	2	0	0	.500	.000
MINOR LEAGUE TOTALS			.285	495	1833	257	522	92	29	34	207	199	394	46	.362	.422

30 LUIS MONTANEZ   OF

Born: Dec. 15, 1981. **B-T:** R-R. **Ht.:** 6-2. **Wt.:** 180. **Drafted:** HS—Miami, 2000 (1st round). **Signed by:** Mike Soper.

Montanez won't ever live up to the expectations that come with going third overall in the 2000 draft, but moving from the middle infield to the outfield in mid-2004 resurrected a career that was going nowhere. He broke into pro ball by winning an MVP award in the Arizona League, but defensive woes at shortstop and second base affected him at the plate and he couldn't get past high Class A. Since going to the outfield, he has batted .294/.371/.482 and made it to Double-A and the Futures Game in 2005. Montanez has a good swing and approach, and he finally has started to hit for average and gap power. He controls the strike zone, though he does have a hole up and in. His speed and corner-outfield defense are OK, and he has a strong arm. He may yet make it to the majors as a backup outfielder who could fill in on the infield corners in a pinch. His bat slowed down some in Double-A in the second half of 2005, so he may go back there to start this season.

Year	Club (League)	Class	AVG	G	AB	R	H	2B	3B	HR	RBI	BB	SO	SB	OBP	SLG
2000	Cubs (AZL)	R	.344	50	192	50	66	16	7	2	37	25	42	11	.438	.531
	Lansing (Mid)	A	.138	8	29	2	4	1	0	0	0	3	6	0	.219	.172
2001	Lansing (Mid)	A	.255	124	499	70	127	33	6	5	54	34	121	20	.316	.375
2002	Daytona (FSL)	A	.265	124	487	69	129	21	5	4	59	44	89	14	.333	.353
2003	Daytona (FSL)	A	.253	126	486	51	123	18	3	5	38	33	89	11	.305	.333
2004	Daytona (FSL)	A	.215	21	79	8	17	4	2	1	7	7	16	2	.292	.354
	Boise (NWL)	A	.297	72	266	47	79	15	7	8	48	35	53	5	.381	.496
2005	Peoria (Mid)	A	.305	82	315	54	96	28	2	12	48	32	46	10	.384	.521
	West Tenn (SL)	AA	.268	45	153	20	41	9	1	2	14	12	21	0	.325	.379
MINOR LEAGUE TOTALS			.272	652	2506	371	682	145	33	39	305	225	483	73	.342	.403

CHICAGO
WHITE SOX

BY **PHIL ROGERS**

Like the 2004 Red Sox, the 2005 White Sox were curse-busters.

While ESPN invented the Curse of Shoeless Joe, the force behind the franchise's 88-year championship drought never really had its own identity. But when you've conspired to lose a World Series on purpose since you've last won one, you can't be blamed for always feeling like you've got one foot in quicksand.

That was the case before 2005 for the White Sox, who had lost all five of their postseason series since beating the New York Giants in the 1917 Fall Classic. But this time they blew through October in record fashion, going 11-1 and outscoring the Red Sox, Angels and Astros by a total of 33 runs, the biggest run differential in playoff history. It was a stunning success for a franchise that had known little except disappointment since winning the American League pennant in 1959.

In late September, Chicago was headed for a potential nightmare finish. The White Sox led the Indians by 15 games at the beginning of August and watched their lead all but vanish before sweeping Cleveland to end the season. Instead of being remembered as the team that blew the largest lead ever, they won 16 of their last 17 games and will go down along with the 1927 Yankees as the only teams to win a regular-season title wire-to-wire and then sweep the World Series.

Lefthander **Mark Buehrle**, third baseman Joe Crede and center fielder Aaron Rowand were the only homegrown regulars. But the organization's commitment to scouting and development has allowed general manager Ken Williams to boldly deal for key players such as Neal Cotts, Carl Everett, Freddy Garcia, Scott Podsednik and Juan Uribe. Previous GM Ron Schueler had dealt farm-system products to get Jon Garland and Paul Konerko.

The system also contributed a pair of valuable pitchers for the stretch drive. Bobby Jenks, claimed on waivers from the Angels during the offseason, replaced injured closer Dustin Hermanson and nailed down four saves in the postseason, including one for Garcia in a combined shutout that clinched the World Series. Brandon McCarthy, a 17th-round pick, replaced Orlando Hernandez in the September rotation and was Chicago's second-best starter in the final month.

Winning a World Series didn't stop Williams from being aggressive in the offseason. With 2003 first-rounder Brian Anderson ready for the big league outfield, Williams traded Rowand and two of the top left-handers in the system (Gio Gonzalez and Daniel Haigwood) to the Phillies for Jim Thome in November.

More talent is on the way to help the big league club or serve as trade bait. The White Sox' recent drafts have been fruitful, and three of their top four farm teams earned spots in the playoffs in 2005, with Kannapolis winning the Class A South Atlantic League title.

TOP 30 PROSPECTS

1. Bobby Jenks, rhp	16. Jeff Bajenaru, rhp
2. Chris Young, of	17. Aaron Cunningham, of
3. Brian Anderson, of	18. Tyler Lumsden, lhp
4. Ryan Sweeney, of	19. Chris Stewart, c
5. Josh Fields, 3b	20. Pedro Lopez, ss/2b
6. Jerry Owens, of	21. Tom Collaro, of
7. Robert Valido, ss	22. Chris Carter, 3b/1b
8. Ray Liotta, lhp	23. Daniel Cortes, rhp
9. Lance Broadway, rhp	24. Carlos Torres, rhp
10. Francisco Hernandez, c	25. Clayton Richard, lhp
11. Sean Tracey, rhp	26. Adam Russell, rhp
12. Casey Rogowski, 1b	27. Ricardo Nanita, of
13. Brandon Allen, 1b	28. Arnie Munoz, lhp
14. Charles Haeger, rhp	29. Gustavo Molina, c
15. Chris Getz, 2b/ss	30. Kris Honel, rhp

ORGANIZATION OVERVIEW

General manager: Kenny Williams. **Farm director:** David Wilder. **Scouting director:** Duane Shaffer.

2005 PERFORMANCE

Class	Team	League	W	L	Pct.	Finish*	Manager(s)
Majors	Chicago	American	99	63	.611	+1st (14)	Ozzie Guillen
Triple-A	Charlotte Knights	International	57	87	.396	13th (14)	Nick Leyva/Manny Trillo
Double-A	Birmingham Barons	Southern	82	57	.590	2nd (10)	Razor Shines
High A	Winston-Salem Warthogs	Carolina	77	64	.546	3rd (8)	Chris Cron
Low A	Kannapolis Intimidators	South Atlantic	74	59	.556	+4th (16)	Nick Capra
Rookie	Great Falls White Sox	Pioneer	32	44	.421	8th (8)	John Orton
Rookie	Bristol White Sox	Appalachian	30	36	.455	6th (10)	Jerry Hairston
OVERALL 2005 MINOR LEAGUE RECORD			352	347	.504	12th (30)	

*Finish in overall standings (No. of teams in league). +League champion.

ORGANIZATION LEADERS

BATTING   *Minimum 250 at-bats
*AVG	Hall, Noah, Winston-Salem	.332
R	Hall, Noah, Winston-Salem	112
H	Owens, Jerry, Birmingham	173
TB	Daigle, Leo, Charlotte/Winston-Salem	293
2B	Young, Chris, Birmingham	41
3B	Valido, Robert, Winston-Salem	7
HR	Daigle, Leo, Charlotte/Winston-Salem	31
RBI	Daigle, Leo, Charlotte/Winston-Salem	120
BB	Hall, Noah, Winston-Salem	86
SO	Collaro, Tom, Winston-Salem	153
SB	Valido, Robert, Winston-Salem	52
*OBP	Hall, Noah, Winston-Salem	.459
*SLG	Hall, Noah, Winston-Salem	.633

PITCHING   #Minimum 75 innings
W	Four tied at	14
L	Munoz, Arnie, Charlotte	14
#ERA	Liotta, Ray, Kannapolis/Winston-Salem	1.64
G	Smith, Matt, Charlotte	66
CG	Egbert, Jack, Kannapolis	4
SV	Zaleski, Matt, Kannapolis	22
IP	Haeger, Charles, Birmingham/Winston-Salem	167
	Rodriguez, Ryan, Winston-Salem	167
BB	Haeger, Charles, Birmingham/Winston-Salem	85
SO	Gonzalez, Gio, Kannapolis/Winston-Salem	163

BEST TOOLS

Best Hitter for Average	Jerry Owens
Best Power Hitter	Chris Young
Best Strike-Zone Discipline	Ricardo Nanita
Fastest Baserunner	Jerry Owens
Best Athlete	Chris Young
Best Fastball	Bobby Jenks
Best Curveball	Bobby Jenks
Best Slider	Tyler Lumsden
Best Changeup	Jack Egbert
Best Control	Ray Liotta
Best Defensive Catcher	Gustavo Molina
Best Defensive Infielder	Robert Valido
Best Infield Arm	Angel Gonzalez
Best Defensive Outfielder	Chris Young
Best Outfield Arm	Ryan Sweeney

PROJECTED 2009 LINEUP

Catcher	A.J. Pierzynski
First Base	Josh Fields
Second Base	Tadahito Iguchi
Third Base	Joe Crede
Shortstop	Jose Uribe
Left Field	Ryan Sweeney
Center Field	Chris Young
Right Field	Brian Anderson

Designated Hitter	Paul Konerko
No. 1 Starter	Mark Buehrle
No. 2 Starter	Jose Contreras
No. 3 Starter	Brandon McCarthy
No. 4 Starter	Freddy Garcia
No. 5 Starter	Jon Garland
Closer	Bobby Jenks

LAST YEAR'S TOP 20 PROSPECTS

1. Brian Anderson, of
2. Ryan Sweeney, of
3. Brandon McCarthy, rhp
4. Josh Fields, 3b
5. Tadahito Iguchi, 2b
6. Sean Tracey, rhp
7. Chris Young, of
8. Gio Gonzalez, lhp
9. Francisco Hernandez, c
10. Pedro Lopez, ss
11. Kris Honel, rhp
12. Ray Liotta, lhp
13. Tyler Lumsden, lhp
14. Robert Valido, ss
15. Casey Rogowski, 1b/of
16. Arnie Munoz, lhp
17. Wes Whisler, lhp
18. Antoin Gray, 2b/3b
19. Daniel Haigwood, lhp
20. Micah Schnurstein, 3b

TOP PROSPECTS OF THE DECADE

Year	Player, Pos.	2005 Org.
1996	Chris Snopek, ss/3b	Out of baseball
1997	Mike Cameron, of	Mets
1998	Mike Caruso, ss	Out of baseball
1999	Carlos Lee, 3b	Brewers
2000	Kip Wells, rhp	Pirates
2001	Jon Rauch, rhp	Nationals
2002	Joe Borchard, of	White Sox
2003	Joe Borchard, of	White Sox
2004	Joe Borchard, of	White Sox
2005	Brian Anderson, of	White Sox

TOP DRAFT PICKS OF THE DECADE

Year	Player, Pos.	2005 Org.
1996	*Bobby Seay, lhp	Rockies
1997	Jason Dellaero, ss	Out of baseball
1998	Kip Wells, rhp	Pirates
1999	Jason Stumm, rhp	White Sox
2000	Joe Borchard, of	White Sox
2001	Kris Honel, rhp	White Sox
2002	Royce Ring, lhp	Mets
2003	Brian Anderson, of	White Sox
2004	Josh Fields, 3b	White Sox
2005	Lance Broadway, rhp	White Sox

*Did not sign.

ALL-TIME LARGEST BONUSES

Joe Borchard, 2000	$5,300,000
Jason Stumm, 1999	$1,750,000
Royce Ring, 2002	$1,600,000
Brian Anderson, 2003	$1,600,000
Lance Broadway, 2005	$1,570,000

MINOR LEAGUE DEPTH CHART

Chicago White Sox

Rank: 12

STRENGTH: Outfield. The White Sox have talent throughout the system and enough depth to use for trades.

WEAKNESS: Starting pitching. Dealing left-handers Gio Gonzalez and Daniel Haigwood drained the White Sox' previously solid depth.

*Depth charts prepared by **John Manuel** and **Chris Kline**. Numbers in parentheses indicate prospect rankings.*

LF
Jerry Owens (6)
Tom Collaro (21)
Ricardo Nanita (27)
David Cook
Evan Tartaglia

CF
Chris Young (2)
Brian Anderson (3)
Mike Spidale

RF
Ryan Sweeney (4)
Aaron Cunningham (17)
Salvador Sanchez

3B
Josh Fields (5)
Micah Schnurstein
Christian Acosta
Tim Hummel
Jose De Los Santos

SS
Robert Valido (7)
Pedro Lopez (20)
Andy Gonzalez
Leonardo Acosta

2B
Chris Getz (15)
Antoin Gray
Michael Myers
Boomer Berry

1B
Casey Rogowski (12)
Brandon Allen (13)
Chris Carter (22)
Clint King
Travis Hinton

C
Francisco Hernandez (10)
Chris Stewart (19)
Gustavo Molina (29)
Donny Lucy
Adam Ricks
Carlos Lee

RHP

Starters	Relievers
Lance Broadway (9)	Bobby Jenks (1)
Sean Tracey (11)	Jeff Bajenaru (16)
Charles Haeger (14)	Matt Smith
Daniel Cortes (23)	Dwayne Pollok
Carlos Torres (24)	Ehren Wasserman
Adam Russell (26)	Ryan Rote
Kris Honel (30)	Matt Zaleski
Jack Egbert	Michael Moat
Ricky Brooks	Josh Fields
Lucas Harrell	Orionny Lopez
Frank Viola, Jr.	Nick Lemon

LHP

Starters	Relievers
Ray Liotta (8)	Arnie Munoz (28)
Tyler Lumsden (18)	Paulino Reynoso
Clayton Richard (25)	Jim Bullard
Ryan Rodriguez	
Wes Whisler	
Corwin Malone	
Heath Phillips	
Israel Chirino	
Logan Williamson	
Yunior Novoa	

DRAFT ANALYSIS

2005

Best Pro Debut: 2B/SS Chris Getz (4) batted .304-1-28 with 11 steals at low Class A Kannapolis. OF Aaron Cunningham (6) was a Rookie-level Appalachian League all-star, hitting .315-5-25.

Best Athlete: Cunningham had little fanfare before 2005, when scouts discovered him while scouting Everett (Wash.) CC pitchers Zach Simons and J.T. Zink. Cunningham has plus power and slightly above-average speed and arm strength. LHP Clayton Richard (8) was a backup quarterback on Michigan's football team. RHP Lance Broadway (1) is a very good athlete for a pitcher.

Best Pure Hitter: Getz controls the strike zone and has a gift for making contact. He drew 36 walks and struck out just 12 times in 238 pro at-bats. Cunningham hits the ball with more authority.

Best Raw Power: 3B Chris Carter (15) is a 6-foot-4, 210-pounder whom scouts considered raw. Yet he managed to hit .283 with 10 homers in the Appy League. Power is Cunningham's best tool.

Fastest Runner: Getz has plus speed and is an even better baserunner because he has excellent instincts.

Best Defensive Player: Getz has the hands and range to play shortstop but an arm better suited to second base.

Best Fastball: RHP Ryan Rote (5) has a 94-95 mph fastball but got tagged for a 7.33 ERA in his pro debut because he's still working on his secondary pitches. Richard and RHPs Daniel Cortes (7) and Derek Rodriguez (13) all top out at 94.

Best Breaking Ball: Broadway had one of the best curveballs in the draft and commands it exceptionally well.

SPORTS ON FILM

Cunningham

Most Intriguing Background: Getz and RHP Ricky Brooks (3) were Chicago's highest unsigned picks from the 2002 and 2003 drafts, respectively. RHP Stephen Squires' (49) father Mike was a Gold Glove first baseman for the White Sox and currently scouts for the Cardinals. Unsigned OF Jordan Danks' (19) brother John was the Rangers' first-round pick in 2003. LHP Brian Flores (37), a draft-and-follow candidate for this spring, was named most outstanding pitcher at the 2005 Junior College World Series and led national juco pitchers with 147 strikeouts in 110 innings. Chicago also took Flores in the 21st round the previous year.

Closest To The Majors: Broadway was the hottest pitcher in college baseball down the stretch and could ride a similar roll to Chicago. Brooks has similar polish, though he lacks Broadway's putaway bender.

Best Late-Round Pick: Carter.

The One Who Got Away: Danks would have gone by the end of the supplemental first round. But he wrote teams a letter asking them not to select him because he wanted to play at Texas, and he remained true to his word.

Assessment: Broadway and Brooks both play to the strengths of the big league club, throwing strikes and letting their defense make plays. Cunningham, Richard and Carter offer interesting upside for late-round choices.

2004 There may not be a superstar, but all three first-rounders— 3B Josh Fields, LHPs Gio Gonzalez (part of the Jim Thome trade) and Tyler Lumsden— look solid. LHP Ray Liotta (2), has two ERA titles in two years. *GRADE:* B

2003 The White Sox thought enough of OF Brian Anderson (1) to trade Aaron Rowand this offseason. OF Ryan Sweeney (2) and SS Robert Valido (4) are part of the club's future. Unsigned 3B Wes Hodges (13) should be one of the first hitters drafted in June. *GRADE:* B+

2002 LHP Royce Ring (1, now with the Mets) is nothing special, but this draft got much better after the first round. Chicago has traded OF Jeremy Reed (2), RHP Josh Rupe (3) and LHP Daniel Haigwood (16) but wisely has held onto RHP Brandon McCarthy (17). *GRADE:* B+

2001 First-round RHPs Kris Honel and Wyatt Allen (now with the Pirates) haven't panned out. But Chris Young (16) has developed into the most exciting outfield prospect the White Sox have had in years. *GRADE:* B+

Draft analysis prepared by Jim Callis. Numbers in parentheses indicate draft rounds.

BOBBY
JENKS

RHP

CARL KLINE

Born: March 14, 1981
Ht.: 6-3. **Wt.:** 270.
Bats: R. **Throws:** R.
Drafted: HS—Spirit Lake, Idaho,
2000 (5th round)
Signed by: Jack Uhey (Angels)

On the recommendation of pro scouts Gary Pellant and Bill Young, the White Sox were one of several teams to put in a claim on Jenks after the Angels finally had enough of his shenanigans and placed him on waivers in December 2004. Los Angeles invested five seasons trying to develop Jenks, who was as rough off the field as his stuff was raw on the mound. The Angels suspended him for violating team rules in 2002, an ESPN The Magazine article revealed several disturbing incidents from his past in 2003, and the final straw came when he beat up a teammate while rehabbing his elbow in the fall of 2004. At that point, Jenks also had been shut down three times in two seasons because of a stress reaction in his elbow, which required surgery in August 2004. Jenks was a new man with the White Sox. Marriage and fatherhood helped him mature, as did the continuing support of Mark Potoshnik, a coach at the Northwest Baseball Academy in Lynwood, Wash., who has been his mentor. Sent to Double-A Birmingham, Jenks took off immediately. He led the Southern League in saves when the Sox promoted him to the big leagues in July. Manager Ozzie Guillen put him in low-stress situations at the start, but Jenks supplanted Dustin Hermanson as closer by September. He wound up with 10 saves, including four in the post-season—closing out the Indians, Red Sox, Angels and Astros in clinching opportunities.

No pitcher takes the mound with two more powerful pitches. Jenks' fastball topped out at 102 mph with the White Sox, and he blew 99-100 mph heat by Jeff Bagwell in his six-pitch strikeout in Game One of the World Series. He complements the fastball with a power snapdragon curve clocked at 85-89 mph. His curve is unhittable when he throws it for strikes. Jenks also owns a hard slider and a decent changeup—leftovers from his years as a starter—but rarely needs to throw them. His mound presence was particularly impressive in his big league debut, as was his ability to bounce back from blown saves.

Though he has matured, Jenks needs supervision and still has to be considered a high risk. His weight could become a problem if he doesn't maintain some semblance of conditioning. His fastball doesn't always have a lot of movement, allowing hitters to zero in on it if they can foul off a few pitches and time it. His control never has been a strong suit.

Given Jenks' rocky road to the big leagues, he'll have to prove he's more than a one-year sensation. He appeared in 73 games last season and could feel wear and tear in 2006. If he holds together, he'll give Guillen a bullpen anchor for years to come.

Year	Club (League)	Class	W	L	ERA	G	GS	CG	SV	IP	H	R	ER	HR	BB	SO	AVG
2000	Butte (Pio)	R	1	7	7.86	14	12	0	0	53	61	57	46	2	44	42	.290
2001	Cedar Rapids (Mid)	A	3	7	5.27	21	21	0	0	99	90	74	58	10	64	98	.245
	Arkansas (TL)	AA	1	0	3.60	2	2	0	0	10	8	5	4	0	5	10	.200
2002	Arkansas (TL)	AA	3	6	4.66	10	10	1	0	58	49	34	30	2	44	58	.234
	Rancho Cucamonga (Cal)	A	3	5	4.82	11	10	1	0	65	50	42	35	4	46	64	.212
2003	Angels (AZL)	R	0	0	0.00	1	1	0	0	4	2	0	0	0	0	5	.154
	Arkansas (TL)	AA	7	2	2.17	16	16	0	0	83	56	23	20	2	51	103	.191
2004	Salt Lake (PCL)	AAA	0	1	8.78	3	3	0	0	12	19	15	12	1	6	13	.358
	Angels (AZL)	R	0	0	8.18	1	1	0	0	3	2	3	3	0	3	5	.182
	Rancho Cucamonga (Cal)	A	0	1	19.46	1	1	0	0	4	5	8	8	0	7	3	.385
2005	Birmingham (SL)	AA	1	2	2.85	35	0	0	19	41	34	17	13	1	20	48	.224
	Chicago (AL)	MLB	1	1	2.75	32	0	0	6	39	34	15	12	3	15	50	.225
MAJOR LEAGUE TOTALS			1	1	2.75	32	0	0	6	39	34	15	12	3	15	50	.225
MINOR LEAGUE TOTALS			19	31	4.77	115	77	2	19	432	376	278	229	22	290	449	.235

2 CHRIS YOUNG
OF

Born: Sept. 5, 1983. **B-T:** R-R. **Ht.:** 6-2. **Wt.:** 180. **Drafted:** HS—Bellaire, Texas, 2001 (16th round). **Signed by:** Joe Butler/Paul Provas.

After going 50-for-50 stealing bases as a senior at Bellaire High in suburban Houston, Young shattered his left forearm in an outfield collision three days before the 2001 draft. Chicago stole him in the 16th round and has watched him blossom into one of the top outfield prospects in the minors. He skipped a level last year and led the Southern League in runs, homers and extra-base hits (70) despite missing two weeks after pulling a muscle in his side during the Futures Game. Young is a dynamic offensive player who sparks comparisons to Eric Davis. He has the power and speed to be a 30-30 man in the big leagues and has proven his ability to make adjustments. Double-A pitchers victimized Young with a steady diet of low curveballs and high fastballs early in the season, but by midseason he forced pitchers to throw him strikes and made them pay when they did. He's an outstanding defensive center fielder. The only thing keeping Young from being a five-tool player is his arm. It's playable in center field but likely would prevent him from moving to right field. He strikes out a lot, but does so without compromising his production and also draws a lot of walks. The White Sox have a center-field opening after trading Aaron Rowand to the Phillies, but they'll likely give it to Brian Anderson and let Young open the season at Triple-A Charlotte. He should be ready by midseason.

Year	Club (League)	Class	AVG	G	AB	R	H	2B	3B	HR	RBI	BB	SO	SB	OBP	SLG
2002	White Sox (AZL)	R	.217	55	184	26	40	13	1	5	17	19	54	7	.308	.380
2003	Bristol (Appy)	R	.290	64	238	47	69	18	3	7	28	23	40	21	.357	.479
	Great Falls (Pio)	R	.176	10	34	5	6	3	0	0	0	1	10	0	.200	.265
2004	Kannapolis (SAL)	A	.262	135	465	83	122	31	5	24	56	66	145	31	.365	.505
2005	Birmingham (SL)	AA	.277	126	466	100	129	41	3	26	77	70	129	32	.377	.545
MINOR LEAGUE TOTALS			.264	390	1387	261	366	106	12	62	178	179	378	91	.357	.492

3 BRIAN ANDERSON
OF

Born: March 11, 1982. **B-T:** R-R. **Ht.:** 6-3. **Wt.:** 200. **Drafted:** Arizona, 2003 (1st round). **Signed by:** John Kazanas.

Regarded as the system's top prospect heading into 2005, Anderson had a solid Triple-A season and spent the last month and a half in the majors. He reached Chicago little more than two years after signing for $1.6 million as a first-round draft pick, with minor injuries the only thing that slowed him down. Anderson is a well-rounded player. He can drive the ball to all fields and could develop into a 25-homer guy at hitter-friendly U.S. Cellular Field. He's a good outfielder with a strong arm, and he has been solid in center field since his college days at Arizona. Anderson is a good athlete with decent speed but isn't a basestealing threat. While he's not terribly impatient at the plate, he doesn't draw a lot of walks. He stayed healthy in 2005, though he had off-season surgery to remove a plate and some screws from his right wrist, remnants of a 2003 operation. Anderson is ready to take the next step, which is why the White Sox were willing to include Aaron Rowand in the Jim Thome trade. Anderson should get the first half of the season to settle in, but then could be challenged by prospects behind him like Chris Young and Jerry Owens.

Year	Club (League)	Class	AVG	G	AB	R	H	2B	3B	HR	RBI	BB	SO	SB	OBP	SLG
2003	Great Falls (Pio)	R	.388	13	49	6	19	2	1	2	13	9	10	3	.492	.592
2004	Winston-Salem (Car)	A	.319	69	254	43	81	22	4	8	46	29	44	10	.394	.531
	Birmingham (SL)	AA	.270	48	185	26	50	9	3	4	27	19	30	3	.346	.416
2005	Charlotte (IL)	AAA	.295	118	448	71	132	24	3	16	57	44	115	4	.360	.469
	Chicago (AL)	MLB	.176	13	34	3	6	1	0	2	3	0	12	1	.176	.382
MAJOR LEAGUE TOTALS			.176	13	34	3	6	1	0	2	3	0	12	1	.176	.382
MINOR LEAGUE TOTALS			.301	248	936	146	282	57	11	30	143	101	199	20	.369	.482

4 RYAN SWEENEY OF

Born: Feb. 20, 1985. **B-T:** L-L. **Ht.:** 6-5. **Wt.:** 205. **Drafted:** HS—Cedar Rapids, Iowa, 2003 (2nd round). **Signed by:** Nathan Durst.

Coming out of Iowa as a prepster, Sweeney wasn't the most likely candidate to jump on the fast track. But when the White Sox needed an extra outfielder in big league camp in 2004 and he responded by hitting .367, they skipped him a level. He spent 2005 in Double-A as a 20-year-old and played through a wrist injury all year, which helps explain his modest numbers. Sweeney is a smart hitter with a sweet swing. Longtime executive and scout Roland Hemond compares him to Harold Baines. Sweeney hits the ball hard to all fields and has the bat speed to handle plus fastballs. A pitching prospect in high school, he has a plus arm and his right-field play is solid. Despite his fast rise, Sweeney has room to improve as a hitter. The White Sox expect him to develop 15-20 home run power, but he has just 10 in three seasons. Though he controls the strike zone, he could stand to be more patient. Sweeney has been impressive in each of the last two major league spring camps and has moved quickly. It wouldn't hurt him to repeat Double-A and pound pitchers after two years facing constant adjustments.

Year	Club (League)	Class	AVG	G	AB	R	H	2B	3B	HR	RBI	BB	SO	SB	OBP	SLG
2003	Bristol (Appy)	R	.313	19	67	11	21	3	0	2	5	7	10	3	.387	.448
	Great Falls (Pio)	R	.353	10	34	0	12	2	0	0	4	2	3	0	.389	.412
2004	Winston-Salem (Car)	A	.283	134	515	71	146	22	3	7	66	40	65	8	.342	.379
2005	Birmingham (SL)	AA	.298	113	429	64	128	22	3	1	47	35	53	6	.357	.371
MINOR LEAGUE TOTALS			.294	276	1045	146	307	49	6	10	122	84	131	17	.353	.381

5 JOSH FIELDS 3B

Born: Dec. 14, 1982. **B-T:** R-R. **Ht.:** 6-2. **Wt.:** 210. **Drafted:** Oklahoma State, 2004 (1st round). **Signed by:** Alex Slattery/Nathan Durst.

A two-sport standout at Oklahoma State, Fields still holds the Cowboys' record for career passing touchdowns with 55. He comes from an athletic family, as his mother Rhonda was the first female athlete to earn a full scholarship to Oklahoma State. Signed for $1.55 million as the 18th overall pick in 2004, he spent his first full pro season in Double-A. Fields has above-average bat speed and strength, which could help him develop into a middle-of-the-order presence. He has the strong arm and leadership expected from a former Big 12 Conference quarterback. Because he divided his attention between two sports in college, Fields still has a lot of rough edges. He made strides defensively in the Arizona Fall League, but he still can appear mechanical at times. His plate discipline is below-average and didn't show much improvement in 2005, in part because he can do damage on pitches off the plate. While the White Sox have been aggressive with several of their recent top draft picks, they can afford to let Fields repeat Double-A. With Joe Crede entrenched in Chicago after a strong postseason, Fields seems a good bet to get another 500 to 1,000 minor league at-bats before being a serious consideration.

Year	Club (League)	Class	AVG	G	AB	R	H	2B	3B	HR	RBI	BB	SO	SB	OBP	SLG
2004	Winston-Salem (Car)	A	.285	66	256	36	73	12	4	7	39	18	74	0	.333	.445
2005	Birmingham (SL)	AA	.252	134	477	76	120	27	0	16	79	55	142	7	.341	.409
MINOR LEAGUE TOTALS			.263	200	733	112	193	39	4	23	118	73	216	7	.339	.422

6 JERRY OWENS OF

Born: Feb. 16, 1981. **B-T:** L-L. **Ht.:** 6-3. **Wt.:** 195. **Drafted:** The Masters (Calif.) College, 2003 (2nd round). **Signed by:** Tony Arango (Expos).

The White Sox grabbed Alex Escobar in an August 2004 waiver claim and used him to steal Owens from the Nationals in a February 2005 trade. Owens made an immediate impression on Chicago manager Ozzie Guillen in spring training and went on to win the Southern League batting title, reaching base in 37 consecutive games in one stretch. Owens had enough speed to play wide receiver at UCLA before a broken foot caused him to sour on football. He makes solid contact to drive the ball past drawn-in infielders, who must respect his quickness and bunting ability. He handles the bat well, working counts and drawing walks. He profiles in center field. Owens is inexperienced for his age, and he's still learning the nuances of basestealing and defense. He doesn't drive the ball much now but could develop gap power. His arm is fringe average. Owens spent the winter chasing another batting title in Venezuela, where he collected 18 hits in his first 36 at-bats. He'll start 2006 in Triple-A but isn't too far from challenging Brian Anderson for the center-field job.

Year	Club (League)	Class	AVG	G	AB	R	H	2B	3B	HR	RBI	BB	SO	SB	OBP	SLG
2003	Vermont (NY-P)	A	.125	2	8	0	1	0	0	0	0	0	2	1	.125	.125
2004	Savannah (SAL)	A	.292	108	418	69	122	17	2	1	37	46	59	30	.365	.349
2005	Birmingham (SL)	AA	.331	130	522	99	173	21	6	2	52	52	72	38	.393	.406
MINOR LEAGUE TOTALS			.312	240	948	168	296	38	8	3	89	98	133	69	.378	.379

7 ROBERT VALIDO SS

STEVE MOORE

Born: May 16, 1985. **B-T:** R-R. **Ht.:** 6-1. **Wt.:** 175. **Drafted:** HS—Miami, 2003 (4th round). **Signed by:** Jose Ortega.

Valido reached high Class A Winston-Salem before he turned 20, but he made more headlines when he drew a 15-game suspension last May after testing positive for performance-enhancing substances. He came back to set career highs in most categories and finished the year strong in the Arizona Fall League. Valido has the speed and hitting skills to earn top-of-the-order consideration in the future. Defensively, he has the makings of a Gold Glover. He ranges well to both sides and has soft hands and a plus arm. He reduced his errors from 27 in 2004 to 12 in 2005. He has learned to read pitchers and get good jumps, leading the Carolina League in steals while getting caught just five times last year. Valido needs to prove his performance hasn't been the product of steroids. He won't be able to bat leadoff unless he recognizes the value of drawing walks. Juan Uribe is signed for two more years, after which Valido should be ready. He's in position to become the White Sox' first homegrown regular at shortstop since Bucky Dent.

Year	Club (League)	Class	AVG	G	AB	R	H	2B	3B	HR	RBI	BB	SO	SB	OBP	SLG
2003	Bristol (Appy)	R	.307	58	215	39	66	15	2	6	31	17	28	17	.364	.479
2004	Kannapolis (SAL)	A	.252	122	456	65	115	25	0	4	43	35	59	28	.313	.333
2005	Winston-Salem (Car)	A	.288	119	513	86	148	28	7	8	59	21	64	52	.320	.417
MINOR LEAGUE TOTALS			.278	299	1184	190	329	68	9	18	133	73	151	97	.325	.396

8 RAY LIOTTA LHP

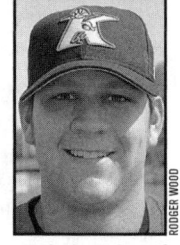
RODGER WOOD

Born: April 3, 1983. **B-T:** L-L. **Ht.:** 6-3. **Wt.:** 220. **Drafted:** Gulf Coast (Fla.) CC, 2004 (2nd round). **Signed by:** Warren Hughes.

Liotta was drafted by the Brewers in the 12th round out of high school, but ended up at Tulane for a year before transferring to Gulf Coast (Fla.) CC. His first two seasons as a pro have yielded a pair of ERA titles, the most recent in the low Class A South Atlantic League. He was even more impressive after a late-season promotion to high Class A. Liotta's best pitch is a 12-to-6 curveball with tight, downward rotation. He has improved the command of his curve, throwing it for strikes in all counts last season. He also has a low-90s fastball that gets on hitters quickly. He induces a lot of groundballs and has surrendered just seven homers in 229 pro innings. Liotta's delivery is a bit mechanical and long, which scouts say could lead to inconsistency, though he hasn't had any problems thus far. His changeup improved last season but has yet to become a weapon. The inclusion of Gio Gonzalez in the Jim Thome trade made Liotta the White Sox' top pitching prospect in the minors. He has earned a trip to Double-A for 2006.

Year	Club (League)	Class	W	L	ERA	G	GS	CG	SV	IP	H	R	ER	HR	BB	SO	AVG
2004	Great Falls (Pio)	R	5	1	2.54	14	11	0	0	64	59	27	18	1	28	65	.250
2005	Kannapolis (SAL)	A	8	3	2.26	20	20	1	0	115	108	39	29	5	35	107	.252
	Winston-Salem (Car)	A	6	2	1.45	8	8	0	0	50	46	11	8	1	16	37	.254
MINOR LEAGUE TOTALS			19	6	2.16	42	39	1	0	229	213	77	55	7	79	209	.252

9 LANCE BROADWAY RHP

RODGER WOOD

Born: Aug. 20, 1983. **B-T:** R-R. **Ht.:** 6-4. **Wt.:** 195. **Drafted:** Texas Christian, 2005 (1st round). **Signed by:** Keith Staab.

A product of Grand Prairie (Texas) High, which also produced big leaguers Kerry Wood and Kevin Walker, Broadway began his college career at Dallas Baptist before transferring to Texas Christian and earning All-America honors in 2005. He allowed just two earned runs in his last 48 innings, causing his draft stock to soar down the stretch, and tied for the NCAA Division I lead with 15 wins. The 15th overall pick in June, he signed for $1.57 million. Broadway's out pitch is a plus-plus curveball that he commands to both sides of the plate. It's a hard curve with a sharp, late break and he can throw it for strikes or bury it in the dirt as a chase pitch. He's a polished pitcher who locates his average fastball very well and understands how to get outs. While Broadway has an ideal pitcher's build, he's not overpowering and his fastball sits at 88-90 mph. His changeup is basically a show-me pitch, though it's improving and he's learning to believe in it. Broadway's polish should help him move rapidly. He went straight to high Class A, where he'll probably return to begin 2006.

Year	Club (League)	Class	W	L	ERA	G	GS	CG	SV	IP	H	R	ER	HR	BB	SO	AVG
2005	Winston-Salem (Car)	A	1	3	4.58	11	11	0	0	55	68	31	28	4	20	58	.306
MINOR LEAGUE TOTALS			1	3	4.58	11	11	0	0	55	68	31	28	4	20	58	.306

10   FRANCISCO HERNANDEZ   C

BILL MITCHELL

Born: Feb. 4, 1986. **B-T:** B-R. **Ht.:** 5-9. **Wt.:** 160. **Signed:** Dominican Republic, 2002. **Signed by:** Denny Gonzalez/Miguel Ibarra.

After Hernandez handled the Rookie-level Appalachian League in 2004, the White Sox promoted him to low Class A Kannapolis last year but the jump proved to be too much. He showed immaturity by losing composure at times, though he got himself back together after a demotion to the Rookie-level Pioneer League. Hernandez is a strong defensive catcher, using his plus arm and quick release to throw out 45 percent of basestealers last season. He still has the potential to grow into a force at the plate as well. He uses a simple approach to make solid contact from both sides of the plate. He's a better hitter from the left side but shows some raw power from the right side. At times, Hernandez can seem like his own worst enemy. He put too much pressure on himself early last season and wasn't able to snap out of his slump. His receiving and game-calling have lagged behind the rest of his defense. Hernandez should be more grounded this season than he was a year ago and could have a breakout season that gets him noticed as one of the top catching prospects in the game. He should have better results in low Class A this time around.

Year	Club (League)	Class	AVG	G	AB	R	H	2B	3B	HR	RBI	BB	SO	SB	OBP	SLG
2003	White Sox (DSL)	R	.296	66	216	34	64	14	0	6	29	23	9	.412	.444
2004	Bristol (Appy)	R	.326	53	181	32	59	13	1	5	30	13	32	0	.372	.492
	Kannapolis (SAL)	A	.333	3	12	0	4	1	0	0	0	0	3	0	.333	.417
2005	Kannapolis (SAL)	A	.222	44	153	15	34	5	0	3	18	13	29	0	.292	.314
	Great Falls (Pio)	R	.349	58	212	37	74	19	0	6	34	19	25	0	.405	.524
MINOR LEAGUE TOTALS			.304	224	774	118	235	52	1	20	111	84	112	9	.377	.451

11   SEAN TRACEY   RHP

Born: Nov. 14, 1980. **B-T:** L-R. **Ht.:** 6-3. **Wt.:** 210. **Drafted:** UC Irvine, 2002 (8th round). **Signed by:** Joe Butler/Matt Hattabaugh.

Considered to have one of the best arms in the White Sox system, Tracey captured interest with his pure velocity in 2004. He refined his skills last year, when his fastball lost a foot or so, tying for the Southern League lead in wins. Tracey has a durable arm and lives for his time on the mound. He's willing to pitch inside and challenge hitters every way possible. His fastball is his best pitch, but it was more often in the low 90s in the 2005, as opposed to the mid-90s in the past. His hard sinker is a decent pitch. Tracey's secondary pitches and his approach both still need work as he enters his fifth pro season. He doesn't change speeds well, which leads to lots of long at-bats as hitters foul off fastballs until they get one they can handle. His control is streaky. Tracey probably will start in Triple-A in 2006, but his profile and aggressiveness seem better suited for the bullpen. The White Sox have a deep rotation and are more in need of relief help, and he could get a callup in that role this year. He eventually could become a top set-up man, if not a closer.

Year	Club (League)	Class	W	L	ERA	G	GS	CG	SV	IP	H	R	ER	HR	BB	SO	AVG
2002	Bristol (Appy)	R	5	2	3.01	13	12	0	0	66	57	27	22	4	19	50	.241
2003	Kannapolis (SAL)	A	2	7	9.50	14	9	0	0	42	51	54	44	4	46	28	.305
	Great Falls (Pio)	R	8	5	3.69	16	12	1	0	93	90	45	38	5	22	74	.259
2004	Winston-Salem (Car)	A	9	8	2.73	27	27	0	0	148	108	60	45	5	69	130	.213
2005	Birmingham (SL)	AA	14	6	4.07	28	28	2	0	164	154	80	74	13	76	106	.257
MINOR LEAGUE TOTALS			38	28	3.92	98	88	3	0	512	460	266	223	31	232	388	.247

12   CASEY ROGOWSKI   1B

Born: May 1, 1981. **B-T:** L-L. **Ht.:** 6-3. **Wt.:** 230. **Drafted:** HS—Redford, Mich., 1999 (13th round). **Signed by:** Nathan Durst.

Added to the 40-man roster after the 2004 season, Rogowski finally escaped Class A last year. He hit just .211 in big league camp but impressed the major league staff with his potential. A shoulder injury in 2002 contributed to his slow rise, but he's a headstrong player who believes in himself and will keep pushing. He won a Michigan high school wrestling championship as a heavyweight, two more state titles in football and the state's Mr. Baseball award in 1999. While Rogowski's home run output suffered at Birmingham's pitcher-friendly Hoover Metropolitan Stadium in 2005, he finished with career highs in doubles and extra-base hits as well as batting average. He has solid strike-zone awareness, though he wasn't as disciplined last year as in the past. He's a below-average runner, but he's very athletic for a first baseman and has seen some time in left field. Still trying to make up for lost time, Rogowski landed a job in the Dominican Winter League and proved himself further as a run producer. He'll try to do the same in Triple-A this year.

Year	Club (League)	Class	AVG	G	AB	R	H	2B	3B	HR	RBI	BB	SO	SB	OBP	SLG
1999	White Sox (AZL)	R	.288	52	160	23	46	7	2	0	27	26	34	2	.384	.356
2000	Burlington (Mid)	A	.231	122	412	62	95	19	1	6	41	47	89	11	.315	.325
2001	Kannapolis (SAL)	A	.287	130	439	66	126	18	3	14	69	62	95	16	.382	.437
2002	White Sox (AZL)	R	.484	8	31	4	15	6	0	2	8	1	5	2	.485	.871
	Winston-Salem (Car)	A	.255	55	184	27	47	5	0	3	23	28	46	16	.358	.332
2003	Winston-Salem (Car)	A	.246	116	357	46	88	20	1	7	38	53	73	18	.354	.367
2004	Winston-Salem (Car)	A	.286	136	465	88	133	28	2	18	90	91	94	16	.401	.471
2005	Birmingham (SL)	AA	.293	134	505	83	148	37	6	9	78	58	111	20	.374	.444
MINOR LEAGUE TOTALS			.273	753	2553	399	698	140	15	59	374	366	547	101	.369	.409

13 BRANDON ALLEN
1B

Born: Feb. 12, 1986. **B-T:** L-R. **Ht.:** 6-4. **Wt.:** 205. **Drafted:** HS—Montgomery, Texas, 2004 (5th round). **Signed by:** Paul Provas/Keith Staab.

A raw baseball talent, Allen bypassed a shot at Division I-A football scholarships as a linebacker to take a $175,000 bonus as a 2004 fifth-round pick. The bonus might have been a lot higher had he had a strong high school senior season, but he had too many strikeouts and too few home runs (two) to fulfill expectations that he could be a first- or second-rounder. The White Sox took him on projections that he could develop into a Ryan Howard-type offensive presence, and they were happy to see he showed immediate improvement as a full-time baseball player. Allen has plenty of brute strength and he'll become even more of a power threat if he can make more consistent contact. Offspeed stuff gave him trouble early in 2005 before he made adjustments, and he needs to figure out a way to be more effective against low pitches. Allen is a good athlete and runner for his size, and should become at least an average defender at first base. Chicago is toying with the idea of trying him in the outfield. But ultimately it's his hitting that will dictate how quickly he moves, and his ceiling is considerable. He's ready for low Class A.

Year	Club (League)	Class	AVG	G	AB	R	H	2B	3B	HR	RBI	BB	SO	SB	OBP	SLG
2004	Bristol (Appy)	R	.205	58	185	17	38	9	1	3	23	16	60	2	.280	.314
2005	Great Falls (Pio)	R	.264	66	231	41	61	11	2	11	42	32	69	7	.366	.472
MINOR LEAGUE TOTALS			.238	124	416	58	99	20	3	14	65	48	129	9	.329	.401

14 CHARLES HAEGER
RHP

Born: Sept. 19, 1983. **B-T:** R-R. **Ht.:** 6-1. **Wt.:** 202. **Drafted:** HS—Plymouth, Mich., 2001 (25th round). **Signed by:** Ken Stauffer/Nathan Durst.

Going nowhere with a high-80s fastball, Haeger became so discouraged with his lack of development that he left the organization in 2003, playing golf for Madonna University in his native Livonia, Mich., where his brother Greg is the baseball coach. But Haeger didn't give up on baseball completely. He worked on a knuckleball that had been suggested by minor league pitching coach Chris Sinacori and decided to give pitching another shot. Haeger rejoined the White Sox as a knuckleball specialist in 2004 and broke through with 14 wins last year. He can make in-game adjustments when the knuckler isn't dancing as well as he would like. He uses a cut fastball to keep hitters off balance. As with most knuckleballers, his control can get dicey, but he holds runners surprisingly well. Fifteen of 24 basestealers were caught on Haeger's watch in 2005. He's mature for his age. The White Sox thought enough of Haeger to protect him on their 40-man roster this winter. His next stop is Triple-A.

Year	Club (League)	Class	W	L	ERA	G	GS	CG	SV	IP	H	R	ER	HR	BB	SO	AVG
2001	White Sox (AZL)	R	0	3	6.39	13	4	0	0	31	44	29	22	2	17	17	.336
2002	White Sox (AZL)	R	1	4	4.17	25	0	0	6	41	46	25	19	2	13	24	.295
2003	Did not play																
2004	Bristol (Appy)	R	1	6	5.18	10	10	0	0	57	70	41	33	6	22	23	.303
	Kannapolis (SAL)	A	1	3	2.01	5	5	0	0	31	31	17	7	0	12	21	.270
2005	Winston-Salem (Car)	A	8	2	3.19	14	13	0	0	82	82	33	29	3	40	64	.267
	Birmingham (SL)	AA	6	3	3.78	13	13	3	0	86	84	43	36	1	45	48	.263
MINOR LEAGUE TOTALS			17	21	4.01	80	45	3	6	328	357	188	146	14	149	197	.284

15 CHRIS GETZ 2B/SS

Born: Aug. 30, 1983. **B-T:** L-R. **Ht.:** 6-0. **Wt.:** 175. **Drafted:** Michigan, 2005 (4th round). **Signed by:** Mike Shirley.

The White Sox coveted Getz for years, drafting him in the sixth round out of high school in 2002 only to watch him head to Wake Forest. He transferred to Michigan after his freshman season, and established himself as one of the best hitters for average in the 2005 draft. Chicago finally nabbed him last June, signing him for $225,000 as a fourth-rounder. He has a short, quick swing with uncanny hand-eye coordination and tremendous plate discipline. He struck out only 47 times in his three seasons in college and walked three times as much as he whiffed in his pro debut. Getz doesn't project to ever develop power with his approach, but his on-base skills and plus speed still will make him an offensive contributor. At second base, he's a plus defender with arm strength, range and soft hands. While he figures to stay at second, the Sox think he throws well enough to fill in at shortstop or third base if needed as a utility player. Getz will hit his way to the big leagues, likely starting in high Class A for his first full season.

Year	Club (League)	Class	AVG	G	AB	R	H	2B	3B	HR	RBI	BB	SO	SB	OBP	SLG
2005	Great Falls (Pio)	R	.333	6	24	3	8	1	0	0	4	1	2	2	.346	.375
	Kannapolis (SAL)	A	.304	55	214	38	65	13	2	1	28	35	10	11	.407	.397
MINOR LEAGUE TOTALS			.307	61	238	41	73	14	2	1	32	36	12	13	.401	.395

16 JEFF BAJENARU RHP

Born: March 21, 1978. **B-T:** R-R. **Ht.:** 6-1. **Wt.:** 190. **Signed:** NDFA/Oklahoma, 2000. **Signed by:** John Kazanas.

Bajenaru has paid his dues and is pounding on the door for a chance in the Chicago bullpen after making sporadic big league appearances the last two years. The White Sox drafted him in the 36th round in 1999, and they retained his rights because he was a fifth-year senior in 2000. They failed to sign him before the draft, but came to terms with him as a nondrafted free agent. A former two-way star at Oklahoma, he achieved immediate results when he became a full-time pitcher, but blew out his elbow and missed the entire 2002 season after Tommy John surgery. Bajenaru relies on a low-90s fastball with sinking action and a quality splitter. He ranked second among Triple-A International League relievers with a .185 opponent average and third with a .548 opponent OPS last year. After nibbling too much during his brief callup in 2004, he made it a point to throw strikes during last September's cameo—and paid for it by serving up two homers. He has value to the White Sox but could be most useful as trade bait.

Year	Club (League)	Class	W	L	ERA	G	GS	CG	SV	IP	H	R	ER	HR	BB	SO	AVG
2000	Bristol (Appy)	R	1	1	3.78	12	0	0	5	14	10	6	6	2	5	31	.179
	Winston-Salem (Car)	A	2	0	4.39	10	0	0	2	12	7	6	6	1	5	15	.167
2001	Birmingham (SL)	AA	0	0	0.00	2	0	0	0	4	4	0	0	0	3	5	.222
	Winston-Salem (Car)	A	2	4	3.35	35	0	0	10	40	32	16	15	3	21	51	.216
2002	Did not play—Injured																
2003	Birmingham (SL)	AA	4	2	3.20	50	0	0	14	65	53	29	23	2	28	62	.225
2004	Birmingham (SL)	AA	2	0	1.34	32	0	0	12	34	19	9	5	3	11	51	.157
	Charlotte (IL)	AAA	1	2	1.80	16	0	0	10	20	12	6	4	2	3	16	.167
	Chicago (AL)	MLB	0	1	10.84	9	0	0	0	8	15	10	10	0	6	8	.405
2005	Charlotte (IL)	AAA	4	6	1.41	61	0	0	19	70	45	14	11	4	29	83	.185
	Chicago (AL)	MLB	0	0	6.28	4	0	0	0	4	4	3	3	2	0	3	.222
MAJOR LEAGUE TOTALS			0	1	9.24	13	0	0	0	13	19	13	13	2	6	11	.345
MINOR LEAGUE TOTALS			16	15	2.42	218	0	0	72	260	182	86	70	17	105	314	.194

17 AARON CUNNINGHAM OF

Born: April 24, 1986. **B-T:** R-R. **Ht.:** 5-11. **Wt.:** 195. **Drafted:** Everett (Wash.) CC, 2005 (6th round). **Signed by:** Adam Virchis.

Cunningham went undrafted out of high school and didn't start to gain scouts' attention until the fall of 2004 at Everett (Wash.) Community College. He still was a relative unknown heading into the spring, when he proceeded to destroy the Northwest Athletic Association of Community Colleges. He almost won the conference triple crown, finishing with a .465 average and 10 home runs in the wood-bat league. Scouts flocked to see Everett pitchers Zach Simons (Colorado, second round) and J.T. Zink (Boston, eighth round) and Cunningham took advantage of his opportunity to shine. He swatted two long home runs with the Major League Scouting Bureau's film crew in attendance and his stock soared. Cunningham continued to hit after signing quickly for $140,000 as a sixth-round pick. He was an Appalachian League all-star and earned a late promotion to low

Class A, where he finally ran out of gas. He has a knack for hitting the ball hard in all directions with strong, quick hands that generate outstanding bat speed. Undersized coming out of high school, he has added muscle without losing his plus speed. His raw arm strength is above-average, though he needs to work on shortening his release and improving his accuracy. He played second base in high school, where his arm and speed were wasted, and his instincts in the outfield need work. He should go back to low Class A for his first full season as a pro.

Year	Club (League)	Class	AVG	G	AB	R	H	2B	3B	HR	RBI	BB	SO	SB	OBP	SLG
2005	Bristol (Appy)	R	.315	56	222	41	70	10	2	5	25	16	45	6	.392	.446
	Kannapolis (SAL)	A	.115	10	26	7	3	0	0	0	2	3	7	1	.207	.115
MINOR LEAGUE TOTALS			.294	66	248	48	73	10	2	5	27	19	52	7	.373	.411

18 TYLER LUMSDEN   LHP

Born: May 9, 1983. **B-T:** R-L. **Ht.:** 6-4. **Wt.:** 205. **Drafted:** Clemson, 2004 (1st round supplemental). **Signed by:** Nick Hostetler.

The first of four lefthanders the White Sox took in the 2004 draft—ahead of Gio Gonzalez (since traded), Wes Whisler and Ray Liotta—Lumsden signed for $975,000 as a supplemental first-round pick. Scouts see some Andy Pettitte in him, but they didn't see Lumsden at all in 2005. He had pitched with pain in his elbow for a year, and missed the entire 2005 season after arthroscopic surgery to remove a bone spur in January. He generally worked with a 90-92 mph fastball at Clemson, but it jumped into the mid-90s when Chicago sent him straight to high Class A for his debut. Before he got hurt, he had a power curveball that was almost unhittable when he located it in the strike zone. He also had a tough cut fastball and a promising changeup. A good athlete who played basketball in high school and can throw 80 mph righthanded, Lumsden will be handled carefully when he returns. He'll be 100 percent for spring training.

Year	Club (League)	Class	W	L	ERA	G	GS	CG	SV	IP	H	R	ER	HR	BB	SO	AVG
2004	Winston-Salem (Car)	A	3	1	4.12	15	3	0	0	39	45	25	18	2	20	31	.280
2005	Did not play—Injured																
MINOR LEAGUE TOTALS			3	1	4.12	15	3	0	0	39	45	25	18	2	20	31	.280

19 CHRIS STEWART   C

Born: Feb. 19, 1982. **B-T:** R-R. **Ht.:** 6-5. **Wt.:** 205. **Drafted:** Riverside (Calif.) CC, 2001 (12th round). **Signed by:** Joe Butler/Mark Salas.

The White Sox have respected Stewart's gamecalling and receiving skills for years. In 2005, they trusted him to play a role in the development of a varied cast of prospects from the powerful Bobby Jenks to knuckleballer Charles Haeger. With his strong arm, Stewart led Southern League catchers by throwing out 52 percent of basestealers. While repeating Double-A, he also had a breakout season at the plate, hitting 11 homers after totaling four in his first three seasons. His .286 average was a career high and 55 points higher than his previous average. He's a below-average runner but not bad for a catcher. His performance earned him a spot on the 40-man roster and a starting job in the Dominican League. While Stewart will have to prove he can hit again this year in Triple-A, Chicago's backup catching job could be awaiting him in 2007.

Year	Club (League)	Class	AVG	G	AB	R	H	2B	3B	HR	RBI	BB	SO	SB	OBP	SLG
2002	Bristol (Appy)	R	.278	42	158	25	44	9	0	1	12	14	23	0	.350	.354
2003	Winston-Salem (Car)	A	.207	76	217	18	45	8	2	2	27	27	29	1	.294	.290
2004	Charlotte (IL)	AAA	.071	5	14	1	1	1	0	0	1	1	3	0	.188	.143
	Birmingham (SL)	AA	.231	83	260	26	60	11	2	1	17	22	59	2	.299	.300
2005	Birmingham (SL)	AA	.286	95	311	39	89	21	0	11	51	24	37	3	.341	.460
MINOR LEAGUE TOTALS			.249	301	960	109	239	50	4	15	108	88	151	6	.318	.356

20 PEDRO LOPEZ   SS/2B

Born: April 28, 1984. **B-T:** R-R. **Ht.:** 6-1. **Wt.:** 160. **Signed:** Dominican Republic, 2000. **Signed by:** Denny Gonzalez.

Lopez caught manager Ozzie Guillen's eye in spring training last year, which earned him a brief promotion to the big leagues in May, but otherwise was unproductive in 2005. Trying to jump to Triple-A after just seven games above Class A proved to be too much. A .291 career hitter entering the season, Lopez batted .202 in 55 games with Charlotte and never quite got himself back together when he was demoted to Double-A. Bat control is Lopez' strength, but he was overmatched and started chasing too many pitches. He has a contact approach with no power to speak of. Even while struggling at the plate, Lopez did contribute with his slick fielding. He's a skilled defender with good range and an adequate arm. He was passed by Robert Valido in the organization's pecking order at shortstop and needs a strong 2006 season to re-establish himself. Another trip to Double-A is in the cards.

Year	Club (League)	Class	AVG	G	AB	R	H	2B	3B	HR	RBI	BB	SO	SB	OBP	SLG
2001	White Sox (AZL)	R	.312	50	199	26	62	11	3	1	19	16	24	12	.359	.412
2002	Bristol (Appy)	R	.319	63	260	42	83	11	0	0	35	20	27	22	.370	.362
2003	Kannapolis (SAL)	A	.264	109	390	40	103	23	0	0	33	26	43	24	.314	.323
	Winston-Salem (Car)	A	.231	4	13	1	3	0	0	0	0	1	0	0	.286	.231
2004	Winston-Salem (Car)	A	.288	111	430	62	124	13	0	4	35	23	35	12	.328	.347
	Birmingham (SL)	AA	.217	7	23	3	5	0	1	0	0	5	2	2	.379	.304
2005	Chicago (AL)	MLB	.286	2	7	1	2	0	0	0	2	0	1	0	.286	.286
	Charlotte (IL)	AAA	.202	55	188	14	38	6	0	3	17	7	24	1	.236	.282
	Birmingham (SL)	AA	.238	68	239	26	57	7	1	3	24	13	29	0	.287	.314
MAJOR LEAGUE TOTALS			.286	2	7	1	2	0	0	0	2	0	1	0	.286	.286
MINOR LEAGUE TOTALS			.273	467	1742	214	475	71	5	11	163	111	184	73	.320	.338

21 TOM COLLARO OF

Born: April 4, 1983. **B-T:** R-R. **Ht.:** 6-4. **Wt.:** 210. **Drafted:** Palm Beach (Fla.) CC, D/F 2001 (27th round). **Signed by:** Ken Stauffer/Jose Ortega.

Power is Collaro's drawing card. He hits monster home runs and is developing into a better hitter, though he still has holes in both his swing and his approach. After three years in Rookie ball, he probably belonged in low Class A last season. The White Sox' aggressive philosophy challenged him with a jump to high Class A, and outside of leading the Carolina League in strikeouts, he held his own. He tied Winston-Salem teammate Leo Daigle for the home run crown and finished second behind Daigle in the RBI race. Collaro's long-term success depends on his bat, specifically his ability to make enough consistent contact. He doesn't run well or cover much ground in left field, though he has an average arm. His best position might be first base, though Chicago is set there for the next few years with Paul Konerko. Collaro figures to move up to Double-A in 2006.

Year	Club (League)	Class	AVG	G	AB	R	H	2B	3B	HR	RBI	BB	SO	SB	OBP	SLG
2002	White Sox (AZL)	R	.213	39	127	22	27	4	3	7	29	14	45	3	.292	.457
2003	Bristol (Appy)	R	.226	45	146	17	33	9	1	8	28	4	46	1	.252	.466
2004	Great Falls (Pio)	R	.287	66	268	48	77	7	6	18	66	13	82	4	.331	.560
2005	Winston-Salem (Car)	A	.264	133	531	68	140	27	3	29	100	25	153	5	.299	.490
MINOR LEAGUE TOTALS			.258	283	1072	155	277	47	13	62	223	56	326	13	.300	.500

22 CHRIS CARTER 3B/1B

Born: Dec. 18, 1986. **B-T:** R-R. **Ht.:** 6-4. **Wt.:** 210. **Drafted:** HS—Las Vegas, 2005 (15th round). **Signed by:** George Kachigian.

Like Micah Schnurstein, another White Sox third-base prospect from Las Vegas, Carter shot onto the radar in his pro debut. Considered a project when he signed as a 15th-round pick last June, he had little problem against older pitchers in the Appalachian League. He generates impressive power with his strong 6-foot-4, 210-pound frame and finished fourth in the Appy home run chase. He'll need to tighten his strike zone at higher levels, however. Carter also has to find a position. He's a decent athlete and moves well for his size, but he struggled at third base, committing 13 errors in 38 games. He also saw time at first base, which might be a better fit but also would reduce his value. If he has a good spring, he could start the season in low Class A.

Year	Club (League)	Class	AVG	G	AB	R	H	2B	3B	HR	RBI	BB	SO	SB	OBP	SLG
2005	Bristol (Appy)	R	.283	65	233	33	66	17	0	10	37	17	64	2	.350	.485
MINOR LEAGUE TOTALS			.283	65	233	33	66	17	0	10	37	17	64	2	.350	.485

23 DANIEL CORTES RHP

Born: March 4, 1987. **B-T:** R-R. **Ht.:** 6-5. **Wt.:** 205. **Drafted:** HS—Pomona, Calif., 2005 (7th round). **Signed by:** Dan Ontiveros.

San Diego State baseball coach Tony Gwynn thought he had found a sleeper recruit in Cortes. But after signing his letter of intent, Cortes grew three inches to 6-foot-5 and saw his fastball velocity jump by 5 mph. That got him drafted in the seventh round last June, and he signed for $115,000. Internally, the White Sox compare him to Jon Garland. Like Garland, Cortes has a long, lanky pitcher's body and has polished a curveball to go with his fastball, which parks at 88-91 mph and peaks at 94. Chicago believes his velocity will increase as he continues to develop physically, which could make him a real steal. A good student, he's extremely coachable, which will help him in his attempt to pick up a change-up. He has the maturity to handle a jump to low Class A at age 19.

Year	Club (League)	Class	W	L	ERA	G	GS	CG	SV	IP	H	R	ER	HR	BB	SO	AVG
2005	Bristol (Appy)	R	1	4	5.17	15	7	0	0	38	44	23	22	2	13	38	.289
MINOR LEAGUE TOTALS			1	4	5.17	15	7	0	0	38	44	23	22	2	13	38	.289

24 CARLOS TORRES
RHP

Born: Oct. 22, 1982. **B-T:** R-R. **Ht.:** 6-1. **Wt.:** 185. **Drafted:** Kansas State, 2004 (15th round). **Signed by:** Keith Staab/Paul Provas.

An unheralded 15th-round pick in the 2004 draft, Torres used a strong senior season at Kansas State to catch the White Sox' attention. He pitched at four colleges in four years, moving from Allan Hancock (Calif.) Junior College to Grossmont (Calif.) Junior College to San Jose State before joining the Wildcats. He has benefited from the stability provided in the Sox system, where the pitching coaches work well together. Torres began 2005 in extended spring training and ended the season with nine strong starts in low Class A, including a win in the South Atlantic League playoffs. He finished up with a strong showing in instructional league, where he went back to a full windup after working exclusively out of the stretch during the season. Torres has a live arm that delivers 92-93 mph fastballs. He also has a solid slider and an improving changeup. Very disciplined and possessing a strong work ethic, he'll move up to high Class A in 2006.

Year	Club (League)	Class	W	L	ERA	G	GS	CG	SV	IP	H	R	ER	HR	BB	SO	AVG
2004	Bristol (Appy)	R	2	2	4.74	19	0	0	1	38	43	30	20	2	12	28	.281
2005	Great Falls (Pio)	R	1	1	2.88	5	5	0	0	25	18	8	8	1	8	26	.205
	Kannapolis (SAL)	A	1	3	3.53	8	8	0	0	43	28	20	17	4	23	54	.179
MINOR LEAGUE TOTALS			4	6	3.81	32	13	0	1	106	89	58	45	7	43	108	.224

25 CLAYTON RICHARD
LHP

Born: Sept. 12, 1983. **B-T:** L-L. **Ht.:** 6-5. **Wt.:** 225. **Drafted:** Michigan, 2005 (8th round). **Signed by:** Mike Shirley.

The White Sox have an affinity for football players. They drafted Joe Borchard (Stanford quarterback) and Josh Fields (Oklahoma State quarterback) in the first round, and lost another first-rounder, Brian West, when he quit baseball to become a defensive end at Louisiana State. They even took a flier on future NFL wide receiver Freddie Mitchell. Chicago found another quarterback when it took Richard with an eighth-round pick last June and signed him for $78,000. He was a coveted high school baseball prospect, but went undrafted because he had a football commitment to Michigan. Richard redshirted in his first year with the Wolverines football program and threw just 15 passes in his second, so he decided to resurrect his baseball career last spring. He was Michigan's co-closer and his durability could give him upside as a reliever, but the Sox want to see how he develops as a starter. His fastball sat in the high 80s when he started as a pro, and parked in the low 90s and touched 94 when he relieved in college. It has natural sinking action that produces groundballs. His curveball and changeup need improvement, but Chicago saw encouraging progress in instructional league. Though Richard has a strong body and is very athletic, scouts always have fretted over his stiff arm action, which may hinder the development of his secondary pitches. He'll begin his first full pro season in low Class A, where he ended 2005.

Year	Club (League)	Class	W	L	ERA	G	GS	CG	SV	IP	H	R	ER	HR	BB	SO	AVG
2005	Great Falls (Pio)	R	2	1	2.85	10	9	0	0	41	37	19	13	2	12	39	.240
	Kannapolis (SAL)	A	0	1	5.24	3	2	0	0	10	14	7	6	1	1	8	.326
MINOR LEAGUE TOTALS			2	2	3.33	13	11	0	0	51	51	26	19	3	13	47	.259

26 ADAM RUSSELL
RHP

Born: April 14, 1983. **B-T:** R-R. **Ht.:** 6-8. **Wt.:** 250. **Drafted:** Ohio, 2004 (6th round). **Signed by:** Larry Grefer/Nathan Durst.

A 26th-round pick by the Marlins out of high school in 2001, Russell may have wished he turned pro when he had little success at Ohio. In three seasons with the Bobcats, he pitched in just 38 games and posted a 6.28 ERA, but a late surge in his junior season nevertheless got him drafted in the sixth round. His huge frame and easy arm action attracted scouts, and Russell has made a smooth transition into pro ball. He earned a spot in the Kannapolis rotation out of spring training and held it all season, helping the Intimidators win the South Atlantic League title. Russell has a lively sinker that sits at 88-90 mph and touches 92. He doesn't have much in the way of complementary pitches, so the White Sox tried him in late-inning relief during instructional league and were encouraged by the results. He likely would gain more velocity if used in shorter bursts, and a bullpen role suits his aggressive nature. He'll probably pitch in the rotation this year in high Class A, though, so he can get some much-needed innings.

Year	Club (League)	Class	W	L	ERA	G	GS	CG	SV	IP	H	R	ER	HR	BB	SO	AVG
2004	Great Falls (Pio)	R	4	0	2.37	15	4	0	0	38	31	11	10	2	18	33	.228
	Kannapolis (SAL)	A	0	2	9.00	2	2	0	0	10	18	11	10	3	7	3	.409
2005	Kannapolis (SAL)	A	9	7	3.78	24	24	0	0	126	116	61	53	10	55	82	.246
MINOR LEAGUE TOTALS			13	9	3.77	41	30	0	0	174	165	83	73	15	80	118	.253

27 RICARDO NANITA   OF

Born: June 12, 1981. **B-T:** L-L. **Ht.:** 6-0. **Wt.:** 202. **Drafted:** Florida International, 2003 (14th round). **Signed by:** Jose Ortega.

Nanita entered pro ball with a Pioneer League-record 30-game hitting streak in 2003, but he broke the hamate bone in his right wrist at the end of the year and took a while to recapture his stroke. After struggling in high Class A in 2004, he thrived there last season, hitting for average and controlling the strike zone. He has gap power and encouraged the White Sox with the progress he made in driving the ball. He can bunt, too. The other parts of the game don't come as easily to Nanita as hitting does. He has good speed but hasn't learned to read pitchers and isn't much of a basestealing threat. He's an adequate outfielder with an average arm. Ticketed for Double-A, Nanita profiles as a fourth outfielder. He fits best defensively in left field but doesn't have the power associated with the position.

Year	Club (League)	Class	AVG	G	AB	R	H	2B	3B	HR	RBI	BB	SO	SB	OBP	SLG
2003	Great Falls (Pio)	R	.384	47	185	38	71	7	4	5	37	17	28	11	.445	.546
2004	Winston-Salem (Car)	A	.241	55	187	21	45	8	1	2	28	23	46	7	.327	.326
	Kannapolis (SAL)	A	.316	61	225	32	71	12	2	1	31	26	32	5	.391	.400
2005	Winston-Salem (Car)	A	.292	120	415	73	121	36	2	9	54	61	53	14	.392	.453
MINOR LEAGUE TOTALS			.304	283	1012	164	308	63	9	17	150	127	159	37	.389	.435

28 ARNIE MUNOZ   LHP

Born: June 21, 1982. **B-T:** L-L. **Ht.:** 5-9. **Wt.:** 170. **Signed:** Dominican Republic, 1998. **Signed by:** Denny Gonzalez.

No longer the choirboy sensation with the mother of all curveballs, the little Dominican lefthander has reached the point of now or never with the White Sox. Had he remained on the career path he was on before 2004, he could have been Chicago's No. 5 starter last year, or possibly filled the lefty-reliever role Neal Cotts handled so well. But Munoz never has seemed to recover from the shock of being pummeled by the Expos in his big league debut in June 2004. He earned the promotion after dominating in Double-A but hasn't shown the same ability since. His curve, once a lights-out weapon, has become inconsistent. His control and command haven't been as good either. Munoz also throws an average 90-mph fastball, plus a slider and a changeup. Unless he has a huge spring, he's a candidate to be traded or placed on waivers.

Year	Club (League)	Class	W	L	ERA	G	GS	CG	SV	IP	H	R	ER	HR	BB	SO	AVG
1999	White Sox (AZL)	R	0	2	5.25	14	0	0	1	12	13	10	7	1	8	12	.255
2000	Burlington (MWL)	A	2	3	6.81	22	0	0	0	38	45	34	29	2	25	44	.294
2001	Kannapolis (SAL)	A	6	3	2.48	60	0	0	12	80	41	24	22	2	42	115	.161
2002	Birmingham (SL)	AA	6	0	2.61	51	0	0	6	72	62	29	21	6	29	78	.231
2003	Charlotte (IL)	AAA	4	3	4.75	49	0	0	6	55	52	35	29	7	27	63	.254
2004	Birmingham (SL)	AA	7	2	2.05	13	13	0	0	75	52	24	17	1	22	68	.198
	Charlotte (IL)	AAA	2	6	5.68	13	13	0	0	70	81	48	44	11	29	60	.289
	Chicago (AL)	MLB	0	1	10.07	11	1	0	0	14	20	16	16	4	12	11	.339
2005	Charlotte (IL)	AAA	8	14	4.27	40	18	0	1	133	150	79	63	16	60	109	.287
MAJOR LEAGUE TOTALS			0	1	10.07	11	1	0	0	14	20	16	16	4	12	11	.339
MINOR LEAGUE TOTALS			35	33	3.91	262	44	0	26	534	496	283	232	46	242	549	.248

29 GUSTAVO MOLINA   C

Born: Feb. 24, 1982. **B-T:** R-R. **Ht.:** 6-2. **Wt.:** 210. **Signed:** Venezuela, 2000. **Signed by:** Roberto Espinoza.

Molina's story is similar to Chris Stewart's. For years, he built his reputation with his work behind the plate. That continued in 2005, when managers rated him the top defensive catcher in the Carolina League. He led the CL by throwing out 53 percent of basestealers, showcasing a plus arm and quality receiving skills. Also like Stewart, Molina came alive with the bat last season. A career .235 hitter with 17 homers in five seasons before 2005, he continued to make progress learning the strike zone and started to show some pop. He'll probably never hit for a high average, but at least he can do some damage when pitchers make a mistake. He offers little speed on the bases. Molina will try to make more gains with his bat while providing his usual quality defense in Double-A this year.

Year	Club (League)	Class	AVG	G	AB	R	H	2B	3B	HR	RBI	BB	SO	SB	OBP	SLG
2000	White Sox (AZL)	R	.243	31	115	15	28	10	0	1	22	13	13	3	.323	.357
2001	Bristol (Appy)	R	.283	46	166	18	47	9	0	2	24	9	26	3	.333	.373
2002	Kannapolis (SAL)	A	.226	94	310	37	70	13	1	2	34	27	61	7	.301	.294
2003	Kannapolis (SAL)	A	.229	96	315	30	72	15	1	5	41	17	56	5	.287	.330
2004	Kannapolis (SAL)	A	.162	37	105	16	17	3	0	4	17	12	24	2	.273	.305
	Winston-Salem (Car)	A	.286	25	77	10	22	6	0	3	14	5	16	0	.333	.481
2005	Winston-Salem (Car)	A	.261	109	345	38	90	20	1	11	41	30	47	1	.328	.420
MINOR LEAGUE TOTALS			.241	438	1433	164	346	76	3	28	193	113	243	21	.310	.357

30 KRIS HONEL   RHP

Born: Nov. 7, 1982. **B-T:** R-R. **Ht.:** 6-5. **Wt.:** 180. **Drafted:** HS—New Lenox, Ill., 2001 (1st round). **Signed by:** Ken Stauffer/Nathan Durst.

Honel was the 16th overall pick in 2001, making him the highest-drafted Illinois high school pitcher since Bob Kipper went eighth in 1982. Honel ranked No. 2 on this list after tearing through high Class A as a 20-year-old in 2003, but little has gone right since. He pitched just six innings in 2004 while battling inflammation in his elbow, which started bothering him sporadically shortly after he turned pro. Honel was able to pitch 93 innings last season, but had arthrocopic elbow surgery afterward. The White Sox hope he'll be able to pitch again early in 2006 and at this point they don't know what to expect from him. At his best, Honel had a low-90s fastball and a nasty knuckle-curve. But in the last two years, he has lost velocity and command while his knuckle-curve ceased being an out pitch. He never has had much of a changeup. If Honel can ever regain his health and stuff, he could benefit from what he's learned about pitching and himself while battling adversity.

Year	Club (League)	Class	W	L	ERA	G	GS	CG	SV	IP	H	R	ER	HR	BB	SO	AVG
2001	White Sox (AZL)	R	2	0	1.80	3	1	0	0	10	9	3	2	0	3	8	.257
	Bristol (Appy)	R	2	3	3.13	8	8	0	0	46	41	19	16	4	9	45	.240
2002	Kannapolis (SAL)	A	9	8	2.82	26	26	0	0	153	128	57	48	12	52	152	.228
	Winston-Salem (Car)	A	0	0	1.70	1	1	0	0	5	3	2	1	0	3	8	.150
2003	Birmingham (SL)	AA	1	0	3.75	2	2	0	0	12	9	6	5	2	6	13	.205
	Winston-Salem (Car)	A	9	7	3.11	24	24	3	0	133	122	51	46	7	42	122	.248
2004	Birmingham (SL)	AA	0	1	9.00	3	1	0	0	6	4	6	6	1	5	7	.190
	Bristol (Appy)	R	0	0	120.00	1	1	0	0	0	1	4	4	0	3	0	.500
2005	Birmingham (SL)	AA	5	7	5.88	21	18	0	0	93	101	68	61	10	64	70	.278
MINOR LEAGUE TOTALS			28	26	3.70	89	82	3	0	459	418	216	189	36	187	425	.244

CINCINNATI
REDS

BY **J.J. COOPER**

When Carl Lindner led the charge that bought Marge Schott out of her majority ownership of the Reds, he seemed like a white knight charging in to save the team.

In 1999, Lindner's first year as the team's CEO, Cincinnati went 96-57 and lost a National League wild-card playoff game to the Mets. Before his second year, the Reds landed Ken Griffey Jr. in a trade with the Mariners. With a push for a new stadium getting under way, the club's future seemed bright.

But Griffey got hurt, manager Jack McKeon was let go in a messy squabble after the 96-win season and the Reds quickly found themselves near the NL Central's basement, dreaming of a .500 season. Cincinnati has endured its worst stretch in 50 years, putting up losing records for five straight seasons.

If there's any hope for the franchise now, it's the thought that a new ownership group, led by local businessman Robert Castellini (a minority investor in the Cardinals), will provide the financial backing and the direction to get the Reds back on track. By the time the sale was announced in November, Lindner was a lightning rod for fan dissatisfaction.

There's plenty of work to be done. The Reds got a short-term attendance jump and some increased revenues out of the move to the Great American Ball Park in 2003. But their payroll remains in the bottom half of the NL, and a $19 million spending spree before the 2005 season proved foolish. Cincinnati lavished nearly $35 million in contracts on Eric Milton, Ramon Ortiz and

LARRY GOREN

Paul Wilson, who went a combined 18-31, 6.15. Milton's 6.47 ERA nearly set a record for worst ever by an NL starter.

The blame for the misguided pitching binge can be pointed squarely at the Reds' inability to develop starting pitching in recent years. The farm system has delivered enough position players (such as Adam Dunn, **Edwin Encarnacion** and Wily Mo Pena) to form the building blocks of a contender. But being a Cincinnati pitching prospect has been hazardous. Ricardo Aramboles, Bobby Basham, Phil Dumatrait, Richie Gardner, Chris Gruler, Josh Hall, Ty Howington, Luke Hudson and Thomas Pauly all have had their careers delayed or derailed by arm problems.

In an attempt to stanch the bleeding, general manager Dan O'Brien instituted a tandem-starter system with strict 75-pitch limits for the lower levels of the system. That didn't stop Gardner or Pauly from going down in 2005, but the Reds believe they're cutting down on the number of injuries.

The added caution, plus Cincinnati's emphasis on arms in recent drafts, could be a key to turning the team around. But while Homer Bailey, Travis Wood and Rafael Gonzalez give the team hope for the future, they're at least a few years away. The Reds will have to plug holes from outside the system, as few prospects in the higher levels are ready to contribute.

TOP 30 PROSPECTS

1. Homer Bailey, rhp
2. Jay Bruce, of
3. Travis Wood, lhp
4. B.J. Szymanski, of
5. Chris Denorfia, of
6. Rafael Gonzalez, rhp
7. Miguel Perez, c
8. Tyler Pelland, lhp
9. Joey Votto, 1b
10. Travis Chick, rhp
11. William Bergolla, 2b/ss
12. Philip Dumatrait, lhp
13. Zach Ward, rhp
14. Paul Janish, ss
15. Adam Rosales, ss
16. Richie Gardner, rhp
17. Thomas Pauly, rhp
18. Brandon Roberts, of
19. Chris Dickerson, of
20. Philippe Valiquette, lhp
21. Justin Germano, rhp
22. James Avery, rhp
23. Sam LeCure, rhp
24. Bobby Basham, rhp
25. Javon Moran, of
26. David Shafer, rhp
27. Mike Burns, rhp
28. Calvin Medlock, rhp
29. Tonys Gutierrez, 1b
30. Elizardo Ramirez, rhp

ORGANIZATION OVERVIEW

General manager: Dan O'Brien. **Farm director:** Tim Naehring. **Scouting director:** Terry Reynolds.

2005 PERFORMANCE

Class	Team	League	W	L	Pct.	Finish*	Manager(s)
Majors	Cincinnati	National	73	89	.451	13th (16)	D. Miley/J. Narron
Triple-A	Louisville RiverBats	International	66	78	.458	11th (14)	Rick Sweet
Double-A	Chattanooga Lookouts	Southern	53	83	.390	10th (10)	Jayhawk Owens
High A	Sarasota Reds	Florida State	65	67	.492	8th (12)	Edgar Caceres
Low A	Dayton Dragons	Midwest	60	79	.432	14th (14)	Alonzo Powell
Rookie	Billings Mustangs	Pioneer	43	33	.566	2nd (8)	Rick Burleson
Rookie	GCL Reds	Gulf Coast	22	32	.407	11th (12)	Luis Aguayo
OVERALL 2005 MINOR LEAGUE RECORD			309	372	.454	28th (30)	

*Finish in overall standings (No. of teams in league).

ORGANIZATION LEADERS

BATTING   *Minimum 250 at-bats

*AVG	Rosales, Adam, Billings/Dayton	.325
R	Denorfia, Chris, Chattanooga/Louisville	90
H	Denorfia, Chris, Chattanooga/Louisville	162
TB	Denorfia, Chris, Chattanooga/Louisville	269
2B	Smitherman, Stephen, Chattanooga/Louisville	39
3B	Anderson, Drew, Dayton/Louisville	10
HR	Piepkorn, Jeremiah, Dayton/Sarasota	25
RBI	Piepkorn, Jeremiah, Dayton/Sarasota	90
BB	Jimenez, D'Angelo, Chattanooga	69
SO	Schramek, Mark, Sarasota	143
SB	Roberts, Brandon, Billings	32
*OBP	Hanigan, Ryan, Chattanooga	.418
*SLG	Rosales, Adam, Billings/Dayton	.558

PITCHING   #Minimum 75 innings

W	Basham, Bobby, Chattanooga/Sarasota	10
	Lohse, Erik, Sarasota	10
L	Dumatrait, Phil, Chattanooga/Sarasota	12
#ERA	Edens, Kyle, Sarasota	2.10
G	Booker, Chris, Louisville	59
CG	Five tied at	1
SV	Booker, Chris, Louisville	20
IP	Kozlowski, Ben, Chattanooga/Louisville	156
BB	Dumatrait, Phil, Chattanooga/Sarasota	73
SO	Bailey, Homer, Dayton	125

BEST TOOLS

Best Hitter for Average	Jay Bruce
Best Power Hitter	Jay Bruce
Best Strike-Zone Discipline	Chris Denorfia
Fastest Baserunner	Brandon Roberts
Best Athlete	Chris Dickerson
Best Fastball	Homer Bailey
Best Curveball	Homer Bailey
Best Slider	Zach Ward
Best Changeup	Travis Wood
Best Control	Bobby Basham
Best Defensive Catcher	Miguel Perez
Best Defensive Infielder	Paul Janish
Best Infield Arm	Adam Rosales
Best Defensive Outfielder	Chris Dickerson
Best Outfield Arm	Jay Bruce

PROJECTED 2009 LINEUP

Catcher	Jason LaRue
First Base	Adam Dunn
Second Base	Ryan Freel
Third Base	Edwin Encarnacion
Shortstop	Felipe Lopez
Left Field	Austin Kearns
Center Field	Wily Mo Pena
Right Field	Jay Bruce

No. 1 Starter	Homer Bailey
No. 2 Starter	Travis Wood
No. 3 Starter	Aaron Harang
No. 4 Starter	Brandon Claussen
No. 5 Starter	Rafael Gonzalez
Closer	Ryan Wagner

LAST YEAR'S TOP 20 PROSPECTS

1. Homer Bailey, rhp
2. Edwin Encarnacion, 3b
3. Richie Gardner, rhp
4. Joey Votto, 1b
5. B.J. Szymanski, of
6. Thomas Pauly, rhp
7. Todd Coffey, rhp
8. William Bergolla, 2b
9. Tyler Pelland, lhp
10. Paul Janish, ss
11. Elizardo Ramirez, rhp
12. Chris Dickerson, of/3b
13. David Shafer, rhp
14. Kevin Howard, 2b
15. Ben Kozlowski, lhp
16. Miguel Perez, c
17. Javon Moran, of
18. Steve Kelly, rhp
19. Dane Sardinha, c
20. Rafael Gonzalez, rhp

TOP PROSPECTS OF THE DECADE

Year	Player, Pos.	2005 Org.
1996	Pokey Reese, ss	Mariners
1997	Aaron Boone, 3b	Indians
1998	Damian Jackson, ss/2b	Padres
1999	Rob Bell, rhp	Devil Rays
2000	Gookie Dawkins, ss	Tigers
2001	Austin Kearns, of	Reds
2002	Austin Kearns, of	Reds
2003	Chris Gruler, rhp	Reds
2004	Ryan Wagner, rhp	Reds
2005	Homer Bailey, rhp	Reds

TOP DRAFT PICKS OF THE DECADE

Year	Player, Pos.	2005 Org.
1996	John Oliver, of	Out of baseball
1997	Brandon Larson, 3b	Rangers
1998	Austin Kearns, of	Reds
1999	Ty Howington, lhp	Reds
2000	David Espinosa, ss	Tigers
2001	*Jeremy Sowers, lhp	Indians
2002	Chris Gruler, rhp	Reds
2003	Ryan Wagner, rhp	Reds
2004	Homer Bailey, rhp	Reds
2005	Jay Bruce, of	Reds

*Did not sign.

ALL-TIME LARGEST BONUSES

Chris Gruler, 2002	$2,500,000
Homer Bailey, 2004	$2,300,000
Austin Kearns, 1998	$1,950,000
Jay Bruce, 2005	$1,800,000
Ty Howington, 1999	$1,750,000

MINOR LEAGUE DEPTH CHART

Cincinnati Reds

Rank: **29**

STRENGTH: Outfield. Unfortunately, that's also the team's strength in Cincinnati.

WEAKNESS: Infield. None of the Reds' infielders projects as an above-average regular.

*Depth charts prepared by **John Manuel** and **Chris Kline**. Numbers in parentheses indicate prospect rankings.*

LF
Jeremiah Piepkorn

CF
B.J. Szymanski (4)
Chris Denorfia (5)
Brandon Roberts (18)
Chris Dickerson (19)
Javon Moran (25)

RF
Jay Bruce (2)
Cody Strait
Kenny Kelly

3B
Michael Jones
Brad Key
Ronny Delgado
Habelito Hernandez

SS
Paul Janish (14)
Adam Rosales (15)

2B
William Bergolla (11)
Drew Anderson
Mayker Sandoval

1B
Joey Votto (9)
Tonys Gutierrez (29)

C
Miguel Perez (7)
Dane Sardinha
Craig Tatum
Justin Tordi
John Purdom
Javier Rumbos

RHP

Starters	Relievers
Homer Bailey (1)	Thomas Pauly (17)
Rafael Gonzalez (6)	David Shafer (26)
Travis Chick (10)	Mike Burns (27)
Zach Ward (13)	Carlos Guevara
Richie Gardner (16)	Abe Woody
Justin Germano (21)	Allan Simpson
James Avery (22)	Bubba Nelson
Sam LeCure (23)	Terrell Young
Bobby Basham (24)	Bo Lanier
Calvin Medlock (28)	Jose Rojas
Elizardo Ramirez (30)	
Steve Kelly	
Jeff Stevens	
Chris Gruler	

LHP

Starters	Relievers
Travis Wood (3)	Omar Segovia
Tyler Pelland (8)	
Phil Dumatrait (12)	
Philippe Valiquette (20)	

DRAFT ANALYSIS
2005

Best Pro Debut: LHP Travis Wood (2) went a combined 2-0, 1.29 with 67 strikeouts in 49 innings. SS Adam Rosales (12) batted .325-14-46, including .328 with nine homers in 32 games at low Class A. Some scouts questioned how he'd hit with wood bats, but area scout Rick Sellers believed in him. OF Jay Bruce (1) ranked as the No. 1 prospect in the Rookie-level Pioneer League and hit .266-9-38 for two Rookie clubs. OF Brandon Roberts (7) was an all-star in the same league, batting .318-4-36 with 32 steals.

Best Athlete: Bruce has plus tools across the board and probably will settle into right field. Area scout Steve Kring unearthed another interesting athlete in SS Michael Jones (8), who's much more raw.

Best Pure Hitter: Bruce, who has been compared to Larry Walker and Jeremy Hermida.

Best Raw Power: Bruce's power is his best tool. When 3B Angel Colon (35) catches up to a pitch, he can drive it a long way.

Fastest Runner: Roberts goes from the left side of the plate to first base in 4.0 seconds. Bruce might beat him in a 60-yard dash, and his speed plays better than his stopwatch time on the bases and in the outfield because of his instincts.

Best Defensive Player: Bruce or Rosales, who has well above-average arm strength. Michael Griffin (14) and Michael DeJesus (15) are good defenders at second base.

Best Fastball: Both Wood and RHP Bo Lanier (10) reached 95 mph during the spring. Wood is lefthanded and has better command of his heater, which sat at 88-91 mph for much of the spring before taking off. RHPs Zach Ward (3), Sam LeCure (4),

LeCure

James Avery (5) and Carlos Fisher (11) all can get into the 93-94 mph range.

Best Breaking Ball: Ward has a good, hard slider. LeCure has a solid slider, while Avery and RHP Jeff Stevens (6) have promising curveballs.

Most Intriguing Background: DeJesus' brother David plays for the Royals. SS/2B Kevyn Feiner's (18) brother Korey catches in the Twins system. Unsigned OF Jake Christensen (50) is a backup quarterback at the University of Iowa. His father Jeff is a former NFL quarterback.

Closest To The Majors: LeCure and Avery. LeCure didn't pitch for College World Series champion Texas during the spring because he was academically ineligible, but he had little difficulty finding his good stuff.

Best Late-Round Pick: Rosales and RHP Abe Woody (31), who has nice life on a fastball that has average velocity.

The One Who Got Away: Cincinnati knew Christensen was a longshot but felt he was worth taking. He's a power-hitting, athletic right fielder with a 6-foot-1, 205-pound frame. The Reds signed every pick in the first 21 rounds, except ninth-round draft-and-follow Milton Loo.

Assessment: Bruce and Wood immediately become two of the better prospects in a thin Reds farm system. After that pair, Cincinnati picked up several hard-throwing righthanders.

2004 RHP Homer Bailey (1) and OF B.J. Szymanski (2) are two of the few bright spots in one of baseball's worst systems, and even they haven't done much. The Reds also have hopes for RHP Rafael Gonzalez (4), SS Paul Janish (5) and LHP Philippe Valiquette (7).   *GRADE:* B

2003 This group looked promising a year ago. But then RHPs Ryan Wagner (1), Thomas Pauly (2) and Richie Gardner (6) all got hurt in 2005, leaving OF Chris Dickerson (16) as the best healthy prospect.   *GRADE:* D

2002 Both first-round picks, RHP Chris Gruler and 3B Mark Schramek, aren't going to make it, with injuries playing a role in Gruler's demise. 1B Joey Votto (2) went backward in 2005, so OF Chris Denorfia (19) might be as good as it gets. Failing to sign OF/LHP Nick Markakis (23) was a blunder.   *GRADE:* D

2001 The Reds spent their first-rounder on LHP Jeremy Sowers (1) and made no attempt to sign him. RHP Bobby Basham (7) is the best signee, and his stuff has slipped.   *GRADE:* F

Draft analysis prepared by Jim Callis. Numbers in parentheses indicate draft rounds.

HOMER
BAILEY

Born: May 3, 1986.
Ht.: 6-3. **Wt.:** 190.
Bats: R. **Throws:** R.
Drafted: HS—LaGrange, Texas,
2004 (1st round).
Signed by: Mike Powers.

B ailey has been pitching in pressure games since before he started shaving. He out-dueled Ryan Wagner in the Texas 3-A state championship game as a freshman, and capped his high school career with a second state title as a senior. He ranked No. 1 on this list a year ago after signing for a $2.3 million bonus as the seventh overall pick in 2004, when he was also named BA's High School Player of the Year. The Reds are exercising extreme caution with him, hoping he can avoid the injury bug that has claimed so many of their best pitching prospects in recent years. He pitched just 12 innings after signing in 2004, and was limited by a tandem-starter system with a strict 75-pitch limit in 2005. He worked six innings in a start only once all season and went as many as five innings in just five other outings, yet still managed to claim the title of top pitching prospect in the low Class A Midwest League. He was sidelined for a couple of weeks in April as he worked back from minor knee surgery, a problem that had nagged him since high school. While his first full season was unremarkable statistically, he showed glimpses of his promise in the final month with a pair of scoreless five-inning outings, including an 11-strikeout two-hitter.

Bailey has front-of-the-rotation stuff. He's armed with two plus pitches—a 92-94 mph fastball that touches 96-97 with good life, and a hard 12-to-6 curveball with potential to be a 70 on the 20-80 scouting scale. He pounds the bottom of the strike zone and usually hits his spots. His control will be another plus. Though he did issue more than his share of walks in 2005, the Reds attribute that to their insistence that he work on his secondary pitches. A former basketball player, Bailey is a natural athlete with an effortless arm action and clean delivery that bode well for future projection. He should get stronger, as there's room to pack more weight on his 6-foot-3, 190-pound frame.

Bailey's changeup always will lag behind his two knockout pitches. It's presently a below-average pitch with just a little sink. He did make it a point to throw the changeup more in 2005, and he did a better job of delivering it with the same arm speed he uses with his fastball. Bailey doesn't always stay on top of his curveball. He also needs to improve his consistency and show that he can pitch effectively on nights where he doesn't have his best stuff. Like many dominant high school starters, he didn't have to work on such nuances as holding runners and quickening his move to the plate. He has made steady improvement in both areas, and he has addressed his rhythm and tempo on the mound. Bailey has admitted that baseball is more of a job than a passion. To achieve his potential as an ace, he'll have to stay focused as he moves up the ladder.

While the Reds have yet to turn Bailey loose, they may challenge him with a jump to Double-A Chattanooga in 2006. Though he's not required to be on the 40-man roster until after the 2007 season, he has been invited to big league camp to get a taste of what awaits him. He could be poised for a breakthrough season.

Year	Club (League)	Class	W	L	ERA	G	GS	CG	SV	IP	H	R	ER	HR	BB	SO	AVG
2004	Reds (GCL)	R	0	1	4.38	6	3	0	0	12	14	7	6	0	3	9	.275
2005	Dayton (Mid)	A	8	4	4.43	28	21	0	0	104	89	64	51	5	62	125	.232
MINOR LEAGUE TOTALS			8	5	4.42	34	24	0	0	116	103	71	57	5	65	134	.237

JAY BRUCE   OF

Born: April 3, 1987. **B-T:** L-L. **Ht.:** 6-2. **Wt.:** 206. **Drafted:** HS—Beaumont, Texas, 2005 (1st round). **Signed by:** Brian Wilson.

Bruce went from unknown to prospect during the summer of 2004, and his surge continued last spring as he emerged as the cream of a quality crop of Texas high school outfielders. He went No. 12 to the Reds and signed for $1.8 million. He ranked as the No. 1 prospect in the Rookie-level Pioneer League in his debut. Bruce draws comparisons to Larry Walker and Jeremy Hermida for his sweet stroke, above-average arm and athleticism. He profiles as a power-hitting right fielder, but the Reds intend to keep him in center until he grows out of the position. He can turn on a fastball, but he also has shown the ability to use the entire field with good bat speed. He has plus speed and good overall instincts. Like many young players, Bruce needs to work on the finer aspects of the game, such as reading pitchers and honing his basestealing technique. He occasionally gets antsy at the plate instead of sitting back and waiting on pitches to drive. Bruce will make his full-season debut at low Class A Dayton. A five-tool talent, his bat will dictate how rapidly he advances.

Year	Club (League)	Class	AVG	G	AB	R	H	2B	3B	HR	RBI	BB	SO	SB	OBP	SLG
2005	Reds (GCL)	R	.270	37	122	29	33	9	2	5	25	11	31	4	.331	.500
	Billings (Pio)	R	.257	17	70	16	18	2	0	4	13	11	22	2	.358	.457
MINOR LEAGUE TOTALS			.266	54	192	45	51	11	2	9	38	22	53	6	.341	.484

TRAVIS WOOD   LHP

Born: Feb. 6, 1987. **B-T:** R-L. **Ht.:** 6-0. **Wt.:** 165. **Drafted:** HS—Alexander, Ark., 2005 (2nd round). **Signed by:** Mike Keenan.

Wood is the highest-drafted Arkansas high school pitcher since the Reds took Dustin Moseley in 1999's supplemental first round. Wood intrigued teams by reaching 95 mph with his fastball as the draft approached, and he dominated two Rookie leagues after signing for $600,000. Wood's changeup drops off the table and already rates as a 70 on the 20-80 scouting scale. He fools hitters by repeating the same arm speed and motion as when he throws his fastball. He regularly hit 93-94 mph and threw to both sides of the plate with good life during the summer. He also features a cutter. Wood's curveball isn't as developed as his other pitches. The Reds have made refining his curve a point of emphasis, and they promoted him to Rookie-level Billings to work with curveball specialist Butch Henry. Wood has some effort in his delivery. Wood aced his introduction to pro ball and seems more than ready for low Class A. He has considerable upside, though coming up with a reliable breaking ball will be crucial.

Year	Club (League)	Class	W	L	ERA	G	GS	CG	SV	IP	H	R	ER	HR	BB	SO	AVG
2005	Reds (GCL)	R	0	0	0.75	8	7	0	0	24	13	3	2	0	7	45	.157
	Billings (Pio)	R	2	0	1.82	6	4	0	0	25	15	6	5	0	13	22	.174
MINOR LEAGUE TOTALS			2	0	1.29	14	11	0	0	49	28	9	7	0	20	67	.166

B.J. SZYMANSKI   OF

Born: Oct. 1, 1982. **B-T:** B-R. **Ht.:** 6-5. **Wt.:** 215. **Drafted:** Princeton, 2004 (2nd round). **Signed by:** Mike Misuraca.

A two-sport star at Princeton, Szymanski was the football team's leading receiver and led the baseball team to the Ivy League title as a junior in 2003-04. Already lacking experience thanks to his dual-sport commitment, he has been hampered by injuries as a pro. A quadriceps injury shortened his 2004 debut, and he missed time in 2005 because of arthroscopic knee surgery and a broken hand. When healthy, Szymanski showcases three impact tools, including explosive raw power from both sides of the plate. He has 30-homer potential in the majors. A chiseled athlete, he can fly around the bases and cover the gaps in center field. His arm is average. Szymanski's swing gets long, and strikeouts and a lower batting average will be a tradeoff for his power. He's still raw and must improve in the fine points of the game, such as getting jumps and running the bases. Injuries have limited him to just 272 pro at-bats. Coming into 2005, Szymanski looked poised for a breakout season. Ticketed for high Class A Sarasota, he's again a prime candidate if he can stay in the lineup.

Year	Club (League)	Class	AVG	G	AB	R	H	2B	3B	HR	RBI	BB	SO	SB	OBP	SLG
2004	Billings (Pio)	R	.259	22	81	13	21	4	2	3	17	9	26	2	.330	.469
2005	Dayton (Mid)	A	.262	50	191	32	50	8	1	10	26	21	57	7	.332	.471
MINOR LEAGUE TOTALS			.261	72	272	45	71	12	3	13	43	30	83	9	.331	.471

5 CHRIS DENORFIA
OF

Born: July 15, 1980. **B-T:** R-R. **Ht.:** 6-1. **Wt.:** 185. **Drafted:** Wheaton (Mass.), 2002 (19th round). **Signed by:** John Brickley.

With his September callup, Denorfia ensured his title as the top male athlete in Wheaton (Mass.) College history. He earned Division III all-America honors in 2002, when he batted .467. He doesn't have overwhelming tools, but Denorfia has surprised scouts with his improved hitting and power the last two seasons. He displays a good feel for the strike zone and works counts in his favor. He's a solid runner with enough range to play center field. He's average defensively in center field and he has enough arm strength to play right. Denorfia doesn't have many glaring weaknesses. He doesn't have exceptional bat speed and his swing doesn't naturally produce loft power. He's already getting everything out of his ability, so there isn't much projection left to him. Denorfia is ready to contribute in Cincinnati after a strong Arizona Fall League performance. He may not be more than a fourth outfielder, especially with the Reds' position depth.

Year	Club (League)	Class	AVG	G	AB	R	H	2B	3B	HR	RBI	BB	SO	SB	OBP	SLG
2002	Reds (GCL)	R	.340	57	200	38	68	9	2	0	19	31	23	18	.425	.405
	Chattanooga (SL)	AA	.429	3	7	0	3	2	1	0	0	2	1	0	.556	1.000
	Dayton (Mid)	A	.000	3	10	2	0	0	0	0	0	0	3	0	.000	.000
2003	Potomac (Car)	A	.236	128	470	60	111	10	5	4	39	54	106	20	.317	.304
2004	Potomac (Car)	A	.312	75	269	52	84	18	4	11	51	48	66	10	.416	.532
	Chattanooga (SL)	AA	.249	61	221	30	55	10	2	6	27	30	42	5	.340	.394
2005	Chattanooga (SL)	AA	.330	46	188	40	62	17	3	7	26	17	38	4	.391	.564
	Louisville (IL)	AAA	.310	91	323	50	100	12	6	13	61	41	54	8	.391	.505
	Cincinnati (NL)	MLB	.263	18	38	8	10	3	0	1	2	6	9	1	.364	.421
MAJOR LEAGUE TOTALS			.263	18	38	8	10	3	0	1	2	6	9	1	.364	.421
MINOR LEAGUE TOTALS			.286	464	1688	272	483	78	23	41	223	223	333	65	.371	.432

6 RAFAEL GONZALEZ
RHP

Born: March 21, 1986. **B-T:** R-R. **Ht.:** 6-1. **Wt.:** 232. **Drafted:** HS—New York, 2004 (4th round). **Signed by:** Jason Baker.

Gonzalez signed with the Yankees out of the Dominican Republic in 2003, but that deal was voided because he was a U.S. citizen who had played at Manhattan's George Washington High before moving to the Dominican as a junior. After signing for $315,000 as a fourth-round pick in 2004, he disappointed the Reds by showing up out of shape for spring training, leaving him unprepared to handle low Class A. His stuff is just a tick behind Homer Bailey's for the best in the system. Gonzalez throws 92-94 mph and peaks at 97, and he also shows a plus curveball and an average changeup at times. Gonzalez has a soft, thick lower half and struggles to keep his weight under control. His stamina and stuff suffered in 2005 until he dedicated more time to cardiovascular work. His secondary pitches and control are very inconsistent. The Reds hope Gonzalez learned his lesson and will be better equipped to succeed in low Class A in 2006. He flashes top-of-the-rotation stuff but must dedicate himself to realize his potential.

Year	Club (League)	Class	W	L	ERA	G	GS	CG	SV	IP	H	R	ER	HR	BB	SO	AVG
2004	Reds (GCL)	R	1	6	4.20	12	8	0	0	41	38	25	19	3	18	32	.259
2005	Billings (Pio)	R	3	0	3.43	11	6	0	1	42	36	18	16	7	23	37	.234
	Dayton (Mid)	A	3	5	9.35	10	5	0	0	26	24	29	27	5	24	22	.250
MINOR LEAGUE TOTALS			7	11	5.13	33	19	0	1	109	98	72	62	15	65	91	.247

7 MIGUEL PEREZ
C

Born: Sept. 25, 1983. **B-T:** R-R. **Ht.:** 6-3. **Wt.:** 190. **Signed:** Venezuela, 2000. **Signed by:** Jorge Oquendo.

Though he has hit just .240 above Rookie ball, Perez made his big league debut before he turned 22 in September. His defensive ability has helped him land jobs in the Venezuela Winter League the past two off-seasons. Perez is the organization's best defensive catcher, with well above-average throwing and receiving skills. He erased 44 percent of basestealers in 2005 and likes to pick off runners with snap throws to first base. He handles pitchers well and runs well for a catcher. Perez' bat hasn't caught up with his catch-and-throw skills and may relegate him to a backup role. He has limited power (eight homers in five pro seasons) and plate discipline, though the Reds think he could hit 10-15 homers annually. When he keeps his hands back, he does a better job of driving the ball. After his short September audition, Perez will go to Double-A in 2006. With the productive tandem of Jason LaRue and Javier Valentin, the Reds don't need to rush Perez.

Year	Club (League)	Class	AVG	G	AB	R	H	2B	3B	HR	RBI	BB	SO	SB	OBP	SLG
2001	Caguas (VSL)	R	.331	48	163	20	54	3	1	0	19	12	33	6	.377	.362
2002	Caguas (VSL)	R	.213	34	108	14	23	4	0	2	18	9	23	1	.320	.306
	Reds (GCL)	R	.360	26	86	12	31	1	0	0	11	2	9	3	.396	.372
2003	Dayton (Mid)	A	.172	20	58	3	10	0	0	0	3	4	19	1	.273	.172
	Billings (Pio)	R	.339	60	227	46	77	11	2	1	25	18	27	1	.410	.419
2004	Dayton (Mid)	A	.237	74	249	22	59	7	0	1	22	16	62	2	.309	.277
	Potomac (Car)	A	.232	18	69	7	16	2	0	0	5	1	12	1	.239	.261
2005	Sarasota (FSL)	A	.268	80	291	36	78	11	0	4	33	16	63	7	.305	.347
	Cincinnati (NL)	MLB	.000	2	3	0	0	0	0	0	0	0	1	0	.000	.000
MAJOR LEAGUE TOTALS			.000	2	3	0	0	0	0	0	0	0	1	0	.000	.000
MINOR LEAGUE TOTALS			.278	360	1251	160	348	39	3	8	136	78	248	22	.337	.333

8 TYLER PELLAND
LHP

Born: Oct. 9, 1983. **B-T:** R-L. **Ht.:** 6-0. **Wt.:** 200. **Drafted:** HS—Bristol, Vt., 2002 (9th round). **Signed by:** Ray Fagnant (Red Sox).

Cincinnati acquired lefties Phil Dumatrait and Pelland from the Red Sox for Scott Williamson at the July 2003 trade deadline. While Dumatrait has been waylaid by Tommy John surgery, Pelland quickly emerged as the top lefty in the Reds system. After posting an 8.66 ERA in low Class A in 2004, he made a successful transition to full-season ball, jumping to high Class A, in 2005. Pelland throws his four-seam fastball at 92-93 mph and can dial it up to 95 at times, and he also has a lively two-seamer. He commands his fastball well, and shows the ability to spin a plus curveball. He's a good athlete who has dominated in spurts. Pelland's curve is inconsistent. When it's not on, hitters can sit on his fastball because his circle changeup is below average and hasn't developed as expected. At 22, he's still far from a refined product, as his control numbers suggest, although as a Northeastern pitcher, he doesn't have many innings on his arm. Pelland has a fresh arm, but needs to take a significant step forward as he approaches Double-A. If he can't improve his secondary pitches, a future in the bullpen awaits him.

Year	Club (League)	Class	W	L	ERA	G	GS	CG	SV	IP	H	R	ER	HR	BB	SO	AVG
2003	Red Sox (GCL)	R	3	4	1.62	11	8	0	0	39	26	12	7	0	18	34	.186
	Reds (GCL)	R	0	0	0.00	1	1	0	0	3	3	0	0	0	0	1	.273
2004	Dayton (Mid)	A	1	7	8.66	14	10	0	0	45	66	49	43	6	20	38	.328
	Billings (Pio)	R	9	3	3.42	18	12	0	0	74	67	36	28	3	39	82	.248
2005	Sarasota (FSL)	A	5	8	4.05	30	15	0	0	102	103	52	46	5	63	103	.270
MINOR LEAGUE TOTALS			18	22	4.25	74	46	0	0	262	265	149	124	14	140	258	.264

9 JOEY VOTTO
1B

Born: Sept. 10, 1983. **B-T:** L-L. **Ht.:** 6-3. **Wt.:** 200. **Drafted:** HS—Toronto, 2002 (2nd round). **Signed by:** John Castleberry.

The Reds tried to cut costs in the 2002 draft with disastrous results, as Denorfia and Votto are the lone bright spots from that crop. After establishing himself as the system's best power prospect, Votto had a disappointing 2005 and continued to struggle in the Arizona Fall League. Votto can launch balls out of sight in batting practice. He drew 90 walks in 2004, showing a disciplined, mature approach. For a big man and former catcher, Votto runs the bases well, and he has grown into a solid defensive first baseman with an above-average arm for the position. Votto lacks plus bat speed and his swing lengthened in 2005. Perhaps too passive in the past, he seemed to start guessing, finding himself behind fastballs and ahead of offspeed offerings. He especially struggled against lefties, hitting .193 with a .315 slugging percentage. Votto's prospect stock has taken a hit, though he's still the top first-base prospect in the system. He needs to rediscover his short stroke and trust his natural hitting instincts in Double-A in 2006.

Year	Club (League)	Class	AVG	G	AB	R	H	2B	3B	HR	RBI	BB	SO	SB	OBP	SLG
2002	Reds (GCL)	R	.269	50	175	29	47	13	3	9	33	21	45	7	.342	.531
2003	Dayton (Mid)	A	.231	60	195	19	45	8	0	1	20	34	64	2	.348	.287
	Billings (Pio)	R	.317	70	240	47	76	17	3	6	38	56	80	4	.452	.488
2004	Dayton (Mid)	A	.302	111	391	60	118	26	2	14	72	79	110	9	.419	.486
	Potomac (Car)	A	.298	24	84	11	25	7	0	5	20	11	21	1	.385	.560
2005	Sarasota (FSL)	A	.256	124	464	64	119	23	2	17	83	52	122	4	.330	.425
MINOR LEAGUE TOTALS			.278	439	1549	230	430	94	10	52	266	253	442	27	.379	.452

10 TRAVIS CHICK RHP

STEVE MOORE

Born: June 10, 1984. **B-T:** R-R. **Ht.:** 6-3. **Wt.:** 220. **Drafted:** HS—Whitehouse, Texas, 2002 (14th round). **Signed by:** Dennis Cardoza (Marlins).

Four years into his pro career, Chick has played for three organizations. A little-known Marlins prospect when he was traded for Ismael Valdez in 2004, he quickly blossomed for the Padres and was one of the surprises of spring training in 2005. After he stalled in Double-A, San Diego sent him and Justin Germano to Cincinnati for Joe Randa last July. Though Chick's velocity was down in 2005, he still had a 91-92 mph fastball that touched 94. His hard slider has good bite and is an average pitch with above-average potential. Chick has a solid pitcher's frame. After dominating low Class A in 2004, Chick couldn't handle jumping to Double-A. He was a victim of big innings all season, unable to get out of jams. His slider was inconsistent, while his changeup remained below-average. He's more of a thrower than a pitcher. Chick has to hone his slider and maintain his mechanics to get back on track. He'll probably repeat Double-A in 2006. Unless his changeup develops, he projects as a power middle reliever.

Year	Club (League)	Class	W	L	ERA	G	GS	CG	SV	IP	H	R	ER	HR	BB	SO	AVG
2002	Marlins (GCL)	R	3	2	2.76	12	8	0	1	46	40	16	14	1	19	39	.227
2003	Jamestown (NY-P)	A	1	2	5.71	13	10	0	0	52	63	41	33	3	26	48	.301
2004	Greensboro (SAL)	A	6	4	4.04	28	11	0	0	91	79	51	41	11	27	112	.228
	Fort Wayne (Mid)	A	5	0	2.13	7	7	0	0	42	32	12	10	4	9	55	.216
2005	Mobile (SL)	AA	2	9	5.27	19	19	1	0	97	107	65	57	12	40	92	.279
	Chattanooga (SL)	AA	2	2	4.86	8	8	0	0	46	47	25	25	5	27	21	.270
MINOR LEAGUE TOTALS			19	19	4.32	87	63	1	1	375	368	210	180	36	148	367	.256

11 WILLIAM BERGOLLA 2B/SS

Born: Feb. 4, 1983. **B-T:** R-R. **Ht.:** 6-0. **Wt.:** 175. **Signed:** Venezuela, 1999. **Signed by:** Johnny Almaraz.

Bergolla has been groomed to be the Reds' second baseman of the future, but the offseason acquisition of Tony Womack was an indication they didn't think he was ready yet. He got his first taste of the big leagues in 2005, as he was called up for two short stints. Bergolla's glove is major league ready, thanks to his fluid actions, good range and average arm. He can slide over to shortstop in a pinch, but his arm is a little short to handle the position every day. At the plate, Bergolla has a compact swing that allows him to spray line drives to all fields. Though the Venezuelan has gained 25 pounds since coming to the States, Bergolla is strictly a singles hitter with little gap power. He doesn't strike out much, as his bat control allows him to fight off tough pitches. He's working on improving his bunting ability. He doesn't walk a lot, which is a concern for a player whose speed is his best asset. Bergolla is one of the Reds' best basestealers, with above-average wheels and a knack for reading pitchers. After averaging 61 steals from 2002-04, he didn't swipe as many bases last year, partly because he was on the shuttle back and forth to Cincinnati, but he still stole at an 84 percent clip. Bergolla still could earn a backup role in Cincinnati with a strong spring, but the Reds wouldn't be dismayed if he were a little more time at Triple-A Louisville.

Year	Club (League)	Class	AVG	G	AB	R	H	2B	3B	HR	RBI	BB	SO	SB	OBP	SLG
2000	Reds (GCL)	R	.182	8	22	2	4	0	0	0	0	4	2	3	.308	.182
	Cagua (VSL)	R	.372	13	43	6	16	3	2	0	5	8	3	1	.481	.535
2001	Billings (Pio)	R	.323	57	232	47	75	5	3	4	24	24	21	22	.387	.422
2002	Dayton (Mid)	A	.248	68	274	38	68	13	1	3	23	16	36	13	.291	.336
	Billings (Pio)	R	.352	53	210	35	74	9	1	3	29	24	26	16	.408	.448
2003	Potomac (Car)	A	.272	128	523	77	142	25	3	2	31	29	59	52	.309	.342
2004	Chattanooga (SL)	AA	.283	116	466	79	132	26	1	4	38	40	63	36	.342	.369
2005	Cincinnati (NL)	MLB	.132	17	38	3	5	0	0	0	1	0	10	0	.132	.132
	Louisville (IL)	AAA	.293	98	400	59	117	23	5	2	38	19	39	16	.325	.390
MAJOR LEAGUE TOTALS			.132	17	38	3	5	0	0	0	1	0	10	0	.132	.132
MINOR LEAGUE TOTALS			.289	541	2170	343	628	104	16	18	188	164	249	159	.339	.377

12 PHILIP DUMATRAIT
LHP

Born: July 12, 1981. **B-T:** R-L. **Ht.:** 6-2. **Wt.:** 170. **Drafted:** Bakersfield (Calif.) JC, 2000 (1st round). **Signed by:** Ed Roebuck (Red Sox).

Acquired from the Red Sox in the Scott Williamson trade in 2003, Dumatrait was one of the system's top prospects before he was derailed by Tommy John surgery that forced him to miss all of the 2004 season. He encouraged the Reds by staying fully healthy and showing that his stuff was starting to bounce back last year. He throws a high-80s fastball that touches 91 and has good life, an average changeup and an average curveball. He's athletic and has an easy delivery that he repeats well. While Dumatrait's stuff came back, his command did not. He never had exceptional control, but he struggled to throw strikes all season, struggling through deep counts and way too many walks. He did show the ability to battle without great stuff, and he kept the ball down, allowing just four homers. Dumatrait's solid-average repertoire and ability to hamstring lefties give him the ability to be a solid lefty reliever if needed, but he'll have several more chances to prove he can be a starter. Command is often the last thing to return after Tommy John surgery, and Cincinnati hopes he'll show more this year in Triple-A.

Year	Club (League)	Class	W	L	ERA	G	GS	CG	SV	IP	H	R	ER	HR	BB	SO	AVG
2000	Red Sox (GCL)	R	0	1	1.65	6	6	0	0	16	10	6	3	0	12	12	.172
2001	Red Sox (GCL)	R	3	0	2.76	8	8	0	0	33	27	10	10	0	9	33	.229
	Lowell (NY-P)	A	1	1	3.48	2	2	0	0	10	9	4	4	0	4	15	.225
2002	Augusta (SAL)	A	8	5	2.77	22	22	1	0	120	109	44	37	5	47	108	.249
	Sarasota (FSL)	A	0	2	3.86	4	4	0	0	14	10	9	6	0	15	16	.192
2003	Sarasota (FSL)	A	7	5	3.02	21	20	0	1	104	74	41	35	4	59	74	.204
	Potomac (Car)	A	4	1	3.35	7	7	1	0	38	36	17	14	2	14	32	.248
2004	Did not play—Injured																
2005	Sarasota (FSL)	A	0	0	2.70	3	2	0	0	10	8	4	3	0	3	13	.211
	Chattanooga (SL)	AA	4	12	3.17	24	24	0	0	128	115	58	45	4	70	101	.245
MINOR LEAGUE TOTALS			27	27	2.99	97	95	2	1	473	398	193	157	15	233	404	.231

13 ZACH WARD
RHP

Born: Jan. 14, 1984. **B-T:** R-R. **Ht.:** 6-3. **Wt.:** 235. **Drafted:** Gardner-Webb, 2005 (3rd round). **Signed by:** Perry Smith.

Ward hardly attracted a second look coming out of high school, but jumped from a mid-80s project as an incoming freshman to a mid-90s fireballer in the course of one year after Gardner-Webb coaches worked on developing his arm strength. He dominated the Cape Cod League in 2004 and became Gardner-Webb's highest-drafted player ever as a third-rounder in 2005. After being used heavily in the spring, Ward didn't pitch in the minors after signing for $420,000. When he did take the mound during instructional league, the Reds were impressed with his 93-94 mph fastball and his plus slider, which sits around 86-87 mph. His changeup has a long ways to go, though it could become a usable third pitch. The concerns about Ward stem from his mechanics. Ward has a "bow-and-arrow" delivery in which he simply rears back and fires. He also short-arms the ball, reminding some scouts of Red Sox reliever Keith Foulke. Despite that, Ward was durable in college and has a strong frame. The Reds plan to see if he can develop into a middle-of-the-rotation starter. If that doesn't work, his fastball-slider combo could make him a closer or late-inning setup man. He'll probably make his pro debut in low Class A.

Year	Club (League)	Class	W	L	ERA	G	GS	CG	SV	IP	H	R	ER	HR	BB	SO	AVG
2005	Did not play—Signed 2006 contract																

14 PAUL JANISH
SS

Born: Oct. 12, 1982. **B-T:** R-R. **Ht.:** 6-2. **Wt.:** 180. **Drafted:** Rice, 2004 (5th round). **Signed by:** Mike Powers.

Janish probably wishes he could have skipped 2005 altogether. He got off to a slow start in low Class A, and just as he started to come out of it with a 17-for-43 stretch, he tore an elbow ligament in a collision at first base on June 5. He was shut down for the remainder of the year and had to have Tommy John surgery. Before the injury, Janish's arm strength was one of his best tools—he hit 93 mph off the mound in the past—and he also had great hands and good actions at shortstop. If his arm bounces back as expected, Janish has few questions about his ability to handle shortstop. He also has outstanding leadership ability. The questions start at the plate. Janish never will be a top-of-the-order threat, but he has to get stronger to be even a useful No. 7 or 8 hitter. He has a long swing and lacks power. To his credit, he'll take pitches the other way and he has a good understanding of the strike zone. He's an average runner. The natural progression would be for Janish to move up to high Class A, but Adam Rosales also is ready for that level after an outstanding pro debut.

Year	Club (League)	Class	AVG	G	AB	R	H	2B	3B	HR	RBI	BB	SO	SB	OBP	SLG
2004	Billings (Pio)	R	.263	66	205	39	54	11	0	2	22	45	45	7	.406	.346
2005	Dayton (Mid)	A	.245	55	208	30	51	10	2	5	29	29	38	5	.346	.385
Minor League Totals			.254	121	413	69	105	21	2	7	51	74	83	12	.376	.366

15 ADAM ROSALES   SS

Born: May 20, 1983. **B-T:** R-R. **Ht.:** 6-2. **Wt.:** 195. **Drafted:** Western Michigan, 2005 (12th round). **Signed by:** Rick Sellers.

Rosales was the Reds' first-day find of the 2005 draft. Area scout Rick Sellers was adamant that the Western Michigan senior was being sold short, and Cincinnati was able to take Rosales in the 12th round. Rosales made Sellers look wise, batting .325 with 14 homers and a system-best .946 on-base plus slugging percentage in his pro debut after hitting .309 with six homers as a college senior. Some area scouts questioned whether Rosales would hit with wood bats, but he showed the ability to center the ball and hit for power. He has solid bat speed and his swing is compact, but it isn't pretty. He swings on a downward plane, yet is able to loft the ball when needed. He also has average speed and plus arm strength. Rosales' range at shortstop could be a question as he gets older and bigger, but he has good hands and currently covers enough ground. He far exceeded expectations in his first pro year, which should earn him a promotion to high Class A.

Year	Club (League)	Class	AVG	G	AB	R	H	2B	3B	HR	RBI	BB	SO	SB	OBP	SLG
2005	Billings (Pio)	R	.321	34	140	29	45	14	0	5	25	13	37	2	.396	.529
	Dayton (Mid)	A	.328	32	134	24	44	8	0	9	21	10	24	3	.378	.590
MINOR LEAGUE TOTALS			.325	66	274	53	89	22	0	14	46	23	61	5	.388	.558

16 RICHIE GARDNER   RHP

Born: Feb. 1, 1982. **B-T:** R-R. **Ht.:** 6-3. **Wt.:** 185. **Drafted:** Arizona, 2003 (6th round). **Signed by:** Jeff Barton.

Gardner, the Reds' 2004 minor league pitcher of the year, didn't seem right at the start of last season. He didn't have his usual good stuff and was rocked on a regular basis by Double-A batters. At first, Cincinnati thought he just had a tired arm. Reds medical director Dr. Tim Kremchek eventually found a cyst in Gardner's shoulder that had to be removed, performing arthroscopic surgery to repair a torn labrum in early August. The Reds hope he'll be back on the mound by the middle of 2006, though Luke Hudson missed an entire season after similar surgery in 2003. This is just the latest setback in a hard-luck career for Gardner, who was slowed by mononucleosis and then by a concussion during his time at Santa Rosa (Calif.) JC. Before his shoulder problems he was the most polished pitcher in the system, with three above-average pitches: a 90-94 sinker, a slider and a changeup. As good as his pitches were, Gardner's feel for pitching and solid makeup impressed the organization even more. The Reds left him off of their 40-man roster, a further indication that he won't return to the mound for some time.

Year	Club (League)	Class	W	L	ERA	G	GS	CG	SV	IP	H	R	ER	HR	BB	SO	AVG
2004	Potomac (Car)	A	8	3	2.50	18	12	0	1	86	77	31	24	3	13	80	.231
	Chattanooga (SL)	AA	5	2	2.56	11	11	0	0	70	68	24	20	7	13	59	.249
2005	Chattanooga (SL)	AA	3	6	5.73	13	13	0	0	66	80	46	42	6	24	47	.309
MINOR LEAGUE TOTALS			16	11	3.48	42	36	0	1	223	225	101	86	16	50	186	.260

17 THOMAS PAULY   RHP

Born: July 28, 1981. **B-T:** R-R. **Ht.:** 6-1. **Wt.:** 195. **Drafted:** Princeton, 2003 (2nd round). **Signed by:** Steve Mondile.

Like Richie Gardner, Pauly entered 2005 as one of the system's top pitching prospects and ended it on the mend after shoulder surgery. After his torn labrum was repaired in May, the Reds initially thought he'd be back for instructional league but ultimately shut him down until 2006. Growing up, Pauly was a swimmer who happened to play baseball on the side. As a high school junior, he converted from an outfielder into a sidearm pitcher. That was enough to get him into Princeton, where head coach and former big league catcher Scott Bradley moved his arm slot back up to overhand. He was one of the three main subjects in Jim Collins' 2004 book "The Last Best League," which portrayed Pauly as a very smart but somewhat goofy pitcher with one of the best fastballs in the Cape Cod League. Pauly was primarily a reliever until his junior season at Princeton, but he quickly settled into a starting role with the Reds, leading the high Class A Carolina League in strikeouts in 2004. Before his injury, Pauly featured one of the system's best fastballs, a 91-93 mph heater that had good life. He also had a potentially plus if erratic changeup and a similarly promising slider. The recovery rate from labrum surgeries isn't particularly good, which explains why Cincinnati left Pauly off its 40-man roster after the season.

Year	Club (League)	Class	W	L	ERA	G	GS	CG	SV	IP	H	R	ER	HR	BB	SO	AVG
2003	Dayton (Mid)	A	2	5	4.02	12	12	0	0	47	45	26	21	5	10	36	.247
2004	Potomac (Car)	A	8	7	2.97	28	19	0	0	121	96	47	40	12	26	135	.219
2005	Did not play—Injured																
MINOR LEAGUE TOTALS			10	12	3.26	40	31	0	0	168	141	73	61	17	36	171	.227

18 BRANDON ROBERTS   OF

Born: Nov. 9, 1984. **B-T:** L-R. **Ht.:** 6-0. **Wt.:** 185. **Drafted:** Cal Poly, 2005 (7th round). **Signed by:** Mike Misuraca.

Roberts is a case where the Reds believe they may have gotten more than they paid for. When they signed him for $137,000 as a seventh-round pick last June, they viewed him as a speedy leadoff hitter. Most scouting reports knocked his defense and arm strength, but Cincinnati was pleasantly surprised to find that he gets decent jumps and covers gaps well enough to be an average center fielder, with enough of an arm (45 on the 20-80 scouting scale) to stay there. That's important, because Roberts' speed game doesn't play as well on an outfield corner. He gets from the left side of the plate to first base in 4.0 second and can run a 6.4-second 60-yard dash. He stole at will at Billings, succeeding in 32 of 39 attempts. Roberts understands how to make best use of his quickness. He bunts well and tries to work the ball to the left side of the field, and he has enough speed to hit .290-.300 by keeping the ball on the ground. He has enough functional strength to be more than just a slap hitter and bolstered his stock by leading the Alaska League with a .373 average in the summer of 2004 while using wood bats. He'll move up to Class A this year.

Year	Club (League)	Class	AVG	G	AB	R	H	2B	3B	HR	RBI	BB	SO	SB	OBP	SLG
2005	Billings (Pio)	R	.318	68	274	50	87	9	6	4	36	24	44	32	.386	.438
MINOR LEAGUE TOTALS			.318	68	274	50	87	9	6	4	36	24	44	32	.386	.438

19 CHRIS DICKERSON   OF

Born: April 10, 1982. **B-T:** L-L. **Ht.:** 6-4. **Wt.:** 212. **Drafted:** Nevada, 2003 (16th round). **Signed by:** Keith Chapman.

Dickerson has had one of the highest ceilings in the Reds system since signing in 2003, but the Reds are still waiting for him to turn that potential into production. Dickerson showed signs of putting it all together during the first half of last season. He won the MVP award at the high Class A Florida State League all-star game, and he reached double digits in both homers and steals by the end of June. But his early power surge actually may have hurt his development, as he got pull-happy and stopped going with pitches. Dickerson hit just .212 with one homer over the final two months. He needs to get a better feel for the strike zone and pitch recognition, as pitchers got him to chase pitches out of the zone. While he scuffled in the second half of the season, there still are reasons for hope. Dickerson is the best athlete and the best defensive outfielder in the system, and he has basestealing ability. He has range in all directions in center field, as well as an average arm. Dickerson's struggles leave the Reds with an interesting decision. With B.J. Szymanski ready for high Class A and Jay Bruce slated for low Class A, Dickerson would fit best in Double-A but has yet to show he can handle advanced pitching.

Year	Club (League)	Class	AVG	G	AB	R	H	2B	3B	HR	RBI	BB	SO	SB	OBP	SLG
2003	Billings (Pio)	R	.244	58	201	36	49	6	4	6	38	39	66	9	.376	.403
2004	Dayton (Mid)	A	.303	84	314	50	95	15	3	4	34	51	92	27	.410	.408
	Potomac (Car)	A	.200	15	45	5	9	2	0	0	5	7	14	3	.321	.244
2005	Sarasota (FSL)	A	.236	119	436	68	103	17	7	11	43	53	124	19	.325	.383
MINOR LEAGUE TOTALS			.257	276	996	159	256	40	14	21	120	150	296	58	.363	.389

20 PHILIPPE VALIQUETTE   LHP

Born: Feb. 14, 1987. **B-T:** L-L. **Ht.:** 6-0. **Wt.:** 175. **Drafted:** HS—Montreal, 2004 (7th round). **Signed by:** Jason Baker.

Valiquette is both one of the most raw and most intriguing players in the system. A native of Pierrefonds, Quebec, he's blessed with an uncommon left arm. Despite a very slight, 6-foot, 175-pound frame and relatively easy motion, he can touch 95 mph with his fastball. But he's still pure projection and has no usable secondary pitches yet, as his curveball and changeup are well below average. As a Canadian high school product, he has few innings under his belt, though he did pitch for the Canadian junior national team. A visa shortage kept Valiquette from making his pro debut until 2005, when the Reds inexplicably sent him to low Class A to begin his career. Predictably, he was torched by older hitters who feasted on his one-pitch approach. Cincinnati thought he had the makeup to risk the lofty assignment, and he seemed to hold up mentally. A native French speaker, he also has handled the language adjustment well. Valiquette is years away from the majors, but the Reds believe he's athletic enough to pick up solid secondary pitches. He'll likely return to low Class A this year.

Year	Club (League)	Class	W	L	ERA	G	GS	CG	SV	IP	H	R	ER	HR	BB	SO	AVG
2005	Dayton (Mid)	A	2	5	6.30	19	16	0	0	64	81	54	45	3	44	42	.315
	Billings (Pio)	R	2	1	6.43	7	3	0	0	21	23	16	15	1	10	18	.291
MINOR LEAGUE TOTALS			4	6	6.33	26	19	0	0	85	104	70	60	4	54	60	.310

21 JUSTIN GERMANO   RHP

Born: Aug. 6, 1982. **B-T:** R-R. **Ht.:** 6-2. **Wt.:** 190. **Drafted:** HS—Claremont, Calif., 2000 (13th round). **Signed by:** Jim Woodward (Padres).

Picked up with Travis Chick in the Joe Randa deal from the Padres at last year's trade deadline, Germano is pretty close to a finished product. He made his major league debut at 21 two years ago but failed to establish himself in opportunities to join the San Diego rotation. None of his pitches stands out, though he'll flash a plus curveball. He has good movement on a high-80s fastball and an average changeup. Germano's strength is his feel for pitching, as he'll add or subtract velocity to get outs. He's a solid athlete with a fluid delivery and excellent command. That command got him in trouble at the major league level, as he nibbled too much. If he can improve his curveball, he has a chance to be a back-of-the-rotation starter. Unless injuries crop up to create an opening with the Reds, he's slated to start 2006 in Triple-A.

Year	Club (League)	Class	W	L	ERA	G	GS	CG	SV	IP	H	R	ER	HR	BB	SO	AVG
2000	Padres (AZL)	R	5	5	4.59	17	8	0	1	67	65	36	34	4	9	67	.249
2001	Fort Wayne (Mid)	A	2	6	4.98	13	13	0	0	65	80	47	36	7	16	55	.302
	Eugene (NWL)	A	6	5	3.49	13	13	2	0	80	77	35	31	5	11	74	.246
2002	Fort Wayne (Mid)	A	12	5	3.18	24	24	1	0	156	166	63	55	14	19	119	.269
	Lake Elsinore (Cal)	A	2	0	0.95	3	3	0	0	19	12	3	2	1	5	18	.174
2003	Lake Elsinore (Cal)	A	9	5	4.23	19	19	1	0	111	127	61	52	4	25	78	.287
	Mobile (SL)	AA	2	5	4.34	9	9	1	0	58	60	34	28	6	13	44	.268
2004	Mobile (SL)	AA	2	1	2.51	5	5	0	0	32	31	11	9	3	7	20	.258
	Portland (PCL)	AAA	9	5	3.38	20	20	2	0	123	113	48	46	12	25	98	.249
	San Diego (NL)	MLB	1	2	8.86	7	5	0	0	21	31	24	21	2	14	16	.341
2005	Portland (PCL)	AAA	7	6	3.70	19	19	1	0	112	111	56	46	13	32	100	.259
	Louisville (IL)	AAA	3	2	4.01	8	8	0	0	49	62	27	22	7	5	38	.313
MAJOR LEAGUE TOTALS			1	2	8.86	7	5	0	0	21	31	24	21	2	14	16	.341
MINOR LEAGUE TOTALS			59	45	3.73	150	141	8	1	871	904	421	361	76	167	711	.267

22 JAMES AVERY   RHP

Born: June 10, 1984. **B-T:** R-R. **Ht.:** 6-1. **Wt.:** 210. **Drafted:** Niagara, 2005 (5th round). **Signed by:** Jason Baker.

Avery is one of three Canadians on this top 30 list, and like Joey Votto and Philippe Valiquette he played for the national junior team. Unlike those two, Avery was scouted in the United States before the Reds signed him. A Saskatchewan native, he got exposure in three years at Niagara University and in the Cape Cod League before signing as a fifth-round pick last June for $170,000. He impressed Reds officials with a 90-92 mph fastball that touches 94, and an above-average changeup. He flashed an average 12-to-6 curveball after signing, but his inability to develop consistency with that pitch as an amateur kept him from going higher in the draft. Avery showed good mound presence in his pro debut. While many scouts thought he profiled as only a reliever coming out of college, Cincinnati thinks he'll have the three-pitch repertoire necessary to start. He's strong enough to handle the role, which he'll fill with one of the Reds' Class A affiliates this year.

Year	Club (League)	Class	W	L	ERA	G	GS	CG	SV	IP	H	R	ER	HR	BB	SO	AVG
2005	Reds (GCL)	R	0	1	2.12	6	5	0	0	17	16	7	4	0	3	18	.239
	Dayton (Mid)	A	1	1	3.94	5	2	0	0	16	17	8	7	1	6	8	.274
MINOR LEAGUE TOTALS			1	2	3.00	11	7	0	0	33	33	15	11	1	9	26	.256

23 SAM LeCURE   RHP

Born: May 4, 1984. **B-T:** R-R. **Ht.:** 6-1. **Wt.:** 190. **Drafted:** Texas, 2005 (4th round). **Signed by:** Brian Wilson.

After serving as the No. 2 starter on the Texas team that lost in the 2004 College World Series championship series, LeCure was slated to be the Longhorns' ace last year. But he was declared academically ineligible just before the season and missed out on Texas' national championship. The Reds kept scouting him, took him in the fourth round and signed him for $260,000. He shook off the rust of inactivity, sitting at 90-91 mph with his fastball. He touched 93 at times while showing the ability to add and subtract as needed. His slider is average as well, while his changeup projects as a potentially average pitch. He showed the ability to pound the zone at the knees and throw strikes with a clean delivery. He'll get his first taste of full-season ball in 2006. Because he has strong mound presence and polish, he could end up in high Class A before too long.

Year	Club (League)	Class	W	L	ERA	G	GS	CG	SV	IP	H	R	ER	HR	BB	SO	AVG
2005	Billings (Pio)	R	5	1	3.27	13	6	0	0	41	43	18	15	2	15	44	.272
MINOR LEAGUE TOTALS			5	1	3.27	13	6	0	0	41	43	18	15	2	15	44	.272

24 BOBBY BASHAM RHP

Born: March 7, 1980. **B-T:** R-R. **Ht.:** 6-3. **Wt.:** 205. **Drafted:** Richmond, 2001 (7th round). **Signed by:** Perry Smith.

Among the several Cincinnati pitching prospects who have been hampered by injuries, Basham has had the quickest rise and fall. After his dominating performance in low Class A in 2002, several Reds officials considered him the system's top pitching prospect. But his velocity and his once-dominating slider disappeared in 2003. An MRI found no damage, though eventually he was diagnosed with a torn labrum in his shoulder. He has surgery to repair that tear and to remove bone spurs, sidelining him for the entire 2004 season. When he returned to the mound last year, the former Richmond backup quarterback showed steady progress. He built up arm strength, working at 87-90 mph for most of the season and touching 92-93 mph in his later starts. He had a 90-93 mph fastball before he got hurt. His slider wasn't as nasty as it once was, but it was showing signs of being at least an average pitch. His changeup is usable, and he threw strikes with his usual ease. Basham pitched well in Double-A in the second half, earning his first shot at Triple-A in 2006.

Year	Club (League)	Class	W	L	ERA	G	GS	CG	SV	IP	H	R	ER	HR	BB	SO	AVG
2001	Billings (Pio)	R	1	2	4.85	6	6	0	0	30	36	23	16	2	17	37	.300
2002	Dayton (Mid)	A	6	4	1.64	13	13	4	0	88	64	25	16	4	9	97	.195
2003	Chattanooga (SL)	AA	5	10	5.17	17	17	0	0	94	133	72	54	16	24	56	.331
	Potomac (Car)	A	0	1	2.70	1	1	0	0	7	5	3	2	0	1	1	.200
2004	Did not play—Injured																
2005	Sarasota (FSL)	A	5	2	3.75	10	10	0	0	50	60	22	21	3	6	42	.309
	Chattanooga (SL)	AA	5	3	2.98	10	10	0	0	51	52	20	17	5	9	46	.275
MINOR LEAGUE TOTALS			22	22	3.55	57	57	4	0	320	350	165	126	30	66	279	.278

25 JAVON MORAN OF

Born: Sept. 30, 1982. **B-T:** R-R. **Ht.:** 5-11. **Wt.** 175. **Drafted:** Auburn, 2003 (5th round). **Signed by:** Mike Stauffer (Phillies).

Moran, righthander Elizardo Ramirez and lefty Joe Wilson came to the Reds when they sent Cory Lidle to the Phillies in August 2004. His first full season in the Cincinnati system was just like his first two in pro ball. He hit for average and stole some bases, but drew few walks and showed even less power. He split time between center and left field in high Class A, largely because he was on the same team as Chris Dickerson, one of the system's top center fielders. But Moran has the range to play center field, albeit with a slightly below-average arm. He needs to improve his patience and basestealing ability to truly profile as a leadoff hitter. His instincts on the bases aren't as good as his speed. He does bunt well and make contact, spraying line drives around the field. Moran will play in Double-A this year.

Year	Club (League)	Class	AVG	G	AB	R	H	2B	3B	HR	RBI	BB	SO	SB	OBP	SLG
2003	Batavia (NY-P)	A	.284	60	250	33	71	9	3	1	12	16	32	27	.326	.356
2004	Lakewood (SAL)	A	.285	101	421	73	120	18	9	2	38	24	78	39	.340	.385
	Dayton (Mid)	A	.383	25	94	11	36	2	0	0	7	10	15	11	.448	.404
2005	Sarasota (FSL)	A	.329	53	210	35	69	4	2	2	23	14	32	13	.378	.395
	Chattanooga (SL)	AA	.301	23	83	14	25	5	1	0	2	5	21	7	.341	.386
MINOR LEAGUE TOTALS			.303	262	1058	166	321	38	15	5	82	69	178	97	.354	.382

26 DAVID SHAFER RHP

Born: March 7, 1982. **B-T:** R-R. **Ht.:** 6-2. **Wt.:** 180. **Drafted:** Central Arizona JC, D/F 2001 (32nd round). **Signed by:** Mark Corey.

Shafer pitched with Oakland's Rich Harden at Central Arizona Junior College in 2001, then was part of a Junior College World Series championship in 2002 before signing as a draft-and-follow. He got off to a quick start last year, not allowing a run in 10 high Class A outings to earn a promotion to Double-A, where he held his own. He was effective as a part-time closer, but his 88-92 mph fastball, average slider and improving changeup mean that he profiles more as a setup man or middle reliever. Shafer keeps the ball down and did a good job of throwing strikes before he got to Double-A. He has a resilient arm that has stood up well to the rigors of bullpen work. Shafer doesn't have a high ceiling, but the Reds need relief help and he could contribute in the near future.

Year	Club (League)	Class	W	L	ERA	G	GS	CG	SV	IP	H	R	ER	HR	BB	SO	AVG
2002	Reds (GCL)	R	1	0	1.29	3	0	0	1	7	3	2	1	0	2	7	.125
	Billings (Pio)	R	5	2	1.72	19	0	0	4	31	30	14	6	0	11	30	.242
2003	Billings (Pio)	R	0	3	3.04	25	0	0	13	24	25	13	8	1	3	32	.253
2004	Dayton (Mid)	A	5	3	2.92	31	7	0	5	77	60	32	25	8	16	84	.216
	Potomac (Car)	A	0	0	0.00	3	0	0	3	4	5	0	0	0	0	5	.278
2005	Sarasota (FSL)	A	1	0	0.00	10	0	0	5	14	9	0	0	0	2	18	.188
	Chattanooga (SL)	AA	1	6	4.08	34	0	0	6	40	31	21	18	3	24	41	.217
MINOR LEAGUE TOTALS			13	14	2.65	125	7	0	37	197	163	82	58	12	58	217	.222

27 MIKE BURNS   RHP

Born: July 14, 1978. **B-T:** R-R. **Ht.:** 6-1. **Wt.:** 190. **Drafted:** Cal State Los Angeles, 2000 (30th round). **Signed by:** Doug Deutsch (Astros).

The Astros put Burns on waivers while trying to clear space on their 40-man roster in November, and the Reds picked him up and will give him the chance to win a spot in their bullpen. A 30th-round pick, Burns is an overachiever who breezed through Houston's system as a starter until hitting the wall in Double-A in 2003. He returned to that level, became a full-time reliever and earned Texas League all-star honors in 2004, then spent most of last year in Houston's bullpen. Burns' best assets are his control and his competitive makeup. His go-to offering is his slider, which has a quick, short break. He also works with an average 89-92 mph fastball that lacks movement, and an erratic but deceptive curveball. His changeup is a below-average pitch, which has led to troubles with lefties.

Year	Club (League)	Class	W	L	ERA	G	GS	CG	SV	IP	H	R	ER	HR	BB	SO	AVG
2000	Martinsville (Appy)	R	2	7	4.52	12	12	0	0	66	75	52	33	12	9	51	.281
2001	Michigan (Mid)	A	7	7	3.95	29	21	1	1	132	131	67	58	10	27	108	.260
2002	Michigan (Mid)	A	14	9	2.49	28	28	3	0	181	146	59	50	12	29	126	.218
2003	Round Rock (TL)	AA	2	13	6.13	38	14	0	0	106	129	80	72	15	30	89	.297
2004	Round Rock (TL)	AA	11	3	1.67	56	0	0	9	81	63	18	15	1	15	94	.209
2005	Round Rock (PCL)	AAA	2	1	2.10	25	0	0	13	30	22	7	7	4	4	34	.200
	Houston (NL)	MLB	0	0	4.94	27	0	0	0	31	29	18	17	6	8	20	.238
MAJOR LEAGUE TOTALS			0	0	4.94	27	0	0	0	31	29	18	17	6	8	20	.238
MINOR LEAGUE TOTALS			38	40	3.55	188	75	4	23	595	566	283	235	54	114	502	.247

28 CALVIN MEDLOCK   RHP

Born: Nov. 8, 1982. **B-T:** R-R. **Ht.:** 5-10. **Wt.:** 175. **Drafted:** North Central Texas CC, D/F 2002 (39th round). **Signed by:** Jimmy Gonzales.

Few pitchers in the system made more strides in 2005 than Medlock. In his first taste of high Class A the year before, he struggled to keep the ball down and showed little feel for his curveball. In his return trip, he dominated batters with a live 88-92 mph fastball that seemed to jump on hitters. He showed added arm speed and tweaked his arm angle. That allowed him to get more downward plane on his fastball, always a challenge for the 5-foot-10 righthander. His curveball returned to effectiveness, his changeup improved and he threw more strikes than ever. Used mostly as a starter, Medlock better fits the profile of a middle reliever. But he has earned the right to remain in the rotation as he advances to Double-A.

Year	Club (League)	Class	W	L	ERA	G	GS	CG	SV	IP	H	R	ER	HR	BB	SO	AVG
2003	Reds (GCL)	R	0	0	0.00	3	0	0	0	5	5	1	0	0	0	3	.263
	Billings (Pio)	R	1	0	1.88	19	0	0	1	29	25	7	6	1	9	31	.234
2004	Dayton (Mid)	A	8	3	2.57	22	15	0	0	95	74	33	27	5	21	111	.214
	Potomac (Car)	A	3	4	6.36	11	9	0	1	47	49	36	33	8	22	46	.268
2005	Sarasota (FSL)	A	6	3	3.06	25	17	0	0	109	95	42	37	6	22	98	.234
MINOR LEAGUE TOTALS			18	10	3.27	80	41	0	2	284	248	119	103	20	74	289	.234

29 TONYS GUTIERREZ   1B

Born: Aug. 18, 1983. **B-T:** L-L. **Ht.:** 6-2. **Wt.:** 225. **Signed:** Venezuela, 2000. **Signed by:** Felix Delgado.

One of the few Reds prospects signed out of Latin America during the latter days of the Jim Bowden era, Gutierrez has been one of the system's most consistent hitters since the day he first put on a pro uniform. His hand-eye coordination and discriminating batting eye rank with the best among Cincinnati farmhands. In his first taste of full-season ball last year, Gutierrez earned Midwest League all-star recognition after finishing second in the batting race. He has gained 45 pounds since signing, but his hitting approach hasn't changed and thus he has yet to develop power. He sprays line drives to all fields, which has led to high averages and on-base percentages. The Reds believe he can become a power hitter if he'll focus more on using his legs more and driving the ball. Gutierrez is a good defensive first baseman with surprising agility for his size, and he's an average runner. He'll move up to high Class A this year.

Year	Club (League)	Class	AVG	G	AB	R	H	2B	3B	HR	RBI	BB	SO	SB	OBP	SLG
2001	Cagua (VSL)	R	.332	54	199	29	66	9	1	4	33	22	26	2	.447	.398
2002	Cagua (VSL)	R	.307	34	101	12	31	6	1	1	19	11	16	3	.416	.410
2003	Reds (GCL)	R	.303	46	155	21	47	12	4	3	18	20	22	1	.490	.399
	Billings (Pio)	R	.200	3	10	1	2	1	0	0	1	0	1	0	.300	.200
2004	Reds (GCL)	R	.275	12	40	2	11	3	2	1	7	8	5	0	.525	.380
	Billings (Pio)	R	.339	18	59	12	20	3	0	2	12	12	15	2	.492	.466
2005	Dayton (Mid)	A	.324	109	410	65	133	21	5	7	48	40	71	6	.396	.451
MINOR LEAGUE TOTALS			.318	276	974	142	310	55	13	18	138	113	156	14	.400	.457

30 ELIZARDO RAMIREZ   RHP

Born: Jan. 28, 1983. **B-T:** L-R. **Ht.:** 6-0. **Wt.:** 180. **Signed:** Dominican Republic, 1999. **Signed by:** Wil Tejeda (Phillies).

Ramirez is one of the rare pitchers who may throw too many strikes. Picked up with Javon Moran and Joe Wilson from the Phillies in the Cory Lidle trade in August 2004, he has earned short stints in the majors during each of the past two seasons. The results haven't been pretty, primarily because big leaguers have discovered that he's always around the plate with hittable stuff. He currently lacks an out pitch, and he doesn't do a good job of expanding the zone to get batters to chase pitches. He especially has troubles against lefties, who hit .386 off him in the majors and .303 in Triple-A in 2005. But Ramirez does have three very usable pitches: an 88-92 mph fastball, an average curveball and an average changeup. He throws them all with a loose and easy motion and nearly flawless mechanics. He's working on adding a cutter or developing some sink to his fastball. He'll work on refining his stuff in Triple-A to begin the season.

Year	Club (League)	Class	W	L	ERA	G	GS	CG	SV	IP	H	R	ER	HR	BB	SO	AVG
2000	Phillies (DSL)	R	5	2	1.88	11	9	0	1	57	47	19	12	1	5	67	.216
2001	Phillies (DSL)	R	10	1	1.26	14	14	1	0	93	71	26	13	0	9	81	.208
2002	Phillies (GCL)	R	7	1	1.10	11	11	2	0	73	44	18	9	3	2	73	.165
2003	Clearwater (FSL)	A	13	9	3.78	27	25	1	0	157	181	85	66	4	33	101	.290
2004	Clearwater (FSL)	A	5	1	2.44	9	9	1	0	59	55	17	16	3	8	33	.255
	Philadelphia (NL)	MLB	0	0	4.80	7	0	0	0	15	17	8	8	3	5	9	.283
	Reading (EL)	AA	2	5	6.68	8	8	1	0	34	51	34	25	4	14	20	.362
	Chattanooga (SL)	AA	1	0	3.19	5	5	1	0	31	35	11	11	6	4	23	.289
2005	Louisville (IL)	AAA	7	7	3.77	21	21	0	0	131	150	63	55	14	18	82	.287
	Cincinnati (NL)	MLB	0	3	8.46	6	4	0	0	22	33	22	21	5	10	9	.344
MAJOR LEAGUE TOTALS			0	3	6.99	13	4	0	0	37	50	30	29	8	15	18	.321
MINOR LEAGUE TOTALS			50	26	2.93	106	102	7	1	636	634	273	207	35	93	480	.259

CLEVELAND
INDIANS

BY **CHRIS KLINE**

LARRY GOREN

Mark Shapiro took over as Indians general manager in November 2001 and promptly dismantled a team that had won six American League Central titles in seven seasons. The big league club was aging and overpaid, while the farm system was thin.

Cleveland fans weren't happy, but Shapiro assured them that the Indians would rebuild the right way—by developing their own talent—and set a timetable of 2005 for the club to contend again.

Let's just say his ETA was right on schedule.

The Indians finished 2005 with 93 wins, the sixth-most in the majors and more than every other National League club except the Cardinals. Cleveland has improved from 68 to 80 to 93 victories over the last three seasons, thanks to homegrown prospects and key trades.

Shapiro's signature deal remains shipping Bartolo Colon to the Expos in June 2002 for Grady Sizemore, Cliff Lee, Brandon Phillips and Lee Stevens. Sizemore and Lee are now part of a young nucleus that also includes Coco Crisp (part of a Chuck Finley trade with the Cardinals in July 2002), Travis Hafner (stolen from the Rangers in a deal for Einar Diaz in December 2002), Victor Martinez (signed out of Venezuela in 1996), **Jhonny Peralta** (signed out of the Dominican Republic in 1999) and C.C. Sabathia (drafted in the first round in 1998). None of that group is older than 28.

While the Indians have emerged from their rebuilding phase, the system continues to develop talent. Another wave of prospects in the upper minors is nearly ready to make an impact in Cleveland. Lefthander Jeremy Sowers, righthanders Fernando Cabrera and Fausto Carmona and first baseman/catcher Ryan Garko all could contribute to the big league club in 2006, and Brad Snyder and Franklin Gutierrez are on hand should an outfield opening arise.

Double-A Akron won the Eastern League title behind up-and-coming managerial candidate Torey Lovullo. Cleveland has had success promoting managers as well as players from within—most notably with big league skipper Eric Wedge and third-base coach Joel Skinner—and Lovullo could be the next in that line. In addition to developing players, managers and coaches, Cleveland also is grooming future general managers. Assistant GM Chris Antonetti turned down the opportunity to interview for Boston's GM job, and farm director John Farrell's name also surfaced in connection with the position. Assistant GM/scouting director John Mirabelli also is a future GM candidate.

Not all of the news from the minors was good. The Indians' top two prospects from a year ago, righthander Adam Miller and first baseman Michael Aubrey, had serious injuries. Miller missed the first half of 2005 with an elbow strain but came back in the second half to reclaim the No. 1 spot on this list. Aubrey had back problems that limited him to just 28 games, and there are some fears they may be chronic.

TOP 30 PROSPECTS

1. Adam Miller, rhp	16. Nick Pesco, rhp
2. Jeremy Sowers, lhp	17. Cody Bunkelman, rhp
3. Brad Snyder, of	18. J.D. Martin, rhp
4. Fausto Carmona, rhp	19. Jensen Lewis, rhp
5. Ryan Garko, 1b/c	20. Edward Mujica, rhp
6. Franklin Gutierrez, of	21. Dan Denham, rhp
7. Fernando Cabrera, rhp	22. Jason Cooper, of
8. Trevor Crowe, of	23. Kevin Kouzmanoff, 3b
9. Stephen Head, 1b	24. Jake Dittler, rhp
10. Michael Aubrey, 1b	25. Justin Hoyman, rhp
11. Chuck Lofgren, lhp	26. Ryan Mulhern, 1b
12. John Drennen, of	27. Nick Weglarz, of
13. Rafael Perez, lhp	28. Scott Lewis, lhp
14. Tony Sipp, lhp	29. Matt Whitney, 3b
15. Andrew Brown, rhp	30. Carlton Smith, rhp

ORGANIZATION OVERVIEW

General manager: Mark Shapiro. **Farm director:** John Farrell. **Scouting director:** John Mirabelli.

2005 PERFORMANCE

Class	Team	League	W	L	Pct.	Finish*	Manager(s)
Majors	Cleveland	American	93	69	.574	5th (14)	Eric Wedge
Triple-A	Buffalo Bisons	International	82	62	.569	2nd (14)	Marty Brown
Double-A	Akron Aeros	Eastern	84	58	.592	+1st (12)	Torey Lovullo
High A	Kinston Indians	Carolina	76	64	.543	4th (8)	Luis Rivera
Low A	Lake County Captains	South Atlantic	72	66	.522	t-6th (16)	Mike Sarbaugh
Short-season	Mahoning Valley Scrappers	New York-Penn	33	43	.434	10th (14)	Rouglas Odor
Rookie	Burlington Indians	Appalachian	25	43	.368	10th (10)	Sean McNally/Lee May Jr.
OVERALL 2005 MINOR LEAGUE RECORD			372	336	.525	6th (30)	

*Finish in overall standings (No. of teams in league). +League champion.

ORGANIZATION LEADERS

BATTING *Minimum 250 at-bats
*AVG	Kouzmanoff, Kevin, Akron/Kinston/Mahoning Valley	.333
R	Snyder, Brad, Akron/Kinston	92
H	Reyes, Argenis, Kinston/Lake County	154
TB	Mulhern, Ryan, Akron/Kinston	258
2B	Kinkade, Mike, Buffalo	35
3B	Inglett, Joe, Buffalo	9
HR	Mulhern, Ryan, Akron/Kinston	32
RBI	Cooper, Jason, Akron/Buffalo	100
BB	Panther, Nathan, Akron/Kinston	67
SO	Snyder, Brad, Akron/Kinston	158
SB	Torres, Eider, Akron	33
*OBP	Barton, Brian, Kinston/Lake County	.442
*SLG	Mulhern, Ryan, Akron/Kinston	.640

PITCHING #Minimum 75 innings
W	Sowers, Jeremy, Akron/Buffalo/Kinston	14
L	Traber, Billy, Akron/Buffalo/Kinston	11
#ERA	Roehl, Scott, Akron/Kinston/Lake County	1.39
G	Collins, Kyle, Kinston/Lake County	57
CG	12 tied at	1
SV	Mattison, Kieran, Buffalo/Kinston/Lake County	25
IP	Carmona, Fausto, Akron/Buffalo	174
BB	Smith, Sean, Kinston	71
SO	Sowers, Jeremy, Akron/Buffalo/Kinston	149

BEST TOOLS

Best Hitter for Average	Ryan Garko
Best Power Hitter	Brad Snyder
Best Strike-Zone Discipline	Michael Aubrey
Fastest Baserunner	Alfred Ard
Best Athlete	Brad Snyder
Best Fastball	Adam Miller
Best Curveball	J.D. Martin
Best Slider	Rafael Perez
Best Changeup	Nick Pesco
Best Control	Jeremy Sowers
Best Defensive Catcher	Javi Herrera
Best Defensive Infielder	Ivan Ochoa
Best Infield Arm	Matt Whitney
Best Defensive Outfielder	Franklin Gutierrez
Best Outfield Arm	Ryan Goleski

PROJECTED 2009 LINEUP

Catcher	Victor Martinez
First Base	Ryan Garko
Second Base	Ronnie Belliard
Third Base	Kevin Kouzmanoff
Shortstop	Jhonny Peralta
Left Field	Coco Crisp
Center Field	Grady Sizemore
Right Field	Brad Snyder

Designated Hitter	Travis Hafner
No. 1 Starter	C.C. Sabathia
No. 2 Starter	Cliff Lee
No. 3 Starter	Adam Miller
No. 4 Starter	Jake Westbrook
No. 5 Starter	Jeremy Sowers
Closer	Fernando Cabrera

LAST YEAR'S TOP 20 PROSPECTS

1.	Adam Miller, rhp	11.	Jake Dittler, rhp
2.	Michael Aubrey, 1b	12.	Francisco Cruceta, rhp
3.	Franklin Gutierrez, of	13.	Juan Valdes, of
4.	Brad Snyder, of	14.	Chuck Lofgren, lhp
5.	Jeremy Sowers, lhp	15.	Mike Butia, of
6.	Fausto Carmona, rhp	16.	Justin Hoyman, rhp
7.	Fernando Cabrera, rhp	17.	Matt Whitney, 3b
8.	Ryan Garko, c/1b	18.	Dan Cevette, lhp
9.	Nick Pesco, rhp	19.	Scott Lewis, lhp
10.	Andrew Brown, rhp	20.	Jason Cooper, of

TOP PROSPECTS OF THE DECADE

Year	Player, Pos.	2005 Org.
1996	Bartolo Colon, rhp	Angels
1997	Bartolo Colon, rhp	Angels
1998	Sean Casey, 1b	Reds
1999	Russell Branyan, 3b	Brewers
2000	C.C. Sabathia, lhp	Indians
2001	C.C. Sabathia, lhp	Indians
2002	Corey Smith, 3b	Padres
2003	Brandon Phillips, ss/2b	Indians
2004	Grady Sizemore, of	Indians
2005	Adam Miller, rhp	Indians

TOP DRAFT PICKS OF THE DECADE

Year	Player, Pos.	2005 Org.
1996	Danny Peoples, 1b/of	Out of baseball
1997	Tim Drew, rhp	Rockies
1998	C.C. Sabathia, lhp	Indians
1999	Will Hartley, c (2nd round)	Out of baseball
2000	Corey Smith, 3b	Padres
2001	Dan Denham, rhp	Indians
2002	Jeremy Guthrie, rhp	Indians
2003	Michael Aubrey, 1b	Indians
2004	Jeremy Sowers, lhp	Indians
2005	Trevor Crowe, of	Indians

LARGEST BONUSES IN CLUB HISTORY

Danys Baez, 1999	$4,500,000
Jeremy Guthrie, 2002	$3,000,000
Jeremy Sowers, 2004	$2,475,000
Michael Aubrey, 2003	$2,010,000
Dan Denham, 2001	$1,860,000

MINOR LEAGUE DEPTH CHART

Cleveland Indians

Rank: **11**

STRENGTH: Pitching, both lefthanded and righthanded, led by Adam Miller and Jeremy Sowers.

WEAKNESS: After graduating Victor Martinez to the majors in 2003, the catching remains thin.

Depth charts prepared by John Manuel and Chris Kline. Numbers in parentheses indicate prospect rankings.

LF
Jason Cooper (22)
Mike Butia
Jon Van Every

CF
Franklin Gutierrez (6)
Trevor Crowe (8)
John Drennen (12)
Brian Barton
Jose Constanza
Juan Valdes

RF
Brad Snyder (3)
Nick Weglarz (27)
Ryan Goleski
Nathan Panther

3B
Kevin Kouzmanoff (23)
Matt Whitney (29)
Jake Gautreau
Pat Osborn

SS
Ivan Ochoa
Bryan Finegan

2B
Argenis Reyes
Matt Fornasiere
Eider Torres
Joe Inglett
Brandon Pinckney

1B
Ryan Garko (5)
Stephen Head (9)
Michael Aubrey (10)
Ryan Mulhern (26)

C
Javi Herrera
Wyatt Toregas
David Wallace

RHP

Starters	Relievers
Adam Miller (1)	Fernando Cabrera (7)
Fausto Carmona (4)	Andrew Brown (15)
Nick Pesco (16)	Edward Mujica (20)
Cody Bunkelman (17)	Kaz Tadano
J.D. Martin (18)	Travis Foley
Jensen Lewis (19)	Brian Slocum
Dan Denham (21)	Kyle Collins
Jake Dittler (24)	Scott Roehl
Justin Hoyman (25)	
Carlton Smith (30)	
Kyle Denney	
Jeremy Guthrie	
Jason Young	
Bear Bay	
Tom Mastny	
James Deters	
Joe Ness	

LHP

Starters	Relievers
Jeremy Sowers (2)	Rafael Perez (13)
Chuck Lofgren (11)	Tony Sipp (14)
Scott Lewis (28)	Brian Tallet
Aaron Laffey	Mariano Gomez
Ryan Edell	Chris Cooper
Justin Pekarek	

DRAFT ANALYSIS
2005

Best Pro Debut: 1B Stephen Head (2) hit .432 with six homers in 10 games at short-season Mahoning Valley, then .286-4-36 in high Class A. RHP Joe Ness (6) went 4-2, 1.67 with 68 strikeouts in 59 innings at Mahoning Valley.

Best Athlete: The best pure athlete is OF Brent Thomas (32). He's a well above-average runner and a good defender in center field. He's not as polished as OF Trevor Crowe (1), who has all-around skills and is also a former national racquetball champion.

Best Pure Hitter: Crowe, OF John Drennen (1) and Head all have the chance to be elite hitters.

Best Raw Power: 1B Nick Weglarz (3) is the best power prospect to come out of Canada since the Braves made Scott Thorman a first-round pick in 2000. Head is strong enough to hit the ball out of any part of the park.

Fastest Runner: Thomas, though he was hampered by a severe hamstring injury.

Best Defensive Player: 3B Nick Petrucci (11) does a solid job. 2B/SS Matt Fornasiere (12) stands out with his hands, arm and instincts.

Best Fastball: RHP Mike Finocchi (14) can reach 95 mph. RHP Kevin Dixon (5) can do the same, though he was tired after playing both ways at Minnesota State-Mankato and was working at 88-90 mph in instructional league. RHP Neil Wagner (21) may have the most velocity. His delivery broke down last spring at North Dakota State, and he pitched at 88-92 mph. Before he signed with Cleveland, he got going again in the college Northwoods League, where his fastball hit 96 in 2004.

Best Breaking Ball: RHP Ryan Edell's (8)

Lewis

curveball. Edell threw his curveball as well as his average fastball and changeup for strikes.

Most Intriguing Background: Fornasiere played for his dad Rob, the assistant head coach at the University of Minnesota. Unsigned RHP Barry Laird (13) is a tight end on the University of Houston football team.

Closest To The Majors: Crowe and Head are advanced college hitters, and Crowe has fewer adjustments to make. RHP Jensen Lewis (3) came into pro ball with a reputation for pitching well with average stuff. When Cleveland slowed down his delivery, his fastball started to touch 94 mph.

Best Late-Round Pick: Finocchi or Wagner.

The One Who Got Away: The Indians pursued several tough signs unsuccessfully. RHP Cody Satterwhite (37, now at Mississippi) might have been a first-round pick if that decision was based solely on talent. RHP Tim Lincecum (42, returned to Washington) dominated in the Cape Cod League but wanted nearly $1 million to sign. Cleveland came closer to signing Laird and RHP Aaron Shafer (16, Wichita State).

Assessment: Several teams coveted Crowe in the middle of the first round and Drennen in the supplemental first round, and the Indians landed them both. They also got a huge value in the second round in Head, who seemed like a lock first-rounder entering 2005 and played like one after signing.

2004 LHP Jeremy Sowers (1) has been exactly what he was supposed to be and should reach the majors in 2006. Two other southpaws, Chuck Lofgren (4) and Tony Sipp (45), have intriguing upside as well. **GRADE: B**

2003 The Indians went 3-for-3 with their first-rounders—1B Michael Aubrey, OF Brad Snyder and RHP Adam Miller—though Aubrey and Miller had injury concerns last year. 1B/C Ryan Garko (3) won't stop hitting. **GRADE: B+**

2002 RHP Jeremy Guthrie (1) has been a waste of $4 million, and he has done more than two other first-rounders, 3B Matt Whitney and 2B Micah Schilling. RHP Nick Pesco (25) has been the highlight of this crop so far. **GRADE: D**

2001 Four first-rounders yielded little: RHP Dan Denham and OF Michael Conroy have moved slowly, RHP Alan Horne didn't sign and RHP J.D. Martin has fought injuries. OF Luke Scott (9) reached the majors with Houston. **GRADE: C**

Draft analysis prepared by Jim Callis. Numbers in parentheses indicate draft rounds.

ADAM
MILLER

RHP

Born: Nov. 26, 1984.
Ht.: 6-4. **Wt.:** 190.
Bats: R. **Throws:** R.
Drafted: HS—McKinney, Texas,
2003 (1st round supplemental).
Signed by: Matt Ruebel.

Miller came into 2005 off a strong first full season, which he finished by not allowing an earned run in 14 innings and touching 101 mph with his explosive fastball during the high Class A Carolina League playoffs. There were whispers during spring training that he could reach Cleveland in 2005 after starting the year at Double-A Akron, paying quick dividends on the 2003 supplemental first-round pick received for the loss of Jim Thome to free agency. But those ambitious plans were put on hold two weeks into spring training when Miller was shut down with a strained ligament in his elbow after long-tossing. He didn't require surgery but lost nearly three months of development time. Miller sat out for three weeks before throwing bullpen sessions in extended spring training. He joined short-season Mahoning Valley at the end of June and was greeted rudely by opposing hitters, who touched him for a .405 average. He never gained confidence in his secondary pitches and continued to struggle after moving up to high Class A Kinston. He pitched better in the Arizona Fall League than his 5.68 ERA would indicate.

When he's healthy, Miller has all the components of a frontline major league starter. Garnering comparisons to Kevin Brown and Bret Saberhagen, he features a heavy 92-97 mph fastball with great life and armside movement. Though he sat at 91-93 mph for much of 2005, his velocity increased as the season wore on. He complements his fastball with a hard-biting, 87-88 mph slider than can dominate lefties and righties alike. His changeup showed significant improvement when he used it. He has an advanced feel for pitching, combining those instincts with power stuff and moxie. Managers and scouts rave about his makeup.

The health of Miller's elbow is a major concern, but he stayed healthy and didn't experience any further problems after his three-month layoff. His mechanics are usually free and easy, so they shouldn't cause him difficulty in the future. Miller's problems on the mound last year can be traced to his secondary pitches. While his slider still had its usual velocity, he lacked the command he showed with the pitch in 2004. He lacked confidence in his changeup, so hitters sat on his fastball. His ability to locate his slider and changeup improved late in the season. With all the time off, Miller developed a hitch in his delivery, dropping his lead arm. That caused him to lower his arm angle, affecting his leverage and deception, but he smoothed out the problem toward the end of the year. Though he earns points for his poise and his work ethic, Miller did get frustrated at times when things didn't go his way.

Miller isn't quite on the same path he was a year ago, when he was regarded as one of the premier pitching prospects in the game. But he still has a huge ceiling and might not be much more than a season away from joining the Indians. They say he's 100 percent healthy and ready for a full season in 2006. Barring any setbacks, he'll head to Double-A to start the year and could take off from there.

Year	Club (League)	Class	W	L	ERA	G	GS	CG	SV	IP	H	R	ER	HR	BB	SO	AVG
2003	Burlington (Appy)	R	0	4	4.95	10	10	0	0	33	30	20	18	2	9	23	.250
2004	Lake County (SAL)	A	7	4	3.36	19	19	1	0	91	79	39	34	7	28	106	.240
	Kinston (Car)	A	3	2	2.08	8	8	0	0	43	29	17	10	1	12	46	.193
2005	Mahoning Valley (NY-P)	A	0	0	5.05	3	3	0	0	11	17	6	6	0	4	6	.405
	Kinston (Car)	A	2	4	4.82	12	12	0	0	60	76	43	32	5	17	45	.318
MINOR LEAGUE TOTALS			12	14	3.79	52	52	1	0	237	231	125	100	15	70	226	.263

2 JEREMY SOWERS
LHP

CARL KLINE

Born: May 17, 1983. **B-T:** L-L. **Ht.:** 6-1. **Wt.:** 175. **Drafted:** Vanderbilt, 2004 (1st round). **Signed by:** Scott Barnsby.

Growing up, Sowers was more into chess than sports, and that may be the best metaphor for his approach to pitching—a strategic match of wits. A two-time first-round pick who turned down the Reds out of high school before signing for $2.475 million as the sixth pick in 2004, he finished his first pro season in Triple-A Buffalo. The Indians gave him their Bob Feller Award as their minor league pitcher of the year. Sowers doesn't overpower hitters with his 88-92 mph fastball, so he relies on his intelligence to gain an edge to keep them guessing. He locates his fastball to all four quadrants of the strike zone, and shows excellent command of both his short slider and his changeup. He scrapped his curveball in favor of the slider, which features a more cutter-like action. Though Sowers locates his changeup well, it lacks depth at times and his arm speed is inconsistent. He needs to do a better job of repeating his arm slot with his slider, as he tends to arch his back, throwing off its overall effectiveness and late bite. Several Tribe officials felt Sowers could have won in the big leagues last year, and they view him as a future 15-20 game winner in the mold of John Tudor. Sowers probably will return to Triple-A to begin 2006, but he could be the first starter Cleveland summons from the minors.

Year	Club (League)	Class	W	L	ERA	G	GS	CG	SV	IP	H	R	ER	HR	BB	SO	AVG
2005	Kinston (Car)	A	8	3	2.78	13	13	0	0	71	60	25	22	5	19	75	.223
	Akron (EL)	AA	5	1	2.08	13	13	0	0	82	74	25	19	8	9	70	.241
	Buffalo (IL)	AAA	1	0	1.58	1	1	0	0	6	7	1	1	0	1	4	.292
MINOR LEAGUE TOTALS			14	4	2.37	27	27	0	0	159	141	51	42	13	29	149	.235

3 BRAD SNYDER
OF

RICH ABEL

Born: May 25, 1982. **B-T:** L-L. **Ht.:** 6-3. **Wt.:** 200. **Drafted:** Ball State, 2003 (1st round). **Signed by:** Bob Mayer/Chuck Ricci.

Snyder has come a long way since a car accident sidetracked his career during his freshman year at Ball State. He rebounded to become the Mid-American Conference player of the year and a first-round pick in 2003, but then missed spring training in 2004 with an eye infection that set back his development. He found his stride in Double-A last year, helping Akron win the Eastern League championship. Snyder has drawn comparisons to Paul O'Neill and Fred Lynn for his wide base of tools. He has the sweetest swing and the best power in the organization, with plus bat speed that produces easy pop to all fields. He's an above-average runner with good instincts on the bases. While he has the speed and range to play center field, his tools are best suited for right. He has average arm strength that plays up thanks to his accuracy and instincts. Snyder's lack of strike-zone discipline hampers him at the plate. He fanned 158 times last year, and big league pitchers could exploit his tendency to swing and miss. He struggles with breaking balls down and away, and he's still learning how to stay back and drive balls consistently. Snyder will head back to Double-A to further hone his approach and tighten up his zone. He should earn a Triple-A promotion by midseason.

Year	Club (League)	Class	AVG	G	AB	R	H	2B	3B	HR	RBI	BB	SO	SB	OBP	SLG
2003	Mahoning Valley (NY-P)	A	.284	62	225	52	64	11	6	6	31	41	82	14	.393	.467
2004	Lake County (SAL)	A	.280	79	304	52	85	15	5	10	54	48	78	11	.382	.461
	Kinston (Car)	A	.355	29	110	20	39	7	1	6	21	13	28	4	.424	.600
2005	Kinston (Car)	A	.278	58	209	36	58	10	2	6	28	24	64	12	.365	.431
	Akron (EL)	AA	.280	75	304	56	85	21	5	16	54	25	94	5	.345	.539
MINOR LEAGUE TOTALS			.287	303	1152	216	331	64	19	44	188	151	346	46	.376	.490

4 FAUSTO CARMONA
RHP

STEVE MOORE

Born: Dec. 7, 1983. **B-T:** R-R. **Ht.:** 6-4. **Wt.:** 190. **Signed:** Dominican Republic, 2000. **Signed by:** Josue Herrera.

Carmona has won 40 games in his three full seasons, tying for the minor league lead with 17 victories in 2003. He struggled in Double-A in both 2004 and 2005, but he recovered to pitch well in Triple-A last year. Carmona enjoyed increased velocity in Triple-A, jumping up to 93-94 mph while topping out at 96. His high-80s slider can be nasty when he commands it, and his deceptive changeup with late action gives him a third plus pitch. Command always has been his forte, as he likes to pound the zone with heavy sinkers and values groundballs as much as strikeouts. Carmona still doesn't miss a lot of bats and probably never will. But someone with his stuff shouldn't be nearly as hittable as he has been in the upper minors. He needs to become more consistent with his mechanics. The Indians envision him developing along the lines of Jake Westbrook. Carmona has the necessary pitches to become a frontline starter, but he still has plenty of development remaining before he's ready. He'll probably spend at least another half-season in Triple-A, as Jeremy Sowers is in line for the first callup.

Year	Club (League)	Class	W	L	ERA	G	GS	CG	SV	IP	H	R	ER	HR	BB	SO	AVG
2001	Indians (DSL)	R	4	2	3.11	14	13	0	0	75	69	36	26	0	12	47	.234
2002	Burlington (Appy)	R	2	4	3.30	13	11	0	1	76	89	36	28	4	10	42	.295
	Mahoning Valley (NY-P)	A	0	0	0.00	3	0	0	0	4	2	0	0	0	1	0	.182
2003	Akron (EL)	AA	0	0	4.50	1	1	0	0	6	8	3	3	1	0	3	.308
	Lake County (SAL)	A	17	4	2.06	24	24	1	0	148	117	48	34	10	14	83	.214
2004	Kinston (Car)	A	5	2	2.83	12	12	0	0	70	68	28	22	6	20	57	.251
	Akron (EL)	AA	4	8	4.97	15	15	0	0	87	114	52	48	3	21	63	.329
2005	Akron (EL)	AA	6	5	4.07	14	14	0	0	91	100	46	41	7	20	57	.276
	Buffalo (IL)	AAA	7	4	3.25	13	12	1	0	83	76	32	30	10	15	49	.244
MINOR LEAGUE TOTALS			45	29	3.26	109	102	2	1	641	643	281	232	41	113	401	.260

5 RYAN GARKO   1B/C

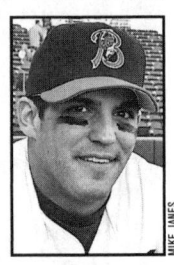

Born: Jan. 2, 1981. **B-T:** R-R. **Ht.:** 6-2. **Wt.:** 225. **Drafted:** Stanford, 2003 (3rd round). **Signed by:** Don Lyle.

Garko's bat never has been in question. But after he went undrafted following his junior year at Stanford, Garko dropped 15 pounds to address concerns over his lack of mobility behind the plate. His stock soared and he earned All-America honors as a senior, and he hit his way to the big leagues little more than two years after turning pro. Garko is short to the ball with an efficient stroke, allowing him to adjust to pitches in any location. He uses the whole field and shows above-average power. His makeup and leadership skills are among the best in the system. The only thing holding Garko back is his defensive deficiencies. The Indians committed to getting him as much work as possible behind the plate in 2005 but have since wavered, realizing backup Josh Bard is a much better defender than Garko ever will be. Though his actions at first base have gotten better, he's still mechanical at times and adequate at best. He's a liability on the basepaths. Garko worked exclusively at first base in the Arizona Fall League. He could push for incumbent Ben Broussard's first-base job in 2006 if he can prove himself serviceable defensively.

Year	Club (League)	Class	AVG	G	AB	R	H	2B	3B	HR	RBI	BB	SO	SB	OBP	SLG
2003	Mahoning Valley (NY-P)	A	.273	45	165	23	45	8	1	4	16	12	19	1	.337	.406
2004	Kinston (Car)	A	.328	65	238	44	78	17	1	16	57	26	34	4	.425	.609
	Akron (EL)	AA	.331	43	172	29	57	15	0	6	38	14	28	1	.397	.523
	Buffalo (IL)	AAA	.350	5	20	2	7	1	0	0	4	2	3	0	.391	.400
2005	Buffalo (IL)	AAA	.303	127	452	75	137	25	3	19	77	44	92	1	.384	.498
	Cleveland (AL)	MLB	.000	1	1	0	0	0	0	0	0	0	1	0	.000	.000
MAJOR LEAGUE TOTALS			.000	1	1	0	0	0	0	0	0	0	1	0	.000	.000
MINOR LEAGUE TOTALS			.309	285	1047	173	324	66	5	45	192	98	176	7	.389	.511

6 FRANKLIN GUTIERREZ   OF

Born: Feb. 21, 1983. **B-T:** R-R. **Ht.:** 6-2. **Wt.:** 180. **Signed:** Venezuela, 2000. **Signed by:** Camilo Pascual (Dodgers).

After hitting 24 homers in a breakout 2003 season, Gutierrez has totaled just 17 longballs in the Indians system since coming over from the Dodgers in the Milton Bradley trade in April 2004. Nagging injuries have been the problem. He had minor elbow surgery in 2004, and he sprained a knee in April and dislocated his left middle finger in June last year. Gutierrez generates tremendous bat speed and crushes inside pitches, and he also shows the ability to take balls the other way through improved pitch recognition. He moved back in the box and raised his hands slightly to improve his load at the plate and did well once he adjusted to the changes. Indians officials consider him the best defensive outfielder in the system, with above-average speed and range to play center and a plus arm. Gutierrez still has a tendency to expand his strike zone, and his lack of discipline has some scouts thinking that his ceiling is nothing more than becoming Juan Encarnacion. If he hadn't lost so much development time during the last two years, Gutierrez might be knocking on the door to Cleveland. He could make the Indians as a fourth outfielder in spring training. But he has yet to prove himself in Triple-A and needs regular at-bats, so he likely will start the year in Buffalo.

Year	Club (League)	Class	AVG	G	AB	R	H	2B	3B	HR	RBI	BB	SO	SB	OBP	SLG
2001	Dodgers (GCL)	R	.269	56	234	38	63	16	0	4	30	16	39	9	.324	.389
2002	South Georgia (SAL)	A	.283	92	361	61	102	18	4	12	45	31	88	13	.344	.454
	Las Vegas (PCL)	AAA	.300	2	10	2	3	2	0	0	2	1	4	0	.364	.500
2003	Vero Beach (FSL)	A	.282	110	425	65	120	28	5	20	68	39	111	17	.345	.513
	Jacksonville (SL)	AA	.313	18	67	12	21	3	2	4	12	7	20	3	.387	.597
2004	Buffalo (IL)	AAA	.148	7	27	4	4	1	0	1	3	1	11	0	.179	.296
	Akron (EL)	AA	.302	70	262	38	79	24	2	5	35	23	77	6	.372	.466
2005	Akron (EL)	AA	.261	95	383	70	100	25	2	11	42	30	77	14	.322	.423
	Buffalo (IL)	AAA	.254	19	67	10	17	6	2	0	7	6	13	2	.320	.403
	Cleveland (AL)	MLB	.000	7	1	2	0	0	0	0	0	1	0	0	.500	.000
MAJOR LEAGUE TOTALS			.000	7	1	2	0	0	0	0	0	1	0	0	.500	.000
MINOR LEAGUE TOTALS			.277	469	1836	300	509	123	17	57	244	154	440	64	.340	.456

7 FERNANDO CABRERA RHP

Born: Nov. 16, 1981. **B-T:** R-R. **Ht.:** 6-4. **Wt.:** 170. **Drafted:** HS—Bayamon, P.R., 1999 (10th round). **Signed by:** Henry Cruz.

The Indians had a poor draft in 1999, as their top pick (second-round-er Will Hartley) never made it out of Rookie ball and just one player signed in the first 20 rounds made it past Double-A. That exception is Cabrera, who reached Double-A as a starter but has been groomed as a late-inning reliever since mid-2003. He has been impressive in late-season callups the last two years. Cabrera operates with two plus pitches, a lively 92-96 mph fastball and a hard, diving splitter. His fastball command has improved since his days as a starter, and he pitches effectively to both sides of the plate. He has both the stuff and the demeanor to close. Cabrera's slider and changeup aren't nearly as effective as his other two offerings. When he stays on top of his slider and doesn't slow down his arm speed with his changeup, both pitches grade out as major league average. He rarely concerns himself with holding runners close to first base. There's no question that Cabrera is Cleveland's closer of the future. The Indians will ease him into the role, however, after re-signing all-star Bob Wickman to finish games in 2006. Cabrera will help set up Wickman this season.

Year	Club (League)	Class	W	L	ERA	G	GS	CG	SV	IP	H	R	ER	HR	BB	SO	AVG
2000	Burlington (Appy)	R	3	7	4.61	13	13	0	0	68	64	42	35	4	20	50	.252
2001	Columbus (SAL)	A	5	6	3.61	20	20	0	0	95	89	49	38	7	37	96	.242
2002	Kinston (Car)	A	6	8	3.52	21	21	0	0	110	83	48	43	7	40	107	.206
	Akron (EL)	AA	1	2	5.33	7	4	0	1	27	26	16	16	1	12	29	.252
2003	Akron (EL)	AA	9	4	2.97	36	15	0	5	109	96	41	36	8	40	115	.237
2004	Buffalo (IL)	AAA	4	3	3.84	44	0	0	5	75	57	37	32	9	43	92	.203
	Cleveland (AL)	MLB	0	0	3.40	4	0	0	0	5	3	3	2	0	1	6	.167
2005	Buffalo (IL)	AAA	6	1	1.23	30	0	0	3	51	36	8	7	3	11	68	.196
	Cleveland (AL)	MLB	2	1	1.47	15	0	0	0	31	24	7	5	1	11	29	.212
MAJOR LEAGUE TOTALS			2	1	1.75	19	0	0	0	36	27	10	7	1	12	35	.206
MINOR LEAGUE TOTALS			34	31	3.48	171	73	0	14	535	451	241	207	39	203	557	.226

8 TREVOR CROWE OF

RODGER WOOD

Born: Nov. 17, 1983. **B-T:** B-R. **Ht.:** 6-0. **Wt.:** 200. **Drafted:** Arizona, 2005 (1st round). **Signed by:** Joe Graham.

A natural athlete with good bloodlines, Crowe is a former junior national racquetball champion and his father David was a professional golfer. Crowe earned All-America honors last spring by hitting .403 and leading NCAA Division I with 15 triples (the second-most in D-I history) and 49 extra-base hits. He went 14th overall in the 2005 draft—the highest-selected University of Arizona player since Eddie Leon went ninth in 1965—and signed for $1.695 million. A switch-hitter with quick hands, Crowe is a slightly better hitter from the left side while displaying more power from the right. He has a history of hitting with wood bats with Team USA and in the Cape Cod League. He makes quick adjustments and has the ability to center the ball and use the whole field. The Indians grade his speed as above-average and believe he can handle the defensive responsibilities of center field. Crowe can be undisciplined at times at the plate and lacks raw power. Some scouts question whether he had the quickness to play center, and his arm is below average. He had trouble staying out of the training room in his pro debut, with an abdominal strain and a freak injury when he was hit in the thumb by a line drive while running the bases. Though he finished 2005 in Double-A, Crowe likely will start in high Class A this year. He's quite similar to Cleveland's current left fielder, Coco Crisp.

Year	Club (League)	Class	AVG	G	AB	R	H	2B	3B	HR	RBI	BB	SO	SB	OBP	SLG
2005	Mahoning Valley (NY-P)	A	.255	12	51	9	13	2	1	1	6	6	8	4	.345	.392
	Lake County (SAL)	A	.258	44	178	18	46	8	2	0	23	18	25	7	.327	.326
	Akron (EL)	AA	.100	3	10	1	1	0	0	0	0	0	3	0	.100	.100
MINOR LEAGUE TOTALS			.251	59	239	28	60	10	3	1	29	24	36	11	.322	.331

9 STEPHEN HEAD — 1B

RICH ABEL

Born: Jan. 13, 1984. **B-T:** L-L. **Ht.:** 6-3. **Wt.:** 220. **Drafted:** Mississippi, 2005 (2nd round). **Signed by:** Scott Barnsby.

Head projected as more of a pitcher coming out of high school and starred as a two-way player at Mississippi. He set the Rebels career saves record with 26, and his 165 RBIs were three shy of another school mark. He entered 2005 projected as an early first-round pick, but dropped to the Indians in the second round because of concerns about his power ceiling. He signed for $605,000 and hit six homers in his first 10 pro games. Head has the strength to hit balls out of the park, generating most of his pop with his lower half. He destroys inside pitches and his long arms enable him to cover the outer half. If he maintains a consistent approach, he can hit for average with 20-30 homers annually. He's a solid defender at first base, with soft hands and good range. Head's upper body isn't great, but he should fill out with more conditioning. He needs to tighten up his strike zone and identify breaking balls better. He also tends to get a little long in his swing and becomes too pull-conscious at times. He's a below-average runner. By jumping Head to high Class A after 10 pro games, the Indians displayed their faith in his advanced bat. He could return there to start 2006 or move up to Double-A if Michael Aubrey isn't healthy.

Year	Club (League)	Class	AVG	G	AB	R	H	2B	3B	HR	RBI	BB	SO	SB	OBP	SLG
2005	Mahoning Valley (NY-P)	A	.432	10	37	11	16	4	0	6	14	8	5	0	.533	1.027
	Kinston (Car)	A	.286	47	203	31	58	15	0	4	36	8	33	4	.310	.419
MINOR LEAGUE TOTALS			.308	57	240	42	74	19	0	10	50	16	38	4	.349	.513

10 MICHAEL AUBREY — 1B

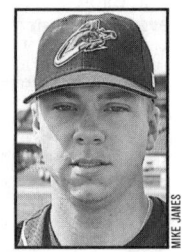

MIKE JAMES

Born: April 15, 1982. **B-T:** L-L. **Ht.:** 6-0. **Wt.:** 195. **Drafted:** Tulane, 2003 (1st round). **Signed by:** Scott Meaney.

Aubrey jumped to Double-A in 2004 after just 98 games as a pro. But a hamstring injury that July sidelined him for five weeks, and he played just one game after May 9 last year after he hurt his back. The injury could be chronic, as back problems also ended his career as a pitcher at Tulane. Aubrey's quick hands allow him to control the barrel of the bat, and he drives balls into the gaps with regularity. He recognizes pitches well and rarely swings and misses. He's a premium defender with good footwork around the bag, soft hands and a plus arm for a first baseman. There's some question about how much power Aubrey will hit for in the majors. He profiles as a gap hitter with occasional pop, and he needs to improve at turning on inside fastballs. After the back injury, he had trouble getting his front foot down without feeling any pain as he went into the turn in his swing. His speed is below-average, though he's not a baseclogger. Aubrey has the highest ceiling of any corner infielder in the system. His health will have a huge role in whether he reaches it. He'll probably return to Double-A in 2006.

Year	Club (League)	Class	AVG	G	AB	R	H	2B	3B	HR	RBI	BB	SO	SB	OBP	SLG
2003	Lake County (SAL)	A	.348	38	138	22	48	13	0	5	19	14	22	0	.409	.551
2004	Kinston (Car)	A	.339	60	218	34	74	14	1	10	60	27	26	3	.438	.550
	Akron (EL)	AA	.261	38	134	13	35	7	0	5	22	15	18	0	.340	.425
2005	Akron (EL)	AA	.283	28	106	17	30	5	1	4	20	7	18	1	.336	.462
MINOR LEAGUE TOTALS			.314	164	596	86	187	39	2	24	121	63	84	4	.392	.507

11 CHUCK LOFGREN — LHP

Born: Jan. 29, 1986. **B-T:** L-L. **Ht.:** 6-4. **Wt.:** 200. **Drafted:** HS—San Mateo, Calif., 2004 (4th round). **Signed by:** Don Lyle.

Lofgren comes from a strong line of athletes at Serra High that includes Barry Bonds, Jim Fregosi, Gregg Jefferies and Patriots quarterback Tom Brady. Lofgren was a standout two-way player in high school, and most clubs liked his bat better than his arm. The Indians were in the minority, and after putting a clause in his $650,000 bonus contract that said he could DH in his 2004 debut, they have him focused solely on pitching now. Lofgren has power stuff, beginning with a heavy 93-94 mph fastball that peaks at 96. His changeup has developed into an effective weapon. He just needs to find a reliable breaking ball to become a quality starter. Lofgren throws a curveball, but it's inconsistent and he struggles to command it. He may scrap the curve and try a slider in 2006. An aggressive competitor, he has adjusted his mechanics to get more leverage and downhill plane to the plate. He has the stuff, makeup and savvy to move quickly. He'll begin 2005 in high Class A.

Year	Club (League)	Class	W	L	ERA	G	GS	CG	SV	IP	H	R	ER	HR	BB	SO	AVG
2004	Burlington (Appy)	R	0	0	6.05	9	9	0	0	22	25	16	15	4	13	23	.294
2005	Lake County (SAL)	A	5	5	2.81	18	18	0	0	93	73	31	29	6	43	89	.218
MINOR LEAGUE TOTALS			5	5	3.43	27	27	0	0	115	98	47	44	10	56	112	.233

12 JOHN DRENNEN OF

Born: Aug. 26, 1986. **B-T:** L-L. **Ht.:** 5-11. **Wt.:** 185. **Drafted:** HS—San Diego, 2005 (1st round supplemental). **Signed by:** Jason Smith.

Drennen was one of the most coveted high school hitters in the 2005 draft. He's a product of San Diego's Rancho Bernardo High, which has produced more premium prospects than any other prep program in the nation over the last decade. Scouts says Drennen resembles former Bronco Danny Putnam, who went to Stanford and was drafted 36th overall by Oakland in 2004. Both Drennen (who went 33rd overall last June and signed for $1 million) and Putnam have compact builds, powerful bats and gamer makeup. Though he isn't physically imposing, Drennen is strong and the ball jumps off his bat. He has plus bat speed with good extension through his swing. He's still pull-conscious against righthanders, though he will use the entire field against lefties. He's a slightly above-average runner and gets good jumps in the outfield, but his arm is well-below-average. The Indians will keep him primarily in center field until he plays himself out of the position, but he'll probably wind up in left field. He recovered from a slow start in his pro debut at Rookie-level Burlington to hit .306 with four homers in August. He'll spend his first full season at low Class A Lake County.

Year	Club (League)	Class	AVG	G	AB	R	H	2B	3B	HR	RBI	BB	SO	SB	OBP	SLG
2005	Burlington (Appy)	R	.238	51	168	24	40	7	1	8	29	18	37	6	.325	.435
MINOR LEAGUE TOTALS			.238	51	168	24	40	7	1	8	29	18	37	6	.325	.435

13 RAFAEL PEREZ LHP

Born: May 15, 1982. **B-T:** L-L. **Ht.:** 6-3. **Wt.:** 180. **Signed:** Dominican Republic, 2002. **Signed by:** Rene Gayo.

After winning a Rookie-level Dominican Summer League title in 2002 and Rookie-level Appalachian League pitcher-of-the-year honors in 2003, the lefthander formerly known as Hanlet Ramirez experienced a rough introduction to full-season ball in 2004. As he grew acclimated to the culture and more familiar with hitters in the States, Perez came into his own last season, helping pitch Akron to the Eastern League crown. He has electric stuff, including a 92-94 mph fastball with outstanding late life. He battled command problems with his fastball early in his career, simply because it has so much natural movement. As he fills out his lanky frame, his velocity should increase. Perez' slider grades out as the best in the system and features exceptional bite. His changeup improved in 2005, though it's not very reliable and thus he still profiles as a reliever. As he adds more mass to his lanky frame, his velocity is likely to increase. A breakout candidate, he'll start 2006 back in Double-A.

Year	Club (League)	Class	W	L	ERA	G	GS	CG	SV	IP	H	R	ER	HR	BB	SO	AVG
2002	Indians West (DSL)	R	7	1	0.96	13	13	1	0	75	58	14	8	3	16	81	.208
2003	Burlington (Appy)	R	9	3	1.70	13	12	0	0	69	56	23	13	1	16	63	.220
2004	Lake County (SAL)	A	7	6	4.85	23	22	0	0	115	121	75	62	9	47	99	.277
	Kinston (Car)	A	0	0	11.49	1	1	0	0	5	10	6	6	1	2	3	.435
2005	Kinston (Car)	A	8	5	3.36	14	14	0	0	78	54	33	29	6	32	48	.194
	Akron (EL)	AA	4	3	1.75	15	8	0	1	67	53	22	13	5	12	46	.215
MINOR LEAGUE TOTALS			35	18	2.89	79	70	1	1	408	352	173	131	25	125	340	.232

14 TONY SIPP LHP

Born: July 12, 1983. **B-T:** L-L. **Ht.:** 6-0. **Wt.:** 185. **Drafted:** Clemson, 2004 (45th round). **Signed by:** Tim Moore.

Sipp plummeted to the 45th round of the 2004 draft after his agent scared off teams with excessive bonus demands, but area scout Tim Moore persuaded the Indians that Sipp was worth following over the summer. He performed well in the Cape Cod League and earned a $130,000 bonus, and he has overmatched hitters in pro ball. He moved from the rotation into the bullpen after a mid-2005 promotion to high Class A and flourished. Sipp spent his college career as a two-way player and didn't focus on pitching before last year, but the lack of innings hasn't deterred his development. He creates excellent deception in his delivery with outstanding extension, and his 89-93 mph fastball explodes on hitters. His fastball has late, tailing action. His slider has emerged as a plus pitch, and he also has made strides with his changeup. If he were willing to trust it more, he would have the repertoire to start again. The Indians want to move him quickly as a reliever, and will start him in Double-A this year and could promote him to Triple-A for the second half.

Year	Club (League)	Class	W	L	ERA	G	GS	CG	SV	IP	H	R	ER	HR	BB	SO	AVG
2004	Mahoning Valley (NY-P)	A	3	1	3.16	10	10	0	0	43	33	23	15	5	13	74	.212
2005	Lake County (SAL)	A	4	1	2.22	13	12	0	0	69	47	19	17	5	19	71	.196
	Kinston (Car)	A	2	2	2.66	22	5	0	2	47	34	19	14	4	23	59	.205
MINOR LEAGUE TOTALS			9	4	2.60	45	27	0	2	159	114	61	46	14	55	204	.203

15 ANDREW BROWN   RHP

Born: Feb. 17, 1981. **B-T:** R-R. **Ht.:** 6-6. **Wt.:** 230. **Drafted:** HS—Trinity Christian Academy, Jacksonville, 1999 (6th round). **Signed by:** Marco Paddy (Braves).

Brown has been involved in two high-profile trades. The first sent him from the Braves to the Dodgers as part of a package for Gary Sheffield in January 2002. When Milton Bradley wore out his welcome with Cleveland, Los Angeles acquired Bradley in exchange for Brown and Franklin Gutierrez in April 2004. Brown was a top prospect in the Dodgers system before missing almost the entire 2003 season with elbow problems. He also sat out 2000 recovering from Tommy John surgery, though he has been healthy since joining the Indians. Brown moved to the bullpen last year, where his effortless 92-97 mph fastball and power slider work well and he no longer has to worry about honing his changeup. While there were concerns about Brown's mental toughness, he was much more aggressive coming out of the bullpen. He struggled with his delivery early in 2005 until Buffalo pitching coach Ken Rowe helped him stay more upright so he can just drop and drive toward home plate. The results were encouraging as he posted a 1.43 ERA and allowed just 12 hits in his final 31 innings. Brown's maximum velocity comes on high fastballs, and he sometimes took that to the extreme, getting too far underneath the ball. He'll be in the mix for a spot in the big league bullpen, but might need further seasoning in Triple-A.

Year	Club (League)	Class	W	L	ERA	G	GS	CG	SV	IP	H	R	ER	HR	BB	SO	AVG
1999	Braves (GCL)	R	1	1	2.34	11	11	0	0	42	40	15	11	4	16	57	.247
2000	Did not play—Injured																
2001	Jamestown (NY-P)	A	3	4	3.92	14	12	0	0	64	50	29	28	5	31	59	.215
2002	Vero Beach (FSL)	A	10	10	4.11	25	24	1	0	127	97	63	58	13	62	129	.215
2003	Jacksonville (SL)	AA	0	0	0.00	1	1	0	0	1	0	0	0	0	0	1	.000
2004	Jacksonville (SL)	AA	1	3	4.02	8	8	0	0	40	36	23	18	5	14	58	.235
	Buffalo (IL)	AAA	1	0	0.00	1	1	0	0	5	4	0	0	0	3	4	.222
	Akron (EL)	AA	3	6	4.66	17	17	0	0	77	66	44	40	7	36	67	.234
2005	Buffalo (IL)	AAA	4	2	3.36	49	0	0	4	70	52	28	26	7	19	81	.204
MINOR LEAGUE TOTALS			23	26	3.81	126	74	1	4	427	345	202	181	41	181	456	.222

16 NICK PESCO   RHP

Born: Sept. 17, 1983. **B-T:** R-R. **Ht.:** 6-6. **Wt.:** 200. **Drafted:** Cosumnes River (Calif.) JC, 2002 (25th round). **Signed by:** Don Lyle.

The Indians aren't afraid to spend on draft-and-follows. They gave Sean Smith $1.1 million in 2002, the same year they drafted Pesco in the 25th round. He got the same amount a year later and has established himself as one of the top righthanders in the system. Pesco struggled with his command through the first half of 2005 and his velocity varied throughout the year, forcing him to learn how to compete without his best stuff. He usually pitches at 90-94 mph, though his fastball dipped into the upper 80s at times. His changeup, the best in the system, has deceptive downward movement. His slider became an effective weapon as he added more tilt and increased power to the pitch. Consistency is his greatest challenge, and he still needs to improve his stamina. Pesco will move up a level to Double-A, where he'll anchor the staff with his close friend and top prospect Adam Miller.

Year	Club (League)	Class	W	L	ERA	G	GS	CG	SV	IP	H	R	ER	HR	BB	SO	AVG
2003	Burlington (Appy)	R	3	1	1.82	13	13	0	0	54	36	16	11	0	22	55	.188
2004	Lake County (SAL)	A	6	7	3.91	21	21	0	0	106	96	49	46	10	30	97	.245
	Akron (EL)	AA	1	0	0.00	1	1	0	0	5	3	0	0	0	1	10	.188
	Kinston (Car)	A	1	2	3.21	3	3	0	0	14	15	9	5	0	4	12	.283
2005	Kinston (Car)	A	11	10	3.82	27	26	0	0	153	168	77	65	15	39	101	.281
MINOR LEAGUE TOTALS			22	20	3.44	65	64	0	0	333	318	151	127	25	96	275	.254

17 CODY BUNKELMAN   RHP

Born: Feb. 6, 1985. **B-T:** R-R. **Ht.:** 6-3. **Wt.:** 210. **Drafted:** Itasca (Minn.) JC, 2004 (6th round). **Signed by:** Les Pajari.

When the Indians drafted Bunkelman out of Itasca (Minn.) Community College, he was a relatively unknown commodity with a raw power arm. Even he was caught off guard when the Indians selected him in 2004's sixth round, but he was so impressive in predraft workouts that they felt they couldn't wait any longer. A star wide receiver at Chippewa Falls (Wis.) High, he was limited to just two games on the gridiron at Itasca because of a foot injury. While he's still raw on the mound, Bunkelman has made impressive strides and could move quickly. He's equipped with a heavy 95 mph fastball and complements it with a wipeout slider. His slider command has improved to the point where he'll use it in any count. His changeup lags behind his other two offerings and will determine whether he winds up as a starter or reliever. For now, he's the most physical starter in the system. Scouts compare his lower half to that of Mark Prior, as Bunkelman has strong legs and huge calves. He repeats his delivery and has great balance and good deception. He'll begin the season in high Class A.

Year	Club (League)	Class	W	L	ERA	G	GS	CG	SV	IP	H	R	ER	HR	BB	SO	AVG
2004	Burlington (Appy)	R	2	1	6.53	17	0	0	0	30	32	26	22	3	11	23	.260
2005	Lake County (SAL)	A	5	5	4.09	16	16	0	0	79	75	43	36	5	39	61	.251
MINOR LEAGUE TOTALS			7	6	4.76	33	16	0	0	110	107	69	58	8	50	84	.254

18 J.D. MARTIN   RHP

Born: Jan. 2, 1983. **B-T:** R-R. **Ht.:** 6-4. **Wt.:** 180. **Drafted:** HS—Ridgecrest, Calif., 2001 (1st round). **Signed by:** Jason Smith.

The Indians had four picks before the second round of the 2001 draft and spent the first three on pitchers. Dan Denham has been inconsistent and Alan Horne didn't sign, and while Martin has been the best thus far, elbow problems have delayed his progress. He went 24-9 in his first two-plus seasons before being shut down in July 2003 with a strained ligament. He avoided surgery at that point and finished strong in 2004, only to further hurt his elbow and require Tommy John surgery last July. Martin's arsenal improved significantly over the last two years. He throws two- and four-seam fastballs, a cutter, a changeup and a curveball that has ranked as the best in the system for a while. As good as his true 12-6 curveball is, his cutter has developed into his best weapon. Lean and wiry, Martin could add more velocity to his 89-91 mph fastball if he can add more weight on his frame. Durability and stamina always have clouded Martin's projection, and those concerns were only magnified after surgery. After his rehabilitation, he'll begin the season in extended spring training and is scheduled to join Mahoning Valley when camp breaks in June.

Year	Club (League)	Class	W	L	ERA	G	GS	CG	SV	IP	H	R	ER	HR	BB	SO	AVG
2001	Burlington (Appy)	R	5	1	1.38	10	10	0	0	46	26	9	7	3	11	72	.164
2002	Columbus (SAL)	A	14	5	3.90	27	26	0	0	138	141	76	60	12	46	131	.266
2003	Kinston (Car)	A	5	3	4.28	16	16	0	0	86	95	50	41	7	30	57	.281
2004	Buffalo (IL)	AAA	0	0	10.80	1	1	0	0	5	9	6	6	1	2	2	.375
	Kinston (Car)	A	11	10	4.39	25	25	2	0	148	139	75	72	15	41	98	.258
2005	Akron (EL)	AA	3	1	2.38	10	10	0	0	57	42	17	15	3	8	63	.201
MINOR LEAGUE TOTALS			38	20	3.77	89	88	2	0	480	452	233	201	41	138	423	.251

19 JENSEN LEWIS   RHP

Born: Sept. 26, 1983. **B-T:** R-R. **Ht.:** 6-0. **Wt.:** 180. **Drafted:** Vanderbilt, 2005 (3rd round). **Signed by:** Scott Barnsby.

The Tribe first drafted Lewis out of high school in the 33rd round in 2002, but the righthander opted for Vanderbilt, where he emerged as a third-rounder three years later. After signing for $375,000, he saw his fastball velocity improve during his pro debut. Despite pitching 152 innings between the spring and summer, he still was strong at the end, throwing in the low 90s more consistently than ever while at Mahoning Valley. Whether the quicker fastball is a better fastball is debatable, because he tends to get better life when he works in the high 80s. Much like former Commodores teammate Jeremy Sowers, Lewis is an extremely savvy pitcher. He can add and subtract velocity from his fastball, and he commands it with precision. His best secondary pitch is his changeup, with good sink and the same easy arm action as his fastball. His slider still needs work. It's short and has late bite, but not enough depth. He does a very good job of throwing strikes and locating his pitches, but he must remember not to rush his delivery, which causes him to leave the ball up in the zone. He's athletic and profiles as a third or fourth starter. One Indians official called him the quiet Sowers' nemesis because Lewis has a gregarious personality—his dream job outside of baseball is cooking alongside Emeril Lagasse or being a big league play-by-play announcer. He's ticketed for low Class A to begin 2006, and he has the polish to advance quickly.

Year	Club (League)	Class	W	L	ERA	G	GS	CG	SV	IP	H	R	ER	HR	BB	SO	AVG
2005	Mahoning Valley (NY-P)	A	4	2	3.20	13	11	0	0	59	58	24	21	6	11	59	.253
MINOR LEAGUE TOTALS			4	2	3.20	13	11	0	0	59	58	24	21	6	11	59	.253

20

EDWARD MUJICA

RHP

Born: May 10, 1984. **B-T:** R-R. **Ht.:** 6-2. **Wt.:** 180. **Signed:** Venezuela, 2001. **Signed by:** Luis Aponte.

Mujica's pro career got off to an inauspicious start when he strained his elbow during his 2002 debut in the Rookie-level Venezuelan Summer League. He didn't miss much time, however, and he took off last year when the Indians made him a full-time closer. He led the system with 24 regular-season saves and recorded four more in the Eastern League playoffs. Mujica brings power stuff with a 93-94 mph fastball and an 86-87 mph slider. He goes right after hitters, and the Indians rave about his fearlessness and short memory. His control is remarkable, as he issued just seven walks in 60 innings last season. He needs to be more effective against lefthanders, who hit .309 against him in Double-A, and coming up with an offspeed pitch might do the trick. Mujica will have a chance to close in Triple-A this year, putting him on the doorstep to Cleveland, an unlikely scenario just two years back.

Year	Club (League)	Class	W	L	ERA	G	GS	CG	SV	IP	H	R	ER	HR	BB	SO	AVG
2002	San Felipe (VSL)	R	2	0	1.78	10	5	0	1	30	22	7	6	0	5	18	.202
2003	Burlington (Appy)	R	2	6	4.36	14	10	0	0	56	57	31	27	3	20	41	.275
2004	Lake County (SAL)	A	7	7	4.65	26	19	1	2	124	130	77	64	18	32	89	.278
2005	Kinston (Car)	A	1	0	2.08	25	0	0	14	26	17	6	6	3	2	32	.183
	Akron (EL)	AA	2	1	2.89	27	0	0	10	34	36	11	11	2	5	33	.273
MINOR LEAGUE TOTALS			14	14	3.80	102	34	1	27	270	262	132	114	26	64	213	.260

21

DAN DENHAM

RHP

Born: Dec. 24, 1982. **B-T:** R-R. **Ht.:** 6-2. **Wt.:** 190. **Drafted:** HS—Antioch, Calif., 2001 (1st round). **Signed by:** Paul Cogan.

Denham was the first of four Indians first-rounders in 2001, signing for a $1.86 million bonus. Cleveland also signed Denham's younger brother Jason as an outfielder in the 13th round of the 2004 draft. Dan's development path has been frustrating at times, but he shows enough for scouts and club officials to maintain high expectations for his future. On his way up the ladder, Denham has needed to repeat each full-season level along the way. He had a tendency to overthrow early in his pro career, but he has good body control and a clean, compact delivery now. His fastball typically is clocked in the low 90s and peaked at 94 last season. Improving his cut fastball once again has elevated his prospect status. He still lacks deception, however, which was one of the main problems in Triple-A. With the addition of his cutter, Denham's arsenal of an above-average fastball, average curveball and slider is that much more dangerous. His changeup isn't effective, which could mean he'll wind up in the bullpen. He'll head back to Buffalo for 2006.

Year	Club (League)	Class	W	L	ERA	G	GS	CG	SV	IP	H	R	ER	HR	BB	SO	AVG
2001	Burlington (Appy)	R	0	4	4.40	8	8	0	0	31	30	21	15	5	26	31	.256
2002	Columbus (SAL)	A	9	8	4.76	28	28	0	0	125	123	76	66	7	65	109	.265
2003	Lake County (SAL)	A	5	2	3.08	14	14	0	0	73	75	28	25	4	22	63	.263
	Kinston (Car)	A	5	5	4.50	14	14	1	0	72	82	42	36	2	27	39	.298
2004	Kinston (Car)	A	7	4	4.18	13	13	0	0	71	73	34	33	6	29	62	.278
	Akron (EL)	AA	5	4	5.33	14	14	1	0	76	88	55	45	12	31	50	.295
2005	Akron (EL)	AA	9	7	3.15	21	21	1	0	140	115	55	49	6	30	108	.222
	Buffalo (IL)	AAA	0	2	10.80	3	3	0	0	10	16	13	12	3	8	6	.381
MINOR LEAGUE TOTALS			40	36	4.23	115	115	3	0	597	602	324	281	45	238	468	.266

JASON COOPER

OF

Born: Dec. 6, 1980. **B-T:** L-L. **Ht.:** 6-3. **Wt.:** 180. **Drafted:** Stanford, 2002 (3rd round). **Signed by:** Don Lyle.

Cooper was part of one of the most heralded prep lineups in recent memory, as Moses Lake (Wash.) High produced three picks in the first two rounds of the 1999 draft. Outfielder B.J. Garbe went fifth overall to the Twins and hasn't lived up to his billing, while catcher Ryan Doumit went to the Pirates in the second round and reached the majors in 2005. Cooper, who went four picks after Doumit to the Phillies, opted to attend Stanford but never got untracked in college as he was plagued by injuries. He's coming off his best professional season, setting career highs with 25 homers and a system-best 100 RBIs. He worked out in the offseason with Paul Konerko, who showed him a better way to load his hands into his swing. Cooper still struggles to make contact and may never hit for much of an average, but the Indians hope to utilize his power in some role. He needs to implement a more patient approach and do a better job of picking out pitches he can drive. Though he's a good athlete who was a backup punter on Stanford's football team, Cooper is a below-average left fielder. He hasn't thrown well since hurting his shoulder in college, and his route-running is suspect. With the depth of outfielders in the system, Cooper faces a make-or-break 2006.

Year	Club (League)	Class	AVG	G	AB	R	H	2B	3B	HR	RBI	BB	SO	SB	OBP	SLG
2002	Columbus (SAL)	A	.255	17	55	9	14	5	0	4	17	6	17	0	.339	.564
2003	Lake County (SAL)	A	.297	69	263	50	78	17	7	12	36	32	52	3	.385	.551
	Kinston (Car)	A	.307	61	218	36	67	17	2	9	36	25	46	3	.380	.528
2004	Akron (EL)	AA	.239	111	422	54	101	24	6	14	69	47	106	2	.321	.424
	Buffalo (IL)	AAA	.176	16	51	6	9	1	0	3	7	9	15	1	.300	.373
2005	Akron (EL)	AA	.254	57	205	41	52	9	2	11	42	30	67	3	.359	.478
	Buffalo (IL)	AAA	.257	73	253	43	65	12	3	14	58	23	76	1	.317	.494
MINOR LEAGUE TOTALS			.263	404	1467	239	386	85	20	67	265	172	379	13	.346	.485

23 KEVIN KOUZMANOFF   3B

Born: July 25, 1981. **B-T:** R-R. **Ht.:** 6-1. **Wt.:** 200. **Drafted:** Nevada, 2003 (6th round). **Signed by:** Don Lyle.

The Indians have been successful mining the University of Nevada for talent. Kouzmanoff, who transferred from Arkansas-Little Rock after his junior year, hopes to follow former Tribe prospect Ryan Church to the big leagues. Cleveland farmhands Chris Gimenez and Joe Inglett also hail from Nevada. Kouzmanoff doesn't have one tool that stands out. He's a throwback of sorts who makes all the routine plays at third base and religiously breaks down his swing searching for ways to improve. He's more upright at the plate than ever, maximizing the use of his lower half and making consistent hard, line-drive contact to all fields. He's a below-average runner who's an average defender at best, so his bat will have to carry him. In part because he signed as a college senior, Kouzmanoff has played just seven games above Class A despite being 24. He lost two months of development time last year when a back injury caused him to be shut down in June and July. The injury can be traced to his stint in the Arizona Fall League in 2004, when he fell into a dugout chasing a foul ball. His back bothered him throughout spring training and sapped much of his ability to drive the ball. He should be healthy to start this season in Double-A.

Year	Club (League)	Class	AVG	G	AB	R	H	2B	3B	HR	RBI	BB	SO	SB	OBP	SLG
2003	Mahoning Valley (NY-P)	A	.272	54	206	31	56	8	1	8	33	21	36	2	.342	.437
2004	Akron (EL)	AA	.208	7	24	3	5	1	1	1	6	2	5	0	.259	.458
	Lake County (SAL)	A	.330	123	473	74	156	35	5	16	87	44	75	5	.394	.526
2005	Mahoning Valley (NY-P)	A	.143	3	7	0	1	0	0	0	0	1	2	0	.250	.143
	Kinston (Car)	A	.339	68	254	47	86	20	4	12	58	24	51	3	.401	.591
MINOR LEAGUE TOTALS			.315	255	964	155	304	64	11	37	184	92	169	10	.380	.520

24 JAKE DITTLER   RHP

Born: Nov. 24, 1982. **B-T:** R-R. **Ht.:** 6-4. **Wt.:** 220. **Drafted:** HS—Henderson, Nev., 2001 (2nd round). **Signed by:** Doug Baker.

Another early-round pitching pick from the 2001 draft, Dittler jumped ahead of first-rounders J.D. Martin and Dan Denham by 2003, but two mediocre seasons in Double-A later have him heading in the wrong direction. The most frustrating part is that he still shows quality stuff. He has a heavy fastball that sits in the low 90s and has been clocked as high as 95 mph. His curveball is a plus pitch at times and his changeup gives him a decent third pitch. Dittler doesn't have trouble finding the strike zone, but he has been hittable because his command isn't as good as his control. He can lose the release point on his curveball, which results in vulnerable pitches up in the strike zone. Though Dittler led the system in innings last year, his stamina became an issue by midseason. He lost too much weight and lost velocity on his fastball, though he bounced back by the end of the year through a stringent conditioning program. He'll get his first taste of Triple-A this season.

Year	Club (League)	Class	W	L	ERA	G	GS	CG	SV	IP	H	R	ER	HR	BB	SO	AVG
2001	Burlington (Appy)	R	1	2	3.68	6	5	0	0	22	25	14	9	0	12	20	.287
2002	Columbus (SAL)	A	5	11	4.28	25	25	0	0	128	127	77	61	4	51	108	.257
2003	Lake County (SAL)	A	6	4	2.63	17	17	1	0	89	86	39	26	4	20	82	.244
	Kinston (Car)	A	5	1	2.40	8	8	1	0	49	47	17	13	2	11	32	.257
2004	Akron (EL)	AA	5	12	5.01	21	20	1	0	108	119	73	60	7	40	85	.278
2005	Akron (EL)	AA	10	9	3.64	28	27	0	0	173	187	94	70	12	61	107	.270
MINOR LEAGUE TOTALS			32	39	3.78	105	102	3	0	569	591	314	239	29	195	434	.264

25 JUSTIN HOYMAN   RHP

Born: April 17, 1982. **B-T:** R-R. **Ht.:** 6-3. **Wt.:** 195. **Drafted:** Florida, 2004 (2nd round). **Signed by:** Chris Jefts.

Though he's a pitcher, Hoyman is one of the best natural athletes in the system. He was a standout soccer player at Cocoa (Fla.) High, and he also punted for the football team before an opponent broke the femur in his right leg trying to block one of his kicks. The injury stunted the growth plates in his right leg, leaving it shorter than his left leg and leading to back problems while he was at Florida. Hoyman, who now wears inserts in his right shoe, was a second-round pick in 2004, making him the highest Gator selected since Brad Wilkerson was a first-rounder in 1998. Hoyman has pitched very well as a pro, but he has worked just 61 innings because he strained an elbow ligament and was shut down last May. He works consistently down in the zone with a sinking 89-92 mph fastball. While he topped out at 95 in college, he hadn't approached that number prior to his injury. Hoyman also throws a slurvy breaking ball and a deceptive changeup. He works fast and holds runners well. He pitched in instructional league after his elbow inflammation subsided and should be fully healthy for 2006. He has shown enough to advance to high Class A.

Year	Club (League)	Class	W	L	ERA	G	GS	CG	SV	IP	H	R	ER	HR	BB	SO	AVG
2004	Mahoning Valley (NY-P)	A	0	0	2.08	5	5	0	0	13	9	3	3	1	4	8	.191
2005	Lake County (SAL)	A	2	0	3.00	9	9	0	0	48	44	23	16	3	18	36	.242
MINOR LEAGUE TOTALS			2	0	2.80	14	14	0	0	61	53	26	19	4	22	44	.231

26 RYAN MULHERN   1B

Born: Nov. 29, 1980. **B-T:** R-R. **Ht.:** 6-2. **Wt.:** 195. **Drafted:** South Alabama, 2003 (11th round). **Signed by:** Chris Jefts.

Cleveland's 2005 Lou Boudreau Award winner as its minor league player of the year, Mulhern established his bona fides as a power hitter long ago. He led national juco hitters with 28 homers at Trinidad State (Colo.) CC in 2000, then set a South Alabama career mark with 43 longballs in three seasons. He hit just 12 homers in his first 162 pro games before exploding for 32 in 2005. He made some adjustments to his swing last year—he's not nearly as long or pull-happy as he was in college—and they paid off. He's now more focused on hitting to the middle of the field and driving balls. He made adjustments to get his hands inside pitches better, generating more backspin and carry. Mulhern has decent strike-zone discipline. His only setback last year came when he was hit in the face with a pitch in May, causing him to miss four weeks. There's some concern on pitchers tying him up on inside fastballs, but like Kevin Kouzmanoff, Mulhern is obsessive about breaking down film of his swing. Drafted as an outfielder, he's far from a finished product at first base, though he has improved there. He took advantage of Michael Aubrey being out of the Akron lineup in 2005, and Mulhern could win the first-base job in Triple-A this spring.

Year	Club (League)	Class	AVG	G	AB	R	H	2B	3B	HR	RBI	BB	SO	SB	OBP	SLG
2003	Mahoning Valley (NY-P)	A	.279	59	229	32	64	25	1	5	30	19	68	6	.340	.463
2004	Lake County (SAL)	A	.255	103	372	48	95	28	1	7	42	32	87	3	.319	.392
2005	Kinston (Car)	A	.321	45	159	32	51	11	0	17	48	19	50	2	.395	.711
	Akron (EL)	AA	.311	67	244	40	76	18	3	15	46	28	64	4	.386	.594
MINOR LEAGUE TOTALS			.285	274	1004	152	286	82	5	44	166	98	269	15	.353	.508

27 NICK WEGLARZ   OF

Born: Dec. 16, 1987. **B-T:** L-L. **Ht.:** 6-3. **Wt.:** 215. **Drafted:** HS—Stevensville, Ontario, 2005 (3rd round). **Signed by:** Les Pajari.

The first Canadian high school player drafted in 2005, Weglarz went in the third round and signed for $435,000. Scouts said he was the best power hitter Canada has produced since the Braves made Scott Thorman a first-round pick in 2000. However, Weglarz' profile more closely resembles that of another Canadian, Justin Morneau, for the size and raw power in his bat. Weglarz left Burlington before the season ended to play for Canada's junior national team, helping it win a bronze medal at the Pan-Am Junior Championships in Mexico. He has long arms and solid bat speed with good leverage. The Tribe worked to make fundamental adjustments in his swing in instructional league, getting his hands further back to get maximum effort from his swing, which he tended to cut off through the zone. Weglarz' bat will have to carry him. He's a below-average runner and was drafted as a first baseman, though he spent his pro debut in right field. His range and arm weren't bad but may not be enough to stick there for the long term. Weglarz is considered a bit of a project, but at 17 he was the youngest player in the Appalachian League last summer. He'll probably start 2006 in extended spring before joining Mahoning Valley in June.

Year	Club (League)	Class	AVG	G	AB	R	H	2B	3B	HR	RBI	BB	SO	SB	OBP	SLG
2005	Burlington (Appy)	R	.231	41	147	22	34	11	0	2	13	17	42	2	.313	.347
MINOR LEAGUE TOTALS			.231	41	147	22	34	11	0	2	13	17	42	2	.313	.347

28 SCOTT LEWIS   LHP

Born: Sept. 26, 1983. **B-T:** B-L. **Ht.:** 6-0. **Wt.:** 190. **Drafted:** Ohio State, 2004 (3rd round). **Signed by:** Bob Mayer.

Lewis' commitment to Ohio State scared teams off him in the 2001 draft, though the

Angels took a flier on him in the 33rd round and made a run at him. As a Buckeyes sophomore, he struck out 16 and 20 in consecutive starts and looked like a sure first-rounder for 2004. He blew out his elbow late that spring, however, and needed Tommy John surgery. Lewis was back on the mound 11 months after the operation, and the Indians saw enough to take him in 2004's third round and sign him for $460,000. While he showed signs of regaining his pre-injury form in his pro debut—topping out at 92 mph and showing good secondary pitches—Lewis took a step back in 2005. Cleveland handled him carefully and kept him on tight pitch counts at Mahoning Valley, but he came down with tightness in his bicep after just three outings and missed six weeks. He totaled just 16 innings for the summer. Lewis has a clean, effortless delivery and has a very deceptive release point. He's added depth and power to his slurvy breaking ball, which has morphed from a plus curveball in college to a faster pitch with 11-to-5 break. He needs to work on his changeup, which is fringe-average at best. Lewis will pitch in low Class A this year as the Indians hope he can have a completely healthy season.

Year	Club (League)	Class	W	L	ERA	G	GS	CG	SV	IP	H	R	ER	HR	BB	SO	AVG
2004	Mahoning Valley (NY-P)	A	0	2	5.09	3	3	0	0	5	5	3	3	0	1	13	.250
2005	Mahoning Valley (NY-P)	A	0	1	4.59	7	6	0	0	16	13	8	8	2	6	24	.224
MINOR LEAGUE TOTALS			0	3	4.71	10	9	0	0	21	18	11	11	2	7	37	.231

29 MATT WHITNEY   3B

Born: Feb. 13, 1984. **B-T:** R-R. **Ht.:** 6-4. **Wt.:** 190. **Drafted:** HS—Palm Beach Gardens, Fla., 2002 (1st round). **Signed by:** Jim Gabella.

Whitney was one of three Indians picks before the second round of the 2002 draft. While righthander Jeremy Guthrie and second baseman Micah Schilling have been extreme disappointments, it's too early to put Whitney in the same category even though he hasn't gotten past low Class A. He broke his left leg while playing basketball at spring training in 2003, which cost him the entire season and limited him to DH duties in 2004. The break required two surgeries, and his development has been circuitous ever since. He returned to low Class A last season, where he played third base extensively for the first time in three years. He has a solid approach at the plate, producing power to all fields. He showed the same explosiveness and fluid, rhythmic approach as he did as an amateur after building up strength in his lower half again. He has plus arm strength and good actions at the hot corner, and scouts rated him as a solid-average defender in 2005. While most of his draft class has passed him by, Whitney will make his long-awaited high Class A debut this season.

Year	Club (League)	Class	AVG	G	AB	R	H	2B	3B	HR	RBI	BB	SO	SB	OBP	SLG
2002	Burlington (Appy)	R	.286	45	175	33	50	12	1	10	33	18	49	5	.359	.537
	Columbus (SAL)	A	.111	6	18	0	2	0	0	0	0	3	4	0	.238	.111
2003	Did not play—Injured															
2004	Lake County (SAL)	A	.256	55	195	21	50	11	0	5	31	23	81	0	.347	.390
2005	Lake County (SAL)	A	.242	74	277	38	67	7	0	6	27	34	64	0	.332	.332
MINOR LEAGUE TOTALS			.254	180	665	92	169	30	1	21	91	78	198	5	.341	.397

30 CARLTON SMITH   RHP

Born: Jan. 23, 1986. **B-T:** L-R. **Ht.:** 6-1. **Wt.:** 200. **Drafted:** Okaloosa-Walton (Fla.) CC, D/F 2004 (21st round). **Signed by:** Scott Barnsby/Chuck Ricci.

The Indians took Smith's older brother Corey with the 26th overall pick in the 2000 draft. Corey ranked No. 1 on this list in 2002 but stalled and was traded to the Padres for another disappointing first-round pick, Jake Gautreau, in February 2005. Carlton had much less fanfare as an amateur, going in the 21st round in 2004 and signing as a draft-and-follow after spending a year at Okaloosa-Walton (Fla.) CC. There were significant questions about his older brother's makeup, but there are no such issues with Carlton's aptitude and willingness to respond to instruction. Smith throws two- and four-seam fastballs, usually sitting in the low 90s and topping out at 93 mph. While he locates his fastball well on the right side of the plate, he's not as effective pitching to the other corner. His late-breaking slider has the potential to be an above-average pitch with good depth and sharpness, and he's also developing a changeup. His mechanics are clean, though he still has somewhat of an upright finish and needs to work on his balance and separation to get the most out of his delivery. Smith had surgery to repair the meniscus in his right knee near the end of his debut but will be ready for spring training. He likely will spend 2006 at Mahoning Valley.

Year	Club (League)	Class	W	L	ERA	G	GS	CG	SV	IP	H	R	ER	HR	BB	SO	AVG
2005	Burlington (Appy)	R	0	2	4.77	9	9	0	0	28	30	16	15	3	5	25	.261
MINOR LEAGUE TOTALS			0	2	4.76	9	9	0	0	28	30	16	15	3	5	25	.261

COLORADO
ROCKIES

BY **TRACY RINGOLSBY**

The Rockies' rebuilding began in earnest in 2005. While enduring their fifth straight losing season and tying the Pirates for the worst record in the National League, they used a franchise-record 19 rookies, including nine from last year's top 30 list. Rookies made more starts (584) and appearances (942) for Colorado than for any other team.

Clint Barmes took over at shortstop and emerged as a rookie-of-the-year favorite before he fell down a flight of stairs and broke his left collarbone. Jeff Francis joined revitalized Aaron Cook and Jason Jennings to give the Rockies three homegrown arms at the front of the rotation. Third baseman Garrett Atkins, right fielder Brad Hawpe and center fielder Cory Sullivan all became regulars, with varying degrees of success, with only catcher J.D. Closser a disappointment. Marcos Carvajal and Scott Dohmann had their moments pitching in relief.

Though the influx of talent in Colorado drained the system of much of its depth at the upper levels, the Rockies do have more prospects on the verge of contributing. First baseman/outfielder Ryan Shealy, right-hander Ryan Speier and outfielder Ryan Spilborghs all could play roles for the Rockies in 2006. So too could infielder Omar Quintanilla, acquired in a midseason trade with the Athletics.

Most of Colorado's next wave of impact talent spent 2005 at high Class A Modesto, one of the two affiliates to make the postseason. Third baseman Ian Stewart and shortstop Troy Tulowitzki are elite players and the organization's top two prospects.

GEORGE BOLKOVICH

Other standouts include righthanders Ubaldo Jimenez and Juan Morillo, catcher Chris Iannetta and shortstop Matt Macri.

Scouting director Bill Schmidt and his staff turned in another promising draft in 2005, starting with Tulowitzki. Expected to go to the Mariners with the No. 3 overall pick before the draft, he fell to the Rockies at No. 7. Righthander Chaz Roe (supplemental first round) asserted himself as one of the system's best pitching prospects, and a pair of middle-rounders starred in the Rookie-level Pioneer League. Infielder Corey Wimberly (sixth) followed up an NCAA Division I batting title with a pro crown by hitting .381, while righty Andrew Johnston (ninth) used a heavy sinker to tie a league mark with 18 saves.

The Rockies' Latin American scouting department continues to thrive under the guidance of Rolando Fernandez. Dominicans Franklin Morales, Jimenez, Morillo, Samuel Deduno and Manuel Corpas all have flashed mid- to upper-90s fastballs. Australian righty Shane Lindsay, another hard thrower, ranked as the top prospect in the short-season Northwest League. After failing miserably by trying to import free-agent pitching—the Rockies lavished $172 million in contracts for Mike Hampton and Denny Neagle, who went 40-51 for Colorado—they're trying to find a different solution.

TOP 30 PROSPECTS

1. Ian Stewart, 3b
2. Troy Tulowitzki, ss
3. Franklin Morales, lhp
4. Chaz Roe, rhp
5. Ubaldo Jimenez, rhp
6. Chris Iannetta, c
7. Juan Morillo, rhp
8. Ryan Shealy, 1b
9. Chris Nelson, ss
10. Dexter Fowler, of
11. Omar Quintanilla, ss/2b
12. Matt Macri, ss
13. Shane Lindsay, rhp
14. Jeff Baker, 3b
15. Seth Smith, of
16. Jim Miller, rhp
17. Jeff Salazar, of
18. Samuel Deduno, rhp
19. Joe Koshansky, 1b
20. Ryan Spilborghs, of
21. Ching-Lung Lo, rhp
22. Corey Wimberly, inf
23. Andrew Johnston, rhp
24. Ryan Speier, rhp
25. Manuel Corpas, rhp
26. Luis Gonzalez, lhp
27. Ryan Mattheus, rhp
28. Jason Van Kooten, ss/2b
29. Joe Gaetti, of
30. Matt Miller, of

ORGANIZATION OVERVIEW

General manager: Dan O'Dowd. **Farm director:** Bill Geivett. **Scouting director:** Bill Schmidt.

2005 PERFORMANCE

Class	Team	League	W	L	Pct.	Finish*	Manager
Majors	Colorado	National	67	95	.414	15th (16)	Clint Hurdle
Triple-A	Colorado Springs Sky Sox	Pacific Coast	65	78	.455	15th (16)	Marv Foley
Double-A	Tulsa Drillers	Texas	75	65	.536	3rd (8)	Tom Runnells
High A	Modesto Nuts	California	72	67	.518	5th (10)	Stu Cole
Low A	Asheville Tourists	South Atlantic	71	67	.514	10th (16)	Joe Mikulik
Short-season	Tri-City Dust Devils	Northwest	36	40	.474	5th (8)	Ron Gideon
Rookie	Casper Rockies	Pioneer	38	38	.500	t-4th (8)	P.J. Carey
OVERALL 2005 MINOR LEAGUE RECORD			357	355	.501	14th (30)	

*Finish in overall standings (No. of teams in league).

ORGANIZATION LEADERS

BATTING
*Minimum 250 at-bats
*AVG	Wimberly, Corey, Casper	.381
R	Miller, Tony, Tulsa	102
H	Miller, Matt, Asheville/Modesto	170
TB	Koshansky, Joe, Asheville/Tulsa	294
	Miller, Matt, Asheville/Modesto	294
2B	Spilborghs, Ryan, Colorado Springs/Tulsa	46
3B	Three tied at	8
HR	Koshansky, Joe, Asheville/Tulsa	38
RBI	Koshansky, Joe, Asheville/Tulsa	115
BB	Miller, Tony, Tulsa	87
SO	Davies, Michael, Modesto	145
SB	Wimberly, Corey, Casper	36
*OBP	Wimberly, Corey, Casper	.427
*SLG	Gaetti, Joe, Modesto	.605

PITCHING
#Minimum 75 innings
W	Nin, Sandy, Modesto/Tulsa	14
L	Hampson, Justin, Colorado Springs	13
#ERA	Ulloa, Enmanuel, Tulsa	2.38
G	Miller, Jim, Modesto/Tulsa	64
CG	Asahina, Jon, Tulsa	4
	Nin, Sandy, Modesto/Tulsa	4
SV	Miller, Jim, Modesto/Tulsa	34
IP	Asahina, Jon, Tulsa	170
BB	Morillo, Juan, Asheville/Modesto	78
SO	Morillo, Juan, Asheville/Modesto	144

BEST TOOLS

Best Hitter for Average	Ian Stewart
Best Power Hitter	Ian Stewart
Best Strike-Zone Discipline	Chris Iannetta
Fastest Baserunner	Corey Wimberly
Best Athlete	Chris Nelson
Best Fastball	Juan Morillo
Best Curveball	Ubaldo Jimenez
Best Slider	Steven Register
Best Changeup	Mike Esposito
Best Control	Jon Asahina
Best Defensive Catcher	Chris Iannetta
Best Defensive Infielder	Troy Tulowitzki
Best Infield Arm	Troy Tulowitzki
Best Defensive Outfielder	Jeff Salazar
Best Outfield Arm	Dexter Fowler

PROJECTED 2009 LINEUP

Catcher	Chris Iannetta
First Base	Todd Helton
Second Base	Chris Nelson
Third Base	Ian Stewart
Shortstop	Troy Tulowitzki
Left Field	Matt Holliday
Center Field	Dexter Fowler
Right Field	Brad Hawpe
No. 1 Starter	Aaron Cook
No. 2 Starter	Jeff Francis
No. 3 Starter	Franklin Morales
No. 4 Starter	Chaz Roe
No. 5 Starter	Jason Jennings
Closer	Brian Fuentes

LAST YEAR'S TOP 20 PROSPECTS

1. Ian Stewart, 3b	11. Clint Barmes, ss
2. Chris Nelson, ss	12. Dexter Fowler, of
3. Jeff Francis, lhp	13. Garrett Atkins, 3b
4. Chin-Hui Tsao, rhp	14. J.D. Closser, c
5. Ubaldo Jimenez, rhp	15. Ryan Shealy, 1b
6. Juan Morillo, rhp	16. Chris Narveson, lhp
7. Jeff Baker, 3b	17. Jim Miller, rhp
8. Seth Smith, of	18. Matt Macri, 3b/2b
9. Jeff Salazar, of	19. Brad Hawpe, of
10. Jayson Nix, 2b	20. Scott Dohmann, rhp

TOP PROSPECTS OF THE DECADE

Year	Player, Pos.	2005 Org.
1996	Derrick Gibson, of	Braves
1997	Todd Helton, 1b	Rockies
1998	Todd Helton, 1b	Rockies
1999	Choo Freeman, of	Rockies
2000	Choo Freeman, of	Rockies
2001	Chin-Hui Tsao, rhp	Rockies
2002	Chin-Hui Tsao, rhp	Rockies
2003	Aaron Cook, rhp	Rockies
2004	Chin-Hui Tsao, rhp	Rockies
2005	Ian Stewart, 3b	Rockies

TOP DRAFT PICKS OF THE DECADE

Year	Player, Pos.	2005 Org.
1996	Jake Westbrook, rhp	Indians
1997	Mark Mangum, rhp	Out of baseball
1998	Choo Freeman, of	Rockies
1999	Jason Jennings, rhp	Rockies
2000	*Matt Harrington, rhp	Fort Worth (Central)
2001	Jayson Nix, ss	Rockies
2002	Jeff Francis, lhp	Rockies
2003	Ian Stewart, 3b	Rockies
2004	Chris Nelson, ss	Rockies
2005	Troy Tulowitzki, ss	Rockies

*Did not sign.

ALL-TIME LARGEST BONUSES

Jason Young, 2000	$2,750,000
Troy Tulowitzki, 2005	$2,300,000
Chin-Hui Tsao, 1999	$2,200,000
Chris Nelson, 2004	$2,150,000
Ian Stewart, 2003	$1,950,000

MINOR LEAGUE DEPTH CHART

Colorado Rockies

Rank: 9

STRENGTH: Middle infield. That happens with back-to-back picks of shortstops in the first round.

WEAKNESS: Starting pitching. The Rockies' top arms are either very young, injury prone or not performing up to expectations.

*Depth charts prepared by **John Manuel** and **Chris Kline**. Numbers in parentheses indicate prospect rankings.*

LF
Seth Smith (15)
Joe Gaetti (29)
Jud Thigpen
Cole Garner
Sean Barker
Michael Paulk

CF
Dexter Fowler (10)
Jeff Salazar (17)
Tony Miller
Jordan Czarnecki
Choo Freeman

RF
Ryan Spilborghs (20)
Matt Miller (30)
Daniel Carte

3B
Ian Stewart (1)
Jeff Baker (14)
Corey Slavik

SS
Troy Tulowitzki (2)
Chris Nelson (9)
Omar Quintanilla (11)
Matt Macri (12)
Jason Van Kooten (28)
Radames Nazario

2B
Corey Wimberly (22)
Jayson Nix
Jonathan Herrera
Luis Guance
Eric Young Jr.

1B
Ryan Shealy (8)
Joe Koshansky (19)

C
Chris Iannetta (6)
Alvin Colina
Neil Wilson
James Sweeney

RHP

Starters	Relievers
Chaz Roe (4)	Juan Morillo (7)
Ubaldo Jimenez (5)	Jim Miller (16)
Shane Lindsay (13)	Andrew Johnston (23)
Samuel Deduno (18)	Ryan Speier (24)
Ching-Lung Lo (21)	Manuel Corpas (25)
Ryan Mattheus (27)	Steven Register
Sandy Nin	Eduardo Sierra
Zach Simons	Ramon Ramirez
Jon Asahina	
Mike Esposito	

LHP

Starters	Relievers
Franklin Morales (3)	Luis Gonzalez (26)
Zach Parker	Josh Newman
	Brandon Durden
	Aaron Marsden

DRAFT ANALYSIS
2005

Best Pro Debut: INF Corey Wimberly (6) led the Rookie-level Pioneer League with a .381 average and 107 hits while also stealing 36 bases. RHP Andrew Johnston (9) tied a Pioneer League record with 18 saves and had a 1.06 ERA. 1B Chris Cook (36) led the PL in homers, while RHP Chaz Roe (1) made the all-star team after going 5-2, 4.17 with 55 strikeouts in 50 innings.

Best Athlete: Not only does Troy Tulowitzki (1) have the defensive skills to play shortstop, but he also has enough offensive ability that the Brewers considered taking him fifth overall to fill their hole at third base. Tulowitzki's makeup is outstanding as well. OF Daniel Carte (2) was BA's Summer College Player of the Year in 2004, when he became the sixth player in Cape Cod League history to reach double figures in homers and steals.

Best Pure Hitter: Though Wimberly won the NCAA Division I batting title (.462 at Alcorn State), Tulowitzki gets the nod.

Best Raw Power: Long Beach State's Blair Field, a pitcher's best friend, helped mask Tulowitzki's power in college. But he has the swing and strength to hit 25-30 homers annually in the majors. Often compared to Bobby Crosby, his predecessor as 49ers shortstop, Tulowitzki has more pop.

Fastest Runner: Wimberly is the fastest player in the system. A switch-hitter, he can go from home to first in 3.9 seconds from the left side and 4.0 from the right.

Best Defensive Player: Tulowitzki has more arm strength and range than Crosby. Chris Frey's (11) instincts in center field remind Colorado of Cory Sullivan.

Carte

Best Fastball: For sheer velocity, it's Roe, who pitches in the low 90s and tops out at 95. For movement, it's Johnston, who has a 92-93 mph sinker that's difficult to lift.

Best Breaking Ball: Longtime minor league manager Tom Kotchman compared Roe's curveball to former Angels star Mike Witt's.

Most Intriguing Background: RHP Sean Ruthven's (27, Dick), unsigned RHP Rod Scurry's (39, Rod) and unsigned 3B Jeremy Farrell's (41, John) fathers all pitched in the big leagues. The elder Ferrell is now Cleveland's farm director. RHP Josh Sullivan (5) is a former Auburn quarterback.

Closest To The Majors: A quadriceps pull slowed Tulowitzki in his first summer as a pro, but he's not going to waste much time getting to Colorado.

Best Late-Round Pick: Travis Becktel (15) or SS Radhames Nazario (22), a defensive standout.

The One Who Got Away: SS Reese Havens (29) might have been a first-round pick if he didn't have a seven-figure asking price. He should make an immediate impact at South Carolina. RHP Kyle Hancock (3) left the organization almost immediately after signing, but Colorado hopes he'll return.

Assessment: The Rockies were elated to get Tulowitzki with the No. 7 pick after it looked like the Mariners were zeroing in on him at No. 3.

2004 Hamstring injuries and a lackluster performance dimmed SS Chris Nelson's (1) star in 2005. But this deep draft still has OF Seth Smith (2), C Chris Iannetta (4), SS Matt Macri (5), 1B Joe Koshansky (6), RHP Jim Miller (8) and OF Dexter Fowler (14). **GRADE: B+**

2003 3B Ian Stewart (1) represents a good draft by himself. RHP Ryan Mattheus (19), a $700,000 draft-and-follow, has started slowly. **GRADE: B+**

2002 LHP Jeff Francis (1) is better than his Coors Field-marred numbers would indicate after his rookie season. 3B Jeff Baker (4) and 1B Ryan Shealy (11) all have a chance to become big league regulars. **GRADE: C+**

2001 2B Jayson Nix (1) has regressed after creating optimism earlier in his career and has fallen off the Rockies prospect list. OF Cory Sullivan (7) is as good as this draft gets. **GRADE: D**

Draft analysis prepared by Jim Callis. Numbers in parentheses indicate draft rounds.

IAN
STEWART

BILL MITCHELL

Born: April 5, 1985.
Ht.: 6-3. **Wt.:** 205.
Bats: L. **Throws:** R.
Drafted: HS—Garden Grove, Calif., 2003 (1st round).
Signed by: Todd Blyleven.

In their first 11 drafts, the Rockies took a position player in the first round just once— Todd Helton in 1995. Since then, they have taken Stewart with the 10th overall pick in 2003, followed by shortstops Chris Nelson in 2004 and Troy Tulowitzki in 2005. Before signing for $1.95 million, Stewart starred as an amateur, winning a bronze medal with Team USA at the 2002 World Junior Championships and leading La Quinta (Calif.) High to a No. 3 national ranking in 2003. He ranked as the No. 1 prospect in the Rookie-level Pioneer League in 2003 and No. 2 in the low Class A South Atlantic League in 2004 before facing adversity for the first time in 2005. A pulled hamstring forced him to spend April in extended spring training, and a sprained right wrist cost him a week in June. But he reinforced Colorado's confidence in his potential by rallying to hit .299-11-52 in his final 60 games at high Class A Modesto to rate as the fourth-best prospect in the California League. He batted .333-3-12 in 12 Arizona Fall League games before reinjuring his wrist sliding into second base.

Stewart should be a quality run producer in the middle of a big league lineup. He has quick hands that allow him to wait on pitches, and his pitch recognition is strong. He's a natural hitter with bat speed, strength and a slight uppercut which generates loft power. He can drive balls out of the park to the opposite field. He handles lefthanded pitching better than most lefty hitters, in part because his father is a southpaw and has thrown him batting practice for years. Stewart is driven to be an elite player, and he makes no qualms that he expects to become not only an all-star, but also a Gold Glover. He has average speed and plus arm strength.

Stewart's swing can get a little long, but his bat is quick enough to compensate. He did have some problems early on in 2005 when pitchers fed him a steady diet of breaking balls and offspeed pitches. He showed the ability to adjust and took advantage of that pitching pattern later in the season. Stewart's third-base defense needs the most work. He made impressive strides in 2004 but seemed to level off in 2005. He reacts a little slowly and has trouble with hard-hit balls directly at him. If Garrett Atkins builds on his rookie season in Colorado, it's possible that Stewart could move to right field, a shift some scouts thought was inevitable when he was in high school. However, he has improved and won't change positions any time soon.

Stewart didn't suffer any structural damage when he reinjured his wrist and is expected to be 100 percent by spring training. He'll move to Double-A Tulsa and could reach Triple-A Colorado Springs by midseason if he stays healthy. If all goes according to plan, his bat could earn him a trip to the majors in September, but a more likely scenario is a mid-2007 arrival at Coors Field. He should follow in Helton's footsteps and become the organization's second homegrown star.

Year	Club (League)	Class	AVG	G	AB	R	H	2B	3B	HR	RBI	BB	SO	SB	OBP	SLG
2003	Casper (Pio)	R	.317	57	224	40	71	14	5	10	43	29	54	4	.401	.558
2004	Asheville (SAL)	A	.319	131	505	92	161	31	9	30	101	66	112	19	.398	.594
2005	Modesto (Cal)	A	.274	112	435	83	119	32	7	17	86	52	113	2	.353	.497
MINOR LEAGUE TOTALS			.302	300	1164	215	351	77	21	57	230	147	279	25	.382	.551

2 TROY TULOWITZKI

SS

Born: Oct. 10, 1984. **B-T:** R-R. **Ht.:** 6-3. **Wt.:** 205. **Drafted:** Long Beach State, 2005 (1st round). **Signed by:** Todd Blyleven.

Tulowitzki has been compared to Bobby Crosby since succeeding him at shortstop for Long Beach State. The seventh overall pick in the 2005 draft, he signed for $2.3 million. He went straight to high Class A, and the only negative in his pro debut was a torn quadriceps that limited him to 22 games. Most scouts think Tulowitzki is slightly ahead of Crosby, the 2004 American League rookie of the year, at the same stage of their careers and a better fit at shortstop. Tulowitzki has the stroke, strength and bat speed to hit 25-30 homers annually. Though he's big, he doesn't sacrifice any athleticism. He has above-average range and arm strength, and his exceptional instincts allow him to extend his range. Tulowitzki sometimes can get out of control and too aggressive at the plate. He could control the strike zone a little better. A broken hamate bone in the spring and the torn quad restricted his development in 2005. Despite the injury, Tulowitzki should be able to handle the jump to Double-A for his first full season. He could be Colorado's starter by 2007.

Year	Club (League)	Class	AVG	G	AB	R	H	2B	3B	HR	RBI	BB	SO	SB	OBP	SLG
2005	Modesto (Cal)	A	.266	22	94	17	25	6	0	4	14	9	18	1	.343	.457
MINOR LEAGUE TOTALS			.266	22	94	17	25	6	0	4	14	9	18	1	.343	.457

3 FRANKLIN MORALES

LHP

Born: Jan. 24, 1986. **B-T:** L-L. **Ht.:** 6-0. **Wt.:** 170. **Signed:** Dominican Republic, 2002. **Signed by:** Francisco Cartaya.

The Rockies brought Morales along slowly in his first full season in the United States. Signed out of the Dominican Republic at 16, he worked in relief early in 2005 before moving into the low Class A Asheville rotation. He improved greatly from his 7.62 ERA at Rookie-level Casper in his U.S. debut. Morales has a live arm. His fastball ranges from 92-98 mph and sits at 94-95. Working from a three-quarters arm slot, he shows a good curveball and an average changeup already. He's tough to run on. He demonstrates a flair and confidence beyond his youth on the mound. Like most young pitchers, Morales lacks consistency. He tends to overthrow when he gets in trouble, costing him control. He needs to throw more strikes, especially when he faces more advanced hitters who will wait him out. He has the basics of a good delivery, though he doesn't always maintain it. Morales will open 2006 in high Class A. The Rockies have shown a willingness to be patient with young Latin pitchers, but they think he has a chance to be special and could accelerate his timetable.

Year	Club (League)	Class	W	L	ERA	G	GS	CG	SV	IP	H	R	ER	HR	BB	SO	AVG
2003	Rockies (DSL)	R	9	3	2.18	13	13	0	0	78	58	24	19	0	34	69	.211
2004	Casper (Pio)	R	6	4	7.62	15	15	1	0	65	92	61	55	8	39	82	.338
2005	Asheville (SAL)	A	8	4	3.08	21	15	0	1	96	73	40	33	6	48	108	.214
MINOR LEAGUE TOTALS			23	11	4.02	49	43	1	1	240	223	125	107	14	121	259	.251

4 CHAZ ROE

RHP

Born: Oct. 9, 1986. **B-T:** R-R. **Ht.:** 6-5. **Wt.:** 180. **Drafted:** HS—Lexington, Ky., 2005 (1st round supplemental). **Signed by:** Scott Corman.

Roe had a chance to follow in the footsteps of his father Donald and play football at Kentucky, but he decided to focus on baseball after having two concussions in high school. The Twins and Braves considerd him in the late first round of the 2005 draft, but he slipped to the Rockies with the 32nd pick. He signed for $1.025 million and made the Pioneer League all-star team in his debut. Roe has a low-90s fastball with hard downward movement and tops out at 95. He has the makings of a down-right nasty curveball, which one national crosschecker called the best he'd seen from a high school pitcher in the last decade. Loose and athletic, he has the ideal build for future projection. His work ethic and feel for the game stood out in Rookie ball. Roe's curveball is still inconsistent and gets slurvy at times. He also needs to polish up his changeup. He's also working on his control, which is hindered when he rushes his delivery and loses balance. He can get too aggressive at times. If everything clicks, Roe can be a front-of-the-rotation starter. He'll probably open his first full season in low Class A.

Year	Club (League)	Class	W	L	ERA	G	GS	CG	SV	IP	H	R	ER	HR	BB	SO	AVG
2005	Casper (Pio)	R	5	2	4.17	12	12	0	0	50	31	25	23	2	36	55	.175
MINOR LEAGUE TOTALS			5	2	4.17	12	12	0	0	50	31	25	23	2	36	55	.175

5 UBALDO JIMENEZ RHP

STEVE MOORE

Born: Jan. 22, 1984. **B-T:** R-R. **Ht.:** 6-4. **Wt.:** 200. **Signed:** Dominican Republic, 2001. **Signed by:** Rolando Fernandez.

Jimenez was on a roll in high Class A in 2004 when the Rockies discovered the beginnings of a stress fracture in his right shoulder. He started slowly in 2005 but earned a promotion to Double-A and adapted well by season's end. Jimenez is a pure power pitcher capable of reaching 96-98 mph, and he worked consistently around 92-94 in 2005. His 12-to-6 curveball is a swing-and-miss pitch, and he has the confidence to throw it when he's behind in the count. He flashes a plus changeup at times. His confidence has grown with his mastery of English. Jimenez' mechanics had to be overhauled to get him back into a compact motion directed at the plate. He still needs to improve his command and his changeup. Though his shoulder woes appear behind him, questions about his health and his delivery prompt some to project him as a future closer. He'll return to Double-A to begin 2006, but could finish the season in Colorado. He has shown too much potential as a starter to consider moving him to the bullpen at this time.

Year	Club (League)	Class	W	L	ERA	G	GS	CG	SV	IP	H	R	ER	HR	BB	SO	AVG
2001	Rockies (DSL)	R	2	5	4.88	13	13	0	0	48	41	36	26	1	44	36	.225
2002	Casper (Pio)	R	3	5	6.53	14	14	0	0	62	72	46	45	6	29	65	.288
	Rockies (DSL)	R	2	0	0.00	3	3	0	0	18	10	1	0	0	6	25	.152
2003	Asheville (SAL)	A	10	6	3.46	27	27	0	0	154	129	67	59	11	67	138	.230
	Visalia (Cal)	A	1	0	0.00	1	0	0	0	5	3	0	0	0	1	7	.176
2004	Visalia (Cal)	A	4	1	2.23	9	9	1	0	44	29	15	11	1	12	61	.184
2005	Modesto (Cal)	A	5	3	3.98	14	14	0	0	72	61	35	32	5	40	78	.232
	Tulsa (TL)	AA	2	5	5.43	12	11	0	0	63	58	40	38	12	31	53	.243
MINOR LEAGUE TOTALS			29	25	4.07	93	91	1	0	467	403	240	211	36	230	463	.232

6 CHRIS IANNETTA C

BILL MITCHELL

Born: April 8, 1983. **B-T:** R-R. **Ht.:** 5-11. **Wt.:** 195. **Drafted:** North Carolina, 2004 (4th round). **Signed by:** Jay Matthews.

North Carolina has produced big league catchers Dwight Lowry, Scott Bradley, B.J. Surhoff, Matt Merullo and Jesse Levis in the last three decades, and Iannetta is the next in line. Rockies pitcher Aaron Cook raved about his receiving ability while on a rehab assignment at Modesto. Iannetta played in the Futures Game in his first full season. Iannetta has a compact swing and good pitch recognition, and his bat has been a pleasant surprise. He should hit for average with gap power. His calling card is his defense. He has soft hands, good agility and a plus arm with a strong release. His poise and leadership enable him to help pitchers work through tough situations. Iannetta can tie himself up when he gets technical with his approach. He tried to play with a broken left hand late in the season, but he couldn't grip the bat properly and his performance suffered. Iannetta will stay in Double-A to start 2006, but he should be able to make another midseason jump. There's no one standing in his way to becoming Colorado's starting catcher in 2007.

Year	Club (League)	Class	AVG	G	AB	R	H	2B	3B	HR	RBI	BB	SO	SB	OBP	SLG
2004	Asheville (SAL)	A	.314	36	121	23	38	5	1	5	17	27	29	0	.454	.496
2005	Modesto (Cal)	A	.276	74	261	51	72	17	3	11	58	45	61	1	.381	.490
	Tulsa (TL)	AA	.233	19	60	7	14	3	1	2	11	8	15	0	.329	.417
MINOR LEAGUE TOTALS			.281	129	442	81	124	25	5	18	86	80	105	1	.395	.482

7 JUAN MORILLO RHP

STEVE MOORE

Born: Nov. 5, 1983. **B-T:** R-R. **Ht.:** 6-3. **Wt.:** 190. **Signed:** Dominican Republic, 2001. **Signed by:** Rolando Fernandez.

The Rockies have developed Morillo cautiously, keeping him in Rookie and short-season leagues for his first four years. He made his full season debut in 2005 and advanced to high Class A after six weeks. Morillo fires easy, effortless gas, and the White Sox reportedly clocked him at 104 mph in 2004. He regularly pops 100 mph and pitches at 95-97. Durable and resilient, he never has missed a start as a pro. He may light up radar guns, but Morillo is primarily a one-pitch pitcher. He still needs to learn to command his fastball and improve his secondary pitches. He has a hard slider and a changeup, but he doesn't have enough command to throw them with confidence. His slider reaches the upper 80s, but he'll try to throw it too hard and lose break. He led the California League in walks, and even when he throws strikes he often leaves his pitches up in the zone. Because he only has one reliable pitch, several scouts foresee Morillo moving to the bullpen, where he could develop into a big league closer. He'll stay in the rotation in Double-A in 2006.

Year	Club (League)	Class	W	L	ERA	G	GS	CG	SV	IP	H	R	ER	HR	BB	SO	AVG
2001	Rockies (DSL)	R	2	4	6.81	14	7	0	0	36	35	31	27	1	38	20	.248
2002	Rockies (DSL)	R	1	5	4.75	14	11	0	0	55	49	44	29	1	33	43	.230
2003	Casper (Pio)	R	1	6	5.91	15	15	0	0	64	85	73	42	6	40	44	.318
2004	Tri-City (NWL)	A	3	2	2.98	14	14	0	0	66	56	34	22	0	41	73	.226
2005	Asheville (SAL)	A	1	3	4.54	7	7	0	0	34	40	24	17	2	13	43	.290
	Modesto (Cal)	A	6	5	4.41	20	20	0	0	112	107	69	55	10	65	101	.258
MINOR LEAGUE TOTALS			14	25	4.71	84	74	0	0	367	372	275	192	20	230	324	.262

8 RYAN SHEALY   1B

Born: Aug. 29, 1979. **B-T:** R-R. **Ht.:** 6-5. **Wt.:** 240. **Drafted:** Florida, 2002 (11th round). **Signed by:** Mike Day.

The Rockies took Shealy in the fifth round out of high school in 1998 but didn't sign him until drafting him again as a college senior. He won two home run titles in his first three pro seasons and would have challenged for the Triple-A Pacific Coast League crown in 2005 if not for his big league time. Shealy has tremendous strength and makes pitchers pay if they miss on the inner third of the plate. He has the patience to work counts and is comfortable hitting the ball the other way. He has soft hands and has improved at first base. The last job for Shealy is to turn on pitches more regularly. Though he's a big man with limited range and speed, he has lost 30 pounds since spring training in 2005. Blocked at first base by Todd Helton, he hopes his work on conditioning and agility will make him an option as a corner outfielder. Coming off an inspiring showing with the Rockies, Shealy has earned a spot on the roster. Finding regular playing time will be a bigger challenge.

Year	Club (League)	Class	AVG	G	AB	R	H	2B	3B	HR	RBI	BB	SO	SB	OBP	SLG
2002	Casper (Pio)	R	.368	69	231	55	85	21	1	19	70	50	52	0	.497	.714
2003	Visalia (Cal)	A	.299	93	341	70	102	31	1	14	73	42	72	0	.391	.519
2004	Tulsa (TL)	AA	.318	132	469	88	149	32	3	29	99	61	123	1	.411	.584
2005	Colorado Springs (PCL)	AAA	.328	108	411	85	135	30	2	26	88	41	81	4	.393	.601
	Colorado (NL)	MLB	.330	36	91	14	30	7	0	2	16	13	22	1	.413	.473
MAJOR LEAGUE TOTALS			.330	36	91	14	30	7	0	2	16	13	22	1	.413	.473
MINOR LEAGUE TOTALS			.324	402	1452	298	471	114	7	88	330	194	328	5	.417	.594

9 CHRIS NELSON   SS

Born: Sept. 3, 1985. **B-T:** R-R. **Ht.:** 5-11. **Wt.:** 176. **Drafted:** HS—Decatur, Ga., 2004 (1st round). **Signed by:** Damon Iannelli.

The Orioles planned on taking Nelson with the eighth overall pick in 2004 until owner Peter Angelos mandated they choose a college pitcher. The Rockies gladly selected him at No. 9 and signed him for $2.15 million. He never got untracked in 2005 while battling groin and hamstring injuries. Nelson is a line-drive hitter with plus speed. The Rockies think he can hit 25-plus homers on an annual basis once he matures physically and develops lift in his swing. One of the best athletes in the system, he has the size, instincts, quick feet and arm to play shortstop. Nelson's plate discipline left something to be desired in 2005, robbing him of the ability to drive the ball with authority. He also developed a bit of a hitch in his throwing motion, a possible side effect after having Tommy John surgery prior to his senior year in high school. He didn't square up to the target on throws during the regular season and focused on correcting that during instructional league. Nelson profiles at shortstop, but so does Tulowitzki, who should beat him to Colorado. Nelson, who will open 2006 in high Class A, could move to second base or center field if needed.

Year	Club (League)	Class	AVG	G	AB	R	H	2B	3B	HR	RBI	BB	SO	SB	OBP	SLG
2004	Casper (Pio)	R	.347	38	147	36	51	6	3	4	20	20	42	6	.432	.510
2005	Asheville (SAL)	A	.241	79	315	51	76	13	3	3	38	25	88	7	.304	.330
MINOR LEAGUE TOTALS			.275	117	462	87	127	19	6	7	58	45	130	13	.346	.387

10   DEXTER FOWLER   OF

BILL MITCHELL

Born: March 22, 1986. **B-T:** B-R. **Ht.:** 6-4. **Wt.:** 173. **Drafted:** HS—Alpharetta, Ga., 2004 (14th round). **Signed by:** Damon Iannelli.

A projected second-round pick out of high school, Fowler slipped in the 2004 draft because he had the options of playing basketball at Harvard and baseball at Miami. The Rockies' strategy to take a 14th-round flier on him paid off when they freed up money by dealing Larry Walker at the 2004 trade deadline, then landed Fowler with a $925,000 bonus. Because he signed late, he didn't play in a pro game until last year. Compared to Andre Dawson and Andruw Jones for his raw talent and athleticism, Fowler had a solid debut, especially considering he began to switch-hit for the first time. His swing can get lengthy, tying him up at times and leading to strikeouts, but the natural righty still managed to bat .258 from the left side of the plate. Like most young players he has trouble with inside pitches but drives balls on the outer half to all fields. A talented athlete with fluid actions, Fowler still is filling out and figures to get stronger as he matures. He glides in the outfield, and his well above-average speed helps him project as a plus defensive center fielder in the future. His arm is just fringe average. He has a bright future, and the Rockies will try to follow a step-by-step approach knowing that his development will require patience. He'll play in low Class A this year.

Year	Club (League)	Class	AVG	G	AB	R	H	2B	3B	HR	RBI	BB	SO	SB	OBP	SLG
2005	Casper (Pio)	R	.273	62	220	43	60	10	4	4	23	27	73	18	.357	.409
MINOR LEAGUE TOTALS			.273	62	220	43	60	10	4	4	23	27	73	18	.357	.409

11   OMAR QUINTANILLA   SS/2B

Born: Oct. 24, 1981. **B-T:** L-R. **Ht.:** 5-9. **Wt.:** 190. **Drafted:** Texas, 2003 (1st round). **Signed by:** Tim Holt (Athletics).

Looking for a quality middle infielder, the Rockies jumped at the opportunity to pick up Quintanilla in the Joe Kennedy-Eric Byrnes trade last July. Quintanilla never had played above Double-A and was rushed to the majors after 13 Triple-A games because Colorado needed bodies. In a perfect world, he'd get at least a half-season of Triple-A seasoning in 2006, but he may earn a spot on the big league roster by default because of the Rockies' limited infield depth. A sparkplug on Texas' 2002 College World Series championship club, he has the makeup to handle the challenge if needed. A career .320 hitter in the minors, Quintanilla not only can hit for average but also can sting the ball into the gaps. Scouts like the way he uses the opposite field, though he got into trouble in the majors by becoming too pull-conscious, leading to problems with breaking pitches. He controls the strike zone and is aggressive because of the confidence he has in his ability to handle the bat. Quintanilla doesn't have the range teams look for at shortstop, but he makes plays thanks to his quick hands and strong instincts. He had no problem adapting to second base at the big league level. He has average speed and is a smart baserunner.

Year	Club (League)	Class	AVG	G	AB	R	H	2B	3B	HR	RBI	BB	SO	SB	OBP	SLG
2003	Vancouver (NWL)	A	.341	32	129	22	44	5	4	0	14	12	20	7	.401	.442
	Modesto (Cal)	A	.417	8	36	9	15	3	0	2	6	3	6	0	.462	.667
2004	Midland (TL)	AA	.351	23	94	20	33	10	0	2	20	10	9	2	.419	.521
	Modesto (Cal)	A	.314	108	452	75	142	32	5	11	72	37	54	1	.370	.480
2005	Midland (TL)	AA	.293	78	294	46	86	14	2	4	25	23	40	2	.347	.395
	Colorado Springs (PCL)	AAA	.346	13	52	14	18	3	2	1	7	3	8	0	.375	.538
	Colorado (NL)	MLB	.219	39	128	16	28	1	1	0	7	9	15	2	.270	.242
MAJOR LEAGUE TOTALS			.219	39	128	16	28	1	1	0	7	9	15	2	.270	.242
MINOR LEAGUE TOTALS			.320	262	1057	186	338	67	13	20	144	88	137	12	.375	.465

12   MATT MACRI   SS

Born: May 29, 1982. **B-T:** R-R. **Ht.:** 6-2. **Wt.:** 200. **Drafted:** Notre Dame, 2004 (5th round). **Signed by:** Scott Corman.

Macri was a two-way standout and a potential first-round draft choice out of high school, but he intended to fulfill his scholarship commitment to Notre Dame. The Twins still drafted him in the 17th round in 2001 as a backup plan in case No. 1 overall pick Joe Mauer didn't sign. Macri's career with the Fighting Irish was sidetracked by Tommy John surgery during his freshman year. He went undrafted as a sophomore-eligible in 2003, and went in the fifth round a year later because concerns about his bat arose after he hit .172 with wood in the Cape Cod League. He has answered those questions with two solid years as a pro. After using an inside-out swing in college, he has begun to turn on pitches and show budding power in the minors. He still strikes out too much, which may be his undoing at higher levels. A good athlete who earned Iowa Mr. Football honors in 2000, he has average speed and is one of the top defensive infielders in the system. Where he'll wind up remains in question. He played third base at Notre Dame and in his debut, but the Rockies are loaded at the hot corner, starting with No. 1 overall prospect Ian Stewart. As a result, Macri moved to shortstop in 2005, but Colorado's last two first-round picks (Chris Nelson and Troy Tulowitzki) are better suited for the position than he is. He has good hands, and while his arm action isn't smooth in the wake of his elbow surgery, he has plenty of arm strength. Macri is a true professional, working hard to improve and showing a very good feel for the game. His biggest problem as a pro has been staying healthy. He missed time in 2004 with plantar fasciitis in his foot, and again in 2005 with a sprained left wrist. He's ticketed for Double-A along with Stewart and Tulowitzki, so Macri could move to second base this year.

Year	Club (League)	Class	AVG	G	AB	R	H	2B	3B	HR	RBI	BB	SO	SB	OBP	SLG
2004	Tri-City (NWL)	A	.333	52	195	33	65	17	4	7	43	23	52	4	.410	.569
2005	Modesto (Cal)	A	.283	64	244	40	69	16	1	7	34	33	67	6	.381	.443
	Tulsa (TL)	AA	.000	1	3	1	0	0	0	0	0	1	0	0	.250	.000
MINOR LEAGUE TOTALS			.303	117	442	74	134	33	5	14	77	57	119	10	.393	.495

13 SHANE LINDSAY   RHP

Born: Jan. 25, 1985. **B-T:** R-R. **Ht.:** 6-1. **Wt.:** 205. **Signed:** Australia, 2003. **Signed by:** Phil Allen.

The first major Australian free agent signed by the Rockies, Lindsay emerged as the short-season Northwest League's top prospect in 2005. He led the league in strikeouts while ranking second in wins and third in ERA. He left the league a week early to pitch at the World Cup. After making so much progress, Lindsay received bad news about his shoulder during the offseason. An MRI exam in Australia revealed what the Rockies believed was a torn labrum, though they planned a further examination in January. If he needs surgery, he would miss the entire 2006 season. Lindsay is aggressive with his fastball, which sits at 91-92 mph. As a game goes on, his velocity will climb as high as 95-97 mph. He features a good spike curveball that he used with better judgment after throwing it too often in his shaky 2004 pro debut. His circle change should become a solid third pitch. Command issues were a major problem for Lindsay in his 2004 debut. A back problem led to bad mechanics that he since has ironed out, but like most of the Rockies' top arms he'll have to throw more strikes. His ability to locate his curve comes and goes. He's hesitant to throw his changeup, which he'll need to be a dominant starter. If Lindsay is healthy, his next challenge is to prove he can excel at the full-season level. But that's a big if.

Year	Club (League)	Class	W	L	ERA	G	GS	CG	SV	IP	H	R	ER	HR	BB	SO	AVG
2004	Casper (Pio)	R	1	1	6.75	17	0	0	0	21	22	24	16	1	19	31	.256
2005	Tri-City (NWL)	A	6	1	1.89	13	13	0	0	67	37	21	14	1	34	107	.163
MINOR LEAGUE TOTALS			7	2	3.07	30	13	0	0	88	59	45	30	2	53	138	.188

14 JEFF BAKER   3B

Born: June 21, 1981. **B-T:** R-R. **Ht.:** 6-2. **Wt.:** 210. **Drafted:** Clemson, 2002 (4th round). **Signed by:** Jay Matthews.

Baker is headed into the final year of a four-year, $2 million contract he signed as a fourth-rounder in 2002, after plummeting from first-round status because of his contract demands coupled with a poor history in wood bat leagues. Plagued by injuries, he never has played in more than 96 games in any of his three seasons as a pro. Problems with his left wrist limited him during his first two years, requiring three surgeries, and bad luck got the best of him in 2005. He started the year at third base as an emergency replacement for Garrett Atkins and would have returned to the big leagues when Clint Barmes went on the disabled list, but Baker was suffering from a deep bone bruise on his right thumb. A month later, he broke his left thumb when a batted ball struck him during batting practice. Clemson's all-time leader with 59 home run—breaking Matthew LeCroy's mark—Baker understands hitting and employs a solid approach. He stays back well on offspeed stuff and consistently drives the ball to the big part of the field. He doesn't have overwhelming raw power and isn't going to hit tape-measure shots, but he's a legitimate homer threat who smokes hard line drives. Strikeouts always have been a tradeoff for his power. He has played mostly third base, but he'll probably move to right field with Atkins in the big leagues and Ian Stewart coming up behind him. Baker has the speed and arm to handle the outfield and looked comfortable there during workouts last spring with big league coach Dave Collins. Baker likely will head back to Triple-A in 2006.

Year	Club (League)	Class	AVG	G	AB	R	H	2B	3B	HR	RBI	BB	SO	SB	OBP	SLG
2003	Asheville (SAL)	A	.289	70	263	44	76	17	0	11	44	30	79	4	.377	.479
2004	Visalia (Cal)	A	.330	72	267	60	88	23	1	11	64	47	70	1	.439	.547
	Tulsa (TL)	AA	.297	24	91	10	27	5	1	4	20	7	22	1	.343	.505
2005	Colorado (NL)	MLB	.211	12	38	6	8	4	0	1	4	5	12	0	.302	.395
	Colorado Springs (PCL)	AAA	.303	61	228	40	69	16	1	10	41	16	44	3	.348	.513
MAJOR LEAGUE TOTALS			.211	12	38	6	8	4	0	1	4	5	12	0	.302	.395
MINOR LEAGUE TOTALS			.306	227	849	154	260	61	3	36	169	100	215	9	.387	.512

15 SETH SMITH   OF

Born: Sept. 30, 1982. **B-T:** L-L. **Ht.:** 6-3. **Wt.:** 215. **Drafted:** Mississippi, 2004 (2nd round). **Signed by:** Damon Iannelli.

The Rockies have had success with quarterbacks giving up football for baseball, with Todd Helton and Matt Holliday as the prime examples. Now comes Smith, who served as Eli Manning's backup at Mississippi, though he never took a snap in his three years. Colorado was pleased to land him in the second round in 2004. He overmatched the Pioneer League in his pro debut but wasn't nearly as dominant in the hitter-friendly California League last year. Smith has a smooth swing and he stays inside the ball. He has to guard against getting power-conscious, a problem that caused some concerns during his junior year at Mississippi and caused him to slip out of the first round. He didn't control the strike zone very well in 2005. His homer output (nine) also was disappointing, but he did hit 45 doubles and should have more over-the-fence power as he matures as a hitter. Smith is a strong athlete who runs well underway but doesn't figure to be a basestealing threat. His arm is average, though he needs a lot of work defensively in the outfield. A center fielder in college, he played primarily in right field last year. The Rockies would like to see him show a better work ethic to address his shortcomings in Double-A this year.

Year	Club (League)	Class	AVG	G	AB	R	H	2B	3B	HR	RBI	BB	SO	SB	OBP	SLG
2004	Casper (Pio)	R	.369	56	233	46	86	21	3	9	61	25	47	9	.427	.601
	Tri-City (NWL)	A	.259	9	27	6	7	1	1	2	5	1	3	0	.276	.593
2005	Modesto (Cal)	A	.300	129	533	87	160	45	6	9	72	44	115	5	.353	.458
MINOR LEAGUE TOTALS			.319	194	793	139	253	67	10	20	138	70	165	14	.374	.504

16 JIM MILLER   RHP

Born: April 28, 1982. **B-T:** R-R. **Ht.:** 6-1. **Wt.:** 200. **Drafted:** Louisiana-Monroe, 2004 (8th round). **Signed by:** Damon Iannelli.

Miller went undrafted as a junior in 2003 at Louisiana-Monroe, and he turned down free-agent opportunities after starring at the National Baseball Congress World Series because he wanted to complete his mathematics degree. After graduating in 2004, he signed for $12,000 as an eighth-round pick and led the Northwest League in saves during his pro debut. He tallied 34 more to lead the system last year, when he was untouchable following a second-half promotion to Double-A. He can overpower hitters with a 93-95 mph fastball. It doesn't have much life, but he can blow his fastball by hitters up in the zone and locate it on both sides of the plate. He also uses a slider and an occasional changeup, though he hasn't shown the confidence to throw either consistently. Despite his success thus far, he'll have to refine a second pitch to use against more advanced hitters. If he can do that, he could reach Colorado by September.

Year	Club (League)	Class	W	L	ERA	G	GS	CG	SV	IP	H	R	ER	HR	BB	SO	AVG
2004	Tri-City (NWL)	A	1	1	0.97	34	0	0	17	37	21	6	4	1	11	65	.159
2005	Modesto (Cal)	A	1	3	3.78	48	0	0	25	48	39	22	20	3	17	68	.213
	Tulsa (TL)	AA	1	1	0.60	16	0	0	9	15	6	5	1	2	8	19	.118
MINOR LEAGUE TOTALS			3	5	2.26	98	0	0	51	100	66	33	25	6	36	152	.180

17 JEFF SALAZAR   OF

Born: Nov. 24, 1980. **B-T:** L-L. **Ht.:** 6-0. **Wt.:** 180. **Drafted:** Oklahoma State, 2002 (8th round). **Signed by:** Dar Cox.

An eighth-round senior sign like Jim Miller, Salazar narrowly missed a 30-30 season and led the South Atlantic League in homers and RBIs in his first full year as a pro in 2003. He reached Triple-A last year and continued to show flashes of being a total-package center fielder, but his previous consistency was missing. For the first time in pro ball, he struck out more than he walked. Salazar needs to learn to stay back on pitches and use the opposite field if he wants to reach his potential. A top-of-the-lineup candidate, he offers power and speed as well as good on-base and bunting ability. Defensively, he has excellent instincts and the confidence that's mandatory for a center fielder. His arm is below-average. He could prove to be a nice fit in Colorado, possibly by midseason. Cory Sullivan impressed the

Rockies with his hustle and defense as a rookie last year, but Salazar offers more upside.

Year	Club (League)	Class	AVG	G	AB	R	H	2B	3B	HR	RBI	BB	SO	SB	OBP	SLG
2002	Tri-City (NWL)	A	.235	72	268	38	63	5	4	4	21	47	43	10	.351	.328
2003	Asheville (SAL)	A	.284	129	486	109	138	23	4	29	98	77	74	28	.387	.527
	Visalia (Cal)	A	.000	1	5	1	0	0	0	0	0	0	0	0	.000	.000
2004	Visalia (Cal)	A	.347	75	314	79	109	18	9	13	44	38	33	17	.419	.586
	Tulsa (TL)	AA	.223	58	224	39	50	13	2	1	17	35	31	10	.331	.313
2005	Tulsa (TL)	AA	.278	69	266	47	74	13	2	6	35	44	49	12	.381	.410
	Colorado Springs (PCL)	AAA	.263	59	236	42	62	17	3	6	26	32	58	5	.349	.436
MINOR LEAGUE TOTALS			.276	463	1799	355	496	89	24	59	241	273	288	82	.373	.450

18 SAMUEL DEDUNO   RHP

Born: July 2, 1983. **B-T:** R-R. **Ht.:** 6-1. **Wt.:** 156. **Signed:** Dominican Republic, 2003. **Signed by:** Felix Feliz.

Deduno had an encouraging U.S. debut in 2004 and won his first five starts in 2005, then fell prey to inconsistency. Minor shoulder soreness sidelined him for much of May and June, and he lost eight of his final 11 decisions. Upon returning from the disabled list, he developed some bad habits with his mechanics. He started separating his hands too early, throwing off his timing and affecting his command and pitch quality. He got to the point where the only pitch he had confidence in throwing for strikes was his curveball. Deduno did make adjustments and got back on track in the Rockies' Dominican instructional league program. Besides his hard curveball, he also has a plus fastball that sits at 92-94 mph and has good cutting action. He can dominate hitters, averaging 12.4 strikeouts per nine innings over the past two seasons. To remain a starter, Deduno will have to make significant improvement to his changeup. He also needs to stop worrying about being too fine with his pitches and just let his natural stuff work for him. If he doesn't begin 2006 in high Class A, he should get there later in the season.

Year	Club (League)	Class	W	L	ERA	G	GS	CG	SV	IP	H	R	ER	HR	BB	SO	AVG
2003	Rockies (DSL)	R	3	4	2.47	12	12	0	0	69	53	26	19	1	26	61	.202
2004	Casper (Pio)	R	6	4	3.18	15	15	0	0	76	62	40	27	3	32	118	.219
2005	Asheville (SAL)	A	8	8	5.62	20	20	1	0	90	82	67	56	9	65	110	.248
MINOR LEAGUE TOTALS			17	16	3.90	47	47	1	0	235	197	133	102	13	123	289	.225

19 JOE KOSHANSKY   1B

Born: May 26, 1982. **B-T:** L-L. **Ht.:** 6-4. **Wt.:** 225. **Drafted:** Virginia, 2004 (6th round). **Signed by:** Jay Matthews.

Koshansky went undrafted after leading Virginia in homers and pitching wins as a junior in 2003, and responded by tearing up the Valley League that summer and winning Atlantic Coast Conference player-of-the-year honors in 2004. Since signing for $40,000 as a sixth-round pick, he has hit 50 homers in 198 pro games, including 38 to rank second in the minors last year. He did much of his damage at Asheville's McCormick Field, where the cozy right-field porch plays to the strengths of a 6-foot-4, 225-pound lefthanded slugger like Koshansky. He hit .355 with 25 homers in 61 games in Asheville, as compared to .227 with 11 homers in 59 road games in the South Atlantic League. There was some thought he was just an older hitter taking advantage of younger pitchers and his ballpark, and even the Rockies were somewhat skeptical. They resisted promoting him until late August, but when they did Koshansky held his own in a short stint in Double-A. He has huge lefthanded power, and though his swing can get long, he can catch up to good fastballs. He does strike out a lot but is willing to take a walk. Koshansky is a good defender at first base, with surprising agility for his size and a plus arm for his position. He is a well-below-average runner, however. He may be a lefty version of Ryan Shealy, and Koshansky could get a chance to further prove himself in Double-A this year.

Year	Club (League)	Class	AVG	G	AB	R	H	2B	3B	HR	RBI	BB	SO	SB	OBP	SLG
2004	Tri-City (NWL)	A	.234	66	239	41	56	18	0	12	43	31	84	1	.330	.460
2005	Asheville (SAL)	A	.291	120	453	92	132	31	1	36	103	53	122	6	.373	.603
	Tulsa (TL)	AA	.267	12	45	5	12	3	0	2	12	2	15	0	.292	.467
MINOR LEAGUE TOTALS			.271	198	737	138	200	52	1	50	158	86	221	7	.355	.548

20 RYAN SPILBORGHS   OF

Born: Sept. 5, 1979. **B-T:** R-R. **Ht.:** 6-1. **Wt.:** 190. **Drafted:** UC Santa Barbara, 2002 (7th round). **Signed by:** Billy Eppler.

Spilborghs was a two-time all-Big West Conference selection at UC Santa Barbara. He couldn't match Rockies farm director Bill Geivett's .412 average for the Gauchos in 1985, but Spilborghs hit .375 and set a school record with a 35-game hitting streak as a sophomore

in 2001. He didn't hit much in his first three years as a pro and looked more like an organizational player. He became more consistent with his approach in 2005 and took off, batting .340 between Double-A and Triple-A. He even earned a surprise one-day callup to
Colorado on July 15 and went 2-for-4 with an RBI against the Reds. Now the Rockies are
talking about him being a fourth outfielder in 2006. Spilborghs did a better job last year of
recognizing which pitches he can turn on. He's also willing to stay back and drive balls to
the opposite field. He's capable at all three spots, and enhances average arm strength with
a quick release and impressive accuracy.

Year	Club (League)	Class	AVG	G	AB	R	H	2B	3B	HR	RBI	BB	SO	SB	OBP	SLG
2002	Tri-City (NWL)	A	.230	71	261	34	60	11	1	4	34	29	61	11	.313	.326
2003	Asheville (SAL)	A	.281	119	434	78	122	22	2	15	61	63	96	10	.379	.445
2004	Visalia (Cal)	A	.259	125	444	59	115	26	3	8	57	64	98	8	.357	.385
2005	Tulsa (TL)	AA	.341	71	255	52	87	23	3	6	54	42	49	10	.435	.525
	Colorado (NL)	MLB	.500	1	4	0	2	0	0	0	1	0	1	0	.500	.500
	Colorado Springs (PCL)	AAA	.339	60	227	49	77	23	5	5	30	22	53	7	.405	.551
MAJOR LEAGUE TOTALS			.500	1	4	0	2	0	0	0	1	0	1	0	.500	.500
MINOR LEAGUE TOTALS			.284	446	1621	272	461	105	14	38	236	220	357	46	.375	.437

21 CHING-LUNG LO   RHP

Born: Aug. 20, 1985. **B-T:** R-R. **Ht.:** 6-6. **Wt.:** 190. **Signed:** Taiwan, 2001. **Signed by:** Kent
Blasingame.

The Rockies have been protective of Lo since signing him for $1.4 million out of Taiwan's
Kolo Yuan High, also the alma mater of Chin-Hui Tsao. That strategy hasn't paid off, as Lo
repeated low Class A last season and yet made little progress. He developed looseness in his
shoulder, and his fastball dropped from 94 mph at the end of spring training to 86 by the
end of the season. After not allowing him to throw his splitter in his first three years as a
pro, Colorado gave it back to him in 2005, but it didn't help much. His slider is still inconsistent, and he uses the splitter for the most part in lieu of a changeup. The one area in
which he did make notable progress was command, as he cut his walk rate per nine innings
from 4.3 to 2.8. Lo probably needs a third year in Asheville, which wouldn't be the worst
thing in the world because he's still just 20.

Year	Club (League)	Class	W	L	ERA	G	GS	CG	SV	IP	H	R	ER	HR	BB	SO	AVG
2002	Casper (Pio)	R	2	4	3.20	14	9	0	0	45	44	22	16	3	22	21	.246
2003	Tri-City (NWL)	A	3	7	2.85	14	14	0	0	76	66	27	24	1	27	48	.237
2004	Asheville (SAL)	A	4	3	5.05	17	9	0	1	62	70	49	35	9	30	49	.293
2005	Asheville (SAL)	A	7	9	5.65	24	24	1	0	121	148	90	76	23	38	91	.303
MINOR LEAGUE TOTALS			16	23	4.47	69	56	1	1	304	328	188	151	36	117	209	.277

22 COREY WIMBERLY   INF

Born: Oct. 26, 1983. **B-T:** B-R. **Ht.:** 5-8. **Wt.:** 180. **Drafted:** Alcorn State, 2005 (6th round).
Signed by: Damon Iannelli.

The first player drafted out of Alcorn State since the Blue Jays selected outfielder Kevin
Campbell in the 12th round in 1991, Wimberly made a strong impression with his speed
and versatility. His size and explosive speed prompted comparisons to Chone Figgins, whom
the Rockies signed as a fourth-rounder in 1997. Wimberly flies down the first-base line in
3.9 seconds form the left side and 4.0 from the right, making him the fastest player in the
system. He won two batting titles in 2005, leading NCAA Division I with a .462 average and
the Pioneer League with a .381 mark. A natural righthanded hitter, he didn't begin switch-
hitting until he got to Alcorn State and made the adjustment quickly. He still needs to work
on hitting the ball hard on the ground to best utilize his skills. He focuses on making contact and using the middle of the field, and he stays back on pitches well. Like Figgins,
Wimberly could be groomed as a super-utility player. He saw extensive action at third base,
second base and shortstop last summer, and also worked out in center field during instructional league. He's still raw defensively and made 22 errors in 67 games, but he has quick
hands and an average if erratic arm. He should move up to low Class A this year.

Year	Club (League)	Class	AVG	G	AB	R	H	2B	3B	HR	RBI	BB	SO	SB	OBP	SLG
2005	Casper (Pio)	R	.381	67	281	58	107	10	0	1	22	18	27	36	.427	.427
MINOR LEAGUE TOTALS			.381	67	281	58	107	10	0	1	22	18	27	36	.427	.427

23 ANDREW JOHNSTON   RHP

Born: April 20, 1984. **B-T:** R-R. **Ht.:** 6-5. **Wt.:** 205. **Drafted:** Missouri, 2005 (9th round). **Signed
by:** Mark Germann.

Johnston's sterling relief work helped Missouri to its best season since 1996 and continued after he signed for $72,500 as a ninth-round pick. He tied a Pioneer League record with 18 saves last summer while posting a 1.06 ERA. Johnston operated primarily with one pitch, but it's a nasty one: a power 92-94 mph sinker that's tough to pick up from his low three-quarters arm slot. He's a groundball machine who didn't allow a homer and had a 3.8 groundball/flyball ratio in his pro debut. He has a resilient arm that can handle multiple innings or appearances on consecutive days. Johnston backs up his sinker with a slider and changeup, but neither is trustworthy because he struggles to stay on top of them. He'll continue to develop in the minors as a closer, but he'll likely fit in as a middle reliever at the big league level. He'll jump to one of Colorado's Class A affiliates in 2006.

Year	Club (League)	Class	W	L	ERA	G	GS	CG	SV	IP	H	R	ER	HR	BB	SO	AVG
2005	Casper (Pio)	R	1	2	1.06	30	0	0	18	34	22	10	4	0	7	24	.171
MINOR LEAGUE TOTALS			1	2	1.06	30	0	0	18	34	22	10	4	0	7	24	.171

24 RYAN SPEIER
RHP

Born: July 24, 1979. **B-T:** R-R. **Ht.:** 6-7. **Wt.:** 200. **Signed:** NDFA/Radford, 2001. **Signed by:** Jay Matthews.

A feel-good story, Speier wasn't recruited out of high school and went undrafted after three years at Radford, where he went 8-14, 5.09. Following his junior season, Speier finally garnered the attention of scouts by setting a Cape Cod League record with 16 saves while not allowing a run all summer. He was inked for $10,000 as a free agent by area scout Jay Matthews, and he joined Jeff Baker and Cory Sullivan as rookies signed by Matthews on Colorado's 2005 Opening Day roster. Speier thrives on deception, stepping across his body and varying his slots from a funky three-quarters slot to a drop-down submarine look. His pure stuff is ordinary, consisting of an 88-90 mph fastball with life, a slider and a changeup. He struggled in the big leagues at the start of last year because he wasn't finishing off his delivery, leaving pitches up in the strike zone. He ironed out that flaw when he returned to the minors in May, though he still battled control issues in September with the Rockies. Like many righties who throw across their body, Speier can be very tough on righthanders but has trouble with lefties. They hit .367 off him in Triple-A and reached base at a .467 clip against him in the majors. Improving his changeup might solve that problem, and he also needs to hone the command of his fastball. He should spend most if not all of 2006 in the majors.

Year	Club (League)	Class	W	L	ERA	G	GS	CG	SV	IP	H	R	ER	HR	BB	SO	AVG
2001	Casper (Pio)	R	1	2	3.16	17	0	0	1	26	19	12	9	2	9	24	.196
2002	Asheville (SAL)	A	3	1	3.93	28	0	0	1	37	32	21	16	3	13	39	.235
	Salem (Car)	A	2	2	3.94	24	0	0	4	32	35	21	14	0	11	33	.285
2003	Visalia (Cal)	A	4	2	1.53	56	0	0	18	59	50	14	10	2	17	73	.226
2004	Tulsa (TL)	AA	3	1	2.04	61	0	0	37	62	33	14	14	3	25	70	.151
2005	Colorado Springs (PCL)	AAA	2	2	4.99	45	0	0	6	52	70	30	29	2	18	45	.327
	Colorado (NL)	MLB	2	1	3.65	22	0	0	0	25	26	12	10	0	13	10	.277
MAJOR LEAGUE TOTALS			2	1	3.65	22	0	0	0	25	26	12	10	0	13	10	.277
MINOR LEAGUE TOTALS			15	10	3.10	231	0	0	67	267	239	112	92	12	93	284	.237

25 MANUEL CORPAS
RHP

Born: Dec. 3, 1982. **B-T:** R-R. **Ht.:** 6-3. **Wt.:** 170. **Signed:** Panama, 1999. **Signed by:** Tim Ireland.

He has yet to spend a day above the Class A level, but Corpas received the Rockies' lone offseason promotion to the 40-man roster. His power fastball and strong finish in 2005 created fears that he could be targeted in the major league Rule 5 draft if left unprotected. Corpas regularly throws 95-97 mph from a low three-quarters slot. He has a tendency to get too low, slinging the ball at times. He creates better movement and sink on his fastball when he stays on top of the pitch. His second pitch, a slider, is more of a hard slurve. Corpas answered concerns about his command last year. He also did a good job of keeping the ball on the ground and in the park. His changeup is not a factor, which leaves Corpas destined for bullpen duty. If he can learn to repeat his arm slot and delivery, he has the potential to dominate in the late innings. He'll move up a level to Double-A.

Year	Club (League)	Class	W	L	ERA	G	GS	CG	SV	IP	H	R	ER	HR	BB	SO	AVG
2000	Venoco (VSL)	R	0	1	15.43	1	0	0	0	2	5	4	4	0	0	3	.385
2001	Rockies (DSL)	R	2	1	2.24	15	5	0	2	56	56	23	14	0	17	41	.248
2002	Casper (Pio)	R	2	4	5.73	29	0	0	2	33	37	24	21	4	18	42	.274
2003	Tri-City (NWL)	A	5	6	5.79	15	15	0	0	84	98	61	54	7	22	47	.292
2004	Asheville (SAL)	A	2	2	3.05	43	0	0	3	44	48	20	15	3	13	52	.267
2005	Modesto (Cal)	A	3	2	3.78	47	0	0	2	69	83	33	29	2	14	52	.299
MINOR LEAGUE TOTALS			14	16	4.27	150	20	0	9	289	327	165	137	16	84	237	.280

26 LUIS GONZALEZ
LHP

Born: Feb. 27, 1983. **B-T:** L-L. **Ht.:** 6-0. **Wt.:** 190. **Drafted:** HS—Melbourne, Fla., 2001 (11th round). **Signed by:** Doug Carpenter (Dodgers).

It would have been easy to slip through the cracks with Jacksonville, Baseball America's 2005 Minor League Team of the Year, but Gonzalez did get noticed after his performance out of the Suns bullpen—so much so that when the Dodgers didn't protect him on their 40-man roster, the Rockies took him in the major league Rule 5 draft. He has to stick on Colorado's big league roster throughout 2006, or else clear waivers and be offered back to Los Angeles for half his $50,000 draft price. An outfielder and a high school teammate of Brewers prospect Prince Fielder in high school, Gonzalez moved full-time to the mound as a pro. He diligently has crafted a three-pitch repertoire, highlighted by a 91-94 mph fastball. Gonzalez has a sturdy, durable frame and a simple delivery with some deception. He relies heavily on his fastball, which he spots well to all four quadrants of the strike zone. His 79-81 mph slider is an average offering that's effective against lefties. He has developed a slightly above-average changeup that has good fade against righties. Gonzalez has some feel for pitching, and when he gets on top of the ball, some life to his stuff. He struggled in his first taste of Triple-A in July, and will get another chance there in 2006. He profiles as a middle reliever or lefty specialist in the big leagues.

Year	Club (League)	Class	W	L	ERA	G	GS	CG	SV	IP	H	R	ER	HR	BB	SO	AVG
2001	Dodgers (GCL)	R	4	2	3.55	13	2	0	0	25	25	15	10	0	14	25	.248
2002	Great Falls (Pio)	R	0	1	7.71	4	3	0	0	12	18	12	10	1	5	15	.346
	Dodgers (GCL)	R	1	1	3.07	6	2	0	0	15	13	5	5	1	6	9	.245
2003	South Georgia (SAL)	A	2	2	3.30	19	0	0	3	30	25	13	11	2	11	31	.221
	Vero Beach (FSL)	A	2	3	1.48	21	0	0	3	30	25	6	5	0	11	19	.231
2004	Jacksonville (SL)	AA	1	3	4.73	45	1	0	0	65	73	41	34	9	47	66	.278
2005	Jacksonville (SL)	AA	7	2	2.21	41	0	0	7	61	35	17	15	1	34	46	.165
	Las Vegas (PCL)	AAA	0	1	9.31	10	0	0	0	10	13	10	10	3	11	10	.342
MINOR LEAGUE TOTALS			17	15	3.64	159	8	0	13	247	227	119	100	17	139	221	.241

27 RYAN MATTHEUS
RHP

Born: Nov. 10, 1983. **B-T:** R-R. **Ht.:** 6-3. **Wt.:** 220. **Drafted:** Sacramento CC, D/F 2003 (19th round). **Signed by:** Gary Wilson.

The Rockies selected Mattheus (pronounced Matthews) in the 34th round out of high school in 2002, and then again in the 19th round the following year out of Sacramento CC. One of the top draft-and-follows in the spring of 2004, Mattheus gave up a commitment to Arizona State to sign for $700,000. He has yet to live up to that lofty bonus, perhaps because Colorado tried to change his motion. Mattheus had success as an amateur despite separating his hands very early in delivery, which isn't ideal but created some hesitation and deception. The Rockies tried to make his mechanics more fluid, but he was hit hard in low Class A last year. His raw stuff remains intriguing, however. Mattheus relies on a hard sinker-slider combination, and he can top out at 94 mph with a four-seam fastball. His changeup is below average. Colorado is now trying to help him regain his old delivery and may have him repeat low Class A.

Year	Club (League)	Class	W	L	ERA	G	GS	CG	SV	IP	H	R	ER	HR	BB	SO	AVG
2004	Casper (Pio)	R	3	3	4.94	7	7	0	0	27	27	16	15	2	14	16	.262
2005	Asheville (SAL)	A	7	6	5.82	23	23	0	0	128	142	90	83	16	52	102	.278
MINOR LEAGUE TOTALS			10	9	5.67	30	30	0	0	156	169	106	98	18	66	118	.275

28 JASON VAN KOOTEN
SS/2B

Born: Sept. 1, 1984. **B-T:** R-R. **Ht.:** 6-0. **Wt.:** 170. **Drafted:** Seward County (Kan.) CC, D/F 2003 (46th round). **Signed by:** Mike Ericson.

Van Kooten first registered on the Rockies' radar through special assistant to the general manager Walt Weiss, who volunteers time at Regis High in the Denver suburb of Aurora. Weiss worked with Van Kooten at Regis, and Colorado took him in the 46th round in 2003 as a draft-and-follow. He signed after one season at Seward County (Kan.) CC, where he was the Jayhawk Conference freshman of the year. Van Kooten is a good athlete who draws comparisons to Rockies shortstops past (Weiss) and present (Clint Barmes). He's also solid at second base and has played some third base as well. He has soft hands and gets excellent reads on balls, though he has had to work on learning to trust his backhand. He also has a little twist in his wrist when he throws but doesn't lose any accuracy. Offensively, Van Kooten profiles as a No. 2 hitter. His priorities are making contact and getting on base, and he's a good bunter. His speed is average. With all the middle-infield talent in the system, Van Kooten's eventual role with the Rockies figures to be as a utilityman. He'll get his first shot at full-season ball this year in Asheville.

Year	Club (League)	Class	AVG	G	AB	R	H	2B	3B	HR	RBI	BB	SO	SB	OBP	SLG
2004	Tri-City (NWL)	A	.236	16	55	10	13	1	0	0	1	5	10	0	.364	.255
	Casper (Pio)	R	.311	26	106	21	33	3	0	2	16	13	14	7	.390	.396
2005	Tri-City (NWL)	A	.299	64	251	34	75	14	2	5	36	14	57	2	.350	.430
MINOR LEAGUE TOTALS			.294	106	412	65	121	18	2	7	53	32	81	9	.363	.398

29 JOE GAETTI
OF

Born: Oct. 16, 1981. **B-T:** R-R. **Ht.:** 5-11. **Wt.:** 205. **Drafted:** North Carolina State, 2003 (12th round). **Signed by:** Jay Matthews.

The son of former all-star third baseman Gary Gaetti, Joe hit just .270 with 14 home runs as a junior for North Carolina State in 2003. Scouts questioned his bat, but his bloodlines and a solid performance in the Northwoods League the previous summer got him drafted in the 12th round. Gaetti has played himself into prospect status since signing. Much like his father, there's nothing smooth about his approach at the plate or in the field, but he produces. He has a short stroke with power, and he learned to trust his quick hands last year. He also stopped pushing himself quite so hard after burying himself when he struggled in his first two pro seasons. Gaetti will work counts and draw walks. His range and arm are just adequate, so he projects as a left fielder, though he has played some center and right as a pro. Headed for Double-A, he'll have to keep producing to one day earn a shot as an extra outfielder.

Year	Club (League)	Class	AVG	G	AB	R	H	2B	3B	HR	RBI	BB	SO	SB	OBP	SLG
2003	Tri-City (NWL)	A	.276	34	116	15	32	7	2	4	9	14	38	1	.348	.474
2004	Asheville (SAL)	A	.257	111	370	62	95	24	1	16	55	55	107	16	.370	.457
2005	Modesto (Cal)	A	.332	113	395	90	131	29	8	21	87	52	114	5	.418	.605
MINOR LEAGUE TOTALS			.293	258	881	167	258	60	11	41	151	121	259	22	.389	.526

30 MATT MILLER
OF

Born: Dec. 26, 1982. **B-T:** R-R. **Ht.:** 6-2. **Wt.:** 210. **Drafted:** Texas State, 2004 (13th round). **Signed by:** Jeff Edwards.

Asheville has produced the last two South Atlantic League MVPs. He isn't the top prospect that 2004 winner Ian Stewart is, but Miller chased the SAL triple crown in his first full season. He was helped by Asheville's McCormick Field, batting .366 with 20 homers in 65 home games, but he has legitimate hitting ability. After a dislocated right shoulder limited him in his pro debut, Miller soared in 2005 after refining his two-strike approach. He maintained his aggressiveness but didn't chase as many pitches and started using the whole field. He doesn't walk much, in part because he makes contact so easily. Miller has average speed and a strong arm, but he played mostly left field last year because he needs to improve his reads and routes on flyballs. The Rockies may skip him a level and send him to Double-A this year.

Year	Club (League)	Class	AVG	G	AB	R	H	2B	3B	HR	RBI	BB	SO	SB	OBP	SLG
2004	Tri-City (NWL)	A	.269	43	167	17	45	8	0	8	25	13	18	0	.337	.461
2005	Asheville (SAL)	A	.331	127	508	79	168	34	0	30	100	26	71	9	.375	.575
	Modesto (Cal)	A	.400	1	5	0	2	0	0	0	1	0	0	0	.400	.400
MINOR LEAGUE TOTALS			.316	171	680	96	215	42	0	38	126	39	89	9	.366	.546

DETROIT
TIGERS

BY **JOHN MANUEL**

The Tigers haven't had a winning season since 1993. The only members of that team who were active major leaguers in 2005 were Chris Gomez and David Wells.

So it's understandable if owner Mike Ilitch wants to spend free-agent money to find a short-term fix for his big league team. That worked in 2004, when Detroit improved to 72 victories and respectability after establishing an American League record for futility with 119 losses in 2003.

The Tigers didn't make further progress in 2005, however, winning just 71 times as they couldn't keep key players such as Carlos Guillen and free-agent signees Magglio Ordonez and Troy Percival healthy. After a smashing Detroit debut in 2004, catcher Ivan Rodriguez slumped badly. His 11 walks were part of a team-wide problem, as the Tigers drew just 384 free passes, the lowest total in the majors since 2002, and ranked 12th in the AL in on-base percentage.

The stagnant offense, as well as a stagnant clubhouse, cost manager and former club icon Alan Trammell his job after three seasons. For the second time in his career as a general manager, Dave Dombrowski turned to Jim Leyland to manage his high-payroll team. While the Tigers perhaps have lower expectations than the 1997 Marlins—a winning season would be a good start—they have the kind of veteran talent Leyland is accustomed to working with.

A poor season had some bright spots, and many of them were provided by a rebounding farm system. Chris Shelton, whom the Pirates somehow left unprotected in the 2003 Rule 5 draft, was Detroit's most consistent hitter and a much-needed potent righthanded bat. Outfielder **Curtis Granderson**, last year's No. 1 prospect, got a chance at consistent playing time and seized it, slugging eight home runs in 162 at-bats and playing a competent center field.

The Tigers, who entered 2005 slotted 29th in Baseball America's farm-system rankings, had their best year in the minors since winning BA's Organization of the Year award in 1997. The downers were injuries and poor performances by top draft picks Kyle Sleeth (third overall pick, 2003), who had Tommy John surgery, and Eric Beattie (second round, 2004), who has major control problems.

The organization's affectation for hard throwers finally paid off as Justin Verlander and Joel Zumaya had breakout seasons. Verlander, the No. 2 overall pick in 2004, took off after the Tigers altered his delivery slightly, started the Futures Game at Comerica Park and pitched in the big leagues three months into his pro career. Zumaya reached Triple-A as a 20-year-old and helped Toledo win the International League championship. The Mud Hens led the minor leagues with 89 wins.

Verlander began the year at high Class A Lakeland, but spent barely half a season there. Lakeland piled up 85 wins, second to Toledo. Overall, the Tigers topped all organizations in minor league winning percentage at .555.

TOP 30 PROSPECTS

1. Justin Verlander, rhp	16. Jair Jurrjens, rhp
2. Joel Zumaya, rhp	17. Juan Francia, 2b
3. Cameron Maybin, of	18. Ryan Raburn, 2b
4. Brent Clevlen, of	19. Donald Kelly, 3b/ss
5. Wilkin Ramirez, 3b	20. Kyle Sleeth, rhp
6. Humberto Sanchez, rhp	21. P.J. Finigan, rhp
7. Jordan Tata, rhp	22. Michael Hollimon, ss
8. Tony Giarratano, ss	23. Sendy Vasquez, rhp
9. Jeff Larish, 1b	24. Audy Ciriaco, ss
10. Kevin Whelan, rhp	25. Chris Robinson, c
11. Kody Kirkland, 3b	26. Virgil Vasquez, rhp
12. Jeff Frazier, of	27. Matt Joyce, of
13. Dallas Trahern, rhp	28. Brent Dlugach, ss
14. Clete Thomas, of	29. Nate Bumstead, rhp
15. Eulogio de la Cruz, rhp	30. Vince Blue, of

ORGANIZATION OVERVIEW

General manager: Dave Dombrowski. **Farm director:** Dan Lunetta. **Scouting director:** David Chadd.

2005 PERFORMANCE

Class	Farm Team	League	W	L	Pct.	Finish*	Manager
Majors	Detroit	American	71	91	.438	11th (14)	Alan Trammell
Triple-A	Toledo Mud Hens	International	89	55	.618	+1st (14)	Larry Parrish
Double-A	Erie SeaWolves	Eastern	63	79	.444	t-11 (12)	Duffy Dyer
High A	Lakeland Tigers	Florida State	85	48	.639	1st (12)	Mike Rojas
Low A	West Michigan Whitecaps	Midwest	73	67	.521	3rd (14)	Matt Walbeck
Short-season	Oneonta Tigers	New York-Penn	48	27	.640	2nd (14)	Tom Brookens
Rookie	GCL Tigers	Gulf Coast	24	30	.444	t-9th (12)	Kevin Bradshaw
OVERALL 2005 MINOR LEAGUE RECORD			382	306	.555	1st (30)	

*Finish in overall standings (No. of teams in league). +League champion

ORGANIZATION LEADERS

BATTING *Minimum 250 at-bats
*AVG	Thames, Marcus, Toledo	.340
R	Frazier, Jeff, West Michigan	79
	Granderson, Curtis, Toledo	79
H	Francia, Juan, Erie/Lakeland	170
TB	Frazier, Jeff, West Michigan	243
2B	Frazier, Jeff, West Michigan	45
3B	Granderson, Curtis, Toledo	13
HR	Hessman, Mike, Toledo	28
RBI	Clevlen, Brent, Lakeland	102
BB	Espinosa, David, Erie/Toledo	74
SO	Hessman, Mike, Toledo	154
SB	Francia, Juan, Erie/Lakeland	41
*OBP	Thames, Marcus, Toledo	.427
*SLG	Thames, Marcus, Toledo	.679

PITCHING #Minimum 75 innings
W	Tata, Jordan, Lakeland	13
L	Cornejo, Nate, Erie	12
#ERA	Verlander, Justin, Erie/Lakeland	1.11
G	Karnuth, Jason, Toledo	63
CG	Grilli, Jason, Toledo	3
	Kauten, Josh, Lakeland/West Michigan	3
SV	Almonte, Edwin, Erie	33
IP	Grilli, Jason, Toledo	167
BB	Zumaya, Joel, Erie/Toledo	76
SO	Zumaya, Joel, Erie/Toledo	199

BEST TOOLS

Best Hitter for Average	Brent Clevlen
Best Power Hitter	Wilkin Ramirez
Best Strike-Zone Discipline	Jeff Larish
Fastest Baserunner	Vince Blue
Best Athlete	Cameron Maybin
Best Fastball	Justin Verlander
Best Curveball	Justin Verlander
Best Slider	Dallas Trahern
Best Changeup	Joel Zumaya
Best Control	Jordan Tata
Best Defensive Catcher	Chris Robinson
Best Defensive Infielder	Tony Giarratano
Best Infield Arm	Kody Kirkland
Best Defensive Outfielder	Cameron Maybin
Best Outfield Arm	Cameron Maybin

PROJECTED 2009 LINEUP

Catcher	Brandon Inge
First Base	Chris Shelton
Second Base	Placido Polanco
Third Base	Wilkin Ramirez
Shortstop	Carlos Guillen
Left Field	Curtis Granderon
Center Field	Cameron Maybin

Right Field	Brent Clevlen
Designated Hitter	Magglio Ordonez
No. 1 Starter	Jeremy Bonderman
No. 2 Starter	Justin Verlander
No. 3 Starter	Joel Zumaya
No. 4 Starter	Humberto Sanchez
No. 5 Starter	Jordan Tata
Closer	Kevin Whelan

LAST YEAR'S TOP 20 PROSPECTS

1. Curtis Granderson, of	11. Wilkin Ramirez, 3b
2. Kyle Sleeth, rhp	12. Roberto Novoa, rhp
3. Justin Verlander, rhp	13. Dallas Trahern, rhp
4. Joel Zumaya, rhp	14. Brent Clevlen, of
5. Humberto Sanchez, rhp	15. Juan Tejeda, 1b
6. Tony Giarratano, ss	16. Bo Flowers, of
7. Jeff Frazier, of	17. Eric Beattie, rhp
8. Ryan Raburn, 2b	18. Collin Mahoney, rhp
9. Eulogio de la Cruz, rhp	19. Kody Kirkland, 3b
10. Chris Shelton, 1b/c	20. Scott Moore, 3b

TOP PROSPECTS OF THE DECADE

Year	Player, Pos.	2005 Org.
1996	Mike Drumright, rhp	Out of baseball
1997	Mike Drumright, rhp	Out of baseball
1998	Juan Encarnacion, of	Marlins
1999	Gabe Kapler, of	Red Sox
2000	Eric Munson, 1b/c	Devil Rays
2001	Brandon Inge, c	Tigers
2002	Nate Cornejo, rhp	Tigers
2003	Jeremy Bonderman, rhp	Tigers
2004	Kyle Sleeth, rhp	Tigers
2005	Curtis Granderson, of	Tigers

TOP DRAFT PICKS OF THE DECADE

Year	Player, Pos.	2005 Org.
1996	Seth Greisinger, rhp	Braves
1997	Matt Anderson, rhp	Rockies
1998	Jeff Weaver, rhp	Dodgers
1999	Eric Munson, 1b/c	Devil Rays
2000	Matt Wheatland, rhp	San Diego (Golden Lg.)
2001	Kenny Baugh, rhp	Tigers
2002	Scott Moore, ss	Cubs
2003	Kyle Sleeth, rhp	Tigers
2004	Justin Verlander, rhp	Tigers
2005	Cameron Maybin, of	Tigers

ALL-TIME LARGEST BONUSES

Eric Munson, 1999	$3,500,000
Kyle Sleeth, 2003	$3,350,000
Justin Verlander, 2004	$3,120,000
Cameron Maybin, 2005	$2,650,000
Matt Anderson, 1997	$2,505,000

MINOR LEAGUE DEPTH CHART

Detroit Tigers

Rank: 14

STRENGTH: Power arms. With 100-mph throwers like Justin Verlander and Joel Zumaya at the top of the class, power pitchers make this list go.

WEAKNESS: Catchers. Detroit needs receivers who can handle big-time heat.

*Depth charts prepared by **John Manuel** and **Chris Kline**. Numbers in parentheses indicate prospect rankings.*

LF
Jeff Frazier (12)
Matt Joyce (27)
David Espinosa
Garth McKinney

CF
Cameron Maybin (3)
Clete Thomas (14)
Vince Blue (30)
Victor Mendez

RF
Brent Clevlen (4)

3B
Wilkin Ramirez (5)
Kody Kirkland (11)
Donald Kelly (19)
Cory Middleton

SS
Tony Giarratano (8)
Michael Hollimon (22)
Audy Ciriaco (24)
Brent Dlugach (28)

2B
Juan Francia (17)
Ryan Raburn (18)
Will Rhymes

1B
Jeff Larish (9)
Kelly Hunt
Ryan Roberson

C
Chris Robinson (25)
Max St. Pierre
Danilo Sanchez

RHP

Starters	Relievers
Justin Verlander (1)	Kevin Whalen (10)
Joel Zumaya (2)	Eulogio de la Cruz (15)
Humberto Sanchez (6)	P.J. Finigan (21)
Jordan Tata (7)	Mark Woodyard
Dallas Trahern (13)	Jeff Hahn
Jair Jurrjens (16)	Jay Sborz
Kyle Sleeth (20)	Collin Mahoney
Sendy Vasquez (23)	Eddie Bonine
Virgil Vasquez (26)	Freddy Dolsi
Nate Bumstead (29)	Ricky Steik
Zach Miner	Kevin Ardoin
Josh Rainwater	
Preston Larrison	
Josh Kauten	
Andrew Kown	
Burke Badenhop	
Jose Fragoso	
Brendan Wise	
Randor Bierd	

LHP

Starters	Relievers
Lucas French	Danny Zell
Erik Averill	

DRAFT ANALYSIS
2005

Best Pro Debut: RHP Kevin Whelan (4) was untouchable, going 1-1, 1.48 with 15 saves between short-season Oneonta and low Class A West Michigan. He fanned 41 in 24 innings while permitting just six hits. SS Michael Hollimon (16) batted .277-13-53 and led the short-season New York-Penn League with 66 runs and 10 triples.

Best Athlete: OF Cameron Maybin (1) was one of the best athletes available in the draft. RHP P.J. Finigan (7), now a full-time pitcher, was a solid shortstop offensively and defensively at Southern Illinois.

Best Pure Hitter: 1B Jeff Larish (5) was one of college baseball's most feared hitters in 2003 but slumped badly in 2004, when he had a wrist injury. Larish rebounded as a senior and batted .280-6-17 in 24 pro games after signing late. OF Clete Thomas (6) hit .311-1-25 with 20 steals, spending the majority of his time in low Class A.

Best Raw Power: Larish tied a College World Series record with three homers in one game in June, and he went deep in each of his first three games following his promotion to the NY-P. Maybin will be a home run threat as well, and he already has added 15 pounds since the draft. Six-foot-6, 240-pound 1B Ryan Roberson (30) also packs plenty of pop.

Fastest Runner: Adding strength hasn't slowed down Maybin, who was clocked in 4.1 seconds from the right side of the plate to first base during instructional league.

Best Defensive Player: Maybin can make all the plays in center. Chris Robinson (3) has a plus arm, average receiving skills and the leadership teams want in a catcher.

Best Fastball: Whelan has a 95-96 mph fastball.

RICH ABEL

Hollimon

Best Breaking Ball: Finigan's slider. Area scouts saw a lot of similarities between Finigan and another former Missouri Valley Conference two-way star, Southwest Missouri State's Shaun Marcum, who needed just two years to reach the majors with Toronto after focusing on pitching.

Most Intriguing Background: Maybin is the cousin of Rashad McCants, who helped North Carolina win the NCAA basketball title before going in the first round of the 2005 NBA draft. Unsigned 3B Alex Avila's (34) father Al is an assistant general manager for the Tigers. Unsigned C Ben Petralli's (15) dad Geno caught in the big leagues.

Closest To The Majors: Whelan could wind up in Detroit's bullpen in the very near future. Larish's bat also could take him to Comerica Park quickly.

Best Late-Round Pick: Hollimon. RHP Jeff Hahn (35) is 6-foot-5 and has an 88-89 mph fastball with late life. He went 8-2, 1.99 between two pro stops.

The One Who Got Away: SS David Adams (21) would have gone in the top three rounds if he hadn't been strongly committed to Virginia.

Assessment: The Tigers had hoped to get the chance to take RHP Mike Pelfrey with the 10th overall choice, but Maybin (BA's No. 3-rated drafted prospect) was a sweet consolation prize. At this point, Whelan and Larish look like steals for where Detroit got them.

2004 RHP Justin Verlander (1) led the minors in ERA and reached Detroit in his debut season. OF Jeff Frazier (3) and RHP Dallas Trahern (34) also have potential. *GRADE: A*

2003 The Tigers may have ruined RHP Kyle Sleeth (1), the No. 3 overall pick, by trying to change his mechanics. He had Tommy John surgery in 2005. SS Tony Giarratano (3) is solid, while RHP Jordan Tata (16) has exceeded expectations. *GRADE: C*

2002 3B Scott Moore (1) didn't start hitting until Detroit traded him to the Cubs. But the Tigers kept plenty of talent in hard-throwing RHP Joel Zumaya (11) and OFs Brent Clevlen (2) and Curtis Granderson (3). *GRADE: B+*

2001 Injuries ruined the first-round picks, RHP Kenny Baugh (now with the Padres) and 2B Michael Woods. Detroit may salvage something with 2B Ryan Raburn (5), 3B/SS Don Kelly (8) and RHP Humberto Sanchez (31). *GRADE: C*

---

*Draft analysis prepared by **Jim Callis**. Numbers in parentheses indicate draft rounds.*

JUSTIN
VERLANDER

RHP

RICK BATTLE

Born: Feb. 20, 1983.
Ht.: 6-5. **Wt.:** 200.
Bats: R. **Throws:** R.
Drafted: Old Dominion, 2004
(1st round).
Signed by: Bill Buck.

Verlander was considered a possible top-five-round talent out of high school, but his commitment to Old Dominion, strong grades and raw arm prompted him to pass through the 2001 draft untouched, much to his disappointment. He went to Old Dominion and became the No. 1 starter instantly. While his college career included several highs, such as pitching for Team USA in 2003 and setting school and Colonial Athletic Association strikeout records, he posted a modest 21-18 record and all three Monarchs teams he played for posted losing records. The Padres considered Verlander with the No. 1 overall pick in 2004 but he wasn't in their final trio of choices, leaving him available for the Tigers at No. 2. Negotiations broke off in October before his father stepped in, called the Tigers and got the contract settled. Verlander signed for a $3.12 million bonus and $4.5 million guaranteed major league contract. His late signing delayed his pro debut until 2005, when he was spectacular. Verlander led the minors in ERA (giving up only one run in 33 innings at Double-A Erie), started the Futures Game in Comerica Park and made his major league debut at Jacobs Field on Independence Day.

Verlander has one of the best arms in the minors and features both the best fastball and curveball in the organization. Tall, lithe and athletic, he generates tremendous arm speed that gives him an electric fastball with both above-average velocity and life. His heater sits at 93-96 mph and touches 99. He commanded his fastball—and all of his pitches, for that matter—much better as a pro than he had in college. Most scouts had noticed that as an amateur, Verlander landed on a stiff front leg, cutting off his follow-through and leading to a tendency to leave his pitches up in the strike zone. The Tigers deemed this flaw correctable, but what impressed them most was how quickly Verlander took to his new delivery. He rarely if ever reverted to his old form. Verlander's curveball is a true knee-buckler, a power breaker with excellent depth and late bite down in the zone. He has excellent arm speed on his late-moving changeup, which also improved with his new delivery and ranks among the best in the organization.

Stuff-wise, Verlander has no weaknesses. His changeup helped him shackle lefthanded hitters in the minors (.175 average, no homers in 171 at-bats). He didn't have that kind of success in his first two big league starts against the Indians and Twins, as lefties went 10-for-30 against him and drew four walks. The Tigers attribute much of that to nerves and inexperience, though. Verlander did recover from a three-run first inning in his first big league game to later retire 12 of 13 batters. As an amateur, he had the reputation of responding to adversity by trying to throw harder, and opponents thought he could be easily rattled. Neither was evident in his first pro season, however.

The Tigers already have one power righty in their big league rotation in Jeremy Bonderman, who is just four months older than Verlander. He should join Bonderman full-time in the rotation in 2006, if not out of spring training then shortly thereafter. If Verlander learns the nuances of pitching to go with his electric stuff, he could supplant Bonderman as Detroit's No. 1 starter.

Year	Club (League)	Class	W	L	ERA	G	GS	CG	SV	IP	H	R	ER	HR	BB	SO	AVG
2005	Lakeland (FSL)	A	9	2	1.67	13	13	2	0	86	70	19	16	3	19	104	.230
	Detroit (AL)	MLB	0	2	7.17	2	2	0	0	11	15	9	9	1	5	7	.313
	Erie (EL)	AA	2	0	0.28	7	7	0	0	33	11	1	1	1	7	32	.103
MAJOR LEAGUE TOTALS			0	2	7.17	2	2	0	0	11	15	9	9	1	5	7	.313
MINOR LEAGUE TOTALS			11	2	1.29	20	20	2	0	119	81	20	17	4	26	136	.197

2 JOEL ZUMAYA RHP

RICH ABEL

Born: Nov. 9, 1984. **B-T:** R-R. **Ht.:** 6-3. **Wt.:** 215. **Drafted:** HS—Chula Vista, Calif., 2002 (11th round). **Signed by:** Rob Wilfong.

Zumaya has added 25 pounds to his frame since high school, when he threw in the upper 80s with a delivery charitably described as raw. Through his added strength and refined mechanics, he has become one of the minors' hardest throwers, regularly touching 100 mph. Scouts in and out of the organization no longer describe Zumaya's delivery as maximum-effort. Now they use the term strong. More under control than ever, Zumaya unleashes a plus-plus fastball and much-improved change-up with similar arm speed, helping him rank second in the minors in strikeouts and opponent average. His curveball also is a plus pitch with depth and low-80s velocity. Some scouts still believe Zumaya's delivery will force a shift to the bullpen. He missed two starts with back pain in 2005. His curve can flatten out, as he tends to drop his elbow. Zumaya is starting to believe he can dominate better hitters, and his improved changeup and less-violent mechanics give him a chance not just to start but to be a frontline starter. He'll compete with Justin Verlander for an opening in the 2006 rotation.

Year	Club (League)	Class	W	L	ERA	G	GS	CG	SV	IP	H	R	ER	HR	BB	SO	AVG
2002	Tigers (GCL)	R	2	1	1.93	9	8	0	0	37	21	9	8	2	11	46	.163
2003	West Michigan (Mid)	A	7	5	2.79	19	19	0	0	90	69	35	28	3	38	126	.209
2004	Lakeland (FSL)	A	7	6	4.15	19	19	1	0	111	81	55	51	9	55	104	.214
	Erie (EL)	AA	2	2	6.30	4	4	0	0	20	19	20	14	6	10	29	.250
2005	Erie (EL)	AA	8	3	2.77	18	18	0	0	107	71	40	33	8	52	143	.187
	Toledo (IL)	AAA	1	2	2.66	8	8	1	0	44	30	13	13	2	24	56	.194
MINOR LEAGUE TOTALS			27	19	3.23	77	76	2	0	410	291	172	147	30	190	504	.201

3 CAMERON MAYBIN OF

TONY FARLOW

Born: April 4, 1987. **B-T:** R-R. **Ht.:** 6-3. **Wt.:** 195. **Drafted:** HS—Arden, N.C. (1st round). **Signed by:** Bill Buck.

Maybin has been around the pro game since his early teenage days, when he served as a batboy for the Class A Asheville Tourists, his local team. He was Baseball America's Youth Player of the Year in 2004 after leading the Midland Redskins to the Connie Mack World Series title. Negotiations with the Tigers were difficult, but he signed for $2.65 million in time to go to instructional league. His cousin Rashad McCants was a first-round NBA draft pick after helping North Carolina win the national championship last spring. Maybin does it all and invites comparisons to players such as Joe Carter and Andre Dawson for his game and physique. He's a graceful runner and defender, and nearly can match Dawson's arm strength. Maybin has wicked raw power and launched a 450-blast that was the talk of instructional league. He fit right in with his new teammates, reinforcing the organization's belief in his quality makeup. He didn't face the toughest high school competition, so there were concerns that Maybin's bat might lag behind his other tools. He started to put those to rest in instructional league, where he showed the ability to make quick adjustments and use the whole field. He had hamstring issues that slowed him late in camp, but they aren't a long-term concern. The Tigers like Maybin even more after seeing him in instructional league. If his spring performance matches what he showed in the fall, he'll easily make the low Class A West Michigan roster and could move faster than initially expected.

Year	Club (League)	Class	AVG	G	AB	R	H	2B	3B	HR	RBI	BB	SO	SB	OBP	SLG
2005	Did not play—Signed 2006 contract															

4 BRENT CLEVLEN OF

STEVE MOORE

Born: Oct. 27, 1983. **B-T:** R-R. **Ht.:** 6-2. **Wt.:** 190. **Drafted:** HS—Cedar Park, Texas, 2002 (2nd round). **Signed by:** Tim Grieve.

After playing well in his first full season, Clevlen struggled for most of 2004, never finding a groove in high Class A. He repeated the level in 2005, however, and rarely slumped on his way to the Florida State League MVP award while helping Lakeland post the best record in the minors among full-season clubs. Clevlen learned how to grind out a season and avoid protracted slumps, allowing his confidence to remain high and his tools to come out. He fits the profile for a big league right fielder. He's athletic, has above-average power potential, runs a tick above-average and has a plus throwing arm. During his cataclysmic 2004 season, Clevlen pressed when good at-bats didn't yield good results. He needs to remember to let the game come to him. He can get pull-conscious, though like most hitters, he's best when he uses the whole field. If Clevlen makes consistent contact like he did last season, the next league he'll repeat is the American. The Tigers already are paying their right fielder (Magglio Ordonez) handsomely, so they won't rush Clevlen. He'll spend 2006 in Double-A and projects to become a full-time big leaguer in 2008.

Year	Club (League)	Class	AVG	G	AB	R	H	2B	3B	HR	RBI	BB	SO	SB	OBP	SLG
2002	Tigers (GCL)	R	.330	28	103	14	34	2	3	3	21	8	24	2	.372	.495
2003	West Michigan (Mid)	A	.260	138	481	67	125	22	7	12	63	72	111	6	.359	.410
2004	Lakeland (FSL)	A	.224	117	420	49	94	23	6	6	50	44	127	2	.300	.350
2005	Lakeland (FSL)	A	.302	130	494	77	149	28	4	18	102	65	118	14	.387	.484
MINOR LEAGUE TOTALS			.268	413	1498	207	402	75	20	39	236	189	380	24	.353	.423

5 WILKIN RAMIREZ 3B

STEVE MOORE

Born: Oct. 25, 1985. **B-T:** R-R. **Ht.:** 6-2. **Wt.:** 190. **Signed:** Dominican Republic, 2003. **Signed by:** Ramon Pena.

After an intriguing debut in the Rookie-level Gulf Coast League in 2003, Ramirez missed the entire 2004 season after right shoulder surgery to repair a torn labrum. He returned to play his first full season last year, though he spent the majority of his time playing DH in deference to his defense and his shoulder. Until Cameron Maybin signed, Ramirez was the closest thing the Tigers had to a five-tool player. He has the most raw power in the organization, able to drive the ball out of any part of virtually any park thanks to excellent bat speed. His arm strength has returned to above-average, and he's one of the organization's better runners. Ramirez has good hands, enough range and plenty of arm to play third base, but his rust and poor footwork led to 26 errors in just 57 games. The Tigers aren't in a hurry to move him, and he's athletic enough for an outfield corner if needed. His lack of plate discipline and a consistent approach resulted in him leading the low Class A Midwest League in strikeouts last season. Ramirez should start 2006 in high Class A. If the Tigers think his bat is ready for an early promotion, don't be surprised if a position switch follows soon thereafter.

Year	Club (League)	Class	AVG	G	AB	R	H	2B	3B	HR	RBI	BB	SO	SB	OBP	SLG
2003	Tigers (GCL)	R	.275	54	200	34	55	6	7	5	35	13	51	6	.321	.450
2004	Did not play—Injured															
2005	West Michigan (Mid)	A	.262	131	493	69	129	21	2	16	65	35	143	21	.317	.410
MINOR LEAGUE TOTALS			.266	185	693	103	184	27	9	21	100	48	194	27	.318	.421

6 HUMBERTO SANCHEZ RHP

KEVIN PATAKY

Born: May 28, 1983. **B-T:** R-R. **Ht.:** 6-6. **Wt.:** 230. **Drafted:** Connors State (Okla.) JC, D/F 2001 (31st round). **Signed by:** Rob Guzik.

Born in the Dominican Republic, Sanchez moved to New York City when he was 10. The Tigers drafted him out of a New York junior college in 2001, and he signed for $1 million as a draft-and-follow after facing better competition at Connors State (Okla.) JC. He missed the first two months of the 2005 season with muscle spasms and an oblique strain, as well as most of August with a groin injury, but he finished strong as one of the top starters in the Arizona Fall League. At his best, Sanchez has stuff just a shade behind Verlander's and Zumaya's. Sanchez' fastball often sits at 93-95 mph. His low-80s curveball is a plus pitch with excellent depth. He uses his size for power, to intimidate hitters and to keep his stuff down in the zone. Sanchez can get out of sync with his mechanics, which contributed to his early injury problems and to the fact that he was never quite right all year. He needs to keep himself in better shape and repeat his delivery more consistently. His changeup is just fair. If Sanchez puts it all together, his big fastball and power should make him a solid middle-of-the-rotation starter. He also could be a factor in the Detroit bullpen fairly soon if needed. He'll return to the Double-A rotation to begin 2006.

Year	Club (League)	Class	W	L	ERA	G	GS	CG	SV	IP	H	R	ER	HR	BB	SO	AVG
2002	Oneonta (NY-P)	A	2	2	3.62	9	9	0	0	32	29	18	13	1	21	26	.244
2003	West Michigan (Mid)	A	7	7	4.42	23	23	0	0	116	107	71	57	3	78	96	.249
2004	Lakeland (FSL)	A	7	11	5.21	19	19	3	0	105	103	67	61	9	51	115	.263
	Erie (EL)	AA	1	0	2.13	2	2	0	0	13	10	5	3	1	6	15	.213
2005	Erie (EL)	AA	3	5	5.56	15	11	0	0	65	72	42	40	10	27	65	.283
MINOR LEAGUE TOTALS			20	25	4.73	68	64	3	0	331	321	203	174	24	183	317	.259

7 JORDAN TATA RHP

Born: Sept. 20, 1981. **B-T:** R-R. **Ht.:** 6-6. **Wt.:** 220. **Drafted:** Sam Houston State, 2003 (16th round). **Signed by:** Tim Grieve.

A two-way player at Sam Houston State, where he also played the outfield, Tata first opened the Tigers' eyes when he touched 93 mph in his first instructional league in 2003. He flew under the radar on West Michigan's 2004 championship club, before breaking out as the Florida State League's 2005 pitcher of the year. Tata has good size and good arm speed, giving him an above-average 90-93 mph fastball with excellent sink. He complements it with a cut fastball that he throws just as hard as his fastball, and one club official said he saw Tata throwing 94-mph cutters late in the year. He can pitch to all four quadrants of the strike zone using his fastball and cutter 90 percent of the time. Cleaner mechanics gave him much better control last year than he had in the past. At 24, Tata has yet to pitch above Class A. His slurvy curveball lags behind his other offerings, but when he throws it for strikes, it's usually an effective change of pace. Tata's breakout year was rewarded with a spot on the 40-man roster. The organization's faith in his sinking and cutting fastballs will be tested when he takes his first spin through Double-A this year.

Year	Club (League)	Class	W	L	ERA	G	GS	CG	SV	IP	H	R	ER	HR	BB	SO	AVG
2003	Oneonta (NY-P)	A	4	3	2.58	16	12	0	1	73	64	32	21	1	20	60	.236
2004	West Michigan (Mid)	A	8	11	3.36	28	28	1	0	166	167	77	62	7	68	116	.272
2005	Lakeland (FSL)	A	13	2	2.79	25	25	2	0	155	138	55	48	12	41	134	.239
MINOR LEAGUE TOTALS			25	16	2.99	69	65	3	1	395	369	164	131	20	129	310	.252

8 TONY GIARRATANO SS

Born: Nov. 29, 1982. **B-T:** B-R. **Ht.:** 6-0. **Wt.:** 180. **Drafted:** Tulane, 2003 (3rd round). **Signed by:** Steve Taylor.

Injuries hit Giarratano again last season, short-circuiting a campaign that saw him get his first big league promotion in early June when Carlos Guillen went down with a pulled hamstring. Giarratano went out with a sports hernia in August, and he was limited to rehabilitation work in Lakeland during instructional league in the fall. When he's healthy, Giarratano grades out as above-average in four tools. He has a quick bat and covers the strike zone with a compact stroke, spraying line drives from pole to pole. He's a plus defender thanks to his range and strong, accurate arm. He also runs well. Giarratano needs to get stronger to keep from getting the bat knocked out of his hands by quality inside fastballs. He figures to never hit for much power anyway. Injuries have affected him three of the last four years going back to his sophomore year at Tulane, including postseason shoulder surgery in 2004, so his durability is a major concern. His 2005 callup shows what the Tigers think of Giarratano's defense. For his offense to keep him in the majors, he'll need to stay healthy and get more at-bats. His spring performance will determine if he returns to Double-A Erie or graduates to Triple-A Toledo this year.

Year	Club (League)	Class	AVG	G	AB	R	H	2B	3B	HR	RBI	BB	SO	SB	OBP	SLG
2003	Oneonta (NY-P)	A	.328	47	189	31	62	11	4	3	27	12	22	9	.369	.476
2004	West Michigan (Mid)	A	.285	43	165	20	47	6	1	1	13	25	22	11	.383	.352
	Lakeland (FSL)	A	.376	53	202	30	76	11	0	5	25	16	38	14	.421	.505
2005	Detroit (AL)	MLB	.143	15	42	4	6	0	0	1	4	5	7	1	.234	.214
	Erie (EL)	AA	.266	89	346	40	92	22	3	3	32	32	75	12	.334	.373
MAJOR LEAGUE TOTALS			.143	15	42	4	6	0	0	1	4	5	7	1	.234	.214
MINOR LEAGUE TOTALS			.307	232	902	121	277	50	8	12	97	85	157	46	.370	.420

9 JEFF LARISH 1B

Born: Oct. 11, 1982. **B-T:** L-R. **Ht.:** 6-2. **Wt.:** 200. **Drafted:** Arizona State, 2005 (5th round). **Signed by:** Brian Reid.

After an All-America season in 2003, Larish slumped as a junior in 2004 because of a wrist injury. He spurned a $650,000 offer from the Dodgers as a 13th-round pick and returned for his senior season, leading Arizona State to its first College World Series trip since 1998. He tied a CWS record with a three-homer game against Nebraska and hit six in 24 pro games after signing for $220,000. Larish generates big-time power with a swing that has excellent leverage, allowing him to drive balls to any part of the park. He can catch up to good fastballs when healthy. He has a determined approach that allows him to wait pitchers out, seeking a pitch he can drive. The Tigers raved about his work ethic after seeing him in instructional league. He has more athleticism and arm strength than most first basemen. When he struggled in 2004, Larish's swing was called mechanical by scouts, and it can get long. It's not a textbook stroke, but Larish has been effective with it. A long swing and patient approach will translate to plenty of strikeouts. It's easy to live with whiffs if a hitter mashes like Larish can. He's set to join the fast track as a college senior with an advanced approach, starting 2006 in high Class A.

Year	Club (League)	Class	AVG	G	AB	R	H	2B	3B	HR	RBI	BB	SO	SB	OBP	SLG
2005	Tigers (GCL)	R	.222	6	18	1	4	1	0	0	4	4	5	0	.375	.278
	Oneonta (NY-P)	A	.297	18	64	16	19	3	0	6	13	13	6	0	.430	.625
MINOR LEAGUE TOTALS			.280	24	82	17	23	4	0	6	17	17	11	0	.417	.549

10 KEVIN WHELAN RHP

Born: Jan. 8, 1984. **B-T:** R-R. **Ht.:** 6-0. **Wt.:** 200. **Drafted:** Texas A&M, 2005 (4th round). **Signed by:** Tim Grieve.

Whelan took control of his career in the Jayhawk League in 2003, asking his coach to move him from catcher to pitcher, but had to move back behind the plate at Texas A&M due to injuries to the Aggies' other backstops. He exploded as a pitching prospect in the Cape Cod League in 2004 with a 0.42 ERA and a league-best 11 saves. He finally became a full-time pitcher in 2005, signed for $265,000 as a fourth-round pick and had a sterling pro debut. Whelan has classic closer stuff. His four-seam fastball tops out at 96 mph, and his two-seamer has wicked sink. When he widens his grip on the two-seamer, it morphs into a mid-80s splitter that buries hitters. His delivery has some deception as well, complicating matters for hitters even more. He's a dogged competitor. Just 6 feet tall, Whelan has to make sure he maintains his over-the-top delivery to keep his fastball from flattening out. He generally succeeds. He continues to pick up pitching nuances as he gains experience on the mound. Whelan has yet to pitch above low Class A, but few in the organization will be shocked if he reaches Detroit in a set-up role this year. With no defined closer in Detroit, he could step forward and seize the role by 2007.

Year	Club (League)	Class	W	L	ERA	G	GS	CG	SV	IP	H	R	ER	HR	BB	SO	AVG
2005	Oneonta (NY-P)	A	1	1	2.25	11	0	0	4	12	2	4	3	1	6	19	.051
	West Michigan (Mid)	A	0	0	0.73	14	0	0	11	12	4	1	1	0	2	22	.098
MINOR LEAGUE TOTALS			1	1	1.48	25	0	0	15	24	6	5	4	1	8	41	.075

11 KODY KIRKLAND 3B

Born: June 9, 1983. **B-T:** R-R. **Ht.:** 6-4. **Wt.:** 200. **Drafted:** JC of Southern Idaho, 2001 (30th round). **Signed by:** Kevin Clouser (Pirates).

Kirkland signed with Pittsburgh as a draft-and-follow out of the College of Southern Idaho and remains involved with the program, teaching hitting there in offseason camps. In a regrettable deal for the Pirates, they sent him and pitchers Roberto Novoa and Adrian Burnside to the Tigers for Randall Simon in November 2002. Kirkland was part of the talented and successful Lakeland club in 2005, though he generally batted sixth or seventh on a team that had several veteran sluggers in the lineup. His season was a vast improvement over his struggles in low Class A the year before. Detroit likes Kirkland's tools and work ethic, and can't quite put its finger on why he hasn't put it all together. He has solid-average raw power and a strong throwing arm suited for third base. He lacks consistency, however, in all phases of the game. He never has hit for average, and while his plate discipline improved last year, it still has a ways to go. His hands at third are a bit stiff despite his above-average athleticism. Kirkland made a step in translating his solid tools into consistent performance, capped by a .293 performance as a taxi-squad player in the Arizona Fall League. Now he's ready for Double-A.

Year	Club (League)	Class	AVG	G	AB	R	H	2B	3B	HR	RBI	BB	SO	SB	OBP	SLG
2002	Pirates (GCL)	R	.306	46	157	22	48	10	2	0	18	14	39	2	.373	.395
2003	Oneonta (NY-P)	A	.303	67	254	46	77	15	11	4	49	25	60	14	.390	.496
2004	West Michigan (Mid)	A	.236	129	496	50	117	30	11	10	61	15	149	6	.276	.401
2005	Lakeland (FSL)	A	.266	125	443	78	118	24	9	16	65	36	102	12	.342	.470
MINOR LEAGUE TOTALS			.267	367	1350	196	360	79	33	30	193	90	350	34	.332	.441

12 JEFF FRAZIER OF

Born: Aug. 10, 1982. **B-T:** R-R. **Ht.:** 6-3. **Wt.:** 195. **Drafted:** Rutgers, 2004 (3rd round). **Signed by:** Derrick Ross.

Frazier has two brothers in baseball, with younger brother Todd a prime 2007 draft target as the shortstop at Rutgers. Older brother Charlie spent six years in the Marlins organiza-tion. Naturally, the Tigers like to describe their Frazier as a "baseball player" who loves the game and has an excellent work ethic. Still, they aren't sure where he fits into their future plans. He had a solid first full season in the minors, leading the Midwest League with 45 doubles while ranking third in hits and total bases. Frazier has a big frame and can get long with his swing, but he's a steady hitter who makes consistent contact. He doesn't have any tools that are significantly deficient, though his fringe-average arm and speed limit him to left field. However, none of his tools grade out as above-average, either. Frazier likely will move one step at a time, which would take him to high Class A this year. He'll have to tweak his swing to either find more power or hit for a higher average to profile as a big league reg-ular on a contender.

Year	Club (League)	Class	AVG	G	AB	R	H	2B	3B	HR	RBI	BB	SO	SB	OBP	SLG
2004	Oneonta (NY-P)	A	.304	20	79	15	24	5	1	1	13	9	11	2	.387	.430
2005	West Michigan (Mid)	A	.287	137	537	79	154	45	4	12	81	46	86	16	.349	.453
MINOR LEAGUE TOTALS			.289	157	616	94	178	50	5	13	94	55	97	18	.354	.450

13 DALLAS TRAHERN   RHP

Born: Nov. 29, 1985. **B-T:** R-R. **Ht.:** 6-3. **Wt.:** 190. **Drafted:** HS—Owasso, Okla., 2004 (34th round). **Signed by:** Steve Taylor.

Detroit got Trahern in the 34th round of the 2004 draft, thanks to good work by area scout Steve Taylor and some good fortune. A two-way star on nationally ranked and state 6-A champion Owasso (Okla.) High, Trahern committed to Oklahoma. But when the Sooners fired pitching coach and recruiting coordinator Ray Hayward, a former Tigers scout, Taylor saw an opening and signed Trahern for $160,000, the equivalent of fifth-round money. In his first full pro season in 2005, he lost five of his first six decisions before finding his groove in low Class A. Athletic and blessed with the ability to repeat an easy delivery, Trahern has two above-average pitches. His 90-92 mph fastball has run and sink, and he's improving his ability to spot it. His slider isn't a strikeout pitch but stays down in the zone and helps him produces scads of groundballs. He had a 2.4 groundball/flyball ratio last year. Trahern's changeup is solid, but like his fastball and slider, it's not quite a swing-and-miss pitch. Trahern either must continue his extreme groundball tendencies or, better yet, improve the depth on his slider to get some strikeouts. He'll move up to high Class A in 2006.

Year	Club (League)	Class	W	L	ERA	G	GS	CG	SV	IP	H	R	ER	HR	BB	SO	AVG
2004	Tigers (GCL)	R	1	2	0.59	7	6	0	0	31	22	8	2	1	7	24	.198
2005	West Michigan (Mid)	A	7	11	3.58	26	26	2	0	156	158	78	62	9	50	66	.265
MINOR LEAGUE TOTALS			8	13	3.09	33	32	2	0	187	180	86	64	10	57	90	.255

14 CLETE THOMAS   OF

Born: Nov. 14, 1983. **B-T:** L-R. **Ht.:** 5-11. **Wt.:** 195. **Drafted:** Auburn, 2005 (6th round). **Signed by:** Jerome Cochran.

Thomas was a fifth-round pick out of high school in 2002 but didn't sign with the Twins. The Tigers were excited to get him as a sixth-rounder in 2005 because he's a college player with two tools hard to find in college—arm strength and speed. Signed for $150,000, he grades out as above-average in both area for most scouts. While Thomas played almost exclusively in right field at Auburn, Detroit believes he profiles best in center field. That's in part because of his speed, and in part because of his slashing style at the plate, as he proj-ects to hit for just average power at best. The Tigers adjusted his hands in his swing to try to give him more of a load and more power. Detroit isn't overflowing with center fielders in the organization, though Cameron Maybin could end up there. Thomas will need to make better reads and get better jumps in the outfield, and his positioning will have to improve as he gains more experience in center. His maturity and polish should keep him a level ahead of Maybin in the short term, and Thomas is slated to start in center in high Class A this year.

Year	Club (League)	Class	AVG	G	AB	R	H	2B	3B	HR	RBI	BB	SO	SB	OBP	SLG
2005	Oneonta (NY-P)	A	.386	18	70	19	27	5	1	1	14	12	11	9	.488	.529
	West Michigan (Mid)	A	.284	51	194	39	55	8	5	0	11	21	37	11	.356	.376
MINOR LEAGUE TOTALS			.311	69	264	58	82	13	6	1	25	33	48	20	.393	.417

15 EULOGIO DE LA CRUZ   RHP

Born: March 12, 1984. **B-T:** R-R. **Ht.:** 5-11. **Wt.:** 175. **Signed:** Dominican Republic, 2001. **Signed by:** Ramon Pena.

While he's not as big as Justin Verlander, Joel Zumaya, Humberto Sanchez and most of the other hard throwers in the system, de la Cruz may have the hardest fastball of the group. He has hit 100 mph out of the bullpen. The Tigers wanted him to try to broaden his repertoire in 2005, and as he moved up to high Class A, he also moved into the rotation. Roving pitching instructor Jon Matlack wanted de la Cruz to get as much work as possible, and he used the additional innings to work on his secondary pitches. De la Cruz throws both a curveball and a changeup, and while they're solid at times, he hasn't shown he can command either pitch. He can throw his fastball for strikes and that has worked for him as a reliever, a role he returned to after 10 starts at Lakeland. He posted a 5.13 ERA in the rotation, compared to 2.11 out of the bullpen last year. De la Cruz, who pitched for Estrellas in the Dominican League over the winter, was added to the 40-man roster and will advance to Double-A for 2006, most likely as a reliever. If one of his secondary pitches improves, his projection would upgrade from setup man to closer.

Year	Club (League)	Class	W	L	ERA	G	GS	CG	SV	IP	H	R	ER	HR	BB	SO	AVG
2002	Tigers (GCL)	R	1	1	2.63	20	0	0	1	38	40	24	11	0	21	46	.260
	Oneonta (NY-P)	A	0	0	23.48	2	0	0	0	2	7	8	6	0	4	4	.500
2003	Tigers (GCL)	R	2	2	2.59	22	0	0	7	24	18	10	7	0	15	30	.205
	Oneonta (NY-P)	A	0	0	10.91	2	0	0	0	3	6	4	4	0	1	4	.400
2004	West Michigan (Mid)	A	2	4	3.83	54	0	0	17	54	51	30	23	2	33	44	.239
2005	Erie (EL)	AA	0	1	15.88	1	0	0	0	2	2	3	3	0	4	0	.286
	Lakeland (FSL)	A	4	3	3.39	40	10	0	5	96	66	46	36	5	36	97	.191
MINOR LEAGUE TOTALS			9	11	3.70	141	10	0	30	219	190	125	90	7	114	225	.227

16 JAIR JURRJENS
RHP

Born: Jan. 29, 1986. **B-T:** R-R. **Ht.:** 6-1. **Wt.:** 160. **Signed:** Curacao, 2003. **Signed by:** Greg Smith.

Jurrjens signed in 2003 out of Curacao and took his first stab at full-season ball in 2005. He was West Michigan's best starter, ranking sixth in the Midwest League in ERA as the Whitecaps had the league's third-best record and best ERA (3.63). His success has the Tigers projecting him as a No. 4 starter if everything falls into place. Jurrjens works primarily off his fastball, which has modest movement but has seen a boost in velocity to the low 90s. He has shown the ability to pound the lower half of the strike zone with his fastball, which tops out at 94 mph. Some scouts can see him throwing much harder as he fills out, particularly if he moves to a relief role down the line, which is a possibility. His second pitch is a good changeup that he throws for strikes. His curveball remains slurvy and could stand a lot of work. His feel for pitching, however, will keep him a starter for now in high Class A.

Year	Club (League)	Class	W	L	ERA	G	GS	CG	SV	IP	H	R	ER	HR	BB	SO	AVG
2003	Tigers (GCL)	R	2	1	3.21	7	2	0	0	28	33	16	10	3	3	20	.292
2004	Tigers (GCL)	R	4	2	2.27	6	6	2	0	40	25	16	10	2	10	39	.171
	Oneonta (NY-P)	A	1	5	5.31	7	7	0	0	39	50	25	23	0	10	31	.311
2005	West Michigan (Mid)	A	12	6	3.41	26	26	0	0	143	132	62	54	5	36	108	.246
MINOR LEAGUE TOTALS			19	14	3.50	46	41	2	0	249	240	119	97	10	59	198	.251

17 JUAN FRANCIA
2B

Born: Jan. 4, 1982. **B-T:** B-R. **Ht.:** 5-9. **Wt.:** 145. **Signed:** Venezuela, 1998. **Signed by:** Ramon Pena.

Francia had two games to remember in 2005. On May 24, Francia collected his first three extra-base hits of the season—two homers and a double. After a promotion to Double-A, he hit safely in 17 of 20 games and hit for the cycle Aug. 9. His improvement last season prompted the Tigers to re-sign the six-year free agent before instructional league. Francia has shown some plus tools throughout his career, most notably his well above-average speed, and he has made small strides in becoming a more efficient basestealer. He'll never hit for much power and fits the Luis Castillo profile as a leadoff or No. 2 hitter who runs well, handles the bat and draws an occasional walk. Francia still plays out of control at times and has to learn to maintain his concentration throughout both a game and the long season. He's settled into being a second baseman. He can play shortstop in a pinch, but his arm fits much better at second. He'll head back to Double-A for 2006 but could reach Detroit soon as a utility player thanks to his speed.

Year	Club (League)	Class	AVG	G	AB	R	H	2B	3B	HR	RBI	BB	SO	SB	OBP	SLG
1999	San Felipe (VSL)	R	.321	37	84	20	27	6	0	0	15	15	29	9	.457	.393
2000	Tigers (GCL)	R	.268	53	194	34	52	5	3	0	14	19	43	23	.336	.325
	Lakeland (FSL)	A	.225	11	40	3	9	2	0	0	0	7	9	5	.340	.275
2001	Oneonta (NY-P)	A	.340	47	191	30	65	5	2	0	8	11	32	17	.380	.387
2002	West Michigan (Mid)	A	.270	128	503	94	136	13	5	2	41	53	94	53	.346	.328

			AVG	G	AB	R	H	2B	3B	HR	RBI	BB	SO	SB	OBP	SLG
2003	West Michigan (Mid)	A	.240	118	405	49	97	7	6	0	27	42	78	31	.316	.286
2004	West Michigan (Mid)	A	.320	111	413	73	132	11	3	0	32	34	44	37	.384	.361
2005	Lakeland (FSL)	A	.325	60	255	39	83	5	0	3	29	27	34	26	.399	.380
	Erie (EL)	AA	.290	72	300	38	87	9	6	3	27	17	43	15	.336	.390
MINOR LEAGUE TOTALS			.288	637	2385	380	688	63	25	8	193	225	406	216	.358	.346

18 RYAN RABURN 2B

Born: April 17, 1981. **B-T:** R-R. **Ht.:** 6-0. **Wt.:** 185. **Drafted:** South Florida CC, 2001 (5th round). **Signed by:** Steve Nichols.

Raburn achieved one key goal in 2005 by remaining healthy. Raburn stayed off the disabled list and played a career-best 130 games, then had enough left to help Toledo win the International League title. He batted .348 in the playoffs during the Mud Hens' Governor's Cup run. Otherwise, Raburn didn't have a tremendous season, and with the arrival of Placido Polanco in Detroit, his window of opportunity with the Tigers is closing. He was outrighted off the 40-man roster prior to the Winter Meetings. Raburn, whose brother Johnny was a utilityman in the Devil Rays system last year, always has been a player who will only go as far as his bat will take him. He's not a gifted defensive player, and while he's athletic, he has lost some athleticism since dislocating his hip in an all-terrain vehicle mishap that sidelined him for most of 2002. He doesn't run well and isn't fluid at second base, where he led the IL with 21 errors. The Tigers are considering moving him to the outfield, and he has enough power to make the switch. He was hitting .197 in late May but came on in the second half to finish third on the Mud Hens in homers and RBIs. Just a solid bat, though, won't do it for Raburn. He'll return to Triple-A and try to be more consistent in order to earn a big league look.

Year	Club (League)	Class	AVG	G	AB	R	H	2B	3B	HR	RBI	BB	SO	SB	OBP	SLG
2001	Tigers (GCL)	R	.155	19	58	4	9	2	0	1	5	9	19	2	.300	.241
	Oneonta (NY-P)	A	.363	44	171	25	62	17	8	8	42	17	42	1	.418	.696
2002	Tigers (GCL)	R	.300	8	30	4	9	3	1	1	5	3	7	0	.364	.567
	West Michigan (Mid)	A	.220	40	150	27	33	10	1	6	28	16	46	0	.306	.420
2003	West Michigan (Mid)	A	.351	16	57	14	20	7	0	3	12	6	14	1	.431	.632
	Lakeland (FSL)	A	.222	95	325	52	72	14	3	12	56	45	89	2	.332	.394
2004	Lakeland (FSL)	A	.273	3	11	1	3	1	0	1	3	1	6	0	.333	.636
	Erie (EL)	AA	.301	98	366	66	110	29	4	16	63	47	96	3	.390	.533
	Detroit (AL)	MLB	.138	12	29	4	4	1	0	0	1	2	15	1	.194	.172
2005	Toledo (IL)	AAA	.253	130	471	62	119	22	4	19	64	45	109	8	.323	.437
MAJOR LEAGUE TOTALS			.138	12	29	4	4	1	0	0	1	2	15	1	.194	.172
MINOR LEAGUE TOTALS			.267	453	1639	255	437	105	21	67	278	189	428	17	.352	.479

19 DONALD KELLY 3B/SS

Born: Feb. 15, 1980. **B-T:** L-R. **Ht.:** 6-4. **Wt.:** 190. **Drafted:** Point Park (Pa.) College, 2001 (8th round). **Signed by:** Lou Laslo.

Kelly won't be an impact big leaguer unless his power spikes significantly, but he can be a valuable utilityman with a solid bat and the ability to play all over the field. Kelly had his best year as a pro in 2005, raking his way through Double-A before finishing up playing shortstop for Toledo's International League championship club. He hit .300 with seven RBIs in the IL playoffs to cap his first full year above Class A. He missed most of the 2004 season with a nerve injury in his right shoulder that required surgery but played injury-free in 2005. He also played in the Arizona Fall League at shortstop after Tony Giarratano's injuries precluded him from going there. Kelly lacks the range, quickness and agility to be an everyday shortstop and is better suited for third base with his solid arm and good hands. Offensively, Kelly sprays line drives to the gaps, has shown pull power and covers the plate well, making him tough to strike out. He has a chance to open the season as a big league utilityman, but more likely will head to Triple-A as the everyday third baseman.

Year	Club (League)	Class	AVG	G	AB	R	H	2B	3B	HR	RBI	BB	SO	SB	OBP	SLG
2001	Oneonta (NY-P)	A	.286	67	262	41	75	8	3	0	25	25	16	8	.345	.340
2002	West Michigan (Mid)	A	.286	128	455	72	130	21	5	1	59	59	40	9	.368	.360
2003	Lakeland (FSL)	A	.317	87	303	48	96	17	4	1	38	45	25	15	.401	.409
	Erie (EL)	AA	.265	22	83	14	22	5	1	1	13	15	9	0	.378	.386
2004	Erie (EL)	AA	.228	28	101	17	23	6	2	0	9	15	13	3	.331	.327
	Tigers (GCL)	R	.400	3	10	2	4	0	0	0	0	0	2	1	.400	.400
2005	Erie (EL)	AA	.340	82	329	54	112	22	3	9	54	36	43	10	.402	.508
	Toledo (IL)	AAA	.250	43	160	22	40	8	0	1	13	13	15	8	.306	.319
MINOR LEAGUE TOTALS			.295	460	1703	270	502	87	18	13	211	208	163	54	.370	.390

20 KYLE SLEETH   RHP

Born: Dec. 20, 1981. **B-T:** R-R. **Ht.:** 6-5. **Wt.:** 205. **Drafted:** Wake Forest, 2003 (1st round). **Signed by:** Bill Buck.

When Sleeth was drafted the Tigers hoped he would never rank this low on a prospect list, but the No. 3 overall pick in the 2003 draft hasn't worked out as expected. Sleeth signed for $3.35 million after winning an NCAA-record-tying 26 consecutive decisions during his decorated career at Wake Forest. In college, he flashed a fastball that touched 96 mph, two average to above-average breaking balls and excellent athleticism and poise. Scouts who questioned Sleeth didn't like that he threw across his body, but the majority felt he was strong enough physically and athletic enough to avoid injury despite his less-than-perfect mechanics. They also believed his delivery gave his pitches movement. Sleeth's pro career got off to a solid start at high Class A in 2004, but when he struggled in Double-A later that year, the Tigers decided to smooth out his crossfire finish. Sleeth had trouble adjusting to his new delivery, and last year came down with an elbow injury that required Tommy John surgery in June. If his rehab goes well, he'll start throwing on the side in spring training. His 2006 season will be about getting healthy. Detroit won't know how his elbow and stuff will bounce back until 2007.

Year	Club (League)	Class	W	L	ERA	G	GS	CG	SV	IP	H	R	ER	HR	BB	SO	AVG
2004	Lakeland (FSL)	A	3	4	3.67	9	9	1	0	54	47	26	22	3	15	55	.230
	Erie (EL)	AA	4	4	6.30	13	13	0	0	80	93	58	56	14	34	57	.297
2005	Did not play—Injured																
MINOR LEAGUE TOTALS			7	8	5.24	22	22	1	0	134	140	84	78	17	49	112	.271

21 P.J. FINIGAN   RHP

Born: Sept. 30, 1982. **B-T:** R-R. **Ht.:** 6-0. **Wt.:** 185. **Drafted:** Southern Illinois, 2005 (7th round). **Signed by:** Marty Miller.

Finigan was Southern Illinois' most important player for three seasons, working as both the team's starting shortstop and as a pitcher. After two years as a reliever, Finigan moved into the Salukis' rotation in 2005 and went 9-3, 3.24 with four complete games. He also had his best offensive season, winning the Missouri Valley Conference batting title at .388 while ranking second with a .461 on-base percentage. The consensus was that the MVC player of the year's pro future was on the mound, and the Tigers concurred after signing him for a low-end $27,500 bonus as a seventh-round pick in June. He came cheap because he was a college senior, and it was the first time that Finigan had been drafted. He has athleticism that produces a fluid, easy arm action that he repeats. He pounds the strike zone with 89-93 mph fastballs. Detroit believes he'll develop more velocity as he focuses on pitching and hones his mechanics. His slider is an above-average offering that showed improved depth and movement after he turned pro, and he has shown a feel for a solid-average changeup. Finigan's athleticism, two-way background and MVC roots earn him comparisons to Blue Jays farmhand Shaun Marcum, though the Tigers want to keep Finigan in the bullpen instead of moving him to the rotation as Toronto did with Marcum. Finigan projects as a solid setup man and should start 2006 in high Class A.

Year	Club (League)	Class	W	L	ERA	G	GS	CG	SV	IP	H	R	ER	HR	BB	SO	AVG
2005	West Michigan (Mid)	A	2	2	2.39	25	0	0	4	38	35	11	10	0	7	32	.243
MINOR LEAGUE TOTALS			2	2	2.39	25	0	0	4	38	35	11	10	0	7	32	.243

22 MICHAEL HOLLIMON   SS

Born: June 14, 1982. **B-T:** B-R. **Ht.:** 6-1. **Wt.:** 185. **Drafted:** Oral Roberts, 2005 (16th round). **Signed by:** Steve Taylor.

Four years ago, Hollimon was a freshman at Texas, undrafted after a ballyhooed high school career. He was considered a potential first-round pick, but went undrafted amid reports that he wanted a $2 million bonus. Hollimon was the Longhorns' top recruit, roomed with 2005 Rookie of the Year Huston Street, and was expected to be a college star. He started most of the 2002 season at shortstop but hit just .276 and lost his job to junior-college transfer Brandon Fahey as Texas won the College World Series. Hollimon's confidence plunged as he struggled defensively on Texas' artificial-turf infield and offensively with a steady diet of breaking balls. After two more seasons of part-time duty, he transferred to Oral Roberts, where he had a solid senior season in 2005. Area scout Steve Taylor stuck with Hollimon, and the Tigers are glad he did after signing him for $5,000 as a 16th-round pick. He led the short-season New York-Penn League in runs and triples in his pro debut, showing solid tools across the board. Hollimon is athletic enough to repeat his swing from both sides of the plate, though he has more leverage and power from the left side. He has the speed and arm to be an average defender at shortstop in the big leagues. He's not overly physical and will need to work to keep his strength up over the course of an entire season. Hollimon is already 23, so the Tigers probably will accelerate his timetable to see if he can be an everyday player. More likely, he profiles as a utilityman, still excellent value for where he was drafted.

Year	Club (League)	Class	AVG	G	AB	R	H	2B	3B	HR	RBI	BB	SO	SB	OBP	SLG
2005	Oneonta (NY-P)	A	.277	72	256	66	71	13	10	13	53	48	76	8	.389	.559
MINOR LEAGUE TOTALS			.277	72	256	66	71	13	10	13	53	48	76	8	.389	.559

23 SENDY VASQUEZ   RHP

Born: Aug. 10, 1982. **B-T:** B-R. **Ht.:** 6-1. **Wt.:** 160. **Signed:** Dominican Republic, 2003. **Signed by:** Ramon Pena.

Most top Dominican players who turn into stars sign as teenagers. Vasquez was nearly 21 when he signed in 2003, however, and he fell further behind when he spent most of his first two seasons in the Gulf Coast League. He won all seven of his decisions at short-season Oneonta last year, tying for second in the New York-Penn League in wins. Vasquez' calling card is a mid-90s fastball. He has excellent arm speed that provides his fastball velocity, and he maintains the same arm speed on his changeup. He has shown some feel for his change-up and flashed the ability to spin a breaking ball. His secondary stuff and his control have a lot of improvement to make, so the Tigers took a calculated gamble that they wouldn't have to protect him on their 40-man roster this offseason. After slipping through the major league Rule 5 draft, Vasquez could skip a level and jump to high Class A.

Year	Club (League)	Class	W	L	ERA	G	GS	CG	SV	IP	H	R	ER	HR	BB	SO	AVG
2003	Tigers (GCL)	R	2	2	7.45	11	1	0	0	16	18	13	13	0	11	12	.290
	Tigers (DSL)	R	0	0	3.21	4	2	0	1	14	7	7	5	1	10	14	.152
2004	Tigers (GCL)	R	2	2	5.46	17	2	0	3	28	29	19	17	0	21	32	.266
2005	Oneonta (NY-P)	A	7	0	3.63	15	11	0	0	67	53	30	27	4	34	60	.218
MINOR LEAGUE TOTALS			11	4	4.48	47	16	0	4	125	107	69	62	5	76	118	.233

24 AUDY CIRIACO   SS

Born: June 16, 1987. **B-T:** R-R. **Ht.:** 6-3. **Wt.:** 195. **Signed:** Dominican Republic, 2005. **Signed by:** Ramon Pena.

The Tigers have a few young Latin American players they have hopes for, none more so than Ciriaco, who signed for $175,000 last February. He struggled at first in extended spring training, then made enough adjustments to earn an assignment to the Gulf Coast League. He got off to a hot start in the GCL before fading, and how he develops physically in the offseason will determine where he starts the 2006 season. Ciriaco's skills could land him on a full-season roster. He has a long, lanky frame closer to that of Shawon Dunston or fellow Tigers farmhand Brent Dlugach, rather than the typical waterbug Latin American shortstop. He has fluid actions with good quickness, soft hands and an above-average arm that plays well at short. He has good bat speed, a sound stroke and some strength, though he needs more. The Tigers project him to hit for power in the future. Ciriaco remains raw and undisciplined at the plate, and he needs to prove he can maintain his play over a long period of time. Nevertheless, the Tigers are excited about his future.

Year	Club (League)	Class	AVG	G	AB	R	H	2B	3B	HR	RBI	BB	SO	SB	OBP	SLG
2005	Tigers (GCL)	R	.250	40	152	20	38	3	4	5	23	10	46	5	.299	.421
MINOR LEAGUE TOTALS			.250	40	152	20	38	3	4	5	23	10	46	5	.299	.421

25 CHRIS ROBINSON   C

Born: May 12, 1984. **B-T:** R-R. **Ht.:** 6-0. **Wt.:** 200. **Drafted:** Illinois, 2005 (3rd round). **Signed by:** Marty Miller.

Detroit hasn't needed great catching depth recently after developing defensive stalwart Brandon Inge and signing all-star Ivan Rodriguez as a free agent. After Rodriguez' horrid 2005 season and Inge's improvement offensively after a move to third base, the Tigers have started to think harder about their future behind the plate. To that end, they used their second pick in the 2005 draft, a third-round selection, to pick Robinson. A native of Canada who played on several junior national teams, Robinson led Illinois to the 2005 Big Ten Conference regular-season title, its first since 1998, before signing for $422,000. His pro career get off to a horrible 2-for-34 start before a four-hit game July 11, after which he batted .299. He has a solid approach and projects as a fringe-average hitter who handles the bat well, with the ability to make consistent contact and hit-and-run. Defensively, he has a plus arm and average receiving skills. His leadership ability also earns praise from scouts.

Robinson could earn a job in high Class A this year considering the organization's lack of depth at catcher.

Year	Club (League)	Class	AVG	G	AB	R	H	2B	3B	HR	RBI	BB	SO	SB	OBP	SLG
2005	Oneonta (NY-P)	A	.154	4	13	2	2	0	0	0	1	1	3	0	.200	.154
	West Michigan (Mid)	A	.257	41	148	16	38	8	1	2	18	15	39	0	.329	.365
MINOR LEAGUE TOTALS			.248	45	161	18	40	8	1	2	19	16	42	0	.318	.348

26 VIRGIL VASQUEZ   RHP

Born: June 7, 1982. **B-T:** R-R. **Ht.:** 6-3. **Wt.:** 205. **Drafted:** UC Santa Barbara, 2003 (7th round). **Signed by:** Tom Hinkle.

Vasquez was a Rangers seventh-round pick out of high school in 2000 but didn't sign, instead attending UC Santa Barbara. Known at Matt Vasquez in college (Matthew is his middle name), he went in the seventh round again in 2003. He was part of a strong Lakeland pitching staff in 2005, joining fellow starters Justin Verlander, Jordan Tata, Eulogio de la Cruz and Nate Bumstead on this Top 30 list. Several other Lakeland pitchers, including lefthanders Lucas French and Danny Zell and righthanders Randor Beird and Preston Larrison, also are on the organization's radar screen. Vasquez moved up to Double-A after just eight starts in high Class A. While he threw eight one-hit innings in his first Erie outing, he won only once thereafter. The Tigers see him as a pitchability righthander, a No. 5 starter with control as good as any pitcher in the system. His stuff remains fringy, though, as he owns an upper-80s fastball, a solid curveball and a decent changeup. He must live down in the strike zone, because when he leaves his stuff up, he gets punished for extra-base hits. He'll return to Double-A in 2006.

Year	Club (League)	Class	W	L	ERA	G	GS	CG	SV	IP	H	R	ER	HR	BB	SO	AVG
2003	Oneonta (NY-P)	A	3	4	6.92	11	11	0	0	53	76	43	41	5	10	35	.328
2004	West Michigan (Mid)	A	14	6	3.64	27	27	0	0	168	156	73	68	14	34	120	.252
2005	Lakeland (FSL)	A	4	1	4.21	8	8	1	0	47	52	23	22	6	7	31	.289
	Erie (EL)	AA	2	8	5.27	15	15	0	0	84	93	59	49	10	14	53	.281
MINOR LEAGUE TOTALS			23	19	4.60	61	61	1	0	352	377	198	180	35	65	239	.277

27 MATT JOYCE   OF

Born: Aug. 3, 1984. **B-T:** L-R. **Ht.:** 6-2. **Wt.:** 185. **Drafted:** Florida Southern, 2005 (12th round). **Signed by:** Steve Nichols.

The Tigers first noticed Joyce when they played against his Florida Southern team, which is based down the street from Detroit's Lakeland spring-training complex. In a scrimmage before spring-training exhibitions began in 2004, Joyce homered against the Tigers. He went on to have a strong sophomore season but struggled as a junior as the Moccasins won the Division II College World Series. Joyce recoved to have a fine pro debut, showing athleticism, a solid bat and good plate discipline. He's still young for his draft class and has room to fill out physically. Joyce has average tools across the board to go with a quiet approach that lets him make consistent contact while using the whole field. His arm might be a tick above average. He also has excellent makeup and a strong work ethic. Joyce has a thin frame that could stand to add muscle, and he'll need more power to play right field, his best position, at higher levels. He'll start his first full year in low Class A.

Year	Club (League)	Class	AVG	G	AB	R	H	2B	3B	HR	RBI	BB	SO	SB	OBP	SLG
2005	Oneonta (NY-P)	A	.331	65	245	51	81	10	4	4	45	30	29	9	.397	.453
MINOR LEAGUE TOTALS			.331	65	245	51	81	10	4	4	45	30	29	9	.397	.453

28 BRENT DLUGACH   SS

Born: March 3, 1983. **B-T:** R-R. **Ht.:** 6-4. **Wt.:** 200. **Drafted:** Memphis, 2004 (6th round). **Signed by:** Harold Zonder.

Dlugach is best summed up as atypical. While he's tall and lanky, he's often described as a smooth-fielding shortstop. Though he has fringy speed and range, has a knack for being in the right place, getting good hops and making plays. He soaked up the experience of his coach at Memphis, former big league shortstop Dave Anderson, who managed at the Triple-A level in the Tigers system as recently as 2000. Dlugach's best assets defensively are his extreme athleticism and exceptional hands. He also has a strong arm and is adept at making accurate throws from different arm angles. Offensively, Dlugach has some potential but his bat probably will never equal his glove. His long frame lends itself to a long swing, and while he has some strength and power, he's not likely to hit for a consistent average. If he makes enough contact to bat .250-.260, he could contribute 10-15 homers. His best-case profile is to become a Kevin Elster. Ticketed for high Class A, Dlugach will move as fast as his bat dictates.

Year	Club (League)	Class	AVG	G	AB	R	H	2B	3B	HR	RBI	BB	SO	SB	OBP	SLG
2004	Oneonta (NY-P)	A	.213	47	183	17	39	7	2	1	12	8	59	5	.256	.290
2005	West Michigan (Mid)	A	.283	124	488	54	138	26	5	5	61	19	121	13	.317	.387
MINOR LEAGUE TOTALS			.264	171	671	71	177	33	7	6	73	27	180	18	.300	.361

29 NATE BUMSTEAD   RHP

Born: May 5, 1982. **B-T:** R-R. **Ht.:** 6-2. **Wt.:** 215. **Drafted:** Louisiana State, 2004 (32nd round). **Signed by:** Jerome Cochran.

Bumstead is the classic case of a pitcher who will have to prove himself at every level, but so far the former 32nd-pound pick has reached high Class A while going 15-5, 2.43 in two pro seasons. He had an uneven career at Louisiana State after transferring from the College of Southern Idaho, where he played with Detroit farmhand Kody Kirkland. Bumstead went 21-7 in two seasons at LSU but his strikeout rate fell, and his draft stock dropped along with it. He has a fringy 86-89 mph fastball and comes nearly straight over the top in his delivery, which makes it hard to project much more velocity. However, his delivery helps Bumstead's best pitch, a 12-to-6 curveball. He also locates his changeup and made great strides in his fastball command in 2005, helping him rank third in the Florida State League in ERA, second in wins and third in innings. Bumstead tired late in the season and the command of all his pitches faltered. He profiles as no more than a fifth starter, and he could become a solid middle reliever because his curveball helps him attack righthanders. They hit just .209 against him in 2005. Bumstead will move up to Double-A for 2006.

Year	Club (League)	Class	W	L	ERA	G	GS	CG	SV	IP	H	R	ER	HR	BB	SO	AVG
2004	Oneonta (NY-P)	A	3	1	2.03	11	9	0	0	58	47	21	13	3	15	75	.226
2005	Lakeland (FSL)	A	12	4	2.58	25	25	2	0	161	136	61	46	11	58	111	.227
MINOR LEAGUE TOTALS			15	5	2.43	36	34	2	0	218	183	82	59	14	73	186	.227

30 VINCE BLUE   OF

Born: Feb. 8, 1983. **B-T:** L-R. **Ht.:** 6-2. **Wt.:** 180. **Drafted:** HS—Houston, Texas, 2001 (10th round). **Signed by:** Tim Grieve.

One of the best defensive outfielders in the system, Blue was an all-state performer in Texas in 2001 along with Brent Clevlen, whom he played beside in the Lakeland outfield last year. Blue has progressed slowly with the bat and didn't make it to full-season ball until his fourth pro season, but he made significant progress in 2005. He'll never hit for much power and compares to current Tigers center fielder Nook Logan. Blue has top-of-the-line speed, getting down to first base in as quick as 3.8 seconds from the left side. Blue isn't afraid to go deep in counts and work a walk, but his slap-hitting approach doesn't scare pitchers either. He can be handled with hard stuff inside and lacks bat speed. While he can fly, he's an inefficient basestealer who must improve his reads and jumps after leading the minors last year with 29 caught stealings in 69 tries. He also needs to become a better bunter to take even more advantage of his speed. Blue stands out defensively with good range and a fearless approach, though his arm is below average. He's ready for his first taste of Double-A in 2006.

Year	Club (League)	Class	AVG	G	AB	R	H	2B	3B	HR	RBI	BB	SO	SB	OBP	SLG
2001	Tigers (GCL)	R	.248	42	113	16	28	2	2	0	4	24	24	8	.380	.301
2002	Tigers (GCL)	R	.219	56	183	20	40	5	4	0	7	17	38	20	.282	.290
2003	Oneonta (NY-P)	A	.288	70	233	47	67	7	8	2	26	38	56	13	.388	.412
2004	West Michigan (Mid)	A	.260	134	497	66	129	19	4	2	43	49	97	19	.328	.326
2005	Lakeland (FSL)	A	.297	124	498	67	148	17	3	0	50	47	84	40	.356	.343
MINOR LEAGUE TOTALS			.270	426	1524	216	412	50	21	4	130	175	299	100	.345	.339

FLORIDA
MARLINS

BY **MIKE BERARDINO**

The Marlins thought they loaded up for a playoff run with the offseason signing of first baseman Carlos Delgado to a four-year, $52 million deal. Delgado held up his end of the bargain with his typical 30-homer, 100-RBI output, but that didn't lead to his first postseason appearance. The Marlins lost 10 of their last 15 games to short-circuit their wild-card bid.

That may be the closest the Marlins come to the playoffs for a while. And it probably will be a long time before Florida lavishes another $52 million contract on a player.

Frustrated in their attempts to get public funding for a baseball-only stadium, the Marlins started tearing their club apart on Thanksgiving. They completed deals that sent Delgado to the Mets and former World Series MVP Josh Beckett, Mike Lowell and Guillermo Mota to the Red Sox. By the end of the Winter Meetings, Florida had traded Luis Castillo to the Twins, Paul Lo Duca to the Mets and Juan Pierre to the Cubs, while A.J. Burnett had joined the Blue Jays via free agency. Burnett's $55 million contract may be double his former club's 2006 payroll.

Club president David Samson began scouting possible new homes at owner Jeffrey Loria's behest. Florida's lease to play at Dolphins Stadium expires after 2007, though they can renew it annually through 2010. The Marlins have said they won't play there after 2010.

For now, Florida fans can take solace in Miguel Cabera, Dontrelle Willis and a suddenly deep farm system. The replenishing began in June. Loaded with compensatory

ED WOLFSTEIN

draft picks for the free-agent losses of Carl Pavano, Armando Benitez and Mike Redmond after the 2004 season, the Marlins had five of the first 44 picks and eight of the top 96 in the 2005 draft. Six were spent on pitching, including the top five, with first-rounders Chris Volstad and Aaron Thompson showing the most immediate promise.

The flurry of trades brought in players that the Marlins hope will have a swifter impact. Hanley Ramirez, the top shortstop prospect on the trade market, will get a chance to replace Alex Gonzalez. Anibal Sanchez, Yusmeiro Petit, Ricky Nolasco, Renyel Pinto and Sergio Mitre are fodder for a decimated rotation. Mike Jacobs could take over for Delgado at first base, while Travis Bowyer will factor into the bullpen.

As usual, the system produced several key contributors during the 2005 season. Lefthander **Jason Vargas**, a second-round pick in 2004, made the biggest impact after soaring from low Class A Greensboro to the majors by mid-July. Right fielder Jeremy Hermida tore up the Double-A Southern League, yet he still had to wait until Aug. 31 to make his big league debut. Lefthander Scott Olsen, catcher/first baseman Josh Willingham, shortstop Robert Andino and righthanders Chris Resop and Randall Messenger are other farmhands who could get more extensive playing time in 2006 after brief looks last year.

TOP 30 PROSPECTS

1. Jeremy Hermida, of
2. Hanley Ramirez, ss
3. Anibal Sanchez, rhp
4. Scott Olsen, lhp
5. Yusmeiro Petit, rhp
6. Josh Johnson, rhp
7. Chris Volstad, rhp
8. Ricky Nolasco, rhp
9. Gaby Hernandez, rhp
10. Aaron Thompson, lhp
11. Josh Willingham, c/1b
12. Mike Jacobs, 1b/c
13. Renyel Pinto, lhp
14. Taylor Tankersley, lhp
15. Kris Harvey, 3b/of
16. Ryan Tucker, rhp
17. Robert Andino, ss
18. Eric Reed, of
19. Jason Stokes, 1b
20. Sean West, lhp
21. J.T. Restko, of
22. Brad McCann, 1b
23. Chris Resop, rhp
24. Jesus Delgado, rhp
25. Jose Garcia, rhp
26. Jacob Marceaux, rhp
27. Travis Bowyer, rhp
28. Harvey Garcia, rhp
29. Dan Uggla, inf
30. Jeff Allison, rhp

ORGANIZATION OVERVIEW

General manager: Larry Beinfest. **Farm director:** Brian Chattin. **Scouting director:** Stan Meek.

2005 PERFORMANCE

Class	Team	League	W	L	Pct.	Finish*	Manager
Majors	Florida	National	83	79	.512	t-5th (16)	Jack McKeon
Triple-A	Albuquerque Isotopes	Pacific Coast	78	66	.542	5th (16)	Dean Treanor
Double-A	Carolina Mudcats	Southern	77	57	.575	3rd (10)	Gary Allenson
High A	Jupiter Hammerheads	Florida State	64	71	.474	9th (12)	Tim Cossins
Low A	Greensboro Grasshoppers	South Atlantic	67	71	.486	11th (16)	Brandon Hyde
Short-season	Jamestown Jammers	New York-Penn	31	44	.413	12th (14)	Mike Mordecai
Rookie	GCL Marlins	Gulf Coast	24	30	.444	t-9th (12)	Edwin Rodriguez
OVERALL 2005 MINOR LEAGUE RECORD			341	339	.501	15th (30)	

*Finish in overall standings (No. of teams in league).

ORGANIZATION LEADERS

BATTING   *Minimum 250 at-bats
*AVG	Dillon, Joe, Albuquerque	.360
R	Wilson, Josh, Albuquerque	88
H	McCann, Brad, Carolina/Greensboro	141
TB	McCann, Brad, Carolina/Greensboro	264
2B	McCann, Brad, Carolina/Greensboro	35
3B	De Aza, Alejandro, Jupiter	9
	Shanks, James, Albuquerque/Carolina	9
HR	McCann, Brad, Carolina/Greensboro	28
RBI	McCann, Brad, Carolina/Greensboro	106
BB	Hermida, Jeremy, Carolina	111
SO	Mitchell, Lee, Jupiter	142
SB	Reed, Eric, Albuquerque/Carolina	40
*OBP	Dillon, Joe, Albuquerque	.459
*SLG	Dillon, Joe, Albuquerque	.631

PITCHING   #Minimum 75 innings
W	Johnson, Josh, Carolina/Jupiter	12
	Russ, James, Carolina/Jupiter	12
L	Castillo, Frank, Albuquerque	11
#ERA	Vargas, Jason, Carolina/Greensboro/Jupiter	2.08
G	Nestor, Scott, Greensboro	58
CG	Walrond, Les, Albuquerque	2
SV	Mobley, Chris, Greensboro	34
IP	Russ, James, Carolina/Jupiter	167
BB	Fulchino, Jeff, Albuquerque	67
SO	Russ, James, Carolina/Jupiter	148

BEST TOOLS

Best Hitter for Average	Jeremy Hermida
Best Power Hitter	Mike Jacobs
Best Strike-Zone Discipline	Jeremy Hermida
Fastest Baserunner	Jose Campusano
Best Athlete	Jai Miller
Best Fastball	Travis Bowyer
Best Curveball	Allen Baxter
Best Slider	Scott Olsen
Best Changeup	Anibal Sanchez
Best Control	Yusmeiro Petit
Best Defensive Catcher	Brett Hayes
Best Defensive Infielder	Hanley Ramirez
Best Infield Arm	Hanley Ramirez
Best Defensive Outfielder	Eric Reed
Best Outfield Arm	Brett Carroll

PROJECTED 2009 LINEUP

Catcher	Brett Hayes
First Base	Mike Jacobs
Second Base	Robert Andino
Third Base	Miguel Cabrera
Shortstop	Hanley Ramirez
Left Field	Josh Willingham
Center Field	Eric Reed

Right Field	Jeremy Hermida
No. 1 Starter	Dontrelle Willis
No. 2 Starter	Anibal Sanchez
No. 3 Starter	Scott Olsen
No. 4 Starter	Yusmeiro Petit
No. 5 Starter	Josh Johnson
Closer	Ryan Tucker

LAST YEAR'S TOP 20 PROSPECTS

1. Jeremy Hermida, of
2. Scott Olsen, lhp
3. Yorman Bazardo, rhp
4. Jason Stokes, 1b
5. Josh Willingham, c/1b
6. Eric Reed, of
7. Taylor Tankersley, lhp
8. Jason Vargas, lhp
9. Robert Andino, ss
10. Trevor Hutchinson, rhp
11. Josh Johnson, rhp
12. Josh Wilson, ss
13. Luke Hagerty, lhp
14. Randall Messenger, rhp
15. Rick Vanden Hurk, rhp
16. Jai Miller, of
17. Greg Burns, of
18. Logan Kensing, rhp
19. Jamar Walton, of
20. Chris Resop, rhp

TOP PROSPECTS OF THE DECADE

Year	Player, Pos.	2005 Org.
1996	Edgar Renteria, ss	Red Sox
1997	Felix Heredia, lhp	Yankees
1998	Mark Kotsay, of	Athletics
1999	A.J. Burnett, rhp	Marlins
2000	A.J. Burnett, rhp	Marlins
2001	Josh Beckett, rhp	Marlins
2002	Josh Beckett, rhp	Marlins
2003	Miguel Cabrera, 3b	Marlins
2004	Jeremy Hermida, of	Marlins
2005	Jeremy Hermida, of	Marlins

TOP DRAFT PICKS OF THE DECADE

Year	Player, Pos.	2005 Org.
1996	Mark Kotsay, of	Athletics
1997	Aaron Akin, rhp	Out of baseball
1998	Chip Ambres, of	Royals
1999	Josh Beckett, rhp	Marlins
2000	Adrian Gonzalez, 1b	Rangers
2001	Garrett Berger, rhp (2nd round)	Tigers
2002	Jeremy Hermida, of	Marlins
2003	Jeff Allison, rhp	Marlins
2004	Taylor Tankersley, lhp	Marlins
2005	Chris Volstad, rhp	Marlins

ALL-TIME LARGEST BONUSES

Josh Beckett, 1999	$3,625,000
Adrian Gonzalez, 2000	$3,000,000
Livan Hernandez, 1996	$2,500,000
Jason Stokes, 2000	$2,027,000
Jeremy Hermida, 2002	$2,012,500

MINOR LEAGUE DEPTH CHART

Florida Marlins

Rank: **2**

STRENGTH: Depth. This is the kind of farm system a fire sale can produce.

WEAKNESS: Middle infield. The Marlins addressed shortstop (Hanley Ramirez) and second base (Dan Uggla) via trade and the Rule 5 draft.

*Depth charts prepared by **John Manuel** and **Chris Kline**. Numbers in parentheses indicate prospect rankings.*

LF
J.T. Restko (21)
Jamar Walton

CF
Eric Reed (18)
Greg Burns
Reggie Abercrombie
Jai Miller
Alejandro De Aza
James Shanks

RF
Jeremy Hermida (1)
Chris Aguila
Angel Molina
Brett Carroll

3B
Kris Harvey (15)
Grant Psomas
Gabriel Sanchez

SS
Hanley Ramirez (2)
Robert Andino (17)
Josh Wilson
Jose Campusano

2B
Dan Uggla (29)
Brian Cleveland

1B
Mike Jacobs (12)
Jason Stokes (19)
Brad McCann (22)

C
Josh Willingham (11)
Brett Hayes
Bradley Davis
Ryan Jorgensen

RHP		LHP	
Starters	**Relievers**	**Starters**	**Relievers**
Anibal Sanchez (3)	Chris Resop (23)	Scott Olsen (4)	Taylor Tankersley (14)
Yusmeiro Petit (5)	Jesus Delgado (24)	Aaron Thompson (10)	Luke Lockwood
Josh Johnson (6)	Jose Garcia (25)	Renyel Pinto (13)	Zach McCormack
Chris Volstad (7)	Travis Bowyer (27)	Sean West (20)	Manuel Olivera
Ricky Nolasco (8)	Harvey Garcia (28)	Adam Bostick	Matt Yourkin
Gaby Hernandez (9)	Randall Messenger	Jon-Michael Nickerson	
Ryan Tucker (16)	Lincoln Holdzkom	Paul Mildren	
Jacob Marceaux (26)	Carlos Martinez	Matthew Goyen	
Jeff Allison (30)	Logan Kensing	Mike Megrew	
Rick Vanden Hurk	Carlos Martinez		
Allen Baxter	David Humen		
Kyle Winters	Rafael Galbizo		
Nic Ungs	Scott Tyler		

2005

Best Pro Debut: After sitting out the spring with a suspension at the University of Miami, 3B Gaby Sanchez (4) won the short-season New York-Penn League batting title (.355). He showed enough promise as a catcher for the Marlins to give him more time there. RHP Chris Volstad (1) ranked as the best pitching prospect in both the NY-P and the Rookie-level Gulf Coast League, going a combined 4-3, 2.22. OF Matt Kutler (24) made the GCL all-star team by hitting .337-1-25, then batted .448 in eight NY-P games.

Best Athlete: 3B/OF Kris Harvey's (2) most obvious tool is his power, but he also has above-average speed and arm strength. As a two-way player at Clemson, he showed a mid-90s fastball in relief.

Best Pure Hitter: The Marlins were impressed Sanchez hit so well after his long layoff. He made very good contact and showed some power potential.

Best Raw Power: Harvey, whose 25 homers were one short of the NCAA Division I lead. The ball jumps off his bat.

Fastest Runner: Harvey has plus speed, though he's better underway than out of the box because he takes a big swing.

Best Defensive Player: C Brett Hayes (2) is very athletic behind the plate and delivers consistent 1.9-second pop times to second base.

Best Fastball: The Marlins had five picks before the second round and used them all on pitchers, so they landed some quality arms. RHP Ryan Tucker (1) has the best velocity, sitting at 92-95 mph and topping out at 97. Volstad can reach 94 mph and has nice sink. Six-foot-8 LHP Sean West (1) has a

RICH ABEL

Harvey

swing-and-miss fastball that runs from 90-94 mph. RHP Jacob Marceaux (1) has a 92-93 mph two-seamer and a 94-95 mph four-seamer. RHP Chris Leroux (7), who had Tommy John surgery before the draft, hit 96-97 mph in the Cape Cod League in 2004.

Best Breaking Ball: LHP Aaron Thompson's (1) slider is a little better than that of Marceaux.

Most Intriguing Background: Harvey's dad Bryan saved 45 games for Florida and was an all-star in the franchise's inaugural 1993 season. RHP Rafael Galbizo (20) is a Cuban defector.

Closest To The Majors: Volstad is very mature for his age and has unusual command for a 6-foot-7 pitcher.

Best Late-Round Pick: Galbizo, 19, has a fastball that can reach 92-93 mph to go with a good curveball. Florida hopes to turn 3B Andy Jenkins (11), the co-MVP of Oregon State's College World Series team, into a catcher. OF Jeff Van Houten (14) may be just 5-foot-9, but his bat plays bigger than that and he hit .283-7-36 in the NY-P.

The One Who Got Away: The Marlins signed their first 12 picks but couldn't come to terms with North Carolina State 1B Aaron Bates (8), who won the home run derby at the Cape Cod League's 2005 all-star game.

Assessment: The Marlins couldn't pass up the arms that kept falling to them. All five of their first-round pitchers have huge ceilings.

2004 LHP Jason Vargas (2) nearly helped pitch the Marlins into the 2005 playoffs and now is one of the team's most experienced pitchers. LHP Taylor Tankersley (1) could contribute in relief soon, while 1B Brad McCann (6) has power in his bat. *GRADE:* B

2002 One of the best drafts in recent years. OF Jeremy Hermida (1) is a stud, and Scott Olsen (6) is one of the game's top lefty prospects. RHP Josh Johnson (4) is a sleeper, OF Eric Reed (9) could start for Florida in 2006 and SS Robert Andino (2) is a slick fielder. *GRADE:* A

2003 RHP Jeff Allison (1) looked like a steal when he fell to Florida at No. 16, but drug problems nearly killed him and he has made baby steps in his comeback. For now, OF J.T. Restko (10) is the best of this group. *GRADE:* D

2001 The Marlins had no first-round pick and their top two choices, RHPs Garrett Berger (2) and Allen Baxter (3), have had arm injuries. RHP Chris Resop (4) surfaced in Florida after converting from the outfield. *GRADE:* F

Draft analysis prepared by Jim Callis. Numbers in parentheses indicate draft rounds.

HERMIDA

OF

ROBERT GURGANUS

Born: Jan. 30, 1984.
Ht.: 6-4. **Wt.:** 200.
Bats: L. **Throws:** R.
Drafted: HS—Marietta, Ga., 2002
(1st round).
Signed by: Joel Smith.

As a high school standout in the Atlanta area, Hermida was ticketed for Clemson along with local rival Jeff Francoeur until the Marlins took him 11th overall in the 2002 draft. Hermida earned Baseball America's nod as the top pure hitter on the prep level and the fourth-best position player overall. Scouts compared him to Eric Chavez, Paul O'Neill and Andy Van Slyke, though Hermida himself preferred Shawn Green as a role model. He signed without acrimony for $2,012,500. His father groomed his hitting stroke from a young age, converting him from a righthanded batter to a lefty at age 4. Hermida was working with wood bats at age 13 and counted former big leaguer Terry Harper among his early private instructors. All those lessons paid further dividends in 2005, when he played in the Futures Game, was MVP of the Southern League all-star game and hit a grand slam off Cardinals righthander Al Reyes in his first big league plate appearance on Aug. 31. That made Hermida the first big leaguer to do that since "Frosty" Bill Duggleby in 1898. This is Hermida's third straight winter atop this list, a first in franchise history.

After he totaled just 16 homers in his first three pro seasons, Hermida's power showed up in 2005. Working with Double-A Carolina hitting coach Steve Phillips and roving instructor John Mallee, Hermida was able to add more lift to his swing and started to pull inside pitches for power. His slight frame continued to fill out. His biggest selling point, though, is a tremendous ability to control the strike zone. As his power increased and his reputation spread, Southern League pitchers routinely avoided throwing him strikes. To his credit, Hermida refused to expand his zone and piled up the third-highest walk total in the minors. For the first time as a pro, he walked more than he struck out. He also runs well and has been caught stealing just 10 times in 77 career chances. His arm is average.

Nagging injuries remain a concern, as he battled minor knee and hamstring problems in the middle of 2005. Earlier in his career he dealt with an ankle problem (2002), a heel injury (2003) and a pulled right hamstring (2004). A left wrist injury delayed his promotion to the majors in late August but he downplayed its role in some of his initial struggles with the Marlins. He continues to make defensive progress, but Hermida is still working to improve his jumps, routes, throwing accuracy and arm strength.

Everything has gone according to plan so far. The next step is for Hermida to take over for free agent Juan Encarnacion as the starting right fielder on Opening Day 2006. If given 500 at-bats as expected, he should challenge to become the Marlins' second National League rookie of the year in four seasons.

Year	Club (League)	Class	AVG	G	AB	R	H	2B	3B	HR	RBI	BB	SO	SB	OBP	SLG
2002	Marlins (GCL)	R	.224	38	134	15	30	7	3	0	14	15	25	5	.316	.321
	Jamestown (NY-P)	A	.319	13	47	8	15	2	1	0	7	7	10	1	.407	.404
2003	Greensboro (SAL)	A	.284	133	468	73	133	23	5	6	49	80	100	28	.387	.393
	Albuquerque (PCL)	AAA	.000	1	3	0	0	0	0	0	0	0	3	0	.000	.000
2004	Jupiter (FSL)	A	.297	91	340	53	101	17	1	10	50	42	73	10	.377	.441
2005	Carolina (SL)	AA	.293	118	386	77	113	29	2	18	63	111	89	23	.457	.518
	Florida (NL)	MLB	.293	23	41	9	12	2	0	4	11	6	12	2	.383	.634
MAJOR LEAGUE TOTALS			.293	23	41	9	12	2	0	4	11	6	12	2	.383	.634
MINOR LEAGUE TOTALS			.284	394	1378	226	392	78	12	34	183	255	300	67	.399	.433

HANLEY RAMIREZ SS

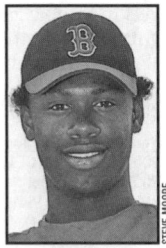

Born: Dec. 23, 1983. **B-T:** B-R. **Ht.:** 6-1. **Wt.:** 170. **Signed:** Dominican Republic, 2000. **Signed by:** Levy Ochoa (Red Sox).

Since reaching full-season ball in 2003, Ramirez has not had a breakout year to match his considerable tools. There was no comparable shortstop on the trade market this offseason, though, and he became the key for Florida in the Josh Beckett trade with Boston. Ramirez has the bat speed, raw power and pitch recognition to hit .300 with 20-plus homers a season. He's aggressive at the plate but doesn't strike out a lot because he easily makes contact. Thanks to his strong wrists, the ball jumps off his bat to all fields. The missing ingredient for Ramirez may be a lack of focus and preparation. He has matured since a few behavioral incidents early in his career, but he needs to develop a game plan at the plate and attach importance to each at-bat. The rest of his game is coming together nicely. He has plus speed, his arm rates a 70 on the 20-80 scouting scale, and his hands and range are above-average as well. He has become much more consistent in the field, cutting his errors to a career-low 19 last year. Ramirez could use more seasoning at Triple-A Albuquerque, but the Marlins need a shortstop and will give him a look in spring training.

Year	Club (League)	Class	AVG	G	AB	R	H	2B	3B	HR	RBI	BB	SO	SB	OBP	SLG
2001	Red Sox (DSL)	R	.345	54	197	32	68	18	2	5	34	15	22	13	.397	.533
2002	Red Sox (GCL)	R	.341	45	164	29	56	11	3	6	26	16	15	8	.402	.555
	Lowell (NY-P)	A	.371	22	97	17	36	9	2	1	19	4	14	4	.400	.536
2003	Augusta (SAL)	A	.275	111	422	69	116	24	3	8	50	32	73	36	.327	.403
2004	Sarasota (FSL)	A	.310	62	239	33	74	8	4	1	24	17	39	12	.364	.389
	Portland (EL)	AA	.310	32	129	26	40	7	2	5	15	10	26	12	.360	.512
2005	Portland (EL)	AA	.271	122	465	66	126	21	7	6	52	39	62	26	.335	.385
	Boston (AL)	MLB	.000	2	2	0	0	0	0	0	0	0	2	0	.000	.000
MAJOR LEAGUE TOTALS			.000	2	2	0	0	0	0	0	0	0	2	0	.000	.000
MINOR LEAGUE TOTALS			.301	448	1713	272	516	98	23	32	220	133	251	111	.352	.441

ANIBAL SANCHEZ RHP

Born: Feb. 27, 1984. **B-T:** R-R. **Ht.:** 6-0. **Wt.:** 180. **Signed:** Venezuela, 2001. **Signed by:** Carlos Ramirez (Red Sox).

The Marlins tried to pry lefthander Jon Lester from the Red Sox in the Josh Beckett blockbuster, but Boston instead gave up Sanchez, a premium prospect in his own right. Since missing all of 2003 after having surgery to transpose a nerve in his elbow, he has dominated minor league hitters. He had an 88-90 mph fastball before his elbow operation, and now he sits at 93-95. Even with the life on his heater and his ability to command it, some scouts think his plus changeup is his best pitch. It has good cutting action, and he throws it with the same arm speed as his fastball. Sanchez' third pitch is his curveball, which is inconsistent and in need of tightening. He has a fluid delivery, though at times he'll fly open with his shoulder, which results in flatter stuff sitting higher in the strike zone. He has good control, mound presence and an understanding of how to get hitters out. In an ideal world, Sanchez would open 2006 in Triple-A, but Florida has a desperate need for starters and may be tempted to bring him to the big leagues.

Year	Club (League)	Class	W	L	ERA	G	GS	CG	SV	IP	H	R	ER	HR	BB	SO	AVG
2001	San Joaquin (VSL)	R	4	3	3.19	24	1	0	3	54	40	23	19	0	23	64	—
2002	Ciudad Alianza (VSL)	R	5	3	3.50	11	11	1	0	62	50	31	24	3	11	73	.222
2003	Did not play—Injured																
2004	Lowell (NY-P)	A	4	4	1.77	15	15	0	0	76	43	24	15	3	29	101	.160
2005	Wilmington (Car)	A	6	1	2.40	14	14	0	0	79	53	25	21	7	24	95	.187
	Portland (EL)	AA	3	5	3.45	11	11	0	0	57	53	28	22	5	16	63	.244
MINOR LEAGUE TOTALS			22	16	2.77	75	52	1	3	328	239	131	101	18	103	396	.200

SCOTT OLSEN LHP

Born: Jan. 12, 1984. **B-T:** L-L. **Ht.:** 6-4. **Wt.:** 200. **Drafted:** HS—Crystal Lake, Ill., 2002 (6th round). **Signed by:** Scot Engler.

Considered a project out of high school, Olsen cost just $160,000 in bonus money. Jeff Schwarz, his pitching coach in the Rookie-level Gulf Coast League, made a few mechanical adjustments and soon Olsen was roaring through the system. He pitches at 91-93 mph and tops out in the mid-90s. His fastball has late life and he has shown a vicious slider at times. It tends to drop straight down like a changeup or a split when it's really on. He has a bulldog demeanor. Olsen tends to overthrow when he gets in trouble and still needs to learn when to subtract velocity instead of adding it. He has gotten better at controlling his emotions and has packed more muscle on his naturally slight frame, but he can improve further in both areas. Shut down for the final six weeks of the season with elbow inflammation, Olsen is expected to be fine in spring training. He will compete for a spot at the back end of a rotation that must be rebuilt after Florida's fire sale.

Year	Club (League)	Class	W	L	ERA	G	GS	CG	SV	IP	H	R	ER	HR	BB	SO	AVG
2002	Marlins (GCL)	R	2	3	2.96	13	11	0	0	52	39	18	17	0	17	50	.204
2003	Greensboro (SAL)	A	7	9	2.81	25	24	0	0	128	101	51	40	4	59	129	.220
2004	Jupiter (FSL)	A	7	6	2.97	25	25	1	0	136	127	57	45	8	53	158	.252
2005	Carolina (SL)	AA	6	4	3.92	14	14	1	0	80	75	38	35	7	27	94	.251
	Florida (NL)	MLB	1	1	3.98	5	4	0	0	20	21	13	9	5	10	21	.259
MAJOR LEAGUE TOTALS			1	1	3.98	5	4	0	0	20	21	13	9	5	10	21	.259
MINOR LEAGUE TOTALS			22	22	3.11	77	74	2	0	397	342	164	137	19	156	431	.235

5 YUSMEIRO PETIT
RHP

Born: Nov. 22, 1984. **B-T:** R-R. **Ht.:** 6-0. **Wt.:** 230. **Signed:** Venezuela, 2001. **Signed by:** Gregorio Machado (Mets).

The best of the three prospects received from the Mets for Carlos Delgado, Petit had been the best pitching prospect in New York's system the last two years. He continued to dominate in 2005 with a repertoire that's typically deemed ordinary. Though he struggled in a late callup to Triple-A, he fanned 14 in a playoff start there. Petit's four-pitch attack plays up because of his above-average command and deception. Some grade his 88-90 mph fastball as a plus because of its movement and his ability to hide the ball well. He complements the fastball with a solid changeup, a slider and a curve. With stuff that is a tick better than average, scouts continue to question whether he has enough to succeed in the majors. While he mows down righthanders, he struggled in 2005 against lefties, who slugged .525 against him. At 6 feet and 230 pounds, he must watch his weight. Petit's numbers suggest a frontline starter, but his raw stuff profiles him toward the back of a rotation. He too could use time in Triple-A, but the Marlins are looking to fill several holes in their rotation.

Year	Club (League)	Class	W	L	ERA	G	GS	CG	SV	IP	H	R	ER	HR	BB	SO	AVG
2002	Universidad (VSL)	R	3	5	2.43	12	11	0	0	56	53	25	15	1	16	62	.252
2003	Kingsport (Appy)	R	3	3	2.32	12	12	0	0	62	47	19	16	2	8	65	.219
	Brooklyn (NY-P)	A	1	0	2.19	2	2	0	0	12	5	3	3	0	2	20	.119
2004	Capital City (SAL)	A	9	2	2.39	15	15	0	0	83	47	29	22	8	22	122	.162
	St. Lucie (FSL)	A	2	3	1.22	9	9	1	0	44	27	9	6	0	14	62	.174
	Binghamton (EL)	AA	1	1	4.50	2	2	0	0	12	10	6	6	0	5	16	.233
2005	Binghamton (EL)	AA	9	3	2.91	21	21	2	0	118	90	41	38	15	18	130	.209
	Norfolk (IL)	AAA	0	3	9.20	3	3	0	0	15	24	16	15	5	6	14	.375
MINOR LEAGUE TOTALS			28	20	2.71	76	75	3	0	402	303	148	121	31	91	491	.209

6 JOSH JOHNSON
RHP

Born: Jan. 31, 1984. **B-T:** L-R. **Ht.:** 6-7. **Wt.:** 240. **Drafted:** HS—Tulsa, Okla., 2002 (4th round). **Signed by:** Darrell Brown.

Signed for $300,000 out of high school, Johnson just keeps improving. He has yet to repeat a minor league stop and reached the majors after just 359 pro innings. He uses his size to create a good downward plane in his delivery. His best pitch is a 91-93 mph fastball that tops out at 95. His changeup and slider continue to show progress. He has strong makeup and mound presence. For the second time in four pro seasons, Johnson missed time with shoulder tendinitis, this time in May. He's around the strike zone so much that he can be hittable at times, and his secondary pitches still need work. After getting a September callup, Johnson will compete in the spring for a spot in Florida's rotation. He got some of his big league jitters out of the way during a wild-card race and figures to be a fixture as a Marlins starter, provided his shoulder cooperates.

Year	Club (League)	Class	W	L	ERA	G	GS	CG	SV	IP	H	R	ER	HR	BB	SO	AVG
2002	Marlins (GCL)	R	2	0	0.60	4	3	0	0	15	8	3	1	0	3	11	.154
	Jamestown (NY-P)	A	0	2	12.38	2	2	0	0	8	15	15	11	0	7	5	.385
2003	Greensboro (SAL)	A	4	7	3.61	17	17	0	0	82	69	44	33	5	29	59	.223
2004	Jupiter (FSL)	A	5	12	3.38	23	22	1	0	114	124	63	43	4	47	103	.285
2005	Carolina (SL)	AA	12	4	3.87	26	26	1	0	140	139	67	60	4	50	113	.261
	Florida (NL)	MLB	0	0	3.65	4	1	0	0	12	11	5	5	0	10	10	.256
MAJOR LEAGUE TOTALS			0	0	3.66	4	1	0	0	12	11	5	5	0	10	10	.256
MINOR LEAGUE TOTALS			23	25	3.71	72	70	2	0	359	355	192	148	13	136	291	.260

7 CHRIS VOLSTAD RHP

Born: Sept. 23, 1986. **B-T:** R-R **Ht.:** 6-7. **Wt.:** 190. **Drafted:** HS—Palm Beach Gardens, Fla., 2005 (1st round). **Signed by:** John Martin.

Volstad struggled in his final high school start, throwing just 48 strikes in 92 pitches in a Florida state playoff loss, and that allowed him to fall to the Marlins as the 16th overall pick in the 2005 draft. After signing for a $1.6 million bonus, he ranked as the top pitching prospect in both the GCL and the short-season New York-Penn League. For his experience level, Volstad is polished. He shows good poise, sound mechanics, an easy and repeatable delivery and a willingness to take instruction. He pitches at 89-91 mph and tops out at 94 mph. He can bury his curveball when necessary or throw it for strikes. He has a solid changeup for his age and generally keeps the ball down in the strike zone. At times Volstad will slow his arm speed when he throws his changeup, and he'll also overthrow his curve. Adding strength would help him add velocity, and that should come with time. Volstad should start 2006 at low Class A Greensboro. From there he could move quickly through a system that knows how to develop starting pitching.

Year	Club (League)	Class	W	L	ERA	G	GS	CG	SV	IP	H	R	ER	HR	BB	SO	AVG
2005	Marlins (GCL)	R	1	1	2.33	6	6	0	0	27	25	14	7	1	4	26	.243
	Jamestown (NY-P)	A	3	2	2.13	7	7	0	0	38	43	19	9	0	11	29	.279
MINOR LEAGUE TOTALS			4	3	2.22	13	13	0	0	65	68	33	16	1	15	55	.265

8 RICKY NOLASCO RHP

Born: Dec. 13, 1982. **B-T:** R-R. **Ht.:** 6-2. **Wt.:** 220. **Drafted:** HS—Rialto, Calif., 2001 (4th round). **Signed by:** Spider Jorgensen (Cubs).

For years, Nolasco had been overshadowed by fellow 2001 Cubs draftees Mark Prior, Andy Sisco and Sergio Mitre, as well as several other young arms in Chicago's pitching-heavy system. Nolasco, whose brother Dave pitched in the Brewers system, joined Mitre and Renyel Pinto in the Cubs' deal to get Juan Pierre at the Winter Meetings in December. Nolasco is coming off his best season as a pro, having been named Double-A Southern League pitcher of the year after leading the league in wins and strikeouts. He has two above-average pitches with his low-90s fastball and his curveball, and he throws his changeup for strikes. Managers rated his command the best in the Southern League, and he has a tremendous feel for pitching. When Nolasco was sent to Triple-A before he was ready in 2004, he didn't handle it well. He dropped down with his breaking ball, trying to aim it for strikes, and didn't have the confidence to use his changeup. After spending most of the last two seasons in Double-A, Nolasco is ready for Triple-A. The Marlins decimated their big league rotation, so he could make his major league debut in 2006.

Year	Club (League)	Class	W	L	ERA	G	GS	CG	SV	IP	H	R	ER	HR	BB	SO	AVG
2001	Cubs (AZL)	R	1	0	1.50	5	4	0	0	18	11	3	3	0	5	23	.175
2002	Boise (NWL)	A	7	2	2.48	15	15	0	0	91	72	32	25	1	25	92	.214
2003	Daytona (FSL)	A	11	5	2.96	26	26	1	0	149	129	58	49	7	48	136	.232
2004	Iowa (PCL)	AAA	2	3	9.30	9	9	0	0	41	68	42	42	7	16	28	.393
	West Tenn (SL)	AA	6	4	3.70	19	19	0	0	107	104	50	44	13	37	115	.260
2005	West Tenn (SL)	AA	14	3	2.89	27	27	1	0	162	151	57	52	13	46	173	.245
MINOR LEAGUE TOTALS			41	17	3.41	101	100	2	0	567	535	242	215	41	177	567	.250

9 GABY HERNANDEZ RHP

Born: May 21, 1986. **B-T:** R-R. **Ht.:** 6-3. **Wt.:** 215. **Drafted:** HS—Miami, 2004 (3rd round). **Signed by:** Joe Salermo (Mets).

After getting Yusmeiro Petit in the Carlos Delgado trade, the Marlins came back and got Hernandez, the Mets' second-best pitching prospect, in the Paul Lo Duca deal. After dominating the Gulf Coast League in his 2004 pro debut, Hernandez did the same in the low Class A South Atlantic League as a teenager. He no-hit West Virginia on Father's Day to clinch a share of the Northern Division first-half title, then beat top Astros prospect Troy Patton in a one-game playoff to win it. Hernandez commands a two-seam fastball with low-90s velocity and excellent life. He also has the makings of a plus changeup. He employs an effortless delivery that bodes well for his command, and he's not afraid to challenge hitters. His grasp of the game is well beyond his youth. Hernandez' curveball is a work in progress. It lacks depth and he tends to reveal it early. He's not overpowering enough to survive without a good breaking ball, a point more advanced hitters drove home following his promotion to the high Class A Florida State League.

Hernandez will get another shot at the FSL, this time in Jupiter, in 2006. He projects as a middle-of-the-rotation starter if his curve develops.

Year	Club (League)	Class	W	L	ERA	G	GS	CG	SV	IP	H	R	ER	HR	BB	SO	AVG
2004	Mets (GCL)	R	3	3	1.09	10	9	2	0	50	25	10	6	1	12	58	.151
	Brooklyn (NY-P)	A	1	0	0.00	1	0	0	0	3	2	0	0	0	0	6	.200
2005	Hagerstown (SAL)	A	6	1	2.43	18	18	1	0	93	59	29	25	4	30	99	.179
	St. Lucie (FSL)	A	2	5	5.74	10	10	0	0	42	48	28	27	1	10	32	.298
MINOR LEAGUE TOTALS			12	9	2.78	39	37	3	0	188	134	67	58	6	52	195	.201

10 AARON THOMPSON
LHP

RICH ABEL

Born: Feb. 28, 1987. **B-T:** L-L. **Ht.:** 6-3. **Wt.:** 195. **Drafted:** HS—Houston, 2005 (1st round). **Signed by:** Dennis Cardoza.

One of Thompson's biggest baseball influences has been Kevin Millar, whom he has known since he was 5. Thompson's grandparents served as Millar's host family when he played at Lamar, and Thompson was a Lamar batboy. Thompson committed to Texas A&M and was considered a tough sign until the Aggies fired their coaching staff, which made his decision to accept a $1.225 million bonus easier. Some say Thompson has a higher ceiling than Chris Volstad. Thompson shows good poise, savvy and competitiveness on the mound. His fastball sits at 90-92 mph and he has a solid changeup and slider. Like most young pitchers, he needs better command of his secondary pitches. He also could stand to improve his pickoff move and attention to detail. He has a good frame but will need to add strength. Thompson figures to join Volstad at Greensboro to start 2006, and the Marlins won't hold them back if they dominate hitters there.

Year	Club (League)	Class	W	L	ERA	G	GS	CG	SV	IP	H	R	ER	HR	BB	SO	AVG
2005	Marlins (GCL)	R	2	4	4.50	8	8	0	0	32	42	20	16	1	10	41	.316
	Jamestown (NY-P)	A	1	2	3.10	5	5	0	0	20	25	13	7	1	10	17	.301
MINOR LEAGUE TOTALS			3	6	3.96	13	13	0	0	52	67	33	23	2	20	58	.310

11 JOSH WILLINGHAM
C/1B

Born: Feb. 17, 1979. **B-T:** R-R. **Ht.:** 6-1. **Wt.:** 200. **Drafted:** North Alabama, 2000 (17th round). **Signed by:** Larry Keller.

Willingham's stock rose significantly after he tried catching in instructional league in 2002. He has spent limited time in the majors each of the past two seasons, though he missed most of the second half of 2005 when he came down with a stress fracture in his forearm in June. Willingham has molded himself into one of the best pure hitters in the system. He shows a short swing, power to all fields and tremendous command of the strike zone. His game-calling has improved and his arm strength is average. Despite all his hard work, though, most view Willingham as a DH stuck in the wrong league. He threw out just 13 percent of basestealers in 2005. Previous knee problems have left him with below-average speed. He entered the offseason blocked by a pair of players signed to long-term contracts, but with Paul Lo Duca and Carlos Delgado now shipped to the Mets, Willingham could get the chance to replace one of them. New manager Joe Girardi has talked about giving him a chance to catch regularly, but few scouts think that would work out. More likely, he'll have to beat out trade acquisition Mike Jacobs at first base to make it into the lineup.

Year	Club (League)	Class	AVG	G	AB	R	H	2B	3B	HR	RBI	BB	SO	SB	OBP	SLG
2000	Utica (NY-P)	A	.263	65	205	37	54	16	0	6	29	39	55	9	.400	.429
2001	Kane County (Mid)	A	.259	97	320	57	83	20	2	7	36	53	85	24	.382	.400
2002	Jupiter (FSL)	A	.274	107	376	72	103	21	4	17	69	63	88	18	.394	.487
2003	Jupiter (FSL)	A	.264	59	193	46	51	17	1	12	34	46	42	9	.422	.549
	Marlins (GCL)	R	.429	2	7	3	3	1	0	1	3	1	2	0	.500	1.000
	Carolina (SL)	AA	.299	22	67	15	20	2	1	5	14	13	20	0	.434	.582
2004	Florida (NL)	MLB	.200	12	25	2	5	0	0	1	1	4	8	0	.310	.320
	Carolina (SL)	AA	.281	112	338	81	95	24	0	24	76	91	87	6	.449	.565
2005	Jupiter (FSL)	A	.222	2	9	1	2	1	0	0	1	0	2	0	.300	.333
	Albuquerque (PCL)	AAA	.324	66	219	56	71	14	3	19	54	47	54	5	.455	.676
	Florida (NL)	MLB	.304	16	23	3	7	1	0	0	4	2	5	0	.407	.348
MAJOR LEAGUE TOTALS			.250	28	48	5	12	1	0	1	5	6	13	0	.357	.333
MINOR LEAGUE TOTALS			.278	532	1734	368	482	116	11	91	316	353	435	71	.417	.515

12 MIKE JACOBS
1B/C

Born: Oct. 30, 1980. **B-T:** L-R. **Ht.:** 6-2. **Wt.:** 2000. **Drafted:** Grossmont (Calif.) JC, 1999 (38th round). **Signed by:** Bob Minor (Mets).

The Mets' minor league player of the year in 2003, Jacobs missed most of the following season with a torn labrum. He came back to win the Eastern League MVP and organization player of the year awards in 2005, and he also became the first big leaguer ever to homer four times in his first four games. But when New York had the chance to acquire Carlos Delgado in the offseason, it didn't hesitate to include Jacobs in the trade. He's primarily a pull hitter with power, but he can drive the ball to the opposite field on occasion. He has a smooth lefthanded stroke and is a purely offensive player. Though the Mets benched him against lefties, he posting an .896 OPS against them in Double-A. While he came up as a catcher, Jacobs split time behind the plate and at first base in Double-A and only played first with New York. He has below-average catch-and-throw skills but is adequate at first base. His swing can get long at times, and plate discipline never has been his strong suit. He'll probably wind up competing with Josh Willingham for Florida's first-base job, and if the Marlins settle on a platoon arrangement, Jacobs will get more at-bats because he hits lefthanded.

Year	Club (League)	Class	AVG	G	AB	R	H	2B	3B	HR	RBI	BB	SO	SB	OBP	SLG
1999	Mets (GCL)	R	.333	44	147	18	49	12	0	4	30	14	30	2	.383	.497
2000	Columbia (SAL)	A	.214	18	56	1	12	5	0	0	8	6	19	1	.290	.304
	Kingsport (Appy)	R	.270	59	204	28	55	15	4	7	40	33	62	6	.371	.485
2001	Brooklyn (NY-P)	A	.288	19	66	12	19	5	0	1	15	6	11	1	.364	.409
	Columbia (SAL)	A	.278	46	180	18	50	13	0	2	26	13	46	0	.328	.383
2002	St. Lucie (FSL)	A	.251	118	467	62	117	26	1	11	64	25	95	2	.291	.381
2003	Binghamton (EL)	AA	.329	119	407	56	134	36	1	17	81	28	87	0	.376	.548
2004	Norfolk (IL)	AAA	.177	27	96	8	17	3	0	2	6	9	30	0	.245	.271
2005	Binghamton (EL)	AA	.321	117	433	66	139	37	2	25	93	35	94	1	.376	.589
	New York (NL)	MLB	.310	30	100	19	31	7	0	11	23	10	22	0	.375	.710
MAJOR LEAGUE TOTALS			.310	30	100	19	31	7	0	11	23	10	22	0	.375	.710
MINOR LEAGUE TOTALS			.288	567	2056	269	592	152	8	69	363	169	474	13	.344	.470

13 RENYEL PINTO LHP

Born: July 8, 1982. **B-T:** L-L. **Ht.:** 6-4. **Wt.:** 190. **Signed:** Venezuela, 1999. **Signed by:** Alberto Rondon (Cubs).

Pinto should have carried a lot of positive momentum into 2005. He was coming off a breakout season in which he led the Southern League in ERA and was the Cubs minor league pitcher of the year. But visa problems made him the last man on Chicago's 40-man roster to report to big league camp, and when he arrived he wasn't in good shape. He wasn't able to handle a jump to Triple-A and had to return to Double-A. Before the Cubs included him in the Juan Pierre trade, Pinto had arguably the best stuff in their system. He has a darting 91-94 mph fastball, a plus changeup with sink and fade, and a hard breaking ball that's closer to a slider than a curveball. His low three-quarters delivery makes his pitches difficult to pick up. What he doesn't have is control and command. Pinto has trouble finding the strike zone, and even when he does he doesn't always put the ball where he wants. Triple-A hitters pounded him by refusing to chase pitches and then teeing off when he laid one over the plate. If he figures everything out, Pinto could pitch toward the front of a big league rotation. But he still has a great deal of work to do. Like most of the pitchers the Marlins acquired during the offseason, Pinto has yet to prove himself in Triple-A but could be pressed into big league duty in 2006.

Year	Club (League)	Class	W	L	ERA	G	GS	CG	SV	IP	H	R	ER	HR	BB	SO	AVG
1999	Cubs (DSL)	R	4	5	4.38	13	13	1	0	64	70	35	31	5	22	62	.289
2000	Cubs (AZL)	R	0	2	6.30	9	4	0	0	30	42	29	21	3	16	23	.326
2001	Lansing (Mid)	A	4	8	5.22	20	20	1	0	88	94	64	51	9	44	69	.278
2002	Daytona (FSL)	A	3	3	5.51	7	7	0	0	33	45	23	20	5	11	24	.338
	Lansing (MWL)	A	7	5	3.31	17	16	0	0	98	79	39	36	9	28	92	.221
2003	Daytona (FSL)	A	3	8	3.22	20	19	0	0	115	91	47	41	4	45	104	.221
2004	West Tenn (SL)	AA	11	8	2.92	25	25	0	0	142	107	50	46	10	72	179	.216
	Iowa (PCL)	AAA	1	1	7.71	2	2	0	0	9	9	9	8	2	8	9	.257
2005	Iowa (PCL)	AAA	1	2	9.53	6	6	0	0	23	31	30	24	3	24	24	.348
	West Tenn (SL)	AA	10	3	2.71	22	21	1	0	130	101	43	39	3	58	123	.223
MINOR LEAGUE TOTALS			44	45	3.91	141	133	3	0	730	669	369	317	53	328	709	.249

14 TAYLOR TANKERSLEY LHP

Born: March 7, 1983. **B-T:** L-L. **Ht.:** 6-2. **Wt.:** 225. **Drafted:** Alabama, 2004 (1st round). **Signed by:** Dave Dangler.

Tankersley's father is a nuclear physicist and his paternal grandfather pitched briefly in the minors. It was Earl Tankersley who taught his grandson the importance of pitching inside at an early age. The lessons paid off with a $1.3 million bonus in 2004. Tankersley is a strike thrower with a bulldog mentality. He pitches at 88-90 mph and tops out at 92 mph with a fastball he releases from a low three-quarters arm slot that makes him particularly tough on lefties. His breaking ball is a slurve with good depth. His changeup is making progress after he started throwing it more. After dropping too much weight last offseason, Tankersley missed two months with shoulder tendinitis. He struggled at times after his return, especially with a breaking ball that needs more variation in speed from his fastball. His stuff isn't overpowering, so he must be solid with his location. Tankersley switched to the bullpen full-time in the Arizona Fall League after the season. He figures to stay in a relief role in 2006, when he'll probably open at high Class A Jupiter.

Year	Club (League)	Class	W	L	ERA	G	GS	CG	SV	IP	H	R	ER	HR	BB	SO	AVG
2004	Jamestown (NY-P)	A	1	1	3.38	6	6	0	0	27	21	14	10	2	8	32	.210
2005	Greensboro (SAL)	A	2	7	5.18	12	12	0	0	66	74	45	38	12	25	63	.279
	Jupiter (FSL)	A	1	0	3.38	4	4	1	0	24	21	10	9	1	9	19	.247
MINOR LEAGUE TOTALS			4	8	4.40	22	22	1	0	117	116	69	57	15	42	114	.258

15 KRIS HARVEY   3B/OF

Born: Jan. 5, 1984. **B-T:** R-R. **Ht.:** 6-2. **Wt.:** 195. **Drafted:** Clemson, 2005 (2nd round). **Signed by:** Joel Matthews.

Harvey's father Bryan is a former all-star and the first closer in Marlins history. A two-way standout in college, Kris hit 97 mph on the mound and finished second in NCAA Division I with 25 homers last spring. Harvey has easy power and the ability to handle high breaking balls. He can turn around quality fastballs, and the ball seems to jump off his bat. Playing right field was no problem for Harvey, who showed a strong, accurate arm. Late in the season Harvey moved to third base, where he showed enough potential to remain for the near future. The Marlins were surprised to discover he has above-average speed, and he has the makeup to match his athleticism. Harvey's pitch selection needs improvement. So far he has gotten by on natural strength, but he could stand to add muscle to a thin frame. He had to shorten his arm action at third base. Harvey figures to start 2006 in low Class A. With his college background and the system's void at third base, he could move up the ladder quickly.

Year	Club (League)	Class	AVG	G	AB	R	H	2B	3B	HR	RBI	BB	SO	SB	OBP	SLG
2005	Jamestown (NY-P)	A	.300	65	263	34	79	14	3	9	38	9	60	4	.320	.479
MINOR LEAGUE TOTALS			.300	65	263	34	79	14	3	9	38	9	60	4	.320	.479

16 RYAN TUCKER   RHP

Born: Dec. 12, 1986. **B-T:** R-R. **Ht.:** 6-3. **Wt.:** 190. **Drafted:** HS—Temple City, Calif., 2005 (1st round supplemental). **Signed by:** John Cole.

Tucker's draft stock gathered steam behind a plus fastball that had scouts drooling all spring. Several clubs, including the Cardinals, considered taking Tucker as a first-rounder but he fell to the Marlins as a sandwich pick. They signed him for $975,000 as a compensation choice for the loss of free agent Armando Benitez. Tucker's fastball sits at 92-95 mph and touches 97 with late life. He shows great competitiveness on the mound. A good athlete, he has a loose, fluid delivery and isn't afraid to pitch inside. Because his fastball always has been so dominant, Tucker hasn't needed to develop a consistent breaking ball. The Marlins took his curveball away temporarily and asked him to concentrate on a slider with mixed results. He's listed at 6-foot-3 but is closer to 6 feet tall. Some view Tucker as a future closer while others would like to see him given a chance to develop as a starter. He was hit hard at short-season Jamestown and could be sent back there in 2006.

Year	Club (League)	Class	W	L	ERA	G	GS	CG	SV	IP	H	R	ER	HR	BB	SO	AVG
2005	Marlins (GCL)	R	3	3	3.69	8	7	0	0	32	35	13	13	0	16	23	.315
	Jamestown (NY-P)	A	1	1	8.36	4	4	0	0	14	21	14	13	3	8	18	.323
MINOR LEAGUE TOTALS			4	4	5.12	12	11	0	0	46	56	27	26	3	24	41	.318

17 ROBERT ANDINO   SS

Born: April 25, 1984. **B-T:** R-R. **Ht.:** 6-0. **Wt.:** 170. **Drafted:** HS—Miami, 2002 (2nd round). **Signed by:** John Martin.

Andino signed for $750,000 as a second-round pick in 2002 despite organizational division on his real worth. He started performing midway through 2004, then came up last September and started a number of games in the National League wild-card race. But just when he was positioning himself to take over for Alex Gonzalez in 2006, Andino turned in a subpar performance in the Arizona Fall League. In fact, he showed so little effort that the Marlins dispatched vice president of player personnel Dan Jennings to Arizona to deliver a stern reprimand. Andino stands out mostly on defense. He has tremendous range, a plus arm and the ability to make the highlight play. His bat speed has improved and he has done a better job of staying back on offspeed pitches after significant work with Double-A hitting coach Steve Phillips and hitting coordinator John Mallee. He was an effective basestealer in the minors. Andino still makes too many errors, sometimes losing focus on routine plays.

At the plate, he appeared overmatched at times in the majors. He must improve his upper-body strength and pitch recognition. His AFL stint and the Marlins' trade for Hanley Ramirez have diminished Andino's chances of opening 2006 as the club's shortstop. But Florida is looking to fill both parts of its double-play combination, so it's still possible.

Year	Club (League)	Class	AVG	G	AB	R	H	2B	3B	HR	RBI	BB	SO	SB	OBP	SLG
2002	Marlins (GCL)	R	.259	9	27	2	7	0	0	0	2	5	6	3	.364	.259
	Jamestown (NY-P)	A	.167	9	36	2	6	1	1	0	3	1	9	1	.189	.250
2003	Greensboro (SAL)	A	.188	119	416	45	78	17	2	2	27	46	128	6	.266	.252
2004	Greensboro (SAL)	A	.281	76	295	27	83	10	1	8	46	18	83	9	.321	.403
	Jupiter (FSL)	A	.281	49	196	18	55	7	2	0	15	7	43	6	.304	.337
2005	Carolina (SL)	AA	.269	127	516	63	139	30	0	5	48	37	111	22	.324	.357
	Florida (NL)	MLB	.159	17	44	4	7	4	0	0	1	5	8	1	.245	.250
MINOR LEAGUE TOTALS			.248	389	1486	157	368	65	6	15	141	114	380	47	.302	.330
MAJOR LEAGUE TOTALS			.159	17	44	4	7	4	0	0	1	5	8	1	.245	.250

18 ERIC REED   OF

Born: Dec. 2, 1980. **B-T:** L-L. **Ht.:** 5-11. **Wt.:** 170. **Drafted:** Texas A&M, 2002 (9th round). **Signed by:** Dennis Cardoza.

Reed opened eyes with a Cape Cod League batting title 2001 but fell in the 2002 draft after a disappointing junior season at Texas A&M. He has battled injuries as a pro, missing the second half in 2004 after breaking his wrist in a bar fight, and struggling in 2005 following hernia surgery and a rib injury suffered when he ran into an outfield wall. Reed's speed remains his top tool, as he has been timed at 3.8 seconds to first. Many believe he's faster and a better defender than Juan Pierre, whom he'll replace as Florida's center fielder this year. Reed also is an excellent bunter and has an average arm. To hit near the top of the line-up, he still needs to control the strike zone better. He has limited power. Though his body fat is just 3 percent, he still could add more muscle to his upper half. He also needs to get better jumps as a basestealer.

Year	Club (League)	Class	AVG	G	AB	R	H	2B	3B	HR	RBI	BB	SO	SB	OBP	SLG
2002	Jamestown (NY-P)	A	.308	60	250	35	77	5	1	0	17	17	30	19	.348	.336
	Kane County (Mid)	A	.360	12	50	11	18	1	0	0	2	3	11	7	.396	.380
2003	Jupiter (FSL)	A	.300	134	514	86	154	15	8	0	25	52	83	53	.367	.360
2004	Carolina (SL)	AA	.306	55	222	32	68	9	6	3	14	14	55	24	.345	.441
2005	Carolina (SL)	AA	.255	71	271	35	69	9	0	1	15	17	62	23	.305	.299
	Albuquerque (PCL)	AAA	.310	39	171	19	53	5	4	1	20	3	31	17	.335	.404
MINOR LEAGUE TOTALS			.297	371	1478	218	439	44	19	5	93	106	272	143	.347	.363

19 JASON STOKES   1B

Born: Jan. 23, 1982. **B-T:** R-R. **Ht.:** 6-4. **Wt.:** 225. **Drafted:** HS—Coppell, Texas, 2000 (2nd round). **Signed by:** Bob Laurie.

Still armed with the best raw power in the system, Stokes remains a mystery. His nagging problems with a balky left wrist have given way to a condition typically seen in elderly patients that causes his left thumb to come out of joint easily and without warning. He wears a brace on the field but was limited to just 46 at-bats in 2005. Signed for $2.027 million out of high school, Stokes is a good situational hitter who can handle quality pitches when healthy. He runs well for a big man and has made significant strides in the field. He worked extensively with Marlins infield coach Perry Hill at big league spring training last year and improved his footwork and reactions. Despite the Carlos Delgado trade, Stokes still has obstacles ahead of him in Josh Willingham and offseason acquisition Mike Jacobs. He likely will head to Triple-A to begin 2006.

Year	Club (League)	Class	AVG	G	AB	R	H	2B	3B	HR	RBI	BB	SO	SB	OBP	SLG
2001	Utica (NY-P)	A	.231	35	130	12	30	2	1	6	19	11	48	0	.299	.400
2002	Kane County (Mid)	A	.341	97	349	73	119	25	0	27	75	47	96	1	.421	.645
2003	Jupiter (FSL)	A	.258	121	462	67	119	31	3	17	89	36	135	6	.312	.448
2004	Marlins (GCL)	R	.250	3	8	1	2	1	0	1	1	3	3	0	.333	.750
	Carolina (SL)	AA	.272	106	394	66	107	26	0	23	78	42	121	5	.345	.513
2005	Albuquerque (PCL)	AAA	.283	13	46	12	13	1	1	5	15	3	16	2	.340	.674
MINOR LEAGUE TOTALS			.281	375	1389	231	390	86	5	79	277	140	419	14	.350	.521

20 SEAN WEST   LHP

Born: June 15, 1986. **B-T:** L-L. **Ht.:** 6-8. **Wt.:** 200. **Drafted:** HS—Shreveport, La., 2005 (1st round supplemental). **Signed by:** Ryan Fox.

West might have the highest ceiling of the five pitchers the Marlins took in the top 44 picks last June. He signed for $775,000 out of a Louisiana high school, ending his prep career with a 17-strikeout loss in the state 5-A quarterfinals. At 6-foot-8, he would become the tallest pitcher in club history should he make the majors. He pitches at 90-92 and touches 94 mph with his fastball, which is a swing-and-miss weapon with late life. He saw his fastball jump from 85-86 mph before his senior year and projects to add velocity as he grows into his body. He's a strike-thrower who has little trouble repeating his delivery, but his overall approach and grasp of situations could improve. His curveball could become a second plus pitch, and his changeup is far less advanced. He'll pitch in low Class A this year.

Year	Club (League)	Class	W	L	ERA	G	GS	CG	SV	IP	H	R	ER	HR	BB	SO	AVG
2005	Marlins (GCL)	R	2	3	2.35	9	8	0	0	38	33	12	10	2	7	40	.229
	Jamestown (NY-P)	A	0	2	5.73	3	3	0	0	11	17	7	7	1	5	14	.362
MINOR LEAGUE TOTALS			2	5	3.10	12	11	0	0	49	50	19	17	3	12	54	.262

21 J.T. RESTKO   OF

Born: Dec. 15, 1984. **B-T:** R-R. **Ht.:** 6-5. **Wt.:** 190. **Drafted:** HS—Tinley Park, Ill., 2003 (10th round). **Signed by:** Scot Engler.

Restko made huge strides in 2005, showing a new willingness to take pitches and work counts and showing commensurate gains in average and on-base percentage. Tall and slender like Mariners slugger Richie Sexson, the wiry Restko extends the comparison with some of the best raw power in the system. He's tough to whiff and spoils two-strike pitches that would put away most young hitters. Some would like to see him be more aggressive early in counts, but his overall approach is excellent. A Chicagoland product, he worked out last winter at a nearby hitting school run by hitting coordinator John Mallee. It was typical for him to put in 15 straight days at the facility before Mallee would force him to take a day off. Restko is a below-average defender in left field and could wind up at first base. Florida wants to see if he can't make the necessary improvements in the outfield, though his arm and range are just adequate. Restko will play left field in high Class A in 2006.

Year	Club (League)	Class	AVG	G	AB	R	H	2B	3B	HR	RBI	BB	SO	SB	OBP	SLG
2003	Marlins (GCL)	R	.249	49	177	15	44	6	0	4	19	16	43	0	.320	.350
2004	Jupiter (FSL)	A	.227	7	22	1	5	2	0	0	2	3	5	0	.320	.318
	Jamestown (NY-P)	A	.235	72	294	40	69	11	1	6	46	16	75	0	.282	.340
2005	Greensboro (SAL)	A	.313	115	403	69	126	22	3	15	70	53	91	3	.414	.494
MINOR LEAGUE TOTALS			.272	243	896	125	244	41	4	25	137	88	214	3	.352	.411

22 BRAD McCANN   1B

Born: Dec. 9, 1982. **B-T:** R-R. **Ht.:** 6-3. **Wt.:** 190. **Drafted:** Clemson, 2004 (6th round). **Signed by:** Joel Matthews.

Fourteen months older than his brother, Braves catcher Brian, McCann announced his presence in his first full pro season. He was drafted as a third baseman out of Clemson, where he was a teammate of 2005 Marlins second-rounder Kris Harvey and missed an Atlantic Coast Conference batting title by six points as a junior. McCann settled in at first base in 2005 and blasted his way to the Marlins' minor league player of the year award. After hitting just three homers in his pro debut, McCann ripped 28 at Greensboro. He did this despite making no major mechanical changes to his swing or his set-up. Using a line-drive stroke, he showed power to all fields and the ability to take close pitches. McCann punishes hanging breaking balls and is an all-around professional hitter. He has good makeup and the mature approach one would expect from a college product. He also made solid strides defensively under roving coordinator Ed Romero, though he'll probably never be much of a defender. His speed, range and arm strength are adequate at best. McCann probably will open this year in high Class A, with a chance to reach Double-A at some point in 2006.

Year	Club (League)	Class	AVG	G	AB	R	H	2B	3B	HR	RBI	BB	SO	SB	OBP	SLG
2004	Jamestown (NY-P)	A	.287	28	108	16	31	6	2	3	13	7	15	0	.339	.463
2005	Greensboro (SAL)	A	.295	123	478	67	141	35	2	28	106	37	97	1	.355	.552
MINOR LEAGUE TOTALS			.294	151	586	83	172	41	4	31	119	44	112	1	.352	.536

23 CHRIS RESOP   RHP

Born: Nov. 4, 1982. **B-T:** R-R. **Ht.:** 6-3. **Wt.:** 200. **Drafted:** HS—Naples, Fla., 2001 (4th round). **Signed by:** Mike Tosar.

It took Resop less than two years to reach the majors after making the conversion from outfield in July 2003. Former farm director Marc DelPiano saved a career that was going nowhere at the plate, where Resop hit .193 with just one homer in 269 at-bats over three pro seasons. He showed a bulldog attitude in his first taste of the majors, but he wasn't able to work his way into many pressure situations as the club futilely chased a wild-card spot. With a fastball that sits at 92-95 mph and tops out at 97, Resop will get every opportunity to make the front end of a revamped Marlins bullpen in 2006. He has the makings of a plus curveball but hasn't used it enough. He has shown a liking for the closer's role in the past and could work his way into a prominent role under new manager Joe Girardi, but first Resop must prove he belongs in the majors. Being more aggressive and throwing more strikes, which weren't problems in the minors, would be a step in the right direction.

Year	Club (League)	Class	AVG	G	AB	R	H	2B	3B	HR	RBI	BB	SO	SB	OBP	SLG
2001	Marlins (GCL)	R	.116	26	86	5	10	2	0	0	5	7	34	0	.189	.140
	Utica (NY-P)	A	.333	2	3	0	1	0	0	0	0	0	2	0	.333	.333
2002	Marlins (GCL)	R	.264	28	91	7	24	5	2	0	11	5	21	1	.323	.363
2003	Greensboro (SAL)	A	.191	37	89	6	17	4	1	1	8	1	29	0	.209	.292
MINOR LEAGUE TOTALS			.193	93	269	18	52	11	3	1	24	13	86	1	.243	.268

Year	Club (League)	Class	W	L	ERA	G	GS	CG	SV	IP	H	R	ER	HR	BB	SO	AVG
2003	Greensboro (SAL)	A	0	1	4.97	11	0	0	0	13	11	7	7	1	5	15	.224
2004	Greensboro (SAL)	A	3	1	1.94	41	0	0	13	42	26	11	9	1	7	68	.173
2005	Carolina (SL)	AA	3	2	2.57	43	0	0	24	49	47	15	14	2	16	56	.242
2005	Florida (NL)	MLB	2	0	8.47	15	0	0	0	17	22	16	16	1	9	15	.324
MAJOR LEAGUE TOTALS			2	0	8.47	15	0	0	0	17	22	16	16	1	9	15	.324
MINOR LEAGUE TOTALS			6	4	2.61	95	0	0	37	103	84	33	30	4	28	139	.214

24 JESUS DELGADO   RHP

Born: April 19, 1984. **B-T:** R-R. **Ht.:** 6-1. **Wt.:** 198. **Signed:** Venezuela, 2001. **Signed by:** Ben Cherington (Red Sox).

The third of four Red Sox prospects acquired in the Josh Beckett blockbuster, Delgado had one of the best pure arms in the Boston system. The Red Sox discovered him as an outfielder in Venezuela but immediately converted him to the mound. After making his debut in the Rookie-level Dominican Summer League, he blew out his elbow and missed the 2002 and 2003 seasons while recovering from Tommy John surgery. Since coming back, Delgado has lit up radar guns, sitting at 95-96 mph and peaking at 98. The Red Sox handled him cautiously, and he remains raw. He relied on his fastball as a reliever in 2005, though he did a better job of keeping hitters off balance with his curveball and changeup in the Arizona Fall League. His changeup is his No. 2 pitch now, though his curve occasionally is a swing-and-miss pitch. How well he develops his secondary stuff will determine whether Delgado returns to the rotation or stays in the bullpen, where he has closer ceiling. He doesn't throw with a lot of effort, though Boston was trying to clean up his delivery. Delgado is ready for high Class A, and Florida may put him in the rotation to get him more innings.

Year	Club (League)	Class	W	L	ERA	G	GS	CG	SV	IP	H	R	ER	HR	BB	SO	AVG
2001	Red Sox (DSL)	R	0	2	5.34	10	8	0	0	32	31	25	19	1	14	19	.240
2002	Did not play—Injured																
2003	Did not play—Injured																
2004	Augusta (SAL)	A	1	5	5.22	21	16	0	0	59	61	40	34	10	26	34	.275
	Red Sox (GCL)	R	0	0	10.80	1	0	0	0	2	4	2	2	0	0	2	.500
2005	Greenville (SAL)	A	7	3	3.50	33	0	0	2	72	57	30	28	3	39	69	.215
MINOR LEAGUE TOTALS			8	10	4.55	65	24	0	2	164	153	97	83	14	79	124	.245

25 JOSE GARCIA   RHP

Born: Jan. 7, 1985. **B-T:** R-R. **Ht.:** 5-11. **Wt.:** 165. **Signed:** Dominican Republic, 2001. **Signed by:** Cesar Santiago.

After spending his first three pro seasons in the Dominican Summer League, Garcia came to the United States and his career picked up steam in 2005. Though undersized, he makes up for it with a good feel for pitching and a strong mound presence. His fastball sits at 90-93 mph and tops out at 95. He shows a solid changeup for his experience level, and has the potential for a plus slider. Some see a little bit of Pedro Martinez in him, though they are careful not to predict the same Cooperstown track. Through four seasons, Garcia has shown the ability to command the strike zone, striking out six batters for every one he's walked. Popular with teammates, he has an easygoing personality, good energy and an apparent love for being on the mound. He figures to return to low Class A, where he should be part of a prospect-laden rotation that includes 2005 draftees Chris Volstad, Aaron Thompson and Ryan Tucker. In the long term, Garcia could wind up in the bullpen as a durable set-up man.

Year	Club (League)	Class	W	L	ERA	G	GS	CG	SV	IP	H	R	ER	HR	BB	SO	AVG
2002	Marlins (DSL)	R	3	2	1.16	15	1	0	3	39	25	18	5	0	13	42	.179
2003	Marlins (DSL)	R	2	6	2.83	12	12	2	0	70	78	37	22	3	14	87	.284
2004	Marlins (DSL)	R	5	3	1.43	14	10	0	0	69	43	16	11	2	10	84	.176
2005	Greensboro (SAL)	A	3	0	1.27	5	4	0	0	28	11	5	4	1	4	39	.115
	Marlins (GCL)	R	0	0	0.00	1	1	0	0	2	1	0	0	0	1	3	.167
	Jupiter (FSL)	A	0	0	18.00	1	1	0	0	2	2	4	4	0	2	0	.286
MINOR LEAGUE TOTALS			13	11	1.97	48	29	2	3	210	160	80	46	6	44	255	.208

26 JACOB MARCEAUX

RHP

Born: Feb. 14, 1984. **B-T:** R-R. **Ht.:** 6-1. **Wt.:** 195. **Drafted:** McNeese State, 2005 (1st round). **Signed by:** Dennis Cardoza.

Florida's third pick in the first round last June, Marceaux was the only college arm scouting director Stan Meek took with his five picks in the top 44. Marceaux' stock took off after a strong showing in the Texas Collegiate League the summer before his junior season. Former all-star closer Mike Henneman was his pitching coach and taught him a pair of breaking balls, proper mechanics and the mindset needed to succeed. Marceaux used those lessons to become the highest draft pick in McNeese State history and signed for $1 million. Much to his surprise, Marceaux struggled mightily in his pro debut. His two-seam fastball still sat at 92-93 mph and topped out at 94-95, but he showed a nagging tendency to fall behind hitters and overthrow. The Marlins blame themselves for making an adjustment to Marceaux' delivery, getting him to close his front side. They told him to revert to his old mechanics, and he began to get his confidence back late in the summer. All four of his pitches have graded out as plus at times. He also throws a mid-80s slider, a mid-70s spike curveball and a changeup. He has enough pitches and the command to be a starter, but his bulldog mentality profiles him as a short reliever. He'll pitch in low Class A this year.

Year	Club (League)	Class	W	L	ERA	G	GS	CG	SV	IP	H	R	ER	HR	BB	SO	AVG
2005	Jamestown (NY-P)	A	3	5	5.55	10	10	0	0	47	56	33	29	5	13	32	.287
	Greensboro (SAL)	A	0	3	12.36	5	5	0	0	20	40	32	27	4	9	12	.426
MINOR LEAGUE TOTALS			3	8	7.56	15	15	0	0	67	96	65	56	9	22	44	.332

27 TRAVIS BOWYER

RHP

Born: Aug. 3, 1981. **B-T:** R-R. **Ht.:** 6-3. **Wt.:** 220. **Drafted:** HS—Bedford, Va., 1999 (20th round). **Signed by:** John Wilson (Twins).

When the Marlins jettisoned Luis Castillo to Minnesota, they received righthanders Bowyer and Scott Tyler in exchange. A former 20th-rounder who fought his way onto the roster after the 2004 season, Bowyer saw his profile rise markedly in 2005 with a strong year in Triple-A. He made the Futures Game, earned a September callup and was assigned to the Arizona Fall League. In both the majors and the AFL, Bowyer got hit hard. He has the biggest fastball in the system, pitching at 95-97 mph and touching 100 in Arizona. His fastball has late life and boring action, though too often it's the only pitch he can command. His frame is strong and durable, which bodes well for nightly relief work. He shows a good work ethic and has a quiet, low-maintenance personality. However, as Bowyer's fastball has improved, jumping from 86-87 mph back in 1999, his secondary pitches have suffered. That's especially true of his changeup, which has all but disappeared. He has a slurvy breaking ball he throws at 85-87 mph but it's not a finished product. If he doesn't stage a breakthrough with a secondary pitch, Bowyer could soon hit a development wall. But given the Marlins' needs at the big league level, he also could emerge as their closer in 2006.

Year	Club (League)	Class	W	L	ERA	G	GS	CG	SV	IP	H	R	ER	HR	BB	SO	AVG
1999	Twins (GCL)	R	1	0	0.00	1	0	0	0	1	0	0	0	0	0	1	.000
2000	Twins (GCL)	R	3	5	4.07	12	12	1	0	55	55	31	25	2	22	36	.255
2001	Elizabethton (Appy)	R	2	5	6.10	9	8	0	0	38	38	30	26	3	20	34	.266
2002	Quad City (Mid)	A	4	4	2.16	39	9	0	3	92	74	28	22	2	46	90	.224
2003	Fort Myers (FSL)	A	5	2	3.83	45	0	0	1	80	68	43	34	1	56	70	.244
2004	Fort Myers (FSL)	A	3	0	0.30	17	0	0	2	30	18	6	1	0	17	32	.168
	New Britain (EL)	AA	6	3	1.76	31	0	0	3	61	42	17	12	3	38	65	.188
2005	Rochester (IL)	AAA	4	2	2.78	59	0	0	23	74	51	23	23	4	40	96	.195
	Minnesota (AL)	MLB	0	1	5.59	8	0	0	0	10	10	6	6	3	3	12	.270
MAJOR LEAGUE TOTALS			0	1	5.59	8	0	0	0	10	10	6	6	3	3	12	.270
MINOR LEAGUE TOTALS			28	21	2.98	213	29	1	32	432	346	178	143	15	239	424	.221

28 HARVEY GARCIA

RHP

Born: March 16, 1984. **B-T:** R-R. **Ht.:** 6-2. **Wt.:** 170. **Signed:** Venezuela, 2000. **Signed by:** Miguel Garcia/Louie Eljaua (Red Sox).

When the Josh Beckett trade expanded to send Guillermo Mota to Boston, the Red Sox added Garcia on their end. It's actually his second tour of duty with the Marlins, as Florida's former director of Latin American scouting Louie Eljaua originally signed Garcia in 2002. When the Marlins released Garcia in mid-2002, Eljaua had moved onto the Red Sox and quickly snapped him up. Garcia is very similar to Jesus Delgado, another piece of the Beckett deal. Both are Venezuelans who throw in the mid-90s, top out at 98 and have a lot of work to do with their secondary pitches. Garcia throws a little consistently harder than Delgado, but his offspeed stuff is a little less advanced. As with Delgado, Garcia's changeup is better than his hard curveball. Garcia is trying to simplify his delivery in order to gain more consistency. He has good control but still is learning that just laying the ball over the plate isn't going to work. He'll move up to high Class A with Delgado this year, and he could see time in the rotation there.

Year	Club (League)	Class	W	L	ERA	G	GS	CG	SV	IP	H	R	ER	HR	BB	SO	AVG
2001	Ciudad Alianza (VSL)	R	2	2	3.58	12	4	0	0	33	36	20	13	0	18	23	—
2002	San Joaquin (VSL)	R	0	2	6.08	4	3	0	0	13	16	11	9	3	8	12	.320
	Ciudad Alianza (VSL)	R	2	3	2.68	9	7	0	0	40	32	15	12	0	14	31	.221
2003	Red Sox North (DSL)	R	0	2	1.20	3	3	0	0	15	10	4	2	0	3	10	.172
	Red Sox (GCL)	R	3	0	1.89	9	8	0	0	33	21	11	7	2	12	32	.179
2004	Lowell (NY-P)	A	4	6	5.16	14	14	0	0	61	61	40	35	8	30	54	.268
2005	Greenville (SAL)	A	3	5	2.01	32	0	0	6	45	49	18	10	3	18	54	.275
MINOR LEAGUE TOTALS			14	20	3.30	83	39	0	6	240	225	119	88	16	103	216	.244

29 DAN UGGLA   INF

Born: March 11, 1980. **B-T:** R-R. **Ht.:** 5-11. **Wt.:** 195. **Drafted:** Memphis, 2001 (11th round). **Signed by:** Scott Jaster (Diamondbacks).

Uggla was the first of Florida's two major league Rule 5 draft picks at the Winter Meetings, preceding the choice of lefty Mike Megrew from the Dodgers. Before the Marlins can send either to the minors in 2006, they would have to clear waivers and then be offered back to their original teams for half the $50,000 draft price. Uggla has had an up-and-down career since being drafted out of Memphis, alternating good seasons with bad. He had his best year yet in 2005, leading Tennessee in several categories in his return to Double-A. Strong and stocky, Uggla has advanced hitting skills and above-average power. His swing can get a little long at times, leaving him behind on plus fastballs, and most of his power (18 of 21 homers) came against righthanders. Uggla has settled in defensively at second base and has soft hands and good instincts there. He also got extensive action last year at the other three infield positions. While he's versatile with the glove, he's no better than average at any of the positions he can play. Uggla has average speed. Scouts love his makeup, and he gives it his all both in games and in drills. He'll be 26 this season, so it's unlikely he'll be more than a utility player. But the Marlins have nothing but question marks in their middle infield, so he could get plenty of big league playing time.

Year	Club (League)	Class	AVG	G	AB	R	H	2B	3B	HR	RBI	BB	SO	SB	SLG	OBP
2001	Yakima (NWL)	A	.277	72	278	39	77	21	0	5	40	20	52	8	.406	.341
2002	Lancaster (Cal)	A	.228	54	184	21	42	7	2	3	16	21	51	3	.337	.311
	South Bend (Mid)	A	.199	53	171	16	34	5	1	2	10	23	34	0	.275	.291
2003	Lancaster (Cal)	A	.290	134	534	104	155	31	7	23	90	46	105	24	.504	.355
2004	El Paso (TL)	AA	.259	83	294	29	76	12	2	4	30	15	55	10	.354	.302
	Lancaster (Cal)	A	.336	37	140	29	47	13	3	6	38	17	21	2	.600	.422
2005	Tennessee (SL)	AA	.297	135	498	88	148	33	3	21	87	52	103	15	.502	.378
MINOR LEAGUE TOTALS			.276	568	2099	326	579	122	18	64	311	194	421	62	.443	.347

30 JEFF ALLISON   RHP

Born: Nov. 7, 1984. **B-T:** R-R. **Ht.:** 6-2. **Wt.:** 195. **Drafted:** HS—Peabody, Mass., 2003 (1st round). **Signed by:** Steve Payne.

Allison's travails are well documented, but the 16th overall pick in the 2003 draft went a long way toward re-establishing his career last year. Amid great curiosity and after a 21-month-plus layoff, he made it back to the mound in low Class A by early May. Living at first with Greensboro pitching coach Steve Foster, a youth minister and former big league pitcher, Allison stayed clean and put his past problems with heroin and painkillers behind him. He stayed in the rotation the rest of the year, except for a six-week absence due to a strained muscle in his upper back. By the end of 2005 he was regularly turning in six or seven innings a start. His stuff was down a notch or two from the 97 mph fastball he once flashed, but he still had the big-breaking curve and the mound presence that once inspired comparisons to Josh Beckett. The Marlins will continue to take things slowly with Allison's comeback, but he figures to start 2006 in high Class A.

Year	Club (League)	Class	W	L	ERA	G	GS	CG	SV	IP	H	R	ER	HR	BB	SO	AVG
2003	Marlins (GCL)	R	0	2	1.00	3	3	0	0	9	7	2	1	0	4	11	.206
2004	Did not play—Restricted list																
2005	Greensboro (SAL)	A	5	4	4.18	17	17	0	0	95	86	49	44	13	40	83	.242
MINOR LEAGUE TOTALS			5	6	3.91	20	20	0	0	104	93	51	45	13	44	94	.239

HOUSTON
ASTROS

BY **JIM CALLIS**

Tim Purpura's first year as Astros general manager got off to an ominous start. His predecessor, Gerry Hunsicker, declined Jeff Kent's $9 million option for 2005 shortly before his abrupt resignation, and Purpura was unable to re-sign Kent.

Then Purpura was held hostage by free agent Carlos Beltran, who waited until a  January deadline before turning down a club-record $105 million contract offer. At that point, no other comparable options remained, and Houston already had concerns about Lance Berkman's right knee and Jeff Bagwell's right shoulder. The Astros' offense never truly recovered, finishing 11th in the National League in scoring and dead last in road games.

Houston started the year 15-30, giving it the game's third-worst record on May 24. But just like they had in 2004, the Astros made a stunning comeback, going 74-43 the rest of the way—the best record in baseball—to earn their second straight wild-card berth. They reached the World Series for the first time in the franchise's 44 seasons, losing to the White Sox.

The club's farm system has slipped in recent years because of unproductive drafts and increased competition for talent in Venezuela, an arena Houston once dominated. Yet the Astros' first-ever World Series club had a predominantly homegrown flavor. They signed and developed their four best hitters (Berkman, Craig Biggio, Morgan Ensberg, Jason Lane), as well as 20-game winner Roy Oswalt and closer Brad Lidge.

Though Baseball America rated the talent in the system 22nd among the 30 organizations entering 2005, six rookies made the World Series roster. The top three players on this list a year ago—second baseman/outfielder Chris Burke, righthander Ezequiel Astacio and outfielder Willy Taveras—all became regulars in the second half. **Chad Qualls** proved to be a valuable set-up man, and lefty Wandy Rodriguez and outfielder Luke Scott also made contributions.

Whether many of them will become more than role players remains to be seen. The system also doesn't have much to offer in the near future beyond righthanders Jason Hirsh and Fernando Nieve. It may be two or three years before a homegrown position player can challenge for a spot in the lineup.

Concerned about the talent drain, Hunsicker reassigned former scouting director David Lakey after the 2004 draft and promoted coordinator of pro scouting Paul Ricciarini to replace him. Ricciarini used his 2005 first-round pick on Brian Bogusevic, addressing the lack of talented lefthanders in the system, then focused on high-ceiling athletes. Outfielders Eli Iorg (supplemental first round) and Josh Flores (fourth) join Bogusevic on this Top 10 list.

It will take more than one draft to rebuild their system, though the Astros bought goodwill with their fans during the last two years. To sustain that momentum, they'll have to use trades and free agents in the short term.

TOP 30 PROSPECTS

1. Jason Hirsh, rhp
2. Troy Patton, lhp
3. Fernando Nieve, rhp
4. Jimmy Barthmaier, rhp
5. Eli Iorg, of
6. Hunter Pence, of
7. Felipe Paulino, rhp
8. Juan Gutierrez, rhp
9. Brian Bogusevic, lhp
10. Josh Flores, of
11. J.R. Towles, c
12. Matt Albers, rhp
13. Josh Anderson, of
14. Taylor Buchholz, rhp
15. Luke Scott, of
16. Ben Zobrist, ss
17. Chance Douglass, rhp
18. Koby Clemens, 3b
19. Mitch Einertson, of
20. Ryan Mitchell, rhp
21. Lou Santangelo, c
22. Chad Reineke, rhp
23. Hector Gimenez, c
24. Paul Estrada, rhp
25. Jared Gothreaux, rhp
26. Mitch Talbot, rhp
27. Mark McLemore, lhp
28. Tommy Manzella, ss
29. Wladimir Sutil, ss/2b
30. Brooks Conrad, 2b

ORGANIZATION OVERVIEW

General manager: Tim Purpura. **Farm director:** Ricky Bennett. **Scouting director:** Paul Ricciarini.

2005 PERFORMANCE

Class	Team	League	W	L	Pct.	Finish*	Manager
Majors	Houston	National	89	73	.549	+3rd (16)	Phil Garner
Triple-A	Round Rock Express	Pacific Coast	74	70	.514	7th (16)	Jackie Moore
Double-A	Corpus Christi Hooks	Texas	64	76	.457	7th (8)	Dave Clark
High A	Salem Avalanche	Carolina	67	74	.475	5th (8)	Ivan DeJesus
Low A	Lexington Legends	South Atlantic	81	58	.583	1st (16)	Tim Bogar
Short-season	Tri-City ValleyCats	New York-Penn	34	42	.447	9th (14)	Gregg Langbehn
Rookie	Greeneville Astros	Appalachian	29	37	.439	7th (10)	Russ Nixon
OVERALL 2005 MINOR LEAGUE RECORD			349	357	.494	18th (30)	

*Finish in overall standings (No. of teams in league). +League champion.

ORGANIZATION LEADERS

BATTING   *Minimum 250 at-bats
*AVG	Sellers, Neil, Tri-City	.344
R	Conrad, Brooks, Corpus Christi/Round Rock	97
H	Ash, Jonny, Lexington/Salem	154
TB	Pence, Hunter, Lexington/Salem	271
2B	Saccomanno, Mark, Corpus Christi	36
3B	Anderson, Josh, Corpus Christi	9
	Rodriguez, Mike, Corpus Christi	9
HR	Pence, Hunter, Lexington/Salem	31
	Scott, Luke, Round Rock	31
RBI	Coolbaugh, Mike, Round Rock	101
BB	Zobrist, Ben, Lexington/Salem	84
SO	Jimerson, Charlton, Corpus Christi/R. Rock	152
SB	Anderson, Josh, Corpus Christi	50
*OBP	Zobrist, Ben, Lexington/Salem	.437
*SLG	Scott, Luke, Round Rock	.603

PITCHING   #Minimum 75 innings
W	Hirsh, Jason, Corpus Christi	13
	Martinez, Ronnie, Lexington	13
L	Four tied at	12
#ERA	Escobar, Rodrigo, Salem	1.75
G	Wigdahl, Jeff, Lexington/Salem	52
CG	Three tied at	2
SV	Wigdahl, Jeff, Lexington/Salem	17
	Williams, Aaron, Corpus Christi/Salem	17
IP	Hirsh, Jason, Corpus Christi	172
BB	Englebrook, Evan, Lexington	65
SO	Nieve, Fernando, Corpus Christi/Round Rock	171

BEST TOOLS

Best Hitter for Average	Hunter Pence
Best Power Hitter	Luke Scott
Best Strike-Zone Discipline	Ben Zobrist
Fastest Baserunner	Josh Flores
Best Athlete	Charlton Jimerson
Best Fastball	Felipe Paulino
Best Curveball	Jimmy Barthmaier
Best Slider	Jared Gothreaux
Best Changeup	Mitch Talbot
Best Control	Jason Hirsh
Best Defensive Catcher	J.R. Towles
Best Defensive Infielder	Tommy Manzella
Best Infield Arm	Tommy Manzella
Best Defensive Outfielder	Charlton Jimerson
Best Outfield Arm	Charlton Jimerson

PROJECTED 2009 LINEUP

Catcher	J.R. Towles
First Base	Lance Berkman
Second Base	Chris Burke
Third Base	Morgan Ensberg
Shortstop	Adam Everett
Left Field	Jason Lane

Center Field	Willy Taveras
Right Field	Eli Iorg
No. 1 Starter	Roy Oswalt
No. 2 Starter	Jason Hirsh
No. 3 Starter	Troy Patton
No. 4 Starter	Andy Pettitte
No. 5 Starter	Ezequiel Astacio
Closer	Brad Lidge

LAST YEAR'S TOP 20 PROSPECTS

1. Chris Burke, 2b	11. Chad Qualls, rhp
2. Ezequiel Astacio, rhp	12. Juan Gutierrez, rhp
3. Willy Taveras, of	13. Tommy Whiteman, ss
4. Mitch Einertson, of	14. Hector Gimenez, c
5. Troy Patton, lhp	15. Jimmy Barthmaier, rhp
6. Matt Albers, rhp	16. Ben Zobrist, ss
7. Taylor Buchholz, rhp	17. Luke Scott, of
8. Fernando Nieve, rhp	18. Lou Santangelo, c
9. Josh Anderson, of	19. Jordan Parraz, of
10. Hunter Pence, of	20. Chad Reineke, rhp

TOP PROSPECTS OF THE DECADE

Year	Player, Pos.	2005 Org.
1996	Billy Wagner, lhp	Phillies
1997	Richard Hidalgo, of	Rangers
1998	Richard Hidalgo, of	Rangers
1999	Lance Berkman, of	Astros
2000	Wilfredo Rodriguez, lhp	Rangers
2001	Roy Oswalt, rhp	Astros
2002	Carlos Hernandez, lhp	Astros
2003	John Buck, c	Royals
2004	Taylor Buchholz, rhp	Astros
2005	Chris Burke, 2b	Astros

TOP DRAFT PICKS OF THE DECADE

Year	Player, Pos.	2005 Org.
1996	Mark Johnson, rhp	Tigers
1997	Lance Berkman, 1b	Astros
1998	Brad Lidge, rhp	Astros
1999	Mike Rosamond, of	Braves
2000	Robert Stiehl, rhp	Astros
2001	Chris Burke, ss	Astros
2002	Derick Grigsby, rhp	Out of baseball
2003	Jason Hirsh, rhp (2nd round)	Astros
2004	Hunter Pence, of (2nd round)	Astros
2005	Brian Bogusevic, lhp	Astros

ALL-TIME LARGEST BONUSES

Chris Burke, 2001	$2,125,000
Brian Bogusevic, 2005	$1,375,000
Robert Stiehl, 2000	$1,250,000
Derick Grigsby, 2002	$1,125,000
Brad Lidge, 1998	$1,070,000

MINOR LEAGUE DEPTH CHART

Houston Astros

Rank: **20**

STRENGTH: Power pitchers. The Astros light up radar guns with righties and lefties.

WEAKNESS: Infield. No Astros infielder cracked the organization's top 10.

*Depth charts prepared by **John Manuel** and **Chris Kline**. Numbers in parentheses indicate prospect rankings.*

LF
Hunter Pence (6)
Luke Scott (15)

CF
Josh Flores (10)
Josh Anderson (13)
Charlton Jimerson

RF
Eli Iorg (5)
Mitch Einertson (19)
Francisco Caraballo
Jordan Parraz

3B
Koby Clemens (18)
Drew Sutton
Billy Hart

SS
Ben Zobrist (16)
Tommy Manzella (28)
Wladimir Sutil (29)
Edwin Maysonet

2B
Brooks Conrad (30)
Jonny Ash
Eric King

1B
Neil Sellers
Scott Robinson

C
J.R. Towles (11)
Lou Santangelo (21)
Hector Gimenez (23)
Ralph Henriquez

RHP

Starters	Relievers
Jason Hirsh (1)	Felipe Paulino (7)
Fernando Nieve (3)	Chad Reineke (22)
Jimmy Barthmaier (4)	Paul Estrada (24)
Juan Gutierrez (8)	Jared Gothreaux (25)
Matt Albers (12)	Jailen Peguero
Taylor Buchholz (14)	Samuel Gervacio
Chance Douglass (17)	Jamie Merchant
Ryan Mitchell (20)	Evan Englebrook
Mitch Talbot (26)	German Melendez
Ronnie Martinez	Brandon Stricklen
Chris Sampson	Sean Walker
Ryan McKeller	Ben Diggins

LHP

Starters	Relievers
Troy Patton (2)	Josh Muecke
Brian Bogusevic (9)	Victor Garate
Mark McLemore (27)	Jeff Wigdahl
Sergio Severino	Philip Barzilla

DRAFT ANALYSIS
2005

Best Pro Debut: OF Josh Flores (4) made the Rookie-level Appalachian League all-star team by batting .335-8-25 with 20 steals and a league-best 83 hits. The Astros sent OF Eli Iorg (1) to the same Greeneville club so he could nurse a foot injury close to his home in Tennessee. Old for the league at 22, Iorg hit as expected, batting .333-7-34 with 12 steals.

Best Athlete: Flores, who's making the transition from shortstop to center field, has top-of-the-line speed and some power. 3B Billy Hart (5) was a backup quarterback on Southern California's 2003 and 2004 national championship football teams.

Best Pure Hitter: Iorg is this crop's most advanced hitter at this point, but 3B Koby Clemens (8) eventually could overtake him.

Best Raw Power: Clemens has shown more hitting ability and pop than the Astros realized he had. Iorg has plus raw power, as does switch-hitting C Ralph Henriquez (2).

Fastest Runner: Flores gets down the first-base line from the right side in 3.9 seconds, and he always runs hard.

Best Defensive Player: SS Tommy Manzella (3) has plus hands and instincts to go with average range and arm strength.

Best Fastball: Though he was worn out after doubling as a pitcher and outfielder on Tulane's College World Series team, LHP Brian Bogusevic (1) still threw some 95 mph fastballs while working as a reliever after signing. He usually works at 89-93 mph as a starter. RHPs Ryan Mitchell (20) and Brandon Stricklen (42) both can touch 94.

Best Breaking Ball: Bogusevic's slider can be nasty at times. It's a harder curve than LHP Cory Lapinski's (11), which helped him lead NCAA Division III with

RODGER WOOD

Henriquez

16.0 strikeouts per nine innings for Illinois Wesleyan in 2005.

Most Intriguing Background: Clemens' father Roger is a future first-ballot Hall of Famer who led the majors in ERA for the Astros at age 42. OF Matt Cunningham's (36) dad Tim is an associate scout for Houston and was one of the regular bar patrons on "Cheers." Iorg's father Garth and uncle Dane played in the majors, his older brother Isaac played in the minors and his younger brother Cale (a University of Alabama shortstop now on a two-year Mormon mission) could be a premium pick in the 2007 draft. RHP Matt Hirsh's (30) brother Jason is one of the system's top pitching prospects. Henriquez' dad Ralph Sr. was his high school coach and is a roving catching instructor for the Braves.

Closest To The Majors: As a lefthander with three pitches he throws for strikes, Bogusevic should move rapidly.

Best Late-Round Pick: The Astros planned on making Mitchell a draft-and-follow, then pounced once they realized he was ready to sign.

The One Who Got Away: Houston failed to sign two righthanders it wanted—Josh Lindblom (3, now at Tennessee) and Jordan Meaker (9, Dallas Baptist).

Assessment: The Astros focused on high-ceiling athletes and improved their position-player depth. Losing out on Lindblom and Meaker hurt the pitching haul, though.

2004 The Astros did a great job of gauging the signability of LHP Troy Patton (9). They had no first-round pick and the consensus was that their top choice, OF Hunter Pence (2), was a reach—but he hasn't played like it. *GRADE:* B

2003 Houston didn't have a first-rounder in this draft, either. They took a first-round talent in OF Drew Stubbs (3) but didn't sign him. Stubbs will go early in the 2006 draft. RHPs Jason Hirsh (2) and Jimmy Barthmaier (13) are two of the best arms in the system. *GRADE:* C+

2002 RHP Derick Grigsby (1) pitched poorly before leaving baseball to battle depression. RHP Chance Douglass (16) led the Carolina League in ERA last year. *GRADE:* D

2001 2B/OF Chris Burke (1) was a playoff hero in October after he eased into big league duty last season, while RHPs Kirk Saarloos (3) and D.J. Houlton (11) pitched in the rotations for other clubs. RHP Matt Albers (23) has a high-ceiling arm but needs better focus to reach his potential. *GRADE:* C+

*Draft analysis prepared by **Jim Callis**. Numbers in parentheses indicate draft rounds.*

JASON
HIRSH

Born: Feb. 20, 1982.
Ht.: 6-8. **Wt.:** 245.
Bats: R. **Throws:** R.
Drafted: California Lutheran, 2003 (2nd round).
Signed by: Mel Nelson.

Despite his size, Hirsh drew little interest out of high school because he threw just 86-88 mph. He went undrafted, and no NCAA Division I programs wanted him, so he wound up at Division III Cal Lutheran. Hirsh blossomed with the Kingsmen, setting school records for career wins (26) and single-game strikeouts (18), but the number that got him noticed was his improved velocity. By his junior season in 2003, his fastball repeatedly touched 97 mph and his slider was peaking in the mid-80s. The Astros lacked a first-round pick that June after signing Jeff Kent as a free agent, and they made Hirsh their top pick as a second-rounder, signing him for $625,000. He blew away short-season New York-Penn League hitters in his debut but struggled at high Class A Salem in his first full season in 2004. Assigned the task of improving his secondary pitches, Hirsh struggled to do so and lost the edge on his fastball. Undeterred, Houston promoted him to Double-A Corpus Christi in 2005 and he responded by becoming Texas League pitcher of the year. A good year got even better for Hirsh when the Astros drafted and signed his brother Matt, another Cal Lutheran righty, in the 30th round. Matt went 1-2, 5.61 as a swingman at Rookie-level Greeneville.

Hirsh's metamorphosis from 2004 to 2005 was astounding. A year after looking like he might not be more than a set-up man, he became a potential frontline starter. He has an intimidating frame at 6-foot-8 and 245 pounds, and he's athletic for his size. That allows him to repeat his delivery and his arm slot, which helped him gain the feel of a hard 80-86 mph slider that's much more consistent than it was in the past. Managers rated it the best breaking ball in the Texas League. Hirsh also has improved the sink on his fastball, opting for a two-seamer that sits at 91-93 mph. He can still reach the mid-90s when needed, but he's more concerned with the location and movement on his fastball. His changeup made strides as well, and is an average pitch. He's not afraid to pitch inside and throws strikes to both sides of the plate. As one scout with an American League club said, "To make that much progress in one year tells you about his makeup and aptitude."

Having gone from owning no reliable pitch to now possessing three of them, Hirsh just needs to do some fine-tuning. He can still improve his command, which is average now but should become a plus with more experience. Likewise, his changeup can get better and is the least trustworthy of his three offerings.

If Hirsh pitches as well at Triple-A Round Rock as he did in Double-A, he'll get called up to Houston in short order. With the Astros deciding not to offer Roger Clemens arbitration, Hirsh could get an opportunity to make the big league rotation in spring training. It's also possible that he could break into the majors as a middle reliever should the Astros develop a need in their bullpen. Hirsh's fastball-slider combination could allow him to excel in that role, but his long-term future is as a No. 2 or 3 starter.

Year	Club (League)	Class	W	L	ERA	G	GS	CG	SV	IP	H	R	ER	HR	BB	SO	AVG
2003	Tri-City (NY-P)	A	3	1	1.95	10	8	0	0	32	22	10	7	0	7	33	.190
2004	Salem (Car)	A	11	7	4.01	26	23	0	0	130	128	66	58	8	57	96	.269
2005	Corpus Christi (TL)	AA	13	8	2.87	29	29	1	0	172	137	63	55	12	42	165	.218
MINOR LEAGUE TOTALS			27	16	3.22	65	60	1	0	335	287	139	120	20	106	294	.235

2 TROY PATTON
LHP

Born: Sept. 3, 1985. **B-T:** B-L. **Ht.:** 6-1. **Wt.:** 185. **Drafted:** HS—Magnolia, Texas, 2004 (9th round). **Signed by:** Rusty Pendergrass.

Considered a tough sign after committing to the University of Texas, Patton turned pro for $550,000—easily the highest bonus in 2004's ninth round. In his first full season, he set a low Class A Lexington record with 32 straight scoreless innings, pitched in the Futures Game and reached high Class A. Patton can get strikes with his power curveball both by throwing it over the plate or by getting hitters to chase it out of the strike zone. He also can locate his 90-94 mph fastball all over the zone, and it has average life. He has very good control and a nasty competitive streak. Patton needs to get stronger and battled some mild shoulder tendinitis in 2005. He must improve the command of his changeup, which lags partly because he doesn't use it enough. His arm slot tends to wander, and he flattens out his curve when he gets under it. There's debate within the Astros' front office as to whether Jason Hirsh or Patton is the system's top prospect. Patton isn't as polished or as physical, but he's lefthanded and 3½ years younger. He could open 2006 in Double-A at age 20.

Year	Club (League)	Class	W	L	ERA	G	GS	CG	SV	IP	H	R	ER	HR	BB	SO	AVG
2004	Greeneville (Appy)	R	2	2	1.93	6	6	0	0	28	23	8	6	1	5	32	.225
2005	Lexington (SAL)	A	5	2	1.94	15	15	0	0	79	59	24	17	3	20	94	.211
	Salem (Car)	A	1	4	2.63	10	9	0	0	41	34	12	12	2	8	38	.227
MINOR LEAGUE TOTALS			8	8	2.13	31	30	0	0	148	116	44	35	6	33	164	.218

3 FERNANDO NIEVE
RHP

Born: July 15, 1982. **B-T:** R-R. **Ht.:** 6-0. **Wt.:** 200. **Signed:** Venezuela, 1999. **Signed by:** Andres Reiner.

After signing in 1999, Nieve didn't make it past low Class A until his sixth pro season. A Texas League all-star in 2005, he spent the second half in Triple-A and might have earned a September callup if his appendix hadn't ruptured. Nieve has two plus pitches, a 93-95 mph fastball with good riding life that managers rated the best in the Texas League, and a hard slider that's not as consistent. Despite being just 6 feet tall, he pitches on a good downward plane. He repeats his delivery well, enhancing his ability to throw strikes. Nieve's arm action is long, allowing lefthanders to get a good look at his pitches. They batted .273 against him in 2005, and he's working on a splitter to combat them. A changeup would help, but he doesn't have faith in the pitch. He can lose his focus and pitch backwards, and at times he'll use a curveball to the detriment of his slider. Nieve is close to helping the Astros. Some scouts envision him becoming a No. 3 starter, while others see him as a late-innings reliever in the mold of Ugueth Urbina.

Year	Club (League)	Class	W	L	ERA	G	GS	CG	SV	IP	H	R	ER	HR	BB	SO	AVG
1999	La Pradera (VSL)	R	0	6	4.50	11	7	0	0	32	31	22	16	0	16	41	—
2000	Venoco (VSL)	R	3	4	2.71	14	13	0	0	80	56	29	24	5	28	64	.199
2001	Martinsville (Appy)	R	4	2	3.79	12	8	1	0	38	27	20	16	2	21	49	.197
2002	Martinsville (Appy)	R	4	1	2.39	13	13	0	0	68	46	23	18	5	27	60	.185
	Lexington (SAL)	A	0	1	6.00	1	1	0	0	3	6	5	2	0	0	2	.353
2003	Lexington (SAL)	A	14	9	3.65	28	28	1	0	150	133	69	61	10	65	144	.238
2004	Salem (Car)	A	10	6	2.96	24	24	2	0	149	136	52	49	9	40	117	.251
	Round Rock (TL)	AA	2	0	1.56	3	3	0	0	17	12	4	3	0	8	17	.203
2005	Corpus Christi (TL)	AA	4	3	2.65	14	14	0	0	85	62	27	25	7	29	96	.203
	Round Rock (PCL)	AAA	4	4	4.83	13	13	2	0	82	92	45	44	10	33	75	.281
MINOR LEAGUE TOTALS			45	36	3.30	133	124	6	0	704	601	296	258	48	267	665	.230

4 JIMMY BARTHMAIER
RHP

Born: Jan. 6, 1984. **B-T:** R-R. **Ht.:** 6-4. **Wt.:** 210. **Drafted:** HS—Roswell, Ga., 2003 (13th round). **Signed by:** Ellis Dungan.

A high school quarterback, Barthmaier drew interest from several college football programs but didn't commit to one because he didn't want to scare off baseball teams. He slid in the 2003 draft anyway before signing for $750,000, a record for a 13th-rounder. Strong and athletic, Barthmaier projects as an innings-eater. He has a chance to have three plus pitches, and his fastball and curveball already are that good. He throws his fastball at 91-93 mph and peaks at 95, and his power curve is the best in the system. His changeup also is making progress. Barthmaier doesn't have the same feel as Jason Hirsh or Troy Patton, and he's still learning to locate his fastball where he wants. His mechanics have gotten better since he signed, but they still could use some more smoothing. There are some minor questions about his maturity. Barthmaier is on the verge of putting it all together, and once he does he'll move quickly to Houston. Ticketed for high Class A to begin 2006, he could reach Double-A by midseason.

Year	Club (League)	Class	W	L	ERA	G	GS	CG	SV	IP	H	R	ER	HR	BB	SO	AVG
2003	Martinsville (Appy)	R	1	1	2.49	8	3	0	0	22	19	9	6	0	7	18	.226
2004	Greeneville (Appy)	R	4	3	3.78	13	13	0	0	69	70	32	29	3	22	65	.262
2005	Lexington (SAL)	A	11	6	2.27	25	25	0	0	135	108	41	34	3	55	142	.220
	Salem (Car)	A	1	0	1.50	1	0	0	0	6	4	4	1	1	1	6	.167
MINOR LEAGUE TOTALS			17	10	2.72	47	41	0	0	231	201	86	70	7	85	231	.232

5 ELI IORG   OF

Born: March 14, 1983. **B-T:** R-R. **Ht.:** 6-3. **Wt.:** 200. **Drafted:** Tennessee, 2005 (1st round supplemental). **Signed by:** Mike Rosamond.

Iorg was the first outfielder drafted in the first round by the Astros since 1999, when they took Mike Rosamond—the son of the area scout who signed Iorg for $950,000. Iorg has baseball relatives as well, as his father Garth and uncle Dane played in the majors; older brother Isaac played in the Braves system; and younger brother Cale could go early in the 2007 draft. Iorg has a quick, sound swing and a strong frame that should allow him to hit for both power and average. He has slightly above-average speed and good instincts, giving him 20-20 potential in the majors. He has solid range and a plus arm in right field. His intensity is another asset. Iorg, who spent 2003 on a Mormon mission to Argentina, was too old for Rookie ball at 22, but went to Greeneville so he could recover from a stress fracture in his right foot while close to his Tennessee home. He could use more patience at the plate and better accuracy on his throws. Houston might send Iorg to low Class A to start 2006. He needs a sterner test and should reach high Class A before too long.

Year	Club (League)	Class	AVG	G	AB	R	H	2B	3B	HR	RBI	BB	SO	SB	OBP	SLG
2005	Greeneville (Appy)	R	.333	35	138	36	46	7	2	7	34	9	27	12	.391	.565
MINOR LEAGUE TOTALS			.333	35	138	36	46	7	2	7	34	9	27	12	.391	.565

6 HUNTER PENCE   OF

Born: April 13, 1986. **B-T:** R-R. **Ht.:** 6-5. **Wt.:** 210. **Drafted:** Texas-Arlington, 2004 (2nd round). **Signed by:** Rusty Pendergrass.

The Astros made Pence their top pick in 2004. He has done nothing but hit, tying for the system lead in homers in 2005 while finishing second in hitting (.327) and RBIs despite a strained left quadriceps. Pence doesn't look pretty at the plate, choking up on the bat and employing a hitch in his swing, but he has quick hands that enable him to get into good hitting position. He punishes fastballs and has power to all fields. Managers rated him the best hitter and the best power hitter in the South Atlantic League. His speed and athleticism are solid. Some scouts wonder if more advanced pitchers will take advantage of Pence's hitch by pounding him inside. Though he has played primarily center field in the minors, he's destined for left. He doesn't get good jumps and reads on fly balls, and his arm is below-average. Pence has been old for his leagues and needs to be challenged. He'll move up to Double-A in 2006.

Year	Club (League)	Class	AVG	G	AB	R	H	2B	3B	HR	RBI	BB	SO	SB	OBP	SLG
2004	Tri-City (NY-P)	A	.296	51	199	36	59	18	1	8	37	23	30	3	.369	.518
2005	Lexington (SAL)	A	.338	80	302	59	102	14	3	25	60	38	53	8	.413	.652
	Salem (Car)	A	.305	41	151	24	46	8	1	6	30	18	37	1	.374	.490
MINOR LEAGUE TOTALS			.317	171	652	119	207	40	5	39	127	79	120	12	.392	.574

7 FELIPE PAULINO   RHP

Born: Oct. 5, 1983. **B-T:** R-R. **Ht.:** 6-2. **Wt.:** 180. **Signed:** Venezuela, 2001. **Signed by:** Andres Reiner/Omar Lopez.

Like Fernando Nieve, Paulino signed out of Venezuela, has a power arm and has been brought along slowly. He has intrigued scouts ever since his first pitch in the United States—a 96 mph fastball at Rookie-level Martinsville in 2003. The Astros have seen Paulino throw as hard as 100 mph, other organizations have clocked him at 102 and he usually pitches from 90-98. Batters not only have to contend with his velocity, but also heavy boring and riding action on his fastball. He changed the grip on his curveball in 2005 and came up with a plus 80-85 mph breaker. Paulino is still raw as a pitcher. He's still discovering how to control his curveball, and his overall command can improve. He's reluctant to throw his changeup, stunting the development of the third pitch he needs to remain a starter. Paulino will pitch in the Salem rotation in 2006. It's easier to project him as a reliever once he reaches the majors, and he has the stuff to become a closer.

Year	Club (League)	Class	W	L	ERA	G	GS	CG	SV	IP	H	R	ER	HR	BB	SO	AVG
2002	Venoco (VSL)	R	0	0	1.29	4	0	0	0	7	4	1	1	1	6	4	.182
2003	Venoco (VSL)	R	1	0	5.57	5	0	0	0	10	6	6	6	0	12	13	.194
	Martinsville (Appy)	R	2	2	5.60	16	0	0	1	26	23	20	16	0	19	27	.235
2004	Greeneville (Appy)	R	1	3	7.59	10	10	0	0	32	30	30	27	4	22	37	.246
2005	Tri-City (NY-P)	A	2	2	3.81	13	2	0	1	31	21	15	13	2	11	34	.189
	Lexington (SAL)	A	1	1	1.85	7	5	0	0	24	21	8	5	2	6	30	.233
MINOR LEAGUE TOTALS			7	8	4.73	55	17	0	2	129	105	80	68	9	76	145	.222

8 JUAN GUTIERREZ   RHP

Born: July 14, 1983. **B-T:** R-R. **Ht.:** 6-3. **Wt.:** 200. **Signed:** Venezuela, 2000. **Signed by:** Andres Reiner/Pablo Torrealba/Rafael Lara.

Gutierrez repeated both the Rookie-level Venezuelan Summer and Appalachian leagues, so the Astros had to protect him on the 40-man roster before he reached full-season ball. He accomplished that mission in 2005, even making it to high Class A in August. Yet another Venezuelan power pitcher in the system, Gutierrez has a 90-96 mph fastball and a big-breaking, 77-78 mph curveball that he uses as his out pitch. He'll even flash a plus changeup at times. His curveball was more consistent in 2005, and he showed much better control and feel than he had in Rookie ball. Strong and durable, he should be able to accumulate innings. Gutierrez still needs to grasp the art of changing speeds. His changeup has its moments, but it's a distant third pitch. His mechanics break down at times, costing him control and command. He needs to improve his conditioning and tone down his on-field antics. If Gutierrez continues to improve like he did in 2005, he could soar through the rest of the minors. The Astros will start him off back in high Class A in 2006.

Year	Club (League)	Class	W	L	ERA	G	GS	CG	SV	IP	H	R	ER	HR	BB	SO	AVG
2001	Venoco (VSL)	R	1	0	1.78	10	3	0	4	25	23	8	5	0	8	17	—
2002	Venoco (VSL)	R	3	2	2.13	13	7	0	1	38	35	14	9	0	12	28	.252
2003	Martinsville (Appy)	R	1	2	4.76	16	3	0	2	34	42	22	18	2	13	30	.302
2004	Greeneville (Appy)	R	8	2	3.70	13	13	0	0	66	74	31	27	4	30	59	.294
2005	Lexington (SAL)	A	9	5	3.21	22	21	1	0	121	106	55	43	10	43	100	.239
	Salem (Car)	A	1	1	3.00	3	2	0	0	12	10	4	4	1	8	9	.233
MINOR LEAGUE TOTALS			23	12	3.23	77	49	1	7	296	290	134	106	17	114	243	.263

9 BRIAN BOGUSEVIC   LHP

Born: Feb. 18, 1984. **B-T:** L-L. **Ht.:** 6-3. **Wt.:** 211. **Drafted:** Tulane, 2005 (1st round). **Signed by:** Mike Rosamond.

Bogusevic led Tulane to the 2005 College World Series by going 13-3, 3.25 on the mound and batting .328 as a right fielder. Most teams preferred him on the mound, and the Astros concurred after taking him 24th overall and signing him for $1.375 million. Worn out by his two-way efforts and a hamstring injury in college, he was kept on a 45-pitch limit in his pro debut. Even while tired, Bogusevic still hit 95 mph out of the bullpen at short-season Tri-City and generally works at 89-93 mph with his fastball. His slider can be nasty, his changeup is average and he throws strikes with all three of his pitches. His days as an outfielder are over, but he has plus hitting ability, raw power and speed. Bogusevic needs to get stronger after fading in 2005 as well as 2004, when he hit .183 in the Cape Cod League. He needs to turn his slider into a more consistently plus pitch to work in the middle of a big league rotation. The Astros have few quality lefties in their system, so Bogusevic will get the opportunity to move quickly. He should be able to handle a jump to high Class A.

Year	Club (League)	Class	W	L	ERA	G	GS	CG	SV	IP	H	R	ER	HR	BB	SO	AVG
2005	Tri-City (NY-P)	A	0	2	7.59	13	0	0	3	21	30	20	18	2	9	17	.316
MINOR LEAGUE TOTALS			0	2	7.59	13	0	0	3	21	30	20	18	2	9	17	.316

10   JOSH FLORES   OF

Born: Nov. 18, 1985. **B-T:** R-R. **Ht.:** 6-0. **Wt.:** 195. **Drafted:** Triton (Ill.) JC, 2005 (4th round). **Signed by:** Kevin Stein.

Some clubs soured on Flores after he turned down six-figure offers from the Braves as a 24th-rounder out of high school and again as a draft-and-follow last spring. He won the national juco batting title with a .519 average, and area scout Kevin Stein and regional supervisor Gerry Craft lobbied hard to draft him. After signing for $217,500, Flores earned Greeneville MVP and Appalachian League all-star honors. The fastest player in the system, Flores goes from the right side of the plate to first base in 3.9 seconds. More than just a speedster, he's an all-around athlete with hitting ability and surprising power. He has good range and a playable arm in center field. Though he led the Appy League in hits, Flores still needs to tighten his strike zone and do a better job recognizing breaking balls. A shortstop until he turned pro, he's still learning outfield nuances such as taking good routes and getting in position to throw. Flores will play in low Class A in 2006. He's a few years away, but he offers more upside than Astros incumbent Willy Taveras.

Year	Club (League)	Class	AVG	G	AB	R	H	2B	3B	HR	RBI	BB	SO	SB	OBP	SLG
2005	Greeneville (Appy)	R	.335	59	248	49	83	12	5	8	25	16	57	20	.384	.520
	Lexington (SAL)	A	.278	5	18	1	5	2	0	0	1	1	4	4	.316	.389
MINOR LEAGUE TOTALS			.331	64	266	50	88	14	5	8	26	17	61	24	.380	.511

11   J.R. TOWLES   C

Born: Feb. 11, 1984. **B-T:** R-R. **Ht.:** 6-2. **Wt.:** 175. **Drafted:** North Central Texas JC, 2004 (20th round). **Signed by:** Pat Murphy.

Towles turned down the Athletics twice, as a 32nd-rounder in 2002 and a 23rd-rounder in 2003, before signing with the Astros as a 20th-rounder in 2004. After he had a lackluster pro debut at Rookie-level Greenville and needed surgery on the tip of his right index finger after getting hit by a foul ball in instructional league, Houston started him in extended spring training last season. The plan was to have him repeat Rookie ball or maybe go to Tri-City. But when Lou Santangelo went down with a torn labrum in June, Towles was needed in low Class A, and he responded by emerging as the system's best catching prospect since John Buck. Towles put on 15 pounds of muscle and moved closer to the plate, and he looked like a different hitter than he had in 2004. He started driving the ball and handled the bat much better. Athletic for a catcher, Towles has average speed and showed bunting and base-stealing abililty. He's also the best all-around defensive catcher in the system. His receiving and blocking skills are strong, and he has arm strength. Towles' pop times from his mitt to second base generally sit at an average 2.0 seconds because he has a long release, though he did throw out 33 percent of basestealers last year. Besides his obvious tools, he also has good instincts and a strong work ethic. Towles could open this year back in Lexington if the Astros want to give him regular action behind the plate, or could move up to high Class A if they don't mind a timeshare arrangement with Santangelo.

Year	Club (League)	Class	AVG	G	AB	R	H	2B	3B	HR	RBI	BB	SO	SB	OBP	SLG
2004	Greeneville (Appy)	R	.243	39	111	17	27	6	0	0	8	12	23	4	.370	.297
2005	Lexington (SAL)	A	.346	45	162	35	56	14	2	5	23	16	29	11	.436	.549
MINOR LEAGUE TOTALS			.304	84	273	52	83	20	2	5	31	28	52	15	.409	.447

12   MATT ALBERS   RHP

Born: Jan. 20,1983. **B-T:** L-R. **Ht.:** 6-0. **Wt.:** 205. **Drafted:** San Jacinto (Texas) JC, D/F 2001 (23rd round). **Signed by:** Rusty Pendergrass.

A local product who played for a suburban Houston high school and nearby juco power San Jacinto, Albers has one of the best arms in the system. But he learned in 2005 that won't mean much if he doesn't improve his dedication. He has yet to place much value on preparing for starts or working on his off days, and his mechanics and command wandered throughout last season. So did his confidence. If he takes his career more seriously, he could be a frontline starter. Albers works consistently at 93-94 mph and touches 97 with his fastball, and both his curveball and slider show the potential to become plus pitches. He doesn't throw his average changeup enough. He needs to get more consistent with his secondary pitches and his control. He was hittable last year because he rarely pitched inside and struggled to keep the ball down. Albers had a soft body when he signed, and while he has gotten in better shape it's still a concern. The Astros suspended him for a month after an alcohol-related incident at a South Atlantic League all-star game function in 2004. He has gotten his life in order, and now must do the same with his career. Some club officials wonder if he lacks the focus to be a starter and might be more effective as a reliever. He'll remain in the rotation for now, though he could repeat high Class A as a wakeup call.

Year	Club (League)	Class	W	L	ERA	G	GS	CG	SV	IP	H	R	ER	HR	BB	SO	AVG
2002	Martinsville (Appy)	R	2	3	5.13	13	13	0	0	60	61	38	34	2	38	72	.274
2003	Tri-City (NY-P)	A	5	4	2.92	15	14	0	0	86	69	37	28	1	25	94	.214
2004	Lexington (SAL)	A	8	3	3.32	22	21	0	0	111	95	51	41	3	57	140	.237
2005	Salem (Car)	A	8	12	4.66	28	27	0	0	149	161	86	77	15	62	146	.278
MINOR LEAGUE TOTALS			23	22	3.99	78	75	0	0	406	386	212	180	21	182	452	.253

13 JOSH ANDERSON   OF

Born: Aug. 10, 1982. **B-T:** L-R. **Ht.:** 6-2. **Wt.:** 195. **Drafted:** Eastern Kentucky, 2003 (4th round). **Signed by:** Nick Venuto.

Anderson led the minors in stolen bases in 2004 and topped the Texas League in 2005, but he needs to show more well-rounded offensive skills if he's to be a big league regular. Since he tore up low Class A at the beginning of 2004, his hitting, gap power and plate discipline have regressed at higher levels. He has leadoff speed but must develop the on-base ability to match. He doesn't need to worry about hitting home runs, but driving a few balls in the gaps and being able to fight off inside fastballs would keep pitchers more honest. Managers rated Anderson the fastest baserunner and the best defensive outfielder in the Texas League, though he could use more polish in both areas. He was caught stealing 19 times last year and sometimes tries to swipe bags in less-than-opportune situations. He doesn't always read line drives well and relies on his speed to make up for his mistakes. His arm is average. He has upside and more pop than Astros incumbent Willy Taveras, though he's not as refined, as fast or as gifted defensively. Anderson needs to tone down his aggressiveness in every aspect of the game and enhance what he does best. After a strong Arizona Fall League performance, he'll move up to Triple-A in 2006.

Year	Club (League)	Class	AVG	G	AB	R	H	2B	3B	HR	RBI	BB	SO	SB	OBP	SLG
2003	Tri-City (NY-P)	A	.286	74	297	44	85	11	4	3	30	16	53	26	.339	.380
2004	Lexington (SAL)	A	.324	73	299	69	97	12	3	4	31	33	47	31	.402	.425
	Salem (Car)	A	.268	66	280	45	75	13	6	2	21	13	53	31	.314	.379
2005	Corpus Christi (TL)	AA	.282	127	524	67	148	16	9	1	26	29	80	50	.329	.353
MINOR LEAGUE TOTALS			.289	340	1400	225	405	52	22	10	108	91	233	154	.344	.379

14 TAYLOR BUCHHOLZ   RHP

Born: Oct. 13, 1981. **B-T:** R-R. **Ht.:** 6-4. **Wt.:** 220. **Drafted:** HS—Springfield, Pa., 2000 (6th round). **Signed by:** Ken Hultzapple (Phillies).

Buchholz was the key player from the Astros' perspective in their Billy Wagner trade with the Phillies in November 2003, but Ezequiel Astacio since has passed him in that regard. Little has gone right for Buchholz in his two seasons in the Houston system. He went 0-5, 7.92 in his first six starts and was just coming out of that slump when he went down with a strained shoulder in July 2004. He had arthroscopic surgery on his labrum and his biceps in November 2004, and seemed hesitant to cut loose last season. Once again, he had to be shut down as he was starting to get on a roll, missing most of the second half with a sore shoulder. He came back at the end of August and did look strong in the Arizona Fall League. It's hard to know what to make of Buchholz. He still has one of the best curveballs in the system, but his velocity ranged from 84-86 to 92-94 mph in 2005. He throws from a high three-quarters angle, robbing his fastball of life and leaving it hittable when he doesn't keep it down. Confidence may be the key with Buchholz. He doesn't aggressively put hitters away, too often laying the ball over the plate after he gets ahead in the count. He needs to use his changeup to get lefthanders out, but he doesn't trust it enough. Staying healthy is also important, as Buchholz had shoulder problems and bone chips in his elbow in 2003. The Astros will send Buchholz to Triple-A for the third straight season, and they'd like to see him develop a mean streak and force his way to Houston.

Year	Club (League)	Class	W	L	ERA	G	GS	CG	SV	IP	H	R	ER	HR	BB	SO	AVG
2000	Phillies (GCL)	R	2	3	2.25	12	7	0	0	44	46	22	11	2	14	41	.269
2001	Lakewood (SAL)	A	9	14	3.36	28	26	5	0	177	165	83	66	8	57	136	.250
2002	Clearwater (FSL)	A	10	6	3.29	23	23	4	0	159	140	66	58	11	51	129	.233
	Reading (EL)	AA	0	2	7.43	4	4	0	0	23	29	19	19	5	6	17	.315
2003	Reading (EL)	AA	9	11	3.55	25	24	1	0	145	136	62	57	14	33	114	.249
2004	New Orleans (PCL)	AAA	6	7	5.23	20	17	1	0	98	107	60	57	16	29	74	.279
2005	Round Rock (PCL)	AAA	6	0	4.81	20	14	0	0	77	79	41	41	14	27	45	.275
MINOR LEAGUE TOTALS			42	43	3.85	132	115	11	0	722	702	353	309	70	217	556	.256

15 LUKE SCOTT   OF

Born: June 25, 1978. **B-T:** L-R. **Ht.:** 6-0. **Wt.:** 210. **Drafted:** Oklahoma State, 2001 (9th round).
Signed by: Chad MacDonald (Indians).

As if getting the rights to Willy Taveras for Jeriome Robertson weren't enough, the Astros also got Scott in a March 2004 deal with the Indians. With Lance Berkman sidelined with a knee injury, Scott became a surprise Opening Day starter for Houston in 2005. He went down to Triple-A in May and led the Pacific Coast League in homers despite playing in just 103 games, then came back up in August and made the National League Division Series roster. He has huge lefthanded power, a commodity the Astros valued coming off their bench, and can crush balls out of the park to all fields. He's an incredibly streaky hitter, and he'll sometimes get himself out when he's going good, needlessly making adjustments because he fears pitchers will do the same. He controls the strike zone well for a slugger, and he holds his own in left field. Scott's speed and arm are both below-average tools but not liabilities. The 27-year-old doesn't figure to win a regular job with Houston, but he should be able to claim a reserve role in spring training.

Year	Club (League)	Class	AVG	G	AB	R	H	2B	3B	HR	RBI	BB	SO	SB	OBP	SLG
2001	Did not play—Injured															
2002	Columbus (SAL)	A	.257	49	171	28	44	15	4	7	32	21	58	9	.345	.515
	Kinston (Car)	A	.239	48	163	22	39	7	1	8	30	16	47	2	.326	.442
2003	Kinston (Car)	A	.278	67	241	37	67	12	1	13	44	27	62	6	.360	.498
	Akron (EL)	AA	.273	50	183	21	50	13	1	7	37	11	37	0	.317	.470
2004	Salem (Car)	A	.278	66	241	45	67	20	1	8	35	41	58	6	.376	.469
	Round Rock (TL)	AA	.298	63	208	45	62	17	0	19	62	33	43	0	.401	.654
2005	Round Rock (PCL)	AAA	.286	103	398	69	114	25	4	31	87	43	96	2	.363	.603
	Houston (NL)	MLB	.188	34	80	6	15	4	2	0	4	9	23	1	.270	.288
MAJOR LEAGUE TOTALS			.188	34	80	6	15	4	2	0	4	9	23	1	.270	.288
MINOR LEAGUE TOTALS			.276	446	1605	267	443	109	12	93	327	192	401	25	.359	.533

16 BEN ZOBRIST   SS

Born: May 26, 1981. **B-T:** B-R. **Ht.:** 6-3. **Wt.:** 200. **Drafted:** Dallas Baptist, 2004 (6th round).
Signed by: Rusty Pendergrass.

Zobrist, the shortstop for Team USA at the 2005 World Cup in the Netherlands, has performed well at all three of his minor league stops, including leading the New York-Penn League in batting and on-base percentage in his 2004 pro debut, but he always has been old for his league. He got a later start on his pro career than most players because he was 19 when he graduated high school and spent four years in college between Olivet Nazarene (Ill.), where he started out as a pitcher, and Dallas Baptist. A switch-hitter who excels at handling the bat, Zobrist has solid-average tools across the board, with the exception of power. Managers rated him as having the best strike-zone discipline in the South Atlantic League last year, and no one controls the zone better in the Houston system. His swing is a little longer from the right side, but he's effective from both sides of the plate. He's bigger and doesn't have the range of a typical shortstop, but his instincts enable him to make the plays required at the position. He also made just 15 errors in 102 games at short in 2005. He continues to remind the Astros of quintessential utilityman Bill Spiers, but they also say it's too early to write off Zobrist as a regular shortstop. They need to push him more, and he'll begin 2006 in Double-A with a chance for a midseason promotion to Triple-A.

Year	Club (League)	Class	AVG	G	AB	R	H	2B	3B	HR	RBI	BB	SO	SB	OBP	SLG
2004	Tri-City (NY-P)	A	.339	68	257	50	87	14	3	4	45	43	31	15	.438	.463
2005	Lexington (SAL)	A	.304	68	247	45	75	17	2	2	32	47	35	16	.415	.413
	Salem (Car)	A	.333	42	141	25	47	12	1	3	13	37	17	2	.475	.496
MINOR LEAGUE TOTALS			.324	178	645	120	209	43	6	9	90	127	83	33	.437	.451

17 CHANCE DOUGLASS   RHP

Born: Feb. 24, 1984. **B-T:** R-R. **Ht.:** 6-1. **Wt.:** 200. **Drafted:** HS—Amarillo, Texas, 2002 (12th round). **Signed by:** Rusty Pendergrass.

It's difficult to sway high school players from a commitment to Rice, but the Astros did that with Douglass after taking him in the 12th round in 2002 and giving him a bonus of $225,000. He did little to justify that bonus in his first three pro seasons, spending two years in Rookie ball before getting torched in low Class A. Douglass broke through in 2005, however, leading the Carolina League in innings and ERA while earning the organization's Salem MVP award. He relies on command and sink. Douglass throws his two-seam fastball in the low 90s and locates it well in the strike zone. He throws two breaking balls, and his slider has some crispness at times. He'd be better off relying on the slider and relegating his curveball to a show pitch. His changeup is below-average now, but it's improving and has good downward movement at times. He's intelligent and a tough competitor. With a strong frame and an easy delivery, he can hold his stuff through games. Projected as a No. 4 or 5 starter, Douglass will advance to Double-A this year.

Year	Club (League)	Class	W	L	ERA	G	GS	CG	SV	IP	H	R	ER	HR	BB	SO	AVG
2002	Martinsville (Appy)	R	2	1	3.66	12	9	0	0	44	45	19	18	4	23	34	.269
2003	Martinsville (Appy)	R	5	1	2.34	10	10	0	0	58	50	17	15	1	10	48	.242
2004	Lexington (SAL)	A	9	10	5.33	29	24	0	0	137	156	99	81	18	73	106	.298
2005	Salem (Car)	A	12	9	2.90	27	27	1	0	168	157	59	54	7	44	128	.249
MINOR LEAGUE TOTALS			28	21	3.72	78	70	1	0	406	408	194	168	30	150	316	.267

18 KOBY CLEMENS 3B

Born: Dec. 4, 1986. **B-T:** R-R. **Ht.:** 5-11. **Wt.:** 193. **Drafted:** HS—Houston, 2005 (8th round). **Signed by:** Rusty Pendergrass.

Most Texas area scouts regarded Roger Clemens' eldest son as a decent player who'd be best off following through on his commitment to Texas rather than turning pro. So it was somewhat of a surprise when Houston took him in the eighth round and signed him for $380,000, the equivalent of late third-round money. But Koby proved to be better than scouts had thought and more than a nepotism pick. Though he threw two no-hitters and flashed a low-90s fastball as a high school senior, Clemens won't follow his dad to the mound. His best tool is his power, and he showed more pop and hitting ability than even the Astros realized he had. Growing up around the game enabled him to make an easy transition to pro ball, and he showed a feel for making adjustments. He has a sound swing and began to use the opposite field. Clemens has his father's build but in a 5-foot-11 frame, so he's not a tremendous athlete. He has the arm strength to play at third base, but will have to exert himself to maintain the range and agility to stay there. That's not an issue because his work ethic (like Roger's) is off the charts. He had back surgery in 2004, so he might move to a less demanding position eventually. If Clemens can remain at the hot corner, he could develop into a big league regular. He has the makeup to handle an assignment to low Class A in 2006.

Year	Club (League)	Class	AVG	G	AB	R	H	2B	3B	HR	RBI	BB	SO	SB	OBP	SLG
2005	Greeneville (Appy)	R	.297	33	111	14	33	8	0	4	17	18	26	4	.398	.477
	Tri-City (NY-P)	A	.281	9	32	3	9	1	2	0	6	4	5	1	.361	.438
MINOR LEAGUE TOTALS			.294	42	143	17	42	9	2	4	23	22	31	5	.387	.469

19 MITCH EINERTSON OF

Born: April 4, 1986. **B-T:** R-R. **Ht.:** 5-11. **Wt.:** 185. **Drafted:** HS—Oceanside, Calif., 2004 (5th round). **Signed by:** Mark Ross.

Einertson's first full season was the exact opposite of his pro debut. An unheralded fifth-round pick in 2004, he tied a 44-year-old Appalachian League home run record, went deep twice more as Greeneville won the playoffs and won the MVP award after also leading the league in extra-base hits, RBIs, total bases and slugging percentage. One scout said no Astros prospect had the ball jump off the bat like Einertson since Jeff Bagwell. Einertson's encore was a huge disappointment, however. He started 2005 in a 3-for-32 slump, didn't homer until May 11 and took four weeks off in midsummer to resolve personal issues. With that behind him, Houston hopes he'll revert to his previous form in 2006. The power potential is still in there, though he has a long way to go with pitch recognition. Even when he was crushing Appy League pitching, he struck out in nearly one-third of his at-bats, so he has to close a lot of holes in his swing. Einertson got some time at second base in instructional league after the 2004 season, but had footwork problems and will stay in the outfield. His range, arm and instincts are all fine for right field. He'll get a second chance to prove himself in low Class A this year.

Year	Club (League)	Class	AVG	G	AB	R	H	2B	3B	HR	RBI	BB	SO	SB	OBP	SLG
2004	Greeneville (Appy)	R	.308	63	227	53	70	15	0	24	67	32	70	4	.413	.692
	Tri-City (NY-P)	A	.143	2	7	1	1	0	0	1	1	0	2	0	.143	.571
2005	Lexington (SAL)	A	.234	101	355	52	83	19	1	7	45	52	99	5	.353	.352
MINOR LEAGUE TOTALS			.261	166	589	106	154	34	1	32	113	84	171	9	.374	.486

20 RYAN MITCHELL RHP

Born: Aug. 13, 1987. **B-T:** R-R. **Ht.:** 6-5. **Wt.:** 235. **Drafted:** HS—Magnolia, Texas, 2005 (20th round). **Signed by:** Rusty Pendergrass

As a projectable 6-foot-4 high school sophomore, Mitchell tore up the summer showcase circuit in 2003 and looked like a first-round pick for the 2005 draft. He made little progress over the next two years, however, and seemed likely to attend juco power San Jacinto (Texas) when the Astros took him in the 20th round last June as a draft-and-follow. Instead, he proved an easier sign than expected and turned pro for $35,000. Mitchell has the potential to rocket up this list in the future. He already throws 90-92 mph, touches 94 and can add more velocity as he gets stronger. He throws his curveball and changeup for strikes and has uncanny command for his age and size. How much he can improve the quality of his secondary pitches will determine how good he becomes. Mitchell is fearless on the mound and has baseball savvy. His arm action has some funk to it, as he has a short arm stroke and sometimes gets too far out in front, but he showed the aptitude to clean it up under the tutelage of Houston's minor league staff. Like Koby Clemens, who took Mitchell under his wing at Greeneville, he won't be overwhelmed by low Class A as a teenager.

Year	Club (League)	Class	W	L	ERA	G	GS	CG	SV	IP	H	R	ER	HR	BB	SO	AVG
2005	Greeneville (Appy)	R	3	1	3.34	11	8	0	0	35	30	15	13	0	14	33	.219
MINOR LEAGUE TOTALS			3	1	3.34	11	8	0	0	35	30	15	13	0	14	33	.219

21 LOU SANTANGELO   C

Born: March 16, 1983. **B-T:** R-R. **Ht.:** 6-1. **Wt.:** 200. **Drafted:** Clemson, 2004 (4th round). **Signed by:** Brian Keegan.

Santangelo has a pair of outstanding tools with his raw power and arm strength, but he's still learning how to get the most out of them. He can hit the ball farther than any Houston farmhand except for Luke Scott, but Santangelo tends to do most of his damage against mistakes hung over the plate. He doesn't recognize breaking balls well and has struggled to hit for average or make contact dating back to his college days at Clemson and Seton Hall. He never topped .300 with metal bats. He has shortened his swing as a pro, but the same problems persist. Even though he had a tear in his labrum that cost him six weeks in the second half and forced him to share time with J.R. Towles in the second half, Santangelo threw out 43 percent of basestealers in 2005. He has a quick release and good accuracy to go with his strong arm, and he'd be even better if he got into a better position to throw. He's a lazy receiver who doesn't shift his body to get in front of balls. He works hard, but he also takes his natural gifts for granted at times. He has below-average speed but runs well for a catcher. His shoulder didn't require surgery and isn't expected to give him problems in the future. He could jump to Double-A depending on how much the Astros decide to spread out their catching talent, but Santangelo would be best off by starting 2006 in high Class A.

Year	Club (League)	Class	AVG	G	AB	R	H	2B	3B	HR	RBI	BB	SO	SB	OBP	SLG
2004	Tri-City (NY-P)	A	.201	47	164	28	33	5	2	6	20	21	58	2	.299	.366
2005	Lexington (SAL)	A	.268	70	239	43	64	14	2	14	39	24	86	4	.336	.519
MINOR LEAGUE TOTALS			.241	117	403	71	97	19	4	20	59	45	144	6	.321	.457

22 CHAD REINEKE   RHP

Born: April 9, 1982. **B-T:** R-R. **Ht.:** 6-6. **Wt.:** 210. **Drafted:** Miami (Ohio), 2004 (13th round). **Signed by:** Nick Venuto.

College senior signs Eric Bruntlett, Morgan Ensberg, Mike Gallo, Jason Lane and Chad Qualls all played roles in Houston's run to the World Series, and the Astros may have another find in Reineke. He was a 13th-round pick in 2004 after going an uninspiring 13-9, 4.63 in four seasons at Miami (Ohio). But his velocity picked up when he moved into a short-relief role as a senior, and he has maintained a consistent 93-94 mph fastball as a pro. Reineke also throws a plus slider that can reach the upper 80s. He uses his 6-foot-7 frame to hide the ball and to throw on a good downward plane. Reineke moved to the rotation in mid-July to get more innings and work on a third pitch. He improved his feel for his changeup but it still has a long ways to go. He was more hittable as a starter but did a better job of throwing strikes. He has toned down the effort in his delivery but still battles his command. He may get some more starts this year in high Class A, but he projects as a late-inning reliever.

Year	Club (League)	Class	W	L	ERA	G	GS	CG	SV	IP	H	R	ER	HR	BB	SO	AVG
2004	Tri-City (NY-P)	A	1	2	2.45	23	0	0	3	37	27	13	10	0	23	52	.197
2005	Lexington (SAL)	A	10	8	3.52	42	11	0	4	102	84	46	40	5	49	108	.230
MINOR LEAGUE TOTALS			11	10	3.24	65	11	0	7	139	111	59	50	5	72	160	.221

23 HECTOR GIMENEZ   C

Born: Sept. 28, 1982. **B-T:** B-R. **Ht.:** 5-10. **Wt.:** 180. **Signed:** Venezuela, 1999. **Signed by:** Andres Reiner.

When the Astros included John Buck in the Carlos Beltran trade in June 2004, Gimenez became the best catcher in the system. He since has been passed by J.R. Towles and Lou Santangelo, and 2005 second-round pick Ralph Henriquez is in his rearview mirror. But after Gimenez' bat stagnated in 2003-04, he bounced back while repeating Double-A last year. For the first time in his pro career, his batting average didn't decline from the previous season. His offense won't be his strength, but Houston still thinks Gimenez might hit enough to warrant consideration as a regular. He's a switch-hitter with some pop. He lacks the bat speed or strike-zone control to hit for much of an average or slot in the upper half of a line-up. He offers little speed on the basepaths. Gimenez' work behind the plate is his ticket to the big leagues. He has a plus arm and a quick release to go with solid receiving skills and agility. He threw out 41 percent of basestealers last year and likes to try to pick off runners. His game-calling skills have improved along with his English, and he has learned not to let his offensive struggles affect his defense. Gimenez will head to Triple-A this year with an eye on supplanting Raul Chavez as Brad Ausmus' backup in 2007.

Year	Club (League)	Class	AVG	G	AB	R	H	2B	3B	HR	RBI	BB	SO	SB	OBP	SLG
2000	Venoco (VSL)	R	.297	34	91	9	27	8	0	1	13	12	21	0	.396	.418
2001	Venoco (VSL)	R	.278	42	144	27	40	12	3	5	34	26	30	4	.388	.507
2002	Lexington (SAL)	A	.263	85	297	41	78	16	1	11	42	25	78	2	.320	.434
2003	Salem (Car)	A	.247	109	381	41	94	17	1	7	54	29	75	2	.304	.352
2004	Round Rock (TL)	AA	.245	97	331	38	81	16	3	6	46	18	64	2	.284	.366
2005	Corpus Christi (TL)	AA	.273	121	454	47	124	19	1	12	58	32	88	2	.322	.399
MINOR LEAGUE TOTALS			.261	488	1698	203	444	88	9	42	247	142	356	12	.320	.398

24 PAUL ESTRADA RHP

Born: Sept. 10, 1982. **B-T:** R-R. **Ht.:** 6-1. **Wt.:** 215. **Signed:** Venezuela, 1999. **Signed by:** Andres Reiner.

Like most of the Venezuelan power pitchers in the system, Estrada has developed at a slow pace. He spent four years in Rookie ball and another at short-season Tri-City before finally advancing to low Class A in 2005. He's still raw and has been used mainly in relief, but on the right night Estrada can show two pitches that grade out as 70s on the 20-80 scouting scale. He can run his fastball up to 95 mph and also flash a knee-buckling curveball. He usually pitches at 92-94 mph with his four-seam fastball, and at 88-90 mph with some sink on his two-seamer. His curve isn't consistently dominating, and he's still searching for a dependable third pitch. He never showed any feel for a changeup, so he switched to a splitter last year and the pitch has good tumble. Estrada's control still needs some work, but he's no longer walking a batter an inning, as he did in his first two U.S. seasons. He sometimes rushes his delivery and leaves pitches up in the zone. He's durable enough to start if he fleshes out his repertoire, and he may pitch out of the rotation this year in high Class A.

Year	Club (League)	Class	W	L	ERA	G	GS	CG	SV	IP	H	R	ER	HR	BB	SO	AVG
2000	Venoco (VSL)	R	1	0	7.14	16	1	0	0	29	38	33	23	1	28	27	.311
2001	Venoco (VSL)	R	2	2	4.20	14	9	0	3	41	35	24	19	0	29	50	—
2002	Martinsville (Appy)	R	2	2	11.64	14	6	0	0	32	45	45	41	2	36	42	.326
2003	Martinsville (Appy)	R	1	0	5.49	12	1	0	1	21	19	17	13	2	22	25	.235
2004	Tri-City (NY-P)	A	5	1	2.81	23	0	0	8	42	26	13	13	4	17	56	.172
2005	Lexington (SAL)	A	6	7	2.69	46	3	0	3	90	65	31	27	6	34	94	.202
MINOR LEAGUE TOTALS			17	12	4.81	125	20	0	15	255	228	163	136	15	166	294	.237

25 JARED GOTHREAUX RHP

Born: Jan. 27, 1980. **B-T:** R-R. **Ht.:** 6-0. **Wt.:** 200. **Drafted:** McNeese State, 2002 (16th round). **Signed by:** James Farrar.

After hitting the wall in the upper minors the last two years and requiring surgery to repair ligament damage in his elbow, Gothreaux was removed from the 40-man roster in November. But the Astros still believe he can contribute, probably in a relief role after spending most of his career as a starter. Gothreaux' out pitch is a slider that has a lot of tilt and ranks as the best in the system. His fastball ranges from 88-92 mph when he pitches out of the rotation, though scouts have seen him touch 94 and project that he'd add 2-3 mph coming out of the bullpen. His fastball also has some nice, late armside sink. Gothreaux hasn't had much success keeping more advanced lefthanded hitters honest with his changeup, and he also has tried a splitter with the same results. Though he has a long arm action, he repeats his delivery well and has good command. At times, he can throw too many strikes. He's just 6 feet tall, so his stuff can flatten out and ride high in the zone when he doesn't stay on top of it. Gothreaux has the competitive makeup to pitch in the late innings, and he may shift to the bullpen this year in Triple-A. He made just one start in the second half of last season but was soft-tossing again in November and should be 100 percent for spring training.

Year	Club (League)	Class	W	L	ERA	G	GS	CG	SV	IP	H	R	ER	HR	BB	SO	AVG
2002	Tri-City (NY-P)	A	2	3	2.72	28	0	0	4	46	55	23	14	3	12	53	.288
2003	Salem (Car)	A	13	4	2.82	29	22	1	1	147	144	54	46	4	26	85	.259
2004	Round Rock (TL)	AA	9	7	3.96	27	24	2	0	157	172	82	69	16	35	110	.283
2005	Round Rock (PCL)	AAA	3	8	4.29	15	15	0	0	86	87	45	41	8	29	47	.269
MINOR LEAGUE TOTALS			27	22	3.51	99	61	3	5	436	458	204	170	31	102	295	.273

26 MITCH TALBOT RHP

Born: Oct. 17, 1983. **B-T:** R-R. **Ht.:** 6-2. **Wt.:** 175. **Drafted:** HS—Cedar City, Utah, 2002 (2nd round). **Signed by:** Doug Deutsch.

Talbot hasn't grown into the velocity the Astros expected when they made him a second-round pick in 2002, and he receives mixed reviews from club officials. Yet he's still an interesting pitching prospect with the best changeup in the system. He throws it with excellent arm action and it drops straight down. He'll occasionally hit 94 mph on the radar gun, but he usually pitches at 88-90 with a two-seam fastball and 91-92 with a four-seamer. He's athletic and has a clean delivery and arm action, so it's possible he could add more velocity in the future. Those attributes allow him to throw strikes with ease. Talbot never has had much success with a breaking ball. He has tried both a slider and curveball, and usually winds up with a mediocre slurve. His best option may be a pitch that's closer to a cut fastball than a true slider. His job in Double-A this year remains the same as it was in 2005: to find a dependable third pitch.

Year	Club (League)	Class	W	L	ERA	G	GS	CG	SV	IP	H	R	ER	HR	BB	SO	AVG
2003	Martinsville (Appy)	R	4	4	2.83	12	12	0	0	54	45	26	17	1	11	46	.224
2004	Lexington (SAL)	A	10	10	3.83	27	27	1	0	153	145	78	65	16	49	115	.252
2005	Salem (Car)	A	8	11	4.34	27	27	1	0	151	169	90	73	15	46	100	.280
MINOR LEAGUE TOTALS			22	25	3.90	66	66	2	0	358	359	194	155	32	106	261	.260

27 MARK McLEMORE LHP

Born: Oct. 9, 1980. **B-T:** L-L. **Ht.:** 6-2. **Wt.:** 220. **Drafted:** Oregon State, 2002 (4th round). **Signed by:** Dan Houston.

McLemore never has had a winning record in three seasons at Oregon State or in four seasons as a pro. He was starting to come into his own and ranked second in the Texas League in ERA last June when he had to be shut down with shoulder problems. He had surgery to repair his labrum in late July, and the Astros kept him on their 40-man roster rather than risk exposing him to the major league Rule 5 draft. Before he got hurt, McLemore was throwing three solid pitches as a starter. He had an 88-92 mph fastball with good sink, a tight slider with late tilt and a deceptive changeup. When his shoulder started bothering him, he got away from throwing his secondary pitches. McLemore's health and command will determine how far he goes. He has trouble maintaining a consistent release point, leading to deep counts and too many pitches up in the zone. Regaining his confidence, which took years to build, is another key. Houston expects him to be ready to go for spring training and likely will start him back in Double-A.

Year	Club (League)	Class	W	L	ERA	G	GS	CG	SV	IP	H	R	ER	HR	BB	SO	AVG
2002	Martinsville (Appy)	R	0	1	1.80	4	2	0	0	10	9	3	2	0	5	11	.237
	Tri-City (NY-P)	A	1	5	14.09	9	6	0	0	23	42	37	36	2	17	16	.393
2003	Lexington (SAL)	A	2	11	4.58	36	7	0	0	92	84	57	47	4	55	101	.243
2004	Salem (Car)	A	7	7	3.67	37	14	1	6	93	80	38	38	8	44	79	.231
2005	Corpus Christi (TL)	AA	5	6	2.81	15	15	1	0	74	59	34	23	5	34	65	.220
MINOR LEAGUE TOTALS			15	30	4.49	101	44	2	6	292	274	169	146	19	155	272	.248

28 TOMMY MANZELLA SS

Born: April 16, 1983. **B-T:** R-R. **Ht.:** 6-2. **Wt.:** 190. **Drafted:** Tulane, 2005 (3rd round). **Signed by:** Mike Rosamond.

Manzella's 2005 pro debut couldn't have been more trying. Hurricane Katrina destroyed his family's home in Chalmette, La., but Manzella gritted it out until Tri-City completed its schedule even after the Astros offered to let him leave. He had a tough time adjusting to wood bats and dealt with a balky elbow that required arthroscopic surgery in the offseason. He has the makeup to bounce back from adversity, and he did just that after he had a mediocre junior season at Tulane that left him undrafted in 2004. As a senior, he emerged as the Green Wave's No. 3 hitter and RBI leader, helping them reach the College World Series. A third-round pick that came from the Mets as part of the compensation for Carlos Beltran, Manzella signed for $289,000. He's a better hitter than he showed in his first taste of pro ball, but he'll have to make adjustments to a long swing that's more tailored for metal bats. He had trouble fighting off inside pitches or lifting the ball. He has enough aptitude and strength to hit .275 with gap power and average speed. The Astros think he'll hit as much as Adam Everett and if that happens, Manzella's glove is good enough to make him a big league regular. He's the best defensive infielder in the system. He has good hands, a strong arm and fine instincts at shortstop, and he made just six errors in 45 pro games. Manzella likely will open 2006 in low Class A to help rebuild his confidence.

Year	Club (League)	Class	AVG	G	AB	R	H	2B	3B	HR	RBI	BB	SO	SB	OBP	SLG
2005	Tri-City (NY-P)	A	.232	53	220	24	51	6	4	0	18	9	40	5	.260	.295
MINOR LEAGUE TOTALS			.232	53	220	24	51	6	4	0	18	9	40	5	.260	.295

29 WLADIMIR SUTIL   SS/2B

Born: Oct. 31, 1984. **B-T:** R-R. **Ht.:** 5-10. **Wt.:** 155. **Signed:** Venezuela, 2003. **Signed by:** Andres Reiner.

Sutil has batted .312 in his two seasons in the United States, showing a contact-oriented swing and a willingness to use all fields. There's some question as to how he'll fare at more advanced levels, however. Listed at 5-foot-10 and 155 pounds, he has little strength. Better pitchers may be able to just blow him away with good fastballs, so he's going to have to get stronger. If Sutil can adapt and get on base enough, he can be a useful player. He has slightly above-average speed and doesn't try to do too much at the plate. He's a good defender who has the range and arm to play shortstop, and he slid over to second base when he teamed with Tommy Manzella last summer. Sutil was steady at both positions, committing just five errors in 58 games. He positions himself well and has good instincts. The next logical step for him is low Class A, which could mean playing second base alongside Manzella again. If Sutil can fend for himself at the plate, he could have a big league future as a utilityman.

Year	Club (League)	Class	AVG	G	AB	R	H	2B	3B	HR	RBI	BB	SO	SB	OBP	SLG
2003	Venoco (VSL)	R	.266	45	154	35	41	11	1	1	21	22	21	11	.378	.370
2004	Greeneville (Appy)	R	.298	53	188	31	56	9	0	0	29	17	24	24	.372	.346
2005	Tri-City (NY-P)	A	.329	59	231	42	76	13	0	0	21	22	12	13	.395	.385
	Lexington (SAL)	A	.261	6	23	2	6	1	0	0	3	0	5	2	.261	.304
MINOR LEAGUE TOTALS			.300	163	596	110	179	34	1	1	74	61	62	50	.379	.366

30 BROOKS CONRAD   2B

Born: Jan. 16, 1980. **B-T:** B-R. **Ht.:** 5-11. **Wt.:** 190. **Drafted:** Arizona State, 2001 (8th round). **Signed by:** Andrew Cotner.

In 2005, Conrad did what he has done throughout his pro career. He moved up a level and proved himself again. He got left off the 40-man roster and didn't get a sniff in the major league Rule 5 draft for the third straight year, yet he's an organization favorite. The Astros love his makeup and his ability to play above his tools. "Everybody loves Brooks Conrad," said Jackie Moore, his manager at Round Rock, "except for the equipment manager because he has to wash his uniform every night. He gets a lot dirtier than most players because he always gives 100 percent." Conrad also has more pop than most middle infielders, setting a career high with 23 homers last year, and he's a switch-hitter to boot. His swing can get long at times, but he has the eye to draw walks. He has average speed and the instincts to steal an occasional base. Conrad's defense lags behind his offense and limits his potential. There's nothing wrong with his hands, as he made just 10 errors in 130 games and led Pacific Coast League second basemen with a .987 fielding percentage last year. But his arm is a little short, even at second base, his footwork isn't smooth and he lacks the range to play shortstop. He's going to have a difficult time beating out Craig Biggio or Chris Burke at second base in Houston, and his lack of versatility limits his ability as a utilityman. He'll probably repeat Triple-A this year.

Year	Club (League)	Class	AVG	G	AB	R	H	2B	3B	HR	RBI	BB	SO	SB	OBP	SLG
2001	Pittsfield (NY-P)	A	.280	65	232	41	65	16	5	4	39	26	52	14	.375	.444
2002	Michigan (MWL)	A	.287	133	499	94	143	25	14	14	94	62	102	18	.368	.477
2003	Lexington (SAL)	A	.186	38	140	20	26	5	2	3	11	17	25	7	.288	.314
	Salem (Car)	A	.284	99	345	50	98	24	3	11	61	42	60	4	.369	.467
2004	Round Rock (TL)	AA	.290	129	480	84	139	38	6	13	83	63	105	8	.365	.475
2005	Corpus Christi (TL)	AA	.234	22	77	13	18	6	1	2	11	16	15	8	.372	.416
	Round Rock (PCL)	AAA	.263	113	418	84	110	22	3	21	57	52	104	12	.347	.481
MINOR LEAGUE TOTALS			.273	599	2191	386	599	136	34	68	356	278	463	71	.359	.460

KANSAS CITY
ROYALS

BY **WILL KIMMEY**

The Royals led the Indians 7-2 entering the top of the ninth inning Aug. 9 before an 11-run Cleveland rally—helped by three errors—sent Kansas City to a 13-7 loss, its 11th straight. The skid swelled to a club-record 19 games, the longest in the majors since 1988, before the Royals beat Barry Zito and the Athletics to snap the streak. The win inspired a celebration that included champagne.

That marked the high point for a Kansas City team that lost 106 times in 2005, the most in baseball and the most in franchise history. That came on the heels of a 104-loss season and three years after a 100-loss campaign. It marked the fourth time in five years the team set or tied a franchise record for losses.

That time period corresponds directly with the tenure of Allard Baird as general manager, which began in June 2000. While Baird has played his part, the downward spiral began in 1993 when former Wal-Mart president and CEO David Glass bought the club and began running it like a discount store. The Royals have topped the .500 mark only once in his tenure, an 83-79 finish in 2003. Glass allowed Baird $22 million to spend on free agents this offseason, but a thin crop of available talent and the team's haplessness mean they couldn't bring any franchise-changing talent aboard.

The Royals' frugality has forced Baird to trade all-star outfielders Carlos Beltran, Johnny Damon and Jermaine Dye since 2001, and the club failed to acquire a quality big leaguer in any of those deals. Expensive misses in the 2000 and 2001 drafts—Colt Griffin, anyone?—thinned the organization's minor league talent. Scouting director Deric Ladnier's last four first-round picks (Zack Greinke, Chris Lubanski, Billy Butler and Alex Gordon) look stronger, but the system offers little beyond that group.

Injuries and ineffectiveness in Kansas City have further depleted the system's depth by hastening the timetables for prospects rushed through the system to fill holes. Eleven Royals made their major league debuts in 2005 after a club-record 14 did so in 2004. Despite the influx of youth, journeymen Emil Brown and Terrence Long commanded 1,000 at-bats in 2005 while players such as Justin Huber and Shane Costa never got regular playing time during their big league stints. Meanwhile, Greinke got pounded and promising young arms such as J.P. Howell and Leo Nunez were abused by major league hitters.

Bright spots were few, though **David DeJesus** cemented his status as a solid regular and Mike MacDougal started to regain the form that made him an all-star in 2003. Rookies Ambiorix Burgos and Andrew Sisco showed promise in the bullpen. John Buck and Mark Teahen, two pieces of the Beltran trade, hit well late in the year. But all of those players are only complementary parts and not the star players the Royals so desperately need. Kansas City will spend the 2006 draft trying to bolster an underwhelming crop of pitchers, starting with the No. 1 overall pick.

TOP 30 PROSPECTS

1. Alex Gordon, 3b
2. Billy Butler, of
3. Justin Huber, 1b
4. Chris Lubanski, of
5. Jeff Bianchi, ss
6. Luis Cota, rhp
7. Chris McConnell, ss
8. Mitch Maier, of
9. Donnie Murphy, 2b
10. Shane Costa, of
11. Billy Buckner, rhp
12. Brian Bass, rhp
13. Adam Donachie, c
14. Angel Sanchez, ss
15. Danny Christensen, lhp
16. Erik Cordier, rhp
17. Joe Dickerson, of
18. Jose Duarte, of
19. Chris Nicoll, rhp
20. Kila Kaaihue, 1b
21. Brent Fisher, lhp
22. Esteban German, inf
23. Mike Aviles, inf
24. Mario Lisson, 3b
25. Chris Demaria, rhp
26. Greg Atencio, rhp
27. Matt Campbell, lhp
28. Dusty Hughes, lhp
29. Paul Raglione, rhp
30. Matt Kniginyzky, rhp

LARRY GOREN

ORGANIZATION OVERVIEW

General Manager: Allard Baird. **Farm director:** Shaun McGinn. **Scouting director:** Deric Ladnier.

2005 PERFORMANCE

Class	Team	League	W	L	Pct.	Finish*	Manager(s)
Majors	Kansas City	American	56	106	.346	14th (14)	Tony Pena/Buddy Bell
Triple-A	Omaha Royals	Pacific Coast	72	72	.500	8th (16)	Mike Jirschele
Double-A	Wichita Wranglers	Texas	68	72	.486	6th (8)	Frank White
High A	High Desert Mavericks	California	75	65	.536	t-3rd (10)	Billy Gardner
Low A	Burlington Bees	Midwest	65	75	.464	t-11th (14)	Jim Gabella
Rookie	Idaho Falls Chukars	Pioneer	34	42	.447	t-6th (8)	Brian Rupp
Rookie	AZL Royals	Arizona	34	22	.607	2nd (9)	Lloyd Simmons
OVERALL 2005 MINOR LEAGUE RECORD			348	348	.500	15th (30)	

*Finish in overall standings (No. of teams in league)

ORGANIZATION LEADERS

BATTING   *Minimum 250 at-bats
*AVG	Diaz, Matt, Omaha/Wichita	.366
R	Brown, Adrian, Omaha	104
H	Sanchez, Angel, High Desert	183
TB	Butler, Billy, High Desert/Wichita	300
2B	Maier, Mitch, High Desert/Wichita	47
3B	Stocker, Mel, High Desert/Wichita	11
HR	Four tied at	30
RBI	Lubanski, Chris, High Desert	116
BB	Kaaihue, Kila, High Desert	97
SO	Moye, Alan, Burlington/High Desert	154
SB	Falu, Irving, Burlington/Wichita	34
*OBP	Maestrales, Pete, Burlington/High Desert	.445
*SLG	Diaz, Matt, Omaha/Wichita	.624

PITCHING   #Minimum 75 innings
W	Gragg, John, High Desert	13
L	Buckner, Billy, Burlington/High Desert	13
#ERA	Demaria, Chris, High Desert/Wichita	1.70
G	Demaria, Chris, High Desert/Wichita	58
CG	Baerlocher, Ryan, Omaha/Wichita	2
SV	Demaria, Chris, High Desert/Wichita	20
IP	Middleton, Kyle, Wichita	171
BB	Buckner, Billy, Burlington/High Desert	63
	Cota, Luis, Burlington	63
SO	Buckner, Billy, Burlington/High Desert	152

BEST TOOLS

Best Hitter for Average	Alex Gordon
Best Power Hitter	Billy Butler
Best Strike-Zone Discipline	Alex Gordon
Fastest Baserunner	Jeff Bianchi
Best Athlete	Mitch Maier
Best Fastball	Luis Cota
Best Curveball	Billy Buckner
Best Slider	Greg Atencio
Best Changeup	Chris Demaria
Best Control	Chris Nicoll
Best Defensive Catcher	Adam Donachie
Best Defensive Infielder	Angel Sanchez
Best Infield Arm	Angel Sanchez
Best Defensive Outfielder	Mitch Maier
Best Outfield Arm	Jose Duarte

PROJECTED 2009 LINEUP

Catcher	John Buck
First Base	Justin Huber
Second Base	Jeff Bianchi
Third Base	Alex Gordon
Shortstop	Angel Berroa
Left Field	Chris Lubanski
Center Field	David DeJesus
Right Field	Mitch Maier

Designated Hitter	Billy Butler
No. 1 Starter	Zack Greinke
No. 2 Starter	Denny Bautista
No. 3 Starter	Luis Cota
No. 4 Starter	Runelvys Hernandez
No. 5 Starter	J.P. Howell
Closer	Ambiorix Burgos

LAST YEAR'S TOP 20 PROSPECTS

1. Billy Butler, 3b
2. Denny Bautista, rhp
3. Mark Teahen, 3b
4. Chris Lubanski, of
5. Justin Huber, c
6. Ambiorix Burgos, rhp
7. Luis Cota, rhp
8. Shane Costa, of
9. Mitch Maier, 3b
10. Donnie Murphy, 2b
11. J.P. Howell, lhp
12. Andrew Sisco, lhp
13. Brian McFall, of
14. Leo Nunez, rhp
15. Billy Buckner, rhp
16. Matt Campbell, lhp
17. Santiago Ramirez, rhp
18. Andres Blanco, ss
19. Brian Bass, rhp
20. Miguel Vega, 1b/3b

TOP PROSPECTS OF THE DECADE

Year	Player, Pos.	2005 Org.
1996	Jim Pittsley, rhp	Out of baseball
1997	Glendon Rusch, lhp	Cubs
1998	Dee Brown, of	Nationals
1999	Carlos Beltran, of	Mets
2000	Dee Brown, of	Nationals
2001	Chris George, lhp	Royals
2002	Angel Berroa, ss	Royals
2003	Zack Greinke, rhp	Royals
2004	Zack Greinke, rhp	Royals
2005	Billy Butler, 3b	Royals

TOP DRAFT PICKS OF THE DECADE

Year	Player, Pos.	2005 Org.
1996	Dee Brown, of	Nationals
1997	Dan Reichert, rhp	Mariners
1998	Jeff Austin, rhp	Out of baseball
1999	Kyle Snyder, rhp	Royals
2000	Mike Stodolka, lhp	Royals
2001	Colt Griffin, rhp	Royals
2002	Zack Greinke, rhp	Royals
2003	Chris Lubanski, of	Royals
2004	Billy Butler, 3b	Royals
2005	Alex Gordon, 3b	Royals

ALL-TIME LARGEST BONUSES

Alex Gordon, 2005	$4,000,000
Jeff Austin, 1998	$2,700,000
Mike Stodolka, 2000	$2,500,000
Zack Greinke, 2002	$2,475,000
Colt Griffin, 2001	$2,400,000

MINOR LEAGUE DEPTH CHART

Kansas City Royals

Rank: 23

STRENGTH: Impact bats. Almost by default in a thin system, but Alex Gordon, Billy Butler and Justin Huber are clearly the organization's three best prospects.

WEAKNESS: Pitching. After rushing Zack Greinke, Ambiorix Burgos and others to the big leagues, there isn't much to get excited about on the mound.

*Depth charts prepared by **John Manuel** and **Chris Kline**. Numbers in parentheses indicate prospect rankings.*

LF
Billy Butler (2)
Shane Costa (10)
Jose Duarte (18)
Alvi Morel

CF
Chris Lubanski (4)
Mitch Maier (8)
Joe Dickerson (17)
Ethien Santana

RF
Brian McFall
Oscar Gonzalez
Alan Moye

3B
Alex Gordon (1)
Mario Lisson (24)
Shawn Hayes

SS
Jeff Bianchi (5)
Chris McConnell (7)
Angel Sanchez (14)
Mike Aviles (23)

2B
Donnie Murphy (9)
Esteban German (22)
Adam Keim
Irving Falu

1B
Justin Huber (3)
Kila Kaaihue (20)
Miguel Vega

C
Adam Donachie (13)
Matt Tupman
Paul Phillips
Kiel Thibault

RHP

Starter	Relievers
Luis Cota (6)	Chris Demaria (25)
Billy Buckner (11)	Greg Atencio (26)
Brian Bass (12)	Matt Kniginyzky (30)
Erik Cordier (16)	Jonah Bayliss
Chris Nicoll (19)	Chad Blackwell
Paul Raglione (29)	Devon Lowery
Brandon Weeden	Ryan Braun
John Gragg	Henry Barrera
Ryan Baerlocher	

LHP

Starters	Relievers
Danny Christensen (15)	Juan Cedeno
Brent Fisher (21)	
Matt Campbell (27)	
Dusty Hughes (28)	

DRAFT ANALYSIS

2005

Best Pro Debut: SS Jeff Bianchi (2) was leading the Rookie-level Arizona League in the triple-crown categories until he pulled a muscle in his back. He finished with .408-6-30 totals in 28 games. OF Joe Dickerson (4) batted .294 and led the AZL with nine triples and 40 RBIs.

Best Athlete: Bianchi's tools proved to be better than the Royals expected. 3B Alex Gordon (1) stands out most with his bat, but he also can play solid defense and steal some bases. C Nick Doscher (8) received NCAA Division I-A offers as a quarterback.

Best Pure Hitter: Gordon, BA's College Player of the Year, has far more offensive potential than Darin Erstad, the only Nebraska player ever taken higher in the draft (No. 1 to Gordon's No. 2). Bianchi's efficient swing allowed him to make a quick transition to wood bats.

Best Raw Power: Gordon.

Fastest Runner: Bianchi has plus-plus speed. He can get from the right side of the plate to first base in 4.1 seconds.

Best Defensive Player: Some teams projected Bianchi as a second baseman because of his average arm strength, but Kansas City is sold on him playing shortstop. Built like a young Jim Edmonds, Dickerson has very good instincts in center field. C Kyle Thibault (9), a good receiver, threw out 36 percent of basestealers in his pro debut.

Best Fastball: RHP Matt Kniginyzky (23), the first player drafted out of High Point since 1991, tops out at 94 mph. RHP Kevin Bulger (25) can get up to 92-93 mph.

Best Breaking Ball: LHP Brent Fisher's (7) curveball gets the edge over Kniginyzky's.

Most Intriguing Background: 2B

BILL MITCHELL

Dickerson

Jeremy Jirschele's (30) father Mike manages the organization's Triple-A Omaha affiliate. Bulger's brother Jason was a Diamondbacks first-round pick in 2001 and made his big league debut in 2005. 1B Jase Turner (27) is the grandson of the late Jesse Gonder, a former big league catcher. RHP Michael Dubee (32), a prime draft-and-follow candidate, is the son of Phillies pitching coach Rich Dubee.

Closest To The Majors: Gordon signed in time to report to the Arizona Fall League, so his holdout shouldn't hold him back. He'll probably break into pro ball in Double-A and reach Kansas City at some point in 2006. RHP Chris Nicoll (3), who has good command and feel, also should move quickly.

Best Late-Round Pick: Paul Raglione (18) is a projectable 6-foot-5 righthander who already has an 88-92 mph fastball.

The One Who Got Away: SS Justin Bristow (22) had prototype third-base tools and also showed a 91-92 mph heater on the mound. He had a chance to go in the first round, but wasn't considered signable when he didn't go that high. He's at Auburn. The Royals signed their first 16 picks.

Assessment: The Royals paid $4 million to land the best college hitter available. Gordon quickly should become one of their few bright spots. The Royals will have the No. 1 pick for the first time in their history this year.

2004 OF Billy Butler (1) has no position and most clubs thought he was a reach at No. 14, but can he hit. The Royals rushed LHP J.P. Howell (1) to the majors last year, while another first-round lefty, Matt Campbell, had labrum surgery. *GRADE:* B+

2003 None of them are franchise cornerstones, but OFs Chris Lubanski (1), Mitch Maier (1) and Shane Costa (2) and RHP Luis Cota (10) all made our Royals top 10 list. *GRADE:* C

2002 RHP Zack Greinke (1) looked like an ace in the making until he got drilled throughout 2005. He carries the weight of this draft class on his shoulders, though 2B Donnie Murphy (5) has played in the majors. *GRADE:* C+

2001 This class could be one of the great draft disasters of all time. Kansas City spent $4.15 million on RHP Colt Griffin (1) and OF Roscoe Crosby (2), two high-ceiling prospects who bottomed out quickly. *GRADE:* F

Draft analysis prepared by Jim Callis. Numbers in parentheses indicate draft rounds.

ALEX
GORDON

BILL MITCHELL

Born: Feb. 10, 1984.
Ht.: 6-1. **Wt.:** 215.
Bats: L. **Throws:** R.
Drafted: Nebraska, 2005
(1st round).
Signed by: Phil Huttmann.

Born and raised in Lincoln, Neb., Gordon grew up making family road trips to Kansas City to see a certain third baseman—whom his brother Brett is named for. He starred as a third baseman and defensive back in high school before following his father Mike in playing baseball at Nebraska. Gordon developed into a two-time Big 12 Conference player of the year and won Baseball America's 2005 College Player of the Year award by hitting .372/.518/.715 with 19 homers and 23 steals as the Cornhuskers advanced to the College World Series. Gordon also won the 2005 Golden Spikes Award as the top amateur player in the United States. Before his banner junior season, he captured offensive MVP honors as he helped Team USA to a gold medal at the 2004 World University Championship in Taiwan. When Arizona took Justin Upton with the No. 1 overall selection in the 2005 draft, Gordon was an obvious choice for the Royals at No. 2. It was the earliest draft pick the Royals have ever had—though they'll pick first in 2006—surpassing their fourth overall selections in 1998 (Jeff Austin) and 2000 (Mike Stodolka). Rumors were prevalent that they would focus on budget more than ability, but they took the best player on the board. Gordon held out until late September, when he accepted a $4 million bonus that shattered Austin's club record of $2.7 million. He signed too late to play in the minors but did get 50 at-bats in the Arizona Fall League, hitting .260 with two homers.

Gordon treats hitting like an art and constantly works to improve his craft. He even borrowed the coach's keys to Nebraska's practice facility in order to hit during summer and Christmas breaks. That work ethic has produced a hitter with great patience and a finely tuned swing. Gordon has the best bat speed in the organization. He hits for average and power to all fields. One scout compared him to Chipper Jones. While he's known mostly for his bat, Gordon isn't a one-dimensional player. Terrific baserunning instincts allowed the solid-average runner to swipe 23 bags in 26 tries as a junior, surpassing his total from his first two years in college. Gordon shows an above-average arm and solid hands at third base. He played first base in his pro debut in the Arizona Fall League only because he replaced Justin Huber on the roster and the club needed someone to man that spot. He also played first base with Team USA, but that was in deference to Gold Glove-caliber third baseman Ryan Zimmerman.

Gordon's biggest flaws should be easily correctable. He can improve his pre-pitch preparation. The Royals had him working on fielding balls from the balls of his feet, with a wider base and further in front of his body.

The Royals initially slated Gordon to make his pro debut at high Class A High Desert, but his AFL showing has given them the confidence to start him at Double-A Wichita. He should develop into a potent middle-of-the-order bat and a fine lefthanded complement to righthanded-hitting Billy Butler, the system's other blue-chip prospect. Mark Teahen poses little obstacle to Gordon, who will take over at third base in Kansas City as soon as he's ready. That could happen at some point in 2006.

Year	Club (League)	Class	AVG	G	AB	R	H	2B	3B	HR	RBI	BB	SO	SB	OBP	SLG
2005	Did not play—Signed 2006 contract															

2 BILLY BUTLER

OF

Born: June 7, 2004. **B-T:** R-R. **Ht.:** 6-2. **Wt.:** 225. **Drafted:** HS—Jacksonville, Fla., 2004 (1st round). **Signed by:** Cliff Pastornicky.

When the Royals drafted Butler 14th overall in 2004, most clubs viewed it as a signability pick—his $1.45 million bonus was $250,000 less than MLB's slot recommendation. He and righthander Eric Hurley, who went 30th to the Rangers, made Jacksonville's Wolfson High the fifth high school to produce a pair of first-rounders in the same draft. Butler has more than justified his selection, and he ranked third in the minors with 300 total bases and fifth with 71 extra-base hits in 2005. Butler is such a mature hitter already that instructors leave him alone and he's able to make adjustments on his own between at-bats. He succeeds because of his impressive bat speed, strength, vision, balance and confidence at the plate. He centers the ball well, uses the whole field and generates above-average power without sacrificing the ability to hit for average. Butler controls the strike zone and attacks pitches in his wheelhouse. He reached 90 mph as a prep pitcher, so he has arm strength. Drafted as a third baseman, Butler lacked the athleticism and footwork for the position, so he moved to left field, where the hope is that he can become adequate. He's a below-average runner. His hitting mechanics aren't typical—his stance is open and spread out with his hands held high, and he uses a toe tap for timing—but they work for him. Butler should develop into an all-star-caliber offensive player along the lines of Travis Hafner. Left field is Butler's position for now, but most scouts think he's destined for first base or DH. He'll begin 2006 in Double-A, and the Royals don't know what they'll do if his bat becomes major league ready before his defense is passable.

Year	Club (League)	Class	AVG	G	AB	R	H	2B	3B	HR	RBI	BB	SO	SB	OBP	SLG
2004	Idaho Falls (Pio)	R	.373	74	260	74	97	22	3	10	68	57	63	5	.488	.596
2005	High Desert (Cal)	A	.348	92	379	70	132	30	2	25	91	42	80	0	.419	.636
	Wichita (TL)	AA	.313	29	112	14	35	9	0	5	19	7	18	0	.353	.527
MINOR LEAGUE TOTALS			.352	195	751	158	264	61	5	40	178	106	161	5	.435	.606

3 JUSTIN HUBER

1B

Born: July 1, 1982. **B-T:** R-R. **Ht.:** 6-2. **Wt.:** 200. **Signed:** Australia, 2000. **Signed by:** Omar Minaya (Mets).

Huber came to the Royals for third-base prospect Jose Bautista as part of the three-team deal that sent Kris Benson to the Mets in July 2004. In his last game in the New York system, Huber hurt his left knee and required arthroscopic surgery, knocking him off Australia's Olympic team and delaying his Royals debut until 2005. The injury also cinched the decision to move him from catcher to first base. He made his major league debut in place of an injured Mike Sweeney in June and won MVP honors in his third Futures Game with a two-run double in July. Huber is a pure hitter with a strong grasp of the strike zone. He stays inside the ball well and can spray hits from gap to gap while offering 20-homer power. He has more athleticism than expected from a former catcher. Huber is still learning how to play first base, fighting his catcher's instinct to block balls with his body rather than field them. He should become adequate, though never an asset defensively. He's a slightly below-average runner. Huber resembles Sweeney in many ways, and Sweeney's presence in Kansas City could mean Huber goes to Triple-A Omaha for regular duty unless the two end up in a first base/DH tradeoff. An Achilles injury canceled Huber's 2005 trip to the Arizona Fall League, but he'll be ready for spring training.

Year	Club (League)	Class	AVG	G	AB	R	H	2B	3B	HR	RBI	BB	SO	SB	OBP	SLG
2001	St. Lucie (FSL)	A	.000	2	6	0	0	0	0	0	0	0	2	0	.000	.000
	Kingsport (Appy)	R	.314	47	159	24	50	11	1	7	31	17	42	4	.415	.528
	Brooklyn (NY-P)	A	.000	3	9	0	0	0	0	0	0	0	4	0	.000	.000
2002	St. Lucie (FSL)	A	.270	28	100	15	27	2	1	3	15	11	18	0	.370	.400
	Columbia (SAL)	A	.291	95	330	49	96	22	2	11	78	45	81	1	.408	.470
2003	St. Lucie (FSL)	A	.284	50	183	26	52	15	0	9	36	17	30	1	.370	.514
	Binghamton (EL)	AA	.264	55	193	16	51	13	0	6	36	19	54	0	.350	.425
2004	St. Lucie (FSL)	A	.245	14	49	10	12	2	0	2	8	5	8	1	.327	.408
	Binghamton (EL)	AA	.271	70	236	44	64	16	1	11	33	46	57	2	.404	.487
	Norfolk (IL)	AAA	.313	5	16	3	5	2	0	0	3	3	3	0	.421	.438
2005	Wichita (TL)	AA	.343	88	335	68	115	22	3	16	74	51	70	7	.432	.570
	Omaha (PCL)	AAA	.274	32	113	19	31	6	1	7	23	16	33	3	.374	.531
	Kansas City (AL)	MLB	.218	25	78	6	17	3	0	0	6	5	20	0	.271	.256
MAJOR LEAGUE TOTALS			.218	25	78	6	17	3	0	0	6	5	20	0	.265	.256
MINOR LEAGUE TOTALS			.291	489	1729	274	503	111	9	72	337	230	402	19	.394	.490

CHRIS LUBANSKI   OF

Born: March 24, 1985. **B-T:** L-L. **Ht.:** 6-3. **Wt.:** 206. **Drafted:** HS—Schwenksville, Pa., 2003 (1st round). **Signed by:** Sean Rooney.

Lubanski was pegged as a mid-first-rounder in 2003, but the Royals took him fifth overall and signed him for $2.1 million—$400,000 below MLB's slot recommendation. He has proven a second-half player in his brief career, especially in 2005, when he hit .354-18-85 in the last three months to finish second in the minors with 116 RBIs and fourth with 294 total bases and 72 extra-base hits. Yes, the Royals know High Desert is a hitter's haven and that Lubanski hit .359-19-71 at home and .245-9-45 on the road. But he started making better contact and his natural loft power started to shine in the second half, which he capped by going 13-for-15 in the high Class A California League playoffs. He's an aggressive hitter but began to take more pitches and showed a freer, looser swing. A plus runner, he was caught stealing just once in 15 tries. Lubanski covered so much ground as a high school center fielder that his timidity and poor routes as a pro puzzle observers. His arm rates just below-average and he needs to use his legs more when he throws. If he doesn't improve, he'll have to move to left field. Some club officials wanted Lubanski to cede High Desert's center-field job to Mitch Maier, but Maier's promotion ended that possibility. They'll start 2006 together again in Double-A, with Lubanski likely remaining in center. He could develop into a No. 5 hitter with basestealing speed.

Year	Club (League)	Class	AVG	G	AB	R	H	2B	3B	HR	RBI	BB	SO	SB	OBP	SLG
2003	Royals 1 (AZL)	R	.326	53	221	41	72	4	6	4	27	18	50	9	.382	.452
2004	Burlington (Mid)	A	.275	127	483	64	133	26	7	9	56	43	104	16	.336	.414
2005	High Desert (Cal)	A	.301	126	531	91	160	38	6	28	116	38	131	14	.349	.554
MINOR LEAGUE TOTALS			.296	306	1235	196	365	68	19	41	199	99	285	39	.350	.481

JEFF BIANCHI   SS

Born: Oct. 5, 1986. **B-T:** R-R. **Ht.:** 6-2. **Wt.:** 190. **Drafted:** HS—Lampeter, Pa, 2005 (2nd round). **Signed by:** Sean Rooney.

Bianchi was a lightly crosschecked high school player, but he generated so much late buzz that Royals scouting director Deric Ladnier eschewed trips to college conference tournaments to see him. The Royals were happy to nab him in the second round for $690,000. Bianchi pushed for the Rookie-level Arizona League triple crown before a lower back strain ended his season and his Arizona Fall League hopes. Bianchi's efficient hitting mechanics and quick, short swing produce impressive results. He uses the whole field and flashes average power. He has plus-plus speed, getting from the right side of the plate to first base in 4.1 seconds. He's athletic and instinctive defensively, and plays a polished overall game. He had an easy transition to pro ball because his high school coach, Todd Garber, is the brother of Kansas City coordinator of minor league instruction Jeff Garber and incorporates many of the Royals' principles. Bianchi hasn't played enough yet for the Royals to discover any warts. His arm isn't the strongest and some teams projected him as a second baseman, but he's able to make plays from the hole. His back had no structural damage and isn't a long-term concern. Bianchi reminds the Royals of Texas shortstop Michael Young with less arm. He could make a jump to full-season ball, but that would mean sharing the low Class A Burlington shortstop job with Chris McConnell. Bianchi likely will end up at Rookie-level Idaho Falls.

Year	Club (League)	Class	AVG	G	AB	R	H	2B	3B	HR	RBI	BB	SO	SB	OBP	SLG
2005	Royals (AZL)	R	.408	28	98	29	40	7	4	6	30	16	22	5	.484	.745
MINOR LEAGUE TOTALS			.408	28	98	29	40	7	4	6	30	16	22	5	.484	.745

LUIS COTA   RHP

Born: Aug. 19, 1985. **B-T:** R-R. **Ht.:** 6-0. **Wt.:** 193. **Drafted:** South Mountain (Ariz.) CC, D/F 2003 (10th round). **Signed by:** Mike Brown.

The younger brother of Diamondbacks first-base prospect Jesus Cota, Luis played mostly shortstop at Tucson's Sunnyside High. The Royals liked his arm strength enough to gamble a 10th-round choice on him in 2003, and he blossomed into the Arizona juco player of the year the next spring. Kansas City signed him as a draft-and-follow for $1.05 million, a record for a 10th-rounder. Cota tops out at an easy 93-95 mph and works at 91-92. His four-seam fastball features so much life that it gets mistaken for a two-seamer as its bores in on righthanders. His power slider sits in the mid-80s and should become a second plus pitch once he refines his command of it. His changeup can be inconsistent, but it improved during the season. Cota needs more consistency with his delivery. He gets underneath the ball too much, leaving his fastball straight and his slider flat. The mechanical correction also would give him better control, allowing him to get ahead of hitters and put them away easier. The Royals view Cota as a power arm with the potential for three plus pitches atop a rotation. He'll need to improve his command and feel as his mental toughness gets checked in the pitcher's wasteland of High Desert this year.

Year	Club (League)	Class	W	L	ERA	G	GS	CG	SV	IP	H	R	ER	HR	BB	SO	AVG
2004	Idaho Falls (Pio)	R	2	1	5.81	14	12	0	0	48	61	37	31	5	21	40	.313
2005	Burlington (Mid)	A	5	8	4.01	26	26	0	0	148	143	75	66	10	63	137	.253
MINOR LEAGUE TOTALS			7	9	4.45	40	38	0	0	196	204	112	97	15	84	177	.268

7 CHRIS McCONNELL   SS

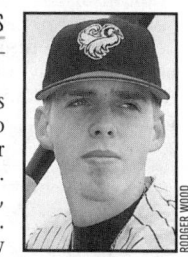

Born: Dec. 18, 1985. **B-T:** R-R. **Ht.:** 5-11. **Wt.:** 170. **Drafted:** HS—Franklinville, N.J., 2004 (9th round). **Signed by:** Sean Rooney.

Area scout Sean Rooney took game tapes he got from McConnell's mother to Kansas City's draft room and used them to support his case to draft the fast-twitch, slick-fielding infielder. McConnell signed for $40,000 as a ninth-round pick instead of attending Louisburg (N.C.) JC. The Royals knew of McConnell's defensive skills—plus range, plus arm, quick feet, soft hands—but his bat has produced more than expected. Though he has an unorthodox stance with a high back elbow and low crouch, his hand-eye coordination and quick hands have produced a .333 average in pro ball. Added strength from maturing physically now allows him to drive the ball into gaps, and he should produce average power for a middle infielder. Instinctive and fluid defensively, McConnell must improve on the bases. He has slightly above-average speed but needs to learn the nuances of baserunning and basestealing. Otherwise, inexperience is his only negative at this point. McConnell's arm strength would push Jeff Bianchi to second base if the duo played together. That won't happen immediately, as McConnell is set for Burlington and Bianchi ticketed for Idaho Falls.

Year	Club (League)	Class	AVG	G	AB	R	H	2B	3B	HR	RBI	BB	SO	SB	OBP	SLG
2004	Royals (AZL)	R	.339	37	124	22	42	5	0	3	11	17	19	8	.420	.452
2005	Idaho Falls (Pio)	R	.331	70	275	56	91	17	8	6	39	31	34	7	.403	.516
MINOR LEAGUE TOTALS			.333	107	399	78	133	22	8	9	50	48	53	15	.408	.496

8 MITCH MAIER   OF

Born: June 30, 1982. **B-T:** L-R. **Ht.:** 6-3. **Wt.:** 200. **Drafted:** Toledo, 2003 (1st round). **Signed by:** Jason Bryans.

Maier, who went 30th overall in 2003 in part because he'd sign for $900,000, has moved from catching in college to third base and now the outfield as a pro. Toledo's all-time leading hitter with a .414 average, he has started each of his two full pro seasons with a flourish and then leveled off following promotions. Maier's hand-eye coordination makes for consistent contact. He gets good leverage in his swing when it works right, so he has more power potential than he has shown. An above-average runner with solid instincts on the bases, he covers plenty of ground in center field. He improved so much at tracking balls that some Royals officials believe he's a better center fielder than Chris Lubanski. Maier's arm is good for center field and average for right. Maier's hands often drift forward as a pitch approaches, costing him power as he gets ahead of his body. Better balance could boost his home run totals and reduce his strikeouts. More patience at the plate also would help. Some scouts liken Maier to Paul O'Neill as a hitter and run producer. He'll work to fine-tune his swing this year in Double-A.

Year	Club (League)	Class	AVG	G	AB	R	H	2B	3B	HR	RBI	BB	SO	SB	OBP	SLG
2003	Royals 1 (AZL)	R	.350	51	203	41	71	14	6	2	45	18	25	7	.403	.507
2004	Burlington (Mid)	A	.300	82	317	41	95	24	3	4	36	27	51	34	.354	.432
	Wilmington (Car)	A	.264	51	174	25	46	9	2	3	17	15	29	9	.326	.391
2005	High Desert (Cal)	A	.336	50	211	42	71	26	1	8	32	12	43	6	.370	.583
	Wichita (TL)	AA	.255	80	322	55	82	21	5	7	49	15	47	10	.289	.416
MINOR LEAGUE TOTALS			.297	314	1227	204	365	94	17	24	179	87	195	66	.344	.460

9 DONNIE MURPHY   2B

Born: March 10, 1983. **B-T:** R-R. **Ht.:** 5-10. **Wt.:** 180. **Drafted:** Orange Coast (Calif.) JC, 2002 (5th round). **Signed by:** Gary Johnson.

A right ankle sprain sidelined Murphy in May, but he recovered and received extended big league time after Tony Graffanino was traded to the Red Sox in July. Murphy sputtered offensively in semi-regular duty before a broken right ring finger ended his season in late August. Murphy shows the discerning eye and gap power to profile as an offensive second baseman. He fields well enough with solid hands and a strong arm. The Royals believe his struggles in the majors came from dipping into survival mode rather than relaxing and playing his usual game. Murphy rotates his wrists to point his bat head toward first base before swinging, a hitch that makes him late on some fastballs and susceptible to offspeed pitches. He has limited range at second base and is a below-average runner. Murphy's arm is playable at third base and he ultimately could become a utility infielder, bowing to younger prospects Jeff Bianchi and Chris McConnell. After his disappointing big league stint, he'll open 2006 in Triple-A.

Year	Club (League)	Class	AVG	G	AB	R	H	2B	3B	HR	RBI	BB	SO	SB	OBP	SLG
2002	Spokane (NWL)	A	.303	28	109	20	33	10	2	0	15	6	17	0	.356	.431
	Burlington (Mid)	A	.225	33	120	12	27	6	3	0	15	11	31	0	.300	.325
2003	Burlington (Mid)	A	.313	132	504	77	158	29	6	5	98	65	78	15	.397	.425
2004	Wilmington (Car)	A	.256	129	485	67	124	32	5	10	75	52	96	1	.328	.404
	Kansas City (AL)	MLB	.185	7	27	1	5	3	0	0	3	0	7	1	.185	.296
2005	Wichita (TL)	AA	.313	50	214	33	67	13	1	10	32	13	32	1	.362	.523
	Kansas City (AL)	MLB	.156	32	77	4	12	5	0	1	8	9	23	0	.241	.260
MAJOR LEAGUE TOTALS			.163	39	104	5	17	8	0	1	11	9	30	1	.230	.269
MINOR LEAGUE TOTALS			.286	372	1432	209	409	90	17	25	235	147	254	17	.357	.425

10 SHANE COSTA   OF

Born: Dec. 12, 1981. **B-T:** L-R. **Ht.:** 6-0. **Wt.:** 220. **Drafted:** Cal State Fullerton, 2003 (2nd round). **Signed by:** Gary Johnson.

In need of a left fielder, the Royals called up Costa ahead of schedule May 31 and started him for much of June. He hit homers off Jeff Weaver and Carlos Silva, but Costa wasn't ready for the majors and went down to Triple-A July 20 after Kansas City traded Tony Graffanino to the Red Sox for Chip Ambres. Costa's strike-zone discipline and short, efficient swing makes him a candidate to hit for a high average with low strikeout numbers. He handles all types of pitching well and can use the whole field. He's a heads-up baserunner with average speed and plenty of intensity. Costa has the strength to hit 20 homers annually, but he doesn't have much load to his swing and seems content to serve line drives to the opposite field. His below-average arm limits him to left field. Costa once drew Brian Giles comparisons, and while he's a stocky player with a keen eye, he'll never have Giles' power. If he doesn't hit for more pop, Costa may be nothing more that a fourth outfielder. He'll spend much of 2006 in Triple-A.

Year	Club (League)	Class	AVG	G	AB	R	H	2B	3B	HR	RBI	BB	SO	SB	OBP	SLG
2003	Royals 2 (AZL)	R	.386	23	88	22	34	6	4	1	24	6	7	4	.444	.580
	Wilmington (Car)	A	.143	3	7	1	1	1	0	0	0	0	2	1	.400	.286
2004	Wilmington (Car)	A	.308	123	451	70	139	20	4	7	59	32	43	9	.364	.417
2005	Kansas City (AL)	MLB	.235	27	81	13	19	2	0	2	7	5	11	0	.287	.333
	Wichita (TL)	AA	.282	75	277	37	78	18	2	8	43	24	23	5	.349	.448
	Omaha (PCL)	AAA	.188	4	16	1	3	1	0	0	1	0	1	0	.188	.250
MAJOR LEAGUE TOTALS			.235	27	81	13	19	2	0	2	7	5	11	0	.279	.333
MINOR LEAGUE TOTALS			.304	228	839	131	255	46	10	16	127	64	75	18	.365	.440

11 BILLY BUCKNER   RHP

Born: Aug. 27, 1983. **B-T:** R-R. **Ht.:** 6-2. **Wt.:** 210. **Drafted:** South Carolina, 2004 (2nd round). **Signed by:** Spencer Graham.

Though he was the third of four pitchers the Royals took in the first two rounds of the 2004 draft, Buckner has the brightest future of the group, which also includes Matt Campbell, J.P. Howell and Erik Cordier. Buckner isn't related to the former big league batting champion of the same name. His dad taught him how to throw a knuckle-curve, and it has developed into a plus 12-to-6 downer. It's a great swing-and-miss pitch that he's working to throw for called strikes more consistently. He fed college hitters a steady diet of curves, but Kansas City has urged Buckner to work more off his fastball as a pro. By doing so, Buckner has built up his arm strength and now reaches the low 90s with consistency. When he's on, he can work both sides of the plate with his fastball. His changeup could become an average pitch. Buckner's overall command varies from excellent to so-so depending on how well he maintains his alignment during delivery. He must work down in the zone more often. Projected as a middle-of-the-rotation starter, Buckner will move to Double-A for 2006.

Year	Club (League)	Class	W	L	ERA	G	GS	CG	SV	IP	H	R	ER	HR	BB	SO	AVG
2004	Idaho Falls (Pio)	R	2	1	3.30	7	5	0	0	30	36	14	11	4	4	37	.303
2005	Burlington (Mid)	A	3	7	3.88	11	11	0	0	60	66	36	26	9	17	60	.268
	High Desert (Cal)	A	5	6	5.36	17	17	0	0	94	105	65	56	10	46	92	.285
MINOR LEAGUE TOTALS			10	14	4.54	35	33	0	0	184	207	115	93	23	67	189	.282

12 BRIAN BASS RHP

Born: Jan. 6, 1982. **B-T:** R-R. **Ht.:** 6-0. **Wt.:** 200. **Drafted:** HS—Montgomery, Ala., 2000 (6th round). **Signed by:** Dennis Woody.

The Arizona Fall League has proven a desert oasis for Bass. An elbow strain limited him to 32 innings in 2004, but he regained his fastball velocity in the AFL. Bass struggled with his mound tempo in 2005, working too slowly and giving up too many hits and walks after getting ahead in early counts. A quicker pace made him more aggressive and gave him the confidence to finish hitters by the end of the year, and Bass opened the AFL with 12 scoreless innings over three appearances and didn't walk a batter in 24 innings in Arizona. His fastball sits around 90 mph and reaches 93 with sinking action that makes it a plus pitch at times. Bass' knee-buckling curveball and tight slider are both solid offerings that are different enough to give hitters trouble, and he also works in a changeup. At his best, he throws all four pitches for strikes. Bass earned a spot on Team USA's Olympic qualifying team and could compete for a job in a thin Kansas City rotation during spring training. He'd probably be better off with some time in Triple-A, however.

Year	Club (League)	Class	W	L	ERA	G	GS	CG	SV	IP	H	R	ER	HR	BB	SO	AVG
2000	Royals (GCL)	R	3	5	3.89	12	9	0	0	44	36	27	19	0	18	44	.211
	Charleston, W.Va. (SAL)	A	0	0	6.75	1	1	0	0	4	6	3	3	0	0	1	.333
2001	Burlington (Mid)	A	3	10	4.65	26	26	1	0	139	138	82	72	16	53	75	.257
2002	Burlington (Mid)	A	5	7	3.83	20	20	1	0	110	103	57	47	8	31	60	.246
2003	Wilmington (Car)	A	9	8	2.84	26	26	2	0	152	129	59	48	7	43	119	.229
2004	Royals (AZL)	R	0	1	2.54	5	5	0	0	18	17	6	5	0	3	23	.246
	Wichita (TL)	AA	0	4	7.44	10	10	0	0	36	53	30	30	4	22	20	.351
2005	Wichita (TL)	AA	12	8	5.24	27	27	0	0	165	185	106	96	14	53	102	.286
MINOR LEAGUE TOTALS			32	43	4.30	127	124	4	0	669	667	370	320	49	223	444	.259

13 ADAM DONACHIE C

Born: March 3, 1984. **B-T:** R-R. **Ht.:** 6-1. **Wt.:** 200. **Drafted:** HS—Orlando, Fla., 2002 (2nd round). **Signed by:** Cliff Pastornicky.

Donachie led all Florida high school players with 15 homers in 2002, and parlayed that power and a prototypical catcher's skill set into an $800,000 bonus as a second-round pick. His pop was slow to come in pro ball, as he spent two years in complex leagues and had his 2004 full-season debut marred by a fractured skull. While they were standing in the on-deck circle during a July 16 game, Burlington teammate Kila Kaaihue hit him in the head with a practice swing, and Donachie had to be airlifted to a hospital. He finally broke out in high Class A last year, and he hit just as well on the road as he did at High Desert. Maturity and dropping switch-hitting to bat strictly righthanded led to his progress. Donachie still is adjusting to breaking pitches down and away from righthanders, after not having much experience batting righthanded against them. He projects as at least an average offensive catcher in terms of power and average, and his defensive skills draw the most plaudits. He's the organization's most well-rounded defender behind the plate. Donachie's above-average arm strength and quick release helped him lead California League regulars by erasing 52 percent of basestealers. He also blocks balls and calls games well. His performance in Double-A this year will indicate whether his improvement is for real.

Year	Club (League)	Class	AVG	G	AB	R	H	2B	3B	HR	RBI	BB	SO	SB	OBP	SLG
2002	Royals (GCL)	R	.206	21	68	7	14	3	0	0	3	9	12	0	.304	.250
2003	Royals 2 (AZL)	R	.444	2	9	3	4	1	0	0	0	1	4	0	.500	.556
	Royals 1 (AZL)	R	.222	20	63	8	14	3	1	0	7	9	12	0	.338	.302
2004	Burlington (Mid)	A	.189	67	228	17	43	7	0	1	21	21	41	5	.261	.232
2005	High Desert (Cal)	A	.294	95	347	64	102	24	0	12	48	43	78	1	.375	.467
MINOR LEAGUE TOTALS			.248	205	715	99	177	38	1	13	79	83	147	6	.330	.358

14 ANGEL SANCHEZ   SS

Born: Sept. 20, 1983. **B-T:** R-R. **Ht.:** 6-2 **Wt.:** 180. **Drafted:** HS—Las Piedras, P.R., 2001 (11th round). **Signed by:** Johnny Ramos.

Sanchez always impressed the Royals with his swing mechanics and ability to make contact, but they wondered if he'd ever develop the strength necessary to be anything more than a slap-hitting utility infielder. While he could stand to build more muscle, he already has added 15 pounds since signing at age 17—and the results have been obvious. He led the minors in hits and ranked second in the California League in runs while serving as High Desert's leadoff man last year. He had 42 extra-base hits after collecting just 34 in his first 1,015 pro at-bats. The physical maturity also enhanced Sanchez' speed. He went from an average runner to above-average. He rates as at least an average defender with solid range, hands and feet, while his arm strength can be a tick above average at times. This year in Double-A, Sanchez will try to prove his breakout season wasn't simply a product of High Desert and the California League.

Year	Club (League)	Class	AVG	G	AB	R	H	2B	3B	HR	RBI	BB	SO	SB	OBP	SLG
2001	Royals (GCL)	R	.242	30	95	10	23	4	0	0	6	6	28	3	.287	.284
2002	Royals (GCL)	R	.251	49	175	21	44	4	0	0	12	10	24	9	.302	.274
2003	Burlington (Mid)	A	.270	106	408	54	110	8	1	2	35	28	52	14	.321	.309
2004	Burlington (Mid)	A	.252	90	337	34	85	12	1	2	24	15	47	16	.300	.312
2005	High Desert (Cal)	A	.313	133	585	102	183	33	4	5	70	39	54	10	.356	.409
MINOR LEAGUE TOTALS			.278	408	1600	221	445	61	6	9	147	98	205	52	.325	.341

15 DANNY CHRISTENSEN   LHP

Born: Aug. 10, 1983. **B-T:** L-L. **Ht.:** 6-1. **Wt.:** 205. **Drafted:** HS—Brooklyn, N.Y., 2002 (4th round). **Signed by:** Steve Connelly.

Christensen had a promising pro debut in 2002, but his next couple of years were ugly. He arrived in spring training out of shape in 2003 and went 1-12 in low Class A, then worked just three innings in 2004 before needing Tommy John surgery. The injury and rehab process brought Christensen perspective, and he came to spring training in excellent shape last year. Though he won just three games for a mediocre Burlington team, he had the best season of his career and finished it off by ringing up 27 strikeouts in 15 innings over his last three starts. He's at his best when he's painting both sides of the plate with his 91-92 mph fastball early in the count, then sending hitters back to the dugout with a curveball that features 1-to-7 tilt. Christensen throws both pitches for strikes and shows a good feel for pitching. His changeup is average, but he's gaining confidence and command with it. He's around the plate a lot, so leaving pitches up in the zone remains a dangerous proposition. He'll move to the rotation at High Desert, where making a bad pitch can offer even scarier results. He profiles as a No. 4 starter.

Year	Club (League)	Class	W	L	ERA	G	GS	CG	SV	IP	H	R	ER	HR	BB	SO	AVG
2002	Royals (GCL)	R	1	3	3.10	7	6	0	0	29	20	13	10	2	14	28	.196
	Spokane (NWL)	A	2	0	1.10	6	6	0	0	33	24	6	4	3	14	23	.198
2003	Burlington (Mid)	A	1	12	5.92	17	16	0	0	79	83	62	52	11	31	46	.269
	Royals 1 (AZL)	R	0	0	2.25	4	2	0	0	12	8	4	3	0	5	12	.178
2004	Burlington (Mid)	A	0	1	15.00	1	1	0	0	3	6	8	5	0	3	2	.353
2005	Burlington (Mid)	A	3	7	3.54	26	21	0	1	109	100	54	43	9	53	110	.238
MINOR LEAGUE TOTALS			7	23	3.97	61	52	0	1	265	241	147	117	25	120	221	.238

16 ERIK CORDIER   RHP

Born: Feb. 25, 1986. **B-T:** R-R. **Ht.:** 6-3. **Wt.:** 195. **Drafted:** HS—Sturgeon Bay, Wisc., 2004 (2nd round). **Signed by:** Phil Huttmann.

Cordier drew some first-round interest before going in the second round in 2004, becoming the highest-drafted player out of Wisconsin since the Angels selected Jarrod Washburn 31st overall nine years before. Cordier has a ceiling as a No. 2 starter, but he has pitched just 35 innings as a pro and didn't make it to the mound last season. Knee pain forced the Royals to shut down Cordirer in August 2004, but it subsided after rest. When his knee locked up again, he had surgery that September to clean up abnormal bone formation. Ever enthusiastic, he called Royals officials and trainers nearly every week during the 2005 season seeking medical clearance to pitch again, which he finally received in November. In high school, Cordier exhibited poise, smooth mechanics and the potential for three plus pitches. He works at 90-92 mph and touches 93-94 with his fastball. He throws his changeup with good arm speed, and he can snap off a solid curveball. Cordier would have gone to Idaho Falls in 2005, and could wind up there or in low Class A this year.

Year	Club (League)	Class	W	L	ERA	G	GS	CG	SV	IP	H	R	ER	HR	BB	SO	AVG
2004	Royals (AZL)	R	2	4	5.19	11	11	0	0	35	38	27	20	1	21	22	.279
2005	Did not play—Injured																
MINOR LEAGUE TOTALS			2	4	5.19	11	11	0	0	35	38	27	20	1	21	22	.279

17 JOE DICKERSON OF

Born: Oct. 3, 1986. **B-T:** L-L. **Ht.:** 6-1. **Wt.:** 190. **Drafted:** HS— Yorba Linda, Calif., 2005 (4th round). **Signed by:** John Ramey.

A fourth-round pick in June, Dickerson chose a $250,000 bonus over attending Texas. He immediately slapped his name all over the Arizona League's leader boards, ranking first in RBIs and triples, second in extra-base hits, third in hits and fifth in slugging. His offensive accolades were impressive because he entered pro ball known more for his above-average speed and defense. Dickerson didn't disappoint in those areas, either, rating as one of the system's best defensive outfielders because of his ability to get good reads and jumps to cover lots of ground in center field. His only knock as a defender is his below-average arm, which is still playable in center. Dickerson's line-drive swing is quick to the ball, but he swings and misses a lot against breaking balls, something that could improve with experience. He can also be very pull-conscious, a remnant from his since-adjusted high school stance where he stood so close to the plate that his left foot was almost in front of it. He still can smoke fastballs on the inner half, but needs to work on staying back on pitches on the outer half so he can drive them for power. Dickerson's overall approach drew comparisons to that of Mark Kotsay, who played his college ball at Cal State Fullerton, just down the road from where Dickerson grew up in Yorba Linda. Dickerson moves up to Idaho Falls for 2006.

Year	Club (League)	Class	AVG	G	AB	R	H	2B	3B	HR	RBI	BB	SO	SB	OBP	SLG
2005	Royals (AZL)	R	.294	56	214	27	63	12	9	4	40	27	46	9	.371	.491
MINOR LEAGUE TOTALS			.294	56	214	27	63	12	9	4	40	27	46	9	.371	.491

18 JOSE DUARTE OF

Born: March 7, 1985. **B-T:** R-R. **Ht.:** 5-10. **Wt.:** 165. **Signed:** Venezuela, 2004. **Signed by:** Juan Indriago.

With five tools that all rate at least average, Duarte stands at the front of a nice collection of young Latin outfielders (Alvi Morel, O.D. Gonzalez) who debuted in the Arizona League in 2005 and shared time with Joe Dickerson. Duarte looks young but his skills are advanced. He needed only one year at the Royals' Dominican academy before his game and his English were ready for a U.S. league. Royals instructors say they can tell when Duarte takes batting practice because the ball sounds different coming off his bat. He has big power but his swing tends to get long, especially when he's expecting a fastball in an advantageous count, but he has plenty of time to work that out. Duarte played mostly left field in 2005, but rates as an above-average defender with the arm to play right field and the speed to play center. That versatility will serve him well as he plays multiple outfield positions in Idaho Falls this year.

Year	Club (League)	Class	AVG	G	AB	R	H	2B	3B	HR	RBI	BB	SO	SB	OBP	SLG
2004	Royals (DSL)	R	.317	58	221	51	70	12	4	2	40	42	39	10	.428	.434
2005	Royals (AZL)	R	.309	47	178	33	55	7	6	3	36	25	32	11	.388	.466
MINOR LEAGUE TOTALS			.313	105	399	84	125	19	10	5	76	67	71	21	.411	.449

19 CHRIS NICOLL RHP

Born: Oct. 30, 1983. **B-T:** R-R. **Ht.:** 6-2. **Wt.:** 190. **Drafted:** UC Irvine, 2005 (3rd round). **Signed by:** John Ramey.

A 43rd-round pick by the Blue Jays out of high school in 2002, Nicoll improved his draft stock 40 rounds after three years at UC Irvine. He went 6-4, 2.50 with a 113-24 strikeout-walk ratio in 112 innings as a junior, beating Jays first-rounder Ricky Romero and then-No. 1 Cal State Fullerton in one start and holding Arizona's powerful offense hitless for six innings in another. Signed for $445,000, Nicoll doesn't offer a dominant pitch, but he succeeds with above-average command, feel and confidence. His fastball usually operates in the high 80s, but he throws it to both sides of the plate and keeps it knee-high nearly all the time. His slider and changeup are average, though he'll need one to improve if he's going to be anything more than a long reliever. The Royals took Nicoll for his polish and believe he'll move quickly through a system thin on advanced pitching talent. He could jump to high Class A to begin his first full season.

Year	Club (League)	Class	W	L	ERA	G	GS	CG	SV	IP	H	R	ER	HR	BB	SO	AVG
2005	Idaho Falls (Pio)	R	0	3	3.63	7	7	0	0	27	26	14	11	4	9	34	.250
MINOR LEAGUE TOTALS			0	3	3.63	7	7	0	0	27	26	14	11	4	9	34	.250

20 KILA KAAIHUE 1B

Born: March 29, 1984. **B-T:** L-R. **Ht.:** 6-3. **Wt.:** 233. **Drafted:** HS—Honolulu, 2002 (15th round). **Signed by:** Eric Tokunaga.

Scouting director Deric Ladnier spotted Kaaihue on a 2001 scouting trip to Hawaii to watch Bronson Sardinha and Brandon League. They went in the first two rounds that year, and the Royals took Kaaihue in the 15th round in 2002. His father Kala was a longtime minor league catcher who topped out in Triple-A during the mid-1970s, and his brother, also named Kala, is a catcher in the Braves system. Kila always had shown lots of raw power and a patient approach, but before 2005 he had a timid swing geared more toward not striking out than packing a punch. The Royals urged him to remain disciplined while attacking the pitches at which he chose to swing. Kaaihue did just that and enjoyed his best season yet. A pitcher and quarterback in high school, he has a strong arm and decent hands at first base, but he leaves a lot to be desired in terms of speed and range. He has earned a shot at Double-A this year.

Year	Club (League)	Class	AVG	G	AB	R	H	2B	3B	HR	RBI	BB	SO	SB	OBP	SLG
2002	Royals (GCL)	R	.259	43	139	15	36	8	0	3	21	26	35	0	.381	.381
2003	Burlington (Mid)	A	.238	114	395	53	94	21	1	11	63	67	87	1	.355	.380
2004	Burlington (Mid)	A	.246	125	390	57	96	23	2	15	62	64	98	1	.361	.431
2005	High Desert (Cal)	A	.304	132	493	84	150	31	2	20	90	97	97	2	.428	.497
MINOR LEAGUE TOTALS			.265	414	1417	209	376	83	5	49	236	254	317	4	.385	.435

21 BRENT FISHER LHP

Born: Aug. 6, 1987. **B-T:** L-L. **Ht.:** 6-2. **Wt.:** 190. **Drafted:** HS—Goodyear, Ariz., 2005 (7th round). **Signed by:** Mike Brown.

Fisher didn't draw a lot of attention from scouts because he doesn't have overpowering stuff, but the Royals took him in the seventh round last June and signed him for $130,000 because they liked his mature approach and his polish. Those attributes allowed him to succeed right away in the Arizona League at age 17. Fisher ranked third in the AZL in strikeouts by attacking hitters aggressively and demonstrating a feel for throwing the right pitch at the right time. His fastball works at 87-91 mph with good sinking action, and his easy delivery makes it deceptive because it gets on hitters quicker than they expect. He could pick up more velocity as he fills out. Fisher registered most of his strikeouts with a 12-to-6 curveball that he regularly throws for strikes. He also uses a changeup that still needs more work. Slated for Idaho Falls in 2006, he could shoot up this list if he continues to succeed.

Year	Club (League)	Class	W	L	ERA	G	GS	CG	SV	IP	H	R	ER	HR	BB	SO	AVG
2005	Royals (AZL)	R	5	2	3.04	13	8	0	1	50	48	20	17	2	13	69	.249
MINOR LEAGUE TOTALS			5	2	3.04	13	8	0	1	50	48	20	17	2	13	69	.249

22 ESTEBAN GERMAN INF

Born: Jan. 26, 1978. **B-T:** R-R. **Ht.:** 5-9. **Wt.:** 165. **Signed:** Dominican Republic, 1996. **Signed by:** Santiago Villalona (Athletics).

The Royals used the first pick in the major league Rule 5 draft at the Winter Meetings to take White Sox lefty Fabio Castro, whom they traded to the Rangers in a prearranged deal for German. He was the Athletics' 2001 minor league player of the year, but never could win a regular job with Oakland. He signed with Texas as a minor league free agent after the 2004 season. German excels at getting on base via his line-drive bat, patient eye and bunting ability, posing a career .404 OBP in the minors. He also has plus speed and has led his leagues in steals three times, including the Triple-A Pacific Coast League last year. He has little power but recognizes that and focuses on putting the ball in play. German's lack of defensive skills have hurt his ability to stick in the majors. His below-average arm makes second base his best position, and he lacks a quick first step, so he possesses just average range despite his speed. He played four different positions in 2005, and his best hope to make the Royals may be as a utilityman.

Year	Club (League)	Class	AVG	G	AB	R	H	2B	3B	HR	RBI	BB	SO	SB	OBP	SLG
1997	Athletics East (DSL)	R	.317	69	249	69	79	17	1	2	29	73	30	58	.474	.418
1998	Athletics West (DSL)	R	.313	10	32	9	10	1	1	0	4	7	2	1	.436	.406
	Athletics (AZL)	R	.307	55	202	52	62	3	10	2	28	33	43	40	.413	.450
1999	Modesto (Cal)	A	.311	128	501	107	156	16	12	4	52	102	128	40	.428	.415
2000	Midland (TL)	AA	.213	24	75	13	16	1	0	1	6	18	21	5	.379	.267
	Visalia (Cal)	A	.264	109	428	82	113	14	10	2	35	61	86	78	.361	.357
2001	Midland (TL)	AA	.284	92	335	79	95	20	3	6	30	63	66	31	.415	.415
	Sacramento (PCL)	AAA	.373	38	150	40	56	8	0	4	14	18	20	17	.457	.507
2002	Sacramento (PCL)	AAA	.275	121	458	72	126	16	4	2	43	78	66	26	.390	.341
	Oakland (AL)	MLB	.200	9	35	4	7	0	0	0	0	4	11	1	.300	.200

			AVG	G	AB	R	H	2B	3B	HR	RBI	BB	SO	SB	OBP	SLG
2003	Sacramento (PCL)	AAA	.306	115	467	86	143	20	8	3	51	56	64	32	.379	.403
	Oakland (AL)	MLB	.250	5	4	0	1	0	0	0	1	0	1	0	.250	.250
2004	Oakland (AL)	MLB	.250	31	60	9	15	1	1	0	7	4	13	0	.297	.300
	Sacramento (PCL)	AAA	.329	55	231	33	76	8	4	2	29	19	28	18	.380	.424
2005	Oklahoma (PCL)	AAA	.313	117	489	103	153	27	6	5	68	65	74	43	.400	.423
	Texas (AL)	MLB	.750	5	4	3	3	1	0	0	1	0	1	2	.750	1.000
MAJOR LEAGUE TOTALS			.252	50	103	16	26	2	1	0	9	8	26	3	.313	.291
MINOR LEAGUE TOTALS			.300	933	3617	745	1085	151	59	33	389	593	628	389	.404	.402

23 MIKE AVILES INF

Born: March 13, 1981. **B-T:** R-R. **Ht.:** 5-11. **Wt.:** 198. **Drafted:** Concordia (N.Y.) College, 2003 (7th round). **Signed by:** Steve Connelly.

Looking to save money in the 2003 draft, Kansas City selected college seniors with its fifth- through ninth-round picks and signed them for $1,000 each. The best of that group, Aviles won NCAA Division II player-of-the-year honors that spring and the Arizona League MVP award that summer. His uncle Ramon, a former big leaguer, managed the Brewers' low Class A West Virginia affiliate in 2005. The Royals believe Aviles can develop into a solid utility player similar to Jose Hernandez. Aviles rarely misses a fastball and has average power for a middle infielder. He usually makes solid contact, though he doesn't walk much. Breaking balls can give him trouble, as he often fails to recognize them and can't lay off them. Defensively, Aviles doesn't offer enough range or consistency (he made 41 errors in 2005) to win an everyday job, but he'd be a fine fit as a utility player capable of playing any infield spot and offering some pop. He has hit at each level, and there's no reason to think he won't play well enough at Triple-A this year to merit a late look in Kansas City.

Year	Club (League)	Class	AVG	G	AB	R	H	2B	3B	HR	RBI	BB	SO	SB	OBP	SLG
2003	Royals 1 (AZL)	R	.363	52	212	51	77	19	5	6	39	13	28	11	.404	.585
2004	Wilmington (Car)	A	.300	126	463	66	139	40	4	6	69	39	57	2	.352	.443
2005	Wichita (TL)	AA	.280	133	521	79	146	33	6	14	80	30	64	11	.318	.447
MINOR LEAGUE TOTALS			.303	311	1196	196	362	92	15	26	188	82	149	24	.347	.470

24 MARIO LISSON 3B

Born: May 31, 1984. **B-T:** R-R. **Ht.:** 6-2. **Wt.:** 193. **Signed:** Venezuela, 2002. **Signed by:** Juan Indriago.

Signed following a tip from a former junior college teammate of farm director Shaun McGinn, Lisson quickly became one of general manager Allard Baird's favorite prospects for his athleticism and raw tools. Lisson has grown from a skinny kid with long arms and a high waist into a very physical player. His 2005 season ended in July when he tore the labrum in his left (non-throwing) shoulder while diving for a ball. When he played, he again showcased a patient approach to go with above-average speed and basestealing savvy. There's still hope that Lisson's above-average raw power will translate into homers, but he didn't get enough time last year to adjust a mechanical flaw. He often tucks in his front shoulder while awaiting a pitch, limiting his bat speed and power. He also strikes out in bunches and must be careful not to fall behind in the count because he's taking too many pitches. A plus arm and soft hands make Lisson a solid third baseman, though 2005 first-round pick Alex Gordon has now laid claim to that position. Lisson also has played catcher, first base and shortstop in the minors. He could return to low Class A to begin 2006.

Year	Club (League)	Class	AVG	G	AB	R	H	2B	3B	HR	RBI	BB	SO	SB	OBP	SLG
2002	Royals (GCL)	R	.200	6	10	0	2	0	0	0	0	4	4	0	.467	.200
	Royals (DSL)	R	.198	30	81	12	16	2	0	0	9	16	22	1	.330	.222
2003	Royals (DSL)	R	.290	62	210	26	61	11	1	3	28	35	36	9	.416	.395
2004	Idaho Falls (Pio)	R	.289	71	256	60	74	10	2	8	49	44	82	15	.398	.438
2005	Burlington (Mid)	A	.250	78	260	57	65	15	4	6	36	53	68	23	.386	.408
MINOR LEAGUE TOTALS			.267	247	817	155	218	38	7	17	122	152	212	48	.393	.393

25 CHRIS DEMARIA RHP

Born: Sept. 28, 1980. **B-T:** B-R. **Ht.:** 6-3. **Wt.:** 210. **Drafted:** Long Beach State, 2002 (17th round). **Signed by:** Mike Kendall (Pirates).

The Rule 5 draft proved one of few areas of success for the Royals in 2005. Andrew Sisco, taken in the major league phase, earned a regular role in the bullpen in 2005 and for the future. Demaria, plucked from the Pirates with the first Triple-A pick, became the only player selected in the minor league phase to reach the majors last year. Demaria's 2.23 ERA for High Desert (including 1.11 at home) was the best of any pitcher who worked at least 50 innings at the launching pad. Demaria's success stems from commanding a straight changeup that rates as the best in the organization. It's so effective because he throws it with the exact arm speed he uses with his 88-mph fastball. Demaria commands those two pitches well, and has a usable breaking ball he can mix in if he's becoming too predictable. He'll probably open the season in Triple-A.

Year	Club (League)	Class	W	L	ERA	G	GS	CG	SV	IP	H	R	ER	HR	BB	SO	AVG
2002	Williamsport (NY-P)	A	1	1	4.35	16	0	0	1	31	34	20	15	6	4	15	.272
2003	Williamsport (NY-P)	A	6	3	2.68	25	1	0	3	47	36	15	14	3	10	48	.209
2004	Hickory (SAL)	A	8	3	2.94	40	0	0	10	80	62	29	26	5	20	101	.209
2005	High Desert (Cal)	A	4	2	2.22	48	0	0	19	61	57	19	15	8	10	73	.247
	Wichita (TL)	AA	0	1	1.76	10	0	0	1	15	12	3	3	3	2	19	.218
	Kansas City (AL)	MLB	1	0	9.00	8	0	0	0	9	14	10	9	3	5	11	.359
MAJOR LEAGUE TOTALS			1	0	9.00	8	0	0	0	9	14	10	9	3	5	11	.359
MINOR LEAGUE TOTALS			19	10	2.81	139	1	0	34	234	201	86	73	25	46	256	.229

26 GREG ATENCIO
RHP

Born: July 15, 1981. **B-T:** R-R. **Ht.:** 6-3. **Wt.:** 210. **Drafted:** Lamar (Colo.) JC, 2002 (10th round). **Signed by:** Mike Brown.

Atencio knew nothing but success as an amateur, winning consecutive New Mexico 5-A state titles at Albuquerque's El Dorado High before helping Lamar (Colo.) Junior College reach the 2002 Junior College World Series. At Lamar, he and the White Sox' Brandon McCarthy served as co-aces. While McCarthy excelled immediately in the minors, Atencio struggled. He got hammered in his pro debut in the short-season Northwest League, earning a demotion to the Arizona League in 2003. He led the low Class A Midwest League with 14 losses in 2004. Atencio seemed more comfortable when he moved to the bullpen full-time last season. His statistics weren't extraordinary, but his fastball jumped to 94-96 mph with heavy sink when he worked in shorter stints. Atencio also throws a slider that reaches the upper 80s, and his power two-pitch combo could take him to the majors if he can improve his command. His biggest problem is that he gets offline to the plate with his mechanics and fails to finish his pitches. He leaves fastballs above the belt too often, and move advanced hitters will punish them. He'll head to Double-A this season.

Year	Club (League)	Class	W	L	ERA	G	GS	CG	SV	IP	H	R	ER	HR	BB	SO	AVG
2002	Spokane (NWL)	A	4	7	6.07	14	12	0	0	59	70	45	40	8	16	35	.297
2003	Royals 2 (AZL)	R	2	5	3.91	12	12	0	0	71	62	40	31	4	17	62	.236
	Burlington (Mid)	A	0	1	12.38	2	0	0	0	8	15	12	11	3	5	7	.385
2004	Burlington (Mid)	A	7	14	5.61	28	28	0	0	149	157	109	93	12	68	118	.274
2005	Burlington (Mid)	A	5	2	4.16	17	2	0	0	43	33	22	20	0	18	40	.209
	High Desert (Cal)	A	3	1	5.64	19	1	0	0	37	43	28	23	4	24	36	.287
MINOR LEAGUE TOTALS			21	30	5.33	92	55	0	0	368	380	256	218	31	148	298	.268

27 MATT CAMPBELL
LHP

Born: Dec. 27, 1982. **B-T:** L-L. **Ht.:** 6-2. **Wt.:** 170. **Drafted:** South Carolina, 2004 (1st round). **Signed by:** Spencer Graham.

Kansas City selected Campbell and J.P. Howell two picks apart at Nos. 29 and 31 in 2004, but their career arcs have been vastly different. Howell won his major league debut June 11, less than a year after signing, while Campbell made just two starts after that date before having season-ending labrum surgery. The Royals believe Campbell threw too many curveballs at South Carolina, where he pitched the Gamecocks to three College World Series in his three seasons, but don't think that's totally to blame for his shoulder troubles. Campbell should be ready for spring training, though he might need some time to regain his arm strength after surgery. Signed for $1.1 million, he hasn't displayed consistent velocity as a pro because of his shoulder problems. His fastball has topped out at 92 mph but also peaked at 82 on other occasions. When healthy, he features a fastball with average velocity, plus command and tailing life away from righthanders. His curve's big 2-to-7 break makes it a plus pitch. His changeup has the potential to become an average offering. The Royals selected Campbell for his polish and poise, thinking he'd move quickly. That won't happen now, and he won't start 2006 above high Class A.

Year	Club (League)	Class	W	L	ERA	G	GS	CG	SV	IP	H	R	ER	HR	BB	SO	AVG
2004	Idaho Falls (Pio)	R	0	2	8.41	4	4	0	0	11	11	10	10	1	10	10	.282
2005	Burlington (Mid)	A	1	5	4.66	13	12	0	0	64	74	41	33	3	37	48	.291
MINOR LEAGUE TOTALS			1	7	5.21	17	16	0	0	74	85	51	43	4	47	58	.290

28 DUSTY HUGHES
LHP

Born: June 29, 1982. **B-T:** L-L. **Ht.:** 5-10. **Wt.:** 187. **Drafted:** Delta State (Miss.), 2003 (11th round). **Signed by:** Mark Willoughby.

Averaging 12.4 strikeouts per nine innings in NCAA Division II three years ago got

Hughes drafted. Opening 2004 with eight no-hit innings got him noticed. But spending 2005 in High Desert's notorious Mavericks Stadium got him scared. He must locate his fastball early and down in the zone to have success, and he fell behind too often. His forte is working both sides of the plate with an 84-90 mph fastball that's average at best. When he didn't locate his pitches well—and sometimes even when he did—opponents teed off, causing Hughes to lose his confidence. An elbow sprain ended his season in mid-July, and in retrospect, it might have been just as well to get him out of High Desert. Hughes likes to work inside and throws a quick, tight cutter as his go-to pitch. He also has a changeup and relies on mixing his pitches, speeds and location. The Royals think Hughes can bounce back this year in Double-A, where his success will determine whether he has a future as a No. 5 starter or just as a lefty specialist.

Year	Club (League)	Class	W	L	ERA	G	GS	CG	SV	IP	H	R	ER	HR	BB	SO	AVG
2003	Royals 1 (AZL)	R	5	2	2.84	11	6	0	0	51	38	21	16	4	18	54	.207
2004	Burlington (Mid)	A	4	2	1.56	8	8	0	0	52	39	12	9	2	15	36	.213
	Wilmington (Car)	A	5	5	2.41	18	18	0	0	108	95	37	29	5	31	68	.245
2005	High Desert (Cal)	A	5	7	5.67	19	19	0	0	92	119	74	58	13	45	87	.319
MINOR LEAGUE TOTALS			19	16	3.33	56	51	0	0	303	291	144	112	24	109	245	.258

29 PAUL RAGLIONE   RHP

Born: Jan. 15, 1987. **B-T:** R-R. **Ht.:** 6-5. **Wt.:** 195. **Drafted:** HS—Portland, Ore., 2005 (18th round). **Signed by:** Greg Smith.

Raglione's numbers weren't pretty after he signed as an 18th-round pick in June, but his projectable frame makes him worth keeping an eye on. He played at the Metro Baseball Academy in Portland, Ore., which also produced Indians first-round pick Trevor Crowe, and would have gone in the first 10 rounds if not for a commitment to Washington State. Raglione is an athletic 6-foot-5, 195-pounder with a clean arm stroke. His height creates a steep downward plane for a fastball that currently sits at 88-89 mph and tops out at 92. Once he grows into his body, he could pitch in the low to mid-90s. Raglione's secondary pitches are still works in progress. His changeup rates as his second-best offering now, but his slider could surpass it once it becomes tighter and more consistent. He'll flash an above-average slider and follow it up with one well below average. Raglione will need time to develop, but the Royals are willing to wait for what could become an impressive payoff. He'll likely start 2006 in the Idaho Falls rotation.

Year	Club (League)	Class	W	L	ERA	G	GS	CG	SV	IP	H	R	ER	HR	BB	SO	AVG
2005	Royals (AZL)	R	3	4	5.94	13	7	0	1	47	66	40	31	4	18	37	.332
MINOR LEAGUE TOTALS			3	4	5.94	13	7	0	1	47	66	40	31	4	18	37	.332

30 MATT KNIGINYZKY   RHP

Born: Oct. 5, 1982. **B-T:** L-R. **Ht.:** 6-3. **Wt.:** 185. **Drafted:** High Point (N.C.), 2005 (23rd round). **Signed by:** Spencer Graham.

A 43rd-round choice of the Blue Jays in 2000 out of high school in Mississauga, Ontario, Kniginyzky took a circuitous route to the Royals. He pitched at Lake City (Fla.) Community College and at Northeastern Oklahoma A&M Junior College (where he came down with elbow tendinitis) before transferring to High Point University. After two years as a starter for the Panthers, he found his niche in the bullpen last spring. When Kansas City took him in the 23rd round, he became the first player drafted out of High Point since 1991. At 6-foot-5, he gets an excellent downhill plane on a 90-94 mph fastball and also throws a hard curveball. He rarely uses his changeup in games, though it does have some potential. His key will be repeating his delivery. At different times, he'll throw across his body, fly open or drop his arm slot. The Royals may use him as a starter in low Class A this year to get him more innings, but they project him as a late-inning reliever.

Year	Club (League)	Class	W	L	ERA	G	GS	CG	SV	IP	H	R	ER	HR	BB	SO	AVG
2005	Idaho Falls (Pio)	R	2	5	4.66	21	0	0	5	29	35	22	15	0	13	40	.287
MINOR LEAGUE TOTALS			2	5	4.66	21	0	0	5	29	35	22	15	0	13	40	.287

LOS ANGELES
ANGELS

BY **ALAN MATTHEWS**

In the Angels' first 40 years, the franchise made just three postseason appearances. In 2005, they won their second straight American League West title and secured their third postseason appearance in the last four years, continuing a run that started with a World Series title in 2002.

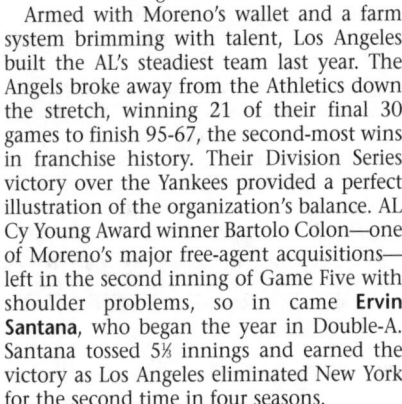

A franchise once mired in mediocrity has become one of baseball's best. Under the aggressive ownership of Arte Moreno and the baseball leadership of general manager Bill Stoneman and manager Mike Scoscia, the Angels show no signs of decline.

Armed with Moreno's wallet and a farm system brimming with talent, Los Angeles built the AL's steadiest team last year. The Angels broke away from the Athletics down the stretch, winning 21 of their final 30 games to finish 95-67, the second-most wins in franchise history. Their Division Series victory over the Yankees provided a perfect illustration of the organization's balance. AL Cy Young Award winner Bartolo Colon—one of Moreno's major free-agent acquisitions—left in the second inning of Game Five with shoulder problems, so in came **Ervin Santana**, who began the year in Double-A. Santana tossed 5⅓ innings and earned the victory as Los Angeles eliminated New York for the second time in four seasons.

The Angels will continue to be major players on the free-agent market. But Stoneman can also rely on the farm system, which is what should give the organization staying power. There isn't an organization in baseball that has more potential star position players waiting in the wings.

Casey Kotchman officially graduated from the minors in 2005 and is ready to play regularly at first base. Dallas McPherson was plagued by back problems last year, but he's another run-producer for the middle of the lineup. Santana established himself as a reliable starter. None of those three qualify for the prospect list any longer.

But the farm system is still loaded. The middle-infield situation is indicative of the Angels' depth in the majors and minors. No. 1 prospect Brandon Wood set an Angels minor league record with 43 homers in 2005. He plays shortstop, as do No. 3 prospect Erick Aybar and Orlando Cabrera, both of whom are further up the organizational ladder. No. 2 prospect Howie Kendrick has a .359 career average as a pro, and he has big leaguer Adam Kennedy and No. 8 prospect Alberto Callaspo looming ahead of him.

Catcher Jeff Mathis will get big league playing time after Bengie Molina declared free agency. Righthander Jered Weaver and lefty Joe Saunders could factor into the rotation, and don't rule out Cuban defector Kendry Morales claiming some at-bats at first base or DH. The Angels aren't as strong with pitching prospects, a shortcoming they've tried to address in scouting director Eddie Bane's two drafts.

Call them what you like. The Angels have a new identity and have become the pre-eminent team in Southern California.

TOP 30 PROSPECTS

1. Brandon Wood, ss	16. Hainley Statia, ss
2. Howie Kendrick, 2b	17. Jose Arredondo, rhp
3. Erick Aybar, ss	18. Stephen Marek, rhp
4. Jeff Mathis, c	19. Nick Gorneault, of
5. Jered Weaver, rhp	20. Tommy Murphy, of
6. Nick Adenhart, rhp	21. Rafael Rodriguez, rhp
7. Kendry Morales, 1b	22. Bobby Wilson, c
8. Alberto Callaspo, 2b	23. Sean Rodriguez, ss
9. Joe Saunders, lhp	24. Peter Bourjos, of
10. Tommy Mendoza, rhp	25. Ryan Mount, ss
11. Mike Napoli, c	26. Jake Woods, lhp
12. Mark Trumbo, 1b	27. Bob Zimmermann, rhp
13. Trevor Bell, rhp	28. Reggie Willits, of
14. P.J. Phillips, ss/3b	29. Nick Green, rhp
15. Steven Shell, rhp	30. Gustavo Espinoza, lhp

ORGANIZATION OVERVIEW

General manager: Bill Stoneman. **Farm director:** Tony Reagins. **Scouting director:** Eddie Bane.

2005 PERFORMANCE

Class	Team	League	W	L	Pct.	Finish*	Manager
Majors	Los Angeles	American	95	67	.586	t-2nd (14)	Mike Scioscia
Triple-A	Salt Lake Stingers	Pacific Coast	79	65	.549	4th (16)	Dino Ebel
Double-A	Arkansas Travelers	Texas	71	69	.507	+4th (8)	Tom Gamboa
High A	Rancho Cucamonga Quakes	California	62	77	.446	8th (10)	Tyrone Boykin
Low A	Cedar Rapids Kernels	Midwest	65	75	.464	t-11th (14)	Bobby Magallanes
Rookie	Orem Owlz	Pioneer	38	38	.500	+t-4th (8)	Tom Kotchman
Rookie	AZL Angels	Arizona	25	31	.446	7th (9)	Brian Harper
OVERALL 2005 MINOR LEAGUE RECORD			340	355	.489	23rd (30)	

*Finish in overall standings (No. of teams in league). +League champion.

ORGANIZATION LEADERS

BATTING
*Minimum 250 at-bats
*AVG	Kendrick, Howie, Arkansas/Rancho Cucamonga	.367
R	Wood, Brandon, Rancho Cucamonga/Salt Lake	110
H	Wood, Brandon, Rancho Cucamonga/Salt Lake	178
TB	Wood, Brandon, Rancho Cucamonga/Salt Lake	370
2B	Wood, Brandon, Rancho Cucamonga/Salt Lake	53
3B	Prieto, Chris, Salt Lake	12
HR	Wood, Brandon, Rancho Cucamonga/Salt Lake	43
RBI	Wood, Brandon, Rancho Cucamonga/Salt Lake	116
BB	Napoli, Mike, Arkansas	88
SO	Napoli, Mike, Arkansas	140
SB	Aybar, Erick, Arkansas	49
	Casilla, Alexi, Arkansas/Cedar Rapids/Salt Lake	49
*OBP	Prieto, Chris, Salt Lake	.418
*SLG	Wood, Brandon, Rancho Cucamonga/Salt Lake	.667

PITCHING
#Minimum 75 innings
W	Davidson, Daniel, Arkansas	13
L	Hunter, Chris, Rancho Cucamonga/Salt Lake	10
	Rodriguez, Fernando, Cedar Rapids	10
	Torres, Joe, Cedar Rapids/Rancho Cucamonga	10
#ERA	Lee, Corey, Salt Lake	2.27
G	Austen, David, Arkansas/Rancho Cucamonga	56
	Wilhite, Matt, Arkansas	56
CG	Rodriguez, Fernando, Cedar Rapids	4
SV	Zimmermann, Bob, Rancho Cucamonga	17
IP	Saunders, Joe, Arkansas/Salt Lake	161
BB	Torres, Joe, Cedar Rapids/Rancho Cucamonga	92
SO	Holcomb, James, Rancho Cucamonga	128
	Rodriguez, Fernando, Cedar Rapids	128

BEST TOOLS

Best Hitter for Average	Howie Kendrick
Best Power Hitter	Brandon Wood
Best Strike-Zone Discipline	Sean Rodriguez
Fastest Baserunner	Peter Bourjos
Best Athlete	Tommy Murphy
Best Fastball	Tommy Mendoza
Best Curveball	Nick Adenhart
Best Slider	Von Stertzbach
Best Changeup	Nick Green
Best Control	Jered Weaver
Best Defensive Catcher	Jeff Mathis
Best Defensive Infielder	Erick Aybar
Best Infield Arm	Erick Aybar
Best Defensive Outfielder	Tommy Murphy
Best Outfield Arm	Warner Madrigal

PROJECTED 2009 LINEUP

Catcher	Jeff Mathis
First Base	Casey Kotchman
Second Base	Howie Kendrick
Third Base	Brandon Wood
Shortstop	Erick Aybar
Left Field	Dallas McPherson
Center Field	Chone Figgins
Right Field	Vladimir Guerrero
Designated Hitter	Kendry Morales
No. 1 Starter	Ervin Santana
No. 2 Starter	John Lackey
No. 3 Starter	Bartolo Colon
No. 4 Starter	Jered Weaver
No. 5 Starter	Nick Adenhart
Closer	Francisco Rodriguez

LAST YEAR'S TOP 20 PROSPECTS

1. Casey Kotchman, 1b	11. Mark Trumbo, 3b/1b
2. Dallas McPherson, 3b	12. Baltazar Lopez, 1b
3. Erick Aybar, ss	13. Joe Saunders, lhp
4. Jeff Mathis, c	14. Sean Rodriguez, 2b/ss
5. Kendry Morales, of/1b	15. Dustin Moseley, rhp
6. Brandon Wood, ss	16. Maicer Izturis, ss/2b
7. Ervin Santana, rhp	17. Rafael Rodriguez, rhp
8. Howie Kendrick, 2b	18. Jake Woods, lhp
9. Alberto Callaspo, 2b/ss	19. Kevin Jepsen, rhp
10. Steven Shell, rhp	20. Nick Adenhart, rhp

TOP PROSPECTS OF THE DECADE

Year	Player, Pos.	2005 Org.
1996	Darin Erstad, of	Angels
1997	Jarrod Washburn, lhp	Angels
1998	Troy Glaus, 3b	Diamondbacks
1999	Ramon Ortiz, rhp	Reds
2000	Ramon Ortiz, rhp	Reds
2001	Joe Torres, lhp	Angels
2002	Casey Kotchman, 1b	Angels
2003	Francisco Rodriguez, rhp	Angels
2004	Casey Kotchman, 1b	Angels
2005	Casey Kotchman, 1b	Angels

TOP DRAFT PICKS OF THE DECADE

Year	Player, Pos.	2005 Org.
1996	Chuck Abbott, ss (2nd round)	Out of baseball
1997	Troy Glaus, 3b	Diamondbacks
1998	Seth Etherton, rhp	Athletics
1999	John Lackey, rhp (2nd round)	Angels
2000	Joe Torres, lhp	Angels
2001	Casey Kotchman, 1b	Angels
2002	Joe Saunders, lhp	Angels
2003	Brandon Wood, ss	Angels
2004	Jered Weaver, rhp	Angels
2005	Trevor Bell, rhp	Angels

ALL-TIME LARGEST BONUSES

Jered Weaver, 2004	$4,000,000
Kendry Morales, 2004	$3,000,000
Troy Glaus, 1997	$2,250,000
Joe Torres, 2000	$2,080,000
Casey Kotchman, 2001	$2,075,000

MINOR LEAGUE DEPTH CHART

Los Angeles Angels

Rank: **3**

STRENGTH: Infielders, particularly in the middle of the diamond. The Angels have several varieties to choose from, too.

WEAKNESS: Lefthanded pitching. Joe Saunders could be a big league starter, but the group doesn't inspire otherwise.

*Depth charts prepared by **John Manuel** and **Chris Kline**. Numbers in parentheses indicate prospect rankings.*

LF
Andrew Toussaint
Aaron Peel
Blake Balkcom

CF
Tommy Murphy (20)
Peter Bourjos (24)
Reggie Willits (28)
Stantrel Smith
Josh LeBlanc
Jerome Moore

RF
Nick Gorneault (19)
Warner Madrigal

3B
P.J. Phillips (14)
Freddy Sandoval
Greg Porter
Dallas Morris

SS
Brandon Wood (1)
Erick Aybar (3)
Hainley Statia (16)
Sean Rodriguez (23)
Ryan Mount (25)

2B
Howie Kendrick (2)
Alberto Callaspo (8)
Brian Specht
Eric Rodland

1B
Kendry Morales (7)
Mark Trumbo (12)
Baltazar Lopez
Mike Collins
Matt Ryan

C
Jeff Mathis (4)
Mike Napoli (11)
Bobby Wilson (22)
Brett Martinez
Martin Maldonado

RHP

Starters	Relievers
Jered Weaver (5)	Jose Arredondo (17)
Nick Adenhart (6)	Stephen Marek (18)
Tommy Mendoza (10)	Bob Zimmermann (27)
Trevor Bell (13)	Bobby Mosebach
Steven Shell (15)	Von Sterzbach
Rafael Rodriguez (21)	Ryan Aldridge
Nick Green (29)	Scott Dunn
Bobby Cassevah	Mitchell Arnold
Chris Bootcheck	Bill Edwards
Dustin Moseley	Matt Hensley
Anthony Ortega	Kevin Lynch
Francisco Cordova	David Austen
Kevin Jepsen	
Felipe Arredondo	
James Holcomb	

LHP

Starters	Relievers
Joe Saunders (9)	Anthony Whittington
Jake Woods (26)	Jon Rouwenhorst
Gustavo Espinoza (30)	
Dan Davidson	
Kelly Shearer	

DRAFT ANALYSIS

2005

Best Pro Debut: RHP Tommy Mendoza (5) earned Rookie-level Arizona League all-star honors by going 3-3, 1.55 with 56 strikeouts in 52 innings. The Angels used him to fill a hole in the high Class A California League at season's end. Mendoza threw three perfect innings to earn a save in his first outing and threw seven shutout frames to win his lone start.

Best Athlete: OF Jeremy Moore (6) starred as a running back in football, a guard in basketball and a sprinter in track while in high school. OF Cody Fuller (48) played two sports at Texas Tech, suiting up as a wide receiver in football.

Best Pure Hitter: P.J. Phillips (2) could outgrow shortstop but has the bat to fit most anywhere on the diamond.

Best Raw Power: 1B Ryan Pressley (17), though he's still raw at the plate.

Fastest Runner: The Angels signed a lot of speed. OF Peter Bourjos (10), who can cover 60 yards in 6.45 seconds, would edge Moore in a race. Fuller is a plus runner.

Best Defensive Player: Bourjos, a center fielder. SS Ryan Mount (2) stands out most for his offensive potential, but Los Angeles also believes he can stay at short.

Best Fastball: Both RHP Trevor Bell (1) and Mendoza consistently hit 95 mph. The Angels still have the rights to draft-and-follow RHP Sean O'Sullivan (3), who can do the same. RHP Stephen Marek (40 in 2004), who signed for $800,000 as a draft-and-follow, threw 97-98 mph as a reliever in college and 96 as a starter as a pro.

Best Breaking Ball: Mendoza's curveball. O'Sullivan has an impressive slider and curve.

Most Intriguing Background: Bell's

Bell

grandfather Bob was Bozo the Clown, a legend on Chicago television shows for 24 years. Bell's mother Barbara is a casting director for "That '70s Show" on Fox. Phillips' brother Brandon is an Indians infielder, and his sister Porsha is one of the nation's top women's basketball recruits. Bourjos' father Chris played in the majors and is a scout for the Brewers.

Closest To The Majors: The Angels didn't draft a four-year player before C Greg Dini (12), who has decent skills and could get to Los Angeles first because of his position. Mendoza is very advanced for a teenager just out of high school.

Best Late-Round Pick: Bourjos, who got $325,000 as a 10th-rounder.

The One Who Got Away: The Angels and LHP Brian Matusz (4) never got on the same page, and he wound up at the University of San Diego. He reminds scouts of Mark Buehrle with better stuff. SS Matt Hall (8, now at Arizona State), OF Tim Murphy (11, UCLA), 3B Brad Suttle (21, Texas), RHP Duente Heath (23, Tennessee), C Brent Milleville (39, Stanford) and RHP Buster Posey (50, Florida State) all could be premium picks down the road.

Assessment: The Angels didn't hit on as many gambles as they did in 2004 and failed to sign six of their first 14 picks. They still came away with a nice collection of athletes and arms, and signing O'Sullivan would give them an extra boost.

2004 RHP Jered Weaver (1) fell to the Angels at No. 12 because of signability, but he was worth the wait, as was RHP Nick Adenhart (14), who has made a quick recovery from Tommy John surgery. *GRADE:* B+

2003 SS Brandon Wood (1) has become one of the game's truly elite prospects, hitting 43 homers in the 2005 regular season and 14 more in the Arizona Fall League. *GRADE:* A

2002 2B Howie Kendrick (10) is one of the minors' best pure hitters. LHP Joe Saunders (1) overcame shoulder problems and is on the verge of joining the big league rotation. *GRADE:* A

2001 We've been touting this draft for four years and won't stop now. 1B Casey Kotchman (1), C Jeff Mathis (1) and 3B Dallas McPherson (2) all could start for Los Angeles in 2006 and have a chance to become stars. *GRADE:* A

Draft analysis prepared by Jim Callis. Numbers in parentheses indicate draft rounds.

BRANDON WOOD

SS

DAVID STONER

Born: March 2, 1985.
Ht.: 6-3. **Wt.:** 185.
Bats: R. **Throws:** R.
Drafted: HS—Scottsdale, Ariz., 2003 (1st round).
Signed by: Jeff Scholzen.

When Wood was a good-fielding, light-hitting freshman at Horizon High (Scottsdale, Ariz.) in 2000, he wore No. 4, not because he liked the number but because it was the only jersey small enough to fit him. He since has filled out to become one of the game's top power prospects. By 2003 he hit 20 homers as a Horizon senior and became a first-round choice, signing for $1.3 million. Wood hit a modest .263 with 16 homers in his first two pro seasons before breaking out in 2005. He slammed 58 homers between the minors, the Arizona Fall League and Team USA. He led the minors in doubles, homers (breaking the Angels' minor league record), total bases and extra-base hits, becoming the first minor leaguer to do so since Len Tucker in 1956. Then he set an AFL mark with 14 homers in 29 games, going deep four times in one contest. He capped his year with one more homer and earned all-tournament honors as Team USA won an Olympic regional qualifier.

Wood's package of power, hitting, all-around defensive skills and championship-caliber makeup prompted one high Class A California League manager to dub him the next Cal Ripken Jr. Wood is an aggressive hitter who attacks pitches with outstanding bat speed while hitting from a slightly open stance. Early in the 2005 season, he occasionally slid his back hip during his swing, collapsed his back side and got underneath balls. He adjusted quickly and learned to take a more direct path to the ball. Wood's swing has leverage that elicits shots with backspin, loft and plenty of carry. "Out of all those home runs, there may have been one or two balls that just cleared the fence," said James Rowson, Wood's hitting coach at high Class A Rancho Cucamonga. "The other 40 were gone right off the bat." Wood's long, thin frame figures to get stronger as he matures. His soft hands, plus arm and great instincts allow him to make all the plays at shortstop. He presently has average speed.

As Wood gets bulkier, he will slow down and lose range. While he has the tools to compensate and remain at shortstop, he may profile better at third base with the power in his bat and his arm. He can drive balls to all fields but because of his bat speed and set-up, he opts to pull almost everything. That approach makes him vulnerable to pitches on the outer half. He has had trouble with swinging and missing against good changeups, and he could tighten his strike zone in general.

Wood should develop into a perennial all-star infielder at either shortstop or third base. The Angels have more premium middle-infield prospects than any organization, and they'll soon be faced with a difficult shortstop decision with incumbent Orlando Cabrera signed through 2008 and both Erick Aybar and Wood pushing for big league consideration. For now, Wood is ticketed to play shortstop at Double-A Arkansas in 2006. But Los Angeles also doesn't have a clear-cut third baseman, and he quickly could become their solution at the hot corner.

Year	Club (League)	Class	AVG	G	AB	R	H	2B	3B	HR	RBI	BB	SO	SB	OBP	SLG
2003	Angels (AZL)	R	.308	19	78	14	24	8	2	0	13	4	15	3	.349	.462
	Provo (Pio)	R	.278	42	162	25	45	13	2	5	31	16	48	1	.348	.475
2004	Cedar Rapids (Mid)	A	.251	125	478	65	120	30	5	11	64	46	117	21	.322	.404
2005	Rancho Cucamonga (Cal)	A	.321	130	536	109	172	51	4	43	115	48	128	7	.383	.672
	Salt Lake (PCL)	AAA	.316	4	19	1	6	2	1	0	1	0	6	0	.316	.526
MINOR LEAGUE TOTALS			.288	320	1273	214	367	104	14	59	224	114	314	32	.352	.531

2 HOWIE KENDRICK 2B

Born: July 12, 1983. **B-T:** R-R. **Ht.:** 5-10. **Wt.:** 180. **Drafted:** St. John's River (Fla.) CC, 2002 (10th round). **Signed by:** Tom Kotchman.

The Angels originally selected Kendrick as a draft-and-follow, but at the behest of area scout Tom Kotchman they signed him right away for $100,000. Last year he finished second in the minors (.367) and fourth in the Arizona Fall League (.380) in hitting. Kendrick may be the best pure hitter in the minors. His swing is compact, balanced and easily repeated. He lets pitches get deep before centering them and driving them to all fields. His swing doesn't create much loft, but he should hit at least 15-20 homers annually because of his bat speed and penchant for making hard contact. His instincts are exceptional in all phases of the game, which makes him an average baserunner and should allow him to develop into a competent defender. Kendrick's non-hitting tools aren't special. He has fringe-average speed, and his range, arm and defensive footwork are average at best. He makes contact so easily that he rarely walks. Kendrick could win multiple batting titles in the big leagues. Angels starter Adam Kennedy will be a free agent following the 2006 season, at which point Kendrick should take over. He's ready for Triple-A Salt Lake, though Los Angeles also must figure out how to get Alberto Callaspo at-bats.

Year	Club (League)	Class	AVG	G	AB	R	H	2B	3B	HR	RBI	BB	SO	SB	OBP	SLG
2002	Angels (AZL)	R	.318	42	157	24	50	6	4	0	13	7	11	12	.368	.408
2003	Provo (Pio)	R	.368	63	234	65	86	20	3	3	36	24	28	8	.434	.517
2004	Angels (AZL)	R	.250	3	12	1	3	1	0	0	0	1	0	2	.308	.333
	Cedar Rapids (Mid)	A	.367	75	313	66	115	24	6	10	49	12	41	15	.398	.578
2005	Rancho Cucamonga (Cal)	A	.384	63	279	69	107	23	6	12	47	14	42	13	.421	.638
	Arkansas (TL)	AA	.342	46	190	35	65	20	2	7	42	6	20	12	.382	.579
MINOR LEAGUE TOTALS			.359	292	1185	260	426	94	21	32	187	64	142	62	.404	.555

3 ERICK AYBAR SS

Born: Jan. 14, 1984. **B-T:** B-R. **Ht.:** 5-11. **Wt.:** 170. **Signed:** Dominican Republic, 2002. **Signed by:** Leo Perez/Clay Daniel.

When the Angels signed Aybar for $100,000 in 2002, he was considered a lesser prospect than his brother Willy, who had signed with the Dodgers for $1.4 million two years earlier. Erick has developed into a better player and the pure shortstop the Angels hoped, while exceeding expectations for his bat. Though undersized, Aybar packs some pop in his swing. Early in the year he was trying to pull everything out of the park before Angels minor league hitting coordinator Ty Van Burkleo encouraged him to shorten his swing. Aybar got back to doing what he does best: spraying line drives to all fields and using his plus speed to set the table. He has plus actions at shortstop, turns the double play with aplomb and has enough arm strength to make plays deep in the hole. He plays with passion and consistently has been a catalyst. Aybar remains a free swinger. If he's going to reach his ceiling as a leadoff hitter, he must improve his plate discipline and willingness to work counts. He plays with a fearless energy that borders on recklessness. Headed for Triple-A, Aybar is sandwiched between big leaguer Orlando Cabrera and top prospect Brandon Wood. The best—and most cost-effective—solution eventually will be to find a taker for Cabrera, hand shortstop to Aybar and move Wood to third base.

Year	Club (League)	Class	AVG	G	AB	R	H	2B	3B	HR	RBI	BB	SO	SB	OBP	SLG
2002	Provo (Pio)	R	.326	67	273	64	89	15	6	4	29	21	43	15	.395	.469
2003	Cedar Rapids (Mid)	A	.308	125	496	83	153	30	10	6	57	17	54	32	.346	.446
2004	Rancho Cucamonga (Cal)	A	.330	136	573	102	189	25	11	14	65	26	66	51	.370	.485
2005	Arkansas (TL)	AA	.303	134	535	101	162	29	10	9	54	29	51	49	.350	.445
MINOR LEAGUE TOTALS			.316	462	1877	350	593	99	37	33	205	93	214	147	.362	.461

4 JEFF MATHIS C

Born: March 31, 1983. **B-T:** R-R. **Ht.:** 6-0. **Wt.:** 180. **Drafted:** HS—Marianna, Fla., 2001 (1st round supplemental). **Signed by:** Tom Kotchman.

Mathis had a miserable second half in 2004 and was ticketed for a return to Double-A in 2005 when Triple-A catcher Wil Nieves was traded to the Yankees, opening a spot at Salt Lake. Mathis had a fine season, re-establishing himself as one of the game's top catching prospects and making his big league debut in August. Mathis is the consummate defensive catcher. He's athletic, which enables him to block, catch and throw with ease. His arm strength is at least average and plays better because of good footwork and a clean exchange. He threw out 33 percent of basestealers in Triple-A. A true leader, he handles pitchers well. Mathis matured as a hitter last season, shortening his swing and reducing the rotation in his lower half to improve his plate coverage and efficiency. He profiles as a .250-.270 hitter with 15-20 homer potential. While he's a slightly below-average runner, he has good instincts on the basepaths. Mathis needs to do a better job of covering the outer half and laying off breaking balls out of the zone. He tends to over-analyze and press, which got him into trouble in 2004. The Angels never doubted that Mathis had the makeup to rebound from 2004. His bat isn't quite ready for everyday duty, but Bengie Molina's departure means Mathis will play a significant role in Los Angeles.

Year	Club (League)	Class	AVG	G	AB	R	H	2B	3B	HR	RBI	BB	SO	SB	OBP	SLG
2001	Angels (AZL)	R	.304	7	23	1	7	1	0	0	3	2	4	0	.346	.348
	Provo (Pio)	R	.299	22	77	14	23	6	3	0	18	11	13	1	.387	.455
2002	Cedar Rapids (Mid)	A	.287	128	491	75	141	41	3	10	73	40	75	7	.346	.444
2003	Rancho Cucamonga (Cal)	A	.323	97	378	73	122	28	3	11	54	35	74	5	.384	.500
	Arkansas (TL)	AA	.284	24	95	19	27	11	0	2	14	12	16	1	.364	.463
2004	Arkansas (TL)	AA	.227	117	432	57	98	24	3	14	55	49	102	2	.310	.394
2005	Salt Lake (PCL)	AAA	.276	112	427	78	118	26	3	21	73	42	85	4	.340	.499
	Los Angeles (AL)	MLB	.333	5	3	1	1	0	0	0	0	0	1	0	.333	.333
MAJOR LEAGUE TOTALS			.333	5	3	1	1	0	0	0	0	0	1	0	.333	.333
MINOR LEAGUE TOTALS			.279	507	1923	317	536	137	15	58	290	191	369	20	.346	.456

5 JERED WEAVER RHP

BILL MITCHELL

Born: Oct. 4, 1982. **B-T:** R-R. **Ht.:** 6-7. **Wt.:** 205. **Drafted:** Long Beach State, 2004 (1st round). **Signed by:** Bobby DeJardin.

Weaver had one of the most dominant college seasons ever in 2004, going 15-1, 1.63 with 213 strikeouts in 144 innings to win Baseball America's College Player of the Year award. The top-rated prospect for the 2004 draft, he dropped to the Angels at No. 12 because of concerns about his price tag. Weaver held out until a week before the 2005 draft before agreeing to a $4 million bonus. He reached Double-A in his pro debut and later pitched in the Arizona Fall League and the Olympic regional qualifier. His brother Jeff has won 78 big league games in the last seven seasons. Weaver owns the system's best combination of present stuff and command. His arm is loose and fast, and he works from a three-quarters arm slot slightly higher than that of his brother. He relies on a nasty 86-90 mph two-seam fastball, a 91-93 mph four-seamer, a slider and a changeup. He pitches with tenacity and passion. Weaver's command is more notable than his stuff, and some scouts think he's more of a No. 3 starter than a headliner. He's an extreme flyball pitcher and is vulnerable to homers. His slider grades as an above-average pitch at times but lack consistency. A free spirit, he loses his cool at times. Some hyperbolic scouting reports declared Weaver as big league-ready when he entered pro ball, but he is at least another half-season away from joining the Angels. He'll open 2006 in Triple-A.

Year	Club (League)	Class	W	L	ERA	G	GS	CG	SV	IP	H	R	ER	HR	BB	SO	AVG
2005	Rancho Cucamonga (Cal)	A	4	1	3.82	7	7	0	0	33	25	18	14	3	7	49	.205
	Arkansas (TL)	AA	3	3	3.98	8	8	0	0	43	43	22	19	5	19	46	.250
MINOR LEAGUE TOTALS			7	4	3.91	15	15	0	0	76	68	40	33	8	26	95	.231

6 NICK ADENHART RHP

BILL MITCHELL

Born: Aug. 24, 1986. **B-T:** R-R. **Ht.:** 6-4. **Wt.:** 190. **Drafted:** HS— Williamsport, Md., 2004 (14th round). **Signed by:** Dan Radcliff.

When his senior season started in 2004, Adenhart ranked with Homer Bailey as the top high school pitching prospects in the nation. But a few weeks before the draft, Adenhart blew out his elbow and had Tommy John surgery. Seemingly headed for North Carolina, he signed for $710,000 as a 14th-round pick. He came back stronger and earlier than expected in 2005, rating as the No. 2 prospect in the Rookie-level Arizona League. Before his injury, Adenhart was lauded for his polished three-pitch repertoire, the life on his stuff and his mound presence. He already has regained much of his arm strength, pitching at 89-92 mph and touching 94 with his fastball. His 11-to-5 curveball has sharp, late break. He showed a feel for a circle changeup that has potential to be a third plus offering. His quick recovery is indicative of his strong work ethic and make-up. Adenhart's delivery can be deceiving, because his arm action is smooth and easy and the ball jumps out of his hand. But he throws across his body, which helps the life on his pitches but also led to his injury. His command isn't yet as sharp as it was, but that's typical of the Tommy John recovery. If his stuff and command come all the way back, Adenhart has a higher ceiling than Jered Weaver. The Angels won't rush Adenhart and may wait until the weather warms up at low Class A Cedar Rapids before letting him start his 2006 season.

Year	Club (League)	Class	W	L	ERA	G	GS	CG	SV	IP	H	R	ER	HR	BB	SO	AVG
2004	Did not play—Injured																
2005	Angels (AZL)	R	2	3	3.68	13	12	1	0	44	39	26	18	0	24	52	.245
	Orem (Pio)	R	1	0	0.00	1	1	0	0	6	3	1	0	0	0	7	.143
MINOR LEAGUE TOTALS			3	3	3.24	14	13	1	0	50	42	27	18	0	24	59	.233

7 KENDRY MORALES 1B

BILL MITCHELL

Born: June 20, 1983. **B-T:** B-R. **Ht.:** 6-1. **Wt.:** 220. **Signed:** Cuba, 2004. **Signed by:** Clay Daniel/Tito Perez.

Omar Linares and Morales are the best position players developed in post-revolution Cuba. The government banned him from baseball after repeated attempts to defect, and he finally succeeded in June 2004. The Angels boasted Morales would compete for a spot on their Opening Day roster when they signed him in November 2004 to a six-year major league contract that could be worth as much as $10 million. Visa problems prevented him from attending spring training, however. After arriving in the United States in May, he homered on his first swing and quickly earned a promotion from high Class A to Double-A. He also batted .380 in the Arizona Fall League. Morales is a mature hitter with above-average power from both sides of the plate. He repeats his swing better from the left side, where he's more comfortable and makes better contact. When he keeps his hands and weight back, he generates good bat speed and power to all fields. Most scouts say Morales lacks the agility and athleticism to play anywhere but first base. While his hands are OK, his footwork needs to improve. He has too much movement in his swing, and tends to drift and reach for offspeed stuff. He can get pull-conscious. With Darin Erstad and Casey Kotchman ahead of him at first base, Morales might spend another full season in the minors, probably in Triple-A. His best fit with the Angels could be as a DH.

Year	Club (League)	Class	AVG	G	AB	R	H	2B	3B	HR	RBI	BB	SO	SB	OBP	SLG
2005	Rancho Cucamonga (Cal)	A	.344	22	90	18	31	3	0	5	17	6	11	0	.400	.544
	Arkansas (TL)	AA	.306	74	281	47	86	12	0	17	54	17	43	2	.349	.530
MINOR LEAGUE TOTALS			.315	96	371	65	117	15	0	22	71	23	54	2	.362	.534

8 ALBERTO CALLASPO 2B

SHAWN DAVIS

Born: April 19, 1983. **B-T:** B-R. **Ht.:** 5-11. **Wt.:** 173. **Signed:** Venezuela, 2001. **Signed by:** Carlos Porte/Amador Arias.

The Angels shifted Callaspo back to second base last year after he played shortstop in 2004. For the second year in a row, he was the toughest player in the minors to strike out, going 20.4 plate appearances per whiff in 2005. He moved up to Triple-A in July and finished the season riding a 15-game hitting streak. Callaspo improved his bat control and situational hitting last season, integral ingredients to his value as a prospect. He bunts well, and while he doesn't have the aptitude Howie Kendrick possesses, he's a solid hitter. A switch-hitter, Callaspo has a more fluid swing and fewer holes from the left side. The Angels believe Callaspo can handle shortstop, but he's a natural second baseman with smooth, easy motions and an outstanding feel for the position. He has an average, accurate arm, soft hands, good range and a smooth double-play pivot. While he has some raw pop, Callaspo is primarily a singles hitter who doesn't walk much because he makes effortless contact. He hit just .241 from the right side in 2005. Though he has average speed, he lacks basestealing savvy and was caught 13 times in 24 tries last year. Callaspo's chances of becoming Los Angeles' second baseman of the future look limited because his bat just doesn't compare to Kendrick's. The two and Erick Aybar should be teammates in Triple-A this year, so Callaspo may play a variety of positions. If he's not traded, his destiny with the Angels may be as a utilityman.

Year	Club (League)	Class	AVG	G	AB	R	H	2B	3B	HR	RBI	BB	SO	SB	OBP	SLG
2001	Angels (DSL)	R	.356	66	275	55	98	11	4	2	39	22	16	14	.403	.447
2002	Provo (Pio)	R	.338	70	299	70	101	16	10	3	60	17	14	13	.374	.488
2003	Cedar Rapids (Mid)	A	.327	133	514	86	168	38	4	2	67	42	28	20	.377	.428
2004	Arkansas (TL)	AA	.284	136	550	76	156	29	2	6	48	47	25	15	.338	.376
2005	Arkansas (TL)	AA	.297	89	350	53	104	8	0	10	49	28	17	9	.346	.406
	Salt Lake (PCL)	AAA	.316	50	212	28	67	21	2	1	31	10	13	2	.345	.448
MINOR LEAGUE TOTALS			.315	544	2200	368	694	123	22	24	294	166	113	73	.362	.424

9 JOE SAUNDERS   LHP

Born: June 16, 1981. **B-T:** L-L. **Ht.:** 6-2. **Wt.:** 200. **Drafted:** Virginia Tech, 2002 (1st round). **Signed by:** Chris McAlpin.

The Angels passed up Scott Kazmir to take Saunders with the 12th overall pick in 2002 and signed him for $1.825 million. After his first pro summer, he was diagnosed with tears in his rotator cuff and labrum, which didn't require surgery but cost him the entire 2003 season. He steadily has climbed the ladder since, making his major league debut last August. Saunders doesn't have overpowering stuff, relying instead on command and feel. His best pitch is a deceptive changeup that he uses to hold righthanders at bay. His fastball sits at 91-92 mph and he can run it in on hitters effectively. He can cut his fastball, or add and subtract velocity as needed. He repeats his delivery well and hasn't missed a start since coming back from his shoulder injury. Saunders doesn't have a put-away breaking ball and will need to improve the depth and quality of his slurvy curveball to become a No. 3 starter. Saunders likely will open 2006 in Triple-A to work further on his curveball. The only other lefthanded pitcher on the 40-man roster was recent trade acquisition J.C. Romero, so the Angels could need Saunders in a relief role.

Year	Club (League)	Class	W	L	ERA	G	GS	CG	SV	IP	H	R	ER	HR	BB	SO	AVG
2002	Provo (Pio)	R	2	1	3.62	8	8	0	0	32	40	19	13	1	11	21	.305
	Cedar Rapids (Mid)	A	3	1	1.88	5	5	0	0	29	16	7	6	2	9	27	.168
2003	Did not play—Injured																
2004	Rancho Cucamonga (Cal)	A	9	7	3.41	19	19	0	0	106	106	49	40	13	23	76	.265
	Arkansas (TL)	AA	4	3	5.77	8	8	0	0	39	51	26	25	5	14	25	.327
2005	Arkansas (TL)	AA	7	4	3.49	18	18	2	0	106	107	52	41	9	32	80	.263
	Salt Lake (PCL)	AAA	3	3	4.58	9	9	1	0	55	65	38	28	3	21	29	.304
	Los Angeles (AL)	MLB	0	0	7.74	2	2	0	0	9	10	8	8	3	4	4	.270
MAJOR LEAGUE TOTALS			0	0	7.74	2	2	0	0	9	10	8	8	3	4	4	.270
MINOR LEAGUE TOTALS			28	19	3.76	67	67	3	0	366	385	191	153	33	110	258	.274

10 TOMMY MENDOZA   RHP

Born: Aug. 18, 1987. **B-T:** R-R. **Ht.:** 6-2. **Wt.:** 185. **Drafted:** HS— Miami, 2005 (4th round). **Signed by:** Mike Silvestri.

Mendoza was primarily a catcher until his sophomore year at Miami's Monsignor Pace High, and he pitched behind White Sox supplemental first-round pick Gio Gonzalez as a junior in 2004. The Angels took Mendoza in the fifth round last June and signed him for $159,000. He was an Arizona League all-star, then jumped all the way to high Class A and pitched 10 scoreless innings. Mendoza dominated older hitters in the California League with a 92-94 mph fastball that touched 95 all summer. He has good life on his heater and controls it well. His curveball has the makings of a plus breaking ball, while his cutter, slider and changeup all have potential. He's mature beyond his years. When Mendoza tries to overpower hitters, he can leave himself vulnerable by missing up in the zone. He rushes his delivery at times and gets offline, hurting his control. After his fastball and curve, his other pitches lack consistency. His debut eased the sting of Los Angeles' failure to sign its third- (Sean O'Sullivan) and fourth-rounders (Brian Matusz). Better than expected, Mendoza will open 2006 in low Class A.

Year	Club (League)	Class	W	L	ERA	G	GS	CG	SV	IP	H	R	ER	HR	BB	SO	AVG
2005	Angels (AZL)	R	3	3	1.55	13	4	0	0	52	42	14	9	1	13	56	.221
	Rancho Cucamonga (Cal)	A	1	0	0.00	2	1	0	1	10	4	0	0	0	0	12	.121
MINOR LEAGUE TOTALS			4	3	1.30	15	5	0	1	62	46	14	9	1	13	68	.206

11 MIKE NAPOLI   C

Born: Oct. 3, 1981. **B-T:** R-R. **Ht.:** 6-0. **Wt.:** 205. **Drafted:** HS—Pembroke Pines, Fla., 2000 (17th round). **Signed by:** Todd Claus.

After missing much of 2003 with a torn labrum in his right shoulder that required surgery, Napoli was barely on the Angels' radar because of uncertainty he could handle catching full-time. He returned in 2004 to post a career high in home runs and followed suit last season, leading the Texas League in homers and RBIs. Napoli's lone plus tool is tremendous raw power. He generates good bat speed and can drive balls with loft and carry to all fields. His swing gets long at times, as a loop in his load makes it hard for him to hit the top half of the ball. He made adjustments last season, but will always struggle with hard stuff above his hands and probably never will hit for average. Napoli swings and misses often but balances his strikeouts by drawing a lot of walks. He's not much of an athlete or runner, but he has improved behind the plate. His arm strength is average and he has smoothed out his footwork and exchange, allowing him to lead the Texas League by catching 47 percent of basestealers last year. He blocks and receives adequately and calls a good game. Napoli is streaky and he's not polished enough defensively to warrant everyday play as a catcher, as he also topped TL backstops with 14 errors and 13 passed balls. Nevertheless, he could make a nice big league backup to Jeff Mathis in the future. Napoli will spend 2006 in Triple-A.

Year	Club (League)	Class	AVG	G	AB	R	H	2B	3B	HR	RBI	BB	SO	SB	OBP	SLG
2000	Butte (Pio)	R	.231	10	26	3	6	2	0	0	3	8	8	1	.400	.308
2001	Rancho Cucamonga (Cal)	A	.200	7	20	3	4	0	0	1	4	8	11	0	.429	.350
	Cedar Rapids (Mid)	A	.232	43	155	23	36	10	1	5	18	24	54	3	.341	.406
2002	Cedar Rapids (Mid)	A	.251	106	362	57	91	19	1	10	50	62	104	6	.362	.392
2003	Rancho Cucamonga (Cal)	A	.267	47	165	28	44	10	1	4	26	23	32	5	.364	.412
2004	Rancho Cucamonga (Cal)	A	.282	132	482	94	136	29	4	29	118	88	166	9	.393	.539
2005	Arkansas (TL)	AA	.237	131	439	96	104	22	2	31	99	88	140	12	.372	.508
MINOR LEAGUE TOTALS			.255	476	1649	304	421	92	9	80	318	301	515	36	.373	.468

12   MARK TRUMBO   1B

Born: Jan. 16, 1986. **B-T:** R-R. **Ht.:** 6-4. **Wt.:** 220. **Drafted:** HS—Villa Park, Calif., 2004 (18th round). **Signed by:** Tim Corcoran.

Trumbo was a high-profile two-way high school standout whom most teams preferred as a pitcher, but they viewed him as impossible to lure away from his commitment to Southern California. The Angels took him in the 18th round of the 2004 draft and got him signed for $1.425 million, easily a record for his round. After watching him launch a pair of shots off the rocks in left-center field at Angels Stadium during a workout, they opted to play him as a corner infielder. Trumbo's pro debut was lackluster, though he did lead the Pioneer League in doubles and ranked second in extra-base hits. His arm strength and raw power are plus tools, and when his timing is on he can mash towering home runs. He's a pull hitter but began using the middle of the field more late in the season. His swing lacks fluidity, as he hits with a dead lower half. Trumbo also needs to improve his plate discipline and pitch recognition. If he learns how to create better leverage in his swing, he could develop into a 40-homer threat. Trumbo is a well-below-average runner and isn't athletic. Los Angeles originally planned on using him at third base but ultimately assigned him to first base. He could develop into an average defender there, though his range is limited and his hands are adequate at best. He throws better than most first basemen, having touched 96 mph as a prep pitcher. Trumbo should get his first taste of full-season ball in low Class A this year.

Year	Club (League)	Class	AVG	G	AB	R	H	2B	3B	HR	RBI	BB	SO	SB	OBP	SLG
2005	Orem (Pio)	R	.274	71	299	45	82	23	1	10	45	21	67	2	.322	.458
MINOR LEAGUE TOTALS			.274	71	299	45	82	23	1	10	45	21	67	2	.322	.458

13   TREVOR BELL   RHP

Born: Oct. 12, 1986. **B-T:** L-R. **Ht.:** 6-2. **Wt.:** 180. **Drafted:** HS—La Crescenta, Calif., 2005 (1st round supplemental). **Signed by:** Tim Corcoran.

Los Angeles' top pick (a supplemental first-rounder for the loss of free agent Troy Percival) last June, Bell had the most intriguing background in the 2005 draft. He has worked as an actor, appearing in commercials for Hot Wheels, Kellogg's and Old Navy. Show business comes naturally to him, as his grandfather Bob was a folk hero on Chicago television for more than two decades as Bozo the Clown. His mother Barbara is a television casting director. On the diamond, Bell was Baseball America's choice as the top 14-year-old player in the nation in 2001. He leveled off a bit as a high school sophomore and junior, and he was known more for his prodigious power than his arm until last spring, when his velocity climbed into the mid-90s. In one start in front of Angels GM Bill Stoneman, Bell struck out 10 in a complete-game two-hitter and was throwing 90 mph in the final inning. He took awhile to come to terms for a $925,000 bonus, so he pitched just eight innings in Rookie ball. Bell threw 90-93 mph with plus life on his fastball in his limited debut, and he showed the ability to get his solid curveball over for strikes even when he fell behind in the count. Both his curve and his slider have the potential to be above-average pitches, though he probably will be better off if he focuses on one breaking ball. He has started to gain a feel for a circle changeup. Bell has a thick, muscular body and his delivery isn't without effort. He most likely will begin the 2006 season in extended spring training and join Rookie-level Orem at midseason.

Year	Club (League)	Class	W	L	ERA	G	GS	CG	SV	IP	H	R	ER	HR	BB	SO	AVG
2005	Angels (AZL)	R	0	0	4.50	4	4	0	0	8	10	4	4	0	3	7	.313
MINOR LEAGUE TOTALS			0	0	4.50	4	4	0	0	8	10	4	4	0	3	7	.313

14 P.J. PHILLIPS   SS/3B

Born: Sept. 23, 1986. **B-T:** R-R. **Ht.:** 6-3. **Wt.:** 170. **Drafted:** HS—Stone Mountain, Ga., 2005 (2nd round). **Signed by:** Chris McAlpin.

Phillips received plenty of exposure as a junior when he played on the same high school and summer league teams as Chris Nelson, the eighth overall pick in the 2004 draft by the Rockies. Redan High (Stone Mountain, Ga.) also has produced big leaguers Milt Hill, Wally Joyner, Brandon Phillips (P.J.'s older brother) and Everett Stull. Athleticism runs in the Phillips family, as his sister Porsha is one of the nation's top women's basketball recruits. After signing for $505,000 as a second-round pick last June, he'll have to pack on muscle on his skinny frame to improve his strength and stamina. It's easy to dream on Phillips' tools and projection. He's athletic and his quick hands make him a good defender and a better hitter. His raw power grades as 60 on the 20-80 scouting scale. Balls jump off his bat and his swing has good leverage. His stroke gets long at times, and like many hitters straight out of high school, his pitch recognition and plate discipline are rudimentary. He has a plus arm and adequate range. He profiles more as a third baseman because he figures to add at least 25 pounds as he matures. He'll be an average runner down the line. He has championship-caliber makeup and a strong work ethic. He might require 2,000 or more at-bats in the minors before he's ready for the majors, but the Angels believe he'll be worth the wait. They'll be patient with him and could play him at Orem this year.

Year	Club (League)	Class	AVG	G	AB	R	H	2B	3B	HR	RBI	BB	SO	SB	OBP	SLG
2005	Angels (AZL)	R	.291	49	182	25	53	6	6	1	24	9	53	13	.328	.407
MINOR LEAGUE TOTALS			.291	49	182	25	53	6	6	1	24	9	53	13	.328	.407

15 STEVEN SHELL   RHP

Born: March 10, 1983. **B-T:** R-R. **Ht.:** 6-5. **Wt.:** 190. **Drafted:** HS—El Reno, Okla., 2001 (3rd round). **Signed by:** Kevin Ham.

After making strides with his command and pitches while repeating high Class A in 2004, Shell failed to follow suit early last season. He seemed to turn a corner in July, when he threw a shutout and later had a strong seven-inning outing in front of Angels GM Bill Stoneman, but then had more difficulty in August. Shell has a prototypical pitcher's body, delivery and arm speed. But his stuff leveled off in 2005. His fastball sat near 90 mph, though it had good late life and armside run. His curveball was just average, rather than slightly above-average as it had been in the past. He still hasn't grasped the feel of his changeup, a below-average offering, and his splitter is equally inconsistent. Shell tends to lose confidence easily and stops attacking hitters. His command suffers and his breaking ball flattens out when he drops his arm slot from his high three-quarters angle. He still has a ceiling of a No. 3 starter, but he'll have to return to Double-A in 2006.

Year	Club (League)	Class	W	L	ERA	G	GS	CG	SV	IP	H	R	ER	HR	BB	SO	AVG
2001	Angels (AZL)	R	1	0	0.00	3	0	0	0	4	1	0	0	0	2	3	.077
	Provo (Pio)	R	0	3	7.16	14	4	0	1	38	52	31	30	3	15	33	.331
2002	Cedar Rapids (Mid)	A	11	4	3.72	22	21	1	0	121	119	59	50	12	26	86	.255
2003	Rancho Cucamonga (Cal)	A	6	8	4.24	22	21	1	0	127	123	66	60	13	26	100	.248
2004	Rancho Cucamonga (Cal)	A	12	7	3.59	28	28	2	0	165	151	76	66	19	40	190	.248
2005	Arkansas (TL)	AA	10	8	4.56	27	27	1	0	160	175	90	81	18	58	126	.283
MINOR LEAGUE TOTALS			40	30	4.20	116	101	5	1	615	621	322	287	65	167	538	.263

16 HAINLEY STATIA   SS

Born: Jan. 19, 1986. **B-T:** B-R. **Ht.:** 5-11. **Wt.:** 162. **Drafted:** HS—Lake Worth, Fla., 2004 (9th round). **Signed by:** Mike Silvestri.

A native of Curacao, Statia raised his profile when he moved to South Florida, where area scout Mike Silvestri spotted him and signed him for a $90,000 bonus as a ninth-round pick in 2004. His debut was delayed by baseball's visa shortage, and he began his pro career in 2005 as a 19-year-old in high Class A. Statia held his own there before starring in the Pioneer League. He has pure shortstop actions with supple hands and an innate ability to read balls off the bat. He led all PL shortstops with a .959 fielding percentage. His arm is strong and accurate, even when he throws on the move. His bat is behind his glove but still is promising. Statia has a good approach at the plate and makes consistent contact from both sides, spraying line drives to all fields. He doesn't project to hit for much power, though he can sting the ball into the gaps. He needs to refine his strike-zone judgment. He's a slightly above-average runner. He speaks four languages, indicative of his outstanding makeup and thirst for instruction. He should climb the minor league ladder one step at a time, opening 2006 in low Class A.

Year	Club (League)	Class	AVG	G	AB	R	H	2B	3B	HR	RBI	BB	SO	SB	OBP	SLG
2005	Rancho Cucamonga (Cal)	A	.245	23	106	12	26	2	0	1	8	5	13	6	.286	.292
	Orem (Pio)	R	.300	68	277	44	83	17	6	2	41	23	40	12	.360	.426
MINOR LEAGUE TOTALS			.285	91	383	56	109	19	6	3	49	28	53	18	.340	.389

17 JOSE ARREDONDO RHP

Born: March 30, 1984. **B-T:** R-R. **Ht.:** 6-0. **Wt.:** 170. **Signed:** Dominican Republic, 2002. **Signed by:** Leo Perez.

No relation to fellow Angels minor league righthander Felipe Arredondo, Jose was hitting .191 as a shortstop in the Arizona League in 2004 when his arm strength compelled the organization to move him to the mound. He has been a fast study, molding a simple delivery and three-quarters arm slot. Arredondo is undersized but has a quick arm and runs his fastball up to 97 mph, pitching most of the 2005 season at 91-93. His control improved as the season went on, but he doesn't have much feel for the strike zone. His secondary stuff has a ways to go, too, though his slider and changeup have some potential. He tends to get around his slider and slows his arm speed on his changeup. Los Angeles added him to its 40-man roster during the offseason rather than risk losing him in the Rule 5 draft. He'll continue his development in low Class A this year as a starter to get him innings, but his long-term role may be as a reliever.

Year	Club (League)	Class	AVG	G	AB	R	H	2B	3B	HR	RBI	BB	SO	SB	OBP	SLG
2002	Angels (DSL)	R	.256	33	90	12	23	5	1	0	11	5	19	0	.333	.302
2003	Angels (DSL)	R	.273	41	154	18	42	4	3	0	19	7	25	9	.338	.302
2004	Angels (AZL)	R	.191	28	68	6	13	2	0	0	3	1	13	1	.221	.203
MINOR LEAGUE TOTALS			.250	102	312	36	78	11	4	0	33	13	57	10	.311	.281

Year	Club (League)	Class	W	L	ERA	G	GS	CG	SV	IP	H	R	ER	HR	BB	SO	AVG
2004	Angels (AZL)	R	0	0	2.93	8	0	0	1	12	14	10	4	1	4	14	.280
2005	Arkansas (TL)	AA	0	0	3.40	5	0	0	0	5	5	2	2	0	4	4	.278
	Orem (Pio)	R	5	0	4.19	15	13	0	0	69	76	34	32	4	20	60	.285
MINOR LEAGUE TOTALS			5	0	3.96	28	13	0	1	86	95	46	38	5	28	78	.284

18 STEPHEN MAREK RHP

Born: Sept. 3, 1983. **B-T:** L-R. **Ht.:** 6-2. **Wt.:** 220. **Drafted:** San Jacinto (Texas), JC, D/F 2004 (40th round). **Signed by:** Chad McDonald.

Though Marek was used primarily in relief at San Jacinto (Texas) Junior College, he touched 94 mph during the 2004 Junior College World Series, earning most outstanding pitcher honors and convincing the Angels to select him as a draft-and-follow pick. He led the Jayhawk League with eight saves that summer, then continued to build buzz by hitting 98 mph during fall practice. After continuing to light up radar guns last spring, he signed for $800,000. Marek could have gone as high as the second round had he re-entered the draft, and he also had a scholarship to pitch at Texas. Marek has a sturdy build and good mechanics, enabling him to pitch from a good downward plane. He pitched out of the Orem rotation after signing and ran his fastball up to 96 before his velocity tapered off to 89-90 by the end of the summer. He made strides in learning how to pitch in the process, though he's a work in progress and his command has a ways to go. His curveball is a sharp, two-plane hammer that comes in at 78-82 mph. He experimented with a changeup, which presently is a below-average pitch. Marek is still raw, especially for a 22-year-old, and San Jac gave scouts pause by redshirting him in his first year and never warming to him as a starter. He profiles best as a set-up man and should open 2006 in low Class A.

Year	Club (League)	Class	W	L	ERA	G	GS	CG	SV	IP	H	R	ER	HR	BB	SO	AVG
2005	Orem (Pio)	R	1	3	4.50	15	14	0	0	66	74	37	33	7	25	55	.292
MINOR LEAGUE TOTALS			1	3	4.50	15	14	0	0	66	74	37	33	7	25	55	.292

19 NICK GORNEAULT OF

Born: April 19, 1979. **B-T:** R-L. **Ht.:** 6-3. **Wt.:** 220. **Drafted:** Massachusetts, 2001 (19th round). **Signed by:** Jon Bunnell.

Gorneault wasn't heavily scouted as an amateur, but he has hit his way into contention for a major league job since signing as a 19th-round pick in 2001. His homer totals have risen in each of his five years as a pro and he led the Triple-A Pacific Coast League in RBIs last season. Each year, Gorneault wins over more detractors with his natural ability to whip the barrel of the bat through the hitting zone. His swing is unorthodox, but when he centers balls they have tremendous carry and backspin. His stroke lacks much loft, yet he still has been a consistent home run threat. He continues to tighten his strike zone and has more-than-acceptable discipline for a power hitter. The rest of Gorneault's game is fine as well. He has average speed to go with superior baserunning skills. He's a solid outfielder with an accurate arm. He can play all three outfield positions, though he lacks the range of a first-rate center fielder. The Angels are well-stocked with outfielders, so Gorneault is probably looking at another season in Triple-A.

Year	Club (League)	Class	AVG	G	AB	R	H	2B	3B	HR	RBI	BB	SO	SB	OBP	SLG
2001	Provo (Pio)	R	.315	54	168	38	53	12	4	6	30	11	65	5	.373	.542
2002	Cedar Rapids (Mid)	A	.289	103	346	60	100	17	7	10	53	30	106	12	.346	.465
2003	Rancho Cucamonga (Cal)	A	.321	97	374	67	120	36	2	14	72	20	82	11	.363	.540
	Arkansas (TL)	AA	.345	29	110	19	38	6	4	2	19	8	25	2	.395	.527
2004	Arkansas (TL)	AA	.281	130	495	91	139	28	4	21	81	45	128	7	.341	.481
	Salt Lake (PCL)	AAA	.316	6	19	4	6	1	0	1	5	1	7	0	.381	.526
2005	Salt Lake (PCL)	AAA	.293	130	488	106	143	25	11	26	108	58	119	7	.366	.549
MINOR LEAGUE TOTALS			.300	549	2000	385	599	125	32	80	368	173	532	44	.358	.514

20 TOMMY MURPHY   OF

Born: Aug. 27, 1979. **B-T:** R-R. **Ht.:** 6-0. **Wt.:** 185. **Drafted:** Florida Atlantic, 2000 (3rd round). **Signed by:** Todd Claus.

Murphy has been one of the best athletes in the system since signing in 2000 as a third-round pick out of Florida Atlantic, the highest draft choice in school history. But he struggled to make consistent contract as a pro and slid off the prospect map. In 2005, his sixth minor league season and second in Double-A, things finally started to click for Murphy. He didn't reach triple digits in strikeouts for the first time in five years and set career highs in several categories, earning a spot on the 40-man roster after the season. Murphy has five solid tools, most prominently plus speed and arm strength. He has a line-drive stroke from both sides of the plate and gap power. While he did a better job at the plate last year, he still swings and misses too often to profile as a leadoff man. Changeups especially give him trouble. The Angels moved Murphy from shortstop to the outfield in 2004 and he has developed into one of the system's best defensive outfielders. He played some center last year but spent most of his time at Arkansas in right field in deference to Reggie Willits. Murphy's athletic ability should carry him to the big leagues as a valuable and versatile reserve.

Year	Club (League)	Class	AVG	G	AB	R	H	2B	3B	HR	RBI	BB	SO	SB	OBP	SLG
2000	Boise (NWL)	A	.225	55	213	38	48	18	1	2	25	15	52	14	.291	.347
2001	Cedar Rapids (Mid)	A	.204	74	280	32	57	15	3	4	31	16	94	7	.259	.321
	Rancho Cucamonga (Cal)	A	.190	50	200	16	38	8	0	0	11	5	69	7	.214	.230
2002	Cedar Rapids (Mid)	A	.270	128	485	72	131	20	2	3	48	40	115	31	.324	.338
2003	Rancho Cucamonga (Cal)	A	.267	132	565	74	151	25	6	11	43	31	138	24	.313	.391
2004	Arkansas (TL)	AA	.260	129	477	77	124	24	6	7	45	36	113	27	.310	.379
2005	Arkansas (TL)	AA	.288	135	500	85	144	24	11	17	76	43	97	26	.346	.482
MINOR LEAGUE TOTALS			.255	703	2720	394	693	134	29	44	279	186	678	136	.306	.374

21 RAFAEL RODRIGUEZ   RHP

Born: Sept. 24, 1984. **B-T:** R-R. **Ht.:** 6-1. **Wt.:** 175. **Signed:** Dominican Republic, 2001. **Signed by:** Leo Perez.

Since the Angels signed Rodriguez for $780,000 in 2001, his arm has been both electric and erratic. He has spent much of the last three years in low Class A, in part because of a tender elbow ruined his 2004 season. He bounced back to log a career-high 146 innings in 2005, when he pitched well at Cedar Rapids but got shelled in his first taste of high Class A. Rodriguez needs to learn how to pitch because he tries to pile up strikeouts instead of just worrying about getting outs. He toned down his maximum-effort delivery but still struggles to repeat his arm slot, often getting under his breaking ball. But when Rodriguez is going well, he's exciting to watch. His fastball sits between 90-94 mph, and his out pitch is a mid-80s slider with depth. He doesn't always stay on top of his slider, however. If he can't refine his changeup, he'll likely end up in the bullpen. It's time for Rodriguez to turn a corner in his development, or risk slipping into obscurity. He should head back to high Class A in 2006, though he could pitch at Double-A with a strong spring training.

Year	Club (League)	Class	W	L	ERA	G	GS	CG	SV	IP	H	R	ER	HR	BB	SO	AVG
2002	Angels (AZL)	R	2	1	3.99	8	8	0	0	38	37	19	17	4	20	50	.255
	Provo (Pio)	R	1	1	5.95	6	6	0	0	26	26	17	17	3	14	25	.268
2003	Cedar Rapids (Mid)	A	10	11	4.31	26	26	1	0	144	129	85	69	7	59	100	.236
2004	Angels (AZL)	R	0	2	6.47	4	4	0	0	15	18	12	11	1	5	13	.295
	Cedar Rapids (Mid)	A	1	5	6.49	7	7	0	0	33	36	27	24	5	19	35	.273
2005	Cedar Rapids (Mid)	A	5	2	2.79	13	13	0	0	74	61	24	23	5	27	74	.220
	Rancho Cucamonga (Cal)	A	4	4	6.75	14	14	0	0	72	84	58	54	11	33	44	.292
MINOR LEAGUE TOTALS			23	26	4.80	78	78	1	0	403	391	242	215	36	177	341	.253

22 BOBBY WILSON C

Born: April 8, 1983. **B-T:** R-R. **Ht.:** 6-0. **Wt.:** 205. **Drafted:** St. Petersburg (Fla.) CC, D/F, 2002. **Signed by:** Tom Kotchman.

Wilson played with Casey Kotchman and was the MVP on Seminole (Fla.) High's 2001 national championship team. The Giants drafted him in the 26th round that June, but he headed to St. Petersburg Community College, where he became the 2003 Florida junior college player of the year. Wilson's stubby body and unorthodox swing mechanics never have impressed scouts. But he makes sharp contact and has improved his catch-and-throw skills since signing as a draft-and-follow for $150,000. He has good raw power and plenty of upside, especially now that he's improved behind the plate. He has average arm strength and has worked hard to improve his exchange and footwork, allowing him to throw out 45 percent of basestealers in 2005. He tends to overswing, but can really launch the bat head through the hitting zone. He has a good feel for the strike zone. He shortened his leg kick during last season, which improved his balance and shortened his swing. Like most catchers, he's a below-average runner. Wilson will move up to Double-A in 2006.

Year	Club (League)	Class	AVG	G	AB	R	H	2B	3B	HR	RBI	BB	SO	SB	OBP	SLG
2003	Provo (Pio)	R	.284	57	236	36	67	12	0	6	62	18	31	0	.329	.411
2004	Cedar Rapids (Mid)	A	.268	105	396	45	106	23	0	8	64	30	55	4	.320	.386
2005	Rancho Cucamonga (Cal)	A	.290	115	466	66	135	32	1	14	77	30	61	2	.333	.453
MINOR LEAGUE TOTALS			.281	277	1098	147	308	67	1	28	203	78	147	6	.328	.420

23 SEAN RODRIGUEZ SS

Born: April 26, 1985. **B-T:** R-R. **Ht.:** 6-0. **Wt.:** 195. **Drafted:** HS—Miami, 2003 (3rd round). **Signed by:** Mike Silvestri.

Rodriguez transferred from Coral Park High to Braddock High in South Florida prior to his senior season when he was shifted from shortstop to center field to make room for Robert Valido, a fourth-round pick by the White Sox in 2003. The Angels popped Rodriguez in the third round and signed him for $400,000. His best tool is his plus arm, but between the organization's depth at shortstop and Rodriguez' lack of pure shortstop actions, he won't play there much longer. His arm, solid glove and instincts—honed by his father Johnny, a minor league batting coach in the Marlins system—would play in center field, at second base and perhaps best behind the plate. Rodriguez lacks confidence at the plate and hasn't performed well against good pitching since signing. He generates good bat speed thanks to his strong wrists, but he changes his approach from at-bat to at-bat. He has an eye for drawing walks, but he can improve his pitch recognition. He strikes out too much for a player with modest power, average speed and good baserunning instincts. Rodriguez' makeup and versatility bode well for his future, though he may repeat low Class A to start 2006.

Year	Club (League)	Class	AVG	G	AB	R	H	2B	3B	HR	RBI	BB	SO	SB	OBP	SLG
2003	Angels (AZL)	R	.269	54	216	30	58	8	5	2	25	14	37	11	.332	.380
2004	Cedar Rapids (Mid)	A	.250	57	196	35	49	8	4	4	17	18	54	14	.333	.393
	Provo (Pio)	R	.338	64	225	64	76	14	4	10	55	51	62	9	.486	.569
2005	Cedar Rapids (Mid)	A	.250	124	448	86	112	29	3	14	45	78	85	27	.371	.422
MINOR LEAGUE TOTALS			.272	299	1085	215	295	59	16	30	142	161	238	61	.383	.439

24 PETER BOURJOS OF

Born: March 31,1987. **B-T:** R-R. **Ht.:** 6-1. **Wt.:** 165. **Drafted:** HS—Scottsdale, Ariz., 2005 (10th round). **Signed by:** John Gracio.

Scouting director Eddie Bane has shown a willingness to gamble in the two drafts he has run for the Angels. In 2004, he took Jered Weaver 12th overall and the team successfully waited out his exorbitant bonus demands, and Los Angeles also landed late-round studs such as Nick Adenhart and Mark Trumbo. The Angels' most successful gamble in 2005 was Bourjos, a multitooled center fielder who had committed to Grand Canyon (Ariz.) University. Los Angeles took him in the 10th round and signed him late in the summer for $325,000, the equivalent of late third-round money. Bourjos' father Chris played briefly in the majors and scouts for the Brewers, and Peter has the instincts of someone who has grown up around the game. His best tool is his speed, as he's capable of running the 60-yard dash in 6.45 seconds. He's a righthanded hitter, and the Angels are toying with the idea of trying to make more use of his speed by having him switch-hit. Bourjos is a legitimate center fielder with 25-25 potential. Los Angeles can't wait to see him in game action, and he should make his pro debut in Rookie ball in June.

Year	Club (League)	Class	AVG	G	AB	R	H	2B	3B	HR	RBI	BB	SO	SB	OBP	SLG
2005	Did Not Play—Signed 2006 Contract															

25 RYAN MOUNT   SS

Born: Aug. 17, 1986. **B-T:** L-R. **Ht.:** 6-1. **Wt.:** 180. **Drafted:** HS—Chino Hills, Calif., 2005 (2nd round). **Signed by:** Tim Corcoran.

Mount didn't attend any major national showcases the year before and wasn't near the top of many follow lists entering his senior season, and UC Irvine and Cal State Fullerton were the only schools that had recruited him. But teams flocked to see him as he emerged last spring, and he wound up with a $615,000 bonus. Scouts were mixed on him. Those who like him say he'll be an offensive middle infielder with the ability to remain at shortstop. Mount didn't hit much in his pro debut, but he showed the foundation of a good approach and power potential. He has plus speed and arm strength, and the Angels believe he could develop into their best defender from the 2005 draft. Other clubs saw Mount as more of a fifth-rounder, evaluating him as a 'tweener who lacked the defense for shortstop or the bat for third base. With Hainley Statia ticketed for low Class A, Mount will begin 2006 in extended spring training before trying to get his bat going at Orem.

Year	Club (League)	Class	AVG	G	AB	R	H	2B	3B	HR	RBI	BB	SO	SB	OBP	SLG
2005	Angels (AZL)	R	.216	29	102	15	22	7	1	1	17	17	31	4	.325	.333
MINOR LEAGUE TOTALS			.216	29	102	15	22	7	1	1	17	17	31	4	.325	.333

26 JAKE WOODS   LHP

Born: Sept. 3, 1981. **B-T:** L-L. **Ht.:** 6-1. **Wt.:** 190. **Drafted:** Bakersfield (Calif.) JC, 2001 (3rd round). **Signed by:** Bobby DeJardin.

Los Angeles brought lefthander Dusty Bergman to spring training in 2005 in hopes he would give them a reliable lefthanded option out of their bullpen. He wasn't healthy, so Woods got the call, breaking camp with the Angels though his experience and track record suggested he needed another season in the minors. He held his own, earning his first major league win April 23 against Oakland before spending most of the second half in Triple-A. Woods doesn't have an overpowering pitch, and the inconsistency of his curveball eventually got him in trouble in the majors. His curve looked like a possible out pitch when he signed as a third-round pick in 2001, but it has slipped since. Woods' best pitch now is a lively 90-93 mph fastball. His command is only average, and when he misses his spots he gets hit hard. He'll need to develop a reliable second pitch, either his curve or his change-up, before he gets another call to the majors.

Year	Club (League)	Class	W	L	ERA	G	GS	CG	SV	IP	H	R	ER	HR	BB	SO	AVG
2001	Provo (Pio)	R	4	3	5.29	15	14	1	0	65	70	41	38	6	29	84	.275
2002	Cedar Rapids (Mid)	A	10	5	3.05	27	27	1	0	153	128	66	52	12	54	121	.228
2003	Rancho Cucamonga (Cal)	A	12	7	3.99	28	28	2	0	171	178	90	76	9	54	109	.270
2004	Arkansas (TL)	AA	9	2	2.70	14	14	1	0	90	86	29	27	5	19	60	.259
	Salt Lake (PCL)	AAA	6	4	6.07	15	14	1	0	83	107	67	56	13	42	60	.317
2005	Los Angeles (AL)	MLB	1	1	4.55	28	0	0	0	28	30	18	14	7	8	20	.270
	Salt Lake (PCL)	AAA	3	1	5.89	15	5	0	0	37	50	27	24	7	17	36	.314
MAJOR LEAGUE TOTALS			1	1	4.55	28	0	0	0	28	30	18	14	7	8	20	.270
MINOR LEAGUE TOTALS			44	22	4.10	114	102	6	0	599	619	320	273	52	215	470	.269

27 BOB ZIMMERMANN   RHP

Born: Nov. 17, 1981. **B-T:** R-R. **Ht.:** 6-5. **Wt.:** 245. **Drafted:** Southwest Missouri State, 2003 (4th round). **Signed by:** Brian Bridges.

The Angels have several hard-throwing yet inconsistent righthanders who project as back-of-the-rotation starters or middle relievers. Zimmermann is the most advanced of a group that includes Ryan Aldridge, Mitchell Arnold, Billy Edwards and Von Stertzbach. Part of Southwest Missouri State's first-ever College World Series team in 2003, Zimmermann uses a maximum-effort delivery that he struggles to repeat. He tends to pitch from a high, three-quarters arm slot, but a lower angle gives him better deception and life on his pitches. His fastball, which sits between 90-95 mph, has sinking action. His slider is his best offspeed offering, but neither it nor his changeup is especially reliable. Zimmermann has a closer's mentality, but unless he improves his command and secondary stuff, he won't be more than a set-up man. The Angels have been patient with him, but it's time to test him against more advanced hitters in Double-A. Los Angeles declined to protect Zimmermann on its 40-man roster following the season and he went unselected in the major league Rule 5 draft.

Year	Club (League)	Class	W	L	ERA	G	GS	CG	SV	IP	H	R	ER	HR	BB	SO	AVG
2003	Provo (Pio)	R	4	2	4.50	11	10	0	0	48	57	29	24	4	8	37	.285
2004	Cedar Rapids (Mid)	A	4	6	2.26	53	0	0	24	68	48	21	17	3	21	82	.192
2005	Rancho Cucamonga (Cal)	A	6	8	3.32	52	0	0	17	60	50	25	22	3	27	62	.229
MINOR LEAGUE TOTALS			14	16	3.23	116	10	0	41	175	155	75	63	10	56	181	.232

28 REGGIE WILLITS
OF

Born: May 30, 1981. **B-T:** B-R. **Ht.:** 5-11. **Wt.:** 185. **Drafted:** Oklahoma, 2003 (7th round). **Signed by:** Kevin Ham.

A senior sign out of Oklahoma after he led the Big 12 Conference with 37 steals in 2003, Willits has moved quickly as a pro—both on the bases and in his development. He already has reached Double-A and has swiped 98 bags in 317 pro games. He's not the only pro athlete in his family, as his sister Wendi played basketball in the WNBA. The primary center fielder on Arkansas' playoff team last summer, he drew Lenny Dykstra and Rusty Greer comparisons from manager Tom Gamboa for his all-out, gamer approach. Willits isn't a slap hitter, but he has limited power and is at his best when he keeps the ball on the ground to utilize his plus speed. He improved his plate discipline in 2005 but still needs to make more contact to become a big league leadoff man. He worked on his bunting in winter ball in Puerto Rico. Balls down and in give him trouble, especially when he hits from the right side of the plate, and he has trouble handling good changeups as well. He's a solid-average center fielder with an average arm. Willits had laser eye surgery before spring training in 2004, and a second eye operation after last season to decrease his sensitivity to light. He'll advance to Triple-A in 2006.

Year	Club (League)	Class	AVG	G	AB	R	H	2B	3B	HR	RBI	BB	SO	SB	OBP	SLG
2003	Provo (Pio)	R	.300	59	230	53	69	14	4	4	27	37	52	14	.410	.448
2004	Rancho Cucamonga (Cal)	A	.283	135	526	99	149	17	5	5	52	73	112	44	.373	.363
2005	Arkansas (TL)	AA	.304	123	487	75	148	23	6	2	46	54	78	40	.377	.388
MINOR LEAGUE TOTALS			.295	317	1243	227	367	54	15	11	125	164	242	98	.382	.389

29 NICK GREEN
RHP

Born: Aug. 20, 1984. **B-T:** R-R. **Ht.:** 6-4. **Wt.:** 200. **Drafted:** Darton (Ga.) JC, 2004 (35th round). **Signed by:** Chris McAlpin.

Green wasn't even recruited by Abraham Baldwin Junior College in his hometown of Tifton, Ga., so he went to Darton Junior College in nearby Albany. He turned down $80,000 from the Astros when they drafted him in the 11th round after his freshman season in 2003, and wound up signing for $1,500 as an Angels 35th-rounder in 2004. Green joined the Cedar Rapids bullpen last May and moved into the rotation for good in late July, going 3-1, 2.72 in his final seven starts. His main weapon is a changeup that rates as the best in the organization. One scout graded it a 70 on the 20-80 scale because of its late, hard sink. Green gets ahead in the count with an 88-91 mph fastball. He also has a serviceable breaking ball and a splitter. He has good mechanics, though his delivery has some effort to it. He throws strikes but will have to improve his location against more advanced hitters. Green will remain a starter in high Class A this year.

Year	Club (League)	Class	W	L	ERA	G	GS	CG	SV	IP	H	R	ER	HR	BB	SO	AVG
2004	Provo (Pio)	R	4	3	4.03	17	10	0	0	51	56	28	23	4	20	44	.275
2005	Cedar Rapids (Mid)	A	3	3	3.58	26	8	1	2	101	95	47	40	11	14	74	.249
MINOR LEAGUE TOTALS			7	6	3.73	43	18	1	2	152	151	75	63	15	34	118	..258

30 GUSTAVO ESPINOZA
LHP

Born: Sept. 9, 1986. **B-T:** L-L. **Ht.:** 6-0. **Wt.:** 170. **Signed:** Venezuela, 2004. **Signed by:** Carlos Porte.

Any Venezuelan lefthander with a feel for a changeup is going to receive Johan Santana comparisons, and Espinoza is no exception. That's getting way ahead of the game, but he had a promising U.S. debut in 2005, leading the Arizona League in strikeouts. Rookie-ball hitters had no chance against his changeup because he throws it with the same arm speed and arm slot as his fastball. Espinoza repeats his delivery well, has a clean arm action and shows a feel for pitching despite his youth. He works off an average fastball at 87-91 mph, with the potential for more velocity as he grows stronger. He also has some bite on his breaking ball. The Angels could challenge Espinoza with a jump to low Class A if he performs well in spring training.

Year	Club (League)	Class	W	L	ERA	G	GS	CG	SV	IP	H	R	ER	HR	BB	SO	AVG
2004	Angels (DSL)	R	6	2	1.37	14	14	3	0	92	46	17	14	2	16	105	.146
2005	Angels (AZL)	R	5	3	3.84	13	12	0	0	70	72	36	30	3	12	78	.257
	Orem (Pio)	R	0	0	9.00	1	0	0	0	2	3	2	2	0	0	1	.333
	Cedar Rapids (Mid)	A	1	0	1.70	1	1	0	0	5	5	2	1	1	1	3	.238
MINOR LEAGUE TOTALS			12	5	2.49	29	27	3	0	170	126	57	47	6	29	187	.202

LOS ANGELES
DODGERS

BY **ALAN MATTHEWS**

When the 2005 season began, Chavez Ravine was full of optimism. The Dodgers were fresh off their National League West division title in 2004 and a popular pick to return to the playoffs. But after a promising 12-2 start, their season slipped away and they finished at 71-91, the franchise's second-worst record (63-99 in 1992) since moving from Brooklyn in 1958.

Injuries and unsuccessful acquisitions spelled doom in the second season under general manager Paul DePodesta. Los Angeles players missed 1,150 games due to injury, the most on any Dodgers club in two decades.

While Jeff Kent (two years, $19 million) produced as expected, DePodesta's two biggest free-agent acquisitions—J.D. Drew (five years, $55 million) and Derek Lowe (four years, $36 million)—were disappointments. Meanwhile, Kent and Milton Bradley engaged in an ugly clubhouse feud.

All the chaos looked mild compared to the front-office turmoil that began the day after the season ended. DePodesta and manager Jim Tracy opted to part ways, with Tracy surfacing with the Pirates.

DePodesta's search for a new manager abruptly ended four weeks later when owner **Frank McCourt** fired him. While McCourt didn't detail the reasons for the dismissal, he said his criteria for a new GM included communication skills and the ability to evaluate talent. The Dodgers turned to Ned Colletti, assistant GM for the Giants under Brian Sabean for the last nine years.

Asked when he took the job if the Dodgers were capable of putting a division winner on the field, Colletti smiled and said, "No." So he brought in a raft of veteran talent, headed by free-agent shortstop Rafael Furcal, to immediately patch big league holes.

More important, though, he made few long-term commitments to the older players. That's because thanks to the deepest and most talented farm system in baseball, the Dodgers could be on the cusp of becoming perennial contenders.

Double-A Jacksonville cruised to the Southern League championship (the first for a Dodgers affiliate since 2002). The first five players on this prospect list—righthander Chad Billingsley, third baseman Andy LaRoche, shortstop Joel Guzman, catcher Russell Martin and righty Jonathan Broxton—starred for the Suns, Baseball America's Minor League Team of the Year.

Most of the Dodgers' top prospects have been signed since Logan White became scouting director following the 2001 season, though the 2005 draft doesn't initially appear as promising as his first three efforts. Los Angeles forfeited its first-round pick for signing Lowe and spent its first pick on Tennessee righthander Luke Hochevar. After a summer with little give and take, Hochevar switched agents in September and agreed to a $2.98 million bonus, then reneged and falsely accused White of trying to coerce him into signing. The negotiations don't appear salvageable.

TOP 30 PROSPECTS

1. Chad Billingsley, rhp	16. Julio Pimentel, rhp
2. Andy LaRoche, 3b	17. Blake Johnson, rhp
3. Joel Guzman, ss/of	18. Greg Miller, lhp
4. Russell Martin, c	19. Josh Wall, rhp
5. Jonathan Broxton, rhp	20. Juan Rivera, ss
6. Scott Elbert, lhp	21. Cory Dunlap, 1b
7. Blake DeWitt, 3b	22. Willie Aybar, 3b/2b
8. Matt Kemp, of	23. Travis Denker, 2b
9. Etanislau Abreu, 2b	24. Xavier Paul, of
10. Chin-Lung Hu, ss	25. Ivan DeJesus Jr., ss
11. James Loney, 1b	26. Josh Bell, 3b
12. Justin Orenduff, rhp	27. Jamie Hoffmann, of
13. Chuck Tiffany, lhp	28. Steve Schmoll, rhp
14. Hong-Chih Kuo, lhp	29. Chris Malone, rhp
15. Delwyn Young, 2b/of	30. Anthony Raglani, of

ORGANIZATION OVERVIEW

General manager: Ned Colletti. **Farm director:** Terry Collins. **Scouting director:** Logan White.

2005 PERFORMANCE

Class	Team	League	W	L	Pct.	Finish*	Manager
Majors	Los Angeles	National	71	91	.438	14th (16)	Jim Tracy
Triple-A	Las Vegas 51s	Pacific Coast	57	86	.399	16th (16)	Jerry Royster
Double-A	Jacksonville Suns	Southern	79	61	.564	+4th (10)	John Shoemaker
High A	Vero Beach Dodgers	Florida State	77	56	.579	3rd (12)	Scott Little
Low A	Columbus Catfish	South Atlantic	57	79	.419	14th (16)	Travis Barbary
Rookie	Ogden Raptors	Pioneer	39	37	.513	3rd (8)	Juan Bustabad
Rookie	GCL Dodgers	Gulf Coast	25	29	.463	7th (12)	Luis Salazar
OVERALL 2005 MINOR LEAGUE RECORD			334	348	.490	22nd (30)	

*Finish in overall standings (No. of teams in league). +League champion.

ORGANIZATION LEADERS

BATTING
*Minimum 250 at-bats
*AVG	Flores, Jose, Las Vegas	.336
R	Donovan, Todd, Jacksonville/Las Vegas	96
H	Young, Delwyn, Jacksonville/Las Vegas	162
TB	LaRoche, Andy, Jacksonville/Vero Beach	263
2B	Young, Delwyn, Jacksonville/Las Vegas	37
3B	Donovan, Todd, Jacksonville/Las Vegas	11
	Hoffmann, Jamie, Columbus/Vero Beach	11
HR	LaRoche, Andy, Jacksonville/Vero Beach	30
RBI	LaRoche, Andy, Jacksonville/Vero Beach	94
BB	Denker, Travis, Columbus/Vero Beach	82
SO	Guzman, Joel, Jacksonville	128
SB	Donovan, Todd, Jacksonville/Las Vegas	65
*OBP	Flores, Jose, Las Vegas	.435
*SLG	Kemp, Matt, Vero Beach	.569

PITCHING
#Minimum 75 innings
W	Billingsley, Chad, Jacksonville	13
L	Jackson, Edwin, Jacksonville/Las Vegas	11
#ERA	Alvarez, Carlos, Columbus/Jacksonville	2.03
G	Dannemiller, Beau, Jacksonville/Las Vegas	56
CG	Billingsley, Chad, Jacksonville	2
	Malone, Chris, Columbus	2
SV	Alexander, Mark, Vero Beach	23
IP	Billingsley, Chad, Jacksonville	146
	Stults, Eric, Jacksonville/Las Vegas	146
BB	Weeden, Brandon, Columbus	69
SO	Billingsley, Chad, Jacksonville	162

BEST TOOLS

Best Hitter for Average	Blake DeWitt
Best Power Hitter	Joel Guzman
Best Strike-Zone Discipline	Russell Martin
Fastest Baserunner	Trayvon Robinson
Best Athlete	Matt Kemp
Best Fastball	Jonathan Broxton
Best Curveball	Chad Billingsley
Best Slider	Jonathan Broxton
Best Changeup	Julio Pimentel
Best Control	Chad Billingsley
Best Defensive Catcher	Russell Martin
Best Defensive Infielder	Ching-Lung Hu
Best Infield Arm	Andy LaRoche
Best Defensive Outfielder	Cody Ross
Best Outfield Arm	Xavier Paul

PROJECTED 2009 LINEUP

Catcher	Russell Martin
First Base	James Loney
Second Base	Blake DeWitt
Third Base	Andy LaRoche
Shortstop	Rafael Furcal
Left Field	J.D. Drew
Center Field	Milton Bradley

Right Field	Joel Guzman
No. 1 Starter	Chad Billingsley
No. 2 Starter	Brad Penny
No. 3 Starter	Scott Elbert
No. 4 Starter	Derek Lowe
No. 5 Starter	Justin Orenduff
Closer	Eric Gagne

LAST YEAR'S TOP 20 PROSPECTS

1. Joel Guzman, ss
2. Chad Billingsley, rhp
3. Edwin Jackson, rhp
4. James Loney, 1b
5. Andy LaRoche, 3b
6. Russell Martin, c
7. Greg Miller, lhp
8. Blake DeWitt, 3b
9. Jonathan Broxton, rhp
10. Chuck Tiffany, lhp
11. Scott Elbert, lhp
12. Julio Pimentel, rhp
13. Chin-Lung Hu, ss
14. Dioner Navarro, c
15. Yhency Brazoban, rhp
16. Xavier Paul, of
17. Joel Hanrahan, rhp
18. Delwyn Young, 2b
19. Cory Dunlap, 1b
20. Mike Megrew, lhp

TOP PROSPECTS OF THE DECADE

Year	Player, Pos.	2005 Org.
1996	Karim Garcia, of	Orix (Japan)
1997	Paul Konerko, 3b	White Sox
1998	Paul Konerko, 1b	White Sox
1999	Angel Pena, c	Out of baseball
2000	Chin-Feng Chen, of	Dodgers
2001	Ben Diggins, rhp	Brewers
2002	Ricardo Rodriguez, rhp	Rangers
2003	James Loney, 1b	Dodgers
2004	Edwin Jackson, rhp	Dodgers
2005	Joel Guzman, ss/of	Dodgers

TOP DRAFT PICKS OF THE DECADE

Year	Player, Pos.	2005 Org.
1996	Damian Rolls, 3b	Yankees
1997	Glenn Davis, 1b	Out of baseball
1998	Bubba Crosby, of	Yankees
1999	Jason Repko, ss/of	Dodgers
2000	Ben Diggins, rhp	Brewers
2001	Brian Pilkington, rhp (2nd round)	Dodgers
2002	James Loney, 1b	Dodgers
2003	Chad Billingsley, rhp	Dodgers
2004	Scott Elbert, lhp	Dodgers
2005	*Luke Hochevar, rhp	Unsigned

*Has not signed.

ALL-TIME LARGEST BONUSES

Joel Guzman, 2001		$2,250,000
Ben Diggins, 2000		$2,200,000
Hideo Nomo, 1995		$2,000,000
Scott Elbert, 2004		$1,575,000
Kazuhisa Ishii, 2002		$1,500,000
James Loney, 2002		$1,500,000

MINOR LEAGUE DEPTH CHART

Los Angeles Dodgers
Rank: 1

STRENGTH: Third base. Andy LaRoche may force Blake DeWitt to move to second base.

WEAKNESS: Center field. The only position where the Dodgers lack a true impact talent.

*Depth charts prepared by **John Manuel** and **Chris Kline**. Numbers in parentheses indicate prospect rankings.*

LF
Delwyn Young (15)
Anthony Raglani (30)
Justin Ruggiano
Scott Van Slyke
Jon Weber

CF
Jamie Hoffmann (27)
Trayvon Robinson

RF
Joel Guzman (3)
Matt Kemp (8)
Xavier Paul (24)
Sergio Pedroza
Cody Ross

3B
Andy LaRoche (2)
Blake DeWitt (7)
Willy Aybar (22)
Josh Bell (26)
Russ Mitchell
Eduardo Perez
Carlos Santana

SS
Chin-Lung Hu (10)
Juan Rivera (20)
Ivan DeJesus Jr. (25)
David Nicholson

2B
Etanislao Abreu (9)
Travis Denker (23)

1B
James Loney (11)
Cory Dunlap (21)
David Sutherland
Cole Bruce
Dan Batz

C
Russell Martin (4)
Juan Apodaca
Chris Westervelt

RHP

Starters	Relievers
Chad Billingsley (1)	Jonathan Broxton (5)
Justin Orenduff (12)	Steve Schmoll (28)
Julio Pimentel (16)	Chris Malone (29)
Blake Johnson (17)	Casey Hoorelbeke
Josh Wall (19)	Ramon Troncoso
Javy Guerra	Franquelis Osoria
Jesus Castillo	Miguel Ramirez
Mario Alvarez	Jumbo Diaz
Jonathan Meloan	Mark Alexander
Eric Hull	Howar Zuleta
Joel Hanrahan	
Jordan Pratt	
Kyle Wilson	
Steve Johnson	

LHP

Starters	Relievers
Scott Elbert (6)	Hong-Chih Kuo (14)
Chuck Tiffany (13)	Greg Miller (18)
Miguel Sanfler	Carlos Alvarez
Brent Leach	Orlando Rodriguez
	Derek Thompson
	Marlon Arias
	Eric Stults
	Ramon Parades

DRAFT ANALYSIS

2005

Best Pro Debut: LHP Brent Leach (6) led the Rookie-level Pioneer League with a 2.43 ERA and went 5-3 with 77 strikeouts in 67 innings. Leach, who had Tommy John surgery in 2003, has an 87-92 mph fastball and a slurve that can be a plus pitch at times.

Best Athlete: OF Scott Van Slyke (15) is a 6-foot-5, 210-pounder with good all-around tools and instincts in the mold of his father Andy, a former all-star outfielder. OF Trayvon Robinson (10), who's much more raw, offers plenty of speed and also some power potential.

Best Pure Hitter: SS Ivan DeJesus Jr. (2) doesn't have much power but he's an effective line-drive hitter. The Dodgers also expect big things from 3B Josh Bell (4).

Best Raw Power: OFs Sergio Pedroza (3) and Drew Locke (19) reached double figures in homers during their debuts, but neither can drive the ball as consistently far as Bell can. He's a switch-hitter with natural loft in his swing from both sides of the plate.

Fastest Runner: The Dodgers clocked Robinson at 6.29 seconds in the 60-yard dash during instructional league. OF Adam Godwin (11), who also has well above-average wheels, led NCAA Division I with 84 steals in 93 attempts at Troy last spring.

Best Defensive Player: DeJesus' father played 15 years in the majors because of his shortstop defense, and Ivan Jr. has a slick glove as well.

Best Fastball: RHP Josh Wall (3) touches 93 mph and has the room to add a lot of strength to his frame. RHP Jon Meloan (5) pitches at 90-92 mph. The Dodgers saw draft-and-follow RHP Jimmy Gilbert (33 in 2005) hit 97 mph and some clubs clocked him at

CLIFF WELCH

DeJesus

100 last spring before he had Tommy John surgery.

Best Breaking Ball: Meloan's knuckle-curve is the best at this point; Wall's curveball will surpass it if he can learn to command the pitch. RHP Steve Johnson's (11) curve could wind up as the best of the bunch.

Most Intriguing Background: DeJesus and Van Slyke aren't the only sons of big leaguers in this crop. Johnson's father Dave pitched in the majors. Unsigned LHP Jake Debus' (39) uncle Jon was the Dodgers' bullpen coach.

Closest To The Majors: Being a lefty with a likelihood of winding up in the bullpen makes Leach the choice over Meloan.

Best Late-Round Picks: Johnson and Van Slyke.

The One Who Got Away: RHP Luke Hochevar (1) should have been the answer to Best Fastball (90-95 mph), Best Breaking Ball (hard slider) and Closest To The Majors. But after switching agents and agreeing to a $2.98 million bonus, he abruptly reneged and returned to Scott Boras. Hochevar and Boras subsequently charged the Dodgers with trying to coerce him into signing a bad deal, and it appears unlikely the two sides will reach an agreement.

Assessment: Getting Hochevar as a supplemental first-rounder would have been a steal. The Dodgers hope that getting players such as Bell, Johnson and Van Slyke in later rounds will help lessen the sting.

2004 LHP Scott Elbert (1), 3B Blake DeWitt (1) and RHP Justin Orenduff (1) are good prospects who get overshadowed in a deep system. Unsigned LHP/OF Joe Savery (15) and LHP David Price (19) look like first-round picks for 2006. *GRADE: A*

2003 RHP Chad Billingsley (1) and 3B Andy LaRoche (39) are the two best prospects in the organization— and two of the best in the game. LHP Chuck Tiffany (2) and OF Matt Kemp (6) have a lot of upside as well. *GRADE: A*

2002 1B James Loney (1) and oft-injured LHP Greg Miller (1) leveled off, but RHP Jonathan Broxton (2) and C Russell Martin (17) pick up the slack. If the Dodgers signed RHP Luke Hochevar (39), they could have saved themselves some headaches in 2005. *GRADE: A*

2001 RHP Edwin Jackson (6) once looked like a star and made up for the lack of a first-round pick. Now it looks like L.A. did a better job of identifying future NFL players in OF Cedric Benson (12) and 3B Brooks Bollinger (50). *GRADE: C*

Draft analysis prepared by Jim Callis. Numbers in parentheses indicate draft rounds.

CHAD
BILLINGSLEY

RHP

RICK BATTLE

Born: July 29, 1984.
Ht.: 6-2. **Wt.:** 215.
Bats: R. **Throws:** R.
Drafted: HS—Defiance, Ohio, 2003 (1st round).
Signed by: Marty Lamb.

Billingsley was just 13 when parents of teammates gasped in disbelief—not over his pitching prowess, but because of the amount he was throwing. After reading "Nolan Ryan's Pitching Bible," Billingsley's father Jim began playing catch and long-tossing with his son before and after games, even if he was pitching that day. The routine helped Billingsley build the arm strength that led to mid-80s velocity by the time he was 15. A talented three-sport athlete, he ruptured his spleen during football practice as a freshman in high school, prompting him to concentrate on baseball. He and Dodgers lefty Chuck Tiffany were USA Baseball teammates in 2002, when Billingsley won the bronze-medal game at the World Junior Championships in Quebec. Two more top Dodgers prospects, catcher Russell Martin (Canada) and shortstop Chin-Lung Hu (Taiwan) also played in the tournament. One of just two high school righthanders taken in the first round of the 2003 draft, Billingsley has justified his $1.375 million bonus. He skipped past low Class A and has ranked as the top pitching prospect in his league in each of his three pro seasons. He first reached Double-A as a 19-year-old in 2004 and excelled there in 2005, combining with Jonathan Broxton on a no-hitter in the opening game of the Southern League playoffs.

Outside of being a couple of inches shorter than the blueprint, Billingsley is the prototypical power pitcher. He attacks hitters from a high three-quarters arm slot that he repeats well and allows him to pitch downhill. His frame is rigid and durable in the mold of Tom Seaver's. Billingsley made progress with his command, approach and all of his pitches in 2005. His 92-95 mph fastball has good life. Coming into the season, his 85-86 mph slider was considered the best in the organization, but his 82-84 mph curveball gives him a second plus breaking ball and could become Billingsley's primary out pitch. He made strides in 2005 repeating his arm slot on both breaking balls, allowing him to more consistently command them. He works diligently on all phases of pitching.

Billingsley has a tendency to overthrow, causing his fastball to straighten out and miss up in the zone. His arm occasionally struggles to catch up with his lower body, which results in a flatter slider. His changeup, which he grips like his fastball except for sliding his index finger to the side of the ball, improved but remains rudimentary. He can improve on his game management, as he occasionally allows the pace of a game to dictate his rhythm instead of slowing down when runners are on base.

Billingsley profiles as a No. 1 or 2 starter, something Los Angeles desperately needs. The big league pitching staff is littered with holes, and he'll get a chance to show what he can do in big league spring training. Depending on the philosophy of new general manager Ned Colletti, the Dodgers could start Billingsley in the back of their Opening Day rotation.

Year	Club (League)	Class	W	L	ERA	G	GS	CG	SV	IP	H	R	ER	HR	BB	SO	AVG
2003	Ogden (Pio)	R	5	4	2.83	11	11	0	0	54	49	24	17	0	15	62	.243
2004	Vero Beach (FSL)	A	7	4	2.35	18	18	0	0	92	68	32	24	6	49	111	.208
	Jacksonville (SL)	AA	4	0	2.98	8	8	0	0	42	32	16	14	1	22	47	.221
2005	Jacksonville (SL)	AA	13	6	3.51	28	26	2	0	146	116	60	57	12	50	162	.215
MINOR LEAGUE TOTALS			29	14	3.01	65	63	2	0	334	265	132	112	19	136	382	.218

2 ANDY LaROCHE 3B

Born: Sept. 13, 1983. **B-T:** R-R. **Ht.:** 6-1. **Wt.:** 200. **Drafted:** Grayson County (Texas) CC, 2003 (39th round). **Signed by:** Mike Leuzinger.

LaRoche signed for $1 million as a 39th-rounder in 2003, giving up the chance to attend Rice. Before the 2005 season, he and his brother, Braves first baseman Adam, bet a fishing trip on who would hit the most homers. Andy won, leading Dodgers farmhands in homers and RBIs. LaRoche plays the game with passion to go along with three plus tools. His power comes from a compact, controlled stroke. He turns around the liveliest fastballs. He's a solid defender and owns the organization's best infield arm. His instincts boost his average range and his hands are dependable. LaRoche's speed is his lone below-average tool. Most of his power is presently to the pull side, and he'll need to cover the outer half better as he faces more advanced pitching. His swing can get long at times. The Dodgers have an immediate need for an everyday third baseman, and LaRoche could fill it, though they'll probably ship him to Triple-A after he attends major league spring training.

Year	Club (League)	Class	AVG	G	AB	R	H	2B	3B	HR	RBI	BB	SO	SB	OBP	SLG
2003	Ogden (Pio)	R	.211	6	19	1	4	1	0	0	5	1	4	0	.238	.263
2004	Columbus (SAL)	A	.283	65	244	52	69	20	0	13	42	29	30	12	.375	.525
	Vero Beach (FSL)	A	.237	62	219	26	52	13	0	10	34	17	42	2	.295	.434
2005	Vero Beach (FSL)	A	.333	63	249	54	83	14	1	21	51	19	38	6	.380	.651
	Jacksonville (SL)	AA	.273	64	227	41	62	12	0	9	43	32	54	2	.367	.445
MINOR LEAGUE TOTALS			.282	260	958	174	270	60	1	53	175	98	168	22	.354	.513

3 JOEL GUZMAN SS/OF

Born: Nov. 24, 1984. **B-T:** R-R. **Ht.:** 6-5. **Wt.:** 225. **Signed:** Dominican Republic, 2001. **Signed by:** Pablo Peguero.

Signed for a club- and Dominican-record $2.25 million in 2001, Guzman used a breakout 2004 season to rank atop this list a year ago. He wasn't as consistent in 2005, teasing the Dodgers with potential he has yet to fully achieve. Yet he more than held his own and batted .316 during Jacksonville's playoff run. Guzman's hitting ability and power are well-above-average. He keeps his hands inside the ball well and uncorks tape-measure blasts when he makes contact. He's a dangerous low-ball hitter. A good athlete, he has a plus arm and average speed. Guzman's pitch recognition and plate discipline still need improvement, and like most big players he has a hole on the inner half. He lacks first-step quickness and his defensive actions are too long, which eventually will prompt a move from shortstop. He saw time at third base in 2005, but right field is his likely destination. With a strong spring, Guzman could win a corner-infield job in 2006, though a full year in Triple-A might be the best thing for his development. The Dodgers' signing of Rafael Furcal further reinforced the notion that Guzman isn't long for shortstop.

Year	Club (League)	Class	AVG	G	AB	R	H	2B	3B	HR	RBI	BB	SO	SB	OBP	SLG
2002	Dodgers (GCL)	R	.212	10	33	4	7	2	0	0	2	5	8	1	.316	.273
	Great Falls (Pio)	R	.252	43	151	19	38	8	2	3	27	18	54	5	.331	.391
2003	South Georgia (SAL)	A	.235	58	217	33	51	13	0	8	29	9	62	4	.263	.406
	Vero Beach (FSL)	A	.246	62	240	30	59	13	1	5	24	11	60	0	.279	.371
2004	Vero Beach (FSL)	A	.307	87	329	52	101	22	8	14	51	21	78	8	.349	.550
	Jacksonville (SL)	AA	.280	46	182	25	51	11	3	9	35	13	44	1	.325	.522
2005	Jacksonville (SL)	AA	.287	122	442	63	127	31	2	16	75	42	128	7	.351	.475
MINOR LEAGUE TOTALS			.272	428	1594	226	434	100	16	55	243	119	434	26	.323	.459

4 RUSSELL MARTIN C

Born: Feb. 15, 1983. **B-T:** R-R. **Ht.:** 5-11. **Wt.:** 202. **Drafted:** Chipola (Fla.) JC, 2002 (17th round). **Signed by:** Clarence Johns.

Area scout Clarence Johns (now with the Rockies) scouted Martin as a third baseman and immediately projected him to catch. Martin has become one of the best catching prospects in the game, thanks to his athleticism and ability to absorb instruction. Martin employs a patient approach at the plate and uses the entire field. His swing is compact and simple, he stays through the ball well and he's a good situational hitter. He's comfortable behind the plate and his blocking and receiving skills are advanced for such an inexperienced catcher. He has a strong, accurate arm, good footwork and an efficient exchange on throws. Martin has yet to show much power, though he can drive balls out of the park when he stays back. Some scouts believe he'll be a 15-20 homer threat in time. He has slightly below-average speed, but he's fast for a catcher and isn't afraid to take an extra base. Martin is similar to former Dodgers catcher Paul LoDuca, with better defensive skills and slightly less offensive ability. He'll probably begin 2006 in Triple-A but could reach Los Angeles in the second half.

Year	Club (League)	Class	AVG	G	AB	R	H	2B	3B	HR	RBI	BB	SO	SB	OBP	SLG
2002	Dodgers (GCL)	R	.286	41	126	22	36	3	3	0	10	23	18	7	.412	.357
2003	South Georgia (SAL)	A	.286	25	98	15	28	4	1	3	14	9	11	5	.343	.439
	Ogden (Pio)	R	.271	52	188	25	51	13	0	6	36	26	26	3	.368	.436
2004	Vero Beach (FSL)	A	.250	122	416	74	104	24	1	15	64	72	54	9	.368	.421
2005	Jacksonville (SL)	AA	.311	129	409	83	127	17	1	9	61	78	69	15	.430	.423
MINOR LEAGUE TOTALS			.280	369	1237	219	346	61	6	33	185	208	178	39	.391	.419

5 JONATHAN BROXTON
RHP

STEVE MOORE

Born: June 16, 1984. **B-T:** R-R. **Ht.:** 6-4. **Wt.:** 240. **Drafted:** HS—Waynesboro, Ga., 2002 (2nd round). **Signed by:** Lon Joyce.

Because of his powerful fastball-slider mix, dogged demeanor and husky frame, Broxton long has been targeted as a future closer. When Eric Gagne went down for the season, the Dodgers moved Broxton to the bullpen in Double-A and called him up five weeks later. Albert Pujols was his first strikeout victim. Broxton's heavy, sinking fastball climbed from 92-94 mph to 96-98 and he touched triple digits when he moved to the bullpen. His filthy slider sits near 88 mph with good tilt. He'll flash a two-seamer against lefthanders. His delivery is fluid. He pounds the strike zone. Broxton is still learning how to pitch and set up hitters. As a reliever, he didn't use his changeup often. It's a fringe-average pitch that could help him against lefties. He's a big man and will have to watch his weight closely. Gagne is expected to be ready for spring training and the Dodgers have a strong complement of relievers with more experience than Broxton. Nonetheless, he should win a job in their bullpen out of spring camp and become Gagne's eventual successor as closer.

Year	Club (League)	Class	W	L	ERA	G	GS	CG	SV	IP	H	R	ER	HR	BB	SO	AVG
2002	Great Falls (Pio)	R	2	0	2.76	11	6	0	2	29	22	9	9	0	16	33	.212
2003	South Georgia (SAL)	A	4	2	3.13	9	8	0	0	37	27	15	13	1	22	30	.208
2004	Vero Beach (FSL)	A	11	6	3.23	23	23	1	0	128	110	49	46	7	43	144	.237
	Jacksonville (SL)	AA	5	3	3.17	33	13	0	5	97	79	36	34	4	31	107	.223
2005	Los Angeles (NL)	MLB	1	0	5.93	14	0	0	0	14	13	11	9	0	12	22	.245
MAJOR LEAGUE TOTALS			1	0	5.93	14	0	0	0	14	13	11	9	0	12	22	.245
MINOR LEAGUE TOTALS			22	11	3.15	76	50	1	7	292	238	109	102	12	112	314	.226

6 SCOTT ELBERT
LHP

STEVE MOORE

Born: May 13, 1985. **B-T:** L-L. **Ht.:** 6-2. **Wt.:** 190. **Drafted:** HS—Seneca, Mo., 2004 (1st round). **Signed by:** Mitch Webster.

As a running back, Elbert amassed 2,449 rushing yards and scored 36 touchdowns as a junior before giving up football. The first prep lefty drafted in 2004, he signed for $1.575 million. After getting knocked around in his pro debut, he rated as the No. 1 prospect in the low Class A South Atlantic League in 2005. Elbert's stuff, body and makeup resemble Billingsley's, plus he's lefthanded. Elbert isn't as polished, but he has a live 88-93 mph fastball, a two-plane breaking ball and future-average changeup. He still was touching 94 in instructional league after his first full pro season. He has outstanding mound presence and an aggressive approach. Elbert's breaking ball, which lies somewhere between a curve and a slider, has inconsistent break. He tends to rush his lower half during his delivery and yanks his arm across his body, getting around and under the ball. He's still refining his circle changeup. While some scouts envision Elbert's power repertoire profiling best at the back of a bullpen, others believe his athleticism will allow him to repeat his delivery and become a frontline starter. He'll open 2006 at high Class A Vero Beach.

Year	Club (League)	Class	W	L	ERA	G	GS	CG	SV	IP	H	R	ER	HR	BB	SO	AVG
2004	Ogden (Pio)	R	2	3	5.26	12	12	0	0	50	47	33	29	5	30	45	.270
2005	Columbus (SAL)	A	8	5	2.66	25	24	1	0	115	83	37	34	8	57	128	.200
MINOR LEAGUE TOTALS			10	8	3.44	37	36	1	0	165	130	70	63	13	87	173	.221

7 BLAKE DeWITT 3B

Born: Aug. 20, 1985. **B-T:** L-R. **Ht.:** 5-11. **Wt.:** 195. **Drafted:** HS—Sikeston, Mo., 2004 (1st round). **Signed by:** Mitch Webster.

The consensus best high school hitting prospect in the 2004 draft class, DeWitt has justified the hype since signing for $1.2 million. A career .289 hitter, he finished his first full season by hitting .419 in high Class A and adding a homer in the Florida State League playoffs. DeWitt's classic lefthanded swing is smooth and controlled, and he repeats it easily. He sets his hands with a good load and generates good bat speed and leverage, the main ingredients of his plus raw power. He shows a feel for the strike zone, though he can improve his pitch recognition and ability to use all fields. He has a slightly above-average arm. DeWitt's swing gets loopy when he doesn't trust his hands. He tends to drift on breaking balls from lefthanders. He's a below-average runner and an adequate defensive third baseman. With Andy LaRoche ahead of him, DeWitt got a look at second base during instructional league and fared well. His instincts and aptitude should allow him to handle the move if necessary. He'll continue his development at third base in high Class A in 2006.

Year	Club (League)	Class	AVG	G	AB	R	H	2B	3B	HR	RBI	BB	SO	SB	OBP	SLG
2004	Ogden (Pio)	R	.284	70	299	61	85	19	3	12	47	28	78	1	.350	.488
2005	Columbus (SAL)	A	.283	120	481	61	136	31	3	11	65	34	79	0	.333	.428
	Vero Beach (FSL)	A	.419	8	31	4	13	3	0	1	7	1	3	0	.438	.613
MINOR LEAGUE TOTALS			.289	198	811	126	234	53	6	24	119	63	160	1	.344	.457

8 MATT KEMP OF

Born: Sept. 23, 1984. **B-T:** R-R. **Ht.:** 6-4. **Wt.:** 215. **Drafted:** HS—Midwest City, Okla., 2003 (6th round). **Signed by:** Mike Leuzinger.

Coming out of high school, Kemp was known mostly for his prowess on the basketball court, but the Dodgers liked his potential and signed him. He made as much improvement as anyone in the organization last season. He broke Adrian Beltre's Vero Beach franchise record for homers, though 22 of his 27 came at home. Kemp has big-time raw power and an aggressive approach. He has strong, quick hands and good bat speed. He kept collapsing on his back side early in 2005, causing him to pop up balls, but he adjusted and later hit the top half of the ball consistently. He shows good instincts in the outfield, above-average speed and a plus arm that plays in right field, where he likely will play more often as he fills out and loses some quickness. Kemp's pitch recognition is rudimentary at best. He's a dead-fastball hitter early in counts, making him vulnerable to changeups. He has a tendency to stride off the ball. Kemp's ceiling is considerable and he could develop into a .275 hitter with 25-30 homers annually. He'll continue refining his game at Double-A in 2006.

Year	Club (League)	Class	AVG	G	AB	R	H	2B	3B	HR	RBI	BB	SO	SB	OBP	SLG
2003	Dodgers (GCL)	R	.270	43	159	11	43	5	2	1	17	7	25	2	.298	.346
2004	Columbus (SAL)	A	.288	111	423	67	122	22	8	17	66	24	100	8	.330	.499
	Vero Beach (FSL)	A	.351	11	37	5	13	5	0	1	9	4	12	2	.405	.568
2005	Vero Beach (FSL)	A	.306	109	418	76	128	21	4	27	90	25	92	23	.349	.569
MINOR LEAGUE TOTALS			.295	274	1037	159	306	53	14	46	182	60	229	35	.336	.506

9 ETANISLAU ABREU 2B

Born: Nov. 13, 1984. **B-T:** B-R. **Ht.:** 5-11. **Wt.:** 172. **Signed:** Dominican Republic, 2002. **Signed by:** Pablo Peguero.

Abreu got off to a slow start until hitting coordinator George Hendrick and Vero Beach hitting coach Dan Radison moved him off the plate, which made Abreu less pull-conscious. He won the Florida State League batting title, thanks in part to a .438 average in June. Abreu has a live body and good tools across the board. His excellent hand-eye coordination allows him to make consistent sharp contact, and he has the strong wrists and bat speed to hit 15-plus homers annually in the big leagues. Defensively, Abreu has outstanding actions, soft hands, good range and enough arm to play shortstop. He is an above-average runner. Abreu needs to shorten his swing from the right side. He also has a tendency to get his front foot down a tick late when he swings. He must become more selective and get stronger. If the Dodgers move Blake DeWitt to second base, they could be faced with a difficult decision in 2008, as both he and Abreu profile as solid everyday players who should require no more than two more seasons in the minors. Abreu is headed to Double-A for now.

Year	Club (League)	Class	AVG	G	AB	R	H	2B	3B	HR	RBI	BB	SO	SB	OBP	SLG
2003	Dodgers (GCL)	R	.294	45	163	30	48	7	5	0	20	11	24	9	.358	.399
	Vero Beach (FSL)	A	.000	3	10	0	0	0	0	0	0	1	2	0	.091	.000
2004	Columbus (SAL)	A	.301	104	359	50	108	21	8	8	54	8	59	16	.326	.471
	Vero Beach (FSL)	A	.419	11	43	8	18	3	1	0	3	1	8	4	.435	.535
2005	Vero Beach (FSL)	A	.327	96	394	54	129	23	7	4	43	15	56	14	.356	.452
	Jacksonville (SL)	AA	.250	24	96	10	24	3	2	0	9	4	21	0	.284	.323
MINOR LEAGUE TOTALS			.307	283	1065	152	327	57	23	12	129	40	170	43	.341	.438

10 CHIN-LUNG HU   SS

Born: Feb. 2, 1984. **B-T:** R-R. **Ht.:** 5-9. **Wt.:** 150. **Signed:** Taiwan, 2003. **Signed by:** Pat Kelly/Vincent Liao.

One scout described Vero Beach's double-play combo of Hu and Etanislau Abreu as "the traveling circus show" because of their penchant for defensive highlights. Hu finished second to Abreu in the Florida State League batting race, then hit .343 for Taiwan at the World Cup tournament following the season. While Abreu is a plus defender, Hu is off the charts. He's slightly undersized but wiry strong with outstanding body control and has pure shortstop actions. His range is extraordinary, as are his hands, and his arm and speed are both above average. Hu made an adjustment at the plate, curtailing his leg kick, which improved his balance and prevented him from flying open during his swing. He has surprising pop, uses the whole field and has a feel for the strike zone. Hu has a tendency to bail on good breaking balls and he needs to become more selective. His small frame doesn't lend considerable room for projection. Hu should be a .270 hitter with 10 home runs annually in the big leagues. Ticketed for Double-A, he should reach Los Angeles by the end of 2007.

Year	Club (League)	Class	AVG	G	AB	R	H	2B	3B	HR	RBI	BB	SO	SB	OBP	SLG
2003	Ogden (Pio)	R	.305	53	220	34	67	9	5	3	23	14	33	5	.343	.432
2004	Columbus (SAL)	A	.298	84	332	58	99	15	4	6	25	20	50	17	.342	.422
	Vero Beach (FSL)	A	.307	20	75	12	23	4	1	0	10	5	6	3	.350	.387
2005	Vero Beach (FSL)	A	.313	116	470	80	147	29	1	8	56	19	40	23	.347	.430
MINOR LEAGUE TOTALS			.306	273	1097	184	336	57	11	17	114	58	129	48	.345	.425

11 JAMES LONEY   1B

Born: May 7, 1984. **B-T:** L-L. **Ht.:** 6-3. **Wt.:** 200. **Drafted:** HS—Missouri City, Texas, 2002 (1st round). **Signed by:** Chris Smith.

Following three seasons marred by wrist and finger injuries, Loney finally stayed healthy in 2005, leading the Southern League in games. But he hit just 11 homers, and scouts continue to wonder if he'll have enough power to be a regular first baseman in the big leagues. That's really the only question about his game. Loney has a good feel for the strike zone, patience, excellent hand-eye coordination and the willingness to uses the entire field. He shows raw power in batting practice, enough for his boosters to project that he'll eventually hit 25 homers on an annual basis, but it has yet to translate in games. Loney's swing gets long at times and he has a tendency to collapse his back side. If the power doesn't come, he could be a Mark Grace type, hitting for high average and playing Gold Glove defense at first base. Loney is athletic for his position, and as a two-way star in high school—he led Elkins High in suburban Houston to the 2002 national title—he drew more interest from pro clubs as a lefthanded pitcher. He has exceptional hands, plus arm strength and average range. He doesn't have a lot of speed but compensates with good instincts on the basepaths. Moving up to Triple-A in 2006, Loney will play in a Las Vegas ballpark conducive to homers.

Year	Club (League)	Class	AVG	G	AB	R	H	2B	3B	HR	RBI	BB	SO	SB	OBP	SLG
2002	Great Falls (Pio)	R	.371	47	170	33	63	22	3	5	30	25	18	5	.457	.624
	Vero Beach (FSL)	A	.299	17	67	6	20	6	0	0	5	6	10	0	.356	.388
2003	Vero Beach (FSL)	A	.276	125	468	64	129	31	3	7	46	43	80	9	.337	.400
2004	Jacksonville (SL)	AA	.238	104	395	39	94	19	2	4	35	42	75	5	.314	.327
2005	Jacksonville (SL)	AA	.284	138	504	74	143	31	2	11	65	59	87	1	.357	.419
MINOR LEAGUE TOTALS			.280	431	1604	216	449	109	10	27	181	175	270	20	.352	.411

12 JUSTIN ORENDUFF   RHP

Born: May 27, 1983. **B-T:** R-R. **Ht.:** 6-4. **Wt.:** 205. **Drafted:** Virginia Commonwealth, 2004 (1st round). **Signed by:** Clair Rierson.

The Dodgers received two compensation choices in the 2004 draft when the Yankees signed Paul Quantrill. Los Angeles used the first one on Blake DeWitt and then popped Orenduff five picks later. At 33rd overall, he was the highest-drafted college pitcher by the Dodgers since they took Ben Diggins 17th overall in 2000. Orenduff was tired and had a lackluster pro debut but rebounded to reach Double-A in his first full season. His slider is his bread and butter. He tends to overuse it, as he throws it for strikes more consistently than his other pitches, but it has sharp bite at 82-84 mph when he stays on top of it. His fastball sits near 91-92 mph with boring action. His changeup has some late fade, though he doesn't have great feel for it. Orenduff's delivery is smooth and he's at his best when working from a three-quarters arm slot. He drops his arm angle at times, hindering his overall command. He experienced shoulder inflammation late in 2005, and Los Angeles would like to see him improve his stamina. He has a ceiling as an innings-eating, middle-of-the-rotation starter and could open 2006 in Triple-A.

Year	Club (League)	Class	W	L	ERA	G	GS	CG	SV	IP	H	R	ER	HR	BB	SO	AVG
2004	Ogden (Pio)	R	2	3	4.74	13	10	0	0	44	46	26	23	4	25	57	.272
2005	Vero Beach (FSL)	A	5	3	2.24	12	12	1	0	60	35	21	15	3	26	81	.167
	Jacksonville (SL)	AA	5	2	4.07	14	13	0	0	66	59	33	30	6	24	65	.241
MINOR LEAGUE TOTALS			12	8	3.59	39	35	1	0	170	140	80	68	13	75	203	.225

13 CHUCK TIFFANY   LHP

Born: Jan. 25, 1985. **B-T:** L-L. **Ht.:** 6-1. **Wt.:** 195. **Drafted:** HS—Charter Oak, Calif., 2003 (2nd round). **Signed by:** Scott Groot.

To lure Tiffany away from Cal State Fullerton, it cost the Dodgers $1.1 million, the second-highest bonus given to a second-rounder in 2003. He began the 2005 season with five dominant starts, but it wasn't until he was roughed up that he started to maximize his advanced feel for pitching and utilize his secondary pitches. Tiffany features a fastball, curveball and changeup that are average to slightly above average, and they all play up because of his command. His fastball ranges from 85-93 mph. He spots it on both corners of the plate, will elevate it in the zone, and adds and subtract velocity. His breaking ball ranges from 74-78 mph with tumbling break, similar to a splitter but with curveball rotation. He likes to back-door it against righthanders. He also has good feel for his changeup, which he'll throw in any count. Most scouts believe Tiffany's ceiling is as a No. 4 or 5 starter, and give him a high probability of attaining it. Maturity and experience are his biggest needs. He'll continue to move one level at a time and spend 2006 in Double-A

Year	Club (League)	Class	W	L	ERA	G	GS	CG	SV	IP	H	R	ER	HR	BB	SO	AVG
2003	Ogden (Pio)	R	0	0	10.13	3	0	0	0	3	4	4	3	0	2	4	.364
2004	Columbus (SAL)	A	5	2	3.70	22	22	1	0	100	76	42	41	11	40	141	.212
2005	Vero Beach (FSL)	A	11	7	3.93	22	21	0	0	110	91	52	48	17	43	134	.226
MINOR LEAGUE TOTALS			16	9	3.90	47	43	1	0	212	171	98	92	28	85	279	.222

14 HONG-CHIH KUO   LHP

Born: July 23, 1981. **B-T:** L-L. **Ht.:** 6-0. **Wt.:** 200. **Signed:** Taiwan, 1999. **Signed by:** Jack Zduriencik/Acey Kohrogi.

Kuo's comeback was one of the minors' most remarkable stories of 2005. The first Taiwanese player to sign with a U.S. team out of high school, he blew out his elbow while striking out seven of the 10 batters he faced in his first pro game in 2000. After Tommy John surgery, he returned in June 2001 but made just 14 appearances before requiring the operation again in 2003. When he came back in 2004, he lasted six innings before needing more surgery to clean out scar tissue. Vero Beach pitching coach Marty Reed encouraged Kuo to push himself to recover and his work paid off. Kuo stayed healthy throughout 2005, reaching the majors on the strength of an 89-98 mph fastball that rises and runs. His smooth, simple delivery enables the ball to get on hitters quickly. He's aggressive and challenges hitters up in the zone. His breaking ball ranges from 78-83 mph and has a 10-to-4 break. It's in between a curveball and slider right now but has the makings of an average pitch. Understandably, Kuo lacked feel for his breaking ball and rudimentary changeup last year. Though he struggled with his command in the majors, he still struck out 10 of the 26 batters he faced. If he remains healthy and throws strikes, he could open 2006 in Los Angeles.

Year	Club (League)	Class	W	L	ERA	G	GS	CG	SV	IP	H	R	ER	HR	BB	SO	AVG
2000	San Bernardino (Cal)	A	0	0	0.00	1	1	0	0	3	0	0	0	0	0	7	.000
2001	Dodgers (GCL)	R	0	0	2.33	7	6	0	0	19	13	5	5	0	4	21	.186
2002	Dodgers (GCL)	R	0	0	4.50	3	3	0	0	6	4	3	3	0	1	9	.200
	Vero Beach (FSL)	A	0	1	6.75	4	4	0	0	8	11	6	6	0	2	8	.324
2003	Did not play—Injured																
2004	Columbus (SAL)	A	1	0	4.50	3	0	0	0	6	8	3	3	0	4	10	.308

Year	Club (League)	Class	W	L	ERA	G	GS	CG	SV	IP	H	R	ER	HR	BB	SO	AVG
2005	Vero Beach (FSL)	A	1	1	2.08	11	3	0	0	26	19	7	6	2	10	42	.202
	Jacksonville (SL)	AA	1	1	1.91	17	0	0	3	28	22	7	6	1	11	44	.210
	Los Angeles (NL)	MLB	0	1	6.75	9	0	0	0	5	5	4	4	1	5	10	.238
MAJOR LEAGUE TOTALS			0	1	6.75	9	0	0	0	5	5	4	4	1	5	10	.238
MINOR LEAGUE TOTALS			3	3	2.70	46	17	0	3	97	77	31	29	3	32	141	.215

15 DELWYN YOUNG   2B/OF

Born: June 30, 1982. **B-T:** B-R. **Ht.:** 5-10. **Wt.:** 180. **Drafted:** Santa Barbara (Calif.) CC, 2002 (4th round). **Signed by:** James Merriweather.

Young got his first taste of the upper minors in 2005 and did what he always had done in his first three pro seasons—rake. When he reached Triple-A in July, he collected 10 hits in his first 25 at-bats, and he put together a 17-game hitting streak in August. An aggressive hitter from both sides of the plate, Young is up there looking to hack. He hits from an open stance and feasts on fastballs early in counts, lashing line drives to all fields. His swing can get long at times and he needs to improve his plate discipline. Young has hit for power throughout his career and he'd make a good offensive second baseman—if he could play second base. He's slow and heavy-footed, and his hands are shaky. He does have a strong arm, which will serve him well when he makes a necessary move to the outfield. That could come this year in Triple-A, because the Dodgers already have Jeff Kent at second base and will use Cesar Izturis there when he returns from Tommy John surgery.

Year	Club (League)	Class	AVG	G	AB	R	H	2B	3B	HR	RBI	BB	SO	SB	OBP	SLG
2002	Great Falls (Pio)	R	.300	59	240	42	72	18	1	10	41	27	60	4	.380	.508
2003	South Georgia (SAL)	A	.323	119	443	67	143	38	7	15	73	36	87	5	.381	.542
2004	Vero Beach (FSL)	A	.281	129	470	76	132	36	3	22	85	57	134	11	.364	.511
2005	Jacksonville (SL)	AA	.296	95	371	52	110	25	1	16	62	27	86	1	.346	.499
	Las Vegas (PCL)	AAA	.325	36	160	23	52	12	0	4	14	8	35	0	.361	.475
MINOR LEAGUE TOTALS			.302	438	1684	260	509	129	12	67	275	155	402	21	.367	.512

16 JULIO PIMENTEL   RHP

Born: Dec. 14, 1985. **B-T:** R-R. **Ht.:** 6-1. **Wt.:** 190. **Signed:** Dominican Republic, 2003. **Signed by:** Santana Peguero.

Signed for $70,000 as an outfielder, Pimentel wasn't hitting much at the club's Dominican academy when his athleticism, frame and arm strength prompted a move to the mound. He surprised the Dodgers with an outstanding spring training in 2004, and followed up with an impressive full-season debut that summer. He stagnated last year and got shellacked in his final five starts. Like many raw Latin pitchers, Pimentel developed the bad habit of over-throwing and flying open with his front side in his delivery. Without staying closed in his delivery, he lost deception and command, leaving his pitches up in the zone. His fastball topped out at 93 mph, at times showing boring and running action, but late in the year he pitched at 88. He flashes a 75-77 mph slurvy breaking ball with late, downward break. Pimentel's 80 mph changeup has potential to be an above-average offering and is a tick ahead of his breaking ball. When he got hit hard, he lost confidence and regressed mechanically. He needs to improve his strength and mental approach, and he has the makeup and work ethic to do it. He likely will return to high Class A to begin 2006.

Year	Club (League)	Class	W	L	ERA	G	GS	CG	SV	IP	H	R	ER	HR	BB	SO	AVG
2003	Dodgers (DSL)	R	1	1	4.09	8	3	0	0	22	17	12	10	1	13	24	.221
2004	Columbus (SAL)	A	10	8	3.48	23	23	2	0	111	106	56	43	14	47	102	.260
2005	Vero Beach (FSL)	A	8	10	5.08	26	24	1	0	124	149	79	70	9	43	105	.305
MINOR LEAGUE TOTALS			19	19	4.30	57	50	3	0	257	272	147	123	24	103	231	.280

17 BLAKE JOHNSON   RHP

Born: June 14, 1985. **B-T:** R-R. **Ht.:** 6-3. **Wt.:** 185. **Drafted:** HS—Baton Rouge, La., 2004 (2nd round). **Signed by:** Clarence Johns.

Johnson was considered one of the top high school pitchers in the nation after a good showing at the 2003 Area Code Games, but a dip in velocity the following spring caused his stock to slip. He struck out 12 during a dominant performance at the National Classic tournament in Anaheim, with Dodgers special adviser Tommy Lasorda and other Los Angeles scouts in attendance. The Dodgers took him in the second round in 2004 and signed him for $600,000. After a lackluster pro debut, Johnson was much improved in his first full season last year. He's athletic and projectable, with a sturdy if underdeveloped frame in the mold of John Smoltz. Johnson pitches from a high three-quarters arm slot that allows him to get downward plane on his three-pitch repertoire. His fastball sits near 90 mph. His mid-70s curveball has depth, tight spin and sharp downward tilt. His changeup is his third pitch and presently fringe average. Johnson has decent command but tends to cut his fastball too much. Columbus pitching coach Glenn Dishman tried to get him to stay inside the ball and drive it down and in on righthanders instead. Johnson wore down late in the year, and his stuff and velocity tapered off. The Dodgers want him to get stronger and to show more energy and fire. He should start the season in high Class A.

Year	Club (League)	Class	W	L	ERA	G	GS	CG	SV	IP	H	R	ER	HR	BB	SO	AVG
2004	Ogden (Pio)	R	3	3	6.47	13	12	0	0	57	73	46	41	5	19	57	.324
2005	Columbus (SAL)	A	9	4	3.33	24	17	1	0	100	83	47	37	4	36	88	.226
MINOR LEAGUE TOTALS			12	7	4.47	37	29	1	0	157	156	93	78	9	55	145	.264

18 GREG MILLER
LHP

Born: Nov. 3, 1984. **B-T:** L-L. **Ht.:** 6-5. **Wt.:** 195. **Drafted:** HS—Yorba Linda, Calif., 2002 (1st round). **Signed by:** Scott Groot.

Once rated as the top lefthanded pitching prospect in baseball, Miller missed all of 2004 and the first half of 2005 with a shoulder injury that required two surgeries. He finally returned last summer and was back in Double-A by August, showing flashes of his old velocity and stuff. He's far from the same pitcher, however, as his shoulder problems have forced him to drop his arm angle. To loosen up, he sometimes throws sidearm before gradually working up to a low three-quarters slot. His fastball ranges from 89-97 mph, and at times he pitched at 94 with good tailing action. He likes to throw a cutter in on the hands of righthanders. Miller owned a slider and a curveball before his injury, but he now works mainly with the curve. It's a two-plane breaking ball at 76-82 mph, a potential plus offering with depth and diagonal tilt. With his lower arm slot, he struggled to get on top of his curve and to command it. Miller also throws an average changeup at 78-81 mph. His stuff plays up because of his remarkable feel for pitching. He's intelligent and mature, and if Miller stays healthy he still could become a front-of-the-rotation starter. The likelihood of that is in doubt, as he was shut down again in October with shoulder soreness after just four innings in the Arizona Fall League.

Year	Club (League)	Class	W	L	ERA	G	GS	CG	SV	IP	H	R	ER	HR	BB	SO	AVG
2002	Great Falls (Pio)	R	3	2	2.37	11	7	0	0	38	27	14	10	1	13	37	.199
2003	Vero Beach (FSL)	A	11	4	2.49	21	21	1	0	116	103	40	32	5	41	111	.240
	Jacksonville (SL)	AA	1	1	1.01	4	4	0	0	27	15	5	3	1	7	40	.156
2004	Did not play—Injured																
2005	Dodgers (GCL)	R	0	0	2.25	4	3	0	0	12	7	5	3	0	4	14	.159
	Vero Beach (FSL)	A	1	0	0.93	5	3	0	0	10	4	1	1	0	7	10	.138
	Jacksonville (SL)	AA	0	0	2.77	12	0	0	2	13	14	6	4	1	15	17	.275
MINOR LEAGUE TOTALS			16	7	2.22	57	38	1	2	215	170	71	53	8	87	229	.216

19 JOSH WALL
RHP

Born: Jan. 21, 1987. **B-T:** R-R. **Ht.:** 6-6. **Wt.:** 190. **Drafted:** HS—Walker, La., 2005 (2nd round). **Signed by:** Dennis Moeller.

Wall's story was very similar to Blake Johnson's from a year earlier. Like Johnson, Wall is a Louisiana high school righthander whose stock soared when he excelled at a prospect showcase. He threw 95 mph during a Perfect Game showcase in Florida in January 2005. His velocity dipped to 86-88 mph late in the summer, so Los Angeles was able to take him in the third round, signing him away from Louisiana State for $480,000. A half-brother of former Dodgers farmhand Lance Caraccioli, Wall has a projectable frame and athleticism that bode well for his future. Besides his fastball, which sat at 90-93 mph for much of the spring, he also has a power 82 mph curveball and an average changeup. His curve will become an out pitch once he masters command of it. Wall could develop into a durable middle-of-the-rotation starter with three above-average offerings. He likely will spend his first full year in low Class A.

Year	Club (League)	Class	W	L	ERA	G	GS	CG	SV	IP	H	R	ER	HR	BB	SO	AVG
2005	Dodgers (GCL)	R	1	3	3.86	5	4	0	0	14	13	8	6	2	8	5	.245
MINOR LEAGUE TOTALS			1	3	3.86	5	4	0	0	14	13	8	6	2	8	5	.245

20 JUAN RIVERA
SS

Born: March 17, 1987. **B-T:** B-R. **Ht.:** 6-0. **Wt.:** 148. **Signed:** Dominican Republic, 2003. **Signed by:** Pablo Peguero/Angel Santana.

Signed for $400,000 as a 16-year-old out of the Dominican Republic, Rivera has the makings of a standout defensive shortstop. He has good actions, sure hands and plenty of arm strength to make plays deep in the hole. His good instincts help him in all phases of the game. He was young for the Rookie-level Pioneer League last year at 18, and he showed a decent grasp of the strike zone for his age. A switch-hitter, Rivera is a natural righty but makes more consistent contact from the left side. He has good hand-eye coordination but still lacks strength and any pop at the plate. He's an average runner. His toolset frequently draws comparisons to that of former all-star and Gold Glover Tony Fernandez. Rivera still needs lots of refinement, especially as a hitter, and will hone his skills at low Class A Columbus this year.

Year	Club (League)	Class	AVG	G	AB	R	H	2B	3B	HR	RBI	BB	SO	SB	OBP	SLG
2004	Dodgers (GCL)	R	.243	52	185	28	45	6	0	0	14	13	30	5	.296	.276
2005	Ogden (Pio)	R	.251	41	171	27	43	5	0	1	16	14	32	9	.312	.298
MINOR LEAGUE TOTALS			.247	93	356	55	88	11	0	1	30	27	62	14	.304	.287

21   CORY DUNLAP   1B

Born: April 14, 1984. **B-T:** L-L. **Ht.:** 6-1. **Wt.:** 230. **Drafted:** Contra Costa (Calif.) CC, 2004 (3rd round). **Signed by:** Mark Sheehy.

Because he was overweight, Dunlap wasn't drafted out of Encinal High (Alameda, Calif.), where he played with Dontrelle Willis. After Dunlap improved his conditioning and led all California junior college players with a .523 average in 2004, he went in the third round and signed for $430,000. He led the Pioneer League in walks and on-base percentage in his pro debut, then skipped a level and spent 2005 in high Class A. His efficient approach and modest power remind scouts of Tony Gwynn. Unfortunately, Dunlap's body also has been compared to Gwynn's—when Gwynn was at the end of his career. Dunlap's hands work well at the plate and he has good plate discipline, though he has a tendency to swing with his shoulders and lose balance. He added a toe tap that helped him keep his weight back, but his swing remains a work in progress. Until he gains consistent balance, he'll struggle to hit home runs. He does show raw power, especially to the pull side, in batting practice. His bat will have to carry him, because his speed and his range at first base are well-below-average. He does have adequate hands and an average arm. The Dodgers may slow things down for Dunlap a bit by sending him back to high Class A to start 2006.

Year	Club (League)	Class	AVG	G	AB	R	H	2B	3B	HR	RBI	BB	SO	SB	OBP	SLG
2004	Ogden (Pio)	R	.351	71	245	57	86	18	1	7	53	68	40	0	.492	.518
2005	Vero Beach (FSL)	A	.291	121	430	61	125	25	0	7	77	65	64	5	.382	.398
MINOR LEAGUE TOTALS			.313	192	675	118	211	43	1	14	130	133	104	5	.425	.441

22   WILLIE AYBAR   3B/2B

Born: March 3, 1983. **B-T:** B-R. **Ht.:** 6-0. **Wt.:** 190. **Signed:** Dominican Republic, 2000. **Signed by:** Felix Feliz.

After the Dodgers dropped a then-Dominican record $1.4 million bonus to sign Aybar in 2000, he progressed slowly but surely. Promoted in September to fill Los Angeles' season-long hole at third base, he collected seven hits in his first three major league starts and hit safely in 20 of 22 big league starts. The problem is that while he has attractive tools, he doesn't profile well at any position. He uses a patient approach to spray line drives to all fields, and on defense he offers above-average arm strength and sound hands. But he doesn't have the range or agility to handle second base and he hasn't shown the pop teams want at the hot corner, leaving him as a 'tweener. After hitting a career-high 15 homers in 2004, he dropped to five last year at Las Vegas—which features one of the best hitter's parks in the minors. He gets pull-conscious when he's behind in the count. Aybar may get an opportunity to fit into the Dodgers third-base mix in 2006, but he's not the long-term answer.

Year	Club (League)	Class	AVG	G	AB	R	H	2B	3B	HR	RBI	BB	SO	SB	OBP	SLG
2000	Great Falls (Pio)	R	.263	70	266	39	70	15	1	4	49	36	45	5	.349	.372
2001	Wilmington (SAL)	A	.237	120	431	45	102	25	2	4	48	43	64	7	.307	.332
	Vero Beach (FSL)	A	.286	2	7	0	2	0	0	0	0	1	2	0	.375	.286
2002	Vero Beach (FSL)	A	.215	108	372	56	80	18	2	11	65	69	54	15	.339	.363
2003	Vero Beach (FSL)	A	.274	119	445	47	122	29	3	11	74	41	70	9	.336	.427
2004	Jacksonville (SL)	AA	.276	126	482	56	133	27	0	15	77	50	77	8	.346	.425
2005	Las Vegas (PCL)	AAA	.297	108	401	47	119	26	4	5	60	40	56	1	.356	.419
	Los Angeles (NL)	MLB	.326	26	86	12	28	8	0	1	10	18	11	3	.448	.453
MAJOR LEAGUE TOTALS			.326	26	86	12	28	8	0	1	10	18	11	3	.448	.453
MINOR LEAGUE TOTALS			.261	653	2404	290	628	140	12	50	373	280	368	45	.338	.392

23   TRAVIS DENKER   2B

Born: Aug. 5, 1985. **B-T:** R-R. **Ht.:** 5-9. **Wt.:** 170. **Drafted:** HS—Brea, Calif., 2003 (21st round). **Signed by:** Scott Groot.

After Denker's strong predraft workout at Dodger Stadium in 2003, club officials compared him to Ron Cey and Marcus Giles. They were prepared to take him in the seventh round but his bonus demands scared off other clubs, so Los Angeles let him slide until the 21st round and signed him for $100,000. Denker's best tool is his bat. He has a thick, squatty build that gives him good power. He generates good bat speed, drives the ball to all fields and could be a perennial 20-homer player in the big leagues. Where he will play when he gets there is the problem. Denker has poor range, stiff actions and a fringe-average arm. He catches what's hit to him and worked diligently with Dodgers infield instructor Dave Anderson on turning double plays, showing gradual improvement. He's also a below-average runner. He has a strong work ethic and good makeup. Denker could be moved to left field in the future, but should spend 2006 as an infielder in high Class A.

Year	Club (League)	Class	AVG	G	AB	R	H	2B	3B	HR	RBI	BB	SO	SB	OBP	SLG
2003	Dodgers (GCL)	R	.270	39	122	17	33	8	1	3	13	20	16	2	.382	.426
	South Georgia (SAL)	A	.227	8	22	2	5	2	0	0	1	2	6	0	.292	.318
2004	Ogden (Pio)	R	.311	57	225	44	70	17	1	12	43	24	52	2	.372	.556
2005	Columbus (SAL)	A	.310	101	358	65	111	23	1	21	68	67	78	2	.417	.556
	Vero Beach (FSL)	A	.185	31	108	14	20	3	0	2	9	15	26	1	.296	.269
MINOR LEAGUE TOTALS			.286	236	835	142	239	53	3	38	134	128	178	7	.382	.493

24 XAVIER PAUL OF

Born: Feb. 25, 1985. **B-T:** L-R. **Ht.:** 6-0. **Wt.:** 200. **Drafted:** HS—Slidell, La., 2003 (4th round). **Signed by:** Clarence Johns.

Scouts who evaluated Paul as an amateur might not recognize him if they watched him now. He has changed his set-up at the plate, raising his back elbow and closing his stance. His swing has lengthened, sapping his pop and ability to pull the ball. He missed most of last April with a leg injury, then got off to a 2-for-24 start and never got untracked, making for his second straight lackluster season. Paul's pitch recognition is poor and he presses at the plate. He also struggled mightily against lefthanders, going 9-for-67 (.134), prompting him to experiment with switch-hitting in instructional league. He has been slow to grasp the nuances of outfield defense as well, though some scouts still believe he has a chance to become an above-average outfielder in time. He has two plus tools, his arm and speed. Otherwise, Paul's sound athleticism has not yet translated into on-field ability. He made progress in instructional league and will return to high Class A this year. His brother Matt, also an outfielder, played briefly with him there last July.

Year	Club (League)	Class	AVG	G	AB	R	H	2B	3B	HR	RBI	BB	SO	SB	OBP	SLG
2003	Ogden (Pio)	R	.307	69	264	60	81	15	6	7	47	34	58	11	.384	.489
2004	Columbus (SAL)	A	.262	128	465	69	122	26	6	9	72	56	127	10	.341	.402
2005	Vero Beach (FSL)	A	.247	85	288	42	71	15	3	7	41	32	81	1	.328	.392
MINOR LEAGUE TOTALS			.269	282	1017	171	274	56	15	23	160	122	266	22	.349	.422

25 IVAN DeJESUS JR. SS

Born: May 1, 1987. **B-T:** B-R. **Ht.:** 5-11. **Wt.:** 182. **Drafted:** HS—Guaynabo, P.R., 2005 (2nd round). **Signed by:** Manny Estrada.

DeJesus was the highest-profile Puerto Rican prospect since righthander Luis Atilano was drafted in the supplemental first round by the Braves in 2003. The son of former major league shortstop Ivan DeJesus, Ivan Jr. signed quickly for slot money ($675,000 as a second-rounder) and played well in the Rookie-level Gulf Coast League. When Juan Rivera strained a leg muscle in August, DeJesus moved up to Rookie-level Ogden but never settled in at the plate. He has good bat control and a level swing that elicits sharp line drives when his timing is on. A switch-hitter, he has a promising combination of wiry strength, a loose stroke and good hand-eye coordination. He needs to improve his plate discipline and pitch recognition. DeJesus can get too flashy in the field, though he has good hands to go along with an average arm. He's a slightly above-average runner with good instincts on the bases. With Rivera destined for low Class A, DeJesus likely will return to Ogden this summer.

Year	Club (League)	Class	AVG	G	AB	R	H	2B	3B	HR	RBI	BB	SO	SB	OBP	SLG
2005	Dodgers (GCL)	R	.339	33	121	18	41	5	0	0	11	10	22	8	.389	.380
	Ogden (Pio)	R	.208	20	72	4	15	1	0	0	3	6	18	3	.296	.222
MINOR LEAGUE TOTALS			.290	53	193	22	56	6	0	0	14	16	40	11	.354	.321

26 JOSH BELL 3B

Born: Nov. 13, 1986. **B-T:** B-R. **Ht.:** 6-1. **Wt.:** 205. **Drafted:** HS—Lantana, Fla., 2005 (4th round). **Signed by:** Manny Estrada.

Scouting directors selected Bell as a second-teamer on Baseball America's preseason High School All-America squad in 2005, but his mediocre senior season caused many scouts to sour on him. He kept adjusting his approach in an attempt to snap out of it, and he wound up hitting just two homers. Bell flew from Florida to New Orleans for a Dodgers predraft workout, winning over scouting director Logan White with his makeup and plus-plus raw power. Los Angeles took Bell in the fourth round and signed him quickly for $212,000. He held his own in the Gulf Coast League, but he needs to maintain a consistent gameplan. When he widens his stance and remains balanced, his swing from both sides of the plate generates good leverage and loft and he uses the entire field. His swing has some length, though he has a basic understanding of the strike zone and fair pitch recognition. Bell has a thick lower body, and his speed and range already are slightly below-average. He has a plus arm and his hands are adequate, so he should be able to handle third base. The Dodgers could send him to low Class A to begin 2006 if he has a good spring training.

Year	Club (League)	Class	AVG	G	AB	R	H	2B	3B	HR	RBI	BB	SO	SB	OBP	SLG
2005	Dodgers (GCL)	R	.318	45	157	26	50	7	1	1	21	20	33	5	.399	.395
MINOR LEAGUE TOTALS			.318	45	157	26	50	7	1	1	21	20	33	5	.399	.395

27 JAMIE HOFFMANN   OF

Born: Aug. 20, 1984. **B-T:** R-R. **Ht.:** 6-3. **Wt.:** 205. **Signed:** NDFA/HS—New Ulm, Minn., 2003. **Signed by:** Jeff Schugel.

In high school, Hoffmann appeared to have a bright future as a professional athlete—but hockey figured to be his sport. The NHL's Carolina Hurricanes drafted him in the eighth round after he played in the United States Hockey League in 2002-03. Like former all-star catcher Terry Steinbach, Hoffmann had excelled in baseball and hockey at New Ulm High. He was Minnesota's state baseball player of the year as junior and led New Ulm to the state 3-A title as a senior, and signed with the Dodgers as a nondrafted free agent in August 2003. In his pro debut, Hoffmann topped the Gulf Coast League in runs, hits, triples, RBIs and total bases in 2004. He's raw in all phases of the game, but his rugged frame and all-out approach make him intriguing. His plus speed enables him to cover lots of ground and make up for his lack of instincts in center field, where he moved last year after playing third base in 2004, and he also has an average arm. His swing is a little stiff, but he's learning to better incorporate his lower half. Hoffmann makes consistent contact, has gap power and could hit 10-12 home runs annually in the majors as he learns to pull the ball. He has the aptitude to command the strike zone, but presently tends to chase breaking balls out of the zone and gets impatient at the plate. Fastballs in on his hands also give him trouble. Hoffmann opened 2005 with a strong performance in low Class A, then hit the wall after a promotion, meaning he'll return to high Class A this year.

Year	Club (League)	Class	AVG	G	AB	R	H	2B	3B	HR	RBI	BB	SO	SB	OBP	SLG
2004	Dodgers (GCL)	R	.310	60	229	40	71	8	7	4	36	24	38	14	.459	.374
2005	Columbus (SAL)	A	.308	79	321	53	99	13	9	1	24	39	73	10	.383	.414
	Vero Beach (FSL)	A	.241	46	166	26	40	6	2	1	10	10	45	3	.287	.319
MINOR LEAGUE TOTALS			.293	185	716	119	210	27	18	6	70	73	156	27	.359	.406

28 STEVE SCHMOLL   RHP

Born: Feb. 4, 1980. **B-T:** R-R. **Ht.:** 6-2. **Wt.:** 200. **Signed:** NDFA/Maryland, 2003. **Signed by:** Clair Rierson.

The Dodgers' bullpen was in flux in 2005, and Schmoll was one of the beneficiaries. He pitched just three innings in major league spring training, but broke camp with Los Angeles and spent most of the season there. Schmoll signed before the 2003 draft as a fifth-year senior free-agent for $75,000 after ranking fourth in NCAA Division I with 12.7 strikeouts per nine innings. He features one plus pitch, a low-90s cutter with rising life. He pitches from a sidearm slot that isn't quite submarine but provides good deception. Major league hitters weren't fooled often enough, batting .275 against him. Schmoll's slider and changeup are average offerings, and he needs to improve at least one of them to complement his fastball. He frequently pitched behind in the count with the Dodgers and must sharpen his overall command. Schmoll will have a chance to secure a spot in the big league bullpen in 2006, but he doesn't have closer stuff and profiles as a middle reliever.

Year	Club (League)	Class	W	L	ERA	G	GS	CG	SV	IP	H	R	ER	HR	BB	SO	AVG
2003	Ogden (Pio)	R	3	1	3.68	24	1	0	7	37	27	23	15	2	15	53	.200
2004	Vero Beach (FSL)	A	3	3	1.80	37	0	0	10	65	57	18	13	0	18	58	.226
	Jacksonville (SL)	AA	0	2	1.83	11	0	0	2	20	14	7	4	0	7	18	.197
2005	Las Vegas (PCL)	AAA	0	3	4.78	22	0	0	5	26	24	15	14	1	13	31	.253
	Los Angeles (NL)	MLB	2	2	5.01	48	0	0	3	47	47	29	26	4	22	29	.275
MAJOR LEAGUE TOTALS			2	2	5.01	48	0	0	3	47	47	29	26	4	22	29	.275
MINOR LEAGUE TOTALS			6	9	2.80	94	1	0	24	148	122	63	46	3	53	160	.221

29 CHRIS MALONE   RHP

Born: June 28, 1983. **B-T:** R-R. **Ht.:** 6-4. **Wt.:** 230. **Signed:** NDFA/San Joaquin Delta (Calif.) JC, 2004. **Signed by:** Mark Sheehy.

Malone was a pleasant surprise for the Dodgers, as he arrived in spring training without a defined role yet pitched his way into the low Class A rotation by mid-May. The Royals failed to sign him as a 36th-round draft-and-follow in 2003-04, and Los Angeles nabbed him as a nondrafted free agent in 2004 after national crosschecker Tim Hallgren saw him pitch for the Alaska League's Mat-Su Miners. Malone would have attended Tennessee had he not turned pro. He features an aggressive approach and good command of his sinker-slider combination. His fastball sits at 87-88 mph with late, hard sink, inducing plenty of groundballs. He spun back-to-back complete games in May, needing just 91 pitches in one outing, including 80 fastballs. He throws his slurvy slider at 75 mph with a spike grip. He also has a below-average changeup that he often tips off by slowing his arm speed. Malone gets into trouble when he tries to strike out hitters or gets too fine with his pitches. He profiles as a future setup man, and is strong and durable enough to handle the role. He should open 2006 in high Class A.

Year	Club (League)	Class	W	L	ERA	G	GS	CG	SV	IP	H	R	ER	HR	BB	SO	AVG
2005	Columbus (SAL)	A	9	7	3.88	31	21	2	0	142	133	77	61	10	41	127	.248
MINOR LEAGUE TOTALS			9	7	3.88	31	21	2	0	142	133	77	61	10	41	127	.248

30 ANTHONY RAGLANI   OF

Born: April 6, 1983. **B-T:** L-L. **Ht.:** 6-2. **Wt.:** 215. **Drafted:** George Washington, 2004 (5th round). **Signed by:** Clair Rierson.

When the Dodgers took Raglani in the fifth round of the 2004 draft, he became their highest-drafted four-year college hitter since they grabbed Koyie Hill in the fourth round in 2000. Raglani raised his stock in the summer of 2003 by performing well in the Cape Cod League, then hit .333-11-46 as a junior at George Washington despite playing much of the year with a broken hamate bone in his right wrist. Signed for $180,000, Raglani jumped to high Class A for his first full season. His best tool is his bat. He deploys an aggressive approach and has a balanced, short swing that produces solid-average power. He gets pull-happy and doesn't work counts as well as his on-base percentage might suggest, but he makes consistent contact. Raglani isn't overly athletic, as he's a fringe-average runner with a below-average arm. He profiles as a left fielder. The Dodgers envision his ceiling as a Brian Giles with less pop. Raglani should spend 2006 in Double-A.

Year	Club (League)	Class	AVG	G	AB	R	H	2B	3B	HR	RBI	BB	SO	SB	OBP	SLG
2004	Dodgers (GCL	R	.300	6	20	2	6	1	0	0	1	2	4	2	.364	.350
2005	Vero Beach (FSL)	A	.289	124	419	82	121	20	5	19	77	60	98	9	.383	.496
MINOR LEAGUE TOTALS			.289	130	439	84	127	21	5	19	78	62	102	11	.382	.490

MILWAUKEE
BREWERS

BY **JOHN MANUEL**

One more win would have been nice. That way, the Brewers could say they had their first winning season since 1992. Instead, the 2005 team's 81-81 record meant Milwaukee had its first non-losing season since that club, snapping a tie with the Pirates for baseball's longest active streak of sub-.500 seasons at 12.

Undeniably, the Brewers made progress. They attained the .500 mark despite a modest $42 million payroll and staff ace Ben Sheets missing 10 starts. Owner Mark Attanasio, 48, brought a new vibe to the organization, which finally shed its link to commissioner (and former owner) Bud Selig. Attanasio increased payroll from $27 million in 2004, and he thanked fans for their support by giving them free tickets to the season finale.

With success, however modest, comes expectations. The Brewers hope they're passing .500 on the way up, not just visiting.

"One of the best things about getting to .500 is we don't have to hear about it anymore," general manager Doug Melvin told the Milwaukee Journal-Sentinel. "But the biggest thing it creates is new challenges for us. It raises the bar, which I think we all need to do . . . But it's going to be tougher to get to the next level."

Because of a farm system still stocked with talent, even after graduating rookie middle infielders J.J. Hardy and **Rickie Weeks** to Milwaukee in 2005, the Brewers are poised to get better. Top prospect Prince Fielder, versatile Corey Hart and pitchers Jose Capellan and Dana Eveland also got time in the majors and should play larger roles in 2006.

Melvin cleared the way for Fielder by trading Lyle Overbay to the Blue Jays, and the other players will give him some interesting choices. Hart is blocked on the outfield corners by all-star Carlos Lee and Geoff Jenkins, but could be in the mix at third base, where Bill Hall broke through. Eveland could slide into the fifth spot in the rotation, unless Melvin pursues a free agent.

They're all good problems to have. The Brewers have talent at the upper levels of the minors to help now while maintaining depth. Scouting director Jack Zduriencik continues to execute a simple philosophy of drafting the best player available, and Milwaukee continues to pay the market rate for top talent. The latest example came when it signed Ryan Braun, the fifth overall pick in the 2005 draft, for $2.45 million.

Melvin's Brewers have excelled at finding talent wherever they can, from independent leagues to Canadian draftees to the waiver wire, which has produced closer Derrick Turnbow and center fielder Brady Clark to name two. Now they've decided to become more of a player internationally, and international scouting director Fernando Arango came through by signing Rolando Pascual, the most coveted amateur pitcher in the Dominican Republic, for $710,000. As the Pascual signing showed, these aren't the same Brewers anymore. The best evidence yet would be a season over .500.

TOP 30 PROSPECTS

1. Prince Fielder, 1b
2. Mark Rogers, rhp
3. Ryan Braun, 3b
4. Yovani Gallardo, rhp
5. Corey Hart, of/3b
6. Alcides Escobar, ss
7. Dana Eveland, lhp
8. Nelson Cruz, of
9. Jose Capellan, rhp
10. Zach Jackson, lhp
11. Will Inman, rhp
12. Charlie Fermaint, of
13. Manny Parra, lhp
14. Brad Nelson, of
15. Hernan Iribarren, 2b
16. Tim Dillard, rhp
17. Rolando Pascual, rhp
18. Steve Hammond, lhp
19. Ben Hendrickson, rhp
20. Lou Palmisano, c
21. Angel Salome, c
22. Dave Krynzel, of
23. Adam Heether, 3b
24. Dennis Sarfate, rhp
25. Steve Moss, of
26. Mat Gamel, 3b
27. Lorenzo Cain, of
28. Vinny Rottino, util
29. Kevin Roberts, rhp
30. Drew Anderson, of

ORGANIZATION OVERVIEW

General manager: Doug Melvin. **Farm director:** Reid Nichols. **Scouting director:** Jack Zduriencik.

2005 PERFORMANCE

Class	Team	League	W	L	Pct.	Finish*	Manager
Majors	Milwaukee	National	81	81	.500	t-8th (16)	Ned Yost
Triple-A	Nashville Sounds	Pacific Coast	75	69	.521	+6th (16)	Frank Kremblas
Double-A	Huntsville Stars	Southern	60	79	.432	8th (10)	Don Money
High A	Brevard County Manatees	Florida State	63	73	.463	10th (12)	Johnny Narron
Low A	West Virginia Power	South Atlantic	60	78	.435	13th (16)	Ramon Aviles
Rookie	Helena Brewers	Pioneer	46	30	.605	1st (8)	Ed Sedar
Rookie	AZL Brewers	Arizona	22	34	.393	7th (9)	Mike Guerrero
OVERALL 2005 MINOR LEAGUE RECORD			326	363	.473	25th (30)	

*Finish in overall standings (No. of teams in league). +League champion.

ORGANIZATION LEADERS

BATTING *Minimum 250 at-bats
*AVG Salome, Angel, Helena/West Virginia .... .347
R Hart, Corey, Nashville 85
H Anderson, Drew, Brevard County................. 158
TB Cruz, Nelson, Huntsville/Nashville 245
2B Cruz, Enrique, Huntsville 34
  Richardson, Grant, West Virginia 34
3B Ezi, Travis, Brevard County/Huntsville 12
HR Fielder, Prince, Nashville 28
RBI Fielder, Prince, Nashville 86
BB Gwynn, Anthony, Huntsville........................... 76
SO Eure, Jeff, Brevard County 140
SB Iribarren, Hernan, West Virginia 38
*OBP Salome, Angel, Helena/West Virginia .... .399
*SLG Salome, Angel, Helena/West Virginia .... .570
PITCHING #Minimum 75 innings
W Dillard, Tim, Brevard County 12
  Taubenheim, Ty, Brevard County/Huntsville.... 12
L Kloosterman, Gregory, West Virginia 19
#ERA Dillard, Tim, Brevard County....................... 2.01
G Stetter, Mitch, Huntsville/Nashville 59
CG Dillard, Tim, Brevard County 5
SV Hinton, Robert, West Virginia......................... 14
IP Dillard, Tim, Brevard County 185
BB Housman, Jeff, Nashville 72
SO Villanueva, Carlos, Brevard Cty./Huntsville 138

BEST TOOLS

Best Hitter for Average............................... Ryan Braun
Best Power Hitter .... Prince Fielder
Best Strike-Zone Discipline................... Anthony Gwynn
Fastest Baserunner .... Darren Ford
Best Athlete .... Charlie Fermaint
Best Fastball.. Mark Rogers
Best Curveball .... Ben Hendrickson
Best Slider .... Mark Rogers
Best Changeup .... Carlos Villanueva
Best Control .... Tim Dillard
Best Defensive Catcher .... Lou Palmisano
Best Defensive Infielder .... Alcides Escobar
Best Infield Arm.................................... Enrique Cruz
Best Defensive Outfielder.................... Charlie Fermaint
Best Outfield Arm................................... Nelson Cruz

PROJECTED 2009 LINEUP

Catcher... Lou Palmisano
First Base .... Prince Fielder
Second Base .... J.J. Hardy
Third Base .... Ryan Braun
Shortstop.. Alcides Escobar
Left Field .... Carlos Lee
Center Field... Rickie Weeks

Right Field.. Geoff Jenkins
No. 1 Starter .... Ben Sheets
No. 2 Starter .... Mark Rogers
No. 3 Starter .... Chris Capuano
No. 4 Starter .... Doug Davis
No. 5 Starter .... Dana Eveland
Closer .... Derrick Turnbow

LAST YEAR'S TOP 20 PROSPECTS

1. Rickie Weeks, 2b
2. Prince Fielder, 1b
3. J.J. Hardy, ss
4. Jose Capellan, rhp
5. Mark Rogers, rhp
6. Corey Hart, of
7. Ben Hendrickson, rhp
8. Brad Nelson, of
9. Hernan Iribarren, 2b
10. David Krynzel, of
11. Manny Parra, lhp
12. Dana Eveland, lhp
13. Jorge de la Rosa, lhp
14. Nelson Cruz, of
15. Lou Palmisano, c
16. Yovanni Gallardo, rhp
17. Jeff Housman, lhp
18. Dennis Sarfate, rhp
19. Josh Baker, rhp
20. Josh Wahpepah, rhp

TOP PROSPECTS OF THE DECADE

Year	Player, Pos.	2005 Org.
1996	Jeff D'Amico, rhp	Out of baseball
1997	Todd Dunn, of	Out of baseball
1998	Valerio de los Santos, lhp	Marlins
1999	Ron Belliard, 2b	Indians
2000	Nick Neugebauer, rhp	Out of baseball
2001	Ben Sheets, rhp	Brewers
2002	Nick Neugebauer, rhp	Out of baseball
2003	Brad Nelson, 1b	Brewers
2004	Rickie Weeks, 2b	Brewers
2005	Rickie Weeks, 2b	Brewers

TOP DRAFT PICKS OF THE DECADE

Year	Player, Pos.	2005 Org.
1996	Chad Green, of	Out of baseball
1997	Kyle Peterson, rhp	Out of baseball
1998	J.M. Gold, rhp	Out of baseball
1999	Ben Sheets, rhp	Brewers
2000	Dave Krynzel, of	Brewers
2001	Mike Jones, rhp	Brewers
2002	Prince Fielder, 1b	Brewers
2003	Rickie Weeks, 2b	Brewers
2004	Mark Rogers, rhp	Brewers
2005	Ryan Braun, 3b	Brewers

ALL-TIME LARGEST BONUSES

Rickie Weeks, 2003 .... $3,600,000
Ben Sheets, 1999 .... $2,450,000
Ryan Braun, 2005 .... $2,450,000
Prince Fielder, 2002................................. $2,400,000
Mark Rogers, 2004 .... $2,200,000

MINOR LEAGUE DEPTH CHART

Milwaukee Brewers

Rank: **5**

STRENGTH: Outfield. Choose a style of hitter, and the Brewers have him in all three outfield spots.

WEAKNESS: Catcher. While both are prospects, Lou Palmisano and Angel Salome have serious flaws as well.

*Depth charts prepared by **John Manuel** and **Chris Kline**. Numbers in parentheses indicate prospect rankings.*

LF
Corey Hart (5)
Brad Nelson (14)
Lorenzo Cain (27)
Vinny Rottino (28)
Drew Anderson (30)
Hasan Rasheed

CF
Charlie Fermaint (12)
Dave Krynzel (22)
Steve Moss (25)
Michael Brantley
Anthony Gwynn
Darren Ford

RF
Nelson Cruz (8)
Brendan Katin
Stephen Chapman
Freddy Parejo
Adam Mannon

3B
Ryan Braun (3)
Adam Heether (23)
Mat Gamel (26)
Michael Bell
Carlos Hereaud

SS
Alcides Escobar (6)
Enrique Cruz
Ryan Crew

2B
Hernan Iribarren (15)
Callix Crabbe
Kenny Holmberg

1B
Prince Fielder (1)
John Alonso
Brandon Gemoll
Grant Richardson

C
Lou Palmisano (20)
Angel Salome (21)
Carlos Corporan

RHP

Starters	Relievers
Mark Rogers (2)	Jose Capellan (9)
Yovani Gallardo (4)	Dennis Sarfate (24)
Will Inman (11)	Jerome Gamble
Tim Dillard (16)	Robert Hinton
Rolando Pascual (17)	Justin Barnes
Ben Hendrickson (19)	Ben Stanczyk
Kevin Roberts (29)	Omar Aguilar
Carlos Villanueva	Chris Demaria
Josh Baker	
Josh Wahpepah	
Glenn Woolard	
Mat Kretzschmar	
Jose Beltre	
Roque Mercedes	
Alexandre Periard	

LHP

Starters	Relievers
Dana Eveland (7)	Steve Hammond (18)
Zach Jackson (10)	Mitch Stetter
Manny Parra (13)	Jeff Housman
Steve Garrison	
Brandon Parillo	
David Welch	
Ryan Costello	

DRAFT ANALYSIS

2005

Best Pro Debut: Most of the Brewers' draftees started strong. 3B Ryan Braun (1) hit .352-10-45, mostly in low Class A. RHP Will Inman (3) went 6-0, 1.91 with 59 strikeouts in 47 innings. 2B Kenny Holmberg (22) batted .372-12-51 and led the Rookie-level Pioneer League in on-base percentage (.450) and slugging (.623).

Best Athlete: Take your pick between former Miami Hurricanes Braun and OF Brendan Katin (23). Braun is a five-tool player who began his college career as a shortstop, and if he can't polish up his third-base defense he could fit in center field. Katin has surprising athleticism for a 6-foot-1, 238-pounder.

Best Pure Hitter: Braun went fifth overall because of his bat, and he stands out among a fine collection of hitters that also includes 3B Mat Gamel (4), OF Michael Brantley (7), 2B Carlos Hereaud (9) and 3B Mike Bell (15).

Best Raw Power: Braun and Katin both have big raw power, but Braun's shows up during games more often.

Fastest Runner: Braun has plus speed (6.6 seconds in the 60-yard dash) and is a step quicker than Brantley. Draft-and-follow OF Darren Ford (18 in 2004) has top-of-the-line speed, while draft-and-follow OF Lorenzo Cain (17 in 2004) is an above-average runner.

Best Defensive Player: Holmberg, who won the Gold Glove award at the NAIA College World Series, has the instincts one would expect from the son of a baseball lifer. His father Dennis is a manager in the Blue Jays system.

Best Fastball: Inman, RHP Kevin Roberts (5) and LHP Steve Hammond (6) all can touch 94 mph. Roberts has the best life on

Gamel

his fastball and may add more velocity now that he'll focus on pitching full-time after also playing third base at Houston. RHP Omar Aguilar (30) threw 98 mph before coming down with elbow problems in junior college. Doctors prescribed rest rather than surgery.

Best Breaking Ball: Roberts' 12-to-6 curveball. Aguilar had a mid-80s slider when he was healthy.

Most Intriguing Background: Unsigned SS Jemile Weeks' (8) brother Rickie is the Brewers' second baseman and went second overall in the 2003 draft. Unsigned 2B Kyle Eveland's (43) brother Dana made his big league debut with Milwaukee in 2005. Brantley's father Mickey played in the majors and is the Blue Jays hitting coach.

Closest To The Majors: Braun. Hammond, who pitched just 24 innings as a junior setup man for Long Beach State, also could move fast as a lefty with a plus arm.

Best Late-Round Pick: If Aguilar can return to health, he'll be one of the steals of the draft. Bell and LHP David Welch (20) are two more junior college products with upside.

The One Who Got Away: Milwaukee couldn't divert Jemile Weeks from Miami.

Assessment: Scouting director Jack Zduriencik continued to add to a deep farm system with a balance of hitters and pitchers from a blend of colleges, junior colleges and high schools. A strong draft-and-follow class also helped.

2004 RHP Mark Rogers (1) has No. 1 starter stuff, but he's learning how to use it. Unheralded RHP Yovani Gallardo (2) has a quality arm as well. OF Lorenzo Cain (17) was Arizona League MVP in his 2005 pro debut. **GRADE:** C+

2003 2B Rickie Weeks (1) may have the quickest bat since Gary Sheffield's. OF Charlie Fermaint (4) is a talented athlete who's just starting to come into his own. **GRADE:** A

2002 1B Prince Fielder (1), arguably the game's top power prospect, will be driving in Weeks for years to come in Milwaukee. LHP Dana Eveland (16) and RHP Tim Dillard (34) were savvy draft-and-follow selections. **GRADE:** A

2001 RHP Mike Jones (1) looked like a star until elbow and shoulder problems got him. SS J.J. Hardy (2) is a big part of the Brewers' future, and they have hope for OF Brad Nelson. **GRADE:** B

Draft analysis prepared by Jim Callis. Numbers in parentheses indicate draft rounds.

PRINCE
FIELDER

1B

ANDREW WOOLLEY

Born: May 9, 1984.
Ht.: 6-0. **Wt.:** 260.
Bats: L. **Throws:** R.
Drafted: HS—Melbourne, Fla.,
2002 (1st round).
Signed by: Tom McNamara/
Jack Zduriencik.

Fielder first came to the attention of BA readers in 1998, our first Baseball For The Ages issue. He wasn't the top 14-year-old—that honor went to Braves righthander Kyle Davies—but he was featured as the prominent son of a big leaguer. His father Cecil was wrapping up a 319-homer major league career. By then, Prince's power already was the talk of his father's clubhouses, thanks to batting-practice displays he had put on at Tiger Stadium. Fielder has since become a major leaguer, like his father, with a June 2005 promotion so he could DH for the Brewers in interleague play. Between being a pudgy, shy 14-year-old and a confident, 21-year-old big leaguer, Fielder has dealt with his share of adversity. Scouts doubted his bulky, overweight body out of high school, but the Brewers didn't and drafted him seventh overall. He arrived in Double-A as a 19-year-old, only after he had been served with papers stemming from an investigation into his father's gambling debts, problems that led to the family's breakup and Prince's estrangement from his father. He left the Arizona Fall League this offseason when his wife Chanel, whom he wed in June, had medical issues while pregnant with their second child.

Through all his travails, Fielder has hit and hit for power. He has as much raw power as any hitter in the minors due to tremendous bat speed and brute strength. He has power to any part of any park and is at his best when he's using the whole field, letting his strength work for him. He homered in his first two games at Triple-A Nashville before a monthlong slump, and it's the adjustments he made to get going again that have the Brewers so excited. Fielder knows the strike zone well and started picking up on the steady diet of breaking balls he was seeing. Once he started trusting his hands to hit breaking balls left in the strike zone, he punished them. He was productive in a pinch-hitting role in the big leagues due to his ability to focus during those at-bats, and he carried that improved concentration with him when he returned to the minors, hitting .349 with 13 homers in his final 39 games.

Fielder can get pull-conscious, opening his shoulder and giving away the outer half of the plate. Defense is perhaps Fielder's biggest obstacle. He's more comfortable in the batter's box than at first base, and he made 12 errors in 101 games in 2005. He has good hands for the position and more quickness than he's given credit for, but must show more pride in his defense to be rated as average.

Lyle Overbay was one of the Brewers' best hitters the last two seasons, but he was arbitration-eligible and his power was dwarfed by Fielder's. So at the Winter Meetings, general manager Doug Melvin sent Overbay and minor league righthander Ty Taubenheim to the Blue Jays for young big leaguers David Bush and Gabe Gross, plus lefty prospect Zach Jackson. Now that Fielder has a clear path to playing time, he's an instant favorite to be National League rookie of the year.

Year	Club (League)	Class	AVG	G	AB	R	H	2B	3B	HR	RBI	BB	SO	SB	OBP	SLG
2002	Ogden (Pio)	R	.390	41	146	35	57	12	0	10	40	37	27	3	.531	.678
	Beloit (Mid)	A	.241	32	112	15	27	7	0	3	11	10	27	0	.320	.384
2003	Beloit (Mid)	A	.313	137	502	81	157	22	2	27	112	71	80	2	.409	.526
2004	Huntsville (SL)	AA	.272	135	497	70	135	29	1	23	78	65	93	11	.366	.473
2005	Nashville (PCL)	AAA	.291	103	378	68	110	21	0	28	86	54	93	8	.388	.569
	Milwaukee (NL)	MLB	.288	39	59	2	17	4	0	2	10	2	17	0	.306	.458
MAJOR LEAGUE TOTALS			.288	39	59	2	17	4	0	2	10	2	17	0	.306	.458
MINOR LEAGUE TOTALS			.297	448	1635	269	486	91	3	91	327	237	320	24	.398	.524

2 MARK ROGERS

RHP

RODGER WOOD

Born: Jan. 30, 1986. **B-T:** R-R. **Ht.:** 6-2. **Wt.:** 205. **Drafted:** HS—Mount Ararat, Maine, 2004 (1st round). **Signed by:** Tony Blengino.

Rogers had college scholarship offers in hockey (Dartmouth) and soccer (Duke) and had signed with Miami to play baseball before becoming the first Maine high schooler ever drafted in the first round. Two of Rogers' pitches could earn 70s on the 20-80 scouting scale. His fastball tops out at 100 mph and sits at 95-97 mph with some late cutting action. Rogers' breaking ball has improved substantially, as a once-loopy pitch became a hard mid-80s slider that reaches 90. He's one of the best athletes in the organization. Rogers put up ugly numbers in the low Class A South Atlantic League because he's still trying to control his powerful body and has been unable to repeat his delivery. He throws across his body, though he has toned that down, and still needs to get better extension to keep his pitches down. His fastball straightens out at times. Rogers' stuff, tenacity and Northern background have elicited John Smoltz comparisons from Milwaukee officials. He'll go to high Class A Brevard County in 2006. When he harnesses his body and can command his stuff, he'll move rapidly.

Year	Club (League)	Class	W	L	ERA	G	GS	CG	SV	IP	H	R	ER	HR	BB	SO	AVG
2004	Brewers (AZL)	R	0	3	4.73	9	6	0	0	27	30	21	14	0	14	35	.294
2005	West Virginia (SAL)	A	2	9	5.11	25	20	0	1	99	87	65	56	11	70	109	.238
MINOR LEAGUE TOTALS			2	12	5.03	34	26	0	1	125	117	86	70	11	84	144	.250

3 RYAN BRAUN

3B

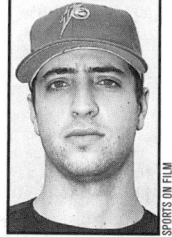

SPORTS ON FILM

Born: Nov. 17, 1983. **B-T:** R-R. **Ht.:** 6-2. **Wt.:** 200. **Drafted:** Miami, 2005 (1st round). **Signed by:** Larry Pardo.

BA's Freshman of the Year in 2003, Braun helped Miami to a pair of College World Series berths in three seasons. He had an All-America season before the Brewers drafted him fifth overall. An elbow strain ended Braun's pro debut two weeks early and limited him to DH duty in instructional league. Braun has all five tools. He works counts waiting for a pitch to hit, then has the bat speed—thanks to very quick hands—to hit for excellent power. His approach and power remind some in the organization of another former Miami third baseman, Pat Burrell. Braun is a plus runner, and his average arm strength should be enough for third base. Braun has a less-than-textbook swing. He could use more balance and a more consistent, less exaggerated load. He needs more repetition at third base, where he'll have to get used to reacting quicker than he did at shortstop, his former position. Braun should reach Double-A Huntsville at some point in 2006. He has enough athleticism and bat to move to an outfield corner if he's not cut out for third base.

Year	Club (League)	Class	AVG	G	AB	R	H	2B	3B	HR	RBI	BB	SO	SB	OBP	SLG
2005	Helena (Pio)	R	.341	10	41	6	14	2	1	2	10	2	6	2	.383	.585
	West Virginia (SAL)	A	.355	37	152	21	54	16	2	8	35	9	34	2	.396	.645
MINOR LEAGUE TOTALS			.352	47	193	27	68	18	3	10	45	11	40	4	.393	.632

4 YOVANI GALLARDO

RHP

BILL MITCHELL

Born: Feb. 27, 1986. **B-T:** R-R. **Ht.:** 6-2. **Wt.:** 190. **Drafted:** HS—Fort Worth, Texas, 2004 (2nd round). **Signed by:** Jim Stevenson.

Gallardo committed to Texas Christian, which hoped to use him as a two-way player, but the Brewers and a $725,000 bonus persuaded him to sign. He thrived in the tandem-starter system at low Class A West Virginia, winning his final eight decisions (all starts). Only Mark Rogers has better stuff in the organization. Gallardo pounds the strike zone with an 89-93 mph fastball that touches 96 with boring action and life down in the zone. He repeats his drop-and-drive delivery well, enabling him to command his fastball, and he can throw his curveball, slider and changeup for strikes. His low-80s slider is at times a plus pitch. The Brewers describe Gallardo's demeanor as quietly intense, while others have chided him as too laid-back. Drop-and-drive pitchers tend to elevate their stuff at times, but he has such downward life on his fastball that it hasn't been a problem. Gallardo's progress in the second half and in instructional league has the Brewers projecting him as a No. 2 starter in the mold of Mike Mussina. He's more polished than Rogers and will join him in high Class A in 2006.

Year	Club (League)	Class	W	L	ERA	G	GS	CG	SV	IP	H	R	ER	HR	BB	SO	AVG
2004	Brewers (AZL)	R	0	0	0.47	6	6	0	0	19	14	3	1	0	4	23	.203
	Beloit (Mid)	A	0	1	12.27	2	2	0	0	7	12	10	10	2	4	8	.400
2005	West Virginia (SAL)	A	8	3	2.74	26	18	0	1	121	100	46	37	5	51	110	.230
MINOR LEAGUE TOTALS			8	4	2.92	34	26	0	1	148	126	59	48	7	59	141	.236

5 COREY HART — OF/3B

Born: March 24, 1982. **B-T:** R-R. **Ht.:** 6-6. **Wt.:** 200. **Drafted:** HS—Bowling Green, Ky., 2000 (11th round). **Signed by:** Mike Gibbons.

Hart played first and third base prior to 2004, earning the Double-A Southern League's MVP award in 2003. He has spent the last two seasons as an outfielder, and he made his first big league start as a center fielder. Hart's athletic ability lends itself to versatility. He can play five positions, and he ranked third in the system in homers and steals in 2005. The organization's best baserunner also ranks near the top in raw power, as he has good leverage in his swing. He has average range and arm strength on the outfield corners. At his size, Hart inevitably has length to his swing and will have periods where he struggles to make contact. Hart is a below-average defender at third, where his range is limited and his throwing motion has to be adjusted. Hart saw Arizona Fall League time at third base, where he'll have to contend with Bill Hall. Hart could also be a solid corner outfielder, though he's blocked by Geoff Jenkins and Carlos Lee, or a utilityman.

Year	Club (League)	Class	AVG	G	AB	R	H	2B	3B	HR	RBI	BB	SO	SB	OBP	SLG
2000	Ogden (Pio)	R	.287	57	216	32	62	9	1	2	30	13	27	6	.332	.366
2001	Ogden (Pio)	R	.340	69	262	53	89	18	1	11	62	26	47	14	.395	.542
2002	High Desert (Cal)	A	.288	100	393	76	113	26	10	22	84	37	101	24	.356	.573
	Huntsville (SL)	AA	.266	28	94	16	25	3	0	2	15	7	16	3	.340	.362
2003	Huntsville (SL)	AA	.302	130	493	70	149	40	1	13	94	28	101	25	.340	.467
2004	Milwaukee (NL)	MLB	.000	1	0	0	0	0	0	0	0	0	1	0	.000	.000
	Indianapolis (IL)	AAA	.281	121	441	68	124	29	8	15	67	41	92	17	.342	.485
2005	Nashville (PCL)	AAA	.308	113	429	85	132	29	9	17	69	48	88	31	.377	.536
	Milwaukee	MLB	.193	21	57	9	11	2	1	2	7	6	11	2	.270	.368
MAJOR LEAGUE TOTALS			.190	22	58	9	11	2	1	2	7	6	12	2	.266	.362
MINOR LEAGUE TOTALS			.298	618	2328	400	694	154	30	82	421	200	472	120	.356	.496

6 ALCIDES ESCOBAR — SS

Born: Dec. 16, 1986. **B-T:** R-R. **Ht.:** 6-1. **Wt.:** 155. **Signed:** Venezuela, 2003. **Signed by:** Epy Guerrero.

Escobar was flirting with a .300 average in early August, but sagged as he wore down. He was shaken by an Aug. 6 incident when his batting-practice line drive hit pitching coach John Curtis in the head, sending him to the hospital. Escobar has the tools to be an above-average defender at shortstop, starting with fluid actions, a strong arm and good hands. His wiry strong body produces some pop at the plate, and his swing is sound. He's a plus runner, getting from home to first in less than 4.2 seconds. Escobar's strike zone is too generous. He improved at recognizing breaking balls in instructional league, and that progress will have to continue for him to make more consistent contact. Escobar's 41 errors ranked third in the minors, but Milwaukee isn't worried about his defense. While the Brewers have J.J. Hardy in the big leagues, Escobar is gaining ground fast. When Hardy couldn't play in the Arizona Fall League, Escobar became the league's youngest player and acquitted himself well. He'll start 2006 in high Class A.

Year	Club (League)	Class	AVG	G	AB	R	H	2B	3B	HR	RBI	BB	SO	SB	OBP	SLG
2004	Helena (Pio)	R	.281	68	231	38	65	8	0	2	24	20	44	20	.348	.342
2005	West Virginia (SAL)	A	.271	127	520	80	141	25	8	2	36	20	90	30	.305	.362
MINOR LEAGUE TOTALS			.274	195	751	118	206	33	8	4	60	40	134	50	.318	.356

7 DANA EVELAND — LHP

Born: Oct. 29, 1983. **B-T:** L-L. **Ht.:** 6-1. **Wt.:** 240. **Signed:** JC of the Canyons (Calif.), D/F 2002 (16th round). **Signed by:** Corey Rodriguez.

Eveland was a draft-and-follow signee in 2003, one year after the Brewers gave Manny Parra $1.5 million as a draft-and-follow. Eveland joined Parra in the Huntsville rotation in 2005, blew past him as a prospect and spent much of the second half in Milwaukee's bullpen. Eveland has a build that evokes David Wells and has some of Wells' pitchability as well. His fastball sits at 88-90 mph, touching 94. Eveland adds and subtracts off his fastball and commands it well. His slider can be a plus pitch, aided by his deceiving, crossfire delivery. His curveball has good depth. Like Wells, Eveland has trouble maintaining his weight. When he became a reliever, his conditioning lagged as he didn't maintain a workout schedule between starts. His changeup is his fourth pitch, though at times it's average. The Brewers hoped Eveland would get back on a conditioning track in the Arizona Fall League, but a knee injury ended his stint. If he's healthy and in shape, he could have the inside track on Milwakee's fifth starter's job.

Year	Club (League)	Class	W	L	ERA	G	GS	CG	SV	IP	H	R	ER	HR	BB	SO	AVG
2003	Helena (Pio)	R	2	1	2.08	19	0	0	14	26	30	9	6	1	8	41	.286
2004	Beloit (Mid)	A	9	6	2.84	22	16	1	2	117	108	48	37	8	24	119	.244
	Huntsville (SL)	AA	0	2	2.28	4	4	0	0	24	23	9	6	0	4	14	.261
2005	Huntsville (SL)	AA	10	4	2.72	18	18	0	0	109	96	42	33	4	38	98	.237
	Milwaukee (NL)	MLB	1	1	5.97	27	0	0	1	32	40	21	21	2	18	23	.317
MAJOR LEAGUE TOTALS			1	1	5.97	27	0	0	1	32	40	21	21	2	18	23	.317
MINOR LEAGUE TOTALS			21	13	2.67	63	38	1	16	276	257	108	82	13	74	272	.247

8 NELSON CRUZ   OF

Born: July 1, 1980. **B-T:** R-R. **Ht.:** 6-3. **Wt.:** 175. **Signed:** Dominican Republic, 1998. **Signed by:** Eddy Toledo (Mets).

After joining the organization in the offseason Keith Ginter trade with Oakland, Cruz played in the Futures Game and was Milwaukee's minor league player of the year. He led Nashville to the Pacific Coast League title, winning the championship series MVP award with three homers in a sweep of Tacoma. Cruz' calling card is well above average raw power. He uses an aggressive swing, strong wrists and quick hands to generate a buggy-whip swing with violent bat speed. But power isn't his only plus tool. He also has a plus arm in right field. Cruz has holes in his swing. Pitchers use his aggressiveness against him with offspeed stuff in fastball counts. They'll also climb the ladder on him because he'll chase high heat. The Brewers say they can live with the strikeouts as long as he makes powerful contact. Cruz figures to take another turn through Triple-A in 2006. He's behind Corey Hart on the depth chart of corner outfielders that already includes Geoff Jenkins and Carlos Lee.

Year	Club (League)	Class	AVG	G	AB	R	H	2B	3B	HR	RBI	BB	SO	SB	OBP	SLG
1998	Mets (DSL)	R	.271	30	70	10	19	0	0	1	13	7	21	6	.363	.314
1999	Mets 1 (DSL)	R	.200	35	90	7	18	4	1	0	11	6	21	6	.255	.267
	Mets 2 (DSL)	R	.278	36	115	20	32	4	1	1	21	16	27	14	.366	.357
2000	Mets East (DSL)	R	.351	69	259	60	91	14	4	15	80	33	56	17	.434	.610
2001	Athletics (AZL)	R	.250	23	88	11	22	3	1	3	16	4	29	6	.283	.409
2002	Vancouver (NWL)	A	.276	63	214	23	59	14	0	4	25	9	58	12	.316	.397
2003	Kane County (Mid)	A	.238	119	470	65	112	26	2	20	85	29	128	10	.292	.430
2004	Modesto (Cal)	A	.345	66	261	54	90	27	1	11	52	24	73	8	.407	.582
	Midland (TL)	AA	.313	67	262	51	82	14	2	14	45	26	69	8	.377	.542
	Sacramento (PCL)	AAA	.231	4	13	4	3	1	0	1	2	1	7	0	.286	.538
2005	Huntsville (SL)	AA	.306	68	248	45	76	19	0	16	54	31	71	10	.388	.577
	Nashville (PCL)	AAA	.269	60	208	33	56	13	0	11	27	30	62	9	.382	.490
	Milwaukee (NL)	MLB	.200	8	5	1	1	1	0	0	0	2	0	0	.429	.400
MAJOR LEAGUE TOTALS			.200	8	5	1	1	1	0	0	0	2	0	0	.429	.400
MINOR LEAGUE TOTALS			.287	640	2298	383	660	139	12	97	431	216	622	106	.357	.485

9 JOSE CAPELLAN   RHP

Born: Jan. 13, 1981. **B-T:** R-R. **Ht.:** 6-4. **Wt.:** 235. **Signed:** Dominican Republic, 1998. **Signed by:** Julian Perez/Rene Francisco (Braves).

After going from Class A to the Braves in 2004, Capellan was the key player in the Dan Kolb trade. While Kolb quickly fizzled in Atlanta, Capellan struggled as a starter in Triple-A before shifting to the bullpen and finishing the season in Milwaukee. Capellan touched 100 mph with his fastball in 2004, but with the Brewers he worked at 92-94 mph as a starter. His velocity spiked back to 95-97 as a reliever, a role he enthusiastically embraced. He generates excellent arm speed, giving his fastball late tail and life up in the strike zone. Lacking confidence in his loopy downer curveball, Capellan switched to a slider as a reliever. It's still slurvy but he was able to throw it for strikes with some consistency. His changeup remains a work in progress, and his conditioning remains a concern. Capellan could return to a starting role if he rediscovers the bite and command on his curve in winter ball or in spring training. He had a 5.16 ERA as a starter and a 1.44 ERA as a reliever in Triple-A. He'll probably open 2006 in a set-up role in Milwaukee.

Year	Club (League)	Class	W	L	ERA	G	GS	CG	SV	IP	H	R	ER	HR	BB	SO	AVG
1999	Braves (DSL)	R	3	3	3.58	14	10	0	2	60	54	31	24	1	28	46	.242
2000	Braves (DSL)	R	3	8	3.69	14	14	0	0	68	58	45	28	0	36	68	.221
2001	Danville (Appy)	R	0	0	1.72	3	3	0	0	16	12	7	3	1	4	25	.200
2002	Did not play—Suspended																
2003	Braves (GCL)	R	0	1	2.65	5	5	0	0	17	18	7	5	0	8	17	.277
	Rome (SAL)	A	1	2	3.80	14	12	1	0	47	43	23	20	2	19	32	.253
2004	Myrtle Beach (Car)	A	5	1	1.94	8	8	1	0	46	27	11	10	0	11	62	.168
	Greenville (SL)	AA	5	1	2.50	9	8	0	0	50	53	15	14	1	19	53	.290
	Richmond (IL)	AAA	4	2	2.51	7	7	0	0	43	33	13	12	0	15	37	.216
	Atlanta (NL)	MLB	0	1	11.25	3	2	0	0	8	14	10	10	2	5	4	.400
2005	Nashville (PCL)	AAA	5	3	3.87	36	12	0	6	91	88	42	39	4	42	76	.257
	Milwaukee (NL)	MLB	1	1	2.87	17	0	0	0	16	17	6	5	1	5	14	.293
MAJOR LEAGUE TOTALS			1	2	5.70	20	2	0	0	24	31	16	15	3	10	18	.333
MINOR LEAGUE TOTALS			26	21	3.18	110	79	2	8	439	386	194	155	9	182	416	.238

10   ZACH JACKSON   LHP

Born: May 13, 1983. **B-T:** L-L. **Ht.:** 6-5. **Wt.:** 220. **Drafted:** Texas A&M, 2004 (1st round supplemental). **Signed by:** Andy Beene (Blue Jays).

Jackson tied for the minor league lead with 16 wins, pitched in the Futures Game and reached Triple-A in his first full season. But when the Blue Jays set their sights on Lyle Overbay, they parted with Jackson and big leaguers David Bush and Gabe Gross in a Winter Meetings trade. Jackson works quickly with a quirky crossfire motion that makes his pitches look faster than they are. Armed with an 83-89 mph cutter, he's able to get it in on the hands of righthanders. He also throws a two-seam fastball at 88-92 mph, a tick above average for a southpaw, and a sweeping curve he uses to expand the zone against lefties. His changeup is average and he controls it well. Jackson makes quick adjustments but proved much more hittable in Triple-A, partly because he relied on his cutter too much. He also seemed to give Triple-A batters too much credit and didn't pitch as aggressively as he did in the lower minors. Jackson is a strike-thrower who keeps his defense in games. His ceiling is as a mid-rotation starter. Expected to open 2006 in Triple-A, he could contribute in Milwaukee before the season is out.

Year	Club (League)	Class	W	L	ERA	G	GS	CG	SV	IP	H	R	ER	HR	BB	SO	AVG
2004	Auburn (NY-P)	A	0	0	5.40	4	4	0	0	15	20	9	9	1	6	11	.323
2005	Dunedin (FSL)	A	8	1	2.88	10	10	0	0	59	56	25	19	3	6	48	.247
	New Hampshire (EL)	AA	4	3	4.00	9	9	0	0	54	57	27	24	3	12	43	.277
	Syracuse (IL)	AAA	4	4	5.14	8	8	0	0	47	61	33	27	3	21	33	.323
MINOR LEAGUE TOTALS			16	8	4.05	31	31	0	0	176	194	94	79	10	45	135	.284

11   WILL INMAN   RHP

Born: Feb. 6, 1987. **B-T:** R-R. **Ht.:** 6-0. **Wt.:** 200. **Signed:** HS—Dry Fork, Va., 2005 (3rd round). **Signed by:** Grant Brittain.

Inman's stellar pro debut was a major coup for area scout Grant Brittain, who stayed on Inman after many other scouts backed off. Inman toned down a maximum-effort delivery in the spring, and set the Virginia high school career strikeout record when his fastball crept into the 90s. Inman's fastball sits at 92-93 and he has big league command of the pitch—rare for a high schooler. His slurvy curveball is a swing-and-miss pitch that Milwaukee wants him to tighten into a slider. The club loves his competitiveness, aptitude and willingness to get better. Not much about Inman is typical. His arm action was likened by one club official to that of a javelin thrower—long in the front and the back. The Brewers were able to improve his extension and quiet his delivery. At times he throws too many breaking balls for someone who throws strikes with a live fastball. Inman has the polish and stuff to move quickly, but the Brewers want to take it slow to make sure he maintains his improved delivery. He'll report to low Class A for his first full season.

Year	Club (League)	Class	W	L	ERA	G	GS	CG	SV	IP	H	R	ER	HR	BB	SO	AVG
2005	Brewers (AZL)	R	0	0	0.00	1	0	0	0	2	0	0	0	0	1	1	.000
	Helena (Pio)	R	6	0	2.00	13	5	0	1	45	29	11	10	5	11	58	.182
MINOR LEAGUE TOTALS			6	0	1.91	14	5	0	1	47	29	11	10	5	12	59	.176

12   CHARLIE FERMAINT   OF

Born: Oct. 11, 1985. **B-T:** R-R. **Ht.:** 5-10. **Wt.:** 170. **Drafted:** HS—Dorado, P.R., 2003 (4th round). **Signed by:** Larry Pardo.

Fermaint has as high a ceiling as any Brewers position player other than Prince Fielder and Ryan Braun, and one Brewers official likens him to Andruw Jones. But it took Fermaint until midway through his third pro season to make it out of Rookie ball, and the progress of his bat will determine how much of his significant potential he reaches. He had hamstring problems in high school in Puerto Rico that helped drive him down to the fourth round of the 2003 draft. He also struggled with shoulder woes and pitch recognition in his first try at Rookie-level Helena in 2004. Like Jones, Fermaint improved as a hitter when he got into a wider, better hitting position to give him more balance against offspeed pitches. That helped him let his bat speed take over, as his hands are quick enough to catch up to any heater and drive it with authority. While he doesn't project to have Jones' power and is more of a top-of-the-order hitter, Fermaint has defensive ability that evokes the young Jones, with a solid-average, accurate arm, effortless range and efficient routes. He's a plus runner, covering 60 yards in 6.5 seconds when healthy. The Brewers liken Fermaint's makeup to that of Corey Hart, as he doesn't get down on himself and is coachable. His ability to adjust to more advanced pitching—South Atlantic Leaguers handled him in his first pass through the league—will determine how quickly he advances.

Year	Club (League)	Class	AVG	G	AB	R	H	2B	3B	HR	RBI	BB	SO	SB	OBP	SLG
2003	Brewers (AZL)	R	.300	25	100	16	30	3	3	1	9	3	19	6	.327	.420
2004	Helena (Pio)	R	.229	58	218	30	50	14	2	5	39	19	83	8	.300	.381
2005	Helena (Pio)	R	.364	31	129	46	47	9	2	12	32	15	28	11	.419	.744
	West Virginia (SAL)	A	.248	27	113	18	28	7	0	5	17	8	39	4	.301	.442
MINOR LEAGUE TOTALS			.277	141	560	110	155	33	7	23	97	45	169	29	.333	.484

13 MANNY PARRA LHP

Born: Oct. 30, 1982. **B-T:** L-L. **Ht.:** 6-3. **Wt.:** 200. **Drafted:** American River (Calif.) JC, D/F 2002 (26th round). **Signed by:** Justin McCray.

In many ways, Parra and Dana Eveland are similar, but Eveland gets the edge as a prospect because of his better health track record, better command and reaching the majors first despite being a year younger than Parra. The Brewers still have significant hopes for Parra, whom they gave a $1.55 million bonus as a draft-and-follow in 2003. His delivery evokes a smaller version of Mark Mulder, but Parra hasn't thrown with the command that helped earn him those Mulder comparisons earlier in his career. He still has excellent stuff when healthy, starting with a darting 88-90 mph two-seam fastball that touches 93. Parra can bump his four-seamer up to 95 mph and work high in the zone with it, then attack hitters with a solid-average splitter or curveball. At times he struggles to control his changeup and two-seamer, throwing fat strikes and leaving him far more hittable than his stuff should allow. Parra also has failed to remain healthy for an entire season as he continues to over-rotate in his delivery, slowing his arm down and leading to nagging injuries. In 2005, he felt it in the back of his shoulder, and while he didn't require surgery, he didn't pitch after June 30. A healthy Parra projects as a No. 3 starter, as does Eveland. Milwaukee thinks Eveland's quick rise has challenged Parra to try to match it. He'll probably open the year in Triple-A.

Year	Club (League)	Class	W	L	ERA	G	GS	CG	SV	IP	H	R	ER	HR	BB	SO	AVG
2002	Brewers (AZL)	R	0	0	4.50	1	1	0	0	2	1	1	1	1	0	4	.143
	Ogden (Pio)	R	3	1	3.21	11	10	0	0	48	59	30	17	3	10	51	.298
2003	Beloit (Mid)	A	11	2	2.73	23	23	1	0	139	127	50	42	9	24	117	.243
2004	High Desert (Cal)	A	5	2	3.48	13	12	1	0	67	76	41	26	3	19	64	.290
	Huntsville (SL)	AA	0	1	3.00	3	3	0	0	6	5	3	2	0	0	10	.217
2005	Huntsville (SL)	AA	5	6	3.96	16	16	0	0	91	111	47	40	4	21	86	.295
MINOR LEAGUE TOTALS			24	12	3.27	67	65	2	0	353	379	172	128	20	74	332	.273

14 BRAD NELSON OF

Born: Dec. 23, 1982. **B-T:** L-R. **Ht.:** 6-2. **Wt.:** 220. **Drafted:** HS—Algona, Iowa, 2001 (4th round). **Signed by:** Harvey Kuenn Jr./Larry Doughty.

Nelson ranked No. 1 on this list after the 2002 season, when he led the minors with 49 doubles and 116 RBIs. His career took its first real step backward in 2005, as he started the year in Triple-A but had to endure a midseason demotion back to Double-A. He moved back up to Nashville for the end of the season and Pacific Coast League playoffs. The Brewers say he handled his demotion well, using it as motivation rather than becoming bitter. Nelson's problems began when he broke his hamate bone in his right wrist in 2003, and his power still has yet to bounce back. His strength and potential are still there, but the Brewers believe he has lost the feel for his swing mechanics and his confidence along with it. Nelson has worked hard to get better in the outfield after Prince Fielder's arrival in the system prompted the Brewers to move him to left field. He runs well enough to play the outfield, and his arm is good enough for him to see action in right. He'll try to rediscover his power stroke in Triple-A this year.

Year	Club (League)	Class	AVG	G	AB	R	H	2B	3B	HR	RBI	BB	SO	SB	OBP	SLG
2001	Brewers (AZL)	R	.302	17	63	10	19	6	1	0	13	8	18	0	.392	.429
	Ogden (Pio)	R	.262	13	42	5	11	4	0	0	10	3	9	0	.298	.357
2002	Beloit (Mid)	A	.297	106	417	70	124	38	2	17	99	34	86	4	.353	.520
	High Desert (Cal)	A	.255	26	102	24	26	11	0	3	17	12	28	0	.333	.451
2003	High Desert (Cal)	A	.311	41	167	23	52	9	1	1	18	12	22	2	.363	.395
	Huntsville (SL)	AA	.210	39	143	15	30	12	0	1	14	11	34	2	.274	.315
2004	Huntsville (SL)	AA	.254	137	500	61	127	31	1	19	77	47	146	11	.321	.434
2005	Huntsville (SL)	AA	.293	55	208	27	61	8	1	6	38	26	42	1	.370	.428
	Nashville (PCL)	AAA	.253	81	281	50	71	16	2	7	39	45	74	4	.359	.399
MINOR LEAGUE TOTALS			.271	515	1923	285	521	135	8	54	325	198	459	24	.342	.434

15   HERNAN IRIBARREN   2B

Born: June 29, 1984. **B-T:** L-R. **Ht.:** 6-1. **Wt.:** 160. **Signed:** Venezuela, 2002. **Signed by:** Epy Guerrero.

Iribarren attracted plenty of attention in 2004, when he won the Rookie-level Arizona League batting title, then had a scintillating 15-game stint at low Class A Beloit. His .637 slugging percentage that year, however, may have given an inaccurate read of the kind of hitter Iribarren is. He was experienced for a Latin player going into the AZL, having spent two years at the Brewers' Dominican academy (which the club since has eliminated in favor of bringing players to the United States sooner). Slender and sleek, he's a slap-and-dash middle infielder whose quick hands and flat swing plane evoke Rod Carew and Luis Castillo. Iribarren just doesn't have much power, and virtually none against lefthanders (three extra-base hits in 100 at-bats last year). He's a plus runner, and he has enough patience and bat control to hit in the No. 2 hole. A solid defender at second, his defensive tools are all a grade or two below those of his West Virginia running mate, Alcides Escobar. They should advance together to high Class A in 2006.

Year	Club (League)	Class	AVG	G	AB	R	H	2B	3B	HR	RBI	BB	SO	SB	OBP	SLG
2002	Brewers (DSL)	R	.314	66	223	35	70	13	2	2	34	19	43	7	.383	.417
2003	Brewers (DSL)	R	.344	64	227	43	78	12	7	2	27	24	36	17	.403	.485
2004	Brewers (AZL)	R	.439	46	189	40	83	6	9	4	36	19	23	15	.490	.630
	Beloit (Mid)	A	.373	15	67	12	25	6	5	1	10	5	16	1	.411	.657
2005	West Virginia (SAL)	A	.290	126	486	72	141	15	8	4	48	51	99	38	.360	.379
MINOR LEAGUE TOTALS			.333	317	1192	202	397	52	31	13	155	118	217	78	.396	.461

16   TIM DILLARD   RHP

Born: July 19, 1983. **B-T:** B-R. **Ht.:** 6-4. **Wt.:** 200. **Drafted:** Itawamba (Miss.) CC, D/F 2002 (34th round). **Signed by:** Doug Reynolds.

The Brewers drafted Dillard in the 15th round in 2001 out of high school, then picked him again out of Itawamba (Miss.) CC, which he helped reach the Junior College World Series. He played catcher and pitched back then, but Milwaukee coveted his power right arm on the mound. Dillard had committed to Mississippi, where his father Steve was an all-American before his own big league career as an infielder, but signed as a draft-and-follow in 2003. The Brewers named Dillard their 2005 minor league pitcher of the year after he led the system's full-season starters in innings, wins and ERA. He has a strong, durable frame and good coordination, and he excels at repeating his low-effort delivery. His slinging arm action helps give him one of the organization's better fastballs. It has heavy sink and boring action, sits at 87-91 mph and touches 94. He averaged an efficient 14 pitches an inning by working on his sinker, and has the best control in the system. Dillard's secondary pitches aren't at his fastball's level, in part because of his relative inexperience as a pitcher. His slider is hard and sweeps a bit but lacks tilt or depth. He tends to drop his arm on his changeup, giving the pitch away. If his secondary stuff can improve to just average, Dillard could be an innings-eating workhorse as a No. 4 starter. He's ready for Double-A.

Year	Club (League)	Class	W	L	ERA	G	GS	CG	SV	IP	H	R	ER	HR	BB	SO	AVG
2003	Brewers (AZL)	R	1	2	3.79	11	4	0	0	36	36	19	15	1	5	32	.261
	Helena (Pio)	R	0	0	0.00	3	0	0	0	5	5	0	0	0	2	6	.250
2004	Beloit (Mid)	A	2	5	3.94	43	1	0	10	78	89	46	34	4	22	61	.280
2005	Brevard County (FSL)	A	12	10	2.48	28	28	5	0	185	150	64	51	9	31	128	.219
MINOR LEAGUE TOTALS			15	17	2.96	85	33	5	10	304	280	129	100	14	60	227	.241

17   ROLANDO PASCUAL   RHP

Born: Feb. 8, 1989. **B-T:** B-R. **Ht.:** 6-6. **Wt.:** 218. **Signed:** Dominican Republic, 2005. **Signed by:** Fernando Arango.

The best evidence of the Brewers' new approach to Latin American scouting, Pascual signed for a $710,000 bonus in September after dogged pursuit by the organization's Latin

American scouting coordinator, Fernando Arango. Milwaukee wants to sign advanced Latin players and bring them to their complex in Arizona, rather than use the academy-based approach that produced Alcides Escobar and Hernan Iribarren but few big leaguers of note (Valerio de los Santos stands out the most). The Brewers consider Pascual, the top Dominican pitcher available in 2005, the equivalent of the second-round pick they forfeited to sign free agent Damian Miller. Pascual had a strong start to his career in instructional league, impressing with his stuff and makeup. He has a long, loose frame with a short upper body and plenty of projection. His fastball sits at 87-90 mph, and he topped out at 92-93 in instructional league. He also showed the ability to spin a breaking ball, though the pitch is still in its nascent stages. The same goes for his changeup. Milwaukee officials praised his work ethic and attitude in instructional league. He should start 2006 in Rookie ball.

Year	Club (League)	Class	W	L	ERA	G	GS	CG	SV	IP	H	R	ER	HR	BB	SO	AVG
2005	Did not play—Signed 2006 contract																

18 STEVE HAMMOND   LHP

Born: April 30, 1982. **B-T:** R-L. **Ht.:** 6-2. **Wt.:** 205. **Drafted:** Long Beach State, 2005 (6th round). **Signed by:** Bruce Seid.

Hammond has a college player's maturity and experience to go with a powerful, relatively fresh left arm. Hammond began his college career at juco power Sacramento City College in 2001, but had bone spurs removed from his elbow that year. He didn't return to full strength until the summer of 2004 in the Central Illinois Collegiate League, then transferred to Long Beach State, where he worked as a lefty specialist. Because he worked just 24 innings during the spring, Milwaukee used him as a starter after he signed for $30,000 as a sixth-round pick. Hammond could move quickly in either a rotation or bullpen role. He has an average 88-92 mph fastball that sits closer to 92-94 when he relieves. He's tweaked his breaking ball, picking up a slider from roving pitching instructor Jim Rooney, and has quickly made it an out pitch. The Brewers have been aggressive with the athletic 23-year-old, giving him time in the Arizona Fall League, and he should begin 2006 as a Double-A starter.

Year	Club (League)	Class	W	L	ERA	G	GS	CG	SV	IP	H	R	ER	HR	BB	SO	AVG
2005	Helena (Pio)	R	1	0	1.06	4	2	0	0	17	13	5	2	1	0	23	.206
	West Virginia (SAL)	A	3	0	2.45	4	1	0	0	15	12	4	4	0	5	11	.235
	Brevard County (FSL)	A	1	3	2.78	8	7	0	0	36	33	17	11	2	9	30	.244
MINOR LEAGUE TOTALS			5	3	2.27	16	10	0	0	67	58	26	17	3	14	64	.233

19 BEN HENDRICKSON   RHP

Born: Feb. 4, 1981. **B-T:** R-R. **Ht.:** 6-4. **Wt.:** 190. **Drafted:** HS—Bloomington, Minn., 1999 (10th round). **Signed by:** Harvey Kuenn Jr.

Hendrickson pitched 46 big league innings in 2004, but his struggles in 2005, Nashville's run to the Pacific Coast League title and Milwaukee's relatively healthy rotation kept him on the farm all season. He has lost luster since he was the Triple-A International League pitcher of the year in 2004. He posted a 10.93 ERA in big league camp last spring, landing him back in Triple-A. He struggled with his mechanics and command from the start in 2005, and his walk total was the highest he had posted since his first full season in 2001. Hendrickson adjusted and challenged hitters more as the year went on, but his stuff—aside from his plus curveball that remains his meal ticket—was too short to overcome constantly being behind hitters. His 88-91 mph fastball had more life last season, but he still pitched backward too often and wasn't as good throwing his curveball and changeup for strikes in fastball counts. His changeup remains his third pitch, though he emphasized it more in 2005. The Brewers say Hendrickson's upside is that of a Jeff Suppan type, a durable fourth or fifth starter. He also profiles similarly to journeyman Dave Eiland, who never quite had the stuff to get big leaguers out consistently. Hendrickson will get a shot at the fifth starter spot in Milwaukee, with Dana Eveland his biggest in-house competition.

Year	Club (League)	Class	W	L	ERA	G	GS	CG	SV	IP	H	R	ER	HR	BB	SO	AVG
2000	Ogden (Pio)	R	4	3	5.68	13	7	0	1	51	50	37	32	7	29	48	.245
2001	Beloit (Mid)	A	8	9	2.84	25	25	1	0	133	122	58	42	3	72	133	.246
2002	High Desert (Cal)	A	5	5	2.55	14	14	0	0	81	61	31	23	3	41	70	.209
	Huntsville (SL)	AA	4	2	2.97	13	13	0	0	70	57	31	23	2	35	50	.231
2003	Huntsville (SL)	AA	7	6	3.45	17	16	0	0	78	82	35	30	6	28	56	.278
2004	Indianapolis (IL)	AAA	11	3	2.02	21	21	2	0	125	114	32	28	6	26	93	.250
	Milwaukee (NL)	MLB	1	8	6.22	10	9	0	0	46	58	33	32	6	20	29	.310
2005	Nashville (PCL)	AAA	6	12	4.97	28	27	1	0	156	176	100	86	17	58	122	.292
MAJOR LEAGUE TOTALS			1	8	6.22	10	9	0	0	46	58	33	32	6	20	29	.310
MINOR LEAGUE TOTALS			45	40	3.42	131	123	4	1	694	662	324	264	44	289	572	.255

20 LOU PALMISANO
C

Born: Sept. 16, 1982. **B-T:** R-R. **Ht.:** 6-1. **Wt.:** 205. **Drafted:** Broward (Fla.) CC, 2003 (3rd round). **Signed by:** Larry Pardo.

The Brewers' dearth of catching caused them to give free agent Damian Miller a three-year contract at age 35, costing them a second-round pick in the 2005 draft. Palmisano is the organization's best hope of developing its own replacement, though Angel Salome is catching up to him. The Rookie-level Pioneer League MVP in his pro debut in 2003, Palmisano hasn't matched his production since. Palmisano, whose brother Nick is a power-hitting first baseman at Stetson, has become a solid receiver by working diligently with roving instructor Charlie Greene. His throwing times to second base come in consistently at or below 2.0 seconds and continue to improve as he enhances his strong arm with technique, including better footwork and a more consistent release point. He hasn't made the same progress at the plate, where he tends to tinker too much. He changes his stance from open to closed, wide to narrow. The Brewers would like him to get more balanced and use his legs more in his swing, the better to bring out his average power potential. He runs well for a catcher. Palmisano is expected to move to Double-A in 2006.

Year	Club (League)	Class	AVG	G	AB	R	H	2B	3B	HR	RBI	BB	SO	SB	OBP	SLG
2003	Helena (Pio)	R	.391	47	174	32	68	13	2	6	43	18	29	13	.458	.592
2004	Beloit (Mid)	A	.293	113	409	59	120	22	3	7	65	43	93	3	.371	.413
2005	Brevard County (FSL)	A	.255	118	432	47	110	16	7	5	49	34	65	3	.314	.359
MINOR LEAGUE TOTALS			.294	278	1015	138	298	51	12	18	157	95	187	19	.363	.421

21 ANGEL SALOME
C

Born: June 8, 1986. **B-T:** R-R. **Ht.:** 5-7. **Wt.:** 190. **Drafted:** HS—New York, 2004 (5th round). **Signed by:** Tony Blengino.

Born in Santo Domingo, Dominican Republic, Salome moved back and forth from the Dominican and New York twice, finally settling into upper Manhattan at age 12. He attended the same high school as Manny Ramirez and hit like Ramirez in high school, surpassing .800 as a senior. Salome hit .415 at Helena last season as his Popeye-like forearms, short swing and powerful stroke helped him get the fat part of the bat on the ball consistently. His swing would be better if he incorporated his lower half more, giving him more power and allowing him to stay back better on breaking balls. His ebullient personality and bilingual ability are both assets as a catcher. Salome still has to adjust to pitchers who throw with velocity and sharp breaking balls he didn't see in high school, both at the plate and behind it. While Salome has a 70 arm on the 20-80 scouting scale and has a prototypical athletic, squat body to catch, he has many adjustments to make defensively. He's still grasping basic receiving fundamentals. He had 18 passed balls in 35 games at catcher and threw out 32 percent of basestealers. He's expected to return to low Class A for 2006.

Year	Club (League)	Class	AVG	G	AB	R	H	2B	3B	HR	RBI	BB	SO	SB	OBP	SLG
2004	Brewers (AZL)	R	.235	20	81	7	19	7	0	0	8	4	14	2	.271	.321
2005	West Virginia (SAL)	A	.254	29	118	15	30	7	1	4	21	8	17	1	.302	.432
	Helena (Pio)	R	.415	37	159	34	66	17	0	8	50	15	16	6	.469	.673
MINOR LEAGUE TOTALS			.321	86	358	56	115	31	1	12	79	27	47	9	.370	.514

22 DAVE KRYNZEL
OF

Born: Nov. 7, 1981. **B-T:** L-L. **Ht.:** 6-1. **Wt.:** 180. **Drafted:** HS—Henderson, Nev., 2000 (1st round). **Signed by:** Bruce Seid.

Krynzel was once one of the Brewers' top prospects as a potential leadoff man and center fielder. He came to spring training last year with a clear shot at the big league job and hit .323, but Brady Clark beat him out. Now Milwaukee has better outfield depth, making Krynzel less a part of the organization's future plans. He has yet to put his considerable tools together. His Pacific Coast League playoff performance was unfortunately too typical, as he tried to do too much and struck out 10 times in 33 at-bats while batting .152. Krynzel typically gets off to fast starts before tailing off in the second half as pitchers adjust. He has average or above-average tools across the board, particularly defensively, and remains one of the organization's fastest baserunners. But his inability to adapt over the course of a season makes him more of a fourth outfielder than a viable candidate as a big league starter.

Year	Club (League)	Class	AVG	G	AB	R	H	2B	3B	HR	RBI	BB	SO	SB	OBP	SLG
2000	Ogden (Pio)	R	.359	34	131	25	47	8	3	1	29	16	23	8	.442	.489
2001	Beloit (Mid)	A	.305	35	141	22	43	1	1	1	19	9	28	11	.364	.348
	High Desert (Cal)	A	.277	89	383	65	106	19	5	5	33	27	122	34	.329	.392
2002	High Desert (Cal)	A	.268	97	365	76	98	13	12	11	45	64	100	29	.391	.460
	Huntsville (SL)	AA	.240	31	129	13	31	2	3	2	13	4	30	13	.269	.349

2003	Huntsville (SL)	AA	.267	124	457	72	122	13	11	2	34	60	119	43	.357	.357
2004	Brewers (AZL)	R	.500	5	16	8	8	1	1	0	0	3	2	2	.600	.688
	Indianapolis (IL)	AAA	.276	69	257	36	71	10	4	6	27	20	65	10	.332	.416
	Milwaukee (NL)	MLB	.220	16	41	6	9	1	0	0	3	3	15	0	.319	.244
2005	Milwaukee (NL)	MLB	.000	5	7	0	0	0	0	0	0	0	3	0	.000	.000
	Nashville (PCL)	AAA	.256	115	450	71	115	25	7	11	51	43	138	24	.324	.416
MAJOR LEAGUE TOTALS			.188	21	48	6	9	1	0	0	3	3	18	0	.278	.208
MINOR LEAGUE TOTALS			.275	599	2329	388	641	92	47	39	251	246	627	174	.352	.405

23 ADAM HEETHER 3B

Born: Jan. 14, 1982. **B-T:** R-R. **Ht.:** 6-0. **Wt.:** 200. **Drafted:** Long Beach State, 2003 (11th round). **Signed by:** Bruce Seid.

After taking Michael Vick in the 30th round of the 2000 draft, the Rockies chose Heether with their next pick. Colorado signed neither, as Heether went to Modesto (Calif.) Junior College before a two-year stint at Long Beach State. Heether was a solid college hitter who has become a solid pro hitter, and the Brewers see him as a possible Jeff Cirillo. Heether's grinder mentality got him through a challenging 2005 season, as he broke his nose in a home-plate collision in the second game of the year. He sat out a week, and later missed a month when a pitch broke a bone in his left hand. Things started to click with Heether's swing last year in instructional league, as he incorporated his lower half into his swing, generating pop to go with his all-fields, line-drive approach. He has quick hands and handles breaking balls when he trusts them to do the work. He battles pitchers and doesn't give away at-bats. His good hands translate as well to the field, where he has solid tools across the board. Heether finished the year strong, hitting safely in 12 of 14 games after a promotion to Double-A, and spent the offseason working out in San Diego with Anthony Gwynn and his father Tony to hone his hitting approach. He'll return to Double-A this year.

Year	Club (League)	Class	AVG	G	AB	R	H	2B	3B	HR	RBI	BB	SO	SB	OBP	SLG
2003	Brewers (AZL)	R	.000	3	11	1	0	0	0	0	0	2	1	0	.214	.000
	Beloit (Mid)	A	.228	47	171	28	39	12	1	2	22	18	28	4	.313	.345
2004	Beloit (Mid)	A	.252	128	476	65	120	35	4	17	72	37	93	2	.313	.450
2005	Brevard County (FSL)	A	.305	93	338	48	103	27	2	6	54	34	48	3	.386	.450
	Huntsville (SL)	AA	.314	14	51	11	16	5	0	0	9	2	8	2	.339	.412
MINOR LEAGUE TOTALS			.266	285	1047	153	278	79	7	25	157	93	178	11	.337	.426

24 DENNIS SARFATE RHP

Born: April 9, 1981. **B-T:** R-R. **Ht.:** 6-4. **Wt.:** 215. **Drafted:** Chandler-Gilbert (Ariz.) CC, 2001 (9th round). **Signed by:** Brian Johnson.

Sarfate has had an uneven pro career, but with his power stuff, a spot in the big league bullpen isn't far away. He hasn't missed a turn in the rotation since having elbow surgery in 2002. Sarfate continued to hone his repertoire last year, focusing on a spike curveball and changeup while shedding his slider. His fastball is among the best in the organization, touching 97 mph and sitting at 92-94 with life. He pitches inside with his fastball relentlessly, daring hitters to try to turn on it, and probably would do well to learn to throw it to the outer half more often. When he leaves his heater over the plate, he tends to get punished. Sarfate's secondary stuff is mediocre at best, and he doesn't throw his curve or changeup with much conviction. None of his three pitches finds the strike zone enough. Scouts believe he profiles best as a power reliever, but if Sarfate improves either of his secondary offerings, he could challenge for Milwaukee's No. 5 starter's job in 2006. Otherwise, he'll get a full taste of Triple-A.

Year	Club (League)	Class	W	L	ERA	G	GS	CG	SV	IP	H	R	ER	HR	BB	SO	AVG
2001	Ogden (Pio)	R	1	2	4.63	9	4	0	1	23	20	13	12	4	10	32	.230
2002	Brewers (AZL)	R	0	0	2.57	5	5	0	0	14	6	4	4	0	7	22	.125
	Ogden (Pio)	R	0	0	9.00	1	1	0	0	2	1	1	1	0	1	2	.400
2003	Beloit (Mid)	A	12	2	2.84	26	26	0	0	140	114	50	44	11	66	140	.227
2004	Huntsville (SL)	AA	7	12	4.05	28	25	0	0	129	128	71	58	12	78	113	.278
2005	Huntsville (SL)	AA	9	9	3.88	24	24	1	0	130	120	65	56	13	59	110	.245
	Nashville (PCL)	AAA	0	1	2.25	2	1	0	0	12	6	3	3	1	4	10	.150
MINOR LEAGUE TOTALS			29	26	3.57	95	85	1	1	449	396	207	178	41	225	429	.242

25 STEVE MOSS OF

Born: Jan. 12, 1984. **B-T:** R-R. **Ht.:** 6-2. **Wt.:** 180. **Drafted:** HS—Sherman Oaks, Calif., 2002 (29th round). **Signed by:** Corey Rodriguez.

After years of waiting for Dave Krynzel to pan out as a center fielder, the Brewers have developed enviable depth at that position, giving them other in-house options if Brady Clark has a short-lived run as the big league starter. Moss is the best intermediate option, a toolsy athlete with significant upside who's ready for his first shot at Double-A. He played a career-best 118 games in 2005, avoiding serious injury for the first time as a pro and just missing 10 days in June with a twisted ankle. Brevard County manager John Tamargo helped Moss understand that even when he's nicked up, he's capable of helping his team win. Moss is a plus runner with above-average power potential. He has bat speed and a quick short swing, but his power has been offset by poor plate discipline. With experience, he'll learn which pitches to drive and which to lay off, and the Brewers project he can hit 20-25 homers annually while staying in center field. His plus arm could allow him to move to right if he slows down too much to stay in center. Moss took on a leadership role in instructional league, setting the pace for younger Brewers with his work ethic and attitude. The organization hopes that's an indication Moss will break out this year in Double-A.

Year	Club (League)	Class	AVG	G	AB	R	H	2B	3B	HR	RBI	BB	SO	SB	OBP	SLG
2002	Brewers (AZL)	R	.292	30	106	20	31	8	2	1	20	22	32	3	.414	.434
	Ogden (Pio)	R	.500	5	8	3	4	2	1	0	3	1	1	0	.538	1.000
2003	Beloit (Mid)	A	.290	57	186	25	54	8	3	1	22	32	44	7	.398	.382
2004	Beloit (Mid)	A	.235	102	362	41	85	17	4	8	34	35	90	6	.318	.370
2005	Brevard County (FSL)	A	.281	118	442	62	124	19	7	9	51	36	113	18	.332	.416
MINOR LEAGUE TOTALS			.270	312	1104	151	298	54	17	19	130	126	280	34	.350	.401

26 MAT GAMEL 3B

Born: July 26, 1985. **B-T:** L-R. **Ht.:** 6-0. **Wt.:** 205. **Drafted:** Chipola (Fla.) JC, 2005 (4th round). **Signed by:** Doug Reynolds.

Gamel is a grinder who can hit, a good combination. He played at Jacksonville high school baseball power Bishop Kenny and didn't start until his senior season, keeping his name under the radar. He spent his first college season at Daytona (Fla.) Community College, and Milwaukee didn't spot him until last year at Chipola, where he played with Brewers draft-and-follow outfielder Darren Ford (now the fastest player in the system). Gamel earned a reputation as one of Florida's top hitters in a down draft year in the Sunshine State, and the Brewers had to grab him in the fourth round. Gamel, who had committed to Louisiana-Monroe, was a juco all-American after hitting .433-14-63, and followed up with a solid pro debut. Chipola coach Jeff Johnson called him the best hitter he had ever coached. Gamel has a good lefthanded stroke that lashes line drives from gap to gap. At times his swing gets a little long, but when his mechanics are right it's a short stroke that should lend itself to good pull power. Gamel's best defensive tool is his arm strength, and the Brewers already have talked of moving him to the outfield. He'll probably open this year in low Class A after finishing 2005 there.

Year	Club (League)	Class	AVG	G	AB	R	H	2B	3B	HR	RBI	BB	SO	SB	OBP	SLG
2005	West Virginia (SAL)	A	.174	8	23	2	4	0	0	1	1	5	9	0	.321	.304
	Helena (Pio)	R	.327	50	199	34	65	15	2	5	37	12	49	7	.375	.497
MINOR LEAGUE TOTALS			.311	58	222	36	69	15	2	6	38	17	58	7	.369	.477

27 LORENZO CAIN OF

Born: April 13, 1986. **B-T:** R-R. **Ht.:** 6-2. **Wt.:** 165. **Drafted:** Tallahassee (Fla.) CC, D/F 2004 (17th round). **Signed by:** Doug Reynolds.

Another one of the Brewers' intriguing outfield prospects, Cain played some center field en route to winning the Arizona League MVP award. However, he profiles more as a corner outfielder and has enough bat to play there. A draft-and-follow, Cain advanced quickly working with AZL hitting coach Joel Youngblood and proved both willing to listen and able to take what he'd learned and apply it quickly. His naturally quick bat is his best tool, and his bat speed and wiry frame have the organization projecting him to hit for future power. He's a plus runner as well and has an average arm. Cain's approach at the plate remains raw, from pitch recognition to his set-up and swing. He had an exaggerated leg kick when he first joined the organization, but toned it down after Milwaukee broke him down on video and showed him just how much of a timing problem the leg kick was causing. He spent much of instructional league working to quiet his approach, with positive results. Cain won't be a fast mover, especially considering the organization's current outfield glut. He has work to do refining such aspects of his game as outfield routes, basestealing and his approach at the plate. He'll have to have a big spring to ensure a spot in full-season ball.

Year	Club (League)	Class	AVG	G	AB	R	H	2B	3B	HR	RBI	BB	SO	SB	OBP	SLG
2005	Brewers (AZL)	R	.356	50	205	45	73	18	5	5	37	20	32	12	.418	.566
	Helena (Pio)	R	.208	6	24	4	5	0	0	0	1	1	6	0	.321	.208
MINOR LEAGUE TOTALS			.341	56	229	49	78	18	5	5	38	21	38	12	.408	.528

28 VINNY ROTTINO
UTIL

Born: April 7, 1980. **B-T:** R-R. **Ht.:** 6-1. **Wt.:** 200. **Signed:** NDFA/Wisconsin-La Crosse, 2003. **Signed by:** Brian Johnson.

Rottino had enrolled in the University of Wisconsin's pharmacy program when he signed with the Brewers, and his drive and intelligence quickly made him an organization favorite. Club officials consider him the hardest worker in the system, and he already has exceeded expectations for a nondrafted free agent. He was Milwaukee's 2004 minor league player of the year and reached Triple-A in 2005. Rottino finished the year as Prince Fielder's replacement in the Arizona Fall League. The Brewers challenged Rottino last year by jumping him to Double-A, then by having him play almost exclusively at catcher to start the season. He never had caught extensively prior to instructional league in 2004, and he impressed enough to get the shot. He still has work to do behind the plate (six passed balls in 22 games), but he has enough arm strength and the body for the position. He's not an everyday option there, however. He's a solid defender at third base, his best position, and can fill in as a corner outfielder. Rottino's power took a hit as he faced more advanced pitching, but he has a low-maintenance, line-drive swing and makes consistent contact. He's not far from being a solid big league utilityman.

Year	Club (League)	Class	AVG	G	AB	R	H	2B	3B	HR	RBI	BB	SO	SB	OBP	SLG
2003	Helena (Pio)	R	.311	64	222	42	69	10	0	1	20	28	25	5	.404	.369
2004	Beloit (Mid)	A	.304	140	529	78	161	25	9	17	124	40	71	5	.352	.482
2005	Huntsville (SL)	AA	.296	120	469	63	139	20	6	6	52	40	68	2	.351	.403
	Nashville (PCL)	AAA	.345	9	29	4	10	1	0	1	2	3	6	0	.406	.483
MINOR LEAGUE TOTALS			.303	333	1249	187	379	56	15	25	198	111	170	12	.362	.432

29 KEVIN ROBERTS
RHP

Born: May 15, 1984. **B-T:** R-R. **Ht.:** 6-0. **Wt.:** 190. **Drafted:** Houston, 2005 (5th round). **Signed by:** Ray Montgomery.

Roberts is another in a recent line of two-way University of Houston stars that includes Brad Sullivan and Jesse Crain, as well as Brad Lincoln, who could go in the first round of the 2006 draft. Unlike Sullivan and Crain, Roberts never put up All-America numbers in college, posting back-to-back 4.00-plus ERAs in his last two seasons. He also led the Cougars in home runs (nine) as a junior. However, his stuff took a jump in the Cape Cod League in 2004, when Roberts focused mainly on pitching. Now that he no longer has to play the infield, his fastball should touch 94 mph more regularly. His curveball is a solid-average pitch that just needs a little more consistency. He has shown flashes of a solid changeup as well. He's not gifted with a perfect pitcher's body, so he'll have to keep his fastball down to be successful. Roberts likely will open in low Class A, where he struggled at the end of his pro debut.

Year	Club (League)	Class	W	L	ERA	G	GS	CG	SV	IP	H	R	ER	HR	BB	SO	AVG
2005	Helena (Pio)	R	1	2	2.82	8	3	0	0	22	19	8	7	0	8	34	.221
	West Virginia (SAL)	A	2	2	4.94	9	3	0	0	27	31	21	15	4	12	20	.272
MINOR LEAGUE TOTALS			3	4	3.99	17	6	0	0	50	50	29	22	4	20	54	.250

30 DREW ANDERSON
OF

Born: June 9, 1981. **B-T:** L-R. **Ht.:** 6-2. **Wt.:** 195. **Drafted:** Nebraska, 2003 (24th round). **Signed by:** Harvey Kuenn Jr.

Anderson played on two Nebraska teams that reached the College World Series and was considered a gritty scrapper, though in his final two seasons he batted just .255 with 14 extra-base hits. He has consistently hit as a pro, however, and his bat and attitude have endeared him to the Brewers. His game is similar to that of Milwaukee's current overachieving center fielder, Brady Clark. Like Clark, Anderson's best tool is his bat. He keeps his swing simple, repeats it well, covers the plate and makes adjustments to keep getting the barrel to the ball. He led the Florida State League in hits and finished fourth in batting last year. He actually has added a tool in pro ball, getting slightly faster so that he now runs a tick above-average, getting to first base in 4.1 seconds from the left side. Anderson makes all the plays in the outfield with a fringy arm and solid range, making him a good bet to be a future fourth outfielder in the majors. Power is his weakest tool and probably will keep him from being an everyday player. He'll make the move to Double-A for 2006.

Year	Club (League)	Class	AVG	G	AB	R	H	2B	3B	HR	RBI	BB	SO	SB	OBP	SLG
2003	Helena (Pio)	R	.318	61	214	33	68	11	3	2	38	35	39	9	.420	.425
2004	Beloit (Mid)	A	.307	123	456	64	140	22	5	5	59	45	95	12	.372	.410
2005	Brevard County (FSL)	A	.311	129	508	69	158	17	7	6	62	39	95	19	.360	.407
MINOR LEAGUE TOTALS			.311	313	1178	166	366	50	15	13	159	119	229	40	.376	.412

MINNESOTA
TWINS

BY MIKE BERARDINO

Their three-year run atop the American League Central came to an end in 2005, but the Twins continued to position themselves as modest-budget contenders for years to come.

The ever-thriving farm system pushed several contributors to the big league team, including **Joe Mauer**, Jesse Crain, Francisco  Liriano, Jason Bartlett and Scott Baker—half of last year's Top 10 Prospects list. Minnesota also replenished the system at the back end with another strong draft under scouting director Mike Radcliff.

Thanks to the free-agent defections of Corey Koskie, Cristian Guzman and Henry Blanco, the Twins owned seven picks in the first three rounds. They spent $4.615 million to sign those picks, which began with hard-throwing Fresno State righthander Matt Garza. Garza was the only 2005 draftee to make the top 10 list this time, but that was a testament to the depth of the organization as well its 2004 draft, which featured five picks before the second round.

Stability remains a Twins hallmark. General manager Terry Ryan signed with the Twins as a high school pitcher, has been in the front office since 1986 and enters his 12th season running the baseball operation. Farm director Jim Rantz has been with the franchise since signing with the then-Washington Senators after winning the final game of the 1960 College World Series. He moved into the front office in 1965 and has been in charge of the farm system since 1986. Radcliff joined the Twins as an area scout in 1987 and became scouting director

in 1994. Assistant GMs Bill Smith and Wayne Krivsky and director of baseball operations Rob Antony all have been with Minnesota for more than a decade. Minnesota's continuity extends to field operations as well, as minor league hitting coordinator Jim Dwyer and pitching coordinator Rich Knapp enter their 10th year in their jobs.

Having such continuity makes it easier to implement a unified philosophy. Minnesota affiliates went a combined 364-316 (.535) in 2005, and the farm system has posted only one losing season (1999) in the past 13 years and just two since 1987. The Twins place a strong emphasis on developing young pitching, and no fewer than 30 of their prospects averaged 90 mph or better with their fastballs in 2005. Baker won the ERA title in the Triple-A International League, Kyle Aselton did the same in the low Class A Midwest League, and Adam Hawes (Appalachian) and Kyle Edlich (Gulf Coast) captured ERA crowns in Rookie ball.

Besides developing their own talent, the Twins have an eye for grabbing it from other organizations. Most famously, they got ace Johan Santana by orchestrating a 1999 Rule 5 draft trade with the Marlins. Top prospect Francisco Liriano was considered the third-best player in the November 2003 A.J. Pierzynski deal with the Giants, in which Minnesota also stole closer Joe Nathan.

TOP 30 PROSPECTS

1. Francisco Liriano, lhp	16. Jose Mijares, lhp
2. Jason Kubel, of	17. David Winfree, 3b
3. Matt Moses, 3b	18. Juan Portes, 2b/of
4. Glen Perkins, lhp	19. Drew Thompson, 2b/ss
5. Anthony Swarzak, rhp	20. Henry Sanchez, 1b
6. Denard Span, of	21. Justin Jones, lhp
7. Matt Garza, rhp	22. Alex Romero, of
8. Jay Rainville, rhp	23. Alexi Casilla, ss/2b
9. Trevor Plouffe, ss	24. Jason Pridie, of
10. Kyle Waldrop, rhp	25. Boof Bonser, rhp
11. Paul Kelly, ss	26. Danny Santiesteban, of
12. Adam Harben, rhp	27. Kyle Edlich, lhp
13. Kevin Slowey, rhp	28. Adam Hawes, rhp
14. J.D. Durbin, rhp	29. Tim Lahey, rhp
15. Eduardo Morlan, rhp	30. Alexander Smit, lhp

MICHAEL WALBY

ORGANIZATION OVERVIEW

General manager: Terry Ryan. **Farm director:** Jim Rantz. **Scouting director:** Mike Radcliff.

2005 PERFORMANCE

Class	Team	League	W	L	Pct.	Finish*	Manager(s)
Majors	Minnesota	American	83	79	.512	7th (14)	Ron Gardenhire
Triple-A	Rochester Red Wings	International	75	69	.521	t-6th (14)	Phil Roof/Rich Miller
Double-A	New Britain Rock Cats	Eastern	70	72	.493	7th (12)	Stan Cliburn
High A	Fort Myers Miracle	Florida State	74	59	.556	4th (12)	Riccardo Ingram
Low A	Beloit Snappers	Midwest	69	71	.493	8th (14)	Kevin Boles
Rookie	Elizabethton Twins	Appalachian	48	19	.716	+1st (10)	Ray Smith
Rookie	GCL Twins	Gulf Coast	28	26	.519	t-4th (12)	Nelson Prada
OVERALL 2005 MINOR LEAGUE RECORD			364	316	.535	5th (30)	

*Finish in overall standings (No. of teams in league). +League champion

ORGANIZATION LEADERS

BATTING
*Minimum 250 at-bats
*AVG	Span, Denard, Fort Myers/New Britain	.307
R	Burns, Deacon, Beloit	90
H	Winfree, David, Beloit	165
TB	Matienzo, Danny, New Britain	259
2B	Burns, Deacon, Beloit	36
	Matienzo, Danny, New Britain	36
3B	Burns, Deacon, Beloit	13
HR	Jones, Garrett, Rochester	24
RBI	Winfree, David, Beloit	101
BB	Deeds, Doug, New Britain	56
SO	Whitrock, Scott, Fort Myers	158
SB	Whitrock, Scott, Fort Myers	25
*OBP	Deeds, Doug, New Britain	.382
*SLG	Matienzo, Danny, New Britain	.488

PITCHING
#Minimum 75 innings
W	Simonitsch, Errol, Fort Myers/New Britain	14
L	Speigner, Levale, New Britain/Rochester	11
	Waldrop, Kyle, Beloit	11
#ERA	Martinez, J.P., Beloit	1.50
G	Kemp, Beau, Rochester	62
CG	Blackburn, Nick, Fort Myers/New Britain/Roch...	3
SV	Neshek, Pat, New Britain	24
IP	Liriano, Francisco, New Britain/Rochester	168
BB	Harben, Adam, Fort Myers	62
SO	Liriano, Francisco, New Britain/Rochester	204

BEST TOOLS

Best Hitter for Average	Jason Kubel
Best Power Hitter	Henry Sanchez
Best Strike-Zone Discipline	Jason Kubel
Fastest Baserunner	Denard Span
Best Athlete	Denard Span
Best Fastball	Francisco Liriano
Best Curveball	Anthony Swarzak
Best Slider	Francisco Liriano
Best Changeup	Kyle Waldrop
Best Control	Kevin Slowey
Best Defensive Catcher	Allan de San Miguel
Best Defensive Infielder	Trevor Plouffe
Best Infield Arm	Paul Kelly
Best Defensive Outfielder	Denard Span
Best Outfield Arm	Danny Santiesteban

PROJECTED 2009 LINEUP

Catcher	Joe Mauer
First Base	Justin Morneau
Second Base	Luis Castillo
Third Base	Michael Cuddyer
Shortstop	Trevor Plouffe
Left Field	Denard Span
Center Field	Torii Hunter
Right Field	Jason Kubel

Designated Hitter	Matt Moses
No. 1 Starter	Johan Santana
No. 2 Starter	Francisco Liriano
No. 3 Starter	Glen Perkins
No. 4 Starter	Anthony Swarzak
No. 5 Starter	Scott Baker
Closer	Joe Nathan

LAST YEAR'S TOP 20 PROSPECTS

1. Joe Mauer, c
2. Jason Kubel, of
3. Jesse Crain, rhp
4. J.D. Durbin, rhp
5. Francisco Liriano, lhp
6. Kyle Waldrop, rhp
7. Anthony Swarzak, rhp
8. Matt Moses, 3b
9. Jason Bartlett, ss
10. Scott Baker, rhp
11. Adam Harben, rhp
12. Trevor Plouffe, ss
13. Glen Perkins, lhp
14. Denard Span, of
15. Jay Rainville, rhp
16. Justin Jones, lhp
17. Matt Fox, rhp
18. Michael Restovich, of
19. Terry Tiffee, 3b
20. Alexander Smit, lhp

TOP PROSPECTS OF THE DECADE

Year	Player, Pos.	2005 Org.
1996	Todd Walker, 2b	Cubs
1997	Todd Walker, 2b	Cubs
1998	Luis Rivas, ss	Twins
1999	Michael Cuddyer, 3b	Twins
2000	Michael Cuddyer, 3b	Twins
2001	Adam Johnson, rhp	Athletics
2002	Joe Mauer, c	Twins
2003	Joe Mauer, c	Twins
2004	Joe Mauer, c	Twins
2005	Joe Mauer, c	Twins

TOP DRAFT PICKS OF THE DECADE

Year	Player, Pos.	2005 Org.
1996	*Travis Lee, 1b	Devil Rays
1997	Michael Cuddyer, ss	Twins
1998	Ryan Mills, lhp	Out of baseball
1999	B.J. Garbe, of	Mariners
2000	Adam Johnson, rhp	Athletics
2001	Joe Mauer, c	Twins
2002	Denard Span, of	Twins
2003	Matt Moses, 3b	Twins
2004	Trevor Plouffe, ss	Twins
2005	Matt Garza, rhp	Twins

*Did not sign.

ALL-TIME LARGEST BONUSES

Joe Mauer, 2001	$5,150,000
B.J. Garbe, 1999	$2,750,000
Adam Johnson, 2000	$2,500,000
Ryan Mills, 1998	$2,000,000
Michael Cuddyer, 1997	$1,850,000

MINOR LEADUE DEPTH CHART

Minnesota Twins

STRENGTH: Starting pitching. Francisco Liriano—a power lefty with upper minors experience—leads a diverse cavalcade of arms.

WEAKNESS: Impact bats. Jason Kubel and Matt Moses—who both have had major injuries—are the Twins' best bets for middle-of-the-order hitters.

Rank: **6**

*Depth charts prepared by **John Manuel** and **Chris Kline**. Numbers in parentheses indicate prospect rankings.*

LF
Alex Romero (22)
Doug Deeds
Trent Oeltjen
Deacon Burns
Scott Whitrock
Erold Andrus

CF
Denard Span (6)
Jason Pridie (24)
Danny Santiesteban (26)
Edward Ovalle
J.W. Wilson
James Tomlin

RF
Jason Kubel (2)
Jeremy Pickrel
Kevin West

3B
Matt Moses (3)
David Winfree (17)

SS
Trevor Plouffe (9)
Paul Kelly (11)
Drew Thompson (19)
J.R. Taylor

2B
Juan Portes (18)
Alexi Casilla (23)
Steven Tolleson
Luke Hughes
Luis Maza

1B
Henry Sanchez (20)
Johnny Woodard
Garrett Jones
Erik Lis
Brock Peterson

C
Allan de San Miguel
Greg Yersich
Caleb Moore
Daniel Matienzo
Rob Bowen
Jose Morales

RHP

Starters	Relievers
Anthony Swarzak (5)	Tim Lahey (29)
Matt Garza (7)	Willie Eyre
Jay Rainville (8)	Beau Kemp
Kyle Waldrop (10)	Patrick Neshek
Adam Harben (12)	Matt Yeatman
Kevin Slowey (13)	J.P. Martinez
J.D. Durbin (14)	Frank Mata
Eduardo Morlan (15)	
Boof Bonser (25)	
Adam Hawes (28)	
Danny Powers	
Alex Burnett	
David Shinskie	
Levale Speigner	
Yohan Pino	
Oswaldo Sosa	

LHP

Starters	Relievers
Francisco Liriano (1)	Alexander Smit (30)
Glen Perkins (4)	Jay Sawatski
Jose Mijares (16)	John Thomas
Justin Jones (21)	Jan Granado
Kyle Edlich (27)	Jason Miller
Errol Simonitsch	Jose Lugo
Ryan Mullins	
Kyle Aselton	
Brian Duensing	
Dave Gassner	

DRAFT ANALYSIS
2005

Best Pro Debut: After leading NCAA Division I in strikeout-walk ratio (134-13 in 136 innings) and fewest walks per nine innings (0.86), RHP Kevin Slowey (2) continued to show pinpoint control as a pro. He went 3-2, 2.12 with an 84-8 K-BB ratio in 72 innings, the bulk of his work coming in low Class A. 1B Erik Lis (9) batted .315-10-41 at Rookie-level Elizabethton.

Best Athlete: SS Paul Kelly (2) rates average or better in all five tools scouts look for in a position player, and he also had a fastball that reached 94-95 mph and a hard slider as a high school pitcher. OF J.W. Wilson (6), who offers a raw combination of power and speed, was a star wide receiver on his high school football team.

Best Pure Hitter: 2B Drew Thompson (2) is a little more polished right now than Kelly, who has to make a few minor adjustments. Minnesota also believes that 6-foot-3, 260-pound 1B Henry Sanchez (1) is a complete hitter, not just a bomber.

Best Raw Power: His power and body have earned Sanchez comparisons to a bigger Andres Galarraga and to Prince Fielder.

Fastest Runner: Wilson runs a tick above average. The fastest players signed by the Twins in 2005 are draft-and-follow OFs Josh Land (38 in 2004) and Danny Santiesteban (39), both plus runners.

Best Defensive Player: Minnesota wanted to improve its middle-infield depth and took Kelly and Thompson a year after taking another high school shortstop, Trevor Plouffe, in the first round. Many clubs projected Thompson as a second baseman, but the Twins think he can remain a shortstop.

Best Fastball: RHP Matt Garza (1) pitch-

PAUL JASIENSKI

Slowey

es at 90-94 mph and touches 96. RHP Alex Burnett (12) can reach 94-95. Both Kelly and C Caleb Moore (4) put up similar radar-gun numbers as amateur pitchers.

Best Breaking Ball: Garza's slider has more velocity than that of RHP Danny Powers (8), the 2005 NCAA Division II player of the year.

Most Intriguing Background: INF Toby Gardenhire's (41) dad Ron manages the Twins and was a former big league infielder, as were the fathers of Thompson (Robby) and Stephen Tolleson (5, Wayne).

Closest To The Majors: Slowey's command should get him to the majors faster than Garza with his power stuff.

Best Late-Round Pick: RHP Brian Kirwan (11) had a chance to go in the first two rounds before tearing up his right knee while playing quarterback for his high school football team. He should be showcasing his low-90s fastball again once he's fully healthy in spring training.

The One Who Got Away: The Twins signed their first 16 picks. Six-foot-7 LHP David Duncan (14) turned down the same $500,000 Kirwan signed for, opting instead to attend Georgia Tech.

Assessment: The Twins once again found a way to not compromise on their extra picks (four in the first three rounds), despite not getting a hugely expanded draft budget. By taking college seniors Moore and Powers, they also saved enough cash to sign Kirwan.

2004 The Twins look like they scored with four of their five first-round picks: SS Trevor Plouffe, LHP Glen Perkins and RHPs Kyle Waldrop and Jay Rainville. RHP Matt Fox has had shoulder problems. RHP Anthony Swarzak (2) could be the best of the group. *GRADE:* B+

2003 3B Matt Moses (1) can rake, while RHP Scott Baker (2) cracked the big league rotation two years after signing. 3B David Winfree (13), discovered while scouting Moses, led the Midwest League in RBIs. *GRADE:* B+

2002 Speedy OF Denard Span's (1) development picked up steam in 2005, and RHP Jesse Crain (2) already is a key member of the big league bullpen. RHP Adam Harben (15) could turn out to be a sleeper. *GRADE:* C+

2001 The Twins had the No. 1 overall pick and got it right with hometown C Joe Mauer. They didn't have much other success and failed to sign LHP Jason Vargas (43), but they didn't need anything else with Mauer, who alone merits its a top grade. *GRADE:* A

Draft analysis prepared by Jim Callis. Numbers in parentheses indicate draft rounds.

FRANCISCO
LIRIANO

Born: Oct. 26, 1983.
Ht.: 6-2. **Wt.:** 185.
Bats: L. **Throws:** L.
Signed: Dominican Republic, 2000.
Signed by: Rick Ragazzo (Giants).

A former outfielder who converted to the mound shortly after signing with the Giants, Liriano has exceeded all expectations. That includes those that accompanied his arrival as an overlooked part of a three-player package sent to the Twins in exchange for catcher A.J. Pierzynski in November 2003. While Joe Nathan has become an all-star closer and Boof Bonser a solid Triple-A starter, Liriano could turn out to be the best of the bunch. He missed part of 2002 and most of 2003 with shoulder problems, but Twins scout Sean Johnson recommended the team grab him after seeing him during instructional league. Liriano has been healthy since switching organizations and was spectacular in 2005, when he was Minnesota's minor league pitcher of the year. He led the minors in strikeouts while ranking as the No. 1 prospect in the Double-A Eastern League and No. 2 (behind Minor League Player of the Year Delmon Young) in the Triple-A International League.

Some scouts say Liriano's stuff is better than that of Twins teammate Johan Santana because Liriano throws harder, has a better slider and owns a changeup that is equal in quality. When he gets rolling, Liriano can dominate for long stretches behind a 94-96 mph fastball that has reached 98 mph and a hard, tight slider that comes in at 89 mph. The fastball and slider grade out as the best in the system. He has thrown a curve in the past, but has pushed it aside for now. Liriano has a reserved personality and shows good baseball aptitude, a strong work ethic and solid makeup. It's not uncommon for him to beat his teammates to the ballpark and start running and long-tossing well before the others arrive. He has learned English well and has no trouble communicating with teammates and coaches.

Liriano's history of shoulder woes means his durability must be monitored. He battled mechanical issues early in 2005, failing to repeat and flying open too often, which caused him to labor noticeably. Once he got to Triple-A, Rochester pitching coach Bobby Cuellar did a good job of keeping Liriano's delivery on track and showing him the benefits of maintaining a smooth motion. He has bouts where he doesn't command or trust his fastball as he should.

After striking out 33 in 24 innings during his first taste of the majors in September, Liriano has been penciled into Minnesota's rotation to begin 2006. Just as the Twins hope location-first righthander Scott Baker will gain from working alongside Brad Radke, they believe Liriano will benefit from pitching with Santana. The pair seemed to hit it off last year. Barring a spring surprise, Liriano's minor league seasoning is complete and he should be on his way to becoming a No. 1 starter.

Year	Club (League)	Class	W	L	ERA	G	GS	CG	SV	IP	H	R	ER	HR	BB	SO	AVG
2001	Giants (AZL)	R	5	4	3.63	13	12	0	0	62	51	26	25	3	24	67	.232
	Salem-Keizer (NWL)	A	0	0	5.00	2	2	0	0	9	7	5	5	2	1	12	.206
2002	Hagerstown (SAL)	A	3	6	3.49	16	16	0	0	80	61	45	31	6	31	85	.210
2003	San Jose (Cal)	A	0	1	51.43	1	1	0	0	1	5	4	4	0	2	0	.714
	Giants (AZL)	R	0	1	4.34	4	4	0	0	8	5	4	4	1	6	9	.192
2004	Fort Myers (FSL)	A	6	7	4.00	21	21	0	0	117	118	56	52	6	43	125	.269
	New Britain (EL)	AA	3	2	3.17	7	7	0	0	40	45	14	14	4	17	49	.287
2005	New Britain (EL)	AA	3	5	3.64	13	13	0	0	77	70	36	31	6	26	92	.242
	Rochester (IL)	AAA	9	2	1.78	14	14	0	0	91	56	25	18	4	24	112	.177
	Minnesota (AL)	MLB	1	2	5.70	6	4	0	0	24	19	15	15	4	7	33	.221
MAJOR LEAGUE TOTALS			1	2	5.70	6	4	0	0	24	19	15	15	4	7	33	.221
MINOR LEAGUE TOTALS			29	28	3.42	91	90	0	0	484	418	215	184	32	174	551	.235

2 JASON KUBEL OF

Born: May 25, 1982. **B-T:** L-R. **Ht.:** 5-11. **Wt.:** 190. **Drafted:** HS--Palmdale, Calif., 2000 (12th round). **Signed by:** Bill Mele.

Kubel reached the majors by the end of 2004, when he hit .352 in the upper minors and even got seven at-bats in the American League Division Series. His banner year ended disastrously, however, when he tore up his left knee in an outfield collision in the Arizona Fall League. He missed the 2005 season. Often compared to a young Brian Giles, Kubel has a tremendous approach at the plate. His plate discipline is the best in the system, while his stroke is quick and compact with some opposite-field power. Defensively, his best tool is a plus right-field arm. Even before the injury, Kubel wasn't considered much of a basestealing threat, though he did swipe 16 bags in 19 tries at Triple-A. He has limited speed and range in the outfield. Like many young hitters, he can become pull-conscious at times. Kubel made it back last year in time for instructional league, where he had to wear a large brace on his knee and couldn't do much running or fielding. The Twins doubt he'll be 100 percent for spring training. Rather than competing for the right-field job, he likely will start the season in Triple-A.

Year	Club (League)	Class	AVG	G	AB	R	H	2B	3B	HR	RBI	BB	SO	SB	OBP	SLG
2000	Twins (GCL)	R	.282	23	78	17	22	3	2	0	13	10	9	0	.367	.372
2001	Twins (GCL)	R	.331	37	124	14	41	10	4	1	30	19	14	3	.422	.500
2002	Quad City (Mid)	A	.321	115	424	60	136	26	4	17	69	41	48	3	.380	.521
2003	Fort Myers (FSL)	A	.298	116	420	56	125	20	4	5	82	48	54	4	.361	.400
2004	New Britain (EL)	AA	.377	37	138	25	52	14	4	6	29	19	19	0	.453	.667
	Rochester (IL)	AAA	.343	90	350	71	120	28	0	16	71	34	40	16	.398	.560
	Minnesota (AL)	MLB	.300	23	60	10	18	2	0	2	7	6	9	1	.358	.433
2005	Did not play—Injured															
MAJOR LEAGUE TOTALS			.300	23	60	10	18	2	0	2	7	6	9	1	.358	.433
MINOR LEAGUE TOTALS			.323	418	1534	243	496	101	18	45	294	171	184	26	.388	.501

3 MATT MOSES 3B

Born: Feb. 20, 1985. **B-T:** L-R. **Ht.:** 6-0. **Wt.:** 210. **Drafted:** HS--Richmond, Va., 2003 (1st round). **Signed by:** John Wilson.

After he was taken 21st overall in the 2003 draft, Moses had a routine physical that revealed a tiny hole in his heart. A 20-minute surgical procedure fixed the problem, and he signed for $1.45 million. But in 2004 he missed nearly four months with a stress fracture in his lower back, a recurrence of an old high school injury. He stayed healthy through 2005 and reached Double-A. One of the best pure hitters in his draft class, Moses has a smooth, compact swing that have drawn comparisons to Hank Blalock's. He was pushed to Double-A and remade his swing at the Twins' suggestion to cut down a pronounced toe tap. He shows a strong work ethic and a grinder's mentality. Some wonder whether Moses' power will follow him up the ladder. He's a below-average runner, and though he has worked hard on defense may have to move to a corner outfield spot in the majors. He has decent range at third base, but his footwork and throws remain a concern. Moses figures to return to Double-A New Britain to start 2006. Michael Cuddyer hasn't been able to seize Minnesota's third-base job, and Moses could challenge him by 2007.

Year	Club (League)	Class	AVG	G	AB	R	H	2B	3B	HR	RBI	BB	SO	SB	OBP	SLG
2003	Twins (GCL)	R	.385	18	65	6	25	5	1	0	11	5	9	0	.417	.492
2004	Twins (GCL)	R	.250	1	4	0	1	0	0	0	1	0	0	0	.250	.250
	Quad City (Mid)	A	.223	29	112	16	25	7	0	3	14	12	25	0	.304	.366
2005	Fort Myers (FSL)	A	.306	73	265	37	81	16	1	7	42	28	59	13	.376	.453
	New Britain (EL)	AA	.210	48	186	25	39	9	1	6	30	14	51	3	.275	.366
MINOR LEAGUE TOTALS			.271	169	632	84	171	37	3	16	98	59	144	16	.337	.415

4 GLEN PERKINS LHP

Born: March 2, 1983. **B-T:** L-L. **Ht.:** 6-0. **Wt.:** 200. **Drafted:** Minnesota, 2004 (1st round). **Signed by:** Mark Wilson.

The last player to sign out of the Twins' 2004 draft class, Perkins accepted a $1.425 million bonus and got right to work. He turned heads with his debut and continued to gain admirers when he reached Double-A in his first full season. His stock continued to rise when he was one of the few starting pitchers to have consistent success in the Arizona Fall League. Perkins got in better shape as a pro and saw his fastball increase from 88-92 to 91-94 mph. That made his advanced changeup even better. He also began throwing two different curveballs, a hard breaker and a slower version to throw off hitters' timing. He has a strong mound presence, good feel for pitching and solid makeup. Perkins isn't much of an athlete and has flat feet, which previously kept him from working out as aggressively as some would have liked. Wearing orthotics has solved that problem. Hit harder than expected in Double-A, Perkins will return there to anchor the rotation. With a successful first half, he could soon find himself in Triple-A.

Year	Club (League)	Class	W	L	ERA	G	GS	CG	SV	IP	H	R	ER	HR	BB	SO	AVG
2004	Elizabethton (Appy)	R	1	0	2.25	3	3	0	0	12	8	3	3	0	4	22	.186
	Quad City (Mid)	A	2	1	1.30	9	9	0	0	48	33	9	7	2	12	49	.205
2005	Fort Myers (FSL)	A	3	2	2.13	10	9	2	0	55	41	14	13	2	13	66	.205
	New Britain (EL)	AA	4	4	4.90	14	14	0	0	79	80	45	43	4	35	67	.263
MINOR LEAGUE TOTALS			10	7	3.06	36	35	2	0	194	162	71	66	8	64	204	.229

5 ANTHONY SWARZAK RHP

Born: Sept. 10, 1985. **B-T:** R-R. **Ht.:** 6-3. **Wt.:** 195. **Drafted:** HS—Fort Lauderdale, Fla., 2004 (2nd round). **Signed by:** Brad Weitzel.

As a senior at Nova High in 2004, Swarzak was the ace for a team that won a Florida 5-A championship, the first state title for a Broward County public high school in 57 years. He was the best pitching prospect on a loaded low Class A Beloit staff last year, and he reached high Class A Fort Myers by the middle of his first full pro season. Swarzak was dominant at times during the first half at Beloit. He pitched at 91-93 mph with his fastball, showing a hard downer curve and a devastating changeup as well. He has touched 95 mph and has electric stuff to go with a prototypical pitcher's frame, loose arm and strong mound presence. He stumbled a bit near midseason, so the Twins promoted him to jar him out of perceived boredom. Pitching close to home in the Florida State League, Swarzak seemed to press at times and developed minor delivery issues. He doesn't trust his changeup enough at times. His body is starting to fill out and he must be careful not to pack on weight in the wrong places. The fifth of six pitchers the Twins took in the first three rounds in 2004, Swarzak remains near the head of that class. He figures to return to high Class A to start 2006, where he'll again head a prospect-laden rotation.

Year	Club (League)	Class	W	L	ERA	G	GS	CG	SV	IP	H	R	ER	HR	BB	SO	AVG
2004	Twins (GCL)	R	5	3	2.63	11	9	0	1	48	46	20	14	1	6	42	.251
2005	Beloit (Mid)	A	9	5	4.04	18	18	0	0	91	81	48	41	7	32	101	.238
	Fort Myers (FSL)	A	3	4	3.66	10	10	0	0	59	72	25	24	3	11	55	.300
MINOR LEAGUE TOTALS			17	12	3.58	39	37	0	1	198	199	93	79	11	49	198	.260

6 DENARD SPAN OF

Born: Feb. 27, 1984. **B-T:** L-L. **Ht.:** 6-1. **Wt.:** 180. **Drafted:** HS—Tampa, 2002 (1st round). **Signed by:** Brad Weitzel.

A star wide receiver in high school, Span received interest from NCAA Division I-A football programs until they realized baseball was his first love. He turned down a 2002 predraft deal to go ninth to the Rockies and wound up signing for $1.7 million as the 20th pick. Nagging injuries to his legs and ankle slowed him in 2003, and a broken hamate bone in his right wrist caused him to miss more than two months in 2004, but he stayed healthy in 2005. The fastest player, best athlete and best defensive outfielder in a deep system, Span improved more than any other Twins farmhand last year. He has been timed at 3.8 seconds to first base and has learned to use his speed. He has sharpened his bunting, taken more pitches, done a better job of keeping the ball out of the air and generally warmed to the role of leadoff hitter. Span doesn't have much power. He sometimes has to rely on his quickness to make up for mistakes on routes in center field. His arm is fringe average at best, though he makes up for it by playing shallow. He gets caught stealing more than he should because he's still perfecting his leads and jumps. With Torii Hunter the subject of trade rumors, Span's window of major league opportunity is drawing closer. Hunter isn't likely to be in Minnesota beyond 2006, at which point the Twins hope Span is ready for his close-up. He'll probably open the season in Triple-A.

Year	Club (League)	Class	AVG	G	AB	R	H	2B	3B	HR	RBI	BB	SO	SB	OBP	SLG
2003	Elizabethton (Appy)	R	.271	50	207	34	56	5	1	1	18	23	34	14	.355	.319
2004	Quad City (Mid)	A	.267	64	240	29	64	4	3	0	14	34	49	15	.363	.308
2005	Fort Myers (FSL)	A	.339	49	186	38	63	3	3	1	19	22	25	13	.410	.403
	New Britain (EL)	AA	.285	68	267	47	76	6	5	0	26	22	41	10	.355	.345
MINOR LEAGUE TOTALS			.288	231	900	148	259	18	12	2	77	101	149	52	.368	.341

7 MATT GARZA
RHP

Born: Nov. 11, 1983. **B-T:** R-R. **Ht.:** 6-4. **Wt.:** 190. **Drafted:** Fresno State, 2005 (1st round). **Signed by:** Kevin Bootay.

Garza has come a long way from the scared kid who went 1-6, 9.55 as a Fresno State freshman in 2003. Afterward, he had eye surgery to correct cloudy vision in his right eye. Over the next two seasons, he went a combined 12-8, 3.99, pitching himself into the first round of the 2005 draft. He signed for $1.35 million as the 25th overall pick. Garza showed a full mix of pitches in his debut, including a 90-94 mph fastball that touches 96, a hard slider at 82-84 mph, a 72-78 mph curveball and a changeup that needs work but shows potential. A hard worker with outstanding makeup, he's a serious pro, a young husband and father who wants to make an impact. His main weakness is a reluctance at times to trust his stuff. Garza will drop down on occasion in an attempt to bury his slider instead of repeating his delivery. The Twins hope he'll be more willing to pitch to contact as he gains experience. Garza needed just four starts in the Rookie-level Appalachian League before moving up to the low Class A Midwest League, where he figures to start out this season. He may not stay there long, as he ranked as the No. 10 prospect in the Mid in 2005.

Year	Club (League)	Class	W	L	ERA	G	GS	CG	SV	IP	H	R	ER	HR	BB	SO	AVG
2005	Elizabethton (Appy)	R	1	1	3.65	4	4	0	0	20	14	10	8	3	6	25	.200
	Beloit (Mid)	A	3	3	3.54	10	10	0	0	56	53	24	22	5	15	64	.251
MINOR LEAGUE TOTALS			4	4	3.57	14	14	0	0	76	67	34	30	8	21	89	.238

8 JAY RAINVILLE
RHP

Born: Oct. 16, 1985. **B-T:** R-R. **Ht.:** 6-3. **Wt.:** 230. **Drafted:** HS—Pawtucket, R.I., 2004 (1st round). **Signed by:** Jay Weitzel.

Drafted out of the same Bishop Hendricken High (Warwick, R.I.) program as Rocco Baldelli, Rainville signed for $875,000 as the fifth of five Twins first-round picks in 2004. He was also an NHL prospect as a defenseman. His brother Michael, a third baseman, signed as a non-drafted free agent with the Devil Rays last summer. A big, physical presence on the mound, Rainville pounds the strike zone with an 88-91 mph fastball, 12-to-6 power curveball and improving changeup. With his strong thighs and intense approach, he reminds some of a young Curt Schilling. Rainville made great strides last year in terms of game management, showing an ability to identify situations that's beyond his years. His command ranks with the best in the system and he posted 3.4 strikeouts for every walk. Rainville's velocity was down a tick or two from the 91-94 mph he reached regularly in his debut. The Twins weren't concerned, attributing that to physical changes anyone his age would experience. Still, his debut season ended with weakness in his throwing shoulder, so durability could be a concern. While he could wind up at the back of the bullpen, Rainville remains a starting prospect now with the potential to be a 230-inning horse. He should start the year back in high Class A as a member of star-studded rotation.

Year	Club (League)	Class	W	L	ERA	G	GS	CG	SV	IP	H	R	ER	HR	BB	SO	AVG
2004	Twins (GCL)	R	3	2	1.84	8	7	0	0	34	39	19	7	1	3	38	.273
2005	Beloit (Mid)	A	8	2	3.77	16	16	0	0	88	83	39	37	14	27	77	.243
	Fort Myers (FSL)	A	4	3	2.67	9	9	1	0	54	54	22	16	7	6	35	.256
MINOR LEAGUE TOTALS			15	7	3.06	33	32	1	0	177	176	80	60	22	36	150	.253

9 TREVOR PLOUFFE
SS

Born: June 15, 1986. **B-T:** R-R. **Ht.:** 6-1. **Wt.:** 175. **Drafted:** HS—Northridge, Calif., 2004 (1st round). **Signed by:** Bill Mele.

A two-way star in high school, Plouffe didn't convince the Twins he was a better position player until March of his draft year. On the mound, he showed a four-pitch mix and could hit 91 mph with command. He went 25-2 his final two seasons, but area scout Bill Mele recommended Plouffe remain at shortstop. He accepted a $1.5 million bonus as the 20th overall pick in the 2004 draft. Plouffe gets the nod as the Twins best defensive infielder, slightly ahead of 2005 second-round pick Paul Kelly, a fellow shortstop. Plouffe's arm is a shade below Kelly's but still rates a solid 60 on the 20-80 scouting scale. Plouffe showed soft hands and good power in 2005, continuing to draw comparisons to former Twins shortstop Greg Gagne. He has average speed. Plouffe got off to a miserable start at Beloit with the bat, struggling with timing because of late activity in his swing. He adjusted in the second half and became a threat at the plate, though he could use more strength on his smallish frame. Defensively, he needs to stay lower on balls and work to improve his balance. With Kelly and second-rounder Drew Thompson entering the system last year, Plouffe suddenly has lots of company at his position. He figures to open the year in high Class A.

Year	Club (League)	Class	AVG	G	AB	R	H	2B	3B	HR	RBI	BB	SO	SB	OBP	SLG
2004	Elizabethton (Appy)	R	.283	60	237	29	67	7	2	4	28	19	34	2	.340	.380
2005	Beloit (Mid)	A	.223	127	466	58	104	18	0	13	60	50	78	8	.300	.345
MINOR LEAGUE TOTALS			.243	187	703	87	171	25	2	17	88	69	112	10	.313	.357

10 KYLE WALDROP   RHP

STEVE MOORE

Born: Oct. 27, 1987. **B-T:** R-R. **Ht.:** 6-4. **Wt.:** 190. **Drafted:** HS—Knoxville, Tenn., 2004 (1st round). **Signed by:** Tim O'Neil.

Kentucky-based Twins scout Tim O'Neil managed Waldrop in the 2003 East Coast Showcase, and that familiarity played a role in Minnesota taking Waldrop 25th overall and signing him for $1 million. Though he went 22-0 over his final two prep seasons, some teams liked him more as a power-hitting first baseman/outfielder. The Twins have no plans to move him off the mound. Waldrop's changeup already is the best in a system that features several polished soft-tossers, and his command is right there with the best of the Twins' prospects. He won't blow hitters away with his 88-91 mph fastball, but he also features a big-breaking curveball and has a slider as well. His work ethic is beyond question and his mound presence is good. His yes-sir, no-sir personality draws comparisons to Peyton Manning's. Waldrop had trouble maintaining his arm slot for most of last season, but he rallied late. He gave up too many hits considering his profile, but some of those were due to mediocre defense behind him. His curveball tends to get loopy at times. Unlike Anthony Swarzak and Jay Rainville, Waldrop stayed in low Class A throughout his first full pro season. He figures to join them in high Class A to begin 2006 and could reach Double-A by midseason if he starts fast.

Year	Club (League)	Class	W	L	ERA	G	GS	CG	SV	IP	H	R	ER	HR	BB	SO	AVG
2004	Twins (GCL)	R	3	2	1.42	7	7	0	0	38	32	9	6	1	4	30	.229
	Elizabethton (Appy)	R	2	0	3.24	4	4	0	0	25	21	10	9	1	3	25	.221
2005	Beloit (Mid)	A	6	11	4.98	27	27	2	0	152	182	93	84	17	23	108	.291
MINOR LEAGUE TOTALS			11	13	4.15	38	38	2	0	215	235	112	99	19	30	163	.273

11 PAUL KELLY   SS

Born: Oct. 19, 1986. **B-T:** R-R. **Ht.:** 6-0. **Wt.:** 185. **Drafted:** HS—Flower Mound, Texas, 2005 (2nd round). **Signed by:** Marty Esposito.

Kelly reminded area scouts of Jesse Crain, a two-way star at the University of Houston and a 2002 Twins second-rounder. Kelly had mound success in high school, showing a 94-95 mph fastball and a hard slider. But Minnesota took him in the second round as a shortstop because of his varied tools. He overcame a blood clot in his shoulder before his senior season and signed for $650,000. Kelly loves to play, shows passion for the game and has a great work ethic. He has the best infield arm in the system, a possible 70 on the 20-80 scouting scale. With the glove, he's a shade behind 2004 first-rounder Trevor Plouffe at this point but could pass him down the line. Kelly is smooth and surehanded in the field and shows plus range. At the plate, he's leaning to stay inside the ball and use his pull-side power better. For now, he has some gap power as well as some quickness on the bases. He got a taste of low Class A at the end of the summer and figures to start there in 2006.

Year	Club (League)	Class	AVG	G	AB	R	H	2B	3B	HR	RBI	BB	SO	SB	OBP	SLG
2005	Twins (GCL)	R	.277	40	137	16	38	6	0	2	20	14	36	3	.358	.365
	Beloit (Mid)	A	.313	5	16	2	5	2	0	1	4	2	3	0	.368	.625
MINOR LEAGUE TOTALS			.281	45	153	18	43	8	0	3	24	16	39	3	.360	.392

12 ADAM HARBEN   RHP

Born: Aug. 19, 1983. **B-T:** R-R. **Ht.:** 6-5. **Wt.:** 210. **Drafted:** Westark (Ark.) CC, 2002 (15th round). **Signed by:** Gregg Miller.

Coming out of Central Arkansas Christian High in Little Rock, the same school that produced A.J. Burnett, Harben didn't sign with the Tigers as a 38th-round afterthought in 2001. Instead, he attended Westark (Ark.) Community College, where he roomed with Toby Gardenhire, whose father Ron manages the Twins. Thanks to a strong recommendation from Toby (who signed with Minnesota as a 41st-round pick in 2005), as well as area scout

Gregg Miller, Harben fell into Minnesota's lap as a 15th-round steal in 2002. His fastball was down a notch to 92-94 mph in 2005, occasionally dropping into the high 80s, in part because of nagging trouble with a strained lat muscle. His slider was inconsistent and he still lacks confidence with his changeup. But he was the mainstay of a talented Fort Myers rotation, tossing a one-hitter against Brevard County in mid-June and impressing Florida State League observers. Harben has a prototypical pitcher's frame, throws downhill and shows a willingness to pitch inside. He has improved his conditioning and mechanics since signing. Added to the 40-man roster for the first time in November, he's ready for Double-A.

Year	Club (League)	Class	W	L	ERA	G	GS	CG	SV	IP	H	R	ER	HR	BB	SO	AVG
2002	Twins (GCL)	R	4	1	3.20	12	3	0	0	25	27	11	9	0	8	27	.270
2003	Quad City (Mid)	A	5	6	4.33	16	15	0	0	87	91	54	42	5	35	77	.259
2004	Quad City (Mid)	A	9	7	3.09	26	26	0	0	143	114	60	49	5	68	171	.226
2005	Fort Myers (FSL)	A	10	5	2.66	25	25	2	0	135	102	52	40	6	62	119	.207
MINOR LEAGUE TOTALS			28	19	3.23	79	69	2	0	391	334	177	140	16	173	394	.231

13 KEVIN SLOWEY   RHP

Born: May 4, 1984. **B-T:** R-R. **Ht.:** 6-3. **Wt.:** 190. **Drafted:** Winthrop, 2005 (2nd round). **Signed by:** Ricky Taylor.

Brad Radke has made a nice career out of locating an average fastball and outsmarting hitters with a devastating changeup. The Twins are hoping Slowey might follow that same path. He signed for $490,000 as a 2005 second-round pick out of Winthrop, where he first put himself on the map with a 19-strikeout game as a freshman. Last spring, he went 11-1, 2.26 and led NCAA Division I in strikeout-walk ratio (134-13 in 136 innings) and fewest walks per nine innings (0.86). Slowey wasted no time in climbing aboard the Twins' fast track, moving into the low Class A rotation and coming within one out of a no-hitter in August. He has the best command in the system and had a better K-BB ratio as a pro (84-8 in 72 innings) than he did in college. Slowey's fastball sits at 87-89 mph and touches 92 mph, but it could add another tick or two as he fills out a wiry frame. He hides the ball well, and that deception adds to the late movement his fastball shows naturally. His slider is solid-average and he made real progress with his changeup during instructional league. He also showed durability despite tossing 208 innings overall, including college. His next step is high Class A, though if the Twins have a logjam of starting candidates at Fort Myers, they could push Slowey to Double-A.

Year	Club (League)	Class	W	L	ERA	G	GS	CG	SV	IP	H	R	ER	HR	BB	SO	AVG
2005	Elizabethton (Appy)	R	0	0	1.17	4	0	0	1	8	2	1	1	1	0	15	.080
	Beloit (Mid)	A	3	2	2.24	13	9	1	0	64	42	18	16	4	8	69	.183
MINOR LEAGUE TOTALS			3	2	2.13	17	9	1	1	72	44	19	17	5	8	84	.173

14 J.D. DURBIN   RHP

Born: Feb. 24, 1982. **B-T:** R-R. **Ht.:** 6-0. **Wt.:** 210. **Drafted:** HS--Scottsdale, Ariz., 2000 (2nd round). **Signed by:** Lee MacPhail.

Two straight years with shoulder problems have raised questions about Durbin's durability and future role. He missed six weeks with shoulder tendinitis last year after May 2004 surgery to shave his labrum and repair a partial tear. A fastball that once hit 101 mph stayed in the 94-96 mph range last year. For a brash type who dubbed himself "Real Deal," this required mental adjustments. Durbin tends to fight himself when things aren't going his way and sometimes gets too caught up in what others think about him. It didn't help when he saw Francisco Liriano and Scott Baker zoom by on their way to the majors. To Durbin's credit, he followed organizational wishes and went to the Venezuelan League in order to work on his changeup, a necessity if he wants to remain a starter. He has shown a hard curveball and tight slider as well, but they remain inconsistent. With all the young starting pitching in their system, the Twins could move Durbin to the bullpen.

Year	Club (League)	Class	W	L	ERA	G	GS	CG	SV	IP	H	R	ER	HR	BB	SO	AVG
2000	Twins (GCL)	R	0	0	0.00	2	0	0	0	2	2	0	0	0	0	4	.222
2001	Elizabethton (Appy)	R	3	2	1.87	8	7	0	0	34	23	13	7	2	17	39	.190
2002	Quad City (Mid)	A	13	4	3.19	27	27	0	0	161	144	66	57	14	51	163	.239
2003	Fort Myers (FSL)	A	9	2	3.09	14	14	0	0	87	73	35	30	3	22	69	.224
	New Britain (EL)	AA	6	3	3.14	14	14	2	0	95	102	39	33	10	29	70	.278
2004	New Britain (EL)	AA	4	1	2.52	13	13	0	0	64	62	21	18	4	22	53	.253
	Rochester (IL)	AAA	3	2	4.54	7	7	0	0	36	49	27	18	4	16	38	.325
	Minnesota (AL)	MLB	0	1	7.40	4	1	0	0	7	12	6	6	0	6	6	.387
2005	Rochester (IL)	AAA	5	5	4.33	22	19	0	0	104	97	52	50	8	51	90	.251
MAJOR LEAGUE TOTALS			0	1	7.40	4	1	0	0	7	12	6	6	0	6	6	.387
MINOR LEAGUE TOTALS			43	19	3.29	107	101	2	0	583	552	253	213	45	208	526	.250

15 EDUARDO MORLAN   RHP

Born: March 1, 1986. **B-T:** R-R. **Ht.:** 6-2. **Wt.:** 210. **Drafted:** HS--Miami, 2004 (3rd round). **Signed by:** Brad Weitzel.

Just before Morlan signed for $420,000 as a third-round pick in 2004, the Twins discovered he had an enlarged heart. He was shut down for a month until the condition was analyzed sufficiently, then he mowed through the Rookie-level Gulf Coast League. Used as a reliever mostly in 2004, he moved into the rotation in his first pro season. Morlan pitched at 90-92 mph and topped out at 94, down a few ticks from his debut. He stayed back in the extended spring program at the start of the year to master a changeup, and he took to it fairly well. He also shows a hard curveball that can be devastating at times. His high-torque delivery deserted him in the middle of the season, but he got it back and continued to make improvements through instructional league. He reminds some of a young Juan Rincon, and a move back to the bullpen remains possible down the road. Morlan figures to open 2006 in low Class A, though he could be pushed to high Class A.

Year	Club (League)	Class	W	L	ERA	G	GS	CG	SV	IP	H	R	ER	HR	BB	SO	AVG
2004	Twins (GCL)	R	1	2	2.85	11	2	0	1	25	25	14	8	1	10	28	.245
2005	Elizabethton (Appy)	R	2	0	0.82	4	4	0	0	22	6	2	2	0	6	30	.085
	Beloit (Mid)	A	4	4	4.39	10	10	0	0	51	39	25	25	5	31	55	.207
MINOR LEAGUE TOTALS			7	6	3.19	25	16	0	1	99	70	41	35	6	47	113	.194

16 JOSE MIJARES   LHP

Born: Oct. 29, 1984. **B-T:** L-L. **Ht.:** 5-10. **Wt.:** 220. **Signed:** Venezuela, 2002. **Signed by:** Jose Leon.

Signed at 17 out of Venezuela, Mijares impressed Midwest League observers last year as the best lefthander in the circuit. Even after moving into the rotation, he maintained the 92-95 mph velocity on his fastball. He gets his curveball over most of the time and has a solid changeup as well. Immaturity remains an issue, as does a tendency to pack weight on a fireplug frame. He failed to make the Beloit roster out of spring training because of conditioning issues but got serious after that setback. He's also going to have to throw more strikes at higher levels. Some view Mijares as a high-maintenance type, but his talent makes him worth the effort. Compared to a young J.C. Romero, whom the Twins traded in December, Mijares could wind up in the bullpen. He pitched for Aragua in the Venezuelan League, and the Twins hope that experience speeds his development. He could return to low Class A as a starter or open 2006 as a swingman on a stacked high Class A staff.

Year	Club (League)	Class	W	L	ERA	G	GS	CG	SV	IP	H	R	ER	HR	BB	SO	AVG
2002	Cagua (VSL)	R	2	5	3.91	13	9	0	0	53	51	29	23	2	27	42	.264
2003	Tronconero 1 (VSL)	R	2	4	1.04	11	7	0	0	52	28	17	6	1	15	58	.159
2004	Twins (GCL)	R	4	0	2.42	19	0	0	5	30	22	9	8	1	15	25	.208
2005	Beloit (Mid)	A	6	3	4.31	20	6	0	2	54	43	28	26	6	40	78	.219
	Fort Myers (FSL)	A	0	0	1.50	5	1	0	0	12	5	4	2	1	5	17	.116
MINOR LEAGUE TOTALS			14	12	2.92	68	23	0	7	201	149	87	65	11	102	220	.209

17 DAVID WINFREE   3B

Born: Aug. 5, 1985. **B-T:** R-R. **Ht.:** 6-3. **Wt.:** 215. **Drafted:** HS--Virginia Beach, Va., 2003 (13th round). **Signed by:** John Wilson.

While scouting Matt Moses as their 2003 first-round pick, the Twins came across Winfree at a rival high school. A prep catcher, Winfree moved to first base after Minnesota took him in the 13th round in 2003, then shifted to third base the last two seasons. That's where he will stay for now after bashing his way to the Twins' minor league player of the year award last summer, when he led the Midwest League in hits, RBIs and total bases. Few players in the system can match Winfree's power or ability to hit quality fastballs. He doesn't strike out excessively but could stand to draw a few more walks. With the organization's urging, he spread out his stance and flattened out his swing more last year. Winfree has strong make-up and a willingness to work, which dates to his decision to leave home after his junior year of high school to play in an advanced summer league in Ohio. A below-average runner, he has a big frame that eventually could land him back at first base. For now he shows average range and a slightly above-average arm at the hot corner. He still struggles with his footwork and decisions defensively. Winfree will advance to high Class A this year.

Year	Club (League)	Class	AVG	G	AB	R	H	2B	3B	HR	RBI	BB	SO	SB	OBP	SLG
2003	Twins (GCL)	R	.129	23	70	4	9	1	2	0	3	2	16	0	.164	.200
2004	Elizabethton (Appy)	R	.286	59	217	31	62	8	0	8	37	18	51	1	.349	.433
2005	Beloit (Mid)	A	.294	135	562	80	165	31	5	16	101	22	93	3	.329	.452
MINOR LEAGUE TOTALS			.278	217	849	115	236	40	7	24	141	42	160	4	.321	.426

18 JUAN PORTES 2B/OF

Born: Nov. 26, 1985. **B-T:** R-R. **Ht.:** 5-11. **Wt.:** 170. **Drafted:** HS--Malden, Mass., 2004 (15th round). **Signed by:** Jay Weitzel.

Born and raised in the Dominican Republic, Portes played limited high school baseball in Massachusetts, then dropped out and spent what would have been his senior year on the showcase circuit. Projected as an early-round pick until he left high school, he slipped to the 15th round of the 2004 draft. Portes received a GED diploma and speaks fluent English. He led the Gulf Coast League in homers and slugging percentage in his debut, then ranked among Appalachian League leaders in those categories during 2005. He projects to add power as he continues to fill out. A shortstop as an amateur, Portes played mostly second base and left field last year. While he showed progress in making the pivot and mastering the intricacies of second, he probably will move to the outfield for good before too long as the Twins have strengthened their middle-infield depth in the past few years. Portes has questionable hands, but he has average speed and arm strength and could merit a look in center field. He'll play in low Class A in 2006.

Year	Club (League)	Class	AVG	G	AB	R	H	2B	3B	HR	RBI	BB	SO	SB	OBP	SLG
2004	Twins (GCL)	R	.327	44	168	24	55	8	1	8	31	12	28	4	.380	.530
2005	Elizabethton (Appy)	R	.286	64	245	40	70	13	1	12	39	22	43	6	.349	.494
MINOR LEAGUE TOTALS			.303	108	413	64	125	21	2	20	70	34	71	10	.361	.508

19 DREW THOMPSON 2B/SS

Born: Nov. 11, 1986. **B-T:** R-R. **Ht.:** 6-1. **Wt.:** 160. **Drafted:** HS--Tequesta, Fla., 2005 (2nd round). **Signed by:** Brad Weitzel.

A second-round pick who signed for $475,000, Thompson was the first of three sons of former big league middle infielders drafted by Minnesota in 2005. His father Robby was an all-star with the Giants and currently is the Indians' bench coach. The Twins also signed Steven Tolleson (Wayne's son) in the fifth round and Toby Gardenhire (whose dad Ron manages the Twins) in the 41st. Thompson is considered more polished than fellow second-round pick Paul Kelly, who went 26 slots ahead of him. A shortstop in high school, Thompson played mostly second in the Gulf Coast League as Kelly stayed at his natural position. Thompson also dealt with a dead-arm period after signing, so the decision was made to leave him at second. Some see him as developing into an offensive second baseman like his father as he fills out, but the Twins believe he can stay at shortstop because of his solid hands and average arm. He's selective and has the potential for gap power. He has a nice, level lefthanded swing and a good idea of the strike zone. Thompson, who wore down by the end of his debut season, figures to open 2006 in extended spring before becoming the starting shortstop at Rookie-level Elizabethton.

Year	Club (League)	Class	AVG	G	AB	R	H	2B	3B	HR	RBI	BB	SO	SB	OBP	SLG
2005	Twins (GCL)	R	.257	35	109	22	28	4	1	2	20	22	22	6	.385	.367
	Fort Myers (FSL)	A	.308	4	13	2	4	1	0	0	1	1	4	0	.357	.385
MINOR LEAGUE TOTALS			.262	39	122	24	32	5	1	2	21	23	26	6	.383	.369

20 HENRY SANCHEZ 1B

Born: Nov. 29, 1986. **B-T:** R-R. **Ht.:** 6-3. **Wt.:** 260. **Drafted:** HS--San Diego, 2005 (1st round supplemental). **Signed by:** John Leavitt.

Slowed by a broken hamate bone in his hand, Sanchez struggled somewhat as a high school senior and dropped to the Twins with the 39th overall pick in the 2005 draft. They signed him for $900,000 and were impressed with his huge raw power, which was on full display at the Area Code Games before his senior year. Compared to a larger Andres Galarraga by some or a taller Prince Fielder by others, Sanchez can reach the seats in all directions. A Mission Bay High (San Diego) teammate of 2004 No. 1 overall pick Matt Bush, Sanchez can become a 35-homer force in the majors. That projection assumes he cuts down on his strikeouts and keeps his weight in check. He has ballooned as high as 300 pounds and came into pro ball at 260 pounds, and his mobility and defense always will be a question. He's a predictably below-average runner but has better footwork around first base than expected. He has worked to shorten up his swing to make more consistent contact, but Minnesota will be careful not to rob him of his natural aggressiveness. Sanchez figures to open the year in extended spring training but could jump to low Class A.

Year	Club (League)	Class	AVG	G	AB	R	H	2B	3B	HR	RBI	BB	SO	SB	OBP	SLG
2005	Twins (GCL)	R	.229	21	70	8	16	2	0	2	11	7	28	0	.300	.343
MINOR LEAGUE TOTALS			.229	21	70	8	16	2	0	2	11	7	28	0	.300	.343

21 JUSTIN JONES

LHP

Born: Sept. 25, 1984. **B-T:** L-L. **Ht.:** 6-4. **Wt.:** 200. **Drafted:** HS--Virginia Beach, 2002 (2nd round). **Signed by:** Billy Swoope (Cubs).

For their part (Doug Mientkiewicz) in the four-team Nomar Garciaparra trade in July 2004, the Twins received Jones from the Cubs. He was shut down with elbow discomfort in 2004 and missed the first half of last season with a strained elbow ligament. Once he got back on the mound, he began to display the ability that drove him as high as No. 2 on the Cubs' prospect list two years ago. With the help of minor league pitching coordinator Rick Knapp, Jones was able to eliminate a mechanical hitch in which his elbow would fly up too high in mid-delivery. As a result, his fastball returned to 92-93 mph and gave him a third weapon to go with his plus curveball and advanced changeup. Jones never had arm surgery, but he missed time in each of the last three seasons and has just 288 innings in four years as a pro. It took him some time to buy into the Twins' mindset, but now that he has he could start to gather momentum if he can stay healthy. He'll see Double-A at some point in 2006.

Year	Club (League)	Class	W	L	ERA	G	GS	CG	SV	IP	H	R	ER	HR	BB	SO	AVG
2002	Cubs (AZL)	R	3	1	1.80	11	11	0	0	50	31	12	10	0	18	63	.181
	Boise (NWL)	A	1	0	1.80	1	1	0	0	5	4	1	1	0	3	4	.211
2003	Lansing (Mid)	A	3	5	2.28	16	16	0	0	71	56	29	18	1	32	87	.215
2004	Lansing (Mid)	A	3	3	3.78	15	15	0	0	64	62	33	27	6	22	59	.270
	Quad City (Mid)	A	0	2	5.32	7	4	0	0	20	20	17	12	2	14	17	.250
2005	Fort Myers (FSL)	A	7	3	3.01	13	13	2	0	78	78	28	26	5	28	54	.268
MINOR LEAGUE TOTALS			17	14	2.93	63	60	2	0	288	251	120	94	14	117	284	.239

22 ALEX ROMERO

OF

Born: Sept. 9, 1983. **B-T:** B-R. **Ht.:** 6-0. **Wt.:** 190. **Signed:** Venezuela, 2000. **Signed by:** Rudy Hernandez.

This isn't what the Twins were expecting when they signed Romero at age 16 out of Venezuela, but they'll take it. As he has added strength and bulk, particularly in his lower half, he has lost the speed portion of his game. He still takes too many risks on the bases, however, as he apparently failed to get the memo. His ability to put the bat on the ball more than makes up for any shortcomings, and he's a switch-hitter to boot. Romero owns a career .306 average despite a reputation as a bad-ball hitter. He more than doubled his previous career high with 15 homers in 2005, and his strikeouts jumped as well. His work ethic and hustle improved last summer after an early-season talk with minor league field coordinator Joe Vavra. Romero projects as a No. 6 hitter, though some believe he could mature into a No. 3 in time. He's an average defender with average arm strength in left field. He should move up to Triple-A in 2006 and could make his big league debut later in the year.

Year	Club (League)	Class	AVG	G	AB	R	H	2B	3B	HR	RBI	BB	SO	SB	OBP	SLG
2001	San Joaquin (VSL)	R	.347	49	167	22	58	9	0	2	30	11	9	10	.388	.437
2002	Twins (GCL)	R	.333	56	186	31	62	13	2	2	42	29	14	16	.423	.457
2003	Quad City (Mid)	A	.296	120	423	50	125	16	3	4	40	43	43	11	.359	.376
2004	Fort Myers (FSL)	A	.292	105	380	59	111	21	2	6	42	54	47	6	.387	.405
2005	New Britain (EL)	AA	.301	139	509	65	153	31	2	15	77	36	69	12	.354	.458
MINOR LEAGUE TOTALS			.306	469	1665	227	509	90	9	29	231	173	182	55	.375	.423

23 ALEXI CASILLA

SS/2B

Born: July 20, 1984. **B-T:** B-R. **Ht.:** 5-9. **Wt.:** 160. **Signed:** Dominican Republic, 2003. **Signed by:** Leo Perez (Angels).

J.C. Romero wore out his welcome with the Twins, who shipped him to the Angels for Casilla in December. Buried behind a slew of talented infielders led by Brandon Wood and Howie Kendrick in the Los Angeles system, Casilla still has his work cut out for him after Minnesota has spent three early-round picks on shortstops in the last two years. He's a high-energy player with above-average speed who keeps the ball on the ground and does the little things to help produce runs. His swing is a little stiff but produces a little gap power. He runs the bases aggressively and has good instincts, finishing fourth in the Midwest League in steals despite playing in just 78 games. Casilla didn't play more because he opened the year filling injury holes at Double-A and Triple-A, then missed the end of the season after breaking his forearm. He was back playing in a low-level Dominican winter league by November. Casilla needs to improve defensively, but has the actions and aptitude to do so as he matures. He should spend most of this year in high Class A.

Year	Club (League)	Class	AVG	G	AB	R	H	2B	3B	HR	RBI	BB	SO	SB	OBP	SLG
2003	Angels (DSL)	R	.298	33	124	21	37	3	2	0	15	16	14	28	.396	.355
2004	Cedar Rapids (Mid)	A	.310	9	29	6	9	2	1	0	1	5	4	1	.412	.448
	Angels (AZL)	R	.258	45	163	29	42	1	4	0	10	15	10	24	.332	.313
	Provo (Pio)	R	.333	4	12	4	4	1	1	0	1	4	0	1	.529	.583
2005	Arkansas (TL)	AA	.211	7	19	4	4	0	0	0	4	2	3	1	.286	.211
	Salt Lake (PCL)	AAA	.256	13	39	3	10	0	0	0	1	3	6	1	.310	.256
	Cedar Rapids (Mid)	A	.325	78	308	62	100	11	3	3	17	29	31	47	.392	.409
MINOR LEAGUE TOTALS			.297	189	694	129	206	18	11	3	49	74	68	103	.375	.367

24 JASON PRIDIE   OF

Born: Oct. 9, 1983. **B-T:** L-R. **Ht.:** 6-1. **Wt.:** 180. **Drafted:** HS—Prescott, Ariz., 2002 (2nd round). **Signed by:** Craig Weissmann (Devil Rays).

A sprained right knee limited Pridie to 29 games in 2005, and when he didn't tear it up in the Arizona Fall League, the Devil Rays gambled by not protecting him on their 40-man roster. Minnesota crossed up Tampa Bay, however, taking Pridie in the major league Rule 5 draft. He can't be sent to the minors in 2006 without clearing waivers and being offered back to the Rays for half his $50,000 draft price. Tampa Bay has a ton of outfield depth in the majors and minors, so the Twins could work out a deal for his rights that would allow them to send him down. Pridie's brother Jon pitched in Minnesota's system from 1998-2004. Jason pitched in high school as well and still boasts plus arm strength, but his sweet swing has made him a full-time outfielder since he signed as a second-rounder in 2002. In his last full season, he topped the low Class A South Atlantic League in runs in 2004. At his best, Pridie has drawn favorable comparisons to Steve Finley from both an offensive and defensive standpoint. He strikes out too much when he gets pull-conscious, and the Devil Rays were trying to get him to focus on making contact and using the opposite field more often. He has solid-average speed to go with excellent instincts in center field.

Year	Club (League)	Class	AVG	G	AB	R	H	2B	3B	HR	RBI	BB	SO	SB	OBP	SLG
2002	Princeton (Appy)	R	.368	67	285	60	105	12	9	7	33	19	35	13	.410	.547
	Hudson Valley (NY-P)	A	.344	8	32	4	11	1	1	1	3	6	0	.400	.531
2003	Charleston, S.C. (SAL)	A	.260	128	530	75	138	28	10	7	48	30	113	26	.302	.391
2004	Charleston, S.C. (SAL)	A	.276	128	515	103	142	27	11	17	86	37	114	17	.327	.470
2005	Visalia (Cal)	A	.500	1	2	0	1	0	0	0	0	0	0	0	.500	.500
	Montgomery (SL)	AA	.213	28	94	15	20	4	2	3	8	8	29	5	.275	.394
MINOR LEAGUE TOTALS			.286	360	1458	257	417	72	33	35	176	97	297	61	.333	.453

25 BOOF BONSER   RHP

Born: Oct. 14, 1981. **B-T:** R-R. **Ht.:** 6-4. **Wt.:** 260. **Drafted:** HS—St. Petersburg, Fla., 2005 (12th round). **Signed by:** Alan Marr (Giants).

Considering the stunning rise of Francisco Liriano, it's hard to remember that Bonser was actually the hotter prospect in November 2003. That's when those two came to the Twins along with Joe Nathan in a package that netted A.J. Pierzynski for the Giants. The reversal of fortune is something that must be monitored with Bonser, who has a tendency to mope at times. To his credit, he put together a strong full season in Triple-A last year, anchoring a Rochester staff that saw Liriano and Scott Baker pass through on their way to the majors. Bonser didn't even rate a September callup, but Minnesota was pleased with his work ethic and the commitment he showed toward improving a lumpy body. He pitches at 89-92 mph, down from the mid-90s range he reached earlier in his career. Bonser, who legally changed his name from John to Boof while in high school, still has a tendency to give up homers. But he has learned to keep hitters off balance by changing speeds and using his plus curveball and decent changeup. He has a ceiling as a back-of-the-rotation starter but likely will break into the majors this year as a middle reliever.

Year	Club (League)	Class	W	L	ERA	G	GS	CG	SV	IP	H	R	ER	HR	BB	SO	AVG
2000	Salem-Keizer (NWL)	A	1	4	6.00	10	9	0	0	33	21	23	22	2	29	41	.188
2001	Hagerstown (SAL)	A	16	4	2.49	27	27	0	0	134	91	40	37	7	61	178	.192
2002	Shreveport (TL)	AA	1	2	5.56	5	5	0	0	24	30	15	15	3	14	23	.316
	San Jose (Cal)	A	8	6	2.88	23	23	0	0	128	89	44	41	9	70	139	.195
2003	Norwich (EL)	AA	7	10	4.00	24	24	1	0	135	122	80	60	11	67	103	.245
	Fresno (PCL)	AAA	1	2	3.13	4	4	0	0	23	17	13	8	4	8	28	.195
2004	New Britain (EL)	AA	12	9	4.37	27	27	0	0	154	160	89	75	22	56	146	.272
	Rochester (IL)	AAA	1	0	1.29	1	1	0	0	7	5	1	1	1	1	7	.200
2005	Rochester (IL)	AAA	11	9	3.99	28	28	0	0	160	153	80	71	22	57	168	.251
MINOR LEAGUE TOTALS			58	46	3.72	149	148	1	0	799	688	385	330	81	363	833	.234

26 DANNY SANTIESTEBAN
OF

Born: Feb. 17, 1985. **B-T:** R-R. **Ht.:** 6-2. **Wt.:** 170. **Drafted:** Palm Beach (Fla.) CC, D/F 2004 (39th round). **Signed by:** Hector Otero.

Santiesteban was one of five draft-and-follows who signed with the Twins last spring, and he's clearly the most advanced in that group. A 39th-round pick in 2004, he returned to Palm Beach (Fla.) Community College for his sophomore season before signing for $10,000. He tore up the Gulf Coast League and was leading the circuit in RBIs and slugging in mid-July when he broke his right pinky on a headfirst slide. Santiesteban presents an intriguing package of tools. He has power and plus speed, and he plays a solid center field along with owning the best outfield arm in the system. He has a long swing and is aggressive at the plate, so he may need to tone things down a bit to hit for average at higher levels. He could end up in right field in the long run. Santiesteban has an intense personality and good leadership skills. He should be able to handle the jump to low Class A if Minnesota chooses to push him.

Year	Club (League)	Class	AVG	G	AB	R	H	2B	3B	HR	RBI	BB	SO	SB	OBP	SLG
2005	Twins (GCL)	R	.307	21	75	16	23	5	1	6	24	7	19	1	.365	.640
MINOR LEAGUE TOTALS			.307	21	75	16	23	5	1	6	24	7	19	1	.365	.640

27 KYLE EDLICH
LHP

Born: March 9, 1986. **B-T:** R-L. **Ht.:** 6-2. **Wt.:** 180. **Signed:** Australia, 2004. **Signed by:** Howard Norsetter.

An Australian import, Edlich was one of four Twins pitchers to win minor league ERA titles in 2005, joining Scott Baker (International), Kyle Aselton (Midwest) and Adam Hawes (Appalachian). Edlich led the Gulf Coast League in his first season in the United States after signing for $60,000. His main pitches are an 88-90 mph fastball and an overhand curve that has the potential to be an out pitch. He now uses a mid-three-quarters delivery after working with minor league pitching coordinator Rick Knapp to lower his arm slot. The Twins changed his posture as well, and that gave his pitches late tail. Edlich is competitive, shows strong mound presence and has made nice progress with his changeup already. He missed two weeks with a midseason health issue that required him to wear a heart monitor, but he checked out fine and returned to action. Edlich projects as a No. 3 or 4 starter, but could be even more if he adds strength to his frame and gets better command of his breaking stuff. He likely will move one level at a time, taking him to Elizabethton in 2006.

Year	Club (League)	Class	W	L	ERA	G	GS	CG	SV	IP	H	R	ER	HR	BB	SO	AVG
2005	Twins (GCL)	R	4	2	1.70	10	9	0	0	48	42	13	9	1	15	53	.243
	Fort Myers (FSL)	A	0	1	6.67	2	0	0	0	3	3	2	2	0	3	3	.273
MINOR LEAGUE TOTALS			4	3	1.97	12	9	0	0	50	45	15	11	1	18	56	.245

28 ADAM HAWES
RHP

Born: April 25, 1983. **B-T:** R-R. **Ht.:** 6-4. **Wt.:** 190. **Drafted:** Connors State (Okla.) CC, 2003 (40th round). **Signed by:** Gregg Miller.

A 40th-round pick in 2003, Hawes didn't make his pro debut until 2005. A Canadian, he didn't sign as a draft-and-follow until 2004, when a shortage of visas for minor league players prevented him from pitching in the United States. To his credit, he voluntarily went to the Dominican Republic for extra work, but fell victim to a parasitic virus and lost weight. After going through extended spring training last year, he won the Appalachian League ERA title. He showed a 92-93 mph riding fastball, the makings of a plus 12-to-6 curveball and an average changeup. He also messes with a slider, but that pitch lags behind the others. Tall and lanky, he uses his leverage well and shows a good feel for pitching. He has a high three-quarters delivery and throws across his body somewhat, but that only adds to his deception and isn't considered a problem for now. He should open this year in the low Class A rotation.

Year	Club (League)	Class	W	L	ERA	G	GS	CG	SV	IP	H	R	ER	HR	BB	SO	AVG
2004	Twins (DSL)	R	0	1	3.71	3	2	0	1	10	11	7	4	2	5	11	.289
2005	Elizabethton (Appy)	R	4	0	1.53	14	9	1	1	59	38	13	10	2	16	68	.183
MINOR LEAGUE TOTALS			4	1	1.83	17	11	1	2	69	49	20	14	4	21	79	.199

29 TIM LAHEY
RHP

Born: Feb. 7, 1982. **B-T:** R-R. **Ht.:** 6-4. **Wt.:** 235. **Drafted:** Princeton, 2004 (20th round). **Signed by:** John Wilson.

Left back at extended spring training last April, Lahey approached minor league field coordinator Joe Vavra and Gulf Coast League pitching coach Steve Mintz with a request:

Could he try pitching? Considering the light-hitting catcher was a 20th-round senior sign out of Princeton, they didn't see the harm in a little experimentation. It took only a few pitches for Lahey to leave behind his catcher's gear for good. With his big, physical frame and surprisingly smooth delivery, he made himself a prospect almost overnight. His heavy fastball hits home at 94-95 mph and shows good boring action. He breaks bats and shows solid command and mound presence. His slider has come along quickly, and he has worked with pitching coordinator Rick Knapp on a changeup and curve. Both show promise, but if he stays in short relief he probably won't need more than two pitches. Lahey proved dominant in the Appalachian League, where he overmatched younger hitters as the closer for a championship club. He'll begin 2006 in low Class A and could move quickly if he continues to do this Troy Percival imitation.

Year	Club (League)	Class	AVG	G	AB	R	H	2B	3B	HR	RBI	BB	SO	SB	OBP	SLG
2004	Elizabethton (Appy)	R	.202	26	84	7	17	2	0	3	11	13	38	0	.317	.333
MINOR LEAGUE TOTALS			.202	26	84	7	17	2	0	3	11	13	38	0	.317	.333

Year	Club (League)	Class	W	L	ERA	G	GS	CG	SV	IP	H	R	ER	HR	BB	SO	AVG
2005	Elizabethton (Appy)	R	0	1	3.56	26	0	0	15	25	21	13	10	0	8	30	.212
MINOR LEAGUE TOTALS			0	1	3.55	26	0	0	15	25	21	13	10	0	8	30	.212

30 ALEXANDER SMIT
LHP

Born: Oct. 2, 1985. **B-T:** L-L. **Ht.:** 6-4. **Wt.:** 205. **Signed:** Netherlands, 2002. **Signed by:** Howard Norsetter.

For the first time in his three-year pro career, Smit struggled in 2005. As usual one of the youngest pitchers in his league, he got hammered in low Class A and had to head back to the Appalachian League, where he pitched the year before. The one thing he did at both levels was rack up strikeouts, averaging 12.3 per nine innings for the season. That's a stunning figure considering his fastball tops out at 92 mph. He did a better job of maintaining his velocity after moving to the bullpen at Elizabethton, after his fastball had dropped to the mid-80s when he tired in the past. Smit also adjusted to throwing a conventional curveball instead of the knuckle-curve he had relied on previously. He's still working on a changeup that's less than reliable. He has a good feel for pitching and an improved understanding of how to set hitters up. Smit, who signed for $800,000, still projects as a No. 3 starter but the bullpen could be his best option. That's where he worked for the Dutch national team at the Athens Olympics. He'll give low Class A another try this year, and at 20 he still has time on his side.

Year	Club (League)	Class	W	L	ERA	G	GS	CG	SV	IP	H	R	ER	HR	BB	SO	AVG
2003	Twins (GCL)	R	3	0	1.18	8	7	0	0	38	19	8	5	0	20	40	.156
2004	Elizabethton (Appy)	R	1	1	2.54	6	5	0	0	28	25	9	8	0	10	43	.248
2005	Beloit (Mid)	A	1	9	5.98	14	10	0	0	50	58	41	33	9	28	54	.283
	Elizabethton (Appy)	R	6	1	1.97	21	0	0	3	46	25	12	10	3	12	86	.157
MINOR LEAGUE TOTALS			11	11	3.12	49	22	0	3	162	127	70	56	12	70	223	.216

NEW YORK METS

BY **MATT MEYERS**

Unlike the year before, the Mets resisted the urge to part with their top prospects at the 2005 trade deadline in an effort to bolster their playoff chances. Ironically, the team was more suited for a postseason run and stayed in the National League wild-card race until late September.

 Omar Minaya made a splash in his first offseason as Mets general manager by signing Pedro Martinez and Carlos Beltran to lavish contracts. While Martinez proved to be the frontline starter the Mets hoped, Beltran was a disappointment.

After standing pat during the season, Minaya jumped back into win-now mode in the offseason. He saved money by trading Mike Cameron to the Padres for Xavier Nady, but then reached deep into his wallet by trading for Carlos Delgado and Paul Lo Duca and signing Billy Wagner as a free agent.

The Mets system has lacked depth for years and continues to do so, particularly on the heels of trading away three of their best prospects in Yusmeiro Petit and first baseman Mike Jacobs (with third baseman Grant Psomas for Delgado) and righthander Gaby Hernandez (with Dante Brinkley for Lo Duca). Though New York's player-development efforts haven't been bountiful, they have yielded impact talents such as Scott Kazmir (sent to Tampa Bay in a horribly shortsighted deal for Victor Zambrano in 2004), Jose Reyes and **David Wright**.

The Mets bolstered their system in 2005 by delving into the Latin American market, which was as strong as it had been in years. They invested $2.1 million in a pair of 16-year-olds, power-hitting Dominican outfielder Fernando Martinez and projectable Venezuelan righthander Deolis Guerra.

Minaya was once the Mets' international scouting director, and seems intent on making his club the dominant force in signing Latin American talent. New York saw the Martinez and Guerra signings as a way to make up for the loss of their second- and third-round picks in the 2005 draft as free-agent compensation.

Minaya also has made an imprint on the scouting department, restructuring it twice since becoming GM. After the 2005 season, 11 scouts were fired or demoted. Russ Bove, who replaced Jack Bowen as scouting director a year earlier, was reassigned as a major league scout. Assistant scouting director Rudy Terrasas was promoted to replace Bove.

Mets officials were miffed they were unable to reach down into their system to promote major league players when injuries hit. It's hard to put all the blame on the scouting department for that lack of depth, however. In three of the last four drafts, the Mets have given up their second- and third-round picks after signing free agents.

Mike Pelfrey, considered the best pitching prospect in the 2005 draft, slipped to New York as the ninth overall pick because of a high price tag. He had yet to sign by the end of the year, but the Mets were expected to work out a deal before spring training.

TOP 30 PROSPECTS

1. Lastings Milledge, of	16. Emmanuel Garcia, ss
2. Philip Humber, rhp	17. Mike Carp, 1b
3. Carlos Gomez, of	18. Hector Pellot, 2b
4. Fernando Martinez, of	19. Matt Durkin, rhp
5. Anderson Hernandez, ss/2b	20. Aarom Baldiris, 2b
6. Brian Bannister, rhp	21. Ambiorix Concepcion, of
7. Alay Soler, rhp	22. Juan Perez, lhp
8. Deolis Guerra, rhp	23. Andy Wilson, 1b/c
9. Jon Niese, lhp	24. Chase Lambin, inf
10. Brett Harper, 1b	25. Matt Lindstrom, rhp
11. Jose Coronado, ss	26. Sean Henry, 2b/ss
12. Jesus Flores, c	27. Corey Ragsdale, ss
13. Jeff Keppinger, 2b	28. Henry Owens, rhp
14. Shawn Bowman, 3b	29. Evan MacLane, lhp
15. Bobby Parnell, rhp	30. Nick Evans, 1b

LARRY GOREN

ORGANIZATION OVERVIEW

General manager: Omar Minaya. **Farm director:** Kevin Morgan. **Scouting director:** Rudy Terrasas.

2005 PERFORMANCE

Class	Team	League	W	L	Pct.	Finish*	Manager
Majors	New York	National	83	79	.512	t-5th (16)	Willie Randolph
Triple-A	Norfolk Tides	International	79	65	.549	3rd (14)	Ken Oberkfell
Double-A	Binghamton Mets	Eastern	63	79	.444	t-11th (12)	Jack Lind
High A	St. Lucie Mets	Florida State	66	68	.493	7th (12)	Tim Teufel
Low A	Hagerstown Suns	South Atlantic	71	66	.518	8th (16)	Gene Richards
Short-season	Brooklyn Cyclones	New York-Penn	40	36	.526	6th (14)	Mookie Wilson
Rookie	Kingsport Mets	Appalachian	28	40	.412	9th (10)	Jesse Levis
Rookie	GCL Mets	Gulf Coast	37	16	.698	1st (12)	Gary Carter
OVERALL 2005 MINOR LEAGUE RECORD			417	400	.510	11th (30)	

*Finish in overall standings (No. of teams in league).

ORGANIZATION LEADERS

BATTING
*Minimum 250 at-bats
*AVG	Keppinger, Jeff, Norfolk	.337
R	Brinkley, Dante, Hagerstown/St. Lucie	84
	Ragsdale, Corey, Binghamton/St. Lucie	84
H	Hernandez, Anderson, Binghamton/Norfolk	168
TB	Harper, Brett, Binghamton/St. Lucie	261
2B	Jacobs, Mike, Binghamton	37
	Psomas, Grant, Hagerstown/St. Lucie	37
	Redman, Prentice, Binghamton/Norfolk	37
3B	Lydon, Wayne, Binghamton/Norfolk	13
HR	Harper, Brett, Binghamton/St. Lucie	36
RBI	Harper, Brett, Binghamton/St. Lucie	102
BB	Psomas, Grant, Hagerstown/St. Lucie	77
SO	Ragsdale, Corey, Binghamton/St. Lucie	169
SB	Gomez, Carlos, Hagerstown	64
*OBP	Brinkley, Dante, Hagerstown/St. Lucie	.427
*SLG	Jacobs, Mike, Binghamton	.589

PITCHING
#Minimum 75 innings
W	Scobie, Jason, Norfolk	15
L	Portobanco, Luz, Binghamton	12
#ERA	Worthington, Tim, Hagerstown/St. Lucie	1.91
G	Lavigne, Tim, Binghamton/Norfolk	53
CG	Five tied at	2
SV	Muniz, Carlos, GCL Mets/Hager./St. Lucie	14
IP	MacLane, Evan, Binghamton/St. Lucie	171
BB	Landing, Jeff, Brooklyn/Hagerstown	61
SO	Petit, Yusmeiro, Binghamton/Norfolk	144

BEST TOOLS

Best Hitter for Average	Lastings Milledge
Best Power Hitter	Brett Harper
Best Strike-Zone Discipline	Andy Wilson
Fastest Baserunner	Carlos Gomez
Best Athlete	Lastings Milledge
Best Fastball	Matt Lindstrom
Best Curveball	Philip Humber
Best Slider	Alay Soler
Best Changeup	Evan MacLane
Best Control	Evan MacLane
Best Defensive Catcher	Drew Butera
Best Defensive Infielder	Anderson Hernandez
Best Infield Arm	Corey Ragsdale
Best Defensive Outfielder	Lastings Milledge
Best Outfield Arm	Carlos Gomez

PROJECTED 2009 LINEUP

Catcher	Jesus Flores
First Base	Carlos Delgado
Second Base	Anderson Hernandez
Third Base	David Wright
Shortstop	Jose Reyes
Left Field	Carlos Beltran
Center Field	Lastings Milledge
Right Field	Victor Diaz
No. 1 Starter	Pedro Martinez
No. 2 Starter	Kris Benson
No. 3 Starter	Philip Humber
No. 4 Starter	Brian Bannister
No. 5 Starter	Alay Soler
Closer	Billy Wagner

LAST YEAR'S TOP 20 PROSPECTS

1. Lastings Milledge, of
2. Yusmeiro Petit, rhp
3. Philip Humber, rhp
4. Gaby Hernandez, rhp
5. Ambiorix Concepcion, of
6. Alay Soler, rhp
7. Shawn Bowman, 3b
8. Victor Diaz, of
9. Jesus Flores, c
10. Matt Lindstrom, rhp
11. Jamar Hill, of
12. Jeff Keppinger, 2b
13. Aarom Baldiris, 3b
14. Matt Durkin, rhp
15. Brian Bannister, rhp
16. Carlos Gomez, of
17. Anderson Hernandez, ss
18. Dae-Sung Koo, lhp
19. Bartolome Fortunato, rhp
20. Craig Brazell, 1b/of

TOP PROSPECTS OF THE DECADE

Year	Player, Pos.	2005 Org.
1996	Paul Wilson, rhp	Reds
1997	Jay Payton, of	Athletics
1998	Grant Roberts, rhp	Yankees
1999	Alex Escobar, of	Nationals
2000	Alex Escobar, of	Nationals
2001	Alex Escobar, of	Nationals
2002	Aaron Heilman, rhp	Mets
2003	Jose Reyes, ss	Mets
2004	Kazuo Matsui, ss	Mets
2005	Lastings Milledge, of	Mets

TOP DRAFT PICKS OF THE DECADE

Year	Player, Pos.	2005 Org.
1996	Robert Stratton, of	Reds
1997	Geoff Goetz, lhp	Nashua (Atlantic)
1998	Jason Tyner, of	Twins
1999	Neal Musser, lhp	Mets
2000	Billy Traber, lhp	Indians
2001	Aaron Heilman, rhp	Mets
2002	Scott Kazmir, lhp	Devil Rays
2003	Lastings Milledge, of	Mets
2004	Philip Humber, rhp	Mets
2005	*Mike Pelfrey, rhp	Unsigned

*Has not signed.

ALL-TIME LARGEST BONUSES

Philip Humber, 2004	$3,000,000
Scott Kazmir, 2002	$2,150,000
Lastings Milledge, 2003	$2,075,000
Geoff Goetz, 1997	$1,700,000
Paul Wilson, 1994	$1,550,000

MINOR LEAGUE DEPTH CHART

New York Mets

Rank: 30

STRENGTH: Outfield. By hanging on to Lastings Milledge, the Mets retained one major impact talent.

WEAKNESS: Pitching. The organization's depth has been gutted by trades.

Depth charts prepared by John Manuel and Chris Kline. Numbers in parentheses indicate prospect rankings.

LF
Courtney Billingslea
Wayne Lydon
Joe Holden

CF
Lastings Milledge (1)
Fernando Martinez (4)
Angel Pagan
Greg Cain

RF
Carlos Gomez (3)
Ambiorix Concepcion (21)
Jamar Hill

3B
Shawn Bowman (14)
Chase Lambin (24)
Rodney Nye
Russ Triplett

SS
Jose Coronado (11)
Emmanuel Garcia (16)
Corey Ragsdale (27)

2B
Anderson Hernandez (5)
Jeff Keppinger (13)
Hector Pellot (18)
Aarom Baldiris (20)
Sean Henry (26)

1B
Brett Harper (10)
Mike Carp (17)
Andy Wilson (23)
Nick Evans (30)
Junior Contreras

C
Jesus Flores (12)
Aaron Hathaway
Drew Butera
Sean McCraw
Yasmil Bucce

RHP

Starters	Reliever
Philip Humber (2)	Matt Lindstrom (25)
Brian Bannister (6)	Henry Owens (28)
Alay Soler (7)	Mitch Wylie
Deolis Guerra (8)	German Marte
Bobby Parnell (15)	Joey Serfass
Matt Durkin (19)	Anderson Garcia
Jose Sanchez	
Jason Scobie	
Eric Junge	
Will Jostock	

LHP

Starters	Relievers
Jon Niese (9)	Juan Perez (22)
Evan MacLane (29)	Tim Hamulack
Neal Musser	Blake McGinley
	Royce Ring
	Eddie Camacho

DRAFT ANALYSIS

2005

Best Pro Debut: RHP Bobby Parnell's (9) 8.86 ERA as a Charleston Southern junior didn't scare off area scout Marlin McPhail, and Parnell led the short-season New York-Penn League with a 1.73 ERA. 3B Matt Anderson (31) earned all-star honors in the Rookie-level Appalachian League by hitting .314-5-30 and was solid after a promotion to the NY-P. Draft-and-follow RHP Jacob Ruckle (41 in 2004) went 8-1, 2.10 and led the Rookie-level Gulf Coast League in victories.

Best Athlete: OF Greg Cain (6) has all five tools, the foremost of which is his speed. He's still raw with the bat.

Best Pure Hitter: 2B Hector Pellot's (4) bat looked promising in instructional league. OF Joe Holden (21), who hit .291 in the NY-P, challenged for the league batting title before slumping in August.

Best Raw Power: OF Courtney Billingslea (10) gets a lot of leverage from his 6-foot-6, 205-pound frame. He's the first player drafted out of Sinclair (Ohio) CC since big leaguer Chris Spurling in 1997.

Fastest Runner: OF Greg Gonzalez (28) gets to first base from the left side of the plate in 4.0 seconds. He batted .324 with 33 steals in 42 attempts in his debut.

Best Defensive Player: C Drew Butera (4) led the NY-P by throwing out 31 base stealers and ranked second among league regulars with a 45 percent success rate.

Best Fastball: RHP Mike Pelfrey (1), the best pitching prospect in the draft, has yet to sign but was expected to eventually reach a deal with the Mets. He has a 92-97 mph heater. Among the players under contract, Parnell has an 88-92 mph sinker, and LHP

Pelfrey

Jon Niese (7) has similar velocity.

Best Breaking Ball: RHP David Koons (27) has a good slider and nice life on his fastball.

Most Intriguing Background: 2B Anthony Manuel's (45) father Jerry played in the majors and coaches first base for the Mets. Butera's dad Sal caught for the Twins and is a special assistant to Blue Jays GM J.P. Ricciardi. LHP Kevin Tomasiewicz (26) was MVP of the 2005 Division III College World Series.

Closest To The Majors: Pelfrey may not need much more than a year in the minors once he signs. Butera's defense could put him on the fast track.

Best Late-Round Pick: Koons was used sparingly and didn't get much exposure at St. Leo (Fla.) College. RHP Will Jostock (49) has a 6-foot-5 frame, a loose arm and an 88-90 mph sinker.

The One Who Got Away: Preston Paramore (22), a switch-hitting offensive catcher, wound up at Arizona State. He had a chance to go as high as the third round before tailing off late in the spring.

Assessment: Russ Bove's first (and last) draft as Mets scouting director was reminiscent of many of the club's recent efforts. New York grabbed a premium talent who slid because of signability (Pelfrey) to make up for the loss of picks as free-agent compensation (second- and third-rounders in 2005).

2004 RHP Philip Humber (1), the No. 3 overall pick, signed late and then needed Tommy John surgery midway through his debut season. The best healthy prospect, RHP Gaby Hernandez (3), went to the Marlins in the Paul Lo Duca trade. **GRADE:** C

2003 OF Lastings Milledge (1) is a budding star. The Mets didn't have second- or third-round picks and got little afterward outside of RHP Brian Bannister (7). **GRADE:** B+

2002 Getting LHP Scott Kazmir (1) with the 15th overall pick was a no-brainer, but dealing him for Victor Zambrano showed no brains. The next-best choice was 1B Ian Bladergroen (44), though he has been hampered by wrist problems and traded to the Red Sox. **GRADE:** A

2001 3B David Wright (1) could be on the road to Cooperstown, and he lasted until the 38th overall pick. RHP Aaron Heilman's (1) 2005 resurgence was a nice cherry on the top. **GRADE:** A

*Draft analysis prepared by **Jim Callis**. Numbers in parentheses indicate draft rounds.*

LASTINGS
MILLEDGE

KEVIN PATAKY

Born: April 5, 1985.
Ht.: 6-1. **Wt.:** 185.
Bats: R. **Throws:** R.
Drafted: HS—Palmetto, Fla., 2003
(1st round).
Signed by: Joe Salermo.

In the Mets' draft room in 2003, the decision came down to Milledge or righthander Jeff Allison. The Mets loved Milledge's talent, but were worried about allegations of sexual misconduct at his high school. They decided they had a positive read on his makeup, and his talent was too tantalizing to pass up. The Mets haven't had any reason to second-guess their decision, as Milledge has established himself as an elite prospect while Allison has battled drug addiction. Milledge's talent has been evident since he played youth baseball, as he led Manatee East to the 1997 Little League World Series. He comes from a baseball family, as his father Tony Sr. and brothers Anthony and Tony Jr. all played professionally. The family has followed Milledge's career throughout the minors in a recreational vehicle affectionately dubbed "Milledgeville." While he was rumored to be involved in a myriad of deadline deals in July, the Mets held onto Milledge and he rewarded them by tormenting Double-A pitching in the second half. He ranked as the top position prospect in the Eastern League.

The first thing scouts mention about Milledge is his lightning-quick bat speed. Milledge boasts one of the fastest bats in the minor leagues, allowing him to wait on pitches longer than most. He uses the entire field and has the strength to hit for average as well as power once he matures as a hitter. He made very good adjustments after he moved from high Class A St. Lucie to Binghamton, improving his pitch recognition. It's still unclear as to whether Milledge profiles better at the top or in the middle of the order. He has above-average speed that he uses to his advantage on the bases and in center field, and he also has a plus arm. With his package of five tools, Milledge has few peers in the minors, and he has produced throughout his minor league career.

The biggest knock on Milledge is his inability to control the strike zone. He's a free swinger prone to chasing breaking balls out of the zone, and he hasn't drawn many walks even though pitchers are wary of him. Though he has the speed to steal bases, his instincts are unrefined and he was caught in 38 percent of his attempts in 2005. He stands up too quickly when he moves toward second base, which slows him down. Milledge has lost time to work on those flaws having played just 204 games in 2½ pro seasons. He held out for most of the summer in 2003, and a broken finger (in 2004) and a shoulder injury (in 2005) cost him playing time the last two seasons.

With Carlos Beltran entrenched in center field at Shea, Milledge might need to try his hand in right. He'll still play center in the minors in 2006, probably at Triple-A Norfolk, and could make his major league debut before the end of the season. With Beltran still in his prime and Milledge, Jose Reyes and David Wright not having reached theirs, the heart of New York's lineup should be in good shape for years to come.

Year	Club (League)	Class	AVG	G	AB	R	H	2B	3B	HR	RBI	BB	SO	SB	OBP	SLG
2003	Kingsport (Appy)	R	.231	7	26	4	6	2	0	0	2	3	4	5	.323	.308
2004	St. Lucie (FSL)	A	.235	22	81	6	19	6	2	2	8	9	21	3	.319	.432
	Capital City (SAL)	A	.337	65	261	66	88	22	1	13	58	17	53	23	.399	.579
2005	St. Lucie (FSL)	A	.302	62	232	48	70	15	0	4	22	19	41	18	.385	.418
	Binghamton (EL)	AA	.337	48	193	33	65	17	0	4	24	14	47	11	.392	.487
MINOR LEAGUE TOTALS			.313	204	793	157	248	62	3	23	114	62	166	60	.382	.485

PHILIP HUMBER

RHP

Born: Dec. 21, 1982. **B-T:** R-R. **Ht.:** 6-4. **Wt.:** 210. **Drafted:** Rice, 2004 (1st round). **Signed by:** Dave Lottsfeldt.

Humber won the final game of the 2003 College World Series and was one of three Rice pitchers to go in the first eight picks in 2004. Considered the safest bet among pitchers in that draft, Humber proved anything but after blowing out his elbow 15 starts into his pro career and had Tommy John surgery in July. Never fully healthy in his pro debut, Humber showed flashes of why he was a No. 3 overall pick. He has two plus pitches, a 12-to-6 curveball and a 91-94 mph fastball. He can vary the break on his curve so it runs in on lefthanders. His changeup eventually could give him a third above-average pitch. The biggest question is how he'll return from reconstructive elbow surgery. He fills the strike zone with all three of his pitches, but his command isn't at the same level of his control. He got hit hard when he left his fastball and changeup up and over the plate. The Mets hope Humber, like many Tommy John survivors, will come back stronger than before. He's scheduled to return to the mound in the second half of 2006.

Year	Club (League)	Class	W	L	ERA	G	GS	CG	SV	IP	H	R	ER	HR	BB	SO	AVG
2005	St. Lucie (FSL)	A	2	6	4.99	14	14	0	0	70	74	41	39	6	18	65	.273
	Binghamton (EL)	AA	0	1	6.75	1	1	0	0	4	4	3	3	0	2	2	.250
MINOR LEAGUE TOTALS			2	7	5.09	15	15	0	0	74	78	44	42	6	20	67	.272

CARLOS GOMEZ

OF

Born: Dec. 4, 1985. **B-T:** R-R. **Ht.:** 6-4. **Wt.:** 190. **Signed:** Dominican Republic, 2002. **Signed by:** Eddy Toledo.

Signed as a speedy but wiry 16-year-old, Gomez has grown into his body and some in the organization think his raw tools might be better than Milledge's. Eight months younger than Milledge, Gomez isn't nearly as polished. Gomez excites scouts with his raw power, speed and arm strength. He can put on a show in batting practice, ranked second in the minors with 64 steals in 2005 and has the best outfield arm in the system. Though he always has been young for his league, he has had no trouble making consistent contact. Still raw, Gomez hasn't shown much power in game situations because he doesn't control the strike zone, tends to let his hands drift to the ball and often overstrides. He's also unrefined on the bases, getting caught stealing 24 times in 2005. He can be erratic as a center and right fielder as well. Gomez flashed enough upside in low Class A that he should begin 2006 in the Florida State League, a pitcher-friendly environment. If everything comes together, he'll be New York's right fielder of the future.

Year	Club (League)	Class	AVG	G	AB	R	H	2B	3B	HR	RBI	BB	SO	SB	OBP	SLG
2003	Mets (DSL)	R	.240	58	208	26	50	7	0	1	10	7	37	13	.283	.288
2004	Kingsport (Appy)	R	.287	38	150	24	43	10	4	1	20	5	29	8	.333	.427
	Mets (GCL)	R	.268	19	71	10	19	7	0	0	11	2	9	9	.303	.366
2005	Hagerstown (SAL)	A	.275	120	487	75	134	13	6	8	48	32	88	64	.331	.376
MINOR LEAGUE TOTALS			.269	235	916	135	246	37	10	10	89	46	163	94	.318	.364

FERNANDO MARTINEZ

OF

Born: October 10, 1988. **B-T:** L-R. **Ht.:** 6-0. **Wt.:** 185. **Signed:** Dominican Republic, 2005. **Signed by:** Rafael Bournigal/Sandy Johnson/Eddy Toledo.

In their first year under Omar Minaya, the Mets were aggressive in mining Latin America. Their biggest splash was Martinez, who signed for $1.4 million. New York, which lacked second- and third-round picks in the draft, believes he matched up with any high school outfielder taken in the draft. Martinez' hitting approach is well beyond his years. He maintains his balance well while keeping his hands back in his stance. His bat and power are both plus tools, and he's a good athlete with solid speed and arm strength. Though he's very advanced for his age, Martinez still will need plenty of time to refine his game and is unproven against pro competition. Currently a center fielder, he projects as a right fielder and his bat will need to carry him if he's to become a star at that position. Because of his precocious hitting skills, the Mets believe Martinez may be able to handle a full-season league in 2006. If they send him to Hagerstown, he'll almost certainly be the youngest player in the South Atlantic League at 17.

Year	Club (League)	Class	AVG	G	AB	R	H	2B	3B	HR	RBI	BB	SO	SB	OBP	SLG
2005	Did not play—Signed 2006 contract															

5 ANDERSON HERNANDEZ — SS/2B

STEVE MOORE

Born: Oct. 30, 1982. **B-T:** B-R. **Ht.:** 5-9. **Wt.:** 170. **Signed:** Dominican Republic, 2001. **Signed by:** Ramon Pena (Tigers).

No player in the organization bolstered his prospect status in 2005 more than Hernandez. After coming over from the Tigers in a trade for Vance Wilson, he shed his good-field/no-hit reputation and emerged as a potential everyday player. A switch-hitter, Hernandez is adept from both sides of the plate. He has learned to focus on using the whole field and to make use of his plus speed. Defensively, he has very soft hands, above-average range and an average, accurate arm. He has excellent body control and lateral mobility. For a player with very little power, Hernandez doesn't control the strike zone, and he needs to do a better job of making contact. For all his defensive gifts, he gets himself into trouble when he tries to be flashy. Hernandez isn't going to move Jose Reyes off of shortstop, but the disappointing Kaz Matsui is vulnerable at second base. Most likely, Hernandez will wind up becoming a dependable utilityman.

Year	Club (League)	Class	AVG	G	AB	R	H	2B	3B	HR	RBI	BB	SO	SB	OBP	SLG
2001	Tigers (GCL)	R	.264	55	216	37	57	5	11	0	18	13	38	34	.303	.389
	Lakeland (FSL)	A	.190	7	21	2	4	0	1	0	1	0	8	0	.190	.286
2002	Lakeland (FSL)	A	.259	123	410	52	106	13	7	2	42	33	102	16	.310	.339
2003	Lakeland (FSL)	A	.229	106	380	47	87	11	4	2	28	27	69	15	.278	.295
2004	Lakeland (FSL)	A	.295	32	122	20	36	4	3	0	11	6	26	7	.326	.377
	Erie (EL)	AA	.274	101	394	65	108	19	3	5	29	26	89	17	.326	.376
2005	Binghamton (EL)	AA	.326	66	273	46	89	14	1	7	24	14	58	11	.360	.462
	Norfolk (IL)	AAA	.303	66	261	34	79	6	4	2	30	22	46	24	.354	.379
	New York (NL)	MLB	.056	6	18	1	1	0	0	0	0	1	4	0	.105	.056
MAJOR LEAGUE TOTALS			.056	6	18	1	1	0	0	0	0	1	4	0	.105	.056
MINOR LEAGUE TOTALS			.273	556	2077	303	566	72	34	18	183	141	436	124	.318	.366

6 BRIAN BANNISTER — RHP

STEVE MOORE

Born: Feb. 28, 1981. **B-T:** R-R. **Ht.:** 6-1. **Wt.:** 205. **Drafted:** Southern California, 2003 (7th round). **Signed by:** Steve Leavitt.

Bannister's father Floyd was the first overall pick in June 1976 and a 134-game winner over 15 major league seasons. His brother Brett pitched with Brian at Southern California and signed with the Mariners as a 19th-round pick in 2005. Brian greatly exceeded expectations in 2005, finishing the year as the No. 1 starter for Team USA at the World Cup. He allowed 13 runs in seven innings over two starts against Nicaragua and Cuba. Refining his cutter helped Bannister take a huge step forward. He spots his cutter and his 90-mph fastball to both sides of the plate. His 12-to-6 curveball can be devastating at times. Despite his success, Bannister still raises some obvious red flags. His fastball's movement is less impressive than its average velocity, and he tends to leave it up in the zone. He doesn't have much feel for a changeup, and his curveball is inconsistent. Bannister held his own in Triple-A and probably will return there in 2006. He'll be among the first in line for a callup in 2006 and could become as much as a No. 4 or 5 starter.

Year	Club (League)	Class	W	L	ERA	G	GS	CG	SV	IP	H	R	ER	HR	BB	SO	AVG
2003	Brooklyn (NY-P)	A	4	1	2.15	12	9	0	1	46	27	12	11	0	18	42	.173
2004	St. Lucie (FSL)	A	5	7	4.24	20	20	0	0	110	111	63	52	6	27	106	.270
	Binghamton (EL)	AA	3	3	4.06	8	8	0	0	44	45	23	20	2	17	28	.283
2005	Binghamton (EL)	AA	9	4	2.56	18	18	1	0	109	91	36	31	11	27	94	.232
	Norfolk (IL)	AAA	4	1	3.18	8	8	0	0	45	48	19	16	0	13	48	.270
MINOR LEAGUE TOTALS			25	16	3.30	66	63	1	1	355	322	153	130	19	102	318	.248

7 ALAY SOLER — RHP

Born: Oct. 9, 1979. **B-T:** R-R. **Ht.:** 6-4. **Wt.:** 240. **Signed:** Cuba, 2004. **Signed by:** Rafael Bournigal.

The biggest mystery in the system, Soler has yet to pitch in pro ball after signing a three-year, $2.8 million contract in September 2004. A Cuban defector who received asylum from the Dominican Republic, he did not get his visa until late October, and spent 2005 at the Mets' Dominican academy. Soler has two plus pitches, a 91-94 mph fastball and a low-80s slider with exceptional depth. The Mets think his big-game experience in Cuba—he helped them win the 2002 World University Games—will serve him well under the bright lights of New York. Using a three-quarters delivery, Soler sometimes gets under his pitches and leaves them high in the strike zone. The harder he throws, the more he struggles with his fastball command. Many Cuban defectors have needed time to adjust to a new culture and lifestyle in the United States. Soler is already 26 and likely will start his pro career in Double-A once he reaches the United States. He has enough stuff to start but also projects as a possible closer, a role the Mets filled by signing Billy Wagner as a free agent.

Year	Club (League)	Class	W	L	ERA	G	GS	CG	SV	IP	H	R	ER	HR	BB	SO	AVG
2005	Did not play—Visa problems																

8 DEOLIS GUERRA RHP

Born: April 17, 1989. **B-T:** R-R. **Ht.:** 6-5. **Wt.:** 200. **Signed:** Venezuela, 2005. **Signed by:** Rafael Bournigal.

Joining Fernando Martinez as the second of the Mets' two major Latin American signings last summer, Guerra agreed to a $700,000 bonus. Regarded as the top amatuer prospect in Venezuela in 2005, he oozes projection and already sits at 90 mph and touches 92 with his fastball, which he throws on a nice downhill plane. He also has an advanced feel for his changeup and a developing power curveball. He operates with a clean delivery and a loose, effortless arm action. Guerra's biggest weakness is an inability to maintain his arm slot. He's at his best when he comes over the top, but he has a tendency to drop down to the side, minimizing the effect of his great extension. The Mets believe Guerra already possesses two plus pitches and see him as a possible front-of-the-rotation starter. Although advanced for his age, he will likely need to cut his teeth in Rookie ball before getting a shot at Brooklyn or Hagerstown.

Year	Club (League)	Class	W	L	ERA	G	GS	CG	SV	IP	H	R	ER	HR	BB	SO	AVG
2005	Did not play—Signed 2006 contract																

9 JON NIESE LHP

Born: Oct. 27, 1986. **B-T:** L-L. **Ht.:** 6-3. **Wt.:** 190. **Drafted:** HS—Defiance, Ohio, 2005 (7th round). **Signed by:** Erwin Bryant.

Niese is a product of the same Defiance (Ohio) High program that also yielded Dodgers 2003 first-rounder Chad Billingsley. Ohio's first-ever back-to-back state high school player of the year, Niese also pitched for the U.S. national team and was considered a tough sign because of his commitment to the University of Cincinnati. Hall of Famer Gary Carter, now New York's Gulf Coast League manager, was so impressed with a tape he saw of Niese pitching in high school that he called him and urged him to sign. Carter's sales pitch worked, as the Mets drafted him in the seventh round and were able to land him for $175,000, the equivalent of early fifth-round money. Niese, born the same day the Mets last won the World Series in 1986, is projectable due to his lanky frame. He offered a glimpse of his future last summer, when he pitched in the low 90s more often than he had as an amateur and touched 94 mph. His secondary stuff requires a lot of refinement, but he showed some feel for his changeup, which is currently ahead of his curveball. The Mets are optimistic about his future and will move him to low Class A this year.

Year	Club (League)	Class	W	L	ERA	G	GS	CG	SV	IP	H	R	ER	HR	BB	SO	AVG
2005	Mets (GCL)	R	1	0	3.65	7	5	0	0	25	23	10	10	1	10	24	.245
MINOR LEAGUE TOTALS			1	0	3.65	7	5	0	0	25	23	10	10	1	10	24	.245

10 BRETT HARPER 1B

Born: July 31, 1981. **B-T:** L-R. **Ht.:** 6-4. **Wt.:** 185. **Drafted:** Scottsdale (Ariz.) JC, 2000 (45th round). **Signed by:** Kevin Frady.

Baseball is in Harper's genes, as his father Brian spent 16 years in the big leagues. Brett has much more pop than his dad ever did, and began to show it in games in 2005. After totaling 22 homers in his first four pro seasons, he finished third in the minors with 36. While his father, now a manager in the Angels minor league system, was known for his ability to put the ball in play with uncanny consistency, Harper employs more of an all-or-nothing approach. It has become clear that his plus-plus power will be his ticket to the big leagues. He always looks for fastballs to drive and continues to struggle mightily with breaking pitches, which leads to alarming strikeout totals. He doesn't run well and his defensive ability is poor. His range is limited at first base and he doesn't look comfortable making even routine plays. His makeup took a hit when he was suspended for two weeks in late June following an altercation at a bar in Port St. Lucie, Fla. Harper proved himself in a half-season at Double-A after struggling there in 2004. He's in line for a promotion to Triple-A, but the Mets trade with Florida that landed Carlos Delgado clouds his future in New York.

Year	Club (League)	Class	AVG	G	AB	R	H	2B	3B	HR	RBI	BB	SO	SB	OBP	SLG
2001	Kingsport (Appy)	R	.336	38	146	24	49	9	1	0	19	8	30	3	.386	.411
	Capital City (SAL)	A	.182	10	33	1	6	1	0	0	4	3	14	0	.250	.212
2002	Brooklyn (NY-P)	A	.279	53	183	21	51	6	0	1	20	14	37	2	.333	.328
2003	St. Lucie (FSL)	A	.205	13	44	5	9	2	0	0	4	5	13	1	.308	.250
	Capital City (SAL)	A	.329	23	79	5	26	6	0	1	9	4	20	1	.376	.443
	Kingsport (Appy)	R	.429	11	35	6	15	8	0	2	10	3	9	0	.500	.829
	Brooklyn (NY-P)	A	.299	28	87	5	26	8	0	1	18	5	12	1	.337	.425
2004	Mets (GCL)	R	.400	2	5	1	2	0	0	1	4	1	1	0	.500	1.000
	St. Lucie (FSL)	A	.350	60	220	32	77	18	1	9	55	35	53	1	.440	.564
	Binghamton (EL)	AA	.247	45	174	24	43	12	0	7	26	14	60	0	.309	.437
2005	St. Lucie (FSL)	A	.280	62	239	35	67	11	1	20	60	21	64	0	.337	.586
	Binghamton (EL)	AA	.273	67	227	37	62	11	0	16	42	26	85	0	.352	.533
MINOR LEAGUE TOTALS			.294	412	1472	196	433	92	3	58	271	139	398	9	.360	.479

11   JOSE CORONADO   SS

Born: April 13, 1986. **B-T:** B-R. **Ht.:** 6-1. **Wt.:** 175. **Signed:** Venezuela, 2003. **Signed by:** Gregorio Machado.

Coronado vaulted up three levels in the system in 2005, beginning in the Gulf Coast League and ending up in Hagerstown, where he hit .280 in the South Atlantic League play-offs. Along the way, he showed impressive range and arm strength, and he has the makings of becoming a solid defensive shortstop. Though he only took up switch-hitting after signing with the Mets in August 2003, he already is competent from both sides of the plate. He shows more patience than most hitters his age. Coronado isn't a burner who projects to steal a lot of bases, but he has above-average speed and excellent instincts in all phases of the game. Because of his small frame, he seldom drives the ball and needs to add bulk. He'll get a chance to prove himself over a full season in low Class A this year.

Year	Club (League)	Class	AVG	G	AB	R	H	2B	3B	HR	RBI	BB	SO	SB	OBP	SLG
2004	Tronconero 2 (VSL)	R	.248	33	121	19	30	6	0	3	17	20	23	0	.354	.372
2005	Mets (GCL)	R	.404	11	47	9	19	1	1	0	4	1	9	1	.429	.468
	Kingsport (Appy)	R	.266	39	139	24	37	5	1	1	8	22	27	6	.382	.338
	Hagerstown (SAL)	A	.225	18	71	4	16	2	1	0	4	7	17	1	.295	.282
MINOR LEAGUE TOTALS			.270	101	378	56	102	14	3	4	33	50	76	8	.362	.354

12   JESUS FLORES   C

Born: Oct. 26, 1984. **B-T:** R-R. **Ht.:** 6-1. **Wt.:** 180. **Signed:** Venezuela, 2002. **Signed by:** Gregorio Machado.

Flores had a breakthrough year in his U.S. debut in 2004, but his encore was basically a lost season. Flores broke his thumb in a big league exhibition game and missed the first month of the season. He didn't get many at-bats in spring training, so he never got into a groove in low Class A. He flashed some power but little else as he continually got himself out by expanding his strike zone. The Mets see him as an offensive-minded catcher, though he holds his own behind the plate and gunned down 40 percent of basestealers in 2005. Flores is extremely hard on himself and seemed to get frustrated by his lack of success, particularly after he had established himself as the best catching prospect in the system. The Mets believe his struggles were a result of his thumb injury, but he still needs to develop his pitch-recognition skills at the plate to avoid chasing pitches out of the zone. He likely will return to low Class A unless he has a huge spring training.

Year	Club (League)	Class	AVG	G	AB	R	H	2B	3B	HR	RBI	BB	SO	SB	OBP	SLG
2002	Universidad (VSL)	R	.203	40	123	10	25	8	0	1	8	10	29	2	.305	.293
	Mets (DSL)	R	.292	19	65	19	19	3	1	3	10	11	14	8	.403	.508
2003	Tronconero 2 (VSL)	R	.255	52	165	25	42	16	0	4	32	21	24	2	.383	.424
2004	Mets (GCL)	R	.319	45	141	16	45	12	3	4	25	8	26	1	.368	.532
	Brooklyn (NY-P)	A	.333	3	6	1	2	0	0	1	3	0	1	0	.333	.833
2005	Hagerstown (SAL)	A	.216	82	319	34	69	18	0	7	42	12	90	2	.250	.339
MINOR LEAGUE TOTALS			.247	241	819	105	202	57	4	20	120	62	184	15	.321	.399

13 JEFF KEPPINGER 2B

Born: April 21, 1980. **B-T:** R-R. **Ht.:** 6-0. **Wt.:** 180. **Drafted:** Georgia, 2001 (4th round). **Signed by:** Jack Powell (Pirates).

Though he hit .337, it was a rough year for Jeff Keppinger. He broke his left kneecap in mid-June when Charlotte's Felix Martinez took him out on a double play, and he didn't play again in 2005. Shortly afterward, Mets second basemen Miguel Cairo and Kazuo Matsui went down with injuries, and Keppinger would have been promoted if healthy. His replacement at Norfolk, Anderson Hernandez, played better than expected and passed him on the organization depth chart. Keppinger's trademark in the minors has been tremendous bat control. He has batted at least .325 in each of the last three seasons and rarely strikes out. Though he homered twice off Southern California ace Mark Prior in a 2001 College World Series game, Keppinger's contact approach means he'll never hit for much power. His value is derived almost entirely from his batting average. His defense at second is average and he saw some time in 2005 at third base and shortstop, his college position. Keppinger probably will return to Triple-A to begin 2006 with hopes of breaking into the majors as a utilityman, though some scouts believe he could handle an everyday assignment.

Year	Club (League)	Class	AVG	G	AB	R	H	2B	3B	HR	RBI	BB	SO	SB	OBP	SLG
2002	Hickory (SAL)	A	.276	126	478	75	132	23	4	10	73	47	33	6	.344	.404
2003	Lynchburg (Car)	A	.325	92	342	55	111	21	2	3	51	23	28	3	.365	.424
2004	Altoona (EL)	AA	.334	82	323	45	108	17	2	1	33	27	17	10	.384	.409
	Binghamton (EL)	AA	.362	14	47	14	17	3	1	0	5	6	2	2	.426	.468
	Norfolk (IL)	AAA	.316	6	19	1	6	1	0	0	2	4	2	0	.458	.368
	New York (NL)	MLB	.284	33	116	9	33	2	0	3	9	6	7	2	.317	.379
2005	Norfolk (IL)	AAA	.337	64	255	40	86	15	3	3	29	16	13	5	.377	.455
MAJOR LEAGUE TOTALS			**.284**	**33**	**116**	**9**	**33**	**2**	**0**	**3**	**9**	**6**	**7**	**2**	**.317**	**.379**
MINOR LEAGUE TOTALS			**.314**	**384**	**1464**	**230**	**460**	**80**	**12**	**17**	**193**	**123**	**95**	**26**	**.367**	**.420**

14 SHAWN BOWMAN 3B

Born: Dec. 9, 1984. **B-T:** R-R. **Ht.:** 6-2. **Wt.:** 206. **Drafted:** HS—Coquitlam, B.C., 2002 (12th round). **Signed by:** Claude Pelletier.

Loaded with tools, Bowman lacks the game experience of many of his peers because he grew up in Canada, where the weather isn't conducive to year-round play. He signed shortly after batting .395 with a team-best four homers for Canada at the 2002 World Junior Championship, but hasn't approached that success as a pro. He's still raw and struck out 110 times last year, even though his season ended in late July when he fractured a bone in his lower back. Bowman has above-average raw power, but he swings and misses too much. His pitch recognition isn't strong and he's too pull-conscious. He did encourage the Mets by showing improvement before he got hurt, hitting .291 with 13 homers after June 1. Already an exceptional defender, Bowman has quick reactions, soft hands and a plus arm. Bowman likely will start this year back in high Class A to work on his offensive approach. While he's blocked at third base by David Wright, it's too early to consider moving Bowman to another position considering his proficiency at third.

Year	Club (League)	Class	AVG	G	AB	R	H	2B	3B	HR	RBI	BB	SO	SB	OBP	SLG
2003	Brooklyn (NY-P)	A	.203	42	138	10	28	7	1	0	5	10	49	2	.260	.268
	Kingsport (Appy)	R	.121	10	33	2	4	1	0	0	3	1	13	0	.216	.152
2004	Capital City (SAL)	A	.258	116	396	66	102	17	1	19	69	39	121	5	.338	.449
2005	St. Lucie (FSL)	A	.221	87	326	44	72	15	1	17	53	22	110	4	.282	.429
MINOR LEAGUE TOTALS			**.231**	**255**	**893**	**122**	**206**	**40**	**3**	**36**	**130**	**72**	**293**	**11**	**.302**	**.403**

15 BOBBY PARNELL RHP

Born: Sept. 8, 1984. **B-T:** R-R. **Ht.:** 6-3. **Wt.:** 180. **Drafted:** Charleston Southern, 2005 (9th round). **Signed by:** Marlin McPhail.

Parnell posted 6.82 and 8.86 ERAs in his last two years at Charleston Southern, yet Mets area scout Marlin McPhail—who signed Ty Wigginton as a 17th-rounder in 1998—had tracked him since high school and liked his live arm and wiry frame. Parnell repaid McPhail's faith by leading the short-season New York-Penn League in ERA. A sinker/slider pitcher, he keeps the ball down and pitches at 88-92 mph with his fastball. He also has a changeup and the confidence to throw any pitch in any count. At Brooklyn, he showed an excellent knack for sticking to his gameplan while being able to make adjustments. Durability is a question for Parnell, who tends to wear down in longer outings. Because of his lack of success in college, he'll need to prove his debut was no fluke. With a strong spring training, he could be fast-tracked to high Class A.

Year	Club (League)	Class	W	L	ERA	G	GS	CG	SV	IP	H	R	ER	HR	BB	SO	AVG
2005	Brooklyn (NY-P)	A	2	3	1.73	15	14	0	0	73	48	20	14	1	29	67	.185
MINOR LEAGUE TOTALS			2	3	1.73	15	14	0	0	73	48	20	14	1	29	67	.185

16 EMMANUEL GARCIA   SS

Born: March 4, 1986. **B-T:** L-R. **Ht.:** 6-2. **Wt.:** 180. **Signed:** NDFA/HS—Montreal, 2004. **Signed by:** Claude Pelletier.

A Canadian high school product, Garcia went undrafted in 2004 when baseball went through a shortage of work visas for minor league players. He signed with the Mets as a non-drafted free agent and impressed them with his improvement during his pro debut last year. He led the Gulf Coast League in runs, hits and on-base percentage while finishing third in hitting. While his ceiling isn't particularly high, Garcia has a mature approach to the game. He controls the strike zone and is a good situational hitter. He has plus speed and good instincts on the bases, succeeding on 17 of his 18 steal attempts in the GCL. Some scouts doubt he has the arm to stick at short, but the Mets still believe Garcia can, citing his soft hands and quick feet. The Mets have a glut of middle infielders at the lower levels, so it's uncertain where he'll play this year.

Year	Club (League)	Class	AVG	G	AB	R	H	2B	3B	HR	RBI	BB	SO	SB	OBP	SLG
2005	Mets (GCL)	R	.339	45	186	43	63	7	0	2	30	21	36	17	.412	.409
	St. Lucie (FSL)	A	.222	2	9	1	2	1	0	0	0	0	2	0	.222	.333
MINOR LEAGUE TOTALS			.333	47	195	44	65	8	0	2	30	21	38	17	.405	.405

17 MIKE CARP   1B

Born: June 30, 1986. **B-T:** L-R. **Ht.:** 6-2. **Wt.:** 205. **Drafted:** HS—Lakewood, Calif., 2004 (9th round). **Signed by:** Steve Leavitt.

Carp burst out of the gate in his full-season debut in 2005, hitting .315 with 11 homers in his first 26 games in low Class A. But he fell into a deep slump afterward, and then had his season end in early August when he hurt his right wrist. Carp's best tool is his plus power. The South Atlantic League adjusted to him after his early power burst and it took him a while to alter his approach. The Mets are working with him to use the whole field and get a better grasp of the strike zone. He heeded their advice in July by hitting .284, but managed just two home runs. Defensively, Carp is average at first base and his main goal is improving his agility and footwork. He's a below-average runner. He'll play in high Class A this year.

Year	Club (League)	Class	AVG	G	AB	R	H	2B	3B	HR	RBI	BB	SO	SB	OBP	SLG
2004	Mets (GCL)	R	.267	57	191	30	51	12	0	4	26	22	51	2	.358	.393
2005	Hagerstown (SAL)	A	.249	89	313	49	78	12	1	19	63	35	96	2	.358	.476
MINOR LEAGUE TOTALS			.256	146	504	79	129	24	1	23	89	57	147	4	.358	.444

18 HECTOR PELLOT   2B

Born: Feb. 8, 1987. **B-T:** R-R. **Ht.:** 5-11. **Wt.:** 185. **Drafted:** HS—Cidra, P.R., 2005 (4th round). **Signed by:** Junior Roman.

Pellot was the second player drafted out of Puerto Rico in 2005, behind only Dodgers second-rounder Ivan DeJesus. Pellot had committed to Santa Clara, and held out for much of the summer before signing for $350,000. After he joined the Mets, he stood out with his bat during instructional league. He has drawn comparisons to Rafael Furcal for his high-energy style and above-average speed. Pellot uses the entire field with a smooth, line-drive stroke and is very aggressive on the bases. A shortstop in high school, he moved to second base as a pro because the Mets think his arm action and tools are better suited there. He still needs to get stronger in order to drive the ball more consistently, as his power is just fringe-average for a second baseman. While Pellot possibly could handle low Class A, he more likely will make his debut in Brooklyn.

Year	Club (League)	Class	AVG	G	AB	R	H	2B	3B	HR	RBI	BB	SO	SB	OBP	SLG
2005	Did not play—Signed 2006 contract															

19 MATT DURKIN, RHP

Born: Feb. 22, 1983. **B-T:** R-R. **Ht.:** 6-4. **Wt.:** 220. **Drafted:** San Jose State, 2004 (2nd round). **Signed by:** Chuck Hensley Jr.

As a client of Scott Boras, Durkin figured to be a tough sign in the 2004 draft. A second-round choice, he didn't sign for $800,000 until the end of the summer. He didn't make his pro debut until 2005 and it was clear that his layoff affected him. His mechanics got out of sync, which led to his stuff becoming just average and his command of it wavering more than usual. Worse yet, he came down with a sore shoulder and missed two months in the middle of the season. Durkin's fastball sat at 90-91 mph, down from 92-94 and a high of 96 in the past. His arm works fast and easy, though he occasionally drops his elbow and loses some extension. Durkin also didn't show the plus curveball that was his trademark when he was successful at San Jose State. He also throws a cutter and changeup. He never made it to high Class A as expected last year, but should at some point in 2006.

Year	Club (League)	Class	W	L	ERA	G	GS	CG	SV	IP	H	R	ER	HR	BB	SO	AVG
2005	Mets (GCL)	R	0	0	0.00	1	1	0	0	3	2	0	0	0	0	4	.200
	Hagerstown (SAL)	A	4	5	3.77	19	14	0	0	76	54	42	32	9	54	79	.205
MINOR LEAGUE TOTALS			4	5	3.63	20	15	0	0	79	56	42	32	9	54	83	.205

20 AAROM BALDIRIS   2B

Born: Jan. 5, 1983. **B-T:** R-R. **Ht.:** 6-2. **Wt.:** 195. **Signed:** Venezuela, 1999. **Signed by:** Gregorio Machado.

The Mets once saw some of Edgardo Alfonzo in Baldiris, but he has stagnated since his breakout 2003 season. He has moved from third base to second because he didn't have the power to profile at the hot corner. Though he became more aggressive at the plate in Double-A, his pop improved only marginally. Baldiris understands the strike zone but struggles with plus velocity. He has a high leg kick that may be more of a detriment than a help to him. The switch to second base didn't come easy for Baldiris. Though he has soft hands and arm strength, he looked stiff at his new position. If Jeff Keppinger returns to Norfolk, Baldiris may have to repeat Double-A.

Year	Club (League)	Class	AVG	G	AB	R	H	2B	3B	HR	RBI	BB	SO	SB	OBP	SLG
2000	Universidad (VSL)	R	.353	44	139	24	49	9	1	7	35	37	23	4	.489	.583
	Kingsport (Appy)	R	.219	32	105	14	23	3	1	2	20	7	20	2	.265	.324
2001	Did not play—Injured															
2002	Kingsport (Appy)	R	.327	58	217	31	71	9	1	3	24	14	24	9	.390	.419
	Brooklyn (NY-P)	A	.303	9	33	5	10	1	0	0	2	1	2	2	.343	.333
2003	Capital City (SAL)	A	.313	107	393	55	123	19	4	6	68	51	55	13	.396	.427
	Brooklyn (NY-P)	A	.364	26	88	20	32	5	2	0	18	14	13	2	.451	.466
2004	St. Lucie (FSL)	A	.305	107	406	57	124	15	5	4	45	46	64	6	.384	.397
	Binghamton (EL)	AA	.222	21	81	8	18	3	1	0	8	6	13	0	.273	.284
2005	Binghamton (EL)	AA	.275	131	495	69	136	35	4	11	63	45	81	7	.341	.416
MINOR LEAGUE TOTALS			.299	535	1957	283	586	99	16	33	283	221	295	45	.377	.417

21 AMBIORIX CONCEPCION   OF

Born: Oct. 15, 1983. **B-T:** R-R. **Ht.:** 6-2. **Wt.:** 180. **Signed:** Dominican Republic, 2000. **Signed by:** Eddy Toledo.

Rated the top prospect in the New York-Penn League in 2004, Concepcion earned a spot on the Mets' 40-man roster. But he took a huge step backward last year, and New York also discovered that he was 19 months older than originally believed. Early in 2005, he tried to pull every pitch he saw in order to put up big power numbers, resulting instead in a lot of weak grounders to shortstop. Low Class A pitchers fed him a steady diet of fastballs in and curveballs away that gave him fits, and his poor grasp of the strike zone and two-strike approach didn't help matters. He has plus raw power but his long swing reduces his ability to make contact. Concepcion has plus speed, outfield range and arm strength, and has split time between center and right field. The Mets will send him to high Class A in 2006 with the hopes he can reaffirm the faith they showed in him when they added him to the 40-man roster.

Year	Club (League)	Class	AVG	G	AB	R	H	2B	3B	HR	RBI	BB	SO	SB	OBP	SLG
2001	Mets (DSL)	R	.264	37	129	17	34	6	0	0	16	9	23	5	.317	.310
2002	Kingsport (Appy)	R	.276	57	228	25	63	13	4	4	31	7	51	6	.302	.421
2003	Kingsport (Appy)	R	.214	45	168	22	36	8	3	0	19	9	35	10	.256	.298
2004	Brooklyn (NY-P)	A	.305	66	259	38	79	14	3	8	46	13	54	28	.338	.475
2005	Hagerstown (SAL)	A	.251	130	521	68	131	29	5	15	61	22	136	35	.289	.413
MINOR LEAGUE TOTALS			.263	335	1305	170	343	70	15	27	173	60	299	84	.300	.402

22 JUAN PEREZ   LHP

Born: Feb. 10, 1981. **B-T:** R-L. **Ht.:** 6-0. **Wt.:** 170. **Signed:** Dominican Republic, 1998. **Signed by:** Levy Ochoa (Red Sox).

One of the more intriguing lefties in the Red Sox system in recent years, Perez became a minor league free agent after the 2005 season and sparked a lot of interest with his strong performance in the Dominican League. The Mets won the bidding for Perez and protected him on their 40-man roster. Known as Luis Perez and thought to be three years younger than his actual birthdate when he first signed with Boston, he represented the Red Sox at the 2004 Futures Game. He throws a tailing, sinking 89-93 mph fastball from a three-quarters angle. His breaking ball, an 80-mph slurve, is a second plus pitch at times. Perez has averaged more than a strikeout per inning for his pro career, but his control and command have been spotty. If he can throw strikes in big league camp, he could make the Mets as a lefty set-up man.

Year	Club (League)	Class	W	L	ERA	G	GS	CG	SV	IP	H	R	ER	HR	BB	SO	AVG
1999	Red Sox (DSL)	R	6	6	1.94	13	13	1	0	70	38	29	15	1	30	107	.159
2000	Red Sox (GCL)	R	3	1	2.36	9	5	0	1	34	24	12	9	2	13	43	.192
2001	Augusta (SAL)	A	8	8	3.58	26	25	0	0	126	118	69	50	14	42	113	.251
2002	Sarasota (FSL)	A	0	6	3.78	16	14	0	0	67	71	34	28	4	19	39	.274
2003	Sarasota (FSL)	A	4	2	2.37	33	0	0	18	38	34	15	10	0	12	37	.230
	Portland (EL)	AA	3	3	3.82	18	0	0	0	31	37	19	13	4	11	24	.306
2004	Portland (EL)	AA	5	1	4.14	46	0	0	6	78	72	46	36	12	37	79	.237
2005	Pawtucket (IL)	AAA	4	5	4.50	40	1	0	1	62	61	31	31	7	29	74	.261
MINOR LEAGUE TOTALS			32	34	3.42	201	58	1	26	505	455	255	192	44	193	516	239

23 ANDY WILSON   1B/C

Born: Nov. 20, 1980. **B-T:** R-R. **Ht.:** 6-2. **Wt.:** 210. **Signed:** NDFA/Stetson, 2003. **Signed by:** Jon Bunnell.

Wilson has done nothing but hit since signing as a nondrafted free agent out of Stetson in 2003. Last season, he led the Florida State League in home runs while finishing second in extra-base hits and slugging, though he was old for high Class A at age 24. He's an excellent mistake hitter who consistently punishes hanging breaking balls or fastballs left over the plate. He also controls the strike zone well. He struggles against quality pitching and has difficulty with pitches on the outer half of the plate, particularly sliders. Wilson isn't much of an athlete and is still looking for a defensive home. He spent most of his time in 2005 at first base, and also played some catcher. The Mets sent him to the Arizona Fall League to work on his catching skills but scouts doubt he can stay behind the plate. His skill set reminds some of Kevin Millar. Wilson will have to prove himself yet again this year in Double-A.

Year	Club (League)	Class	AVG	G	AB	R	H	2B	3B	HR	RBI	BB	SO	SB	OBP	SLG
2003	Kingsport (Appy)	R	.343	10	35	5	12	3	0	1	7	2	5	0	.395	.514
	Brooklyn (NY-P)	A	.250	31	96	15	24	8	4	13	13	19	2	.342	.458
2004	St. Lucie (FSL)	A	.429	5	14	2	6	0	0	2	6	2	2	0	.500	.857
	Capital City (SAL)	A	.286	104	370	63	106	32	0	19	70	43	80	2	.364	.527
2005	St. Lucie (FSL)	A	.284	127	464	81	132	25	3	28	89	68	88	8	.370	.532
	Norfolk (IL)	AAA	.000	3	7	0	0	0	0	0	0	1	0	0	.125	.000
MINOR LEAGUE TOTALS			.284	280	986	166	280	68	3	54	185	129	194	12	.366	.523

24 CHASE LAMBIN   INF

Born: July 7, 1979. **B-T:** B-R. **Ht.:** 6-1. **Wt.:** 180. **Drafted:** Louisiana-Lafayette, 2002 (34th round). **Signed by:** Bob Rossi.

Lambin's minor league career was unremarkable heading into 2005, when he established personal bests in most offensive categories. He dominated the Eastern League after batting an uninspiring .244 there in 2004, and continued to hit in Triple-A. Like Andy Wilson, he was old for his leagues, turning 26 at midseason. A switch-hitter, he employs a gap-to-gap approach and has home run power from both sides of the plate. He still has some trouble with pitch recognition but can drive his pitch when he gets it. Defensively, he has a strong arm and not much else. Lambin played third base, shortstop, second base and left field last season, but none of them particularly well. He also has tried catcher, but his hands hampered his receiving ability and also hurt him as an infielder. He's probably best suited for the outfield and has a solid arm. Lambin profiles as a utilityman who stands out for his bat, rather than his glove or versatility. He'll head to Triple-A and wait for an injury to create an opening for him in New York.

Year	Club (League)	Class	AVG	G	AB	R	H	2B	3B	HR	RBI	BB	SO	SB	OBP	SLG
2002	Brooklyn (NY-P)	A	.279	47	179	25	50	6	3	6	27	8	50	5	.316	.447
2003	St. Lucie (FSL)	A	.289	118	401	58	116	27	2	5	49	46	81	13	.366	.404
2004	Binghamton (EL)	AA	.244	121	410	64	100	22	4	10	64	48	103	4	.331	.390
2005	Binghamton (EL)	AA	.331	53	181	26	60	17	0	14	29	20	38	2	.396	.657
	Norfolk (IL)	AAA	.289	61	211	35	61	16	2	10	34	20	47	2	.350	.526
MINOR LEAGUE TOTALS			.280	400	1382	208	387	88	11	45	203	142	319	26	.351	.457

25 MITCH WYLIE RHP

Born: Jan. 14, 1977. **B-T:** R-R. **Ht.:** 6-3. **Wt.:** 190. **Drafted:** St. Ambrose (Iowa), 1998 (8th round). **Signed by:** Ken Stauffer/Nathan Durst (White Sox).

After eight years in pro ball, Wylie is on the verge of reaching the big leagues after the Mets took him in the major league Rule 5 draft at the Winter Meetings. He has had to persevere through more than his share of adversity to get there. He blew out his elbow in 1999, his first full pro season, and required Tommy John surgery. After starting to build positive momentum by leading the Double-A Southern League with 15 wins and making the White Sox' 40-man roster in 2001, he missed most of the next season with shoulder inflammation. He tried to pitch through a broken right foot in 2004 with little success and couldn't get an offer as a minor league free agent after the season. Wylie opened 2005 with the independent Northern League's Sioux City Explorers, who sold him to the Giants in June. Used as a Triple-A swingman, he showed a 92-95 mph fastball and a quality changeup. His breaking ball always has lagged behind his fastball and changeup. He worked on both a slider and a curveball at Fresno, and the slider is a better pitch. Wylie locates his fastball well and isn't afraid to work inside. He employs a short-arm delivery. New York will give him the chance to make its bullpen. If he doesn't stick on the 25-man roster, he'll have to clear waivers and be offered back to San Francisco for half his $50,000 draft price before the Mets can send him to the minors.

Year	Club (League)	Class	W	L	ERA	G	GS	CG	SV	IP	H	R	ER	HR	BB	SO	AVG
1998	Bristol (Appy)	R	0	2	3.30	20	0	0	6	30	34	12	11	1	11	32	.286
1999	Burlington (Mid)	A	1	0	1.97	6	6	0	0	32	28	11	7	0	11	27	.237
2000	Winston-Salem (Car)	A	3	7	4.34	17	17	0	0	95	112	59	46	8	34	57	.297
2001	Winston-Salem (Car)	A	0	1	3.60	1	1	0	0	5	7	2	2	0	1	4	.318
	Birmingham (SL)	AA	15	4	4.21	24	24	0	0	141	138	70	66	13	46	123	.253
2002	Charlotte (IL)	AAA	2	3	4.76	6	6	0	0	34	43	22	18	6	5	23	.307
2003	Winston-Salem (Car)	A	2	0	3.38	4	0	0	0	8	7	3	3	1	3	7	.233
	Birmingham (SL)	AA	3	5	4.40	14	10	1	0	57	53	33	28	2	17	42	.247
2004	Charlotte (IL)	AAA	1	4	5.74	28	1	0	1	53	63	41	34	8	24	42	.289
2005	Sioux City (Nor)	IND	1	0	3.00	5	5	0	0	33	29	12	11	4	5	22	.236
	Fresno (PCL)	AAA	3	5	4.50	22	9	0	2	66	68	36	33	6	15	58	.261
MINOR LEAGUE TOTALS			30	31	4.28	142	74	1	9	522	553	289	248	45	167	415	.270

26 MATT LINDSTROM RHP

Born: Feb. 11, 1980. **B-T:** R-R. **Ht.:** 6-4. **Wt.:** 205. **Drafted:** Ricks (Idaho) JC, 2002 (10th round). **Signed by:** Jim Reeves.

Lindstrom spent two years on a Mormon mission in Sweden, returning in 2001 to pitch at Ricks (Idaho) JC with his brother Rob. A product of eastern Idaho, his baseball experience already was limited by weather in high school, so he's still raw despite his age. He wowed scouts with his arm strength during the Arizona Fall League in 2004, and as a result the Mets protected him on their 40-man roster. Lindstrom possesses the most explosive arm in the system with a fastball that sits at 94-96 mph and has touched 100. While his heater has impressive velocity, his strikeout numbers are just pedestrian because he lacks movement, command and deception. Hitters get a good look at the ball coming out of his hand. He has a hard time throwing his fastball for strikes, let alone locating it within the zone. He has similar problems with his secondary stuff, as he has yet to find a second pitch he can trust. He has trouble repeating his delivery, which contributes to his inconsistency. New York moved him to relief last June in Double-A, and he posted a 3.12 ERA in that role, compared to 8.18 as a starter. Opponents batted .306 against him when he came out of the bullpen, however, so he still has a great deal of work to accomplish. Nevertheless, his arm strength is intriguing.

Year	Club (League)	Class	W	L	ERA	G	GS	CG	SV	IP	H	R	ER	HR	BB	SO	AVG
2002	Kingsport (Appy)	R	0	6	4.84	12	11	0	0	48	56	45	26	6	21	39	.280
2003	Capital City (SAL)	A	2	3	2.86	12	11	0	0	57	46	21	18	2	33	50	.228
	Brooklyn (NY-P)	A	7	3	3.44	14	14	0	0	65	61	28	25	2	27	52	.250
2004	St. Lucie (FSL)	A	5	5	3.73	14	14	1	0	80	83	44	33	5	20	50	.282
	Capital City (SAL)	A	3	2	3.21	13	12	0	0	56	47	26	20	3	10	64	.230
2005	Binghamton (EL)	AA	2	5	5.40	35	10	0	0	73	90	61	44	11	55	58	.302
MINOR LEAGUE TOTALS			19	24	3.94	100	72	1	0	379	383	225	166	29	166	313	.266

27 SEAN HENRY
2B/SS

Born: Aug. 18, 1985. **B-T:** R-R. **Ht.:** 5-10. **Wt.:** 154. **Drafted:** Diablo Valley (Calif.) CC, 2004 (20th round). **Signed by:** Chuck Hensley Jr.

The Tigers drafted Henry in the 10th round out of high school in 2003, when he spent the summer with the U.S. junior national team. He hit .481, second on a team that included future first-round picks Matt Bush (Padres), Neil Walker (Pirates) and Billy Butler (Royals). Henry opted to attend Diablo Valley (Calif.) JC and declined to sign with Detroit as a draft-and-follow, allowing the Mets to lock him up as a 20th-rounder in 2004. Though he has a small frame and will need to fill out, Henry boasts above-average bat speed and good pop for a middle infielder. He understands the strike zone but has a long swing, which hampers his ability to make contact. Henry signed as a shortstop and has a strong if sometimes inaccurate arm, but he moved to second base at Rookie-level Kingsport to accommodate Jose Coronado. Henry's future lies at second because he lacks true shortstop actions. He's immature and has to answer questions about his work ethic. He needs to distinguish himself in low Class A this year.

Year	Club (League)	Class	AVG	G	AB	R	H	2B	3B	HR	RBI	BB	SO	SB	OBP	SLG
2004	Mets (GCL)	R	.282	56	202	35	57	9	5	4	30	22	43	10	.364	.436
2005	Kingsport (Appy)	R	.255	42	149	24	38	7	1	5	31	22	43	15	.350	.416
MINOR LEAGUE TOTALS			.271	98	351	59	95	16	6	9	61	44	86	25	.358	.427

28 COREY RAGSDALE
SS

Born: Nov. 10, 1982. **B-T:** R-R. **Ht.:** 6-4. **Wt.:** 185. **Drafted:** HS—Jonesboro, Ark., 2001 (2nd round). **Signed by:** Larry Chase.

A career .193 hitter prior to last season, Ragsdale was known more for his impressive athleticism than his performance on the field. The Mets had tried making him a switch-hitter in 2003 in hopes of invigorating his career, but that failed. Ragsdale hit a career-high 19 homers in 2005, inspiring some hope, and he batted .279 with seven homers in August after struggling mightily in his first month in Double-A. But he also struck out a career-high 169 times, and it's unlikely he'll ever make consistent contact. One of the best athletes in the system, Ragsdale has above-average speed and range and plus-plus arm strength. Some scouts have suggested that his best chance of reaching the majors would be as a pitcher. New York will keep him at shortstop for now and probably send him back to Double-A to start this year.

Year	Club (League)	Class	AVG	G	AB	R	H	2B	3B	HR	RBI	BB	SO	SB	OBP	SLG
2001	Kingsport (Appy)	R	.141	23	71	9	10	3	2	1	5	10	38	4	.256	.282
2002	Capital City (SAL)	A	.177	37	124	15	22	1	0	1	12	15	45	8	.262	.210
	Brooklyn (NY-P)	A	.183	66	224	35	41	7	2	2	19	23	72	26	.277	.259
2003	Capital City (SAL)	A	.180	105	355	50	64	11	4	3	27	46	133	31	.297	.259
2004	St. Lucie (FSL)	A	.219	124	421	65	92	19	5	7	38	42	152	24	.303	.337
	Norfolk (IL)	AAA	.250	6	20	1	5	1	0	0	1	4	1	4	.286	.300
2005	St. Lucie (FSL)	A	.260	68	273	51	71	16	8	10	38	33	94	8	.347	.487
	Binghamton (EL)	AA	.226	64	217	33	49	5	3	9	31	21	75	4	.305	.401
MINOR LEAGUE TOTALS			.208	493	1705	259	354	63	24	33	171	191	613	106	.300	.331

29 HENRY OWENS
RHP

Born: April 23, 1979. **B-T:** R-R. **Ht.:** 6-3. **Wt.:** 230. **Signed:** NDFA/Barry (Fla.), 2001. **Signed by:** Delvy Santiago (Pirates).

A backup catcher at NCAA Division II Barry (Fla.), Owens put his medical-school plans on hold when the Pirates signed him as a nondrafted free agent and immediately converted him to the mound. The Mets took him in the Triple-A Rule 5 draft at the 2004 Winter Meetings, and they added him to the 40-man roster after his first season in the organization. Owens stands out for his arm speed, which generates fastballs that run from the low to mid-90s and are lethal when he keeps them down in the strike zone. His slider and his command are fringy, however. If he can refine his slider, it could mean a quick ascent through the upper minors. Owens will move up to Double-A this year.

Year	Club (League)	Class	W	L	ERA	G	GS	CG	SV	IP	H	R	ER	HR	BB	SO	AVG
2001	Pirates (GCL)	R	1	0	1.29	6	0	0	1	7	5	1	1	0	2	8	.192
2002	Williamsport (NY-P)	A	0	3	2.62	23	0	0	7	45	26	18	13	4	16	63	.166
2003	Hickory (SAL)	A	2	1	2.91	22	0	0	9	34	21	14	11	1	17	52	.176
	Lynchburg (Car)	A	1	2	2.45	13	0	0	5	15	9	6	4	0	11	21	.176
2004	Lynchburg (Car)	A	3	4	4.28	39	0	0	4	55	46	26	26	4	26	49	.219
2005	St. Lucie (FSL)	A	2	5	3.15	38	1	0	4	54	49	29	19	2	24	74	.233
MINOR LEAGUE TOTALS			9	15	3.18	141	1	0	30	209	156	94	74	11	96	267	.202

30 EVAN MacLANE

LHP

Born: Nov. 4, 1982. **B-T:** L-L. **Ht.:** 6-2. **Wt.:** 185. **Drafted:** Feather River (Calif.) CC, 2003 (25th round). **Signed by:** Chuck Hensley Jr.

MacLane was able to succeed in the lower minors with only average stuff because he has such a good feel of pitching. He had no problems making the jump to high Class A in 2005, but he ran into trouble in Double-A. MacLane's strengths are his plus command and plus changeup, which sits in the 76-80 mph range. His fastball sits in the mid-80s and touches 87, while his curveball is more notable for his ability to locate it than its break. With below-average velocity, MacLane needs to rely on keeping hitters off balance and controlling their bat speed. If he can improve his curveball, he could be a big leaguer in the mold of Jamie Moyer. He'll work on that in 2006 when he returns to Double-A.

Year	Club (League)	Class	W	L	ERA	G	GS	CG	SV	IP	H	R	ER	HR	BB	SO	AVG
2003	Kingsport (Appy)	R	4	1	2.88	14	6	0	0	56	59	20	18	4	8	57	.271
	Brooklyn (NY-P)	A	1	0	0.00	1	1	0	0	6	3	0	0	0	1	5	.136
2004	Capital City (SAL)	A	5	2	2.39	14	10	0	0	68	57	21	18	9	10	66	.228
	Brooklyn (NY-P)	A	5	2	2.48	12	12	0	0	69	61	27	19	5	6	68	.236
2005	St. Lucie (FSL)	A	8	5	3.20	19	19	1	0	112	96	51	40	14	15	92	.224
	Binghamton (EL)	AA	3	2	4.14	9	9	1	0	59	63	31	27	7	9	48	.266
MINOR LEAGUE TOTALS			26	12	2.97	69	57	2	0	370	339	150	122	39	49	336	.240

NEW YORK
YANKEES

BY **JOHN MANUEL**

Robinson Cano proved it can be done. So did Chien-Ming Wang. The Dominican second baseman and Taiwanese righthander showed that the Yankees can develop homegrown talent and give those players a chance to earn roles in the major leagues. That's still true with a payroll that has soared past $200 million, and with a farm system that hasn't produced in recent years as it once did.

The homegrown core of the club that has won eight consecutive American League East titles and made nine straight playoff appearances (including four World Series titles) is still effective but aging. Bernie Williams, 37, has declined significantly and will take a backup role to new center fielder Johnny Damon. Jorge Posada, 34, has shown signs of slipping. While Derek Jeter, 31, and Mariano Rivera, 36, remain star players of the first order, they need more homegrown help.

The Yankees continue to have the game's highest revenues—around $335 million in 2005—but the New York Daily News reported the club lost between $50 million and $85 million, in part due to revenue-sharing and luxury-tax payments. Responding to reality and fan demand (New York drew an AL-record 4.09 million fans in 2005), the Yankees have raised ticket prices, with top seats fetching $110 a game.

General manager Brian Cashman was expected to leave New York when his contract ended after the 2005 season, but he and manager Joe Torre returned, extending a run of stability dating to 1997. Only Atlanta (John Schuerholz, Bobby Cox) and

St. Louis (Walt Jocketty, Tony La Russa) have had greater continuity in the GM and manager roles.

Cashman and Torre will try to claim the Yankees' 27th World Series crown while holding the line on payroll—relatively speaking of course. However, the graduation of Cano and Wang to New York left the system painfully thin at the upper levels, particularly in Triple-A. Eric Duncan, No. 1 on this list a year ago, was rushed to Double-A and struggled, hitting just .235, but he rebounded with a strong effort in the Arizona Fall League while moving from third base to first. Duncan may be a big leaguer soon, and third base, thanks to AL MVP Alex Rodriguez, is taken.

While Duncan remains a good prospect, he was passed by 2004 first-round pick Philip Hughes, who symbolizes the state of the system. In the last two years, New York has added high-end prospects with international signings and a more aggressive approach in the draft. The organization has potential impact bats such as outfielders Jose Tabata and Austin Jackson and infielders C.J. Henry and Eduardo Nunez, as well as intriguing arms in Hughes, Christian Garcia and Jeff Marquez. Loaded Yankees affiliates won championships in the short-season New York-Penn and Rookie-level Gulf Coast leagues, but most of their best talent has yet to play above the Class A level.

TOP 30 PROSPECTS

1. Philip Hughes, rhp
2. Eric Duncan, 3b/1b
3. Jose Tabata, of
4. C.J. Henry, ss
5. Austin Jackson, of
6. Eduardo Nunez, ss
7. Marcos Vechionacci, 3b/ss
8. Christian Garcia, rhp
9. Jeff Marquez, rhp
10. Tyler Clippard, rhp
11. J. Brent Cox, rhp
12. Tim Battle, of
13. Brett Gardner, of
14. Steven White, rhp
15. Melky Cabrera, of
16. Matt DeSalvo, rhp
17. Alan Horne, rhp
18. Sean Henn, lhp
19. Kevin Howard, 2b/3b
20. Matt Smith, lhp
21. Justin Christian, 2b/of
22. Bronson Sardinha, of
23. Kevin Thompson, of
24. T.J. Beam, rhp
25. Garrett Patterson, lhp
26. Andy Phillips, 1b/3b
27. Rudy Guillen, of
28. Kevin Reese, of
29. Jason Stephens, rhp
30. Jeff Karstens, rhp

ORGANIZATION OVERVIEW

General manager: Brian Cashman. **Farm director:** Pat Roessler. **Scouting director:** Damon Oppenheimer.

2005 PERFORMANCE

Class	Team	League	W	L	Pct.	Finish*	Manager(s)
Majors	New York	American	95	67	.586	t-2nd (14)	Joe Torre
Triple-A	Columbus Clippers	International	77	67	.535	5th (14)	Bucky Dent
Double-A	Trenton Thunder	Eastern	74	68	.521	t-4th (12)	Bill Masse
High A	Tampa Yankees	Florida State	56	79	.415	11th (12)	Joe Breeden
Low A	Charleston Riverdogs	South Atlantic	80	58	.580	2nd (14)	Bill Mosiello
Short-season	Staten Island Yankees	New York-Penn	52	24	.684	+1st (14)	Andy Stankiewicz
Rookie	GCL Yankees	Gulf Coast	33	20	.623	+2nd (12)	Oscar Acosta
OVERALL 2005 MINOR LEAGUE RECORD			372	316	.541	4th (30)	

*Finish in overall standings (No. of teams in league). +League champion.

ORGANIZATION LEADERS

BATTING *Minimum 250 at-bats
*AVG	Nunez, Eduardo, Staten Island	.313
R	Battle, Tim, Charleston	97
H	Thompson, Kevin, Columbus/Trenton	155
TB	Duncan, Shelley, Trenton	263
2B	Thompson, Kevin, Columbus/Trenton	45
3B	Battle, Tim, Charleston	11
HR	Duncan, Shelley, Trenton	34
RBI	Duncan, Shelley, Trenton	92
BB	Thompson, Kevin, Columbus/Trenton	76
SO	Battle, Tim, Charleston	195
SB	Christian, Justin, Charleston/Tampa	55
*OBP	Thompson, Kevin, Columbus/Trenton	.394
*SLG	Phillips, Andy, Columbus	.573

PITCHING #Minimum 75 innings
W	Karstens, Jeff, Trenton	12
L	Jones, Jason, Tampa	13
	Marquez, Jeff, Charleston	13
#ERA	Beam, T.J., Charleston/Tampa	1.62
G	Bean, Colter, Columbus	65
CG	Five tied at	1
SV	Martinez, Mike, Columbus	30
IP	Karstens, Jeff, Trenton	169
BB	Gomez, Abel, Charleston/GCL/Tampa	75
SO	Clippard, Tyler, Charleston/Columbus/Tampa	181

BEST TOOLS

Best Hitter for Average	Jose Tabata
Best Power Hitter	Eric Duncan
Best Strike-Zone Discipline	Kevin Reese
Fastest Baserunner	Brett Gardner
Best Athlete	C.J. Henry
Best Fastball	Philip Hughes
Best Curveball	Christian Garcia
Best Slider	Matt Smith
Best Changeup	Matt DeSalvo
Best Control	Tyler Clippard
Best Defensive Catcher	Omir Santos
Best Defensive Infielder	Marcos Vechionacci
Best Infield Arm	Eduardo Nunez
Best Defensive Outfielder	Brett Gardner
Best Outfield Arm	Rudy Guillen

PROJECTED 2009 LINEUP

Catcher	Jorge Posada
First Base	Eric Duncan
Second Base	Robinson Cano
Third Base	Alex Rodriguez
Shortstop	Derek Jeter
Left Field	C.J. Henry
Center Field	Austin Jackson
Right Field	Jose Tabata

Designated Hitter	Hideki Matsui
No. 1 Starter	Philip Hughes
No. 2 Starter	Chien-Ming Wang
No. 3 Starter	Christian Garcia
No. 4 Starter	Shawn Chacon
No. 5 Starter	Jeff Marquez
Closer	J. Brent Cox

LAST YEAR'S TOP 20 PROSPECTS

1. Eric Duncan, 3b
2. Robinson Cano, 2b
3. Philip Hughes, rhp
4. Steven White, rhp
5. Christian Garcia, rhp
6. Marcos Vechionacci, inf
7. Melky Cabrera, of
8. Bronson Sardinha, 3b/of
9. Chien-Ming Wang, rhp
10. Jeff Marquez, rhp
11. Brett Smith, rhp
12. Rudy Guillen, of
13. Jesse Hoover, rhp
14. Tim Battle, of
15. Matt DeSalvo, rhp
16. Edwardo Sierra, rhp
17. Tyler Clippard, rhp
18. Andy Phillips, 1b/3b
19. Abel Gomez, lhp
20. Jon Poterson, of

TOP PROSPECTS OF THE DECADE

Year	Player, Pos.	2005 Org.
1996	Ruben Rivera, of	Yankees
1997	Ruben Rivera, of	Yankees
1998	Eric Milton, lhp	Reds
1999	Nick Johnson, 1b	Nationals
2000	Nick Johnson, 1b	Nationals
2001	Nick Johnson, 1b	Nationals
2002	Drew Henson, 3b	Out of baseball
2003	Jose Contreras, rhp	White Sox
2004	Dioner Navarro, c	Dodgers
2005	Eric Duncan, 3b	Yankees

TOP DRAFT PICKS OF THE DECADE

Year	Player, Pos.	2005 Org.
1996	Eric Milton, lhp	Reds
1997	*Tyrell Godwin, of	Nationals
1998	Andy Brown, of	Out of baseball
1999	David Walling, rhp	Out of baseball
2000	David Parrish, c	Yankees
2001	John-Ford Griffin, of	Blue Jays
2002	Brandon Weeden, rhp (2nd round)	Dodgers
2003	Eric Duncan, 3b	Yankees
2004	Philip Hughes, rhp	Yankees
2005	C.J. Henry, ss	Yankees

*Did not sign.

ALL-TIME LARGEST BONUSES

Hideki Irabu, 1997	$8,500,000
Jose Contreras, 2002	$6,000,000
Wily Mo Pena, 1999	$2,440,000
Drew Henson, 1998	$2,000,000
Chien-Ming Wang, 2000	$1,900,000

MINOR LEAGUE DEPTH CHART

New York Yankees

Rank: 17

STRENGTH: Athleticism. 2005 draftees C.J. Henry and Austin Jackson would form a nice Division I hoops backcourt.

WEAKNESS: Upper-level talent. Nine of the top 10 prospects have yet to play a full season above Class A.

*Depth charts prepared by **John Manuel** and **Chris Kline**. Numbers in parentheses indicate prospect rankings.*

LF
Melky Cabrera (15)
Kevin Reese (28)
Jon Poterson
Yovany Almario-Cabrera
Evan Tierce

CF
Austin Jackson (5)
Tim Battle (12)
Brett Gardner (13)
Kevin Thompson (23)

RF
Jose Tabata (3)
Bronson Sardinha (22)
Rudy Guillen (27)
Edwar Gonzalez
Ben Himes

3B
Marcos Vechionacci (7)
J.T. LaFountain

SS
C.J. Henry (4)
Eduardo Nunez (6)
Ramiro Pena
Hector Made
Andy Cannizaro

2B
Kevin Howard (19)
Justin Christian (21)
Mario Holmann
Chris Malec

1B
Eric Duncan (2)
Andy Phillips (26)
Mitch Jones
Shelley Duncan
Kyle Larsen

C
Omir Santos
Jose Gil
Irwil Rojas

RHP

Starters	Relievers
Philip Hughes (1)	J. Brent Cox (11)
Christian Garcia (8)	T.J. Beam (24)
Jeff Marquez (9)	Justin Pope
Tyler Clippard (10)	Ferdin Tejada
Steven White (14)	Cory Stuart
Matt DeSalvo (16)	Josh Schmidt
Alan Horne (17)	Mike Martinez
Jason Stephens (29)	Jesse Hoover
Jeff Karstens (30)	
Brett Smith	
Lance Pendleton	
Jim Conroy	
Eric Wordekemper	
Jason Jones	
Evan Hacker	
Keaton Everett	

LHP

Starters	Relievers
Sean Henn (18)	Matt Smith (20)
Abel Gomez	Garrett Patterson (25)
Zack Kroenke	Toni Lara
Chase Wright	
Edgar Soto	

DRAFT ANALYSIS

2005

Best Pro Debut: RHP Josh Schmidt (15) went 5-1, 0.27 with 13 saves and 47 strikeouts in 33 innings at short-season Staten Island. He added two more wins and a save as Staten Island won the New York-Penn League title. RHP Jim Conroy (19), a strikethrower whose best pitch is his changeup, went 5-1, 2.04 with 67 whiffs in 66 NY-P innings.

Best Athlete: The Yankees signed two of the best athletes in the entire draft in SS C.J. Henry (1) and OF Austin Jackson (8), who otherwise would have played college basketball at Kansas and Georgia Tech. Jackson signed for an eighth-round record $800,000.

Best Pure Hitter: Jackson outhit Henry .304 to .249 in the Rookie-level Gulf Coast League, but Henry rates a slight edged based on his performance in instructional league.

Best Raw Power: Unless the Yankees work out a deal with 1B Karl Amonite (11), who's out of college eligibility but recovering from a knee injury, they won't have signed a player whose best tool is power. Henry won a home run derby in instructional league and has 20-25 homer upside.

Fastest Runner: Henry and Jackson are fast, though not as fast as OF Brett Gardner (3). Gardner accelerates so quickly and gets from the left side of the plate to first base in 3.8-3.9 seconds.

Best Defensive Player: Gardner has tremendous range, good instincts and a playable arm in center field.

Best Fastball: Two elbow surgeries and his age (23) caused clubs to back off LHP Garrett Patterson (7), but he threw 90-96 mph last summer. RHP Alan Horne (11) pitched at 92-95 mph in instructional league.

RICH ABEL

Gardner

Best Breaking Ball: RHP J. Brent Cox (2) throws a dastardly slider from a low-three-quarters arm angle.

Most Intriguing Background: For the second straight year the Yankees drafted LHP Clint Priesendorfer (32), whose father Rusty is a noted surfboard shaper and the founder of Rusty Surfboards. 2B Chris Malec (16) beat testicular cancer while at UC Santa Barbara. Unsigned C Matt Wallach's (23) dad Tim made five all-star teams and won three Gold Gloves. Henry comes from a basketball family. His father Carl twice led Kansas in scoring and spent a season in the NBA; his mother Barbara also played for the Jayhawks.

Closest To The Majors: Cox could be setting up games for Mariano Rivera as early as 2006.

Best Late-Round Pick: Horne, a first-round pick of the Indians in 2001 who had Tommy John surgery in 2003, signed late for $400,000. Schmidt uses the same arm angle Cox does and has a good 86-89 mph sinker.

The One Who Got Away: Projectable 6-foot-8 RHP Doug Fister (6) elected to return to Fresno State.

Assessment: First-year scouting director Damon Oppenheimer grabbed quality up-the-middle athletes and used the Yankees' wealth to take some later-round gambles. Local media and fans howled when Oppenheimer selected Henry over St. John's Craig Hansen at No. 17, but Cox should reach the majors nearly as quickly as Hansen did.

2004 RHP Philip Hughes (1) is the system's best prospect, though it would be nice if he could put together a full, healthy season. RHPs Jeff Marquez (1) and Christian Garcia (3) give the Yankees two more talented arms. *GRADE:* B

2003 3B/1B Eric Duncan (1) is the organization's top upper-level prospect and won Arizona Fall League MVP honors. RHP Tyler Clippard (9) keeps putting up numbers. *GRADE:* C+

2002 The Yankees had no first-round pick and top choice/RHP Brandon Weeden's (2) lasting contribution will be as a throw-in in the regrettable Kevin Brown trade. *GRADE:* D

2001 With three first-round choices, the Yankees blew them on OFs John-Ford Griffin and Bronson Sardinha and RHP Jon Skaggs. RHP Philip Humber (29) blossomed into the third overall pick in 2004. *GRADE:* D

Draft analysis prepared by Jim Callis. Numbers in parentheses indicate draft rounds.

PHILIP
HUGHES

RHP

Born: June 24, 1986.
Ht.: 6-5. **Wt.:** 220.
Bats: R. **Throws:** R.
Drafted: HS—Santa Ana., Calif.,
2004 (1st round).
Signed by: Jeff Patterson.

Hughes is a California guy but grew up a Red Sox fan, as his father hails from New England and he had a grandmother who lived in Rhode Island. As a boy, Hughes took trips to visit her in the summer and went to games at Fenway Park regularly. Hughes was one of the nation's top high school arms when the 2004 draft rolled around, but slipped to the Yankees with the 23rd overall pick as teams focused on college players. Signed for $1.4 million, Hughes worked just five innings in his pro debut before he stubbed his toe in his hotel room. Being ultra-cautious and fearing a fracture, New York shut him down. Hughes' first full season also ended early because of a pair of stints on the disabled list, one with shoulder tendinitis and another with a tired arm.

One Yankees official has called Hughes "Mark Prior light" since he joined the organization, and the similarities are striking. He has a sturdy, strong body and relatively effortless delivery, and the ball comes out of his hand easy. His fastball settled into the 92-94 mph range last season and he has more velocity when he needs it. As with Prior, the striking feature of Hughes' fastball is his control and command of it. He throws it for strikes consistently and is honing his ability to put it in just the right spot. He has a hard, late-biting slider that the Yankees wouldn't let him throw last year, but he likes it better than his curveball and has the go-ahead to use it again in 2006. His curve progressed significantly and is now an above-average pitch. New York officials believe he has the poise and intangibles to go with his front-of-the-rotation stuff.

Like Prior, Hughes has not been durable the last two years. He has pitched for three teams as a pro and has ended each stint on the disabled list. Besides the stubbed toe, he also had a mild case of elbow tendinitis in 2004. Hughes hasn't needed surgery, and the Yankees insist the biggest hurdle he must overcome with regard to his health is getting to know his body better. All pitchers get sore, but Hughes has to learn what soreness is to be expected over the course of a season and what's unusual. At times he throws his curve in the low 70s just to get it over, and he needs to throw it in the 78-80 mph range for it to be a plus pitch. He did that as the year progressed but will have to maintain that feel when he reintroduces his slider. His changeup is his fourth pitch, but he has the feel and arm speed for it to be at least average.

The wraps come off Hughes in 2006. The Yankees will start him at high Class A Tampa, and he shouldn't be there long. As he reintroduces his slider, he should become a starter with well-above-average control and above-average command who throws three plus pitches for strikes. In a different organization, a healthy Hughes could reach the major leagues in 2006. Instead, he should be in the mix for a rotation spot in New York in 2007—as long as he stays off the disabled list.

Year	Club (League)	Class	W	L	ERA	G	GS	CG	SV	IP	H	R	ER	HR	BB	SO	AVG
2004	Yankees (GCL)	R	0	0	0.00	3	3	0	0	5	4	0	0	0	0	8	.222
2005	Charleston, S.C. (SAL)	A	7	1	1.97	12	12	1	0	69	46	19	15	1	16	72	.192
	Tampa (FSL)	A	2	0	3.05	5	4	0	0	18	8	6	6	0	4	21	.140
MINOR LEAGUE TOTALS			9	1	2.07	20	19	1	0	91	58	25	21	1	20	101	.184

² ERIC DUNCAN 3B/1B

Born: Dec. 7, 1984. **B-T:** L-R. **Ht.:** 6-3. **Wt.:** 195. **Drafted:** HS—West Orange, N.J., 2003 (1st round). **Signed by:** Cesar Presbott.

One of the youngest players in the Double-A Eastern League last year, Duncan survived a poor start and trade rumors. Then he got beaned in the head by a pitch by Akron's Victor Kleine on Aug. 14 and wasn't right the rest of the season. He bounced back to win the Arizona Fall League's MVP award. Duncan has above-average lefthanded power with enough bat speed to turn on quality fastballs, and he has easy opposite-field power as well. A solid athlete, he also has excellent makeup. He's coachable and willing to make adjustments. Once EL pitchers realized Duncan had trouble with quality breaking balls, they fed him a steady diet of them and rarely gave him fastballs in the strike zone. He needs to trust his hands more on offspeed pitches. He led the EL with 27 errors at third base, mostly due to a fringy arm. With Alex Rodriguez in front of him at third base, Duncan should move to first base sooner than later and began the process in the AFL. The position switch and his modest 2005 season likely will prompt his return to Trenton in 2006.

Year	Club (League)	Class	AVG	G	AB	R	H	2B	3B	HR	RBI	BB	SO	SB	OBP	SLG
2003	Yankees (GCL)	R	.278	47	180	24	50	12	2	2	28	18	33	0	.348	.400
	Staten Island (NY-P)	A	.373	14	59	11	22	5	4	2	13	2	11	1	.413	.695
2004	Battle Creek (Mid)	A	.260	78	288	52	75	23	2	12	57	38	84	7	.351	.479
	Tampa (FSL)	A	.254	51	173	23	44	20	2	4	26	31	47	0	.366	.462
2005	Trenton (EL)	AA	.235	126	451	60	106	15	3	19	61	59	136	9	.326	.408
MINOR LEAGUE TOTALS			.258	316	1151	170	297	75	13	39	185	148	311	17	.346	.447

³ JOSE TABATA OF

Born: Aug. 12, 1988. **B-T:** R-R. **Ht.:** 5-11. **Wt.:** 160. **Signed:** Venezuela, 2005. **Signed by:** Ricardo Finol.

Only Braves shortstop Elvis Andrus was younger than Tabata in the Rookie-level Gulf Coast League last year. He signed for $550,000 and had an exciting debut performance that included a league-best 22 stolen bases. Tabata has plus tools across the board and stands out from young peers such as C.J. Henry and Austin Jackson because of his advanced approach at the plate. He has exceptional hand-eye coordination (he was the second-hardest player to strike out in the GCL) and his swing already puts backspin on the ball to generate loft. That and his plus-plus bat speed have club officials projecting big power. The Yankees are excited about Tabata's total package and see the cultural adjustments of living in the United States and speaking English as his biggest obstacles. He's a center fielder with plus speed now, but as he fills out he should lose a step or two and move to right field, where his arm will fit fine. Tabata's bat is advanced enough to earn him a spot at low Class A Charleston for his full-season debut. His ceiling is as high as any Yankees minor leaguer since Alfonso Soriano.

Year	Club (League)	Class	AVG	G	AB	R	H	2B	3B	HR	RBI	BB	SO	SB	OBP	SLG
2005	Yankees (GCL)	R	.314	44	156	30	49	5	1	3	25	15	14	22	.382	.417
MINOR LEAGUE TOTALS			.314	44	156	30	49	5	1	3	25	15	14	22	.382	.417

⁴ C.J. HENRY SS

Born: May 31, 1986. **B-T:** R-R. **Ht.:** 6-3. **Wt.:** 205. **Drafted:** HS—Putnam City, Okla., 2005 (1st round). **Signed by:** Mark Batchko.

The Yankees needed a $1.575 million bonus to convince Henry that baseball, not basketball, was his future. Though he never signed a hoops scholarship, he would have been a recruited walk-on at Kansas, where his father Carl played before a brief NBA career. His mother Barbara also played for the Jayhawks, and his younger brother Xavier is a top basketball prospect. Henry is a premier athlete, already the best in the system. He has well-above-average raw power and is a plus runner. Despite his strong frame, he's athletic enough to stay at shortstop and impressed the Yankees with his defense in his debut. Henry's swing can get long and mechanical, and he may never hit for a high average. He'll need plenty of minor league at-bats to develop a better feel. If he moves off shortstop, it will be because of his fringe-average arm. Henry's athleticism, competitiveness and presence were too much for the Yankees to pass on. He'll head to low Class A for his first full season. New York is in no rush to find a new shortstop, so Henry will have to be patient.

Year	Club (League)	Class	AVG	G	AB	R	H	2B	3B	HR	RBI	BB	SO	SB	OBP	SLG
2005	Yankees (GCL)	R	.249	48	181	32	45	9	3	3	17	17	39	17	.333	.381
MINOR LEAGUE TOTALS			.249	48	181	32	45	9	3	3	17	17	39	17	.333	.381

5 AUSTIN JACKSON — OF

Born: Feb. 1, 1987. **B-T:** R-R. **Ht.:** 6-1. **Wt.:** 185. **Drafted:** HS—Denton, Texas, 2005 (8th round). **Signed by:** Mark Batchko.

Jackson was set to go to Georgia Tech on a basketball scholarship. Jackson's basketball jones threw off many area scouts, who doubted his desire to play baseball. But Mark Batchko realized Jackson wanted to be a Yankee, having written his first scouting report on him when Jackson was 12. New York signed him quickly in June for $800,000, a record for an eighth-round pick. Jackson rivals C.J. Henry in his athletic ability and competitive nature. At the plate, he exhibits a knack for staying inside the ball and can drive the ball the other way, which along with his wiry frame has elicited some Derek Jeter comparisons. He's an above-average runner and a solid defender. The biggest question for Jackson is his power. He needs to add strength and will have to learn to pull the ball. The top player in his age group at ages 12 (1999) and 15 (2002) in our annual Baseball for the Ages rankings, Jackson has been a prospect since before he was a teenager. He'll spend his first season as a full-time baseball player in low Class A and could move quickly thanks to his advanced offensive approach.

Year	Club (League)	Class	AVG	G	AB	R	H	2B	3B	HR	RBI	BB	SO	SB	OBP	SLG
2005	Yankees (GCL)	R	.304	40	148	32	45	11	2	0	14	18	26	11	.374	.405
MINOR LEAGUE TOTALS			.304	40	148	32	45	11	2	0	14	18	26	11	.374	.405

6 EDUARDO NUNEZ — SS

Born: June 15, 1987. **B-T:** B-R. **Ht.:** 6-0. **Wt.:** 155. **Signed:** Dominican Republic, 2004. **Signed by:** Victor Mata.

Nunez hit just .215 in the Rookie-level Dominican Summer League in 2004, but his bat sizzled in the short-season New-York Penn League, even though he was the league's third-youngest position player. For a teenage middle infielder, not to mention an inexperienced Dominican, Nunez has an advanced feel for hitting that allowed him to skip the Gulf Coast League. He has a level, smooth swing from both sides of the plate and projects to hit for average power. Nunez has a 70 arm on the 20-80 scouting scale and good hands defensively. He's also an above-average runner but has shaky footwork at shortstop, and some question whether he'll have the range or mobility to stay there. He might have to move to second base or the outfield. To fulfill his power projections, he'll have to get stronger. Nunez was so impressive at Staten Island and the organization is so bereft of shortstops that he'll jump to high Class A in 2006. He may have to switch positions eventually, in deference to Derek Jeter ahead of him and C.J. Henry behind him.

Year	Club (League)	Class	AVG	G	AB	R	H	2B	3B	HR	RBI	BB	SO	SB	OBP	SLG
2004	Yankees 1 (DSL)	R	.215	57	191	29	41	9	5	3	20	27	41	16	.324	.361
2005	Staten Island (NY-P)	A	.313	73	281	37	88	11	6	3	46	20	43	6	.365	.427
MINOR LEAGUE TOTALS			.273	130	472	66	129	20	11	6	66	47	84	22	.339	.400

7 MARCOS VECHIONACCI — 3B/SS

Born: Aug. 7, 1986. **B-T:** R-R. **Ht.:** 6-2. **Wt.:** 170. **Signed:** Venezuela, 2002. **Signed by:** Ricardo Finol.

Vechionacci was one of the youngest players in the low Class A South Atlantic League in 2005 and batted third most of the season. He switched from shortstop to third base in June in an attempt to take some of the pressure off him, and he responded with a better second half. Vechionacci has a smooth swing and solid approach at the plate. While he was a solid defender at short, he's a potential Gold Glove winner at third base with good range, soft hands and a well above-average arm. The Yankees believe in profiles, and third base is a power position, but expecting Vechionacci to hit for power in the majors involves a lot of projection. He must get stronger and improve both his pitch recognition and his plate discipline, learning what pitches to lay off, which to drive to the gaps and which to pull for power. Now that he's at third base, he'll hop off the fast track because Alex Rodriguez is in New York. Vechionacci's confidence faltered in Charleston last season, and a successful return there would put a him back on the right track.

Year	Club (League)	Class	AVG	G	AB	R	H	2B	3B	HR	RBI	BB	SO	SB	OBP	SLG
2003	Yankees 1 (DSL)	R	.300	62	200	28	60	10	4	2	30	37	22	4	.410	.420
2004	Tampa (FSL)	A	.250	1	4	1	1	0	0	0	0	0	0	0	.250	.250
	Staten Island (NY-P)	A	.292	19	72	13	21	5	0	0	8	11	13	0	.393	.361
	Yankees (GCL)	R	.336	36	131	24	44	9	1	4	22	12	19	5	.392	.511
2005	Charleston (SAL)	A	.252	128	503	83	127	26	8	2	62	43	83	16	.314	.348
MINOR LEAGUE TOTALS			.278	246	910	149	253	50	13	8	122	103	137	25	.353	.388

8 CHRISTIAN GARCIA RHP

DAVID SCHOFIELD

Born: Aug. 24, 1985. **B-T:** R-R. **Ht.:** 6-4. **Wt.:** 175. **Drafted:** HS—Miami, 2004 (3rd round). **Signed by:** Dan Radison.

Garcia had signed to play catcher at South Carolina. While he played in the Palmetto State in 2005, it was in Charleston as a pitcher for the Yankees, as he signed for $390,000 as a third-round pick after moving to the mound as a high school senior. He missed a month with a right elbow strain but returned to finish his first full season strong. Garcia has the perfect pitcher's frame with wide shoulders, big hands and long limbs. He has a clean arm action that he repeats well. His fastball sits at 92-93 mph and touches 95, and he keeps it down in the strike zone. His curveball is a true hammer, a 12-to-6 pitch with power at 74-78 mph. Inexperience dogs Garcia on the field and off it, as some in the organization question his desire to be great. He relies too heavily on his curve for someone who has such a good fastball. His changeup is rudimentary at this point. Nuances such as setting hitters up and holding runners will have to come with experience. Garcia's upside is tremendous, but he's going to need time and has a lot to learn. He's expected to repeat low Class A in 2006.

Year	Club (League)	Class	W	L	ERA	G	GS	CG	SV	IP	H	R	ER	HR	BB	SO	AVG
2004	Yankees (GCL)	R	3	4	2.84	13	6	0	0	38	26	13	12	1	17	47	.188
2005	Charleston (SAL)	A	5	6	3.91	21	20	0	0	106	102	57	46	3	53	103	.249
MINOR LEAGUE TOTALS			8	10	3.63	34	26	0	0	144	128	70	58	4	70	150	.234

9 JEFF MARQUEZ RHP

STEVE MOORE

Born: Aug. 10, 1984. **B-T:** L-R. **Ht.:** 6-2. **Wt.:** 175. **Drafted:** Sacramento CC, 2004 (1st round supplemental). **Signed by:** Jeff Patterson.

The Yankees sent the top four pitchers they drafted in 2004 to low Class A in 2005, and Marquez won the most games and pitched the most innings of that group. He saw his velocity take off in his freshman year at Sacramento City College in 2004, and the Yankees signed him for $790,000 after making him a supplemental first-round pick. Marquez shows three pitches that could be 55 or 60 offerings on the 20-80 scouting scale. His 89-94 mph two-seam fastball has excellent sink and tails in to righthanders. He holds his velocity well. His downer curveball doesn't quite have true 12-to-6 break but is a swing-and-miss pitch. His firm changeup sinks like his two-seamer. Marquez is still honing his four-seam fastball so he can get inside consistently on lefthanders and to be more consistent with his change. He has some issues with his extension and finishing off pitches, which leads to high walk totals and inconsistent control. If his control and command improve to be major league average, Marquez could top out as a No. 2 or 3 starter. He's slated to move up to high Class A this year.

Year	Club (League)	Class	W	L	ERA	G	GS	CG	SV	IP	H	R	ER	HR	BB	SO	AVG
2004	Yankees (GCL)	R	2	0	0.63	4	2	0	0	14	10	1	1	0	4	18	.189
	Staten Island (NY-P)	A	2	4	3.02	11	11	0	0	51	51	26	17	2	20	36	.267
2005	Charleston (SAL)	A	9	13	3.41	27	27	1	0	140	138	64	53	4	61	107	.257
MINOR LEAGUE TOTALS			13	17	3.12	42	40	1	0	205	199	91	71	6	85	161	.255

10 TYLER CLIPPARD RHP

Born: Feb. 14, 1985. **B-T:** R-R. **Ht.:** 6-4. **Wt.:** 170. **Drafted:** HS—Trinity, Fla., 2003 (9th round). **Signed by:** Scott Pleis.

Clippard pitched near home in 2005 and had a breakthrough season in high Class A. His 181 strikeouts ranked fifth overall in the minors, and he placed seventh with an average of 10.6 strikeouts per nine innings. Clippard always has pounded the strike zone and shown a willingness to pitch inside. He worked with roving pitching coordinator Nardi Contreras to clean up his delivery, which became more consistent. Subsequently all his pitches got better. He now has an 89-92 mph fastball with some life that touches 94, a plus curveball, a slider and a changeup. He has excellent control with improving command. A fly ball pitcher, Clippard is going to give up homers when he misses his spot while trying to work inside. He must maintain and repeat his delivery as he continues to add weight to his lanky frame. Clippard combines a knack for pitching with solid-average stuff and a strikeout pitch. He profiles as a No. 3 starter and could move quickly if he gets off to a strong start in Double-A this season.

Year	Club (League)	Class	W	L	ERA	G	GS	CG	SV	IP	H	R	ER	HR	BB	SO	AVG
2003	Yankees (GCL)	R	3	3	2.88	11	5	0	0	44	33	16	14	3	5	56	.212
2004	Battle Creek (Mid)	A	10	10	3.44	26	25	1	0	149	153	71	57	12	32	145	.264
2005	Charleston (SAL)	A	0	1	7.50	1	1	0	0	6	9	5	5	1	0	10	.333
	Tampa (FSL)	A	10	9	3.18	26	25	0	0	147	118	56	52	12	34	169	.219
	Columbus (IL)	AAA	0	0	0.00	1	0	0	0	1	0	0	0	0	0	2	.000
MINOR LEAGUE TOTALS			23	23	3.32	65	56	1	0	347	313	148	128	28	71	382	.240

11 J. BRENT COX RHP

Born: May 13, 1984. **B-T:** L-R. **Ht.:** 6-3. **Wt.:** 205. **Drafted:** Texas, 2005 (2nd round). **Signed by:** Steve Boros.

Cox was Huston Street's wingman at Texas for two years, setting up the current Athletics closer before taking the reins himself and recording the final out when Texas completed its sweep through the 2005 College World Series. The Yankees love a winner, and that describes Cox, who also pitched for Team USA. They took him in the second round in June and signed him for $550,000. Frequently compared to Street, Cox broke his career appearance record at Texas with 106 while tying the school record for single-season saves with 19, a figure that led NCAA Division I. Like Street, Cox works from a lower arm angle and can throw in the low 90s with a plus slider. Unlike Street, Cox is at his best when he takes something off his fastball, throws it in the upper 80s and gets good sink and armside run in on righthanders. Then he goes down and away with his hard slider, a power pitch that gets plenty of swings and misses. Cox has the intangibles necessary to close, even if his stuff is a little short for the true closer profile. He figures to move quickly through the Yankees organization because of his strike-throwing ability and could debut in New York sometime in 2006.

Year	Club (League)	Class	W	L	ERA	G	GS	CG	SV	IP	H	R	ER	HR	BB	SO	AVG
2005	Tampa (FSL)	A	1	2	2.60	16	0	0	0	28	20	9	8	1	5	27	.206
MINOR LEAGUE TOTALS			1	2	2.60	16	0	0	0	28	20	9	8	1	5	27	.206

12 TIM BATTLE OF

Born: Sept. 10, 1985. **B-T:** R-R. **Ht.:** 6-2. **Wt.:** 185. **Drafted:** HS—Peachtree, Ga., 2003 (3rd round). **Signed by:** Steve Swail.

Battle was diagnosed with lymphoma soon after the Yankees drafted him, and he overcame cancer with surgery and chemotherapy treatments. He made his full-season debut in low Class A last year and led Charleston in extra-base hits, home runs and stolen bases. He also topped the minors in strikeouts—fellow Yankees farmhand Mitch Jones was second—because of his poor pitch recognition. It's not one pitch that flummoxes Battle, who is a decent breaking-ball hitter and has the bat speed to turn on good fastballs. Though he takes his fair share of walks, he'll swing at just about anything. He's a guess hitter, and when he guesses breaking ball and sees one, he swings—whether or not it's hittable. If he tempers his aggressiveness, Battle's prodigious power could explode. He's an 80 runner on the 20-80 scouting scale who continues to improve on the nuances of basestealing. Defensively, Battle has exceptional range in center field and an average arm. Mental lapses keep him from being more than an average defender at present, however. His dedication to the game improved significantly in 2005, as he often was the first River Dog to take early work in the batting cage and shagged extra flies to improve his route-running. His ceiling is significant, and his development hinges on improving his pitch recognition and taming his strikeouts. He'll try to make more strides in that regard in high Class A this year.

Year	Club (League)	Class	AVG	G	AB	R	H	2B	3B	HR	RBI	BB	SO	SB	OBP	SLG
2003	Yankees (GCL)	R	.208	27	106	14	22	5	0	0	5	7	33	5	.270	.255
2004	Yankees (GCL)	R	.320	12	50	11	16	3	3	1	4	4	15	5	.364	.560
	Staten Island (NY-P)	A	.246	53	199	28	49	8	2	1	20	14	74	13	.302	.322
2005	Charleston (SAL)	A	.259	134	525	97	136	33	11	16	60	50	195	40	.335	.455
MINOR LEAGUE TOTALS			.253	226	880	150	223	49	16	18	89	75	317	63	.322	.407

13 BRETT GARDNER OF

Born: Aug. 24, 1983. **B-T:** L-L. **Ht.:** 5-10. **Wt.:** 180. **Drafted:** College of Charleston, 2005 (3rd round). **Signed by:** Steve Swail.

Of the Yankees' 2005 draftees, only righthander J. Brent Cox figures to move faster than

Gardner, who earned raves as an amateur and again in helping lead Staten Island to the New York-Penn League championship. Gardner was a third-team All-American in 2005, when he set College of Charleston records for runs (85) and hits (122, tied for the NCAA Division I lead) in a season while leading the Southern Conference in those categories as well as stolen bases (38). A third-round pick in June who signed for $210,000, Gardner is an 80 runner on the 20-80 scouting scale and has edged Tim Battle as the organization's fastest man. He's also a savvy basestealer. He doesn't have Battle's power, but he has enough juice to earn pitchers' respect and his polish at the plate is obvious. He doesn't try to do too much, spraying line drives from foul pole to foul pole, and isn't afraid to take a walk. He's a good defender in center field with a solid arm. Gardner needs to hone his two-strike approach and could improve his bunting to better take advantage of his speed. He's poised to skip a level and should join Battle in the Tampa outfield.

Year	Club (League)	Class	AVG	G	AB	R	H	2B	3B	HR	RBI	BB	SO	SB	OBP	SLG
2005	Staten Island (NY-P)	A	.284	73	282	62	80	9	1	5	32	39	49	19	.377	.376
MINOR LEAGUE TOTALS			.284	73	282	62	80	9	1	5	32	39	49	19	.377	.376

14 STEVEN WHITE   RHP

Born: June 15, 1981. **B-T:** R-R. **Ht.:** 6-5. **Wt.:** 205. **Drafted:** Baylor, 2004 (4th round). **Signed by:** Steve Boros/Mark Newman.

The way the Yankees' big league season worked out, a healthy White might have had a shot at reaching New York and helping a beleaguered rotation. Instead, he missed nearly two months in the first half with an oblique strain, then spent time in the hospital and missed the Eastern League playoffs with a bout with pancreatitis. White also had pancreatitis as a college sophomore, so he'll have to monitor his health more closely in the future to avoid another flareup. He made up for lost time by pitching in the Arizona Fall League and making the U.S. Olympic qualifying team. In the AFL, his stuff was better than it had been all year, as he threw his fastball at 90-93 mph. White has touched 95-96 mph with his heater in the past, and he's at his best when he works off it, supplemented by an average curveball that has improved since he has turned pro. His injury issues stunted the work he needed to do on his changeup. White will return to Double-A in 2006 and needs to stay healthy to remain ahead of the younger, higher-ceiling arms behind him in the organization.

Year	Club (League)	Class	W	L	ERA	G	GS	CG	SV	IP	H	R	ER	HR	BB	SO	AVG
2004	Battle Creek (Mid)	A	5	2	2.65	9	9	2	0	58	36	19	17	4	26	56	.183
	Tampa (FSL)	A	6	2	2.56	12	12	1	0	60	51	26	17	4	19	44	.232
2005	Tampa (FSL)	A	0	0	3.08	3	2	0	0	12	8	4	4	1	2	8	.195
	Trenton (EL)	AA	2	7	6.44	11	11	0	0	50	61	41	36	9	26	54	.296
MINOR LEAGUE TOTALS			13	11	3.71	35	34	3	0	179	156	90	74	18	73	162	.235

15 MELKY CABRERA   OF

Born: Aug. 11, 1984. **B-T:** B-L. **Ht.:** 5-11. **Wt.:** 170. **Signed:** Dominican Republic, 2001. **Signed by:** Victor Mata/Carlos Rios.

Failing on a stage as public as center field for the Yankees in a series against the Red Sox would kill most prospects' confidence. That's what happened with Cabrera, whom New York turned to in June to fill in for an injured Bernie Williams. Cabrera was overwhelmed, misplaying a Trot Nixon liner into an inside-the-park home run and looking lost at the plate. He was demoted to Triple-A Columbus after just six games and carried his struggles with him, and his performance there prompted a return to Double-A. Cabrera's bat is his best tool. He has excellent hand-eye coordination and a handsy swing that allows him to hammer breaking balls. He could use a better trigger to help him catch up to good fastballs and hit for more power. Cabrera needs to be more aggressive and get better jumps to be an average center fielder, and a dose of confidence wouldn't hurt. He profiles defensively as a corner outfielder but doesn't have the power to play there regularly in the majors at this point. He'll return to Triple-A this year and could rejoin the Yankees as an extra outfielder.

Year	Club (League)	Class	AVG	G	AB	R	H	2B	3B	HR	RBI	BB	SO	SB	OBP	SLG
2002	Yankees W (DSL)	R	.335	60	218	37	73	19	3	3	29	18	23	7	.388	.491
2003	Staten Island (NY-P)	A	.283	67	279	34	79	10	2	2	31	23	36	13	.345	.355
2004	Battle Creek (Mid)	A	.333	42	171	35	57	16	3	0	16	15	23	7	.383	.462
	Tampa (FSL)	A	.288	85	333	48	96	20	3	8	51	23	59	3	.341	.438
2005	New York (AL)	MLB	.211	6	19	1	4	0	0	0	0	0	2	0	.211	.211
	Columbus (IL)	AAA	.248	26	101	15	25	3	0	3	17	9	15	2	.309	.366
	Trenton (EL)	AA	.275	106	426	57	117	22	3	10	60	28	72	11	.322	.411
MAJOR LEAGUE TOTALS			.211	6	19	1	4	0	0	0	0	0	2	0	.211	.211
MINOR LEAGUE TOTALS			.293	386	1528	226	447	90	14	26	204	116	228	43	.346	.421

16   MATT DeSALVO   RHP

Born: Sept. 11, 1980. **B-T:** R-R. **Ht.:** 6-0. **Wt.:** 170. **Signed:** NDFA/Marietta (Ohio), 2003.
Signed by: Mike Gibbons.

DeSalvo was one of the best NCAA Division III pitchers ever, setting NCAA all-division records for wins (53) and strikeouts (603), but his slight frame and a knee injury that forced him to redshirt his fourth year in college caused him to pass through the 2002 draft unclaimed. The Yankees signed him as a fifth-year senior before the 2003 draft, and he was Trenton's ace last year, pitching the Thunder to the Eastern League playoffs. DeSalvo has altered his delivery since college, varying his arm angle to put more movement on his 89-90 mph fastball. When he goes over the top, he gets more velocity, but he rarely does so anymore. Instead, he keeps his fastball down and uses it to set up his plus-plus changeup that fools hitters because of his deceptive arm action and its late sink. DeSalvo also has two solid-average breaking balls, a slider and changeup, and good control of both. Despite fringy stuff, DeSalvo is tough to hit—his .202 opponent average ranked sixth in the minors among starting pitchers. He never gives in to hitters, a trait that endears him to scouts and managers. His bulldog mentality and passion to win make his makeup his best attribute. DeSalvo will rely on the same formula as he moves up to Triple-A this year. He profiles as a fourth or fifth starter.

Year	Club (League)	Class	W	L	ERA	G	GS	CG	SV	IP	H	R	ER	HR	BB	SO	AVG
2003	Staten Island (NY-P)	A	3	3	1.84	10	10	1	0	49	42	18	10	2	19	52	.232
	Battle Creek (Mid)	A	2	0	0.82	3	3	0	0	22	15	5	2	0	5	21	.195
2004	Tampa (FSL)	A	6	3	1.43	13	13	0	0	75	48	20	12	1	30	80	.177
	Trenton (EL)	AA	2	2	6.59	5	5	0	0	27	27	20	20	3	10	24	.262
2005	Trenton (EL)	AA	9	5	3.02	25	24	0	0	149	106	55	50	8	67	151	.202
MINOR LEAGUE TOTALS			22	13	2.62	56	55	1	0	323	238	118	94	14	131	328	.206

17   ALAN HORNE   RHP

Born: Jan. 5, 1983. **B-T:** R-R. **Ht.:** 6-4. **Wt.:** 195. **Drafted:** Florida, 2005 (11th round).
Signed by: Brian Barber.

Horne has lived a baseball lifetime since he played with Angels prospect Jeff Mathis in high school—and he still has yet to make his pro debut. Horne was a first-round pick in 2001 but didn't sign with the Indians, attending Mississippi instead. After a solid freshman year in 2002, Horne hurt his elbow early in his sophomore year and had Tommy John surgery, taking a medical redshirt. He then transferred to Chipola (Fla.) Junior College, where his father had played and where he had known the coach, Jeff Johnson, since he was young. Johnson helped Horne develop a cut fastball that he could throw consistently for strikes. The Angels took Horne in the 30th round of the 2004 draft, but he turned down six-figure offers to go to Florida. He threw better as the spring progressed, sitting at 88-93 mph with his fastball. He also learned to compete better and improved his approach to pitching. Horne made only one start in the College World Series and injured his left hamstring. He flirted with returning to Florida as a fifth-year senior, but signed for $400,000 and attended the Yankees' fall mini-camp. He impressed club officials with his stuff—his fastball was up to 92-95 mph—and mature demeanor. Horne's progress will depend on his health and control of his secondary pitches, which include a curveball that showed improved bite down in the zone in mini-camp, and a changeup. He could make his pro debut in high Class A with a strong spring.

Year	Club (League)	Class	W	L	ERA	G	GS	CG	SV	IP	H	R	ER	HR	BB	SO	AVG
2005	Did not play—Signed 2006 contract																

18   SEAN HENN   LHP

Born: April 23, 1981. **B-T:** R-L. **Ht.:** 6-5. **Wt.:** 200. **Drafted:** McLennan (Texas) JC, 2000 (26th round). **Signed by:** Mark Batchko.

The Yankees finally got a return on their $1.701 million investment in Henn—a record at the time for a draft-and-follow signee—when he made his big league debut in 2005. It didn't go as they hoped, as his control deserted him and he gave up 16 runs in three starts. In the minors, though, he had his best season before a mid-August bout with stiffness in his left forearm ended his season. As a power lefthander, Henn has enough stuff to get by with just enough control, and when he's at his best he's effectively wild. He has enough life on his 90-93 mph fastball to pitch up in the strike zone, and then he can bury his hard slider down in the zone. When he stays on top of the pitch, it's an above-average breaking ball. He was less consistent with his slider in Triple-A and compounded his difficulties when he tried to be too fine. Henn just needs to trust his stuff and attack hitters. He still lacks a real feel for a changeup, and the total package profiles him better as a reliever. The Yankees have resisted making that move yet. He's expected to rejoin the Triple-A rotation in 2006, and his name continues to come up in trade talks.

Year	Club (League)	Class	W	L	ERA	G	GS	CG	SV	IP	H	R	ER	HR	BB	SO	AVG
2001	Staten Island (NY-P)	A	3	1	3.00	9	8	0	1	42	26	15	14	3	15	49	.178
2002	Did not play—Injured																
2003	Yankees (GCL)	R	1	1	2.25	2	1	0	0	8	5	3	2	1	3	10	.167
	Tampa (FSL)	A	4	3	3.61	16	16	0	0	72	69	31	29	3	37	52	.259
2004	Trenton (EL)	AA	6	8	4.41	27	27	0	0	163	173	94	80	11	63	118	.280
2005	Trenton (EL)	AA	2	1	0.71	4	4	0	0	25	16	2	2	1	9	21	.188
	New York (AL)	MLB	0	3	11.15	3	3	0	0	11	18	16	14	3	11	3	.360
	Columbus (IL)	AAA	5	5	3.23	16	16	1	0	86	79	37	31	5	27	64	.254
MAJOR LEAGUE TOTALS			0	3	11.12	3	3	0	0	11	18	16	14	3	11	3	.360
MINOR LEAGUE TOTALS			21	19	3.58	74	72	1	1	397	368	182	158	24	154	314	.253

19 KEVIN HOWARD   2B/3B

Born: June 25, 1981. **B-T:** L-R. **Ht.:** 6-2. **Wt.:** 185. **Drafted:** Miami, 2002 (5th round). **Signed by:** Greg Zunino (Reds).

Howard, acquired from the Reds in a trade for Tony Womack during the Winter Meetings, has hit at almost every stop along a storied career. He was Baseball America's College Freshman of the Year in 2000, when he batted .413, and won a College World Series championship ring with Miami in 2001. He hit .373 in the Arizona Fall League in 2004, then won the AFL batting title with a .409 average this offseason while playing third base. Howard had played just one game at the hot corner as a pro after starring there for the Hurricanes. The move was simply a way to get him at-bats on an AFL team that already had enough second basemen, but it also enhanced his value by showing his versatility. Howard's bat is ready for the majors right now. He has shown a consistent ability to center the ball, with an effective line-drive swing and adequate power from the left side. He has average speed. Howard's defense is what keeps him from profiling as an everyday middle infielder. His actions are a little unorthodox, he doesn't turn the double play particularly well, his range is average and his arm is below average, especially at third base. Howard, who profiles best as a utilityman, likely will spend most of 2006 in Triple-A.

Year	Club (League)	Class	AVG	G	AB	R	H	2B	3B	HR	RBI	BB	SO	SB	OBP	SLG
2003	Dayton (Mid)	A	.285	134	509	80	145	26	3	9	75	50	67	12	.355	.401
2004	Potomac (Car)	A	.286	124	468	68	134	24	0	11	79	58	70	8	.366	.408
2005	Chattanooga (SL)	AA	.296	129	479	63	142	23	2	12	70	33	64	13	.346	.428
MINOR LEAGUE TOTALS			.289	387	1456	211	421	73	5	32	224	141	201	33	.356	.412

20 MATT SMITH   LHP

Born: June 15, 1979. **B-T:** L-L. **Ht.:** 6-5. **Wt.:** 225. **Drafted:** Oklahoma State, 2000 (4th round). **Signed by:** Mark Batchko.

Smith had a high-profile college career at Oklahoma State, where he was the No. 1 starter as a sophomore on the Cowboys' last College World Series entry. He also pitched for Team USA in 1999 in a rotation that also included Mark Prior. Injuries stunted his progress as a pro. He found new life in the bullpen last season and earned a spot on the 40-man roster as well as a second turn with Team USA, this time on the team of professionals in the November regional Olympic qualifier in Arizona. Smith is a different pitcher from the one the Yankees drafted, having battled elbow soreness and a serious blow to his confidence when he struggled in 2002 in his first stab at Double-A. In the bullpen, he has improved the velocity on his formerly flagging fastball, getting it back to 89-92 mph. He has honed his breaking ball, once a slurvy curveball, into a sweeping slider that at times has 1-to-7 depth and bite. One club official rated it a plus pitch, and until Philip Hughes starts throwing his again, Smith has the best slider in the system. The pitch gives him an edge over the likes of Sean Henn and Wayne Franklin to earn a spot as a bullpen lefty in New York in 2006, but he'll have to prove himself to the big league brass and figures to open the year in Triple-A.

Year	Club (League)	Class	W	L	ERA	G	GS	CG	SV	IP	H	R	ER	HR	BB	SO	AVG
2000	Staten Island (NY-P)	A	5	4	2.38	14	14	0	0	76	74	32	20	1	20	59	.261
2001	Greensboro (SAL)	A	5	3	2.59	16	16	1	0	97	69	37	28	1	32	116	.197
	Tampa (FSL)	A	6	2	2.24	11	11	0	0	68	54	21	17	2	22	71	.215
2002	Norwich (EL)	AA	3	8	5.44	17	17	0	0	89	112	63	54	8	37	70	.305
	Tampa (FSL)	A	0	4	6.59	8	6	0	0	27	37	23	20	1	17	20	.330
2003	Tampa (FSL)	A	2	3	2.23	6	6	0	0	32	20	11	8	0	12	25	.175
	Trenton (EL)	AA	2	3	4.26	9	9	0	0	51	57	29	24	6	24	36	.291
2004	Trenton (EL)	AA	4	4	4.96	14	11	0	0	62	67	34	34	5	31	56	.285
2005	Columbus (IL)	AAA	2	0	2.60	25	0	0	1	28	24	9	8	3	13	33	.226
	Trenton (EL)	AA	3	4	2.80	22	4	0	2	55	46	24	17	2	23	59	.230
MINOR LEAGUE TOTALS			32	35	3.54	142	94	1	3	585	560	283	230	29	231	545	.253

21 JUSTIN CHRISTIAN   2B/OF

Born: April 3, 1980. **B-T:** R-R. **Ht.:** 6-1. **Wt.:** 188. **Signed:** NDFA/River City (Frontier), 2004.
Signed by: John Coppolella.

One of the Yankees' most unlikely prospects, Christian is also one of the system's better hitters. His bat has found a home with New York, and the much-traveled Christian could use a home. He played at Skyline (Calif.) Junior College, Auburn and Southeast Missouri State in college, and signed with River City of the independent Frontier League when he wasn't drafted following his junior season in 2003. He hit .374 with 45 steals in parts of two seasons with River City, prompting the Yankees to sign him to fill a roster spot at short-season Staten Island in 2004. He has proven to be more than roster filler, however. Christian can hit with a short, consistent stroke that produces average power. He has excellent plate discipline and is a 6.5-second runner over 60 yards. His speed and excellent instincts helped him lead Yankees farmhands with 55 steals in just 62 attempts in 2005. The total package makes him potentially an impact top-of-the-order hitter. Christian's biggest shortcoming is defense. His below-average arm and modest infield actions limit him to second base, where he's average at best. He earned an invitation to the organization's fall minicamp, where he worked on playing outfield. Christian could become a super utility player and figures to play every day at second base or in left or center field in Double-A this year.

Year	Club (League)	Class	AVG	G	AB	R	H	2B	3B	HR	RBI	BB	SO	SB	OBP	SLG
2003	River City (Fron)	IND	.301	38	123	24	37	5	1	1	15	16	18	19	.390	.382
2004	River City (Fron)	IND	.450	30	120	31	54	11	2	5	22	17	22	26	.518	.700
	Yankees (GCL)	R	.571	3	7	1	4	3	0	0	4	4	0	0	.727	1.000
	Staten Island (NY-P)	A	.274	50	208	29	57	9	2	7	33	19	39	14	.336	.438
2005	Charleston (SAL)	A	.290	29	100	31	29	5	0	3	10	14	12	17	.393	.430
	Tampa (FSL)	A	.306	95	372	52	114	27	6	8	37	33	47	38	.371	.476
MINOR LEAGUE TOTALS				177	687	113	204	44	8	18	84	70	98	69	.369	.463

22 BRONSON SARDINHA   OF

Born: April 6, 1983. **B-T:** L-R. **Ht.:** 6-1. **Wt.:** 195. **Drafted:** HS—Honolulu, Hawaii, 2001 (1st round). **Signed by:** Gus Quattlebaum.

Sardinha found a position in 2005, moving to right field after previous stints at shortstop, third base and two other outfield spots. He took to his new home well and showed a solid-average arm that plays up because of its accuracy. The nuances of right field also started coming to him, as he learned to throw to the right base and take better routes to the ball. He's the youngest of three brothers in the minors: Dane played in the Reds system last season, Duke in the Rockies organization. Bronson's bat was supposed to be his ticket and was the reason the Yankees drafted him in the supplemental first round in 2001, but his offensive progress stalled a bit. He's better off when he uses the whole field, but he tried too hard to hit for power last season, leading to him cheating on fastballs and trying to jerk balls down the line for home runs. Sardinha has a knack for staying inside the ball and using left-center field. His raw power is just average, and he's in danger of becoming a 'tweener. The Yankees want him to focus better on the field and off it in terms of his preparation. Coming off a .344 performance in the Arizona Fall League, he'll get his first shot at Triple-A in 2006 and needs to get back to hitting for average instead of worrying about his power.

Year	Club (League)	Class	AVG	G	AB	R	H	2B	3B	HR	RBI	BB	SO	SB	OBP	SLG
2001	Yankees (GCL)	R	.303	55	188	42	57	14	3	4	27	28	51	11	.398	.473
2002	Greensboro (SAL)	A	.263	93	342	49	90	13	0	12	44	34	78	15	.334	.406
	Staten Island (NY-P)	A	.323	36	124	25	40	8	0	4	16	24	36	4	.433	.484
2003	Tampa (FSL)	A	.193	59	212	23	41	8	2	1	17	24	57	8	.279	.264
	Battle Creek (Mid)	A	.275	71	269	54	74	16	0	8	44	40	40	5	.374	.424
2004	Tampa (FSL)	A	.315	63	248	37	78	12	2	2	33	29	39	9	.389	.403
	Trenton (EL)	AA	.267	72	266	37	71	11	1	6	29	37	65	4	.356	.383
2005	Trenton (EL)	AA	.258	133	503	63	130	30	2	12	68	55	115	11	.338	.398
MINOR LEAGUE TOTALS			.270	582	2152	330	581	112	10	49	275	271	481	67	.356	.400

23 KEVIN THOMPSON   OF

Born: Sept. 18, 1979. **B-T:** R-R. **Ht.:** 5-10. **Wt.:** 185. **Drafted:** Grayson County (Texas) JC, 1999 (31st round). **Signed by:** Mark Batchko.

Thompson started the 2005 season well in Double-A and even earned a start in the Futures Game, but he wasn't as impressive in the second half after a promotion to Triple-A. He remains unrefined for a player of his age and experience level. He's slump-prone in part because of his makeup, as Yankees officials use phrases such as "nervous energy," "edgy" and "emotional" to describe him. Thompson has raw power potential and carries his pop into games when he's aggressive yet disciplined at the plate. The Yankees would like him to play that way defensively. While he has center-field tools, he's tentative with his jumps and still lacks savvy, such as proper positioning, throwing to the right cutoff man and knowing when to dive for a ball. He's one of the organization's faster runners and has improved his basestealing ability. Thompson almost certainly will return to Triple-A in 2006.

Year	Club (League)	Class	AVG	G	AB	R	H	2B	3B	HR	RBI	BB	SO	SB	OBP	SLG
2000	Yankees (GCL)	R	.267	20	75	13	20	7	1	2	9	10	14	2	.356	.467
2001	Staten Island (NY-P)	A	.262	68	260	46	68	11	4	6	33	36	48	11	.360	.404
2002	Greensboro (SAL)	A	.283	62	226	44	64	24	3	3	31	37	42	14	.396	.456
	Tampa (FSL)	A	.184	25	87	10	16	5	0	0	7	13	15	11	.298	.241
	Staten Island (NY-P)	A	.302	36	139	25	42	5	2	4	14	17	24	6	.376	.453
2003	Tampa (FSL)	A	.331	44	163	42	54	13	4	5	25	32	27	16	.433	.552
	Trenton (EL)	AA	.226	86	328	48	74	16	2	5	20	37	57	47	.310	.332
2004	Tampa (FSL)	A	.356	11	45	12	16	4	0	2	6	4	7	9	.420	.578
	Trenton (EL)	AA	.281	69	270	43	76	17	0	9	17	30	40	29	.362	.444
2005	Trenton (EL)	AA	.329	81	313	59	103	28	5	12	43	53	68	25	.432	.565
	Columbus (IL)	AAA	.249	58	209	28	52	17	0	2	28	23	45	18	.335	.359
MINOR LEAGUE TOTALS			.277	560	2115	370	585	147	21	50	233	292	387	188	.371	.437

24   T.J. BEAM   RHP

Born: Aug. 28, 1980. **B-T:** R-R. **Ht.:** 6-7. **Wt.:** 215. **Drafted:** Mississippi, 2003 (10th round). **Signed by:** D.J. Svihlik.

Known as T.J. because he's Theodore Lester Beam Jr., Beam was a solid starter at Mississippi in college, leading the Rebels in wins as a senior. He was a fastball pitcher in the offspeed-heavy Southeastern Conference and got away with it because of his low-90s velocity and the downhill plane he generates from his 6-foot-7 frame. His lack of a quality offspeed pitch caught up with him in pro ball. He made strides with his slider and picked up velocity on his fastball after moving to the bullpen in 2005, and his improvement prompted the Yankees to protect him on their 40-man roster in November. Beam's fastball often sat at 92-96 mph last year, and while it lacks movement, he has enough velocity to pitch up in the zone. His slider greatly improved and became an average pitch. He locates it much better than he used to, and at times it has good tilt and some hard bite. His changeup is just fringe average. Beam profiles as a set-up man and will start this year in Double-A. If his slider continues to improve, he could move quickly.

Year	Club (League)	Class	W	L	ERA	G	GS	CG	SV	IP	H	R	ER	HR	BB	SO	AVG
2003	Staten Island (NY-P)	A	2	1	2.70	9	5	0	1	33	25	14	10	4	9	31	.200
	Battle Creek (Mid)	A	2	1	5.81	5	5	0	0	22	27	16	14	3	8	19	.300
2004	Staten Island (NY-P)	A	2	4	2.56	12	12	1	0	67	61	28	19	4	14	69	.251
	Battle Creek (Mid)	A	2	5	4.36	11	7	0	0	41	34	20	20	8	17	54	.227
2005	Tampa (FSL)	A	1	1	3.12	12	0	0	1	17	14	7	6	2	7	27	.215
	Charleston (SAL)	A	3	3	1.66	35	2	0	2	60	45	15	11	2	18	78	.206
MINOR LEAGUE TOTALS			12	15	3.00	84	31	1	4	240	206	100	80	23	73	278	.231

25   GARRETT PATTERSON   LHP

Born: May 11, 1982. **B-T:** L-L. **Ht.:** 6-2. **Wt.:** 220. **Drafted:** Oklahoma, 2005 (7th round). **Signed by:** Mark Batchko.

Staten Island dominated the New York-Penn League, going 52-24 and winning the playoffs, thanks to a pitching staff that posted a 2.85 ERA to lead the league by a substantial margin. Patterson had an ERA nearly a full run higher than the team mark, but his power left-handed arm makes him Staten Island's top pitching prospect. He had a well-traveled college career due in part to elbow problems. He started his career at Kansas State before transferring first to Grayson County (Texas) Community College and then Oklahoma, where he was a part-time starter and reliever. Patterson has big stuff, with enough power to be effective despite fringy control. His fastball sits at 93-94 and he touched 96 this summer out of the bullpen. His changeup gives him a second plus pitch, though it's a notch below his electric heater. He also has shown the ability to spin a breaking ball, a decent though inconsistent curve. While he has an easy and fairly smooth delivery, he has command and control issues. Patterson's poor conditioning has something to do with it, and he also tends to lose his release point at times. If he comes to spring training in better shape, he'll be given a chance to be a starter in Class A because of his three-pitch mix. Otherwise, he could move quickly as a power lefty reliever in the Alan Embree mold.

Year	Club (League)	Class	W	L	ERA	G	GS	CG	SV	IP	H	R	ER	HR	BB	SO	AVG
2005	Staten Island (NY-P)	A	1	2	3.71	17	11	0	0	51	37	22	21	1	38	71	.204
MINOR LEAGUE TOTALS			1	2	3.71	17	11	0	0	51	37	22	21	1	38	71	.204

26 ANDY PHILLIPS

1B/3B

Born: April 6, 1977. **B-T:** R-R. **Ht.:** 6-0. **Wt.:** 205. **Drafted:** Alabama, 1999 (7th round). **Signed by:** Leon Wurth.

Phillips continue to do what he does best—hit—but it looks like he may never be more than a 4-A player. The Yankees have used him in 32 big league games during the last two years, and Phillips has shown glimpses of the power he has displayed in the minors—six of his eight hits have gone for extra bases. The former Alabama star, who led the Crimson Tide to the 1999 College World Series with a Southeastern Conference-record 36-game hitting streak, had another strong minor league season in 2005. He has slightly above-average pop, and he maximizes his power potential by being an intelligent, disciplined hitter. He'll be 29 this season and may never get consistent at-bats in New York to justify the Kevin Millar comparisons that some scouts have put on him. A college shortstop, Phillips has been held back by his defense as a pro. He's still capable of filling in at second base and played more at third base than he did at first base in Triple-A last year. But his bat comes alive when he's at first, where he's an average defender.

Year	Club (League)	Class	AVG	G	AB	R	H	2B	3B	HR	RBI	BB	SO	SB	OBP	SLG
1999	Staten Island (NY-P)	A	.322	64	233	35	75	11	7	7	48	37	40	3	.417	.519
2000	Tampa (FSL)	A	.287	127	478	66	137	33	2	13	58	46	98	2	.346	.446
	Norwich (EL)	AA	.250	7	28	5	7	2	1	0	3	3	11	1	.323	.393
2001	Norwich (EL)	AA	.268	51	183	23	49	9	2	6	25	21	54	1	.340	.437
	Tampa (FSL)	A	.302	75	288	43	87	17	4	11	50	25	55	3	.353	.503
2002	Norwich (EL)	AA	.305	73	272	58	83	24	2	19	51	33	56	4	.381	.618
	Columbus (IL)	AAA	.263	51	205	32	54	11	1	9	36	10	46	0	.296	.459
2003	Columbus (IL)	AAA	.209	17	67	7	14	4	0	2	5	5	17	0	.264	.358
2004	Trenton (EL)	AA	.357	10	42	8	15	2	1	4	16	3	1	3	.383	.738
	Columbus (IL)	AAA	.318	115	434	83	138	19	6	26	85	51	60	2	.388	.569
	New York (AL)	MLB	.250	5	8	1	2	0	0	1	2	0	1	0	.250	.625
2005	New York (AL)	MLB	.150	27	40	7	6	4	0	1	4	1	13	0	.171	.325
	Columbus (IL)	AAA	.300	75	300	60	90	14	1	22	54	36	61	2	.379	.573
MAJOR LEAGUE TOTALS			.167	32	48	8	8	4	0	2	6	1	14	0	.184	.375
MINOR LEAGUE TOTALS			.296	665	2530	420	749	146	27	119	431	270	499	21	.363	.516

27 RUDY GUILLEN

OF

Born: Nov. 23, 1983. **B-T:** R-R. **Ht.:** 6-3. **Wt.:** 186. **Signed:** Dominican Republic, 2000. **Signed by:** Victor Mata.

Guillen ranked third on this list just two years ago, and the Yankees still see some ceiling in him. Expectations have been lowered, though, as it becomes apparent that he doesn't have quite the power the organization thought would develop. His swing consistently is a little late and a little long. Because power is the last tool to come, the Yankees haven't ruled out that Guillen will shorten up and hit for enough pop to be a starting corner outfielder. He showed improved ability to pull the ball in the club's fall minicamp, a crucial aspect he must add to his game to avoid being pounded inside by fastballs. His plate discipline also hasn't progressed as he has advanced to higher levels. Otherwise, Guillen still has solid tools, with good hands that allow him to steer offspeed pitches to the opposite field with some author- ity. His strong throwing arm remains his best tool. Guillen got his first Double-A experience last season and wasn't overwhelmed. He'll return to the Trenton in 2006, still trying to make the adjustments needed at the plate to avoid being characterized as a fourth outfielder.

Year	Club (League)	Class	AVG	G	AB	R	H	2B	3B	HR	RBI	BB	SO	SB	OBP	SLG
2001	Yankees (DSL)	R	.281	62	231	38	65	13	2	11	41	15	50	11	.337	.498
2002	Yankees (GCL)	R	.306	59	219	38	67	7	2	3	35	14	39	7	.351	.397
2003	Battle Creek (Mid)	A	.260	133	493	64	128	29	4	13	79	32	87	13	.311	.414
2004	Yankees (GCL)	R	.429	4	14	1	6	0	0	0	1	0	0	0	.429	.429
	Tampa (FSL)	A	.264	79	307	40	81	16	2	1	42	22	59	1	.313	.339
2005	Tampa (FSL)	A	.260	100	389	51	101	14	4	6	39	19	70	10	.305	.362
	Trenton (EL)	AA	.257	28	109	12	28	2	0	2	8	5	20	0	.289	.330
MINOR LEAGUE TOTALS			.270	465	1762	244	476	81	14	36	245	107	325	42	.318	.393

28 KEVIN REESE

OF

Born: March 11, 1978. **B-T:** L-L. **Ht.:** 5-11. **Wt.:** 195. **Drafted:** San Diego, 2000 (27th round). **Signed by:** Tim McWilliam (Padres).

The last week of June couldn't have been more memorable for Reese. Two days after he proposed to his longtime girlfriend, Laura Le Gallo, the Yankees finally rewarded his offen- sive talent with a brief big league promotion. He struck out and walked in two plate appear- ances. New York acquired him from the Padres in December 2001 in a trade for Bernie

Castro. Reese is an efficient hitter with a career .299 average in the minors, and he's smart and patient enough to identify and wait for pitches he can drive. He has an excellent two-strike approach. He hangs in well against lefthanders and has power to the gaps, but he doesn't have enough juice to be a corner outfielder on a contender. He's also a good baserunner and efficient basestealer. Defensively, Reese is solid-average on either corner, though his arm profiles best in left. He has played some center field in the minors, mostly in 2004, and grades out as slightly below average. Realistically, Reese will be an extra outfielder for the Yankees and won't get a chance to start until he's in another organization.

Year	Club (League)	Class	AVG	G	AB	R	H	2B	3B	HR	RBI	BB	SO	SB	OBP	SLG
2000	Idaho Falls (Pio)	R	.358	53	201	51	72	14	4	2	36	43	30	12	.474	.498
2001	Fort Wayne (Mid)	A	.329	125	459	84	151	30	6	13	73	54	62	30	.402	.505
2002	Norwich (EL)	AA	.290	138	514	80	149	24	6	4	45	77	87	22	.385	.383
2003	Columbus (IL)	AAA	.218	15	55	11	12	1	0	1	3	6	8	1	.295	.291
	Trenton (EL)	AA	.272	86	309	42	84	13	2	4	21	25	58	27	.328	.366
2004	Trenton (EL)	AA	.298	78	329	57	98	37	4	6	40	23	48	13	.348	.489
	Columbus (IL)	AAA	.323	53	217	41	70	13	3	8	28	12	34	4	.370	.521
2005	New York (AL)	MLB	.000	2	1	0	0	0	0	0	0	1	1	0	.500	.000
	Columbus (IL)	AAA	.276	133	540	92	149	38	7	14	69	63	86	16	.359	.450
MAJOR LEAGUE TOTALS			.000	2	1	0	0	0	0	0	0	1	1	0	.500	.000
MINOR LEAGUE TOTALS			.299	681	2624	458	785	170	32	52	315	303	413	125	.376	.448

29 JASON STEPHENS   RHP

Born: Oct. 10, 1984. **B-T:** R-R. **Ht.:** 6-4. **Wt.:** 190. **Drafted:** HS—Tallmadge, Ohio, 2003 (6th round). **Signed by:** Mike Gibbons.

The Yankees have been waiting for results from Stephens since they signed him for a $500,000 bonus as a 2003 sixth-round pick. At the time, New York scout Gordon Blakeley compared Stephens to Mark Prior, whom the club had drafted out of high school five years before. Stephens doesn't quite have Prior's physique, and the Yankees still have to do some projection on him, as he has yet to play full-season ball. He made significant strides at Staten Island last season, mostly in his mound demeanor. Stephens didn't face much adversity in high school and is learning how to get through tough innings, making big pitches when he needs them and not giving in to hitters. He locates his 89-90 mph fastball well, and the Yankees believe there's more velocity to come once he fills out physically. He's still learning to get more sink on the pitch. His 12-to-6 curveball is his out pitch, and he also throws a changeup. He has good control now and the Yankees expect him to have above-average command down the road. He'll head to low Class A this season for his first shot at full-season ball. This would have been his draft year had he attended Georgia Tech.

Year	Club (League)	Class	W	L	ERA	G	GS	CG	SV	IP	H	R	ER	HR	BB	SO	AVG
2003	Yankees (GCL)	R	0	2	4.55	10	3	1	1	32	42	20	16	1	9	25	.333
2004	Yankees (GCL)	R	5	3	2.61	13	8	0	1	48	55	23	14	1	10	48	.279
	Staten Island (NY-P)	A	0	1	5.40	1	1	0	0	5	10	4	3	1	0	1	.455
2005	Staten Island (NY-P)	A	4	1	2.82	18	10	0	1	67	55	25	21	3	19	52	.229
MINOR LEAGUE TOTALS			9	7	3.20	42	22	1	3	152	162	72	54	6	38	126	.277

30 JEFF KARSTENS   RHP

Born: Sept. 24, 1982. **B-T:** R-R. **Ht.:** 6-3. **Wt.:** 175. **Drafted:** Texas Tech, 2003 (19th round). **Signed by:** Mark Batchko.

Karstens spent two years at Grossmont Junior College and was an all-conference selection in one of California's most competitive community college conferences. He moved on to Texas Tech for a year as a reliever, but New York thinks he can be a back-of-the-rotation starter. A pitchability righthander, Karstens resembles 2005 Yankees savior Aaron Small in some ways, with a tall frame (though less solid than Small's) and the ability to throw all his pitches for strikes. Karstens has an 88-91 mph fastball that he spots to all four quadrants of the strike zone, and he also uses a changeup, curveball and slider. His changeup is his second-best pitch, and he used it to hold lefthanders to a .257 average. Righthanders handled him at a .307 clip. Karstens needs to pitch inside more and keep his modest stuff down in the zone, as he was too hittable last year. But he has shown enough of a knack for pitching to keep the Yankees interested. He'll move up to Triple-A for the first time in 2006.

Year	Club (League)	Class	W	L	ERA	G	GS	CG	SV	IP	H	R	ER	HR	BB	SO	AVG
2003	Staten Island (NY-P)	A	4	2	2.54	14	10	0	0	67	63	22	19	2	16	53	.256
2004	Tampa (FSL)	A	6	9	4.02	24	24	1	0	139	151	70	62	11	31	116	.284
2005	Trenton (EL)	AA	12	11	4.15	28	27	0	0	169	192	91	78	16	42	147	.285
MINOR LEAGUE TOTALS			22	22	3.82	66	61	1	0	375	406	183	159	29	89	316	.280

ATHLETICS
BY KEVIN GOLDSTEIN

So much for rebuilding. Before the 2005 season, the Athletics dealt Tim Hudson and Mark Mulder in a pair of money-saving moves. General manager Billy Beane preached the wisdom of building for the future rather than making incremental moves to keep the major league team in contention.

When Oakland started the year with just 17 wins in its first 49 games, the season seemed over in May. But with huge contributions by rookies, the A's went on a 58-24 run that vaulted them atop the American League West at the end of August. They faded in September, but served notice that they'll continue to contend.

Oakland's most prominent first-year player was **Huston Street**, who made the Opening Day roster after just 26 pro innings. He took over as closer for the injured Octavio Dotel in May and won Baseball America's Rookie of the Year award by saving 23 games with a 1.72 ERA. Rookies Joe Blanton, Nick Swisher and Dan Johnson also made significant contributions.

The graduation of so much talent to Oakland has thinned out the farm system. The A's won't have much of a rookie influx in 2006, with the possible exception of top prospect Daric Barton, who could hit his way into a DH role. Most of the organization's top minor league talent came from the 2005 draft, when Oakland owned five of the first 101 picks. After following their standard operating procedure by taking polished collegians Cliff Pennington and Travis Buck with their first two choices, the A's took three consecutive high school pitchers,

BILL NICHOLS

a college senior and then three more prep arms. That's the risky draft demographic that fans of "Moneyball" rush to disdain on Internet message boards, but a direction Oakland felt it needed to take.

In the end, Beane doesn't care what is written or said about him or the A's—as long as they continue to compete. "We chuckle at everyone's perception of what we do and what we don't do," Beane said. "It's somewhat comical."

While the big league roster was going through turnover, so too was the club's ownership. In March, billionaire John Fisher and managing partner Lewis Wolff led a group that bought the A's from Steve Schott and Ken Hofmann for $180 million. Despite ties to San Jose, Wolff insists he's committed to keeping the team in Oakland and trying to build a new stadium in the Network Associates Coliseum parking lot.

The new owners rewarded Beane with the first ownership stake for a GM in modern big league history. Beane, who received nearly 5 percent of the club, also got a contact extension through 2012.

The A's nearly got a new manager as well. Contract talks between Beane and incumbent Ken Macha broke down after the season, and Macha walked away to pursue the same job with his hometown Pirates. When that didn't work out, Macha returned to Oakland nine days later.

TOP 30 PROSPECTS

1. Daric Barton, 1b
2. Javier Herrera, of
3. Cliff Pennington, ss
4. Andre Ethier, of
5. Travis Buck, of
6. Kevin Melillo, 2b
7. Jairo Garcia, rhp
8. Craig Italiano, rhp
9. Shane Komine, rhp
10. Vince Mazzaro, rhp
11. Kurt Suzuki, c
12. Jared Lansford, rhp
13. Richie Robnett, of
14. Danny Putnam, of
15. Jason Windsor, rhp
16. Gregorio Petit, inf
17. Justin Sellers, ss
18. Jimmy Shull, rhp
19. Dallas Braden, lhp
20. Landon Powell, c
21. Dan Meyer, lhp
22. Jason Ray, rhp
23. Brant Colamarino, 1b
24. Connor Robertson, rhp
25. Brian Stavisky, of
26. Freddie Bynum, of/ss
27. John Rheinecker, lhp
28. Mike Madsen, rhp
29. Ramon Alvarado, of
30. Jeff Baisley, 3b

ORGANIZATION OVERVIEW

General manager: Billy Beane. **Farm director:** Keith Lieppman. **Scouting director:** Eric Kubota.

Class	Team	League	W	L	Pct.	Finish*	Manager
Majors	Oakland	American	88	74	.543	6th (14)	Ken Macha
Triple-A	Sacramento River Cats	Pacific Coast	80	64	.556	t-2nd (16)	Tony DeFrancesco
Double-A	Midland RockHounds	Texas	78	62	.557	+1st (8)	Von Hayes
High A	Stockton Ports	California	78	62	.557	2nd (10)	Todd Steverson
Low A	Kane County Cougars	Midwest	67	72	.482	10th (14)	Dave Joppie
Short-season	Vancouver Canadians	Northwest	46	30	.605	1st (8)	Juan Navarrette
Rookie	AZL Athletics	Arizona	30	26	.536	3rd (9)	Ruben Escalera
OVERALL 2005 MINOR LEAGUE RECORD			379	316	.545	3rd (30)	

*Finish in overall standings (No. of teams in league). +League champion

ORGANIZATION LEADERS

BATTING *Minimum 250 at-bats*
*AVG	Barton, Daric, Midland/Stockton	.317
R	Ethier, Andre, Midland/Sacramento	104
H	Ethier, Andre, Midland/Sacramento	165
TB	Melillo, Kevin, Kane County/Mid./Stockton	268
2B	Majewski, Dustin, Stockton	43
3B	Bynum, Freddie, Sacramento	9
HR	Melillo, Kevin, Kane County/Mid./Stockton	24
RBI	Putnam, Danny, Midland/Stockton	100
BB	Cust, Jack, Sacramento	115
SO	Cust, Jack, Sacramento	153
SB	Herrera, Javier, Kane County/Sacramento	27
*OBP	Barton, Daric, Midland/Stockton	.426
*SLG	Morris, Jed, Midland/Sacramento/Stockton	.538

PITCHING #Minimum 75 innings
W	Braden, Dallas, Midland/Stockton	15
L	Webb, Ryan, Kane County	11
#ERA	Madsen, Mike, Vancouver	1.39
G	Kohn, Shawn, Midland	55
	Robertson, Connor, Kane Co./Sac./Stockton	55
CG	Three tied at	1
SV	Garcia, Jairo, Midland/Sacramento	26
	Santos, Alex, Midland/Sacramento/Stockton	26
IP	Bondurant, Steven, Midland	165
BB	Sharpe, Steven, AZL Athletics/Kane Co./Stock.	61
SO	Ziegler, Brad, Midland/Stockton	164

BEST TOOLS

Best Hitter for Average	Daric Barton
Best Power Hitter	Kevin Melillo
Best Strike-Zone Discipline	Daric Barton
Fastest Baserunner	Freddie Bynum
Best Athlete	Javier Herrera
Best Fastball	Craig Italiano
Best Curveball	Shane Komine
Best Slider	Jairo Garcia
Best Changeup	Jason Windsor
Best Control	Dallas Braden
Best Defensive Catcher	Kurt Suzuki
Best Defensive Infielder	Cliff Pennington
Best Infield Arm	Cliff Pennington
Best Defensive Outfielder	Javier Herrera
Best Outfield Arm	Javier Herrera

PROJECTED 2009 LINEUP

Catcher	Kurt Suzuki
First Base	Dan Johnson
Second Base	Cliff Pennington
Third Base	Eric Chavez
Shortstop	Bobby Crosby
Left Field	Travis Buck
Center Field	Javier Herrera

Right Field	Nick Swisher
Designated Hitter	Daric Barton
No. 1 Starter	Rich Harden
No. 2 Starter	Barry Zito
No. 3 Starter	Dan Haren
No. 4 Starter	Joe Blanton
No. 5 Starter	Craig Italiano
Closer	Huston Street

LAST YEAR'S TOP 20 PROSPECTS

1. Nick Swisher, of	11. Kurt Suzuki, c
2. Daric Barton, 1b/c	12. Landon Powell, c
3. Javier Herrera, of	13. Danny Putnam, of
4. Dan Meyer, lhp	14. John Baker, c/1b
5. Joe Blanton, rhp	15. Brian Snyder, 3b
6. Dan Johnson, 1b	16. Andre Ethier, of
7. Huston Street, rhp	17. Jason Windsor, rhp
8. Jairo Garcia, rhp	18. Brad Knox, rhp
9. Richie Robnett, of	19. Tyler Johnson, lhp
10. Omar Quintanilla, ss	20. Alexi Ogando, of

TOP PROSPECTS OF THE DECADE

Year	Player, Pos.	2005 Org.
1996	Ben Grieve, of	Cubs
1997	Miguel Tejada, ss	Orioles
1998	Ben Grieve, of	Cubs
1999	Eric Chavez, 3b	Athletics
2000	Mark Mulder, lhp	Cardinals
2001	Jose Ortiz, 2b	Out of baseball
2002	Carlos Pena, 1b	Tigers
2003	Rich Harden, rhp	Athletics
2004	Bobby Crosby, ss	Athletics
2005	Nick Swisher, of	Athletics

TOP DRAFT PICKS OF THE DECADE

Year	Player, Pos.	2005 Org.
1996	Eric Chavez, 3b	Athletics
1997	Chris Enochs, rhp	Pirates
1998	Mark Mulder, lhp	Cardinals
1999	Barry Zito, lhp	Athletics
2000	Freddie Bynum, ss (2nd round)	Athletics
2001	Bobby Crosby, ss	Athletics
2002	Nick Swisher, of	Athletics
2003	Brad Sullivan, rhp	Athletics
2004	Landon Powell, c	Athletics
2005	Cliff Pennington, ss	Athletics

ALL-TIME LARGEST BONUSES

Mark Mulder, 1998	$3,200,000
Nick Swisher, 2002	$1,780,000
Barry Zito, 1999	$1,625,000
Cliff Pennington, 2005	$1,475,000
Joe Blanton, 2002	$1,400,000

MINOR LEAGUE DEPTH CHART

Oakland Athletics

Rank: **26**

STRENGTH: Outfield. The Athletics have good depth at all three outfield spots with toolsy players like Javier Herrera and Travis Buck.

WEAKNESS: Depth. Give the A's time to replenish after placing four players on BA's 2005 All-Rookie team.

Depth charts prepared by **John Manuel** *and* **Chris Kline**. *Numbers in parentheses indicate prospect rankings.*

LF
Travis Buck (5)
Danny Putnam (14)
Brian Stavisky (25)
Matt Watson
Jason Perry

CF
Javier Herrera (2)
Freddie Bynum (26)
Steve Stanley

RF
Andre Ethier (4)
Richie Robnett (13)
Ramon Alvarado (29)

3B
Jeff Baisley (30)
Brian Snyder

SS
Cliff Pennington (3)
Justin Sellers (17)
Mike Rouse
Ronnie Merrill

2B
Kevin Mellillo (6)
Gregorio Petit (16)
Mark Kiger
Luke Appert

1B
Daric Barton (1)
Brant Colamarino (23)
Myron Leslie
Vasili Spanos

C
Kurt Suzuki (11)
Landon Powell (20)
Jeremy Brown
Raul Padron

RHP

Starters	Relievers
Shane Komine (9)	Jairo Garcia (7)
Vince Mazzaro (10)	Craig Italiano (8)
Jared Lansford (12)	Jason Ray (22)
Jason Windsor (15)	Connor Robertson (24)
Jimmy Shull (18)	Marcus McBeth
Mike Madson (28)	David Bradley
Brad Knox	Shawn Kown
Mike Rogers	Jared Burton
Scott Deal	Ryan Webb
Brad Sullivan	Chris Mabeus
Matt Roney	

LHP

Starters	Relievers
Dallas Braden (19)	Brad Kilby
Dan Meyer (21)	Brad Davis
John Rheinecker (27)	Ryan Ford
	Steven Bondurant
	Ron Flores

DRAFT ANALYSIS

2005

Best Pro Debut: OF Travis Buck (1) hit .361 at short-season Vancouver and .341 at low Class A Kane County. Vancouver's pitching staff featured several strong debuts. RHP Michael Madsen (21) went 6-1 with a Northwest League-best 1.69 ERA. Deceptive LHP Brad Kilby (29) went 2-0, 1.95 with 14 saves and 38 strikeouts in 28 innings, and hard-throwing setup RHP Jason Ray (8) had a 2.12 ERA and 56 whiffs in 30 innings.

Best Athlete: SS Cliff Pennington (1) is an ultimate gamer who also has very good tools. He can hit for average with gap power, and he has plus speed and arm strength. SS Justin Sellers (6) has a lot of the same traits.

Best Pure Hitter: Buck hits line drives all over the field and hangs in well against left-handers. He has the potential for 20-25 homers annually if he gets stronger and looks to drive the ball more often.

Best Raw Power: C Anthony Recker (18) still needs to adjust to pro pitching, but he's very strong and is dangerous when he makes contact.

Fastest Runner: Pennington, Sellers and OF Mike Massaro (13) all have above-average speed. Pennington has exceptional instincts on the bases as well.

Best Defensive Player: Pennington and Sellers have similar hands and range, but Pennington has the better arm. His rates a 65 on the 20-80 scouting scale, while Sellers' is closer to average.

Best Fastball: No draft prospect lit up radar guns as consistently as RHP Craig Italiano (2) did during the spring, when he threw in the mid-90s and touched 98 mph every time out. Fellow high school RHPs Jared Lansford (2), Vince Mazzaro (3) and

Lansford

Scott Deal (5) all can hit 93 or 94 mph. Ray threw 93-95 mph once he moved to the bullpen as a pro.

Best Breaking Ball: Ray has a hammer curveball. Italiano has improved his breaking ball from a slurve to a true slider, and if it keeps getting better, he could be another Brad Lidge.

Most Intriguing Background: Lansford's father Carney won an American League batting title in 1981 and a World Series with the A's in 1989. His uncles Phil and Joe were both first-round picks, and Joe also reached the majors. Sellers' father Jeff pitched in the big leagues. SS Zeke Parraz' (25) brother Jordan is an outfielder in the Astros system.

Closest To The Majors: Pennington has the skills and savvy to become Bobby Crosby's double-play partner in Oakland at some point in 2007.

Best Late-Round Pick: Madsen doesn't have overwhelming stuff but he wins with his 89-92 mph fastball and decent curve.

The One Who Got Away: 1B Justin Smoak's (16) power, switch-hitting ability and defensive polish would have made him a supplemental first-round pick if not for his $1 million asking price.

Assessment: Known to prefer college players, the A's crossed teams up by taking six high school pitchers in the first seven rounds. Oakland wanted to add some quality arms, and the prepsters were the best ones on their board.

2004 RHP Huston Street (1) not only became Oakland's closer faster than anyone expected, but he also was BA's 2005 Rookie of the Year. OFs Richie Robnett (1) and Danny Putnam (1), C Kurt Suzuki (2) and 2B Kevin Melillo (5) are among the A's best prospects. *GRADE:* A

2003 Of the three first-round picks, only SS/2B Omar Quintanilla looks like he'll pan out—and he was traded to the Rockies. The others, RHP Brad Sullivan and 3B Brian Snyder, barely played in 2005. *GRADE:* C

2002 The famed "Moneyball" draft featured seven first-round picks: two successes (OF Nick Swisher, RHP Joe Blanton), a marginal big leaguer (3B Mark Teahen, traded to the Royals), a fringe prospect (C Jeremy Brown) and three failures (3B/SS John McCurdy, RHPs Ben Fritz and Steve Obenchain). *GRADE:* A

2001 Their best draft from 2001-04, starting with SS Bobby Crosby and RHP Jeremy Bonderman in the first round. LHP Neal Cotts (2) and 1B Dan Johnson (7) were nice bonuses. *GRADE:* A

Draft analysis prepared by Jim Callis. Numbers in parentheses indicate draft rounds.

DARIC
BARTON

1B

LARRY GOREN

Born: Aug. 16, 1985.
Ht.: 6-0. **Wt.:** 205.
Bats: L. **Throws:** R.
Drafted: HS—Huntington Beach, Calif., 2003 (1st round).
Signed by: Dan Ontiveros (Cardinals).

Considered one of the top lefthanded bats in the 2003 draft, Barton fell to the Cardinals with the 28th pick because of his bad body and fringy defensive skills. Signed for $975,000, Barton quickly established himself as the top prospect in the St. Louis system. In his first full season, he led the low Class A Midwest League in on-base percentage and finished fourth in slugging. Looking for a starter to headline their rotation, the Cardinals sent three players to the Athletics for Mark Mulder in December 2004. While Dan Haren would win 14 games for Oakland in 2005, Barton was considered the key player in the deal. General manager Billy Beane called Barton the best pure hitter in the minors after acquiring him. The A's decided the rigors of catching were hindering Barton's development, so they moved him to first base in spring training. He hit just .241 at high Class A Stockton in April but found his groove afterward. He hit .404 in June and earned a promotion to Double-A Midland before his 20th birthday. He went 9-for-16 in his first five games in Double-A and reached base in 50 of his 56 contests there.

Hitting comes easy for Barton, who has natural ability to go along with a mature approach. He has a short swing and picture-perfect mechanics, with a fluid load and quick explosion through the zone. His pitch recognition is off the charts. He draws a large number of walks while still being an aggressive hitter, equally comfortable turning on inside fastballs or slicing outside breaking balls the other way. Barton holds his own against lefthanders. He took well to first base in his first year there and shows the potential for improvement. He has good instincts, soft hands and decent range.

Barton's power potential is the subject of debate among scouts. He has a tendency to drop the barrel of the bat and slice balls into the gaps. The A's are convinced he'll eventually produce 25-30 homers on an annual basis, citing his hitting ability and the scouting axiom that power often is the last tool to develop. Others think he might top out at 15-20 homers, less than ideal production for a first baseman. Questions about his work ethic have dogged Barton in the past. His inability to remain a catcher was due more to lack of effort than lack of ability. He's a below-average runner, and his conditioning could improve.

The A's have no immediate plans to move Barton back behind the plate, where his offensive skills would give him star potential, but they haven't completely ruled it out yet either. While his bat is nearly ready for the big leagues, Barton would need substantial time in the minors if he returned to catching. He'll begin the year playing first base at Triple-A Sacramento, and could make his major league debut before he turns 21 in August. Oakland almost certainly will have to make a decision as to how to get his bat permanently in the lineup by Opening Day 2007.

Year	Club (League)	Class	AVG	G	AB	R	H	2B	3B	HR	RBI	BB	SO	SB	OBP	SLG
2003	Johnson City (Appy)	R	.294	54	170	29	50	10	0	4	29	37	48	0	.420	.424
2004	Peoria (Mid)	A	.313	90	313	63	98	23	0	13	77	69	44	4	.445	.511
2005	Stockton (Cal)	A	.318	79	292	60	93	16	2	8	52	62	49	0	.438	.469
	Midland (TL)	AA	.316	56	212	38	67	20	1	5	37	35	30	1	.410	.491
MINOR LEAGUE TOTALS			.312	279	987	190	308	69	3	30	195	203	171	5	.431	.479

2 JAVIER HERRERA   OF

Born: April 9, 1985. **B-T:** R-R. **Ht.:** 5-11. **Wt.:** 190. **Signed:** Venezuela, 2001. **Signed by:** Julio Franco.

Herrera won MVP honors in the short-season Northwest League in 2004, but his encore was delayed when he was suspended after testing positive for a performance-enhancing substance before Opening Day. Once he returned, his natural talent took over. He earned a one-week May stint in Triple-A when Sacramento was decimated by injuries. Herrera's combination of raw tools outclasses that of any A's farmhand. A true five-tool talent, he can hit for average, flashes plus power and is a well-above-average runner. He took to the Oakland approach in 2005, dramatically improving his walk rate. He's a good center fielder with a plus arm. Herrera is still a work in progress when it comes to translating his tools to performance. He has a tendency to overswing, leading to high strikeout totals. He needs to improve his throwing accuracy and his routes in the outfield, especially on balls hit in front of him. The A's have a rare commodity in Herrera, a potential 30-30 man in center field. His progress will continue one step at a time with an assignment to high Class A in 2006.

Year	Club (League)	Class	AVG	G	AB	R	H	2B	3B	HR	RBI	BB	SO	SB	OBP	SLG
2002	Athletics East (DSL)	R	.286	65	227	40	65	14	5	5	47	23	56	21	.359	.458
2003	Athletics (AZL)	R	.230	17	61	12	14	3	1	2	13	7	19	3	.329	.410
2004	Vancouver (NWL)	A	.331	65	263	50	87	15	4	12	47	24	59	23	.392	.555
2005	Sacramento (PCL)	AAA	.417	5	12	5	5	1	0	1	3	1	1	1	.533	.750
	Kane County (Mid)	A	.275	94	360	70	99	18	2	13	62	47	110	26	.374	.444
MINOR LEAGUE TOTALS			.293	246	923	177	270	51	12	33	172	102	245	74	.375	.481

3 CLIFF PENNINGTON   SS

Born: June 15, 1984. **B-T:** B-R. **Ht.:** 5-11. **Wt.:** 160. **Drafted:** Texas A&M, 2005 (1st round). **Signed by:** Blake Davis.

After starring in the Cape Cod League in 2004 and leading Texas A&M in nearly every offensive category in 2005, Pennington became the first Aggie to be taken in the first round since 1999. Signed for $1.475 million, he was thrust into the leadoff spot at low Class A Kane County, where he scored 49 runs in 69 games. Pennington is a solid hitter who makes contact, occasionally drives the ball and shows a good understanding of the strike zone. He's an above-average runner and a dangerous basestealer with excellent instincts. He's a plus defender with good range to both sides and a strong, accurate arm. Like most top A's draft picks of late, he has outstanding makeup and an infectious enthusiasm for the game. Pennington has a small frame and probably never will hit for much home run power, but he still needs to work harder on driving balls instead of just serving them back up the middle. He can get a little out of control in the field, occasionally rushing his throws. With Bobby Crosby in Oakland, there's no need to rush Pennington, who will begin the year in high Class A. But he should move quickly regardless and likely will move over to second base and play alongside Crosby when he's ready for the majors.

Year	Club (League)	Class	AVG	G	AB	R	H	2B	3B	HR	RBI	BB	SO	SB	OBP	SLG
2005	Kane County (Mid)	A	.276	69	290	49	80	15	0	3	29	39	47	25	.364	.359
MINOR LEAGUE TOTALS			.276	69	290	49	80	15	0	3	29	39	47	25	.364	.359

4 ANDRE ETHIER   OF

Born: April 10, 1982. **B-T:** L-R. **Ht.:** 6-3. **Wt.:** 195. **Drafted:** Arizona State, 2003 (2nd round). **Signed by:** John Kuehl.

Ethier was having a breakout season in 2004 when a stress fracture in his back cut him down in July. He spent the offseason working on his conditioning and earned Double-A Texas League MVP honors in 2005. He hit .361-9-39 in the first two months before pitchers stopped throwing him strikes. A gifted hitter, Ethier has simple swing mechanics, getting the bat into the zone quickly and keeping it there for a long time. He has average power, and he's a good corner outfielder with a solid arm. One of the keys to his breakout season was a change in attitude. Once considered a hothead who was easily flustered, he showed a more mature approach and consistent effort in 2005. He also won an award for his sportsmanship in the Arizona Fall League. Ethier doesn't have the speed to play center field and may not have the power teams desire from an everyday corner outfielder. He can become enamored with his power at times, causing him to over-swing. A walk machine in college, Ethier has yet to show the same plate discipline as a pro. There's no clear opening for Ethier in a crowded Oakland outfield, so he likely will spend the majority of 2006 in Triple-A. Coming off a career year, he also could be useful as trade bait.

Year	Club (League)	Class	AVG	G	AB	R	H	2B	3B	HR	RBI	BB	SO	SB	OBP	SLG
2003	Vancouver (NWL)	A	.390	10	41	7	16	4	1	1	7	3	3	2	.444	.610
	Kane County (Mid)	A	.272	40	162	23	44	10	0	0	11	19	25	2	.355	.333
2004	Modesto (Cal)	A	.313	99	419	72	131	23	5	7	53	45	64	2	.383	.442
2005	Midland (TL)	AA	.319	131	505	104	161	30	3	18	80	48	93	1	.385	.497
	Sacramento (PCL)	AAA	.267	4	15	0	4	1	0	0	2	2	3	0	.353	.333
MINOR LEAGUE TOTALS			.312	284	1142	206	356	68	9	26	153	117	188	7	.382	.455

5 TRAVIS BUCK   OF

Born: Nov. 18, 1983. **B-T:** L-R. **Ht.:** 6-2. **Wt.:** 205. **Drafted:** Arizona State, 2005 (1st round supplemental). **Signed by:** Jeremy Schied.

Buck entered 2005 ranked as one of the top college hitters available in his draft class, but he hit just .246 in his first 15 games. He rebounded to hit .419 afterward, helping Arizona State to the College World Series, but his early slump and disappointing power (six homers) dropped him to the A's with the 36th overall pick. After signing for $950,000, he hit .346 in pro ball. Buck has a knack for hitting, using a compact, line-drive swing to tag balls to all fields. He makes good adjustments from at-bat to at-bat and understands the value of a walk. He's a good outfielder with solid range and arm strength. He draws praise for his work ethic. Buck hit just three home runs in his debut, and needs to get more loft into has swing while incorporating his lower half better. Oakland thinks he can hit 20-25 homers annually once he improves his ability to recognize which pitches he can drive. The A's have a glut of good-hitting corner outfielders in their system, but Buck's bat was too good to pass up. He'll begin the year in high Class A.

Year	Club (League)	Class	AVG	G	AB	R	H	2B	3B	HR	RBI	BB	SO	SB	OBP	SLG
2005	Vancouver (NWL)	A	.361	9	36	7	13	1	0	2	9	5	8	1	.439	.556
	Kane County (Mid)	A	.341	32	123	17	42	13	0	1	22	19	19	3	.427	.472
MINOR LEAGUE TOTALS			.346	41	159	24	55	14	0	3	31	24	27	4	.429	.491

6 KEVIN MELILLO   2B

Born: May 14, 1982. **B-T:** L-R. **Ht.:** 5-11. **Wt.:** 185. **Drafted:** South Carolina, 2004 (5th round). **Signed by:** Michael Holmes.

The A's became excited about Melillo, a high school teammate of Rickie Weeks, when they were scouting 2004 first-round pick Landon Powell at South Carolina. Melillo helped the Gamecocks to three College World Series. As a pro he has provided the kind of power the injured Powell was supposed to deliver, leading the system with 24 homers in his first full season. Melillo has a quick, compact swing and surprising power, thanks to natural loft and a high finish. He has a nice feel for working the count and makes consistent hard contact. He's a good baserunner and can steal bases thanks to excellent reads and jumps. Melillo isn't very athletic and his defense continues to lag behind his bat despite his considerable effort at improving. His speed is average at best, his range is limited and his arm is below-average. While Melillo likely will begin 2006 in Double-A, Oakland doesn't expect him to finish the year there. If he keeps hitting, he could be in line for a big league look in 2007.

Year	Club (League)	Class	AVG	G	AB	R	H	2B	3B	HR	RBI	BB	SO	SB	OBP	SLG
2004	Vancouver (NWL)	A	.340	22	94	22	32	11	2	2	21	11	16	2	.422	.564
2005	Kane County (Mid)	A	.286	78	280	47	80	18	3	8	36	53	40	10	.399	.457
	Stockton (Cal)	A	.400	22	90	21	36	7	1	9	23	12	18	2	.471	.800
	Midland (TL)	AA	.282	35	131	33	37	10	0	7	34	14	23	9	.347	.519
MINOR LEAGUE TOTALS			.311	157	595	123	185	46	6	26	114	90	97	23	.402	.539

7 JAIRO GARCIA

RHP

Born: March 7, 1983. **B-T:** R-R. **Ht.:** 6-0. **Wt.:** 165. **Signed:** Dominican Republic, 2000. **Signed by:** Bernardino Rosario/Raymond Abreu.

Garcia rocketed though the system in 2004 after a conversion to the bullpen, beginning the year at Low A Kane County and reaching Oakland by August. He continued to pile up strikeouts in 2005 but was dogged by inconsistency, including two blown saves in the Triple-A Pacific Coast League playoffs. Garcia's stuff is closer-worthy. He has an upper-90s fastball with plenty of movement and a plus-plus slider with late break that one scout describes as bordering on illegal. He's aggressive with both pitches and likes to pitch inside. He also has a solid changeup. Garcia still can be plagued by command problems at times. He can get flustered on the mound, beginning to nibble at the corners when struggling to throw strikes. While Huston Street is clearly the closer at the big league level for years to come, Garcia could give Oakland a devastating 1-2 punch in the bullpen. He'll return to Triple-A to begin the season, as the A's want his next callup to the bigs be his last.

Year	Club (League)	Class	W	L	ERA	G	GS	CG	SV	IP	H	R	ER	HR	BB	SO	AVG
2000	Athletics East (DSL)	R	6	2	3.26	11	10	0	0	47	33	24	17	2	29	56	.189
2001	Athletics (AZL)	R	4	2	2.85	12	7	0	0	47	37	19	15	2	6	50	.214
2002	Athletics (AZL)	R	2	1	2.44	13	8	0	1	59	56	24	16	5	17	66	.258
	Vancouver (NWL)	A	0	3	7.32	3	3	0	0	12	15	11	10	1	7	16	.300
2003	Kane County (Mid)	A	0	1	2.55	14	9	0	0	42	40	14	12	0	19	28	.250
2004	Kane County (Mid)	A	1	0	0.30	25	0	0	16	30	16	2	1	0	6	49	.150
	Midland (TL)	AA	2	0	1.50	13	0	0	2	18	10	3	3	0	15	32	.156
	Sacramento (PCL)	AAA	1	2	3.94	11	0	0	1	14	10	6	6	1	9	21	.196
	Oakland (AL)	MLB	0	0	12.63	4	0	0	0	6	5	8	8	3	9	5	.227
2005	Midland (TL)	AA	0	0	1.08	10	0	0	6	17	9	3	2	1	9	30	.153
	Sacramento (PCL)	AAA	3	6	4.47	44	0	0	20	48	45	30	24	6	20	73	.239
	Oakland (AL)	MLB	0	0	3.00	3	0	0	0	3	2	1	1	0	1	1	.182
MAJOR LEAGUE TOTALS			0	0	9.35	7	0	0	0	9	7	9	9	3	10	6	.212
MINOR LEAGUE TOTALS			19	17	2.85	156	37	0	46	335	271	136	106	18	137	421	.218

8 CRAIG ITALIANO

RHP

Born: July 22, 1986. **B-T:** R-R. **Ht.:** 6-3. **Wt.:** 190. **Drafted:** HS—Flower Mound, Texas, 2005 (2nd round). **Signed by:** Blake Davis.

Italiano showed more velocity than any pitcher in the 2005 draft, but a bout with shoulder inflammation and questionable mechanics dropped him to the second round. The A's took him, the first of six high school pitchers they took with their next seven picks, and signed him for $725,500. Italiano's fastball immediately became the best in Oakland's system, sitting at 93-95 mph in the Rookie-level Arizona League and touching 96. His heater peaked at 98 in high school. He has refined his slurvy breaking ball into a true slider, which could become a plus pitch. Italiano short-arms the ball and has a maximum-effort delivery, leaving many concerned about his long-term health and projecting him as more of a power reliever. He rarely has thrown a changeup, and his fastball can be a little too straight at times. Italiano will join fellow 2005 draftees Jared Lansford and Vince Mazzaro to create that rarest of happenings in the Oakland system—a low Class A rotation consisting mostly of teenagers. While his future may be in the bullpen, the A's will give him every chance to use his overpowering stuff as a starter.

Year	Club (League)	Class	W	L	ERA	G	GS	CG	SV	IP	H	R	ER	HR	BB	SO	AVG
2005	Athletics (AZL)	R	1	2	6.74	8	3	0	0	19	20	17	14	0	8	27	.267
MINOR LEAGUE TOTALS			1	2	6.74	8	3	0	0	19	20	17	14	0	8	27	.267

9 SHANE KOMINE

RHP

Born: Oct. 18, 1980. **B-T:** R-R. **Ht.:** 5-9. **Wt.:** 175. **Drafted:** Nebraska, 2002 (9th round). **Signed by:** Jim Pransky.

A native of Hawaii, Komine helped put Nebraska's baseball program on the map. He led the Cornhuskers to back-to-back College World Series appearances while going undefeated as a senior in 2002. A heavy college workload resulted in back and shoulder woes, and Komine required Tommy John surgery in mid-2004. He returned last year to dominate in the Texas League playoffs and wow scouts in the Arizona Fall League. Komine has a full arsenal of pitches, starting with a low-90s fastball and a knee-buckling curveball that's his primary out pitch. He also mixes in a slider and change-up. He knows how to set up hitters and has outstanding makeup. Size and health are Komine's biggest obstacles. His listed height of 5-foot-9 may be generous, but he still does a good job of staying on top of his pitches. Whether he has the durability to be a starter remains questionable, though he would make a useful long reliever. Komine will start the year in the Triple-A rotation, but should be on the short list for a callup should the opportunity arise in Oakland. His first taste of the big leagues could come in the bullpen.

Year	Club (League)	Class	W	L	ERA	G	GS	CG	SV	IP	H	R	ER	HR	BB	SO	AVG
2002	Visalia (Cal)	A	1	3	5.95	18	0	0	0	26	23	20	17	2	20	22	.240
2003	Kane County (Mid)	A	6	0	1.82	8	8	1	0	54	45	12	11	1	9	50	.223
	Midland (TL)	AA	4	6	3.75	19	18	1	0	103	108	51	43	6	30	75	.271
2004	Midland (TL)	AA	4	5	4.77	17	17	0	0	94	103	56	50	10	28	65	.281
2005	Athletics (AZL)	R	0	1	9.76	4	4	0	0	8	10	10	9	0	7	11	.294
	Stockton (Cal)	A	0	0	4.14	2	2	0	0	9	10	4	4	0	3	11	.294
	Midland (TL)	AA	2	1	3.16	5	5	0	0	31	27	12	11	5	7	33	.235
MINOR LEAGUE TOTALS			17	16	4.00	73	54	2	0	326	326	165	145	24	104	267	.261

10 VINCE MAZZARO RHP

BILL MITCHELL

Born: Sept. 27, 1986. **B-T:** R-R. **Ht.:** 6-2. **Wt.:** 190. **Drafted:** HS—Rutherford, N.J., 2005 (3rd round). **Signed by:** Jeff Bittiger.

After selecting a pair of high school righthanders in the second round of the 2005 draft, the A's took another in the third with Mazzaro. They paid him a $380,000 bonus to sway him away from pitching at St. John's. While he signed too late to make his pro debut, he outpitched both second-rounders Craig Italiano and Jared Lansford in instructional league. Mazarro's lively, sinking fastball sits at 88-91 mph can touch 94. His corkscrew delivery and high three-quarters arm slot offer plenty of deception. He throws a power curveball with good break. While his makeup was questioned by some in high school, Oakland praises his work ethic. Mazzaro throws across his body, which hurts his control and could pose a long-term health risk. Like many young pitchers, he never really has needed a changeup, so it still ranks well behind his sinker and curveball. Mazzaro's performance in instructional league surprised even the A's, who think he's ready for full-season ball. He'll make his pro debut as a 19-year-old in low Class A.

Year	Club (League)	Class	W	L	ERA	G	GS	CG	SV	IP	H	R	ER	HR	BB	SO	AVG
2005	Did not play—Signed 2006 contract																

11 KURT SUZUKI C

Born: Oct. 4, 1983. **B-T:** R-R. **Ht.:** 6-1. **Wt.:** 200. **Drafted:** Cal State Fullerton, 2004 (2nd round). **Signed by:** Randy Johnson.

Suzuki capped his Cal State Fullerton career in style, hitting .413-16-87 to earn All-America honors and delivering the championship-winning hit at the 2004 College World Series. He was slated to begin 2005 in low Class A until Landon Powell tore up his left knee in January. Bumped to high Class A, Suzuki delivered a solid performance in his first full pro season. Suzuki's offensive abilities are above-average for a catcher. He has a short, level swing and makes consistent contact. He works the count well and has occasional power. Defensively, he has an average arm and threw out 37 percent of basestealers last year. While his throwing is fine, Suzuki needs work on the rest of his defensive game, such as blocking balls and framing pitches. Though his effort and leadership skills are universally praised, he can be a little too headstrong at times. He'll argue with umpires, which doesn't help his pitchers' cause, and visibly shows frustration with poor play by himself or others. Most observers agree Suzuki will reach the majors, but whether it will be as a starter or back-up is still a question. Clearly the top catching prospect in the system, he moves up to Double-A this year.

Year	Club (League)	Class	AVG	G	AB	R	H	2B	3B	HR	RBI	BB	SO	SB	OBP	SLG
2004	Vancouver (NWL)	A	.297	46	175	27	52	10	3	3	31	18	26	0	.394	.440
2005	Stockton (Cal)	A	.277	114	441	85	122	26	5	12	65	63	61	5	.378	.440
MINOR LEAGUE TOTALS			.282	160	616	112	174	36	8	15	96	81	87	5	.383	.440

12 JARED LANSFORD RHP

Born: Oct. 22, 1986. **B-T:** R-R. **Ht.:** 6-2. **Wt.:** 190. **Drafted:** HS—Santa Clara, Calif., 2005 (2nd round). **Signed by:** Scott Kidd.

Lansford's father Carney played in the majors for 15 years, including 10 with Oakland, and his uncles Phil and Jose were first-round picks. Carney indicated to most teams that Jared was only interested in beginning his pro career as a position player, but the A's correctly gauged his willingness to sign as a pitcher and selected him in the second round in June. Signed for $525,000, Lansford has a low-90s fastball that can touch 94, as well as a solid breaking ball and developing changeup. He commands all of his offerings well and shows a mature understanding of his craft, not surprising for a teenager who has spent much of his life exposed to the pro game. Lansford isn't overly physical and is more of a hard worker getting the most out of good stuff than a young arm who offers a lot of projection. He's slated to join fellow 2005 draftees Craig Italiano and Vince Mazzaro in the low Class A rotation.

Year	Club (League)	Class	W	L	ERA	G	GS	CG	SV	IP	H	R	ER	HR	BB	SO	AVG
2005	Athletics (AZL)	R	0	1	1.27	7	6	0	0	21	16	4	3	0	5	20	.216
MINOR LEAGUE TOTALS			0	1	1.27	7	6	0	0	21	16	4	3	0	5	20	.216

13 RICHIE ROBNETT · OF

Born: Sept. 17, 1983. **B-T:** L-L. **Ht.:** 5-10. **Wt.:** 190. **Drafted:** Fresno State, 2004 (1st round). **Signed by:** Scott Kidd.

Robnett received the top bonus ($1.325 million) of any A's 2004 draftee and also got an invite to big league camp, but his first full pro season was a mixed bag as he racked up 40 more strikeouts than hits. He was slowed early by a hamstring problem that kept him from getting into a rhythm. He made some adjustments in the second half, leading to 14 home runs in his last 60 games. Robnett offers one of the best packages of tools among Oakland farmhands. Compact and muscular, he has tremendous bat speed and above-average power, but he needs to make more contact and work the count better to take advantage of it. He has the athleticism to play center field and the arm for right, but he still needs work at both positions because of bad jumps and poor routes. He's an above-average runner, though he already has lost a step since college. The A's were happy with the improvement Robnett made during instructional league and believe he's close to breaking through. He'll likely return to high Class A in 2006.

Year	Club (League)	Class	AVG	G	AB	R	H	2B	3B	HR	RBI	BB	SO	SB	OBP	SLG
2004	Vancouver (NWL)	A	.299	43	164	26	49	14	1	4	36	28	43	1	.395	.470
2005	Stockton (Cal)	A	.243	115	457	77	111	30	0	20	74	56	151	8	.324	.440
MINOR LEAGUE TOTALS			.258	158	621	103	160	44	1	24	110	84	194	9	.344	.448

14 DANNY PUTNAM · OF

Born: Sept. 17, 1982. **B-T:** L-L. **Ht.:** 5-11. **Wt.:** 195. **Drafted:** Stanford, 2004 (1st round). **Signed by:** Scott Kidd.

Like Kurt Suzuki and Richie Robnett, Putnam was a 2004 draft from a premier college program whom the A's felt comfortable sending to high Class A for his first full season. He responded to being pushed by leading Stockton in runs, hits and RBIs. That earned him a promotion to Double-A for the Texas League playoffs, during which he hit .314 in nine games. He made a much better impression than he did in his pro debut. A Stanford product, Putnam played his high school ball at San Diego powerhouse Rancho Bernardo. Coached by Sam Blalock (Oakland GM Billy Beane's high school coach at San Diego's Mount Carmel), Rancho has produced six first-round picks since 1995 (counting Putnam) as well as Hank Blalock. Blessed with natural hitting ability, Putnam has a good approach, a quick bat and tremendous hand-eye coordination. He consistently drives the ball to all fields. The question is whether he'll produce enough to profile as an every day left fielder. His power is no more than average and he's limited to an outfield corner or first base because of a lack of speed and a below-average arm. Short and squat, Putnam will need to pay better attention to his conditioning as he matures. His swing has a lot of moving parts, but it has worked well for him so far. His showing this year in Double-A will help the A's determine if his future is as a starter or as a solid bench bat.

Year	Club (League)	Class	AVG	G	AB	R	H	2B	3B	HR	RBI	BB	SO	SB	OBP	SLG
2004	Vancouver (NWL)	A	.289	11	38	10	11	2	0	2	3	14	8	1	.481	.500
	Kane County (Mid)	A	.219	49	160	29	35	5	2	7	27	29	40	0	.347	.406
2005	Stockton (Cal)	A	.307	131	514	97	158	37	3	15	100	66	92	1	.388	.479
MINOR LEAGUE TOTALS			.287	191	712	136	204	44	5	24	130	109	140	2	.384	.463

15 JASON WINDSOR · RHP

Born: July 16, 1982. **B-T:** R-R. **Ht.:** 6-2. **Wt.:** 209. **Drafted:** Cal State Fullerton, 2004 (3rd round). **Signed by:** Randy Johnson.

Windsor signed for $270,000 as a 2004 third-round pick after pitching Cal State Fullerton to a College World Series title, capping a 24-6, 1.82 two-year career with the Titans. Though he reached Double-A in his first full season, Windsor was plagued by inconsistency and biceps tendinitis, which ended his year in early August. Windsor's pinpoint command and ability to set up hitters make up for his fringe-average stuff. His fastball sits at only 85-87 mph and touches 90 only occasionally, but he spots it well in all four quadrants of the strike zone and can add cutting movement to it. He throws a big-breaking curveball for strikes and mixes in a slider. His out pitch is a plus-plus changeup that's capable of making hitters look foolish. Because he can't overpower hitters, Windsor is forced to pitch backwards, which proved to be a challenge against more experienced hitters in Double-A. Unless he regains the consistent 89-90 mph fastball velocity he showed in college, he projects as no more than a back-of-the-rotation starter or long reliever, though few doubt his ability to get to the majors. Windsor will begin 2006 back in Double-A.

Year	Club (League)	Class	W	L	ERA	G	GS	CG	SV	IP	H	R	ER	HR	BB	SO	AVG
2004	Vancouver (NWL)	A	0	0	0.00	4	0	0	1	5	4	0	0	0	0	5	.211
	Kane County (Mid)	A	1	0	2.77	9	0	0	3	13	11	4	4	0	5	13	.220
2005	Stockton (Cal)	A	2	2	3.58	10	10	0	0	55	52	28	22	5	8	64	.244
	Midland (TL)	AA	3	6	5.71	11	11	0	0	57	69	40	36	5	23	39	.303
MINOR LEAGUE TOTALS			6	8	4.29	34	21	0	4	130	136	72	62	10	36	121	.267

16 GREGORIO PETIT INF

Born: Dec. 10, 1984. **B-T:** R-R. **Ht.:** 5-10. **Wt.:** 160. **Signed:** Venezuela, 2001. **Signed by:** Julio Franco.

Petit wowed Northwest League observers with his defensive prowess at shortstop in 2004, but he got off to a slow start in low Class A last year and missed a month with a fractured finger on his throwing hand. Moved to second base in the second half to accommodate first-round pick Cliff Pennington, Petit came alive with the bat, hitting .305 in the final three months. A good athlete with too much power for his own good, he finally responded to the organization's pleas to use the whole field. He still can turn on mistakes, but no longer tries to jerk every pitch and makes much more consistent contact. Already a plus defender at shortstop, Petit showed little trouble in moving to the other side of the bag and even impressed in some spot starts at third base. He doesn't have the power or on-base skills to profile as a top-of-the-order presence, but with his defensive skills and offensive potential, he has enough tools to emerge as a big league regular. Now on the same development path as Cliff Pennington, he'll stay at second base for now as they both move up to high Class A.

Year	Club (League)	Class	AVG	G	AB	R	H	2B	3B	HR	RBI	BB	SO	SB	OBP	SLG
2002	Athletics West (DSL)	R	.280	63	218	44	61	11	5	1	21	39	44	5	.392	.390
2003	Athletics (AZL)	R	.265	32	117	13	31	6	0	0	12	10	22	3	.323	.316
2004	Vancouver (NWL)	A	.256	68	254	34	65	9	2	4	35	20	67	3	.315	.354
2005	Kane County (Mid)	A	.289	87	287	55	83	10	4	9	33	26	44	8	.349	.446
MINOR LEAGUE TOTALS			.274	250	876	146	240	36	11	14	101	95	177	19	.348	.388

17 JUSTIN SELLERS SS

Born: Feb. 1, 1986. **B-T:** R-R. **Ht.:** 5-10. **Wt.:** 160. **Drafted:** HS--Huntington Beach, Calif., 2005 (6th round). **Signed by:** Randy Johnson.

The son of former big league pitcher Jeff Sellers, Justin played at Marina High (Huntington Beach, Calif.) with top A's prospect Daric Barton. Marina also has produced big leaguers Kevin Elster, Marc Newfield, Steve Springer and Craig Wilson. Sellers' tools and feel for the game impressed many teams, but his lack of size dropped the Cal State Fullerton recruit to the sixth round. One A's official insists that if Sellers were even 6 feet tall, he could have been a late first-round pick. Signed for $150,000, he's fluid in all aspects of the game. He has a smooth, level swing that allows him to hit for a high average. A baseball rat with fantastic instincts, he's an excellent defender with good range to both sides and solid arm strength. He's also an above-average runner. Sellers isn't expected to fill out much because he has a small frame, and he offers little in the way of power. Oakland has worked with him to tame his approach at the plate and help him with his transition from metal to wood bat. With a good spring, he'll be the everyday shortstop in low Class A.

Year	Club (League)	Class	AVG	G	AB	R	H	2B	3B	HR	RBI	BB	SO	SB	OBP	SLG
2005	Vancouver (NWL)	A	.274	47	175	31	48	8	1	0	13	19	24	8	.369	.331
MINOR LEAGUE TOTALS			.274	47	175	31	48	8	1	0	13	19	24	8	.369	.331

18 JIMMY SHULL

RHP

Born: Aug. 21, 1983. **B-T:** R-R. **Ht.:** 6-2. **Wt.:** 185. **Drafted:** Cal Poly, 2005 (4th round). **Signed by:** Rick Magnante.

Shull was an eighth-round pick for the Diamondbacks in 2004, but returned to Cal Poly in an attempt to improve his draft stock. The gambit paid off as Shull found a couple extra ticks on his fastball and was the first college pitcher Oakland drafted in 2005, a fourth-rounder who received a $120,000 bonus. He led a successful short-season Vancouver staff in strikeouts in his pro debut. Shull has excellent command of an 89-92 mph sinker that can touch 94, but his best pitch is a plus slider that gives righthanders fits. His changeup is a work in progress, though it could become an average pitch. Shull can be a victim of his own command at times, becoming overly focused on throwing strikes and leaving too many hittable pitches over the plate. He has to learn he can afford to set up hitters a little better or try to lure them into chasing sliders out of the zone. Because he played four years of college ball, the A's believe Shull is ready for high Class A in his first full pro season.

Year	Club (League)	Class	W	L	ERA	G	GS	CG	SV	IP	H	R	ER	HR	BB	SO	AVG
2005	Vancouver (NWL)	A	4	3	2.47	14	13	0	0	73	65	25	20	3	10	81	.233
MINOR LEAGUE TOTALS			4	3	2.47	14	13	0	0	73	65	25	20	3	10	81	.233

19 DALLAS BRADEN

LHP

Born: Aug. 13, 1983. **B-T:** L-L. **Ht.:** 6-1. **Wt.:** 180. **Drafted:** Texas Tech, 2004 (24th round). **Signed by:** Blake Davis.

Braden grew up in Stockton and played college ball at Texas Tech, not too far from Midland. He played at both stops in 2005, his first full pro season after signing as a 24th-round pick the year before. He quickly merited his promotion to Double-A after recording four consecutive double-digit strikeout games in high Class A. The jump proved to be much more of a challenge for Braden, who was shut down in August with a tired arm. He gets hitters out with guile, command and a trick pitch. His screwball features so much break and deception that less-advanced hitters had no idea how to hit it. Unfortunately for Braden, it's his only above-average pitch. His fastball sits in the mid-80s and can touch 89, and he mixes in a below-average slider and a decent changeup. More advanced hitters were disciplined enough to lay off his breaking stuff and wait for his fastball, so he'll have to find a way to keep more patient hitters more off balance. He'll begin 2006 back in Double-A.

Year	Club (League)	Class	W	L	ERA	G	GS	CG	SV	IP	H	R	ER	HR	BB	SO	AVG
2004	Vancouver (NWL)	A	2	0	2.76	7	0	0	2	16	15	7	5	1	3	26	.250
	Kane County (Mid)	A	2	1	4.70	5	5	0	0	23	22	13	12	2	6	33	.242
2005	Stockton (Cal)	A	6	0	2.68	7	7	1	0	44	31	14	13	4	11	64	.201
	Midland (TL)	AA	9	5	3.90	16	16	0	0	97	104	43	42	5	32	71	.281
MINOR LEAGUE TOTALS			19	6	3.60	35	28	1	2	180	172	77	72	12	52	194	.255

20 LANDON POWELL

C

Born: March 19, 1982. **B-T:** B-R. **Ht.:** 6-3. **Wt.:** 235. **Drafted:** South Carolina, 2004 (1st round). **Signed by:** Michael Holmes.

Powell had two draft dramas earlier in his career. In high school, advised by Scott Boras, he took the GED and became the first prep junior to enter the draft. Teams were hazy on his draft eligibility, and he became a free agent when he went unpicked in 2000. No club met his price, so he attended South Carolina. He had lofty draft aspirations as a junior in 2003, but a lackluster season dropped him to the Cubs in the 25th round. He performed better as a senior, and the A's made him their top draft pick (24th overall) in 2004, signing him for $1 million. Slated to begin 2005 in high Class A, he missed the entire season after tearing the anterior cruciate ligament in his left knee while working out in January. He wasn't ready to catch or run in instructional league, but should be ready to start 2006 at Stockton. Powell offers power potential from both sides of the plate while drawing a good share of walks. He has plus arm strength and is surprisingly nimble for his size behind the plate. Already a well-below-average runner, Powell could be an absolute baseclogger after knee surgery. His weight, always a concern, was up to 270 pounds in the fall, and the A's want him at 240-250 pounds like he was as a college player.

Year	Club (League)	Class	AVG	G	AB	R	H	2B	3B	HR	RBI	BB	SO	SB	OBP	SLG
2004	Vancover (NWL)	A	.244	38	135	24	33	6	1	3	19	26	22	0	.368	.370
2005	Did not play—Injured															
MINOR LEAGUE TOTALS			.244	38	135	24	33	6	1	3	19	26	22	0	.368	.370

21 DAN MEYER
LHP

Born: July 3, 1981. **B-T:** R-L. **Ht.:** 6-3. **Wt.:** 210. **Drafted:** James Madison, 2002 (1st round). **Signed by:** J.J. Picollo (Braves).

Considered the key to the offseason Tim Hudson deal with the Braves, Meyer was expected to immediately step into the big league rotation and contribute. Considered the top left-handed pitching prospect in Triple-A in 2004, he couldn't have been a bigger disappointment. He posted a 7.78 ERA in big league camp and a 5.36 ERA in Triple-A—nearly double his previous career mark. Worse yet, he batted season-long shoulder soreness that never was fully explained. Meyer was the system's biggest enigma, as every aspect of his game took a significant step backwards. Armed with a 91-94 mph fastball in 2004, he rarely hit 90 after the trade. His slider went from a plus pitch to a flat, easily hittable offering. Mechanically, Meyer became unhinged, flying open on nearly every pitch and landing sloppily on his front foot. In less than six months, he went from a projected middle-of-the-rotation starter to a pitcher who couldn't retire minor leaguers with any consistency. The A's aren't sure what to expect from Meyer at this point, but they'd be happy if he could just get 100 percent healthy so they can assign him to Triple-A in an attempt to rediscover his stuff.

Year	Club (League)	Class	W	L	ERA	G	GS	CG	SV	IP	H	R	ER	HR	BB	SO	AVG
2002	Danville (Appy)	R	3	3	2.74	13	13	1	0	66	47	22	20	4	18	77	.198
2003	Rome (SAL)	A	4	4	2.86	15	15	0	0	82	76	35	26	6	15	95	.248
	Myrtle Beach (Car)	A	3	6	2.87	13	13	0	0	78	69	29	25	7	17	63	.236
2004	Greenville (SL)	AA	6	3	2.22	14	13	0	0	65	50	17	16	1	12	86	.216
	Richmond (IL)	AAA	3	3	2.79	12	11	0	0	61	62	23	19	6	25	60	.270
	Atlanta (NL)	MLB	0	0	0.00	2	0	0	0	2	2	0	0	0	1	1	.286
2005	Sacramento (PCL)	AAA	2	8	5.36	19	17	0	0	89	101	64	53	15	43	63	.286
MAJOR LEAGUE TOTALS			0	0	0.00	2	0	0	0	2	2	0	0	0	1	1	.286
MINOR LEAGUE TOTALS			21	27	3.24	86	82	1	0	441	405	190	159	39	130	444	.245

22 JASON RAY
RHP

Born: July 14, 1984. **B-T:** R-R. **Ht.:** 5-11. **Wt.:** 195. **Drafted:** Azusa Pacific (Calif.), 2005 (8th round). **Signed by:** Randy Johnson.

Ray began his college career as a right fielder at San Diego City College, but his arm strength led to an experiment on the mound in his second year. He fired low-90s fastballs and showed a surprisingly effective curveball. Ray transferred to Azusa Pacific (Calif.) as a junior in 2005, becoming a full-time pitcher and seeing his stuff take another step forward. The A's took him in the eighth round—making him the third-highest pick in school history, behind big leaguers Paul Moskau and Jeff Robinson—and signed him for $70,000. Ray struck out nearly two men per inning in his pro debut, including a run of 32 strikeouts over 14 innings in his final 10 games. He has two plus pitches, a 93-95 mph fastball and a big-breaking power curve. Because of his lack of time on the mound, Ray remains extremely raw for a pitcher with college experience. His mechanics are complicated and his control is spotty. He's also on the small side, so his fastball lacks much downward plane. Oakland is excited about Ray's potential but sees him as a reliever only. He'll begin the year in Class A.

Year	Club (League)	Class	W	L	ERA	G	GS	CG	SV	IP	H	R	ER	HR	BB	SO	AVG
2005	Vancouver (NWL)	A	0	1	2.12	20	0	0	0	30	17	8	7	1	23	56	.163
MINOR LEAGUE TOTALS			0	1	2.12	20	0	0	0	30	17	8	7	1	23	56	.163

23 BRANT COLAMARINO
1B

Born: Dec. 4, 1980. **B-T:** L-L. **Ht.:** 5-10. **Wt.:** 221. **Drafted:** Pittsburgh, 2002 (7th round). **Signed by:** Tom Clark.

After a disappointing full-season debut in 2003, Colamarino got into the best shape of his life and had a breakout campaign in 2004. He started strong in Double-A in 2005 but was unable to replicate his success in Triple-A, where he hit just .194 with one home run in his final 25 games. Colamarino has as much in-game power as any player in the system, thanks to a compact swing and tremendous natural strength. He's also the organization's top defensive first baseman, with soft hands and good reactions. Colamarino lost confidence in his abilities at Triple-A and began to press, leading to a pull-conscious approach that left him highly susceptible to good lefties. He's a well below-average runner. Colamarino had surgery on his non-throwing shoulder in the offseason, but is expected to be healthy by the start of spring training. Blocked by an organizational glut of players limited to first base or DH, he'll give Triple-A another shot in 2006.

Year	Club (League)	Class	AVG	G	AB	R	H	2B	3B	HR	RBI	BB	SO	SB	OBP	SLG
2002	Vancouver (NWL)	A	.259	67	228	30	59	6	2	6	41	27	54	3	.348	.382
2003	Kane County (Mid)	A	.259	133	498	68	129	26	0	19	80	59	101	1	.350	.426
2004	Modesto (Cal)	A	.355	50	183	41	65	8	2	11	41	28	23	1	.450	.601
	Midland (TL)	AA	.273	77	304	39	83	22	2	8	50	27	61	0	.333	.438
2005	Midland (TL)	AA	.321	46	187	31	60	13	4	10	45	18	34	0	.377	.594
	Sacramento (PCL)	AAA	.243	74	280	37	68	15	3	11	47	19	76	0	.297	.436
MINOR LEAGUE TOTALS			.276	447	1680	246	464	90	13	65	304	178	349	5	.353	.461

24 CONNOR ROBERTSON
RHP

Born: Sept. 10, 1981. **B-T:** R-R. **Ht.:** 6-3. **Wt.:** 215. **Drafted:** Birmingham-Southern, 2004 (31st round). **Signed by:** Steve Barningham.

Robertson was an offensive star at Birmingham-Southern, finishing his four-year career as the school's all-time leader in home runs (60) and RBIs (239). He also led the Panthers to the NAIA national championship as a freshman, winning MVP honors at the NAIA World Series and homering in the title game. He pitched just six innings in his first three years of college, but he became Birmingham-Southern's closer as senior and tied a school record with nine saves. In 2005, his first full season as a pitcher, Robertson averaged 14.4 strikeouts per nine innings and reached Triple-A briefly. His method of success, like his career path, has been unconventional. He throws an 88-92 mph sinker and a decent slider, and both pitches are very difficult to pick up. He turns to the side in his delivery, all but completely blocking his arm from the hitter's view, while a lightning-quick release adds to his deception. At 24, he's still a bit raw as a pitcher and needs to throw more strikes. He's expected to open 2006 in Double-A and could be a part of the Oakland bullpen in 2007 if his success continues.

Year	Club (League)	Class	W	L	ERA	G	GS	CG	SV	IP	H	R	ER	HR	BB	SO	AVG
2004	Athletics (AZL)	R	2	2	0.92	25	0	0	13	29	17	8	3	2	8	46	.157
	Vancouver (NWL)	A	0	0	3.60	3	0	0	0	5	4	2	2	1	2	5	.211
2005	Kane County (Mid)	A	2	2	2.92	20	0	0	1	28	23	10	9	0	14	47	.232
	Sacramento (PCL)	AAA	0	0	1.80	3	0	0	0	5	2	1	1	0	3	5	.118
	Stockton (Cal)	A	5	2	2.77	32	0	0	1	42	37	17	13	1	23	68	.228
MINOR LEAGUE TOTALS			9	6	2.30	83	0	0	15	109	83	38	28	4	50	171	.205

25 BRIAN STAVISKY
OF

Born: July 6, 1980. **B-T:** L-R. **Ht.:** 6-2. **Wt.:** 210. **Drafted:** Notre Dame, 2002 (6th round). **Signed by:** Rich Sparks.

Stavisky starred at Notre Dame and hit a game-winning homer to eliminate Rice in the 2002 College World Series. He has put together a solid pro career so far, winning high Class A California League MVP honors in 2004 and finishing third in the Texas League in RBIs and on-base percentage last season. Stavisky has excellent pitch recognition and a good feel for contact to go along with average power. He's maniacal in his preparation and a leader in the clubhouse, with some pointing to him as the key influence in Andre Ethier's turnaround. Stavisky isn't athletic, so his on-field value consists entirely of what he can provide with the bat. He's a poor runner and very stiff mechanically. While he hits the ball hard consistently, he has never learned to add loft to his swing, limiting his home run power. He has made some strides in the outfield, but is still well below average and has an arm that rates a 20 on the 20-80 scouting scale. The A's believe his offense alone can get him to the majors, and they'll send him to Triple-A this year.

Year	Club (League)	Class	AVG	G	AB	R	H	2B	3B	HR	RBI	BB	SO	SB	OBP	SLG
2002	Vancouver (NWL)	A	.294	32	102	12	30	10	1	1	15	15	30	5	.407	.441
2003	Kane County (Mid)	A	.266	98	331	54	88	20	2	6	35	62	74	4	.396	.393
2004	Modesto (Cal)	A	.343	130	513	108	176	39	5	19	83	54	89	6	.413	.550
2005	Midland (TL)	AA	.316	135	510	84	161	36	6	11	88	69	84	0	.398	.475
MINOR LEAGUE TOTALS			.313	395	1456	258	455	105	14	37	221	200	277	15	.403	.480

26 FREDDIE BYNUM
OF/SS

Born: March 15, 1980. **B-T:** L-R. **Ht.:** 6-1. **Wt.:** 180. **Drafted:** Pitt County (N.C.) CC, 2000 (2nd round). **Signed by:** Billy Owens.

The A's top pick (second round) in 2000, Bynum has taken a slow, steady path through the system. While his 2005 season was delayed by lingering problems from a blood clot near his ribcage that required offseason surgery, he made his big league debut in September. Though he may not have enough offensive firepower to be an everyday player, Bynum remains one of the top athletes in the system. He's a line-drive hitter with decent plate discipline and the speed to be a disruptive force on the basepaths. Oakland has been grooming him as a super-sub the last two years, giving him time at second base, shortstop, third base and the outfield. While he has the athleticism to play almost anywhere on the field, he's still erratic, even at his original position of shortstop. His winter season in the Dominican Republic was cut short by another blood clot, but assuming he can put that behind him, he'll get a shot at a bench job in spring training.

Year	Club (League)	Class	AVG	G	AB	R	H	2B	3B	HR	RBI	BB	SO	SB	OBP	SLG
2000	Vancouver (NWL)	A	.256	72	281	52	72	10	1	1	26	31	58	22	.341	.310
2001	Modesto (Cal)	A	.261	120	440	59	115	19	7	2	46	41	95	28	.325	.350
2002	Visalia (Cal)	A	.306	135	539	83	165	26	5	3	56	64	116	41	.385	.390
2003	Midland (TL)	AA	.263	132	510	84	134	18	9	5	58	56	135	22	.344	.363
2004	Midland (TL)	AA	.268	65	265	38	71	13	4	1	22	24	56	18	.332	.358
	Sacramento (PCL)	AAA	.283	66	258	42	73	11	2	2	26	19	61	21	.339	.364
2005	Sacramento (PCL)	AAA	.278	102	378	56	105	16	9	2	40	38	83	23	.347	.384
	Oakland (AL)	MLB	.286	7	7	0	2	1	0	0	1	0	3	0	.286	.429
MAJOR LEAGUE TOTALS			.286	7	7	0	2	1	0	0	1	0	3	0	.286	.429
MINOR LEAGUE TOTALS			.275	692	2671	414	735	113	37	16	274	273	604	175	.348	.363

27 JOHN RHEINECKER   LHP

Born: May 29, 1979. **B-T:** L-L. **Ht.:** 6-2. **Wt.:** 215. **Drafted:** Southwest Missouri State, 2001 (1st round). **Signed by:** Jim Pransky.

Rheinecker ranked No. 2 on this list entering 2003, but his command and consistency have slipped since. He seemed to be getting back on track in Triple-A last year, going at least seven innings while allowing no more than two earned runs in six of his seven starts. But then he came down with a mysterious finger injury that prevented him from pitching again in 2005. An irritation in the second joint of his left middle finger on his throwing hand originally was expected to cost him just a few weeks, but the pain never subsided. Even at the end of the season, Rheinecker was unable to even grip a baseball. He began testing the finger on a very light throwing program in instructional league, but it still bothered him, albeit to a lesser extent. At his best, Rheinecker is a crafty lefthander with good stuff. He gets plenty of movement on an 88-90 mph fastball and mixes in a cutter, a sharp-breaking slider and a usable changeup. He usually throws strikes, though he can be around the zone too much and very hittable because his stuff isn't overpowering. The A's hope he'll be fully healed by spring training and able to build on his early 2005 success when he returns to Triple-A.

Year	Club (League)	Class	W	L	ERA	G	GS	CG	SV	IP	H	R	ER	HR	BB	SO	AVG
2001	Vancouver (NWL)	A	0	1	1.59	6	5	0	0	23	13	5	4	0	4	17	.160
	Modesto (Cal)	A	0	1	6.30	2	2	0	0	10	10	7	7	1	5	5	.256
2002	Visalia (Cal)	A	3	0	2.31	9	9	0	0	51	41	16	13	2	10	62	.216
	Midland (TL)	AA	7	7	3.38	20	20	1	0	128	137	63	48	7	24	100	.274
2003	Midland (TL)	AA	9	6	4.74	23	23	1	0	142	186	90	75	13	32	89	.313
	Sacramento (PCL)	AAA	2	0	3.79	6	6	0	0	38	47	19	16	1	12	26	.303
2004	Sacramento (PCL)	AAA	11	9	4.44	28	27	0	0	172	192	102	85	22	51	129	.284
2005	Sacramento (PCL)	AAA	4	0	1.77	7	7	0	0	46	29	15	9	0	14	24	.181
MINOR LEAGUE TOTALS			36	24	3.79	101	99	2	0	610	655	317	257	46	152	452	.273

28 MIKE MADSEN   RHP

Born: Nov. 29, 1982. **B-T:** R-R. **Ht.:** 6-0. **Wt.:** 160. **Drafted:** Ohio State, 2005 (21st round). **Signed by:** Rick Sparks.

Madden had a successful four-year career at Ohio State, going 24-9 overall and starting the 2004 Cape Cod League all-star game. But his small frame turned many scouts off and he wasn't drafted until 2005, when the A's took him in the 21st-round as a bargain-basement senior sign. He won the short-season Northwest League ERA title in his pro debut, allowing two or fewer earned runs in all but one start. While he gets by mostly on command and moxie, Oakland scouting director Eric Kubota describes Madsen's stuff as "anything but late-round pickish." Madsen has an average fastball, sitting at 89-92 mph, as well as a good curveball he throws for strikes at any point in the count. He shows good feel for a changeup that should become an average pitch. Because of his size and age, Madsen offers little in the way of projection. His fastball comes in a little too straight, which could be a problem at higher levels. Because the A's want to get their highly regarded teenage pitchers from the 2005 draft started in the full-season leagues, Madsen most likely will skip a level and begin the season in high Class A.

Year	Club (League)	Class	W	L	ERA	G	GS	CG	SV	IP	H	R	ER	HR	BB	SO	AVG
2005	Vancouver (NWL)	A	6	1	1.69	15	12	0	0	80	56	21	15	2	14	68	.192
MINOR LEAGUE TOTALS			6	1	1.69	15	12	0	0	80	56	21	15	2	14	68	.192

RAMON ALVARADO OF

Born: June 3, 1985. **B-T:** R-R. **Ht.:** 6-1. **Wt.:** 160. **Signed:** Venezuela, 2001. **Signed by:** Julio Franco.

While the A's don't scout Latin America as heavily as other teams, they are excited about a pair of Venezuelan outfielders. Javier Herrera has been turning heads in the United States for three years, while Alvarado made his U.S. debut in 2005 as one of the top power hitters in the Arizona League. He might have won the AZL home run crown had a strained quadriceps not slowed him down in August. Alvarado is still raw, but his tools grade as at least average across the board. Long and lean, he has some juice in his bat, good pitch recognition and enough speed to swipe a few bases. He has a tendency to overswing and get pull-conscious. His arm is above average but his outfield instincts are poor, which may limit him to left field. His performance this spring will determine if he is ready to open the year in low Class A.

Year	Club (League)	Class	AVG	G	AB	R	H	2B	3B	HR	RBI	BB	SO	SB	OBP	SLG
2002	Athletics East (DSL)	R	.276	55	163	19	45	9	3	1	23	17	22	4	.378	.387
2003	Athletics 1 (DSL)	R	.242	43	132	17	32	5	0	2	18	11	22	3	.314	.326
2004	Athletics 1 (DSL)	R	.303	64	195	29	59	12	3	1	27	17	27	7	.379	.410
2005	Athletics (AZL)	R	.296	48	169	37	50	10	3	6	32	23	36	9	.412	.497
MINOR LEAGUE TOTALS			.282	210	659	102	186	36	9	10	100	68	107	23	.375	.410

JEFF BAISLEY 3B

Born: Dec. 19, 1982. **B-T:** R-R. **Ht.:** 6-3. **Wt.:** 210. **Drafted:** South Florida, 2005 (12th round). **Signed by:** Steve Barningham.

The younger brother of righthander Brad Baisley, a 1998 Phillies second-round pick who topped out in Double-A, Jeff attended South Florida, where he started alongside his twin brother Brian. Baisley expected to be drafted as a junior in 2004, but he tried to play through a stress fracture in his left foot and batted just .264. He rebounded to hit .356 with a school-record 26 doubles last spring, which got him drafted in the 12th round. He had a solid pro debut and shined in instructional league, where he earned MVP honors. Baisley's strengths are exactly what the A's like to see in hitters. He has a patient approach at the plate, good contact skills and gap power. While his range at third base is just average, he has soft hands and a plus arm. Baisley may not develop the power to profile as an everyday player at the corner, and at 23 he needs to move quickly through the system. He'll likely begin the year in high Class A, but Oakland would like to get him to high Class A at some point during 2006.

Year	Club (League)	Class	AVG	G	AB	R	H	2B	3B	HR	RBI	BB	SO	SB	OBP	SLG
2005	Vancouver (NWL)	A	.252	61	218	28	55	15	1	6	38	27	27	3	.362	.413
MINOR LEAGUE TOTALS			.252	61	218	28	55	15	1	6	38	27	27	3	.362	.413

PHILADELPHIA
PHILLIES

BY **WILL KIMMEY**

Pushing the eject button on Larry Bowa's managerial career netted the Phillies just two more wins in 2005 than Bowa earned in each of the previous two seasons. Though Philadelphia won 14 of its last 20 games, it still ended up one game behind the Astros in the National League wild-card race.

The 88 wins marked the franchise's most since it advanced to the World Series in 1993 and gave the Phillies three consecutive winning seasons for the first time since 1975-80. But falling short of the playoffs for the eighth straight year cost general manager Ed Wade his job. Team president David Montgomery hired former Blue Jays, Orioles and Mariners GM Pat Gillick as Wade's replacement, passing over in-house candidates Ruben Amaro Jr. and Mike Arbuckle, both assistant GMs.

Gillick inherits a club coming off its best season in a dozen years, highlighted by a number of good individual performances. Jimmy Rollins finished the year on a 36-game hit streak. Double-play partner Chase Utley emerged as a team leader and offensive force. First baseman **Ryan Howard**, the NL rookie of the year, replicated the power production of injured slugger Jim Thome and made Thome expendable. Pat Burrell bounced back with his best season since 2002. Brett Myers developed into a staff ace. Robinson Tejeda and Eude Brito delivered 18 solid starts after injuries to veterans.

Each of those performances came from a player 28 or younger who was originally signed by the Phillies. Factor in catcher Mike Lieberthal, Ryan Madson, Jason

DAVID SCHOFIELD

Michaels and Randy Wolf, and most of the roster is homegrown, a fact not lost on a franchise that's been trying to overtake the Braves, the ultimate homegrown franchise. Though he didn't get the GM job, Arbuckle has helped acquire and/or develop each of those contributors and plenty more in his 13 years in the organization. He became scouting director in 1992, added farm director to his duties in 2000 and became the assistant GM for scouting and player development in 2001.

The system has been thinned out by a lack of draft picks (no club has had fewer picks in the first five rounds since 2000 because of free-agent compensation) and the use of prospects in trades. Each of the Phillies' six U.S.-based minor league affiliates had a losing record in 2005.

"We don't have a lot of top-line guys down there," Arbuckle said. "We've been hurt by not having a lot of picks and we've traded about 20 guys in the last few years to get players like Billy Wagner. Not all 20 were big prospects, but somebody else wanted them, so that says something."

Gillick's first trade added depth to the system. He not only spun Thome to the White Sox for Aaron Rowand while having to pick up just $22 million of the $46 million remaining on Thome's contract, but he also got Chicago to include minor league lefties Gio Gonzalez and Daniel Haigwood.

TOP 30 PROSPECTS

1. Cole Hamels, lhp	16. Carlos Carrasco, rhp
2. Gio Gonzalez, lhp	17. Michael Durant, 1b
3. Greg Golson, of	18. Carlos Ruiz, c
4. Michael Bourn, of	19. J.A. Happ, lhp
5. Scott Mathieson, rhp	20. Jake Blalock, of
6. Daniel Haigwood, lhp	21. Matt Maloney, lhp
7. Welinson Baez, 3b/ss	22. Josh Outman, lhp
8. Mike Costanzo, 3b	23. Louis Marson, c
9. Brad Harman, ss/2b	24. Brett Harker, rhp
10. Jason Jaramillo, c	25. Jeremy Slayden, of
11. Tim Moss, 2b	26. Tim Kennelly, 3b
12. Edgar Garcia, rhp	27. Chris Booker, rhp
13. Chris Roberson, of	28. Kyle Kendrick, rhp
14. Shane Victorino, of	29. Scott Mitchinson, rhp
15. Eude Brito, lhp	30. Yoel Hernandez, rhp

ORGANIZATION OVERVIEW

General manager: Pat Gillick. **Farm director:** Steve Noworyta. **Scouting director:** Marti Wolever.

2005 PERFORMANCE

Class	Team	League	W	L	Pct.	Finish*	Manager
Majors	Philadelphia	National	88	74	.543	4th (16)	Charlie Manuel
Triple-A	Scranton/W-B Red Barons	International	69	75	.479	t-9th (14)	Gene Lamont
Double-A	Reading Phillies	Eastern	69	73	.486	8th (12)	Steve Swisher
High A	Clearwater Threshers	Florida State	41	95	.301	12th (12)	Greg Legg
Low A	Lakewood Blue Claws	South Atlantic	56	83	.403	16th (16)	P.J. Forbes
Short-season	Batavia Muckdogs	New York-Penn	36	39	.480	8th (14)	Manny Amador
Rookie	GCL Phillies	Gulf Coast	24	27	.471	6th (12)	Jim Morrison
OVERALL 2005 MINOR LEAGUE RECORD			295	392	.429	30th (30)	

*Finish in overall standings (No. of teams in league).

ORGANIZATION LEADERS

BATTING   *Minimum 250 at-bats
*AVG   Ruiz, Randy, Reading.................................... .349
R   Victorino, Shane, Scranton.............................. 93
H   Roberson, Chris, Reading............................ 172
TB   Victorino, Shane, Scranton........................ 264
2B   Dzurilla, Michael, Lakewood 33
3B   Victorino, Shane, Scranton.......................... 16
HR   Ruiz, Randy, Reading 27
RBI   Coste, Chris, Scranton 89
     Ruiz, Randy, Reading 89
BB   Orr, Sam, Lakewood 72
SO   Moss, Tim, Clearwater 129
SB   Bourn, Michael, Reading 38
*OBP   Gredvig, Doug, Clearwater/Lakewood .... .413
*SLG   Ruiz, Randy, Reading.................................... .669
PITCHING   #Minimum 75 innings
W   Davis, Allen, Reading/Scranton 14
L   Segovia, Zach, Clearwater 14
     Smith, Mike, Reading/Scranton 14
#ERA   Minix, Travis, Reading/Scranton 1.48
G   Three tied at 58
CG   De la Cruz, Maximino, Lakewood 5
SV   Perez, Franklin, Scranton 23
IP   Davis, Allen, Reading/Scranton 196
BB   Smith, Mike, Reading/Scranton 85
SO   Griffith, Derek, Lakewood 131

BEST TOOLS

Best Hitter for Average .... Brad Harman
Best Power Hitter .... Michael Durant
Best Strike-Zone Discipline .... Michael Bourn
Fastest Baserunner .... Michael Bourn
Best Athlete .... Greg Golson
Best Fastball.. Scott Mathieson
Best Curveball .... Gio Gonzalez
Best Slider .... Daniel Haigwood
Best Changeup .... Cole Hamels
Best Control.. Cole Hamels
Best Defensive Catcher .... Jason Jaramillo
Best Defensive Infielder.............................. Brad Harman
Best Infield Arm .... Welinson Baez
Best Defensive Outfielder .... Michael Bourn
Best Outfield Arm .... Greg Golson

PROJECTED 2009 LINEUP

Catcher... Jason Jaramillo
First Base .... Ryan Howard
Second Base .... Chase Utley
Third Base .... Welinson Baez
Shortstop .... Jimmy Rollins
Left Field .... Pat Burrell
Center Field.. Greg Golson

Right Field.. Bobby Abreu
No. 1 Starter .... Brett Myers
No. 2 Starter .... Cole Hamels
No. 3 Starter .... Randy Wolf
No. 4 Starter .... Gio Gonzalez
No. 5 Starter .... Gavin Floyd
Closer .... Scott Mathieson

LAST YEAR'S TOP 20 PROSPECTS

1. Ryan Howard, 1b
2. Gavin Floyd, rhp
3. Cole Hamels, lhp
4. Greg Golson, of
5. Michael Bourn, of
6. Scott Mathieson, rhp
7. Jake Blalock, of
8. Carlos Carrasco, rhp
9. Edgar Garcia, rhp
10. Scott Mitchinson, rhp
11. Carlos Ruiz, c
12. Chris Roberson, of
13. Jason Jaramillo, c
14. Zach Segovia, rhp
15. Keith Bucktrot, rhp
16. J.A. Happ, lhp
17. Andy Baldwin, rhp
18. Eude Brito, lhp
19. Shane Victorino, of
20. Juan Richardson, 3b

TOP PROSPECTS OF THE DECADE

Year	Player, Pos.	2005 Org.
1996	Scott Rolen, 3b	Cardinals
1997	Scott Rolen, 3b	Cardinals
1998	Ryan Brannan, rhp	Out of baseball
1999	Pat Burrell, 1b	Phillies
2000	Pat Burrell, 1b/of	Phillies
2001	Jimmy Rollins, ss	Phillies
2002	Marlon Byrd, of	Nationals
2003	Gavin Floyd, rhp	Phillies
2004	Cole Hamels, lhp	Phillies
2005	Ryan Howard, 1b	Phillies

TOP DRAFT PICKS OF THE DECADE

Year	Player, Pos.	2005 Org.
1996	Adam Eaton, rhp	Padres
1997	*J.D. Drew, of	Dodgers
1998	Pat Burrell, 1b	Phillies
1999	Brett Myers, rhp	Phillies
2000	Chase Utley, 2b	Phillies
2001	Gavin Floyd, rhp	Phillies
2002	Cole Hamels, lhp	Phillies
2003	Tim Moss, 2b (3rd round)	Phillies
2004	Greg Golson, of	Phillies
2005	Mike Costanzo, 3b (2nd round)	Phillies

*Did not sign.

ALL-TIME LARGEST BONUSES

Gavin Floyd, 2001	$4,200,000
Pat Burrell, 1998	$3,150,000
Brett Myers, 1999	$2,050,000
Cole Hamels, 2002	$2,000,000
Chase Utley, 2000	$1,780,000

MINOR LEAGUE DEPTH CHART

Philadelphia Phillies

Rank: **22**

STRENGTH: Lefthanded pitching. White Sox trade pieces Gio Gonzalez and Daniel Haigwood strengthen an intriguing corps.

WEAKNESS: Power bats. 2005 draftees Mike Costanzo and Jeremy Slayden were needed to shore up this deficiency.

*Depth charts prepared by **John Manuel** and **Chris Kline**. Numbers in parentheses indicate prospect rankings.*

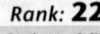

LF
Jake Blalock (20)
Jeremy Slayden (25)
Sean Gamble
Jermaine Williams

CF
Greg Golson (3)
Michael Bourn (4)
Chris Roberson (13)
Shane Victorino (14)

RF
Steve Alexander
Curt Miaso

3B
Welinson Baez (7)
Mike Costanzo (8)
Tim Kennelly (26)
Redne Fuenmayor

SS
Brad Harman (9)
Fidel Hernandez

2B
Tim Moss (11)
Danny Sandoval
Mitch Graham
Cooper Osteen

1B
Michael Durant (17)
Randy Ruiz
Clay Harris
Bryan Hansen

C
Jason Jaramillo (10)
Carlos Ruiz (18)
Louis Marson (23)
Joel Naughton
Tuffy Gosewisch
Aaron Cheesman

RHP	
Starters	**Relievers**
Scott Mathieson (5)	Brett Harker (24)
Edgar Garcia (12)	Chris Booker (27)
Carlos Carrasco (16)	Yoel Hernandez (30)
Kyle Kendrick (28)	Patrick Overholt
Scott Mitchinson (29)	Andy Barb
Maximino De la Cruz	Mark Kelly
Darren Byrd	Ronald Hill
Matt Olson	Nick Evangelista
Pedro Liriano	
Zach Segovia	
Andy Baldwin	

LHP	
Starters	**Relievers**
Cole Hamels (1)	Eude Brito (15)
Gio Gonzalez (2)	
Daniel Haigwood (6)	
J.A. Happ (19)	
Matt Maloney (21)	
Josh Outman (22)	
Derek Griffith	
Justin Blaine	

DRAFT ANALYSIS
2005

Best Pro Debut: RHP Pat Overholt (22) went 2-3, 2.52 with five saves and 51 strikeouts in 34 innings at short-season Batavia. 3B Mike Costanzo (2), Philadelphia's top pick, batted just .184-1-9 in his first 28 games at Batavia, then finished with a .326-10-41 flourish over his final 45 contests.

Best Athlete: The Phillies say OF Jermaine Williams (7) resembles a young Andre Dawson. SS Derek Mitchell (23) earned all-state recognition in Michigan in baseball, football (as a quarterback) and basketball (as a guard). Costanzo and LHP Josh Outman (10) starred as two-way players in college.

Best Pure Hitter: Corner infielder Clay Harris (9), who batted .311-2-40 at Batavia.

Best Raw Power: 1B Michael Durant (4) has the most raw power, while Costanzo has the most current power.

Fastest Runner: OF Dennis Diaz (24), who set the Sun Belt Conference career steals record with 142 in four years at Florida International.

Best Defensive Player: Mitchell has the arm, hands and feet to be a good shortstop.

Best Fastball: Outman was throwing as hard as 93-94 mph after turning pro. Overholt, who had Tommy John surgery in 2004, touched 93 this summer.

Best Breaking Ball: RHP Brett Harker's (5) hard curveball is a plus pitch. Overholt will flash an above-average slider.

Most Intriguing Background: Scouts who saw Outman at St. Louis CC-Forest Park said he had the strangest mechanics they ever had seen, the product of biomechanical and kinetic research by his father, who published a book on the subject. Outman used

Outman

to extend his left arm straight up, bend it to nearly touch his right shoulder and then throw the ball while taking a casual step toward the plate. He had success with his delivery, which is supposed to reduce stress on the arm, but after transferring to Central Missouri State in 2005, the staff there remade his arm action to enhance his chances of getting drafted. Mitchell's uncle Jerry won a Tony award in 2005 for choreographing "La Cage Aux Folles."

Closest To The Majors: LHP Matt Maloney (3) is a lefty who knows how to pitch. His best pitch is his changeup, and he has an 88-91 mph fastball.

Best Late-Round Pick: Outman, Overholt and Mitchell.

The One Who Got Away: All three players the Phillies couldn't sign among their top 20 picks are intriguing prospects. RHP Vance Worley (20) came down with a sore elbow just before the draft. He didn't need surgery and decided to attend Long Beach State. LHP David Huff (19) was another potential early pick until his velocity tailed off late in the spring. He transferred from Cypress (Calif.) JC to UCLA. OF Aja Barto (14) went to Tulane.

Assessment: The Phillies lost their first-rounder as free-agent compensation, so their first pick didn't come until No. 65. They still came away with some interesting athletes and pitchers with savvy.

2004 Philadelphia remains high on OF Greg Golson (1), C Jason Jaramillo (2) and LHP J.A. Happ (3), but they're going to need some time to develop. **GRADE:** C

2003 The Phillies didn't pick in the first two rounds and didn't sign two potential 2006 first-rounders, RHPs Blair Erickson (28) and Greg Reynolds (41). 2B Tim Moss (3), the top choice, showed some signs of life last year, and OF Michael Bourn (4) has some leadoff potential. **GRADE:** D

2002 When Cole Hamels (1) actually has taken the mound, he has been one of the most dynamic left-handed pitchers in the minors. But he has worked just 152 innings in three years. RHP Scott Mathieson (17) looked very good in the Arizona Fall League. **GRADE:** C+

2001 1B Ryan Howard (5) won the 2005 National League rookie of the year award and forced Jim Thome out of Philadelphia. That took a lot of the disappointment off RHP Gavin Floyd's (1) awful Triple-A season. **GRADE:** B+

---

*Draft analysis prepared by **Jim Callis**. Numbers in parentheses indicate draft rounds.*

COLE
HAMELS

LHP

RICK BATTLE

Born: Dec. 27, 1983.
Ht.: 6-2. **Wt.:** 185.
Bats: L. **Throws:** L.
Drafted: HS—San Diego, 2002
(1st round).
Signed by: Darrell Conner.

Hamels broke the humerus in his left arm as a high school sophomore, but despite a full recovery and rehabilitation work with noted pitching guru Tom House, his medical history scared off some clubs in the 2002 draft. He dropped to the Phillies with the 17th overall pick and signed for $2 million, and he hasn't shown any effects from that injury since. However, an assortment of other maladies has limited him to just 28 appearances over three seasons. After holding out in 2002, he showed up out of shape to instructional league and thus wasn't ready for a full-season assignment in 2003, which he began in extended spring training. He pulled a muscle behind his right shoulder at the end of 2003, knocking him off the U.S. Olympic qualifying team. He missed most of 2004 after pulling a right triceps muscle while throwing too hard too early during a stint in major league spring training, during which he struck out Derek Jeter and Alex Rodriguez. The injury worsened when he failed to tell the organization about it in an effort to pitch through the pain. Hamels broke his left hand in a bar fight in January 2005 in Clearwater, Fla. He returned in June and made just six appearances before a stress fracture in his back ended his season and a chance at making up lost time in the Arizona Fall League. When healthy, Hamels has dominated, going 11-3, 1.54 with 208 strikeouts in 152 innings.

Hamels is a lefthander with three above-average pitches and the command, feel and mound presence of a veteran. His changeup, which sinks and fades away from righthanders, is a plus-plus pitch that may be the best in the minors. His fastball hovers around 90 mph and tops out at 93-94 with good life, and he has shown a knack for being able to reach back for extra velocity when needed. His curveball has shown more consistency with its break and location. Hamels maintains an even keel on the mound, never letting his emotions tell the tale of his outing. He's also a very good athlete with clean mechanics and the ability to field his position and hold runners well.

Durability is a major concern with Hamels. The good news is that all his injuries have been unrelated and that only his high school break involved his arm. The bad news is that he has lost so much development time. Had he stayed healthy, he'd be a strong candidate for the major league rotation rather than having pitched just 19 innings above high Class A.

Hamels was working at Double-A Reading when his back forced him out, and he should start 2006 there. His 2004 spring-training success remains in the minds of the Phillies' decision makers, however, keeping him on a very fast track. A quick jump to Triple-A Scranton/Wilkes-Barre and eventually Philadelphia are both possible. Despite the setbacks, the Phillies still envision Hamels as a top-of-the-rotation starter.

Year	Club (League)	Class	W	L	ERA	G	GS	CG	SV	IP	H	R	ER	HR	BB	SO	AVG
2003	Lakewood (SAL)	A	6	1	0.84	13	13	1	0	75	32	8	7	0	25	115	.136
	Clearwater (FSL)	A	0	2	2.73	5	5	0	0	26	29	9	8	0	14	32	.299
2004	Clearwater (FSL)	A	1	0	1.13	4	4	0	0	16	10	2	2	0	4	24	.192
2005	Clearwater (FSL)	A	2	0	2.25	3	3	0	0	16	7	5	4	0	7	18	.137
	Reading (EL)	AA	2	0	2.37	3	3	0	0	19	10	6	5	2	12	19	.159
MINOR LEAGUE TOTALS			11	3	1.54	28	28	1	0	152	88	30	26	2	62	208	.176

2 GIO GONZALEZ
LHP

Born: Sept. 19, 1985. **B-T:** R-L. **Ht.:** 5-11. **Wt.:** 185. **Drafted:** HS—Miami, 2004 (1st round supplemental). **Signed by:** Jose Ortega (White Sox).

A supplemental first-round pick out of a Miami high school in 2004, Gonzalez jumped into full-season ball within two months of signing. He finished his first full year in high Class A and could move even faster after coming to the Phillies in the Jim Thome trade with the White Sox. Gonzalez has clean, effortless mechanics and creates easy velocity into the low 90s, topping out at 93-94. His hard curveball is his go-to pitch and he mixes in a quality changeup. He has gained confidence in his changeup and throws all three pitches at any time in the count. Gonzalez has a lean upper body with the potential to gain some strength, but the question of durability is going to continue to follow him, especially after he encountered back and shoulder problems last year. He figures to make his Double-A debut at age 20, with a shot at reaching Philadelphia at 21 or 22.

Year	Club (League)	Class	W	L	ERA	G	GS	CG	SV	IP	H	R	ER	HR	BB	SO	AVG
2004	Bristol (Appy)	R	1	2	2.25	7	6	0	0	24	17	8	6	0	8	36	.207
	Kannapolis (SAL)	A	1	1	3.03	6	6	0	0	33	30	13	11	1	13	27	.229
2005	Kannapolis (SAL)	A	5	3	1.87	11	10	0	0	57	36	16	12	3	22	84	.175
	Winston-Salem (Car)	A	8	3	3.56	13	13	0	0	73	61	33	29	5	25	79	.228
MINOR LEAGUE TOTALS			15	9	2.78	37	35	0	0	188	144	70	58	9	68	226	.210

3 GREG GOLSON
OF

Born: Sept. 17, 1985. **B-T:** R-R. **Ht.:** 6-0. **Wt.:** 190. **Drafted:** HS—Austin, 2004 (1st round). **Signed by:** Steve Cohen.

The consensus best athlete in the 2004 draft, Golson signed for $1.475 million as the 21st overall pick. Injuries hampered him in 2005, as a high ankle sprain cost him six weeks at the beginning of the year and a sprained knee sidelined him for more than a week in July. Golson boasts five-tool potential, as well as solid baseball instincts and a willingness to learn. He has the bat speed to hit for average and the strength to hit 15-20 homers annually in the majors. His above-average speed makes him a threat on the bases, and that and his plus arm make him a plus defender. Golson still must refine his overall plate discipline and his pitch recognition in particular. He did most of his damage against lefthanders in 2005, hitting .346 compared to .241 against righties. He continues to work on his reads in the outfield. Because Golson lost 150 at-bats to injury, he could begin 2006 back at low Class A Lakewood. If he dominates the South Atlantic League, he'll move up quickly to high Class A Clearwater. There's substantial center-field depth in the system, so he won't be rushed even though he should become the best of the group.

Year	Club (League)	Class	AVG	G	AB	R	H	2B	3B	HR	RBI	BB	SO	SB	OBP	SLG
2004	Phillies (GCL)	R	.295	47	183	34	54	8	5	1	22	10	54	12	.345	.410
2005	Lakewood (SAL)	A	.264	89	375	51	99	19	8	4	27	26	106	25	.322	.389
MINOR LEAGUE TOTALS			.274	136	558	85	153	27	13	5	49	36	160	37	.329	.396

4 MICHAEL BOURN
OF

Born: Dec. 27, 1982. **B-T:** L-R. **Ht.:** 5-11. **Wt.:** 180. **Drafted:** Houston, 2003 (4th round). **Signed by:** Dave Owen.

After Bourn posted a .433 on-base percentage in low Class A in 2004, the Phillies skipped him a level to Double-A. His offensive numbers weren't as robust, but he handled the move well and made adjustments. Managers rated him the Eastern League's most exciting player and he led the system in steals. Bourn offers the quickness, aptitude and offensive approach required of a leadoff hitter. He's the system's best defensive outfielder and also has an above-average arm. The fastest player in the system, he outraced Greg Golson by a step in the 60-yard dash. Bourn's strikeout rate jumped in 2005, though the Phillies aren't as concerned because he faced a two-level jump and pitchers with more advanced command than he had previously seen. His tendency to hit deep in counts also contributed, and he should be able to adapt with more at-bats against better pitchers. Bourn likely will return to Double-A to gain confidence before moving to Triple-A sometime in 2006. He could take over everyday duties in Philadelphia in 2007, though Greg Golson should press him for the center-field job down the road.

Year	Club (League)	Class	AVG	G	AB	R	H	2B	3B	HR	RBI	BB	SO	SB	OBP	SLG
2003	Batavia (NY-P)	A	.280	35	125	12	35	0	1	0	4	23	28	23	.404	.296
2004	Lakewood (SAL)	A	.317	109	413	92	131	20	14	5	53	85	88	57	.433	.470
2005	Reading (EL)	AA	.268	135	544	80	146	18	8	6	44	63	123	38	.348	.364
MINOR LEAGUE TOTALS			.288	279	1082	184	312	38	23	11	101	171	239	118	.388	.396

5 SCOTT MATHIESON
RHP

Born: Feb. 27, 1984. **B-T:** R-R. **Ht.:** 6-4. **Wt.:** 195. **Drafted:** HS—Aldergrove, B.C., 2002 (17th round). **Signed by:** Tim Kissner.

Mathieson has pitched for several Canadian national teams, and he beat Sweden and lost to Cuba (after shutting them out for four innings) at the World Cup in September. He also served as Philadelphia's Futures Game representative in 2005. His grandfather Doug tried out for the Philadelphia Athletics during the Connie Mack era. A projection pick who threw 84 mph as a high school senior, Mathieson now reaches 95-96 regularly and works in the low 90s. He switched from a curveball to a slider midway through 2005, and his new breaking ball has a chance to become his second plus pitch. His down-breaking changeup is solid, as are his mechanics. Though Mathieson showed solid progress in 2005, he must continue to improve his overall command. It's not a question of throwing strikes, but of throwing better strikes. With the makings of three average-or-better pitches, Mathieson could emerge as a No. 2 or 3 starter if all goes well. He also could become a power closer if the Phillies need him to. He'll pitch in Double-A in 2006.

Year	Club (League)	Class	W	L	ERA	G	GS	CG	SV	IP	H	R	ER	HR	BB	SO	AVG
2002	Phillies (GCL)	R	0	2	5.40	7	2	0	0	17	24	11	10	0	6	14	.338
2003	Phillies (GCL)	R	2	7	5.52	11	11	0	0	59	59	42	36	5	13	51	.247
2003	Batavia (NY-P)	A	0	0	0.00	2	0	0	1	6	0	0	0	0	0	7	.000
2004	Lakewood (SAL)	A	8	9	4.32	25	25	1	0	131	130	73	64	7	50	112	.260
2005	Clearwater (FSL)	A	3	8	4.14	23	23	1	0	122	111	62	56	17	34	118	.241
MINOR LEAGUE TOTALS			13	26	4.44	68	61	2	1	334	324	188	165	29	103	302	.252

6 DANIEL HAIGWOOD
LHP

RODGER WOOD

Born: Nov. 19, 1983. **B-T:** B-L. **Ht.:** 6-2. **Wt.:** 200. **Draft:** HS— Pleasant Plains, Ark., 2002 (16th round). **Signed by:** Alex Slattery (White Sox).

Haigwood went 43-1 at Midland High in Arkansas and has continued his winning ways as a pro, going 32-11 in the White Sox system before joining the Phillies in the Jim Thome trade. Despite missing the entire 2003 season following surgery to repair a torn anterior cruciate ligament in his left knee, Haigwood reached Double-A last year as a 21-year-old. He primarily works with fringe-average velocity, but he gained a little extra zip in 2005, topping out in the low 90s with a two-seamer that dives to the bottom of the strike zone. His best pitch is his slider that some call a sharp curveball. His changeup has improved each year. Haigwood can be particularly tough on lefties, though righthanders didn't have any success against him in Double-A, batting .141. He works quickly and has developed a reputation for escaping the toughest of jams. Haigwood is at least a year away but has earned his first trip to big league camp.

Year	Club (League)	Class	W	L	ERA	G	GS	CG	SV	IP	H	R	ER	HR	BB	SO	AVG
2002	White Sox (AZL)	R	8	4	2.28	14	14	0	0	75	69	31	19	2	26	74	.244
2003	Did not play—Injured																
2004	Kannapolis (SAL)	A	10	4	4.76	21	21	0	0	113	97	63	60	10	56	99	.246
2005	Winston-Salem (Car)	A	8	2	3.77	15	15	0	0	76	79	39	32	8	33	84	.265
	Birmingham (SL)	AA	6	1	1.74	11	11	0	0	67	39	14	13	0	31	76	.170
MINOR LEAGUE TOTALS			32	11	3.36	61	61	0	0	332	284	147	124	20	146	333	.236

7 WELINSON BAEZ
3B/SS

RICH ABEL

Born: July 7, 1984. **B-T:** R-R. **Ht.:** 6-3. **Wt.:** 190. **Signed:** Dominican Republic, 2002. **Signed by:** Wil Tejada.

Baez' immense physical gifts, including a power arm that led some scouts to project him as a pitcher, earned him a $250,000 signing bonus. In 2005, he finally shed a reputation for hitting well in extended spring training before fizzling in actual league play. He was short-season Batavia's most dangerous hitter while playing out of position at short-stop to accommodate second-round pick Mike Costanzo. Filling out physically and recognizing breaking balls better allowed Baez to show the first signs of unleashing his plus loft power. His 70 arm strength on the 20-80 scouting scale rates as the organization's best, and he makes accurate throws as well. He charges bunts well and shows soft hands. Baez remains raw and will have to continue to make adjustments. His size means he must work to stay low in his defensive positioning to gather more groundballs. Baez owns one of the highest ceilings in the organization. The Phillies will try to separate him and Costanzo in 2006 so both can play third base, and Baez likely will go to low Class A.

Year	Club (League)	Class	AVG	G	AB	R	H	2B	3B	HR	RBI	BB	SO	SB	OBP	SLG
2003	Phillies (GCL)	R	.246	41	142	20	35	6	1	3	17	12	37	3	.319	.366
2004	Phillies (GCL)	R	.234	51	171	24	40	7	2	4	18	21	62	3	.320	.368
2005	Phillies (GCL)	R	.267	15	45	6	12	4	1	2	6	8	14	1	.400	.533
2005	Batavia (NY-P)	A	.324	45	170	34	55	14	1	6	37	22	45	2	.408	.524
MINOR LEAGUE TOTALS			.269	152	528	84	142	31	5	15	78	63	158	9	.355	.432

8 MIKE COSTANZO 3B

RICH ABEL

Born: Sept. 9, 1983. **B-T:** L-R. **Ht.:** 6-3. **Wt.:** 215. **Drafted:** Coastal Carolina, 2005 (2nd round). **Signed by:** Roy Tanner.

Costanzo grew up a Phillies fan in Springfield, Pa., and came home from the hospital when he was born in a tiny Phillies jacket. Before signing for $570,000 as Philadelphia's top draft pick, he was named Big South Conference athlete of the year. He led Division I in walks (68) while blasting 16 homers and earning 14 saves. The Phillies immediately changed Costanzo's stance when he got to Batavia, making him more upright and open. He started slowly, but his hitting skills and bat speed ultimately shined through as he drove balls to all fields with authority. Defensively, Costanzo offers good body control and agility along with an above-average, accurate arm. Costanzo split time between first and third base in college, so he's still getting used to everyday action at the hot corner. His hard work should help him improve his reads and routes. He batted just .170 with 25 strikeouts in 53 at-bats against lefthanders. Because he's older, Costanzo is more likely than Welinson Baez to open 2006 in high Class A. Costanzo's maturity and approach should allow him to handle skipping a level.

Year	Club (League)	Class	AVG	G	AB	R	H	2B	3B	HR	RBI	BB	SO	SB	OBP	SLG
2005	Batavia (NY-P)	A	.274	73	281	47	77	17	3	11	50	35	89	0	.356	.473
MINOR LEAGUE TOTALS			.274	73	281	47	77	17	3	11	50	35	89	0	.356	.473

9 BRAD HARMAN SS/2B

ANDREW WOOLLEY

Born: Nov. 19, 1985. **B-T:** R-R. **Ht.:** 6-1. **Wt.:** 175. **Signed:** Australia, 2003. **Signed by:** Kevin Hooker.

The Phillies have signed several players from Australia in the last three years, and Harman rates as the best. None have commanded bonuses of more than $50,000, a welcome change from the Latin American market the organization believes has become overpriced. Harman played for Australia in the 2005 World Cup, posting a .412 on-base percentage and playing eight errorless games. An instinctive player, Harman has improved quickly because of his work ethic and ability to learn. His bat speed has increased and he now shows some loft power after filling out a bit. Harman fields balls with sure hands and smooth actions and offers a strong, accurate arm. He's better defensively than Chase Utley. Harman's speed is average at best. This limits his range, so he's working to improve his first-step quickness and reads on grounders. Philadelphia thinks Harman can play shortstop with average range, and he also has worked at second and third base. He'll continue to play mostly shortstop in high Class A in 2006, and he's at least two years away from the majors.

Year	Club (League)	Class	AVG	G	AB	R	H	2B	3B	HR	RBI	BB	SO	SB	OBP	SLG
2004	Clearwater (FSL)	A	.000	1	0	1	0	0	0	0	0	1	0	0	1.000	.000
	Phillies (GCL)	R	.230	51	183	23	42	10	0	2	19	11	41	2	.281	.317
2005	Lakewood (SAL)	A	.303	105	419	63	127	23	1	11	58	45	89	5	.380	.442
MINOR LEAGUE TOTALS			.281	157	602	87	169	33	1	13	77	57	130	7	.352	.404

10   JASON JARAMILLO   C

Born: Oct. 9, 1982. **B-T:** B-R. **Ht.:** 6-0. **Wt.:** 200. **Drafted:** Oklahoma
State, 2004 (2nd round). **Signed by:** Paul Scott.

The Phillies initially drafted Jaramillo in the 42nd round out of a
Wisconsin high school in 2001. Three years later, they picked him 40
rounds earlier and were able to sign him for $585,000. Older brothers
Frankie and Lee both played in the minors. Managers rated him the best
defensive catcher in the South Atlantic League, though his 20 errors led
all minor league catchers. His agility helps him block balls well, and his
above-average arm helped him throw out 34 percent of basestealers. He
made strides in game-calling and handling pitchers. He's a line-drive hitter who started
switch-hitting in high school and is equally adept from either side. Jaramillo doesn't offer
much power and may not hit more than 10-15 homers in a big league season. He projects
as a bottom-of-the-order hitter on a contender, though his defense should make up for what
he lacks offensively. He has below-average speed. Philadelphia's catcher of the future,
Jaramillo will open 2006 in high Class A. He reminds some club officials of former Phillies
farmhand Johnny Estrada.

Year	Club (League)	Class	AVG	G	AB	R	H	2B	3B	HR	RBI	BB	SO	SB	OBP	SLG
2004	Phillies (GCL)	R	.667	1	3	1	2	0	0	0	1	0	0	0	.667	.667
	Batavia (NY-P)	A	.223	31	112	11	25	5	0	1	14	12	27	0	.299	.295
2005	Lakewood (SAL)	A	.304	119	448	46	136	28	4	8	63	44	72	2	.368	.438
MINOR LEAGUE TOTALS			.290	151	563	58	163	33	4	9	78	56	99	2	.355	.410

11   TIM MOSS   2B

Born: Jan. 26, 1982. **B-T:** R-R. **Ht.:** 5-9. **Wt.:** 150. **Drafted:** Texas, 2003 (3rd round). **Signed
by:** Dave Owen.

The Phillies made Moss their top pick (third round) in 2003, a year after he helped Texas
win the College World Series. Though he's an excellent athlete, he was raw for a player from
a top college program. Some club officials were ready to write him off before he exploded in
2005. Moss isn't big but offers surprising power for his size because of his bat speed. His bat
and foot speed actually increased in 2005, when he once again got down the first-base line
in 4.1-4.15 seconds, as he had in college. He's unorthodox in the field, but his speed allows
him to make plays and he's solid on the double-play pivot. One Phillies front-office member questions whether Moss really made any significant improvement in 2005 other than
building confidence after a hot start. He still strikes out too much and needs to do a better
job of getting on base. He struggles on routine defensive plays and has awkward throwing
mechanics. It remains to be seen whether Moss' breakout was a fluke. He'll move to Double-
A in 2006 and try to show that a smallish second baseman can keep punishing baseballs.

Year	Club (League)	Class	AVG	G	AB	R	H	2B	3B	HR	RBI	BB	SO	SB	OBP	SLG
2003	Batavia (NY-P)	A	.150	43	160	10	24	5	2	1	11	11	47	5	.220	.225
2004	Lakewood (SAL)	A	.256	78	273	31	70	15	1	2	28	24	75	10	.342	.341
2005	Clearwater (FSL)	A	.269	123	469	87	126	30	5	17	61	45	129	28	.348	.463
MINOR LEAGUE TOTALS			.244	244	902	128	220	50	8	20	100	80	251	43	.324	.384

12   EDGAR GARCIA   RHP

Born: Sept. 20, 1987. **B-T:** R-R. **Ht.:** 6-2. **Wt.:** 190. **Signed:** Dominican Republic, 2004. **Signed
by:** Sal Agostinelli/Wil Tejada.

The Phillies tracked Garcia for more than a year and signed him right before he played in
the Perfect Game/Baseball America World Wood Bat Championship in the fall of 2004. He
worked out for the Phillies, who were in nearby Clearwater, Fla., for their organizational
meetings, and they signed him for $500,000 before he could boost his stock at the show-
case. He made significant progress in his first year in the system. Garcia features a lively 91-
94 mph fastball along with smooth mechanics and a sturdy build that offer the promise of
more velocity. Garcia's changeup should emerge as a plus pitch, as he sells it with fastball
arm speed and will throw it in any count. His feel and poise are impressive. Garcia's 12-to-
6 curveball is still inconsistent. Given time, he should be able to refine it into at least an
average offering. The Phillies will move Garcia slowly, with Batavia his scheduled stop for
2006. They believe he may be two years before starting to put everything together, after
which he could ascend rapidly and ultimately wind up as a No. 2 or 3 starter.

Year	Club (League)	Class	W	L	ERA	G	GS	CG	SV	IP	H	R	ER	HR	BB	SO	AVG
2005	Phillies (GCL)	R	4	4	3.56	10	10	0	0	56	63	26	22	4	13	42	.284
MINOR LEAGUE TOTALS			4	4	3.56	10	10	0	0	56	63	26	22	4	13	42	.284

13 CHRIS ROBERSON OF

Born: Aug. 23, 1979. **B-T:** R-R. **Ht.:** 6-2. **Wt.:** 175. **Drafted:** Contra Costa (Calif.) CC., 2001 (9th round). **Signed by:** Scott Ramsey.

Roberson gets his tremendous athleticism from his father Will, a former NBA draft pick. After three mediocre pro seasons, Chris finally had a breakthrough in 2004 and proved it wasn't a fluke by repeating his success in 2005. He won the Eastern League's rookie-of-the-year award after leading the league in hits and runs. He also reached career bests in average and homers, because he has improved at identifying pitches he can handle and knowing when to make use of his power. His strikeout rate crept down for the third straight season. He's an above-average runner and got going on the bases again after swiping just 16 bags in 2004. Pushed out of center field by Michael Bourn, Roberson fit nicely in right field. Managers rated his arm the best among EL outfielders. He still must improve some minor things, such as knowing when it's a good time to steal a base and hitting cutoff men more regularly. He continues to flail at hard breaking balls. He's working on learning the different outfield angles after moving from center to right. Roberson is not as instinctive a player as either Greg Golson or Bourn, the outfielders ahead of him on this list. As a 26-year-old, Roberson also doesn't have as high a ceiling as they do. He'll move to Triple-A this year and could return to center field if Shane Victorino sticks in Philadelphia and Bourn remains in Reading. He'd stay in right if either of them are on the Scranton roster and profiles as a fourth outfielder in the long run.

Year	Club (League)	Class	AVG	G	AB	R	H	2B	3B	HR	RBI	BB	SO	SB	OBP	SLG
2001	Phillies (GCL)	R	.248	38	133	17	33	8	1	0	13	16	30	6	.336	.323
2002	Batavia (NY-P)	A	.276	62	214	29	59	8	3	2	24	26	51	17	.377	.369
2003	Lakewood (SAL)	A	.234	132	470	64	110	19	5	2	32	57	108	59	.331	.309
2004	Clearwater (FSL)	A	.307	83	313	52	96	13	6	9	38	27	71	16	.371	.473
2005	Reading (EL)	AA	.311	139	553	90	172	24	8	15	70	40	112	34	.365	.465
MINOR LEAGUE TOTALS			.279	454	1683	252	470	72	23	28	177	166	372	132	.356	.399

14 SHANE VICTORINO OF

Born: Nov. 30, 1980. **B-T:** B-R. **Ht.:** 5-9. **Wt.:** 160. **Drafted:** HS—Wailuku, Hawaii, 1999 (6th round). **Signed by:** Hank Jones (Dodgers)

Victorino twice has been plucked from the Dodgers in the Rule 5 draft. The "Flyin' Hawaiian" became the second Maui native to play in the majors, but the Padres returned him to Los Angeles after 73 at-bats in 2003. He failed to make the Phillies' 25-man roster in 2005, but the Dodgers declined to take him back and he spent the year in Triple-A. Long known for his above-average speed and defense, Victorino emerged as the International League's MVP. The performance surprised the Phillies, who had the same scouting report as everyone else, though Victorino had displayed increased power in 2004. His breakthrough came with the simple change of adjusting his approach to make more contact (to better utilize his fleet feet), and his naturally strong wrists delivered added power as a bonus. Victorino should stick with the Phillies as a low-cost extra outfielder in 2006, but has a chance to play a more prominent role.

Year	Club (League)	Class	AVG	G	AB	R	H	2B	3B	HR	RBI	BB	SO	SB	OBP	SLG
1999	Great Falls (Pio)	R	.280	55	225	53	63	7	6	2	25	20	31	20	.335	.391
2000	Yakima (NWL)	A	.246	61	236	32	58	7	2	2	20	20	44	21	.310	.318
2001	Wilmington (SAL)	A	.283	112	435	71	123	21	9	4	32	36	61	47	.344	.400
	Vero Beach (FSL)	A	.167	2	6	2	1	0	0	0	0	3	1	0	.444	.167
2002	Jacksonville (SL)	AA	.258	122	481	61	124	15	1	4	34	47	49	45	.328	.318
2003	San Diego (NL)	MLB	.151	36	73	8	11	2	0	0	4	7	17	7	.232	.178
	Jacksonville (SL)	AA	.282	66	266	37	75	9	4	2	15	21	41	16	.340	.368
	Las Vegas (PCL)	AAA	.390	11	41	6	16	1	2	1	9	1	5	0	.395	.585
2004	Las Vegas (PCL)	AAA	.235	55	200	28	47	9	1	3	20	11	37	7	.278	.335
	Jacksonville (SL)	AA	.328	75	293	70	96	13	7	16	43	20	64	9	.375	.584
2005	Scranton/W-B (IL)	AAA	.310	126	494	93	153	25	16	18	70	51	74	17	.377	.534
	Philadelphia (NL)	MLB	.294	21	17	5	5	0	0	2	8	0	3	0	.263	.647
MAJOR LEAGUE TOTALS			.178	57	90	13	16	2	0	2	12	7	20	7	.238	.267
MINOR LEAGUE TOTALS			.282	685	2677	453	756	107	48	52	268	230	407	182	.343	.417

15 EUDE BRITO LHP

Born: Sept. 19, 1978. **B-T:** L-L. **Ht.:** 5-11. **Wt.:** 160. **Signed:** Dominican Republic, 1998. **Signed by:** Wil Tejada.

When Brito was in high school, a teacher told him he was too skinny and short to become a major leaguer, and that he should focus on his other passion, singing. Brito became the first major leaguer from Sabana de la Mar in the Dominican Republic. Entering 2005, he was tagged as a situational reliever who would get extra work in the rotation at Triple-A. Yet he wound up filling in as an emergency starter for the Phillies down the stretch and beat the Braves with six shutout innings on Sept. 12. Nevertheless, his inconsistent command caught up with him in his final two starts for Philadelphia and means his future remains in the bullpen. Brito's fastball and power slider have shown flashes of being plus pitches. His fastball gets up to 95-96 mph out of the bullpen, but sits around 90 when he's forced to work longer stretches. It features sinking and tailing action. A jump in velocity during the 2004 season enhanced Brito's prospect status, but his command failed to improve. His changeup did, developing into an average pitch when Brito worked out of the rotation. He's most likely to open 2006 as a middle man in the Phillies bullpen.

Year	Club (League)	Class	W	L	ERA	G	GS	CG	SV	IP	H	R	ER	HR	BB	SO	AVG
1999	Phillies (GCL)	R	0	1	5.02	12	3	0	0	29	39	22	16	0	19	23	.336
2000	Phillies (GCL)	R	3	5	2.54	9	7	0	0	50	38	20	14	1	19	42	.210
	Batavia (NY-P)	A	1	1	5.40	4	3	0	0	18	16	14	11	0	3	11	.225
2001	Lakewood (SAL)	A	4	3	2.73	44	0	0	6	69	53	28	21	7	14	58	.210
2002	Lakewood (SAL)	A	1	1	2.55	11	0	0	1	18	14	5	5	1	6	11	.226
	Clearwater (FSL)	A	3	3	5.71	20	0	0	0	35	40	22	22	5	14	27	.292
2003	Clearwater (FSL)	A	4	3	3.09	36	0	0	6	58	50	21	20	3	27	54	.231
2004	Reading (EL)	AA	8	6	4.42	43	7	1	4	98	95	56	48	10	42	84	.256
2005	Scranton/W-B (IL)	AAA	6	2	4.85	28	15	0	0	98	97	59	53	13	39	76	.266
	Philadelphia (NL)	MLB	1	2	3.68	6	5	0	0	22	20	9	9	2	11	15	.250
MAJOR LEAGUE TOTALS			1	2	3.68	6	5	0	0	22	20	9	9	2	11	15	.250
MINOR LEAGUE TOTALS			30	25	4.00	207	35	1	17	473	442	247	210	40	183	386	.250

16 CARLOS CARRASCO   RHP

Born: March 21, 1987. **B-T:** R-R. **Ht.:** 6-3. **Wt.:** 178. **Signed:** Dominican Republic, 2003. **Signed by:** Sal Agostinelli.

Carrasco signed for $300,000 out of a Venezuelan tryout camp and a strong U.S. debut rocketed him to No. 8 on this list a year ago. It also encouraged Philadelphia enough that it sent him to full-season ball before he was ready. Older hitters punished Carrasco's mistakes, which crushed his confidence and eventually got him sent down to Batavia. The Phillies rarely rush callow prospects up the ladder, so they claim fault here, but were also disappointed with how he handled the situation. His good stuff remained intact despite the struggles, though he fell into the trap of thinking throwing harder was better every time he found trouble. A year older than Edgar Garcia, Carrasco owns a similar repertoire. His fastball, which sits in the low 90s, and changeup are his best offerings, and both are plus pitches. Carrasco's curveball should end up at least average, but it still lacks consistency. He's a good athlete who effectively repeats a smooth delivery. Carrasco will receive a second chance in low Class A this year, and he still owns a ceiling as a No. 2 or 3 starter.

Year	Club (League)	Class	W	L	ERA	G	GS	CG	SV	IP	H	R	ER	HR	BB	SO	AVG
2004	Phillies (GCL)	R	5	4	3.56	11	8	0	0	48	53	23	19	2	15	34	.276
2005	Lakewood (SAL)	A	1	7	7.04	13	13	1	0	63	78	50	49	11	28	46	.302
	Batavia (NY-P)	A	0	3	13.50	4	4	0	0	15	29	25	23	8	5	12	.392
	Phillies (GCL)	R	0	0	1.80	2	2	0	0	5	3	1	1	0	1	2	.176
MINOR LEAGUE TOTALS			6	14	6.32	30	27	1	0	131	163	99	92	21	49	94	.301

17 MICHAEL DURANT   1B

Born: Jan. 2, 1987. **B-T:** R-R. **Ht.:** 6-5. **Wt.:** 230. **Drafted:** HS—Berkeley, Calif., 2005 (4th round). **Signed by:** Joey Davis.

Durant's size and immense power remind the Phillies of a righthanded-hitting Ryan Howard. He hit .450 with 13 home runs in 26 games as a high school senior. At the behest of fellow Oakland native Jimmy Rollins, Durant attended a predraft workout at Citizens Bank Park and jacked nine home runs, including one that went 20 rows deep into the left-field stands and nearly reached the second deck. Durant's mother was 15 when he was born, so his grandmother raised him for five years until she died of cancer. Durant returned to his mother's care until the seventh grade, when the family of one of his junior-high friends adopted him. He lived in a cottage in their backyard from the eighth grade on. Durant passed on a scholarship to Fresno State to sign for a $247,500 bonus. His raw power rates a 70 on the 20-to-80 scale, but he remains a work in progress. Adjusting to breaking balls and making more contact top his to-do list. Durant, who played third base in high school, is surprisingly agile for his size with quick feet and soft hands. He also pitched in high school, so arm strength is not a question. He could emerge as an above-average defender at first base. Durant needs lots of game experience and will start 2006 in extended spring training before moving up to Batavia.

Year	Club (League)	Class	AVG	G	AB	R	H	2B	3B	HR	RBI	BB	SO	SB	OBP	SLG
2005	Phillies (GCL)	R	.190	39	126	21	24	4	0	6	22	16	56	3	.301	.365
MINOR LEAGUE TOTALS			.190	39	126	21	24	4	0	6	22	16	56	3	.301	.365

18 CARLOS RUIZ   C

Born: Jan. 22, 1979. **B-T:** R-R. **Ht.:** 5-10. **Wt.:** 180. **Signed:** Dominican Republic, 1998. **Signed by:** Sal Agostinelli.

Ruiz' strong arm and limited agility drove international scouting director Sal Agostinelli to try him out at catcher. He liked what he saw and signed Ruiz for $8,000, a shrewd invest-ment for a player with a good chance to make the Phillies' big league roster after his second straight strong offensive season in the minors. The Phillies saw Ruiz as little more than a backup catcher during his first five years in the organization. An injury to Russ Jacobson granted Ruiz more than a platoon role in 2004, and he slugged .484 with 17 home runs to greatly enhance his standing. A .458 slugging performance in 2005 reinforced his raw power. He continued to show the ability to make adjustments and control the strike zone while improving how he handled offspeed pitches. Ruiz' defense remains solid, as he has an above-average arm, good feet and a strong lower half. He threw out 31 percent of basesteal-ers in Triple-A. Durability cropped up as a concern in 2005, as he missed time with a possi-ble concussion and later a sore shoulder that pushed him to DH and likely prevented a September callup. Ruiz will contend for a backup role in Philadelphia.

Year	Club (League)	Class	AVG	G	AB	R	H	2B	3B	HR	RBI	BB	SO	SB	OBP	SLG
1999	Phillies (DSL)	R	.305	60	226	39	69	15	5	4	35	9	11	3	.351	.469
2000	Phillies (GCL)	R	.277	38	130	11	36	7	1	1	22	9	9	3	.329	.369
2001	Lakewood (SAL)	A	.261	73	249	21	65	14	3	4	32	10	27	5	.290	.390
2002	Clearwater (FSL)	A	.213	92	342	35	73	18	3	5	32	18	30	3	.264	.327
2003	Clearwater (FSL)	A	.315	15	54	5	17	0	0	2	9	2	5	2	.339	.426
	Reading (EL)	AA	.266	52	169	22	45	6	0	2	16	12	15	1	.321	.337
2004	Reading (EL)	AA	.284	101	349	45	99	15	2	17	50	22	37	8	.338	.484
2005	Scranton/W-B (IL)	AAA	.300	100	347	50	104	25	9	4	40	30	48	4	.354	.458
MINOR LEAGUE TOTALS			.272	531	1866	228	508	100	23	39	236	112	182	29	.321	.413

19 J.A. HAPP   LHP

Born: Oct. 19, 1982. **B-T:** L-L. **Ht.:** 6-5. **Wt.:** 205. **Drafted:** Northwestern, 2004 (3rd round). **Signed by:** Bob Szymkowski.

The first Northwestern player to make the all-Big 10 Conference team three times, Happ is a classic lefthanded control pitcher. According to scouting director Marti Wolever, "Deception is his best pitch." That attribute makes Happ's upper-80s fastball play better than its raw grade of fringe average. Like Randy Wolf, he can elevate his fastball against righthanders and still get them to swing through it. Happ is a thinker with an excellent feel for pitching who knows when and where to throw his plus changeup. He must tighten his slider and throw it harder, as it devolves into a slurve too often. Throwing it more would help, but he prefers to go with his fastball because he always has had success with it. Pulled quadriceps and oblique muscles cost Happ innings in 2005. His polish and athleticism—he left St. Bede Academy (Peru, Ill.) as its all-time leading scorer in basketball—mean he should move quickly, as his dominant September start in Double-A foretold. He'll start 2006 in high Class A and eventually should become a back-of-the-rotation starter.

Year	Club (League)	Class	W	L	ERA	G	GS	CG	SV	IP	H	R	ER	HR	BB	SO	AVG
2004	Batavia (NY-P)	A	1	2	2.02	11	11	0	0	36	22	8	8	1	18	37	.185
2005	Lakewood (SAL)	A	4	4	2.36	14	12	0	0	72	57	26	19	3	26	70	.213
	Reading (EL)	AA	1	0	1.50	1	1	0	0	6	3	1	1	0	2	8	.150
MINOR LEAGUE TOTALS			6	6	2.21	26	24	0	0	114	82	35	28	4	46	115	.202

20 JAKE BLALOCK   OF

Born: Aug. 6, 1983. **B-T:** R-R. **Ht.:** 6-4. **Wt.:** 205. **Drafted:** HS—San Diego, 2002 (5th round). **Signed by:** Darrell Conner.

The younger brother of Rangers all-star third baseman Hank Blalock and a high school teammate of Phillies No. 1 prospect Cole Hamels, Blalock has spent his pro career trying to carve out his own niche. He has moved from third base to left field and earns plaudits from Phillies for his work ethic—which rates among the best in the organization—and his grind-it-out mentality. Though Blalock's slugging percentage hit a three-year low, officials attrib-ute that to the spacious parks of the high Class A Florida State League and expect more homers out of him in 2006. He still projects to hit for above-average power to all fields after closing his stance during 2004. Blalock's strikeout rate declined for the second straight year, though he's still prone to chasing breaking balls despite better overall pitch selection. He works hard on his defense, though he's never likely to be much better than an average left fielder with an average arm. He'll try for a breakout year in Double-A in 2006.

Year	Club (League)	Class	AVG	G	AB	R	H	2B	3B	HR	RBI	BB	SO	SB	OBP	SLG
2002	Phillies (GCL)	R	.250	25	88	13	22	6	0	1	13	10	15	3	.317	.352
2003	Batavia (NY-P)	A	.245	72	261	36	64	23	7	5	31	30	81	9	.323	.444
2004	Lakewood (SAL)	A	.271	131	517	81	140	40	2	16	90	61	126	4	.350	.449
2005	Clearwater (FSL)	A	.279	134	502	50	140	22	0	11	65	60	100	10	.359	.388
MINOR LEAGUE TOTALS			.268	362	1368	180	366	91	9	33	199	161	322	26	.346	.420

21 MATT MALONEY LHP

Born: Jan. 16, 1984. **B-T:** L-L. **Ht.:** 6-4. **Wt.:** 220. **Drafted:** Mississippi, 2005 (3rd round). **Signed by:** Mike Stauffer.

Maloney spent his freshman year at Manatee (Fla.) Junior College before moving to Mississippi as a sophomore. After improving his strength, conditioning and slider he broke out as a junior last spring, when he started the season as the Rebels' closer before emerging as their best starter. His college innings rose from 48 in 2004 to 104 in 2005, so he arrived in pro ball with a dead arm after signing for $400,000 as a third-round pick. The Phillies limited his innings at Batavia and in instructional league, so they don't have a great read yet on what they've got. Physical maturity helped Maloney consistently pitch at 88-91 mph with his fastball. His height allows him to maintain a good downward plane, and his ability to locate the fastball makes up for its lack of life. His changeup is probably his best pitch, though it's no more than a solid-average offering. His slider and curveball can be as good at times, but he must show more consistency with all his secondary offerings. Location, however, isn't a problem and in fact rates as Maloney's greatest strength as a pitcher. He'll start 2006 in low Class A.

Year	Club (League)	Class	W	L	ERA	G	GS	CG	SV	IP	H	R	ER	HR	BB	SO	AVG
2005	Batavia (NY-P)	A	2	1	3.89	8	8	0	0	37	38	20	16	2	15	36	.277
MINOR LEAGUE TOTALS			2	1	3.89	8	8	0	0	37	38	20	16	2	15	36	.277

22 JOSH OUTMAN LHP

Born: Sept. 14, 1984. **B-T:** L-L. **Ht.:** 6-1. **Wt.:** 180. **Drafted:** Central Missouri State, 2005 (10th round). **Signed by:** Jerry Lafferty.

Outman was the fourth of five Central Missouri State pitchers selected in the first 11 rounds of the 2005 draft after the Mules placed third in the NCAA Division II World Series. Scouts had rarely seen a more unorthodox delivery than the one Outman used at St. Louis CC-Forest Park. It was developed by his father Fritz, who wrote a manual on pitching mechanics. Outman extended his arm straight up, bent it down to almost touch his opposite shoulder and then took a walking step—instead of a normal leg kick—before cutting loose. He threw an 86-88 mph fastball and tied for the Division II juco strikeout lead, but coaches at Central Missouri State reworked his mechanics after he transferred there. With a more conventional delivery, his velocity jumped to 90-94 mph. Outman continues to work on refining his mechanics, but he's athletic enough that he should eventually get it together. He posted a 1.059 OPS as an outfielder/DH for the Mules, a perennial Division II World Series participant, and some teams wanted to draft him as a hitter. The Phillies feel they got a steal by taking him in the 10th round and spending just $52,500 to sign him. Outman throws three pitches in addition to his plus fastball: a slider, curveball and changeup. Philadelphia wants him to dump one of the breaking balls because he often gets caught in between and winds up with an ineffective slurve. His slider seems most likely to emerge as a sharp put-away pitch. He's still learning to throw a changeup with regularity. It must become at least average to keep Outman in a rotation. Otherwise, he could become a power reliever capable of blowing away lefties. He'll move to low Class A this year.

Year	Club (League)	Class	W	L	ERA	G	GS	CG	SV	IP	H	R	ER	HR	BB	SO	AVG
2005	Batavia (NY-P)	A	2	1	2.76	11	4	0	0	29	23	14	9	1	14	31	.207
MINOR LEAGUE TOTALS			2	1	2.76	11	4	0	0	29	23	14	9	1	14	31	.207

23 LOUIS MARSON C

Born: July 26, 1986. **B-T:** R-R. **Ht.:** 6-1. **Wt.:** 195. **Drafted:** HS—Scottsdale, Ariz., 2004 (4th round). **Signed by:** Therron Brockish.

A broken collarbone three games into his senior season crushed Marson's shot at playing quarterback in college, but the Phillies liked his package of size, strength and power enough to offer a $265,000 bonus. Despite his pedestrian production in his first two seasons in the system, he has impressed the player-development staff. An infielder and outfielder in high school, Marson has taken to catching quickly. Philadelphia believes he can become an intelligent, dependable receiver with an above-average arm and solid power. He must improve his patience and handling of breaking balls as a hitter. Marson started strong at Batavia, but slowed down over the second half, so he'll need to work on the conditioning needed from an everyday catcher this season in low Class A. His ceiling might be the highest of any catcher in the system, but he's not as sure a bet as Jason Jaramillo.

Year	Club (League)	Class	AVG	G	AB	R	H	2B	3B	HR	RBI	BB	SO	SB	OBP	SLG
2004	Phillies (GCL)	R	.257	38	113	18	29	3	0	4	8	13	18	4	.333	.389
2005	Batavia (NY-P)	A	.245	60	220	25	54	11	3	5	25	27	52	0	.329	.391
MINOR LEAGUE TOTALS			.249	98	333	43	83	14	3	9	33	40	70	4	.331	.390

24 BRETT HARKER
RHP

Born: July 9, 1984. **B-T:** R-R. **Ht.:** 6-3. **Wt.:** 185. **Drafted:** College of Charleston, 2005 (5th round). **Signed by:** Roy Tanner.

Harker's college career took off when he became the College of Charleston's closer as a sophomore in 2004. He set a school record with 13 saves that season and broke it in 2005, when he was named Southern Conference pitcher of the year and led the league with a 2.47 ERA and 15 saves. Harker signed for $165,000 as a fifth-round pick, after which the Phillies limited his innings because he had worked a lot at Charleston and also pulled a muscle in his hip. Harker's money pitch is his power curveball, which breaks late and straight down. His maximum-effort delivery makes it register in the low 80s and it's a knee-buckler that often catches batters looking. He used his fastball mostly to set up his curve in college, but Philadelphia wants him to work on throwing the heater more as a pro. Increased use of his fastball could build strength in an already quick arm, and bump up its peak velocity from its current 92 mph. With one plus pitch already, Harker could emerge as a late-inning option in the majors. He'll close in low Class A this year.

Year	Club (League)	Class	W	L	ERA	G	GS	CG	SV	IP	H	R	ER	HR	BB	SO	AVG
2005	Batavia (NY-P)	A	1	2	5.06	9	7	0	0	37	38	23	21	5	12	15	.257
MINOR LEAGUE TOTALS			1	2	5.06	9	7	0	0	37	38	23	21	5	12	15	.257

25 JEREMY SLAYDEN
OF

Born: July 28, 1982. **B-T:** L-R. **Ht.:** 6-0. **Wt.:** 185. **Drafted:** Georgia Tech, 2005 (8th round). **Signed by:** Chip Lawrence.

Slayden set a Georgia Tech freshman record with 18 home runs in 2002, and despite a sophomore slump, still ranked as a possible first-round pick entering 2004. Slayden lasted just nine games before a torn rotator cuff in his right (throwing) shoulder ended his season. He saw little time in the field as a redshirt junior in 2005, as the shoulder injury rendered his arm below average and a staph infection in his foot cost him three weeks. A 20th-round pick of the Padres out of high school and an 18th-round pick of the Athletics in 2004, Slayden finally signed for $95,000 as an eighth-rounder last June. He showed his power potential and solid approach in his pro debut, but his defensive limitations were also obvious and DHing in college added rust to the equation. Slayden could gain arm strength as he recovers from the shoulder surgery but it never will be better than average. He needs even more work at making better reads and taking better routes on flyballs. At best he'll be a playable outfielder, but his bat could make him worthwhile. He'll see time in left field and at DH in low Class A this year.

Year	Club (League)	Class	AVG	G	AB	R	H	2B	3B	HR	RBI	BB	SO	SB	OBP	SLG
2005	Batavia (NY-P)	A	.268	54	194	35	52	11	0	9	36	28	45	1	.373	.464
MINOR LEAGUE TOTALS			.268	54	194	35	52	11	0	9	36	28	45	1	.373	.464

26 TIM KENNELLY
3B

Born: Dec. 5, 1986. **B-T:** R-R. **Ht.:** 6-0. **Wt.:** 180. **Signed:** Australia, 2004. **Signed by:** Kevin Hooker.

Kennelly is yet another product of the Phillies' increased reliance on the Australian talent market. He earned MVP honors at a Major League Baseball academy there in 2004 before emerging as one of the better players on Philadelphia's Gulf Coast League roster a year later. Like fellow Aussie Brad Harman, Kennelly shows a quick bat, compact swing and solid approach at the plate. He also has the potential to drive the ball and add power as he progresses. Defensively, Kennelly offers solid hands and at least an average arm at third base, but his range is lacking and his fielding can get mechanical. To that end, the Phillies tried him behind the plate in instructional league and feel he eventually could become a solid backstop. The presence of Welinson Baez and Mike Costanzo ahead of him at third base probably rules out a promotion to a full-season league. Kennelly likely will play third base at Batavia in 2006 and might see a little action at catcher.

Year	Club (League)	Class	AVG	G	AB	R	H	2B	3B	HR	RBI	BB	SO	SB	OBP	SLG
2005	Phillies (GCL)	R	.295	38	112	15	33	11	0	1	15	21	16	3	.415	.420
MINOR LEAGUE TOTALS			.295	38	112	15	33	11	0	1	15	21	16	3	.415	.420

27 CHRIS BOOKER
RHP

Born: Dec. 9, 1976. **B-T:** R-R. **Ht.:** 6-3. **Wt.:** 230. **Drafted:** HS—Monroeville, Ala., 1995 (20th round). **Signed by:** Jim Crawford (Cubs).

Booker was a member of four different organizations in the last three months of 2005. He finished the year with the Reds before signing with the Nationals as a six-year free agent. The Tigers selected him with the fifth pick of the major league Rule 5 draft and immediately sent him to the Phillies for cash. Booker's mid-90s fastball always has made him an intriguing reliever, but command issues and the lack of a reliable secondary pitch have held him back. He might be best known for becoming the sixth player in minor league history to strike out five batters in an inning back in 2000. Last year, he added a splitter that's a plus pitch at times and enjoyed his best season, culminating with his major league debut on Sept. 5. He also throws a slider. He rarely surrendered homers as a minor leaguer, but allowed two bombs in two innings for the Reds. Booker figures to stick with the Phillies as a middle reliever.

Year	Club (League)	Class	W	L	ERA	G	GS	CG	SV	IP	H	R	ER	HR	BB	SO	AVG
1995	Cubs (GCL)	R	3	2	2.76	13	7	0	1	42	36	22	13	0	16	43	.232
1996	Daytona (FSL)	A	0	0	0.00	1	1	0	0	2	1	1	0	0	3	2	.125
	Williamsport (NY-P)	A	4	6	5.31	14	14	0	0	61	57	51	36	2	51	52	.246
1997	Williamsport (NY-P)	A	1	5	3.35	24	3	0	1	46	39	20	17	2	25	60	.234
1998	Rockford (Mid)	A	1	2	3.36	44	1	0	4	64	47	32	24	2	53	78	.212
1999	Daytona (FSL)	A	2	5	3.95	42	0	0	6	73	72	45	32	6	37	68	.254
2000	Daytona (FSL)	A	0	2	2.28	31	0	0	10	28	25	12	7	0	14	34	.238
	West Tenn (SL)	AA	1	0	3.68	12	0	0	0	15	10	8	6	1	12	21	.189
2001	West Tenn (SL)	AA	2	6	4.33	45	0	0	1	52	39	29	25	7	36	76	.205
	Chattanooga (SL)	AA	2	0	3.94	16	0	0	1	16	13	7	7	1	11	25	.217
2002	Did not play—Injured																
2003	Dayton (Mid)	A	0	0	9.00	5	0	0	0	5	4	5	5	3	4	6	.211
	Reds (GCL)	R	0	2	8.49	12	0	0	2	12	17	11	11	1	8	11	.327
2004	Chattanooga (SL)	AA	2	0	1.38	28	0	0	5	39	26	6	6	0	25	57	.182
	Louisville (IL)	AAA	0	1	4.50	7	0	0	0	12	10	6	6	2	10	9	.213
2005	Louisville (IL)	AAA	8	4	2.49	59	0	0	20	65	45	20	18	2	28	91	.195
	Cincinnati (NL)	MLB	0	0	31.50	3	0	0	0	2	6	8	7	2	4	2	.545
MAJOR LEAGUE TOTALS			0	0	31.50	3	0	0	0	2	6	8	7	2	4	2	.545
MINOR LEAGUE TOTALS			26	35	3.61	353	26	0	51	532	441	275	213	29	333	633	.224

28 KYLE KENDRICK
RHP

Born: Aug. 26, 1984. **B-T:** R-R. **Ht.:** 6-3. **Wt.:** 185. **Drafted:** HS—Mount Vernon, Wash., 2003 (7th round). **Signed by:** Tim Kissner.

Kendrick's skills as a quarterback and punter earned him a Washington State football scholarship, but he instead signed with Philadephia for $135,000 as a seventh-round pick in 2003. The Phillies envisioned him adding velocity to his fastball as he filled out his lanky but sturdy frame, and his heater now sits at 90-92 mph with good movement. Kendrick took longer than expected to come up with a suitable second pitch. His soft, loopy curveball never developed any bite and he failed to put away hitters when he got ahead in the count. So the Phillies moved him out of low Class A last April and switched him to a slider. Once he got a feel for it, the slider's tight break made Kendrick a different pitcher. He finally owned a strikeout pitch he could trust. Kendrick's changeup is close to average. With everything coming together for him, the Phillies are predicting a big year for him in 2006. Kendrick still needs to improve his overall command, and will start the season back in low Class A.

Year	Club (League)	Class	W	L	ERA	G	GS	CG	SV	IP	H	R	ER	HR	BB	SO	AVG
2003	Phillies (GCL)	R	0	4	5.46	9	5	0	0	31	40	24	19	3	12	26	.305
2004	Lakewood (SAL)	A	3	8	6.08	15	15	0	0	67	85	56	45	9	33	36	.318
	Batavia (NY-P)	A	2	8	5.48	13	12	0	0	71	94	52	43	6	18	53	.330
2005	Clearwater (FSL)	A	0	1	0.00	1	1	0	0	4	5	1	0	0	2	1	.333
	Lakewood (SAL)	A	0	3	9.13	5	5	0	0	23	38	24	23	2	10	11	.369
	Batavia (NY-P)	A	5	4	3.74	14	14	1	0	91	94	49	38	7	22	70	.262
MINOR LEAGUE TOTALS			10	28	5.27	57	52	1	0	287	356	206	168	27	97	197	.307

29 SCOTT MITCHINSON
RHP

Born: Dec. 28, 1984. **B-T:** R-R. **Ht.:** 6-3. **Wt.:** 185. **Signed:** Australia, 2003. **Signed by:** Kevin Hooker.

For $10,000, Mitchinson became the first of an ever-increasing number of Australian teenagers to sign with the Phillies. He led the Gulf Coast League in wins and ranked second in ERA during his U.S. debut in 2004, but his most stunning stat was allowing only one walk in 62 innings. Hampered by a tender arm in extended spring training last year, Mitchinson struggled to find his trademark command. Without it, batters savaged his repertoire of fringe-average pitches. His fastball, which jumped from 85 to 90 mph during his first two years in the organization, didn't pick up any velocity, while his curveball and changeup also plateaued. Mitchinson's command must improve if he's to progress, because it's his feel and ability to locate pitches that previously compensated for his lack of powerful stuff. The Phillies hope a return to health in low Class A will do the trick in 2006.

Year	Club (League)	Class	W	L	ERA	G	GS	CG	SV	IP	H	R	ER	HR	BB	SO	AVG
2004	Phillies (GCL)	R	7	0	1.75	10	10	0	0	62	40	12	12	2	1	60	.182
2005	Phillies (GCL)	R	0	0	0.00	1	1	0	0	3	1	0	0	0	0	4	.100
	Batavia (NY-P)	A	5	6	5.35	13	13	1	0	71	88	49	42	1	16	57	.311
MINOR LEAGUE TOTALS			12	6	3.59	24	24	1	0	135	129	61	54	3	17	121	.251

30 YOEL HERNANDEZ
RHP

Born: April 15, 1980. **B-T:** R-R. **Ht.:** 6-2. **Wt.:** 170. **Signed:** Venezuela, 1998. **Signed by:** Jesus Mendez.

Not to be confused with the standout Cuban hurdler of the same name, Hernandez could find his way to Philadelphia in 2006. He succeeded in the lower levels with precise location of fringe-average stuff but became more hittable as he advanced through the system. Hernandez moved to the bullpen in 2003 and started paring down his repertoire. The short stints also allowed his fastball to reach 90-92 mph after previously sitting in the upper 80s. He was progressing nicely in 2004 before elbow and shoulder problems ended his season in early August. Hernandez didn't immediately regain his strength and velocity, so he started in high Class A in 2005. By the end of May he had worked his way to Triple-A, where he effectively mixed his fastball with a plus slider out of the bullpen. Hernandez' ceiling isn't high, but he should make his big league debut this year, though he might begin the season in Triple-A.

Year	Club (League)	Class	W	L	ERA	G	GS	CG	SV	IP	H	R	ER	HR	BB	SO	AVG
1999	La Victoria (VSL)	R	2	2	3.32	14	11	0	1	60	48	27	22	3	29	57	.226
2000	Phillies (GCL)	R	4	1	1.35	10	9	2	0	60	39	10	9	2	17	46	.183
2001	Lakewood (SAL)	A	6	9	3.47	25	25	1	0	161	153	94	62	7	42	111	.243
2002	Clearwater (FSL)	A	7	16	3.54	28	28	3	0	170	176	76	67	6	54	116	.271
2003	Reading (EL)	AA	6	3	4.26	43	1	0	2	74	100	43	35	4	31	46	.336
	Scranton/W-B (IL)	AAA	0	0	6.00	2	0	0	0	3	5	2	2	0	0	3	.357
2004	Scranton/W-B (IL)	AAA	0	0	6.46	14	2	0	0	31	38	26	22	4	7	18	.333
	Reading (EL)	AA	1	2	2.01	20	0	0	6	31	24	12	7	0	15	33	.203
2005	Clearwater (FSL)	A	1	1	11.81	4	0	0	0	5	8	10	7	1	3	7	.320
	Reading (EL)	AA	2	0	1.32	9	0	0	0	14	12	2	2	0	6	15	.231
	Scranton/W-B (IL)	AAA	6	4	3.40	40	0	0	3	56	53	21	21	5	24	52	.256
MINOR LEAGUE TOTALS			35	38	3.47	209	76	6	12	664	656	323	256	32	228	504	.259

PITTSBURGH
PIRATES

BY **JOHN PERROTTO**

The Pirates have been stressing the importance of a small-market franchise being able to build from within ever since Kevin McClatchy's ownership group took control of the club on the first day of spring training in 1996. After years of trying, Pittsburgh began practicing what it has preached the second half of the 2005 season.

The Pirates began the season without one rookie on their roster. Before their 13th consecutive losing season ended, though, 12 players had made their major league debuts. That began a full-scale youth movement that the Pirates believe eventually can lead them back to respectability.

Pittsburgh's long-suffering fans were enthused by the play of such youngsters as lefthanders **Zach Duke** and Paul Maholm; catcher Ryan Doumit; first baseman Brad Eldred; and outfielders Chris Duffy and Nate McLouth. Duke had the best debut at 8-2, 1.81 and finished fifth in the National League rookie of the year race. Lefty Tom Gorzelanny, righties Bryan Bullington, Matt Capps and Ian Snell, catcher Ronny Paulino, third baseman Jose Bautista and infielder J.J. Furmaniak also made cameo appearances.

"As far as having players who can help us in the future, this is the best position we've been in since I got here," said general manager Dave Littlefield, who replaced Cam Bonifay midway through the 2001 season.

While the focus was on the rookies at the end of 2005, Pittsburgh also saw other players make significant progress in their second full major league seasons.

Left fielder Jason Bay built on his NL

GEORGE GOJKOVICH

rookie-of-the-year award by hitting .306-32-101 with 21 steals in 22 attempts while starting all 162 games. Second baseman Jose Castillo began to develop power, hitting .268-11-53 in 101 games before a knee injury ended his season in late August.

The Pirates also have high hopes for 23-year-old lefthander Oliver Perez, who slipped to 7-5, 5.85 in 20 starts and missed nearly two months with a broken big toe after he kicked a metal laundry cart in frustration. He went 12-10, 2.98 with 239 strikeouts in 196 innings in 2004.

The Pirates stressed patience in player development when Littlefield took over and brought in Brian Graham as farm director and Ed Creech as scouting director. Instead of rushing players to the majors, they moved them one level at a time for the most part. The players who arrived in Pittsburgh in 2005 didn't appear overwhelmed. Under Graham, Pirates farm clubs have posted a combined winning record in each of the last four seasons. Prior to that, they finished above .500 just once in 33 years.

Pittsburgh's strength in recent years clearly has been pitching, but that's starting to change as the Pirates used the 11th overall pick in the last two drafts on a pair of high school position players: catcher Neil Walker (2004) and center fielder Andrew McCutchen (2005). They rank 1-2 on the prospect list this year.

TOP 30 PROSPECTS

1. Neil Walker, c	16. Mike Johnston, lhp
2. Andrew McCutchen, of	17. Josh Sharpless, rhp
3. Tom Gorzelanny, lhp	18. Joe Bauserman, rhp
4. Paul Maholm, lhp	19. Todd Redmond, rhp
5. Jose Bautista, 3b	20. Adam Boeve, of
6. Nate McLouth, of	21. Brent Lillibridge, ss
7. Bryan Bullington, rhp	22. Javier Guzman, ss
8. John Van Benschoten, rhp	23. Matt Swanson, rhp
9. Chris Duffy, of	24. Matt Peterson, rhp
10. Matt Capps, rhp	25. Jason Quarles, rhp
11. Rajai Davis, of	26. Clayton Hamilton, rhp
12. Craig Stansberry, 2b	27. Jonah Bayliss, rhp
13. Ronny Paulino, c	28. Wardell Starling, rhp
14. James Boone, of	29. Eddie Prasch, 3b
15. Brad Corley, of	30. Brian Bixler, ss

ORGANIZATION OVERVIEW

General manager: David Littlefield. **Farm director:** Brian Graham. **Scouting director:** Ed Creech.

2005 PERFORMANCE

Class	Team	League	W	L	Pct.	Finish*	Manager(s)
Majors	Pittsburgh	National	67	95	.414	t-15th (16)	L. McClendon/P. Mackanin
Triple-A	Indianapolis Indians	International	78	66	.542	4th (14)	Trent Jewett
Double-A	Altoona Curve	Eastern	76	66	.535	t-2nd (12)	Tony Beasley
High A	Lynchburg Hillcats	Carolina	78	62	.557	2nd (8)	Tim Leiper
Low A	Hickory Crawdads	South Atlantic	54	80	.403	15th (16)	Jeff Branson
Short-season	Williamsport Crosscutters	New York-Penn	44	32	.579	4th (14)	Tom Prince
Rookie	GCL Pirates	Gulf Coast	28	26	.519	t-4th (12)	Jeff Livesey
OVERALL 2005 MINOR LEAGUE RECORD			358	332	.519	9th (30)	

*Finish in overall standings (No. of teams in league).

ORGANIZATION LEADERS

BATTING
*Minimum 250 at-bats
*AVG	Carlin, Michael, Hickory	.318
R	Magness, Pat, Lynchburg	98
H	Walker, Neil, Hickory/Lynchburg	157
TB	Stansberry, Craig, Altoona/Ind./Lynchburg	251
2B	Magness, Pat, Lynchburg	39
3B	Stansberry, Craig, Altoona/Ind./Lynchburg	13
HR	Eldred, Brad, Altoona/Indianapolis	28
RBI	Bautista, Jose, Altoona/Indianapolis	94
BB	Magness, Pat, Lynchburg	141
SO	Bixler, Brian, Hickory	134
SB	Thompson, Rich, Altoona/Indianapolis	58
*OBP	Magness, Pat, Lynchburg	.481
*SLG	Eldred, Brad, Altoona/Indianapolis	.674

PITCHING
#Minimum 75 innings
W	Duke, Zach, Indianapolis	12
L	Five tied at	10
#ERA	Borner, Brady, Altoona	2.08
G	Corey, Mark, Indianapolis	61
CG	O'Brien, Patrick, Lynchburg	2
	Snell, Ian, Indianapolis	2
SV	Corey, Mark, Indianapolis	28
IP	Hankins, Derek, Hickory	156
BB	Bloom, Kyle, Hickory/Lynchburg	76
SO	Gorzelanny, Tom, Altoona/Indianapolis	124

BEST TOOLS

Best Hitter for Average	Andrew McCutchen
Best Power Hitter	Jose Bautista
Best Strike-Zone Discipline	Andrew McCutchen
Fastest Baserunner	Pedro Powell
Best Athlete	Neil Walker
Best Fastball	Tom Gorzelanny
Best Curveball	Jason Quarles
Best Slider	Josh Sharpless
Best Changeup	Joe Bauserman
Best Control	Paul Maholm
Best Defensive Catcher	Ronny Paulino
Best Defensive Infielder	Brent Lillibridge
Best Infield Arm	Javier Guzman
Best Defensive Outfielder	Andrew McCutchen
Best Outfield Arm	Brad Corley

PROJECTED 2009 LINEUP

Catcher	Neil Walker
First Base	Sean Casey
Second Base	Jose Castillo
Third Base	Jose Bautista
Shortstop	Jack Wilson
Left Field	Jason Bay
Center Field	Andrew McCutchen

Right Field	Nate McLouth
No. 1 Starter	Zach Duke
No. 2 Starter	Oliver Perez
No. 3 Starter	Kip Wells
No. 4 Starter	Tom Gorzelanny
No. 5 Starter	Paul Maholm
Closer	Mike Gonzalez

LAST YEAR'S TOP 20 PROSPECTS

1. Zach Duke, lhp	11. Rajai Davis, of
2. Neil Walker, c	12. Jose Bautista, 3b
3. John Van Benschoten, rhp	13. Freddy Sanchez, 2b/ss
4. Ian Snell, rhp	14. Ryan Doumit, c
5. Tom Gorzelanny, lhp	15. Steve Lerud, c
6. Bryan Bullington, rhp	16. Chris Duffy, of
7. Paul Maholm, lhp	17. Eddie Prasch, 3b
8. Brad Eldred, 1b	18. Blair Johnson, rhp
9. Matt Peterson, rhp	19. Cory Stewart, lhp
10. Nate McLouth, of	20. Brian Bixler, ss

TOP PROSPECTS OF THE DECADE

Year	Player, Pos.	2005 Org.
1996	Jason Kendall, c	Athletics
1997	Kris Benson, rhp	Mets
1998	Kris Benson, rhp	Mets
1999	Chad Hermansen, of	Out of baseball
2000	Chad Hermansen, of	Out of baseball
2001	J.R. House, c	Out of baseball
2002	J.R. House, c	Out of baseball
2003	John Van Benschoten, rhp	Pirates
2004	John Van Benschoten, rhp	Pirates
2005	Zach Duke, lhp	Pirates

TOP DRAFT PICKS OF THE DECADE

Year	Player, Pos.	2005 Org.
1996	Kris Benson, rhp	Mets
1997	J.J. Davis, of	Rockies
1998	Clint Johnston, lhp/of	Blue Jays
1999	Bobby Bradley, rhp	Pirates
2000	Sean Burnett, lhp	Pirates
2001	John Van Benschoten, rhp/of	Pirates
2002	Bryan Bullington, rhp	Pirates
2003	Paul Maholm, lhp	Pirates
2004	Neil Walker, c	Pirates
2005	Andrew McCutchen, of	Pirates

ALL-TIME LARGEST BONUSES

Bryan Bullington, 2002	$4,000,000
John Van Benschoten, 2001	$2,400,000
Bobby Bradley, 1999	$2,225,000
Paul Maholm, 2003	$2,200,000
Kris Benson, 1996	$2,000,000

MINOR LEAGUE DEPTH CHART

Pittsburgh Pirates

Rank: **19**

STRENGTH: Pitching depth. Pirates still have arms after graduating Zach Duke and others to Pittsburgh.

WEAKNESS: Impact talent. Andrew McCutchen and Neil Walker are the only star-quality players in the organization.

*Depth charts prepared by **John Manuel** and **Chris Kline**. Numbers in parentheses indicate prospect rankings.*

LF
Nate McLouth (16)
Victor Igsema

CF
Andrew McCutchen (2)
Chris Duffy (9)
Rajai Davis (11)
James Boone (14)
Antonio Sucre
Nyjer Morgan
Chaz Lytle

RF
Brad Corley (15)
Adam Boeve (20)
Jeff Cook
Ray Sadler

3B
Jose Bautista (5)
Eddie Prasch (29)
Yurendell DeCaster

SS
Brent Lillibridge (21)
Javier Guzman (22)
Brian Bixler (30)

2B
Craig Stansberry (12)
J.J. Furmaniak
Cameron Blair

1B
Steven Pearce

C
Neil Walker (1)
Ronny Paulino (13)
Steve Lerud
Mike McCuiston

RHP

Starters	Relievers
Bryan Bullington (7)	Matt Capps (10)
John Van Benschoten (8)	Josh Sharpless (17)
Joe Bauserman (18)	Matt Swanson (23)
Todd Redmond (19)	Jason Quarles (25)
Matt Peterson (24)	Jonah Bayliss (27)
Clayton Hamilton (26)	Justin Vaclavik
Wardell Starling (28)	Jacob Cuffman
Brad Clapp	Chris Hernandez
Blair Johnson	Jonathan Albaladejo
Kyle Pearson	Chad Blackwell
Matt Guillory	
Derek Hankins	

LHP

Starters	Relievers
Tom Gorzelanny (3)	Mike Johnston (16)
Paul Maholm (4)	Mike Connolly
Kyle Bloom	Shane Youman
Brian Holliday	Brady Borner
Josh Shortslef	

DRAFT ANALYSIS

2005

Best Pro Debut: OF Andrew McCutchen (1) hit .297-2-30 with 13 steals to rank as the top prospect in the Rookie-level Gulf Coast League, then batted .346 in a 13-game stint in the short-season New York-Penn League. 1B Steve Pearce (8) hit .301-7-52 and topped the NY-P with 26 doubles. RHP Matt Swanson (13) went 4-2, 1.61 with six saves and 30 strikeouts in 28 innings in the NY-P.

Best Athlete: The only thing McCutchen really lacks is size. Though he's 5-foot-11 and 175 pounds, his hands and bat are so quick that he has average raw power. All of his other tools except for his arm (which is average) grade out as plus, and his makeup is strong as well. OF James Boone (3) and SS Brent Lillibridge (4) are good athletes too.

Best Pure Hitter: McCutchen can catch up to good fastballs and drills line drives to all fields. The Pirates think OF Brad Corley (2) will take off now that he's recovered from a thumb injury that marred his final season at Mississippi State. They also like Boone's swing, though he needs to cut down on his strikeouts (85 in 68 pro games).

Best Raw Power: It just might be McCutchen, who put on a batting-practice show during a workout at PNC Park. Boone and Corley are his biggest challengers.

Fastest Runner: A Florida state track champion as a relay runner, McCutchen posted a 6.35-second 60-yard dash in a showcase just before the draft.

Best Defensive Player: McCutchen has the range and instincts to be a star center fielder. Boone is good in center; Lillibridge has plus range and arm strength at shortstop.

Best Fastball: RHP Jeff Sues (5) usually

ROGER WOOD

Boone

works at 92-93 mph, and the Pirates clocked him at 97 mph in the spring. RHP Justin Vaclavik (7) and Swanson both can hit 95 mph, while RHP Eric Krebs (16) showed 93-94 mph heat as a junior college reliever.

Best Breaking Ball: Sues backs up his fastball with a hard slider.

Most Intriguing Background: OF Juan Mesa's (23) father Jose is Pittsburgh's closer. OF Ryan Searage's (18) dad Ray pitched in the majors and is a pitching coach in the Pirates system. 3B Tony Mansolino's (26) father Doug is the Astros' third-base coach.

Closest To The Majors: McCutchen is very advanced for a high school player. Corley, Boone or Pearce could beat him to the big leagues if they get their bats going, and don't rule out Vaclavik as a setup man.

Best Late-Round Pick: Swanson was an unexpected surprise, regularly pitching with an 88-93 mph fastball and a good slider.

The One Who Got Away: Jarred Bogany (15), a raw athlete with impressive tools, was part of a banner Texas high school outfield crop. Physically reminiscent of Milton Bradley, he's now at Louisiana State.

Assessment: Ownership mandated college picks in the first round in 2002-03, but for the second straight year scouting director Ed Creech was allowed to pick a toolsy high schooler. The Pirates concentrated on hitters in the draft, taking outfielders with their first three picks.

2004 C Neil Walker (1), a hometown pick, is athletic and off to a nice start in his career, but his value will diminish if he moves from behind the plate. RHP Joe Bauserman (4) is the next-best signee at this point. **GRADE:** C+

2003 LHP Paul Maholm (1) had a 2.18 ERA in his big league debut last year, and LHP Tom Gorzelanny (2) may still end up being better. In the long run, both could take a back seat to unsigned RHP Dallas Buck (19), who should be an early first-round pick in 2006. **GRADE:** B

2002 RHP Bryan Bullington (1) had his best year in 2005 but required shoulder surgery in October. The Pirates will continue to rue using the No. 1 pick on Bullington rather than B.J. Upton. 1B Brad Eldred (6) and RHP Matt Capps (7) have surpassed expectations. **GRADE:** C

2001 LHP Zach Duke (20) had a spectacular rookie season and is Pittsburgh's ace. 1B Chris Shelton (33) was another steal, but the Pirates lost him to the Tigers in the 2004 Rule 5 draft. Signing SS Stephen Drew (11) would have been a spectacular addition. **GRADE:** B+

Draft analysis prepared by Jim Callis. Numbers in parentheses indicate draft rounds.

NEIL
WALKER

C

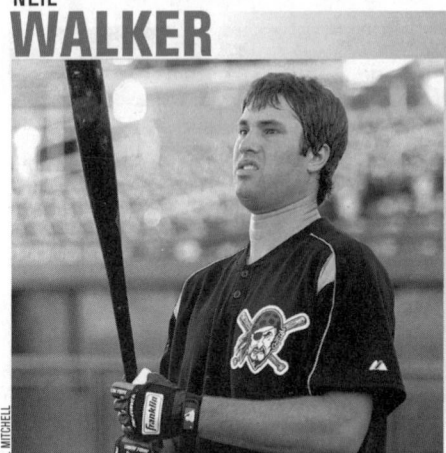

BILL MITCHELL

Born: Sept. 10, 1985.
Ht.: 6-2. **Wt.:** 215.
Bats: B. **Throws:** R.
Drafted: HS—Gibsonia, Pa., 2004
(1st round).
Signed by: Jon Mercurio.

Walker was born to play baseball, and it has been his dream to play in the majors since he attended the 1994 All-Star Game at old Three Rivers Stadium. His father Tom pitched in the big leagues for six seasons with four teams from 1972-77. His uncle, Chip Lang, pitched for the Expos in 1975-76. His brother Matt was an outfielder in the Tigers and Orioles systems. Walker was the first Pittsburgh-area player ever selected in the first round by the Pirates after hitting .657-13-42 in his senior season at Pine-Richland High, and his charismatic nature has enabled him to handle the attention with aplomb. In addition to being a prep All-American in baseball, Walker was an all-state wide receiver in high school and received plenty of interest from major college football programs.

Walker is a rare commodity, a switch-hitter who can produce for both average and power. Though he's a natural righthanded hitter, he showed outstanding power as a lefthanded batter in 2005 and really has no weak side. He relishes the opportunity to hit with runners on base and projects as a middle-of-the-order run producer who should hit in the neighborhood of .300 with 30 homers per season. Walker has a strong arm and threw out 37 percent of runners attempting to steal in 2005. Though not a burner, he also runs well, particularly for a catcher.

Walker could stand to take a few more walks, though he has been able to overcome that by his ability to make consistent hard contact. His defense needs plenty of work. His throwing mechanics are often inconsistent and he occasionally lapses into bad habits where he doesn't move his feet and stabs at pitches. While the Pirates believe Walker can stay behind the plate and reach the majors, they also believe they would receive more long-term production if they removed him from the rigors of catching. With that in mind, Walker began taking ground balls at third base in the Arizona Fall League with an eye on eventually moving to the hot corner or a corner-outfield position. He has the athleticism to handle the transition to any of those spots. Walker tore a ligament in his left wrist while swinging a bat at the end of the AFL season, requiring surgery that forced him to take a couple of months off. The Pirates expect him to be ready for spring training.

How quickly Walker reaches Pittsburgh depends upon what position he ultimately plays. If he stays behind the plate, he likely won't be ready until 2008. If he moves to third base or the outfield, that timetable easily could speed up to 2007. He'll probably open 2006 at high Class A Lynchburg with the likelihood of moving to Double-A Altoona during the season. Walker excelled in his first season of full-season ball in 2005, then held his own as one of the youngest players in the AFL. That leads to the feeling he could get to the majors quickly and provide the Pirates with a sorely needed second elite hitter to go with Jason Bay in the heart of the batting order. They haven't had a starting position player from the Pittsburgh area since third baseman/outfielder Bill Robinson from 1975-82, and the win-starved fans would relish having one of their own to cheer.

Year	Club (League)	Class	AVG	G	AB	R	H	2B	3B	HR	RBI	BB	SO	SB	OBP	SLG
2004	Pirates (GCL)	R	.271	52	192	28	52	12	3	4	20	10	33	3	.313	.427
	Williamsport (NY-P)	A	.313	8	32	2	10	3	0	0	7	2	1	1	.343	.406
2005	Hickory (SAL)	A	.301	120	485	78	146	33	2	12	68	20	71	7	.332	.452
	Lynchburg (Car)	A	.262	9	42	4	11	2	1	0	12	0	12	0	.244	.357
MINOR LEAGUE TOTALS			.292	189	751	112	219	50	6	16	107	32	117	11	.323	.438

2 ANDREW McCUTCHEN OF

Born: Oct. 10, 1986. **B-T:** R-R. **Ht.:** 5-11. **Wt.:** 175. **Drafted:** HS—Fort Meade, Fla., 2005 (1st round). **Signed by:** Rob Sidwell.

The Pirates made McCutchen their top pick after he hit .709-11-28 as a high school senior. He has good athletic genes; his father played football at small-college power Carson-Newman (Tenn.) and his mother played volleyball in junior college in Florida. He ranked as the top prospect in the Rookie-level Gulf Coast League in his debut. McCutchen has a good blend of power and speed, often drawing comparisons to Marquis Grissom. He has wiry strength and his extra-base hit total should increase once his body fills out. He has outstanding speed (he covers 60 yards in 6.35 seconds) and a quick first step, enabling him to cover plenty of ground in center field. McCutchen played at a small rural high school and is still somewhat raw in all aspects of the game. His arm is his weakest tool but still grades out as average. McCutchen is ready to log a full season at low Class A Hickory. His talent and maturity could get him to the major leagues as soon as 2008.

Year	Club (League)	Class	AVG	G	AB	R	H	2B	3B	HR	RBI	BB	SO	SB	OBP	SLG
2005	Pirates (GCL)	R	.297	45	158	36	47	9	3	2	30	29	24	13	.411	.430
	Williamsport (NY-P)	A	.346	13	52	12	18	3	1	0	5	8	6	4	.443	.442
MINOR LEAGUE TOTALS			.310	58	210	48	65	12	4	2	35	37	30	17	.419	.433

3 TOM GORZELANNY LHP

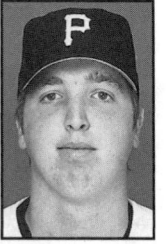

Born: July 12, 1982. **B-T:** L-L. **Ht.:** 6-2. **Wt.:** 207. **Drafted:** Triton (Ill.) JC, 2003 (2nd round). **Signed by:** Mark Germann.

After starting his college career at Kansas, Gorzelanny turned into a high-round pick after academic woes prompted him to transfer to Triton Junior College near his Chicago-area home. He made his big league debut in September, barely more than two years after being drafted, and set a Double-A Altoona record by striking out 13 in an Eastern League playoff game. Gorzelanny throws hard; his fastball sits at 90-92 mph with excellent movement and reaches as high as 95. His slider can be unhittable at times, and he really took a step forward in 2005 after he dramatically improved his changeup. He also has good mound presence and refuses to give in to hitters. Gorzelanny needs to tighten up his breaking ball because it gets slurvy at times. He can solve that problem by developing a more consistent arm slot. Though he got a major league look, Gorzelanny needs to spend the majority of 2006 at Triple-A Indianapolis to become a finished product. He has the chance to become a fine No. 2-3 starter.

Year	Club (League)	Class	W	L	ERA	G	GS	CG	SV	IP	H	R	ER	HR	BB	SO	AVG
2003	Williamsport (NY-P)	A	1	2	1.78	8	8	0	0	30	23	6	6	1	10	22	.215
2004	Hickory (SAL)	A	7	2	2.23	16	15	1	0	93	63	30	23	9	34	106	.194
	Lynchburg (Car)	A	3	5	4.85	10	10	0	0	56	54	31	30	6	19	61	.255
2005	Altoona (EL)	AA	8	5	3.26	23	23	1	0	130	114	50	47	6	46	124	.236
	Pittsburgh (NL)	MLB	0	1	12.00	3	1	0	0	6	10	8	8	1	3	3	.357
MAJOR LEAGUE TOTALS			0	1	12.00	3	1	0	0	6	10	8	8	1	3	3	.357
MINOR LEAGUE TOTALS			19	14	3.09	57	56	2	0	309	254	117	106	22	109	313	.226

4 PAUL MAHOLM LHP

Born: June 25, 1982. **B-T:** L-L. **Ht.:** 6-2. **Wt.:** 225. **Drafted:** Mississippi State, 2003 (1st round). **Signed by:** Everett Russell.

Maholm's 2004 season was cut short when a line drive struck him in the left eye in mid May while he was in high Class A, and his 2005 was eventful as well. An outstanding spring training led to him beginning the season in Double-A. After a trip to the Futures Game and a stopover in Triple-A, Maholm landed in Pittsburgh. Off the field, his mother died of colon cancer and his new house in Holly Springs, Miss., narrowly missed being heavily damaged by Hurricane Katrina. Maholm has outstanding mound presence and very good command of three pitches that can be above average at times. He runs his 88-91 mph fastball in on righthanders. He also has a good curveball and a slider that's improving. Righthanders hit .265 against Maholm—compared to .173 by lefties—in part because the quality of his changeup fluctuates. He's not overpowering, so he doesn't have much margin for error. Maholm showed he's ready to be a major league starter, but the Pirates' depth might force him back to Triple-A to start 2006.

Year	Club (League)	Class	W	L	ERA	G	GS	CG	SV	IP	H	R	ER	HR	BB	SO	AVG
2003	Williamsport (NY-P)	A	2	1	1.83	8	8	0	0	34	25	11	7	1	10	32	.197
2004	Lynchburg (Car)	A	1	3	1.84	8	8	0	0	44	39	11	9	2	15	28	.245
	Pirates (GCL)	R	0	0	2.25	1	0	0	0	4	5	1	1	0	1	2	.294
	Hickory (SAL)	A	0	2	9.49	3	3	0	0	12	17	14	13	2	10	12	.354
2005	Altoona (EL)	AA	6	2	3.20	16	16	0	0	82	73	32	29	5	26	75	.243
	Indianapolis (IL)	AAA	1	1	3.53	6	6	0	0	36	40	19	14	2	12	21	.286
	Pittsburgh (NL)	MLB	3	1	2.18	6	6	0	0	41	31	10	10	2	17	26	.209
MAJOR LEAGUE TOTALS			3	1	2.18	6	6	0	0	41	31	10	10	2	17	26	.209
MINOR LEAGUE TOTALS			10	9	3.10	42	41	0	0	212	199	88	73	12	74	170	.251

5 JOSE BAUTISTA 3B

Born: Oct. 19, 1980. **B-T:** R-R. **Ht.:** 6-0. **Wt.:** 192. **Drafted:** Chipola (Fla.) JC, 2000 (20th round). **Signed by:** Jack Powell.

Bautista got needed at-bats at Double-A in 2005 after getting just 88 while bouncing around the majors with four teams in 2004 as a Rule 5 draft pick. Baltimore selected Bautista from the Pirates, and he wound up going to Tampa Bay and Kansas City on waiver claims before landing back in Pittsburgh in the Kris Benson trade. Bautista got just 165 at-bats in 2003 because of a broken hand. Bautista has a quick bat and began to show plus power in 2005. He has the tools to be an above-average defensive third baseman with good range and a strong arm. An average runner, he's versatile with the ability to play second base and all three outfield positions. He needs to smooth out some rough edges. Bautista lacks plate discipline and can be made to chase bad pitches. His hands are also a little stiff and he makes too many errors on routine plays. The Pirates have a big need at third base but believe Bautista needs to spend at least a half-season in Triple-A. He could get an extended look after the all-star break.

Year	Club (League)	Class	AVG	G	AB	R	H	2B	3B	HR	RBI	BB	SO	SB	OBP	SLG
2001	Williamsport (NY-P)	A	.286	62	220	43	63	10	3	5	30	21	41	8	.364	.427
2002	Hickory (SAL)	A	.301	129	438	72	132	26	3	14	57	67	104	3	.402	.470
2003	Pirates (GCL)	R	.348	7	23	5	8	1	0	1	3	4	7	0	.429	.522
	Lynchburg (Car)	A	.242	51	165	28	40	14	2	4	20	27	48	1	.359	.424
2004	Baltimore (AL)	MLB	.273	16	11	3	3	0	0	0	0	1	3	0	.333	.273
	Tampa Bay (AL)	MLB	.167	12	12	1	2	0	0	0	1	3	7	0	.333	.167
	Pittsburgh (NL)	MLB	.200	23	40	1	8	2	0	0	0	2	18	0	.238	.250
	Kansas City (AL)	MLB	.200	13	25	1	5	1	0	0	1	1	12	0	.231	.240
2005	Altoona (EL)	AA	.283	117	445	63	126	27	1	23	90	48	101	7	.364	.503
	Indianapolis (IL)	AAA	.255	13	51	6	13	3	0	1	4	4	10	1	.309	.373
	Pittsburgh (NL)	MLB	.143	11	28	3	4	1	0	0	1	3	7	1	.226	.179
MAJOR LEAGUE TOTALS			.190	75	116	9	22	4	0	0	3	10	47	1	.254	.224
MINOR LEAGUE TOTALS			.285	379	1342	217	382	81	9	48	204	171	311	20	.375	.466

6 NATE McLOUTH OF

Born: Oct. 28, 1981. **B-T:** L-R. **Ht.:** 5-11. **Wt.:** 186. **Drafted:** HS—Whitehall, Mich., 2000 (25th round). **Signed by:** Duane Gustavson.

McLouth shared Mr. Baseball honors in Michigan in 2000, but teams shied away from drafting him because of his commitment to the University of Michigan. However, the Pirates drafted him in the 25th round and persuaded him to sign for $500,000. He made his big league debut last season and hit four home runs in his final six games. McLouth's tools all grade out at average or a little above. He plays above his tools because of his outstanding work ethic and baseball acumen. He handles the bat well, makes consistent contact, runs well and is an exceptional bunter. A 'tweener, McLouth lacks the desired power for an outfield corner and the range for center field. His best position is probably right field, where his arm is just adequate. He has shown the ability to hit doubles in the minors and needs to translate that into over-the-fence power. McLouth may not have the perfect profile, but he consistently has overcome doubters and should become at least a good fourth outfielder. He'll compete for a big league job in spring training.

Year	Club (League)	Class	AVG	G	AB	R	H	2B	3B	HR	RBI	BB	SO	SB	OBP	SLG
2001	Hickory (SAL)	A	.285	96	351	59	100	17	5	12	54	43	54	21	.371	.464
2002	Lynchburg (Car)	A	.244	114	393	58	96	23	4	9	46	41	48	20	.324	.392
2003	Lynchburg (Car)	A	.300	117	440	85	132	27	2	6	33	55	68	40	.386	.411
2004	Altoona (EL)	AA	.322	133	515	93	166	40	4	8	73	48	62	31	.384	.462
2005	Indianapolis (IL)	AAA	.297	110	397	64	118	20	3	5	39	39	58	34	.364	.401
	Pittsburgh (NL)	MLB	.257	41	109	20	28	6	0	5	12	3	20	2	.305	.450
MAJOR LEAGUE TOTALS			.257	41	109	20	28	6	0	5	12	3	20	2	.305	.450
MINOR LEAGUE TOTALS			.292	570	2096	359	612	127	18	40	245	226	290	146	.367	.427

7 BRYAN BULLINGTON

RHP

Born: Sept. 30, 1980. **B-T:** R-R. **Ht.:** 6-4. **Wt.:** 222. **Drafted:** Ball State, 2002 (1st round). **Signed by:** Duane Gustavson.

Though some members of the organization preferred B.J. Upton, the Pirates made Bullington the No. 1 pick in the 2002 draft and gave him a club-record $4 million bonus. After missing the first six weeks of the 2005 season with a sore shoulder, he had a fine year at Triple-A and made his big league debut in September. However, he needed shoulder surgery to repair damage to his labrum in October and won't be able to pitch until June. Bullington regained the touch on his slider in 2005. With its late break and good tilt, it became his out pitch. He has a smooth delivery and his pitches have good movement coming from a three-quarters arm slot. Bullington's fastball hit 95 mph in college, but he never has thrown that hard since coming into pro ball. The Pirates hope he might regain velocity following his shoulder surgery. Bullington's curveball tends to get loopy and his changeup can be erratic. Bullington will begin the season rehabbing his shoulder, slowing down his timetable. Look for him to spend most of 2006 in the minors, with a September callup to the majors most likely.

Year	Club (League)	Class	W	L	ERA	G	GS	CG	SV	IP	H	R	ER	HR	BB	SO	AVG
2003	Hickory (SAL)	A	5	1	1.39	8	7	0	0	45	25	10	7	3	11	46	.155
	Lynchburg (Car)	A	8	4	3.05	17	17	2	0	97	101	39	33	5	27	67	.270
2004	Altoona (EL)	AA	12	7	4.10	26	26	0	0	145	160	77	66	18	47	100	.289
2005	Indianapolis (IL)	AAA	9	5	3.38	18	18	1	0	109	104	48	41	11	26	82	.251
	Pittsburgh (NL)	MLB	0	0	13.50	1	0	0	0	1	1	2	2	0	1	1	.250
MAJOR LEAGUE TOTALS			0	0	13.50	1	0	0	0	1	1	2	2	0	1	1	.250
MINOR LEAGUE TOTALS			34	17	3.33	69	68	3	0	397	390	174	147	37	111	295	.259

8 JOHN VAN BENSCHOTEN

RHP

Born: April 14, 1980. **B-T:** R-R. **Ht.:** 6-4. **Wt.:** 217. **Drafted:** Kent State, 2001 (1st round). **Signed by:** Duane Gustavson.

Van Benschoten missed the entire 2005 season because of three arthroscopic shoulder surgeries, one on his throwing arm and two on his left arm. He led NCAA Division I with 31 home runs at Kent State in 2001, and the Pirates surprised many clubs by drafting him eighth overall as a pitcher that June. After pitching strictly in relief in college, he reached the majors as a starter in three years. Van Benschoten has the ideal pitcher's build and a consistent 91-94 mph fastball. His best pitch is a late-breaking slider that causes many swings and misses. He also has a solid curveball. Despite trying several grips, Van Benschoten never has gained complete feel for a changeup. Despite his age, he lacks pitching experience because of his college background. His mechanics can wander at times, leading to a loss of location. Van Benschoten should be ready to pitch by the time spring training begins. He went just 4-11, 4.72 in Triple-A in 2004 and needs more time in the minors. He should challenge for a spot in the Pittsburgh rotation in 2007.

Year	Club (League)	Class	W	L	ERA	G	GS	CG	SV	IP	H	R	ER	HR	BB	SO	AVG
2001	Williamsport (NY-P)	A	0	2	3.51	9	9	0	0	26	23	11	10	0	10	19	.247
2002	Hickory (SAL)	A	11	4	2.80	27	27	0	0	148	119	57	46	6	62	145	.219
2003	Lynchburg (Car)	A	6	0	2.22	9	9	0	0	49	33	14	12	1	18	49	.192
	Altoona (EL)	AA	7	6	3.69	17	17	1	0	90	95	46	37	5	34	78	.268
2004	Nashville (PCL)	AAA	4	11	4.72	23	23	0	0	132	135	75	69	16	49	101	.264
	Pittsburgh (NL)	MLB	1	3	6.91	6	5	0	0	29	33	27	22	3	19	18	.300
2005	Did not play—Injured																
MAJOR LEAGUE TOTALS			1	3	6.91	6	5	0	0	29	33	27	22	3	19	18	.300
MINOR LEAGUE TOTALS			28	23	3.52	85	85	1	0	444	405	203	174	28	173	392	.242

9 CHRIS DUFFY

OF

Born: April 20, 1980. **B-T:** B-L. **Ht.:** 5-10. **Wt.:** 183. **Drafted:** Arizona State, 2001 (8th round). **Signed by:** Ted Williams.

Duffy has continued to impress the Pirates since leading the short-season New York-Penn League in steals in his pro debut in 2001. He had a strong big league camp and hit .300 for the fourth time in five years in 2005. Installed as the Pirates' center fielder in mid-July, he hit .341 until his season ended in late August with a torn left hamstring. Duffy has outstanding speed that he uses to his advantage both on the bases and in the field. Though he never batted lefthanded until he got to Arizona State, he has hit consistently throughout the minors. He's an outstanding center fielder who covers both gaps and makes highlight-reel plays. He's also a good basestealer, though he was hesitant to run in the majors. Duffy strikes out a lot for a top-of-the-order hitter who relies on speed. His arm is below average, though he compensates by making accurate throws. The Pirates' center-field job will be Duffy's to lose in spring training. He's their best defensive center fielder since Andy Van Slyke, though his bat will determine his long-term future.

Year	Club (League)	Class	AVG	G	AB	R	H	2B	3B	HR	RBI	BB	SO	SB	OBP	SLG
2001	Williamsport (NY-P)	A	.317	64	221	50	70	12	4	1	24	33	33	30	.440	.421
2002	Lynchburg (Car)	A	.301	132	539	85	162	27	5	10	52	33	101	22	.353	.425
2003	Altoona (EL)	AA	.273	137	494	84	135	23	6	1	42	44	78	34	.355	.350
2004	Altoona (EL)	AA	.309	113	453	84	140	23	6	8	41	33	77	30	.378	.439
2005	Indianapolis (IL)	AAA	.308	78	308	55	95	13	7	7	31	16	57	17	.358	.464
	Pittsburgh (NL)	MLB	.341	39	126	22	43	4	2	1	9	7	22	2	.385	.429
MAJOR LEAGUE TOTALS			.341	39	126	22	43	4	2	1	9	7	22	2	.385	.429
MINOR LEAGUE TOTALS			.299	524	2015	358	602	98	28	27	190	159	346	133	.370	.415

10 MATT CAPPS   RHP

Born: Sept. 3, 1983. **B-T:** R-R. **Ht.:** 6-3. **Wt.:** 231. **Drafted:** HS—Douglasville, Ga., 2002 (7th round). **Signed by:** Jack Powell.

Capps made an amazing rise after posting a 10.07 ERA in eight low Class A Hickory starts in 2004. Converted to a reliever during spring training in 2005, he began the season back at Hickory and finished it in the Pittsburgh bullpen. Capps attacks hitters and doesn't back down, a style that works much better for him in short relief. His fastball routinely hits 95 mph and looks even quicker because he comes straight over the top with it. He does an exceptional job of throwing strikes. Capps hasn't been able to come up with a consistent breaking ball. He'll need another pitch, possibly a splitter, to go with his fastball in order to get major league hitters out. He's more hittable than he should be with his velocity because hitters can sit on his heater. Though Capps got a taste of the major leagues at the end of 2005, he needs more seasoning and will begin 2006 in Double-A. He has a chance to eventually become a major league closer if he can find a complement for his plus fastball.

Year	Club (League)	Class	W	L	ERA	G	GS	CG	SV	IP	H	R	ER	HR	BB	SO	AVG
2002	Pirates (GCL)	R	1	0	0.69	7	0	0	1	13	13	2	1	0	6	8	.271
2003	Lynchburg (Car)	A	0	0	5.40	1	1	0	0	5	3	3	3	0	4	5	.167
	Pirates (GCL)	R	5	1	1.87	10	10	1	0	63	40	16	13	1	9	54	.178
2004	Hickory (SAL)	A	2	3	10.07	12	8	0	0	42	82	55	47	8	16	27	.400
	Williamsport (NY-P)	A	3	5	4.85	11	11	0	0	65	84	43	35	7	4	33	.312
2005	Hickory (SAL)	A	3	4	2.52	35	0	0	14	54	47	15	15	0	5	39	.239
	Altoona (EL)	AA	0	2	2.70	17	0	0	7	20	21	8	6	2	1	26	.250
	Pittsburgh (NL)	MLB	0	0	4.50	4	0	0	0	4	5	2	2	0	0	3	.333
MAJOR LEAGUE TOTALS			0	0	4.50	4	0	0	0	4	5	2	2	0	0	3	.333
MINOR LEAGUE TOTALS			14	15	4.13	93	30	1	22	261	290	142	120	18	45	192	.277

11 RAJAI DAVIS   OF

Born: Oct. 19, 1980. **B-T:** R-R. **Ht.:** 5-11. **Wt.:** 190. **Drafted:** Connecticut-Avery Point JC, 2001 (38th round). **Signed by:** Charlie Sullivan.

To answer the inevitable question, Davis' first name is pronounced "RAHJ-ay" and it means "king" in Sanskrit. He set an Altoona franchise record for stolen bases last season after leading the high Class A Carolina League in hitting and steals in 2004. Davis has a good feel for being a leadoff hitter, though his strikeout-walk ratio declined in 2005. He's willing to take pitches, bunt and slap the ball on the ground to get on base. He has above-average speed and seems to find another gear when he needs to beat out an infield hit or chase down fly balls into the gap. Davis needs to tighten his strike zone a little more and polish his routes in center field, though he often can make up for defensive mistakes with his speed. The Pirates have a similar player in Chris Duffy, who broke into the majors last year and likely will be their starting center fielder in 2006. Davis will spend this season in Triple-A before posing a challenge to Duffy in 2007.

Year	Club (League)	Class	AVG	G	AB	R	H	2B	3B	HR	RBI	BB	SO	SB	OBP	SLG
2001	Williamsport (NY-P)	A	.083	6	12	1	1	0	0	0	0	0	2	4	0	.214	.083
	Pirates (GCL)	R	.262	26	84	19	22	1	0	0	4	13	26	11	.364	.274
2002	Pirates (GCL)	R	.384	58	224	38	86	16	5	4	35	20	25	24	.436	.554
	Williamsport (NY-P)	A	.000	1	4	0	0	0	0	0	0	0	1	0	.000	.000
	Hickory (SAL)	A	.429	6	14	4	6	0	0	0	3	6	2	2	.619	.429
2003	Hickory (SAL)	A	.305	125	478	84	146	21	7	6	54	55	65	40	.383	.416

2004	Lynchburg (Car)	A	.314	127	509	91	160	27	7	5	38	59	60 57	.388	.424
2005	Altoona (EL)	AA	.281	123	499	82	140	22	5	4	34	43	76 45	.351	.369
MINOR LEAGUE TOTALS			.308	472	1824	319	561	87	24	19	168	198	259 179	.382	.413

12 CRAIG STANSBERRY 2B

Born: March 8, 1982. **B-T:** R-R. **Ht.:** 6-0. **Wt.:** 185. **Drafted:** Rice, 2003 (5th round). **Signed by:** Tom Barnard.

Stansberry has been a winner throughout his career. He helped lead North Central (Texas) Community College to the Junior College World Series title in 2002 and Rice to the College World Series championship in 2003. Stanberry also won championship rings in his first two pro stops at Williamsport in 2003 and Hickory in 2004, then helped Altoona reach the Eastern League playoffs last year. Stansberry began to develop pop in 2005 with a combined 21 homers, including 18 in Double-A. He also has outstanding instincts for the game with the defensive skills to play a good second or third base, and enough speed to steal some bases. Stansberry's power surge came with a price, as he became too pull-happy and his batting average plummeted. Once he begins using the whole field again, his average should return to the .280-.300 range. He likely will play second base in Triple-A this year. His path to the majors at that position is blocked by Jose Castillo, but Stansberry is helped by his ability to also play third.

Year	Club (League)	Class	AVG	G	AB	R	H	2B	3B	HR	RBI	BB	SO	SB	OBP	SLG
2003	Williamsport (NY-P)	A	.307	45	166	19	51	9	3	2	21	13	25	5	.370	.434
2004	Hickory (SAL)	A	.286	106	391	57	112	14	5	9	67	52	88	20	.376	.417
2005	Lynchburg (Car)	A	.351	24	94	17	33	7	2	3	19	11	13	7	.430	.564
	Altoona (EL)	AA	.238	116	421	62	100	22	11	18	67	44	114	14	.314	.470
MINOR LEAGUE TOTALS			.276	291	1072	155	296	52	21	32	174	120	240	46	.355	.453

13 RONNY PAULINO C

Born: April 21, 1981. **B-T:** R-R. **Ht.:** 6-3. **Wt.:** 210. **Signed:** Dominican Republic, 1997. **Signed by:** Pablo Cruz.

Paulino went to big league camp with the Royals in 2003 as a major league Rule 5 draft pick, but was returned to the Pirates and then hit a combined .229-7-31 in the mid-minors. He regained his prospect luster with two strong seasons before making his big league debut late in 2005. Paulino is a big guy who's finally starting to realize his power potential, especially since he has learned to use the entire field. He's strong enough to hit the ball out of the park to the opposite field and doesn't have to try to pull everything. Paulino also has a strong arm and threw out 36 percent of basestealers in the minors in 2005. He has greatly improved his rapport with pitchers as his English has gotten better. His swing tends to get long, causing him to strike out in bunches at times. He's also a bit stiff behind the plate and needs to soften his hands. The Pirates have some interesting young catching options in Ryan Doumit and Humberto Cota ahead of Paulino and top prospect Neil Walker coming up behind them. Paulino figures to begin this season in Triple-A.

Year	Club (League)	Class	AVG	G	AB	R	H	2B	3B	HR	RBI	BB	SO	SB	OBP	SLG
1998	Pirates (DSL)	R	.235	53	170	18	40	5	0	4	26	17	27	6	.318	.335
1999	Pirates (GCL)	R	.253	29	83	6	21	2	4	1	13	8	19	1	.319	.410
2000	Hickory (SAL)	A	.289	88	301	38	87	16	2	6	39	27	71	3	.354	.415
2001	Lynchburg (Car)	A	.290	103	352	30	102	16	1	6	51	36	76	4	.353	.392
2002	Lynchburg (Car)	A	.262	119	442	63	116	26	2	12	55	39	87	2	.321	.412
2003	Altoona (EL)	AA	.226	46	159	19	36	6	1	6	19	12	35	0	.283	.390
	Lynchburg (Car)	A	.235	23	81	8	19	3	0	1	12	8	8	1	.308	.309
2004	Altoona (EL)	AA	.285	99	369	54	105	23	2	15	60	32	62	3	.344	.480
2005	Altoona (EL)	AA	.292	43	168	24	49	6	0	6	20	15	30	3	.350	.435
	Indianapolis (IL)	AAA	.315	77	273	49	86	18	2	13	42	26	48	3	.372	.538
	Pittsburgh (NL)	MLB	.500	2	4	1	2	0	0	0	0	1	0	0	.600	.500
MAJOR LEAGUE TOTALS			.500	2	4	1	2	0	0	0	0	1	0	0	.600	.500
MINOR LEAGUE TOTALS			.276	680	2398	309	661	121	14	70	337	220	463	26	.338	.425

14 JAMES BOONE OF

Born: March 16, 1983. **B-T:** B-R. **Ht.:** 6-2. **Wt.:** 175. **Drafted:** Missouri, 2005 (3rd round). **Signed by:** Jimmy Rough.

The Pirates loaded up on college hitters in the 2005 draft, taking five in the first eight rounds. Boone, who signed for $420,000 as a third-rounder, is the best prospect among that group to this point. Passed up by all 30 clubs as a draft-eligible sophomore in 2004, he batted .340-8-72 as a junior at Missouri and continued to hit in his pro debut. Boone is a solid hitter from both sides of the plate. He has more of a line-drive stroke at this stage of his career but his power, which comes primarily from the left side, should increase as he learns to turn on pitches and lift the ball more. He doesn' have blazing speed but shows smarts on the basepaths and is above average defensively in center field. Boone struck out too much in his first taste of pro ball, though the Pirates are confident he'll develop better plate discipline with more experience. If he doesn't make adjustments, he'll get exploited at higher levels. He'll begin his first full season in low Class A and could get to Pittsburgh by 2008 if he gets the strikeouts under control.

Year	Club (League)	Class	AVG	G	AB	R	H	2B	3B	HR	RBI	BB	SO	SB	OBP	SLG
2005	Williamsport (NY-P)	A	.291	68	278	44	81	12	4	8	42	16	85	8	.343	.450
MINOR LEAGUE TOTALS			.291	68	278	44	81	12	4	8	42	16	85	8	.343	.450

15 BRAD CORLEY   OF

Born: Dec. 28, 1983. **B-T:** R-R. **Ht.:** 6-2. **Wt.:** 198. **Drafted:** Mississippi State, 2005 (2nd round). **Signed by:** Everett Russell.

After Corley batted .380-19-55 as a sophomore at Mississippi State in 2004, there was talk he could go in the first round of the 2005 draft. But he broke a thumb while trying out for Team USA in the summer of 2004 and it bothered him last spring, when he hit just .316-5-40 for the Bulldogs, killing his first-round aspirations. Some clubs felt the Pirates overdrafted him in the second round, and he got off to a slow start in the New York-Penn League after signing for $605,000. Once he shortened his swing, however, Corley's power returned and he came on strong at Williamsport before starring in instructional league. He has good power potential and his swing reminds some scouts of Pat Burrell's. Corley also has a strong arm that's suitable for right field. He has average range in the outfield. Pro pitchers were able to find holes in Corley's swing and make him chase pitches out of the strike zone, though he started to make adjustments in August. He'll join James Boone in low Class A this year and will move quickly if he's able to maintain his power stroke.

Year	Club (League)	Class	AVG	G	AB	R	H	2B	3B	HR	RBI	BB	SO	SB	OBP	SLG
2005	Williamsport (NY-P)	A	.279	68	265	29	74	10	6	4	35	16	56	3	.331	.408
MINOR LEAGUE TOTALS			.279	68	265	29	74	10	6	4	35	16	56	3	.331	.408

16 MIKE JOHNSTON   LHP

Born: March 30, 1979. **B-T:** L-L. **Ht.:** 6-3. **Wt.:** 200. **Drafted:** Garrett (Md.) CC, 1998 (20th round). **Signed by:** Craig Kornfeld.

Johnston generated national headlines in 2004 when he made the Pirates out of spring training, making the jump from Double-A and becoming only the second player in major league history to publicly admit he has Tourette's Syndrome. The condition includes visible nervous tics and forced him to drop out of high school in Philadelphia. Johnston made nine straight scoreless appearances to begin his big league career, but he has experienced elbow problems on and off the last two seasons. Johnston's strength is that he's one of the hardest-throwing lefthanders around. His fastball routinely reaches 95 mph and tops out at 98. He also relishes pitching inside and isn't afraid to, as he says, "buzz the tower." Johnston's slider can be devastating but he has problems staying consistent with the pitch and it often becomes slurvy. He also hasn't maintained his conditioning since reaching the majors and must be diligent in watching his weight. Johnston isn't exactly a kid, but he still has a high ceiling because of his power arm. If he gains command of his slider, he could develop into one of the top lefthanded relievers in the game.

Year	Club (League)	Class	W	L	ERA	G	GS	CG	SV	IP	H	R	ER	HR	BB	SO	AVG
1998	Pirates (GCL)	R	1	2	3.34	13	3	0	0	30	28	17	11	1	10	17	.248
	Erie (NY-P)	A	0	0	4.50	2	0	0	0	2	4	4	1	0	1	2	.364
1999	Williamsport (NY-P)	A	3	2	4.25	14	2	0	2	42	46	26	20	5	18	30	.267
2000	Hickory (SAL)	A	4	2	6.22	26	0	0	2	51	66	42	35	2	30	52	.320
2001	Hickory (SAL)	A	4	5	3.38	16	16	0	0	93	88	47	35	5	42	80	.249
	Lynchburg (Car)	A	4	4	3.34	11	10	1	0	62	66	27	23	2	24	44	.272
2002	Lynchburg (Car)	A	4	2	3.63	15	10	0	0	57	50	29	23	2	26	50	.230
2003	Altoona (EL)	AA	6	2	2.12	46	0	0	7	72	49	17	17	4	27	65	.199
2004	Pittsburgh (NL)	MLB	0	3	4.37	24	0	0	0	23	29	16	11	2	15	18	.315
	Nashville (PCL)	AAA	0	0	8.40	19	0	0	0	15	19	14	14	3	13	6	.297
2005	Pittsburgh (NL)	MLB	0	0	36.00	1	0	0	0	1	4	4	4	2	0	2	.571
	Indianapolis (IL)	AAA	2	1	2.97	52	0	0	0	58	43	21	19	5	30	52	.208
MAJOR LEAGUE TOTALS			0	3	5.70	25	0	0	0	24	33	20	15	4	15	20	.333
MINOR LEAGUE TOTALS			28	20	3.70	214	41	1	11	482	459	244	198	29	221	398	.251

17 JOSH SHARPLESS
RHP

Born: Jan. 26, 1981. **B-T:** R-R. **Ht.:** 6-5. **Wt.:** 225. **Drafted:** Allegheny (Pa.) College, 2003 (24th round). **Signed by:** Jon Mercurio.

Sharpless has proven to be quite a find for Pittsburgh since signing as a 24th-round pick out of nearby Allegheny College, an NCAA Division III school. He has averaged 13.5 strikeouts per nine innings as a pro and held opponents to a .107 batting average last year before missing the final two months with a strained elbow. Sharpless has an outstanding slider that is hard and breaks late, leaving hitters to flail at it. His fastball is usually in the 88-91 mph range but looks faster because he throws it from straight over the top. He's still somewhat raw and lost valuable development time because of his elbow, but he pitched pain-free in instructional league. He's not athletic and struggles to repeat his delivery at times. Sharpless doesn't have a whole lot left to prove in the minors beyond his health. Spring training will determine whether he begins 2006 in Double-A or Triple-A, and he very well could make his Pittsburgh debut later in the year.

Year	Club (League)	Class	W	L	ERA	G	GS	CG	SV	IP	H	R	ER	HR	BB	SO	AVG
2003	Williamsport (NY-P)	A	1	1	2.59	22	0	0	5	31	19	9	9	2	17	45	.173
2004	Hickory (SAL)	A	6	2	3.03	44	0	0	4	74	42	28	25	4	55	109	.158
2005	Lynchburg (Car)	A	3	0	0.00	17	0	0	5	27	7	1	0	0	11	46	.081
	Altoona (EL)	AA	1	0	2.89	7	0	0	0	9	6	3	3	0	3	13	.171
MINOR LEAGUE TOTALS			11	3	2.35	90	0	0	14	142	74	41	37	6	86	213	.149

18 JOE BAUSERMAN
RHP

Born: Oct. 4, 1985. **B-T:** R-R. **Ht.:** 6-2. **Wt.:** 220. **Drafted:** HS—Tallahassee, Fla., 2004 (4th round). **Signed by:** Rob Sidwell.

Bauserman was a two-sport, two-state star in high school, playing baseball in Florida and football in Virginia. He chose baseball after high school, signing with the Pirates for $300,000 as a 2004 fourth-round pick and passing up a scholarship to play quarterback at Ohio State. Bauserman has a strong pitcher's body and good loose arm action. The ball comes out of his hand easily and his fastball sits in the 90-92 mph range while reaching 95. His curveball has good downward bite and his changeup has the makings of a plus pitch. Some scouts though Bauserman showed bad body language during his debut season in the Gulf Coast League in 2004. He looked more mature on the mound last season and was one of the best pitchers on the Williamsport staff despite being young for the league. His slider could use some tightening, though it's only his fourth pitch. Bauserman is still somewhat raw and the Pirates see no need to rush him. He'll get his first taste of full-season ball this year in low Class A and isn't likely to reach the majors until the end of 2008 at the earliest.

Year	Club (League)	Class	W	L	ERA	G	GS	CG	SV	IP	H	R	ER	HR	BB	SO	AVG
2004	Pirates (GCL)	R	2	2	2.79	9	8	0	0	39	26	13	12	4	10	35	.187
2005	Williamsport (NY-P)	A	6	2	2.84	14	14	0	0	70	64	30	22	3	26	45	.253
MINOR LEAGUE TOTALS			8	4	2.82	23	22	0	0	108	90	43	34	7	36	80	.230

19 TODD REDMOND
RHP

Born: May 17, 1985. **B-T:** R-R. **Ht.:** 6-3. **Wt.:** 1985. **Drafted:** St. Petersburg (Fla.) JC, D/F 2004 (39th round). **Signed by:** Rob Sidwell.

One of the better draft-and-follows from 2004, Redmond led St. Petersburg Junior College to the Florida state juco championship in 2005 with 18 scoreless innings in the playoffs and a second-place finish at the Junior College World Series before signing with the Pirates. In his debut, he finished second in the New York-Penn League ERA race. Redmond's fastball sits at 91-93 mph and touches 95. His curveball and changeup also have the makings of becoming above-average pitches. What really sets him apart, though, is his outstanding mound presence and bulldog demeanor. Like most young pitchers, Redmond needs to gain consistency with his changeup. His curve also tends to get loopy from time to time. More than anything, he just needs to keep logging innings. Redmond made a seamless transition from juco to short-season ball. There's no reason to think he won't handle the adjustment to pitching in a full-season league this year. If Redmond improves his secondary pitches, his long-term future is a starter. His heater also makes him an intriguing short-relief candidate.

Year	Club (League)	Class	W	L	ERA	G	GS	CG	SV	IP	H	R	ER	HR	BB	SO	AVG
2005	Williamsport (NY-P)	A	1	2	1.98	15	14	0	0	73	62	22	16	2	21	63	.232
MINOR LEAGUE TOTALS			1	2	1.98	15	14	0	0	73	62	22	16	2	21	63	.232

20 ADAM BOEVE OF

Born: June 20, 1980. **B-T:** R-R. **Ht.:** 6-1. **Wt.:** 205. **Drafted:** Northern Iowa, 2003 (12th round). **Signed by:** Mark German.

Boeve, whose name rhymes with movie, was a three-sport star in high school in Doon, Iowa, playing football, basketball and track. He went to Northern Iowa on a football scholarship to play safety but wound up winning Missouri Valley Conference player-of-the-year honors in baseball as a senior in 2003. After a lackluster pro debut at Williamsport that summer, Boeve has shown the ability to hit for both power and average. He has a mature approach at the plate and looks to hit the ball up the middle because he has the power to hit the ball out to the opposite field. Boeve is prone to striking out. He has a high leg kick and Double-A pitchers were able to exploit it at times, so he may have to tone it down. He's an average defender at best, with a bit above-average range and a bit below-average arm. He held his own in the Arizona Fall League at the end of the season. At 25, he's a bit old for a prospect. The Pirates will try to push him to Triple-A in 2006, though he'll probably start the year back in Double-A.

Year	Club (League)	Class	AVG	G	AB	R	H	2B	3B	HR	RBI	BB	SO	SB	OBP	SLG
2003	Williamsport (NY-P)	A	.250	39	132	20	33	9	1	3	16	15	39	6	.353	.402
2004	Hickory (SAL)	A	.290	130	459	93	133	25	2	28	92	61	112	10	.385	.536
2005	Lynchburg (Car)	A	.313	71	249	60	78	15	1	13	47	39	66	12	.419	.538
	Altoona (EL)	AA	.288	47	160	24	46	9	1	5	23	22	54	5	.375	.450
MINOR LEAGUE TOTALS			.290	287	1000	197	290	58	5	49	178	137	271	33	.388	.505

21 BRENT LILLIBRIDGE SS

Born: Sept. 18, 1983. **B-T:** R-R. **Ht.:** 5-11. **Wt.:** 185. **Drafted:** Washington, 2005 (4th round). **Signed by:** Greg Hopkins.

One of the few anthropology majors in pro ball, Lillibridge was a first-team all-Pacific-10 Conference selection in each of his three seasons at Washington. He played every game at shortstop for the Huskies last season after spending time in center field earlier in his career. A fourth-round pick in June, he signed for $262,500. He's an athletic player with a live body and lots of energy. He hits for average and also has gap power. He's an above-average defensive shortstop with excellent range and a good arm, enabling him to make acrobatic plays. He also has above average speed and can steal a base. Lillibridge struggled in making the adjustment to wood bats and was prone to strikeouts even while starring at Washington. He has a big swing, looks for fastballs and doesn't recognize breaking balls well, so he'll have several adjustments to make. He made 13 errors in 42 games in his pro debut, but much of that was attributed to trying too hard to make tough plays. Lillibridge has a lot of upside and could move quickly after beginning 2006 in low Class A.

Year	Club (League)	Class	AVG	G	AB	R	H	2B	3B	HR	RBI	BB	SO	SB	OBP	SLG
2005	Williamsport (NY-P)	A	.243	42	169	19	41	12	4	4	18	14	35	10	.305	.432
MINOR LEAGUE TOTALS			.243	42	169	19	41	12	4	4	18	14	35	10	.305	.432

22 JAVIER GUZMAN SS

Born: May 4, 1984. **B-T:** B-R. **Ht.:** 5-11. **Wt.:** 160. **Signed:** Dominican Republic, 2000. **Signed by:** Jose Luna.

One of several Dominicans who were discovered in 2002 to have falsified their birthdates, Guzman is two years older than he was believed to be entering 2005 because the Pirates failed to update his age on their rosters. After reaching Double-A at midseason last year, he batted .355 in his first 19 games then slumped and hit just .187 in his final 49. He needs to learn to handle breaking and off-speed pitches better and he can be susceptible to fastballs under his hands. That said, he has plenty of tools. Guzman runs well and has outstanding range and an above-average arm. His bat was also a plus until the end of last season, as the switch-hitter has some pop from the left side. Guzman needs to be more consistent at the plate as well as in the field, as he makes too many errors on routine plays. Because he was overmatched in Double-A, he'll have to prove himself there in 2006. How well he redeems himself will go a long way in determining his future.

Year	Club (League)	Class	AVG	G	AB	R	H	2B	3B	HR	RBI	BB	SO	SB	OBP	SLG
2001	Pirates (DSL)	R	.209	57	206	30	43	4	3	0	15	27	49	23	.311	.257
2002	Pirates (GCL)	R	.307	50	199	42	61	6	6	5	20	12	25	13	.347	.472
2003	Williamsport (NY-P)	A	.243	47	173	19	42	9	2	2	14	10	26	4	.283	.353
2004	Hickory (SAL)	A	.306	124	470	75	144	20	12	2	63	20	78	31	.334	.413
2005	Lynchburg (Car)	A	.324	69	256	40	83	13	7	5	35	20	41	13	.374	.488
	Altoona (EL)	AA	.236	68	263	27	62	9	1	3	24	10	46	8	.262	.312
MINOR LEAGUE TOTALS			.278	415	1567	233	435	61	31	17	181	99	265	92	.322	.389

23 MATT SWANSON RHP

Born: Oct. 17, 1982. **B-T:** R-R. **Ht.:** 6-8. **Wt.:** 240. **Drafted:** California, 2005 (13th round). **Signed by:** Jaron Madison.

The Pirates think they got a steal when they grabbed Swanson in the 13th round last June. He held opponents to a .163 average in his pro debut. The 6-foot-7 Swanson learned how to use his size to his advantage last year. He began getting on top of his fastball more and his velocity rose to the low 90s with a peak of 95 mph more often because of his newfound leverage. He also throws a slider and a splitter. Swanson needs to gain more consistency with his split in order to contrast his heater, and his slider also could use some tightening from time to time. He lacks experience after pitching primarily out of the bullpen in college and the Pirates plan to rectify that by having him work as a starter this year in low Class A. He projects more as a set-up man for the long term.

Year	Club (League)	Class	W	L	ERA	G	GS	CG	SV	IP	H	R	ER	HR	BB	SO	AVG
2005	Williamsport (NY-P)	A	4	2	1.61	19	0	0	6	28	16	6	5	2	7	30	.163
MINOR LEAGUE TOTALS			4	2	1.61	19	0	0	6	28	16	6	5	2	7	30	.163

24 MATT PETERSON RHP

Born: Feb. 11, 1982. **B-T:** R-R. **Ht.:** 6-5. **Wt.:** 210. **Drafted:** HS—Alexandria, La., 2000 (2nd round). **Signed by:** Bob Rossi (Mets).

Peterson has perplexed the Pirates ever since they acquired him from the Mets in the mid-2004 Kris Benson trade. He has compiled a 5.66 ERA in 34 games at Double-A since the deal and hasn't shown the form that made him the Mets' 2003 minor league pitcher of the year. Peterson has the makings of a solid starting pitcher, as he has a 90-94 mph fastball and a 12-to-6 curveball that's unhittable when it's on. He also has shown a good feel for a changeup at times, but he has been unable to consistently throw any of his pitches for strikes since coming to the Pirates. He has had particularly trouble controlling his curve. Peterson also has put too much pressure on himself in an effort to try to justify being traded for an established major league pitcher. He'll go back to Double-A for a third straight season, and he's too young and talented to write off as a prospect. However, at some point soon he has to start pitching well to stay in Pittsburgh's plans.

Year	Club (League)	Class	W	L	ERA	G	GS	CG	SV	IP	H	R	ER	HR	BB	SO	AVG
2001	Brooklyn (NY-P)	A	2	2	1.62	6	6	0	0	33	26	7	6	0	14	19	.217
	Capital City (SAL)	A	2	6	4.99	18	14	0	0	79	87	46	44	9	29	72	.275
2002	St. Lucie (FSL)	A	1	0	1.50	1	1	0	0	6	5	2	1	0	2	5	.217
	Capital City (SAL)	A	8	10	3.86	26	26	1	0	138	109	67	59	13	61	153	.221
2003	Binghamton (EL)	AA	1	2	3.45	6	6	0	0	31	29	18	12	2	20	23	.248
	St. Lucie (FSL)	A	9	2	1.71	15	15	1	0	84	65	24	16	2	24	73	.212
2004	Binghamton (EL)	AA	6	4	3.27	19	18	0	0	105	97	44	38	11	45	90	.253
	Altoona (EL)	AA	3	2	6.25	7	7	0	0	36	36	25	25	7	22	29	.277
2005	Altoona (EL)	AA	11	9	5.51	27	26	0	0	144	156	102	88	19	74	87	.281
MINOR LEAGUE TOTALS			43	37	3.96	125	119	2	0	656	610	335	289	63	291	551	.249

25 JASON QUARLES RHP

Born: April 20, 1983. **B-T:** R-R. **Ht.:** 6-0. **Wt.:** 195. **Drafted:** Southern, 2004 (7th round). **Signed by:** Everett Russell.

Quarles became the accidental pitcher at Southern in 2004. He was recruited as an outfielder from Glen Oaks (Mich.) Community College and moved to the mound when he failed to crack Southern's everyday starting lineup. Two months later, he was a seventh-round draft pick. Quarles' velocity is as good as any pitcher in the organization as he routinely hits 98 mph on the gun with his fastball, though it sits at 92-94. His curveball has a huge break, dropping from the hitter's shoulders to his knees. Quarles also has a fresh arm because he didn't pitch much as an amateur. He needs a lot of polish as he's a thrower at this stage of his career. He needs better command of the fastball to both sides of the plate, as he just basically throws it and hopes for the best. He also has a tendency to bounce his curveball. Quarles began last season in extended spring training before being moved to low Class A. He likely will go back there to start 2006 but the Pirates are willing to be patient because of his live arm.

Year	Club (League)	Class	W	L	ERA	G	GS	CG	SV	IP	H	R	ER	HR	BB	SO	AVG
2004	Williamsport (NY-P)	A	0	4	4.56	23	0	0	0	23	30	15	9	1	18	30	.300
2005	Hickory (SAL)	A	0	3	2.61	19	1	0	0	38	31	15	11	2	26	45	.226
MINOR LEAGUE TOTALS			0	7	2.93	42	1	0	0	61	61	30	20	3	44	75	.257

26 CLAYTON HAMILTON RHP

Born: June 15, 1982. **B-T:** R-R. **Ht.:** 6-5. **Wt.:** 200. **Drafted:** Penn State, 2004 (17th round). **Signed by:** Josh Boyd (Padres).

A Pittsburgh native, Hamilton was drafted by the Pirates after his junior year at Penn State but wasn't offered a contract. They finally landed him this offseason, when he came over from the Padres for the disappointing Bobby Hill. Hamilton never posted a winning record nor an ERA under 5.50 in college, though he did pitch well in the Valley League in the summer of 2003. He impressed San Diego enough with his maturity to earn an emergency start at Double-A just months after signing, and he continued to stand out last year. He creates good downward plane on a solid-average 89-91 mph fastball that maxes out at 94. He has developed an average slider after using a curveball until midway through his senior season. Hamilton is aggressive in the zone and pitches intelligently. He doesn't beat himself with walks or homers. His slider is still inconsistent and has a tendency to flatten out. He occasionally tips his changeup early by slowing down his delivery. He struggled with a groin injury late in 2005 that sapped his velocity, and pitching 100-plus innings for the first time also took its toll. Hamilton projects as a No. 5 starter or swingman, and should make the jump to Double-A this year.

Year	Club (League)	Class	W	L	ERA	G	GS	CG	SV	IP	H	R	ER	HR	BB	SO	AVG
2004	Padres (AZL)	R	0	0	2.08	3	0	0	0	4	2	1	1	0	1	3	.125
	Mobile (SL)	AA	1	0	1.80	1	1	0	0	5	5	2	1	0	2	6	.263
	Eugene (NWL)	A	1	1	5.20	8	5	0	0	28	21	21	16	5	13	31	.208
2005	Fort Wayne (Mid)	A	9	6	2.88	20	20	0	0	122	101	44	39	9	36	86	.226
	Lake Elsinore (Cal)	A	2	2	5.14	7	6	0	0	28	39	19	16	2	9	18	.339
MINOR LEAGUE TOTALS			13	9	3.51	39	32	0	0	187	168	87	73	16	61	144	.241

27 JONAH BAYLISS RHP

Born: Aug. 13, 1980. **B-T:** R-R. **Ht.:** 6-2. **Wt.:** 200. **Drafted:** Trinity (Conn.) College, 2002 (7th round). **Signed by:** Steve Connelly (Royals).

One of two righthanders acquired from the Royals for Mark Redman over the winter (the other, Chad Blackwell, just missed this prospect list), Bayliss threw a no-hitter at NCAA Division III Trinity (Conn.) in 2002 and another for low Class A Burlington in 2003. He's not likely to throw another one following a successful move to the bullpen last year after three seasons as a starter. He made his major league debut June 22 with a perfect inning against the White Sox. Working in relief helped Bayliss improve his stuff, and he felt more comfortable in that role that he had in the rotation. His fastball jumped from hovering around 90 mph to an easy, consistent 93 mph. It runs and rides in on righthanders, making it a nice complement to his changeup, which fades and sinks. His slider also improved into a strikeout pitch with depth. His success carried over into the Arizona Fall League, and he should get a chance to make the Pirates in 2006.

Year	Club (League)	Class	W	L	ERA	G	GS	CG	SV	IP	H	R	ER	HR	BB	SO	AVG
2002	Spokane (NWL)	A	4	8	5.35	15	15	0	0	71	70	46	42	9	29	38	.264
2003	Burlington (Mid)	A	7	12	3.86	26	26	2	0	140	129	78	60	11	69	133	.242
2004	Wilmington (Car)	A	6	6	4.93	24	24	0	0	111	119	70	61	11	44	79	.287
2005	Kansas City (AL)	MLB	0	0	4.62	11	0	0	0	12	7	6	6	2	4	10	.167
	Wichita (TL)	AA	1	2	2.84	30	0	0	8	57	43	19	18	5	26	63	.208
MAJOR LEAGUE TOTALS			0	0	4.62	11	0	0	0	12	7	6	6	2	4	10	.167
MINOR LEAGUE TOTALS			18	28	4.30	95	65	2	8	379	361	213	181	36	168	313	.254

28 WARDELL STARLING RHP

Born: March 14, 1983. **B-T:** R-R. **Ht.:** 6-4. **Wt.:** 200. **Drafted:** Odessa (Texas) JC, 2002 (4th round). **Signed by:** Tom Barnard.

Starling helped lead Elkins High (Missouri City, Texas) to a national high school championship as a senior in 2002, but he failed to sign with the Pirates after being drafted in the fourth round. Starling went to Odessa (Texas) Junior College and hit .420-12-80 to rank among the national juco leaders in all three categories before Pittsburgh signed him just before the 2003 draft as a pitcher. Starling has the makings of an above-average pitcher though he has been slow to put it all together. His fastball routinely sits at 92-94 mph with good life and peaks at 97. He also throws a curveball and changeup with both pitches having the potential to be above average. Starling has the rap of being immature and failing to get the most out of his talent. He's young enough to outgrow that but another concern is that he continually seems to fall into mechanical ruts, though his fine athletic ability should allow him to repeat his delivery. Starling will likely go back to high Class A to start this season unless he has a lights-out spring training. He won't move up until he proves he's ready.

Year	Club (League)	Class	W	L	ERA	G	GS	CG	SV	IP	H	R	ER	HR	BB	SO	AVG
2003	Pirates (GCL)	R	4	1	3.94	11	11	0	0	48	47	23	21	5	13	52	.247
2004	Hickory (SAL)	A	11	8	4.11	26	26	1	0	140	132	84	64	10	51	114	.253
2005	Lynchburg (Car)	A	10	10	5.22	28	28	1	0	153	168	98	89	18	55	102	.279
MINOR LEAGUE TOTALS			25	19	4.59	65	65	2	0	341	347	205	174	33	119	268	.264

29 EDDIE PRASCH 3B

Born: Jan. 25, 1986. **B-T:** L-R. **Ht.:** 6-1. **Wt.:** 180. **Drafted:** HS—Alpharetta, Ga., 2004 (3rd round). **Signed by:** Jack Powell.

Prasch was one of the top draft prospects in the talent-rich Atlanta area in 2004 and the Pirates gave him a $500,000 bonus as a third-round pick. He has managed to play in just 73 games and log only 263 at-bats in his two pro seasons because of a variety of injuries, including a strained back that sidelined him for most of 2005. When healthy, Prasch has a pretty line-drive stroke from the left side. He's short to the ball and generates plenty of bat speed. However, his swing got longer and slower last season, a symptom of his back problems. Prasch showed the ability to hit both lefties and righties as an amateur but has yet to get untracked in the pros. He has yet to homer, though he projects to hit 15-25 annually once his body fills out and if he stays healthy. His feet are slow and his hands aren't overly soft, but Prasch compensates at third base with a strong arm. He doesn't appear ready for full-season ball yet. He likely will remain in extended spring training, then report to Williamsport in June.

Year	Club (League)	Class	AVG	G	AB	R	H	2B	3B	HR	RBI	BB	SO	SB	OBP	SLG
2004	Pirates (GCL)	R	.220	32	118	11	26	6	2	0	21	12	27	1	.301	.305
2005	Pirates (GCL)	R	.302	15	53	9	16	2	0	0	6	9	12	0	.403	.340
	Williamsport (NY-P)	A	.217	26	92	11	20	2	0	0	7	12	17	3	.321	.239
MINOR LEAGUE TOTALS			.236	73	263	31	62	10	2	0	34	33	56	4	.329	.289

30 BRIAN BIXLER SS

Born: Oct 22, 1982. **B-T:** R-R. **Ht.:** 6-1. **Wt.:** 188. **Drafted:** Eastern Michigan, 2004 (2nd round). **Signed by:** Duane Gustavson.

Bixler ranked second in NCAA Division I in batting (.453) and on-base percentage (.520) at Eastern Michigan in 2004. While he has hit for a decent average as a pro, his on-base skills have declined. That detracts from his ability to use his best tool, his speed. He's always a threat to steal and can take the extra base on most balls hit to the outfield. Though he showed improved pop in 2005, he needs to worry more about improving his grasp of the strike zone. He swings and misses too much, and pitchers at higher levels will exploit his declining discipline even further. He also needs to be more consistent in the field after making 33 errors last season. Bixler will move to high Class A this season. His tools are intriguing but his production must improve.

Year	Club (League)	Class	AVG	G	AB	R	H	2B	3B	HR	RBI	BB	SO	SB	OBP	SLG
2004	Williamsport (NY-P)	A	.276	59	228	40	63	7	4	0	21	15	51	14	.321	.342
2005	Hickory (SAL)	A	.281	126	502	74	141	23	2	9	50	38	134	21	.343	.388
MINOR LEAGUE TOTALS			.279	185	730	114	204	30	6	9	71	53	185	35	.336	.374

ST. LOUIS
CARDINALS

BY **WILL LINGO**

Though the team fell short of its goal of a World Series title again in 2005, the Cardinals also reached 100 wins and posted the best record in the major leagues for the second year in a row. St. Louis led the National League in ERA and finished third in scoring, showing once again that the front office knows how to build a major league roster.

 The Cardinals are built largely around players who came up through other organizations, with such notable exceptions as Albert Pujols. Homegrown catcher **Yadier Molina** did seize the big league job, and righthander Brad Thompson established himself as a reliable set-up man in his rookie season. Otherwise, the big league team was assembled through astute free-agent signings and savvy trades.

To bolster their minor league system, which Baseball America rated the game's worst entering 2005, the Cardinals have taken a hard look at their scouting operation over the last two years. They have made significant changes, both in the structure and responsibilities of the scouting staff and in the use of sophisticated performance analysis through statistics.

The new philosophy resulted in a heavy college approach in the 2004 draft, as St. Louis looked for players who could make quick contributions at the higher levels of the system. The team was also in the early stages of developing its system of statistical analysis, which has become much more sophisticated and is now done almost exclusively in-house, rather than by outside suppliers. St. Louis got an opportunity to test its

new approach with a draft windfall in 2005, getting four extra picks for the loss of free agents Edgar Renteria and Mike Matheny.

The Cardinals' draft showed their willingness to look at all types of players. There were sleepers drafted on college performance, such as outfielder Nick Stavinoha (seventh round), and college players whose performance never seemed to measure up to their tools, such as righthander Mark McCormick (supplemental first). There were toolsy high school players whose projection is based on the judgments of scouts, such as outfielder Daryl Jones (third). St. Louis even spent a couple of early picks on Tyler Herron (supplemental first) and Josh Wilson (second), a pair of prep righthanders—considered the riskiest demographic in the draft.

The Cardinals also are making a renewed commitment to Latin America, opening a new academy in the Dominican Republic two years after vacating a substandard facility there, and working on a Venezuelan academy to open in 2006. The organization has committed to looking for talent wherever it can be found, which should pay dividends for a farm system thin on premium talent.

Fortunately for St. Louis, the major league team has few immediate holes that need to be plugged by minor leaguers. But as the Cardinals move into a new Busch Stadium, they have the hope of introducing new homegrown talent in the coming years as well.

TOP 30 PROSPECTS

1. Anthony Reyes, rhp
2. Colby Rasmus, of
3. Tyler Greene, ss
4. Chris Lambert, rhp
5. Mark McCormick, rhp
6. Adam Wainwright, rhp
7. Travis Hanson, 3b
8. Cody Haerther, of
9. Nick Webber, rhp
10. Stuart Pomeranz, rhp
11. Daryl Jones, of
12. Tyler Herron, rhp
13. Brendan Ryan, ss
14. Tyler Johnson, lhp
15. Chris Duncan, 1b/of
16. Juan Mateo, rhp
17. Juan Lucena, ss
18. Nick Stavinoha, of
19. Skip Schumaker, of
20. Rick Ankiel, of
21. Mark Worrell, rhp
22. Eric Haberer, lhp
23. Josh Wilson, rhp
24. Mark Michael, rhp
25. Blake Hawksworth, rhp
26. Mike Parisi, rhp
27. Cory Doyne, rhp
28. Jose Martinez, 2b/ss
29. Mike Ferris, 1b
30. Kenny Maiques, rhp

ORGANIZATION OVERVIEW

General manager: Walt Jocketty. **Farm director:** Bruce Manno. **Scouting director:** Jeff Luhnow.

2005 PERFORMANCE

Class	Team	League	W	L	Pct.	Finish*	Manager
Majors	St. Louis	National	100	62	.617	1st (16)	Tony La Russa
Triple-A	Memphis Redbirds	Pacific Coast	71	72	.497	9th (16)	Danny Sheaffer
Double-A	Springfield Cardinals	Texas	70	70	.500	5th (8)	Chris Maloney
High A	Palm Beach Cardinals	Florida State	69	71	.493	+6th (12)	Ron Warner
Low A	Swing of the Quad Cities	Midwest	72	67	.518	t-4th (14)	Joe Cunningham
Short-season	New Jersey Cardinals	New York-Penn	37	39	.487	7th (14)	Mark DeJohn
Rookie	Johnson City Cardinals	Appalachian	28	39	.418	8th (10)	Tommy Kidwell
OVERALL 2005 MINOR LEAGUE RECORD			347	358	.492	19th (30)	

*Finish in overall standings (No. of teams in league). +League champion.

ORGANIZATION LEADERS

BATTING *Minimum 250 at-bats*

*AVG	Stavinoha, Nick, Quad Cities	.344
R	Minges, Tyler, New Jersey/Springfield	98
H	Hanson, Travis, Springfield	155
TB	Hanson, Travis, Springfield	250
2B	Minges, Tyler, New Jersey/Springfield	34
3B	Haerther, Cody, Palm Beach/Springfield	8
HR	Four tied at	21
RBI	Hanson, Travis, Springfield	97
BB	Shepherd, Matt, Quad Cities	87
SO	Nelson, John, Memphis	141
SB	Lemanczyk, Matt, Quad Cities	48
*OBP	Shepherd, Matt, Quad Cities	.402
*SLG	Minges, Tyler, New Jersey/Springfield	.564

PITCHING #Minimum 75 innings

W	Leek, Randy, Memphis/Springfield	15
L	Three tied at	11
#ERA	Webber, Nick, New Jersey/Quad Cities	1.93
G	Torres, Jaymie, Palm Beach/Quad Cities	59
CG	Leek, Randy, Memphis/Springfield	3
SV	Worrell, Mark, Palm Beach	35
IP	Leek, Randy, Memphis/Springfield	192
BB	Lambert, Chris, Palm Beach/Springfield	63
SO	Wainwright, Adam, Memphis	147

BEST TOOLS

Best Hitter for Average	Colby Rasmus
Best Power Hitter	Chris Duncan
Best Strike-Zone Discipline	John Gall
Fastest Baserunner	Daryl Jones
Best Athlete	Daryl Jones
Best Fastball	Anthony Reyes
Best Curveball	Adam Wainwright
Best Slider	Anthony Reyes
Best Changeup	Phillip Anderson
Best Control	Anthony Reyes
Best Defensive Catcher	Mike Mahoney
Best Defensive Infielder	Juan Lucena
Best Infield Arm	John Nelson
Best Defensive Outfielder	Skip Schumaker
Best Outfield Arm	Rick Ankiel

PROJECTED 2009 LINEUP

Catcher	Yadier Molina
First Base	Albert Pujols
Second Base	Travis Hanson
Third Base	Scott Rolen
Shortstop	Tyler Greene
Left Field	Cody Haerther
Center Field	Daryl Jones
Right Field	Colby Rasmus

No. 1 Starter	Chris Carpenter
No. 2 Starter	Mark Mulder
No. 3 Starter	Anthony Reyes
No. 4 Starter	Chris Lambert
No. 5 Starter	Adam Wainwright
Closer	Nick Webber

LAST YEAR'S TOP 20 PROSPECTS

1. Anthony Reyes, rhp
2. Adam Wainwright, rhp
3. Blake Hawksworth, rhp
4. Chris Lambert, rhp
5. Stuart Pomeranz, rhp
6. Brad Thompson, rhp
7. Brendan Ryan, ss
8. Chris Duncan, 1b
9. Cody Haerther, of
10. Carmen Cali, lhp
11. Reid Gorecki, of
12. Mike Ferris, 1b
13. Brandon Yarbrough, c
14. Donnie Smith, rhp
15. Juan Lucena, ss
16. Mark Michael, rhp
17. Mike Parisi, rhp
18. Travis Hanson, 2b/3b
19. John Gall, of/1b
20. Skip Schumaker, of

TOP PROSPECTS OF THE DECADE

Year	Player, Pos.	2005 Org.
1996	Alan Benes, rhp	Cardinals
1997	Matt Morris, rhp	Cardinals
1998	Rick Ankiel, lhp	Cardinals
1999	J.D. Drew, of	Dodgers
2000	Rick Ankiel, lhp	Cardinals
2001	Bud Smith, lhp	Twins
2002	Jimmy Journell, rhp	Cardinals
2003	Dan Haren, rhp	Athletics
2004	Blake Hawksworth, rhp	Cardinals
2005	Anthony Reyes, rhp	Cardinals

TOP DRAFT PICKS OF THE DECADE

Year	Player, Pos.	2005 Org.
1996	Braden Looper, rhp	Mets
1997	Adam Kennedy, ss	Angels
1998	J.D. Drew, of	Dodgers
1999	Chance Caple, rhp	Out of baseball
2000	Shaun Boyd, of	Cardinals
2001	Justin Pope, rhp	Yankees
2002	Calvin Hayes, ss (3rd round)	Cardinals
2003	Daric Barton, c	Athletics
2004	Chris Lambert, rhp	Cardinals
2005	Colby Rasmus, of	Cardinals

ALL-TIME LARGEST BONUSES

J.D. Drew, 1998	$3,000,000
Rick Ankiel, 1997	$2,500,000
Chad Hutchinson, 1998	$2,300,000
Shaun Boyd, 2000	$1,750,000
Braden Looper, 1996	$1,675,000

MINOR LEAGUE DEPTH CHART

St. Louis Cardinals

Rank: **21**

STRENGTH: New faces. The Cardinals had nowhere to go but up, and a strong 2005 draft class got the process started well.

WEAKNESS: Hitters. Almost all the Cardinals position players who have significant upside were drafted in 2005.

*Depth charts prepared by **John Manuel** and **Chris Kline**. Numbers in parentheses indicate prospect rankings.*

LF
Cody Haerther (8)
John Gall
Shaun Boyd

CF
Colby Rasmus (2)
Daryl Jones (11)
Skip Schumaker (19)
Reid Gorecki

RF
Nick Stavinoha (18)
Rick Ankiel (20)
Edgar Lara
Jairo Martinez

3B
Travis Hanson (7)
Gabe Johnson

SS
Tyler Greene (3)
Brendan Ryan (13)
Juan Lucena (17)
John Nelson
Donovan Solano

2B
Jose Martinez (28)
Kevin Estrada
Calvin Hayes
Jose Delgado
Matt Shepherd
Jarrett Hoffpauir

1B
Chris Duncan (15)
Mike Ferris (29)
Andy Schutzenhofer

C
Brandon Yarbrough
Bryan Anderson

RHP

Starters	Relievers
Anthony Reyes (1)	Nick Webber (9)
Chris Lambert (4)	Juan Mateo (16)
Mark McCormick (5)	Mark Worrell (21)
Adam Wainwright (6)	Kenny Maiques (30)
Stuart Pomeranz (10)	Dennis Dove
Tyler Herron (12)	Josh Kinney
Josh Wilson (23)	Rhett Parrott
Mark Michael (24)	
Blake Hawksworth (25)	
Mike Parisi (26)	
Cory Doyne (27)	
Mitch Boggs	
Donnie Smith	
Phillip Andersen	
Shaun Garceau	
Matt Scherer	
Jordan Pals	
Tyler Leach	

LHP

Starters	Relievers
Eric Haberer (22)	Tyler Johnson (14)
Zach Zuercher	Carmen Cali
Jaime Garcia	Kevin Ool
Chris Narveson	Adam Daniels

DRAFT ANALYSIS

2005

Best Pro Debut: OF Nick Stavinoha (7) immediately became one of the most feared hitters in the low Class A Midwest League, batting .344-14-53.

Best Athlete: OF Daryl Jones (3) had NCAA Division I-A football offers as a wide receiver, and he was thought to be a tough sign because he committed to Rice. But St. Louis got him for $450,000, the equivalent of second-round money. OF Colby Rasmus (1) isn't as fast as Jones, but he's a better hitter and another five-tool center fielder. And SS Tyler Greene (1) is a five-tool shortstop.

Best Pure Hitter: Rasmus, who hit .296-7-27 with 13 steals at Rookie-level Johnson City, has a higher ceiling than Stavinoha.

Best Raw Power: Stavinoha over Rasmus. Jones is just scratching the surface of his power potential, but both of his long-balls at Johnson City were bombs.

Fastest Runner: Jones runs the 60-yard dash in 6.4 seconds, and OF Malcolm Owens (13) is just as quick.

Best Defensive Player: Greene can be inconsistent, but he has the above-average arm and range to be a good shortstop. Rasmus has good instincts in center field.

Best Fastball: RHP Mark McCormick (1) hit 98 mph during the spring and pitched at 91-96 mph through instructional league. RHP Nick Webber (2) has a 91-94 mph fastball that's more notable for its sink and movement than its velocity. RHPs Tyler Herron (1), Josh Wilson (2), Mitch Boggs (5), Jason Cairns (8) and Kenny Maiques (37) all have touched 94.

Best Breaking Ball: McCormick, Herron and LHP Jaime Garcia (22) all have good curveballs at times. Maiques has a hard slider when healthy.

MIKE JANES

Jones

Most Intriguing Background: OF Wilfrido Pujols (6) is the cousin of Cardinals superstar Albert Pujols. 1B A.J. Van Slyke's (23) father was a former Cardinals first-round pick and a big league all-star, and his brother Scott was a 15th-round pick of the Dodgers. Unsigned 2B Jesse Schoendienst's (40) great uncle Red is a Hall of Famer who played for and managed the Cardinals. LHP Josh Schwartz (42) won his final 37 decisions for Rowan (N.J.), setting an NCAA record. Boggs played quarterback at Tennessee-Chattanooga and Stavinoha was a long snapper at Houston before both transferred to focus on baseball.

Closest To The Majors: Webber's sinker and his role as a reliever make him the front runner.

Best Late-Round Pick: The Cardinals thought they'd have to take Maiques in the supplemental first round until he blew out his elbow and needed Tommy John surgery.

The One Who Got Away: LHP Miers Quigley (19) had a 92-94 mph fastball before coming down with biceps tendinitis. He didn't bounce back enough for St. Louis to meet his asking price, so he's now at Alabama.

Assessment: After the Cardinals failed to sign a high school player in 2004, first-year scouting director Jeff Luhnow drafted a blend of collegians and prepsters, hitters and pitchers. The position players were most welcome in a system with few who project as big league regulars.

2004 The industry immediately panned this draft, and nothing has changed a year later. RHP Chris Lambert (1) is the best of the 41 players signed, all out of colleges. **GRADE:** D

2003 The Cardinals used 1B Daric Barton (1) to trade for Mark Mulder, and found another possible ace in RHP Anthony Reyes (15). They let two more get away, as RHPs Ian Kennedy (14) and Max Scherzer (43) will be two of the first pitchers drafted in 2006 **GRADE:** A

2002 St. Louis didn't pick until the third round, and SS Calvin Hayes (3) has yet to get past low Class A. RHP Brad Thompson (16) helped the bullpen last year, while OF Cody Haerther (6) and 3B Travis Hanson (9) are two of the system's better position players. **GRADE:** C

2001 RHP Dan Haren (2), another piece of the Mulder trade, is a solid big league starter. The Cardinals had similar hopes for RHP Blake Hawksworth (28), but he can't stay healthy. **GRADE:** B

Draft analysis prepared by Jim Callis. Numbers in parentheses indicate draft rounds.

ANTHONY REYES

RHP

NIKKI BOERTMAN

Born: Oct. 16, 1981.
Ht.: 6-2. **Wt.:** 215.
Bats: R. **Throws:** R.
Drafted: Southern California, 2003 (15th round).
Signed by: Nakia Hill.

Reyes is looking more and more like the steal of the 2003 draft. Persistent injuries plagued him throughout his career at Southern California, but the Cardinals bet he could return to the dominant form he showed as a sophomore if he could get healthy. They took him in the 15th round, and by and large they've been right. Reyes has been bothered by occasional shoulder inflammation as a pro, but he has suffered no major injuries and has moved quickly through the system in just two seasons. In an organization that didn't have such a well-stocked major league pitching staff, Reyes could have been pressed into service in 2005. But the Cardinals had five reliable starters and were happy to keep him at Triple-A Memphis for more seasoning. He did get a spot start in August and allowed just two hits in 6⅓ shutout innings against the Brewers, then returned to Memphis and struck out 15 in his next start. He was often dominant in the Pacific Coast League, ranking first in baserunners per nine innings (10.0), second in strikeouts per nine (9.5) and third in opponent average.

While he's probably not a No. 1 starter, Reyes has the frame, stuff and command to pitch toward the front of a major league rotation. He makes hitters put the ball in play, trusts his defense and doesn't beat himself. He pitches consistently at 92-93 mph and occasionally reaches into the mid-90s, and his slider and changeup are effective complements to his fastball. His changeup has late sink and improved significantly as the season went on. He also worked on getting more movement on his fastball and began using a two-seamer effectively to get more sink. His command, which managers rated the best in the PCL, makes all of his pitches more effective. He not only stays ahead and avoids walks but also spots his pitches to both sides of the plate and keeps hitters off balance.

Reyes has no obvious flaws in his repertoire. He continues to work on improving his durability, but until he stays completely healthy for a full season that will remain a question. He worked 142 innings in 2005, but he missed three weeks after spraining a joint in his shoulder in May and often took more than four days between starts. The elbow problems that bothered him at Southern California haven't returned, but his shoulder has bothered him in each of his two pro seasons. Some scouts worry that his arm action will always lead to injury problems.

With the Cardinals losing free agent Matt Morris to the Giants, Reyes will be the frontrunner for a spot in the big league rotation. If no opening exists, he could compete for a bullpen job. He's easily the next pitcher in line for the St. Louis staff, and his combination of stuff and aptitude should allow him to be a contributor right away.

Year	Club (League)	Class	AVG	G	AB	R	H	2B	3B	HR	RBI	BB	SO	SB	OBP	SLG
2004	Palm Beach (FSL)	A	3	0	4.66	7	7	0	0	37	41	21	19	5	7	38	.297
	Tennessee (SL)	AA	6	2	2.91	12	12	0	0	74	62	27	24	3	13	102	.230
2005	Memphis (PCL)	AAA	7	6	3.64	23	23	2	0	129	105	55	52	13	34	136	.222
	St. Louis (NL)	MLB	1	1	2.71	4	1	0	0	13	6	4	4	2	4	12	.133
MAJOR LEAGUE TOTALS			1	1	2.71	4	1	0	0	13	6	4	4	2	4	12	.133
MINOR LEAGUE TOTALS			16	8	3.57	42	42	2	0	240	208	103	95	21	54	276	.236

COLBY RASMUS
OF

Born: Aug. 11, 1986. **B-T:** L-L. **Ht.:** 6-1. **Wt.:** 175. **Drafted:** HS—Phenix City, Ala., 2005 (1st round). **Signed by:** Scott Nichols.

Rasmus has a baseball pedigree that stacks up with just about anyone's. His father Tony was a 10th-round draft pick in January 1986 and now is the coach at Russell County High in Alabama, which won the 2005 national championship behind Colby and his younger brother Cory, a premium prospect for the 2006 draft. The Cardinals took Colby 28th overall and signed him for $1 million. Rasmus' tools are average or better across the board, but it's his baseball savvy and desire that make him stand out. He has a sweet lefthanded swing and the ability to put a charge in the ball. He has the arm and speed to play center field, and he's a threat on the bases. Strikeouts were Rasmus' biggest problem in his pro debut as he struggled to recognize offspeed pitches, though he showed the willingness to take a walk. He needs to add strength to his rail-thin frame. He's the best all-around outfield prospect St. Louis has brought in since J.D. Drew. Rasmus will open his first full season at low Class A Quad Cities and could progress quickly.

Year	Club (League)	Class	AVG	G	AB	R	H	2B	3B	HR	RBI	BB	SO	SB	OBP	SLG
2005	Johnson City (Appy)	R	.296	62	216	47	64	16	5	7	27	21	73	13	.362	.514
MINOR LEAGUE TOTALS			.296	62	216	47	64	16	5	7	27	21	73	13	.362	.514

TYLER GREENE
SS

Born: Aug. 17, 1983. **B-T:** R-R. **Ht.:** 6-2. **Wt.:** 185. **Drafted:** Georgia Tech, 2005 (1st round). **Signed by:** Roger Smith.

Greene had an up-and-down career at Georgia Tech, alternating success with struggles on both offense and defense. He showed better hitting aptitude with wood, batting a team-best .431 for Team USA in 2003 and .296 in the Cape Cod League in 2004. His junior season was delayed by a broken jaw, but he still went 30th overall in the 2005 draft and earned a $1.1 million bonus. When in a groove, Greene hits to all fields and shows pop. The Cardinals regard him as a pure shortstop with a plus arm and good range. He's an impressive specimen with legs that look like a sprinter's, and an above-average runner who's an efficient basestealer. Greene's ultimate value will be determined by what he does with the bat. He tends to be streaky and needs to use his hands better. He gets erratic with his defensive footwork at times, leading to throwing errors. Greene has impressive tools to go with great makeup and a willingness to learn, so he should move quickly if he hits. He'll return to high Class A Palm Beach to start 2006.

Year	Club (League)	Class	AVG	G	AB	R	H	2B	3B	HR	RBI	BB	SO	SB	OBP	SLG
2005	New Jersey (NY-P)	A	.261	35	138	28	36	12	0	1	18	15	37	13	.352	.370
	Palm Beach (FSL)	A	.271	20	85	17	23	4	0	2	5	5	28	6	.326	.388
MINOR LEAGUE TOTALS			.265	55	223	45	59	16	0	3	23	20	65	19	.343	.377

CHRIS LAMBERT
RHP

Born: March 8, 1983. **B-T:** R-R. **Ht.:** 6-1. **Wt.:** 205. **Drafted:** Boston College, 2004 (1st round). **Signed by:** Joe Rigoli.

Though he's a college pitcher, Lambert doesn't have much experience on the mound. He comes from cold-weather New England and concentrated more on hockey in high school. He built on a solid first full season by pitching in the Arizona Fall League and for Team USA in an Olympic qualifying tournament. After looking tired in his first pro summer, Lambert was stronger in 2005. He consistently worked at 91-94 mph and showed better movement with his fastball. He has a good changeup and a potentially dominating curveball. Lambert's curveball is inconsistent, as are his control and his mechanics. There's some effort to his delivery, which affects his ability to repeat it and throw strikes. After moving up to Double-A Springfield, he learned he couldn't just get hitters out with his fastball. Pitchers from the Northeast often struggle with the adjustment to pro ball, but Lambert's performance in the early part of 2005 showed his potential. He'll return to Double-A to start 2006 but should finish the year in the Triple-A rotation.

Year	Club (League)	Class	W	L	ERA	G	GS	CG	SV	IP	H	R	ER	HR	BB	SO	AVG
2004	Peoria (Mid)	A	1	1	2.58	9	9	0	0	38	31	15	11	2	24	46	.218
2005	Palm Beach (FSL)	A	7	1	2.63	10	10	0	0	55	53	20	16	4	15	46	.255
	Springfield (TL)	AA	3	8	6.35	18	18	0	0	85	97	69	60	10	48	69	.291
MINOR LEAGUE TOTALS			11	10	4.40	37	37	0	0	178	181	104	87	16	87	161	.265

5 MARK McCORMICK RHP

Born: Oct. 15, 1983. **B-T:** R-R. **Ht.:** 6-2. **Wt.:** 195. **Drafted:** Baylor, 2005 (1st round supplemental). **Signed by:** Joe Almaraz.

McCormick has been throwing in the mid-90s since he was in high school, but he dropped to the Orioles in the 11th round because of questions about his signability, immaturity and complementary pitches. He went to Baylor and didn't start to shed that rap until 2005, when the Cardinals drafted him 43rd overall and signed him for $800,000. McCormick had one of the best power arms in the 2005 draft, pitching consistently at 92-95 mph and topping out at 97-98 all year long. His hammer curveball can be a plus pitch when it's on and his changeup should be average. Because he still is working on his control, McCormick doesn't always dominate as his stuff would indicate. His complementary pitches are inconsistent, and righthanders tee off on his curveball when it's not sharp. He worked on changeup grips last summer. Cardinals scouts loved McCormick's arm, and their stat analysis loved his college strikeout rates. If his power package comes together, he could be a dominant starter. He'll open 2006 at one of St. Louis' Class A stops.

Year	Club (League)	Class	W	L	ERA	G	GS	CG	SV	IP	H	R	ER	HR	BB	SO	AVG
2005	New Jersey (NY-P)	A	0	0	0.00	2	2	0	0	6	1	0	0	0	3	10	.053
	Quad Cities (Mid)	A	1	2	5.48	9	9	0	0	43	41	27	26	4	28	45	.253
MINOR LEAGUE TOTALS			1	2	4.81	11	11	0	0	49	42	27	26	4	31	55	.232

6 ADAM WAINWRIGHT RHP

Born: Aug. 30, 1981. **B-T:** R-R. **Ht.:** 6-7. **Wt.:** 205. **Drafted:** HS—Brunswick, Ga., 2000 (1st round). **Signed by:** Rob English (Braves).

Wainwright came to the Cardinals in the J.D. Drew trade before the 2004 season and continued his steady ascent through the minors in 2005, earning a September callup. He led the Pacific Coast League in innings, as well as hits allowed and wild pitches (12). After battling an elbow strain in 2004, Wainwright was a workhorse in 2005 and dominated early in the season. His fastball is solid-average and sometimes better than that, running up to 93 mph with good sink. He has a good feel for a changeup, and it may have become his second-best pitch ahead of his curveball and slider. He did a better job of pitching downhill in 2005. Wainwright struggled when he got away from working off his fastball. He has a hard time putting hitters away when his breaking pitches aren't on. His slider gets flat and his curveball gets slow too often for his own good. Wainwright is ready for a big league opportunity, but it may have to come in the bullpen because Anthony Reyes is ahead of him. He still projects as a starter down the road.

Year	Club (League)	Class	W	L	ERA	G	GS	CG	SV	IP	H	R	ER	HR	BB	SO	AVG
2000	Braves (GCL)	R	4	0	1.13	7	5	0	0	32	15	5	4	1	10	42	.136
	Danville (Appy)	R	2	2	3.69	6	6	0	0	29	28	13	12	3	2	39	.252
2001	Macon (SAL)	A	10	10	3.77	28	28	1	0	165	144	89	69	9	48	184	.230
2002	Myrtle Beach (Car)	A	9	6	3.31	28	28	1	0	163	149	67	60	7	66	167	.240
2003	Greenville (SL)	AA	10	8	3.37	27	27	1	0	150	133	59	56	9	37	128	.242
2004	Memphis (PCL)	AAA	4	4	5.37	12	12	0	0	64	68	47	38	12	28	64	.280
2005	Memphis (PCL)	AAA	10	10	4.40	29	29	0	0	182	204	98	89	18	51	147	.280
	St. Louis (NL)	MLB	0	0	13.50	2	0	0	0	2	2	3	3	1	1	0	.250
MAJOR LEAGUE TOTALS			0	0	13.50	2	0	0	0	2	2	3	3	1	1	0	.250
MINOR LEAGUE TOTALS			49	40	3.76	137	135	3	0	785	741	378	328	59	242	771	.248

7 TRAVIS HANSON 3B

Born: Jan. 24, 1981. **B-T:** L-R. **Ht.:** 6-2. **Wt.:** 197. **Drafted:** Portland, 2002 (9th round). **Signed by:** Dane Walker.

A broken ankle derailed Hanson in 2004, but he bounced back with his best pro season in 2005. He was the Double-A Texas League's all-star third baseman and led Cardinals farmhands in RBIs and total bases (250). Like Chris Lambert, he finished the year in the AFL and with Team USA in the Olympic qualifier. For the first time, Hanson showed power that had only been potential in the past. His powerful swing generates a lot of leverage off the back side, and the timing came together in 2005, showing that he can be a run producer. Before he got hurt in 2004, he was a slick fielder at third base and had seen time at second. In part because of his injury, Hanson's footwork was poor when he returned. He led Texas League third basemen with 36 errors, though he did look better as the season went on. With Hanson's defensive struggles and Scott Rolen's presence in St. Louis, the Cardinals will continue to try him at other positions. His offensive performance merits a move up to Triple-A, and he could break into the big leagues as a utility player.

Year	Club (League)	Class	AVG	G	AB	R	H	2B	3B	HR	RBI	BB	SO	SB	OBP	SLG
2002	New Jersey (NY-P)	A	.294	75	272	31	80	17	5	4	40	12	55	1	.326	.438
2003	Peoria (Mid)	A	.277	136	527	70	146	31	5	9	78	35	104	3	.325	.406
2004	Palm Beach (FSL)	A	.259	57	224	26	58	11	0	2	35	19	38	2	.321	.335
2005	Springfield (TL)	AA	.284	137	546	82	155	29	3	20	97	54	99	2	.347	.458
MINOR LEAGUE TOTALS			.280	405	1569	209	439	88	13	35	250	120	296	8	.332	.419

8 CODY HAERTHER   OF

Born: July 14, 1983. **B-T:** L-R. **Ht.:** 6-1. **Wt.:** 198. **Drafted:** HS—Chatsworth, Calif., 2002 (6th round). **Signed by:** Steve Gossett.

Haerther was in the midst of a breakout season in 2004 before getting derailed by a stress fracture in his left leg. He got back on track in 2005, jumping to Double-A and playing in the Arizona Fall League. His brother Casey is a top Southern California high school prospect for the 2006 draft. In a system thin on impact bats, Haerther is a lefthanded hitter with power potential, and he showed a lot more of that potential in 2005. The ball jumps off his bat, and he has a smooth stroke, a good approach and the ability to control the strike zone. He has average speed and savvy on the basepaths. Haerther's defense is a work in progress and he went to instructional league in an effort to improve it. He has the ability to play a passable left field if he continues to improve, though he split time between left and DH in 2005. Haerther has few roadblocks ahead of him in the farm system, and even in the big leagues the Cardinals have relied on aging veterans and marginal players. He'll return to Double-A to begin 2006.

Year	Club (League)	Class	AVG	G	AB	R	H	2B	3B	HR	RBI	BB	SO	SB	OBP	SLG
2003	Johnson City (Appy)	R	.332	63	226	31	75	12	6	3	39	22	30	2	.390	.478
2004	Peoria (Mid)	A	.316	86	326	48	103	20	2	5	45	32	59	7	.383	.436
2005	Palm Beach (FSL)	A	.318	47	173	29	55	8	7	8	30	17	31	8	.380	.584
	Springfield (TL)	AA	.298	65	208	30	62	10	1	10	37	9	44	0	.333	.500
MINOR LEAGUE TOTALS			.316	261	933	138	295	50	16	26	151	80	164	17	.373	.488

9 NICK WEBBER   RHP

Born: May 9, 1984. **B-T:** R-R. **Ht.:** 6-7. **Wt.:** 210. **Drafted:** Central Missouri State, 2005 (2nd round). **Signed by:** Scott Melvin.

Central Missouri State is a powerhouse NCAA Division II program that set a division record 16 shutouts in 2005, with Webber serving as the Mules' closer. The Cardinals used him as a starter after signing him for $425,000, and he quickly jumped to low Class A. Webber's fastball is one of the best in the organization, not just because of its 91-94 mph velocity but more because it has heavy sink and unbelievable movement. He relied almost exclusively on his fastball in college and had similar success with it at short-season New Jersey. If Webber is to make it as a starter, he'll need to develop his slider and changeup. He had a hard time maintaining his velocity, throwing in the high 80s in some outings, and will need to sharpen his command. Webber has the one dominant pitch and makeup to be a closer. Nevertheless, St. Louis will keep using him as a starter in high Class A in 2006, because his value will be enhanced if he shows an aptitude for it.

Year	Club (League)	Class	W	L	ERA	G	GS	CG	SV	IP	H	R	ER	HR	BB	SO	AVG
2005	New Jersey (NY-P)	A	5	2	1.87	10	9	0	0	53	35	18	11	2	15	43	.179
	Quad Cities (Mid)	A	0	4	3.41	5	5	1	0	29	28	15	11	1	9	11	.250
MINOR LEAGUE TOTALS			5	6	2.41	15	14	1	0	82	63	33	22	3	24	54	.205

10 STUART POMERANZ   RHP

Born: Dec. 17, 1984. **B-T:** R-R. **Ht.:** 6-7. **Wt.:** 245. **Drafted:** HS—Collierville, Tenn., 2003 (2nd round). **Signed by:** Marty Denton.

Pomeranz pitched the entire 2005 season as a 20-year-old and earned a promotion to Double-A in May. He didn't post good numbers there but earned praise from some Texas League observers as the best arm on the Springfield staff, ahead of Chris Lambert. Pomeranz has the size and pitches to be an innings-eater. He's a solid 6-foot-7 with a fastball that now sits in the low 90s, a knuckle-curve and a changeup. His fastball has good sink and late movement that bores in on righthanders. Pomeranz needs to refine his command so he can avoid getting behind hitters and start missing more bats. He shows good arm speed with his changeup but still needs to improve the pitch to make it an effective third option. The Cardinals were impressed with Pomeranz' aptitude, confidence and consistency in Double-A, though his numbers weren't impressive. He'll probably go back to Springfield to open 2006 but could see Triple-A by the end of the year. If his changeup doesn't come around, his future will be in the bullpen.

Year	Club (League)	Class	W	L	ERA	G	GS	CG	SV	IP	H	R	ER	HR	BB	SO	AVG
2003	Johnson City (Appy)	R	1	1	6.12	4	3	0	0	15	13	10	10	2	4	14	.236
2004	Peoria (Mid)	A	12	4	3.55	17	17	0	0	101	95	59	40	10	25	88	.251
2005	Palm Beach (FSL)	A	2	5	3.35	8	8	0	0	48	56	26	18	1	10	29	.296
	Springfield (TL)	AA	5	6	5.29	18	18	0	0	99	110	65	58	12	40	66	.278
MINOR LEAGUE TOTALS			20	16	4.31	47	46	0	0	263	274	160	126	25	79	197	.269

11 DARYL JONES   OF

Born: June 25, 1987. **B-T:** L-L. **Ht.:** 5-11. **Wt.:** 180. **Drafted:** HS—Spring, Texas, 2005 (3rd round). **Signed by:** Joe Almaraz.

A third-round pick in June, Jones didn't make a strong impression in his pro debut. He's raw as a baseball player and was overmatched even in the advanced Rookie-level Appalachian League, the lowest rung on the Cardinals' minor league ladder. But he has as much speed and athletic ability as anyone in the system, as well as a passion for baseball. As a wide receiver in high school, he caught 20 touchdown passes over his last two seasons, and his 4.5-second speed in the 40-yard dash attracted NCAA Division I-A football scholarship offers. He turned those down to accept a baseball ride from Rice. Most clubs thought it would be nearly impossible to get him into pro ball, but area scout Joe Almaraz got a good read on Jones and the Cardinals signed him quickly for $450,000. His most notable tool is his speed, but he also shows intriguing raw power. He needs to refine both to put them into use in games, however. His speed and frame prompted scouts to compare him to Kenny Lofton, though he has more power potential than Lofton. He definitely has the range to play center field, but slid over to right field at Johnson City because St. Louis wanted to play Colby Rasmus in center. Jones' arm fit fine in right. He has a lot of work to do, particularly with his hitting approach, but he has the aptitude to make fast improvement now that he's focusing on baseball. He'll start the year in extended spring training before heading to one of the Cardinals' short-season affiliates in June.

Year	Club (League)	Class	AVG	G	AB	R	H	2B	3B	HR	RBI	BB	SO	SB	OBP	SLG
2005	Johnson City (Appy)	R	.209	61	182	36	38	6	1	2	10	15	41	10	.311	.286
MINOR LEAGUE TOTALS			.209	61	182	36	38	6	1	2	10	15	41	10	.311	.286

12 TYLER HERRON   RHP

Born: Aug. 5, 1986. **B-T:** R-R. **Ht.:** 6-3. **Wt.:** 190. **Drafted:** HS—Wellington, Fla., 2005 (1st round supplemental). **Signed by:** Steve Turco.

Herron comes out of one of Florida's cradles of pitching, Wellington High, which produced Pirates first-rounders Bobby Bradley (1999) and Sean Burnett (2000), as well as Justin Pope, a first-round pick of the Cardinals in 2001 after he spent three years at Central Florida. Herron grabbed attention last spring with two duels against Chris Volstad, who went 16th overall to the Marlins, and the Cardinals took him 30 picks later and signed him for $675,000. Herron shows a good feel for pitching, and the stuff and intensity to pitch at the front of a rotation. His fastball touched 94 mph during his high school season but sat more at 87-91 during his debut. He should eventually settle into the low 90s. His curveball is consistent, thought at times it rates as a 70 on the 20-80 scouting scale. He showed advanced aptitude for a changeup. As a former shortstop, he's athletic with a projectable frame. Herron needs to refine all his pitches, and especially improve his fastball command to set up his secondary pitches. He should jump to low Class A this year.

Year	Club (League)	Class	W	L	ERA	G	GS	CG	SV	IP	H	R	ER	HR	BB	SO	AVG
2005	Johnson City (Appy)	R	0	3	5.61	13	13	0	0	50	47	35	31	11	27	49	.245
MINOR LEAGUE TOTALS			0	3	5.62	13	13	0	0	50	47	35	31	11	27	49	.245

13 BRENDAN RYAN   SS

Born: March 26, 1982. **B-T:** R-R. **Ht.:** 6-2. **Wt.:** 195. **Drafted:** Lewis-Clark State (Idaho), 2003 (7th round). **Signed by:** Dane Walker.

Rated as the top position prospect in the organization going into last season, Ryan has been passed by 2005 draft picks with more upside and some holdovers who had better seasons. Ryan still has plenty of potential, however, and held his own after a midseason promotion to Double-A. He put together a positive season despite the death of his father just before spring training. He said he knew his father would want him on the field, so he reported to camp on time. Ryan remains one of the best athletes in the organization, and he's still trying to harness his tools to make himself a consistently productive player. He has a nice swing and is willing to take a walk. He's also a plus runner, though he didn't run much in 2005 because of a sore hamstring. He hustles all the time and plays with energy and enthusiasm that's contagious. Ryan also has the tools to remain at shortstop, though he committed 29 errors last season because of ill-advised throws and bad footwork. He still has to show more than just flashes of brilliance, but the Cardinals were encouraged by his progress in 2005. He'll go back to Double-A to open 2006.

Year	Club (League)	Class	AVG	G	AB	R	H	2B	3B	HR	RBI	BB	SO	SB	OBP	SLG
2003	New Jersey (NY-P)	A	.311	53	193	20	60	14	4	0	13	14	25	11	.363	.425
2004	Peoria (Mid)	A	.322	105	426	72	137	21	4	2	59	24	42	30	.356	.404
2005	Palm Beach (FSL)	A	.303	49	188	29	57	17	0	1	16	15	20	8	.355	.410
	Springfield (TL)	AA	.273	43	154	28	42	8	1	2	9	15	19	6	.343	.377
MINOR LEAGUE TOTALS			.308	250	961	149	296	60	9	5	97	68	106	55	.355	.405

14 TYLER JOHNSON   LHP

Born: June 7, 1981. **B-T:** B-L. **Ht.:** 6-2. **Wt.:** 180. **Drafted:** Moorpark (Calif.) JC, D/F 2000 (34th round). **Signed by:** Chuck Fick.

The Cardinals gambled that Johnson wouldn't be able to stick in the big leagues by leaving him off their 40-man roster after the 2004 season, and the gamble paid off. The Athletics took him in the major league Rule 5 draft but couldn't keep him, so he came back to St. Louis after spring training and made his big league debut in September. Johnson's goofy, carefree attitude has always made him a hard player for coaches and managers to figure out. It makes them wonder if he's focused, yet it also means he won't wilt in pressure situations and can put bad outings behind him quickly. He has the stuff to be an effective lefty reliever, with a natural, loopy curveball that grades as a plus-plus pitch when he locates it well. He complements the curve with an 88-91 mph fastball with late tail, and he throws both pitches with a natural, effortless motion. The Cardinals didn't gamble by leaving Johnson off the big league roster again, and with Ray King gone he'll have a golden opportunity to win a bullpen job in spring training.

Year	Club (League)	Class	W	L	ERA	G	GS	CG	SV	IP	H	R	ER	HR	BB	SO	AVG
2001	Johnson City (Appy)	R	1	1	2.65	9	9	0	0	41	26	17	12	1	21	58	.181
	Peoria (Mid)	A	0	1	3.94	3	3	0	0	14	14	9	6	1	10	15	.255
2002	Peoria (Mid)	A	15	3	2.00	22	18	0	0	121	96	35	27	7	42	132	.218
2003	Palm Beach (FSL)	A	5	5	3.08	22	10	0	0	79	79	29	27	2	38	81	.262
	Tennessee (SL)	AA	1	0	1.65	20	0	0	0	27	16	7	5	1	15	39	.168
2004	Tennessee (SL)	AA	2	2	4.80	53	0	0	4	56	48	32	30	4	37	77	.221
2005	Memphis (PCL)	AAA	2	1	4.27	57	0	0	7	59	51	31	28	6	26	77	.232
	St. Louis (NL)	MLB	0	0	0.00	5	0	0	0	3	3	0	0	0	3	4	.300
MAJOR LEAGUE TOTALS			0	0	0.00	5	0	0	0	3	3	0	0	0	3	4	.300
MINOR LEAGUE TOTALS			26	13	3.06	186	40	0	11	397	330	160	135	22	189	479	.224

15 CHRIS DUNCAN   1B/OF

Born: May 5, 1981. **B-T:** L-R. **Ht.:** 6-5. **Wt.:** 210. **Drafted:** HS—Tucson, 1999 (1st round supplemental). **Signed by:** Manny Guerra.

People could have argued that Duncan, whose father Dave is the Cardinals' longtime pitching coach, was a nepotism pick before the last two seasons, when he started to realize his power potential. He made his major league debut in September, homering off Brandon Claussen on the final day of the season and making for a proud father in the dugout. Duncan's power is clearly his best tool, and he has gotten shorter and quicker to the ball in the last couple of years. He led Memphis in both homers and RBIs last season. His adjustments have also helped his overall hitting approach, though he'll always have high strikeout numbers and hit no better than .260-.270. Defense remains his biggest weakness. He has worked hard to get better at first base but still committed 17 errors in 2005. He got some time in left field in Triple-A and in the Mexican Pacific League, but he'll have to work hard to be adequate there. There are opportunities in the outfield, however, so if he can hold his own on defense he could get a long look there during spring training. If not, he won't beat out Albert Pujols at first base, so he'll either become trade bait or head back to Triple-A.

Year	Club (League)	Class	AVG	G	AB	R	H	2B	3B	HR	RBI	BB	SO	SB	OBP	SLG
1999	Johnson City (Appy)	R	.214	55	201	23	43	8	1	6	34	25	62	3	.300	.353
2000	Peoria (Mid)	A	.256	122	450	52	115	34	0	8	57	36	111	1	.318	.384
2001	Potomac (Car)	A	.179	49	168	12	30	6	0	3	16	10	47	4	.229	.268
	Peoria (Mid)	A	.306	80	297	44	91	23	2	13	59	36	55	13	.386	.529
2002	Peoria (Mid)	A	.271	129	487	58	132	25	4	16	75	44	118	5	.337	.437

Year	Club (League)	Class	AVG	G	AB	R	H	2B	3B	HR	RBI	BB	SO	SB	OBP	SLG
2003	Palm Beach (FSL)	A	.254	121	425	26	108	20	0	2	42	44	115	4	.322	.315
	Tennessee (SL)	AA	.200	10	25	1	5	1	0	1	3	0	6	0	.200	.360
2004	Tennessee (SL)	AA	.289	120	387	57	112	23	0	16	65	64	94	8	.393	.473
2005	Memphis (PCL)	AAA	.265	128	431	57	114	21	2	21	73	63	104	1	.358	.469
	St. Louis (NL)	MLB	.200	9	10	2	2	1	0	1	3	0	5	0	.200	.600
MAJOR LEAGUE TOTALS			.200	9	10	2	2	1	0	1	3	0	5	0	.200	.600
MINOR LEAGUE TOTALS			.261	814	2871	330	750	161	9	86	424	322	712	39	.339	.413

16 JUAN MATEO   RHP

Born: Dec. 17, 1982. **B-T:** R-R. **Ht.:** 6-2. **Wt.:** 180. **Signed:** Dominican Republic, 2001. **Signed by:** Jose Serra (Cubs).

Though they're going to contend again in 2006, the Cardinals decided Mateo was too tempting to pass up in the major league Rule 5 draft at the Winter Meetings. They'll have to keep him on their active big league roster all season, or else they'll have to put him on waivers and offer him back to the Cubs for half his $50,000 draft price. Mateo may have the most upside of the 12 players taken in the big league Rule 5 draft. He throws strikes with a 91-94 mph fastball, an improving slider and a rudimentary changeup. Mostly a reliever for his first three seasons in the Chicago system, Mateo moved to the rotation last May. After taking a few starts to adapt, he went 4-1, 1.79 over his final 10 outings. He'll pitch out of the bullpen in 2006 for the Cardinals, who should be able to find him enough innings so it won't be a totally wasted year of development.

Year	Club (League)	Class	W	L	ERA	G	GS	CG	SV	IP	H	R	ER	HR	BB	SO	AVG
2002	Cubs (DSL)	R	3	0	3.18	11	4	0	3	28	24	15	10	1	10	22	.214
2003	Cubs (AZL)	R	4	1	4.46	18	0	0	2	36	42	25	18	2	14	35	.288
2004	Lansing (Mid)	A	4	1	3.28	53	1	0	9	74	61	28	27	3	19	60	.216
2005	Daytona (FSL)	A	10	5	3.21	32	16	1	2	109	99	47	39	9	27	123	.240
MINOR LEAGUE TOTALS			21	7	3.41	114	21	1	16	248	226	115	94	15	70	240	.237

17 JUAN LUCENA   SS

Born: Jan. 20, 1984. **B-T:** R-R. **Ht.:** 5-10. **Wt.:** 155. **Signed:** Venezuela, 2002. **Signed by:** Enrique Brito.

Lucena is one of the few legitimate Latin American prospects in the system, a shortcoming that should change as the team makes a renewed commitment to international scouting under scouting director Jeff Luhnow. The Cardinals opened a new academy in the Dominican Republic over the winter and have several Latin American players at the lowest levels of the system that they'll monitor closely this year. The most advanced Latin prospect is Lucena, who won the Appalachian League batting title in his 2004 U.S. debut and handled the jump to low Class A last year. He has a simple line-drive swing that allows him to make contact almost at will. He struck out just once every 32.7 plate appearances in 2005, a rate that would have topped the minors if he had enough playing time to qualify. However, he needs to take more pitches and draw more walks because he'll never show much power. Lucena is a solid shortstop and the best defensive infielder in the system. He has sure hands and average arm strength, as well as the versatility to play other positions in case he has to become a utilityman. Lucena will take the next step to high Class A in 2006.

Year	Club (League)	Class	AVG	G	AB	R	H	2B	3B	HR	RBI	BB	SO	SB	OBP	SLG
2002	Cardinals (VSL)	R	.191	16	47	4	9	1	0	0	3	1	2	0	.208	.213
2003	Cardinals (DSL)	R	.234	64	248	44	58	11	6	0	18	14	9	6	.287	.327
2004	Johnson City (Appy)	R	.332	56	205	35	68	8	1	4	30	11	16	7	.365	.439
2005	Quad Cities (Mid)	A	.301	99	332	39	100	10	0	2	43	12	11	9	.329	.349
MINOR LEAGUE TOTALS			.282	235	832	122	235	30	7	6	94	38	38	22	.318	.357

18 NICK STAVINOHA   OF

Born: May 3, 1982. **B-T:** R-R. **Ht.:** 6-2. **Wt.:** 225. **Drafted:** Louisiana State, 2005 (7th round). **Signed by:** Steve Gossett.

With four extra picks at the top of the 2005 draft, the Cardinals had to save money in the middle rounds and found a bargain in Stavinoha. A seventh-round college senior who signed for $15,000, he jumped right to low Class A and led the system in hitting. Stavinoha began his college career as a linebacker recruit at Houston, and he became a long snapper in order to get playing time. After his freshman year he decided he wanted to play baseball, and he spent two seasons as a catcher at San Jacinto (Texas) Junior College before moving to Louisiana State. He was a DH for his junior season but moved into the outfield as a senior last spring, when he was the Tigers' top hitter at .370-18-65. Stavinoha is a polished hitter who should be able to hit for power and average. The major questions about Stavinoha are his age—because of his extended college career he'll play most of 2006 at 24—and his position. He doesn't have the tools to be a pro catcher, so St. Louis will try him at both outfield corners. He already is one of the most advanced hitting prospects in the organization and could jump to Double-A to start the season.

Year	Club (League)	Class	AVG	G	AB	R	H	2B	3B	HR	RBI	BB	SO	SB	OBP	SLG
2005	Quad Cities (Mid)	A	.344	65	250	54	86	9	2	14	53	23	25	4	.398	.564
MINOR LEAGUE TOTALS			.344	65	250	54	86	9	2	14	53	23	25	4	.398	.564

19 SKIP SCHUMAKER
OF

Born: Feb. 3, 1980. **B-T:** L-R. **Ht.:** 5-10. **Wt.:** 175. **Drafted:** UC Santa Barbara, 2001 (5th round). **Signed by:** Steve Gossett.

A two-way player at UC Santa Barbara, Schumaker hit 92 mph off the mound for the Gauchos before becoming a full-time outfielder as a pro. It took a few years for his swing to get dialed in, but once it did in 2004 he moved quickly, making his major league debut last year and playing his way into the big league club's plans. Schumaker is a plus runner and the best defensive outfielder in the organization, and he'd have the best outfield arm if former pitcher Rick Ankiel also weren't in the outfield now. Schumaker started to make leaps when hitting coach Steve Balboni changed the position of his hands and his hitting approach when he was in Double-A, and he has been a more consistent offensive performer ever since. He even showed a small dose of pop last season, though his game will be putting the ball in play. To make himself a legitimate top-of-the-order hitter, Schumaker must continue to develop his plate discipline and draw more walks. He's also learning to make the best use of his speed, as he doesn't steal bases often enough and isn't efficient when he does run. Schumaker had surgery to repair the bursa sac in his right knee after the season, but he's expected to be healthy for spring training. He could win a reserve outfield job solely with his defense, but he'd be best served by going back to Triple-A to refine his offensive game.

Year	Club (League)	Class	AVG	G	AB	R	H	2B	3B	HR	RBI	BB	SO	SB	OBP	SLG
2001	New Jersey (NY-P)	A	.253	49	162	22	41	10	1	0	14	29	33	11	.368	.327
2002	Potomac (Car)	A	.287	136	551	71	158	22	4	2	44	45	84	26	.342	.352
2003	Tennessee (SL)	AA	.251	91	342	43	86	20	3	2	22	37	54	6	.330	.345
2004	Tennessee (SL)	AA	.316	138	516	78	163	29	6	4	43	60	61	19	.389	.419
2005	Memphis (PCL)	AAA	.287	115	443	66	127	24	3	7	34	29	54	14	.330	.402
	St. Louis (NL)	MLB	.250	27	24	9	6	1	0	0	1	2	2	1	.308	.292
MINOR LEAGUE TOTALS			.286	529	2014	280	575	105	17	15	157	200	286	76	.352	.377
MAJOR LEAGUE TOTALS			.250	27	24	9	6	1	0	0	1	2	2	1	.308	.292

20 RICK ANKIEL
OF

Born: July 19, 1979. **B-T:** L-L. **Ht.:** 6-1. **Wt.:** 215. **Drafted:** HS—Port St. Lucie, Fla., 1997 (2nd round). **Signed by:** John Dipuglia.

If Ankiel can make it back to the big leagues as an outfielder, it would be a heartwarming story. He had two-way ability in high school, but his arm was so good that it was clear he would be a pitcher after he signed for $2.5 million as a second-round pick in 1997. He made his big league debut in 1999, held the No. 1 spot on Baseball America's Top 100 Prospects list that offseason and spent all of 2000 in St. Louis. He went 11-7, 3.50 and was dominant at times during the regular season, but his control suddenly deserted him in the playoffs—he had 11 walks and nine wild pitches in four innings—never to return. (He qualifies for this prospect list because he hasn't exceeded the rookie limit of 130 major league at-bats.) Ankiel was a terrific hitter as an amateur, and he starred as a two-way player for the U.S. junior national team for two summers. Teammates and scouts who saw him take batting practice even when he was pitching said he could have been one of the best hitting prospects in the minors. Once he committed to hitting full-time again in 2005, it didn't take him long to knock off the rust. He showed the same smooth swing and power potential he had as an amateur, and his 21 homers tied for the system lead even though he missed the first month recovering from a strained back he suffered in spring training. Ankiel opened his season by going 1-for-20 in Double-A, then was demoted to low Class A so he could have success and find a groove. When he returned to Double-A, he hit 10 homers and drove in 30 runs in his final 28 games. His speed is close to average and he's still learning the nuances of outfield play, but he clearly has an outstanding arm. Scouts who saw him last year said he had a chance to become a platoon outfielder in the majors. Age is his biggest negative at this point, and at 26 he'll get a long look in spring training. The Cardinals obviously saw something last year, because they restored him to the 40-man roster after removing him in spring training. He'll probably open 2006 in Triple-A, but if he hits he'll be back in St. Louis soon.

Year	Club (League)	Class	W	L	ERA	G	GS	CG	SV	IP	H	R	ER	HR	BB	SO	AVG
1998	Peoria (Mid)	A	3	0	2.06	7	7	0	0	35	15	8	8	0	12	41	.134
	Prince William (Car)	A	9	6	2.79	21	21	1	0	126	91	46	39	8	38	181	.205
1999	Arkansas (TL)	AA	6	0	0.91	8	8	1	0	49	25	6	5	2	16	75	.145
	Memphis (PCL)	AAA	7	3	3.16	16	16	0	0	88	73	37	31	7	46	119	.223
	St. Louis (NL)	MLB	0	1	3.27	9	5	0	1	33	26	12	12	2	14	39	.215
2000	St. Louis (NL)	MLB	11	7	3.50	31	30	0	0	175	137	80	68	21	90	194	.219
2001	St. Louis (NL)	MLB	1	2	7.13	6	6	0	0	24	25	21	19	7	25	27	.275
	Memphis (PCL)	AAA	0	2	20.93	3	3	0	0	4	3	10	10	0	17	4	.200
	Johnson City (Appy)	R	5	3	1.33	14	14	1	0	88	42	20	13	1	18	158	.140
2002	Did not play—Injured																
2003	Tennessee (SL)	AA	2	6	6.30	20	10	1	0	54	45	42	38	5	49	64	.232
2004	Palm Beach (FSL)	A	0	1	2.07	3	3	0	0	9	5	4	2	0	0	11	.167
	Tennessee (SL)	AA	1	0	0.00	2	2	0	0	9	3	1	0	0	2	7	.100
	Memphis (PCL)	AAA	1	0	0.00	1	1	0	0	6	1	1	0	0	0	5	.053
	St. Louis (NL)	MLB	1	0	5.40	5	0	0	0	10	10	6	6	2	1	9	.256
MAJOR LEAGUE TOTALS			13	10	3.90	51	41	0	1	242	198	119	105	32	130	269	.226
MINOR LEAGUE TOTALS			34	21	2.80	95	85	4	0	469	303	175	146	23	198	665	.184

Year	Club (League)	Class	AVG	G	AB	R	H	2B	3B	HR	RBI	BB	SO	SB	OBP	SLG
1999	Arkansas (TL)	AA	.400	8	10	1	4	0	0	1	1	1	0	0	.455	.700
	Memphis (PCL)	AAA	.286	16	21	3	6	2	0	0	4	0	3	0	.273	.381
	St. Louis (NL)	MLB	.100	9	10	0	1	0	0	0	0	0	3	0	.100	.100
2000	St. Louis (NL)	MLB	.250	35	68	8	17	1	1	2	9	4	20	0	.292	.382
2001	St. Louis (NL)	MLB	.000	6	8	1	0	0	0	0	0	1	5	0	.111	.000
	Johnson City (Appy)	R	.286	41	105	21	30	7	0	10	35	11	26	0	.364	.638
2002	Did not play—Injured															
2003	Tennessee (SL)	AA	.240	30	25	2	6	1	0	1	5	1	2	0	.269	.400
2004	Tennessee (SL)	AA	.000	2	4	0	0	0	0	0	0	0	0	0	.000	.000
	St. Louis (NL)	MLB	.000	5	1	0	0	0	0	0	0	1	1	0	.500	.000
2005	Quad Cities (Mid)	A	.270	51	185	33	50	10	1	11	45	27	37	0	.368	.514
	Springfield (TL)	AA	.243	34	136	18	33	7	0	10	30	10	29	0	.295	.515
MAJOR LEAGUE TOTALS			.207	55	87	9	18	1	1	2	9	6	29	0	.258	.310
MINOR LEAGUE TOTALS			.265	182	486	78	129	27	1	33	120	50	97	0	.338	.529

21 MARK WORRELL   RHP

Born: March 18, 1982. **B-T:** R-R. **Ht.:** 6-1. **Wt.:** 200. **Drafted:** Florida International, 2004 (12th round). **Signed by:** Steve Turco.

Worrell led the minors with 35 saves in 2005 and helped propel Palm Beach to the high Class A Florida State League championship, but any discussion about his ability always starts with his unorthodox delivery. Concerns about his mechanics depressed his draft stock coming out of high school and college, though he has thrown in the low 90s since he was a teenager. Worrell never throws from a windup, barely has a leg kick and keeps his upper body back until the moment his arm forces it to open to the plate. He also slings the ball from several sidearm angles and tends to pull off toward first base after he throws. But he has been durable as a reliever and his delivery deceives hitters, so the Cardinals have no plans to mess with it. He developed it himself with little instruction, so it's natural for him and doesn't create stress on his arm. He's also able to bounce back quickly from outing to outing. Worrell throws his fastball at 91-92 mph, using a sidearm version against righthanders and a more conventional two-seamer against lefties. He also throws a slider and occasionally mixes in a changeup against lefties. He has the makeup to be a closer and was nails in crucial situations for Palm Beach, doubling the franchise save record and adding three more in the playoffs. He needs to refine his command, but otherwise he should move quickly through the system, opening 2006 as the closer in Double-A.

Year	Club (League)	Class	W	L	ERA	G	GS	CG	SV	IP	H	R	ER	HR	BB	SO	AVG
2004	Johnson City (Appy)	R	1	0	1.21	17	0	0	6	22	12	3	3	1	7	35	.152
	Peoria (Mid)	A	0	2	4.29	12	0	0	6	15	9	10	7	2	6	20	.170
2005	Palm Beach (FSL)	A	2	3	2.25	53	0	0	35	56	38	20	14	6	19	53	.191
MINOR LEAGUE TOTALS			3	5	2.32	82	0	0	47	93	59	33	24	9	32	108	.178

22 ERIC HABERER   LHP

Born: Sept. 14, 1982. **B-T:** L-L. **Ht.:** 6-5. **Wt.:** 220. **Drafted:** Southern Illinois, 2004 (3rd round). **Signed by:** Scott Melvin.

If Southern Illinois hadn't been in desperate need of a starter in 2004, St. Louis might not have found one of its most intriguing starting pitching prospects. Haberer had pitched in relief before that season, and his one-pitch repertoire would have driven him straight to the bullpen as a pro. But like the Salukis, the Cardinals gave him a shot to start and he has taken to it. Haberer always has had an effective fastball, throwing it around 90 mph with heavy sink and late life that induces a lot of groundballs. Improved fastball command was the first step to his success, as he delivers quality strikes now instead of just throwing it down the middle. He has also shown aptitude for a changeup and curveball. The changeup is his second-best pitch, while his curveball is currently below average now but showed significant improvement as the season went on. To remain a starter, Haberer will have to refine his command of his secondary pitches as he has with his fastball. He could be an effective lefty specialist if starting doesn't work out, but the early returns are promising. He'll try to win a job in the Double-A rotation during spring training.

Year	Club (League)	Class	W	L	ERA	G	GS	CG	SV	IP	H	R	ER	HR	BB	SO	AVG
2004	Johnson City (Appy)	R	2	2	4.69	9	9	0	0	40	47	30	21	3	13	37	.287
	New Jersey (NY-P)	A	0	0	2.37	3	3	0	0	19	14	7	5	1	9	12	.226
2005	Quad Cities (Mid)	A	4	2	2.12	9	9	0	0	55	52	20	13	0	17	33	.248
	Palm Beach (FSL)	A	8	6	3.71	17	17	1	0	95	96	42	39	2	35	58	.270
MINOR LEAGUE TOTALS			14	10	3.35	38	38	1	0	209	209	99	78	6	74	140	.264

23 JOSH WILSON   RHP

Born: Sept. 6, 1986. **B-T:** R-R. **Ht.:** 5-11. **Wt.:** 180. **Drafted:** HS—Tyler, Texas, 2005 (2nd round). **Signed by:** Joe Almaraz.

Wilson was regarded as a potential first- or second-round pick coming off his Area Code Games performance in the summer of 2004. When his stuff dropped off a bit late last spring, he was seen as a third- or fourth-rounder. But Cardinals scouts always regarded him as a first-round talent, so they were happy to grab him with the second-rounder they received from the Giants for free agent Mike Matheny. Signed for $515,000, Wilson has long arms that generate good downward plane on his pitches, and his 90-92 mph fastball explodes out of his hand and shows good late movement. He already has good control of his two-seamer, which is unusual for a high school pitcher, though he needs to improve the command of all his pitches. His curveball has the potential to be an above-average pitch, but he needs to get more bite on it. He showed good aptitude for a changeup, which he rarely threw in high school, and made noticeable improvement with it over the spring and summer. He has some effort in his delivery, but not enough to create injury concerns. Wilson should make his full-season debut in low Class A this year.

Year	Club (League)	Class	W	L	ERA	G	GS	CG	SV	IP	H	R	ER	HR	BB	SO	AVG
2005	Johnson City (Appy)	R	2	2	4.22	12	12	0	0	53	49	37	25	7	23	32	.250
MINOR LEAGUE TOTALS			2	2	4.22	12	12	0	0	53	49	37	25	7	23	32	.250

24 MARK MICHAEL   RHP

Born: Aug. 25, 1982. **B-T:** R-R. **Ht.:** 6-4. **Wt.:** 215. **Drafted:** Delaware, 2003 (4th round). **Signed by:** Tom Shields.

A two-way star in both high school and college who played third base and shortstop, Michael has dealt with injuries and inconsistency since focusing on the mound as a pro. He came down with shoulder problems in 2004 and had minor surgery to repair fraying in his rotator cuff and a small ligament tear. He worked with a physical therapist in the offseason to get stronger and improve his range of motion, and said he felt better than ever in spring training. Still, he came down with shoulder tendinitis that kept him out for nearly two months in the middle of the season. Michael has very good stuff, working around 93 mph and touching 95 with his lively fastball. He considers his changeup to be his best pitch, though it remains inconsistent, and has an effective curveball. He's athletic, fields his position well and owns a strong pickoff move. Most of his problems are the result of mechanical breakdowns, when he doesn't stay on top of the ball in his delivery. That causes control difficulties—which persisted last year as he had 10 wild pitches and hit 14 batters in 82 innings—and puts stress on his shoulder. Michael showed at the end of 2005 that he was healthy again, so now he needs to put in a full year to work on his delivery and move forward in his development. He'll likely return to high Class A to start the season.

Year	Club (League)	Class	W	L	ERA	G	GS	CG	SV	IP	H	R	ER	HR	BB	SO	AVG
2003	New Jersey (NY-P)	A	1	2	3.17	11	10	0	0	54	50	23	19	0	20	56	.249
2004	Peoria (Mid)	A	6	6	3.36	20	20	1	0	121	117	59	45	9	39	95	.259
2005	Palm Beach (FSL)	A	4	5	4.05	18	17	0	0	82	68	47	37	7	35	57	.224
MINOR LEAGUE TOTALS			11	13	3.54	49	47	1	0	257	235	129	101	16	94	208	.246

25 BLAKE HAWKSWORTH   RHP

Born: March 1, 1983. **B-T:** R-R. **Ht.:** 6-3. **Wt.:** 195. **Drafted:** Bellevue (Wash.) CC, D/F 2001 (28th round). **Signed by:** Dane Walker.

Little has gone right for Hawksworth since he was rated as the Cardinals' best prospect before the 2004 season. Signed as a draft-and-follow in May 2002 for $1.475 million, he started off quickly before injuries derailed him. He had bone spurs in his ankle in 2003, but a more serious problem cropped up in 2004 when a shoulder injury limited him to 11 innings. He had surgery that July to repair a partially torn labrum and remove loose cartilage. The Cardinals were cautious with him and brought him along slowly, and his arm strength never came around in 2005. He kept breaking down with nagging injuries and struggled to put consistent starts together, finally getting shut down after 15 innings in the short-season New York-Penn League. The Cardinals put him on a throwing program and encouraged him to rest because they thought he tried to do too much in his rehab. When healthy, Hawksworth had a fastball that sat in the low 90, one of the best changeups in the system and a good curveball. He had the stuff to pitch at the top of a rotation, but whether he can recover that stuff is now a huge question. He'll get a fresh start in spring training and just try to prove he's healthy enough to break camp with a full-season club.

Year	Club (League)	Class	W	L	ERA	G	GS	CG	SV	IP	H	R	ER	HR	BB	SO	AVG
2002	Johnson City (Appy)	R	2	4	3.14	13	12	0	0	66	58	31	23	8	18	61	.232
	New Jersey (NY-P)	A	1	0	0.00	2	2	0	0	10	6	0	0	0	2	8	.171
2003	Peoria (Mid)	A	5	1	2.30	10	10	0	0	55	37	16	14	0	12	57	.187
	Palm Beach (FSL)	A	1	3	3.94	6	6	0	0	32	28	14	14	2	11	32	.235
2004	Palm Beach (FSL)	A	1	0	5.91	2	2	0	0	11	10	7	7	2	3	11	.250
2005	New Jersey (NY-P)	A	0	3	7.98	7	6	0	0	15	18	18	13	0	10	12	.321
MINOR LEAGUE TOTALS			10	11	3.40	40	38	0	0	188	157	86	71	12	56	181	.225

26 MIKE PARISI   RHP

Born: April 18, 1983. **B-T:** R-R. **Ht.:** 6-3. **Wt.:** 215. **Drafted:** Manhattan, 2004 (9th round). **Signed by:** Joe Rigoli.

Parisi was noted for his strikeouts during his college career, as he twice broke the Manhattan record for strikeouts in a season and set the school's career mark as well (272 in 244 innings). However, he doesn't have the stuff to be a strikeout pitcher as a professional. What he does have is a determined approach and a good feel for pitching that could allow him to pitch in the middle of a rotation. Parisi consistently throws his fastball at 92-93 mph with good movement, and his curveball is also a potentially above-average pitch if he becomes more consistent with it. His changeup shows potential, but he still doesn't use it enough. He has a bulldog makeup on the mound and won't give in to hitters. That works to his detriment at times, as he gives up too many hits. He needs to sharpen his command to keep the ball out of the hitting zone. Parisi also has to focus on staying on top of the ball and throwing downhill. He pitched better last season after a midseason promotion to high Class A, so he'll move up to Double-A to open 2006.

Year	Club (League)	Class	W	L	ERA	G	GS	CG	SV	IP	H	R	ER	HR	BB	SO	AVG
2004	New Jersey (NY-P)	A	4	2	4.46	7	7	0	0	36	40	18	18	3	6	26	.292
	Peoria (Mid)	A	1	1	3.28	6	6	0	0	36	30	16	13	1	15	36	.238
2005	Quad Cities (Mid)	A	5	5	4.08	14	14	0	0	86	98	42	39	5	25	66	.286
	Palm Beach (FSL)	A	5	6	3.23	13	13	1	0	78	79	31	28	6	22	63	.264
MINOR LEAGUE TOTALS			15	14	3.74	40	40	1	0	236	247	107	98	15	68	191	.273

27 CORY DOYNE   RHP

Born: Aug. 13, 1981. **B-T:** R-R. **Ht.:** 6-0. **Wt.:** 210. **Drafted:** HS—Land O' Lakes, Fla., 2000 (8th round). **Signed by:** Chuck Carlson (Astros).

Doyne always has had a premium arm, but it took him awhile to grow up and find his niche. He went to four high schools in four years and had off-field issues that pushed him to the eighth round of the 2000 draft despite a fastball that touched 95 mph. The Astros released him after three unimpressive seasons, and the Padres had him for about a year before cutting him loose in June 2004. The Cardinals signed him, and by the end of the 2005 season he was their Double-A closer after never getting above low Class A in five previous seasons. The proverbial light seemed to go on for Doyne, who realized he was squandering his ability, got in shape and harnessed his explosive fastball. He still touches 95 mph and complements his heater with a hard slider. He has the fearless makeup of a closer and is effectively wild. He has toned down his delivery but still has effort in it, though that's not as much of a concern out of the bullpen. Doyne's newfound maturity put him on the fast track, and if he builds on it this season he could pitch in the big leagues after opening in Triple-A.

Year	Club (League)	Class	W	L	ERA	G	GS	CG	SV	IP	H	R	ER	HR	BB	SO	AVG
2000	Martinsville (Appy)	R	3	6	5.44	12	8	0	0	40	25	27	24	1	35	54	.180
2001	Martinsville (Appy)	R	4	3	3.54	13	13	0	0	61	57	31	24	2	30	56	.251
2002	Michigan (Mid)	A	9	8	4.26	27	26	0	0	142	131	76	67	8	63	101	.243
2003	Lexington (SAL)	A	3	1	2.14	9	9	0	0	55	34	18	13	4	19	48	.177
	Fort Wayne (Mid)	A	4	6	4.21	12	12	0	0	47	44	31	22	2	29	37	.246

Year	Club (League)	Class	W	L	ERA	G	GS	CG	SV	IP	H	R	ER	HR	BB	SO	AVG
2004	New Jersey (NY-P)	A	2	0	2.33	30	0	0	12	39	19	10	10	2	12	48	.141
2005	Quad Cities (Mid)	A	0	0	0.00	2	0	0	0	2	0	0	0	0	0	5	.000
	Palm Beach (FSL)	A	1	0	0.00	6	0	0	0	9	3	0	0	0	2	11	.100
	Springfield (TL)	AA	2	1	1.95	48	0	0	19	55	37	14	12	5	36	53	.188
MINOR LEAGUE TOTALS			28	25	3.45	159	68	0	31	449	350	207	172	24	226	413	.213

28 JOSE MARTINEZ
2B/SS

Born: Jan. 24, 1986. **B-T:** R-R. **Ht.:** 5-11. **Wt.:** 175. **Signed:** Venezuela, 2004. **Signed by:** Enrique Brito.

Martinez is another example of the Cardinals' renewed push into Latin America. They hope to open an academy in Venezuela in 2006, and in the meantime they signed Martinez in December 2004 and sent him straight to the United States, where he had a terrific debut in the Appalachian League. Martinez is one of the best athletes in the organization, with the innate ability to make contact and the bat speed to hit with a little pop. He also showed surprising plate discipline, walking more than he struck out in his pro debut. Martinez has the tools to play solid defense at either middle-infield spot, and while he probably has enough arm for shortstop, his range and actions suggest he'd be better at second base. He has good speed and should learn to steal more bases as he advances. Martinez will have to get stronger and needs polish in every phase, but he was one of the organization's most pleasant surprises in 2005. He'll compete for a job in the Quad Cities infield in spring training.

Year	Club (League)	Class	AVG	G	AB	R	H	2B	3B	HR	RBI	BB	SO	SB	OBP	SLG
2005	Johnson City (Appy)	R	.300	55	150	28	45	8	2	6	31	20	15	9	.387	.500
MINOR LEAGUE TOTALS			.300	55	150	28	45	8	2	6	31	20	15	9	.387	.500

29 MIKE FERRIS
1B

Born: Dec. 31, 1982. **B-T:** L-L. **Ht.:** 6-2. **Wt.:** 225. **Drafted:** Miami (Ohio), 2004 (2nd round). **Signed by:** Tom Shields.

Ferris seemingly came out of nowhere as a Miami (Ohio) junior to bat .361-21-62, earn first team All-America honors and get consideration as a mid-first-round pick before St. Louis grabbed him in the second. His first season and a half as a professional have the Cardinals wondering what they can do to get that hitter back. He had trouble handling low Class A pitching and stayed in Quad Cities all season, and he has struggled to find a consistent hitting approach since signing. The encouraging signs were that he grasped how to use the whole field rather than trying to pull everything by the end of the year, and he showed renewed plate discipline. Ferris has tremendous power potential, but like everything else about his game, he must get more consistent with it. He had a quick, powerful stroke in college but has struggled to adjust to hitting with wood. He's a below-average runner but has been fine defensively at first base. Ferris will move up to high Class A to open 2006 and needs to start producing.

Year	Club (League)	Class	AVG	G	AB	R	H	2B	3B	HR	RBI	BB	SO	SB	OBP	SLG
2004	New Jersey (NY-P)	A	.199	40	146	18	29	5	0	3	14	19	44	2	.295	.295
2005	Quad Cities (Mid)	A	.230	127	439	65	101	26	0	16	69	69	88	2	.334	.399
MINOR LEAGUE TOTALS			.222	167	585	83	130	31	0	19	83	88	132	4	.325	.373

30 KENNY MAIQUES
RHP

Born: June 25, 1985. **B-T:** R-R. **Ht.:** 6-1. **Wt.:** 175. **Drafted:** Rio Hondo (Calif.) JC, 2005 (37th round). **Signed by:** Anup Sinha.

Maiques started his college career at Long Beach State, but with pitchers like Jered Weaver, Jason Vargas and Cesar Ramos ahead of him, he made just 12 appearances as a freshman in 2004. He went to the Alaska League and showed a 95 mph fastball, then decided to enroll at Rio Hondo (Calif.) JC to get more innings and become eligible for the 2005 draft. It looked like a great decision as Maiques became the most dominant juco pitcher in the nation—pitching two seven-inning perfect games and going 49 innings without giving up an earned run—but then he blew out his elbow and had Tommy John surgery. The Cardinals had considered taking him with one of their extra picks in the supplemental first round before he was injured, but instead grabbed him in the 37th round and signed him for $80,000. When healthy, Maiques has two plus pitches: a 91-94 mph fastball and a power slider. He's strong and keeps himself in excellent condition, but his size is a concern, so the Cardinals will watch him carefully when he returns. They expect him to be ready to pitch in spring training, though he'll probably spend most of the year in extended spring training before getting his feet wet with a short-season club.

Year	Club (League)	Class	W	L	ERA	G	GS	CG	SV	IP	H	R	ER	HR	BB	SO	AVG
2005	Did not play—Injured/Signed 2006 contract																

SAN DIEGO
PADRES

BY KEVIN GOLDSTEIN

MICHAEL WALBY

While the Padres won the National League West and visited the postseason for the first time since 1998, it's hard to call 2005 a banner year for the franchise. San Diego had to scrape to finish two games over .500, then was swept by St. Louis in an NL Division Series. The Padres won five fewer games than in 2004, had the lowest winning percentage of any non-strike-year playoff team in baseball history and would have finished closer to last place than first in the NL East or Central.

General manager Kevin Towers began to remake the team even before it wrapped up the division, shipping out malcontent Phil Nevin at the trade deadline. Towers made the first two major deals of the offseason, acquiring Vinny Castilla for Brian Lawrence and Mike Cameron for Xavier Nady in an effort to jump-start the offense. The Padres came up with the money to keep Brian Giles and Trevor Hoffman, but catcher Ramon Hernandez signed with the Orioles as a free agent and Towers then traded Sean Burroughs and Mark Loretta.

A front-office overhaul preceded the roster makeover. Towers explored the GM opening in Arizona and emerged as a candidate in Boston, but remained in San Diego and enters his 11th season at the helm. Owner John Moores brought in heavy hitters to assist him. Former Major League Baseball vice president and Athletics GM Sandy Alderson was made team president, overseeing the entire baseball operation. Credited with molding Billy Beane into a star executive and promoting statistical analysis in Oakland, Alderson started implementing many of the same ideas in San Diego.

Grady Fuson, who worked under Alderson as the scouting director in Oakland, joined the Padres as a special assistant to Towers in spring training and spent the majority of the year evaluating the system's talent as well as evaluating top prospects for the draft. Following the season, his role was expanded to vice president of scouting and development. Fuson, who held the same roles with the Rangers, is in charge of revitalizing a flagging farm system. Longtime farm director Tye Waller was made the new big league first-base coach. Bill Gayton remains scouting director.

Though the system isn't strong, it did provide returns in 2005 as a pair of astute minor league deals began to pay off, a year after producing Baseball America Rookie of the Year **Khalil Greene**. Righthander Clay Hensley, acquired from the Giants for Matt Herges in 2003, emerged as one of San Diego's top relievers and will compete for a rotation spot in the spring. Outfielder Ben Johnson, added in the Carlos Hernandez trade with the Cardinals in 2000, is on the cusp of the big leagues. Beyond that, the system is bordering on barren. The Padres' four full-season affiliates placed just three players on Baseball America's minor league Top 20 Prospects lists, none in the top 10.

TOP 30 PROSPECTS

1. Cesar Carrillo, rhp	16. Joel Santo, rhp
2. George Kottaras, c	17. Ernesto Frieri, rhp
3. Josh Barfield, 2b	18. Josh Geer, rhp
4. Ben Johnson, of	19. Yefri Carvajal, of
5. Chase Headley, 3b	20. Kenny Baugh, rhp
6. Clay Hensley, rhp	21. Leo Rosales, rhp
7. Jared Wells, rhp	22. Jon Knott, of/1b
8. Paul McAnulty, of/1b	23. Billy Killian, c
9. Nick Hundley, c	24. Javis Diaz, of
10. Freddy Guzman, of	25. Drew Macias, of
11. Cesar Ramos, lhp	26. Geoff Vandel, lhp
12. Sean Thompson, lhp	27. Colt Morton, c
13. Matt Bush, ss	28. Evan Meek, rhp
14. Ben Krosschell, rhp	29. Fabian Jimenez, lhp
15. Kyle Blanks, 1b	30. Stephen Andrade, rhp

ORGANIZATION OVERVIEW

General manager: Kevin Towers. **Farm director:** Grady Fuson. **Scouting director:** Bill Gayton.

2005 PERFORMANCE

Class	Team	League	W	L	Pct.	Finish*	Manager
Majors	San Diego	National	82	80	.506	7th (16)	Bruce Bochy
Triple-A	Portland Beavers	Pacific Coast	70	73	.490	10th (16)	Craig Colbert
Double-A	Mobile BayBears	Southern	58	80	.420	9th (10)	Gary Jones
High A	Lake Elsinore Storm	California	70	68	.507	6th (10)	Rick Renteria
Low A	Fort Wayne Wizards	Midwest	65	75	.464	t-11th (14)	Randy Ready
Short-season	Eugene Emeralds	Northwest	34	42	.447	t-6th (8)	Roy Howell
Rookie	AZL Padres	Arizona	29	27	.518	4th (9)	Carlos Lezcano
OVERALL 2005 MINOR LEAGUE RECORD			326	365	.472	26th (30)	

*Finish in overall standings (No. of teams in league).

ORGANIZATION LEADERS

BATTING   *Minimum 250 at-bats
*AVG	Baker, Steve, Lake Elsinore/Mobile	.314
R	Bonvechio, Brett, Lake Elsinore	85
H	Barfield, Josh, Portland	160
TB	Knott, Jon, Portland	243
2B	Kottaras, George, Lake Elsinore/Mobile	36
3B	Dowdy, Brett, Fort Wayne/Lake Elsinore	9
HR	Johnson, Ben, Portland	25
	Knott, Jon, Portland	25
RBI	Johnson, Ben, Portland	83
	Valenzuela, Fernando, Lake Elsinore	83
BB	Bonvechio, Brett, Lake Elsinore	86
SO	Bonvechio, Brett, Lake Elsinore	163
SB	Robinson, Kerry, Portland	26
*OBP	Delucchi, Dustin, Mobile/Portland	.424
*SLG	Johnson, Michael, Lake Elsinore	.618

PITCHING   #Minimum 75 innings
W	Ekstrom, Michael, Fort Wayne	13
	Wells, Jared, Lake Elsinore/Mobile	13
L	Jimenez, Fabian, Eugene/Fort Wayne	14
#ERA	Carter, Brent, Eugene/Fort Wayne	1.42
G	Abraham, Paul, Lake Elsinore/Mobile	65
CG	Oxspring, Chris, Portland	3
SV	Varner, Matt, Fort Wayne/Lake Elsinore	34
IP	Thompson, Mike, Mobile/Portland	175
BB	Oyervidez, Jose, Mobile	82
SO	Thompson, Sean, Lake Elsinore/Mobile	139

BEST TOOLS

Best Hitter for Average	Paul McAnulty
Best Power Hitter	Kyle Blanks
Best Strike-Zone Discipline	Chase Headley
Fastest Baserunner	Freddy Guzman
Best Athlete	Ben Johnson
Best Fastball	Cesar Carrillo
Best Curveball	Sean Thompson
Best Slider	Stephen Andrade
Best Changeup	Leo Rosales
Best Control	Cesar Carrillo
Best Defensive Catcher	Nick Hundley
Best Defensive Infielder	Matt Bush
Best Infield Arm	Matt Bush
Best Defensive Outfielder	Freddy Guzman
Best Outfield Arm	Yordany Ramirez

PROJECTED 2009 LINEUP

Catcher	George Kottaras
First Base	Kyle Blanks
Second Base	Josh Barfield
Third Base	Chase Headley
Shortstop	Khalil Greene
Left Field	Paul McAnulty

Center Field	Mike Cameron
Right Field	Ben Johnson
No. 1 Starter	Jake Peavy
No. 2 Starter	Adam Eaton
No. 3 Starter	Cesar Carrillo
No. 4 Starter	Tim Stauffer
No. 5 Starter	Clay Hensley
Closer	Scott Linebrink

LAST YEAR'S TOP 20 PROSPECTS

1. Josh Barfield, 2b
2. Freddy Guzman, of
3. George Kottaras, c
4. Travis Chick, rhp
5. Tim Stauffer, rhp
6. Matt Bush, ss
7. Justin Germano, rhp
8. Sean Thompson, lhp
9. Brad Baker, rhp
10. Paul McAnulty, of/1b
11. Jon Knott, of
12. Tagg Bozied, 1b
13. Humberto Quintero, c
14. Billy Killian, c
15. Jared Wells, rhp
16. Ben Johnson, of
17. Chris Oxspring, rhp
18. Daryl Jones, 1b
19. Fabian Jimenez, lhp
20. Rusty Tucker, rhp

TOP PROSPECTS OF THE DECADE

Year	Player, Pos.	2005 Org.
1996	Ben Davis, c	White Sox
1997	Derrek Lee, 1b	Cubs
1998	Matt Clement, rhp	Red Sox
1999	Matt Clement, rhp	Red Sox
2000	Sean Burroughs, 3b	Padres
2001	Sean Burroughs, 3b	Padres
2002	Sean Burroughs, 3b	Padres
2003	Xavier Nady, of	Padres
2004	Josh Barfield, 2b	Padres
2005	Josh Barfield, 2b	Padres

TOP DRAFT PICKS OF THE DECADE

Year	Player, Pos.	2005 Org.
1996	Matt Halloran, ss	Out of baseball
1997	Kevin Nicholson, ss	Somerset (Atlantic)
1998	Sean Burroughs, 3b	Padres
1999	Vince Faison, of	Yankees
2000	Mark Phillips, lhp	Out of baseball
2001	Jake Gautreau, 3b	Indians
2002	Khalil Greene, ss	Padres
2003	Tim Stauffer, rhp	Padres
2004	Matt Bush, ss	Padres
2005	Cesar Carrillo, rhp	Padres

ALL-TIME LARGEST BONUSES

Matt Bush, 2004	$3,150,000
Mark Phillips, 2000	$2,200,000
Sean Burroughs, 1998	$2,100,000
Jake Gautreau, 2001	$1,875,000
Cesar Carrillo, 2005	$1,550,000

MINOR LEAGUE DEPTH CHART

San Diego Padres

Rank: **28**

STRENGTH: Catcher. George Kottaras and Nick Hundley are two of the organization's better hitters.

WEAKNESS: Pitching. The Padres tried to address this with their top two picks in the '05 draft but still need more help.

*Depth charts prepared by **John Manuel** and **Chris Kline**. Numbers in parentheses indicate prospect rankings.*

LF
Yefri Carvajal (19)
Jon Knott (22)
Javis Diaz (24)
Will Venable
Dustin Delucchi

CF
Freddy Guzman (10)
Drew Macias (25)
Kennard Jones
Yordany Ramirez
Mike Sansoe

RF
Ben Johnson (4)
Matt Thayer
Steve Baker

3B
Chase Headley (5)
Corey Smith

SS
Matt Bush (13)
Juan Ciriaco

2B
Josh Barfield (3)
Sean Kazmar
Seth Johnston
Peter Ciofrone

1B
Paul McAnulty (8)
Kyle Blanks (15)
Michael Johnson
Tagg Bozied
Fernando Valenzuela Jr.

C
George Kottaras (2)
Nick Hundley (9)
Billy Killian (23)
Colt Morton (27)
Matt Lauderdale
Jose Loboton

RHP

Starters	Relievers
Cesar Carrillo (1)	Joel Santo (16)
Clay Hensley (6)	Leo Rosales (21)
Jared Wells (7)	Evan Meek (28)
Ben Krosschell (14)	Stephen Andrade (30)
Ernesto Frieri (17)	Manny Ayala
Josh Geer (18)	Neil Jamison
Kenny Baugh (20)	Alfredo Fernandez
Michael Ekstrom	Dale Thayer
	Matt Varner
	Jose Oyervidez
	Joaquim Soria

LHP

Starters	Relievers
Cesar Ramos (11)	Rusty Tucker
Sean Thompson (12)	Craig Breslow
Geoff Vandel (26)	Kyle Stutes
Fabian Jimenez (29)	

DRAFT ANALYSIS

2005

Best Pro Debut: LHP Brent Carter (16) went 6-2, 1.71 with a 79-8 K-BB ratio in 84 innings, and he won both his starts in low Class A after beginning at short-season Eugene. RHP Neil Jamison (6) had eight saves, a 1.69 ERA and 43 strikeouts in 37 innings at the same two stops. LHP Geoff Vandel (34) went 1-1, 0.58 with a 43-6 K-BB ratio in 31 innings between the Rookie-level Arizona League and Eugene.

Best Athlete: OF Will Venable (7) was Princeton's basketball MVP the last two seasons. OF Josh Thomas-Dotson (49) was a linebacker at Oregon, which doesn't have a baseball program.

Best Pure Hitter: 3B Chase Headley (2) wowed the Padres in instructional league, piling up quality at-bats and showing pop from both sides of the plate. He has a great eye at the plate, allowing him to rank second in NCAA Division I in walks (63) and fourth in OBP (.530) at Tennessee during the spring.

Best Raw Power: 1B Casey Smith (9) can put on a batting-practice show to rival anyone, but making contact in game situations was a problem in his debut.

Fastest Runner: OF Mike Sansoe (18), who has plus-plus speed, is a step quicker than Venable.

Best Defensive Player: The Padres drafted C Nick Hundley (2) for his skills behind the plate. He has a strong arm, a quick release and good agility. He also offers some power at the plate, so he's not just a defensive specialist.

Best Fastball: RHP Cesar Carrillo (1) may weigh just 177 pounds, but he has a 90-96 mph fastball that he maintained all year and deep into games. He stands out in a

Venable

Padres draft in which most of the pitchers were more notable for their command and offspeed stuff than their velocity.

Best Breaking Ball: Jamison's slider. Carrillo's curveball ranges from an average to a plus pitch.

Most Intriguing Background: Venable's father Max played in the majors and is now San Diego's low Class A hitting coach. Hundley's dad Tim is the defensive coordinator for Texas-El Paso's football team. Unsigned OF Jeremy Shelby's (46) father John is an ex-big leaguer who coached first base for the Dodgers in 2005.

Closest To The Majors: Carrillo finished his first pro summer by going 4-0, 3.23 in five Double-A starts. He could make his big league debut in 2006. LHP Cesar Ramos (1) is also very polished, throwing four pitches for strikes.

Best Late-Round Pick: Carter isn't overpowering, but he's a battler who does a fine job of locating his fastball and changeup. Vandel has a high-80s fastball with sneaky sink and an advanced changeup.

The One Who Got Away: The Padres made a six-figure offer to LHP Josh Romanski (15). He didn't want to give up hitting and won't have to at the University of San Diego.

Assessment: In Carrillo and Ramos, the Padres started their draft with two pitchers who can help them quickly. Headley and Hundley could crack the big league lineup in the near future as well.

2004 SS Matt Bush (1) hasn't hit since the Padres made a late decision to pass up Stephen Drew with the No. 1 overall choice. Whoops. RHP Ben Krosschell (16) and 1B Kyle Blanks (42) have been just as promising. **GRADE:** C

2003 San Diego took RHP Tim Stauffer (1) fourth overall before both sides discovered he had a shoulder injury. Stauffer reached the majors last year, but his stuff hasn't been the same. The rest of this draft has fizzled quickly. **GRADE:** D

2002 SS Khalil Greene (1) has been exactly what the Padres wanted. LHP Sean Thompson (5), OF/1B Paul McAnulty (12), C George Kottaras (20) and RHP Jared Wells (31) are some of the system's top prospects. **GRADE:** B+

2001 2B Josh Barfield (4) is on the verge of becoming a starter in San Diego, and SS Jason Bartlett (13) might have been his double-play partner—if he hadn't been dealt to the Twins. The Padres gave up on 2B/3B Jake Gautreau (1), trading him to the Indians. **GRADE:** B

Draft analysis prepared by Jim Callis. Numbers in parentheses indicate draft rounds.

CESAR
CARRILLO

RHP

ROBERT OLVER

Born: April 29, 1984.
Ht.: 6-3. **Wt.:** 177.
Bats: R. **Throws:** R.
Drafted: Miami, 2005 (1st round).
Signed by: Joe Bochy.

C arrillo was a star both on the mound and as a shortstop at Chicago's Mount Carmel High, which has a rich athletic track record. It has produced pro football stars Donovan McNabb and Simeon Rice, basketball's Antoine Walker and baseball's last 30-game winner, Denny McLain. Scouts knew about Carrillo when he was in high school, but he dropped to the Royals in the 33rd round in 2002 because he committed to Miami and had a bout of biceps tendinitis. After sitting out 2003 in a dispute between the school and the NCAA over his ACT score, Carrillo was the Hurricanes' top pitcher for the next two years, beginning his career with a 24-game winning streak, the fourth-longest in NCAA Division I history. The 18th overall pick in the 2005 draft, he signed for $1.55 million and hopped on the fast track. He started his career at high Class A Lake Elsinore before going 4-0 in five starts for Double-A Mobile. When he returned to Lake Elsinore to pitch out of the bullpen in the California League playoffs, Carrillo was hit hard as the impact of pitching since January took its toll. Between college, the regular season and those playoffs, Carrillo pitched 192 innings in 2005.

Some scouts believe Carrillo could get major leaguers out right now, as he combines the arsenal of a power pitcher with the command of a finesse specialist. His fastball is regularly clocked at 91-94 mph with late life and sinking action, and he can ratchet it up to 96 at times. Despite his slender build, he carries his velocity deep into games, hitting 96 on his 100th pitch in a college game last spring. His curveball has tight downward break, and Carrillo has the ability to drop it into the zone for a strike or bury it in the dirt as a chase pitch. His changeup has the makings of a plus pitch and he throws it with good arm action. He not only throws each of his offerings for strikes, but also works them down in the zone, generating lots of grounders. His arm is loose and quick, and his delivery is effortless. He displays a mature mound presence, pitches with confidence and isn't easily flustered. He's an excellent athlete who fields his position well.

Carrillo lacks the physicality of a classic power pitcher, and his skinny frame offers little in the way of projection. He can become too enamored with his fastball at times, causing him to lose touch on his secondary pitches, both of which can be above-average when he keeps them in the mix. While his changeup is deceptive, it could use a greater difference in velocity from his fastball to keep hitters more off balance.

The Padres targeted a polished college pitcher who could provide help quickly with their first-round pick, and Carrillo is poised to rocket through the system. He'll begin 2006 in Double-A and could make his big league debut later in the year. He should be a fixture in San Diego's rotation for years to come, possibly as a No. 2 starter.

Year	Club (League)	Class	W	L	ERA	G	GS	CG	SV	IP	H	R	ER	HR	BB	SO	AVG
2005	Mobile (SL)	AA	4	0	3.23	5	5	0	0	31	23	11	11	2	7	35	.204
	Lake Elsinore (Cal)	A	1	2	7.01	7	7	0	0	26	30	21	20	3	9	29	.280
MINOR LEAGUE TOTALS			5	2	4.95	12	12	0	0	56	53	32	31	5	16	64	.241

2 GEORGE KOTTARAS C

Born: May 16, 1983. **B-T:** L-R. **Ht.:** 6-0. **Wt.:** 190. **Drafted:** Connors State (Okla.) JC, D/F 2002 (20th round). **Signed by:** Lane Decker.

After signing in May 2003 as a draft-and-follow for early fourth-round money ($375,000), Kottaras played a full season of pro ball for the first time in 2005. He played just 78 games in 2004 because he was a backup on the Greek Olympic team, going 3-for-12 in Athens. Kottaras profiles as an offense-oriented catcher. He displays natural hitting instincts and commands the strike zone. He generates easy line-drive power with a quiet setup and fluid swing, projecting to hit 15-20 home runs annually. He's athletic behind the plate and has plus arm strength. Kottaras has a tendency to get pull-happy, and needs to focus simply on centering the ball and letting his strength work for him naturally. His arm plays only average because of a slow glove-hand exchange and a long release. He's a bit small for a catcher, leaving some to wonder if he can handle the rigors of a full season. Kottaras' bat separates him from the rest of San Diego's catching prospects. He'll begin 2006 back in Double-A and is on schedule to be the starter at the big league level by the end of 2007.

Year	Club (League)	Class	AVG	G	AB	R	H	2B	3B	HR	RBI	BB	SO	SB	OBP	SLG
2003	Idaho Falls (Pio)	R	.259	42	143	27	37	8	1	7	24	19	36	1	.348	.476
2004	Fort Wayne (Mid)	A	.310	78	271	40	84	18	1	7	46	51	41	0	.415	.461
2005	Lake Elsinore (Cal)	A	.303	91	337	54	102	29	0	9	50	50	60	2	.390	.469
	Mobile (SL)	AA	.287	29	101	16	29	7	0	2	15	19	23	0	.397	.416
MINOR LEAGUE TOTALS			.296	240	852	137	252	62	2	25	135	139	160	3	.392	.461

3 JOSH BARFIELD 2B

Born: Dec. 17, 1982. **B-T:** R-R. **Ht.:** 6-0. **Wt.:** 185. **Drafted:** HS—Spring, Texas, 2001 (4th round). **Signed by:** Jimmy Dreyer.

On the heels of a disappointing Double-A performance in 2004, when he was hampered by hamstring troubles, Barfield improved his conditioning. He got off to a slow start at Triple-A Portland in 2005, but recovered to hit .343-11-50 over the final three months. His father Jesse hit 241 career homers in the majors, and his brother Jeremy is a rising high school prospect. Barfield has excellent bat speed and is at his best when he drives the ball to right-center. He has worked to improve his patience at the plate. He made strides defensively and is no longer expected to have to move to left field. Barfield can be unorthodox both at the plate and in the field, yet it's hard to argue with the results. Pitchers can beat him inside, and he pulls off pitches to compensate. He hits better in clutch situations because he concentrates on using the whole field, an approach he should take into every at-bat. The trade of Mark Loretta to Boston for Doug Mirabelli cleared a path to the lineup for Barfield. Unless he flops in spring training, he should be San Diego's Opening Day starter.

Year	Club (League)	Class	AVG	G	AB	R	H	2B	3B	HR	RBI	BB	SO	SB	OBP	SLG
2001	Idaho Falls (Pio)	R	.310	66	277	51	86	15	4	4	53	16	54	12	.350	.437
2002	Fort Wayne (Mid)	A	.306	129	536	73	164	22	3	8	57	26	105	26	.340	.403
	Lake Elsinore (Cal)	A	.087	6	23	2	2	0	0	0	4	1	4	0	.120	.087
2003	Lake Elsinore (Cal)	A	.337	135	549	99	185	46	6	16	128	50	122	16	.389	.530
2004	Mobile (SL)	AA	.248	138	521	79	129	28	3	18	90	48	119	4	.313	.417
2005	Portland (PCL)	AAA	.310	137	516	74	160	25	1	15	72	52	108	20	.370	.450
MINOR LEAGUE TOTALS			.300	611	2422	378	726	136	17	61	404	193	512	78	.351	.445

4 BEN JOHNSON OF

Born: Jan. 18, 1981. **B-T:** R-R. **Ht.:** 6-1. **Wt.:** 200. **Drafted:** HS—Germantown, Tenn., 1999 (4th round). **Signed by:** Randy Benson (Cardinals).

Johnson earned baseball and football scholarships to Mississippi State out of high school before opting to sign with the Cardinals, who sent him to San Diego in a 2000 trade for Carlos Hernandez. He spent parts of three seasons in Double-A but started to take off in mid-2004 and ended 2005 in San Diego, even making a playoff start. Johnson has all the tools to be an everyday outfielder in the big leagues. He has shortened his swing and developed above-average power while improving his grasp of the strike zone. Once a plus-plus runner, he's now just a tick above-average. He's a good right fielder with a solid arm. Johnson has a tendency to overswing, as he did in the postseason. He still has troubles with breaking balls, particularly against righthanders, and some scouts project him as a platoon player. The Padres have been patient and believe Johnson is ready to contribute in San Diego. With Brian Giles' surprising return, however, Johnson doesn't have an obvious opening in the lineup.

Year	Club (League)	Class	AVG	G	AB	R	H	2B	3B	HR	RBI	BB	SO	SB	OBP	SLG
1999	Johnson City (Appy)	R	.330	57	203	38	67	9	1	10	51	29	57	14	.423	.532
2000	Peoria (Mid)	A	.242	93	330	58	80	22	1	13	46	53	78	17	.353	.433
	Fort Wayne (Mid)	A	.193	29	109	11	21	6	2	3	13	7	25	0	.261	.367
2001	Lake Elsinore (Cal)	A	.276	136	503	79	139	35	6	12	63	54	141	22	.358	.441
2002	Mobile (SL)	AA	.241	131	456	58	110	23	4	10	55	65	127	11	.337	.375
2003	Mobile (SL)	AA	.181	44	127	8	23	5	0	1	7	10	36	0	.252	.244
	Lake Elsinore (Cal)	A	.266	52	184	30	49	9	0	8	29	20	49	6	.354	.446
2004	Mobile (SL)	AA	.251	136	475	80	119	28	6	23	85	55	136	5	.334	.480
2005	Portland (PCL)	AAA	.312	107	414	79	129	27	0	25	83	51	88	6	.394	.558
	San Diego (NL)	MLB	.213	31	75	10	16	8	1	3	13	11	23	0	.310	.467
MAJOR LEAGUE TOTALS			.213	31	75	10	16	8	1	3	13	11	23	0	.310	.467
MINOR LEAGUE TOTALS			.263	785	2801	441	737	164	20	105	432	344	737	81	.352	.448

5 CHASE HEADLEY
3B

Born: May 9, 1984. **B-T:** B-R. **Ht.:** 6-2. **Wt.:** 195. **Drafted:** Tennessee, 2005 (2nd round). **Signed by:** Billy Merkel.

Headley led Pacific in hits and the Big West Conference in walks as a freshman in 2003 before transferring to Tennessee, where hamstring problems limited him as a sophomore. He finished second in NCAA Division I in walks (63) last spring before signing for $560,000. Headley is adept from both sides of the plate, showing outstanding pitch recognition and average power. He's a fundamentally sound third baseman with soft hands and an average, accurate arm. A high school valedictorian and academic all-American, he boasts excellent baseball instincts and makeup. Headley's power ceiling has long been a question, leaving some to wonder if he profiles as an everyday third baseman. He makes the routine plays, though his feet are a little slow and restrict his range. He's a below-average runner but not a clogger. Sean Burroughs never worked out at third base, but the Padres believe they have found their long-term answer in Headley. He tore up instructional league and could move fast after starting his first full season in high Class A.

Year	Club (League)	Class	AVG	G	AB	R	H	2B	3B	HR	RBI	BB	SO	SB	OBP	SLG
2005	Eugene (NWL)	A	.268	57	220	29	59	14	3	6	33	34	48	1	.375	.441
	Fort Wayne (Mid)	A	.200	4	15	2	3	0	0	0	1	1	4	0	.250	.200
MINOR LEAGUE TOTALS			.264	61	235	31	62	14	3	6	34	35	52	1	.367	.426

6 CLAY HENSLEY
RHP

Born: Aug. 31, 1979. **B-T:** R-R. **Ht.:** 5-11. **Wt.:** 190. **Drafted:** Lamar, 2002 (8th round). **Signed by:** Tom Korenek (Giants).

Hensley didn't play baseball for nearly four years after graduating from high school in 1997, reappearing as a closer at Alvin (Texas) CC. The Padres acquired him from the Giants for Matt Herges at the 2003 non-waiver trade deadline, and everything clicked once Triple-A pitching coach Gary Lance dropped Hensley's arm slot in 2005. He pitched in all three playoff games for San Diego. Hensley's best pitch is a hard, late-breaking slider. His fastball velocity sits at 90-91 mph, but its darting sink and run and his command make it effective. He consistently works down in the zone, understands how to set up hitters and has great makeup. Hensley doesn't get much downward plane on his pitches and lacks a true strikeout offering. His changeup and curve are merely decent. He needs a better changeup to keep lefthanders at bay. While he has already proven to be a pleasant surprise, Hensley has a new challenge to show he can hold up in the rotation at the big league level. If he can't, he could fall back to being a solid contributor again in the San Diego bullpen.

Year	Club (League)	Class	W	L	ERA	G	GS	CG	SV	IP	H	R	ER	HR	BB	SO	AVG
2002	Salem-Keizer (NWL)	A	7	0	2.53	15	15	1	0	82	72	31	23	3	25	84	.235
2003	Hagerstown (SAL)	A	4	3	3.18	12	12	3	0	68	56	26	24	4	20	74	.223
	San Jose (Cal)	A	2	3	5.83	5	5	0	0	29	38	20	19	4	9	25	.336
	Lake Elsinore (Cal)	A	3	4	3.45	8	8	0	0	44	50	24	17	0	14	40	.286
2004	Mobile (SL)	AA	11	10	4.30	27	27	2	0	159	167	84	76	14	48	125	.281
2005	Portland (PCL)	AAA	2	2	2.99	15	14	0	0	90	63	31	30	8	22	71	.197
	San Diego (NL)	MLB	1	1	1.70	24	1	0	0	48	33	12	9	0	17	28	.195
MAJOR LEAGUE TOTALS			1	1	1.70	24	1	0	0	48	33	12	9	0	17	28	.195
MINOR LEAGUE TOTALS			29	22	3.60	82	81	6	0	473	446	216	189	33	138	419	.253

7 JARED WELLS

RHP

Born: Oct. 31, 1981. **B-T:** R-R. **Ht.:** 6-4. **Wt.:** 200. **Drafted:** San Jacinto (Texas) JC, D/F 2002 (31st round). **Signed by:** Jay Darnell.

Wells had struggled to find consistency in the minors but took a step forward by leading the California League in ERA in 2005. He turned in quality starts in his first four Double-A outings and later was Team USA's top starter in the World Cup in September. Wells has an ideal power pitcher's frame, good arm action and solid stuff. His four-seam fastball runs from 91-93 mph, and his new two-seamer features plenty of sink. He mixes in a hard-breaking slider and commands all of his pitches well. A former high school quarterback, he's a good athlete and a tough competitor. While Wells has the stamina to be an innings-eater, his ability to remain a starter hinges on the development of his changeup, which is currently below-average. He doesn't own a true out pitch, as he has little trust in his slider. He tries to get batters to chase it as opposed to throwing it for strikes. Wells projects as a back-of-the-rotation starter and could end up in the bullpen. Still unrefined, he has his best days ahead of him. He'll return to Double-A in 2006.

Year	Club (League)	Class	W	L	ERA	G	GS	CG	SV	IP	H	R	ER	HR	BB	SO	AVG
2003	Eugene (NWL)	A	4	6	2.75	14	14	0	0	79	77	34	24	6	32	53	.256
2004	Fort Wayne (Mid)	A	4	6	4.09	14	14	1	0	81	91	42	37	6	19	72	.283
	Lake Elsinore (Cal)	A	4	6	4.52	13	12	0	0	72	81	44	36	5	30	38	.290
2005	Lake Elsinore (Cal)	A	11	3	3.44	19	19	2	0	120	116	51	46	6	26	80	.257
	Mobile (SL)	AA	2	5	4.40	7	7	0	0	43	51	25	21	3	16	22	.307
MINOR LEAGUE TOTALS			25	26	3.74	67	66	3	0	395	416	196	164	26	123	265	.274

8 PAUL McANULTY

OF/1B

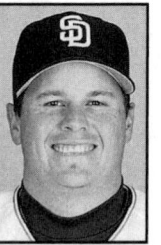

Born: Feb. 24, 1981. **B-T:** L-R. **Ht.:** 5-10. **Wt.:** 220. **Drafted:** Long Beach State, 2002 (12th round). **Signed by:** Jason McLeod.

Former Padres scout Jason McLeod (now Red Sox scouting director) and crosschecker Chris Gwynn fell in love with McAnulty's bat at Long Beach State in 2002, when he hit .360-9-55. He won the Rookie-level Pioneer League batting title in his pro debut and hit his way to the big leagues in three years. McAnulty has a quick bat, quiet swing mechanics and no problem hitting lefties. He shows good patience at the plate and crushes mistakes. He's a gritty player who always gives full effort. Though he's a better athlete than his stocky frame suggests, McAnulty offers little more than his bat. He has below-average speed and arm strength. He lacks the power to profile as an everyday first baseman or corner outfielder, and he's no better than an adequate defender at those spots. McAnulty has little chance at earning a full-time job in spring training, so he's likely ticketed for a return to Triple-A. He could emerge as a valuable bat off San Diego's bench.

Year	Club (League)	Class	AVG	G	AB	R	H	2B	3B	HR	RBI	BB	SO	SB	OBP	SLG
2002	Idaho Falls (Pio)	R	.379	67	235	56	89	29	0	8	51	49	43	7	.488	.604
2003	Fort Wayne (Mid)	A	.273	133	455	48	124	27	0	7	73	67	82	5	.370	.378
2004	Lake Elsinore (Cal)	A	.297	133	495	98	147	36	3	23	87	88	106	3	.404	.521
2005	Mobile (SL)	AA	.282	79	298	39	84	17	2	10	42	34	66	5	.364	.453
	Portland (PCL)	AAA	.344	38	151	27	52	15	0	6	27	16	29	0	.405	.563
	San Diego (NL)	MLB	.208	22	24	4	5	0	0	0	0	3	7	1	.321	.208
MAJOR LEAGUE TOTALS			.208	22	24	4	5	0	0	0	0	3	7	1	.321	.208
MINOR LEAGUE TOTALS			.304	450	1634	268	496	124	5	54	280	254	326	20	.400	.485

9 NICK HUNDLEY

C

Born: Sept. 8, 1983. **B-T:** R-R. **Ht.:** 6-1. **Wt.:** 220. **Drafted:** Arizona, 2005 (2nd round). **Signed by:** Dave Lottsfeldt.

Hundley was a fifth-round pick by the Marlins out of high school, and he did little to improve his draft stock until his junior year at Arizona, where he led the Wildcats in home runs (15) and walks (42). His father Tim is the defensive coordinator for Texas-El Paso's football team. Hundley is a strong, powerful hitter with natural loft in his swing, and he also has good pitch recognition. Behind the plate, he has above-average agility and arm strength. He consistently puts his throws on the bag and threw out 35 percent of basestealers in his pro debut. Hundley is a dead-pull hitter with a power-only approach not conducive to hitting for a high average. Normally fundamentally sound, he often came out of his crouch too early during his pro debut and struggled to block balls. More advanced than 2004 third-round pick, catcher Billy Killian, Hundley will be tested in his first full season with an assignment to high Class A. If he polishes his receiving and blocking skills, he could reach San Diego in two-three years.

Year	Club (League)	Class	AVG	G	AB	R	H	2B	3B	HR	RBI	BB	SO	SB	OBP	SLG
2005	Eugene (NWL)	A	.250	43	148	30	37	7	1	7	22	33	35	1	.391	.453
	Fort Wayne (Mid)	A	.222	10	36	2	8	2	0	0	5	4	9	0	.310	.278
MINOR LEAGUE TOTALS			.245	53	184	32	45	9	1	7	27	37	44	1	.376	.418

10 FREDDY GUZMAN   OF

Born: Jan. 20, 1981. **B-T:** B-R. **Ht.:** 5-10. **Wt.:** 165. **Signed:** Dominican
Republic, 2000. **Signed by:** Bill Clark/Modesto Ulloa.

Guzman was poised to compete for San Diego's center-field job last spring before blowing out his throwing elbow. Tommy John surgery kept him out until he played in the Dominican League over the winter. The elbow injury had no effect on Guzman's best tool—game-changing speed. He impacts the game on the bases and in the field, and he led the minors with 90 steals in 2003. His center-field range borders on exceptional, as he gets good jumps and effortlessly reaches balls in both gaps. He's a contact hitter with decent plate discipline. Guzman's arm already was below-average, and could get worse after surgery. He doesn't always make good reads on balls, relying on his quickness to make up for mistakes. He pressed during his big league stint in 2004 and expanded his strike zone, undermining his ability to make use of his speed. The Padres traded for Mike Cameron, ending any longshot chance Guzman had of starting for them in 2006. He'll open the year in Triple-A and will push for a reserve job in the second half.

Year	Club (League)	Class	AVG	G	AB	R	H	2B	3B	HR	RBI	BB	SO	SB	OBP	SLG
2000	Padres (DSL)	R	.210	49	167	38	35	6	1	1	10	46	38	24	.386	.275
2001	Idaho Falls (Pio)	R	.348	12	46	11	16	4	1	0	5	2	10	5	.388	.478
2002	Lake Elsinore (Cal)	A	.259	21	81	13	21	3	0	1	6	8	12	14	.326	.333
	Fort Wayne (Mid)	A	.279	47	190	35	53	7	5	0	18	18	37	39	.341	.368
	Eugene (NWL)	A	.225	21	80	14	18	2	1	0	8	7	15	16	.293	.275
2003	Lake Elsinore (Cal)	A	.285	70	281	64	80	12	3	2	22	40	60	49	.375	.370
	Mobile (SL)	AA	.271	46	177	30	48	5	2	1	11	26	34	38	.368	.339
	Portland (PCL)	AAA	.300	2	10	1	3	0	0	0	0	0	1	3	.300	.300
2004	Mobile (SL)	AA	.283	35	138	21	39	5	2	1	7	16	28	17	.359	.370
	Portland (PCL)	AAA	.292	66	264	48	77	12	4	1	19	30	46	48	.365	.379
	San Diego (NL)	MLB	.211	20	76	8	16	3	0	0	5	3	13	5	.250	.250
2005	Did Not Play—Injured															
MAJOR LEAGUE TOTALS			.211	20	76	8	16	3	0	0	5	3	13	5	.250	.250
MINOR LEAGUE TOTALS			.272	369	1434	275	390	56	19	7	106	193	281	253	.361	.352

11 CESAR RAMOS   LHP

Born: June 22, 1984. **B-T:** L-L. **Ht.:** 6-2. **Wt.:** 190. **Drafted:** Long Beach State, 2005 (1st round supplemental). **Signed by:** Brendan Hause.

Ramos was drafted in the sixth round by the Devil Rays out of high school, but decided to attend Long Beach State, where he became the winningest lefty in school history and followed fellow 49ers pitchers Abe Alvarez, Jason Vargas and Jered Weaver into the top two rounds of the draft. Ramos showed signs of fatigue late last spring and was pounded in the NCAA regionals. After signing for $950,000, Ramos got knocked around for much of his pro debut as well. He relies on his command and aggressiveness on the mound. His fastball tops out at 91 but sits at 86-88 mph. Ramos mixes in a low-80s two-seamer with good movement. He also has confidence in his slider and changeup, both of which are effective. He commands all of his pitches with pinpoint accuracy, working in all four quadrants of the strike zone. He's not overpowering, and needs to find a pitch to get righthanders out. That might be his changeup, though he all but abandoned it after signing. He'll need to keep an eye on his weight and work habits. He doesn't offer much projection, but his feel for pitching should carry him. He'll begin the year in high Class A and could reach Double-A by midseason.

Year	Club (League)	Class	W	L	ERA	G	GS	CG	SV	IP	H	R	ER	HR	BB	SO	AVG
2005	Eugene (NWL)	A	0	1	6.53	6	4	0	0	21	27	21	15	3	7	13	.303
	Fort Wayne (Mid)	A	3	2	4.19	7	7	1	0	39	42	19	18	0	7	32	.282
MINOR LEAGUE TOTALS			3	3	5.01	13	11	1	0	59	69	40	33	3	14	45	.290

12 SEAN THOMPSON   LHP

Born: Oct. 13, 1982. **B-T:** L-L. **Ht.:** 5-11. **Wt.:** 160. **Drafted:** HS—Denver, Colo., 2002 (5th round). **Signed by:** Darryl Milne.

Coming out of a Denver high school, Thompson needed two years of short-season ball before advancing to low Class A, where he led Fort Wayne in wins and strikeouts in 2004.

He started off last season in lights-out fashion in high Class A but struggled after a promotion to Double-A, though he still led the system in whiffs. Thompson's best pitch is a curveball that rates a 70 on the 20-80 scouting scale, a big breaker that's considered the best in the system. He also flashes a plus changeup at times and works with an 85-88 mph fastball. A good athlete who earned NCAA Division I-A scholarship offers in football, Thompson fields his position well and has a terrific pickoff move. After finding adversity for the first time in Double-A, he needs to set up more experienced hitters for his secondary stuff more efficiently and improve his fastball command. He takes the mentality of a power pitcher on the mound but lacks the fastball to back it up. The Padres see Thompson's ceiling as a potential No. 4 or 5 starter, and at worst he should become a lefty bullpen specialist. He'll return to Double-A to begin 2006.

Year	Club (League)	Class	W	L	ERA	G	GS	CG	SV	IP	H	R	ER	HR	BB	SO	AVG
2002	Idaho Falls (Pio)	R	4	3	3.83	13	11	0	0	56	51	34	24	4	38	69	.249
2003	Eugene (NWL)	A	7	1	2.48	15	15	0	0	80	58	28	22	5	39	97	.204
2004	Fort Wayne (Mid)	A	9	6	3.10	27	27	0	0	148	124	60	51	15	57	157	.239
2005	Lake Elsinore (Cal)	A	4	1	2.16	6	6	0	0	33	26	15	8	4	13	45	.210
	Mobile (SL)	AA	4	5	4.67	20	20	0	0	114	127	67	59	10	55	94	.294
MINOR LEAGUE TOTALS			28	16	3.42	81	79	0	0	431	386	204	164	38	202	462	.247

13 MATT BUSH   SS

Born: Feb. 8, 1986. **B-T:** R-R. **Ht.:** 5-11 **Wt.:** 170 **Drafted:** HS—El Cajon, Calif., 2005 (1st round). **Signed by:** Tim McWilliam.

The Padres narrowed their choices for the No. 1 overall pick in 2004 down to Stephen Drew, Jeff Niemann and Jered Weaver before settling on Drew. But three days before the draft, San Diego's upper management decided Drew wasn't worth his asking price—he eventually signed a $5.5 million major league contract with the Diamondbacks—leaving the scouting department scrambling for an alternative. That turned out to be Bush, a local two-way star and projected top-10 talent. Bush signed quickly for a $3.15 million bonus, but before he even took the field, he was suspended for his role in a fight outside an Arizona nightclub. Then he hit .192 in his pro debut. While he was on his best behavior in 2005, Bush never got going with the bat, collecting more than two hits in a game only once while recording just 18 extra-base hits. He made progress in instructional league after being drafted, but regressed into bad habits last year. He's a good contact hitter, but he tries too hard to pull pitches, doesn't work deep counts and then presses when he falls behind. Bush isn't without tools, however. He's a potential Gold Glove shortstop with plus range to both sides, an excellent double-play pivot and a powerful arm that ranks as a pure 80 on the 20-80 scouting scale. He hit 95 mph as a prep pitcher. Neither the Padres nor scouts have given up on Bush, who draws comparisons to a young Royce Clayton. That's not ideal for the first pick in a draft, and Bush may never live up to that status. The Padres will keep Bush's electric arm in the back of their minds, and he ultimately could end up back on the mound if his bat doesn't improve. He's ticketed for high Class A, where the hitter-friendly parks of the California League could help spur his career.

Year	Club (League)	Class	AVG	G	AB	R	H	2B	3B	HR	RBI	BB	SO	SB	OBP	SLG
2004	Padres (AZL)	R	.181	21	72	12	13	2	1	0	10	11	17	4	.302	.236
	Eugene (NWL)	A	.222	8	27	1	6	2	0	0	3	2	9	0	.276	.296
2005	Fort Wayne (Mid)	A	.221	126	453	56	100	13	3	2	32	33	76	8	.279	.276
MINOR LEAGUE TOTALS			.216	155	552	69	119	17	4	2	45	46	102	12	.282	.272

14 BEN KROSSCHELL   RHP

Born: Oct. 2, 1985. **B-T:** R-R. **Ht.:** 6-1. **Wt.:** 165. **Drafted:** HS—Highlands Ranch, Colo., 2004 (16th round). **Signed by:** Jake Wilson.

Like Sean Thompson, Kroschell was a Colorado prep product the Padres kept in short-season leagues for two years to allow him to get used to the higher level of competition. He looked like one of the best arms in the system in 2004 instructional league, but started slowly at short-season Eugene last season. He came on strong late in the year and again looked sharp in instructional league. Kroschell is all about projection. Long and loose with a quick arm, he has a fastball that sits at 89-91 mph. He flashes 93 at times and San Diego believes he has all the ingredients to pitch with plus velocity as he fills out his skinny frame. His slider is inconsistent but shows the potential to be an above-average pitch, while his changeup, once nonexistent, has come along nicely. Kroschell displays good command for his age. He still needs to improve his offspeed stuff to give him a viable option against lefthanders, who batted .316 off him last year. The Padres are looking forward to what he can do over a full season, and he'll spend 2006 in low Class A.

Year	Club (League)	Class	W	L	ERA	G	GS	CG	SV	IP	H	R	ER	HR	BB	SO	AVG
2004	Padres (AZL)	R	1	3	2.42	14	11	0	0	48	48	21	13	2	19	40	.262
2005	Eugene (NWL)	A	2	7	4.70	16	15	0	0	77	83	50	40	4	18	59	.272
MINOR LEAGUE TOTALS			3	10	3.82	30	26	0	0	125	131	71	53	6	37	99	.268

15 KYLE BLANKS   1B

Born: Sept. 11, 1986. **B-T:** R-R. **Ht.:** 6-6. **Wt.:** 290. **Drafted:** Yavapai (Ariz.) JC, D/F 2004 (42nd round). **Signed by:** Jake Wilson.

Area scout Jake Wilson was one of the few to see Blanks as a prep star in the tiny New Mexico town of Moriarity, and he persuaded the Padres to take him as a draft-and-follow in 2004. Their secret was unearthed at Yavapai (Ariz.) Junior College, as Blanks led the wood-bat Arizona Community College Athletic Conference in batting (.440), doubles (25) and RBIs (47) while earning national juco defensive-player-of-the-year honors. San Diego signed him for $260,000 before the 2005 draft, where Blanks figured to go in the first five rounds if he was available. Blanks hit seven home runs in his first 14 games as a pro, but failed to homer in his final 34 while striking out more than once a game. The seven homers held up for the Rookie-level Arizona Fall League lead, however. His raw power is the best in the organization, and he can punish the ball to all fields. He's a patient hitter who draws walks despite a sizable strike zone. His approach at the plate is single-minded—every swing is designed to hit the ball a mile—causing his swing to get long and leading to high strikeout totals. Scouts joked that the 6-foot-6, 290-pounder would dwarf Frank Thomas, but Blanks exhibits good athleticism for his size. He's an average runner and an excellent defensive first baseman with a strong arm. Some scouts think he even could play left field. The Padres would like to see him get down to 270 pounds, and he has the work ethic and makeup to do it. His combination of size and athleticism has San Diego dreaming about Dave Parker. While Blanks' ceiling is enormous, it also is distant. He'll move up to low Class A this year.

Year	Club (League)	Class	AVG	G	AB	R	H	2B	3B	HR	RBI	BB	SO	SB	OBP	SLG
2005	Padres (AZL)	R	.299	48	164	33	49	10	1	7	30	25	49	3	.420	.500
MINOR LEAGUE TOTALS			.299	48	164	33	49	10	1	7	30	25	49	3	.420	.500

16 JOEL SANTO   RHP

Born: June 4, 1984. **B-T:** R-R. **Ht.:** 6-3. **Wt.:** 194. **Signed:** Dominican Republic, 2002. **Signed by:** Felix Francisco.

The Padres have seen Santo as one of the better pure arms in the system since his strong showing in the Rookie-level Dominican Summer League in 2002. He was finally ready for full-season ball last year, and while he was rarely dominant, his ERA improved every month during the season. Santo is projectable and he's already strong. He operates with smooth mechanics and an effortless delivery. His fastball resides in the low 90s and hits 95. He has good makeup and an aggressive approach, with a strong drive to improve. Santo's offspeed pitches are still a work in progress. He throws his slider too hard, eliminating its downward break, and he has demonstrated little feel for his changeup. He offers considerable upside, but until he refines his secondary stuff he's a likely candidate for an eventual move to the bullpen. His development will require patience, and he'll most likely return to low Class A for 2006.

Year	Club (League)	Class	W	L	ERA	G	GS	CG	SV	IP	H	R	ER	HR	BB	SO	AVG
2002	Padres (DSL)	R	3	2	1.77	12	7	0	0	41	30	11	8	0	22	27	.213
2003	Idaho Falls (Pio)	R	5	5	6.71	16	11	0	0	56	66	53	42	12	23	44	.277
2004	Padres (AZL)	R	0	3	4.60	5	5	0	0	16	20	13	8	1	9	9	.323
	Eugene (NWL)	A	2	2	5.35	7	7	0	0	34	40	25	20	2	23	22	.305
2005	Fort Wayne (Mid)	A	4	11	4.75	27	27	0	0	140	156	90	74	14	51	86	.280
MINOR LEAGUE TOTALS			14	23	4.77	67	57	0	0	287	312	192	152	29	128	188	.276

17 ERNESTO FRIERI   RHP

Born: July 19, 1985. **B-T:** R-R. **Ht.:** 6-2. **Wt.:** 168. **Signed:** Colombia, 2003. **Signed by:** Robert Rowley/Marical DelValle.

The Padres are one of the few teams to scout extensively in Colombia, and they've discovered a few high-ceiling pitchers in Frieri and Fabian Jimenez. Frieri's U.S. debut in 2005 was an eye-opener, as he led the Arizona League in wins and ERA. His fastball has no more than average velocity, but he features two quality breaking balls: a hard, cutting slider and a big, looping curve. Both generated plenty of swings and misses in the AZL. Frieri's penchant for breaking balls has led to a number of nagging hand problems, including an ingrown nail early in the year and a blister problem in instructional league. His command is spotty, and most of his strikeouts came when inexperienced hitters chased pitches out of the zone. He can get away with that now, but Frieri will need to hone his command and learn to throw more quality strikes. San Diego used Frieri in a swingman role to limit his innings and might continue that practice if he jumps to low Class A to start 2006. The other option is to work with him in extended spring training before putting him in the rotation at Eugene.

Year	Club (League)	Class	W	L	ERA	G	GS	CG	SV	IP	H	R	ER	HR	BB	SO	AVG
2003	Tronconero 1 (VSL)	R	1	4	4.00	15	4	0	0	36	36	23	16	0	15	49	.265
2004	Padres (DSL)	R	4	0	1.43	21	1	0	1	50	30	14	8	1	24	59	.167
2005	Lake Elsinore (Cal)	A	0	0	2.70	2	0	0	0	3	3	1	1	1	1	3	.231
	Padres (AZL)	R	7	1	1.17	17	5	0	0	46	21	7	6	0	29	59	.137
MINOR LEAGUE TOTALS			12	5	2.05	55	10	0	1	136	90	45	31	2	69	170	.187

18 JOSH GEER   RHP

Born: June 2, 1983. **B-T:** R-R. **Ht.:** 6-3. **Wt.:** 190. **Drafted:** Rice, 2005 (3rd round). **Signed by:** Bob Laurie.

The Devil Rays made Geer a 19th-round pick in 2003 following his freshman year at Navarro (Texas) Junior College, but couldn't sign him as a draft-and-follow in 2004 and he headed on to Rice. The Owls were rebuilding arguably the best rotation in college history—Philip Humber, Jeff Niemann and Wade Townsend led Rice to a 2003 national title and went in the top eight picks in the 2004 draft—and Geer became the ace, leading them in wins and innings. His polished four-pitch arsenal attracted the Padres, who signed him for $395,000 as a third-round pick. He works consistently in the zone with an 86-90 mph sinker. He throws both a slider and curve, and his best pitch is a deceptive changeup. Geer sat out several weeks before signing, and as a result his velocity was down and his breaking stuff wasn't nearly as sharp in his debut. Scouts are concerned they haven't seen his velocity consistently sit in the low 90s since he was at Navarro. Geer doesn't have overpowering stuff and lacks a true out pitch. He didn't miss many bats as a pro, and he may need to scrap one of his breaking pitches in order to refine the other. His slider has more promise. San Diego hopes Geer just needed the offseason to regain his stuff with rest, and will return in 2006 poised to move quickly through the system. He'll begin the year in Class A.

Year	Club (League)	Class	W	L	ERA	G	GS	CG	SV	IP	H	R	ER	HR	BB	SO	AVG
2005	Eugene (NWL)	A	3	1	3.69	7	6	0	0	32	35	13	13	5	4	13	.285
	Fort Wayne (Mid)	A	1	1	4.25	5	5	0	0	30	29	16	14	3	9	23	.259
MINOR LEAGUE TOTALS			4	2	3.96	12	11	0	0	61	64	29	27	8	13	36	.272

19 YEFRI CARVAJAL   OF

Born: Jan. 22, 1989. **B-T:** R-R. **Ht.:** 5-10. **Wt.:** 190. **Signed:** Dominican Republic, 2005. **Signed by:** Felix Francisco.

The Padres haven't fared well with their Dominican Republic operations. They have yet to develop an everyday player from the Dominican, and owner John Moores was underwhelmed by the club's academy there when he toured it last spring. San Diego tried to take a more aggressive approach in 2005, offering $1 million to outfielder Fernando Martinez, only to lose him to the Mets for $1.4 million. The Padres did land Carvajal for $350,000 in July. His short, stocky frame and lightning-quick bat elicit comparisons to Bill Madlock, Kevin Mitchell and Kirby Puckett. Carvajal has excellent hitting instincts, plus power to all fields and an aggressive approach. While his bat offers plenty of reason for excitement, his other tools are ordinary. He's an average runner with a decent arm, so he projects as a corner outfielder whose bat will have to carry him to the big leagues. Carvajal is currently a little too spread out at the plate, and San Diego is trying to straighten his stance and incorporate his lower half more into his swing. He should make his pro debut in the Arizona League this summer.

Year	Club (League)	Class	AVG	G	AB	R	H	2B	3B	HR	RBI	BB	SO	SB	OBP	SLG
2005	Did not play—Signed 2006 contract															

20 KENNY BAUGH   RHP

Born: Feb. 5, 1979. **B-T:** R-R. **Ht.:** 6-4. **Wt.:** 190. **Drafted:** Rice, 2001 (1st round). **Signed by:** Tim Grieve (Tigers).

Baugh no longer has the look of a first-round pick, but he does have the look of a fringy No. 5 starter who should contribute in the big leagues. The Padres picked him up from the Tigers in a mid-December trade for low Class A righthander Ricky Steik. The 11th overall choice in the 2001 draft, Baugh pitched 205 innings that year between Rice and the minors. The workload took a toll on his shoulder, as he had a torn labrum that required surgery and cost him the entire 2002 season. Baugh has shown improved health and durability the last three seasons, and in 2005 he led the Triple-A International League in starts while ranking second in wins and fifth in ERA. He had two playoff victories to help Toledo win the IL championship as well. Baugh no longer has first-round stuff, as his fastball now sits at 87-89 mph. He does spot his fastball well, however, and generally uses his height well to keep it on a good downward plane. He also throws a spike curveball and an improved changeup that helps him handle lefthanders. San Diego will give Baugh a look in spring training but he could be headed for more time in Triple-A.

Year	Club (League)	Class	W	L	ERA	G	GS	CG	SV	IP	H	R	ER	HR	BB	SO	AVG
2001	West Michigan (Mid)	A	2	1	1.59	6	6	0	0	34	31	14	6	0	10	39	.238
	Erie (EL)	AA	1	3	2.97	5	5	1	0	30	23	16	10	5	6	30	.207
2002	Did not play—Injured																
2003	Lakeland (FSL)	A	3	0	3.86	4	4	0	0	21	21	14	9	2	11	12	.263
	Erie (EL)	AA	7	9	4.59	19	19	1	0	110	111	71	56	16	32	58	.262
2004	Erie (EL)	AA	8	8	3.72	24	24	1	0	143	154	70	59	13	41	107	.280
2005	Toledo (IL)	AAA	12	8	3.38	28	28	1	0	165	159	72	62	13	60	107	.253
MINOR LEAGUE TOTALS			33	29	3.61	86	86	4	0	503	499	257	202	49	160	353	.260

21 LEO ROSALES   RHP

Born: May 28, 1981. **B-T:** R-R. **Ht.:** 6-1. **Wt.:** 185. **Drafted:** Cal State Northridge, 2003 (20th round). **Signed by:** Chris Gwynn.

Rosales was a workhorse starter at Cal State Northridge before blossoming into one of the top relief prospects in the Padres system. He led the low Class A Midwest League in saves in 2004, then repeated the feat in the California League last year. He put an exclamation point on the season by recording a win and two saves in four scoreless postseason appearances. Rosales features the best changeup in the system, a plus-plus offering one scout referred to as a "changeup from hell." His fastball has average velocity, sitting at 89-91 mph, but it's straight and he leaves it up in the zone too often. He does use a curveball but it offers little break. Rosales' mechanics are violent, the main reason his command is spotty. He has the same repertoire that Trevor Hoffman has used for years, though Hoffman threw much harder in his younger days and has top-of-the-line command. Rosales' changeup is good enough to carry him to the majors, but his ability to develop an effective second pitch will define whether his future is as a long reliever or a valuable set-up option. He'll face a big test in Double-A this season.

Year	Club (League)	Class	W	L	ERA	G	GS	CG	SV	IP	H	R	ER	HR	BB	SO	AVG
2003	Eugene (NWL)	A	3	1	2.09	36	0	0	3	43	32	13	10	4	16	58	.201
2004	Fort Wayne (Mid)	A	6	1	1.40	53	1	0	26	58	38	11	9	4	15	66	.177
2005	Lake Elsinore (Cal)	A	8	7	3.18	61	0	0	27	65	53	26	23	5	24	77	.219
MINOR LEAGUE TOTALS			17	9	2.28	150	1	0	56	166	123	50	42	13	55	201	.200

22 JON KNOTT   OF/1B

Born: Aug. 4, 1978. **B-T:** R-R. **Ht.:** 6-3. **Wt.:** 220. **Signed:** NDFA/Mississippi State, 2001. **Signed by:** Mal Fichman.

Knott went undrafted out of Mississippi State because of a leg injury, but he has been one of the system's top run producers since the Padres signed him out of a tryout camp. While his average took a dip when he repeated Triple-A last year, he still led the organization in homers. Knott is a big-bodied slugger, with classic pull power and a good understanding of the strike zone. His swing can get long and he has problems with good lefties. Knott isn't overly gifted physically. He's an average runner once he gets going but a poor defensive player. He often takes bad jumps on flyballs and has a below-average arm. At 27, Knott is running out of time with the Padres. They passed him over for both Paul McAnulty and Ben Johnson when roster spots opened up at the major league level last season. Knott has the skills to be a solid bench player, but that chance may have to come elsewhere, and some see him as better suited for the American League. With no logical spot for him on the San Diego roster, he faces a third year in Triple-A.

Year	Club (League)	Class	AVG	G	AB	R	H	2B	3B	HR	RBI	BB	SO	SB	OBP	SLG
2002	Fort Wayne (Mid)	A	.333	37	126	19	42	12	3	3	18	17	33	2	.411	.548
	Lake Elsinore (Cal)	A	.341	93	367	55	125	33	8	8	73	46	68	5	.414	.540
2003	Mobile (SL)	AA	.252	127	432	83	109	32	0	27	82	82	117	5	.387	.514
	Portland (PCL)	AAA	.346	7	26	5	9	1	0	1	5	4	3	0	.433	.500
2004	San Diego (NL)	MLB	.214	9	14	1	3	2	0	0	1	1	5	0	.267	.357
	Portland (PCL)	AAA	.290	113	435	79	126	22	3	26	85	58	110	5	.376	.533
2005	Portland (PCL)	AAA	.250	134	503	81	126	34	4	25	78	55	112	1	.333	.483
MAJOR LEAGUE TOTALS			.214	9	14	1	3	2	0	0	1	1	5	0	.267	.357
MINOR LEAGUE TOTALS			.284	511	1889	322	537	134	18	90	341	262	443	18	.378	.517

23 BILLY KILLIAN C

Born: June 12, 1986. **B-T:** L-R. **Ht.:** 6-1. **Wt.:** 190. **Drafted:** HS—Stanwood, Mich., 2004 (3rd round). **Signed by:** Jeff Stewart.

The son of Padres part-time scout Bill Killian, Billy ranked as Michigan's top high school player in 2004, so it wasn't nepotism that led the club to take him. San Diego knew Killian would be a long-term project, and he has spent most of his first two years in Rookie ball. He has made progress both at the plate and behind it, and his upside still excites the Padres. He's a lefthanded-hitting catcher who makes hard contact, though he has yet to homer as pro. His best defensive tool is a strong, accurate arm, and he unleashes throws with a lightning-quick exchange and release. While he's still raw behind the plate from a receiving and game-calling standpoint, he has the makeup and athleticism to improve. San Diego wants him to bulk up in order to withstand the grind of a full season. Because he didn't play in a baseball hotbed, Killian has been slow to adjust to the higher level of competition. Now he's ready for a full-season test and will begin 2006 in low Class A.

Year	Club (League)	Class	AVG	G	AB	R	H	2B	3B	HR	RBI	BB	SO	SB	OBP	SLG
2004	Padres (AZL)	R	.230	40	135	17	31	7	2	0	13	11	21	3	.293	.311
	Portland (PCL)	AAA	.143	3	7	0	1	0	0	0	0	1	0	0	.250	.143
2005	Padres (AZL)	R	.287	32	115	6	33	8	2	0	10	3	28	4	.300	.391
	Eugene (NWL)	A	.189	14	37	0	7	0	1	0	4	4	13	0	.286	.243
MINOR LEAGUE TOTALS			.245	89	294	23	72	15	5	0	27	19	62	7	.294	.330

24 JAVIS DIAZ OF

Born: June 25, 1984. **B-T:** L-L. **Ht.:** 5-10. **Wt.:** 165. **Signed:** Dominican Republic, 2003. **Signed by:** Felix Francisco.

Diaz was one of the best prospects on the Padres' Dominican Summer League team in 2003 and 2004, and his U.S. debut last summer confirmed that. He finished among the Arizona League's top five in batting, on-base percentage, slugging and stolen bases. Diaz has a wiry but strong frame, a short swing and a good feel for contact. He can put a surprising charge into the ball for his size, and he's a threat to reach third base every time he rips one into the gap. He bats out of an extreme crouch, and draws a good share of walks because of it. A 70 runner on the 20-80 scouting scale, he's a good basestealer and an excellent bunter. Diaz' outfield work leaves much to be desired, however. While he has the speed to play center field, he's below-average even in left and makes poor reads on balls. His arm is well-below-average. He's 21 and has yet to be tested in a full-season league, though that will change this year when he's sent to low Class A.

Year	Club (League)	Class	AVG	G	AB	R	H	2B	3B	HR	RBI	BB	SO	SB	OBP	SLG
2003	Padres (DSL)	R	.286	64	203	44	58	11	4	0	22	39	27	27	.414	.379
2004	Padres (DSL)	R	.242	68	236	43	57	3	4	1	15	39	42	25	.351	.301
2005	Padres (DSL)	R	.322	20	59	12	19	1	1	2	10	14	8	10	.447	.475
	Padres (AZL)	R	.352	39	145	22	51	5	6	2	24	17	30	19	.425	.510
	Eugene (NWL)	A	.211	5	19	3	4	0	0	0	0	4	4	2	.348	.211
MINOR LEAGUE TOTALS			.285	196	662	124	189	20	15	5	71	113	111	83	.395	.384

25 DREW MACIAS OF

Born: March 7, 1983. **B-T:** L-L. **Ht.:** 6-3. **Wt.:** 175. **Drafted:** Chaffey (Calif.) JC, D/F 2002 (35th round). **Signed by:** Chris Gwynn.

San Diego targeted Macias for years, tabbing him as a draft-and-follow out of both high school and junior college. He has worked his way through the system one level at a time. Macias is a good defensive center fielder, utilizing his plus speed while getting good jumps and taking excellent routes. He's more comfortable coming in on balls than going back, so he plays a deep center field. At the plate, he's a patient hitter with an easy, level, contact-oriented swing and good plate discipline. The wiry Macias offers little in the way of strength, and he struggles against lefties with good breaking balls. He's a grinder who shows up early to the park and works hard on all aspects of his game. The Padres think his frame can handle some muscle and expect him to develop average power as he matures. He has added nearly 15 pounds in the offseason, and will begin the year in Double-A. The Padres envision him as a player in the mold of former big league outfielder Dave Martinez.

Year	Club (League)	Class	AVG	G	AB	R	H	2B	3B	HR	RBI	BB	SO	SB	OBP	SLG
2003	Idaho Falls (Pio)	R	.251	61	239	41	60	10	4	2	13	19	32	15	.318	.351
	Fort Wayne (Mid)	A	.000	1	2	0	0	0	0	0	0	0	1	0	.000	.000
2004	Fort Wayne (Mid)	A	.266	129	478	60	127	18	5	8	55	49	68	16	.340	.374
2005	Lake Elsinore (Cal)	A	.289	128	492	79	142	23	6	6	66	46	78	15	.355	.396
MINOR LEAGUE TOTALS			.272	319	1211	180	329	51	15	16	134	114	179	46	.341	.378

26 GEOFF VANDEL
LHP

Born: June 9, 1987. **B-T:** L-L. **Ht.:** 6-1. **Wt.:** 190. **Drafted:** HS—Columbus, Ga., 2005 (34th round). **Signed by:** Hank King.

Former area scout Hank King (who now works as an agent) had a history of finding diamonds in the rough—including Jonny Gomes in the 18th round and Chad Orvella in the 13th while he was with the Devil Rays—and he may have nailed another late-round gem in Vandel. Few teams were on him entering 2005, and the Padres initially selected him as a 34th-round draft-and-follow, but King correctly gauged his eagerness to sign in the summer despite his plans to play for Chipola (Fla.) Junior College. Vandel was downright dominant in his debut and capped his unlikely summer with a pair of excellent starts at Eugene. He has excellent command of an upper-80s fastball with good sink, and he has a feel for a curveball. His changeup is remarkably advanced for his age, and it's already a plus offering that he confidently throws at any point in the count. Vandel is a little undersized, and his fastball will never have more than average velocity. San Diego is understandably excited about Vandel's possibilities and likes his desire and makeup. He has a shot to make the low Class A rotation out of spring training.

Year	Club (League)	Class	W	L	ERA	G	GS	CG	SV	IP	H	R	ER	HR	BB	SO	AVG
2005	Padres (AZL)	R	1	1	0.43	11	0	0	1	21	12	2	1	0	5	32	.164
	Eugene (NWL)	A	0	0	0.90	2	2	0	0	10	8	1	1	0	1	11	.229
MINOR LEAGUE TOTALS			1	1	0.58	13	2	0	1	31	20	3	2	0	6	43	.185

27 COLT MORTON
C

Born: April 10, 1982. **B-T:** R-R. **Ht.:** 6-5. **Wt.:** 230. **Drafted:** North Carolina State, 2003 (3rd round). **Signed by:** Mike Rikard.

Morton's raw power and arm strength made him one of the more intriguing catchers in the 2003 draft, despite concerns about his ability to make contact. Both the good and the bad were on display during his first two years as a pro, as he entered 2005 with 31 home runs in 150 games, but also 177 strikeouts and a .216 average. He worked hard prior to last season to improve his approach and responded with encouraging results, including six home runs in his first eight California League games. Morton is an immense presence at the plate, with 70 raw power on the 20-80 scouting scale and a patient approach. Despite his size, he's surprisingly agile behind the plate, though his plus arm strength is tempered by a long release. Hitting for average will always be an issue for Morton, and he profiles as a reserve catcher at best. He's prone to chasing breaking balls away, and his loopy swing is designed solely for hitting the ball a long way. Morton struggled with a hamstring injury early in the year and has yet to play more than 104 games or prove himself over the course of a full season. He needs to show that the second half of 2005 wasn't a fluke, and he'll have to do it in the tough offensive environment at Mobile.

Year	Club (League)	Class	AVG	G	AB	R	H	2B	3B	HR	RBI	BB	SO	SB	OBP	SLG
2003	Eugene (NWL)	A	.278	25	97	14	27	6	0	7	20	10	29	0	.346	.557
	Fort Wayne (Mid)	A	.171	22	76	5	13	4	0	2	7	5	28	0	.222	.303
2004	Fort Wayne (Mid)	A	.150	36	127	10	19	5	1	4	11	16	45	0	.260	.299
	Eugene (NWL)	A	.239	66	243	43	58	13	0	17	45	33	75	2	.340	.502
	Mobile (SL)	AA	.333	1	3	1	1	0	0	1	1	1	0	0	.500	1.333
2005	Fort Wayne (Mid)	A	.261	63	222	27	58	15	0	10	46	35	57	0	.362	.464
	Lake Elsinore (Cal)	A	.323	26	96	19	31	4	0	9	19	14	30	0	.407	.646
MINOR LEAGUE TOTALS			.240	239	864	119	207	47	1	50	149	114	264	2	.334	.470

28 EVAN MEEK
RHP

Born: May 12, 1983. **B-T:** R-R. **Ht.:** 6-1. **Wt.:** 190. **Drafted:** Bellevue (Wash.) CC, D/F 2002 (12th round). **Signed by:** Bill Lohr (Twins).

The Padres will try to give Meek a fresh start after he lost his command and was released by the Twins last season. He was a priority draft-and-follow coming out of the 2002 draft for Minnesota, and he signed for $180,000 the next May. Shortly before turning pro, he turned in a no-hitter and a one-hitter in consecutive playoff starts for Bellevue (Wash.) Community College. Meek was outstanding in his pro debut at Elizabethton but came down with a case of the yips in 2004, as his control disappeared and his velocity dropped. Things got worse in 2005, and Minnesota released him after 18 miserable innings in low Class A. Padres pro scout Charley Kerfeld, who lives near Meek in the Seattle area, signed him after one look at his lively arm in a private workout. Meek returned to the mound in instructional league and was once again throwing strikes and touching 97 mph with his fastball. The Padres tinkered with his mechanics to allow his free-working arm to do its job. He's still primarily a one-pitch pitcher, though. He hasn't regained the confidence or command of his power curveball, which once was a dominant swing-and-miss pitch. Meek still has to prove he's beyond the mental lapses that led to his demise with the Twins. His ability to throw strikes in spring training will determine his 2006 destination.

Year	Club (League)	Class	W	L	ERA	G	GS	CG	SV	IP	H	R	ER	HR	BB	SO	AVG
2003	Elizabethton (Appy)	R	7	1	2.47	14	8	0	1	51	33	15	14	2	24	47	.178
2004	Quad City (Mid)	A	0	0	11.12	3	3	0	0	6	7	7	7	0	15	3	.333
	Elizabethton (Appy)	R	1	2	8.06	12	3	0	0	22	18	26	20	1	25	23	.228
2005	Beloit (Mid)	A	0	1	10.00	13	0	0	0	18	15	26	20	0	36	11	.231
MINOR LEAGUE TOTALS			8	4	5.66	42	14	0	1	97	73	74	61	3	100	84	.209

29 FABIAN JIMENEZ LHP

Born: Aug. 27, 1986. **B-T:** L-L. **Ht.:** 6-3. **Wt.:** 170. **Signed:** Colombia, 2002. **Signed by:** Robert Rowley/Marcial DelValle.

San Diego signed Jimenez out of Colombia on his 16th birthday, and his performance in the Rookie-level Venezuelan Summer League in 2003 quickly made him the subject of trade talks involving established major leaguers. The Padres always have loved his upside, which may have led them to be a little too aggressive with him. They sent him to low Class A as an 18-year-old at the start of 2005, and he quickly fizzled after winning three of his first four starts. He went 0-7, 10.58 in his final 10 starts for Fort Wayne before going to Eugene. Long and lanky, Jimenez has intriguing stuff but little feel for his craft. His fastball sits in the low 90s at times and touches 94, but he worked more in the high 80s last year because of sloppy mechanics. He has yet to develop much of a breaking ball, and to call his changeup a work in progress may be giving it too much credit. His control and command also have a long way to go. His raw skills and youth keep the Padres optimistic about Jimenez, who will get another shot at low Class A in 2006.

Year	Club (League)	Class	W	L	ERA	G	GS	CG	SV	IP	H	R	ER	HR	BB	SO	AVG
2003	Tronconero 1 (VSL)	R	2	2	3.30	16	8	0	0	60	48	30	22	3	23	48	.221
2004	Padres (AZL)	R	2	6	6.95	12	9	0	0	45	60	40	35	0	28	28	.330
2005	Fort Wayne (Mid)	A	4	11	7.03	20	20	0	0	90	120	80	70	8	59	38	.331
	Eugene (NWL)	A	1	3	2.22	7	6	0	0	28	31	19	7	0	12	18	.261
MINOR LEAGUE TOTALS			9	22	5.40	55	43	0	0	223	259	169	134	11	122	132	.294

30 STEPHEN ANDRADE RHP

Born: Feb. 6, 1978. **B-T:** R-R. **Ht.:** 6-1. **Wt.:** 220. **Drafted:** Cal State Stanislaus, 2001 (32nd round). **Signed by:** Todd Blyleven (Angels).

When the Padres dealt Sean Burroughs to the Devil Rays for Dewon Brazelton in a swap of failed first-round picks at the Winter Meetings, they were more excited about getting Andrade as the player to be named. (In fact, they did not tender Brazelton a contract after the deal.) Tampa Bay selected Andrade from the Blue Jays system in the major league Rule 5 draft and sent him on to San Diego, meaning the Padres will have to keep him on the major league roster all season. If not, Andrade will have to clear waivers and get offered back to Toronto for half his $50,000 draft price before the Padres can send him to the minors. The Blue Jays got Andrade, who was originally drafted by the Angels, in a waiver claim in December 2004. He put up impressive numbers in Double-A as he has throughout his career, averaging 12.8 strikeouts per nine innings in four and a half seasons. Despite the gaudy strikeout totals, he's not a power reliever. His fastball is average at best, but his slider is a plus-plus offering with two-plane break that often makes hitters look foolish thanks to his awkward, deceptive delivery. He can mix in a curveball and changeup, but rarely needs them, and neither is a big league offering. At 28, Andrade is what he is, but he should be good enough for a big league bullpen job with the Padres.

Year	Club (League)	Class	W	L	ERA	G	GS	CG	SV	IP	H	R	ER	HR	BB	SO	AVG
2001	Provo (Pio)	R	0	0	0.00	1	0	0	0	2	3	0	0	0	0	5	.333
	Cedar Rapids (Mid)	A	2	1	6.52	20	0	0	0	29	33	24	21	3	8	31	.284
2002	Cedar Rapids (Mid)	A	1	1	1.16	46	0	0	11	54	30	7	7	1	16	93	.162
2003	Rancho Cucamonga (Cal)	A	0	0	0.00	3	0	0	1	3	0	0	0	0	3	7	.000
	Arkansas (TL)	AA	5	1	2.65	36	0	0	7	51	26	16	15	2	19	74	.147
2004	Salt Lake (PCL)	AAA	0	1	4.61	12	0	0	3	14	15	7	7	1	8	17	.288
	Arkansas (TL)	AA	2	2	2.44	35	0	0	9	48	37	16	13	4	12	59	.204
2005	New Hampshire (EL)	AA	3	2	1.97	35	0	0	3	50	23	12	11	3	16	71	.134
MINOR LEAGUE TOTALS			13	8	2.65	188	0	0	34	251	167	82	74	14	82	357	.185

SAN FRANCISCO
GIANTS

BY **JOHN MANUEL**

Once again in September, Barry Bonds led the Giants into a series with a playoff spot on the line. Sure, San Francisco was below .500. But Bonds' late return from three knee surgeries and the ineptitude of the National League West gave the Giants a chance at the playoffs when they played the Padres in the season's final week. A victory in the opener pulled them within three games of first place, but San Francisco lost its next five games and finished with a losing record for the first time since 1996—the year before Brian Sabean took over as general manager.

The Giants got a glimpse of the post-Bonds era, and it wasn't a pretty sight. Several rookies who had waited for a big league chance got it, with mixed results. Outfielders Jason Ellison, who had a hot start before fading, and Todd Linden didn't play like long-term answers. First baseman Lance Niekro slumped in the second half but showed power. Relievers **Jeremy Accardo**, Scott Munter and Jack Taschner were part of manager Felipe Alou's aggressively used bullpen.

The most lasting impression, however, was made by No. 1 prospect Matt Cain, who lived up to his billing and posted the big league team's second-best ERA in 46 innings. He's the best example of the Giants' philosophy under Sabean and vice president of player personnel Dick Tidrow, who have stressed developing pitchers both to stock the big league club and to use as a commodity in trades. While the stable front office lost a key member when assistant GM Ned Colletti left to run the rival Dodgers, that philosophy won't change.

San Francisco has traded some live arms of late, including former No. 1 prospects Jesse Foppert (for Randy Winn) and Jerome Williams (for LaTroy Hawkins, since traded himself). The organization still is paying for the 2003 deal that sent Boof Bonser, Francisco Liriano and Joe Nathan to the Twins for catcher A.J. Pierzynski. The Giants released Pierzynski after one difficult season, only to see him become a playoff hero while helping lead the White Sox to the World Series championship. Nathan has been one of baseball's best closers the last two years and Liriano has blossomed into one of the game's top pitching prospects.

The win-now approach, designed to complement Bonds, also has prompted free-agent signings and the accompanying loss of draft picks. San Francisco didn't pick until the fourth round in 2005—132 picks in—and gave up first-round picks in 2003 and 2004. By finishing with the 10th-worst record in baseball in 2005, the Giants will keep their first-round pick in 2006.

In recent years, the Giants have tried to incorporate more hitters into their drafts, focusing on outfielders who could replace Bonds. With better hitting depth, San Francisco affiliates posted the second-best winning percentage (.555) in the minors, including championships in the high Class A California and Rookie-level Arizona leagues.

TOP 30 PROSPECTS

1. Matt Cain, rhp
2. Marcus Sanders, ss/2b
3. Eddy Martinez-Esteve, of
4. Travis Ishikawa, 1b
5. Merkin Valdez, rhp
6. Jonathan Sanchez, lhp
7. Nate Schierholtz, of
8. Fred Lewis, of
9. Kevin Frandsen, 2b/ss
10. Craig Whitaker, rhp
11. Dan Ortmeier, of
12. Brian Wilson, rhp
13. Jeremy Accardo, rhp
14. Clay Timpner, of
15. Pablo Sandoval, 3b
16. Dan Griffin, rhp
17. Scott Munter, rhp
18. Jack Taschner, lhp
19. Waldis Joaquin, rhp
20. Jon Coutlangus, lhp
21. John Bowker, of/1b
22. Alfredo Simon, rhp
23. Ben Copeland, of
24. Jesus Reina, lhp
25. Kelyn Acosta, rhp
26. Justin Knoedler, c
27. Brian Horwitz, of
28. Shairon Martis, rhp
29. Pat Misch, lhp
30. David Maroul, ss/3b

ORGANIZATION OVERVIEW

General manager: Brian Sabean. **Farm director:** Jack Hiatt. **Scouting director:** Dick Tidrow.

2005 PERFORMANCE

Class	Team	League	W	L	Pct.	Finish*	Manager
Majors	San Francisco	National	75	87	.463	12th (16)	Felipe Alou
Triple-A	Fresno Grizzlies	Pacific Coast	68	76	.472	t-11th (16)	Shane Turner
Double-A	#Norwich Navigators	Eastern	71	71	.500	6th (12)	Dave Machemer
High A	San Jose Giants	California	85	55	.607	+1st (10)	Lenn Sakata
Low A	Augusta GreenJackets	South Atlantic	77	59	.566	3rd (16)	Roberto Kelly
Short-season	Salem-Keizer Volcanoes	Northwest	45	31	.592	2nd (8)	Steve Decker
Rookie	AZL Giants	Arizona	39	17	.696	+1st (9)	Bert Hunter
OVERALL 2005 MINOR LEAGUE RECORD			385	309	.555	2nd (30)	

*Finish in overall standings (No. of teams in league). +League champion. #Franchise will be known as Connecticut Defenders in 2006.

ORGANIZATION LEADERS

BATTING   *Minimum 250 at-bats
*AVG	Horwitz, Brian, Augusta/San Jose	.349
R	Frandsen, Kevin, Fresno/Norwich/San Jose	97
H	Frandsen, Kevin, Fresno/Norwich/San Jose	172
TB	Schierholtz, Nate, San Jose	258
2B	Martinez-Esteve, Eddy, San Jose	44
3B	Timpner, Clay, San Jose	12
HR	Linden, Todd, Fresno	30
RBI	Cervenak, Mike, Fresno	103
BB	Martinez-Esteve, Eddy, San Jose	89
SO	Schierholtz, Nate, San Jose	132
SB	Sanders, Marcus, Augusta	57
*OBP	Linden, Todd, Fresno	.437
*SLG	Linden, Todd, Fresno	.682

PITCHING   #Minimum 75 innings
W	Three tied at	12
L	Misch, Pat, Fresno/Norwich	11
#ERA	Bateman, Joe, Fresno/San Jose	1.57
G	Villafuerte, Brandon, Fresno	57
CG	Misch, Pat, Fresno/Norwich	2
	Sack, Darren, Augusta	2
SV	Bateman, Joe, Fresno/San Jose	21
	Wilson, Brian, Augusta/Fresno/Norwich	21
IP	Broshuis, Garrett, Fresno/San Jose	163
	Misch, Pat, Fresno/Norwich	163
BB	Cain, Matt, Fresno	73
SO	Cain, Matt, Fresno	176

BEST TOOLS

Best Hitter for Average	Eddy Martinez-Esteve
Best Power Hitter	Nate Schierholtz
Best Strike-Zone Discipline	Eddy Martinez-Esteve
Fastest Baserunner	Marcus Sanders
Best Athlete	Fred Lewis
Best Fastball	Matt Cain
Best Curveball	Matt Cain
Best Slider	Brian Wilson
Best Changeup	Pat Misch
Best Control	Garrett Broshuis
Best Defensive Catcher	Justin Knoedler
Best Defensive Infielder	Kevin Frandsen
Best Infield Arm	David Maroul
Best Defensive Outfielder	Clay Timpner
Best Outfield Arm	Mike Mooney

PROJECTED 2009 LINEUP

Catcher	Justin Knoedler
First Base	Travis Ishikawa
Second Base	Marcus Sanders
Third Base	Pedro Feliz
Shortstop	Kevin Frandsen
Left Field	Eddy Martinez-Esteve
Center Field	Randy Winn

Right Field	Nate Schierholtz
No. 1 Starter	Matt Cain
No. 2 Starter	Noah Lowry
No. 3 Starter	Jason Schmidt
No. 4 Starter	Matt Morris
No. 5 Starter	Jonathan Sanchez
Closer	Merkin Valdez

LAST YEAR'S TOP 20 PROSPECTS

1. Matt Cain, rhp	11. Pat Misch, lhp
2. Merkin Valdez, rhp	12. Dan Ortmeier, of
3. Fred Lewis, of	13. John Bowker, of
4. Eddy Martinez-Esteve, of	14. Brian Buscher, 3b
5. Nate Schierholtz, of/3b	15. Todd Linden, of
6. Alfredo Simon, rhp	16. Justin Knoedler, c
7. Brad Hennessey, rhp	17. Marcus Sanders, 2b
8. Craig Whitaker, rhp	18. Clay Timpner, of
9. David Aardsma, rhp	19. Jeremy Accardo, rhp
10. Travis Ishikawa, 1b	20. Billy Sadler, rhp

TOP PROSPECTS OF THE DECADE

Year	Player, Pos.	2005 Org.
1996	Shawn Estes, lhp	Diamondbacks
1997	Joe Fontenot, rhp	Out of baseball
1998	Jason Grilli, rhp	Tigers
1999	Jason Grilli, rhp	Tigers
2000	Kurt Ainsworth, rhp	Orioles
2001	Jerome Williams, rhp	Cubs
2002	Jerome Williams, rhp	Cubs
2003	Jesse Foppert, rhp	Mariners
2004	Merkin Valdez, rhp	Giants
2005	Matt Cain, rhp	Giants

TOP DRAFT PICKS OF THE DECADE

Year	Player, Pos.	2005 Org.
1996	*Matt White, rhp	Out of baseball
1997	Jason Grilli, rhp	Tigers
1998	Tony Torcato, 3b	Giants
1999	Kurt Ainsworth, rhp	Orioles
2000	Boof Bonser, rhp	Twins
2001	Brad Hennessey, rhp	Giants
2002	Matt Cain, rhp	Giants
2003	David Aardsma, rhp	Cubs
2004	Eddy Martinez-Esteve, of (2nd)	Giants
2005	Ben Copeland, of (4th)	Giants

*Did not sign.

ALL-TIME LARGEST BONUSES

Jason Grilli, 1997	$1,875,000
David Aardsma, 2003	$1,425,000
Brad Hennessey, 2001	$1,380,000
Matt Cain, 2002	$1,375,000
Osvaldo Fernandez, 1996	$1,300,000
Kurt Ainsworth, 2000	$1,300,000

San Francisco Giants

Rank: **18**

STRENGTH: Relief pitching. The Giants have power bullpen arms both close to the majors and at the lower levels.

WEAKNESS: Catcher. No backstop in the organization profiles as a regular.

Depth charts prepared by **John Manuel** *and* **Chris Kline** *Numbers in parentheses indicate prospect rankings.*

LF
Eddy Martinez-Esteve (3)
John Bowker (21)
Ariel Nunez

CF
Fred Lewis (8)
Clay Timpner (14)
Ben Copeland (23)
Joey Dyche
Antoan Richardson

RF
Nate Schierholtz (7)
Dan Ortmeier (11)
Brian Horwitz (27)
Mike Mooney
Jon Armitage

3B
Pablo Sandoval (15)
Todd Jennings
Brian Buscher
Simon Klink

SS
Marcus Sanders (2)
David Maroul (30)
Sharlon Schoop
Angel Chavez
Jake Wald

2B
Kevin Frandsen (9)
Mark Minicozzi

1B
Travis Ishikawa (4)
Mike Cervenak
Will Thompson

C
Justin Knoedler (26)
Eliezer Alfonzo
Barry Gunther

RHP

Starters	Relievers
Matt Cain (1)	Craig Whitaker (10)
Merkin Valdez (5)	Brian Wilson (12)
Dan Griffin (16)	Jeremy Accardo (13)
Waldis Joaquin (19)	Scott Munter (17)
Shairon Martis (28)	Alfredo Simon (22)
Garrett Broshuis	Kelyn Acosta (25)
Caleb Salankey	Ben Cox
Anthony Moreno	Billy Sadler
Osiris Matos	Justin Hedrick
Mike Musgrave	Joe Bateman
Ryan Shaver	Brian Anderson
	Nick Pereira

LHP

Starters	Relievers
Jonathan Sanchez (6)	Jack Taschner (18)
Jesus Reina (24)	Jon Coutlangus (20)
Pat Misch (29)	Erick Threets
Brian Burres	
Chris Nieto	

DRAFT ANALYSIS
2005

Best Pro Debut: RHP Brian Anderson (14) led the short-season Northwest League with 19 saves, going 3-1, 1.95 with a 42-3 K-BB ratio in 28 innings. OF Antoan Richardson (35) topped the Rookie-level Arizona League in runs (45), steals (40) and on-base percentage (.465) while batting .321. RHP Dan Griffin (5) pitched in both leagues and put up a combined 3-2, 1.99 record with 69 strikeouts in 50 innings.

Best Athlete: OF Ben Copeland (4), San Francisco's top choice. His best tool is his speed. He also has some bat speed and is starting to hit for some power. OF Joey Dyche (7), a former college volleyball player, and Richardson are also good athletes.

Best Pure Hitter: Copeland, who hit .315-5-37 between the AZL and NWL. Dyche, who uses an inside-out swing, set a record at NAIA power Lewis-Clark State (Idaho) by hitting .500 in 2005. He also became the first player ever to hit for the cycle at the NAIA World Series.

Best Raw Power: SS David Maroul (23) is inconsistent at the plate but can launch balls when he connects. He got hot at the right time for the University of Texas in June, winning College World Series MVP honors as the Longhorns captured the national title.

Fastest Runner: Richardson flies down the first-base line in 3.9 seconds from the left side and 4.0 from the right. Copeland, Dyche and 1B Chris Stanton (43) all have above-average wheels.

Best Defensive Player: Maroul was a whiz at third base for the Longhorns but moved to shortstop at Salem-Keizer. Maroul had no problems at the tougher position and will stay there in 2006.

BILL MITCHELL

Copeland

Best Fastball: Griffin can be overpowering, using his 6-foot-7, 225-pound frame to generate 90-94 mph fastballs. That's up from 82-83 mph when he enrolled at Niagara, and there's more velocity in there. RHP Wayne Foltin (31) also can touch 94 mph.

Best Breaking Ball: RHP Robert Grace's (21) curveball. Griffin has the makings of a power curve. RHP Nick Pereira (10) has the best slider.

Most Intriguing Background: Grace is the half-brother of former Giants reliever Scott Eyre, now with the Cubs. RHP Ivan Rusova (26) was born of Russian parents, spent his early years in Cuba and moved to Canada when he was five.

Closest To The Majors: Anderson. He has a good slider, an 88-91 mph fastball and good control. Copeland is the most advanced of the position players.

Best Late-Round Pick: Anderson and Pereira among the pitchers, Maroul and Minicozzi among the hitters.

The One Who Got Away: OF Kurt Lipton (40) took his line-drive bat to Vanderbilt. RHP Brad Cuthbertson (6) and 2B Scotty Bridges (8) remain under Giants control.

Assessment: The Giants were the last team to start drafting, kicking things off with Copeland at No. 132, and didn't land a premium draft-and-follow as they did the previous year with Marcus Sanders. But they always seem to come up with pitchers, and Griffin could be special.

2004 Despite not having a first-round pick, the Giants found some promising bats, led by top pick/OF Eddy Martinez-Esteve (2) and 2B Kevin Frandsen (12). LHP Jonathan Sanchez (27) is a super sleeper. **GRADE:** C+

2003 SS/2B Marcus Sanders (17) is the system's top position player prospect. RHP Craig Whitaker (1) can be erratic but has a live arm and closer potential. So did RHP David Aardsma (1) before he faded quickly and got traded to the Cubs. **GRADE:** C+

2002 RHP Matt Cain (1), arguably the game's best mound prospect, dominated big league hitters in September. RHPs Kevin Correia (4) and Clay Hensley (8) have pitched in the majors, Hensley with the Padres. 1B Travis Ishikawa (21) has developing power. **GRADE:** A

2001 RHP Brad Hennessey (1) and LHP Noah Lowry (1) are in San Francisco's rotation, while OF Todd Linden (1) is a platoon player. RHP Jesse Foppert (2), now with the Mariners, looked like a star before Tommy John surgery. **GRADE:** B

Draft analysis prepared by Jim Callis. Numbers in parentheses indicate draft rounds.

MATT
CAIN

ANDREW WOOLLEY

Born: Oct. 1, 1984.
Ht.: 6-3. **Wt.:** 230.
Bats: R. **Throws:** R.
Drafted: HS—Germantown, Tenn.,
2002 (1st round).
Signed by: Lee Elder.

The Memphis area has become a hotbed for baseball talent, and two of its best prep products reached the major leagues in 2005 as Cain and the Pirates' Paul Maholm broke through. With all due respect to Maholm, Cardinals farmhand Stuart Pomeranz (Cain's former Houston High teammate) and the rest, Cain is clearly the best of that group. He opened 2005 as a 20-year-old in Triple-A and led the Pacific Coast League in strikeouts. He made his big league debut Aug. 29 against the Rockies and was impressive in a 2-1 loss. San Francisco won four of his last six starts as he led the majors in opponent batting average (.148) in September. He became the youngest San Francisco Giant ever to spin a complete game when he two-hit the Cubs on Sept. 9. Cain was the youngest player in the National League all season, and only former PCL foil Felix Hernandez was younger in the majors in 2005.

Hernandez also is one of the few pitchers in Cain's class in terms of upside. The Giants believe he has the stuff and intangibles to be a No. 1 starter. Cain has the kind of fastball that pitchers dream of, because he throws it hard with relative ease. He can throw it for strikes, and the more he uses it, the better he commands it. Cain realized that in the major leagues, pitched off his fastball and found he could dominate with it. His fastball velocity sits at 93-94 mph with good sinking life, and he can dial it up to 97. His curveball also is a plus pitch, a hard downer in the upper 70s. The Giants mandated that Cain use his change-up more often in 2005. He started to trust it more and it has become a solid-average third pitch. His delivery is fairly clean and repeatable, and he's a student of the game who isn't satisfied with being just good enough. After his first big league start, he was more interested to find out what he needed to do for his next outing than in reveling in his accomplishment. He even handles the bat well.

The Giants' biggest worry with Cain is throwing strikes. While he can pitch out of jams, he gets in trouble with walks and also takes himself out of games early because of higher-than-necessary pitch counts. He ranked third in the PCL in walks because he nibbled at hitters too much early in the count, and when he was ahead, he sometimes thought too much about setting them up rather than challenging them. He was more efficient down the stretch as he realized he was better when he attacked hitters relentlessly.

Jesse Foppert is the only homegrown Giants pitcher who has approached Cain's stuff in the last decade. However, Cain's mental toughness, dedication and preparation set him apart from Foppert, who got hurt in 2003 and was traded to the Mariners in 2005. Not only is Cain a lock to start for San Francisco in 2006, but he should front the Giants rotation for years to come. He's the player most likely to be the face of the franchise after Barry Bonds' retirement.

Year	Club (League)	Class	W	L	ERA	G	GS	CG	SV	IP	H	R	ER	HR	BB	SO	AVG
2002	Giants (AZL)	R	0	1	3.73	8	7	0	0	19	13	10	8	1	11	20	.197
2003	Hagerstown (SAL)	A	4	4	2.55	14	14	0	0	74	57	24	21	5	24	90	.209
2004	San Jose (Cal)	A	7	1	1.86	13	13	0	0	73	58	25	15	5	17	89	.216
	Norwich (EL)	AA	6	4	3.35	15	15	0	0	86	73	44	32	7	40	72	.236
2005	Fresno (PCL)	AAA	10	5	4.39	26	26	1	0	146	118	77	71	22	73	176	.218
	San Francisco (NL)	MLB	2	1	2.33	7	7	1	0	46	24	12	12	4	19	30	.151
MAJOR LEAGUE TOTALS			2	1	2.33	7	7	1	0	46	24	12	12	4	19	30	.151
MINOR LEAGUE TOTALS			27	15	3.33	76	75	1	0	398	319	180	147	40	165	447	.219

2 MARCUS SANDERS
SS/2B

Born: Aug. 25, 1985. **B-T:** R-R. **Ht.:** 6-0. **Wt.:** 160. **Drafted:** South Florida CC, D/F 2003 (17th round). **Signed by:** Paul Turco Jr.

Sanders' older brother Frankie reached Triple-A in the Indians system and played with Giants scout Paul Turco Jr. as an amateur. Turco knew Marcus had a high school football injury to his right shoulder but also knew he had athleticism, speed and savvy. The Giants took Sanders in the 17th round in 2003 and signed him a year later as a draft-and-follow. Sanders has game-changing speed. He has excellent instincts on the bases and ranked fifth in the minors in steals while being caught just nine times. When healthy, he has excellent hands and wiry strength, allowing him to drive the ball to all fields. Sanders' bad shoulder didn't make it through the 2005 season. Weakened in the second half, he didn't hit with any power and struggled defensively with 20 arm strength on the 20-80 scale. He had surgery again after the season to clean out the joint. Some scouts see Sanders' arm limiting him to center field, but the Giants want to keep him in the infield—possibly at second base, where he made his pro debut. If he can stay healthy, he should be an impact leadoff hitter. He'll open 2006 at high Class A San Jose.

Year	Club (League)	Class	AVG	G	AB	R	H	2B	3B	HR	RBI	BB	SO	SB	OBP	SLG
2004	Giants (AZL)	R	.292	55	209	54	61	12	4	3	21	35	45	28	.415	.431
2005	Augusta (SAL)	A	.300	111	420	86	126	19	4	5	40	69	90	57	.407	.400
MINOR LEAGUE TOTALS			.297	166	629	140	187	31	8	8	61	104	135	85	.410	.410

3 EDDY MARTINEZ-ESTEVE
OF

Born: July 14, 1983. **B-T:** R-R. **Ht.:** 6-2. **Wt.:** 215. **Drafted:** Florida State, 2004 (2nd round). **Signed by:** Paul Turco Jr.

A Mariners third-round pick out of a Miami high school, Martinez-Esteve didn't sign and had two big seasons at Florida State before the Giants took him with their top pick (second round) in 2004. Martinez-Esteve surprised San Francisco by having offseason shoulder surgery on his own. He was healthy enough to start the 2005 season but didn't play in the outfield until mid-June, and he missed the postseason with a foot injury that isn't considered serious. Martinez-Esteve stands out as the Giants' most polished hitter, with a fluid, efficient swing and a discerning eye at the plate. His bat is quick enough to hit good fastballs, and he's an excellent breaking-ball hitter. He has power to all fields. Being a DH suited Martinez-Esteve too well, considering he's in a National League organization. He lost life in his lower body after a college hamstring injury and has lost arm strength because of his shoulder problems. His lessened athleticism and lack of desire to be a good defender means his entire value stems from his bat. Fortunately for Martinez-Esteve, he really can hit. The Giants will try him at first base and give him a chance in left field at Double-A Connecticut (the Norwich franchise's new name) in 2006.

Year	Club (League)	Class	AVG	G	AB	R	H	2B	3B	HR	RBI	BB	SO	SB	OBP	SLG
2004	Giants (AZL)	R	.357	4	14	2	5	2	0	0	4	0	2	2	.375	.500
	Salem-Keizer (NWL)	A	.286	10	35	5	10	4	0	0	2	6	7	0	.405	.400
	Hagerstown (SAL)	A	.217	13	46	4	10	1	1	1	11	8	8	1	.339	.348
	San Jose (Cal)	A	.420	17	69	11	29	7	2	0	14	4	9	0	.446	.580
2005	San Jose (Cal)	A	.313	132	479	89	150	44	3	17	94	89	82	4	.427	.524
MINOR LEAGUE TOTALS			.317	176	643	111	204	58	6	18	125	107	108	7	.420	.510

4 TRAVIS ISHIKAWA
1B

Born: Sept. 24, 1983. **B-T:** L-L. **Ht.:** 6-3. **Wt.:** 200. **Drafted:** HS—Federal Way, Wash., 2002 (21st round). **Signed by:** Todd Woodward.

Since the Giants bought Ishikawa out of his Oregon State commitment with a $955,000 signing bonus as a 21st-round pick in 2002, they have waited for him to break out. He finally did so in 2005, setting career highs across the board to earn a spot on the 40-man roster. The Giants always have believed in Ishikawa's bat and makeup. He's athletic and repeats a balanced, fluid stroke, and his swing has natural leverage that produces power. He's patient and unafraid to work deep into counts. He actually hit better against lefties (.317) than righties (.273) in 2005. He's an excellent defender at first base, with good footwork and fine hands. Ishikawa will strike out a lot because his swing can get long and has some holes. He can be beaten inside by above-average fastballs, and he's still learning to make better adjustments, such as pulling the ball more consistently. He's slowed some as he has filled out physically and is now a below-average runner. The Giants have been patient with Ishikawa, who finally will reach Double-A in his fifth pro season. He projects as a .275 hitter with 20-30 homers annually.

Year	Club (League)	Class	AVG	G	AB	R	H	2B	3B	HR	RBI	BB	SO	SB	OBP	SLG
2002	Giants (AZL)	R	.279	19	68	10	19	4	2	1	10	7	20	7	.364	.441
	Salem-Keizer (NWL)	A	.307	23	88	14	27	2	1	1	17	5	22	1	.347	.386
2003	Hagerstown (SAL)	A	.206	57	194	20	40	5	0	3	22	33	69	3	.329	.278
	Salem-Keizer (NWL)	A	.254	66	248	53	63	17	4	3	31	44	77	0	.376	.391
2004	Hagerstown (SAL)	A	.256	97	355	59	91	19	2	15	54	45	110	10	.357	.448
	San Jose (Cal)	A	.232	16	56	10	13	7	0	1	10	10	16	0	.353	.411
2005	San Jose (Cal)	A	.282	127	432	87	122	28	7	22	79	70	129	1	.387	.532
MINOR LEAGUE TOTALS			.260	405	1441	253	375	82	16	46	223	214	443	22	.365	.435

5 MERKIN VALDEZ   RHP

BILL MITCHELL

Born: Nov. 10, 1981. **B-T:** R-R. **Ht.:** 6-3. **Wt.:** 220. **Signed:** Dominican Republic, 1999. **Signed by:** Felix Francisco (Braves).

Since being acquired from the Braves in the Russ Ortiz trade prior to 2003, Valdez has tantalized the Giants with his power arm. After earning a brief promotion to the San Francisco bullpen in 2004, he spent most of 2005 as a starter before an elbow strain ended his season in August. At his best, Valdez can be a front-of-the-rotation starter. His fastball can sit in the mid-90s, and if he's throwing strikes with it, he doesn't need much else. His changeup has become his best secondary offering. With a delivery that often gets out of sync, Valdez lacks the body control to throw strikes consistently. His elbow drops when he throws his curveball and slider, neither of which is a dependably average pitch. His mechanics also put too much strain on his elbow, though the injury didn't require surgery. The Giants, often quick to put power arms in the bullpen, have decided to wait and see if Valdez can be an impact starter. Valdez worked on his mechanics in instructional league and was pitching in the Dominican Winter League. He'll start 2006 in the minors but could join the big league rotation later in the year if healthy.

Year	Club (League)	Class	W	L	ERA	G	GS	CG	SV	IP	H	R	ER	HR	BB	SO	AVG
2000	Braves (DSL)	R	1	5	1.57	14	7	0	0	57	52	27	10	2	14	32	.234
2001	Braves 2 (DSL)	R	6	7	2.93	15	14	1	0	92	93	41	30	0	18	48	.258
2002	Braves (GCL)	R	7	3	1.98	12	8	1	0	68	47	18	15	0	12	76	.193
2003	Hagerstown (SAL)	A	9	5	2.25	26	26	2	0	156	119	42	39	11	49	166	.213
2004	Fresno (PCL)	AAA	0	0	7.20	1	1	0	0	5	6	4	4	0	4	5	.316
	San Jose (Cal)	A	3	1	2.52	7	7	0	0	36	30	12	10	4	5	44	.219
	San Francisco (NL)	MLB	0	0	26.47	2	0	0	0	2	4	5	5	1	3	2	.444
	Norwich (EL)	AA	1	4	4.32	10	7	0	1	42	35	21	20	3	15	31	.229
2005	Norwich (EL)	AA	5	6	3.53	24	19	1	0	107	99	48	42	7	45	96	.252
MAJOR LEAGUE TOTALS			0	0	26.47	2	0	0	0	2	4	5	5	1	3	2	.444
MINOR LEAGUE TOTALS			32	31	2.72	109	89	5	1	563	481	213	170	27	162	498	.230

6 JONATHAN SANCHEZ   LHP

BILL MITCHELL

Born: Nov. 19, 1982. **B-T:** L-L. **Ht.:** 6-2. **Wt.:** 165. **Drafted:** Ohio Dominican, 2004 (27th round). **Signed by:** Sean O'Connor.

Sanchez starred at NAIA power Ohio Dominican despite a delivery that left him pushing the ball. Scout Sean O'Connor recognized a player with arm strength and mechanics that could be fixed, and the Giants stole Sanchez in the 27th round in 2004. He finished his first full pro season with two electric starts in the high Class A California League playoffs, helping San Jose win the title. Since Sanchez joined the Giants, he has made dramatic progress incorporating his lower half into his delivery. The change has pushed the velocity on his fastball consistently to the 93-94 mph range with excellent life and sink. He has good arm speed on his changeup, which can be a plus pitch. Sanchez' low arm angle means he must be mechanically sound in order to stay on top of his curveball. When he doesn't, his curve flattens out and is hittable. He still needs to be more consistent with his delivery in order to improve his command. With an arm action and velocity reminiscent of Oliver Perez, Sanchez has excited the Giants and could move quickly. He'll return to high Class A to start 2006.

Year	Club (League)	Class	W	L	ERA	G	GS	CG	SV	IP	H	R	ER	HR	BB	SO	AVG
2004	Giants (AZL)	R	5	0	2.77	9	3	0	1	26	22	9	8	0	9	27	.229
	Salem-Keizer (NWL)	A	2	1	4.84	6	6	0	0	22	16	13	12	3	19	34	.203
2005	Augusta (SAL)	A	5	7	4.08	25	25	0	0	126	122	59	57	8	39	166	.254
MINOR LEAGUE TOTALS			12	8	3.98	40	34	0	1	174	160	81	77	11	67	227	.244

7 NATE SCHIERHOLTZ OF

Born: Feb. 15, 1984. **B-T:** L-R. **Ht.:** 6-2. **Wt.:** 215. **Drafted:** Chabot (Calif.) JC, 2003 (2nd round). **Signed by:** Matt Nerland.

STEVE MOORE

Since being a surprise second-round pick, Schierholtz has made steady progress while switching from third base to right field. In 2005, his first full season in the outfield, he ranked sixth in the California League in batting and tied for the league lead with 15 outfield assists. Schierholtz has above-average raw power from the left side, and should hit more homers as he learns the strike zone and his own swing. His bat speed allows him to wait on his pitch and use the whole field, and he hit .300 or better in every full month of the 2005 season. He runs well for his size. His hand-eye coordination and bat speed make Schierholtz at times too aggressive at the plate, and his strike-out-walk ratio needs improvement. He has a long swing path, but his bat speed has allowed him to succeed with it at lower levels. He took well to the outfield but needs repetitions to become an average defender. Schierholtz also will be worked at first base in case the Giants' outfield glut forces their hand. He'll get his first trip to Double-A in 2006.

Year	Club (League)	Class	AVG	G	AB	R	H	2B	3B	HR	RBI	BB	SO	SB	OBP	SLG
2003	Giants (AZL)	R	.400	11	45	5	18	0	2	0	5	3	8	4	.449	.489
	Salem-Keizer (NWL)	A	.306	35	124	23	38	6	2	3	29	12	15	0	.382	.460
2004	Hagerstown (SAL)	A	.296	58	233	41	69	22	0	15	53	18	52	1	.353	.584
	San Jose (Cal)	A	.295	62	258	39	76	18	9	3	31	15	41	3	.338	.469
2005	San Jose (Cal)	A	.319	128	502	83	160	37	8	15	86	32	132	5	.363	.514
MINOR LEAGUE TOTALS			.311	294	1162	191	361	83	21	36	204	80	248	13	.361	.511

8 FRED LEWIS OF

Born: Dec. 9, 1980. **B-T:** L-R. **Ht.:** 6-2. **Wt.:** 190. **Drafted:** Southern, 2002 (2nd round). **Signed by:** Tom Korenek.

Instead of building on a breakthrough 2004 season, when he led the organization in on-base percentage (.424), walks (89) and steals (34), Lewis got off to a miserable start in his first stint in Double-A. His average sat at .223 in early July before he recovered to hit .339 in his final 58 games. A cousin of big league outfielder Matt Lawton, Lewis played wide receiver at Mississippi Gulf Coast Junior College and Southern. Lewis' bat speed and level swing could make him a .300 hitter, and he could steal 30-40 bases annually with his plus speed. He has the raw power to hit 20 homers a year, and he took better routes and showed a more accurate arm when he moved from center field to left at midseason. Despite three full seasons in the minors, Lewis remains raw. He's far from mastering pitch recognition, which often leaves him letting hittable pitches go by. His power won't come until he starts to pull the ball more often. The Giants' strength is outfield depth, so they can be patient with Lewis. He might repeat Double-A and could get another shot in center field.

Year	Club (League)	Class	AVG	G	AB	R	H	2B	3B	HR	RBI	BB	SO	SB	OBP	SLG
2002	Salem-Keizer (NWL)	A	.322	58	239	43	77	9	3	1	23	26	58	9	.396	.397
2003	Hagerstown (SAL)	A	.250	114	420	61	105	17	8	1	27	68	112	30	.361	.336
2004	San Jose (Cal)	A	.301	115	439	88	132	20	11	8	57	84	109	33	.424	.451
	Fresno (PCL)	AAA	.304	6	23	3	7	1	0	1	2	5	5	1	.429	.478
2005	Norwich (EL)	AA	.273	137	512	79	140	28	7	7	47	69	124	30	.361	.396
MINOR LEAGUE TOTALS			.282	430	1633	274	461	75	29	18	156	252	408	103	.384	.397

9 KEVIN FRANDSEN 2B/SS

Born: May 24, 1982. **B-T:** R-R. **Ht.:** 6-0. **Wt.:** 175. **Drafted:** San Jose State, 2004 (12th round). **Signed by:** Matt Nerland.

BILL MITCHELL

Frandsen grew up 40 miles from Candlestick Park as a Giants fan, then attended San Jose State, where he became the Spartans' career hits leader (250). He bounced back from a broken collarbone to reach Triple-A Fresno and play in the Futures Game during his first full pro season. He finished the year by hitting .367 in the California League playoffs. Frandsen is an organizational favorite for his solid tools and off-the-charts makeup. He's fundamentally sound in the field and at the plate, where he has a simple swing and uses the whole field. His arm and range are excellent at second base and fringy at short. He has the hands to fill in at third base as well. Frandsen is getting the most out of his ability, so there's not much projection left. He can drive the ball to the gaps but has below-average home run power. He's not overly quick or fast. Frandsen reminds some of former all-star Robby Thompson, though with less power. At worst, he fits the profile of a useful utility player and could fill that role in San Francisco in 2006.

Year	Club (League)	Class	AVG	G	AB	R	H	2B	3B	HR	RBI	BB	SO	SB	OBP	SLG
2004	Salem-Keizer (NWL)	A	.296	25	98	22	29	5	0	3	14	9	9	0	.369	.439
2005	San Jose (Cal)	A	.351	75	291	57	102	22	3	2	40	26	22	13	.429	.467
	Norwich (EL)	AA	.287	33	129	22	37	8	0	2	20	4	14	7	.336	.395
	Fresno (PCL)	AAA	.351	20	94	18	33	10	1	2	16	2	5	1	.378	.543
MINOR LEAGUE TOTALS			.328	153	612	119	201	45	4	9	90	41	50	21	.393	.459

10 CRAIG WHITAKER   RHP

Born: Nov. 19, 1984. **B-T:** R-R. **Ht.:** 6-4. **Wt.:** 170. **Drafted:** HS—Lufkin, Texas, 2003 (1st round supplemental). **Signed by:** Tom Korenek.

In his first year in full-season ball, Whitaker barely made it through one month in the low Class A Augusta rotation. He went on the disabled list with a middle back sprain, and when he returned in June, it was as a reliever. He didn't allow a run in his first 11 innings out of the bullpen. The Giants like to say Whitaker has "power equipment." It starts with a mid-90s fastball that he whips to the plate thanks to a very quick arm. He has a feel for spinning a breaking ball and can throw a changeup with the same arm speed he uses on his fastball. Whitaker lacks a feel for his craft. He was tipping his curveball to hitters, using a different delivery than he did for his fastball or change-up, and has switched to a slider, which he was able to throw for strikes more consistently. He needs to improve his focus and mechanics. Whitaker's upside remains significant, as do the obstacles he has to overcome. He's a candidate to return to low Class A to give pitching in the rotation another go, and with an arm this good, the Giants don't mind being patient.

Year	Club (League)	Class	W	L	ERA	G	GS	CG	SV	IP	H	R	ER	HR	BB	SO	AVG
2003	Giants (AZL)	R	0	1	1.70	3	1	0	0	5	2	2	1	0	4	8	.105
2004	Salem-Keizer (NWL)	A	4	2	3.44	15	15	0	0	71	58	33	27	4	43	77	.234
2005	Augusta (SAL)	A	3	4	4.66	29	6	0	5	58	54	36	30	3	39	72	.245
MINOR LEAGUE TOTALS			7	7	3.90	47	22	0	5	134	114	71	58	7	86	157	.234

11 DAN ORTMEIER   OF

Born: May 11, 1981. **B-T:** R-L. **Ht.:** 6-4. **Wt.:** 220. **Drafted:** Texas–Arlington, 2002 (3rd round). **Signed by:** Todd Thomas.

Ortmeier was the Giants' top outfield prospect before they loaded up on outfielders in the last three drafts. He suffered through an injury-plaged season in 2004 but bounced back with a strong 2005 campaign. Ortmeier has a solid all-around game but will go as far as his bat takes him. He did a good job of translating his raw power into game power last year, clubbing 20 homers after totaling 23 over his first three seasons. He also did a better job of making contact. He's aggressive at the plate, on the bases and in the field (hence the collisions that have caused injuries to both shoulders and a concussion). He's an above-average runner, particularly for his size. Ortmeier still must improve his approach and feel for hitting to be an everyday big leaguer. His arm strength hasn't come back since a 2004 injury to his left shoulder and is now fringe average, though he compensates with good accuracy and a quick release. No one in the organization plays harder. Ortmeier had four multihit efforts in six games in the Arizona Fall League before a sore wrist caused him to shut it down for the fall. He looked overmatched in September in his big league trial and will get his first taste of Triple-A Fresno in 2006.

Year	Club (League)	Class	AVG	G	AB	R	H	2B	3B	HR	RBI	BB	SO	SB	OBP	SLG
2002	Salem-Keizer (NWL)	A	.292	49	195	32	57	9	1	5	31	18	37	3	.352	.426
2003	San Jose (Cal)	A	.304	115	408	62	124	32	6	8	56	39	89	13	.378	.471
2004	Norwich (EL)	AA	.252	106	377	55	95	23	6	10	48	47	110	18	.352	.424
2005	Norwich (EL)	AA	.274	135	503	85	138	23	6	20	79	48	115	35	.360	.463
	San Francisco (NL)	MLB	.136	15	22	1	3	0	0	0	1	3	5	1	.269	.136
MAJOR LEAGUE TOTALS			.136	15	22	1	3	0	0	0	1	3	5	1	.240	.136
MINOR LEAGUE TOTALS			.279	405	1483	234	414	87	19	43	214	152	351	69	.362	.450

12 BRIAN WILSON   RHP

Born: March 16, 1982. **B-T:** R-R. **Ht.:** 6-1. **Wt.:** 205. **Drafted:** Louisiana State, 2003 (24th round). **Signed by:** Tom Korenek.

The Giants have waited to see the real Brian Wilson since drafting him less than two months after he had Tommy John surgery in 2003. He signed a 2004 contract because of his elbow injury, meaning San Francisco didn't have to protect him on its 40-man roster this off-season. The Giants certainly would have if needed, because he'll likely reach the majors in 2006. Formerly a No. 1 starter at Louisiana State, Wilson worked mostly in the bullpen trying to build up arm strength in his pro debut and got hammered in low Class A. Humbled by his performance, Wilson changed his diet, hit the weight room and got into the best shape of his life. The results were immediate—a spike in fastball velocity to the mid-90s, a return of his plus curveball and a more effective changeup. Wilson disciplined himself on the mound as well as off the field. He tightened his repertoire, ditching extraneous pitches and focusing on three good ones. His hard downer curve has such bite that it's often mistaken for a split-ter. Wilson zoomed to Triple-A and didn't allow a home run all season. He tired late and wasn't at his best in the Arizona Fall League. If he has another strong offseason, he could start 2006 in San Francisco's bullpen, though a return to Triple-A is more likely.

Year	Club (League)	Class	W	L	ERA	G	GS	CG	SV	IP	H	R	ER	HR	BB	SO	AVG
2004	Hagerstown (SAL)	A	2	5	5.34	23	3	0	3	57	63	37	34	7	22	41	.269
2005	Augusta (SAL)	A	5	1	0.82	26	0	0	13	33	23	7	3	0	7	30	.190
	Norwich (EL)	AA	0	0	0.57	15	0	0	8	16	6	1	1	0	5	22	.115
	Fresno (PCL)	AAA	1	1	3.98	9	0	0	0	11	8	7	5	0	8	13	.190
MINOR LEAGUE TOTALS			8	7	3.30	73	3	0	24	117	100	52	43	7	42	106	.223

13 JEREMY ACCARDO   RHP

Born: Dec. 8, 1981. **B-T:** R-R. **Ht.:** 6-2. **Wt.:** 190. **Signed:** NDFA/Illinois State, 2003. **Signed by:** Doug Mapson.

Accardo has moved rapidly through the system, reaching the major leagues in 2005 as a pitcher just two years after he was Illinois State's shortstop and closer and pitching a perfect inning May 4 in his big league debut. The Giants signed him as a nondrafted free agent after seeing him throw 92-93 mph in the Alaska League in the summer of 2003. Accardo has settled in at 90-93 mph since signing while improving his slider. He threw a true cut fastball with more horizontal action when he signed, and he has added depth to the pitch as a pro. Accardo's fastball jumps on hitters because he has an easy delivery, and he's able to locate it both high and low in the strike zone, keeping them guessing. He showed a durable arm as a big leaguer, though the Giants were careful with him and used him on back-to-back nights just six times. He didn't allow a run in any of those 12 appearances. Accardo doesn't have a guaranteed spot in the San Francisco bullpen because he's still learning the subtleties of pitching, but his live arm, athleticism and continual improvement bode well for his future as a set-up man.

Year	Club (League)	Class	W	L	ERA	G	GS	CG	SV	IP	H	R	ER	HR	BB	SO	AVG
2004	Norwich (EL)	AA	2	1	5.42	7	0	0	1	8	9	5	5	1	2	5	.265
	San Jose (Cal)	A	1	2	4.25	50	0	0	27	55	57	28	26	3	15	43	.257
2005	Norwich (EL)	AA	1	0	0.93	8	0	0	4	10	8	3	1	0	1	15	.211
	San Jose (Cal)	A	0	0	0.00	2	0	0	1	2	1	0	0	0	1	3	.143
	Fresno (PCL)	AAA	2	0	1.95	25	0	0	3	32	25	7	7	0	10	30	.214
	San Francisco (NL)	MLB	1	5	3.94	28	0	0	0	30	26	13	13	2	9	16	.232
MAJOR LEAGUE TOTALS			1	5	3.94	28	0	0	0	30	26	13	13	2	9	16	.232
MINOR LEAGUE TOTALS			6	3	3.27	92	0	0	36	107	100	43	39	4	29	96	.239

14 CLAY TIMPNER   OF

Born: May 13, 1983. **B-T:** L-L. **Ht.:** 6-2. **Wt.:** 195. **Drafted:** Central Florida, 2004 (4th round). **Signed by:** Paul Turco Jr.

As a leadoff man and center fielder, Timpner was a key cog in San Jose's California League championship last year. Lenn Sakata has managed several of the system's top outfielders at San Jose the last two years and believes Timpner is the surest bet of all to be a big leaguer because of his defense and speed. Both of those tools earn 60 grades on the 20-80 scouting scale, and his average arm plays up because of his quick release and accuracy. Timpner needs to make better use of his wheels offensively to become an everyday player in the majors, however. He'll never be much of a home run threat, so he has to improve his jumps and reads to become a more efficient basestealer. He generally stays within himself, spraying the ball to all fields and showing gap power, and he has become a better bunter. He also holds his own against lefthanders. He must show more patience to stay at the top of a lineup, though his college and pro track records don't indicate he'll ever be more than average in that regard. Timpner will move up to Double-A this season.

Year	Club (League)	Class	AVG	G	AB	R	H	2B	3B	HR	RBI	BB	SO	SB	OBP	SLG
2004	Salem-Keizer (NWL)	A	.293	68	294	37	86	7	2	5	28	20	35	16	.339	.381
	San Jose (Cal)	A	.280	6	25	4	7	2	0	0	2	1	2	1	.296	.360
2005	San Jose (Cal)	A	.291	126	549	85	160	22	12	4	39	34	93	34	.334	.397
MINOR LEAGUE TOTALS			.291	200	868	126	253	31	14	9	69	55	130	51	.335	.391

15 PABLO SANDOVAL
3B

Born: Aug. 11, 1986. **B-T:** B-R. **Ht.:** 5-11. **Wt.:** 180. **Signed:** Venezuela, 2002. **Signed by:** Ciro Villalobos.

Ranked No. 27 on this list a year ago, Sandoval moved up 12 spots despite giving up playing a premium position. That's how much the Giants like his switch-hitting bat. Moving to third base helped bring out his bat even more, but to be an everyday third baseman he'll have to hit more homers. His current approach is to use the entire field, and he'll have to learn to pull the ball to bring more of his batting-practice power into games. His swing is consistent and fluid from both sides of the plate, keeping his bat in the hitting zone longer than the average hitter's. While he's a low-ball hitter, a trait more commonly associated with lefthanded hitters, he showed more pop from the right side. His plate coverage and hand-eye coordination should cut down on his strikeouts, though he also doesn't walk much. Defensively, he got off to a solid start at third base, and he has the tools to stick there. His hands and arm are solid-average for the hot corner, though his range is somewhat limited. He's athletic despite a pudgy 5-foot-11 frame that never will look good in a uniform. If he stays in shape and grows into third base with experience, Sandoval could develop into an average defender with a line-drive bat capable of hitting .300.

Year	Club (League)	Class	AVG	G	AB	R	H	2B	3B	HR	RBI	BB	SO	SB	OBP	SLG
2003	Giants (DSL)	R	.354	57	209	36	74	16	2	3	33	13	13	6	.390	.493
2004	Giants (AZL)	R	.266	46	177	21	47	9	5	0	26	5	17	4	.287	.373
2005	Salem-Keizer (NWL)	A	.330	75	294	46	97	15	2	3	50	21	33	2	.383	.425
MINOR LEAGUE TOTALS			.321	178	680	103	218	40	9	6	109	39	63	12	.361	.432

16 DAN GRIFFIN
RHP

Born: Sept. 29, 1984. **B-T:** R-R. **Ht.:** 6-7. **Wt.:** 225. **Drafted:** Niagara, 2005 (5th round). **Signed by:** Sean O'Connor.

Griffin is a perfect example of the raw arms with upside the Giants love to draft. Unlike other pitchers drafted high out of the Albany, N.Y., area, such as Tim Stauffer and former Blue Jays lefthander John Cerutti, Griffin is a power pitcher. He remains raw because he's still growing into his 6-foot-7, 225-pound body, and if he improves his body control then he could rocket up this list. He led NCAA Division I in 2005 by averaging 13.8 strikeouts per nine innings, leading the Metro Atlantic Athletic Conference with 120 whiffs in 78 frames. He won his last five starts of his college career after losing 11 of his first 13 decisions for Niagara, a solid program in a relatively weak, Northern college conference. He redshirted as a freshman to get stronger—his fastball registered 82-84 mph—and improve his mechanics. As he has grown stronger and learned more about pitching, Griffin has increased his velocity to a consistent 90-94 mph and figured out how to use his height to throw downhill. His fastball already had natural sink, and he showed more consistency with his angular delivery in instructional league. Griffin's hard curveball also can be a plus pitch, though it can be inconsistent. His changeup is a third pitch and needs work, but when he's on, his fastball and curve suffice. Griffin is at his best when he works quickly and attacks hitters. He's expected to start 2006 in low Class A.

Year	Club (League)	Class	W	L	ERA	G	GS	CG	SV	IP	H	R	ER	HR	BB	SO	AVG
2005	Giants (AZL)	R	0	0	0.75	4	4	0	0	12	9	2	1	0	6	20	.214
	Salem-Keizer (NWL)	A	3	2	2.39	8	8	0	0	38	33	11	10	1	12	49	.241
MINOR LEAGUE TOTALS			3	2	1.99	12	12	0	0	50	42	13	11	1	18	69	.235

17 SCOTT MUNTER
RHP

Born: March 7, 1980. **B-T:** R-R. **Ht.:** 6-6. **Wt.:** 235. **Drafted:** Butler County (Kan.) CC, 2001 (47th round). **Signed by:** Todd Thomas.

While he wasn't on the prospect radar prior to 2004, Munter has made great strides and worked in 45 big league games last year. He was used heavily until a mid-August elbow injury, described as inflammation, landed him on the disabled list. He pitched just once in September after he returned but didn't have surgery. Munter always has owned a heavy fastball, but in the last two years he has been able to keep his mechanics more consistent, throw more strikes and improve his velocity. His sinker sits in the low 90s, and some nights he pitches at 94-95 mph. His confidence took off when he started challenging hitters and had success, and he showed last year he could be effective with essentially one plus pitch. He allowed only one home run and recorded 83 of his 118 outs via groundballs in 2005. Munter struck out just 11 hitters because he truly lacks a swing-and-miss pitch. His slider has become an adequate breaking ball because he throws it with some power, though it lacks tilt. He's working on a changeup that's getting better, but Munter already has a formula for success with his power sinker. While he needs to watch his weight and stay healthy, he should continue to be a groundball pitcher in a set-up role.

Year	Club (League)	Class	W	L	ERA	G	GS	CG	SV	IP	H	R	ER	HR	BB	SO	AVG
2001	Salem-Keizer (NWL)	A	1	2	5.91	15	0	0	0	35	42	26	23	3	12	28	.296
	Hagerstown (SAL)	A	1	0	3.40	1	1	0	0	5	5	3	2	0	1	2	.278
2002	Salem-Keizer (NWL)	A	1	1	6.97	10	4	0	0	30	33	24	23	0	20	20	.287
	San Jose (Cal)	A	0	0	10.47	3	0	0	0	4	12	5	5	0	4	2	.571
2003	Hagerstown (SAL)	A	3	5	2.36	40	0	0	5	69	61	28	18	3	28	47	.230
2004	Norwich (EL)	AA	2	4	2.35	42	0	0	3	65	63	19	17	4	22	30	.246
	Fresno (PCL)	AAA	1	1	3.44	13	0	0	1	16	20	8	6	1	4	5	.299
2005	Fresno (PCL)	AAA	1	3	5.12	12	0	0	0	12	17	8	7	0	4	5	.362
	San Francisco (NL)	MLB	2	0	2.56	45	0	0	0	39	40	15	11	1	12	11	.280
MAJOR LEAGUE TOTALS			2	0	2.56	45	0	0	0	39	40	15	11	1	12	11	.280
MINOR LEAGUE TOTALS			10	16	3.85	136	5	0	9	236	253	121	101	11	95	139	.272

18 JACK TASCHNER
LHP

Born: April 21, 1978. **B-T:** L-L. **Ht.:** 6-3. **Wt.:** 205. **Drafted:** Wisconsin-Oshkosh, 1999 (2nd round). **Signed by:** Steve Arnieri.

The Giants had high hopes for Taschner and pushed him aggressively in his first full pro season, sending him to high Class A. He was waylaid by injuries, however, including a blown out elbow that required Tommy John surgery that knocked him out for the entire 2002 season. Taschner endured, even through an ugly second half in 2004 when he posted a 9.28 ERA in Triple-A and gave up 14 home runs in 53 innings. He was much better in a return trip to Fresno last season, and his stuff took off when he worked solely in a relief role. His once-average velocity jumped into the low to mid-90s, the hardest he has thrown since he was drafted. His improved fastball and solid changeup helped him shackle righthanders to a .138 average between Triple-A and the majors. His increased velocity was the biggest factor in his ability to handle them. His slider has some depth to it and can be a solid-average pitch if it becomes more consistent. If Taschner were more durable, he'd probably get a chance to start again. But the Giants finally have found a way for him to be productive and will keep him in relief. He figures to be one of the top lefties in their bullpen this year.

Year	Club (League)	Class	W	L	ERA	G	GS	CG	SV	IP	H	R	ER	HR	BB	SO	AVG
1999	Salem-Keizer (NWL)	A	3	2	2.51	7	6	0	0	29	26	12	8	1	10	36	.241
2000	San Jose (Cal)	A	2	2	4.11	10	2	0	1	26	23	17	12	0	17	22	.237
2001	San Jose (Cal)	A	4	4	4.11	14	14	0	0	66	62	33	30	7	29	72	.244
2002	Did not play—Injured																
2003	Norwich (EL)	AA	0	6	5.71	34	12	0	0	76	78	53	48	7	45	46	.269
2004	Norwich (EL)	AA	3	1	2.48	14	10	0	0	58	47	17	16	5	16	55	.233
	Fresno (PCL)	AAA	4	7	9.29	18	9	0	0	53	71	59	55	14	32	44	.323
2005	Fresno (PCL)	AAA	3	0	1.64	44	0	0	10	49	30	9	9	3	24	62	.173
	San Francisco (NL)	MLB	2	0	1.59	24	0	0	0	23	15	5	4	0	13	19	.185
MAJOR LEAGUE TOTALS			2	0	1.59	24	0	0	0	23	15	5	4	0	13	19	.185
MINOR LEAGUE TOTALS			19	22	4.49	141	53	0	11	357	337	200	178	37	173	337	.251

19 WALDIS JOAQUIN
RHP

Born: Dec. 25, 1986. **B-T:** R-R. **Ht.:** 6-2. **Wt.:** 190. **Signed:** Dominican Republic, 2004. **Signed by:** Rick Ragazzo.

After Joaquin posted a 1.61 ERA in the Rookie-level Dominican Summer League in 2004, the Giants highly anticipated his U.S. debut. They weren't disappointed, as he helped their Rookie-level Arizona League affiliate win a championship. Joaquin has an electric arm and one of the highest ceilings in the organization. His lightning arm speed yields consistent mid-90s fastballs, and in his final outing of the year he hit 98 eight times while striking out eight of the 10 batters he faced. He also throws a hard slider that reaches the upper 80s and has some depth, though it needs more consistency. Giants officials try to temper expectations for Joaquin by pointing out that he's still much more of a thrower than a pitcher at this point. His arm action and delivery need plenty of work to become more fluid and reduce the effort he puts into each pitch. Like all teenagers, he needs experience, and his changeup is very rudimentary. Joaquin is raw enough that a jump to full-season ball this year might be asking too much. If he makes significant progress with his offseason drills and throwing program, however, he could make the leap to low Class A.

Year	Club (League)	Class	W	L	ERA	G	GS	CG	SV	IP	H	R	ER	HR	BB	SO	AVG
2004	Giants (DSL)	R	6	1	1.62	14	13	0	0	61	51	21	11	0	28	44	.229
2005	Giants (AZL)	R	1	1	3.64	10	5	0	1	30	28	17	12	1	10	37	.241
MINOR LEAGUE TOTALS			7	2	2.27	24	18	0	1	91	79	38	23	1	38	81	.233

20 JON COUTLANGUS

LHP

Born: Oct. 21, 1980. **B-T:** L-L. **Ht.:** 6-1. **Wt.:** 180. **Drafted:** South Carolina, 2003 (19th round). **Signed by:** Dick Tidrow.

Coutlangus hadn't pitched since high school but always showed above-average arm strength as an above-average defender in center field. When the Giants moved him to the mound after he hit .194 in 2004, he began a quick ascent and earned a spot on the 40-man roster after the 2005 season. Coutlangus hit well in his pro debut but San Francisco didn't hesitate to make him a pitcher once he struggled at the plate, having considered the position change since signing him. His athleticism and raw arm strength helped him take to the new role. At his best last year, Coutlangus threw his fastball at 90-92 mph, though his velocity diminished as the workload got to him. He was able to pound the strike zone and wasn't afraid to pitch inside. Considering his inexperience, he had good command of his fastball, not only throwing it for strikes but also keeping it down. He tightened the slurvy breaking ball he had taught himself into a sweepy slider under the tutelage of San Jose pitching coach Trevor Wilson, and added a cutter. He still has plenty to learn about pitching and may need to cut down his repertoire, which also includes a curveball and changeup. Coutlangus will pitch in Double-A in 2006.

Year	Club (League)	Class	W	L	ERA	G	GS	CG	SV	IP	H	R	ER	HR	BB	SO	AVG
2004	Giants (AZL)	R	0	0	0.00	1	0	0	0	1	1	0	0	0	0	0	.250
2005	San Jose (Cal)	A	4	0	3.04	50	0	0	3	77	64	27	26	3	29	79	.234
MINOR LEAGUE TOTALS			4	0	3.00	51	0	0	3	78	65	27	26	3	29	79	.234

21 JOHN BOWKER

OF/1B

Born: July 8, 1983. **B-T:** L-L. **Ht.:** 6-2. **Wt.:** 190. **Drafted:** Long Beach State, 2004 (3rd round). **Signed by:** Lee Carballo.

Bowker didn't have a bad season in high Class A in 2005, but he didn't distinguish himself from the rest of his outfield competition in the system either. He has more raw power than most other San Francisco farmhands but hit just three homers in the first three months because he became too passive. The spacious right-field area in San Jose's Municipal Stadium also worked against him, as he hit just two homers at home all season. Bowker finished with a flurry, however, homering five times in his final eight games. He has premium lefthanded power, and the key to bringing it out is maintaining his aggressive approach. He had an injury-plagued career at Long Beach State, redshirting as a freshman because of problems with his right wrist, and still is gaining a feel for his all-out swing. He was too passive at the plate early during his poor start and got going once he started being aggressive again. Bowker's bat is his ticket. He's a below-average runner with decent outfield skills and a fringy arm. The Giants played him at first base in instructional league as a possible solution to their outfield logjam. Bowker needs a good spring training to earn a promotion to Double-A, especially if they keep him in the outfield for now.

Year	Club (League)	Class	AVG	G	AB	R	H	2B	3B	HR	RBI	BB	SO	SB	OBP	SLG
2004	Giants (AZL)	R	.512	10	43	14	22	7	1	2	11	7	11	1	.580	.860
	Salem-Keizer (NWL)	A	.323	31	127	23	41	9	2	4	16	8	25	1	.390	.520
2005	San Jose (Cal)	A	.267	121	464	66	124	27	1	13	67	36	108	3	.319	.414
MINOR LEAGUE TOTALS			.295	162	634	103	187	43	4	19	94	51	144	5	.352	.465

22 ALFREDO SIMON

RHP

Born: May 8, 1981. **B-T:** R-R. **Ht.:** 6-4. **Wt.:** 230. **Signed:** Dominican Republic, 1999. **Signed by:** Wil Tejada/Sal Agostinelli (Phillies).

The Phillies were developing Simon—formerly known as Carlos Cabrera and believed to be 21 months younger before baseball's sweeping visa reform in 2003—as a starter who could pitch off his fastball when they sent him to San Francisco in the July 2004 Felix Rodriguez trade. He had little success in the rotation after switching organizations, so the Giants moved him to the bullpen last year. They felt he'd be more aggressive in relief, and he responded by converting 12 of his first 13 save opportunities before faltering late in the season. Simon draws comparisons to a young Armando Benitez for his power fastball, which sits at 93-94 mph and reaches 97. But Simon's fastball lacks deception and he had a bad habit of nibbling as a starter. When he fell behind in the count, hitters sat on his heater with success. San Francisco has worked to improve his offspeed stuff since acquiring him. While Simon throws his changeup, curveball and slider for strikes, none is better than fringe average. He needs to continue making adjustments, such as pitching inside more often and throwing his offspeed offerings in fastball counts. He has fallen behind Brian Wilson in the organization's relief pecking order, not to mention Jeremy Accardo and Scott Munter. Simon must have a good spring to open 2006 in Triple-A.

Year	Club (League)	Class	W	L	ERA	G	GS	CG	SV	IP	H	R	ER	HR	BB	SO	AVG
2000	Phillies (DSL)	R	0	0	1.46	4	4	0	0	12	6	3	2	0	9	10	.136
2001	Phillies (GCL)	R	2	2	2.91	10	8	0	0	43	35	23	14	2	23	40	.220
2002	Batavia (NY-P)	A	9	2	3.59	15	14	0	0	90	79	44	36	5	46	77	.237
2003	Lakewood (SAL)	A	5	0	3.79	14	7	0	2	71	59	32	30	4	25	66	.224
2004	Clearwater (FSL)	A	7	9	3.27	22	21	4	0	135	121	58	49	13	38	107	.242
	San Jose (Cal)	A	1	2	5.68	6	6	0	0	32	44	24	20	7	12	21	.352
2005	Norwich (EL)	AA	3	8	5.03	43	9	0	19	91	104	54	51	6	24	60	.293
MINOR LEAGUE TOTALS			27	23	3.83	114	69	4	21	475	448	238	202	37	177	381	.252

23 BEN COPELAND   OF

Born: Dec. 12, 1983. **B-T:** L-L. **Ht.:** 6-1. **Wt.:** 195. **Drafted:** Pittsburgh, 2005 (4th round). **Signed by:** Sean O'Connor.

Though San Francisco didn't have a pick in the first three rounds of the 2005 draft, the player-development staff was pleased with the talent uncovered by the scouting department. The Giants' first choice came at No. 132 overall, and though offensive outfielders are a strength of the system, Copeland's tools were too good to pass up. So was his production. He led the Big East Conference in hitting, runs, hits, doubles, total bases, slugging percentage and stolen bases in 2005, and he set Pittsburgh single-season records for runs, hits, doubles and triples. He's the highest-drafted player out of the Panthers' resurgent program since 1985, when the Royals took Chris Jelic in the second round. Copeland's quick hands help him make quick adjustments and turn on good fastballs. With more experience he'll learn to trust his hands and wait better on breaking balls. He has solid gap power and is an above-average runner with good instincts on the bases and in the outfield. His arm is fringe average but more than playable in center, and staying in center will be the key to whether Copeland can be an everyday player. He'll report to low Class A for his first full season.

Year	Club (League)	Class	AVG	G	AB	R	H	2B	3B	HR	RBI	BB	SO	SB	OBP	SLG
2005	Giants (AZL)	R	.333	18	60	16	20	4	2	1	14	5	14	2	.388	.517
	Salem-Keizer (NWL)	A	.306	29	121	25	37	5	4	4	23	11	25	2	.364	.512
MINOR LEAGUE TOTALS			.315	47	181	41	57	9	6	5	37	16	39	4	.372	.514

24 JESUS REINA   LHP

Born: April 20, 1984. **B-T:** L-L. **Ht.:** 6-2. **Wt.:** 175. **Signed:** Venezuela, 2001. **Signed by:** Ciro Villalobos.

With the recent successes of Noah Lowry and Jack Taschner, the Giants have made a breakthrough with developing lefthanders. Eager to continue the trend, they protected some of their top lefty arms, such as Jon Coutlangus and Reina, on their 40-man roster this offseason. Reina has been on San Francisco's radar since he made his U.S. debut in 2003. The Venezuelan native has yet to produce consistently, but he has a live arm and stuff. His fastball sits in the low 90s when he's right, with some sink and excellent hard, late tailing action. Reina also has shown a solid-average changeup, and he throws both a slider and an occasional curveball. He showed his stuff in the Venezuelan League after the 2004 season, where his performance made the Giants worry they might lose him in the Rule 5 draft if he wasn't protected. After pitching 55 innings the previous winter, Reina came down with biceps tendinitis that limited him to 68 innings in 2005. An inconsistent release point hinders his control. A healthy Reina could move quickly, but he also has to show he can consistently get minor leaguers out.

Year	Club (League)	Class	W	L	ERA	G	GS	CG	SV	IP	H	R	ER	HR	BB	SO	AVG
2002	Giants (DSL)	R	5	5	2.96	18	15	1	0	91	71	41	30	2	35	90	.214
2003	Giants (AZL)	R	1	1	3.38	11	0	0	0	16	18	9	6	0	11	22	.286
	Salem-Keizer (NWL)	A	0	1	9.73	3	0	0	0	4	5	5	4	0	4	2	.417
2004	Salem-Keizer (NWL)	A	2	6	5.40	15	13	0	0	57	68	42	34	4	20	55	.298
2005	Fresno (PCL)	AAA	0	0	6.28	1	1	0	0	4	3	3	3	0	6	3	.200
	San Jose (Cal)	A	2	4	5.16	18	13	0	0	68	58	48	39	8	42	72	.227
MINOR LEAGUE TOTALS			10	17	4.35	66	42	1	0	240	223	148	116	14	118	244	.246

25 KELYN ACOSTA   RHP

Born: April 24, 1985. **B-T:** R-R. **Ht.:** 6-2. **Wt.:** 195. **Signed:** Dominican Republic, 2002. **Signed by:** Rick Ragazzo.

The Giants continue to try to find power arms in Latin America, with Felix Diaz their best success story in recent years. Most of San Francisco's better Latin pitchers, such as former big leaguers Livan Hernandez and Felix Rodriguez and current minor leaguers Alfredo Simon and Merkin Valdez, originally were signed by other organizations. The Giants liken Acosta to Simon in that he's a big, strong power arm with a body that should make him durable. Acosta has a delivery with some effort, but the result is a fastball that touched 99 mph in the past. He had an elbow injury that required Tommy John surgery in 2004 and returned in 2005 throwing in the low 90s. Acosta did work hard on his rehab and is still rediscovering his stuff. His secondary offerings remain inconsistent—his slider has shown promise—but San Francisco didn't hesitate to protect Acosta on the 40-man roster. This season is crucial for him, and he'll probably pitch at San Jose so the Giants can keep a close eye on him.

Year	Club (League)	Class	W	L	ERA	G	GS	CG	SV	IP	H	R	ER	HR	BB	SO	AVG
2002	Giants (DSL)	R	5	7	3.40	17	16	2	0	85	80	52	32	9	22	64	.235
2003	Giants (AZL)	R	3	4	4.40	10	8	0	0	45	56	28	22	0	16	35	.315
2004	Hagerstown (SAL)	A	4	3	4.41	10	10	0	0	51	61	31	25	5	23	37	.302
2005	Giants (AZL)	R	0	0	9.00	2	0	0	0	3	5	3	3	0	0	1	.417
	Augusta (SAL)	A	0	1	1.42	11	0	0	5	13	10	2	2	0	3	6	.222
MINOR LEAGUE TOTALS			12	15	3.85	50	34	2	5	196	212	116	84	14	64	143	.273

26 JUSTIN KNOEDLER C

Born: July 17, 1980. **B-T:** R-R. **Ht.:** 6-2. **Wt.:** 215. **Drafted:** Miami (Ohio), 2001 (5th round). **Signed by:** Steve Arnieri.

Knoedler reached the major leagues again in 2005. He's just 1-for-11 in brief tours of duty, but that's still quite an accomplishment for someone who began his pro career as a pitcher. Perhaps the Giants were onto something back then, because his bat still has a long way to go for him to become a big league regular. While he's protected on the 40-man roster, San Francisco also likes Eliezer Alfonzo, who's also on the 40-man. Knoedler, whose twin brother Jason is a Tigers minor league outfielder, gets the edge on the prospect list because he's a much better defender and is younger than Alfonzo. Knoedler has a strong body and plus arm strength that helped him throw out 38 percent of basestealers in Triple-A last year, and he did a better job at receiving in 2005. Furthermore, he improved his game-calling skills during his apprenticeship to veteran Mike Matheny when he was called up to the big leagues. Knoedler, who has shown decent power in the past, was relatively powerless in his first stab at Triple-A. He doesn't have much plate discipline or speed, so he offered little at the plate. He also hit just .226 in 53 Arizona Fall League at-bats. With a strong spring, Knoedler could become Matheny's full-time backup in 2006.

Year	Club (League)	Class	AVG	G	AB	R	H	2B	3B	HR	RBI	BB	SO	SB	OBP	SLG
2002	Hagerstown (SAL)	A	.257	86	280	32	72	16	2	5	33	37	56	6	.349	.382
2003	San Jose (Cal)	A	.257	101	354	48	91	25	2	10	43	35	78	13	.326	.424
2004	Norwich (EL)	AA	.274	115	409	64	112	28	3	9	47	32	98	5	.335	.423
	San Francisco (NL)	MLB	.000	1	1	0	0	0	0	0	0	0	0	0	.000	.000
2005	Norwich (EL)	AA	.300	4	10	2	3	0	0	0	2	0	2	2	.417	.300
	Fresno (PCL)	AAA	.272	85	287	35	78	19	1	4	32	26	61	5	.345	.387
	San Francisco (NL)	MLB	.100	8	10	0	1	0	0	0	0	0	1	0	.182	.100
MAJOR LEAGUE TOTALS			.091	9	11	0	1	0	0	0	0	0	1	0	.091	.091
MINOR LEAGUE TOTALS			.266	391	1340	181	356	88	8	28	155	132	293	31	.338	.406

27 BRIAN HORWITZ OF

Born: Nov. 7, 1982. **B-T:** R-R. **Ht.:** 6-1. **Wt.:** 180. **Signed:** NDFA/California, 2004. **Signed by:** Matt Nerland.

Horwitz isn't overly physical, hit just two home runs last season while playing a power position (right field), signed as a nondrafted free agent and lacks a plus tool. What he can do is hit, which he showed by winning the low Class A South Atlantic League batting title, then following it up with an MVP performance in the Cal League championship series. It was his second straight batting crown, as Horwitz topped the short-season Northwest League in his pro debut. Horwitz showed he could hit in college, batting .347 as a junior for California in 2003, but he didn't sign as a 26th-round pick of the Athletics after the season. Instead, he returned for his senior year and struggled, hitting just .288 with 14 extra-base hits. Horwitz has done nothing but hit since turning pro. He stays inside the ball well, covers the whole plate and has a knack for making contact, though his approach doesn't lend itself to power. His instincts stand out at the plate, on the basepaths and in right field, where's he's a solid-average defender with an average, accurate arm. Horwitz joined John Bowker and Jon Armitage as Giants outfielders who worked out as first basemen in instructional league. He'll start 2006 in high Class A and will keep rising as long as he hits.

Year	Club (League)	Class	AVG	G	AB	R	H	2B	3B	HR	RBI	BB	SO	SB	OBP	SLG
2004	Salem-Keizer (NWL)	A	.347	71	268	41	93	24	1	2	44	21	34	3	.407	.466
2005	Augusta (SAL)	A	.349	123	470	77	164	38	4	2	88	50	39	6	.415	.460
MINOR LEAGUE TOTALS			.348	194	738	118	257	62	5	4	132	71	73	9	.412	.462

28 SHAIRON MARTIS
RHP

Born: March 30, 1987. **B-T:** R-R. **Ht.:** 6-1. **Wt.:** 175. **Signed:** Curacao, 2004. **Signed by:** Philip Elhage.

The Giants' Arizona League club was one of the minors' most successful teams, posting a 39-17 record and winning the league title for the second consecutive year. The cast changed and was much younger last season, featuring righthanders Waldis Joaquin and Martis as teenage flamethrowers. Martis and slick-fielding AZL shortstop Sharlon Schoop both signed out of Curacao. Martis looks like the better prospect at this point because of his live arm and Schoop's suspect bat. Martis doesn't quite have Joaquin's arm, but he's not far off with a fastball that reaches the mid-90s. His curveball shows signs of being a solid pitch, and he throws a slider and a changeup as well. While his arm action is relatively smooth and fluid, his delivery has issues in terms of maintaining balance and incorporating his entire body. He'll have to polish his mechanics to earn a spot in low Class A to start the year.

Year	Club (League)	Class	W	L	ERA	G	GS	CG	SV	IP	H	R	ER	HR	BB	SO	AVG
2004	Giants (DSL)	R	4	3	1.79	14	12	0	0	70	55	15	14	2	17	63	.221
2005	Giants (AZL)	R	2	1	1.85	11	5	0	1	34	28	10	7	1	9	50	.226
MINOR LEAGUE TOTALS			6	4	1.81	25	17	0	1	104	83	25	21	3	26	113	.223

29 PAT MISCH
LHP

Born: Aug. 18, 1981. **B-T:** R-L. **Ht.:** 6-2. **Wt.:** 195. **Drafted:** Western Michigan, 2003 (7th round). **Signed by:** Steve Arnieri.

Misch seemed on the verge of breaking through into San Francisco, following Noah Lowry's lead as a finesse lefty who could use his savvy and average stuff to get big leaguers out. But in his second full pro season, Misch got hammered in Triple-A and had to retreat to Double-A to regain his footing. While Lowry is an obvious comparison as a homegrown lefty, Misch has different stuff, with his fastball, curveball, slider and changeup all grading out as average. His curve has become his best pitch, but he doesn't really have a plus offering. That, plus his tendency to nibble, was his undoing at Fresno. Giants officials say Misch was too stubborn for much of the season and didn't make adjustments in how he set up hitters, who figured out his pitch patterns and punished him. He recovered a bit in Double-A, but not enough to earn a spot on the 40-man roster. Misch made it through the Rule 5 draft but will have to earn San Francisco's trust again with a more successful stint in Triple-A this year.

Year	Club (League)	Class	W	L	ERA	G	GS	CG	SV	IP	H	R	ER	HR	BB	SO	AVG
2003	Salem-Keizer (NWL)	A	7	5	2.18	14	14	0	0	87	78	33	21	3	20	61	.247
2004	Norwich (EL)	AA	7	6	3.06	26	26	4	0	159	138	61	54	13	35	123	.243
2005	Fresno (PCL)	AAA	3	9	6.35	19	19	1	0	102	135	80	72	18	40	69	.325
	Norwich (EL)	AA	4	2	3.52	9	9	1	0	61	63	25	24	7	7	43	.270
MINOR LEAGUE TOTALS			21	22	3.76	68	68	6	0	409	414	199	171	41	102	296	.270

30 DAVID MAROUL
SS/3B

Born: Feb. 15, 1983. **B-T:** R-R. **Ht.:** 6-2. **Wt.:** 210. **Drafted:** Texas, 2005 (23rd round). **Signed by:** Tom Korenek.

Maroul became the latest in a recent line of surprise Most Outstanding Players at the College World Series. He somewhat resembles Astros outfielder Charlton Jimerson, the 2001 CWS MOP for Miami, as a college senior draft from a prominent program who nevertheless remains raw and toolsy. Maroul's best tool is his arm, and if he doesn't succeed in the field, he could follow in the footsteps of Jon Coutlangus and move to the mound. He threw in the low 90s in workouts at Texas. He has a bit more going for him as a position player than Coutlangus, though, starting with easy power. While Maroul makes inconsistent contact because of his long swing, the ball jumps off his bat. He's also one of the best defensive infielders in the system already, as his arm plays well at either spot on the left side of the infield. He's the best defensive third baseman in the organization, but he moved to shortstop at short-season Salem-Keizer to accommodate Pablo Sandoval. Maroul looked solid at short during the summer and again in instructional league. He has soft hands and enough agility for the Giants to continue playing him at shortstop this season, likely in low Class A.

Year	Club (League)	Class	AVG	G	AB	R	H	2B	3B	HR	RBI	BB	SO	SB	OBP	SLG
2005	Giants (AZL)	R	.345	8	29	6	10	5	0	1	5	1	7	0	.355	.621
	Salem-Keizer (NWL)	A	.263	44	175	20	46	8	1	5	27	4	61	0	.288	.406
MINOR LEAGUE TOTALS			.275	52	204	26	56	13	1	6	32	5	68	0	.298	.436

SEATTLE
MARINERS

BY JIM CALLIS

Bill Bavasi's second year on the job as Seattle general manager wasn't much better than the first. After the Mariners bottomed out in 2004 by going 63-99—their first last-place finish since 1992 and worst record since 1983—they didn't stand pat. Attempting to upgrade the American League's worst offense, they spent $114 million on free agents Adrian Beltre and Richie Sexson.

Sexson performed as expected in 2005, but Beltre was a disappointment and so were the Mariners again. They scored one more run than they did in 2004 and went 69-93, finishing in the cellar in consecutive years for the first time ever. Seattle's record-tying 116-win season in 2001 seems much more distant than five years in the past.

There were a few silver linings, almost all of them provided by the farm system. Ultrahyped **Felix Hernandez** lived up to his billing, becoming one of the best pitchers in the major leagues the instant he set foot in Seattle on Aug. 4. Ten of his 12 outings were quality starts, and he finished 4-4, 2.67 with 77 strikeouts in 84 innings. And he did all that at age 19.

After hitting .327 in the minors and .397 in a September 2004 callup, Jeremy Reed batted a soft .254. But he proved he could handle center field at Safeco Field, which had been in question, and his bat should come around. Yuniesky Betancourt signed in January and reached Seattle in July. Multiple veteran scouts called him the best defensive shortstop they ever had seen.

The bad news, as if there already wasn't enough, is that the system can't offer any more immediate hope. A series of poor drafts has caught up to the Mariners, who forfeited four first-round picks and failed to sign another (John Mayberry Jr., who became the 19th overall choice in 2005) from 2000-04. Their decision to take Michael Garciaparra 36th overall in 2001, after he barely played as a high school senior because of a football knee injury, remains one of the most puzzling choices in recent draft history. Signed for $2 million, Nomar's little brother has yet to rise above high Class A.

Since taking Alex Rodriguez with the No. 1 overall pick in 1993, the Mariners have drafted and signed exactly two players who performed well in the majors in 2005. Those two, Jason Varitek (first round, 1994) and Brian Fuentes (25th round, 1995), were traded before they were big league-ready and didn't blossom until after they left Seattle.

If not for their efforts on the international market, the Mariners' situation would be far worse. Five of their top eight prospects come from five different nations: catcher Kenji Johjima (Japan), outfielder Chris Snelling (Australia), infielder Asdrubal Cabrera (Venezuela), righthander Emiliano Fruto (Colombia) and outfielder Shin-Soo Choo (Korea).

Seattle hasn't made many upgrades this offseason. Signing Johjima filled a hole, but Bavasi's next move was to get Carl Everett. A third-straight last-place finish looms as a distinct possibility.

TOP 30 PROSPECTS

1. Jeff Clement, c	16. Ryan Feierabend, lhp
2. Adam Jones, of/ss	17. Cesar Jimenez, lhp
3. Kenji Johjima, c	18. Bobby Livingston, lhp
4. Chris Snelling, of	19. Sebastien Boucher, of
5. Matt Tuiasosopo, ss	20. T.J.Bohn, of
6. Asdrubal Cabrera, ss/2b	21. Rene Rivera, c
7. Shin-Soo Choo, of	22. Travis Blackley, lhp
8. Emiliano Fruto, rhp	23. Renee Cortez, rhp
9. Clint Nageotte, rhp	24. Michael Wilson, of
10. Rob Johnson, c	25. Francisco Cruceta, rhp
11. Wladimir Balentien, of	26. Yung-Chi Chen, 3b/2b
12. Michael Saunders, of	27. Oswaldo Navarro, 2b/ss
13. Yorman Bazardo, rhp	28. George Sherrill, lhp
14. Luis Valbuena, 2b	29. Bryan LaHair, 1b
15. Stephen Kahn, rhp	30. Anthony Varvaro, rhp

ORGANIZATION OVERVIEW

General manager: Bill Bavasi. **Farm director:** Frank Mattox. **Scouting director:** Bob Fontaine.

2005 PERFORMANCE

Class	Team	League	W	L	Pct.	Finish*	Manager
Majors	Seattle	American	69	93	.426	12th (14)	Mike Hargrove
Triple-A	Tacoma Rainiers	Pacific Coast	80	64	.556	t-2nd (16)	Dan Rohn
Double-A	San Antonio Missions	Texas	76	64	.543	2nd (8)	Dave Brundage
High A	Inland Empire 66ers	California	58	82	.414	9th (10)	Daren Brown
Low A	Wisconsin Timber Rattlers	Midwest	76	63	.547	2nd (14)	Scott Steinmann
Short-season	Everett AquaSox	Northwest	42	34	.553	3rd (8)	Pedro Grifol
Rookie	AZL Mariners	Arizona	27	29	.482	t-5th (9)	Dana Williams
OVERALL 2005 MINOR LEAGUE RECORD			396	359	.525	7th (30)	

*Finish in overall standings (No. of teams in league).

ORGANIZATION LEADERS

BATTING
*Minimum 250 at-bats
*AVG	Boucher, Sebastien, I. Empire/Wisconsin	.340
R	Wilson, Michael, Wisconsin	93
H	Bohn, T.J., San Antonio/Tacoma	161
TB	Balentien, Wladimir, Inland Empire	272
2B	Balentien, Wladimir, Inland Empire	38
3B	Cabrera, Asdrubal, I. Empire/Tacoma/Wis.	10
HR	Balentien, Wladimir, Inland Empire	25
RBI	LaHair, Bryan, Inland Empire	113
BB	Nunez, Abraham, Tacoma	71
SO	Balentien, Wladimir, Inland Empire	160
SB	Bubela, Jaime, San Antonio	40
*OBP	Boucher, Sebastien, Inland Empire/Wisconsin	.434
*SLG	Balentien, Wladimir, Inland Empire	.553

PITCHING
#Minimum 75 innings
W	Livingston, Bobby, Everett/S.A./Tacoma	14
L	Jensen, Aaron, Wisconsin	13
#ERA	Key, Chris, Inland Empire/S.A./Tacoma	1.78
G	Green, Sean, San Antonio/Tacoma	54
CG	Lorraine, Andrew, Tacoma	2
SV	Kida, Masao, Tacoma	22
IP	Mackintosh, Jason, Inland Empire	180
BB	Rivera, Mumba, Inland Empire/Wisconsin	76
SO	Mackintosh, Jason, Inland Empire	141

BEST TOOLS

Best Hitter for Average	Chris Snelling
Best Power Hitter	Jeff Clement
Best Strike-Zone Discipline	Chris Snelling
Fastest Baserunner	Sebastien Boucher
Best Athlete	Adam Jones
Best Fastball	Stephen Kahn
Best Curveball	Emiliano Fruto
Best Slider	Clint Nageotte
Best Changeup	Emiliano Fruto
Best Control	Bobby Livingston
Best Defensive Catcher	Rene Rivera
Best Defensive Infielder	Oswaldo Navarro
Best Infield Arm	Asdrubal Cabrera
Best Defensive Outfielder	T.J. Bohn
Best Outfield Arm	Adam Jones

PROJECTED 2009 LINEUP

Catcher	Jeff Clement
First Base	Richie Sexson
Second Base	Jose Lopez
Third Base	Adrian Beltre
Shortstop	Yuniesky Betancourt
Left Field	Adam Jones
Center Field	Jeremy Reed
Right Field	Ichiro Suzuki
Designated Hitter	Chris Snelling

No. 1 Starter	Felix Hernandez
No. 2 Starter	Rafael Soriano
No. 3 Starter	Jesse Foppert
No. 4 Starter	Joel Pineiro
No. 5 Starter	Emiliano Fruto
Closer	Clint Nageotte

LAST YEAR'S TOP 20 PROSPECTS

1. Felix Hernandez, rhp
2. Jeremy Reed, of
3. Shin-Soo Choo, of
4. Clint Nageotte, rhp
5. Matt Tuiasosopo, ss
6. Travis Blackley, lhp
7. Chris Snelling, of
8. Adam Jones, ss
9. Yuniesky Betancourt, ss/2b
10. Wladimir Balentien, of
11. Asdrubal Cabrera, ss/2b
12. Jamal Strong, of
13. George Sherrill, lhp
14. Greg Dobbs, 3b
15. Justin Leone, inf/of
16. Cha Seung Baek, rhp
17. Ryan Feierabend, lhp
18. Cesar Jimenez, lhp
19. Mike Morse, ss
20. Rich Dorman, rhp

TOP PROSPECTS OF THE DECADE

Year	Player, Pos.	2005 Org.
1996	Jose Cruz Jr.	Dodgers
1997	Jose Cruz Jr.	Dodgers
1998	Ryan Anderson, lhp	Brewers
1999	Ryan Anderson, lhp	Brewers
2000	Ryan Anderson, lhp	Brewers
2001	Ryan Anderson, lhp	Brewers
2002	Ryan Anderson, lhp	Brewers
2003	Rafael Soriano, rhp	Mariners
2004	Felix Hernandez, rhp	Mariners
2005	Felix Hernandez, rhp	Mariners

TOP DRAFT PICKS OF THE DECADE

Year	Player, Pos.	2005 Org.
1996	Gil Meche, rhp	Mariners
1997	Ryan Anderson, lhp	Brewers
1998	Matt Thornton, lhp	Mariners
1999	Ryan Christianson, c	Mariners
2000	Sam Hays, lhp (4th round)	Out of baseball
2001	Michael Garciaparra, ss	Mariners
2002	*John Mayberry Jr., of	Rangers
2003	Adam Jones, ss/rhp	Mariners
2004	Matt Tuiasosopo, ss	Mariners
2005	Jeff Clement, c	Mariners

*Did not sign.

ALL-TIME LARGEST BONUSES

Ichiro Suzuki, 2000	$5,000,000
Jeff Clement, 2005	$3,400,000
Matt Tuiasosopo, 2004	$2,290,000
Ryan Anderson, 1997	$2,175,000
Ryan Christianson, 1999	$2,100,000

MINOR LEAGUE DEPTH CHART

Seattle Mariners

Rank: **27**

STRENGTH: Catcher. The addition of Japanese veteran Kenji Johjima bought 2005 first-rounder Jeff Clement some time.

WEAKNESS: Starting pitching. The Mariners' talent fell off a cliff after graduating Felix Hernandez.

Depth charts prepared by **John Manuel** *and* **Chris Kline**. *Numbers in parentheses indicate prospect rankings.*

LF
Chris Snelling (4)
Jaime Bubela
Brent Johnson
Casey Craig

CF
Adam Jones (2)
Sebastien Boucher (19)
T.J. Bohn (20)
Jamal Strong

RF
Shin-Soo Choo (7)
Wladimir Balentien (11)
Michael Saunders (12)
Michael Wilson (24)
Chris Colton
Eddy Hernandez

3B
Matt Tuiasosopo (5)
Jesus Guzman
Hunter Brown
Erick Monzon

SS
Asdrubal Cabrera (6)
Oswaldo Navarro (27)
Michael Garciaparra

2B
Luis Valbuena (14)
Yung-Chi Chen (26)

1B
Bryan LaHair (29)
Jeff Flaig

C
Jeff Clement (1)
Kenji Johjima (3)
Rob Johnson (10)
Rene Rivera (21)

RHP

Starters	Relievers
Emiliano Fruto (8)	Clint Nageotte (9)
Yorman Bazardo (13)	Stephen Kahn (15)
Francisco Cruceta (25)	Renee Cortez (23)
Anthony Varvaro (30)	Scott Atchison
Aaron Jensen	Jon Lockwood
Jon Huber	Mike Flannery
Jorge Campillo	Edgar Guaramato
Rich Dorman	Mark Lowe

LHP

Starters	Relievers
Ryan Feierabend (16)	Cesar Jimenez (17)
Bobby Livingston (18)	George Sherrill (28)
Travis Blackley (22)	Erik O'Flaherty
Justin Thomas	
Tom Oldham	
Robert Rohrbaugh	
Steve Uhlmansiek	
Harold Williams	

DRAFT ANALYSIS

2005

Best Pro Debut: Drafted No. 3 overall for his offense, C Jeff Clement (1) didn't disappoint, hitting .319-6-20 in 30 games in low Class A. 1B Andy Hargrove (47) earned all-star recognition in the Rookie-level Arizona League by batting .314-3-25 with a .464 on-base percentage.

Best Athlete: OF/3B Bryan Sabatella (9) moves well for a 6-foot-4, 220-pounder and has intriguing power, arm and speed tools. Draft-and-follow OF Michael Saunders (11 in 2004) has better all-around tools and has been compared to Shawn Green. He hit .270-7-39 as an 18-year-old in the short-season Northwest League.

Best Pure Hitter: Clement made great strides as a hitter in 2005, beginning to use the entire field while showing improved discipline and plate coverage.

Best Raw Power: Clement had more raw power than any college player available in the draft. He still holds the national high school career home run record with 75, and his 46 longballs at Southern California were the second-most in the storied program's history behind Mark McGwire's 54.

Fastest Runner: Sabatella rates a 55 on the 20-80 scouting scale. The Mariners didn't draft much speed.

Best Defensive Player: 3B Ronnie Prettyman (10) has fairly ordinary physical tools, but his exceptional instincts allow him to make all the plays. Clement's defense took a step forward last year under the tutelage of Trojans volunteer coach Chad Kreuter, a former big leaguer.

Best Fastball: RHP Stephen Kahn (5) pitched at 95 mph and topped out at 97-98 with explosive life when the Mariners moved him to the bullpen as a pro. His fastball command still needs work. RHP

Clement

Anthony Varvaro (12) had a 92-94 mph heater before he succumbed to Tommy John surgery in May.

Best Breaking Ball: Varvaro showed a power curveball before blowing out his elbow. Kahn has a hard curve, while LHP Justin Thomas (4) has the best slider.

Most Intriguing Background: Hargrove's father Mike manages the Mariners and was the 1974 American League rookie of the year. RHP Brett Bannister's (19) father Floyd was the No. 1 overall pick in the June 1976 draft and an all-star for Seattle in 1982. His brother Brian pitches in the Mets system. Unsigned RHP John Holdzkom's (15) brother Lincoln pitches in the Marlins system.

Closest To The Majors: The signing of Japanese free agent Kenji Johjima buys him time, but Clement should be ready to catch in Seattle within two years.

Best Late-Round Pick: The Mariners again used their 12th-rounder on a pitcher who needed Tommy John surgery. In 2004 it was Steve Uhlmansiek, and this time it was Varvaro, who would have gone in the second or third round if healthy.

The One Who Got Away: RHP Lance Lynn (6) could become a two-way star at Mississippi and develop into a higher draft pick by 2008.

Assessment: Clement was the Mariners' earliest draft pick since 1995 (third, Jose Cruz Jr.). Seattle forfeited its second- and third-rounders as free-agent compensation, but made up for it by signing Saunders and Varvaro.

2004 The Mariners didn't have picks in the first two rounds, and they spent $2.29 million to buy SS Matt Tuiasosopo (3) away from college football. **GRADE:** C+

2003 Many teams would have used OF/SS Adam Jones (1) on the mound, but Seattle couldn't be more pleased with his development. LHP Ryan Feierabend (3) is a quality starter prospect in a system that has few. **GRADE:** C+

2002 A disaster. The Mariners failed to sign OFs John Mayberry Jr. (1) and Eddy Martinez-Esteve (3), with Mayberry and OF Travis Buck (23) becoming first-rounders in 2005. OF T.J. Bohn (30) is as good as this crop gets. **GRADE:** F

2001 SS Michael Garciaparra was the most stunning first-round pick in recent draft history. C Rene Rivera (2) and LHP Bobby Livingston (4) are low-level prospects. **GRADE:** D

Draft analysis prepared by Jim Callis. Numbers in parentheses indicate draft rounds.

JEFF
CLEMENT

C

BILL MITCHELL

Born: Aug. 21, 1983.
Ht.: 6-1. **Wt.:** 215.
Bats: L. **Throws:** R.
Drafted: Southern California, 2005
(1st round).
Signed by: Greg Whitworth.

In 2002, Clement had a chance to become the first Iowa high school player ever drafted in the first round. But his lackluster performance at the Perfect Game predraft showcase in mid-May dropped his stock enough that he wasn't going to give up on his commitment to Southern California. Considered unsignable at that point, he went in the 12th round to the Twins. After the draft, Clement finished his prep career by leading Marshalltown to the Iowa state 4-A title and breaking Drew Henson's national high school career home run record with 75. With the Trojans, he set a school freshman record with 21 homers and hit 46 in three years, eight short of Mark McGwire's career mark. With the No. 3 overall pick in June—their earliest choice in a decade—the Mariners were zeroing in on Long Beach State shortstop Troy Tulowitzki. But the weekend before the draft, Seattle decided it already was deep in shortstops, switched gears and opted for Clement. He held out until late July before signing for $3.4 million, a club record for a drafted player. It took him a couple of weeks to get his bat going, but he finished the summer on a 25-for-68 (.368) tear that included five homers, then played well in the Arizona Fall League.

Clement has been known for his light-tower power since he was chasing Henson's record in high school. Very few catchers in baseball history can match his lefthanded pop, and he should be a more complete hitter than the more recent candidates, such as Todd Hundley and Mickey Tettleton. After batting just .298 and .293 in his first two seasons at USC, Clement made some adjustments as a junior and improved to .348. He now has a shorter and sounder swing, stays inside the ball better and generates good backspin. He also tightened his strike zone and covered more of the plate. He's content to use the entire field because he realizes he doesn't have to pull pitches to smoke them out of the park. His bat always has been ahead of his defense, but he made significant strides behind the plate last year as well after working with USC volunteer assistant Chad Kreuter, a former big leaguer who's also the son-in-law of Trojans head coach Mike Gillespie. Clement has put to rest any doubts that he can stay behind the plate. He has average arm strength, his receiving and game-calling skills are fine and he blocks balls well. He has the leadership ability desired of a catcher and the work ethic to get better.

Clement, who threw out 29 percent of basestealers in his pro debut, can improve his throwing. He needs to refine his footwork and transfer because his release gets long, costing him time and accuracy. He won't be a Gold Glover, though he should be more than adequate defensively. He's going to accumulate some strikeouts, but that's an acceptable trade-off for his power, and he'll also draw his share of walks. Typical for a catcher, he's a below-average runner.

After signing Japanese all-star Kenji Johjima in November, the Mariners don't need to rush Clement. But Clement, who has a higher ceiling, could be ready toward the end of 2007. He'll probably open the year at high Class A Inland Empire and could be pushing for a promotion to Double-A San Antonio by midseason.

Year	Club (League)	Class	AVG	G	AB	R	H	2B	3B	HR	RBI	BB	SO	SB	OBP	SLG
2005	Wisconsin (Mid)	A	.319	30	113	17	36	5	0	6	20	12	25	1	.386	.522
MINOR LEAGUE TOTALS			.319	30	113	17	36	5	0	6	20	12	25	1	.386	.522

2 ADAM JONES
OF/SS

Born: Aug. 1, 1985. **B-T:** R-R. **Ht.:** 6-2. **Wt.:** 180. **Drafted:** HS—San Diego, 2003 (1st round supplemental). **Signed by:** Joe Boehringer.

Many clubs wanted to make Jones a pitcher after he hit 96 mph in high school, but the Mariners granted his wish to play every day after signing him for $925,000. Jones was developing nicely as a shortstop, but Yuniesky Betancourt's fielding wizardry led to a change in plans. Seattle had Jones play center field in the Arizona Fall League and will keep him there. He reminded the Mariners a lot of Mike Cameron when he changed positions. Both are premium athletes with plus speed, solid power and strong arms. Jones improved with the bat in 2005, showing more discipline and consistency. His arm is still a cannon, and he could play shortstop if needed. Jones can get out of control at the plate when he tries to do too much. Breaking balls still can give him trouble. Jones hit well in Double-A last year, but Seattle may send him back there because he pressed at the plate while adjusting to center field in the AFL. If Jeremy Reed doesn't start hitting, Jones could make a play for his job in 2007.

Year	Club (League)	Class	AVG	G	AB	R	H	2B	3B	HR	RBI	BB	SO	SB	OBP	SLG
2003	Mariners (AZL)	R	.284	28	109	18	31	5	1	0	8	5	19	5	.368	.349
	Everett (NWL)	A	.462	3	13	2	6	1	0	0	4	1	3	0	.467	.538
2004	Wisconsin (Mid)	A	.267	130	510	76	136	23	7	11	72	33	124	8	.314	.404
2005	Inland Empire (Cal)	A	.295	68	271	43	80	20	5	8	46	29	64	4	.374	.494
	San Antonio (TL)	AA	.298	63	228	33	68	10	3	7	20	22	48	9	.365	.461
MINOR LEAGUE TOTALS			.284	292	1131	172	321	59	16	26	150	90	258	26	.346	.433

3 KENJI JOHJIMA
C

Born: June 8, 1976. **B-T:** R-R. **Ht.:** 6-0. **Wt.:** 200. **Signed:** Japan, 2005. **Signed by:** Yasushi Yamamoto/Ted Heid/Bob Engle/Hide Sueyoshi.

The first Japanese catcher to sign with a U.S. team, Johjima agreed to a three-year, $16.5 million contract in November. A perennial all-star and Gold Glover in Japan, he was the Pacific League MVP in 2003 and batted .378 as Japan won a bronze medal in the 2004 Olympics. Johjima should be a solid all-around catcher in the States. He controls the strike zone well and should produce for average as well as gap power. Defensively, he's an agile receiver with good catch-and-throw skills. He loves to run a pitching staff, and he's learning English quickly. Having polished his game during nine seasons in the Japanese majors, Johjima has no glaring flaws. He's a below-average runner, but so are most catchers. He doesn't draw many walks because he puts the ball in play so easily. He missed time in 2005 with shoulder tendinitis and hairline fracture in his fibula, though neither is a long-term concern. Johjima won't make an Ichiro-like impact, but he should fill a position at which Seattle has gotten little production for years.

Year	Club (League)	Class	AVG	G	AB	R	H	2B	3B	HR	RBI	BB	SO	SB	OBP	SLG
1995	Fukuoka (PL)	JAP	.167	12	12	2	2	0	0	0	1	1	4	0	.231	.167
1996	Fukuoka (PL)	JAP	.241	17	58	5	14	2	0	4	9	3	9	1	.290	.483
1997	Fukuoka (PL)	JAP	.308	120	432	49	133	24	2	15	68	22	62	6	.343	.477
1998	Fukuoka (PL)	JAP	.251	122	395	53	99	19	0	16	58	27	67	5	.309	.420
1999	Fukuoka (PL)	JAP	.306	135	493	65	151	33	1	17	77	31	61	6	.356	.481
2000	Fukuoka (PL)	JAP	.310	84	303	38	94	22	2	9	50	27	48	10	.377	.485
2001	Fukuoka (PL)	JAP	.258	140	534	63	138	18	0	31	95	31	55	9	.305	.466
2002	Fukuoka (PL)	JAP	.293	115	416	60	122	18	0	25	74	30	41	8	.348	.517
2003	Fukuoka (PL)	JAP	.330	140	551	101	182	39	2	34	119	51	50	9	.399	.593
2004	Fukuoka (PL)	JAP	.338	116	498	91	144	25	1	36	91	49	45	6	.432	.655
2005	Fukuoka (PL)	JAP	.309	116	411	70	127	22	4	24	57	33	32	3	.381	.557
TOTALS			.299	1117	4031	597	1206	222	12	211	699	307	474	63	.360	.517

4 CHRIS SNELLING
OF

Born: Dec. 3, 1981. **B-T:** L-L. **Ht.:** 5-10. **Wt.:** 205. **Signed:** Australia, 1999. **Signed by:** Barry Holland.

The story never changes with Snelling. In 2005, he hit .370 to raise his career average to .323. He also tore the meniscus in his left knee in spring training, costing him the first two weeks of the year, and sprained the same knee shortly after a big league callup in August, ending his season. Former Seattle manager Lou Piniella wanted Snelling on his Opening Day roster in 2001—when he was 19—and he has been ready to hit in the majors for years. His quick hands, discerning eye and tremendous instincts have allowed him to rake everywhere he ever has played. He has solid gap power and average arm strength. Snelling hasn't had a healthy season since his 1999 pro debut, and he has played in more than 72 games in a season just once. His litany of injuries includes a broken left hand and ligament damage in his left wrist (2000), a stress fracture in his right ankle (2001), a broken right thumb and blown-out left knee (2002), more problems with his left knee (2003) and a deep bone bruise in his right wrist (2004). Knee surgeries have left him with slightly below-average speed, relegating him to an outfield corner, where his 15-20 homer power is fringy. If Snelling can stay healthy, he'd be an asset in the Seattle lineup. But that's such a big "if" that the Mariners can't count on him. They signed Carl Everett this offseason, meaning Snelling will have to start the year at Triple-A Tacoma.

Year	Club (League)	Class	AVG	G	AB	R	H	2B	3B	HR	RBI	BB	SO	SB	OBP	SLG
1999	Everett (NWL)	A	.306	69	265	46	81	15	3	10	50	33	24	8	.388	.498
2000	Wisconsin (Mid)	A	.305	72	259	44	79	9	5	9	56	34	34	7	.386	.483
2001	San Bernardino (Cal)	A	.336	114	450	90	151	29	10	7	73	45	63	12	.418	.491
2002	San Antonio (TL)	AA	.326	23	89	10	29	9	2	1	12	12	11	5	.429	.506
	Seattle (AL)	MLB	.148	8	27	2	4	0	0	1	3	2	4	0	.207	.259
2003	San Antonio (TL)	AA	.333	47	186	24	62	12	2	3	25	8	30	1	.371	.468
	Tacoma (PCL)	AAA	.269	18	67	11	18	2	0	3	10	5	12	1	.333	.433
2004	Mariners (AZL)	R	.313	10	32	8	10	4	1	0	9	7	3	1	.476	.500
2005	Tacoma (PCL)	AAA	.370	65	246	50	91	17	2	8	46	36	43	2	.452	.553
	Seattle (AL)	MLB	.276	15	29	4	8	2	0	1	1	5	2	0	.382	.448
MAJOR LEAGUE TOTALS			.214	23	56	6	12	2	0	2	4	7	6	0	.302	.357
MINOR LEAGUE TOTALS			.327	418	1594	283	521	97	25	41	281	180	220	37	.406	.496

5 MATT TUIASOSOPO SS

Born: May 10, 1986. **B-T:** R-R. **Ht.:** 6-2. **Wt.:** 210. **Drafted:** HS—Woodinville, Wash., 2004 (3rd round). **Signed by:** Phil Geisler.

The Mariners didn't have picks in the first two rounds of the 2004 draft, so they swung for the fences with their third-rounder. They took Tuiasosopo and bought him out of a football scholarship to play quarterback at Washington with a $2.29 million bonus. Both his father Manu and brother Marques have played in the NFL. With his bat speed and strength, Tuiasosopo projects as a middle-of-the-order run producer. He handled low Class A well as a teenager. A fine all-around athlete, he has good speed and a strong arm. He also shows soft hands on defense. Though Seattle has kept Tuiasosopo at shortstop so far, scouts don't think he has the actions or quickness to stay there. He'll slow down as he fills out, eventually forcing a move to third base or the outfield. He hasn't reached much of his power potential yet, as he has an inside-out swing and has a ways to go with his pitch recognition. He'll continue to play shortstop in high Class A. Adrian Beltre's contract runs through 2009, buying Tuiasosopo plenty of time to develop.

Year	Club (League)	Class	AVG	G	AB	R	H	2B	3B	HR	RBI	BB	SO	SB	OBP	SLG
2004	Mariners (AZL)	R	.412	20	68	18	28	5	2	4	12	13	14	1	.528	.721
	Everett (NWL)	A	.248	29	101	18	25	6	1	2	14	10	36	4	.336	.386
2005	Wisconsin (Mid)	A	.276	107	409	72	113	21	3	6	45	44	96	8	.359	.386
MINOR LEAGUE TOTALS			.287	156	578	108	166	32	6	12	71	67	146	13	.377	.426

6 ASDRUBAL CABRERA SS/2B

Born: Nov. 13, 1985. **B-T:** B-R. **Ht.:** 6-0. **Wt.:** 170. **Signed:** Venezuela, 2002. **Signed by:** Emilio Carrasquel.

An all-star shortstop in each of his first two seasons, Cabrera ceded the position to Matt Tuiasosopo at low Class A Wisconsin and dazzled at second base. Promoted to high Class A when Adam Jones moved to Double-A, Cabrera returned to shortstop and didn't miss a beat. He finished the season as Tacoma's starting shortstop in the Pacific Coast League playoffs. Managers rated Cabrera the best defensive second baseman in the Midwest League, and some voted for him at shortstop. He's an acrobat with plus range, arm strength, hands and instincts. Offensively, he's a switch-hitter who makes contact and has some pop. His speed is average. Cabrera can get too aggressive at the plate and needs to draw more walks to bat near the top of a lineup. Some scouts wonder how much offense he'll provide in the majors. His bat speed is just average, and he doesn't stand out in terms of on-base skills, power or basestealing ability. Seattle wants to spread out its shortstop prospects, so Cabrera could return to Triple-A at age 20. He'll eventually have to beat out Yuniesky Betancourt at shortstop or Jose Lopez at second base to start for the Mariners.

Year	Club (League)	Class	AVG	G	AB	R	H	2B	3B	HR	RBI	BB	SO	SB	OBP	SLG
2003	Aguirre (VSL)	R	.283	55	198	31	56	12	4	0	29	16	31	5	.367	.384
2004	Everett (NWL)	A	.272	63	239	44	65	16	3	5	41	21	43	7	.330	.427
2005	Wisconsin (Mid)	A	.318	51	192	26	61	12	3	4	30	30	32	2	.407	.474
	Inland Empire (Cal)	A	.284	55	225	31	64	15	6	1	26	15	47	3	.325	.418
	Tacoma (PCL)	AAA	.217	6	23	4	5	0	1	0	3	1	4	0	.250	.304
MINOR LEAGUE TOTALS			.286	230	877	136	251	55	17	10	129	83	157	17	.353	.422

7 SHIN-SOO CHOO OF

Born: July 13, 1982. **B-T:** L-L. **Ht.:** 5-11. **Wt.:** 178. **Signed:** Korea, 2000. **Signed by:** Jae Lee/Jim Colborn.

The MVP of the 2000 World Junior Championships as a two-way star who dominated more as a pitcher, Choo became a full-time outfielder after signing for $1.335 million. He breezed through the minors until 2005, when he scuffled in Triple-A. He did play in his third straight Futures Game, homering off Toronto's Zach Jackson. Choo still offers an impressive array of tools. He consistently has hit for average, and the Mariners continue to believe his strength will translate into 20-25 homers annually. He has good speed and the instincts to steal bases. He led Pacific Coast League outfielders with 24 assists, and managers rated his arm as the league's best. A natural right fielder, he moved to left in 2005 because of Ichiro's presence in Seattle. Scouts from other organizations aren't as optimistic about Choo's power. They think his inside-out swing and approach will limit him to 10-15 homers per year, which isn't enough for a regular corner outfielder. He tried to hit for more power last season and got too pull-conscious. Choo will have to repeat Triple-A, though he's still just 23. In the fight to become Seattle's left fielder, Chris Snelling is a better hitter but Choo is a more well-rounded player.

Year	Club (League)	Class	AVG	G	AB	R	H	2B	3B	HR	RBI	BB	SO	SB	OBP	SLG
2001	Mariners (AZL)	R	.302	51	199	51	60	10	10	4	35	34	49	12	.420	.513
	Wisconsin (Mid)	A	.462	3	13	1	6	0	0	0	3	1	3	2	.533	.462
2002	Wisconsin (Mid)	A	.302	119	420	69	127	24	8	6	48	70	98	34	.417	.440
	San Bernardino (Cal)	A	.308	11	39	14	12	5	1	1	9	9	9	3	.460	.564
2003	Inland Empire (Cal)	A	.286	110	412	62	118	18	13	9	55	44	84	18	.365	.459
2004	San Antonio (TL)	AA	.315	132	517	89	163	17	7	15	84	56	97	40	.382	.462
2005	Tacoma (PCL)	AAA	.282	115	429	73	121	21	5	11	54	69	97	20	.382	.431
	Seattle (AL)	MLB	.056	10	18	1	1	0	0	0	1	3	4	0	.190	.056
MAJOR LEAGUE TOTALS			.056	10	18	1	1	0	0	0	1	3	4	0	.190	.056
MINOR LEAGUE TOTALS			.299	541	2029	359	607	95	44	46	288	283	437	129	.393	.457

8 EMILIANO FRUTO RHP

Born: June 6, 1984. **B-T:** R-R. **Ht.:** 6-3. **Wt.:** 240. **Signed:** Colombia, 2000. **Signed by:** Curtis Wallace.

Signed for $250,000 out of Colombia, Fruto was an enigma during his first four seasons in the system. His arm was intriguing, but his lack of focus or command left his managers reluctant to use him in close games. He matured in 2005, when managers rated him the best relief prospect in the Double-A Texas League. Fruto easily has the best stuff in a farm system hurting for pitching prospects. His curveball and changeup are the best in the system. Both are plus pitches, as is his fastball, which jumped from the low 90s to the mid-90s last year when he started using it more often. His control improved as well. His slider gives him a fourth pitch that's average. Fruto has more than enough stuff to start, but the Mariners have mostly used him in relief because of questions about his maturity and poise. His weight has risen from 170 pounds to 240 since he signed, though he still has retained his athleticism. After breaking through in Double-A last year, he was shelled in Triple-A. Seattle is toying with the idea of giving Fruto another shot as a starter, a role he hasn't filled since early 2003. His upside is huge—and so is his potential to flame out quickly.

Year	Club (League)	Class	W	L	ERA	G	GS	CG	SV	IP	H	R	ER	HR	BB	SO	AVG
2001	Mariners (AZL)	R	5	3	5.83	12	12	0	0	62	73	45	40	3	22	51	.291
2002	Wisconsin (Mid)	A	6	6	3.55	33	13	0	1	112	101	57	44	6	55	99	.239
2003	Tacoma (PCL)	AAA	1	0	0.00	1	0	0	0	4	1	0	0	0	2	2	.083
	Inland Empire (Cal)	A	7	8	3.77	42	4	0	7	79	80	43	33	5	38	83	.267
2004	San Antonio (TL)	AA	3	3	5.67	43	1	0	1	68	77	47	43	6	37	56	.277
2005	San Antonio (TL)	AA	2	3	2.56	40	0	0	12	67	56	22	19	6	22	63	.231
	Tacoma (PCL)	AAA	1	2	13.09	9	0	0	0	11	11	17	16	1	11	12	.268
MINOR LEAGUE TOTALS			25	25	4.37	180	30	0	21	402	399	231	195	27	187	366	.258

9 CLINT NAGEOTTE RHP

Born: Oct. 25, 1980. **B-T:** R-R. **Ht.:** 6-3. **Wt.:** 225. **Drafted:** HS—Brooklyn, Ohio, 1999 (5th round). **Signed by:** Ken Madeja.

Nageotte has hit speed bumps since leading the minors in strikeouts in 2002 and topping the Texas League in 2003. He got crushed in his 2004 major league debut and became a reliever last year after missing most of the first three months with a strained forearm. Nageotte's stuff is still good, but it has taken a downturn in the last two years. He used to own one of the nastiest sliders in the game, but it has lost velocity and sharpness and now grades as a 65 rather than an 80 on the 20-80 scouting scale. His fastball has lost 2-3 mph, sitting at 91-92 mph as he has tried to add sink and command. Most pitchers see their stuff improve when they work shorter stints out of the bullpen, so Nageotte's slippage raises a red flag. He has had health issues over the last three seasons, including elbow tendinitis in 2003 and a lower-back strain in 2004. His control still needs to improve. He never came up with a trustworthy changeup as a starter. Desperate for pitching help, Seattle could move Nageotte back to the rotation. He has a chance to make the Mariners out of spring training but more Triple-A innings wouldn't hurt.

Year	Club (League)	Class	W	L	ERA	G	GS	CG	SV	IP	H	R	ER	HR	BB	SO	AVG
2000	Mariners (AZL)	R	4	1	2.16	12	7	0	1	50	29	15	12	0	28	59	.167
2001	Wisconsin (Mid)	A	11	8	3.13	28	26	0	0	152	141	65	53	10	50	187	.246
2002	San Bernardino (Cal)	A	9	6	4.54	29	29	1	0	165	153	101	83	10	68	214	.241
2003	San Antonio (TL)	AA	11	7	3.10	27	27	2	0	154	127	60	53	6	67	157	.224
2004	Tacoma (PCL)	AAA	6	6	4.46	14	14	0	0	81	78	42	40	9	35	63	.257
	Seattle (AL)	MLB	1	6	7.36	12	5	0	0	37	48	31	30	3	27	24	.324
2005	Mariners (AZL)	R	0	0	0.00	1	1	0	0	3	0	0	0	0	0	6	.000
	Seattle (AL)	MLB	0	0	6.75	3	0	0	0	4	6	3	3	0	1	1	.353
	Tacoma (PCL)	AAA	2	1	2.65	19	0	0	2	34	21	16	10	2	22	35	.176
MAJOR LEAGUE TOTALS			1	6	7.30	15	5	0	0	41	54	34	33	3	28	25	.327
MINOR LEAGUE TOTALS			43	29	3.54	130	104	3	3	639	549	299	251	37	270	721	.230

10 ROB JOHNSON C

Born: July 22, 1983. **B-T:** R-R. **Ht.:** 6-1. **Wt.:** 200. **Drafted:** Houston, 2004 (4th round). **Signed by:** Kyle Van Hook.

He doesn't get as much attention as Jeff Clement and Kenji Johjima, but Johnson is a fine catching prospect in his own right. Managers rated him the best defensive catcher in the Midwest League in 2005, his first full pro season. He was the starting backstop for the Team USA at the World Cup, where he hit .273. Johnson makes consistent contact at the plate, drilling line drives to both gaps. He's a quality receiver with a strong arm, and he threw out 37 percent of basestealers last year. He's a better athlete than Clement or Johjima and runs the bases well for a catcher. His leadership skills are strong as well. Johnson has the frame and strength to hit homers, but never has shown the pop scouts expected. His power is more evident in batting practice than during games. He can get impatient at the plate, and it's not a sure thing that he'll have enough bat to be a quality regular. Johnson probably will open 2006 in Double-A, but Clement could be pushing for regular time there by midseason.

Year	Club (League)	Class	AVG	G	AB	R	H	2B	3B	HR	RBI	BB	SO	SB	OBP	SLG
2004	Everett (NWL)	A	.234	20	77	17	18	3	1	1	7	4	10	6	.286	.338
	Mariners (AZL)	R	.222	8	27	4	6	1	0	0	1	3	7	1	.323	.259
2005	Wisconsin (Mid)	A	.272	77	305	41	83	19	1	9	51	20	31	10	.319	.430
	Inland Empire (Cal)	A	.314	19	70	15	22	3	0	2	12	10	14	2	.381	.443
MINOR LEAGUE TOTALS			.269	124	479	77	129	26	2	12	71	37	62	19	.324	.407

11 WLADIMIR BALENTIEN OF

Born: July 2, 1984. **B-T:** R-R. **Ht.:** 6-1. **Wt.:** 210. **Signed:** Curacao, 2000. **Signed by:** Karel Williams.

There aren't many minor league hitters who are more fun to watch than Balentien. He has as much raw power as just about anyone—more than top Mariners prospect Jeff Clement, though Clement's is more usable—and he never deviates from his John Daly approach: grip it and rip it. Predictably, this approach yields a lot of homers (68 in 371 pro games) and a lot more strikeouts (402, about one for every three at-bats). Whether it will work above high Class A remains to be seen. A member of the 2004 Dutch Olympic team, Balentien offers more than just power. He has a plus arm and average speed. He makes good reads and gets nice jumps on defense, so his primary position the last two years has been center field. In the long term, he's better suited for right. Balentien chases too many balls off the plate and tries to pull everything. He swings so hard that he routinely pulls his head out of proper hitting position. His effort and conditioning also have been questioned. Balentien has one of the highest ceilings in the system, and Seattle will monitor his progress closely this year at San Antonio.

Year	Club (League)	Class	AVG	G	AB	R	H	2B	3B	HR	RBI	BB	SO	SB	OBP	SLG
2001	Aguirre (VSL)	R	.206	53	131	27	27	2	1	0	9	25	48	7	.333	.237
2002	Aguirre (VSL)	R	.279	59	197	41	55	13	4	10	39	34	52	6	.390	.538
2003	Mariners (AZL)	R	.283	50	187	42	53	12	5	16	52	22	55	4	.363	.658
2004	Wisconsin (Mid)	A	.277	76	260	39	72	12	3	15	46	12	77	10	.315	.519
	Inland Empire (Cal)	A	.289	10	38	5	11	1	0	2	5	4	10	1	.357	.474
2005	Inland Empire (Cal)	A	.291	123	492	76	143	38	8	25	93	33	160	9	.338	.553
MINOR LEAGUE TOTALS			.277	371	1305	230	361	78	21	68	244	130	402	37	.346	.525

12 MICHAEL SAUNDERS OF

Born: Nov. 19, 1986. **B-T:** L-R. **Ht.:** 6-4. **Wt.:** 205. **Drafted:** Tallahassee (Fla.) CC, D/F 2004 (11th round). **Signed by:** Phil Geisler.

The Mariners drafted Saunders out of a British Columbia high school in 2004, when baseball's visa shortage would have made it impossible for him to launch his pro career. He decided to attend Tallahassee (Fla.) Community College, then signed as a draft-and-follow for $237,500. During his impressive pro debut at short-season Everett, he drew comparisons to Shawn Green. Saunders has a sweet lefthanded swing with natural loft that gives him plus power potential. A good athlete, Saunders showed NHL potential as a teenager and also starred in basketball, lacrosse and soccer. He also was a legitimate prospect as a pitcher, showing an 88-91 mph fastball and a loose arm. Saunders has solid speed once he gets going and plus arm strength. He's adapting well to right field after being drafted as a third baseman. He struck out excessively in his debut, so he'll have to adjust in low Class A this year.

Year	Club (League)	Class	AVG	G	AB	R	H	2B	3B	HR	RBI	BB	SO	SB	OBP	SLG
2005	Everett (NWL)	A	.270	56	196	24	53	13	3	7	39	27	74	2	.361	.474
MINOR LEAGUE TOTALS			.270	56	196	24	53	13	3	7	39	27	74	2	.361	.474

13 YORMAN BAZARDO RHP

Born: July 11, 1984. **B-T:** R-R. **Ht.:** 6-2. **Wt.:** 200. **Signed:** Venezuela, 2000. **Signed by:** Miguel Garcia (Marlins).

Mariners general manager Bill Bavasi did a nice job at the 2005 trade deadline, spinning spare parts for useful pitching—Bazardo, Mike Flannery, Jesse Foppert and Natanael Mateo—and journeyman catchers Miguel Ojeda and Yorvit Torrealba. Foppert was an elite prospect before Tommy John surgery in 2003, while Bazardo is the best of the three minor league righties acquired. Bazardo touched 98 mph in the Marlins system, but pitched at 91-92 and peaked at 94 following the trade. He made progress with his slider and curveball, and his changeup remains his best secondary pitch. His numbers never have matched the quality of his stuff because he lacks consistent command. Bazardo doesn't struggle to throw strikes but must realize the importance of locating his pitches within the strike zone. His velocity dipped at the end of 2004 as well, so he'll need to get stronger. Unless he can develop a couple of truly reliable pitches to go with his heat, Bazardo faces a future in the bullpen. He'll stay in the rotation for now, probably opening the season in Double-A.

Year	Club (League)	Class	W	L	ERA	G	GS	CG	SV	IP	H	R	ER	HR	BB	SO	AVG
2001	Ciudad Alianza (VSL)	R	7	2	2.43	12	12	1	0	70	59	26	19	0	18	62	—
2002	Jamestown (NY-P)	A	5	0	2.73	25	0	0	6	36	39	11	11	0	6	26	.275
2003	Greensboro (SAL)	A	9	8	3.12	21	21	4	0	130	132	56	45	8	26	70	.261
2004	Jupiter (FSL)	A	5	9	3.27	25	25	2	0	154	161	78	56	3	30	95	.274
2005	Florida (NL)	MLB	0	0	21.60	1	0	0	0	2	5	5	4	0	2	2	.500
	Carolina (SL)	AA	8	7	3.99	19	19	0	0	108	108	60	48	12	36	73	.263
	San Antonio (TL)	AA	3	1	4.27	6	6	0	0	34	38	16	16	4	11	26	.295
MAJOR LEAGUE TOTALS			0	0	21.60	1	0	0	0	2	5	5	4	0	2	2	.500
MINOR LEAGUE TOTALS			37	27	3.29	108	83	7	6	533	537	247	195	27	127	352	.269

14 LUIS VALBUENA 2B

Born: Nov. 30, 1985. **B-T:** L-R. **Ht.:** 5-10. **Wt.:** 160. **Signed:** Venezuela, 2002. **Signed by:** Emilio Carrasquel.

Valbuena ranked as the No. 6 prospect in the short-season Northwest League in 2005 and earned all-star honors after leading the league in homers and RBIs. The year before, he won the MVP award and batting title in the Rookie-level Venezuelan Summer League. Of his predecessors as standout Everett middle infielders, he most closely resembles Ismael Castro, who hasn't enjoyed much success in full-season ball. Valbuena, who has been likened to Ray Durham, is an offensive second baseman. He has a quick bat and makes good contact, though Everett Memorial Stadium magnified his power (11 of his 12 homers last year came at home). Valbuena has average speed and defensive skills, and Seattle would like to see him improve with the glove. Though he topped NWL second basemen with a .978 fielding percentage, his hands are somewhat stiff. The Mariners trusted him enough to use him as an emergency fill-in in Triple-A last year, and they'll turn him loose in low Class A in 2006.

Year	Club (League)	Class	AVG	G	AB	R	H	2B	3B	HR	RBI	BB	SO	SB	OBP	SLG
2003	Aguirre (VSL)	R	.228	50	167	26	38	11	4	1	22	20	25	3	.323	.359
2004	Aguirre (VSL)	R	.361	61	216	44	78	24	6	2	34	27	15	11	.444	.556
2005	Tacoma (PCL)	AAA	.000	3	4	0	0	0	0	0	0	1	2	0	.200	.000
	Everett (NWL)	A	.261	74	287	47	75	10	3	12	51	31	37	14	.333	.443
MINOR LEAGUE TOTALS			.283	188	674	117	191	45	13	15	107	79	79	28	.366	.455

15 STEPHEN KAHN   RHP

Born: Dec. 14, 1983. **B-T:** L-R. **Ht.:** 6-3. **Wt.:** 215. **Drafted:** Loyola Marymount, 2005 (5th round). **Signed by:** Greg Whitworth.

An eighth-round pick of the Brewers out of high school in 2002, Kahn didn't sign and attended Loyola Marymount. After winning West Coast Conference pitcher-of-the-year honors and pitching for Team USA in 2004, Kahn projected as a possible first-round pick for 2005. But he lost his fastball command and went just 5-6, 5.60 as a junior, sliding to the Mariners in the fifth round. After signing for $190,000, Kahn moved to the bullpen and took to his new role. His maximum-effort delivery is better suited for shorter stints, as is his aggressive nature. When he pitched in relief, his fastball sat at 95 mph and topped out at 98 with explosive life. It's the best fastball in the system. His second pitch is a 12-to-6 curveball that can get loopy at times. Kahn's curve needs more consistency, and he might be better off switching to a slider. Despite his initial success, he still has to improve his ability to throw both strikes and quality strikes. If he can locate two quality pitches, he'll have closer potential. Seattle could challenge Kahn by jumping him to high Class A in 2006.

Year	Club (League)	Class	W	L	ERA	G	GS	CG	SV	IP	H	R	ER	HR	BB	SO	AVG
2005	Mariners (AZL)	R	0	0	0.00	1	0	0	0	1	1	0	0	0	1	1	.333
	Everett (NWL)	A	3	0	3.93	17	0	0	12	18	14	9	8	1	14	22	.209
MINOR LEAGUE TOTALS			3	0	3.72	18	0	0	12	19	15	9	8	1	15	23	.214

16 RYAN FEIERABEND   LHP

Born: Aug. 22, 1985. **B-T:** L-L. **Ht.:** 6-3. **Wt.:** 190. **Drafted:** HS—Grafton, Ohio, 2003 (3rd round). **Signed by:** Ken Madeja.

Feierabend has arguably the best pickoff move in the minors. A year after leading Midwest League pitchers with 16 basestealers caught, he topped the California League with 18 in 2005—when he gave up only one successful steal. Feierabend also was the youngest starting pitcher in the Cal League and more than held his own as a teenager in high Class A. He finished strong for the second straight year, going 6-2, 2.55 in his final 13 starts. His fastball bumped up a notch to 89-90 mph, occasionally topping out at 92. He's still young and projectable, so it's possible he could add velocity. His curveball and circle changeup are average, and his whole repertoire plays up because of his command and ability to keep hitters off balance by mixing his pitches. Feierabend doesn't have a huge ceiling, but he has passed every test so far and could become a No. 4 starter. He'll advance to Double-A this season.

Year	Club (League)	Class	W	L	ERA	G	GS	CG	SV	IP	H	R	ER	HR	BB	SO	AVG
2003	Mariners (AZL)	R	2	3	2.61	6	5	0	1	21	23	11	6	0	6	12	.288
2004	Wisconsin (Mid)	A	9	7	3.63	26	26	1	0	161	158	78	65	17	44	106	.263
2005	Inland Empire (Cal)	A	8	7	3.88	29	29	0	0	151	186	80	65	16	51	122	.310
MINOR LEAGUE TOTALS			19	17	3.68	61	60	1	1	332	367	169	136	33	101	240	.286

17 CESAR JIMENEZ   LHP

Born: Nov. 12, 1984. **B-T:** L-L. **Ht.:** 5-11. **Wt.:** 180. **Signed:** Venezuela, 2001. **Signed by:** Emilio Carrasquel.

Primarily a starter in his first two pro seasons, Jimenez has advanced rapidly since becoming a full-time reliever in 2004, reaching Triple-A last year as a 20-year-old. He goes after hitters with three solid pitches: an 88-89 mph fastball that tops out at 92, a curveball that improved in 2005 and a changeup that ranks among the best in the system. He does a good job of throwing strikes and keeping the ball down. Jimenez doesn't have a dominant pitch, so he's probably not going to be a late-inning reliever, but with three effective offerings he could be a starter. The last time he was in that role, he made the Midwest League midseason all-star team in 2003 but saw his fastball drop to the mid-80s as he lost seven of his final nine starts. The Mariners are considering putting him back in the rotation after adding him to the 40-man roster, but Jimenez probably will relieve in Triple-A this year.

Year	Club (League)	Class	W	L	ERA	G	GS	CG	SV	IP	H	R	ER	HR	BB	SO	AVG
2002	Aguirre (VSL)	R	7	1	0.83	11	11	2	0	65	37	6	6	0	12	67	.167
	Mariners (AZL)	R	0	0	3.33	1	0	0	0	3	3	2	1	0	0	3	.300
	Everett (NWL)	A	2	1	2.70	8	0	0	1	20	12	7	6	2	5	25	.174
2003	Wisconsin (Mid)	A	8	11	2.94	28	20	0	0	126	134	61	41	7	46	76	.273
2004	Inland Empire (Cal)	A	6	7	2.29	43	2	0	6	86	80	28	22	3	19	81	.241
2005	Tacoma (PCL)	AAA	0	0	9.35	4	0	0	0	8	9	8	8	5	1	9	.290
	San Antonio (TL)	AA	3	5	2.62	45	1	0	4	69	64	21	20	3	24	54	.250
MINOR LEAGUE TOTALS			26	25	2.49	140	34	2	11	376	339	133	104	20	107	315	.241

18 BOBBY LIVINGSTON
LHP

Born: Sept. 3, 1982. **B-T:** L-L. **Ht.:** 6-3. **Wt.:** 193. **Drafted:** HS—Lubbock, Texas, 2001 (4th round). **Signed by:** Kyle Van Hook.

At this point, the low-90s fastball Livingston showed as a high school senior isn't going to come back. His velocity dropped to 86-87 mph before the 2001 draft, and it hasn't gotten any better. But Livingston hasn't needed to be able to throw the ball by hitters to thrive. In 2005, he led the Texas League in ERA and won six of his 10 Triple-A starts. He got knocked around in the Pacific Coast League at first, but allowed five runs over his final four starts and fanned a career-high 14 in his last outing. Seattle placed him on its 40-man roster during the offseason, though scouts remain skeptical as to whether Livingston can succeed in the majors. At times his fastball drops to 82-85 mph, though he enhances it with good sink and even better command. No pitcher in the system locates his pitches as well as Livingston. He also throws a curveball and a changeup, and he'll use a cutter against righthanders. None of his pitches is close to special, but he's a strike machine with tremendous feel for his craft. The Mariners love finesse lefties (see Jamie Moyer), but they've seen lefties such as Craig Anderson and Travis Blackley succeed in the lower minors and falter at the top. Livingston likely will open 2006 in Triple-A and should get his first big league opportunity later in the year.

Year	Club (League)	Class	W	L	ERA	G	GS	CG	SV	IP	H	R	ER	HR	BB	SO	AVG
2002	Everett (NWL)	A	6	5	3.03	15	14	0	0	80	80	33	27	2	14	76	.255
2003	Wisconsin (Mid)	A	15	7	2.73	26	26	1	0	178	176	72	54	10	28	105	.259
2004	Inland Empire (Cal)	A	12	6	3.57	28	27	1	0	187	187	90	74	15	30	141	.262
2005	San Antonio (TL)	AA	8	4	2.86	18	18	0	0	116	103	45	37	7	27	78	.242
	Tacoma (PCL)	AAA	6	2	4.70	10	10	0	0	52	53	31	27	2	15	41	.260
MINOR LEAGUE TOTALS			47	24	3.22	97	95	2	0	613	599	271	219	36	114	441	.256

19 SEBASTIEN BOUCHER
OF

Born: Oct. 19, 1981. **B-T:** L-R. **Ht.:** 6-0. **Wt.:** 190. **Drafted:** Bethune-Cookman, 2004 (7th round). **Signed by:** Mark Leavitt.

Like Michael Saunders, Boucher is a Canadian who was caught in baseball's visa crunch in 2004. The Mid-Eastern Athletic Conference player of the year that spring, he signed for $90,000 but wasn't permitted to join a minor league team. He made his pro debut last year at age 23 and made up for lost time. Boucher led all Mariners farmhands with a .340 average and .434 on-base percentage, and he also swiped 26 bases in 30 attempts. He has the best speed in the system, rating a 70 on the 20-80 scouting scale. His quickness is also an asset in center field. Boucher is a line-drive hitter who uses the whole field. He doesn't have much power and presently strikes out too much. But he understands getting on base and creating havoc is his game, and he does a good job drawing walks. His arm is below-average but playable in center. Boucher finished the year by playing for Team Canada in the World Cup and in an Olympic regional qualifying tournament. His next step is Double-A.

Year	Club (League)	Class	AVG	G	AB	R	H	2B	3B	HR	RBI	BB	SO	SB	OBP	SLG
2005	Wisconsin (Mid)	A	.326	48	178	37	58	14	2	2	31	26	34	11	.411	.461
	Inland Empire (Cal)	A	.352	52	213	54	75	14	3	2	21	36	49	15	.453	.474
MINOR LEAGUE TOTALS			.340	100	391	91	133	28	5	4	52	62	83	26	.434	.468

20 T.J. BOHN
OF

Born: Jan. 17, 1980. **B-T:** R-R. **Ht.:** 6-5. **Wt.:** 205. **Drafted:** Bellevue (Neb.), 2002 (30th round). **Signed by:** Mark Lummus.

Bohn has had one of the system's better packages of tools since coming out of NCAA Division II Bellevue (Neb.) in 2002. He transferred to Bellevue after Iowa State shuttered its program in 2001. He finally delivered a performance to match his tools last year, reaching Triple-A (where he bashed three homers in the Pacific Coast League playoffs) and getting added to the 40-man roster. Bohn has hitting aptitude and a fair amount of power in his 6-foot-5, 205-pound frame. He has become more aggressive about looking for pitches to drive, and he'd hit more homers if he had more loft in his swing. Improved selectivity and contact also would help. He has good speed for his size and runs well once he gets going on the bases. Bohn's long strides allow him to cover enough ground to play center field, and his jumps and routes are strong as well. He's the system's best defensive outfielder and also has one of the best arms, making him a good fit in right field. He's 26 and may not become a regular in the majors, but he could have a career as a fourth outfielder with pop in the Gabe Kapler/Jayson Werth mold. Bohn will attend his first big league camp this spring.

Year	Club (League)	Class	AVG	G	AB	R	H	2B	3B	HR	RBI	BB	SO	SB	OBP	SLG
2002	Everett (NWL)	A	.245	62	212	28	52	10	0	3	20	29	53	7	.340	.335
2003	Wisconsin (Mid)	A	.272	128	471	75	128	31	2	13	70	70	131	16	.371	.429
2004	Inland Empire (Cal)	A	.283	71	240	46	68	9	3	7	37	44	61	6	.412	.433
	San Antonio (TL)	AA	.264	62	220	24	58	9	4	7	29	22	46	6	.336	.436
2005	San Antonio (TL)	AA	.308	113	438	67	135	30	2	12	57	35	96	27	.365	.468
	Tacoma (PCL)	AAA	.321	22	81	15	26	3	0	1	7	2	23	4	.360	.395
MINOR LEAGUE TOTALS			.281	458	1662	255	467	92	11	43	220	202	410	66	.367	.427

21 RENE RIVERA   C

Born: July 31, 1983. **B-T:** R-R. **Ht.:** 5-10. **Wt.:** 190. **Drafted:** HS—Bayamon, P.R., 2001 (2nd round). **Signed by:** Pedro Grifol.

Rivera was the MVP of the 2001 Excellence Games, an annual showcase for Puerto Rican draft prospects, boosting him into the second round that year. He continues to make a living off his work behind the plate, as managers have rated him his league's best defensive catcher for three years running. He led the Texas League by throwing out 54 percent of basestealers in 2005. Though he has a chunky body, he's agile and has good receiving skills. He spent a month in Seattle last year as a big league backup, and that's his long-term role, especially with Jeff Clement, Kenji Johjima and Rob Johnson in the organization. Rivera hasn't hit enough to project as a regular, though the Mariners note that they've rushed him. He has some raw power, but he owns a long swing, chases too many pitches and struggles against breaking balls. He's also a well-below-average runner. Though Rivera has just 115 at-bats above Double-A and needs much more work on his hitting, he and Johjima are the only catchers on the big league roster. Rivera could open 2006 as Johjima's backup in Seattle.

Year	Club (League)	Class	AVG	G	AB	R	H	2B	3B	HR	RBI	BB	SO	SB	OBP	SLG
2001	Everett (NWL)	A	.089	15	45	3	4	1	0	2	3	1	19	0	.106	.244
	Mariners (AZL)	R	.338	21	71	13	24	4	0	2	12	2	11	0	.360	.479
2002	Everett (NWL)	A	.242	62	227	29	55	18	1	1	26	16	38	5	.314	.344
2003	Wisconsin (Mid)	A	.275	116	407	39	112	19	0	9	54	38	81	2	.344	.388
2004	Tacoma (PCL)	AAA	.400	4	15	3	6	1	0	1	1	0	3	0	.400	.667
	Inland Empire (Cal)	A	.235	107	379	41	89	22	1	6	53	28	70	0	.300	.346
	Seattle (AL)	MLB	.000	2	3	0	0	0	0	0	0	0	1	0	.000	.000
2005	San Antonio (TL)	AA	.278	57	212	20	59	14	1	2	21	7	35	1	.305	.382
	Tacoma (PCL)	AAA	.204	14	49	3	10	3	0	1	6	2	12	0	.235	.327
	Seattle (AL)	MLB	.396	16	48	3	19	3	0	1	6	1	11	0	.408	.521
MAJOR LEAGUE TOTALS			.373	18	51	3	19	3	0	1	6	1	12	0	.385	.490
MINOR LEAGUE TOTALS			.256	396	1405	151	359	82	3	24	176	94	269	8	.312	.369

22 TRAVIS BLACKLEY   LHP

Born: Nov. 4, 1982. **B-T:** L-L. **Ht.:** 6-3. **Wt.:** 190. **Signed:** Australia, 2000. **Signed by:** Jim Colborn.

While the Mariners were tracking Shin-Soo Choo at the 2000 World Junior Championship, they also found Blackley pitching for Australia. His younger brother Adam pitches in the Red Sox system. Travis moved rapidly after coming to the United States, leading the minors with 17 wins as a 20-year-old in Double-A in 2003. But little has gone right for him since. Promoted to Seattle the following July, he changed his approach and tried to pitch away from contact. He lost command and velocity and ended 2004 on the Tacoma disabled list with shoulder tendinitis. Doctors subsequently discovered two small tears in his labrum. He missed all of the 2005 season after February surgery but should be ready for spring training. When he was going well, Blackley drew Mark Buehrle comparisons while keeping hitters off balance with a four-pitch mix. His changeup was his best pitch, and he also used an 87-92 mph fastball with natural cutting action, a curveball and a slider. His stuff didn't give him much margin for error, so if it doesn't come all the way back, he could be in trouble.

Year	Club (League)	Class	W	L	ERA	G	GS	CG	SV	IP	H	R	ER	HR	BB	SO	AVG
2001	Everett (NWL)	A	6	1	3.32	14	14	0	0	79	60	34	29	7	29	90	.211
2002	San Bernardino (Cal)	A	5	9	3.49	21	20	1	0	121	102	52	47	11	44	152	.227

2003	San Antonio (TL)	AA	17	3	2.61	27	27	0	0	162	125	55	47	11	62	144	.215
2004	Tacoma (PCL)	AAA	8	6	3.83	19	18	2	0	110	100	49	47	14	47	80	.251
	Seattle (AL)	MAJ	1	3	10.04	6	6	0	0	26	35	31	29	9	22	16	.321
2005	Did not play—Injured																
MAJOR LEAGUE TOTALS			1	3	10.04	6	6	0	0	26	35	31	29	9	22	16	.321
MINOR LEAGUE TOTALS			36	19	3.24	81	79	3	0	473	387	190	170	43	182	466	.226

23 RENEE CORTEZ   RHP

Born: Dec. 9, 1982. **B-T:** R-R. **Ht.:** 6-4. **Wt.:** 180. **Signed:** Venezuela, 2000. **Signed by:** Pedro Avila.

Cortez' season began with a 15-day suspension in April after testing positive for performance-enhancing drugs, but finished on a positive note when the Mariners added him to the 40-man roster. He has one of the better arms in the system, delivering 93-94 mph fastballs that peak at 97. He blew away Jeff Bagwell with his heat, striking him out during Bagwell's rehab assignment to Double-A in September. Cortez engenders mixed reviews from scouts, however. Those who like him rate his slider as an average to plus pitch and give him credit for maturing. His detractors don't think he stays on top of his slider enough and believe he still gets too emotional on the mound. He's fiddling with a splitter as a third pitch. Cortez still has a lot of effort to his delivery but has improved his control. After two years in San Antonio, he'll move up to Triple-A and could surface in the Seattle bullpen later in 2006.

Year	Club (League)	Class	W	L	ERA	G	GS	CG	SV	IP	H	R	ER	HR	BB	SO	AVG
2000	San Felipe (VSL)	R	2	3	1.80	14	2	0	3	35	32	19	7	1	27	22	.237
2001	Mariners (AZL)	R	2	0	4.42	11	9	0	0	53	60	34	26	4	10	52	.278
2002	Mariners (AZL)	R	1	3	3.56	7	5	0	0	43	47	22	17	0	6	54	.269
	Wisconsin (Mid)	A	5	8	4.12	17	17	0	0	98	102	62	45	12	32	67	.265
2003	Wisconsin (Mid)	A	4	2	2.92	28	0	0	4	46	40	20	15	3	16	51	.237
	Inland Empire (Cal)	A	0	1	1.66	15	0	0	3	22	10	5	4	0	6	16	.133
2004	San Antonio (TL)	AA	2	5	4.44	36	0	0	3	53	61	29	26	7	24	46	.279
2005	San Antonio (TL)	AA	5	3	3.96	44	1	0	10	64	61	32	28	4	23	62	.253
MINOR LEAGUE TOTALS			21	25	3.66	172	34	0	23	414	413	223	168	31	144	370	.256

24 MICHAEL WILSON   OF

Born: June 29, 1983. **B-T:** R-R. **Ht.:** 6-2. **Wt.:** 215. **Drafted:** HS—Tulsa, 2001 (2nd round). **Signed by:** Mark Lummus.

Matt Tuiasosopo isn't the only blue-chip football recruit in the system. Wilson was headed to play linebacker for Oklahoma until the Mariners took him in the second round of the 2001 draft and offered him $900,000. They also signed outfielder Matt Ware to a two-sport deal as a 21st-rounder that year but eventually lost him to the NFL's Philadelphia Eagles. Wilson didn't make it to a full-season league until 2005 but turned a corner in low Class A. Inserted in the middle of the Wisconsin lineup, he batted .280-11-51 over the final two months. He started seeing the ball better and laid off pitches he used to chase in the past. He stopped switch-hitting in 2004 and has fared better while batting solely righthanded. Strong and powerful, he's one of the best athletes in the system. Wilson can make plays in center field, though he profiles better in right. He has corrected what was once a horrible arm action and now has average arm strength. He still has holes in his swing, but Seattle is enthused about his progress and his leadership ability. He's headed for high Class A.

Year	Club (League)	Class	AVG	G	AB	R	H	2B	3B	HR	RBI	BB	SO	SB	OBP	SLG
2002	Mariners (AZL)	R	.238	41	143	28	34	5	0	4	19	18	52	4	.357	.357
2003	Mariners (AZL)	R	.311	48	177	33	55	9	3	3	25	20	46	6	.391	.446
2004	Everett (NWL)	A	.259	66	239	45	62	15	0	9	51	25	61	10	.357	.435
2005	Wisconsin (Mid)	A	.266	127	463	93	123	29	3	19	84	57	107	10	.360	.464
MINOR LEAGUE TOTALS			.268	282	1022	199	274	58	6	35	179	120	266	30	.364	.439

25 FRANCISCO CRUCETA   RHP

Born: July 4, 1981. **B-T:** R-R. **Ht.:** 6-2. **Wt.:** 180. **Signed:** Dominican Republic, 1999. **Signed by:** Pablo Peguero (Dodgers).

When Cleveland got both Cruceta and righthander Ricardo Rodriguez from the Dodgers while dumping Paul Shuey's contract in July 2002, it looked like a coup. But neither panned out with the Indians, who placed Cruceta on waivers last August. Short on quality arms, the Mariners claimed him. Cruceta has an 89-92 mph sinker that maxes out at 94. He added a splitter in 2004 and it quickly became his No. 2 pitch, ahead of his slider and rudimentary changeup. Cruceta still is learning to pitch, however. He throws strikes but his location isn't consistent. He tends to work high in the zone, leaving him vulnerable when he makes mistakes. Primarily a starter for most of his career, he worked as a swingman last year. Seattle will decide his role in spring training, and he'll begin the season in Triple-A. The Mariners took him off their 40-man roster, but he found no takers in the major league Rule 5 draft.

Year	Club (League)	Class	W	L	ERA	G	GS	CG	SV	IP	H	R	ER	HR	BB	SO	AVG
1999	Dodgers (DSL)	R	3	2	7.56	14	1	0	0	25	33	34	21	4	15	21	.308
2000	Dodgers (DSL)	R	4	2	3.31	21	6	0	3	49	33	29	18	1	36	49	.180
2001	Dodgers (DSL)	R	0	4	1.50	11	9	0	0	48	35	24	8	1	24	47	.200
2002	South Georgia (SAL)	A	8	5	2.80	20	20	3	0	113	98	42	35	7	34	111	.231
	Kinston (Car)	A	2	0	2.49	7	7	0	0	40	31	13	11	2	25	37	.217
2003	Akron (EL)	AA	13	9	3.09	27	25	6	0	163	141	70	56	7	66	134	.232
2004	Akron (EL)	AA	4	8	5.28	15	15	1	0	89	89	58	52	11	33	45	.261
	Buffalo (IL)	AAA	6	5	3.25	14	14	1	0	83	78	35	30	6	36	62	.259
	Cleveland (AL)	MLB	0	1	9.35	2	2	0	0	8	10	9	8	1	4	9	.303
2005	Buffalo (IL)	AAA	6	4	5.19	30	13	1	0	102	123	65	59	16	32	92	.297
	Tacoma (PCL)	AAA	1	1	5.00	2	2	0	0	9	11	6	5	3	3	10	.297
MAJOR LEAGUE TOTALS			0	1	9.35	2	2	0	0	8	10	9	8	1	4	9	.303
MINOR LEAGUE TOTALS			47	40	3.68	161	112	12	3	721	672	376	295	58	304	608	.246

26 YUNG-CHI CHEN   3B/2B

Born: July 13, 1983. **B-T:** R-R. **Ht.:** 5-11. **Wt.:** 172. **Signed:** Taiwan, 2004. **Signed by:** Jamey Storvick.

A veteran of international play with Taiwan, Chen started at third base in the 2004 Olympics and at second base in the 2005 World Cup. He batted .438 to earn all-tournament honors at the latter event. Hitting is what Chen does best. His strong wrists and his knack for centering the ball on the bat give him surprising pop for his size. He makes consistent line-drive contact, using the entire field with a solid approach. Nothing else about Chen's game really stands out, but he doesn't have a glaring weakness either. He has average speed and the instincts to steal an occasional base. His hands, range and arm are ordinary, which is enough to get the job done in the field. His best position is second base because he doesn't have the power for third. The main reason he has seen so much time at the hot corner is that he has been on teams with Asdrubal Cabrera, Oswaldo Navarro and Matt Tuiasosopo, who have shared second and shortstop. Chen is ticketed for high Class A in 2006 and will be the everyday second baseman if Cabrera and Navarro are promoted ahead of him.

Year	Club (League)	Class	AVG	G	AB	R	H	2B	3B	HR	RBI	BB	SO	SB	OBP	SLG
2004	Everett (NWL)	A	.300	49	200	37	60	13	1	3	34	16	36	25	.353	.420
2005	Wisconsin (Mid)	A	.292	121	503	77	147	27	7	7	80	37	76	15	.339	.416
MINOR LEAGUE TOTALS			.294	170	703	114	207	40	8	10	114	53	112	40	.343	.417

27 OSWALDO NAVARRO   2B/SS

Born: Oct. 2, 1984. **B-T:** B-R. **Ht.:** 6-0. **Wt.:** 155. **Signed:** Venezuela, 2001. **Signed by:** Emilio Carrasquel.

If the Mariners could somehow combine Navarro and Yung-Chi Chen, they'd have a valuable middle infielder. While Chen's hitting is the most notable part of his otherwise ordinary game, Navarro stands out with his glove but has a questionable bat. He edges Asdrubal Cabrera as the best infield defender in the system. Navarro's middle-infield actions, instincts and hands all are above-average, and he has enough arm to make plays from shortstop. Like most of Seattle's infield prospects, he has seen time at a variety of positions to enhance his versatility. That's especially valuable to Navarro because most scouts project him as a utilityman. He has a smooth, flat swing that's tailored to contact, but at times he'll try to hit for power. While he surprised the Mariners with 29 doubles and nine homers in 2005, he needs to stop swinging for the fences and just worry about getting on base. He has some speed but isn't a huge basestealing threat. Navarro is an organization favorite, a gamer who plays with constant energy. Seattle added him to the 40-man roster this offseason and could skip him a level to Double-A, though his bat probably isn't ready for that jump.

Year	Club (League)	Class	AVG	G	AB	R	H	2B	3B	HR	RBI	BB	SO	SB	OBP	SLG
2002	Aguirre (VSL)	R	.261	37	119	13	31	4	1	0	9	12	21	3	.338	.311
2003	Everett (NWL)	A	.258	61	233	42	60	12	1	0	23	10	39	16	.302	.318
2004	Wisconsin (Mid)	A	.211	40	109	13	23	4	0	0	7	11	19	4	.295	.248
	Everett (NWL)	A	.273	68	267	38	73	27	1	1	30	21	59	17	.331	.393
2005	Wisconsin (Mid)	A	.269	120	450	57	121	29	0	9	69	39	60	11	.329	.393
MINOR LEAGUE TOTALS			.261	326	1178	163	308	76	3	10	138	93	198	51	.322	.357

28 GEORGE SHERRILL   LHP

Born: April 19, 1977. **B-T:** L-L. **Ht.:** 6-0. **Wt.:** 220. **Signed:** NDFA/Winnipeg (Northern), 2003. **Signed by:** Charley Kerfeld.

The Mariners spent a first-round pick on Matt Thornton in 1998, but they may have found a more effective lefty reliever when they signed Sherrill out of the independent

Northern League in mid-2003. Sherrill spent five years in three indy leagues before hooking on with Seattle, in part because his weight ballooned to 300 pounds at one point and scared clubs off. Sherrill isn't as imposing or as overpowering as Thornton, but he's very deceptive. Using a slow, stiff delivery, Sherrill short-arms the ball and releases it from behind his ear, making it difficult to pick up his pitches. His velocity was down a tick to 90-91 mph last season, still more than enough for a lefty. His best pitch is his slider, and he's death on left-handers (.143 average against in Triple-A, .156 with Seattle). He'd be more effective against righthanders if he could refine a changeup, and until that happens, he'll be a lefty special-ist. He competes hard and keeps the ball down. Sherrill spent the last two months of 2005 in the majors, pitching well until allowing four runs without recording an out against the A's in the final game. He'll have to battle for a big league job again in spring training.

Year	Club (League)	Class	W	L	ERA	G	GS	CG	SV	IP	H	R	ER	HR	BB	SO	AVG
1999	Evansville (Fron)	IND	2	4	3.15	22	4	1	2	40	40	20	14	3	18	33	.268
2000	Evansville (Fron)	IND	3	5	4.66	13	13	1	0	75	71	45	39	5	35	61	.250
2001	Sioux Falls (Nor)	IND	4	4	2.45	48	2	0	0	59	53	20	16	3	14	45	.249
2002	Winnipeg (Nor)	IND	3	5	3.07	38	0	0	2	41	35	16	14	6	13	61	.227
2003	Winnipeg (Nor)	IND	1	0	1.13	16	0	0	1	16	8	2	2	0	4	30	.151
	San Antonio (TL)	AA	3	0	0.33	16	0	0	0	27	19	2	1	1	12	31	.198
2004	Tacoma (PCL)	AAA	4	2	2.33	36	0	0	13	50	42	13	13	4	9	62	.219
	Seattle (AL)	MLB	2	1	3.80	21	0	0	0	24	24	12	10	3	9	16	.258
2005	Mariners (AZL)	R	0	0	0.00	3	2	0	0	4	0	0	0	0	0	5	.000
	Tacoma (PCL)	AAA	1	3	2.28	22	0	0	7	24	19	7	6	0	6	38	.209
	Seattle (AL)	MLB	4	3	5.21	29	0	0	0	19	13	12	11	3	7	24	.194
MAJOR LEAGUE TOTALS			6	4	4.43	50	0	0	0	43	37	24	21	6	16	40	.231
MINOR LEAGUE TOTALS			8	5	1.71	77	2	0	20	105	80	22	20	5	27	136	.205

29 BRYAN LaHAIR 1B

Born: Nov. 5, 1982. **B-T:** L-R. **Ht.:** 6-5. **Wt.:** 215. **Drafted:** St. Petersburg (Fla.) JC, D/F 2002 (39th round). **Signed by:** Mark Leavitt.

LaHair had a classic breakout season in 2005. After batting .273 with eight homers over his first two pro seasons, he exploded to hit .310-22-113 and earn all-star honors in the California League. He also starred with Team USA, batting .361-3-8 in 10 games at the World Cup in September and .444-1-3 in three contests at an Olympic regional qualifying tourna-ment in November. LaHair made a key adjustment to his swing mechanics, allowing him to get his front foot down quicker and improve his timing. Big and strong, he has legitimate lefthanded power. He doesn't lose any pop against southpaws, but his .218 average against them last year may mean his ceiling is as a platoon player. LaHair has played outfield in the past, but he has below-average speed and athleticism, prompting him to become a full-time first baseman. While he's not smooth around the bag, he did lead California League first basemen with a .996 fielding percentage. The Mariners aren't quite sure he's for real, and he'll have to prove himself again in Double-A after being left off the 40-man roster.

Year	Club (League)	Class	AVG	G	AB	R	H	2B	3B	HR	RBI	BB	SO	SB	OBP	SLG
2003	Everett (NWL)	A	.244	57	201	26	49	14	0	2	20	11	40	4	.286	.343
2004	Everett (NWL)	A	.440	7	25	5	11	6	0	1	7	1	3	0	.464	.800
	Wisconsin (Mid)	A	.279	67	262	30	73	24	0	5	28	16	66	0	.323	.427
2005	Inland Empire (Cal)	A	.310	126	509	81	158	28	2	22	113	51	125	0	.373	.503
MINOR LEAGUE TOTALS			.292	257	997	142	291	72	2	30	168	79	234	4	.345	.458

30 ANTHONY VARVARO RHP

Born: Oct. 31, 1984. **B-T:** R-R. **Ht.:** 6-0. **Wt.:** 180. **Drafted:** St. John's, 2005 (12th round). **Signed by:** David May.

In his two years running Seattle's drafts, scouting director Bob Fontaine has used his 12th-round picks on college prospects who faced Tommy John surgery. He took Wichita State lefty Steve Uhlmansiek in 2004, and Uhlmansiek returned to the mound last June, days after the Mariners took Varvaro. Before he blew out his elbow in May, Varvaro projected as a sec-ond- or third-round pick. Signed for $500,000, he ranked sixth in NCAA Division I with 12.1 strikeouts per nine innings last spring. That was a better rate than that of his more herald-ed St. John's teammate, Craig Hansen (11.9), who went in the first round to the Red Sox. Some scouts said Varvaro was a more complete pitcher than Hansen, and he carved up col-lege hitters with a 92-94 mph fastball and a hard curveball. Once he returns to health, Varvaro should have the best curveball in the system. He'll have to tone down his delivery and work on his changeup. The Mariners expect he'll be able to pitch by midseason.

Year	Club (League)	Class	W	L	ERA	G	GS	CG	SV	IP	H	R	ER	HR	BB	SO	AVG
2005	Did not play—Injured/Signed 2006 contract																

TAMPA BAY
DEVIL RAYS

BY BILL BALLEW

During what proved to be his final season as general manager of the Devil Rays, Chuck LaMar actually said, "The only thing that keeps this organization from being recognized as one of the finest in baseball is wins and losses at the major league level."

Yet most Baseball America readers understood what LaMar was getting at. After all, the only area Tampa Bay can consider a success while failing to top 70 wins in each of its first eight years of existence is its development of position players. While the Rays were at times forced to operate with a big league payroll only slightly higher than Alex Rodriguez' annual salary, they have produced Rocco Baldelli, Jorge Cantu, Carl Crawford, **Jonny Gomes**, Toby Hall and Aubrey Huff.

After finishing in last place for the seventh time in eight seasons, Tampa Bay went for a full makeover at the end of the season. Stuart Sternberg, who purchased 48 percent of the franchise in 2004, replaced Vince Naimoli as managing partner. Sternberg immediately fired LaMar, the only GM in club history, along with a significant chunk of his front office, including assistant GM Scott Proefrock, director of player personnel Cam Bonifay and director of international scouting Rudy Santin. Manager Lou Piniella, who criticized Sternberg's ownership for being more concerned about the future than the present during the season, was bought out of the final year of his contract.

To replace LaMar, Sternberg promoted Andrew Friedman. Friedman, 28, worked on Wall Street before joining the team in 2004 as an assistant for baseball development. He

hired former Astros GM Gerry Hunsicker as his second-in-command and Angels bench coach Joe Maddon as manager.

Sternberg has worked hard to change the Rays' image, trying to win over fans with lower ticket prices and free parking. He is playing up the nucleus of homegrown players with an "under construction" advertising campaign. But while Tampa Bay has impressive young talent in the majors and more on the way, it will be a tall order to contend in the American League East.

The Devil Rays may have had the two best position players in the minors last year in shortstop B.J. Upton (who no longer qualifies for BA's prospect list) and outfielder Delmon Young, Baseball America's 2005 Minor League Player of the Year. LaMar's regime antagonized both players by declining to promote them in September in order to delay their eligibility for arbitration and free agency.

Beyond that pair, the farm system may be deeper than ever. Special assistant Tim Wilken, who left to become Cubs scouting director in December, played a major role in the club's 2004 draft and ran the 2005 effort, both of which have yielded several promising prospects. Last year's crop could get even stronger with the eventual signing of third-round righthander Bryan Morris, who is at Motlow State (Tenn.) Community College and can negotiate again once his juco season ends.

TOP 30 PROSPECTS

1. Delmon Young, of
2. Jeff Niemann, rhp
3. Jason Hammel, rhp
4. Reid Brignac, ss
5. Elijah Dukes, of
6. Wade Davis, rhp
7. Wes Bankston, 1b
8. Chad Orvella, rhp
9. Matt Walker, rhp
10. Chris Mason, rhp
11. Shawn Riggans, c
12. Jamie Shields, rhp
13. Fernando Perez, of
14. Wade Townsend, rhp
15. John Jaso, c/dh
16. Jacob McGee, lhp
17. Shaun Cumberland, of
18. Elliot Johnson, 2b
19. Jeremy Hellickson, rhp
20. Andy Sonnanstine, rhp
21. Jose de la Cruz, rhp
22. James Houser, lhp
23. Andrew Lopez, of
24. Chris Seddon, lhp
25. Carlos Hines, rhp
26. Brian Stokes, rhp
27. Juan Salas, rhp
28. John Matulia, of
29. Derek Feldkamp, rhp
30. Francisco Leandro, of

ORGANIZATION OVERVIEW

General manager: Andrew Friedman. **Farm director:** Mitch Lukevics. **Scouting director:** R.J. Harrison.

2005 PERFORMANCE

Class	Team	League	W	L	Pct.	Finish*	Manager
Majors	Tampa Bay	American	67	95	.414	13th (14)	Lou Piniella
Triple-A	Durham Bulls	International	65	79	.451	12th (14)	Bill Evers
Double-A	Montgomery Biscuits	Southern	67	70	.489	5th (10)	Charlie Montoyo
High A	Visalia Oaks	California	55	85	.393	10th (10)	Steve Livesey
Low A	SW Michigan Devil Rays	Midwest	72	67	.518	t-4th (14)	Joe Szekely
Short-season	Hudson Valley Renegades	New York-Penn	31	43	.419	11th (14)	Dave Howard
Rookie	Princeton Devil Rays	Appalachian	34	31	.523	3rd (10)	Jamie Nelson
OVERALL 2005 MINOR LEAGUE RECORD			324	375	.464	27th (30)	

*Finish in overall standings (No. of teams in league).

ORGANIZATION LEADERS

BATTING
*Minimum 250 at-bats
*AVG	Leandro, Francisco, Southwest Michigan/Visalia	.329
R	Upton, B.J., Durham	98
H	Young, Delmon, Durham/Montgomery	176
TB	Young, Delmon, Durham/Montgomery	294
2B	Leandro, Francisco, Southwest Michigan/Visalia	44
3B	Perez, Fernando, Southwest Michigan	13
HR	Snyder, Earl, Durham	29
RBI	Young, Delmon, Durham/Montgomery	99
BB	Leandro, Francisco, Southwest Michigan/Visalia	82
SO	Cuevas, Aneudi, Visalia	141
SB	Perez, Fernando, Southwest Michigan	57
*OBP	Leandro, Francisco, Southwest Michigan/Visalia	.433
*SLG	Laforest, Pete, Durham	.578

PITCHING
#Minimum 75 innings
W	Sonnanstine, Andy, Southwest Michigan/Visalia	14
L	Prochaska, Mike, Durham/Visalia	12
#ERA	Davis, Wade, Hudson Valley	2.19
G	De la Cruz, Jose, Southwest Michigan	50
CG	Hammel, Jason, Durham/Montgomery	3
SV	De la Cruz, Jose, Southwest Michigan	19
IP	Sonnanstine, Andy, Southwest Michigan/Visalia	181
BB	Lavergne, Jarrad, Southwest Michigan	70
SO	Sonnanstine, Andy, Southwest Michigan/Visalia	178

BEST TOOLS

Best Hitter for Average	Delmon Young
Best Power Hitter	Delmon Young
Best Strike-Zone Discipline	Francisco Leandro
Fastest Baserunner	Fernando Perez
Best Athlete	Elijah Dukes
Best Fastball	Wade Davis
Best Curveball	Matt Walker
Best Slider	Jeff Niemann
Best Changeup	Jamie Shields
Best Control	Jason Hammel
Best Defensive Catcher	Shawn Riggans
Best Defensive Infielder	Neil Walton
Best Infield Arm	Neil Walton
Best Defensive Outfielder	Fernando Perez
Best Outfield Arm	Delmon Young

PROJECTED 2009 LINEUP

Catcher	Toby Hall
First Base	Wes Bankston
Second Base	Jorge Cantu
Third Base	Reid Brignac
Shortstop	B.J. Upton
Left Field	Carl Crawford
Center Field	Rocco Baldelli
Right Field	Delmon Young

Designated Hitter	Jonny Gomes
No. 1 Starter	Scott Kazmir
No. 2 Starter	Jeff Niemann
No. 3 Starter	Jason Hammel
No. 4 Starter	Wade Davis
No. 5 Starter	Matt Walker
Closer	Chad Orvella

LAST YEAR'S TOP 20 PROSPECTS

1. Delmon Young, of
2. Scott Kazmir, lhp
3. Jeff Niemann, rhp
4. Joey Gathright, of
5. Jason Hammel, rhp
6. Reid Brignac, ss
7. James Houser, lhp
8. Elijah Dukes, of
9. Chad Orvella, rhp
10. Seth McClung, rhp
11. Wes Bankston, 1b/of
12. Elliot Johnson, 2b
13. Jason Pridie, of
14. Wade Davis, rhp
15. Travis Schlichting, 3b
16. Chris Seddon, lhp
17. Jonny Gomes, of
18. Angel Garcia, rhp
19. Gabby Martinez, 1b/3b
20. Matt Diaz, of

TOP PROSPECTS OF THE DECADE

Year	Player, Pos.	2005 Org.
1997	Matt White, rhp	Out of baseball
1998	Matt White, rhp	Out of baseball
1999	Matt White, rhp	Out of baseball
2000	Josh Hamilton, of	Devil Rays
2001	Josh Hamilton, of	Devil Rays
2002	Josh Hamilton, of	Devil Rays
2003	Rocco Baldelli, of	Devil Rays
2004	B.J. Upton, ss	Devil Rays
2005	Delmon Young, of	Devil Rays

TOP DRAFT PICKS OF THE DECADE

Year	Player, Pos.	2005 Org.
1996	Paul Wilder, of	Out of baseball
1997	Jason Standridge, rhp	Reds
1998	Josh Pressley, 1b (4th round)	Royals
1999	Josh Hamilton, of	Devil Rays
2000	Rocco Baldelli, of	Devil Rays
2001	Dewon Brazelton, rhp	Devil Rays
2002	B.J. Upton, ss	Devil Rays
2003	Delmon Young, of	Devil Rays
2004	Jeff Niemann, rhp	Devil Rays
2005	Wade Townsend, rhp	Devil Rays

ALL-TIME LARGEST BONUSES

Matt White, 1996	$10,200,000
Rolando Arrojo, 1997	$7,000,000
B.J. Upton, 2002	$4,600,000
Dewon Brazelton, 2001	$4,200,000
Josh Hamilton, 1999	$3,960,000

MINOR LEAGUE DEPTH CHART

Tampa Bay Devil Rays

Rank: **10**

STRENGTH: Impact talent. From Delmon Young and Elijah Dukes in the outfield to Jeff Niemann and Jason Hammel on the mound, the Rays could produce several future all-stars.

WEAKNESS: Third base. No wonder the Rays were linked to Andy Marte in trade talks during the winter.

*Depth charts prepared by **John Manuel** and **Chris Kline**. Numbers in parentheses indicate prospect rankings.*

LF
Shaun Cumberland (17)
Francisco Leandro (30)
Chris Cunningham
Maiko Loyola

CF
Fernando Perez (13)
John Matulia (28)

RF
Delmon Young (1)
Elijah Dukes (5)
Andrew Lopez (23)
Garrett Groce

3B
Gabby Martinez
Mike McCormick
Travis Schlichting

SS
Reid Brignac (4)
Neil Walton

2B
Elliot Johnson (18)
Fernando Cortez

1B
Wes Bankston (7)
Chris Nowak
Henry Wrigley
Matt Fields

C
Shawn Riggans (11)
John Jaso (15)
Pete LaForest

RHP

Starters	Relievers
Jeff Niemann (2)	Chad Orvella (8)
Jason Hammel (3)	Jose de la Cruz (21)
Wade Davis (6)	Carlos Hines (25)
Matt Walker (9)	Juan Salas (27)
Chris Mason (10)	Tim Corcoran
Jamie Shields (12)	Matt Rico
Wade Townsend (14)	Celso Rondon
Jeremy Hellickson (19)	
Andy Sonnanstine (20)	
Brian Stokes (26)	
Derek Feldkamp (29)	
Greg Reinhard	
John Webb	
Woods Fines	
Jason Clayton	

LHP

Starters	Relievers
Jacob McGee (16)	Chris Seddon (24)
James Houser (22)	Jeff Ridgway
Mike Wlodarczyk	Yorkin Ferreras
Brandon Mann	Jason Cromer
	Jarrad Lavergne

DRAFT ANALYSIS

2005

Best Pro Debut: RHP Derek Feldkamp (9) led the short-season New York-Penn League with 15 saves, going 1-2, 4.05 with 35 strikeouts in 27 innings. OF Garrett Groce (41) batted .322-9-35 with 12 steals in the NY-P.

Best Athlete: RHP Chris Mason (2), who was also a regular third baseman at UNC Greensboro. His mechanics, fielding and pickoff move are all smooth. As a position player, he had plus power, speed and defensive ability. Among the everyday players, the pick is OF John Matulia (10). He has speed, hitting ability and pop, and he plays center field well.

Best Pure Hitter: OF Andrew Lopez (8) is a natural hitter who batted .325-4-21 at Rookie-level Princeton. It cost $300,000, the equivalent of third-round money, to divert him from attending Long Beach State.

Best Raw Power: 1B Henry Wrigley (14) was consistently driving pitches in instructional league after signing late.

Fastest Runner: Matulia has above-average speed, though he was caught in 10 of his 18 steal attempts.

Best Defensive Player: SS Neil Walton (16) pushed skilled defenders Justin Turner and Ronnie Prettyman to other positions at Cal State Fullerton. He has enough arm strength to pitch if the Devil Rays want to try him on the mound.

Best Fastball: Feldkamp, Mason and RHPs Jeremy Hellickson (4) and Greg Reinhard (6) all have 91-95 mph fastballs. So does RHP Bryan Morris (3), who's expected to sign as a draft-and-follow this spring. The Devil Rays agreed to a reported $1.3 million deal with Morris, but didn't close it in time to keep him from attending Motlow State (Tenn.) CC.

Townsend

Best Breaking Ball: Mason and Morris both have terrific curveballs. RHP Wade Townsend's (1) signature pitch is his spike curveball, but he won't be throwing it for at least a year after blowing out his elbow in the Arizona Fall League. RHP Ryan Zimmerman (12) also has a power curve but is recuperating from Tommy John surgery.

Most Intriguing Background: Morris' father Ricky is an assistant coach at Motlow State. Matulia's dad Michael is the head coach at Lake Sumter (Fla.) CC. Zimmerman started at quarterback for Southern Utah before moving to Salt Lake CC and focusing on baseball. Unsigned 1B/LHP Ike Davis' (19) father Ron was an all-star reliever.

Closest To The Majors: Mason, who has strong makeup to go with all of his physical gifts.

Best Late-Round Pick: Zimmerman, who also had an 88-92 mph fastball, could be a steal once he makes a full recovery from Tommy John surgery. Wrigley and Groce have legitimate hitting potential.

The One Who Got Away: Davis, now at Arizona State, could be a star as either a hitter or a pitcher.

Assessment: Former team president Vince Naimoli and GM Chuck LaMar didn't do the Rays any favors by insisting on the choice of Townsend at No. 8 overall or by holding up the Morris deal. There's still plenty of depth to salvage this draft, and Morris can be signed this spring.

2004 RHP Jeff Niemann (1) has had shoulder problems, but if healthy could be the ace Tampa Bay needs. It was also a very deep draft. **GRADE:** B+

2003 OF Delmon Young is the game's No. 1 prospect—exactly what you'd hope for from a No. 1 overall pick. Unsigned LHP Andrew Miller (3) could be the first overall pick in 2006. C/DH John Jaso (12) and RHP Chad Orvella (13) were nice finds. **GRADE:** A

2002 SS B.J. Upton (1) still needs a position but should become a superstar. Tampa Bay also has high hopes for OF Elijah Dukes (3), 1B Wes Bankston (4) and RHP Jason Hammel (10). **GRADE:** A

2001 Tampa Bay whiffed on RHP Dewon Brazelton (1) but found OFs Jonny Gomes (18) and Joey Gathright (32) deep in the draft. Another late gem, RHP Thomas Diamond (38), became a 2004 first-rounder. **GRADE:** B

Draft analysis prepared by Jim Callis. Numbers in parentheses indicate draft rounds.

DELMON
YOUNG

Born: Sept. 14, 1985.
Ht.: 6-3. **Wt.:** 205.
Bats: R. **Throws:** R.
Drafted: HS—Camarillo, Calif.,
2003 (1st round).
Signed by: Rich Aude.

Young did nothing in 2005 to argue against the predominant belief that he's the top prospect in the minor leagues. After signing a major league contract with a $3.7 million bonus as the first overall pick in the 2003 draft, Young led the low Class A South Atlantic League in hits and RBIs while making his pro debut in 2004. Last season, he would have had a solid shot at capturing the Double-A Southern League triple crown as a teenager had he not been promoted to Triple-A Durham in mid-July. He had to settle for Baseball America's Minor League Player of the Year award. Young was at times a man among boys at the Double-A level, and won the Southern League MVP award despite his early departure. He ranked fourth in the minors in hits and total bases (294) and finished four home runs short of a 30-30 season. He and his brother, Tigers DH Dmitri Young (the fourth choice in 1991), were the highest-drafted siblings ever until 2005. When Arizona took Justin Upton No. 1 overall, he and Devil Rays shortstop B.J. Upton (No. 2 in 2002) passed the Youngs.

Young packs a punch from the right side of the plate with a powerful and consistent stroke. His knowledge of the strike zone is advanced for his age, and coupled with his bat control allows him to make repeated hard contact. He's strong enough that he doesn't have to pull balls to drive them out of the park. He has average speed but makes things happen in terms of stealing bags and taking the extra base. Defensively, Young has above-average range for right field, plus the arm strength and accuracy to play the position at the major league level. With virtually no chinks in his armor, it's easy to see why managers tabbed him the Southern League's best batting prospect, best power hitter, best outfield arm and most exciting player. Because he's close to his brother, he grew up around the game and honed his instincts at a young age.

Young has few faults on the field. He occasionally takes bad routes on fly balls and sometimes gets overaggressive at the plate. He could use some more patience at the plate after walking four times in 52 Triple-A games and 29 times overall last year. Though there are no questions about his makeup, he crossed the line twice in 2005. He drew a three-game suspension after chest-bumping Southern League umpire Jeff Latter in late April. When the Devil Rays declined to promote him in September, he ripped the organization (though he later recanted).

Young has all the tools to be an all-star for years to come. Tampa Bay believes he'll channel his desire in the right direction instead of holding a grudge over what he felt was a slap in the face last fall. The Devil Rays are loaded with outfielders, but they'll hand him their right-field job when he's ready. He has little left to prove in the minors and could force his way into the lineup in spring training. It's also possible he could spend the first half in Triple-A refining his plate discipline and getting a little more prepared.

Year	Club (League)	Class	AVG	G	AB	R	H	2B	3B	HR	RBI	BB	SO	SB	OBP	SLG
2004	Charleston, S.C. (SAL)	A	.320	131	513	95	164	26	5	25	115	53	120	21	.386	.536
2005	Montgomery (SL)	AA	.336	84	330	59	111	13	4	20	71	25	66	25	.386	.582
	Durham (IL)	AAA	.285	52	228	33	65	13	3	6	28	4	33	7	.303	.447
MINOR LEAGUE TOTALS			.317	267	1071	187	340	52	12	51	214	82	219	53	.370	.531

JEFF NIEMANN

RHP

Born: Feb. 28, 1983. **B-T:** R-R. **Ht.:** 6-9. **Wt.:** 260. **Drafted:** Rice, 2004 (1st round). **Signed by:** Jonathan Bonifay.

Niemann might have gone No. 1 in the 2004 draft had he not been coming off arthroscopic elbow surgery and a groin strain. He went fourth overall and held out until January 2005, when he signed a $5.2 million major league deal. A tender shoulder and more groin problems limited him in his pro debut, and he had minor surgery to shave the joint between his collarbone and shoulder in October. Niemann has great size and mound presence. He's learning how to work off his 92-96 mph fastball. His slider has sharp, cutting action and was deemed the best breaking pitch in the 2004 draft. He has an excellent feel for pitching and good body control. Niemann needs innings and will have to avoid the injuries that have plagued his young career. His changeup and spike curveball need more consistency to give him a complete repertoire. Provided he stays healthy, Niemann should move fast. He may open the season back in Double-A Montgomery, but could receive his first taste of the big leagues later in the year. The Rays envision Niemann joining Scott Kazmir as a potent 1-2 punch.

Year	Club (League)	Class	W	L	ERA	G	GS	CG	SV	IP	H	R	ER	HR	BB	SO	AVG
2005	Visalia (Cal)	A	0	1	3.99	5	5	0	0	20	12	10	9	3	10	28	.167
	Montgomery (SL)	AA	0	1	4.37	6	3	0	0	10	7	7	5	0	5	14	.184
MINOR LEAGUE TOTALS			0	2	4.11	11	8	0	0	31	19	17	14	3	15	42	.173

JASON HAMMEL

RHP

Born: Sept. 2, 1982. **B-T:** R-R. **Ht.:** 6-6. **Wt.:** 200. **Drafted:** Treasure Valley (Ore.) CC, 2002 (10th round). **Signed by:** Paul Kirsch.

Tampa Bay failed to sign Hammel as a 19th-round draft-and-follow in 2001, then drafted him again and signed him in 2002. After breaking through in the second half of 2004, he was shelved for the first month of last season with a strained elbow. He didn't miss a start the rest of the way and could have been called up in September, but the Devil Rays didn't want to start his service-time clock ticking. Hammel's lively fastball sits in the 91-94 mph range and gets on hitters quickly thanks to his tremendous extension. He also throws a hard curveball in the 75-79 mph range, and he has shown considerable improvement with his changeup. He has the best command in the system. Hammel's curveball is inconsistent. While his fastball has good life down in the zone, it straightens out when he leaves it up. His projectable frame is filling out, but he still needs to add strength. Hammel will get a shot at earning a job on the major league club in spring training. He should be a significant building block as a middle-of-the-rotation starter in the Rays' building project.

Year	Club (League)	Class	W	L	ERA	G	GS	CG	SV	IP	H	R	ER	HR	BB	SO	AVG
2002	Princeton (Appy)	R	0	0	0.00	2	0	0	1	5	7	0	0	0	0	5	.318
	Hudson Valley (NY-P)	A	1	5	5.22	13	10	0	1	52	71	41	30	0	14	38	.314
2003	Charleston, S.C. (SAL)	A	6	2	3.40	14	12	1	0	77	70	32	29	2	27	50	.246
2004	Charleston, S.C. (SAL)	A	4	7	3.23	18	18	0	0	95	94	54	34	7	27	88	.257
	Bakersfield (Cal)	A	6	2	1.89	11	11	0	0	71	52	18	15	4	20	65	.211
2005	Montgomery (SL)	AA	8	2	2.66	12	12	3	0	81	70	26	24	5	19	76	.235
	Durham (IL)	AAA	3	2	4.11	10	10	0	0	55	57	31	25	8	27	48	.264
MINOR LEAGUE TOTALS			28	20	3.24	80	73	4	2	436	421	202	157	26	134	370	.254

REID BRIGNAC

SS

Born: Jan. 16, 1986. **B-T:** L-R. **Ht.:** 6-1. **Wt.:** 185. **Drafted:** HS—St. Amant, La., 2004 (2nd round). **Signed by:** Benny Latino.

Brignac's first full season wasn't as spectacular as his 2004 pro debut, but he more than held his own against older competition in the low Class A Midwest League. The Devil Rays believe he answered any questions about his ability to play shortstop with a strong showing in all phases of the game. Brignac has a live bat with a sweet, smooth swing from the left side. Balls jump off his bat and he has natural loft in his stroke. He could produce 25-plus homers annually down the road. Brignac uses the entire field and has a plan at the plate. His speed, arm, hands and footwork are solid. He showed the mental toughness to handle a challenging assignment last year. Some scouts think Brignac lacks the athleticism to stay at shortstop, though Tampa Bay will give him every chance to prove otherwise. He's discovering plate discipline. He gives away too many at-bats, which led to 131 strikeouts in 2005. While his baserunning is improving, it still needs work. Brignac has made impressive progress at a young age. Plans call for a promotion to high Class A Visalia this year.

Year	Club (League)	Class	AVG	G	AB	R	H	2B	3B	HR	RBI	BB	SO	SB	OBP	SLG
2004	Princeton (Appy)	R	.361	25	97	16	35	4	2	1	25	9	10	2	.413	.474
	Charleston, S.C. (SAL)	A	.500	3	14	3	7	1	0	0	5	1	2	0	.533	.571
2005	Southwest Michigan (Mid)	A	.264	127	512	77	135	29	2	15	61	40	131	5	.319	.416
MINOR LEAGUE TOTALS			.284	155	623	96	177	34	4	16	91	50	143	7	.339	.429

5 ELIJAH DUKES   OF

Born: June 26, 1984. **B-T:** B-R. **Ht.:** 6-2. **Wt.:** 225. **Drafted:** HS—Tampa, 2002 (3rd round). **Signed by:** Kevin Elfering.

MIKE JANES

Dukes continues to move through the minors and have disciplinary problems along the way. He set career highs in several categories in 2005 but was suspended twice and ejected from five games. He also had legal problems in Tampa, declined an invitation to the Southern League all-star game because he wasn't selected to start and missed the Arizona Fall League in order to complete anger-management classes. Dukes is an incredible athlete with all-star ability. He makes solid contact, has at least 20-homer power and plays with all-out aggression. He has plus speed and range, as well as one of the strongest arms in the organization. He has demonstrated improved control of the strike zone. If he can't accept authority and develop discipline, Dukes will fall short of his potential. That said, he's dedicated to the game. His average suffers when he tries too hard to hit for power. From a tools standpoint, everything is in place for Dukes to be a prototype right fielder. The Devil Rays are working with him to help him reach that potential. On the field, Delmon Young will be a formidable roadblock to Dukes playing right field in Tampa Bay.

Year	Club (League)	Class	AVG	G	AB	R	H	2B	3B	HR	RBI	BB	SO	SB	OBP	SLG
2003	Charleston, S.C. (SAL)	A	.245	117	383	51	94	17	4	7	53	45	130	33	.338	.366
2004	Charleston, S.C. (SAL)	A	.288	43	163	26	47	12	2	2	15	18	47	14	.368	.423
	Bakersfield (Cal)	A	.332	58	211	44	70	16	2	8	34	26	50	16	.416	.540
2005	Montgomery (SL)	AA	.287	120	446	73	128	21	5	18	73	45	83	19	.355	.478
MINOR LEAGUE TOTALS			.282	338	1203	194	339	66	13	35	175	134	310	82	.362	.446

6 WADE DAVIS   RHP

Born: Sept. 7, 1985. **B-T:** R-R. **Ht.:** 6-5. **Wt.:** 220. **Drafted:** HS—Lake Wales, Fla., 2004 (3rd round). **Signed by:** Kevin Elfering.

MICKEY WEINSTEIN

Most teams thought Davis was headed to the University of Florida, but area scout Kevin Elfering did his homework and persuaded the Devil Rays to take him in 2004's third round. Davis signed quickly for $475,000 and showed first-round ability in 2005, when he led the short-season New York-Penn League in strikeouts. Davis is a big, power pitcher with a smooth delivery and easy arm action. He throws on a downward plane. He drives his fastball low in the zone at 92-98 mph. His hard curveball became more consistent last year, and his slider is a solid-average pitch. He has had no problem throwing strikes as a pro. He still could use an offspeed pitch, and Davis is working on a changeup that needs more consistent fade and depth. He can fall into lapses of concentration on the mound, though that should decrease with maturity. Davis looks more like the total pitching package every time he takes the mound. The Rays are confident he will develop into a frontline starter. His next stop is low Class A Southwest Michigan, and he could move quickly.

Year	Club (League)	Class	W	L	ERA	G	GS	CG	SV	IP	H	R	ER	HR	BB	SO	AVG
2004	Princeton (Appy)	R	3	5	6.08	13	13	0	0	58	71	46	39	8	19	38	.301
2005	Hudson Valley (NY-P)	A	7	4	2.72	15	15	0	0	86	75	35	26	5	23	97	.234
MINOR LEAGUE TOTALS			10	9	4.07	28	28	0	0	144	146	81	65	13	42	135	.262

7 WES BANKSTON 1B

LARRY GOREN

Born: Nov. 23, 1983. **B-T:** R-R. **Ht.:** 6-4. **Wt.:** 210. **Drafted:** HS—Plano, Texas, 2002 (4th round). **Signed by:** Milt Hill.

Bankston continues his methodical climb through the organization. After ranking among the South Atlantic League leaders in homers, RBIs and extra-base hits in 2004, he received a midseason promotion to Double-A last year and helped pick up the slack in Montgomery after Delmon Young's departure. Bankston shows as much raw power as anyone in the organization. He's learning how to harness that pop in game action. He has made impressive strides in hitting to the opposite field with authority. His pitch selection and plate discipline should get better with experience. Injuries have plagued Bankston, including a knee injury that cost him six weeks at the start of 2005. A right fielder until mid-2004, he has improved at first base but remains merely adequate there. His lower body has gotten thicker in the past two years, reducing his speed and overall athleticism. Bankston reminds some scouts of former all-star Glenn Davis. He'll move up to Triple-A in 2006 and should get his first taste of the big leagues by September.

Year	Club (League)	Class	AVG	G	AB	R	H	2B	3B	HR	RBI	BB	SO	SB	OBP	SLG
2002	Princeton (Appy)	R	.301	62	246	48	74	10	1	18	57	18	46	2	.346	.569
	Hudson Valley (NY-P)	A	.303	8	33	2	10	1	0	0	1	0	6	1	.294	.333
2003	Charleston, S.C. (SAL)	A	.256	103	375	46	96	18	1	12	60	53	94	2	.346	.405
2004	Charleston, S.C. (SAL)	A	.289	127	470	82	136	30	3	23	101	73	104	9	.390	.513
2005	Visalia (Cal)	A	.387	17	62	15	24	4	1	3	23	15	17	0	.513	.629
	Montgomery (SL)	AA	.292	82	301	42	88	17	2	12	47	30	64	3	.362	.482
MINOR LEAGUE TOTALS			.288	399	1487	235	428	80	8	68	289	189	331	17	.370	.490

8 CHAD ORVELLA RHP

Born: Oct. 1, 1980. **B-T:** R-R. **Ht.:** 5-11. **Wt.:** 190. **Drafted:** North Carolina State, 2003 (13th round). **Signed by:** Hank King.

Mainly a shortstop in college, Orvella made it to the majors as a pitcher less than two years after he turned pro. He was unhittable in the minors, posting a 1.22 ERA, .159 opponent average and 160-17 K-BB ratio in 111 innings. He assumed a late-inning set-up role with the Devil Rays, though he didn't pitch after Sept. 16 because of a sore shoulder. When he was a shortstop, Orvella's best tool was his arm, which now delivers consistent 92-94 mph fastballs with late life. Hitters can't sit on his heater because he has a plus changeup, which is a nifty weapon against lefthanders. His numbers testify to his ability to locate the ball where he wants. Orvella's slider can be a plus pitch at times, but it lacks consistency and is significantly behind his fastball and changeup. While his shoulder problem was diagnosed as mild irritation, he's not big and never has worked more than 75 innings in a season. Orvella and Lance Carter once again should serve as Danys Baez' primary set-up men. Baez continually gets mentioned in trade talks, and Orvella is his likely successor should Baez get dealt.

Year	Club (League)	Class	W	L	ERA	G	GS	CG	SV	IP	H	R	ER	HR	BB	SO	AVG
2003	Hudson Valley (NY-P)	A	0	0	0.00	10	0	0	8	12	6	0	0	0	1	15	.140
2004	Charleston, S.C. (SAL)	A	1	0	1.33	22	0	0	4	47	28	9	7	4	5	76	.164
	Bakersfield (Cal)	A	0	1	3.06	15	0	0	4	18	13	7	6	2	4	24	.197
	Montgomery (SL)	AA	0	0	0.00	6	0	0	4	7	0	0	0	0	0	14	.000
	Durham (IL)	AAA	0	0	5.40	2	0	0	0	2	1	1	1	1	1	2	.167
2005	Montgomery (SL)	AA	0	0	0.36	16	0	0	9	25	15	1	1	0	6	29	.169
	Tampa Bay (AL)	MLB	3	3	3.60	37	0	0	1	50	47	26	20	4	23	43	.246
MAJOR LEAGUE TOTALS			3	3	3.60	37	0	0	1	50	47	26	20	4	23	43	.246
MINOR LEAGUE TOTALS			1	1	1.22	71	0	0	29	111	63	18	15	7	17	160	.159

9 MATT WALKER RHP

ROBERT GURGANUS

Born: Aug. 16, 1986. **B-T:** R-R. **Ht.:** 6-3. **Wt.:** 193. **Drafted:** HS—Baton Rouge, La., 2004 (10th round). **Signed by:** Benny Latino.

Walker seemed to have more potential as a quarterback entering his senior season of high school. His baseball stock surged in the spring of 2004, but he tailed off late and dropped to the 10th round. Still, the Devil Rays coughed up $600,000 to sign him. He made his pro debut in 2005 and while his numbers weren't pretty, Rookie-level Appalachian League observers were impressed. Walker is a power pitcher who has added 15 pounds since signing. His fastball ranges from 89-96 mph with good life.

His overhand power curveball has a sharp break and is the best in the system. He's mentally tough and battles on the mound. He has a ways to go to become a true pitcher. Walker is ironing out his mechanics. He overthrows at times, trying to overpower hitters instead of using his head to get the out. A more consistent changeup and added maturity will take him a long way. Yet another high-ceiling pitcher, Walker will pitch in low Class A this year at 19. While the Devil Rays are grooming him as a starter, he also profiles well as a reliever.

Year	Club (League)	Class	W	L	ERA	G	GS	CG	SV	IP	H	R	ER	HR	BB	SO	AVG
2005	Hudson Valley (NY-P)	A	0	0	10.91	1	1	0	0	3	5	4	4	0	4	5	.357
	Princeton (Appy)	R	2	3	5.30	13	12	0	1	58	63	39	34	2	22	71	.274
MINOR LEAGUE TOTALS			2	3	5.61	14	13	0	1	61	68	43	38	2	26	76	.279

10 CHRIS MASON   RHP

Born: July 1, 1984. **B-T:** R-R. **Ht.:** 6-0. **Wt.:** 185. **Drafted:** UNC Greensboro, 2005 (2nd round). **Signed by:** Brad Matthews.

Mason broke Kevin Millwood's Bessemer City (N.C.) High strikeout record, then set another mark with 135 whiffs at UNC Greenboro last spring. An excellent two-way player in college, Mason displayed above-average defensive skills at third base while showing electricity in his bat. Though he's just 6 feet tall, Mason generates 91-95 mph velocity and plus movement on his fastball thanks to a lightning-quick arm. He has a power curveball and started to develop a good changeup during instructional league. His pickoff move and defense are among the best in the organization, and his aggressiveness is unmatched. Mason's curveball can get slurvy, though he usually locates it so well that it's not a huge issue. The Rays were cautious with him last season, limiting him to 40 pitches per outing because he worked hard and played both ways in college, but he has been durable. The Devil Rays will give Mason the opportunity to jump into their Double-A rotation in 2006. He relishes the chance to hit as a pro, but he's too talented a pitcher for Tampa Bay to consider it.

Year	Club (League)	Class	W	L	ERA	G	GS	CG	SV	IP	H	R	ER	HR	BB	SO	AVG
2005	Hudson Valley (NY-P)	A	1	1	2.40	9	0	0	2	15	11	4	4	0	8	14	.220
	Southwest Michigan (Mid)	A	1	0	1.44	10	0	0	0	19	17	8	3	0	5	16	.246
MINOR LEAGUE TOTALS			2	1	1.87	19	0	0	2	34	28	12	7	0	13	30	.235

11 SHAWN RIGGANS   C

Born: July 25, 1980. **B-T:** R-R. **Ht.:** 6-2. **Wt.:** 190. **Drafted:** Indian River (Fla.) JC, 2000 (24th round). **Signed by:** Kevin Elfering.

Injuries bit Riggans again in 2005, as he missed three weeks after suffering a high left ankle sprain in mid-May, but he was healthy otherwise and collected a career-high 313 at-bats. He had Tommy John surgery shortly after signing in 2001, and elbow problems bothered him again in 2004. A solid defensive catcher, Riggans has good bounce behind the plate. His catch-and-throw skills and arm strength are above average. He has a quick release and good awareness, and he threw out 32 percent of basestealers last year. He receives high marks for his ability to work with pitchers and call a game. Riggans' hitting steadily has improved, and the Rays believe he'll provide some pop in the lower half of the lineup. He remains too pull-conscious at the plate, however, and falls into the habit of uppercutting too many pitches. He also tends to surrender the outside part of the plate. A more disciplined approach could mean the difference between being a platoon player and a starter in the major leagues. Riggans is expected to be the starting catcher in Triple-A in 2006, with a likely promotion to Tampa in September.

Year	Club (League)	Class	AVG	G	AB	R	H	2B	3B	HR	RBI	BB	SO	SB	OBP	SLG
2001	Princeton (Appy)	R	.345	15	58	15	20	4	0	8	17	9	18	1	.433	.828
2002	Hudson Valley (NY-P)	A	.263	73	266	34	70	13	0	9	48	32	72	2	.343	.414
2003	Charleston, S.C. (SAL)	A	.280	68	232	33	65	17	0	3	34	19	35	3	.340	.392
	Orlando (SL)	AA	.274	22	62	7	17	6	0	1	11	4	14	0	.319	.419
2004	Bakersfield (Cal)	A	.346	34	127	20	44	11	0	5	22	15	23	0	.417	.551
	Montgomery (SL)	AA	.222	10	36	3	8	1	0	2	7	2	14	0	.282	.417
2005	Montgomery (SL)	AA	.310	89	313	40	97	21	0	8	53	26	69	1	.365	.454
MINOR LEAGUE TOTALS			.293	311	1094	152	321	73	0	36	192	107	245	7	.359	.459

12 JAMIE SHIELDS   RHP

Born: Dec. 20, 1981. **B-T:** R-R. **Ht.:** 6-3. **Wt.:** 215. **Drafted:** HS—Newhall, Calif., 2000 (16th round). **Signed by:** Fred Repke.

After battling shoulder tendinitis in 2004 and not taking the mound last season until the end of May, Shields put together an outstanding campaign. He did not surrender more than four earned runs in any of his 16 starts and held opponents to two runs or less in 10 of those outings. Though not overpowering for a righthander, Shields showed he has the overall package to be a solid fourth starter in the big leagues. He has good run on his 89-92 mph fastball, and he controls and commands it well. His changeup is his best offering, possessing excellent deception and fade. Shields works with two breaking balls, a curveball and a slurvy slider. He uses the curve to change planes on hitters, and his slider as a chase pitch down and away to righthanders. He needs to sharpen one of the breaking balls in order to have a solid third pitch. Shields also has a little length to his arm action and could add some strength to his tall and slender frame. He worked on those elements during a strong effort in the Arizona Fall League, where he ranked second with a 1.74 ERA, and will open 2006 in Triple-A.

Year	Club (League)	Class	W	L	ERA	G	GS	CG	SV	IP	H	R	ER	HR	BB	SO	AVG
2001	Hudson Valley (NY-P)	A	2	1	2.31	5	5	0	0	27	27	8	7	1	5	25	.255
	Charleston, S.C. (SAL)	A	4	5	2.65	10	10	2	0	71	63	24	21	7	10	60	.236
2002	Did not play—Injured																
2003	Bakersfield (Cal)	A	10	10	4.45	26	24	0	1	144	161	85	71	19	38	119	.279
2004	Montgomery (SL)	AA	0	3	7.87	4	4	0	0	18	24	16	16	4	8	14	.329
	Bakersfield (Cal)	A	8	5	4.23	20	20	1	0	117	119	61	55	13	33	92	.273
2005	Montgomery (SL)	AA	7	5	2.80	17	16	0	0	109	95	36	34	6	31	104	.244
	Durham (IL)	AAA	1	0	6.00	1	1	0	0	6	9	4	4	0	3	6	.346
MINOR LEAGUE TOTALS			32	29	3.80	83	80	3	1	493	498	234	208	50	128	420	.266

13 FERNANDO PEREZ   OF

Born: April 28, 1983. **B-T:** R-R. **Ht.:** 6-1. **Wt.:** 195. **Drafted:** Columbia, 2004 (7th round). **Signed by:** Brad Matthews.

The highest-drafted player ever out of Columbia University (seventh round in 2004), Perez solidified his status as one of Tampa Bay's top prospects in his first full pro season. He led the Midwest League in steals and overcame an early-season slump. Batting just .239 at the end of May, he raised his average to .289 by season's end. Perez has struggled at times making contact, though he gave switch-hitting a try during instructional league and had success. He has a good eye at the plate, which enhances his ability to use his speed. That's easily his best tool, as managers rated him the best and fastest baserunner in the MWL. He has an incredible first step and can run with anyone in the minor leagues. Perez is a strong defensive outfielder with plus-plus range in center field. He also tied for fourth in the MWL with 13 outfield assists. The Rays love his even-keeled approach and his exceptional intelligence. He wants to learn everything possible about the game. He's still discovering the nuances of running the bases and taking the right angle on balls in the outfield, but there's no question he has the talent to develop those skills. A full season in high Class A awaits in 2006.

Year	Club (League)	Class	AVG	G	AB	R	H	2B	3B	HR	RBI	BB	SO	SB	OBP	SLG
2004	Hudson Valley (NY-P)	A	.232	69	267	46	62	8	5	2	20	30	70	24	.314	.322
2005	Southwest Michigan (Mid)	A	.289	134	522	93	151	17	13	6	48	58	80	57	.361	.406
MINOR LEAGUE TOTALS			.270	203	789	139	213	25	18	8	68	88	150	81	.345	.378

14 WADE TOWNSEND   RHP

Born: Feb. 22, 1983. **B-T:** R-R. **Ht.:** 6-4. **Wt.:** 230. **Drafted:** Dripping Springs, Texas, 2005 (1st round). **Signed by:** Jonathan Bonifay.

The Devil Rays' former upper-management team overruled the scouting department and mandated that the club take Townsend with the eighth overall pick in the 2005 draft. He appealed to them because he had little bargaining power and would sign for below market value—he agreed to $1.5 million, a savings of $700,000 in the eighth slot—and theoretically would move quickly through the minors. But his first taste of pro ball went poorly. Townsend strained his neck the day after making his debut and pitched poorly in the New York-Penn League. Assigned to the Arizona Fall League, he tore an elbow ligament in his first outing and is expected to miss the entire 2006 season while recovering from Tommy John surgery. Townsend also went eighth overall in the 2004 draft, when he and Rice rotation-mates Philip Humber and Jeff Niemann all went in the top eight to become the highest-drafted trio ever off one team. But the Orioles lowballed Townsend in bonus talks, leading to acrimony that never got resolved. He returned to school to complete his degree, gambling that he could still negotiate after renouncing his eligibility, but MLB ruled against him. Forced to re-enter the draft after nearly a year on the sidelines, he spent much of April and May working out for clubs. At his best at Rice, he pitched at 90-92 mph with his fastball and dominated hitters with a spike curveball. But last year, his velocity ranged anywhere from 85-92 and his curve lacked its trademark bite. He didn't have much of a fastball in the NY-P, relying on his curveball and changeup to try to get hitters out. Townsend is an intense competitor, and a lot of scouts think his fire would work better if he were used as a reliever. Tampa Bay sees him as a starter, but he won't get back on the mound until 2007.

Year	Club (League)	Class	W	L	ERA	G	GS	CG	SV	IP	H	R	ER	HR	BB	SO	AVG
2005	Hudson Valley (NY-P)	A	0	4	5.50	12	10	0	0	39	44	28	24	4	24	33	.275
MINOR LEAGUE TOTALS			0	4	5.50	12	10	0	0	39	44	28	24	4	24	33	.275

15 JOHN JASO
C/DH

Born: Sept. 19, 1983. **B-T:** L-R. **Ht.:** 6-2. **Wt.:** 205. **Drafted:** Southwestern (Calif.) JC, 2003 (12th round). **Signed by:** Craig Weissmann.

Some members of the Tampa Bay scouting department predicted a breakout year for Jaso in 2005, and he did just that despite battling a rotator-cuff problems. He made just one catching appearance during the last two months of the season and didn't play after Aug. 7 because he was limited by his shoulder. After arthroscopic surgery, he's expected to be at full strength for spring training. An excellent contact hitter with a good approach from the left side, Jaso could produce 25-plus homers annually at higher levels. His body is maturing and adding strength, turning some of his doubles into homers last year. He also drove the ball with more backspin and showed the ability to take pitches to the opposite field. Jaso is a good low-ball hitter. His primary weakness is a tendency to roll his wrists on breaking balls. Midwest League observers didn't get to see enough of Jaso behind the plate to know if he could stay behind the plate, but the Devil Rays say he has the catch-and-throw skills to make it work. He's more athletic and has more speed and agility than most catchers, and even with a bad shoulder he threw out 36 percent of basestealers. He could have an even bigger year in the hitter-friendly high Class A California League in 2006.

Year	Club (League)	Class	AVG	G	AB	R	H	2B	3B	HR	RBI	BB	SO	SB	OBP	SLG
2003	Hudson Valley (NY-P)	A	.227	47	154	20	35	7	0	2	20	25	26	2	.344	.312
2004	Hudson Valley (NY-P)	A	.302	57	199	34	60	17	2	2	35	22	32	1	.378	.437
2005	Southwest Michigan (Mid)	A	.307	92	332	61	102	25	1	14	50	42	53	3	.383	.515
MINOR LEAGUE TOTALS			.288	196	685	115	197	49	3	18	105	89	111	6	.373	.447

16 JACOB McGEE
LHP

Born: Aug. 6, 1986. **B-T:** L-L. **Ht.:** 6-3. **Wt.:** 200. **Drafted:** HS—Sparks, Nev., 2004 (5th round). **Signed by:** Fred Repke.

A fifth-round pick in 2004, McGee was Rookie-level Princeton's pitcher of the year in his pro debut and followed up by finishing second to Wade Davis in the New York-Penn League strikeout race in 2005. McGee has added 15 pounds to his 6-foot-3 frame since signing without sacrificing the good body control that allows him to repeat his delivery. He also has improved the quality of his pitches and his confidence. McGee has one of the best curveballs in the minors, an overhand bender that can be unhittable. He adds and subtracts from his curve, varying its velocity from 69-77 mph. His only problem with the pitch is that it breaks so much that lower-level umpires don't always call it for strikes. McGee does a good job of getting ahead in counts with his 88-92 mph fastball. His changeup needs work but could become a solid-average pitch. McGee's biggest need other than innings is staying on top of his delivery. His future appears bright, and his first shot in a full-season league will come in low Class A this year.

Year	Club (League)	Class	W	L	ERA	G	GS	CG	SV	IP	H	R	ER	HR	BB	SO	AVG
2004	Princeton (Appy)	R	4	1	3.97	12	12	0	0	57	49	30	25	5	25	53	.244
2005	Hudson Valley (NY-P)	A	5	4	3.64	15	14	0	0	77	64	32	31	4	23	89	.226
MINOR LEAGUE TOTALS			9	5	3.78	27	26	0	0	133	113	62	56	9	48	142	.233

17 SHAUN CUMBERLAND
OF

Born: Aug. 1, 1984. **B-T:** L-R. **Ht.:** 6-2. **Wt.:** 185. **Drafted:** HS—Milton, Fla., 2003 (10th round). **Signed by:** Skip Bundy.

Cumberland's strong second half in 2005—he had eight homers and 45 RBIs in the last two months—left the Devil Rays believing he has the overall package to become a starting right fielder at the major league level. Scouts drool over his picture-perfect swing from the left side of the plate. He has quick wrists and sprays line drives to all fields, though he'll need to reduce his strikeouts. Tampa Bay thinks he'll develop above-average power as his body gains strength. Cumberland runs the bases well and his good speed also gives him good range in right field. He also has the arm strength for the position as well. Most important,

Cumberland displayed more maturity last year. Competitive almost to a fault, he still needs to channel his emotions in a more positive manner. The Rays believe he'll continue to improve in that regard with more experience. He'll play this season in high Class A.

Year	Club (League)	Class	AVG	G	AB	R	H	2B	3B	HR	RBI	BB	SO	SB	OBP	SLG
2003	Princeton (Appy)	R	.252	62	218	28	55	11	5	1	32	19	41	12	.314	.362
2004	Hudson Valley (NY-P)	A	.329	50	164	25	54	7	4	1	11	11	23	9	.375	.439
2005	Southwest Michigan (Mid)	A	.268	119	436	62	117	22	3	13	69	37	100	23	.326	.422
MINOR LEAGUE TOTALS			.276	231	818	115	226	40	12	15	112	67	164	44	.333	.410

18 ELLIOT JOHNSON   2B

Born: March 9, 1984. **B-T:** B-R. **Ht.:** 6-0. **Wt.:** 171. **Signed:** NDFA/HS—Thatcher, Ariz., 2002. **Signed by:** Craig Weissmann.

Johnson emerged as a bona-fide prospect in 2004 and built on that reputation while making an in-season jump to Double-A last summer. The second baseman created havoc on the basepaths in the California League, stealing 28 bases in 33 attempts, though nagging leg injuries tempered his aggressiveness after he moved up. Signed by scout Craig Weissmann as a nondrafted free agent in 2002, Johnson is a solid all-around player. In addition to his plus speed, he should develop consistent extra-base power once his body fills out more completely and adds some strength. Though he's not a big home run threat, he's one of just two players in professional baseball history to hit three homers in the first three innings of a game. He pulled off that feat on May 28, 2004, joining Carl Reynolds of the 1930 White Sox. Johnson needs to reduce his strikeouts by cutting down on his somewhat long swing. Defensively, he has plenty of range and arm strength at second base, yet must improve upon his fielding mechanics and his consistency. A gritty, hard-nosed performer, Johnson could be a starting second baseman in the big leagues, but is more likely to be a utilityman. He should make the jump to Triple-A during the 2006 season.

Year	Club (League)	Class	AVG	G	AB	R	H	2B	3B	HR	RBI	BB	SO	SB	OBP	SLG
2002	Princeton (Appy)	R	.263	42	152	21	40	10	1	1	13	18	48	14	.345	.362
2003	Charleston, S.C. (SAL)	A	.212	54	151	22	32	4	0	0	15	38	32	8	.370	.238
2004	Charleston, S.C. (SAL)	A	.262	126	503	92	132	22	7	6	41	54	91	43	.339	.370
2005	Visalia (Cal)	A	.273	56	227	42	62	10	3	8	33	24	49	28	.350	.449
	Montgomery (SL)	AA	.261	63	264	31	69	9	6	3	21	13	68	15	.305	.375
MINOR LEAGUE TOTALS			.258	341	1297	208	335	55	17	18	123	147	288	108	.338	.369

19 JEREMY HELLICKSON   RHP

Born: April 8, 1987. **B-T:** R-R. **Ht.:** 6-1. **Wt.:** 185. **Drafted:** HS— Des Moines, Iowa, 2005 (4th round). **Signed by:** Tom Couston.

Projected to go in the first two rounds of the 2005 draft, Hellickson dropped to the fourth because clubs worried about his bonus demands and his commitment to Louisiana State. He signed for $500,000, easily the highest bonus in his round, after an accomplished amateur career that included serving as the ace of the U.S. national team that won the 2003 World Youth Championship in Taiwan. Hellickson's arm works easy in his smooth, mechanically sound delivery and produces 91-95 mph fastballs with plus movement. He surprises hitters with the way his fastball explodes and gets on top of them. His curveball has some power and sits around 74-78 mph with the potential to become a plus pitch. He also shows an excellent feel for a changeup that could become average with time. The biggest concern about Hellickson is his undersized frame for a righthander, which at 6 feet and 170 pounds isn't the definition of projectable. If he were bigger, he might have been the first Iowa prep player ever drafted in the first round. He missed his junior season in high school because of a fractured growth plate in his right shoulder, but was strong as a senior and after reporting to Princeton in mid-August. Impressive during instructional league, Hellickson should be a member of the Southwest Michigan rotation this year.

Year	Club (League)	Class	W	L	ERA	G	GS	CG	SV	IP	H	R	ER	HR	BB	SO	AVG
2005	Princeton (Appy)	R	0	0	6.00	4	0	0	0	6	6	4	4	1	1	11	.240
MINOR LEAGUE TOTALS			0	0	6.00	4	0	0	0	6	6	4	4	1	1	11	.240

20 ANDY SONNANSTINE   RHP

Born: March 18, 1983. **B-T:** L-R. **Ht.:** 6-3. **Wt.:** 185. **Drafted:** Kent State, 2004 (13th round). **Signed by:** James Bonnici.

Sonnanstine won the system's pitching triple crown in 2005, leading all Tampa Bay farmhands in wins, strikeouts and ERA. His most eye-popping number was his 178-18 K-BB rato, and managers rated him as having the best control in the Midwest League. He has proven durable, setting a Kent State record with 125 innings in 2004 and working a total of

363 frames over the last two years, including a system-best 181 last year. Sonnanstine doesn't have overwhelming stuff, but he maintains it over the course of a game and stays ahead of hitters. His changeup is his best pitch, and he also throws an 88-92 mph fastball and a backdoor slurve. He also fields his position well and does all the little things to help himself win games. While his command and feel are very good, he does struggle to maintain a consistent arm slot. He'll begin the year in Double-A.

Year	Club (League)	Class	W	L	ERA	G	GS	CG	SV	IP	H	R	ER	HR	BB	SO	AVG
2004	Hudson Valley (NY-P)	A	3	1	1.00	9	2	0	1	27	18	4	3	0	3	24	.176
	Charleston, S.C. (SAL)	A	2	0	0.59	8	5	0	0	31	18	5	2	0	7	42	.167
2005	Southwest Michigan (Mid)	A	10	4	2.54	18	18	1	0	117	103	42	33	10	11	103	.232
	Visalia (Cal)	A	4	1	3.80	10	10	0	0	64	71	29	27	5	7	75	.277
MINOR LEAGUE TOTALS			19	6	2.45	45	35	1	1	238	210	80	65	15	28	244	.231

21 JOSE DE LA CRUZ   RHP

Born: Sept. 23, 1983. **B-T:** R-R. **Ht.:** 6-7. **Wt.:** 245. **Signed:** Dominican Republic, 2002. **Signed by:** Junior Ramirez.

De la Cruz has intimidating mound presence. Standing 6-foot-7 and weighing in excess of 240 pounds, the righthander physically resembles Antonio Alfonseca, only larger, and is nicknamed "The Aircraft Carrier." He delivers his pitches with good power and improving body control, coming at hitters with arms and legs flying in different directions, making them all the more leery of digging in. De la Cruz fires a 91-95 mph fastball with nice movement and is developing a slider with good tilt and bite. He has made major strides with the slider but it still lacks consistency. Once that happens, he'll bring two dominating pitches out of the bullpen. In the meantime, de la Cruz' finesse is still catching up with his power. He needs to improve both his control and command, yet rarely do hitters get a good hack at his offerings. He keeps the ball in the park, allowing just three home runs in 130 innings as a pro. Though still a work in progress, he's taking the steps toward becoming a potential closer. He'll advanced to high Class A in 2006.

Year	Club (League)	Class	W	L	ERA	G	GS	CG	SV	IP	H	R	ER	HR	BB	SO	AVG
2003	Princeton (Appy)	R	0	2	1.33	15	1	0	1	27	25	8	4	1	9	15	.248
2004	Hudson Valley (NY-P)	A	2	0	1.10	17	0	0	7	41	28	8	5	0	11	42	.185
2005	Southwest Michigan (Mid)	A	3	6	3.94	50	0	0	19	62	51	33	27	2	35	60	.224
MINOR LEAGUE TOTALS			5	8	2.50	82	1	0	27	130	104	49	36	3	55	117	.217

22 JAMES HOUSER   LHP

Born: Dec. 15, 1984. **B-T:** L-L. **Ht.:** 6-4. **Wt.:** 185. **Drafted:** HS—Sarasota, Fla., 2003 (2nd round). **Signed by:** Kevin Elfering.

No. 7 on this list last year and No. 4 two years ago, Houser has fallen because of questions about his health and the projectability of his stuff. He dropped to the second round of the 2003 draft mainly because he has a heart murmur that scared teams off. He made just seven starts in 2004 before he was shut down with shoulder stiffness that didn't require surgery. He came down with shoulder problems again last season, sidelining him for most of July. Houser did manage to toss a career-high 115 innings in 2005, but his pitches and overall strength haven't improved as much as the Devil Rays hoped. He still has plenty of potential, however, and club officials won't be surprised if he has a breakthrough season in high Class A this year. Though he's slender, Houser throws a 91-94 mph fastball from a low three-quarters slot. He needs to develop his secondary pitches, as his curveball and changeup are inconsistent. He throws two versions of his curve, one of which backdoors righthanders. His delivery is smooth and easy, but maintaining his release point is key.

Year	Club (League)	Class	W	L	ERA	G	GS	CG	SV	IP	H	R	ER	HR	BB	SO	AVG
2003	Princeton (Appy)	R	0	4	3.73	10	10	0	0	41	43	23	17	1	13	44	.262
2004	Charleston, S.C. (SAL)	A	3	1	2.20	7	7	0	0	33	27	9	8	1	13	27	.239
2005	Southwest Michigan (Mid)	A	8	8	3.76	22	22	0	0	115	100	50	48	12	31	109	.239
MINOR LEAGUE TOTALS			11	13	3.48	39	39	0	0	189	170	82	73	14	57	180	.244

23 ANDREW LOPEZ   OF

Born: Jan. 18, 1987. **B-T:** R-R. **Ht.:** 6-1. **Wt.:** 185. **Drafted:** HS—Elk Grove, Calif., 2005 (8th round). **Signed by:** Carlos Delgado.

Some Devil Rays officials say Delmon Young is the only hitter in the system with a better approach than Lopez, an eighth-round pick in June. Several teams were wary of his commitment to Long Beach State, but he signed for $300,000, the equivalent of late third-round money. Not only did he hit .325 in his pro debut, but he also raked against older pitchers during instructional league, where he reminded veteran scouts of Magglio Ordonez. Lopez has a line-drive stroke and quick wrists that should allow him to clear fences consistently in the future. He tends to get a bit upright in his stance at the plate, and while he has a good eye, he can do a better job of making contact. While his baserunning ability is fringe average, he has good range and plus arm strength in right field. He'll spend his first full pro season in low Class A.

Year	Club (League)	Class	AVG	G	AB	R	H	2B	3B	HR	RBI	BB	SO	SB	OBP	SLG
2005	Princeton (Appy)	R	.325	34	120	21	39	10	2	4	21	11	40	1	.403	.542
MINOR LEAGUE TOTALS			.325	34	120	21	39	10	2	4	21	11	40	1	.403	.542

24 CHRIS SEDDON LHP

Born: Oct. 13, 1983. **B-T:** L-L. **Ht.:** 6-3. **Wt.:** 190. **Drafted:** HS—Santa Clara, Calif., 2001 (5th round). **Signed by:** Fred Repke.

Five years into his pro career, Seddon reached Triple-A at the age of 21. He has been more and more hittable as he moves up the ladder, but he keeps advancing and earning comparisions to Kirk Rueter and other crafty lefthanders. Seddon has more velocity than Rueter. While his fastball varies from 84-92 mph, it sits toward the high end of that range. His changeup is a solid-average pitch, but neither his curveball nor his delivery were as good last year as they had been in the past. He has good control but doesn't always locate his pitches where he wants within the strike zone. He has a habit of elevating his pitches, which is when he gets in the most trouble. No one questions the overall quality of Seddon's effort and makeup. If he can make the necessary adjustments, especially with his command, he could find a role in Tampa Bay's bullpen.

Year	Club (League)	Class	W	L	ERA	G	GS	CG	SV	IP	H	R	ER	HR	BB	SO	AVG
2001	Princeton (Appy)	R	1	2	5.12	4	2	0	0	12	15	7	7	2	6	18	.300
2002	Charleston, S.C. (SAL)	A	6	8	3.62	26	20	0	1	117	93	63	47	7	68	88	.218
2003	Bakersfield (Cal)	A	9	11	5.00	26	26	0	0	133	147	93	74	12	54	95	.279
2004	Bakersfield (Cal)	A	5	0	0.65	7	7	0	0	41	30	4	3	0	8	41	.207
	Montgomery (SL)	AA	9	10	4.39	21	21	1	0	119	129	67	58	19	44	102	.284
2005	Montgomery (SL)	AA	6	1	4.82	10	10	0	0	52	58	31	28	4	20	46	.284
	Durham (IL)	AAA	4	9	5.45	19	19	0	0	96	114	74	58	11	43	70	.295
MINOR LEAGUE TOTALS			40	41	4.33	113	105	1	1	571	586	339	275	55	243	460	.267

25 CARLOS HINES RHP

Born: Sept. 26, 1980. **B-T:** R-R. **Ht.:** 6-3. **Wt.:** 190. **Drafted:** HS—Smithfield, N.C., 1999 (24th round). **Signed by:** Steve Kring (Reds).

Hines was originally drafted by the Reds, who released him after just three months in the organization. He didn't play at all in 2000, and the Devil Rays signed him in the middle of the 2001 season. Durham pitching coach Joe Coleman raved about the way Hines pitched for the Bulls during the final month of the 2005 season. In his last 11 outings, Hines surrendered just one earned run in 19⅔ innings, and the Devil Rays were most impressed with the way he responded in pressure situations. They have hope he may finally live up to the potential he has teased them with for the past several seasons. Hines has a fast arm that produces a powerful 92-97 mph fastball. His improvement at Durham came when he came up with a more effective slider, a pitch that has some power in the upper 70s. As always, consistency and maintaining the feel for his two main pitches as well as a modest changeup are crucial. His control slipped last year, and he's going to have to do a better job of throwing strikes. Hines could make Tampa Bay as a middle reliever in spring training and might develop into a set-up man down the road.

Year	Club (League)	Class	W	L	ERA	G	GS	CG	SV	IP	H	R	ER	HR	BB	SO	AVG
1999	Reds (GCL)	R	0	0	8.10	5	0	0	0	10	15	12	9	0	8	7	.349
2000	Did not play																
2001	Princeton (Appy)	R	2	3	4.44	13	7	0	0	49	51	33	24	3	17	56	.260
2002	Hudson Valley (NY-P)	A	2	2	3.96	5	5	0	0	25	28	13	11	3	7	12	.295
	Charleston, S.C. (SAL)	A	1	3	5.22	24	7	0	2	48	54	29	28	1	15	26	.287
	Orlando (SL)	AA	0	0	16.36	3	0	0	0	3	8	9	6	0	5	3	.400
2003	Charleston, S.C. (SAL)	A	1	0	1.46	30	0	0	16	37	25	6	6	2	9	25	.195
	Bakersfield (Cal)	A	1	1	2.77	25	0	0	8	26	22	10	8	0	13	23	.220
	Orlando (SL)	AA	0	1	9.00	2	0	0	0	3	5	3	3	0	1	2	.417
2004	Montgomery (SL)	AA	4	2	4.40	43	1	0	5	80	82	43	39	4	22	64	.257
2005	Montgomery (SL)	AA	0	2	3.71	22	0	0	6	34	28	17	14	1	16	24	.237
	Durham (IL)	AAA	3	1	3.28	26	0	0	0	36	39	16	13	1	17	22	.277
MINOR LEAGUE TOTALS			14	15	4.13	198	20	0	37	351	357	191	161	15	130	264	.263

26 BRIAN STOKES
RHP

Born: Sept. 7, 1979. **B-T:** R-R. **Ht.:** 6-1. **Wt.:** 205. **Signed:** NDFA/Riverside (Calif.) CC, 1998. **Signed by:** Craig Weissmann.

Like Elliot Johnson, Stokes was signed as a nondrafted free agent by area scout Craig Weissmann. Stokes hasn't progressed nearly as fast as Johnson, having repeated high Class A and missing all of 2004 following Tommy John surgery, and he has yet to reach Triple-A at age 26. But he returned to the mound last year, kept battling and is on the verge of knocking on the door to the big leagues. Stokes' best pitch is a mid-70s curveball, and his 89-92 mph fastball can feature heavy sink when he keeps it down in the zone. When he throws it belt-high, it straightens out. His changeup could use some more depth. Stokes is usually around the strike zone, yet isn't very hittable. A starter for the last five seasons, he projects as more of a middle reliever in the majors.

Year	Club (League)	Class	W	L	ERA	G	GS	CG	SV	IP	H	R	ER	HR	BB	SO	AVG
1999	Princeton (Appy)	R	2	3	3.89	33	0	0	9	37	33	20	16	2	21	39	.239
2000	Charleston, S.C. (SAL)	A	5	6	2.56	46	0	0	5	70	45	24	20	1	34	66	.179
2001	Bakersfield (Cal)	A	8	6	3.92	32	20	1	1	129	118	65	56	11	64	92	.244
2002	Bakersfield (Cal)	A	10	7	3.26	28	28	1	0	166	156	79	60	13	57	152	.248
2003	Orlando (SL)	AA	2	5	3.20	10	10	0	0	51	55	26	18	2	13	33	.274
2005	Visalia (Cal)	A	1	2	4.24	4	4	0	0	17	15	8	8	3	5	21	.231
	Montgomery (SL)	AA	4	6	3.47	16	16	1	0	93	82	36	36	8	28	70	.238
MINOR LEAGUE TOTALS			32	35	3.42	169	78	3	15	563	504	258	214	40	222	473	.238

27 JUAN SALAS
RHP

Born: Nov. 7, 1978. **B-T:** R-R. **Ht.:** 6-2. **Wt.:** 210. **Signed:** Dominican Republic, 1998. **Signed by:** Rudy Santin.

A coveted amateur free agent, Salas signed out of the Dominican Republic for $600,000 in 1998. He consistently showed an 80 arm on the 20-80 scouting scale at the hot corner, but his power never developed as expected. He batted .264 with 28 homers in six years before moving to the mound in mid-2004, and since then he has made rapid progress. Salas' arm has translated well to pitching, as he can overpower hitters with 91-96 mph heat. However, he's strictly a one-speed pitcher at this point. He has been tinkering with a hard slider that could develop into at least an average pitch down the road. Predictably, his overall pitching package is raw. He's still learning how to pitch inside and his control and delivery aren't consistent. He does show excellent body control, thanks in part to his days as an infielder. A return to Double-A to open 2006 is the most likely scenario for Salas.

Year	Club (League)	Class	AVG	G	AB	R	H	2B	3B	HR	RBI	BB	SO	SB	SLG	OBP
1999	Princeton (Appy)	R	.259	53	193	19	50	9	0	2	15	13	50	1	.314	.337
2000	Charleston, S.C. (SAL)	A	.241	60	220	25	53	11	0	1	26	3	50	6	.270	.305
	Hudson Valley (NY-P)	A	.284	38	134	22	38	7	1	2	14	9	31	3	.333	.396
2001	Charleston, S.C. (SAL)	A	.228	135	500	53	114	25	3	7	62	17	93	9	.255	.332
2002	Bakersfield (Cal)	A	.323	66	260	32	84	13	0	4	25	9	59	6	.349	.419
2003	Bakersfield (Cal)	A	.321	37	137	26	44	6	1	6	30	7	30	1	.365	.511
	Orlando (SL)	AA	.272	75	279	30	76	8	2	3	41	10	43	1	.297	.348
2004	Montgomery (SL)	AA	.246	78	284	26	70	13	3	3	29	9	68	2	.277	.345
MINOR LEAGUE TOTALS			.264	542	2007	233	529	92	10	28	242	77	424	29	.296	.361

Year	Club (League)	Class	W	L	ERA	G	GS	CG	SV	IP	H	R	ER	HR	BB	SO	AVG
2004	Princeton (Appy)	R	1	0	4.84	8	0	0	0	9	10	7	5	2	6	6	.263
2005	Visalia (Cal)	A	2	1	3.52	25	0	0	1	38	30	19	15	6	18	47	.216
	Montgomery (SL)	AA	1	0	3.68	15	0	0	0	22	25	12	9	2	12	18	.281
MINOR LEAGUE TOTALS			4	1	3.75	48	0	0	1	70	65	38	29	10	36	71	.244

28 JOHN MATULIA
OF

Born: Aug. 19, 1986. **B-T:** L-L. **Ht.:** 6-0. **Wt.:** 175. **Drafted:** HS—Eustis, Fla., 2005 (10th round). **Signed by:** Rudy Santin.

One Devil Rays coach describes Matulia as "tougher than a one-dollar steak." A 10th-round pick last June, he signed for $75,000 after making it clear he wanted to play for Tampa Bay. Matulia's family has a long relationship with Tim Wilken, the scouting director who drafted him (and who since has departed for the Cubs). Wilken scouted John's father Mike, the head coach at Lake Sumter (Fla.) Community College, when he played at The Citadel in the early 1980s. The fact that Matulia was raised in a baseball family is evident in his hard-nosed approach to the game. He's a tough out who makes sharp contact. He has above-average speed that should allow him to develop into a catalyst atop the lineup. His power should develop as his body matures, yet his game centers around getting on base with his keen batting eye and good strike-zone discipline. His instincts in the outfield make him a natural center fielder. Matulia needs to learn the nuances of baserunning after getting caught stealing in 10 of his 18 pro attempts, and upgrading his bunting ability would boost his stock as a leadoff hitter. After showing little difficulty making the adjustment to pro ball, Matulia should spend a full season in low Class A this year.

Year	Club (League)	Class	AVG	G	AB	R	H	2B	3B	HR	RBI	BB	SO	SB	OBP	SLG
2005	Princeton (Appy)	R	.362	27	105	19	38	6	2	2	15	14	18	8	.437	.514
	Hudson Valley (NY-P)	A	.189	9	37	4	7	0	0	0	1	4	9	0	.268	.189
MINOR LEAGUE TOTALS			.317	36	142	23	45	6	2	2	16	18	27	8	.394	.430

29 DEREK FELDKAMP   RHP

Born: May 9, 1983. **B-T:** R-R. **Ht.:** 6-4. **Wt.:** 210. **Drafted:** Michigan, 2005 (9th round). **Signed by:** James Bonnici.

The Devil Rays are ecstatic about the potential demonstrated by Feldkamp after he led the New York-Penn League in saves during his pro debut. A ninth-round pick who signed for $75,000, he surrendered runs in only four of his first 19 professional outings before fatigue struck late in the season. He was more consistent in pro ball than he was at Michigan, where he pitched his way out of the rotation last spring. Feldkamp's stuff plays very well when he's used in relief, a role in which he shows a 91-95 mph fastball and an 82-84 mph slider. His fastball is fairly straight, however, so it can get hittable. He showed a good changeup in instructional league, but didn't use it in the NY-P and must work it in more against lefthanders. Tampa Bay is uncertain whether Feldkamp will be a starter or a reliever down the road, but is leaning toward putting him in the rotation at one of its Class A affiliates this year.

Year	Club (League)	Class	W	L	ERA	G	GS	CG	SV	IP	H	R	ER	HR	BB	SO	AVG
2005	Hudson Valley (NY-P)	A	1	2	4.04	23	0	0	15	27	20	14	12	3	11	35	.206
MINOR LEAGUE TOTALS			1	2	4.04	23	0	0	15	27	20	14	12	3	11	35	.206

30 FRANCISCO LEANDRO   OF

Born: July 19, 1980. **B-T:** L-L. **Ht.:** 5-10. **Wt.:** 180. **Drafted:** Central Missouri State, 2004 (24th round). **Signed by:** Ricky Drexler.

Tampa Bay's improving minor league depth has been evidenced by the performance of the prospects ranked 30th on this list the previous two years. Second baseman Elliot Johnson (2004) and catcher John Jaso (2005) both have significantly elevated their status since, and Leandro has the potential to do the same. Leandro has hit .320 in two pro seasons since signing as a 24th-round pick out of NCAA Division II power Central Missouri State. Managers rated his strike-zone judgment the best in the Midwest League last year, and he didn't miss a beat after a midseason promotion to high Class A, where he quickly put together a 24-game hitting streak. Leandro puts solid wood on the ball and has a knack for recording extra-base hits in bunches. His strength continues to increase and should produce enough power to allow him to play on an outfield corner in the majors. Leandro runs the bases well and has slightly above-average range to go with average speed. His arm fits best in left field. In addition to his tools, the Rays also like Leandro's strong desire to excel, which he showed by playing winter ball in his native Venezuela. He should move up to Double-A in 2006.

Year	Club (League)	Class	AVG	G	AB	R	H	2B	3B	HR	RBI	BB	SO	SB	OBP	SLG
2004	Hudson Valley (NY-P)	A	.266	40	143	20	38	8	1	1	18	18	26	3	.359	.357
	Charleston, S.C. (SAL)	A	.349	31	106	30	37	10	1	2	19	19	11	7	.448	.519
2005	Southwest Michigan (Mid)	A	.304	73	253	44	77	21	1	3	39	45	33	11	.417	.431
	Visalia (Cal)	A	.355	60	248	53	88	23	3	8	40	37	24	9	.449	.569
MINOR LEAGUE TOTALS			.320	204	750	147	240	62	6	14	116	119	94	30	.421	.475

TEXAS
RANGERS

BY **AARON FITT**

The Rangers followed up their surprising 89-win 2004 campaign with their fifth losing season in the last six years. The exciting young infield core of Mark Teixeira, Alfonso Soriano, **Hank Blalock** and Michael Young produced excellent numbers again, as Texas' 260 homers were just four shy of the major league record.

LARRY GOREN

But as usual, pitching was the problem for the Rangers. They scored the third-most runs in baseball but gave up the fifth-most. They jettisoned three-fifths of their Opening Day rotation by the end of July and entered the offseason looking for answers.

The identity of the man responsible for finding those answers changed in the offseason. Former general manager John Hart originally was to step down after the 2004 season, turning the reins over to assistant general manager Grady Fuson, who also ran the farm and scouting departments. But Hart and manager Buck Showalter persuaded owner Tom Hicks that Hart should return for 2005, leading to Fuson's departure.

Hart stepped down as GM after the 2005 season, moving into a consultant role after Texas went 311-337 on his watch. Jon Daniels, 28, was promoted from assistant GM to become the youngest general manager in baseball history. Daniels hired Rockies director of baseball operations Thad Levine to be his assistant, and tabbed Rockies pro scout Scott Servais to replace Dom Chiti as farm director, with Chiti becoming bullpen coach. Daniels retained Ron Hopkins, who succeeded Fuson as scouting director.

Daniels' first major move was trying to swing a deal for Josh Beckett, which would have given the Rangers a young ace who was a Texas native to boot. That trade fell through when the Red Sox swooped in and acquired Beckett. Daniels did pull off a blockbuster at the Winter Meetings, acquiring Brad Wilkerson, pitching prospect Armando Galarraga and journeyman Terrmel Sledge from the Nationals for Soriano, who becomes a free agent after 2006.

In the near future, the Rangers hope they won't have to go outside the organization for mound help. Five of their top seven prospects are pitchers, and the depth is largely the result of Fuson's drafts. With all the arms on hand, Hopkins had the freedom to focus on position players in the 2005 draft. Texas used its first three picks on a premium athlete (outfielder John Mayberry Jr.), a pure hitter (third baseman Johnny Whittleman) and a Gold Glove-caliber defender (Taylor Teagarden), and later added some promising high school pitchers.

Texas also continued to expand its presence in Latin America. While the Rangers are making progress in Venezuela, they're making a bigger impact in the Dominican Republic. Second baseman Jose Vallejo is establishing himself as a legitimate prospect, while Texas signed catcher Cristian Santana, shortstop Johan Yan and righthander Fabio Castillo to six-figure bonuses in 2005.

TOP 30 PROSPECTS

1. Edison Volquez, rhp	16. Fabio Castro, lhp
2. John Danks, lhp	17. Travis Metcalf, 3b
3. Thomas Diamond, rhp	18. Vince Sinisi, of
4. Joaquin Arias, ss	19. John Hudgins, rhp
5. Eric Hurley, rhp	20. Jose Vallejo, 2b
6. Ian Kinsler, 2b	21. Cristian Santana, c
7. Armando Galarraga, rhp	22. Kevin Mahar, of
8. Jason Botts, of	23. John Bannister, rhp
9. Taylor Teagarden, c	24. Anthony Webster, of
10. John Mayberry Jr., of	25. Mike Nickeas, c
11. Johnny Whittleman, 3b	26. Steve Murphy, of
12. Josh Rupe, rhp	27. Omar Beltre, rhp
13. Michael Schlact, rhp	28. Drew Meyer, inf/of
14. C.J. Wilson, lhp	29. Omar Poveda, rhp
15. Scott Feldman, rhp	30. Manuel Pina, c

ORGANIZATION OVERVIEW

General manager: John Hart. **Farm director:** Scott Servais. **Scouting director:** Ron Hopkins.

2005 PERFORMANCE

Class	Team	League	W	L	Pct.	Finish*	Manager
Majors	Texas	American	79	83	.488	9th (14)	Buck Showalter
Triple-A	Oklahoma RedHawks	Pacific Coast	80	63	.559	1st (16)	Bobby Jones
Double-A	Frisco RoughRiders	Texas	58	82	.414	8th (8)	Darryl Kennedy
High A	Bakersfield Blaze	California	68	72	.486	7th (10)	Arnie Beyeler
Low A	Clinton LumberKings	Midwest	71	69	.507	6th (14)	Carlos Subero
Short-season	Spokane Indians	Northwest	37	39	.487	+4th (8)	Greg Riddoch
Rookie	AZL Rangers	Arizona	27	29	.482	t-5th (9)	Pedro Lopez
OVERALL 2005 MINOR LEAGUE RECORD			341	354	.491	21st (30)	

*Finish in overall standings (No. of teams in league). +League champion.

ORGANIZATION LEADERS

BATTING   *Minimum 250 at-bats
*AVG	Gonzalez, Adrian, Oklahoma	.338
R	German, Esteban, Oklahoma	103
H	Arias, Joaquin, Frisco	157
TB	Botts, Jason, Oklahoma	266
2B	Webster, Anthony, Bakersfield	36
3B	Webster, Anthony, Bakersfield	11
HR	Botts, Jason, Oklahoma	25
RBI	Botts, Jason, Oklahoma	102
BB	Hulett, Tug, Clinton	90
SO	Botts, Jason, Oklahoma	152
SB	German, Esteban, Oklahoma	43
	Yan, Ruddy, AZL Rangers/Frisco/Oklahoma	43
*OBP	Eldridge, Rashad, Frisco/Oklahoma	.415
*SLG	Gonzalez, Adrian, Oklahoma	.561

PITCHING   #Minimum 75 innings
W	Diamond, Thomas, Bakersfield/Frisco	13
L	Danks, John, Bakersfield/Frisco	13
#ERA	Mathis, Doug, Spokane	2.10
G	Veras, Jose, Oklahoma	57
CG	Rodriguez, Ricardo, Oklahoma	3
SV	Veras, Jose, Oklahoma	24
IP	Walker, Andy, Bakersfield/Clinton	178
BB	Diamond, Thomas, Bakersfield/Frisco	69
SO	Diamond, Thomas, Bakersfield/Frisco	169

BEST TOOLS

Best Hitter for Average	Johnny Whittleman
Best Power Hitter	Jason Botts
Best Strike-Zone Discipline	Tug Hulett
Fastest Baserunner	R.J. Anderson
Best Athlete	John Mayberry Jr.
Best Fastball	Edison Volquez
Best Curveball	John Danks
Best Slider	Josh Rupe
Best Changeup	Edison Volquez
Best Control	Scott Feldman
Best Defensive Catcher	Taylor Teagarden
Best Defensive Infielder	Joaquin Arias
Best Infield Arm	Joaquin Arias
Best Defensive Outfielder	Kevin Mahar
Best Outfield Arm	John Mayberry Jr.

PROJECTED 2009 LINEUP

Catcher	Taylor Teagarden
First Base	Mark Teixeira
Second Base	Joaquin Arias
Third Base	Hank Blalock
Shortstop	Michael Young
Left Field	Kevin Mench
Center Field	Brad Wilkerson
Right Field	John Mayberry Jr.

Designated Hitter	Adrian Gonzalez
No. 1 Starter	Edison Volquez
No. 2 Starter	John Danks
No. 3 Starter	Chris Young
No. 4 Starter	Thomas Diamond
No. 5 Starter	Eric Hurley
Closer	Francisco Cordero

LAST YEAR'S TOP 20 PROSPECTS

1. Thomas Diamond, rhp	11. Jason Botts, 1b/of
2. John Danks, lhp	12. Edison Volquez, rhp
3. Joaquin Arias, ss	13. Eric Hurley, rhp
4. Ian Kinsler, ss	14. Juan Senreiso, of
5. Chris Young, rhp	15. Michael Schlact, rhp
6. John Hudgins, rhp	16. Matt Lorenzo, rhp
7. Juan Dominguez, rhp	17. Nick Masset, rhp
8. Adrian Gonzalez, 1b	18. Kameron Loe, rhp
9. Josh Rupe, rhp	19. Wes Littleton, rhp
10. Vince Sinisi, of	20. K.C. Herren, of

TOP PROSPECTS OF THE DECADE

Year	Player, Pos.	2005 Org.
1996	Andrew Vessel, of	Out of baseball
1997	Danny Kolb, rhp	Braves
1998	Ruben Mateo, of	Out of baseball
1999	Ruben Mateo, of	Out of baseball
2000	Ruben Mateo, of	Out of baseball
2001	Carlos Pena, 1b	Tigers
2002	Hank Blalock, 3b	Rangers
2003	Mark Teixeira, 3b	Rangers
2004	Adrian Gonzalez, 1b	Rangers
2005	Thomas Diamond, rhp	Rangers

TOP DRAFT PICKS OF THE DECADE

Year	Player, Pos.	2005 Org.
1996	R.A. Dickey, rhp	Rangers
1997	Jason Romano, 3b	Marlins
1998	Carlos Pena, 1b	Tigers
1999	Colby Lewis, rhp	Tigers
2000	Scott Heard, c	Out of baseball
2001	Mark Teixeira, 3b	Rangers
2002	Drew Meyer, ss	Rangers
2003	John Danks, lhp	Rangers
2004	Thomas Diamond, rhp	Rangers
2005	John Mayberry Jr., of	Rangers

ALL-TIME LARGEST BONUSES

Mark Teixeira, 2001	$4,500,000
John Danks, 2003	$2,100,000
Vince Sinisi, 2003	$2,070,000
Thomas Diamond, 2004	$2,025,000
Drew Meyer, 2002	$1,875,000

MINOR LEAGUE DEPTH CHART

Texas Rangers

Rank: 16

STRENGTH: Catching. The Rangers' weakness last year—so much so Mike Nickeas was rushed to Double-A—is now a point of depth and impact talent.

WEAKNESS: Impact players. The Rangers have depth at almost every position but have no prospects who look like big league stars.

*Depth charts prepared by **John Manuel** and **Chris Kline**. Numbers in parentheses indicate prospect rankings.*

LF
Jason Botts (8)
Vince Sinisi (18)
Steve Murphy (26)
K.C. Herren

CF
Kevin Mahar (22)
Anthony Webster (24)
Ruddy Yan
Brandon Boggs
R.J. Anderson
Jayce Tingler

RF
John Mayberry (10)
Juan Senreiso
Ben Harrison
Will Smith

SS
Joaquin Arias (4)
Drew Meyer (28)
Johan Yan
German Duran

3B
Johnny Whittleman (11)
Travis Metcalf (17)
Marshall McDougall
Emerson Frostad

2B
Ian Kinsler (6)
Jose Vallejo (20)
Tug Hullett

1B
Nate Gold
Jim Fasano
Freddie Thon

C
Taylor Teagarden (9)
Cristian Santana (21)
Mike Nickeas (25)
Manuel Pina (30)
Alberto Martinez

RHP

Starters	Relievers
Edison Volquez (1)	Scott Feldman (15)
Thomas Diamond (3)	Omar Beltre (27)
Eric Hurley (5)	Jesse Chavez
Armando Galarraga (7)	Wes Littleton
Josh Rupe (12)	Kelvin Jimenez
Michael Schlact (13)	John Lujan
John Hudgins (19)	Mark Roberts
John Bannister (23)	Agustin Montero
Omar Poveda (29)	Matt Farnum
Nick Masset	Nate Fogle
Kyle Rogers	
Shane Funk	
Jacob Rasner	
Matt Nevarez	
Fabio Castillo	
Doug Mathis	
Matt Lorenzo	

LHP

Starters	Relievers
John Danks (2)	Fabio Castro (16)
C.J. Wilson (14)	A.J. Murray
Michael Kirkman	Clint Brannon
Zach Phillips	Brian Mattoon
Estelin Soto	Jesse Hall

DRAFT ANALYSIS

2005

Best Pro Debut: OF Steve Murphy (14) won the MVP award in the short-season Northwest League after batting .306-9-37. RHP Jon Wilson (29) also stood out in the NWL, going 3-1, 2.08 with 11 saves and a 49-4 strikeout-walk ratio in 35 innings. The Rangers challenged RHP Kea Kometani (15), sending him to low Class A, and he responded by going 3-2, 2.40 with a 46-13 K-BB ratio in 56 innings.

Best Athlete: OF John Mayberry Jr. (1) was the best college athlete in the draft, a 6-foot-6, 230-pound package of tools. He has huge power potential, plus arm strength and speed. Power separates him from OF R.J. Anderson (9), a blue-chip defensive-back recruit who committed to play football at South Florida before signing with Texas.

Best Pure Hitter: 3B Johnny Whittleman (2), who hit .279-0-35 with 11 steals in the Rookie-level Arizona League, has merited comparisons to Hank Blalock.

Best Raw Power: Mayberry hit 11 homers in the NWL. Though he hit just .253 with 71 strikeouts in as many games, the Rangers say he has started to make adjustments to his swing and found a batting stance he'll stick with.

Fastest Runner: Anderson can cover 60 yards in 6.35 seconds.

Best Defensive Player: Taylor Teagarden (3) was the best defensive catcher in the draft, and he lasted 99 picks only because clubs worried about agent Scott Boras' asking price. One scout called Teagarden, who signed for $725,000, the best catch-and-throw amateur since Joe Mauer. He hit .281 with seven homers in a month in the NWL.

Best Fastball: RHP Matt Nevarez (10) works at 91-92 mph and maxes out at 94.

RODGER WOOD

Whittleman

RHP Shane Funk (4) can reach 93 mph.

Best Breaking Ball: LHP Michael Kirkman (5) mixes four pitches well for a teenager. His 1-to-7 curveball is better than his slider, but that has potential as well. Funk gets good bite on his curve.

Most Intriguing Background: Mayberry's dad John also was a first-round pick and was one of the top power threats in the American League during the mid-1970s. Unsigned C Kevin Gossage's (33) uncle Rich is on the cusp of being voted into the Hall of Fame. RHP Jacob Rasner's (7) cousin Darrell broke into the majors with the Nationals in 2005. SS Renny Osuna (32) was MVP of the Junior College World Series.

Closest To The Majors: Teagarden is on the express route, especially if he continues to hit like he did in his first month as a pro.

Best Late-Round Pick: Nevarez and Murphy.

The One Who Got Away: Texas made a strong run at projectable 6-foot-4 RHP Chris Hicks (35), but not enough to keep him from Georgia Tech. The Rangers will sign their first 16 picks, if RHPs Brad Barragar (8) and Dexter Carter (12) sign in the spring as draft-and-follows.

Assessment: Mayberry is a classic boom-or-bust pick. The Rangers exceeded slot money to sign Whittleman, Teagarden, Rasner and Anderson, and they'll have to open the checkbook again to sign Barragar in the spring.

2004 Always in search of pitching, the Rangers found two keepers in RHPs Thomas Diamond (1) and Eric Hurley (1). Also keep an eye on RHP Michael Schlact (3). **GRADE:** B+

2003 Texas found another pitcher in LHP John Danks (1) and is handing a big league job to 2B Ian Kinsler (17). A $2.07 million investment in OF Vince Sinisi (2) hasn't paid off yet because Sinisi hasn't stayed healthy. **GRADE:** B+

2002 Passing up Jeremy Hermida and Scott Kazmir to take IF/OF Drew Meyer (1) 10th overall was a disaster, and the Rangers didn't pick again until the sixth round. RHP Kameron Loe (20) is the best of this group. **GRADE:** C

2001 Signability dropped 1B Mark Teixeira (1) to Texas as the fifth overall pick. The Rangers took rounds 2-4 off, then got LHP C.J. Wilson (5) with their second choice. **GRADE:** A

*Draft analysis prepared by **Jim Callis**. Numbers in parentheses indicate draft rounds.*

EDISON
VOLQUEZ

BILL MITCHELL

Born: July 3, 1983.
Ht.: 6-1. **Wt.:** 170.
Bats: R. **Throws:** R.
Signed: Dominican Republic, 2001.
Signed by: Rodolfo Rosario.

Volquez draws Pedro Martinez comparisons as much for his electric personality as his electric arm. Though he's a fierce competitor, Volquez often has a big smile on his face when he's not on the mound. He speaks English well and relates well to American players. He's not intimidated pitching in front of 20,000 passionate fans in the Dominican League, and he wasn't intimidated speaking to a group of high-ranking Rangers front-office personnel during an organization banquet. Volquez is even built like Martinez, with a wiry frame and long arms and fingers. Known as Julio Reyes and believed to be 15½ months younger until baseball's visa crackdown, he's still advanced and mature for a 22-year-old. Part of the Rangers' DVD trio, along with John Danks and Thomas Diamond, Volquez surged past the two first-round picks in 2005. He was the first to reach Double-A Frisco and remains the lone member of the group to reach the majors. He got a rude awakening in Texas, losing his first three starts and giving up six runs over two innings in three relief outings.

Though he did not post overwhelming numbers in 2005, Volquez transformed himself from sleeper to top prospect. Both his fastball and changeup rate as the best in the system. His fastball explodes out of his hand and tops out at 97 mph, showing good sink and run when he throws it at 93-95. He holds his velocity late into games, throwing as high as 95 mph in the ninth inning in one outing. His changeup sometimes merits a 70 on the 20-80 scouting scale. Volquez is aggressive and comes right after hitters. He has had little problem throwing strikes as a pro. He has a clean, repeatable delivery and lightning-quick arm action, though there's some effort in it. He isn't the most physical pitcher, but he's athletic and has added 10-15 pounds to his frame since spring training.

For Volquez to stick as a front-of-the-rotation starter rather than a power reliever, he must improve his erratic breaking ball. Sometimes it shows big downward break and looks like a curveball, while other times it features more tilt and looks like a true slider. He uses it more as a third option to cross hitters up. After he missed three weeks in July and August with a strained oblique, Volquez got a callup to the big leagues as the Rangers looked for a spark. He struggled with his fastball command in Texas, and overthrowing only made the problem worse. He tends to buckle plenty of knees with his changeup early in games, but doesn't command it as well in later innings.

Questions remain about Volquez' ability to reach his considerable potential, but his tantalizing package of stuff and makeup can't be overlooked. He should open 2006 with Triple-A Oklahoma but could be pitching in the Rangers rotation by the all-star break if the staff needs help—which it usually does.

Year	Club (League)	Class	W	L	ERA	G	GS	CG	SV	IP	H	R	ER	HR	BB	SO	AVG
2002	Rangers (DSL)	R	1	2	2.68	14	8	0	0	47	45	19	14	1	14	58	.254
2003	Rangers (AZL)	R	2	1	4.00	10	4	0	1	27	24	14	12	1	11	28	.245
2004	Clinton (Mid)	A	4	4	4.21	21	15	0	3	88	82	49	41	8	27	74	.246
	Stockton (Cal)	A	4	1	2.95	8	8	0	0	40	31	16	13	6	14	34	.221
2005	Bakersfield (Cal)	A	5	4	4.18	11	11	1	0	67	64	34	31	9	12	77	.252
	Rangers (AZL)	R	0	0	0.00	1	1	0	0	2	2	0	0	0	0	2	.222
	Frisco (TL)	AA	1	5	4.14	10	10	1	0	59	58	29	27	6	17	49	.258
	Texas (AL)	MLB	0	4	14.17	6	3	0	0	13	25	22	20	3	10	11	.403
MAJOR LEAGUE TOTALS			0	4	14.17	6	3	0	0	13	25	22	20	3	10	11	.403
MINOR LEAGUE TOTALS			17	17	3.78	75	57	2	4	329	306	161	138	31	95	322	.248

JOHN DANKS
LHP

Born: April 15, 1985. **B-T:** L-L. **Ht.:** 6-2. **Wt.:** 190. **Drafted:** HS—Round Rock, Texas, 2003 (1st round). **Signed by:** Randy Taylor.

Danks comes from an athletic family. His father John played basketball at Texas; younger brother Jordan, a slugging outfielder, could have been a 2005 first-round pick if he hadn't committed strongly to the Longhorns; and younger sister Emily is a star volleyball player. The No. 9 overall pick in the 2003 draft, John signed for $2.1 million. Danks' best pitch is a plus curveball that's devastating against lefthanders. He can sneak his 87-93 mph fastball in on the hands of righties, and should pick up velocity as he fills out. He has good feel for his changeup, which the Rangers had him emphasize last year to further its development. He has a free, easy delivery and has improved his leverage from a high three-quarters arm slot. He shows poise beyond his age. Not only would getting stronger give Danks more fastball, it also would help him avoid a late-season fade like he had in 2005. En route to a career-high 156 innings, he went 2-8, 6.46 in the final two months. He needs to continue to develop his changeup and avoid leaving his fastball up in the zone. Danks figures to start 2006 back in Double-A, with a Triple-A promotion likely and a September callup to Texas possible. He looks like a safe bet to develop into a No. 3 starter, and he has a ceiling of a No. 2.

Year	Club (League)	Class	W	L	ERA	G	GS	CG	SV	IP	H	R	ER	HR	BB	SO	AVG
2003	Rangers (AZL)	R	1	0	0.69	5	3	0	0	13	6	3	1	0	4	22	.136
	Spokane (NWL)	A	0	2	8.50	5	5	0	0	13	12	12	12	0	7	13	.267
2004	Clinton (Mid)	A	3	2	2.17	14	8	0	0	50	38	17	12	4	14	64	.210
	Stockton (Cal)	A	1	4	5.24	13	13	0	0	55	62	38	32	5	26	48	.297
2005	Bakersfield (Cal)	A	3	3	2.50	10	10	0	0	58	50	18	16	5	16	53	.228
	Frisco (TL)	AA	4	10	5.49	18	17	0	0	98	117	66	60	12	34	85	.297
MINOR LEAGUE TOTALS			12	21	4.18	65	56	0	0	286	285	154	133	26	101	285	.261

THOMAS DIAMOND
RHP

Born: April 6, 1983. **B-T:** R-R. **Ht.:** 6-3. **Wt.:** 230. **Drafted:** New Orleans, 2004 (1st round). **Signed by:** Randy Taylor.

Signed for $2.025 million as the 10th overall pick in 2004, Diamond dominated at high Class A Bakersfield last year before struggling with his command in Double-A. Diamond was hit hard in his final start of the year after going home to New Orleans to help his family after Hurricane Katrina. Diamond is tough both physically and mentally, with a mean streak that suits his big, physical frame. He is a classic innings-eating power pitcher with a 92-94 mph fastball that can touch 97. He also has an above-average changeup. The biggest question for Diamond is whether he can get comfortable with a third pitch. He flashes a decent curveball now and then, but the Rangers introduced a slider to him halfway through 2005. Scouts think his arm slot is more suited to a slider. Diamond's arm action is smooth but long and not deceptive, and he struggles to repeat his delivery. His fastball is too straight and often dropped to 89-91 mph last year. His command needs to get better. Diamond projects as a solid workhorse if he can improve his command. He could start 2006 in Double-A but figures to see Triple-A at some point.

Year	Club (League)	Class	W	L	ERA	G	GS	CG	SV	IP	H	R	ER	HR	BB	SO	AVG
2004	Spokane (NWL)	A	0	2	2.35	5	3	0	1	15	13	5	4	0	5	26	.220
	Clinton (Mid)	A	1	0	2.05	7	7	0	0	31	18	8	7	1	8	42	.175
2005	Bakersfield (Cal)	A	8	0	1.99	14	14	1	0	81	53	20	18	3	31	101	.191
	Frisco (TL)	AA	5	4	5.35	14	14	0	0	69	66	44	41	8	38	68	.249
MINOR LEAGUE TOTALS			14	6	3.21	40	38	1	1	196	150	77	70	12	82	237	.213

JOAQUIN ARIAS
SS

Born: Sept. 21, 1984. **B-T:** R-R. **Ht.:** 6-2. **Wt.:** 160. **Signed:** Dominican Republic, 2001. **Signed by:** Victor Mata/Carlos Rios/Freddy Tiburcio (Yankees).

Signed out of the Dominican for $300,000, Arias was the player to be named in the February 2004 Alex Rodriguez trade with the Yankees. The Rangers chose him from a list of five prospects that also included Robinson Cano. Typically a slow starter, Arias batted .197 last April before making adjustments and hitting .341 the rest of the way. Like Devon White, Arias is a graceful strider who doesn't look like he's burning, but he's a plus-plus runner who can reach first base in four seconds flat from the right side. His well-above-average arm and above-average range at shortstop allow him to make difficult plays look easy. He has quick, whippy hands and wrists with a good feel for the bat head, letting him control the outer half of the plate. Arias needs to fill out his wiry frame and continue to refine his game. He still can be spastic in the field and butcher routine plays, though his error totals should decrease as he gains experience. He made adjustments after struggling with inside fastballs early in 2005, but he still shows more raw power in batting practice than in games, and he sometimes lets pitchers expand his strike zone. He needs to improve his baserunning instincts. Arias should be a plus defender and has a chance to be a table-setter with gap power. Ticketed for Triple-A this year, he might have to move to second base because the Rangers have all-star Michael Young at shortstop.

Year	Club (League)	Class	AVG	G	AB	R	H	2B	3B	HR	RBI	BB	SO	SB	OBP	SLG
2002	Yankees (GCL)	R	.300	57	203	29	61	7	6	0	21	12	16	2	.338	.394
2003	Battle Creek (Mid)	A	.266	130	481	60	128	12	8	3	48	26	44	12	.306	.343
2004	Stockton (Cal)	A	.300	123	500	77	150	20	8	4	62	31	53	30	.344	.396
2005	Frisco (TL)	AA	.315	120	499	65	157	23	8	5	56	17	46	20	.335	.423
MINOR LEAGUE TOTALS			.295	430	1683	231	496	62	30	12	187	86	159	64	.330	.389

5 ERIC HURLEY RHP

Born: Sept. 17, 1985. **B-T:** R-R. **Ht.:** 6-4. **Wt.:** 195. **Drafted:** HS— Jacksonville, 2004 (1st round). **Signed by:** Guy DeMutis.

Hurley hasn't shot through the minors as quickly as his Wolfson High (Jacksonville) teammate and fellow 2004 first-round pick Billy Butler of the Royals, but he did lead the low Class A Midwest League in strikeouts during his first full pro season. His lean body held up well, and he showed maturity living on his own in Iowa and getting married as a 19-year-old. Hurley was able to dominate high school hitters with only his 92-95 mph fastball, which has good life up in the zone and late boring action down at the knees. He made a lot of progress in 2005 with his late-breaking 78-83 mph slider, which looks like it will become an above-average pitch as well. He's confident on the mound and has good command for his age. Hurley's changeup is still a work in progress but could end up an average pitch. He gets a lot of leverage from his long frame, but needs to grow into it and learn to repeat his delivery better. The next step for Hurley is conquering the hitter-friendly high Class A California League. He's not as advanced or as famous as the DVD trio yet, but he may have a higher ceiling than all of them.

Year	Club (League)	Class	W	L	ERA	G	GS	CG	SV	IP	H	R	ER	HR	BB	SO	AVG
2004	Rangers (AZL)	R	0	1	2.35	6	2	0	0	15	20	8	4	1	4	15	.317
	Spokane (NWL)	A	0	2	5.41	8	6	0	0	28	31	18	17	6	6	21	.295
2005	Clinton (Mid)	A	12	6	3.77	28	28	0	0	155	135	72	65	11	59	152	.234
MINOR LEAGUE TOTALS			12	9	3.89	42	36	0	0	199	186	98	86	18	69	188	.250

6 IAN KINSLER 2B

Born: June 22, 1982. **B-T:** R-R. **Ht.:** 6-0. **Wt.:** 175. **Drafted:** Missouri, 2003 (17th round). **Signed by:** Mike Grouse.

After Kinsler's breakout 2004 season, when he hit .345 with a minor league-high 51 doubles, the Rangers moved him from shortstop to second base so he wouldn't be blocked by Michael Young or Joaquin Arias. Kinsler embraced the move and had a solid year in Triple-A. He wanted to work more on his positioning and fundamentals at second base, so he asked to go to instructional league. He turned down an invitation to join Team USA's Olympic qualifying squad so he could do speed and agility drills, hit in the cage and focus on strength training. Kinsler may be an overachiever, but that doesn't mean he lacks tools. He has a quick bat and is a terrific fastball hitter. He profiles as at least an average hitter in the majors, with a bit of power. Defensively, he has a plus arm and made a lot of progress at second base. Scouts criticized Kinsler for swinging for the fences too much in Triple-A when that really isn't his game. He's a slightly below-average runner and still needs to get better at making routine plays at second. After trading Alfonso Soriano, the Rangers will give Kinsler a chance to win their second-base job. If he fails he still could make Texas as a reserve because he has little left to prove in Triple-A.

Year	Club (League)	Class	AVG	G	AB	R	H	2B	3B	HR	RBI	BB	SO	SB	OBP	SLG
2003	Spokane (NWL)	A	.277	51	188	32	52	10	6	1	15	20	34	11	.352	.410
2004	Clinton (Mid)	A	.402	59	224	52	90	30	1	11	52	25	36	16	.465	.692
	Frisco (TL)	AA	.300	71	277	51	83	21	1	9	46	32	47	7	.400	.480
2005	Oklahoma (PCL)	AAA	.274	131	530	102	145	28	2	23	94	53	89	19	.348	.464
MINOR LEAGUE TOTALS			.304	312	1219	237	370	89	10	44	207	130	206	53	.382	.501

7 ARMANDO GALARRAGA
RHP

Born: Jan. 15, 1982. **B-T:** R-R. **Ht.:** 6-4. **Wt.:** 170. **Signed:** Venezuela, 2000. **Signed by:** Fred Ferreira (Expos).

Brad Wilkerson was easily the biggest name the Rangers received when they traded Alfonso Soriano to the Nationals in December, but the inclusion of Galarraga gave Texas another promising arm. Because of 2002 Tommy John surgery, he pitched just 54 innings in his first three seasons in the United States. He stayed healthier once he began to take baseball more seriously in 2004, and he had his best year yet in 2005, earning a berth in the Futures Game and a promotion to Double-A. Galarraga has a lively 92-94 mph sinker and a hard, sharp slider that he can throw for strikes and use as an out pitch. He has a strong, athletic frame and attacks hitters from a three-quarters arm slot. He's competitive and shows a mean streak. For Galarraga to stick as a starter, he needs to complement his two plus offerings with a third pitch. He must continue to develop his changeup, which shows some promise. He doesn't walk many batters but sometimes misses his spots inside the zone. Galarraga can be a No. 3 starter if his changeup emerges. If that doesn't work out, he could be a powerful bullpen arm. He figures to start 2006 back in Double-A but could earn a big league promotion late in the year.

Year	Club (League)	Class	W	L	ERA	G	GS	CG	SV	IP	H	R	ER	HR	BB	SO	AVG
1999	San Joaquin (VSL)	R	1	2	4.99	21	3	0	2	43	49	37	24	4	28	31	.283
2000	Cagua (VSL)	R	1	5	5.25	14	9	0	1	46	49	35	27	0	22	47	.266
2001	Expos (GCL)	R	1	3	3.11	14	1	0	2	35	37	21	12	2	15	24	.274
2002	Expos (GCL)	R	0	0	2.43	2	2	0	0	4	1	1	1	1	0	1	.083
2003	Expos (GCL)	R	1	1	1.80	5	5	0	0	15	13	5	3	0	5	7	.241
2004	Savannah (SAL)	A	5	5	4.65	23	19	2	0	110	104	64	57	14	31	94	.248
2005	Potomac (Car)	A	3	4	2.48	14	14	0	0	80	69	30	22	7	23	79	.228
	Harrisburg (EL)	AA	3	4	5.19	13	13	1	0	76	80	47	44	10	21	58	.275
MINOR LEAGUE TOTALS			15	24	4.17	106	66	3	5	410	402	240	190	38	145	341	.256

8 JASON BOTTS
OF

Born: July 26, 1980. **B-T:** B-R. **Ht.:** 6-5. **Wt.:** 250. **Drafted:** Glendale (Calif.) JC, D/F 1999 (46th round). **Signed by:** Tim Fortugno.

After bouncing between first base and the outfield for a couple of years, Botts settled in left field in 2005 and posted good power numbers for the second straight year. He held his own in a September callup to Arlington but struggled in the Dominican League. Botts has the body and athleticism of an NFL tight end, and he has more raw power than anyone in the system. He hits for power from both sides of the plate but is a better hitter righthanded. He draws walks and isn't afraid to hit with two strikes. He runs well for his size, particularly once he gets under way. Despite all his athleticism, Botts is brutal defensively and never will be better than adequate in left field. To play every day in the majors, he'll have to hit a lot of homers, but some scouts question how usable his raw power is. He runs into some pitches, but his swing is long and lacks a suitable load, so he has trouble catching up with good fastballs, especially on the inner half. Botts doesn't really have a position, so it's hard to see him playing regularly in the majors in 2006. He should return to Triple-A to continue working on his defense, though he could provide the Rangers with a power boost if needed.

Year	Club (League)	Class	AVG	G	AB	R	H	2B	3B	HR	RBI	BB	SO	SB	OBP	SLG
2000	Rangers (GCL)	R	.319	48	163	36	52	12	0	6	34	26	29	4	.440	.503
2001	Savannah (SAL)	A	.309	114	392	63	121	24	2	9	50	53	88	13	.416	.449
	Charlotte (FSL)	A	.167	4	12	1	2	1	0	0	4	4	0	.375	.250
2002	Charlotte (FSL)	A	.254	116	401	67	102	22	5	9	54	75	99	7	.387	.401
2003	Stockton (Cal)	A	.314	76	283	58	89	14	2	9	61	45	59	12	.409	.473
	Frisco (TL)	AA	.263	55	194	26	51	11	1	4	27	21	45	6	.341	.392
2004	Frisco (TL)	AA	.293	133	481	85	141	25	3	24	92	77	126	7	.399	.507
2005	Oklahoma (PCL)	AAA	.286	133	510	93	146	31	7	25	102	67	152	2	.375	.522
	Texas (AL)	MLB	.296	10	27	4	8	0	0	0	3	3	13	0	.367	.296
MAJOR LEAGUE TOTALS			.296	10	27	4	8	0	0	0	3	3	13	0	.367	.296
MINOR LEAGUE TOTALS			.289	679	2436	429	704	140	20	86	420	368	602	51	.394	.469

9 TAYLOR TEAGARDEN
C

Born: Dec. 21, 1983. **B-T:** B-R. **Ht.:** 6-1. **Wt.:** 200. **Drafted:** Texas, 2005 (3rd round). **Signed by:** Randy Taylor.

Teagarden was a leader on Texas' College World Series championship team last spring and was the best defensive catcher available in the draft. Because of concerns about his bat and his signability—he's a Scott Boras client—the Rangers got him in the third round. He signed for $725,000, which could be a bargain, and hit well at short-season Spokane. Teagarden has amazingly soft hands and good quickness and agility behind the plate. He blocks balls in the dirt well and has a strong, accurate throwing arm with a quick release. He put on an impressive show in instructional league, hitting balls out of the park to all fields, and the Rangers think he will develop at least average power. Long-term wear on Teagarden's elbow led him to have Tommy John surgery after instructional league. The rehab isn't as grueling for position players as it is for pitchers, so Texas considers it just a short-term setback. He has holes in his swing and struck out in one-third of his at-bats during his debut. He's a below-average runner but decent for a catcher. The surgery will cost Teagarden a nonroster invitation to big league camp, but the Rangers think he'll be able to hit early in 2006 and throw by the end of season. It may be easier to get him at-bats as a DH in high Class A.

Year	Club (League)	Class	AVG	G	AB	R	H	2B	3B	HR	RBI	BB	SO	SB	OBP	SLG
2005	Spokane (NWL)	A	.281	31	96	23	27	5	4	7	16	23	32	1	.426	.635
MINOR LEAGUE TOTALS			.281	31	96	23	27	5	4	7	16	23	32	1	.426	.635

10 JOHN MAYBERRY JR.
OF

Born: Dec. 21, 1983. **B-T:** R-R. **Ht.:** 6-6. **Wt.:** 230. **Drafted:** Stanford, 2005 (1st round). **Signed by:** Tim Fortugno.

Mayberry first joined his father John as a first-round pick when the Mariners drafted him 28th overall out of high school in 2002. After three years at Stanford, he went 19th in the 2005 draft and signed with the Rangers for $1.525 million. Now the goal is to follow in his father's footsteps and become an all-star. The best college athlete in the 2005 draft, Mayberry earns 70s on the 20-80 scouting scale for both his raw power and his arm strength. Though he was a slick-fielding first baseman in college, the Rangers think he can be at least an average defender in right field. His speed is above-average. Mayberry never got comfortable at the plate at Stanford, tinkering with his stance too often and trying too hard to hit to the opposite field. His swing is long and lacks rhythm and balance. He shows light-tower power in batting practice but has to cheat on fastballs to generate power in game situations. Many scouts have doubts he'll be a productive major league hitter. Defensively, he needs to work on his jumps. Mayberry is a classic boom-or-bust first-round pick. His upside is enormous, but it will take a lot of time and hard work on his swing for him to reach his potential. He'll spend six weeks at the Rangers' Arizona complex before spring training working on his stroke, then will open the season at low Class A Clinton.

Year	Club (League)	Class	AVG	G	AB	R	H	2B	3B	HR	RBI	BB	SO	SB	OBP	SLG
2005	Spokane (NWL)	A	.253	71	265	51	67	16	0	11	26	26	71	7	.341	.438
MINOR LEAGUE TOTALS			.253	71	265	51	67	16	0	11	26	26	71	7	.341	.438

11 JOHNNY WHITTLEMAN
3B

Born: Feb. 11, 1987. **B-T:** L-R. **Ht.:** 6-2. **Wt.:** 195. **Drafted:** HS—Kingwood, Texas, 2005 (2nd round). **Signed by:** Randy Taylor.

As a shortstop who also doubled as his football team's starting quarterback, Whittleman tied a school record with 10 homers last spring while leading Kingwood High to the Texas state 5-A title. A local kid, he had played for the Rangers' Area Code Games team before signing with Texas for $650,000, better than slot money for the mid-second round. Texas loves Whittleman's baseball-rat mentality. He's a gifted pure hitter who strokes line drives to all fields and projects to have average or better power. He has a very advanced offensive approach for his age, and had more than 20 two-strike hits in the Rookie-level Arizona League. He's a below-average runner but has plus instincts on the bases. Though Whittleman's actions and hands are sound at third base, he lacks range and body control. He's still growing into his size 14 feet, which leads to some inaccurate throws. He tied for the lead among AZL third basemen with 14 errors in 47 games. His arm is strong.

Whittleman has upside but isn't all projection—he can hit already. If it all comes together, he could be a Hank Blalock-type third baseman, or possibly develop into an offensive second baseman. Whittleman is ready offensively and mentally for low Class A.

Year	Club (League)	Class	AVG	G	AB	R	H	2B	3B	HR	RBI	BB	SO	SB	OBP	SLG
2005	Rangers (AZL)	R	.279	51	190	31	53	12	8	0	35	35	42	11	.393	.426
MINOR LEAGUE TOTALS			.279	51	190	31	53	12	8	0	35	35	42	11	.393	.426

12 JOSH RUPE   RHP

Born: Aug. 18, 1982. **B-T:** R-R. **Ht.:** 6-2. **Wt.:** 200. **Drafted:** Louisburg (N.C.) JC, 2002 (3rd round). **Signed by:** John Tumminia (White Sox).

The Rangers still have hope for all three players they got from the White Sox in a July 2003 trade for Carl Everett. Frankie Francisco joined the Texas bullpen in 2004 before hurting his elbow, while outfielder Anthony Webster remains one of the system's best athletes. In the long run, Rupe should be the best of the trio. Scouts who saw him struggle in the first half of 2005 swear he was a completely different pitcher when they saw him relieving for the Rangers in September. Earlier in the year, his fastball sat in the mid-80s without any sink and he couldn't miss bats with any of his offerings. But his approach became much more professional in 2005, and he was able to work through his struggles. His fastball regained its life in the second half, sitting at 91-94 mph and touching 96 with plus sinking action. His best pitch remains his power cutter/slider, which he throws at 85-89 mph with late movement. Rupe's slow, three-quarters curveball and his changeup are decent pitches but lag behind his harder weapons. He doesn't have a big body and his arm might be more suited for a relief role long term. His four-pitch repertoire still could make him an effective starter if he ever harnesses his command—the perennial question with Rupe, who still has difficulty repeating his release point. He'll pitch out of the bullpen for Texas in 2006.

Year	Club (League)	Class	W	L	ERA	G	GS	CG	SV	IP	H	R	ER	HR	BB	SO	AVG
2002	Bristol (Appy)	R	3	3	5.25	17	2	0	0	38	38	23	22	4	22	40	.260
2003	Kannapolis (SAL)	A	5	5	3.01	26	7	2	6	66	50	27	22	0	36	69	.212
	Clinton (Mid)	A	4	1	3.90	6	5	0	0	28	29	14	12	1	7	23	.266
2004	Spokane (NWL)	A	2	0	1.50	4	3	0	0	18	14	3	3	1	3	19	.209
	Stockton (Cal)	A	2	0	0.98	4	3	0	0	18	12	4	2	0	4	14	.182
	Frisco (TL)	AA	2	2	4.38	7	6	0	0	37	41	23	18	5	16	16	.281
2005	Frisco (TL)	AA	4	3	3.74	11	10	0	0	65	64	29	27	7	26	55	.261
	Oklahoma (PCL)	AAA	6	7	6.24	17	17	0	0	94	116	75	65	12	38	62	.306
	Texas (AL)	MLB	1	0	2.78	4	1	0	0	10	7	4	3	0	4	6	.219
MAJOR LEAGUE TOTALS			1	0	2.79	4	1	0	0	10	7	4	3	0	4	6	.219
MINOR LEAGUE TOTALS			28	21	4.24	92	53	2	6	363	364	198	171	30	152	298	.261

13 MICHAEL SCHLACT   RHP

Born: Dec. 9, 1985. **B-T:** R-R. **Ht.:** 6-7. **Wt.:** 205. **Drafted:** HS—Marietta, Ga., 2004 (3rd round). **Signed by:** John Castleberry.

When the Rangers drafted him out of Wheeler High (Marietta, Ga.)—the same school that produced ex-big leaguer Shane Monahan and recent first-round picks Josh Burrus and Jeremy Hermida—Schlact was built like a deer. Since then he has bulked up his shoulders and back, which helped give him the durability to pitch 168 innings in his first full pro season. Despite the heavy workload, his stuff was actually better in August than it was in April. His command improved, his changeup made significant strides, and his ability to hold runners and overall game awareness improved greatly. Schlact lives off his 90-92 mph sinker and pitches with a lot of downhill leverage. He still needs to tighten his slurvy breaking ball. He doesn't consistently miss bats because he lacks a true out pitch, though his changeup may eventually fill that void. He still has room to add strength to his frame. The Rangers see Schlact's grounder-inducing repertoire as a perfect fit for Ameriquest Field in Arlington. He'll pitch in the same rotation as Eric Hurley for the third straight year, this time in high Class A. Schlact could find himself in the middle of the Rangers rotation by mid-2008.

Year	Club (League)	Class	W	L	ERA	G	GS	CG	SV	IP	H	R	ER	HR	BB	SO	AVG
2004	Rangers (AZL)	R	1	1	3.52	10	5	0	0	31	32	18	12	0	9	22	.264
2005	Clinton (Mid)	A	10	7	4.17	28	28	0	0	168	184	85	78	10	37	90	.280
MINOR LEAGUE TOTALS			11	8	4.07	38	33	0	0	199	216	103	90	10	46	112	.278

14 C.J. WILSON   LHP

Born: Nov. 18, 1980. **B-T:** L-L. **Ht.:** 6-2. **Wt.:** 190. **Drafted:** Loyola Marymount, 2001 (5th round). **Signed by:** Tim Fortugno.

Wilson missed the entire 2004 season after having Tommy John surgery the previous

August, but he came back strong last year. He built himself up by making three- to five-inning starts in the minors before getting the call to pitch out of the Texas bullpen in early June. In his second big league outing, he struck out Carlos Delgado with a 94-mph fastball. Wilson reminds the Rangers of Neal Cotts, who like Wilson came up through the minors as a starter. Wilson has an 89-94 mph fastball that jumps out of his hand, and he also relies heavily upon an average 80-84 mph slider. He flashes a fading changeup and a mid-70s curveball, but didn't use either pitch much when he pitched in relief. He deals from a quick delivery from a high arm slot, but sometimes his mechanics are actually too quick and he loses his tempo. He's aggressive but needs to improve his command. Wilson's four-pitch mix could enable him to start down the line, but he'll continue to serve as a reliever for the Rangers in 2006.

Year	Club (League)	Class	W	L	ERA	G	GS	CG	SV	IP	H	R	ER	HR	BB	SO	AVG
2001	Pulaski (Appy)	R	1	0	0.95	8	8	0	0	38	24	6	4	2	9	49	.178
	Savannah (SAL)	A	1	2	3.18	5	5	2	0	34	30	13	12	2	9	26	.252
2002	Charlotte (FSL)	A	10	2	3.06	26	15	0	1	106	86	48	36	4	41	76	.215
	Tulsa (TL)	AA	1	0	1.80	5	5	0	0	30	23	6	6	0	12	17	.211
2003	Frisco (TL)	AA	6	9	5.05	22	21	0	0	123	135	79	69	11	38	89	.276
2004	Did not play—Injured																
2005	Bakersfield (Cal)	A	0	1	3.28	4	4	0	0	14	10	5	5	2	4	14	.189
	Frisco (TL)	AA	0	4	4.43	12	12	0	0	45	51	32	22	7	14	43	.290
	Texas (AL)	MLB	1	7	6.94	24	6	0	1	48	63	39	37	5	18	30	.320
MAJOR LEAGUE TOTALS			1	7	6.94	24	6	0	1	48	63	39	37	5	18	30	.320
MINOR LEAGUE TOTALS			19	18	3.56	82	70	2	1	389	359	189	154	28	127	314	.242

15 SCOTT FELDMAN RHP

Born: Feb. 7, 1983. **B-T:** L-R. **Ht.:** 6-5. **Wt.:** 210. **Drafted:** San Mateo (Calif.) JC, 2003 (30th round). **Signed by:** Tim Fortugno.

Another Tommy John survivor, Feldman pitched just seven innings in 2004 but impressed the Rangers in instructional league that fall by filling the zone with strike after strike. He opened 2005 with a dominating April in high Class A before establishing himself as a force against righthanders in Double-A. Feldman's fastball velocity increased from 88-90 mph early in the year to 91-93 by the time he received a mid-August callup to Texas. His fastball has plus life and good sink, inducing bushels of groundballs. He has a loose, whippy arm and a deceptive sidearm delivery. He shows plus-plus command against righties, moving the ball around the zone but typically keeping it down. Feldman complements his fastball with an average sweeping slider. He also has a changeup to employ against lefthanders as a show pitch. He still needs to improve at getting lefties out, and the Rangers think he eventually will become a middle reliever. For now, he figures to be a right-on-right specialist in Texas.

Year	Club (League)	Class	W	L	ERA	G	GS	CG	SV	IP	H	R	ER	HR	BB	SO	AVG
2003	Rangers (AZL)	R	1	1	4.29	3	1	0	0	6	4	6	3	0	1	7	.138
2004	Rangers (AZL)	R	0	0	0.00	4	3	0	0	7	2	0	0	0	1	5	.091
2005	Bakersfield (Cal)	A	0	0	0.00	6	0	0	3	9	5	2	0	0	2	11	.152
	Frisco (TL)	AA	1	2	2.36	46	0	0	14	61	43	18	16	3	23	41	.202
	Texas (AL)	MLB	0	1	0.97	8	0	0	0	9	9	1	1	0	2	4	.257
MAJOR LEAGUE TOTALS			0	1	0.97	8	0	0	0	9	9	1	1	0	2	4	.257
MINOR LEAGUE TOTALS			2	3	2.05	59	4	0	17	83	54	26	19	3	27	64	.182

16 FABIO CASTRO LHP

Born: Jan. 20, 1985. **B-T:** L-L. **Ht.:** 5-8. **Wt.:** 157. **Signed:** Dominican Republic, 2001. **Signed by:** Denny Gonzalez (White Sox).

The Royals took Castro from the White Sox with the No. 1 pick in the 2005 major league Rule 5 draft, then sent him to the Rangers in a prearranged deal for infielder Esteban German. After Chicago left Castro off its 40-man roster, he raised his profile with a strong winter in the Dominican League. His fastball was better than ever, sitting at 91-93 mph and touching 94. He was nearly untouchable down the stretch in high Class A, not allowing an earned run while striking out 16 in his final 14 innings. Castro complements his fastball with a good changeup that acts like a splitter at times. He also has a tight curveball with downward spin and a good feel for pitching. Despite his slight frame, Castro is durable and wants the ball every day. His delivery is clean and has some deception, though he needs to work on staying more upright so his stuff doesn't flatten out. His stuff is good enough for him to start, but he profiles as a lefthanded power arm out of the bullpen because of his size. As a major league Rule 5 draftee, he can't be sent to the minors in 2006 unless the Rangers pass him through waivers and offer him back to the White Sox for half his $50,000 draft price. Texas should be able to find room for a talented lefty prospect on its staff.

Year	Club (League)	Class	W	L	ERA	G	GS	CG	SV	IP	H	R	ER	HR	BB	SO	AVG
2002	White Sox (DSL)	R	10	2	1.95	25	2	0	8	65	37	17	14	3	23	89	.159
2003	Bristol (Appy)	R	6	2	1.72	19	0	0	2	47	29	14	9	1	19	59	.173
	Kannapolis (SAL)	A	0	2	3.27	2	2	0	0	11	8	5	4	0	5	16	.200
2004	Kannapolis (SAL)	A	4	0	3.00	37	0	0	3	51	44	20	17	2	23	44	.224
	Winston-Salem (Car)	A	1	1	2.35	6	0	0	0	8	2	2	2	0	2	9	.083
2005	Winston-Salem (Car)	A	5	5	2.28	53	0	0	6	79	58	23	20	7	37	75	.209
MINOR LEAGUE TOTALS			26	12	2.28	142	4	0	19	260	178	81	66	13	109	292	,190

17 TRAVIS METCALF
3B

Born: Aug. 17, 1982. **B-T:** R-R. **Ht.:** 6-3. **Wt.:** 2105. **Drafted:** Kansas, 2004 (11th round). **Signed by:** Mike Grouse.

After setting a Kansas record and tying for the Big 12 Conference lead with 18 home runs as a redshirt junior in 2004, Metcalf joined the Rangers as an 11th-round pick. He was signed by area scout Mike Grouse, who also found late-round steals Travis Hafner and Ian Kinsler in previous drafts as well as short-season Northwest League MVP Steve Murphy in 2005. Metcalf led the NWL with 37 extra-base hits in his pro debut, and he encored by winning the organization's minor league player of the year award in 2005. He profiles as an average hitter with potentially above-average power. He draws some walks but strikes out quite a bit because he has some exploitable holes in his swing. He's no speedster, but he has completely recovered from the knee injury he suffered in a 2002 baserunning collision. For his size, Metcalf has good feet and good actions at third base to go along with quick reactions and a strong, accurate arm. He's already a solid defender and could become a real asset with more experience. He'll advance to Double-A this year.

Year	Club (League)	Class	AVG	G	AB	R	H	2B	3B	HR	RBI	BB	SO	SB	OBP	SLG
2004	Spokane (NWL)	A	.269	72	290	48	78	21	1	15	62	37	74	1	.351	.503
2005	Bakersfield (Cal)	A	.291	132	505	80	147	32	7	22	94	49	129	8	.358	.513
MINOR LEAGUE TOTALS			.283	204	795	128	225	53	8	37	156	86	203	9	.355	.509

18 VINCE SINISI
OF

Born: Nov. 7, 1981. **B-T:** L-L. **Ht.:** 6-0. **Wt.:** 195. **Drafted:** Rice, 2003 (2nd round). **Signed by:** Randy Taylor.

Sinisi was the most dangerous hitter on Rice's College World Series championship team in 2003, when he was one of the best pure bats available in the draft. Because he had lots of leverage as a draft-eligible sophomore at a strong academic school, not to mention being represented by Scott Boras, he dropped to the second round. The Rangers lavished a $2.07 million on bonus on Sinisi, but have gotten little return on it so far and didn't bother to protect him on their 40-man roster this offseason. He has yet to play a full season. He broke his left forearm in a collision with Joaquin Arias in 2004. His recovery was slowed because he had to have a metal plate inserted into and later removed from his forearm, and he developed a dangerous bacterial infection that could have killed him. Sinisi couldn't start the 2005 season until mid-May. While he tore up high Class A, his health problems seem to have affected his pop. He lost weight during his downtime and got tired after a promotion to Double-A. Sinisi can hit line drives to all fields and knows the strike zone, though he sometimes gets impatient. His smooth lefthanded stroke is tailored to hit doubles in the gaps, but scouts question if he'll ever have the 20-homer power the Rangers hope he'll develop. Sinisi's bat will have to carry him, because his below-average speed and defensive skills limit him to left field or first base. He'll start 2006 in Double-A and hope for his first fully healthy and fully productive season.

Year	Club (League)	Class	AVG	G	AB	R	H	2B	3B	HR	RBI	BB	SO	SB	OBP	SLG
2003	Stockton (Cal)	A	.258	14	62	9	16	1	0	1	5	3	8	1	.288	.323
2004	Stockton (Cal)	A	.310	63	248	39	77	13	3	7	40	33	45	7	.383	.472
2005	Bakersfield (Cal)	A	.363	35	135	25	49	10	2	6	22	17	19	5	.438	.600
	Frisco (TL)	AA	.258	65	248	27	64	9	0	4	29	15	39	4	.300	.343
MINOR LEAGUE TOTALS			.297	177	693	100	206	33	5	18	96	68	111	17	.357	.437

19 JOHN HUDGINS
RHP

Born: Aug. 31, 1981. **B-T:** R-R. **Ht.:** 6-2. **Wt.:** 195. **Drafted:** Stanford, 2003 (3rd round). **Signed by:** Tim Fortugno.

The Most Outstanding Player at the 2003 College World Series in a losing effort for Stanford, Hudgins is known for his cerebral approach. But he may have out-thought himself in 2005. He got off to a strong start following a quick promotion to Triple-A, but then he tried to pitch to the radar guns too often instead of being his usual efficient, strike-throwing self. He labored and was shut down at the end of July with bone chips in his elbow.

There was no structural damage, however, and he should return healthy in spring training. Hudgins had moved quickly thanks to his ability to throw three pitches for strikes. His best offering is a sinking changeup that he sells with grunts and late violence in his delivery. When he gets in a jam, he can crank his 87-91 mph fastball up to 93. He also has an average curveball that could become a plus pitch. Hudgins is a smart control pitcher with a deceptive delivery that he repeats despite a short, chicken-wing arm action. If he can be more consistent, he can be a No. 5 starter, perhaps as soon as the second half of 2006.

Year	Club (League)	Class	W	L	ERA	G	GS	CG	SV	IP	H	R	ER	HR	BB	SO	AVG
2003	Clinton (Mid)	A	0	0	0.00	1	0	0	0	2	1	0	0	0	0	4	.143
2004	Stockton (Cal)	A	3	1	2.35	15	11	0	2	65	49	19	17	4	18	73	.204
	Frisco (TL)	AA	5	3	3.13	12	12	0	0	69	57	29	24	12	18	64	.232
	Oklahoma (PCL)	AAA	0	1	7.50	3	2	0	0	12	19	10	10	1	5	8	.352
2005	Frisco (TL)	AA	1	2	4.68	3	2	0	0	17	15	9	9	1	8	11	.231
	Oklahoma (PCL)	AAA	3	7	5.87	19	19	1	0	103	127	74	67	12	37	77	.305
MINOR LEAGUE TOTALS			12	14	4.26	53	46	1	2	268	268	141	127	30	86	237	.260

20 JOSE VALLEJO   2B

Born: Sept. 11, 1986. **B-T:** B-R. **Ht.:** 6-0. **Wt.:** 172. **Signed:** Dominican Republic, 2004. **Signed by:** Rodolfo Rosario/Manny Batista.

It is a testament to Vallejo's remarkable makeup that he has persevered through tragedy. His father was killed by a drunken driver a couple of years ago, and his mother died of cancer in the spring of 2005. Yet when the Rangers brought the 18-year-old Vallejo to the United States last year, he handled the challenge with aplomb. He started to learn English and working hard on and off the field. He arrived in Arizona as a righthanded hitter, but special assistant to baseball operations Terry Shumpert suggested he try switch-hitting, and Vallejo took to it. In his first summer as a switch-hitter, he showed the ability to drive balls from the left side, though not as well as he does from the right. He has plus bat speed and does a fine job centering the ball on the bat. He's also a good bunter. Vallejo is an outstanding athlete with plus speed on the bases and nice range at second base. His hands aren't good enough to play shortstop, but he has solid instincts and more than enough arm to stand out at second base. Vallejo is young and needs polish, particularly at the plate, but he'll have a chance to earn the second-base job in low Class A this year.

Year	Club (League)	Class	AVG	G	AB	R	H	2B	3B	HR	RBI	BB	SO	SB	OBP	SLG
2004	Rangers (DSL)	R	.212	52	170	23	36	4	1	1	19	16	52	9	.302	.265
2005	Rangers (AZL)	R	.291	52	203	28	59	7	2	1	15	19	49	18	.364	.360
MINOR LEAGUE TOTALS			.255	104	373	51	95	11	3	2	34	35	101	27	.336	.316

21 CRISTIAN SANTANA   C

Born: June 18, 1989. **B-T:** R-R. **Ht.:** 6-0. **Wt.:** 175. **Signed:** Dominican Republic, 2005. **Signed by:** Jesus Ovalle/Don Welke/Manny Batista.

As a 16-year-old in the Dominican Republic, Santana drew interest from the Braves, Cubs, Mariners, Mets, Red Sox and Yankees before signing with the Rangers for $325,000. He comes from the same town as Rafael Furcal, who served as his adviser during negotiations. Some of the other clubs on Santana's trail wanted to make him a center fielder because he's so athletic. He's a plus runner—not just for a catcher, but for any position player. Texas wants to keep him behind the plate, however, because he has caught all of his life and loves the position. Santana has an above-average arm and impressed the Rangers by throwing behind runners at first base in instructional league, where he was the youngest player in their camp. He's a quick, agile defender with advanced catch-and-throw skills for his age. Santana is still raw in all phases of his game, particularly at the plate. He has quick hands and good bat speed, and he could hit for power as he grows into his body. He likely will debut in the Rookie-level Dominican Summer League.

Year	Club (League)	Class	AVG	G	AB	R	H	2B	3B	HR	RBI	BB	SO	SB	OBP	SLG
2005	Did not play—Signed 2006 contract															

22 KEVIN MAHAR   OF

Born: June 8, 1981. **B-T:** R-R. **Ht.:** 6-5. **Wt.:** 220. **Signed:** NDFA/Indiana, 2004. **Signed by:** Derek Lee.

After he led the Big 10 Conference with 14 homers as a fifth-year senior in 2004, Mahar signed with the Rangers as a free agent before the draft that June. He already has exceeded expectations with a strong performance in high Class A last year, when he bounced back quickly after breaking his left thumb in April. He wasn't even fazed by having to move from his natural position in right field to center after the Rangers released Adam Bourassa.

Mahar's 6-foot-5, 215-pound frame draws comparisons to Dave Winfield's, yet he's athletic enough to play a solid center field. He has power but got too pull-conscious in the second half of 2005, leading to far too many struggles. He runs well for his size and has decent baserunning instincts. He plays the game with abandon and is a hard worker. Mahar struggled in the Arizona Fall League, batting .194 with 24 strikeouts in 67 at-bats, raising questions about his readiness for Double-A. But he's 24, so he's heading to Frisco regardless.

Year	Club (League)	Class	AVG	G	AB	R	H	2B	3B	HR	RBI	BB	SO	SB	OBP	SLG
2004	Rangers (AZL)	R	.280	27	100	20	28	5	1	5	18	9	28	7	.348	.500
	Spokane (NWL)	A	.316	38	152	26	48	9	0	6	22	12	38	5	.379	.493
2005	Bakersfield (Cal)	A	.315	110	447	98	141	27	4	17	63	47	109	17	.396	.508
MINOR LEAGUE TOTALS			.310	175	699	144	217	41	5	28	103	68	175	29	.385	.504

23 JOHN BANNISTER   RHP

Born: Jan. 20, 1984. **B-T:** R-R. **Ht.:** 6-4. **Wt.:** 198. **Signed:** NDFA/HS—Tucson, 2002. **Signed by:** Dave Birecki.

Bannister played at Tucson's Sabino High with J.J. Hardy, but the added exposure didn't get him drafted in 2002. He signed with the Rangers as a nondrafted free agent that August for $17,500 and since has become an intriguing prospect in his own right. In 2005, he learned how to make adjustments and be a professional in an up-and-down season in low Class A. He had some ugly outings, like a one-inning, nine-run disaster in June, but also showed flashes of brilliance, such as an eight-inning, 12-strikeout gem he spun in August. Bannister has a projectable frame, a loose arm and an improving delivery. He has an effective two-seam fastball that sits at 89-92 mph and touches 94, and he sometimes flashes a big league curveball with excellent bite and good depth. His changeup has improved but is still below average, and his command wavers. He's still more thrower than pitcher, though he does show some feel for his craft. He needs to learn how to pitch out of jams better. Bannister figures to pitch in the high Class A rotation in 2006. If his changeup doesn't develop, his future will be as a reliever.

Year	Club (League)	Class	W	L	ERA	G	GS	CG	SV	IP	H	R	ER	HR	BB	SO	AVG
2003	Rangers (AZL)	R	2	4	4.22	13	7	0	1	43	47	31	20	2	16	28	.283
2004	Spokane (NWL)	A	2	2	3.51	16	7	0	0	59	49	29	23	3	28	67	.236
	Clinton (Mid)	A	0	0	1.80	1	1	0	0	5	5	1	1	0	1	5	.263
2005	Clinton (Mid)	A	8	10	4.58	29	28	0	0	157	171	98	80	13	58	127	.275
MINOR LEAGUE TOTALS			12	16	4.23	59	43	0	1	264	272	159	124	18	103	227	.268

24 ANTHONY WEBSTER   OF

Born: April 10, 1983. **B-T:** L-R. **Ht.:** 6-0. **Wt.:** 197. **Drafted:** HS—Parsons, Tenn., 2001 (15th round). **Signed by:** Larry Grefer (White Sox).

Part of the July 2003 Carl Everett trade with the White Sox, Webster was a Tennessee high school football star at tailback. It has taken awhile to translate his athleticism into baseball skills. He played like he expected success to be handed to him in the first half of 2005, prompting the Rangers to tell him to kick himself into gear if he didn't want to be sent home. After batting .222 in the first two months, Webster hit .345 the rest of the way. His best tool is his plus speed, which he used to leg out 11 triples and steal 25 bases in 30 tries. He has average power, particularly to the gaps. He can spray balls to all fields, though his swing tends to get long. His athleticism should make him a better defensive center fielder than he is, but his routes are suspect. His arm is no better than average. Webster likes to have a good time, but if he can refine his work habits and stay focused, he could become a center-field option for Texas in a couple of years. He faces an important year in Double-A.

Year	Club (League)	Class	AVG	G	AB	R	H	2B	3B	HR	RBI	BB	SO	SB	OBP	SLG
2001	White Sox (AZL)	R	.307	55	225	38	69	9	7	0	30	9	33	18	.332	.409
2002	Bristol (Appy)	R	.352	61	244	58	86	7	3	1	30	38	38	16	.448	.418
2003	Kannapolis (SAL)	A	.289	94	363	68	105	18	1	2	33	31	58	20	.353	.361
	Clinton (Mid)	A	.270	18	74	11	20	7	0	1	9	0	8	4	.286	.405
2004	Stockton (Cal)	A	.287	99	380	66	109	20	7	8	44	39	69	20	.363	.439
2005	Bakersfield (Cal)	A	.301	122	498	93	150	36	11	11	73	31	55	25	.346	.484
MINOR LEAGUE TOTALS			.302	449	1784	334	539	97	29	23	219	148	261	103	.362	.428

25 MIKE NICKEAS   C

Born: Feb. 13, 1983. **B-T:** R-R. **Ht.:** 6-0. **Wt.:** 205. **Drafted:** Georgia Tech, 2004 (5th round). **Signed by:** John Castleberry.

Nickeas' father Mark played professional soccer in the North American Soccer League and in England, and Mike is athletic for a thick-bodied catcher. But it was his outstanding make-up more than his physical ability that landed him a spot on the U.S. national team in both high school and college. His strong leadership skills and game-calling ability also led Texas to jump him to Double-A in 2005. Though Nickeas was over his head offensively, the Rangers wanted him to work with their better pitching prospects. He's a good receiver with sound blocking instincts, soft hands and an average arm. He threw out 43 percent of base-stealers last year and didn't let his offensive woes carry over to his defense. Nickeas struggled at the plate all year and missed all of June and half of July after a foul ball broke his right hand. He has a bit of power, but his stiff swing has too many moving parts and he profiles as a below-average hitter. He did go 17-for-40 (.425) in the Arizona Fall League, suggesting he'll be more ready to handle Texas League pitching the second time around.

Year	Club (League)	Class	AVG	G	AB	R	H	2B	3B	HR	RBI	BB	SO	SB	OBP	SLG
2004	Spokane (NWL)	A	.288	62	233	42	67	18	0	10	55	33	53	2	.384	.494
2005	Rangers (AZL)	R	.286	6	21	2	6	1	0	1	6	3	4	0	.400	.476
	Frisco (TL)	AA	.202	68	242	22	49	7	1	5	24	20	43	1	.263	.302
MINOR LEAGUE TOTALS			.246	136	496	66	122	26	1	16	85	56	100	3	.327	.399

26 STEVE MURPHY OF

Born: April 22, 1984. **B-T:** L-R. **Ht.:** 6-2. **Wt.:** 210. **Drafted:** Kansas State, 2005 (14th round). **Signed by:** Mike Grouse.

Murphy played with 2005 Rangers first rounder John Mayberry Jr. at Rockhurst High (Overland Park, Kan.) before winning an NCAA Division II championship at Central Missouri State and finishing his college career at Kansas State. Murphy is the latest late-round find for area scout Mike Grouse, who also signed Travis Hafner, Ian Kinsler and Travis Metcalf. Reunited with Mayberry in his pro debut, Murphy outplayed his more highly touted teammate and won Northwest League MVP honors. His season ended prior to Spokane's playoff run when he broke his hand in a late-August game. Murphy is a classic baseball rat with solid but not eye-catching tools. He has average power to all fields and a controlled, disciplined swing, and he handles lefthanded pitching very well for a lefty hitter. His speed is just fringe average but he's a smart baserunner who goes from first to third well. Murphy's arm is average and he's a decent defender who fits best in left field. He could stand to be more selective at the plate, or else he could face trouble against more advanced pitching. The Rangers could push Murphy to high Class A in 2006.

Year	Club (League)	Class	AVG	G	AB	R	H	2B	3B	HR	RBI	BB	SO	SB	OBP	SLG
2005	Spokane (NWL)	A	.306	62	255	45	78	23	4	9	37	20	71	13	.361	.533
MINOR LEAGUE TOTALS			.306	62	255	45	78	23	4	9	37	20	71	13	.361	.533

27 OMAR BELTRE RHP

Born: Aug. 24, 1981. **B-T:** R-R. **Ht.:** 6-3. **Wt.:** 215. **Signed:** Dominican Republic, 2000. **Signed by:** Rodolfo Rosario.

After signing for a $650,000 bonus in 2000, Beltre ranked as the No. 10 prospect in the Rookie-level Gulf Coast League, just behind Jason Botts and Adrian Gonzalez. But while those players have slugged their way to the majors, Beltre's prospect status slid as he was discovered to be a year older than originally believed, his weight ballooned and he was caught in a visa scandal that forced him to remain in the Dominican Republic and pitch in the Dominican Summer League in 2005. Beltre made the best of his situation, getting his weight back down to 215 pounds and dominating the DSL with a mid-90s fastball that reached 97. He also has decent command of a slider that he used as an out pitch in the summer, plus a splitter he featured more prominently in winter ball. Makeup questions used to dog Beltre, but several Rangers officials have sat down with him in the past year and are convinced he's more focused on his career. He has the electric arm to be an effective late-innings power reliever, but he's 24 years old and has to prove himself in Double-A this year.

Year	Club (League)	Class	W	L	ERA	G	GS	CG	SV	IP	H	R	ER	HR	BB	SO	AVG
2000	Rangers (GCL)	R	5	4	3.54	13	13	0	0	61	54	30	24	2	15	44	.238
2001	Pulaski (Appy)	R	6	3	3.38	13	12	0	0	69	56	28	26	4	23	83	.222
2002	Did not play—Injured																
2003	Clinton (Mid)	A	3	3	2.39	16	5	0	1	49	46	19	13	4	11	27	.250
2004	Stockton (Cal)	A	4	5	2.45	46	0	0	6	59	60	32	16	1	24	47	.255
2005	Rangers (DSL)	R	5	4	1.62	15	10	3	0	72	51	22	13	0	13	94	.188
MINOR LEAGUE TOTALS			23	19	2.67	103	40	3	7	310	267	131	92	11	86	295	.228

28 DREW MEYER INF/OF

Born: Aug. 29, 1981. **B-T:** L-R. **Ht.:** 5-10. **Wt.:** 200. **Drafted:** South Carolina, 2002 (1st round). **Signed by:** Jim Fairey.

At this point, there's little chance Meyer will live up to his status as the 10th overall pick in the 2002 draft, when the next seven picks after him all look like winners: Jeremy Hermida (Marlins), Joe Saunders (Angels), Khalil Greene (Padres), Russ Adams (Blue Jays), Scott Kazmir (Mets), Nick Swisher (Athletics) and Cole Hamels (Phillies). But last year was considerably better for Meyer than his disastrous 2004, when he broke his collarbone and fell out of favor with the Rangers. He hit much better in his second full season in Double-A, and worked hard to lose weight, dropping 15 pounds. He doesn't look like an infielder, but he's an average-to-plus defender at shortstop, second base, third base and all three outfield positions. His plus arm, good hands and feet and smooth actions work at shortstop. He's also an average runner with outstanding baseball instincts. But Meyer just doesn't hit enough to be an everyday player in the big leagues. He has an unorthodox approach and a hitch in his rigid swing. He struggles to get the bat head through the zone and rarely drives the ball. His versatility could make him a useful utilityman, though he'll have to show he can handle Triple-A pitching first.

Year	Club (League)	Class	AVG	G	AB	R	H	2B	3B	HR	RBI	BB	SO	SB	OBP	SLG
2002	Savannah (SAL)	A	.243	54	214	15	52	5	4	1	24	10	53	7	.274	.318
	Tulsa (TL)	AA	.214	4	14	0	3	0	0	0	0	1	5	0	.267	.214
2003	Stockton (Cal)	A	.281	94	398	59	112	16	9	5	53	32	92	24	.330	.405
	Frisco (TL)	AA	.316	26	98	14	31	1	1	0	6	11	23	9	.385	.347
2004	Rangers (AZL)	R	.387	15	62	15	24	2	0	0	5	3	8	4	.415	.419
	Frisco (TL)	AA	.241	59	232	35	56	6	2	2	13	22	43	4	.309	.310
2005	Frisco (TL)	AA	.321	83	321	49	103	14	4	3	45	26	55	12	.372	.417
	Oklahoma (PCL)	AAA	.247	42	178	25	44	11	4	0	19	14	43	5	.301	.354
MINOR LEAGUE TOTALS			.280	377	1517	212	425	55	24	11	165	119	322	65	.331	.370

29 OMAR POVEDA   RHP

Born: Sept. 28, 1987. **B-T:** R-R. **Ht.:** 6-4. **Wt.:** 230. **Signed:** Venezuela, 2004. **Signed by:** Andres Espinosa/Manny Batista.

Poveda signed as a 16-year-old out of Venezuela for $75,000 in July 2004 and went to instructional league that fall, where he showed impressive poise for his age. His 2005 debut in the Rookie-level Arizona League was even more encouraging. His ERA ballooned to 5.61 because of two bad outings and belied his sterling 56-12 K-BB ratio. Big leaguer Gerald Laird caught Poveda during one rehab stint and was amazed at how advanced his command and feel for pitching were for such a young pitcher. Poveda's best pitch is his fastball, which jumped from 86-88 mph early in the summer to the 90-92 range by the fall. He also has a three-quarters breaking ball and a changeup, though both pitches have a ways to go. Poveda has a big, projectable body and already has put on 25 pounds since signing. His legs are very strong, but he's still quite lean from the waist up and needs more upper-body strength. Poveda should skip a level and pitch in low Class A this year.

Year	Club (League)	Class	W	L	ERA	G	GS	CG	SV	IP	H	R	ER	HR	BB	SO	AVG
2005	Rangers (AZL)	R	2	6	5.71	14	9	0	0	52	64	38	33	1	12	56	.305
MINOR LEAGUE TOTALS			2	6	5.71	14	9	0	0	52	64	38	33	1	12	56	.305

30 MANUEL PINA   C

Born: June 5, 1987. **B-T:** R-R. **Ht.:** 5-11. **Wt.:** 165. **Signed:** Venezuela, 2004. **Signed by:** Manny Batista.

Pina has put on about 15 pounds since signing as a 17-year-old Venezuelan shortstop in 2004. The Rangers immediately converted him to catcher, and he progressed rapidly in their Dominican instructional league that fall. Pina has an excellent backstop's build and catch-and-throw skills to go with it. He's a good receiver with great hands, a very strong, accurate arm and a quick release. His pop times to second base have been clocked at 1.87 seconds. Pina has made significant progress in blocking balls in the dirt and at calling games. His makeup is outstanding, as he has learned to speak English and handles a pitching staff well. The question with Pina is whether his offense will catch up to his defense. His strong forearms and wrists generate decent bat speed and his stroke is compact, but he can't touch breaking balls and hasn't shown an ability to hit for power or average. Pina is young enough that his bat could still come around, and even if he never becomes more than a below-average hitter he still could be a big league backup catcher. He'll probably play at short-season Spokane in 2006.

Year	Club (League)	Class	AVG	G	AB	R	H	2B	3B	HR	RBI	BB	SO	SB	OBP	SLG
2005	Rangers (AZL)	R	.247	27	85	13	21	3	1	0	10	7	12	2	.356	.306
MINOR LEAGUE TOTALS			.247	27	85	13	21	3	1	0	10	7	12	2	.356	.306

TORONTO
BLUE JAYS

BY MATT EDDY

The Blue Jays recovered from an abominable, injury-marred 2004 to win 80 games and reclaim third place in the American League East in 2005. They hung around the fringes of the wild-card race late into the season, even after losing ace Roy Halladay to a broken left tibia.

Coming on the heels of a 94-loss season, an 80-82 season had to be considered progress. But Toronto general manager J.P. Ricciardi acknowledged his club was still a few pieces short of contending with the Red Sox and Yankees. "If we bring the whole team back with Halladay healthy we win 85, 87 games," Ricciardi said. "It's our goal to be better than that."

That's just what Ricciardi and the Blue Jays set out to do in the offseason. They identified their biggest needs as two additional hitters and a No. 2 starter. Buoyed by its purchase of SkyDome and the stronger showing of the Canadian dollar, the club's owner, Rogers Communications, budgeted $210 million for the big league payroll over the next three seasons. That's a big step up from the 2005 payroll of $45.7 million, the sixth-lowest in baseball.

Ricciardi didn't hesitate to spend the extra money. He gave out the two biggest contracts to free-agent pitchers, doling out $55 million to A.J. Burnett and $47 million to B.J. Ryan in five-year deals. Then he bolstered the offense by trading young players, including righthander David Bush and lefthander Zach Jackson, to get Lyle Overbay from the Brewers.

Ricciardi had to look outside the organization for answers because while his farm system has depth, it offers precious little frontline talent. But in an encouraging sign, more young players contributed to the Blue Jays in 2005 than at any point in Ricciardi's four-year tenure. Russ Adams, Aaron Hill and Alex Rios established themselves as regulars in the lineup. **Gustavo Chacin** made 34 starts, a club record for rookies, and finished fifth in AL rookie-of-the-year balloting. No. 1 prospect Dustin McGowan, just 14 months recovered from Tommy John surgery, was thrust into the rotation in August.

On the farm, Toronto's affiliates finished with an aggregate winning record for the third straight season, and two teams—high Class A Dunedin and short-season Auburn—made the playoffs. The Blue Jays have shifted their focus in four years under Ricciardi, seeking mature college players capable of climbing the ladder quickly. Toronto also has been more active on the international market, signing big-ticket Taiwanese pitchers Chi-Hung Cheng ($400,000) in 2003 and Po-Hsuan Keng ($225,000) in 2004, and power-hitting Dominican third baseman Leance Soto for $600,000 last spring.

The Blue Jays can't expect to find everything they're shopping for on the free-agent market, and they're prepared to trade prospects as needed. It's no longer about development with the Blue Jays. It's time to win, and they are betting 2005 was a sign of better things to come.

TOP 30 PROSPECTS

1. Dustin McGowan, rhp
2. Ricky Romero, lhp
3. David Purcey, lhp
4. Adam Lind, of
5. Josh Banks, rhp
6. Casey Janssen, rhp
7. Brandon League, rhp
8. Francisco Rosario, rhp
9. Curtis Thigpen, c
10. Vince Perkins, rhp
11. Shaun Marcum, rhp
12. Guillermo Quiroz, c
13. Ryan Patterson, of
14. Chi-Hung Cheng, lhp
15. Kyle Yates, rhp
16. Chip Cannon, 1b
17. Rob Cosby, 3b
18. Ismael Ramirez, rhp
19. Brian Pettway, of
20. Robinzon Diaz, c
21. John Hattig, 3b
22. John-Ford Griffin, of/dh
23. Eric Fowler, lhp
24. Jesse Litsch, rhp
25. Yuber Rodriguez, of
26. Ryan Roberts, 2b
27. Robert Ray, rhp
28. Davis Romero, lhp
29. Jacob Butler, of
30. Wesley Stone, 2b

BILL NICHOLS

ORGANIZATION OVERVIEW

General manager: J.P. Ricciardi. **Farm director:** Dick Scott. **Scouting director:** Jon Lalonde.

2005 PERFORMANCE

Class	Team	League	W	L	Pct.	Finish*	Manager
Majors	Toronto	American	80	82	.494	8th (14)	John Gibbons
Triple-A	Syracuse SkyChiefs	International	71	73	.493	8th (14)	Marty Pevey
Double-A	New Hampshire Fisher Cats	Eastern	68	74	.479	9th (12)	Mike Basso
High A	Dunedin Blue Jays	Florida State	82	58	.586	2nd (12)	Omar Malave
Low A	Lansing Lugnuts	Midwest	70	69	.504	7th (14)	Ken Joyce
Short-season	Auburn Doubledays	New York-Penn	45	30	.600	3rd (14)	Dennis Holmberg
Rookie	Pulaski Blue Jays	Appalachian	34	33	.507	4th (10)	Dave Pano
OVERALL 2005 MINOR LEAGUE RECORD			370	337	.523	7th (30)	

*Finish in overall standings (No. of teams in league).

ORGANIZATION LEADERS

BATTING
*Minimum 250 at-bats
*AVG	Patterson, Ryan, Auburn	.339
R	Roberts, Ryan, Dunedin/New Hampshire	87
H	Lind, Adam, Dunedin	155
TB	Barker, Kevin, New Hampshire/Syracuse	280
2B	Lind, Adam, Dunedin	42
3B	French, Anton, Syracuse	10
HR	Cannon, Chip, Dunedin/Lansing/New Hampshire	32
RBI	Barker, Kevin, New Hampshire/Syracuse	114
BB	Roberts, Ryan, Dunedin/New Hampshire	79
SO	Griffin, John-Ford, Syracuse	140
SB	Klosterman, Ryan, Dunedin/Lansing	30
*OBP	Snavely, Christian, Lansing	.390
*SLG	Patterson, Ryan, Auburn	.595

PITCHING
#Minimum 75 innings
W	Jackson, Zach, Dunedin/New Hampshire	16
L	Ramirez, Ismael, New Hampshire	13
#ERA	Janssen, Casey, Dunedin/Lansing/New Hampshire	1.81
G	Gronkiewicz, Lee, New Hampshire/Syracuse	66
CG	Banks, Josh, New Hampshire	2
	Gaudin, Chad, Syracuse	2
SV	Gronkiewicz, Lee, New Hampshire/Syracuse	30
IP	Banks, Josh, New Hampshire	162
BB	Purcey, David, Dunedin/New Hampshire	81
SO	Purcey, David, Dunedin/New Hampshire	161

BEST TOOLS

Best Hitter for Average	Adam Lind
Best Power Hitter	Chip Cannon
Best Strike-Zone Discipline	Curtis Thigpen
Fastest Baserunner	Miguel Negron
Best Athlete	Yuber Rodriguez
Best Fastball	Dustin McGowan
Best Curveball	Kyle Yates
Best Slider	Dustin McGowan
Best Changeup	Shaun Marcum
Best Control	Josh Banks
Best Defensive Catcher	Erik Kratz
Best Defensive Infielder	Manuel Mayorson
Best Infield Arm	Manuel Mayorson
Best Defensive Outfielder	Miguel Negron
Best Outfield Arm	Miguel Negron

PROJECTED 2009 LINEUP

Catcher	Curtis Thigpen
First Base	Lyle Overbay
Second Base	Orlando Hudson
Third Base	Aaron Hill
Shortstop	Russ Adams
Left Field	Adam Lind
Center Field	Vernon Wells
Right Field	Alex Rios
Designated Hitter	Shea Hillenbrand
No. 1 Starter	Roy Halladay
No. 2 Starter	A.J. Burnett
No. 3 Starter	Dustin McGowan
No. 4 Starter	Gustavo Chacin
No. 5 Starter	Ricky Romero
Closer	B.J. Ryan

LAST YEAR'S TOP 20 PROSPECTS

1. Brandon League, rhp
2. Aaron Hill, ss
3. Guillermo Quiroz, c
4. Francisco Rosario, rhp
5. David Purcey, lhp
6. Russ Adams, ss
7. Dustin McGowan, rhp
8. Zach Jackson, lhp
9. Josh Banks, rhp
10. Gustavo Chacin, lhp
11. Gabe Gross, of
12. Yuber Rodriguez, of
13. Vince Perkins, rhp
14. Shawn Marcum, rhp
15. Curtis Thigpen, c
16. Ismael Ramirez, rhp
17. Adam Lind, of
18. Robinzon Diaz, c
19. Chi-Hung Cheng, lhp
20. Raul Tablado, ss/3b

TOP PROSPECTS OF THE DECADE

Year	Player, Pos.	2005 Org.
1996	Shannon Stewart, of	Twins
1997	Roy Halladay, rhp	Blue Jays
1998	Roy Halladay, rhp	Blue Jays
1999	Roy Halladay, rhp	Blue Jays
2000	Vernon Wells, of	Blue Jays
2001	Vernon Wells, of	Blue Jays
2002	Josh Phelps, c	Devil Rays
2003	Dustin McGowan, rhp	Blue Jays
2004	Alex Rios, of	Blue Jays
2005	Brandon League, rhp	Blue Jays

TOP DRAFT PICKS OF THE DECADE

Year	Player, Pos.	2005 Org.
1996	Billy Koch, rhp	Out of baseball
1997	Vernon Wells, of	Blue Jays
1998	Felipe Lopez, ss	Reds
1999	Alex Rios, of	Blue Jays
2000	Miguel Negron, of	Blue Jays
2001	Gabe Gross, of	Blue Jays
2002	Russ Adams, ss	Blue Jays
2003	Aaron Hill, ss	Blue Jays
2004	David Purcey, lhp	Blue Jays
2005	Ricky Romero, lhp	Blue Jays

ALL-TIME LARGEST BONUSES

Ricky Romero, 2005	$2,400,000
Felipe Lopez, 1998	$2,000,000
Gabe Gross, 2001	$1,865,000
Russ Adams, 2002	$1,785,000
Aaron Hill, 2003	$1,675,000

MINOR LEAGUE DEPTH CHART

Toronto Blue Jays

Rank: **25**

STRENGTH: Lefthanded starting pitching, often a weakness for other clubs, is Toronto's best spot, even after trading Zach Jackson.

WEAKNESS: Middle infielders. After graduating Russ Adams and Aaron Hill to Toronto, not much is left.

*Depth charts prepared by **John Manuel** and **Chris Kline**. Numbers in parentheses indicate prospect rankings.*

LF
Adam Lind (4)
Brian Pettway (19)
John-Ford Griffin (22)
Jacob Butler (29)
Ron Davenport
Cory Patton

CF
Yuber Rodriguez (25)
Miguel Negron

RF
Ryan Patterson (13)
Dustin Majewski
Yohermyn Chavez

3B
Rob Cosby (17)
John Hattig (21)
Christian Snavely
Leance Soto

SS
Ryan Klosterman
Jesus Gonzalez
Manny Mayorson
Raul Tablado

2B
Ryan Roberts (26)
Wesley Stone (30)
Sean Shoffit
Juan Peralta

1B
Chip Cannon (16)
Joey Metropoulos
Paul Franko

C
Curtis Thigpen (9)
Guillermo Quiroz (12)
Robinzon Diaz (20)
Josh Bell
Jonathan Jaspe

RHP

Starters	Relievers
Dustin McGowan (1)	Brandon League (7)
Josh Banks (5)	Francisco Rosario (8)
Casey Janssen (6)	Shaun Marcum (11)
Vince Perkins (10)	Ryan Houston
Kyle Yates (15)	Danny Hill
Ismael Ramirez (18)	Paul Phillips
Jesse Litsch (24)	Reidier Gonzalez
Robert Ray (27)	Eddy Rodriguez
Po-Hsuan Keng	Ty Taubenheim
Shane Benson	Tracy Thorpe
Orlando Trias	Lee Gronkiewicz

LHP

Starters	Relievers
Ricky Romero (2)	Davis Romero (28)
David Purcey (3)	Brad Mumma
Chi-Hung Cheng (14)	Jesse Carlson
Eric Fowler (23)	Matt Foster
Kurt Isenberg	
Wilfreddy Aguirre	

DRAFT ANALYSIS

2005

Best Pro Debut: OF Ryan Patterson (4) batted .339-13-65 and led the short-season New York-Penn League in RBIs, extra-base hits (40) and slugging percentage (.595). OF Jacob Butler (8) made the Rookie-level Appalachian League all-star team by hitting .290-14-52. RHP Paul Phillips (9) went 2-1, 2.29 with 13 saves and 41 strikeouts in 39 NY-P innings.

Best Athlete: 2B Sean Shoffit (15) has a good lefthanded swing with power potential, above-average speed and a plus arm. He was clocked at 92-93 mph while pitching at Cosumnes River (Calif.) JC. The Blue Jays signed a number of prominent two-way players, including OF Brian Pettway (3), C Josh Bell (6), OF Zach Kalter (20) and RHP Dennis Bigley (22).

Best Pure Hitter: Patterson's swing is a little unconventional but it works for him. He won the 2004 Cape Cod League batting title with a .327 average. Butler has more of a traditional stroke and also gets good results. Pettway challenged for the Southeastern Conference batting title with a .383 average at Mississippi, but hit .225 in the NY-P.

Best Raw Power: Pettway has the best pull power, while Bell has the best to the opposite field. Patterson and Butler have good pop, too.

Fastest Runner: OF Matt Cooksey (32) gets from home to first in 4.0 seconds from the left side. Kalter is a step behind Cooksey but still has plus speed.

Best Defensive Player: Cooksey plays a solid center fielder. SS Chris Gutierrez, signed as nondrafted free agent out of Oklahoma State, is a better defender.

Best Fastball: Phillips pitched at 89-95

Pettway

mph all summer out of the bullpen. RHP Reidier Gonzalez (19) also can touch 95. RHP Billy Carnline (12) peaks at 94, while LHP Ricky Romero (1) and RHP Robert Ray (7) deliver the most consistent heat among the starters at 89-93 mph. Ray's fastball has explosive late life.

Best Breaking Ball: Romero's curveball is more effective than LHP Eric Fowler's (5) because Romero commands it so well.

Most Intriguing Background: RHP Josh Sowers' (10) twin brother Jeremy was a two-time first-round pick and pitches in the Indians system. Phillips' father Arnold is a part-time scout for the Devil Rays.

Closest To The Majors: Romero, the top lefty in the draft and the first pitcher selected. He blends the stuff of David Purcey and the command of Zach Jackson, Toronto's first two picks in the 2004 draft. Romero spent most of the summer in high Class A and went 1-0, 3.82 in eight starts.

Best Late-Round Pick: Shoffit, Gonzalez and Kalter.

The One Who Got Away: The Blue Jays didn't come close to signing 1B Brett Wallace (42), now at Arizona State. But they did sign their first 15 picks.

Assessment: The Blue Jays are as dogmatic in the pursuit of college players as any organization. They signed just one high school product (2B Wesley Stone, 11). By focusing on draftees who can advance more quickly, however, Toronto winds up sacrificing ceiling.

2004 Four of the Blue Jays' best prospects came out of this draft: LHP David Purcey (1), C Curtis Thigpen (2), OF Adam Lind (3) and RHP Casey Janssen (4). LHP Zach Jackson (1) was a fifth until getting included in the Lyle Overbay trade. **GRADE:** B

2003 INF Aaron Hill (1) has played as advertised and has already reached Toronto. RHP Shawn Marcum (3) also sped to the majors, and RHP Josh Banks (2) is on his way. **GRADE:** B

2002 SS Russ Adams (1) and RHP David Bush (2) can be steady big leaguers, though Bush also was part of the Overbay deal. RHP Adam Peterson (4) pitched in the majors and was traded for Shea Hillenbrand. **GRADE:** C+

2001 OF Gabe Gross (1), RHP Brandon League (2) and OF Tyrell Godwin (3) have reached the majors but haven't met expectations. Gross was included in the Overbay trade, and Godwin was lost in the Rule 5 draft. **GRADE:** C

Draft analysis prepared by Jim Callis. Numbers in parentheses indicate draft rounds.

DUSTIN
McGOWAN

RHP

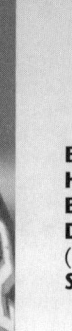

KEVIN PATAKY

Born: March 24, 1982.
Ht.: 6-3. **Wt.:** 220.
Bats: R. **Throws:** R.
Drafted: HS—Ludowici, Ga., 2000
(1st round supplemental).
Signed by: Chris Buckley/Joe Siers.

McGowan ranked as the organization's No. 1 prospect entering 2003, and he finished that season strong by going 7-0 in Double-A. He started strong in 2004 and seemed on the verge of his first big league promotion when a torn elbow ligament halted his progress. He had Tommy John surgery in May 2004 and didn't return to the field until June 2005. Interestingly, the Blue Jays nearly voided his first pro contract ($950,000 as a supplemental first-round pick in 2000) when they discovered he had an inflamed elbow. It's conceivable that he may now be pitching with a healthy elbow for the first time as a pro. McGowan rehabbed vigorously from surgery, as evidenced by his relatively brief 13-month recovery period, working without a ball to refine his mechanics. His focal points were working to stay back during his delivery so his arm could catch up to his body, and getting on top of his pitches to deliver them on more of a downhill plane. McGowan pitched respectably in his first taste of the majors, going 6⅔ innings in his debut to register the win, but seemed more relaxed on the mound when he moved to the bullpen in September to limit his workload. In his final appearance of the year, he struck out all four batters he faced with electric stuff.

McGowan has overpowering frontline stuff and pitches down in the zone with explosive life. He has four major league weapons to attack hitters with, starting with a 92-94 mph four-seam fastball that he frequently dials up to 96 in relief. His fast-developing change is already his second pitch, and it's an effective weapon against lefthanders. He maintains fastball arm speed with the pitch. McGowan's breaking stuff is less consistent but does show promise. He gets good rotation on a downer curve, though his 86-88 mph slider has more the look of a potential out pitch. When it's working for him, his slider features sharp two-plane break. McGowan is athletic, quiet and diligent, and he has shown the aptitude to make adjustments to his level of competition.

Like many young power pitchers, McGowan struggles to command his fastball, and sometimes his heater lacks movement. Big league hitters weren't as prone to chasing his breaking stuff out of the strike zone, so he'll need to get ahead in the count with his fastball. He's also seeking more consistency with his breaking pitches. The Blue Jays believe his curve and slider will be better than average once he learns to command them in the strike zone.

McGowan showed a lot of growth in 2005, but he still has much improvement in front of him. He'll need to refine his fastball command if he's to become the front-of-the-rotation starter the Blue Jays envision. He'll compete for a rotation spot in spring training, but would benefit from a few months pitching at Triple-A Syracuse.

Year	Club (League)	Class	W	L	ERA	G	GS	CG	SV	IP	H	R	ER	HR	BB	SO	AVG
2000	Medicine Hat (Pio)	R	0	3	6.48	8	8	0	0	25	26	21	18	2	25	19	.274
2001	Auburn (NY-P)	A	3	6	3.76	15	14	0	0	67	57	33	28	1	49	80	.234
2002	Charleston, W.Va. (SAL)	A	11	10	4.19	28	28	1	0	148	143	77	69	10	59	163	.251
2003	Dunedin (FSL)	A	5	6	2.85	14	14	1	0	76	62	29	24	1	25	66	.223
	New Haven (EL)	AA	7	0	3.17	14	14	1	0	77	78	28	27	1	19	72	.261
2004	New Hampshire (EL)	AA	2	0	4.06	6	6	0	0	31	24	14	14	4	15	29	.209
2005	Dunedin (FSL)	A	0	1	4.29	5	5	0	0	21	21	12	10	2	5	20	.253
	New Hampshire (EL)	AA	0	2	3.34	6	6	0	0	35	35	16	13	6	10	33	.263
	Toronto (AL)	MLB	1	3	6.36	13	7	0	0	45	49	34	32	7	17	34	.277
MAJOR LEAGUE TOTALS			1	3	6.36	13	7	0	0	45	49	34	32	7	17	34	.277
MINOR LEAGUE TOTALS			28	28	3.81	96	95	3	0	480	446	230	203	27	207	482	.245

RICKY ROMERO LHP

RICH ABEL

Born: Nov. 6, 1984. **B-T:** R-L. **Ht.:** 6-1. **Wt.:** 195. **Drafted:** Cal State Fullerton, 2005 (1st round). **Signed by:** Demerius Pittman.

A second-team All-American as a junior, Romero was the first pitcher selected in the 2005 draft. The Blue Jays took him sixth overall and signed him for a club-record $2.4 million. He was one of Cal State Fullerton's two aces on its 2004 national championship team. Romero is poised on the mound and attacks hitters with command of three above-average pitches. He moves his fastball in and out and usually throws it at 90-92 mph. He gets late action in the zone with his two-seamer. His power downer curve is sometimes his second pitch, while other times it's his changeup, which he uses to combat righthanders. Romero doesn't have dominant stuff. While his delivery is efficient now, the Jays are working to get his fastball on a more downward plane. After a heavy amateur workload, Toronto limited him to a strict 50-60 pitch count during his debut. Romero likely will return to high Class A Dunedin to start 2006; with a strong spring, he could start in Double-A. He should move quickly and is a safe bet to reach his ceiling as a No. 3 starter.

Year	Club (League)	Class	W	L	ERA	G	GS	CG	SV	IP	H	R	ER	HR	BB	SO	AVG
2005	Dunedin (FSL)	A	1	0	3.81	8	8	0	0	31	36	13	13	2	7	22	.283
	Auburn (NY-P)	A	0	0	0.00	1	1	0	0	2	2	0	0	0	1	2	.250
MINOR LEAGUE TOTALS			1	0	3.58	9	9	0	0	33	38	13	13	2	8	24	.281

DAVID PURCEY LHP

KEVIN PATAKY

Born: April 22, 1982. **B-T:** L-L. **Ht.:** 6-5. **Wt.:** 240. **Drafted:** Oklahoma, 2004 (1st round). **Signed by:** Ty Nichols.

After turning down lucrative offers to turn pro with the Mariners (out of high school) and the Yankees (as a draft-eligible sophomore), Purcey signed with the Blue Jays for $1.6 million as the 16th overall pick in 2004. He started his first full season in high Class A and reached Double-A by the end of July. Purcey's 91-93 mph fastball tops out at 95 and explodes on batters as it arrives at the plate. He also generates awkward swings and misses with his plus 12-to-6 curveball, one of the best in the system. He has the makings of a quality changeup and has good arm speed with the pitch, but it's not as advanced as his other offerings. Command has been by far Purcey's biggest stumbling block, in part because he has difficulty repeating his release point. The Blue Jays are also working with him to improve his pitch efficiency and stamina by not maxing out on every pitch. Purcey is a physical pitcher with power stuff. He won't reach his potential as a No. 2 starter if he doesn't consistently throw strikes. He almost certainly will begin 2006 back in Double-A.

Year	Club (League)	Class	W	L	ERA	G	GS	CG	SV	IP	H	R	ER	HR	BB	SO	AVG
2004	Auburn (NY-P)	A	1	0	1.50	3	2	0	0	12	6	2	2	0	1	13	.158
2005	Dunedin (FSL)	A	5	4	3.63	21	21	0	0	94	80	51	38	8	56	116	.229
	New Hampshire (EL)	AA	4	3	2.93	8	8	1	0	43	32	17	14	2	25	45	.205
MINOR LEAGUE TOTALS			10	7	3.25	32	31	1	0	149	118	70	54	10	82	174	.217

ADAM LIND OF

RODGER WOOD

Born: June 17, 1983. **B-T:** L-L. **Ht.:** 6-2. **Wt.:** 195. **Drafted:** South Alabama, 2004 (3rd round). **Signed by:** Joel Grampietro.

One year after Lind signed with the Blue Jays as a draft-eligible sophomore, he has become the best hitting prospect in the organization. He led the high Class A Florida State League in doubles and extra-base hits while ranking second in batting and hits. Lind has the quickest bat in the system, making him Toronto's only position prospect with star potential. Described as a natural-born hitter by one Jays official, he uses a picture-perfect lefthanded swing to make hard contact to all fields. He's doesn't panic when he falls behind, as his advanced two-strike approach allows him to be more selective and get pitches to hit. Lind's desire to improve defensively has been questioned. To his credit, he worked doggedly to improve his left-field play, taking two rounds of batting-practice flyballs a day to hone his jumps and routes. His arm is fringy and he's a below-average runner. Lind is expected to start 2006 at Double-A. The Blue Jays see him as their left fielder of the future and a middle-of-the-order presence capable of hitting .300 with 40 doubles and 20 homers. If his glove proves unplayable in left, he may return to first base.

Year	Club (League)	Class	AVG	G	AB	R	H	2B	3B	HR	RBI	BB	SO	SB	OBP	SLG
2004	Auburn (NY-P)	A	.312	70	266	43	83	23	0	7	50	24	36	1	.371	.477
2005	Dunedin (FSL)	A	.313	126	495	80	155	42	4	12	84	49	77	2	.375	.487
MINOR LEAGUE TOTALS			.313	196	761	123	238	65	4	19	134	73	113	3	.374	.484

5 JOSH BANKS

RHP

RICH ABEL

Born: July 18, 1982. **B-T:** R-R. **Ht.:** 6-3. **Wt.:** 195. **Drafted:** Florida International, 2003 (2nd round). **Signed by:** Tony Arias.

A strained elbow ligament in 2002 and recurring blisters on his pitching hand may have scared teams off, but the Blue Jays snagged Banks in the second round of the 2003 draft. He has shown improvement in each of his first three pro seasons. Banks is one of the minors' finest control pitchers and went eight straight starts without a walk last year. In the second half, he began to pitch down in the zone more effectively, something he didn't do in his first taste of Double-A in 2004. Banks commands both sides of the plate with a solid-average fastball that sits at 90-91 mph and touches 93. His splitter is a major league out pitch. Banks made strides with his fringy curveball late in the season, gaining the confidence to go to it when behind in the count. Less frequently, he'll go to his slider or changeup. He's still perfecting his pitch sequencing. He's vulnerable to homers, perhaps because he is so resistant to giving up walks. The durable Banks finished among Eastern League leaders in innings, strikeouts and complete games. He's bound for Triple-A and the Jays are excited about his future as a No. 3 or 4 starter.

Year	Club (League)	Class	W	L	ERA	G	GS	CG	SV	IP	H	R	ER	HR	BB	SO	AVG
2003	Auburn (NY-P)	A	7	2	2.43	15	15	0	0	67	58	21	18	1	10	81	.233
2004	Dunedin (FSL)	A	7	1	1.80	11	11	0	0	60	49	17	12	4	8	60	.225
	New Hampshire (EL)	AA	6	6	5.03	18	17	1	0	91	89	54	51	15	28	76	.256
2005	New Hampshire (EL)	AA	8	12	3.83	27	27	2	0	162	159	76	69	18	11	145	.256
MINOR LEAGUE TOTALS			28	21	3.55	71	70	3	0	380	355	168	150	38	57	362	.247

6 CASEY JANSSEN

RHP

KEVIN PATAKY

Born: Sept. 17, 1981. **B-T:** R-R. **Ht.:** 6-4. **Wt.:** 205. **Drafted:** UCLA, 2004 (4th round). **Signed by:** Billy Gasparino.

A two-way player at UCLA his first three seasons, Janssen devoted full attention to pitching his senior season. He went from a 49th-round pick by the Orioles in 2003 to a fourth-rounder by the Jays in 2004 to one of the system's best prospects in 2005, when his 2.18 ERA ranked fourth in the minors. Janssen commands four pitches for strikes. He creates good natural cutting movement on his 89-91 mph two-seam fastball. He throws a solid-average slider with good bite, a changeup with tailing action and an average though soft curveball. He follows a gameplan when he pitches, keeps the ball on the ground and is adept at holding runners. None of Janssen's four pitches projects as above average, and it's uncertain how his stuff will play against more advanced hitters who swing and miss less frequently. He wore down a bit as the season progressed, so he needs to get stronger. With his ability to throw strikes, Janssen looks like a future No. 4 starter in the majors. He'll open the season in Double-A.

Year	Club (League)	Class	W	L	ERA	G	GS	CG	SV	IP	H	R	ER	HR	BB	SO	AVG
2004	Auburn (NY-P)	A	3	1	3.48	10	10	0	0	52	47	21	20	2	10	45	.240
2005	Lansing (Mid)	A	4	0	1.37	7	7	0	0	46	27	8	7	0	4	38	.174
	Dunedin (FSL)	A	6	1	2.26	10	10	0	0	60	46	16	15	2	12	51	.216
	New Hampshire (EL)	AA	3	3	2.93	9	9	0	0	43	49	20	14	3	4	47	.288
MINOR LEAGUE TOTALS			16	5	2.52	36	36	0	0	200	169	65	56	7	30	181	.230

7 BRANDON LEAGUE

RHP

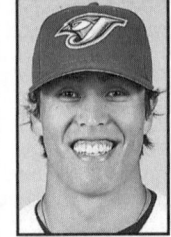

Born: March 16, 1983. **B-T:** R-R. **Ht.:** 6-3. **Wt.:** 190. **Drafted:** HS—Honolulu, 2001 (2nd round). **Signed by:** David Blume.

No. 1 on this list a year ago, League saw his progress stall after his callup to Toronto at the end of 2004. He made the Jays' Opening Day roster in 2005, struggled in the majors and never got back on track in Triple-A. Switching roles from starter to reliever and back probably hasn't helped his development. League has a special arm. He throws everything hard. He popped 101 mph on the radar gun in the big leagues and typically sits at 94-96 mph with diving action in the strike zone when he's on. His hard slider clocks in at 88-91 mph. League's changeup has sinking action and is thrown so hard (88-92 mph) it looks like a two-seam fastball. League gets in trouble when he can't locate his pitches. He can't get away with pitching up in the zone because his stuff flattens out. He doesn't consistently repeat his low three-quarters release point and is far more hittable than he should be with his stuff. The club still thinks League will one day close in the majors. They believe that with pitching coach Brad Arnsberg and a veteran staff, they have the support system in place to facilitate his growth.

Year	Club (League)	Class	W	L	ERA	G	GS	CG	SV	IP	H	R	ER	HR	BB	SO	AVG
2001	Medicine Hat (Pio)	R	2	2	4.65	9	9	0	0	39	36	23	20	3	11	38	.245
2002	Auburn (NY-P)	A	7	2	3.15	16	16	0	0	86	80	42	30	2	23	72	.248
2003	Charleston, W.Va. (SAL)	A	2	3	1.91	12	12	0	0	71	58	15	15	1	18	61	.230
	Dunedin (FSL)	A	4	3	4.75	13	12	0	0	66	76	40	35	3	20	34	.288
2004	New Hampshire (EL)	AA	6	4	3.38	41	10	0	2	104	92	44	39	3	41	90	.237
	Toronto (AL)	MLB	1	0	0.00	3	0	0	0	5	3	0	0	0	1	2	.176
2005	Syracuse (IL)	AAA	4	4	5.71	19	10	0	0	63	78	44	40	7	18	35	.306
	Toronto (AL)	MLB	1	0	6.55	20	0	0	0	36	42	27	26	8	20	17	.302
MAJOR LEAGUE TOTALS			2	0	5.80	23	0	0	0	40	45	27	26	8	21	19	.288
MINOR LEAGUE TOTALS			25	18	3.76	110	69	0	2	428	420	208	179	19	131	330	.258

8 FRANCISCO ROSARIO   RHP

MIKE JANES

Born: Sept. 28, 1980. **B-T:** R-R. **Ht.:** 6-0. **Wt.:** 195. **Signed:** Dominican Republic, 1999. **Signed by:** Tony Arias.

Rosario was just starting to blossom in 2002 when he injured his elbow in the Arizona Fall League and required Tommy John surgery. He hasn't fully recovered the feel for his stuff. The Blue Jays neglected to call him up in 2005 despite the need to bolster their bullpen. Rosario was shifted to the bullpen in August to begin grooming him for a late-inning relief role. He throws his plus fastball at 93-96 mph. To complement his heater, he throws an above-average 86-88 mph changeup with late action and an 85-88 mph slider. All of his pitches were sharper when he worked in relief. Despite his arm strength and velocity, Rosario has a tendency to lose life and command on his fastball. He also lacks feel for his secondary stuff, especially his slider. Some observers think he pitches as if he fears hurting his elbow again. Because he missed the entire 2003 season, Rosario has one option remaining, so he won't have to clear waivers if he doesn't make the big league team in spring training. He should open the season in the Triple-A bullpen.

Year	Club (League)	Class	W	L	ERA	G	GS	CG	SV	IP	H	R	ER	HR	BB	SO	AVG
1999	Blue Jays (DSL)	R	1	0	3.07	18	0	0	3	32	26	16	11	0	11	38	.208
2000	Blue Jays (DSL)	R	2	0	1.21	26	0	0	16	37	21	5	5	0	7	51	.160
2001	Medicine Hat (Pio)	R	3	7	5.59	16	15	0	0	76	79	61	47	8	38	55	.271
2002	Charleston, W.Va. (SAL)	A	6	1	2.56	13	13	1	0	67	50	22	19	5	14	78	.206
	Dunedin (FSL)	A	3	3	1.29	13	12	0	0	63	33	10	9	3	25	65	.151
2003	Did not play—Injured																
2004	Dunedin (FSL)	A	1	1	4.68	6	6	0	0	17	16	12	9	2	11	16	.239
	New Hampshire (EL)	AA	2	4	4.31	12	12	0	0	48	48	25	23	6	16	45	.271
2005	Syracuse (IL)	AAA	2	7	3.95	30	18	0	2	116	111	59	51	16	42	80	.258
MINOR LEAGUE TOTALS			20	23	3.43	134	76	1	21	457	384	210	174	40	164	428	.228

9 CURTIS THIGPEN   C

KEVIN PATAKY

Born: April 19, 1983. **B-T:** R-R. **Ht.:** 5-11. **Wt.:** 190. **Drafted:** Texas, 2004 (2nd round). **Signed by:** Andy Beene.

A member of three College World Series teams in three years at Texas, Thigpen saw more action at first base because the Longhorns had one of college baseball's top defensive catchers in Taylor Teagarden. Thigpen has taken to full-time catching even better than the Blue Jays expected, throwing out 40 percent of basestealers and reaching Double-A in his first full pro season. Strike-zone judgment and athleticism are Thigpen's calling cards. He's a line-drive hitter with a short stroke and gap power. He's a cerebral catcher who studies ways to set up opposing hitters, and he works well with his pitchers. He's versatile enough to play anywhere but shortstop and center field. Thigpen is agile behind the plate and has made strides with his footwork, but still can improve his receiving skills. When his mechanics break down, his arm can rate as slightly below-average. The Jays see Thigpen as an everyday catcher and will give him every opportunity to succeed. His strong finish at Double-A was encouraging. He'll likely start 2006 back with New Hampshire.

Year	Club (League)	Class	AVG	G	AB	R	H	2B	3B	HR	RBI	BB	SO	SB	OBP	SLG
2004	Auburn (NY-P)	A	.301	45	166	34	50	11	2	7	29	23	32	1	.390	.518
2005	Lansing (Mid)	A	.287	79	293	41	84	18	2	5	35	54	34	5	.397	.413
	New Hampshire (EL)	AA	.284	39	141	18	40	8	0	4	15	9	19	0	.340	.426
MINOR LEAGUE TOTALS			.290	163	600	93	174	37	4	16	79	86	85	6	.383	.445

10 VINCE PERKINS RHP

Born: Sept. 27, 1981. **B-T:** L-R. **Ht.:** 6-5. **Wt.:** 220. **Drafted:** Lake City (Fla.) CC, D/F 2000 (18th round). **Signed by:** Chris Buckley/Joe Siers.

Perkins was a Little League and high school teammate of Rich Harden while growing up in Victoria, British Columbia. Perkins reached Double-A in 2005, though he missed time with a strained ribcage after having back and elbow injuries in 2004. Perkins' power arm rivals any in the system. The action on Perkins' heavy 93-96 mph sinking fastball has been likened to a bowling ball, and it's a true out pitch. He throws two average secondary pitches: a hard 86-87 mph slider and a developing change-up. He gets high marks for his mound presence and makeup. Pitch efficiency never has been Perkins' strong suit because he struggles with his command. Despite having a prototypical pitcher's frame, he doesn't have ideal mechanics. He often throws across his body and his shoulder flies open when he uses his slider. He needs to slow the pace of his delivery and repeat his motion. Command is often the last thing to come for power pitchers, and the Blue Jays are optimistic Perkins will figure it out. If not, he could have a bright future in the bullpen. His spring-training performance will determine if he's ready for Triple-A.

Year	Club (League)	Class	W	L	ERA	G	GS	CG	SV	IP	H	R	ER	HR	BB	SO	AVG
2001	Auburn (NY-P)	A	1	4	3.27	14	14	0	0	52	41	23	19	1	37	67	.220
2002	Auburn (NY-P)	A	5	5	3.34	15	15	0	0	73	51	32	27	3	44	85	.198
2003	Charleston, W.Va. (SAL)	A	3	1	1.83	8	8	0	0	44	19	9	9	1	22	60	.136
	Dunedin (FSL)	A	7	6	2.46	18	17	0	0	84	58	32	23	1	53	69	.201
2004	Dunedin (FSL)	A	1	4	3.95	13	9	0	0	55	53	28	24	2	24	47	.269
2005	New Hampshire (EL)	AA	7	7	4.03	26	24	0	0	132	124	65	59	9	51	111	.250
MINOR LEAGUE TOTALS			24	27	3.29	94	87	0	0	440	346	189	161	17	231	439	.221

11 SHAUN MARCUM RHP

Born: Dec. 14, 1981. **B-T:** R-R. **Ht.:** 6-0. **Wt.:** 180. **Drafted:** Southwest Missouri State University, 2003 (3rd round). **Signed by:** Ty Nichols.

Marcum was the starting shortstop and closer for Southwest Missouri State's 2003 College World Series team. He has moved quickly since turning pro and made his major league debut last September by not allowing a run in five relief appearances, including two-inning stints against the Red Sox and Yankees. Marcum doesn't have a knockout pitch, but he commands his stuff and he works ahead of batters. He throws his two-seam fastball at 88-91 mph to both sides of the plate. His changeup, which he uses to combat lefthanders, is a plus pitch because he maintains fastball arm speed. Marcum's late-breaking, 81-83 mph slider is effective and he can spot it when he falls behind in the count. His curveball is fringy and likely to be shelved if he stays in the bullpen. He has a quick arm, and his upright delivery might be best suited for relief. He got into home run trouble at Triple-A when he would catch too much of the plate in fastball counts. It's all about sequencing and location for Marcum, who doesn't have a large margin for error. Despite working mostly as a starter in the minors, he's a strong candidate to rejoin the Toronto bullpen at some point this season.

Year	Club (League)	Class	W	L	ERA	G	GS	CG	SV	IP	H	R	ER	HR	BB	SO	AVG
2003	Auburn (NY-P)	A	1	0	1.32	21	0	0	8	34	15	6	5	1	7	47	.129
2004	Charleston, W.Va. (SAL)	A	7	4	3.19	13	13	1	0	79	64	32	28	7	16	83	.217
	Dunedin (FSL)	A	3	2	3.12	12	12	0	0	69	74	30	24	6	4	72	.279
2005	New Hampshire (EL)	AA	7	1	2.53	9	9	1	0	53	44	15	15	5	10	40	.229
	Syracuse (IL)	AAA	6	4	4.95	18	18	0	0	104	112	59	57	17	18	90	.271
	Toronto (AL)	MLB	0	0	0.00	5	0	0	0	8	6	0	0	0	4	4	.214
MAJOR LEAGUE TOTALS			0	0	0.00	5	0	0	0	8	6	0	0	0	4	4	.214
MINOR LEAGUE TOTALS			24	11	3.42	73	52	2	8	339	309	142	129	36	55	332	.241

12 GUILLERMO QUIROZ C

Born: Nov. 29, 1981. **B-T:** R-R. **Ht.:** 6-1. **Wt.:** 200. **Signed:** Venezuela, 1998. **Signed by:** Emilio Carrasquel.

Quiroz has been largely invisible since his huge 2003 season in Double-A, missing chunks of the past two seasons to injury. It's now uncertain what kind of return the Blue Jays will get on their initial $1.2 million bonus investment in Quiroz. His troubles started during his breakout year, when he suffered a collapsed lung toward the end of the season. He was stricken with the same problem last spring, and had surgery to build scar tissue in an attempt to prevent another reoccurrence. His left hand was broken by a pitch in 2004, and he has played a total of 141 games during the last two years. Quiroz has gotten rusty after the layoff from live pitching, but he has a good batting eye and is capable of delivering big-time power for his position. He does have a long swing, however, and never has hit for much of an average. His receiving looked shoddy in the Arizona Fall League, and though he has plus arm strength and a quick release, he threw out just 29 percent of basestealers in 2005. He has well below-average speed on the bases. Quiroz' injuries have been fluky, and he played through his first collapsed lung for a time, thinking it was just a severe chest cold. But now he's heading into his eighth season in the system, and Curtis Thigpen has passed him in the Jays' long-term plans. Quiroz will have to fight for the big league backup job in spring training, though he may be better served by getting more regular playing time in Triple-A.

Year	Club (League)	Class	AVG	G	AB	R	H	2B	3B	HR	RBI	BB	SO	SB	OBP	SLG
1999	Medicine Hat (Pio)	R	.221	63	208	25	46	7	0	9	28	18	55	0	.296	.385
2000	Hagerstown (SAL)	A	.162	43	136	14	22	4	0	1	12	16	44	0	.269	.213
	Queens (NY-P)	A	.224	55	196	27	44	9	0	5	29	27	48	1	.329	.347
2001	Charleston, W.Va. (SAL)	A	.199	82	261	25	52	12	0	7	25	29	67	5	.294	.326
2002	Dunedin (FSL)	A	.260	111	411	50	107	28	1	12	68	35	91	1	.330	.421
	Syracuse (IL)	AAA	.222	13	45	7	10	4	0	1	6	3	14	0	.271	.378
2003	New Haven (EL)	AA	.282	108	369	63	104	27	0	20	79	45	83	0	.372	.518
2004	Syracuse (IL)	AAA	.227	76	255	32	58	19	1	8	32	28	54	0	.309	.404
	Toronto (AL)	MLB	.212	17	52	2	11	2	0	0	6	2	8	1	.263	.250
2005	Dunedin (FSL)	A	.237	11	38	4	9	1	0	2	6	2	8	0	.326	.421
	Syracuse (IL)	AAA	.229	25	83	11	19	3	0	6	18	9	19	0	.309	.482
	Toronto (AL)	MLB	.194	12	36	3	7	2	0	0	4	2	13	0	.256	.250
MAJOR LEAGUE TOTALS			.205	29	88	5	18	4	0	0	10	4	21	1	.239	.250
MINOR LEAGUE TOTALS			.235	587	2002	258	471	114	2	71	303	212	483	7	.321	.401

13 RYAN PATTERSON
OF

Born: May 2, 1983. **B-T:** R-R. **Ht.:** 5-11. **Wt.:** 205. **Drafted:** Louisiana State University, 2005 (4th round). **Signed by:** Matt Briggs.

A fourth-round pick who signed in June for $162,500, Patterson arrived in pro ball with an impressive hitting résumé. A third-team All-American in 2005, he hit 50 homers as a collegian and led the Cape Cod League with a .327 batting average in 2004 after finishing eighth at .288 the year before. Despite being a little old for the short-season New York-Penn League—he was a senior sign who went undrafted as a junior—Patterson couldn't have made a stronger impression, as he led the league in RBIs, extra-base hits and slugging percentage. He's an aggressive hitter who's locked in at the plate and likes to jump on the first pitch he can handle. Though his swing is somewhat unconventional, it's compact and his bat stays in the hitting zone for a long time. He has shown an ability to hit fastballs and breaking balls in any count. Patterson played center field in college and in his pro debut, but he profiles more as a right fielder. He has the arm strength for right field and he's an average runner. Expected to begin 2006 in high Class A, Patterson will try to make the same jump Adam Lind did last season.

Year	Club (League)	Class	AVG	G	AB	R	H	2B	3B	HR	RBI	BB	SO	SB	OBP	SLG
2005	Auburn (NY-P)	A	.339	71	274	52	93	23	4	13	65	21	53	5	.386	.595
MINOR LEAGUE TOTALS			.339	71	274	52	93	23	4	13	65	21	53	5	.386	.595

14 CHI-HUNG CHENG
LHP

Born: June 20, 1985. **B-T:** L-L. **Ht.:** 6-1. **Wt.:** 180. **Signed:** Taiwan, 2003. **Signed by:** J.P. Ricciardi.

Cheng had a decorated amateur career in Taiwan, pitching for the 1996 Little League World Series championship club and several other national teams. His heavy workload scared off other clubs that scout Asia, but he hasn't had any physical problems since signing for $400,000 following the 2003 World Cup. Cheng led the Rookie-level Appalachian League in strikeouts during his 2004 debut and finished third in the low Class A Midwest League last year, when he was the youngest pitcher on a Jays full-season affiliate. Cheng's out pitch is a plus curveball. He commands it better than his 86-88 mph fastball, which features so much life that he struggles to throw strikes with it. He led the MWL in walks. Cheng is still developing his changeup. He has made great strides acclimating to the U.S. culture and he's learning English rapidly. Toronto would like to see Cheng pitch more to contact and be more aggressive instead of trying to be too fine. He'll tackle high Class A in 2006 and the Jays project him as a future starter. With his curveball, Cheng at least should become a lefty reliever.

Year	Club (League)	Class	W	L	ERA	G	GS	CG	SV	IP	H	R	ER	HR	BB	SO	AVG
2004	Pulaski (Appy)	R	3	1	2.82	14	14	0	0	61	47	27	19	4	35	74	.219
	Auburn (NY-P)	A	0	0	4.50	1	0	0	0	2	1	1	1	1	0	3	.143
2005	Lansing (Mid)	A	7	6	3.15	26	25	0	0	137	109	61	48	8	72	142	.215
MINOR LEAGUE TOTALS			10	7	3.07	41	39	0	0	200	157	89	68	13	107	219	.216

15 KYLE YATES   RHP

Born: Jan. 8, 1983. **B-T:** R-R. **Ht.:** 6-0. **Wt.:** 195. **Drafted:** Texas, 2004 (13th round). **Signed by:** Andy Beene.

The Blue Jays gambled on Yates when he was a nondescript reliever pitching behind the likes of Huston Street and J. Brent Cox at Texas, and it's paying dividends. Yates emerged in 2005, his second pro season, making more progress than any pitcher in the organization save Casey Janssen. Yates's curve is a true 70 pitch on the 20-80 scouting scale and is the best in the system. His 88-90 mph fastball is just fringe average, though he can hit 92 consistently out of the pen. After learning a changeup in instructional league in 2004, Yates was switched to a starting role at low Class A Lansing last year and took to it with aplomb. He took advantage of his starts and side sessions to refine his changeup, which he didn't use in relief. After Yates was promoted to high Class A, pitching coach Rick Langford implored him to mix his pitch sequences and not become too reliant on his curve when going for strikeouts. Yates also needs to be more attentive to how batters are reacting to him, something working with more experienced catchers might correct. He's a safe bet to begin 2006 in high Class A, where he'll continue to get innings as a starter. He may return to the bullpen in the future.

Year	Club (League)	Class	W	L	ERA	G	GS	CG	SV	IP	H	R	ER	HR	BB	SO	AVG
2004	Auburn (NY-P)	A	0	1	6.77	9	0	0	0	9	9	7	7	0	5	11	.243
2005	Lansing (Mid)	A	4	3	4.43	14	14	1	0	81	82	41	40	6	19	81	.265
	Dunedin (FSL)	A	7	3	1.91	14	14	0	0	75	69	30	16	4	19	67	.242
MINOR LEAGUE TOTALS			11	7	3.42	37	28	1	0	166	160	78	63	10	43	159	.254

16 CHIP CANNON   1B

Born: Nov. 30, 1981. **B-T:** L-R. **Ht.:** 6-5. **Wt.:** 215. **Drafted:** The Citadel, 2004 (8th round). **Signed by:** Marc Tramuta.

Area scout Marc Tramuta liked Cannon so much that he advocated drafting him in the second round in 2004. The Blue Jays waited until the eighth round and signed him for $25,000, a discounted rate because he was a college senior. Cannon powered through three full-season leagues in 2005, hitting a total of 32 homers to rank fifth in the minors. He tore up two Class A leagues before finding the going tougher in Double-A. Cannon doesn't pick the ball up well against lefthanders, and Double-A southpaws fanned him 25 times in 48 at-bats. He does have the best pop in the system, as well as the batting eye and patience to take walks. Because he was born with two club feet and had three operations on each foot as a child, Cannon has trouble starting and stopping on the bases and in the field. Limited to first base, he has a well above-average arm for his position and was clocked at 90 mph as a pitcher at The Citadel. After exceeding Toronto's wildest expectations in 2005, he'll take another crack at Double-A this season.

Year	Club (League)	Class	AVG	G	AB	R	H	2B	3B	HR	RBI	BB	SO	SB	OBP	SLG
2004	Auburn (NY-P)	A	.271	62	210	33	57	15	1	10	41	22	55	0	.338	.495
2005	Lansing (Mid)	A	.268	46	168	22	45	9	2	11	36	20	47	0	.351	.542
	Dunedin (FSL)	A	.384	29	112	28	43	4	2	14	39	16	32	0	.465	.830
	New Hampshire (EL)	AA	.247	47	170	15	42	13	1	7	23	10	58	2	.293	.459
MINOR LEAGUE TOTALS			.283	184	660	98	187	41	6	42	139	68	192	2	.352	.555

17 ROB COSBY   3B

Born: April 2, 1981. **B-T:** R-R. **Ht.:** 6-1. **Wt.:** 216. **Drafted:** HS—San Juan, P.R., 1999 (10th round). **Signed by:** Jorge Rivera.

Cosby looked to be on his way up after a solid 2003 performance in high Class A and a stellar spring-training follow-up, but five games into the 2004 season he completely tore the anterior-cruciate ligament in his knee and missed the rest of the year. He showed few ill effects once he returned last year, finishing among the Eastern League leaders in average, doubles and slugging percentage despite playing his home games in the brutal offensive environment of New Hampshire's Fisher Cats Ballpark. He's not patient at the plate, but Cosby makes contact and drives the ball, producing for both power and average.

Defensively, he has quickness, solid hands, a strong arm and average range at third base. He's still working to regain his full speed and agility, and he's still learning how his knee will react to spins and throws on the run. The Blue Jays expect Cosby to be fully recovered in 2006, two years away from his injury, and he destined for Triple-A.

Year	Club (League)	Class	AVG	G	AB	R	H	2B	3B	HR	RBI	BB	SO	SB	OBP	SLG
1999	Medicine Hat (Pio)	R	.270	46	178	22	48	9	1	3	25	12	29	10	.309	.382
2000	Hagerstown (SAL)	A	.237	77	291	31	69	9	0	4	29	16	37	2	.275	.309
	Queens (NY-P)	A	.270	42	163	15	44	8	0	0	22	14	22	4	.326	.319
2001	Charleston, W.Va. (SAL)	A	.228	120	412	48	94	22	1	5	43	32	60	6	.286	.323
2002	Charleston, W.Va. (SAL)	A	.294	109	419	52	123	20	3	5	59	28	55	2	.333	.391
2003	Dunedin (FSL)	A	.277	133	476	53	132	34	2	4	52	46	61	3	.343	.382
2004	New Hampshire (EL)	AA	.529	5	17	2	9	1	0	1	6	0	1	0	.529	.765
2005	New Hampshire (EL)	AA	.308	115	428	56	132	34	0	17	68	24	77	2	.346	.507
MINOR LEAGUE TOTALS			.273	647	2384	279	651	137	7	39	304	172	342	29	.321	.385

18 ISMAEL RAMIREZ RHP

Born: March 3, 1981. **B-T:** R-R. **Ht.:** 6-3. **Wt.:** 200. **Signed:** Venezuela, 1998. **Signed by:** Emilio Carrasquel.

The Florida State League's 2004 pitcher of the year, Ramirez moved up to Double-A last year and was nearly as effective except for becoming much more vulnerable to homers. He sometimes gets lost in the shuffle of Toronto's upper-level pitching prospects, but he has good stuff. He throws a sinking 90-92 mph fastball that can reach 94. His slider and change-up can be plus pitches at times, though he doesn't produce as many groundballs as someone with his sinker/slider combo should. Ramirez uses his changeup as his main weapon against lefthanders, and he'll need to refine it to remain a starter. A streaky pitcher, he gets hit when he falls behind in the count. His mechanics place stress on his elbow—he came down with tendinitis at season's end—and the Blue Jays are working with him to close his delivery, which also will aid him in keeping his pitches down. He employs a slight pause in his windup to help throw off hitters' timing. He may return to Double-A to start 2006, but Toronto would like to see him force his way to Triple-A in his eighth season in the organization.

Year	Club (League)	Class	W	L	ERA	G	GS	CG	SV	IP	H	R	ER	HR	BB	SO	AVG
1999	Chino (VSL)	R	1	0	4.20	3	3	0	0	15	16	10	7	0	1	8	.281
2000	Chino (VSL)	R	2	0	3.15	4	4	0	0	20	20	7	7	4	2	13	.253
	Blue Jays (DSL)	R	3	1	3.72	11	7	0	2	46	51	24	19	1	6	26	.276
2001	Medicine Hat (Pio)	R	5	6	5.35	14	14	0	0	74	77	48	44	12	21	35	.267
2002	Charleston, W.Va. (SAL)	A	0	1	4.85	6	1	0	0	17	20	10	9	2	7	14	.290
	Auburn (NY-P)	A	0	2	7.17	3	3	0	0	11	17	10	9	2	2	7	.354
	Medicine Hat (Pio)	R	4	2	2.98	11	10	0	0	54	51	23	18	4	14	51	.249
2003	Charleston, W.Va. (SAL)	A	6	5	3.02	24	22	1	0	119	110	51	40	6	31	70	.243
2004	Dunedin (FSL)	A	15	6	2.72	28	27	0	0	165	151	57	50	5	25	131	.245
2005	New Hampshire (EL)	AA	8	13	4.12	27	27	0	0	151	155	75	69	19	32	125	.267
MINOR LEAGUE TOTALS			44	36	3.64	131	118	1	2	673	668	315	272	55	141	480	.259

19 BRIAN PETTWAY OF

Born: July 29, 1983. **B-T:** R-R. **Ht.:** 6-1. **Wt.:** 225. **Drafted:** Mississippi, 2005 (3rd round). **Signed by:** Matt Briggs.

Pettway enhanced his draft stock by shedding 20 pounds for a junior season that culminated in second-team All-America honors as he helped Mississippi get within a game of the College World Series. Several Southeastern Conference opponents considered Pettway, and not Indians second-round pick Stephen Head, the Rebels' most dangerous hitter last spring. After Pettway signed for $440,000 as a third-round pick in June, he struggle more than expected against pro pitching. He had trouble making contact, which may be the result of a brief layoff during negotiations and/or a lack of advanced wood bat experience. Pettway is an aggressive hitter who favors swinging at the first pitch, and he was frequently induced to put less-than-optimal pitches in play. He utilizes a level, consistent swing to hit for average and he's expected to develop power—some think he'll have more than Ryan Patterson—as he matures. A two-way player who also relieved at Mississippi, Pettway played catcher when he arrived in college and has enough arm for right field. He has below-average speed and ordinary range, so he profiles more as a left fielder. After working on his selectivity during instructional league, he'll head to low Class A to begin this season.

Year	Club (League)	Class	AVG	G	AB	R	H	2B	3B	HR	RBI	BB	SO	SB	OBP	SLG
2005	Auburn (NY-P)	A	.225	56	200	19	45	10	2	6	25	16	66	0	.288	.385
MINOR LEAGUE TOTALS			.225	56	200	19	45	10	2	6	25	16	66	0	.288	.385

20 ROBINZON DIAZ C

Born: Sept. 19, 1983. **B-T:** R-R. **Ht.:** 5-11. **Wt.:** 195. **Signed:** Dominican Republic, 2000. **Signed by:** Hilario Soriano.

Diaz won the Appalachian League batting title in 2003 and has earned league all-star honors in each of the past two seasons. With quick wrists and hands positioned over the plate, Diaz can get his bat on just about any pitch. He's a classic bad-ball hitter who puts the ball in play nearly every at-bat, resulting in low walk and strikeout totals. A spray hitter with an inside-out swing, he has yet to develop much power. Diaz has a live body and runs surprisingly well for a catcher. He has a strong arm, throwing out 36 percent of basestealers in 2005, and he blocks balls well. His gamecalling needs a lot of improvement, as he needs to work better with his pitchers to formulate gameplans. With Curtis Thigpen moving ahead of him, Diaz may have to repeat high Class A until an everyday job opens in Double-A.

Year	Club (League)	Class	AVG	G	AB	R	H	2B	3B	HR	RBI	BB	SO	SB	OBP	SLG
2001	Blue Jays (DSL)	R	.312	65	253	49	79	17	2	2	45	20	19	4	.374	.419
2002	Dunedin (FSL)	A	.120	10	25	3	3	0	0	0	1	1	4	0	.148	.120
	Medicine Hat (Pio)	R	.297	58	192	29	57	9	0	0	20	13	19	7	.345	.344
2003	Pulaski (Appy)	R	.374	48	182	33	68	20	2	1	44	10	14	1	.407	.522
2004	Charleston, W.Va. (SAL)	A	.287	105	407	62	117	20	2	2	42	27	31	10	.341	.361
2005	Dunedin (FSL)	A	.294	100	388	47	114	17	6	1	65	15	28	5	.325	.376
MINOR LEAGUE TOTALS			.303	386	1447	223	438	83	12	6	217	86	115	27	.348	.389

21 JOHN HATTIG 3B

Born: Feb. 27, 1980. **B-T:** B-R. **Ht.:** 6-2. **Wt.:** 215. **Drafted:** HS—Santa Rita, Guam, 1998 (25th round). **Signed by:** Wally Komatsubara (Red Sox).

The first player ever drafted out of Guam, Hattig joined the Blue Jays in a July 2004 trade for Terry Adams. Hattig was in the midst of a career year that saw him hit 22 homers, but he failed to build on that effort in 2005. He hurt his elbow in spring training, sidelining him for six weeks, before lingering hamstring problems ended his season after 37 games. Hattig has a good swing from both sides of the plate and controls the strike zone, though he rarely has hit for much power with the exception of 2004. Hattig isn't much of an athlete and needs to spend more time on his conditioning, a lingering concern. He's adequate at third base, where his arm is average, but lacks first-step quickness and likely will have to move to first base in the future. He has the makeup to put bad at-bats and errors behind him. His quest to become Guam's first big leaguer will resume in Triple-A this year.

Year	Club (League)	Class	AVG	G	AB	R	H	2B	3B	HR	RBI	BB	SO	SB	OBP	SLG
1999	Red Sox (GCL)	R	.270	50	163	28	44	7	3	1	17	16	20	1	.333	.368
2000	Lowell (NY-P)	A	.289	61	242	30	70	8	1	0	28	20	43	1	.342	.331
2001	Lowell (NY-P)	A	.111	11	45	4	5	0	1	1	5	3	7	1	.184	.222
	Augusta (SAL)	A	.285	50	179	25	51	9	1	1	23	22	42	4	.371	.363
2002	Sarasota (FSL)	A	.247	24	85	6	21	6	0	0	6	7	16	0	.301	.318
	Augusta (SAL)	A	.282	93	347	46	98	20	0	7	56	52	73	1	.377	.401
2003	Sarasota (FSL)	A	.295	114	400	51	118	29	2	6	70	59	70	9	.385	.423
	Portland (EL)	AA	.219	8	32	3	7	2	0	0	1	2	11	0	.265	.281
2004	Portland (EL)	AA	.295	75	264	53	78	21	1	12	35	47	68	3	.411	.519
	New Hampshire (EL)	AA	.296	40	142	24	42	7	0	10	30	12	41	0	.352	.556
2005	Dunedin (FSL)	A	.386	11	44	8	17	3	0	0	5	3	7	0	.417	.455
	Syracuse (IL)	AAA	.316	26	95	15	30	7	0	1	10	10	16	0	.387	.421
MINOR LEAGUE TOTALS			.285	563	2038	293	581	119	9	39	286	253	414	20	.366	.410

22 JOHN-FORD GRIFFIN OF/DH

Born: Nov. 19, 1979. **B-T:** L-L. **Ht.:** 6-2. **Wt.:** 215. **Drafted:** Florida State, 2001 (1st round). **Signed by:** Scott Pleis (Yankees).

Griffin led the Triple-A International League in home runs and RBIs in 2005, finally showing the power three organizations had been looking for since the Yankees drafted him 23rd overall in 2001. New York sent him to Oakland in the Jeff Weaver trade in July 2002, and the A's moved him to the Blue Jays for Jason Perry in January 2003. In college, Griffin was known more for his ability to hit for average. He topped .400 in each of his three seasons at Florida State, set a Seminoles record with a career .427 mark and had coach Mike Martin call him the best pure hitter in the program's history. But after slugging a mere .430 during his first two pro seasons, Griffin spent his next two in Double-A learning to identify which pitches he could drive. The tradeoff for his power has been a drop in batting average and a spike in strikeouts. At least he still draws his share of value. Griffin's value consists entirely of what he can do with the bat. He's a below-average runner, thrower and defender who's limited to left field and first base and may fit best at DH. The Blue Jays rewarded Griffin's

2005 performance with his first major league callup to give him an idea of what he has to do to make the club, and he homered off Kansas City's Jimmy Gobble on the final day of the season. Griffin will get the chance to make Toronto as a reserve outfielder and pinch-hitter this spring.

Year	Club (League)	Class	AVG	G	AB	R	H	2B	3B	HR	RBI	BB	SO	SB	OBP	SLG
2001	Staten Island (NY-P)	A	.311	66	238	46	74	17	1	5	43	40	41	10	.413	.454
2002	Tampa (FSL)	A	.267	65	255	32	68	16	1	3	31	29	45	1	.344	.373
	Norwich (EL)	AA	.328	18	67	17	22	3	0	5	10	8	13	0	.400	.597
	Midland (TL)	AA	.143	2	7	0	1	0	0	0	0	0	3	0	.250	.143
2003	New Haven (EL)	AA	.279	104	373	48	104	23	3	13	75	49	85	2	.361	.461
2004	New Hampshire (EL)	AA	.248	129	467	66	116	28	1	22	81	56	128	1	.330	.454
2005	Syracuse (IL)	AAA	.254	135	512	80	130	21	1	30	103	62	140	1	.335	.475
	Toronto (AL)	MLB	.308	7	13	3	4	2	0	1	6	0	4	0	.308	.692
MAJOR LEAGUE TOTALS			.308	7	13	3	4	2	0	1	6	0	4	0	.308	.692
MINOR LEAGUE TOTALS			.268	519	1919	289	515	108	7	78	343	244	455	15	.352	.454

23 ERIC FOWLER
LHP

Born: March 18, 1983. **B-T:** L-L. **Ht.:** 6-3. **Wt.:** 215. **Drafted:** Mississippi, 2005 (5th round). **Signed by:** Matt Briggs.

A teammate of Brian Pettway's at Mississippi, Fowler was the fifth of five Rebels to go in the first five rounds of the 2005 draft. A fifth-rounder who signed for $182,500, he has a down-breaking curveball that's already a major league pitch. He backs up his curve by using a quick arm action to throw an 88-91 mph fastball, which he locates down in the zone. Fowler's fastball is deceptive in that it looks faster than its velocity and has late life, running in on lefties. His changeup is average at times but remains a work in progress. He'll have to get stronger after tiring down the stretch at short-season Auburn, which affected his control. He'll have to refine his command and maybe add a slider, but otherwise the Blue Jays are pleased with his progress and think he mainly needs experience. He may make a two-level jump to high Class A this year.

Year	Club (League)	Class	W	L	ERA	G	GS	CG	SV	IP	H	R	ER	HR	BB	SO	AVG
2005	Auburn (NY-P)	A	4	2	3.02	15	10	0	0	57	42	24	19	1	29	55	.202
MINOR LEAGUE TOTALS			4	2	3.02	15	10	0	0	57	42	24	19	1	29	55	.202

24 JESSE LITSCH
RHP

Born: March 9, 1985. **B-T:** R-R. **Ht.:** 6-1. **Wt.:** 195. **Drafted:** South Florida CC, D/F 2004 (24th round). **Signed by:** Tony Arias.

The Rockies tried to sign Litsch as a 37th-round draft-and-follow from 2003, and considered redrafting him in 2004. When he declined both offers, the Blue Jays took him in the 24th round in 2004 and came to terms with him as a draft-and-follow after he spent a second season at South Florida Community College. Litsch had a dominant pro debut, over-matching Appy League hitters with four pitches and excellent control. He goes straight after hitters, mixing his 88-92 mph four-seam fastball, which cuts away from righthanders; a slider he throws at 84-86 mph with plus potential; a fading changeup; and a solid-average curve he throws to alter batters' eye levels. He's an aggressive pitcher, though sometimes he'll try to be too fine and throw a perfect slider when he just needs to throw the pitch for a strike. Toronto is trying to get him to throw his pitches on more of a downward plane, as he occasionally loses his direction to the plate. He'll head to low Class A to begin 2006.

Year	Club (League)	Class	W	L	ERA	G	GS	CG	SV	IP	H	R	ER	HR	BB	SO	AVG
2005	Pulaski (Appy)	R	5	1	2.74	11	11	0	0	66	51	22	20	6	10	67	.212
	Auburn (NY-P)	A	0	1	3.60	4	3	0	0	10	11	9	4	0	6	7	.268
MINOR LEAGUE TOTALS			5	2	2.85	15	14	0	0	76	62	31	24	6	16	74	.220

25 YUBER RODRIGUEZ
OF

Born: Nov. 17, 1983. **B-T:** B-R. **Ht.:** 6-0. **Wt.:** 170. **Signed:** Venezuela, 2000. **Signed by:** Raphael Moncada.

Rodriguez struggled out of the gate in his full-season debut in 2005, hitting .173 for the first two months and just reaching the Mendoza Line at season's end. Unlike Lansing teammate Chi-Hung Cheng, who made a smooth transition to his new surroundings, Rodriguez had trouble adapting to the colder temperatures and more extensive travel in the Midwest League. A raw five-tool talent, Rodriguez has a long way to go to harness his physical abilities. The center fielder is the organization's top athlete and he's a plus defender, thrower and runner. But he doesn't yet possess basestealing instincts and needs to improve his leads and jumps. At the plate, he fell into bad habits early and began pressing. He has good bat speed and power potential, but has several adjustments to make at the plate after striking out 114 times in 111 games. Rodriguez will try to get back on track when he repeats low Class A this year.

Year	Club (League)	Class	AVG	G	AB	R	H	2B	3B	HR	RBI	BB	SO	SB	OBP	SLG
2001	Blue Jays (DSL)	R	.182	44	159	21	29	7	0	4	21	13	49	12	.250	.302
2002	Carora (VSL)	R	.272	56	206	33	56	17	2	1	22	7	59	19	.320	.388
2003	Pulaski (Appy)	R	.282	41	131	18	37	11	0	2	15	5	41	1	.333	.412
2004	Pulaski (Appy)	R	.306	62	245	49	75	13	6	8	50	28	70	9	.394	.506
2005	Lansing (Mid)	A	.200	111	375	52	75	15	1	4	43	47	114	13	.293	.277
MINOR LEAGUE TOTALS			.244	314	1116	173	272	63	9	19	151	100	333	54	.319	.367

26 RYAN ROBERTS 2B

Born: Sept. 19, 1980. **B-T:** R-R. **Ht.:** 5-11. **Wt.:** 190. **Drafted:** Texas-Arlington, 2003 (18th round). **Signed by:** Andy Beene.

Drafted as a third baseman in 2003, Roberts was shifted to second base in instructional league that year and the transition has gone smoothly. He didn't distinguish himself in his first crack at high Class A in 2004, but it took him just two months to master the level in 2005 and he didn't stop hitting after a promotion to Double-A. Roberts has an advanced approach at the plate—he placed third in the Eastern League in on-base percentage—and opposite-field power. He'll take a pitcher's pitch on the outside corner and serve it to right field. While he's an offensive-minded second baseman, Roberts has average speed, range and arm strength, solid hands and an effective double-play pivot. He's a high-energy player whom opposing managers commend for his professionalism. He's ready for Triple-A and getting close to his first big league promotion.

Year	Club (League)	Class	AVG	G	AB	R	H	2B	3B	HR	RBI	BB	SO	SB	OBP	SLG
2003	Auburn (NY-P)	A	.278	66	248	52	69	10	3	8	36	35	63	7	.374	.440
2004	Charleston, W.Va. (SAL)	A	.283	64	226	38	64	9	0	13	39	55	50	0	.440	.496
	Dunedin (FSL)	A	.239	59	205	29	49	1	1	7	25	36	51	0	.350	.356
2005	Dunedin (FSL)	A	.287	42	164	33	47	9	0	9	35	24	27	6	.380	.506
	New Hampshire (EL)	AA	.272	92	338	54	92	19	3	15	44	55	94	5	.379	.479
MINOR LEAGUE TOTALS			.272	323	1181	206	321	48	7	52	179	205	285	18	.386	.456

27 ROBERT RAY RHP

Born: Jan. 21, 1984. **B-T:** R-R. **Ht.:** 6-5. **Wt.:** 190. **Drafted:** Texas A&M, 2005 (7th round). **Signed by:** Andy Beene.

Despite an inconsistent junior season at Texas A&M in 2005, the Blue Jays made Ray a seventh-round pick on the strength of his dominant summer the year before in the Cape Cod League. Ray was more consistent as a pro than he had been in the spring, and Toronto believes he can remain a starter after he pitched in multiple roles for the Aggies. His best pitch is an 89-93 mph fastball with late life, and his heater sat at 92-94 when he came out of the bullpen in Cape Cod. His slider rates a 55 on the 20-80 scouting scale, and he also throws an average curve and an in-progress changeup. The Jays were impressed with his feel for changing speeds and attacking hitters. Roving pitching instructor Dane Johnson helped simplify his approach, but Ray will need to improve his command if he's to remain a starter. He also can do a better job of trying to figure out what hitters are attempting to do against him. He'll open his first full pro season in low Class A.

Year	Club (League)	Class	W	L	ERA	G	GS	CG	SV	IP	H	R	ER	HR	BB	SO	AVG
2005	Auburn (NY-P)	A	4	3	2.77	15	13	0	0	62	46	22	19	2	20	58	.204
MINOR LEAGUE TOTALS			4	3	2.77	15	13	0	0	62	46	22	19	2	20	58	.204

28 DAVIS ROMERO LHP

Born: March 30, 1983. **B-T:** L-L. **Ht.:** 5-10. **Wt.:** 156. **Signed:** Panama, 1999. **Signed by:** Giovany Miranda.

Romero generates surprising velocity for a pitcher who's generously listed at 5-foot-10, getting his fastball up to 91-92 mph. He ranked third in the Florida State League in strikeouts last year, and when he's on he throws strikes with his fastball, locates his changeup and puts batters away with his above-average, sweeping curveball. At other times, he'll pitch in the high 80s and be much more hittable. Romero is athletic and very sound mechanically. He's using a new low-three-quarters arm slot, suggested by roving pitching instructor Dane Johnson to improve the width on his curve. Romero struggles at times to set batters up for future at-bats, and he pitched well coming out of the bullpen, suggesting a likely future role of lefty reliever. The Jays would like to see Romero make a run at their Double-A rotation this season.

Year	Club (League)	Class	W	L	ERA	G	GS	CG	SV	IP	H	R	ER	HR	BB	SO	AVG
2000	Blue Jays (DSL)	R	1	0	2.65	13	2	0	4	34	15	10	10	1	10	45	.129
2001	Blue Jays (DSL)	R	4	3	2.47	10	9	0	0	51	35	19	14	1	12	85	.187
2002	Medicine Hat (Pio)	R	3	2	5.19	27	4	0	2	50	49	38	29	7	18	76	.249
2003	Auburn (NY-P)	A	4	1	2.37	30	0	0	2	42	31	13	11	1	8	53	.199
2004	Charleston, W.Va. (SAL)	A	5	4	2.53	32	14	0	1	103	77	36	29	6	30	108	.209
2005	Dunedin (FSL)	A	9	6	3.46	34	18	0	1	125	133	60	48	10	34	136	.273
MINOR LEAGUE TOTALS			26	16	3.13	146	47	0	10	405	340	176	141	26	112	503	.225

29 JACOB BUTLER
OF

Born: Feb. 9, 1983. **B-T:** R-R. **Ht.:** 6-1. **Wt.:** 200. **Drafted:** Nevada, 2005 (8th round). **Signed by:** Brandon Mozley.

Butler led Nevada with a .340 batting average as a senior in 2005, piquing the Blue Jays' interest with his plate discipline and hitting approach. After they nabbed him in the eighth round and signed him for $25,000 last June, Toronto has compared him to former Wolf Pack stars Ryan Church and Kevin Kouzmanoff. Butler was too advanced for the Appalachian League but headed there because the Jays had too many corner outfielders at Auburn. He made the most of his assignment, finishing second in home runs, RBIs, slugging percentage and extra-base hits. Promoted for the New York-Penn League playoffs, Butler had a five-hit, six-RBI game in the semifinals. Butler has sound pitch-recognition skills, making adjustments to offspeed pitches, and plus power. He's limited to left field by an average arm and below-average running speed. The Jays are optimistic about his chances against advanced competition and could push him to high Class A, though he'll probably begin this year in low Class A.

Year	Club (League)	Class	AVG	G	AB	R	H	2B	3B	HR	RBI	BB	SO	SB	OBP	SLG
2005	Pulaski (Appy)	R	.290	55	200	42	58	16	1	14	52	31	60	1	.384	.590
	Auburn (NY-P)	A	.200	11	40	5	8	1	1	2	8	2	7	0	.238	.425
MINOR LEAGUE TOTALS			.275	66	240	47	66	17	2	16	60	33	67	1	.362	.563

30 WESLEY STONE
2B

Born: April 16, 1987. **B-T:** R-R. **Ht.:** 5-10. **Wt.:** 170. **Drafted:** HS—Rialto, Calif., 2005 (11th round). **Signed by:** Demerius Pittman.

The Blue Jays wanted to take an advanced high school hitter early in the 2005 draft, but their targets kept getting taken by other clubs. They settled for Stone in the 11th round, making him only prep player they signed last year and their earliest high school hitter selected during general manager J.P. Ricciardi's tenure. Because they lack a complex league team, Toronto was looking for a polished hitter who could make a quick adjustment to the pros. Stone delivered on both counts before fading in August. His best tool is his bat, though he needs to get stronger to take advantage of his projectable power. The Jays were impressed with Stone's batting eye, but he struggled to make consistent contact in his debut. Quiet and a diligent worker, Stone is capable at second base but could stand to improve his footwork around the bag. While his arm is average, he needs to speed up his pivot to catch up with the faster level of competition. He made strides in that regard during instructional league. He could open 2006 in low Class A if he has a good spring.

Year	Club (League)	Class	AVG	G	AB	R	H	2B	3B	HR	RBI	BB	SO	SB	OBP	SLG
2005	Pulaski (Appy)	R	.272	43	162	23	44	7	0	1	15	22	62	0	.358	.333
MINOR LEAGUE TOTALS			.272	43	162	23	44	7	0	1	15	22	62	0	.358	.333

WASHINGTON
NATIONALS

BY **AARON FITT**

The Nationals' first season in Washington was a success on the field, as the team staged a surprising playoff run and finished .500 despite being the majors' lowest-scoring club. The struggles of free-agent acquisitions Vinny Castilla and Cristian Guzman contributed to the offensive woes, though a trade for outfielder Jose Guillen worked out well. The team's strength was its pitching staff, which finished with the ninth-best ERA in baseball, thanks to a terrific bullpen and the emergence of John Patterson in the rotation.

But while the Nationals came together on the field, their front-office future took longer to materialize. By the end of 2005, there still was no new ownership group in place and Major League Baseball still had not signed a new stadium deal with local leaders as the situation descended into political chaos. MLB still controls the club and it's uncertain how long the appointed general manager, Jim Bowden, will remain with Washington. He was given a six-month extension to get the club through the winter, as the sale of the club waited for the ballpark situation to get resolved.

Bowden dismissed farm director Adam Wogan in October and named vice president of ballpark operations Andy Dunn interim farm director. Wogan's firing came after another difficult year for Nationals affiliates, who combined for a .438 winning percentage, second-worst in baseball. The system's top two prospects entering the year, lefthander Mike Hinckley and first baseman Larry Broadway, suffered from injuries and confidence problems.

Washington tried to reinstitute its instructional league program for the first time in five years, planning on holding it at special assistant to the GM Jose Rijo's complex in the Dominican Republic. But construction on the hotel where the players were to have stayed was behind schedule, and the program was scrapped without the players ever getting on the field.

There was good news. The big league club got help from the top of the farm system, as Ryan Church emerged in the outfield and Gary Majewski was a revelation out of the bullpen. Prospects like Collin Balester, Ian Desmond, Kory Casto and Frank Diaz had breakout years. And first-round pick Ryan Zimmerman zoomed to the majors.

The Guzman and Castilla signings deprived the club of its second- and third-round picks, so scouting director Dana Brown tried to make up for it by drafting high-upside outfielders Justin Maxwell and Ryan DeLaughter before bolstering the organization's pitching depth with college arms. The returns on Brown's recent drafts have been encouraging, particularly given the tight fiscal restraints imposed by MLB when the franchise was in Montreal. But Brown—who received a one-year contract extension—and his scouts still have managed to find talent, signing all-star closer **Chad Cordero** and eight of the players in the organization top 10 in his four years with the team.

TOP 30 PROSPECTS

1. Ryan Zimmerman, 3b	16. Shawn Hill, rhp
2. Collin Balester, rhp	17. Brandon Watson, of
3. Clint Everts, rhp	18. Brendan Harris, 2b/3b
4. Ian Desmond, ss	19. Devin Ivany, c
5. Kory Casto, 3b	20. Leonard Davis, 3b
6. Mike Hinckley, lhp	21. Francisco Guzman, of
7. Bill Bray, lhp	22. Ryan DeLaughter, of
8. Larry Broadway, 1b	23. Edgardo Baez, of
9. Daryl Thompson, rhp	24. Francisco Plasencia, of
10. Frank Diaz, of	25. Tyrell Godwin, of
11. Jason Bergmann, rhp	26. Salomon Manriquez, c
12. Justin Maxwell, of	27. Devin Perrin, rhp
13. Travis Hughes, rhp	28. Andre Enriquez, rhp
14. Josh Whitesell, 1b	29. Marvin Lowrance, of
15. Darrell Rasner, rhp	30. Rogearvin Bernadina, of

ORGANIZATION OVERVIEW

General manager: Jim Bowden. **Farm director:** Andy Dunn. **Scouting director:** Dana Brown.

2005 PERFORMANCE

Class	Team	League	W	L	Pct.	Finish*	Manager
Majors	Washington	National	81	81	.500	t-8th (16)	Frank Robinson
Triple-A	New Orleans Zephyrs	Pacific Coast	64	76	.457	14th (16)	Tim Foli
Double-A	Harrisburg Senators	Eastern	64	78	.451	10th (12)	Keith Bodie
High A	Potomac Nationals	Carolina	63	77	.450	6th (8)	Bob Henley
Low A	Savannah Sand Gnats	South Atlantic	62	76	.449	12th (16)	Randy Knorr
Short-season	#Vermont Expos	New York-Penn	28	48	.368	13th (14)	Bobby Williams
Rookie	GCL Nationals	Gulf Coast	21	32	.396	12th (12)	Wendell Kim
OVERALL 2005 MINOR LEAGUE RECORD			302	387	.438	29th (30)	

*Finish in overall standings (No. of teams in league). #Franchise will be known as Vermont Lake Monsters in 2006.

ORGANIZATION LEADERS

BATTING   *Minimum 250 at-bats
*AVG	Short, Rick, New Orleans	.383
R	Casto, Kory, Potomac	86
H	Diaz, Frank, Potomac	173
TB	Diaz, Frank, Potomac	276
2B	Diaz, Frank, Potomac	45
3B	Davis, Leonard, Vermont	8
HR	Haynes, Dee, Harrisburg/New Orleans	23
RBI	Casto, Kory, Potomac	90
BB	Casto, Kory, Potomac	84
SO	Mortimer, Steve, GCL Nationals/Savannah	142
SB	Watson, Brandon, Harrisburg/New Orleans	38
*OBP	Short, Rick, New Orleans	.456
*SLG	Short, Rick, New Orleans	.569

PITCHING   #Minimum 75 innings
W	O'Connor, Michael, Potomac	10
	Price, Brett, Potomac	10
L	Stevenson, Jason, Harrisburg/Potomac	14
#ERA	Rivera, Saul, Harrisburg	1.92
G	Rueckel, Danny, Harrisburg	53
CG	Five players tied at	2
SV	Campbell, Brett, Potomac/Savannah	20
IP	O'Connor, Michael, Potomac	168
BB	Price, Brett, Potomac	81
SO	O'Connor, Michael, Potomac	158

BEST TOOLS

Best Hitter for Average	Ryan Zimmerman
Best Power Hitter	Larry Broadway
Best Strike-Zone Discipline	Kory Casto
Fastest Baserunner	Brandon Watson
Best Athlete	Justin Maxwell
Best Fastball	Collin Balester
Best Curveball	Clint Everts
Best Slider	Bill Bray
Best Changeup	Clint Everts
Best Control	Darrell Rasner
Best Defensive Catcher	Erick San Pedro
Best Defensive Infielder	Ryan Zimmerman
Best Infield Arm	Ian Desmond
Best Defensive Outfielder	Frank Diaz
Best Outfield Arm	Ryan DeLaughter

PROJECTED 2009 LINEUP

Catcher	Brian Schneider
First Base	Nick Johnson
Second Base	Kory Casto
Third Base	Ryan Zimmerman
Shortstop	Ian Desmond
Left Field	Ryan Church
Center Field	Alfonso Soriano
Right Field	Jose Guillen

No. 1 Starter	Collin Balester
No. 2 Starter	Clint Everts
No. 3 Starter	John Patterson
No. 4 Starter	Livan Hernandez
No. 5 Starter	Mike Hinckley
Closer	Chad Cordero

LAST YEAR'S TOP 20 PROSPECTS

1. Mike Hinckley, lhp
2. Larry Broadway, 1b
3. Ryan Church, of
4. Clint Everts, rhp
5. Brendan Harris, 3b/2b
6. Bill Bray, lhp
7. Daryl Thompson, rhp
8. Darrell Rasner, rhp
9. Kory Casto, 3b
10. Collin Balester, rhp
11. Jerry Owens, of
12. Danny Rueckel, rhp
13. Rogearvin Bernadina, of
14. Edgardo Baez, of
15. J.J. Davis, of
16. Shawn Hill, rhp
17. Josh Karp, rhp
18. Tony Blanco, of/1b
19. Ian Desmond, ss
20. Gary Majewski, rhp

TOP PROSPECTS OF THE DECADE

Year	Player, Pos.	2005 Org.
1996	Vladimir Guerrero, of	Angels
1997	Vladimir Guerrero, of	Angels
1998	Brad Fullmer, 1b	White Sox
1999	Michael Barrett, 3b/c	Cubs
2000	Tony Armas Jr., rhp	Nationals
2001	Donnie Bridges, rhp	Nationals
2002	Brandon Phillips, ss	Indians
2003	Clint Everts, rhp	Nationals
2004	Clint Everts, rhp	Nationals
2005	Mike Hinckley, lhp	Nationals

TOP DRAFT PICKS OF THE DECADE

Year	Player, Pos.	2005 Org.
1996	*John Patterson, rhp	Nationals
1997	Donnie Bridges, rhp	Nationals
1998	Josh McKinley, ss	Out of baseball
1999	Josh Girdley, lhp	Out of baseball
2000	Justin Wayne, rhp	Dodgers
2001	Josh Karp, rhp	Nationals
2002	Clint Everts, rhp	Nationals
2003	Chad Cordero, rhp	Nationals
2004	Bill Bray, lhp	Nationals
2005	Ryan Zimmerman, 3b	Nationals

*Did not sign.

ALL-TIME LARGEST BONUSES

Ryan Zimmerman, 2005	$2,975,000
Justin Wayne, 2000	$2,950,000
Josh Karp, 2001	$2,650,000
Clint Everts, 2002	$2,500,000
Grady Sizemore, 2000	$2,000,000

MINOR LEAGUE DEPTH CHART

Washington Nationals

Rank: 24

STRENGTH: Third base. If Ryan Zimmerman weren't so good, Kory Casto wouldn't have to dabble at second base.

WEAKNESS: Lefthanded pitching. Mike Hinckley's return to 2004 form is the organization's best hope.

*Depth charts prepared by **John Manuel** and **Chris Kline**. Numbers in parentheses indicate prospect rankings.*

LF
Francisco Guzman (21)
Tyrell Godwin (25)
Marvin Lowrance (29)
Mike Daniel
Dee Brown

CF
Frank Diaz (10)
Justin Maxwell (12)
Brandon Watson (17)
Francisco Plasencia (24)
Rogearvin Bernadina (30)

RF
Ryan DeLaughter (22)
Edgardo Baez (23)

3B
Ryan Zimmerman (1)
Kory Casto (5)
Leonard Davis (20)
Ofilio Castro

SS
Ian Desmond (4)
Josh Labandeira
Jean Alvarez

2B
Brendan Harris (18)
Bernie Castro
Shawn Norris

1B
Larry Broadway (8)
Josh Whitesell (14)
Tony Blanco
John Howell

C
Devin Ivany (19)
Salomon Manriquez (26)
Erick San Pedro
Luke Montz
Brian Peacock

RHP

Starters	Relievers
Collin Balester (2)	Jason Bergmann (11)
Clint Everts (3)	Travis Hughes (13)
Daryl Thompson (9)	Devin Perrin (27)
Darrell Rasner (15)	Andre Enriquez (28)
Shawn Hill (16)	Danny Rueckel
Greg Bunn	Brett Campbell
Chris Lugo	Alex Morales
Marco Estrada	Saul Rivera
Josh Karp	Brett Reid

LHP

Starters	Relievers
Mike Hinckley (6)	Bill Bray (7)
Michael O'Connor	Matt White
Ricardo Morales	Coby Mavroulis
Jack Spradlin	David Maust
Brett Price	Joe Horgan

DRAFT ANALYSIS

2005

Best Pro Debut: 3B Ryan Zimmerman (1) hit .336-11-38 in the minors, then hit .397-0-6 in 20 big league games. OF John Michael Howell (9) batted .363-3-18 at short-season Vermont.

Best Athlete: After breaking through in the Cape Cod League in 2003, OF Justin Maxwell (4) projected as a first-round pick. But he has barely played since, instead sidelined by a series of broken bones in his forearm, finger and wrist. He has size (6-foot-5, 225 pounds), power and speed. He signed for $390,000 after turning down $386,000 from the Rangers as a 10th-rounder in 2004.

Best Pure Hitter: Zimmerman hit a Team USA-record .468 in the summer 2004, outperforming seven other 2005 first-round picks on the national team.

Best Raw Power: Six-foot-4, 215-pound OF Ryan DeLaughter (5) edges out former Central Florida teammates Howell and OF Dee Brown (10). The Nationals clocked DeLaughter at 93 mph on the mound as a prep.

Fastest Runner: Maxwell can run a 6.6-second 60-yard dash.

Best Defensive Player: Zimmerman will start winning Gold Gloves at third base once Scott Rolen leaves the National League. His range, arm, hands and footwork are all easily plus defensive tools. Washington even had him play some shortstop in hopes he might fill the biggest hole in the big league lineup. Maxwell is an above-average center fielder.

Best Fastball: RHP Andre Enriquez (13) spent most of his college career as an infielder. But area scouts Larry Izzo and Tony Arango liked his arm more than anything, and Enriquez was throwing 92-95 mph as a full-time pitcher as a pro. RHP

Maxwell

Marco Estrada (6) pitches at 90-93 mph.

Best Breaking Ball: Estrada has a plus curveball and can throw it for strikes.

Most Intriguing Background: Brown's father Jerome was a two-time Pro Bowl defensive lineman in the NFL before he was killed in a 1992 car accident.

Closest To The Majors: Zimmerman was the first position player from the 2005 draft to reach the big leagues.

Best Late-Round Pick: Enriquez. RHP Brad Clark (19) is a 6-foot-6, 200-pounder with a good fastball/slider combination. His draft stock tumbled when he came down with a sore shoulder late in the spring, but the Nationals worked him out in the summer before signing him and think he'll be fine. Clark had gotten more exposure in showcases than in high school because he was academically ineligible for his first three seasons.

The One Who Got Away: Scouts compare OF Marcus Jones (38) to Maxwell, but say Jones is more advanced at the same stage of his career. Like Maxwell, Jones is a top student with good makeup. He'll play at North Carolina State.

Assessment: Washington couldn't have gotten a much more immediate payoff than it got from Zimmerman. Though they lost their second- and third-round picks for signing free agents, the Nationals got equivalent talents by signing Maxwell and Clark in October.

2004 Despite having a limited budget in their last year in Montreal, the Expos came away with LHP Bill Bray (1), SS Ian Desmond (3) and RHP Collin Balester (4). That's good value, and this draft could rise. **GRADE:** C

2003 RHP Chad Cordero (1) saved 47 games in 2005. OF Jerry Owens (2) won the Southern League batting title—after getting traded to the White Sox. At least 3B Kory Casto (3) and RHP Daryl Thompson (8) are still around. **GRADE:** B+

2002 The Nationals remain high on RHP Clint Everts (1) and 1B Larry Broadway (3), though they've been slowed by injuries. RHPs Darrell Rasner (2) and Jason Bergmann (11) pitched in Washington last year. **GRADE:** C

2001 RHP Josh Karp (1) has massively underachieved as a pro even more than he did at UCLA. LHP Mike Hinckley (3) was making up for that disappointment, but he had shoulder issues in 2005. **GRADE:** C

Draft analysis prepared by Jim Callis. Numbers in parentheses indicate draft rounds.

RYAN
ZIMMERMAN

3B

RICH ABEL

Born: Sept. 28, 1984.
Ht.: 6-3. **Wt.:** 220.
Bats: R. **Throws:** R.
Drafted: Virginia, 2005
(1st round).
Signed by: Alex Smith.

Signed for $2.975 million after being drafted No. 4 overall out of Virginia in June, Zimmerman wasted no time asserting himself as the Nationals' top prospect. Washington's scouting department had coveted Zimmerman for almost a year, dating back to his breakout performance for Team USA in the summer of 2004, when he set a national-team record with a .468 average to go with four home runs and 27 RBIs in 77 at-bats. Zimmerman kept up his high level of play for the Cavaliers as a junior, batting .393-6-59 with 17 stolen bases on his way to second-team All-America honors. He already had proven he could excel with a wood bat for Team USA, so his quick adjustment to pro ball wasn't a surprise. Zimmerman got a 17-at-bat tuneup at low Class A Savannah, then hit for power and average at Double-A Harrisburg before being called up to the majors Sept. 1. With Cristian Guzman struggling mightily for their major league team, the Nationals tried Zimmerman out at shortstop—where he had filled in occasionally at Virginia—for eight games at Harrisburg. He showed the ability to play the position, but his best spot is third base and that's where he saw most of his action with Washington.

Zimmerman is a once-in-a-generation defender at the hot corner, where his soft hands, good range to both sides and above-average arm make for a legitimate Brooks Robinson-like package. He makes plays coming in on bunts as well as any current major leaguer, is adept at making backhand plays in the hole, and his throws are crisp and accurate regardless of whether his feet are set or he's throwing on the run. Zimmerman is already a near-Gold Glover, and he should be a star at the plate as well. He's a polished hitter with excellent pitch recognition and a patient approach. He doesn't chase pitches out of the zone and isn't afraid to work the count, but if he gets a pitch he likes he attacks it. He hits hard line drives to all fields, and he also has over-the-fence power and projects to hit 20 homers annually to go along with a .300-plus batting average. His speed is average. Zimmerman's makeup is off the charts, as he carries himself with a quiet confidence and never gets rattled.

Zimmerman just needs to keep playing to fine-tune his offensive game. Shortly after signing, he made a minor adjustment, quieting down some of the movement with his lower half and getting his hands into position a little earlier rather than dropping them down. As a result, his hands are more direct to the ball. There are no other holes in his game.

He got to the big leagues in a hurry, and Zimmerman could hold the Nationals' third-base job for the next decade. There's a chance he could begin the season at Triple-A New Orleans, and a couple hundred more minor league at-bats couldn't hurt him, but he's just about ready to start in the majors now. He's a perennial Gold Glove winner and all-star in waiting.

Year	Club (League)	Class	AVG	G	AB	R	H	2B	3B	HR	RBI	BB	SO	SB	OBP	SLG
2005	Savannah (SAL)	A	.471	4	17	5	8	2	1	2	6	0	3	0	.471	1.059
	Harrisburg (EL)	AA	.326	63	233	40	76	20	0	9	32	15	34	1	.371	.528
	Washington (NL)	MLB	.397	20	58	6	23	10	0	0	6	3	12	0	.419	.569
MAJOR LEAGUE TOTALS			.397	20	58	6	23	10	0	0	6	3	12	0	.419	.569
MINOR LEAGUE TOTALS			.336	67	250	45	84	22	1	11	38	15	37	1	.377	.564

COLLIN BALESTER RHP

Born: June 6, 1986. **B-T:** R-R. **Ht.:** 6-5. **Wt.:** 190. **Drafted:** HS—Huntington Beach, Calif., 2004 (4th round). **Signed by:** Tony Arango.

In his first full pro season, Balester established himself as the system's best pitching prospect. The son of a surfboard shop owner in California, he shows a laid-back, unflappable demeanor as well as excellent work habits. Balester attacks hitters with a steady diet of 92-94 mph fastballs on a steep downhill angle. Already a physical pitcher with a resilient arm, he holds his velocity deep into games and could add more as he continues to fill out. His power curveball, an average pitch at times, is further along than the Nationals expected and could end up being a plus offering. Balester needs a better feel for throwing his curveball to righthanders and further development of his changeup to reach his potential as a frontline starter. Washington encouraged Balester to throw at least 10 changeups per game last year, and it began to show signs of developing into an average pitch. Balester will open 2006 as a 19-year-old at high Class A Potomac. After being limited to 125 innings in 2005, he'll have free reign to pitch deep into games and deep into the season. He profiles as a No. 2 starter in the majors as soon as 2008.

Year	Club (League)	Class	W	L	ERA	G	GS	CG	SV	IP	H	R	ER	HR	BB	SO	AVG
2004	Expos (GCL)	R	1	2	2.19	5	4	0	0	25	20	8	6	0	5	21	.215
2005	Savannah (SAL)	A	8	6	3.67	24	23	1	0	125	105	62	51	11	42	95	.222
MINOR LEAGUE TOTALS			9	8	3.43	29	27	1	0	150	125	70	57	11	47	116	.221

CLINT EVERTS RHP

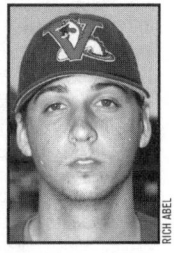

Born: Aug. 10, 1984. **B-T:** R-R. **Ht.:** 6-3. **Wt.:** 180. **Drafted:** HS—Houston, 2002 (1st round). **Signed by:** Ray Corbett.

The system's No. 1 prospect in 2003 and 2004, Everts was derailed by Tommy John surgery in September 2004. During his layoff, he grew a couple of inches and added 10-15 pounds of muscle. He came back ahead of schedule, returning to the mound in late June. Everts has a changeup that rates as a current 70 on the 20-80 scouting scale, and his curveball is also well above average, though for the most part he was only allowed to throw it in bullpen sessions. In order to build his arm strength back up, the Nationals made Everts throw almost exclusively fastballs, which topped out around 87 mph, and capped his outings at 50 pitches. The key for Everts will be continuing to regain his arm strength and improve his fastball command. He needs to be forced to throw a fastball-heavy diet and hope his heater regains its previous low-90s velocity. He also must develop better conditioning and work habits, as well as learn how to pitch inside. With two plus-plus offspeed pitches, Everts can still be a frontline starter if his velocity returns. He'll start 2006 at Potomac.

Year	Club (League)	Class	W	L	ERA	G	GS	CG	SV	IP	H	R	ER	HR	BB	SO	AVG
2003	Vermont (NY-P)	A	2	4	4.17	10	10	0	0	54	49	26	25	4	35	50	.247
	Savannah (SAL)	A	0	3	3.46	5	5	0	0	26	23	13	10	1	10	21	.230
2004	Savannah (SAL)	A	7	3	2.49	17	17	1	0	90	67	29	25	3	21	103	.208
	Brevard County (FSL)	A	2	2	2.25	4	4	0	0	20	16	5	5	2	10	19	.239
2005	Nationals (GCL)	R	0	1	3.38	7	7	0	0	16	18	9	6	0	8	15	.269
	Vermont (NY-P)	A	0	1	3.79	8	1	0	0	19	21	12	8	0	12	21	.266
MINOR LEAGUE TOTALS			11	14	3.16	51	44	1	0	225	194	94	79	10	96	229	.233

IAN DESMOND SS

Born: Sept. 20, 1985. **B-T:** R-R. **Ht.:** 6-2. **Wt.:** 185. **Drafted:** HS—Sarasota, Fla., 2004 (3rd round). **Signed by:** Russ Bove.

The more the Nationals see of Desmond, the more excited they get. He spent his first full pro season in Class A at age 19, showing enough maturity to earn a midseason promotion to Potomac. Desmond's actions simply make people believe he'll succeed. He has an athletic frame and plays with passion and confidence. His soft hands, aggressive instincts, plus range and plus-plus arm strength should make him an above-average defender at shortstop with a little time. Desmond occasionally tries to force plays in the field, resulting in 39 errors in 2005, but the Nationals aren't concerned about his defense. He still has plenty of work to do offensively, however. Desmond choked the bat, limiting his bat speed and extension, so he had to rotate his grip. After making the adjustment, his swing was shorter and quicker but he still chased too many pitches, struggled to recognize offspeed pitches and had problems with inside fastballs. Desmond should start 2006 back in high Class A. His bat remains uncertain, yet the Nats see him as their shortstop of the future.

Year	Club (League)	Class	AVG	G	AB	R	H	2B	3B	HR	RBI	BB	SO	SB	OBP	SLG
2004	Expos (GCL)	R	.227	55	216	28	49	11	0	1	27	10	40	13	.272	.292
	Vermont (NY-P)	A	.250	4	12	2	3	0	0	1	1	0	2	0	.308	.500
2005	Savannah (SAL)	A	.247	73	296	37	73	10	2	4	23	13	60	20	.291	.334
	Potomac (Car)	A	.256	55	219	37	56	13	3	3	15	21	53	13	.325	.384
MINOR LEAGUE TOTALS			.244	187	743	104	181	34	5	9	66	44	155	46	.296	.339

5 KORY CASTO   3B

Born: Dec. 8, 1981. **B-T:** L-R. **Ht.:** 6-1. **Wt.:** 200. **Drafted:** Portland, 2003 (3rd round). **Signed by:** Doug McMillan.

Casto's prospect status jumped when he converted from the outfield to third base and had a solid offensive year in 2004. Now his star is even brighter after he made more strides on offense while vastly improving his defense, which was voted the best in the high Class A Carolina League by managers. Casto's bat remains his best tool, as he hits for power and average and uses all fields. He showed much better pitch selection in 2005, nearly tripling his walk total from the previous season. Defensively, he's solid coming in on slow rollers, making backhand plays and starting double plays. His slightly above-average arm became more accurate after he changed his arm slot. Casto still needs to work a bit on his first step at third base. He's a very streaky hitter who can get into funks when he tries to make too many adjustments after an 0-for-4 day. He needs to relax. With Ryan Zimmerman entrenched at third base, the Nationals planned to experiment with Casto at second base in the offseason. His bat should play in the big leagues even if Zimmerman pushes him to the outfield. Casto should play third base in Double-A in 2006.

Year	Club (League)	Class	AVG	G	AB	R	H	2B	3B	HR	RBI	BB	SO	SB	OBP	SLG
2003	Vermont (NY-P)	A	.239	71	259	26	62	14	2	4	28	30	47	1	.322	.355
2004	Savannah (SAL)	A	.286	124	483	67	138	35	4	16	88	31	70	1	.337	.474
2005	Potomac (Car)	A	.290	135	500	86	145	36	4	22	90	84	98	6	.394	.510
MINOR LEAGUE TOTALS			.278	330	1242	179	345	85	10	42	206	145	215	8	.358	.464

6 MIKE HINCKLEY   LHP

Born: Oct. 5, 1982. **B-T:** R-L. **Ht.:** 6-3. **Wt.:** 170. **Drafted:** HS—Moore, Okla., 2001 (3rd round). **Signed by:** Darrell Brown.

The system's top prospect entering 2005, Hinckley went to big league camp in the spring with a chance to earn a spot on the Opening Day roster. He began overthrowing and his arm action got longer, which caused him to strain his shoulder and miss the first month of the season. He spent the rest of the year stuck in high Class A trying to regain his rhythm and stuff before going home to get married. The completely healthy Hinckley of years past featured outstanding command of three solid pitches—a low-90s fastball, a hard-breaking curveball and a changeup. His makeup always has drawn praise. Hinckley's fastball velocity never quite returned to normal in 2005, peaking at about 89 mph. His curveball wasn't as sharp and he struggled to find his command all season, even after he was given a clean bill of health. Hinckley needs to start fresh and learn lessons from his first taste of injury and adversity. If he's healthy, he has the work ethic and stuff to be a quality mid-rotation starter in the majors, perhaps even in 2006. He'll probably start the year in Double-A.

Year	Club (League)	Class	W	L	ERA	G	GS	CG	SV	IP	H	R	ER	HR	BB	SO	AVG
2001	Expos (GCL)	R	2	2	5.24	8	5	0	0	34	46	23	20	1	12	28	.329
2002	Vermont (NY-P)	A	6	2	1.37	16	16	0	0	92	60	19	14	4	30	66	.188
2003	Savannah (SAL)	A	9	5	3.64	23	23	2	0	121	124	54	49	4	41	111	.271
	Brevard County (FSL)	A	4	0	0.72	4	4	1	0	25	14	2	2	1	1	23	.159
2004	Brevard County (FSL)	A	6	2	2.61	10	10	0	0	62	47	23	18	6	18	51	.211
	Harrisburg (EL)	AA	5	2	2.87	16	16	0	0	94	83	34	30	5	23	80	.250
2005	Potomac (Car)	A	3	9	4.93	22	21	1	0	128	151	90	70	10	51	80	.293
MINOR LEAGUE TOTALS			35	22	3.29	99	95	4	0	556	525	245	203	31	176	439	.253

7 BILL BRAY
LHP

Born: June 5, 1983. **B-T:** L-L. **Ht.:** 6-3. **Wt.:** 215. **Drafted:** William & Mary, 2004 (1st round). **Signed by:** Alex Smith.

The Nationals spent consecutive first-round picks on college relievers, hitting big with Chad Cordero in 2003 and having high hopes for Bray, the 13th overall choice in 2004. Tightness in his back sidelined him until late May in his first full season, but he rose to Triple-A and showed no ill effects once he returned. Bray is a strong ox of a lefthander with a pair of plus pitches: a heavy 91-94 mph fastball with darting movement and a tight 81-84 mph slider. He's effective against lefties and righties and is not afraid to pitch inside. His slider can still be inconsistent, though Bray generally commands it well. Washington had toyed with the idea of making him a starter, but his change-up still has a long way to go because he used it little in college. His biggest key is staying healthy. More than a mere lefthanded specialist, Bray can be a factor in the late innings. He'll get the chance to begin 2006 with the Nationals and serve as Cordero's set-up man.

Year	Club (League)	Class	W	L	ERA	G	GS	CG	SV	IP	H	R	ER	HR	BB	SO	AVG
2004	Brevard County (FSL)	A	0	2	4.91	6	0	0	1	7	9	5	4	0	1	6	.290
2005	Potomac (Car)	A	1	0	2.13	8	0	0	3	13	8	3	3	1	3	18	.170
	Harrisburg (EL)	AA	1	0	6.35	3	0	0	1	6	10	4	4	1	1	6	.385
	New Orleans (PCL)	AAA	1	4	5.06	23	0	0	2	21	23	16	12	3	9	25	.271
MINOR LEAGUE TOTALS			3	6	4.40	40	0	0	7	47	50	28	23	5	14	55	.265

8 LARRY BROADWAY
1B

Born: Dec. 17, 1980. **B-T:** L-L. **Ht.:** 6-4. **Wt.:** 230. **Drafted:** Duke, 2002 (3rd round). **Signed by:** Dana Brown.

Broadway got off to a characteristically slow start in 2005 before straining a knee ligament fielding a ground ball. An injury to first baseman Nick Johnson caused Broadway to try to rush his return, setting him back further. A bulky knee brace hindered him when he returned, though he did hit nine homers in August. Broadway has above-average power to all fields, and his pop stands out in a system desperate for some. He also hits for a decent average and draws his share of walks. He's a solid defensive first baseman, overcoming his lack of range with smooth actions, sure hands and an above-average arm. In order to make more consistent contact, Broadway needs to stay behind the ball better. He could flourish if he can drive more pitches to the opposite field. At 25, Broadway heads into a pivotal season. He could compete for a big league job if he can get completely healthy by spring training, and he still can become a 30-homer man in the majors.

Year	Club (League)	Class	AVG	G	AB	R	H	2B	3B	HR	RBI	BB	SO	SB	OBP	SLG
2002	Expos (GCL)	R	.250	4	8	1	2	0	0	0	0	4	4	0	.500	.250
	Vermont (NY-P)	A	.315	35	127	13	40	3	0	4	23	13	33	0	.379	.433
2003	Savannah (SAL)	A	.307	83	290	56	89	25	4	14	51	44	70	3	.400	.566
	Brevard County (FSL)	A	.224	25	76	8	17	7	1	1	7	18	20	0	.367	.382
	Harrisburg (EL)	AA	.321	21	78	13	25	3	0	5	18	7	15	0	.371	.551
2004	Harrisburg (EL)	AA	.270	131	477	70	129	20	0	22	72	68	103	2	.362	.451
2005	New Orleans (PCL)	AAA	.193	18	57	4	11	3	0	0	5	7	17	2	.281	.246
	Nationals (GCL)	R	.429	8	28	3	12	5	0	1	4	7	3	0	.543	.714
	Harrisburg (EL)	AA	.269	52	186	29	50	14	0	12	24	17	37	0	.329	.538
MINOR LEAGUE TOTALS			.283	377	1327	197	375	80	5	59	204	185	302	7	.370	.484

9 DARYL THOMPSON
RHP

Born: Nov. 2, 1985. **B-T:** R-R. **Ht.:** 6-1. **Wt.:** 170. **Drafted:** HS— Mechanicsville, Md., 2003 (8th round). **Signed by:** Alex Smith.

In his second straight season as a teenager in the low Class A South Atlantic League, Thompson showed his electric stuff can translate into results, as he lowered his ERA by 1.73 runs from 2004. But his breakout season was sidetracked in July when he was shut down for minor cleanup surgery on his shoulder. Like Collin Balester, Thompson is mature, has a great frame and loves to pitch with his fastball. He's beginning to fill out and held the velocity on his 91-94 mph fastball longer than he did in the past. His 11-to-5 curveball continued to be an average pitch most of the time, and his changeup improved a great deal. Thompson's physical maturation will be hastened if he learns to eat right and develop better work habits. His health shouldn't be an issue in 2006, as the Nationals expect him to enter the spring at 100 percent. He just needs to continue refining his secondary pitches. Thompson figures to be another power arm in the Potomac rotation in 2006. He could be a fixture in Washington's rotation by 2008.

Year	Club (League)	Class	W	L	ERA	G	GS	CG	SV	IP	H	R	ER	HR	BB	SO	AVG
2003	Expos (GCL)	R	1	2	2.15	12	10	0	0	46	49	16	11	1	11	18	.288
2004	Savannah (SAL)	A	4	9	5.08	25	21	0	0	103	117	66	58	13	30	79	.296
2005	Savannah (SAL)	A	2	3	3.35	11	11	0	0	54	46	23	20	3	24	48	.232
MINOR LEAGUE TOTALS			7	14	3.96	48	42	0	0	202	212	105	89	17	65	145	.278

10 FRANK DIAZ   OF

Born: Oct. 6, 1983. **B-T:** R-R. **Ht.:** 6-2. **Wt.:** 180. **Signed:** Venezuela, 2000. **Signed by:** Carlos Acosta.

A converted pitcher who switched to the outfield in 2001, Diaz struggled against more advanced competition until the Nationals allowed him to repeat high Class A in 2005. He had a career year that included a trip to the Futures Game. He benefited immensely from the guidance of Potomac manager Bob Henley and roving hitting instructor Mitchell Page, as well as many hours in the batting cage. Page shortened Diaz' swing by removing his front arm bar, which had caused him to commit too early and struggle against inside fastballs. He began hitting line drives to all fields, showing doubles power to right-center and home run pop to left-center. Defensively, he shifted from right to center field in winter ball after the 2004 season, and he became the Carolina League's best defensive outfielder, showing an above-average arm, good first-step quickness and range. Most notably, he took charge in center, aggressively calling off other defenders and making plays. He still needs to learn the strike zone and improve his pitch recognition a bit, but with five average or better tools, Diaz has a chance to be an everyday center fielder. How he responds to Double-A competition this year will be a big barometer.

Year	Club (League)	Class	AVG	G	AB	R	H	2B	3B	HR	RBI	BB	SO	SB	OBP	SLG
2001	Expos (GCL)	R	.219	38	128	10	28	5	1	0	8	12	27	10	.297	.273
2002	Expos (GCL)	R	.277	51	173	33	48	8	2	5	24	19	28	8	.370	.434
	Brevard County (FSL)	A	.226	10	31	3	7	2	0	0	1	6	4	3	.351	.290
2003	Savannah (SAL)	A	.270	122	440	63	119	28	4	7	49	15	73	19	.298	.400
2004	Brevard County (FSL)	A	.242	114	413	46	100	17	8	8	57	31	76	16	.303	.380
2005	Potomac (Car)	A	.312	134	554	85	173	45	5	16	74	20	67	14	.342	.498
MINOR LEAGUE TOTALS			.273	469	1739	240	475	105	20	36	213	103	275	70	.321	.419

11 JASON BERGMANN   RHP

Born: Sept. 25, 1981. **B-T:** R-R. **Ht.:** 6-4. **Wt.:** 205. **Drafted:** Rutgers, 2002 (11th round). **Signed by:** Larry Izzo.

Bergmann's career took off after he moved to the bullpen midway through the 2004 season. He tore through Double-A and Triple-A in 2005 before being called up to Washington. He proved a reliable late-innings option for the Nationals in the season's final month. Bergmann has loose arm action and gets full extension from a three-quarters arm slot. He works fast and attacks hitters with a 92-94 mph fastball that touches 95, a curveball that sometimes freezes hitters and a power slider he added in 2005 and reaches 86. He even mixes in a changeup now and then. He needs to find a more effective way of combating left-handers, though. They hit .283 against him in Triple-A and .355 in the majors. Bergmann still needs to fine-tune his control, but he's ready to stick in the majors and figures to be an important part of the Nationals' bullpen this season.

Year	Club (League)	Class	W	L	ERA	G	GS	CG	SV	IP	H	R	ER	HR	BB	SO	AVG
2002	Vermont (NY-P)	A	7	4	2.89	14	14	0	0	72	48	27	23	4	33	57	.194
2003	Savannah (SAL)	A	6	11	4.29	23	22	1	0	109	108	57	52	8	53	82	.264
2004	Savannah (SAL)	A	3	7	4.85	13	13	0	0	65	67	43	35	6	34	58	.269
	Brevard County (FSL)	A	3	2	1.14	24	0	0	8	32	20	7	4	0	18	28	.177
	Harrisburg (EL)	AA	0	2	9.00	2	0	0	0	4	7	5	4	3	2	3	.368
2005	Harrisburg (EL)	AA	2	0	1.22	21	0	0	5	37	27	7	5	3	16	37	.201
	New Orleans (PCL)	AAA	3	2	3.16	20	0	0	2	37	26	15	13	5	13	39	.203
	Washington (NL)	MLB	2	0	2.75	15	1	0	0	20	14	6	6	1	11	21	.200
MAJOR LEAGUE TOTALS			2	0	2.74	15	1	0	0	20	14	6	6	1	11	21	.200
MINOR LEAGUE TOTALS			24	28	3.44	117	49	1	15	355	303	161	136	29	169	304	.233

12 JUSTIN MAXWELL   OF

Born: Nov. 6, 1983. **B-T:** R-R. **Ht.:** 6-5. **Wt.:** 225. **Drafted:** Maryland, 2005 (4th round). **Signed by:** Alex Smith.

An excellent student who graduated high school with a 4.0 grade-point average and chose Maryland over Harvard, Maxwell is even more gifted athletically. An exciting, toolsy talent, he burst onto the prospect landscape in 2003 by leading Maryland in the triple-crown categories and stolen bases as a sophomore and then lighting up the Cape Cod League. Projected as a possible 2004 first-rounder, Maxwell saw his junior season end before it began when he was hit by a pitch in an intrasquad game and broke his right arm. The Rangers still took him in the 10th round and planned to follow him in the Cape League, but he was hit by another pitch and broke his little finger. Injuries continued to plague him in 2005, as he missed most of the college season after breaking the hamate bone in his hand while hitting a ball on the barrel of the bat seven games into the season. The Nationals signed him for $390,000 as a fourth-rounder and considered him the equivalent of the second-rounder they forfeited for signing Vinny Castilla. Maxwell is an above-average runner who has been clocked down the first-base line in 4.15 seconds from the right side, and he has plus raw power. He's a plus defender, though his arm is no better than average. Until he proves otherwise, his health will be a concern. If he stays healthy, Maxwell could be an impact big league center fielder in two or three years. He'll make his pro debut with one of Washington's Class A affiliates in 2006.

Year	Club (League)	Class	AVG	G	AB	R	H	2B	3B	HR	RBI	BB	SO	SB	OBP	SLG
2005	Did not play—Signed 2006 contract															

13 TRAVIS HUGHES RHP

Born: May 25, 1978. **B-T:** R-R. **Ht.:** 6-5. **Wt.:** 235. **Drafted:** Cowley County (Kan.) CC, 1997 (19th round). **Signed by:** Mike Grouse (Rangers).

Based on the recommendation of director of major league administration Lee MacPhail, the Nationals claimed Hughes off waivers from the Rangers following the 2004 season. Hughes was a starter in the Texas system until moving to the bullpen in mid-2003, and the Nationals view him as a power reliever. Out of the pen, Hughes is a max-effort pitcher with the strongest arm in the system. He has mostly stopped throwing his changeup since shifting to relief, relying solely on a 94-96 mph fastball that tops out at 98 and a plus high-80s slider. He displays only a limited feel for commanding either pitch, however. A high-energy player with a great clubhouse presence, he sometimes gets too amped up and loses his composure and command. New Orleans pitching coach Charlie Corbell did a nice job getting Hughes to stay within himself. He'll need to learn to harness his power arsenal before he's ready for a full-time middle-relief role in the majors. If everything clicks, he has the stuff to be a set-up man or closer in another year.

Year	Club (League)	Class	W	L	ERA	G	GS	CG	SV	IP	H	R	ER	HR	BB	SO	AVG
1998	Pulaski (Appy)	R	2	6	3.89	22	3	0	2	42	30	25	18	2	25	48	.189
1999	Savannah (SAL)	A	11	7	2.81	30	23	1	2	157	127	60	49	9	54	150	.221
2000	Charlotte (FSL)	A	9	9	4.42	39	14	1	9	126	122	76	62	9	54	96	.254
2001	Tulsa (TL)	AA	5	7	4.64	47	5	0	8	87	91	52	45	8	45	86	.270
2002	Tulsa (TL)	AA	9	7	3.52	26	26	1	0	143	139	68	56	11	82	137	.255
2003	Oklahoma (PCL)	AAA	1	3	5.46	11	11	0	0	58	79	41	35	4	27	36	.329
	Frisco (TL)	AA	4	8	4.99	24	10	1	0	74	81	47	41	6	26	58	.277
2004	Frisco (TL)	AA	3	6	3.69	40	0	0	7	63	63	34	26	4	33	68	.253
	Oklahoma (PCL)	AAA	1	2	5.26	13	0	0	0	26	21	15	15	2	9	24	.214
	Texas (AL)	MAJ	0	0	13.50	2	0	0	0	1	4	2	2	0	2	4	.500
2005	New Orleans (PCL)	AAA	2	5	3.02	52	0	0	13	60	47	25	20	3	25	73	.214
	Washington (NL)	MLB	1	1	5.54	14	0	0	0	13	18	8	8	4	8	8	.333
MAJOR LEAGUE TOTALS			1	1	6.29	16	0	0	0	14	22	10	10	4	10	12	.355
MINOR LEAGUE TOTALS			47	60	3.95	304	92	4	41	836	800	443	367	58	380	776	.250

14 JOSH WHITESELL 1B

Born: April 14, 1982. **B-T:** L-L. **Ht.:** 6-3. **Wt.:** 220. **Drafted:** Loyola Marymount, 2003 (6th round). **Signed by:** Tony Arango.

One of the strongest players in the system, Whitesell improved in every significant offensive category except strikeouts in 2005. He strikes out a lot because he's not afraid to work deep into counts and wait for his pitch or draw walks. He knows his strike zone very well and gives away many fewer at-bats than he used to. Whitesell shows the ability to hit for average, but his well above average power is his best tool. He can drive balls from line to line and might be strongest to the opposite field. He still needs to fine-tune his swing so there's less movement getting into hitting position, but he has become much more consistent. Whether he ever becomes an adequate defender at first base is still in question. He has worked hard to improve his agility around the bag, though he still profiles more as a DH at this point. He'll play first base in Double-A this year.

Year	Club (League)	Class	AVG	G	AB	R	H	2B	3B	HR	RBI	BB	SO	SB	OBP	SLG
2003	Vermont (NY-P)	A	.246	49	167	13	41	10	1	5	19	28	53	0	.365	.407
2004	Savannah (SAL)	A	.250	113	380	56	95	29	0	16	54	58	91	0	.351	.453
2005	Potomac (Car)	A	.293	113	389	59	114	32	2	18	66	74	125	1	.416	.524
MINOR LEAGUE TOTALS			.267	275	936	128	250	71	3	39	139	160	269	1	.381	.474

15 DARRELL RASNER RHP

Born: Jan. 13, 1981. **B-T:** R-R. **Ht.:** 6-3. **Wt.:** 210. **Drafted:** Nevada, 2002 (2nd round). **Signed by:** Keith Snider.

Rasner impressed the Nationals with his composure and maturity in major league spring training camp, then put up another solid, consistent performance in his first full Double-A season to earn a September callup. Command is his forte, as he doesn't walk many batters and does a good job mixing his pitches. He has a clean arm action and compact, repeatable delivery. Though he still lacks a legitimate out pitch, Rasner works off his heavy 86-91 mph sinker. He threw a slider in college at Nevada, abandoned it in favor of a curveball in his first few pro seasons, then went back to the slider in the second half of last year. It became a better pitch for him than his inconsistent curve and changeup. Rasner still gives up too many hits and doesn't miss enough bats to be a top starter, but he could be ready for a No. 5 starter job or long-relief role for Washington in 2006.

Year	Club (League)	Class	W	L	ERA	G	GS	CG	SV	IP	H	R	ER	HR	BB	SO	AVG
2002	Vermont (NY-P)	A	2	5	4.33	10	10	0	0	44	44	27	21	1	18	49	.262
2003	Savannah (SAL)	A	7	7	4.19	22	22	2	0	105	106	53	49	8	36	90	.268
2004	Brevard County (FSL)	A	6	5	3.17	22	21	0	0	119	133	55	42	6	31	88	.295
	Harrisburg (EL)	AA	1	1	1.21	5	5	0	0	30	21	4	4	1	9	15	.221
2005	Harrisburg (EL)	AA	6	7	3.59	27	26	1	0	150	150	66	60	10	29	96	.260
	Washington (NL)	MLB	0	1	3.68	5	1	0	0	7	5	3	3	0	2	4	.192
MAJOR LEAGUE TOTALS			0	1	3.68	5	1	0	0	7	5	3	3	0	2	4	.192
MINOR LEAGUE TOTALS			22	25	3.53	86	84	3	0	448	454	205	176	26	123	338	.269

16 SHAWN HILL RHP

Born: April 28, 1981. **B-T:** R-R. **Ht.:** 6-2. **Wt.:** 185. **Drafted:** HS—Georgetown, Ont., 2000 (6th round). **Signed by:** Alex Agostino.

Hill first injured his elbow in high school and pitched with discomfort for years before it finally caught up with him in 2004. After posting his second straight solid Double-A season and making his big league debut, Hill went 1-0, 1.64 in 11 innings for Team Canada in the Olympics. Upon his return to the organization, he needed Tommy John surgery that kept him out for all of 2005. The Nationals expect him to be ready to pitch by spring training. When he was healthy, Hill commanded a heavy low-90s sinker that induced plenty of groundballs, and he complemented it with a good curveball and decent changeup. Hill has an athletic frame and draws comparisons to a stonger version of Jake Westbrook because of his size and stuff. He's mature and ready to compete for a spot in the big league rotation once his recovery is complete. Hill has a chance to be a back-of-the-rotation starter by 2007.

Year	Club (League)	Class	W	L	ERA	G	GS	CG	SV	IP	H	R	ER	HR	BB	SO	AVG
2000	Expos (GCL)	R	1	3	4.81	7	7	0	0	24	25	17	13	0	10	20	.250
2001	Vermont (NY-P)	A	2	2	2.27	7	7	0	0	36	22	12	9	0	8	23	.172
2002	Clinton (Mid)	A	12	7	3.44	25	25	0	0	147	149	75	56	7	35	99	.261
2003	Brevard County (FSL)	A	9	4	2.56	22	21	2	0	127	118	47	36	3	26	66	.248
	Harrisburg (EL)	AA	3	1	3.54	4	4	0	0	20	23	12	8	0	11	12	.280
2004	Harrisburg (EL)	AA	5	7	3.39	17	17	2	0	88	90	39	33	4	20	53	.274
	Montreal (NL)	MLB	1	2	16.00	3	3	0	0	9	17	16	16	1	7	10	.415
2005	Did not play—Injured																
MAJOR LEAGUE TOTALS			1	2	16.00	3	3	0	0	9	17	16	16	1	7	10	.415
MINOR LEAGUE TOTALS			32	24	3.16	82	81	4	0	441	427	202	155	14	110	273	.253

17 BRANDON WATSON OF

Born: Sept. 30, 1981. **B-T:** L-R. **Ht.:** 6-1. **Wt.:** 170. **Drafted:** HS—Los Angeles, 1999 (9th round). **Signed by:** Mark Baca.

Watson's slow starts have become an annual occurrence, and 2005 was no exception. Demoted to Double-A after spending all of 2004 in Triple-A, he stumbled to a .247 average through mid-May. But after moving back to Triple-A, he flipped a switch and once again became a hitting machine, as he was in the second half of his previous two seasons. Watson is a pure hitter who makes good contact and gives third basemen fits with his ability to flare balls over their heads or drop down bunts in front of them. He's a well-above-average runner and an exceptional bunter. Watson has good hand-eye coordination and an unorthodox, Ichiro-like hitting approach, sometimes almost stepping out of the box as he's swinging. That style costs him most of his power, as he has hit just six homers in seven pro seasons. A solid defensive center fielder, Watson does a good job charging shallow flyballs and has an average arm. To be an everyday player and leadoff man in the majors, Watson needs to take more walks and improve his baserunning, as he still gets caught stealing too often. For now, he profiles more as a fourth outfielder, a role he could fill for the Nationals in 2006.

Year	Club (League)	Class	AVG	G	AB	R	H	2B	3B	HR	RBI	BB	SO	SB	OBP	SLG
1999	Expos (GCL)	R	.303	33	119	15	36	2	0	0	12	11	11	4	.361	.319
2000	Vermont (NY-P)	A	.291	69	278	53	81	9	1	0	30	25	38	26	.354	.331
2001	Clinton (Mid)	A	.327	117	489	74	160	16	9	2	38	29	65	33	.364	.409
2002	Brevard County (FSL)	A	.267	111	424	57	113	16	2	0	24	27	53	22	.314	.314
	Harrisburg (EL)	AA	.333	2	6	2	2	0	0	0	0	1	0	0	.429	.333
2003	Harrisburg (EL)	AA	.319	139	565	86	180	17	6	1	39	38	60	18	.362	.375
2004	Edmonton (PCL)	AAA	.293	139	526	74	154	17	3	2	41	31	68	22	.332	.348
2005	Harrisburg (EL)	AA	.247	34	146	13	36	1	0	0	6	7	21	7	.290	.253
	New Orleans (PCL)	AAA	.355	88	372	69	132	15	3	1	25	28	33	31	.400	.419
	Washington (NL)	MLB	.175	25	40	8	7	1	1	1	5	4	8	0	.250	.325
MAJOR LEAGUE TOTALS			.175	25	40	8	7	1	1	1	5	4	8	0	.250	.325
MINOR LEAGUE TOTALS			.306	732	2925	443	894	93	24	6	215	197	349	163	.351	.360

18 BRENDAN HARRIS 2B/3B

Born: Aug. 26, 1980. **B-T:** R-R. **Ht.:** 6-1. **Wt.:** 200. **Drafted:** William & Mary, 2001 (5th round). **Signed by:** Billy Swoope (Cubs).

Just two years ago, Harris was projected as the Cubs' answer at third base, but Aramis Ramirez' emergence closed that door. When Chicago and Boston were scrambling to complete the four-team Nomar Garciaparra-Orlando Cabrera deal minutes before the 2004 trading deadline, the Red Sox tried to finalize it by sending outfield prospect Matt Murton to the then-Expos. But Montreal general manager Omar Minaya balked at taking Murton, so Cubs GM Jim Hendry took Murton and sent Harris to the Expos. While Murton batted .321 in 51 games as a rookie last season, Harris had a down year. He made the full-time transition from third base to second in mid-May, and he seemed to take to the role, at least defensively. A career .301 hitter in four minor league seasons entering 2005, Harris wasn't as productive at New Orleans. He still has a solid line-drive stroke with some gap power. He has a strong arm and good infield instincts, though he doesn't do anything in spectacular fashion. He doesn't hit for enough power to stick at third base, and he wouldn't beat out Ryan Zimmerman anyway. Harris still is in the Nationals' plans as a versatile utilityman who has an outside chance to be an everyday second baseman.

Year	Club (League)	Class	AVG	G	AB	R	H	2B	3B	HR	RBI	BB	SO	SB	OBP	SLG
2001	Lansing (Mid)	A	.274	32	113	25	31	5	1	4	22	17	26	5	.370	.442
2002	Daytona (FSL)	A	.329	110	425	82	140	35	6	13	54	43	57	16	.395	.532
	West Tenn (SL)	AA	.321	13	53	8	17	4	1	2	11	2	5	1	.345	.547
2003	West Tenn (SL)	AA	.280	120	435	56	122	34	7	5	52	51	72	6	.364	.425
2004	Chicago (NL)	MLB	.222	3	9	0	2	1	0	0	1	1	1	0	.300	.333
	Iowa (PCL)	AAA	.311	69	254	48	79	21	1	11	35	16	40	0	.353	.531
	Edmonton (PCL)	AAA	.285	33	123	20	35	6	0	6	24	10	21	0	.345	.480
	Montreal (NL)	MLB	.160	20	50	4	8	2	0	1	2	2	11	0	.208	.260
2005	Washington (NL)	MLB	.333	4	9	1	3	1	0	1	3	0	0	0	.400	.778
	New Orleans (PCL)	AAA	.270	127	470	67	127	22	4	13	81	40	77	9	.329	.417
MAJOR LEAGUE TOTALS			.191	27	68	5	13	4	0	2	6	3	12	0	.247	.338
MINOR LEAGUE TOTALS			.294	504	1873	306	551	127	20	54	279	179	298	37	.360	.470

19 DEVIN IVANY C

Born: July 27, 1982. **B-T:** R-R. **Ht.:** 6-2. **Wt.:** 185. **Drafted:** South Florida, 2004 (6th round). **Signed by:** Russ Bove.

One of the most improved players in the system in 2005, Ivany reinvented his swing through individual hard work during the offseason. He came out of college with no set-up or trigger and a bat that was dead and slow through the zone, so Washington sent him home at the end of his rough pro debut with instructions to improve his offensive rhythm. He returned in spring training with a shorter swing with much improved flow, and he started hitting the ball solidly to all fields. He has a flat swing plane more suited for doubles than homers, though he does have a bit of pull power. Ivany's defense remains considerably more advanced than his offense. He's a tough, physical catcher with quick feet and a solid-average arm. He threw out 39 percent of basestealers last year thanks to his 1.90-1.95-second pop times. Drafted out of high school in the ninth round as a shortstop, he still needs a little work at game-calling. His durability must improve, as he wore down late in the season, hitting .163 in August. At the plate, he needs to get his lower half involved, because he still uses his hands and arms too much and doesn't get through the ball enough. While he makes decent contact, he draws few walks. Ivany should spend 2006 in high Class A, and he profiles as a reliable big league backup catcher with a chance to be a regular.

Year	Club (League)	Class	AVG	G	AB	R	H	2B	3B	HR	RBI	BB	SO	SB	OBP	SLG
2004	Vermont (NY-P)	A	.125	12	48	4	6	0	0	0	1	1	5	1	.143	.125
	Savannah (SAL)	A	.170	32	106	7	18	4	0	0	4	8	21	2	.239	.208
2005	Savannah (SAL)	A	.262	113	409	52	107	27	1	13	54	25	65	7	.315	.428
MINOR LEAGUE TOTALS			.233	157	563	63	131	31	1	13	59	34	91	10	.286	.361

20 LEONARD DAVIS 3B

Born: Dec. 24, 1983. **B-T:** L-R. **Ht.:** 5-10. **Wt.:** 195. **Drafted:** Fresno (Calif.) CC, 2004 (8th round). **Signed by:** Doug McMillan.

Football is in Davis' blood. His older brothers Marque and Rodney starred at Fresno State, and Marque went to training camp with the NFL's Seattle Seahawks in 2005. Leonard played one season as a safety at Fresno City College before switching to baseball as a sophomore. A right fielder when the Expos drafted him in 2004, he moved to third base as a pro. A prototype long-term project, he developed more rapidly than expected last season, particularly on offense. Davis put too much pressure on himself early and got off to a 3-for-23 start at short-season Vermont before batting .318 the rest of the way. A stocky athlete built similarly to Charlie Hayes and Terry Pendleton, Davis stands out most with his huge raw power, especially to the opposite field. He can get into trouble when he tries to pull balls down the right-field line, but he has gotten better at handling inside pitches and has shortened his swing by six to 10 inches. He has a tendency to chase balls up out of the zone and needs to improve his pitch selection. Davis is an average runner with good range and agility at third base. His arm is strong but inaccurate, and his hands are too hard. He has plenty of natural talent but a long way to go. He'll begin 2006 in low Class A.

Year	Club (League)	Class	AVG	G	AB	R	H	2B	3B	HR	RBI	BB	SO	SB	OBP	SLG
2004	Expos (GCL)	R	.182	42	143	18	26	6	1	3	14	19	58	2	.295	.301
2005	Vermont (NY-P)	A	.300	67	237	34	71	8	8	7	35	12	64	8	.348	.489
MINOR LEAGUE TOTALS			.255	109	380	52	97	14	9	10	49	31	122	10	.327	.418

21 FRANCISCO GUZMAN OF

Born: Dec. 21, 1983. **B-T:** R-R. **Ht.:** 6-4. **Wt.:** 195. **Signed:** Dominican Republic, 2003. **Signed by:** Ismael Cruz.

Major League Baseball didn't allocate any money for the Expos to sign international players in 2002 or 2003, yet director of Latin American operations Ismael Cruz was able to sign Guzman for no bonus. A former basketball player, Guzman has had little baseball instruction and remains raw at age 22. An energetic, happy-go-lucky player with good work habits, he plays with flair but sometimes seems to have no idea what he's doing, mimicking bad big league habits because he doesn't know any better. His bat will be his ticket. A free swinger, Guzman has raw plus power to all fields and can get the bat on the ball anywhere in the zone, though he can get out of control. He has shortened his swing but needs to reduce an extremely pronounced leg kick. The Nationals played him in center field in order to get him more action and speed up his development, but his future is at a corner spot and he'll need to make huge strides to become a passable defender. Guzman has a strong arm and average speed, though he has long, awkward strides and runs the bases poorly. He already has started to improve at a rapid clip and could blossom if he's allowed to play every day in low Class A this year.

Year	Club (League)	Class	AVG	G	AB	R	H	2B	3B	HR	RBI	BB	SO	SB	OBP	SLG
2003	Expos (DSL)	R	.282	41	131	10	37	3	2	1	16	1	33	3	.317	.359
2004	Expos (DSL)	R	.289	67	239	36	69	13	0	5	29	15	27	14	.347	.406
2005	Nationals (GCL)	R	.344	40	154	20	53	6	0	7	24	5	20	0	.393	.519
	Vermont (NY-P)	A	.469	9	32	8	15	2	0	2	7	0	4	0	.485	.719
MINOR LEAGUE TOTALS			.313	157	556	74	174	24	2	15	76	21	84	17	.360	.444

22 RYAN DeLAUGHTER OF

Born: Dec. 31, 1986. **B-T:** R-R. **Ht.:** 6-3. **Wt.:** 210. **Drafted:** HS—Denton, Texas, 2005 (5th round). **Signed by:** Ray Corbett.

DeLaughter was a two-way star in high school who touched 93 mph off the mound, but the Nationals drafted him as a right fielder. Scouts in Texas were split on his best future role, though the consensus was that he was better off as a power-hitting right fielder. That's the role Washington chose for him, and he bears a physical resemblance to Ryan Church. Confident and outgoing, DeLaughter showed off above-average power potential and a plus arm in the Rookie-level Gulf Coast League. He's a good fastball hitter and can go to the opposite field, but he struggles to hit breaking balls and his swing needs to be shortened. He might never hit for much of an average. He didn't run well in his debut because of an old football knee injury, though he could end up being an average defender. DeLaughter figures to start 2006 in extended spring training, followed by a trip to Vermont in June.

Year	Club (League)	Class	AVG	G	AB	R	H	2B	3B	HR	RBI	BB	SO	SB	OBP	SLG
2005	Nationals (GCL)	R	.248	33	125	18	31	3	1	6	21	6	39	1	.304	.432
MINOR LEAGUE TOTALS			.248	33	125	18	31	3	1	6	21	6	39	1	.304	.432

23 EDGARDO BAEZ OF

Born: July 12, 1985. **B-T:** R-R. **Ht.:** 6-2. **Wt.:** 190. **Drafted:** HS—Dorado, P.R., 2003 (4th round). **Signed by:** Delvy Santiago.

The Nationals grew frustrated with Baez in 2005 after he failed to make adjustments in his second stint in the Sally League. After hitting .347 with four homers in April, he reverted to bad habits and batted just .226 with seven longballs the rest of the way. He let pitchers dictate at-bats and chased too many bad pitches, he tinkered with his swing and set-up, and he wasn't particularly receptive to instruction. Much of Baez' problem is with his lower half. He has quick hands but gets beaten because his weight is shifted over his front side. Roving hitting instructor Mitchell Page is trying to force him to stay back, and if the lessons take Baez could become a Jose Guillen type someday. He still possesses the pure physical tools that made him a fourth-round pick in 2003, including the ability to hit for average, plus raw power and a strong right-field arm. But this year he'll need to earn his way into a lineup, probably back in low Class A again, and put in the effort to be a better outfielder and more disciplined hitter.

Year	Club (League)	Class	AVG	G	AB	R	H	2B	3B	HR	RBI	BB	SO	SB	OBP	SLG
2003	Expos (GCL)	R	.274	34	117	12	32	7	1	3	15	9	31	1	.323	.427
2004	Savannah (SAL)	A	.178	50	191	16	34	10	0	5	29	19	56	1	.264	.309
	Vermont (NY-P)	A	.248	46	165	18	41	6	1	7	27	20	34	2	.332	.424
2005	Savannah (SAL)	A	.246	125	447	62	110	21	6	11	64	55	128	11	.329	.394
MINOR LEAGUE TOTALS			.236	255	920	108	217	44	8	26	135	103	249	15	.315	.386

24 FRANCISCO PLASENCIA OF

Born: June 19, 1984. **B-T:** L-L. **Ht.:** 6-1. **Wt.:** 192. **Signed:** Venezuela, 2000. **Signed by:** Epy Guerrero (Brewers).

Plasencia has average tools across the board, but he struggled to translate them into production while with the Brewers from 2001-03. Milwaukee released him early in 2004, and Nationals director of Latin American operations Ismael Cruz rediscovered him that fall playing in an unaffiliated Venezuelan league. Plasencia went to extended spring training last year and shortened his stroke while eliminating excess movement in his stance before the pitch. A gap-to-gap hitter with the ability to pull the ball out of the park, Plasencia is a good defender with average speed, good instincts and a strong, accurate arm in center field. He needs to continue to improve his pitch selection and not chase breaking balls in the dirt, and Washington would like to see him hit fewer fly balls and more line drives. The Nationals may try to push him to high Class A this year to see if he can become more than just a spare outfielder.

Year	Club (League)	Class	AVG	G	AB	R	H	2B	3B	HR	RBI	BB	SO	SB	OBP	SLG
2001	Brewers (AZL)	R	.270	49	200	38	54	7	1	0	19	31	46	10	.368	.315
2002	Brewers (AZL)	R	.348	17	66	15	23	2	1	1	14	8	13	4	.427	.455
	Ogden (Pio)	R	.183	34	104	15	19	3	1	0	9	11	29	7	.261	.231
2003	Brewers (AZL)	R	.283	47	187	30	53	11	3	2	21	19	43	14	.356	.406
2004	Did not play															
2005	Vermont (NY-P)	A	.300	72	280	43	84	16	4	11	56	29	60	14	.367	.504
MINOR LEAGUE TOTALS			.278	219	837	141	233	39	10	14	119	98	191	49	.357	.399

25 TYRELL GODWIN OF

Born: July 10, 1979. **B-T:** L-R. **Ht.:** 6-0. **Wt.:** 200. **Drafted:** North Carolina, 2001 (3rd round). **Signed by:** Charles Aliano (Blue Jays).

Acquired from the Blue Jays in the major league Rule 5 draft after the 2004 season, Godwin had his best full-season performance to date in his first taste of Triple-A last year. A two-time first-round pick—by the Yankees in 1997 out of high school and the Rangers in 2000—he didn't sign until the Blue Jays took him in the third round of the 2001 draft. He always has had some juice in his bat, but this was the first time it translated into extra-base hits, thanks in part to ditching his high leg kick in favor of a more natural move with his front foot. He remains a plus runner, though he needs to improve his basestealing skills as he was caught 12 times in 34 tries. A former University of North Carolina running back, he's a more physical player than fellow Triple-A speedster Brandon Watson, but Godwin is 26 and doesn't have much projection left in him. Despite his speed and average arm, he's not a good defensive outfielder, even in left field. At this point he looks like an extra outfielder, and he might not get that chance with the Nationals because of their crowded outfield.

Year	Club (League)	Class	AVG	G	AB	R	H	2B	3B	HR	RBI	BB	SO	SB	OBP	SLG
2001	Auburn (NY-P)	A	.368	33	117	26	43	8	2	2	15	19	27	9	.464	.521
2002	Charleston, W.Va. (SAL)	A	.281	48	185	31	52	8	5	0	16	20	23	10	.364	.378
2003	Dunedin (FSL)	A	.273	97	322	52	88	16	0	1	33	29	39	20	.348	.332
	New Haven (EL)	AA	.309	33	123	20	38	6	3	1	13	3	27	6	.328	.431
2004	New Hampshire (EL)	AA	.253	133	521	85	132	21	7	6	40	52	110	42	.326	.355
2005	Washington (NL)	MLB	.000	3	3	0	0	0	0	0	0	0	1	0	.000	.000
	New Orleans (PCL)	AAA	.321	129	499	83	160	22	6	9	48	50	77	22	.387	.443
MAJOR LEAGUE TOTALS			.000	3	3	0	0	0	0	0	0	0	1	0	.000	.000
MINOR LEAGUE TOTALS			.290	473	1767	297	513	81	23	19	165	173	303	109	.361	.394

26 SALOMON MANRIQUEZ

C

Born: Sept. 15, 1982. **B-T:** R-R. **Ht.:** 6-1. **Wt.:** 190. **Signed:** Venezuela, 1999. **Signed by:** Randy Kierce.

Manriquez spent a few years as a utility player before finally getting a chance to catch every day at Potomac last year after Erick San Pedro was lost for the season in May. Manriquez wasted little time establishing himself as a good offensive catcher once he stopped looking over his shoulder. He's a solid gap-to-gap hitter who doesn't overswing and has some power, though he projects more as a doubles hitter with the ability to hit for average if he can cut down his strike zone a bit. Defense is the big question with Manriquez. He showed an average arm, throwing out 28 percent of basestealers, and improved at blocking balls under the tutelage of Potomac manager and former big league catcher Bob Henley. He still needs to improve his receiving skills and handle pitchers better. Playing every day could help Manriquez become a serviceable backup catcher with a decent bat off the bench. He'll likely start 2006 in Double-A.

Year	Club (League)	Class	AVG	G	AB	R	H	2B	3B	HR	RBI	BB	SO	SB	OBP	SLG
2000	Cagua (VSL)	R	.167	11	24	1	4	1	0	0	0	1	6	0	.200	.208
	Expos (DSL)	R	.253	54	190	31	48	12	1	1	32	17	26	5	.324	.342
2001	Expos (GCL)	R	.217	34	120	8	26	9	0	0	8	7	30	0	.277	.292
2002	Expos (GCL)	R	.282	41	131	21	37	10	0	4	26	12	29	0	.344	.450
2003	Savannah (SAL)	A	.239	37	117	14	28	12	0	3	22	4	25	0	.280	.419
	Vermont (NY-P)	A	.196	45	168	14	33	4	0	2	11	10	41	0	.243	.256
2004	Harrisburg (EL)	AA	.148	11	27	2	4	1	0	1	2	0	4	0	.148	.296
	Brevard County (FSL)	A	.250	16	52	5	13	5	0	1	2	1	14	0	.264	.404
	Savannah (SAL)	A	.264	33	121	12	32	7	0	3	19	8	33	0	.311	.397
	Vermont (NY-P)	A	.290	10	31	2	9	3	0	1	5	2	3	0	.333	.484
2005	Potomac (Car)	A	.287	119	443	64	127	36	2	15	68	30	86	0	.336	.479
MINOR LEAGUE TOTALS			.254	411	1424	174	361	100	3	31	195	92	297	5	.305	.393

27 DEVIN PERRIN

RHP

Born: May 14, 1981. **B-T:** R-R. **Ht.:** 6-7. **Wt.:** 225. **Drafted:** Grand Canyon, 2003 (7th round). **Signed by:** Tony Arango.

On paper, Perrin's season as a 24-year-old in high Class A doesn't look impressive. He struggled as a starter, going 2-5, 5.54 with more walks than strikeouts, until he took a line drive off his shin and went on the disabled list in early July. When he returned, Perrin moved to the bullpen and his fastball velocity jumped to 93-95 mph. He abandoned his ineffective curveball and replaced it with an 82-84 mph slider, and dabbled with a change-up. Perrin pitches downhill thanks to his long frame and straight over-the-top delivery. He still walks too many, but his command improved after the shift to relief because he did a better job attacking hitters. With his frame and velocity, Perrin has a chance to be a dominant reliever if he can harness his fastball command and refine his secondary stuff. His development isn't expected to be fast, but he could take off now that he's in the pen, as Jason Bergmann did after his conversion. Perrin should open this year in Double-A.

Year	Club (League)	Class	W	L	ERA	G	GS	CG	SV	IP	H	R	ER	HR	BB	SO	AVG
2003	Vermont (NY-P)	A	2	4	3.27	11	11	0	0	52	47	23	19	3	23	36	.251
2004	Savannah (SAL)	A	5	6	4.50	36	15	0	0	122	112	64	61	9	62	108	.249
2005	Potomac (Car)	A	3	7	4.99	28	14	0	3	92	96	54	51	7	58	66	.275
MINOR LEAGUE TOTALS			10	17	4.43	75	40	0	3	266	255	141	131	19	143	210	.259

28 ANDRE ENRIQUEZ   RHP

Born: May 15, 1984. **B-T:** R-R. **Ht.:** 6-3. **Wt.:** 210. **Drafted:** Le Moyne, 2005 (13th round).
Signed by: Tony Arango/Larry Izzo.

Enriquez hit 27 home runs in three years as a third baseman at LeMoyne, good for third place on the school's all-time list. He threw just eight innings as a pitcher in college, but the Nationals happened to see him touch 96 mph in one of his relief appearances in 2005. He reminded them of another infielder from a small New York school with a strong arm and almost no collegiate pitching experience: Joe Nathan. Enriquez has a fresh power arm and an athletic, physical frame. He pitched just 10 pro innings after arriving late in the Gulf Coast League because of a knee injury, but he impressed Washington with his lively 92-95 mph fastball, which some scouts think eventually could top out near 100. He's still raw on the mound and relies solely on his fastball. Enriquez is working on a short slider but it has a long way to go. He was reluctant to throw breaking balls after tweaking his elbow prior to his junior season. Enriquez simply needs to learn how to pitch. If he can, his electric arm could carry him all the way to a big league closer's job, though it's a longshot. He has a chance to start 2006 at Savannah but is more likely to wind up in Vermont.

Year	Club (League)	Class	W	L	ERA	G	GS	CG	SV	IP	H	R	ER	HR	BB	SO	AVG
2005	Nationals (GCL)	R	0	0	0.87	7	0	0	1	10	11	2	1	0	2	10	.275
MINOR LEAGUE TOTALS			0	0	0.87	7	0	0	1	10	11	2	1	0	2	10	.275

29 MARVIN LOWRANCE   OF

Born: July 16, 1984. **B-T:** L-L. **Ht.:** 6-0. **Wt.:** 215. **Drafted:** Golden West (Calif.) JC, 2004 (7th round). **Signed by:** Tony Arango.

Shortly after drafting him in 2004, scouting director Dana Brown said Lowrance's swing had a high finish that reminded him of Mo Vaughn, Brown's former Seton Hall teammate. The Nationals expected big things out of Lowrance in 2005, but he missed more than two months after fracturing his kneecap when he ran into the left-field wall in April. He's a natural hitter who does a good job getting his hands through the zone and putting the barrel of the bat on the ball consistently. He uses the opposite field well and has an intense approach, seldom giving away at-bats. He's strong, but his power has yet to develop because he needs to do a better job turning on the ball. He could use more plate discipline as well. Lowrance has below-average speed and defensive skills, and he'll have to work hard just to be adequate in left field. He'll play in high Class A in 2006.

Year	Club (League)	Class	AVG	G	AB	R	H	2B	3B	HR	RBI	BB	SO	SB	OBP	SLG
2004	Vermont (NY-P)	A	.289	53	187	23	54	6	1	3	20	28	40	1	.393	.380
2005	Savannah (SAL)	A	.288	57	212	27	61	15	1	4	35	16	50	2	.353	.425
	Nationals (GCL)	R	.321	8	28	4	9	1	0	2	9	3	2	0	.387	.571
MINOR LEAGUE TOTALS			.290	118	427	54	124	22	2	9	64	47	92	3	.373	.415

30 ROGEARVIN BERNADINA   OF

Born: June 12, 1984. **B-T:** L-L. **Ht.:** 6-0. **Wt.:** 175. **Signed:** Netherlands, 2001. **Signed by:** Fred Ferreira.

In three seasons at low Class A, Bernadina has yet to post an average higher than .238. He remains naturally gifted but unrefined, and the "limited baseball experience" excuse is starting to wear thin. He has plus raw power, but his hitting approach is a mess. Formerly a free swinger, Bernadina has gone too far in the opposite direction and now needs to be more aggressive at the plate. He takes too many called third strikes. He's rigid and mechanical at the plate and doesn't release his hands through the zone. He tried a leg kick last year, but it didn't help. He just needs a freer, more fluid swing, and he needs to eliminate his occasional tendency to dog it. Bernadina is an outstanding defensive center field with plus speed and range to go with a strong, accurate arm, though he could still stand to improve his routes on flyballs. Time is starting to tick away, so the Nationals will get Bernadina as many at-bats as possible and hope something clicks for him in high Class A this year.

Year	Club (League)	Class	AVG	G	AB	R	H	2B	3B	HR	RBI	BB	SO	SB	OBP	SLG
2002	Expos (GCL)	R	.276	57	196	22	54	7	0	3	18	19	25	1	.348	.357
2003	Savannah (SAL)	A	.237	77	278	36	66	12	3	4	39	19	53	11	.292	.345
2004	Savannah (SAL)	A	.238	129	450	67	107	24	7	7	66	60	113	24	.338	.369
2005	Savannah (SAL)	A	.233	122	417	64	97	15	3	12	54	75	92	35	.356	.369
MINOR LEAGUE TOTALS			.242	385	1341	189	324	58	13	26	177	173	283	71	.336	.362

APPENDIX

The last two first-round picks from the 2005 draft to sign, Justin Upton (No. 1 overall, Diamondbacks) and Mike Pelfrey (No. 9, Mets), came to terms too late to be included with their teams in the Prospect Handbook, but we present their scouting reports here. Upton would have ranked No. 1 for Arizona (ahead of Stephen Drew) and Pelfrey would have ranked No. 2 for New York (between Lastings Milledge and Philip Humber).

JUSTIN UPTON
SS, DIAMONDBACKS

Born: Aug. 25, 1987. **B-T:** R-R. **Ht.:** 6-2. **Wt.:** 187. **Drafted:** HS—Chesapeake, Va., 2005 (1st round). **Signed by:** Greg Lonigro.

When Upton went No. 1 overall in the 2005 draft, he and his older brother B.J. (the No. 2 pick by the Devil Rays in 2002) became the highest-selected siblings in draft history. Justin had been billed as 2005's potential top pick ever since he starred as a 14-year-old at the 2002 Area Code Games, and he never faltered throughout his high school career. He was Baseball America's 2005 High School Player of the Year after hitting .519-11-32 in 54 at-bats. After Arizona chose him, Upton held out until January before signing for a $6.1 million bonus, shattering the previous draft record of $5.3 million set by Joe Borchard in 2000. Few high school players in recent memory can compare to Upton, who's considered a more advanced prospect than B.J. was. Stronger, faster and more advanced offensively than his older brother at the same age, Upton demonstrates excellent patience at the plate and a quick stroke. His well-defined, muscular upper body attests to his plus power potential, and he has top-of-the-line speed. His 6.23-second time in the 60-yard dash at a Perfect Game showcase in 2004 is the quickest in the scouting service's history. Upton moves well defensively and shows clean actions at shortstop, but like his brother he has inconsistent mechanics that have led to inaccuracy and throwing errors. Arm strength isn't a question, as he has been clocked at 94 mph off the mound. While some scouts have said they would move Upton to center field and envision him becoming the next Ken Griffey Jr., the Diamondbacks have no plans to change his position yet. At some point either Upton or Stephen Drew will have to move, but they probably won't be on the same team for a couple of years. Upton's five-tool ability draws so much attention that his quality character and work ethic are sometimes overshadowed. Upton will make his pro debut at low Class A South Bend. B.J. reached the majors with the Devil Rays during his second pro season, and Justin is talented enough to do the same with the Diamondbacks.

MIKE PELFREY
RHP, METS

Born: Jan. 14, 1984. **B-T:** R-R. **Ht.:** 6-7. **Wt.:** 210. **Drafted:** Wichita State, 2005 (1st round). **Signed by:** Larry Chase.

Baseball America's top-rated pitching prospect in the 2005 draft, Pelfrey received consideration from the Diamondbacks as the No. 1 overall choice. Arizona ultimately chose Justin Upton, and other teams were wary of Pelfrey's price tag, so the Mets were able to nab him with the ninth pick. He held out until January and was the last first-rounder to sign. Pelfrey received a club-record $3.55 million bonus as part of a four-year major league contract worth a guaranteed $5.25 million. Easily attained roster bonuses could push the value of the deal to $6.6 million, and there are performance and award incentives as well. Pelfrey starred for three seasons at Wichita State, going 33-7 with a 2.18 ERA that broke Darren Dreifort's school record. Shockers pitching coach Brent Kemnitz called him the best pitching prospect in school history, a rich tradition that includes seven other first-rounders. Pelfrey suffered from draftitis in 2002, when he entered his senior season of high school in Wichita as a projected first-round pick, but that wasn't the case last year. He blew away hitters consistently with a 92-97 mph fastball that's as notable for its sink as for its velocity. He's adept at getting grounders or strikeouts, depending on the situation. He has refined a straight changeup that will be a plus pitch and keeps lefthanders in check. He also has tightened his curveball and become more consistent with it. Add in a perfect pitcher's frame, good control and a competitive makeup, and there's not much to quibble with. Pelfrey likely will start his pro career at high Class A St. Lucie and may not need much more than a year in the minors before he's ready for New York.

SIGNING BONUSES

EVOLUTION of the BONUS RECORD

DOMESTIC PLAYERS ONLY

Pre-Draft Record

Year	Team, Player, Pos., School	Bonus
1964	Angels. Rick Reichart, of, Wisconsin	$205,000

Draft Era Record

Year	Team, Player, Pos., School, Round	Bonus
1965	Athletics. Rick Monday, of, Arizona State (1)	$100,000
1975	Angels. Danny Goodwin, c, Southern (1)	125,000
1978	Braves. Bob Horner, 3b, Arizona State (1)	162,000
	Tigers. Kirk Gibson, of, Michigan State (1)	150,000
1979	Giants. Bill Bordley, lhp, Southern California (1/January)	200,000
	Yankees. Todd Demeter, 1b, HS—Oklahoma City (2)	208,000
1988	Padres. Andy Benes, rhp, Evansville (1)	235,000
1989	Braves. Tyler Houston, c, HS—Las Vegas (1)	241,000
	Orioles. #Ben McDonald, rhp, Louisiana State (1)	350,000
	Blue Jays. John Olerud, 1b, Washington State (3)	575,000
1991	Braves. Mike Kelly, of, Arizona State (1)	575,000
	Yankees. Brien Taylor, lhp, HS—Beaufort, N.C. (1)	1,550,000
1994	Mets. Paul Wilson, rhp, Florida State (1)	1,550,000
	Marlins. Josh Booty, 3b, HS—Shreveport, La. (1)	1,600,000
1996	Pirates. Kris Benson, rhp, Clemson (1)	2,000,000
	*Diamondbacks. Travis Lee, 1b, San Diego State U. (1)	10,000,000
	*Devil Rays. Matt White, rhp, HS—Chambersburg, Pa. (1)	10,200,000

Round indicated in parentheses.

*Declared free agent on contract tendering technicality.

#Signed major league contract (For players signed to major league contracts, the amount is only the stated bonus in the contract. For players signed to standard minor league contracts, the amount is the full compensation to be paid out over the life of the contract.).

LARGEST BONUSES in DRAFT HISTORY

FOR PLAYERS SIGNING WITH THE TEAM THAT DRAFTED THEM

Rank	Club, Year. Player, Pos., School	Bonus
1.	Diamondbacks, 2005. Justin Upton, ss, HS—Chesapeake, Va.	$6,100,000
2.	White Sox, 2000. Joe Borchard, of, Stanford	5,300,000
3.	Twins, 2001. Joe Mauer, c, HS—St. Paul	5,150,000
4.	Devil Rays, 2002. B.J. Upton, ss, HS—Chesapeake, Va.	4,600,000
5.	Rangers, 2001. #Mark Teixeira, 3b, Georgia Tech	4,500,000
6.	Devil Rays, 2001. #Dewon Brazelton, rhp, Middle Tennessee State	4,200,000
	Phillies, 2001. Gavin Floyd, rhp, HS—Severna Park, Md.	4,200,000
8.	Cubs, 2001. #Mark Prior, rhp, Southern California	4,000,000
	Pirates, 2002. Bryan Bullington, rhp, Ball State	4,000,000
	Angels, 2004. Jered Weaver, rhp, Long Beach State	4,000,000
	Diamondbacks, 2004. #Stephen Drew, ss, Florida State	4,000,000
	Royals, 2005. Alex Gordon, 3b, Nebraska	4,000,000
13.	Devil Rays, 1999. Josh Hamilton, of, HS—Raleigh, N.C.	3,960,000
14.	Cubs, 1998. Corey Patterson, of, HS—Kennesaw, Ga.	3,700,000
	Devil Rays, 2003. #Delmon Young, of, HS—Camarillo, Calif.	3,700,000
16.	Marlins, 1999. #Josh Beckett, rhp, HS—Spring, Texas	3,625,000
17.	Brewers, 2003. #Rickie Weeks, 2b, Southern	3,600,000
18.	Mets, 2005. #Mike Pelfrey, rhp, Wichita State	3,550,000
19.	Tigers, 1999. #Eric Munson, c, Southern California	3,500,000
20.	Mariners, 2005. Jeff Clement, c, Southern California	3,400,000

Signed major league contract (For players signed to major league contracts, the amount is only the stated bonus in the contract. For players signed to standard minor league contracts, the amount is the full compensation to be paid out over the life of the contract.).

SIGNING BONUSES
2005 DRAFT

TOP 100 PICKS

FIRST ROUND

No. Team. Player, Pos.	Bonus
1. Diamondbacks. Justin Upton, ss	$6,100,000
2. Royals. Alex Gordon, 3b	4,000,000
3. Mariners. Jeff Clement, c	3,400,000
4. Nationals. Ryan Zimmerman, 3b	2,975,000
5. Brewers. Ryan Braun, 3b	2,450,000
6. Blue Jays. Ricky Romero, lhp	2,400,000
7. Rockies. Troy Tulowitzki, ss	2,300,000
8. Devil Rays. Wade Townsend, rhp	1,500,000
9. Mets. Mike Pelfrey, rhp	3,550,000
10. Tigers. Cameron Maybin, of	2,650,000
11. Pirates. Andrew McCutchen, of	1,900,000
12. Reds. Jay Bruce, of	1,800,000
13. Orioles. Brandon Snyder, c	1,700,000
14. Indians. Trevor Crowe, of	1,695,000
15. White Sox. Lance Broadway, rhp	1,570,000
16. Marlins. Chris Volstad, rhp	1,600,000
17. Yankees. C.J. Henry, ss	1,575,000
18. Padres. Cesar Carrillo, rhp	1,550,000
19. Rangers. John Mayberry, of	1,525,000
20. Cubs. Mark Pawelek, lhp	1,750,000
21. Athletics. Cliff Pennington, ss	1,475,000
22. Marlins. Aaron Thompson, lhp	1,225,000
23. Red Sox. Jacoby Ellsbury, of	1,400,000
24. Astros. Brian Bogusevic, lhp	1,375,000
25. Twins. Matt Garza, rhp	1,350,000
26. Red Sox. Craig Hansen, rhp	1,325,000
27. Braves. Joey Devine, rhp	1,300,000
28. Cardinals. Colby Rasmus, of	1,000,000
29. Marlins. Jacob Marceaux, rhp	1,000,000
30. Cardinals. Tyler Greene, ss	1,100,000

SUPPLEMENTAL FIRST ROUND

No. Team. Player, Pos.	Bonus
31. Diamondbacks. Matt Torra, rhp	$1,025,000
32. Rockies. Chaz Roe, rhp	1,025,000
33. Indians. John Drennen, of	1,000,000
34. Marlins. Ryan Tucker, rhp	975,000
35. Padres. Cesar Ramos, lhp	950,000
36. Athletics. Travis Buck, of	950,000
37. Angels. Trevor Bell, rhp	925,000
38. Astros. Eli Iorg, of	900,000
39. Twins. Henry Sanchez, 1b	900,000
40. Dodgers. Luke Hochevar, rhp	Unsigned
41. Braves. Beau Jones, lhp	$825,000
42. Red Sox. Clay Buchholz, rhp	800,000
43. Cardinals. Mark McCormick, rhp	800,000
44. Marlins. Sean West, lhp	775,000
45. Red Sox. Jed Lowrie, 2b	762,500
46. Cardinals. Tyler Herron, rhp	675,000
47. Red Sox. Michael Bowden, rhp	730,000
48. Orioles. Garrett Olson, lhp	650,000

SECOND ROUND

No. Team. Player, Pos.	Bonus
49. Diamondbacks. Matt Green, rhp	$500,000
50. Royals. Jeff Bianchi, ss	690,000
51. Dodgers. Ivan De Jesus, ss	$675,000
52. Rockies. Daniel Carte, of	670,000
53. Athletics. Craig Italiano, rhp	725,500
54. Twins. Paul Kelly, ss	650,000
55. Rockies. Zach Simons, rhp	635,000
56 Devil Rays. Chris Mason, rhp	630,000
57. Red Sox. Jon Egan, c	625,000
58. Angels. Ryan Mount, ss	615,000
59. Pirates. Brad Corley, of	605,000
60. Reds. Travis Wood, lhp	600,000
61. Orioles. Nolan Reimold, of	590,000
62. Indians. Stephen Head, 1b	605,000
63. Yankees. J. Brent Cox, rhp	550,000
64. Marlins. Kris Harvey, of	575,000
65. Phillies. Mike Costanzo, 3b	570,000
66. Padres. Chase Headley, 3b	560,000
67. Rangers. Johnny Whittleman, 3b	650,000
68. Cubs. Donald Veal, lhp	530,000
69. Athletics. Jared Lansford, rhp	525,000
70. Cardinals. Josh Wilson, rhp	515,000
71. Angels. P.J. Phillips, ss	505,000
72. Astros. Ralph Henriquez, c	485,000
73. Twins. Kevin Slowey, rhp	490,000
74. Dodgers. Josh Wall, rhp	480,000
75. Braves. Yunel Escobar, ss	475,000
76. Padres. Nick Hundley, c	465,000
77. Braves. Jeff Lyman, rhp	460,000
78. Cardinals. Nick Webber, rhp	425,000

SUPPLEMENTAL SECOND ROUND

No. Team. Player, Pos.	Bonus
79. Marlins. Brett Hayes, c	$450,000
80. Twins. Drew Thompson, ss	475,000

THIRD ROUND

No. Team. Player, Pos.	Bonus
81. D'backs. Jason Neighborgall, rhp	$500,000
82. Royals. Chris Nicoll, rhp	445,000
83. D'backs. Micah Owings, rhp	440,000
84. Twins. Brian Duensing, lhp	400,000
85. Brewers. Will Inman, rhp	500,000
86. Blue Jays. Brian Pettway, of	440,000
87. Rockies. Kyle Hancock, rhp	Contract voided
88. Devil Rays. Bryan Morris, rhp	Unsigned
89. Astros. Tommy Manzella, ss	$289,000
90. Tigers. Chris Robinson, c	422,000
91. Pirates. James Boone, of	420,000
92. Reds. Zach Ward, rhp	420,000
93. Orioles. Brandon Erbe, rhp	415,000
94. Indians. Nick Weglarz, 1b	435,000
95. White Sox. Ricky Brooks, rhp	300,000
96. Marlins. Matt Goyen, lhp	340,000
97. Phillies. Matt Maloney, lhp	400,000
98. Padres. Josh Geer, rhp	395,000
99. Rangers. Taylor Teagarden, c	725,000
100. Cubs. Mark Holliman, rhp	385,000

SIGNING BONUSES
2004 DRAFT

FIRST ROUND

No. Player, Pos.	Bonus
1. Padres. Matt Bush, ss	$3,150,000
2. Tigers. Justin Verlander, rhp	3,150,000
3. Mets. Philip Humber, rhp	3,000,000
4. Devil Rays. Jeff Niemann, rhp	3,200,000
5. Brewers. Mark Rogers, rhp	2,200,000
6. Indians. Jeremy Sowers, lhp	2,475,000
7. Reds. Homer Bailey, rhp	2,300,000
8. Orioles. Wade Townsend, rhp	Did not sign
9. Rockies. Chris Nelson, ss	2,150,000
10. Rangers. Thomas Diamond, rhp	2,025,000
11. Pirates. Neil Walker, c	1,950,000
12. Angels. Jered Weaver, rhp	4,000,000
13. Expos. Bill Bray, lhp	1,750,000
14. Royals. Billy Butler, 3b	1,400,000
15. Diamondbacks. Stephen Drew, ss	4,000,000
16. Blue Jays. David Purcey, lhp	1,600,000
17. Dodgers. Scott Elbert, lhp	1,575,000
18. White Sox. Josh Fields, 3b	1,550,000
19. Cardinals. Chris Lambert, rhp	1,525,000
20. Twins. Trevor Plouffe, ss	1,500,000
21. Phillies. Greg Golson, of	1,475,000
22. Twins. Glen Perkins, lhp	1,425,000
23. Yankees. Philip Hughes, rhp	1,400,000
24. Athletics. Landon Powell, c	1,000,000
25. Twins. Kyle Waldrop, rhp	1,000,000
26. Athletics. Richie Robnett, of	1,325,000
27. Marlins. Taylor Tankersley, lhp	1,300,000
28. Dodgers. Blake Dewitt, 3b	1,200,000
29. Royals. Matt Campbell, lhp	1,100,000
30. Rangers. Eric Hurley, rhp	1,050,000

SUPPLEMENTAL FIRST-ROUND

No. Player, Pos.	Bonus
31. Royals. J.P. Howell, lhp	1,000,000
32. Blue Jays. Zach Jackson, lhp	1,017,500
33. Dodgers. Justin Orenduff, rhp	1,000,000
34. White Sox. Tyler Lumsden, lhp	975,000
35. Twins. Matt Fox, rhp	950,000
36. Athletics. Danny Putnam, of	950,000
37. Yankees. Jon Poterson, of	925,000
38. White Sox. Gio Gonzalez, lhp	850,000
39. Twins. Jay Rainville, rhp	875,000
40. Athletics. Huston Street, rhp	800,000
41. Yankees. Jeff Marquez, rhp	790,000

SECOND ROUND

No. Player, Pos.	Bonus
42. Yankees. Brett Smith, rhp	800,000
43. Tigers. Eric Beattie, rhp	800,000
44. Mets. Matt Durkin, rhp	800,000
45. Devil Rays. Reid Brignac, ss	795,000
46. Brewers. Yovani Gallardo, rhp	725,000
47. Indians. Justin Hoyman, rhp	725,000
48. Reds. B.J. Szymanski, of	725,000
49. Athletics. Michael Rogers, rhp	700,000

No. Player, Pos.	Bonus
50. Rockies. Seth Smith, of	690,000
51. Rangers. K.C. Herren, of	675,000
52. Pirates. Brian Bixler, ss	670,000
53. White Sox. Wes Whisler, lhp	660,000
54. Expos. Erick San Pedro, c	650,000
55. Royals. Billy Buckner, rhp	635,000
56. Diamondbacks. Jon Zeringue, of	630,000
57. Blue Jays. Curtis Thigpen, c	625,000
58. Dodgers. Blake Johnson, rhp	600,000
59. White Sox. Donny Lucy, c	525,000
60. Cardinals. Mike Ferris, 1b	600,000
61. Twins. Anthony Swarzak, rhp	575,000
62. Phillies. Jason Jaramillo, c	585,000
63. Royals. Eric Cordier, rhp	575,000
64. Astros. Hunter Pence, of	575,000
65. Red Sox. Dustin Pedroia, ss	575,000
66. Cubs. Grant Johnson, rhp	1,260,000
67. Athletics. Kurt Suzuki, c	550,000
68. Marlins. Jason Vargas, lhp	525,000
69. White Sox. Ray Liotta, lhp	499,000
70. Giants. Eddy Martinez-Esteve, of	537,500
71. Braves. Eric Campbell, 3b	500,000

THIRD ROUND

No. Player, Pos.	Bonus
72. Padres. Billy Killian, c	450,000
73. Tigers. Jeff Frazier, of	500,000
74. Mets. Gaby Hernandez, rhp	480,000
75. Devil Rays. Wade Davis, rhp	475,000
76. Brewers. Josh Wahpepah, rhp	400,000
77. Indians. Scott Lewis, lhp	460,000
78. Reds. Craig Tatum, c	450,000
79. Orioles. Jeff Fiorentino, of	450,000
80. Rockies. Steven Register, rhp	450,000
81. Rangers. Michael Schlact, rhp	455,000
82. Pirates. Eddie Prasch, 3b	500,000
83. Blue Jays. Adam Lind, 1b/of	445,000
84. Expos. Ian Desmond, ss	430,000
85. Royals. Josh Johnson, ss	410,000
86. Diamondbacks. Garrett Mock, rhp	440,000
87. Blue Jays. Danny Hill, rhp	275,000
88. Dodgers. Cory Dunlap, 1b	430,000
89. White Sox. Grant Hansen, rhp	430,000
90. Cardinals. Eric Haberer, lhp	422,500
91. Twins. Eduardo Morlan, rhp	420,000
92. Phillies. J.A. Happ, lhp	420,000
93. Mariners. Matt Tuiasosopo, ss	2,290,000
94. Astros. Jordan Parraz, of	400,000
95. Red Sox. Andrew Dobies, lhp	400,000
96. Cubs. Mark Reed, c	650,000
97. Athletics. Jason Windsor, rhp	270,000
98. Marlins. Greg Burns, of	395,000
99. Yankees. Christian Garcia, rhp	390,000
100. Giants. John Bowker, of	405,000

SIGNING BONUSES
2003 DRAFT

FIRST ROUND

No. Player, Pos.	Bonus
1. Devil Rays. Delmon Young, of	$3,700,000
2. Brewers. Rickie Weeks, 2b	3,600,000
3. Tigers. Kyle Sleeth, rhp	3,350,000
4. Padres. Tim Stauffer, rhp	750,000
5. Royals. Chris Lubanski, of	2,100,000
6. Cubs. Ryan Harvey, of	2,400,000
7. Orioles. Nick Markakis, of/lhp	1,850,000
8. Pirates. Paul Maholm, lhp	2,200,000
9. Rangers. John Danks, lhp	2,100,000
10. Rockies. Ian Stewart, 3b	1,950,000
11. Indians. Michael Aubrey, 1b	2,010,000
12. Mets. Lastings Milledge, of	2,075,000
13. Blue Jays. Aaron Hill, ss	1,675,000
14. Reds. Ryan Wagner, rhp	1,400,000
15. White Sox. Brian Anderson, of	1,600,000
16. Marlins. Jeff Allison, rhp	1,850,000
17. Red Sox. David Murphy, of	1,525,000
18. Indians. Brad Snyder, of	1,525,000
19. Diamondbacks. Conor Jackson, 3b	1,500,000
20. Expos. Chad Cordero, rhp	1,350,000
21. Twins. Matt Moses, 3b	1,450,000
22. Giants. David Aardsma, rhp	1,425,000
23. Angels. Brandon Wood, ss	1,300,000
24. Dodgers. Chad Billingsley, rhp	1,375,000
25. Athletics. Brad Sullivan, rhp	1,360,000
26. Athletics. Brian Snyder, 3b	1,325,000
27. Yankees. Eric Duncan, 3b	1,250,000
28. Cardinals. Daric Barton, c	975,000
29. Diamondbacks. Carlos Quentin, of	1,100,000
30. Royals. Mitch Maier, c	900,000

SUPPLEMENTAL FIRST-ROUND

No. Player, Pos.	Bonus
31. Indians. Adam Miller, rhp	1,025,000
32. Red Sox. Matt Murton, of	1,010,000
33. Athletics. Omar Quintanilla, ss	992,500
34. Giants. Craig Whitaker, rhp	975,000
35. Braves. Luis Atilano, rhp	950,000
36. Braves. Jarrod Saltalamacchia, c	950,000
37. Mariners. Adam Jones, ss	925,000

SECOND ROUND

No. Player, Pos.	Bonus
38. Devil Rays. James Houser, lhp	900,000
39. Brewers. Anthony Gwynn, of	875,000
40. Tigers. Jay Sborz, rhp	865,000
41. Padres. Daniel Moore, lhp	800,000
42. Royals. Shane Costa, of	775,000
43. Braves. Jo Jo Reyes, lhp	800,000
44. Orioles. Brian Finch, rhp	750,000
45. Pirates. Tom Gorzelanny, lhp	775,000
46. Rangers. Vince Sinisi, 1b	2,070,000
47. Rockies. Scott Beerer, rhp	725,000
48. Indians. Javi Herrera, c	710,000
49. Red Sox. Abe Alvarez, lhp	700,000
50. Blue Jays. Josh Banks, rhp	650,000

No. Player, Pos.	Bonus
51. Reds. Thomas Pauly, rhp	660,000
52. White Sox. Ryan Sweeney, of	785,000
53. Marlins. Logan Kensing, rhp	675,000
54. Red Sox. Mickey Hall, of	800,000
55. Giants. Todd Jennings, c	620,000
56. Mariners. Jeff Flaig, 3b	710,000
57. Expos. Jerry Owens, of	600,000
58. Twins. Scott Baker, rhp	600,000
59. Astros. Jason Hirsh, rhp	625,000
60. Angels. Anthony Whittington, lhp	650,000
61. Dodgers. Chuck Tiffany, lhp	1,100,000
62. Athletics. Andre Ethier, of	580,000
63. Giants. Nate Schierholtz, 3b	572,000
64. Yankees. Estee Harris, of	725,000
65. Cardinals. Stuart Pomeranz, rhp	570,000
66. Diamondbacks. Jamie D'Antona, 3b	560,000
67. Braves. Paul Bacot, rhp	550,000

THIRD ROUND

No. Player, Pos.	Bonus
68. Devil Rays. Andrew Miller, lhp	Did not sign
69. Brewers. Lou Palmisano, c	500,000
70. Tigers. Tony Giarratano, ss	500,000
71. Padres. Colt Morton, c	500,000
72. Royals. Brian McFall, 1b	385,000
73. Cubs. Jake Fox, c	500,000
74. Orioles. Chris Ray, rhp	485,000
75. Pirates. Steve Lerud, c	512,500
76. Rangers. John Hudgins, rhp	490,000
77. Rockies. Aaron Marsden, lhp	462,500
78. Indians. Ryan Garko, c	270,000
79. Braves. Jake Stevens, lhp	475,000
80. Blue Jays. Shaun Marcum, rhp	449,000
81. Reds. Jose Ronda, ss	440,000
82. White Sox. Clint King, of	440,000
83. Marlins. Jonathan Fulton, ss	440,000
84. Red Sox. Beau Vaughan, rhp	250,000
85. Phillies. Tim Moss, 2b	440,000
86. Mariners. Ryan Feierabend, lhp	437,500
87. Expos. Kory Casto, of	410,000
88. Twins. John Woodard, 1b	425,000
89. Astros. Drew Stubbs, of	Did not sign
90. Angels. Sean Rodriguez, ss	400,000
91. Dodgers. Cory VanAllen, lhp	Did not sign
92. Athletics. Dustin Majewski, of	220,000
93. Giants. Brian Buscher, 3b	215,000
94. Yankees. Tim Battle, of	425,000
95. Cardinals. Dennis Dove, rhp	400,000
96. Diamondbacks. Matt Chico, lhp	365,000
97. Braves. Matt Harrison, lhp	395,000

FOURTH ROUND

No. Player, Pos.	Bonus
98. Devil Rays. Travis Schlichting, ss	400,000
99. Brewers. Charlie Fermaint, of	295,000
100. Tigers. Josh Rainwater, rhp	300,000

COLLEGE TOP 100   *CLASS OF 2006*

Rank Player	Pos.	Class	B-T	HT	WT	College	Hometown	Prev. Drafted
1. Andrew Miller	LHP	Jr.	L-L	6-6	210	North Carolina	Gainesville, Fla.	Devil Rays '03 (3)
2. Drew Stubbs	OF	Jr.	R-R	6-4	190	Texas	Atlanta	Astros '03 (3)
3. Max Scherzer	RHP	Jr.	R-R	6-1	208	Missouri	Chesterfield, Mo.	Cardinals '03 (43)
4. Daniel Bard	RHP	Jr.	R-R	6-4	200	North Carolina	Charlotte, N.C.	Yankees '03 (20)
5. Ian Kennedy	RHP	Jr.	R-R	6-0	180	Southern California	Huntington Beach, Ca.	Cardinals '03 (14)
6. Evan Longoria	SS/3B	Jr.	R-R	6-2	185	Long Beach State	Downey, Calif.	Never drafted
7. Matt LaPorta	1B	Jr.	R-R	6-0	210	Florida	Port Charlotte, Fla.	Cubs '03 (14)
8. Wes Hodges	3B	Jr.	R-R	6-2	185	Georgia Tech	Ooltewah, Tenn.	White Sox '03 (13)
9. Brandon Morrow	RHP	Jr.	R-R	6-3	185	California	Rohnert Park, Calif.	Angels '03 (40)
10. Dallas Buck	RHP	Jr.	R-R	6-2	190	Oregon State	Newberg, Ore.	Pirates '03 (19)
11. Kyle McCulloch	RHP	Jr.	R-R	6-3	170	Texas	Houston	Mets '03 (18)
12. Joba Chamberlain	RHP	Jr.	R-R	6-4	225	Nebraska	Lincoln, Neb.	Never drafted
13. Brad Lincoln	RHP	Jr.	L-R	6-0	200	Houston	Clute, Texas	Rangers '03 (28)
14. Mark Melancon	RHP	Jr.	R-R	6-2	205	Arizona	Golden, Colo.	Dodgers '03 (30)
15. Jared Hughes	RHP	Jr.	R-R	6-7	230	Long Beach State	Laguna Niguel, Calif.	Devil Rays '03 (16)
16. Greg Reynolds	RHP	Jr.	R-R	6-8	220	Stanford	Pacifica, Calif.	Phillies '03 (41)
17. Jason Donald	SS	Jr.	R-R	6-1	190	Arizona	Clovis, Calif.	Angels '03 (20)
18. Blair Erickson	RHP	Jr.	R-R	6-1	205	UC Irvine	Fair Oaks, Calif.	Phillies '03 (28)
19. Colin Curtis	OF	Jr.	L-L	6-1	195	Arizona State	Issaquah, Wash.	Reds '03 (50)
20. Brennan Boesch	OF	Jr.	L-L	6-6	210	California	Los Angeles	Never drafted
21. Brian Jeroloman	C	Jr.	L-R	6-0	190	Florida	Wellington, Fla.	Never drafted
22. Chris Perez	RHP	Jr.	R-R	6-4	223	Miami	Holmes Beach, Fla.	Never drafted
23. Justin Masterson	RHP	Jr.	R-R	6-6	235	San Diego State	Beaver Creek, Ohio	Never drafted
24. Gary Daley	RHP	Jr.	R-R	6-3	200	Cal Poly	Grass Valley, Calif.	Never drafted
25. Chad Tracy	C	Jr.	R-R	6-3	175	Pepperdine	Claremont, Calif.	Never drafted
26. Josh Rodriguez	SS	Jr.	R-R	6-0	180	Rice	Houston	Never drafted
27. Matt Antonelli	3B	Jr.	R-R	6-0	185	Wake Forest	Peabody, Mass.	Dodgers '03 (19)
28. Wade LeBlanc	LHP	Jr.	L-L	6-3	195	Alabama	Lake Charles, La.	Devil Rays '03 (36)
29. Shane Robinson	OF	Jr.	R-R	5-9	165	Florida State	Tampa	Never drafted
30. Jon Jay	OF	Jr.	L-L	6-0	200	Miami (Fla.)	Miami	Never drafted
31. Tim Lincecum	RHP	Jr.	L-R	6-0	160	Washington	Renton, Wash.	Indians '05 (42)
32. Adam Davis	2B	Jr.	B-R	5-9	180	Florida	Fort Myers, Fla.	Never drafted
33. Mark Hamilton	1B	Jr.	L-L	6-3	207	Tulane	Bellaire, Texas	Never drafted
34. Chris Errecart	OF	Jr.	B-L	6-1	210	California	Stockton, Calif.	Never drafted
35. Aaron Bates	1B	Jr.	R-R	6-4	232	North Carolina State	La Selva Beach, Calif.	Marlins '05 (8)
36. David Huff	LHP	Jr.	B-L	6-3	200	UCLA	Huntington Beach, Ca.	Phillies '05 (19)
37. Hunter Mense	OF	Jr.	L-L	5-11	185	Missouri	Liberty, Mo.	Never drafted
38. Chris Coghlan	3B	Jr.	L-R	6-1	197	Mississippi	Tarpon Springs, Fla.	D'backs '03 (18)
39. Keith Weiser	LHP	Jr.	R-L	6-2	190	Miami (Ohio)	Hamilton, Ohio	Braves '03 (18)
40. Brooks Brown	RHP	Jr.	R-R	6-3	205	Georgia	Portal, Ga.	Braves '03 (21)
41. Nate Boman	LHP	Jr.	L-L	5-11	165	San Diego	San Diego	Angels '03 (39)
42. Brett Sinkbeil	RHP	Jr.	R-R	6-4	185	Missouri State	Sand Springs, Okla.	Cardinals '03 (38)
43. John Shelby	2B	Jr.	R-R	5-10	175	Kentucky	Lexington, Ky.	Never drafted
44. Jordan Newton	C	Jr.	R-R	5-11	185	Western Kentucky	Hodgenville, Ky.	Mets '03 (33)
45. Brant Rustich	RHP	Jr.	R-R	6-6	215	UCLA	El Cajon, Calif.	Twins '03 (46)
46. Josh Morris	1B	Jr.	R-R	6-5	235	Georgia	Cartersville, Ga.	Red Sox '03 (20)
47. Mike Ambort	C	Jr.	R-R	6-2	210	Lamar	Rockville Centre, N.Y.	Expos '03 (44)
48. Scott Sizemore	2B	Jr.	R-R	6-0	180	Va. Commonwealth	Chesapeake, Va.	Never drafted
49. Jonah Nickerson	RHP	Jr.	R-R	6-1	190	Oregon State	Oregon City, Ore.	Never drafted
50. Pat Bresnehan	RHP	Jr.	R-R	6-1	205	Arizona State	Sherborn, Mass.	Royals '03 (23)

51.	Jason Berken	RHP	Jr.	R-R	6-0	175	Clemson	DePere, Wis.	Never drafted
52.	Nick Moresi	OF	Jr.	R-R	6-4	190	Fresno State	Clayton, Calif.	Never drafted
53.	John Gaub	LHP	Jr.	L-L	6-2	205	Minnesota	South St. Paul, Minn.	Twins '03 (25)
54.	Casey Hudspeth	RHP	Jr.	R-R	6-0	185	South Florida	Sarasota, Fla.	Devil Rays '03 (21)
55.	Harold Mozingo	RHP	Jr.	R-R	6-1	185	Va. Commonwealth	Tappahannock, Va.	Mets '03 (15)
56.	Jim Negrych	2B	Jr.	L-R	5-9	175	Pittsburgh	Buffalo, N.Y.	Never drafted
57.	Danny Dorn	OF	Sr.	L-L	6-2	205	Cal State Fullerton	Diamond Bar, Calif.	Devil Rays '05 (23)
58.	Doug Fister	RHP	Sr.	R-R	6-8	195	Fresno State	Merced, Calif.	Yankees '05 (6)
59.	Sergio Perez	RHP	Jr.	R-R	6-2	220	Tampa	Tampa	Never drafted
60.	Ben Snyder	LHP	So.	L-L	6-2	190	Ball State	Bellevue, Ohio	Dodgers '03 (24)
61.	Justin Cassel	RHP	Jr.	R-R	6-2	207	UC Irvine	Northridge, Calif.	Athletics '03 (30)
62.	Blake Davis	SS	Jr.	L-R	5-11	155	Cal State Fullerton	Fountain Valley, Calif.	Indians '05 (46)
63.	Tim Gustafson	RHP	Jr.	R-R	6-2	195	Georgia Tech	Lilburn, Ga.	Never drafted
64.	Nate Culp	LHP	Jr.	L-L	6-1	180	Missouri	Glen Carbon, Ill.	Never drafted
65.	Cyle Hankerd	OF	Jr.	R-R	6-2	205	Southern California	Covina, Calif.	Cubs '03 (44)
66.	Josh Butler	RHP	Jr.	R-R	6-5	180	San Diego	Danville, Calif.	Never drafted
67.	Dustin Evans	RHP	Jr.	R-R	6-4	215	Georgia Southern	Taylorsville, Ga.	Reds '03 (28)
68.	Brett Pill	1B	Jr.	R-R	6-4	205	Cal State Fullerton	Covina, Calif.	Yankees '05 (45)
69.	Derrik Lutz	RHP	Jr.	R-R	6-0	210	George Washington	Grantville, Pa.	Never drafted
70.	Jon Still	C	Jr.	R-R	6-2	205	North Carolina State	Madison, Miss.	Never drafted
71.	Kris Johnson	LHP	Jr.	L-L	6-3	170	Wichita State	Blue Springs, Mo.	Angels '03 (50)
72.	Mike McBryde	OF	Jr.	R-R	6-1	170	Florida Atlantic	North Palm Beach, Fla.	Red Sox '03 (38)
73.	Cory VanAllen	LHP	Jr.	L-L	6-3	180	Baylor	Sugar Land, Texas	Dodgers '03 (3)
74.	Carson Kainer	OF	Jr.	R-R	6-1	195	Texas	Tomball, Texas	Never drafted
75.	Jeff Manship	RHP	Jr.	R-R	6-1	175	Notre Dame	San Antonio	D'backs '03 (50)
76.	Bud Norris	RHP	Jr.	R-R	6-0	200	Cal Poly	Novato, Calif.	Never drafted
77.	Emmanuel Burris	SS	Jr.	B-R	6-0	160	Kent State	Washington, D.C.	Never drafted
78.	Blake Holler	LHP	Jr.	L-L	6-4	180	Stanford	Terre Haute, Ind.	Never drafted
79.	Michael Campbell	OF	Jr.	L-L	6-1	190	South Carolina	Winchester, Va.	Never drafted
80.	John Hester	C	Sr.	R-R	6-4	220	Stanford	Roswell, Ga.	Never drafted
81.	Tyler Norrick	LHP	Sr.	L-L	6-3	210	Southern Illinois	Festus, Mo.	Blue Jays '05 (17)
82.	Steven Wright	RHP	Jr.	R-R	6-3	210	Hawaii	Moreno Valley, Calif.	Padres '03 (26)
83.	Daniel McCutchen	RHP	Sr.	R-R	6-2	195	Oklahoma	Norman, Okla.	Cardinals '05 (12)
84.	Andy D'Alessio	1B	Jr.	L-R	6-4	220	Clemson	Naples, Fla.	Reds '03 (10)
85.	Zech Zinicola	RHP	Jr.	R-R	6-2	205	Arizona State	San Bernardino, Calif.	Braves '03 (43)
86.	Justin Turner	2B	Sr.	R-R	5-11	175	Cal State Fullerton	Lakewood, Calif.	Yankees '05 (29)
87.	Chase Lirette	RHP	Jr.	R-R	6-4	214	South Florida	Tallahassee, Fla.	Never drafted
88.	Jimmy Van Ostrand	1B	Sr.	R-R	6-4	225	Cal Poly	Richmond, B.C.	Never drafted
89.	Alex Presley	OF	Jr.	L-L	5-11	180	Mississippi	Monroe, La.	Never drafted
90.	Chris Valaika	SS	Jr.	R-R	6-1	180	UC Santa Barbara	Newhall, Calif.	Never drafted
91.	Adam Ottavino	RHP	Jr.	R-R	6-5	215	Northeastern	Brooklyn, N.Y.	Devil Rays '03 (30)
92.	Kyle Parker	RHP	Jr.	R-R	6-3	195	Washington	Yakima, Wash.	Never drafted
93.	Paul Coleman	LHP	Sr.	L-L	6-4	190	Pepperdine	Canyon Lake, Calif.	Tigers '05 (9)
94.	Jeff Samardzija	RHP	Jr.	R-R	6-5	215	Notre Dame	Valparaiso, Ind.	Never drafted
95.	Garrett Olson	3B	Jr.	R-R	6-2	200	Franklin Pierce	Norway, Maine	Never drafted
96.	Daniel Perales	OF	Sr.	L-L	6-1	180	Southern California	Orange, Calif.	Never drafted
97.	Blake Wood	RHP	Jr.	R-R	6-4	215	Georgia Tech	Suwanee, Ga.	Never drafted
98.	Jordan Abruzzo	C	Jr.	B-R	6-2	230	San Diego	El Cajon, Calif.	Never drafted
99.	Shelby Ford	3B	Jr.	B-R	6-3	190	Oklahoma State	Fort Worth, Texas	Never drafted
100.	Eric Gunderson	LHP	Jr.	R-L	5-10	160	Oregon State	Portland, Ore.	Never drafted

DRAFT PROSPECTS
HIGH SCHOOL TOP 100

CLASS OF 2006

Rank Player	Pos.	B-T	HT	WT	High School	Hometown	Commitment
1. Jordan Walden	RHP	R-R	6-4	185	Mansfield	Mansfield, Texas	Texas
2. Chris Marrero	3B	R-R	6-3	205	Monsignor Pace	Miami	Miami
3. Brett Anderson	LHP	L-L	6-4	215	Stillwater	Stillwater, Okla.	Oklahoma State
4. Matt Latos	RHP	R-R	6-5	200	Coconut Creek	Margate, Fla.	
5. Dellin Betances	RHP	R-R	6-8	210	Grand Street	New York	
6. Kyle Drabek	RHP/SS	R-R	5-11	175	The Woodlands	The Woodlands, Texas	
7. Chris Tillman	RHP	R-R	6-7	185	Fountain Valley	Fountain Valley, Calif.	Cal State Fullerton
8. Jeremy Jeffress	RHP	R-R	6-1	170	Halifax County	South Boston, Va.	
9. Cody Johnson	OF/1B	L-R	6-4	200	Mosley	Panama City, Fla.	Florida State
10. Hank Conger	C	B-R	6-0	210	Huntington Beach	Huntington Beach, Calif.	Southern California
11. Chris Parmelee	OF/1B	L-L	6-1	200	Chino Hills	Chino Hills, Calif.	Cal State Fullerton
12. Kasey Kiker	LHP	L-L	5-11	175	Russell County	Phenix City, Ala.	South Alabama
13. Ryan Adams	SS	R-R	5-11	175	Jesuit	Mandeville, La.	Louisiana State
14. Max Sapp	C	L-R	6-1	225	Bishop Moore	Windermere, Fla.	Florida State
15. Colton Willems	RHP	R-R	6-4	190	John Carroll Catholic	Fort Pierce, Fla.	Florida
16. Carmine Giardina	LHP	R-L	6-2	225	Durant	Valrico, Fla.	Texas
17. Grant Green	SS	R-R	6-3	170	Canyon	Anaheim	Southern California
18. Jason Stoffel	RHP	R-R	6-2	202	Agoura	Agoura Hills, Calif.	Arizona
19. Devin Shepherd	OF	R-R	6-4	230	Oxnard	Agoura Hills, Calif.	Oklahoma
20. Riley Cooper	OF	R-R	6-3	200	Seminole	Clearwater, Fla.	
21. Jason Place	OF	R-R	6-3	205	Wren	Easley, S.C.	South Carolina
22. Shawn Tolleson	RHP	R-R	6-2	215	Allen	Fairview, Texas	Baylor
23. Nick Akins	SS	R-R	6-1	185	El Camino Real	Los Angeles	San Diego State
24. Cory Rasmus	RHP	R-R	6-0	195	Russell County	Phenix City, Ala.	Auburn
25. Travis Snider	1B	L-L	6-1	220	Jackson	Everett, Wash.	Arizona State
26. Derrick Robinson	OF	B-L	5-11	168	P.K. Yonge	Archer, Fla.	Florida
27. Aaron Miller	LHP/OF	L-L	6-3	205	Channelview	Channelview, Texas	Baylor
28. Nate Bridges	SS	R-R	6-1	170	Villa Park	Yorba Linda, Calif.	Cal State Fullerton
29. Clayton Kershaw	LHP	L-L	6-4	210	Highland Park	Dallas	Texas A&M
30. Ryan Jackson	SS	R-R	6-1	160	Florida Christian	Miami Springs, Fla.	Miami
31. Kevin Chapman	LHP	L-L	6-3	195	Westminster Academy	Coral Springs, Fla.	Florida
32. Bill Rowell	SS	L-R	6-5	195	Bishop Eustace Prep	Sewell, N.J.	Alabama
33. Jeff Rapoport	OF	R-R	6-0	175	Westlake	Westlake Village, Calif.	UCLA
34. Brandon Belt	LHP	L-L	6-5	188	Hudson	Lufkin, Texas	Texas
35. Josh Thrailkill	RHP	R-R	6-4	185	T.C. Roberson	Arden, N.C.	Clemson
36. Matthew Petiton	LHP	L-L	6-0	180	Garden City	Garden City, N.Y.	North Carolina
37. Mark Sobolewski	SS	R-R	5-11	185	Sarasota	Sarasota, Fla.	Miami
38. Nathan Karns	RHP	R-R	6-3	198	Martin	Arlington, Texas	
39. David Christensen	OF	R-R	6-0	190	Stoneman Douglas	Parkland, Fla.	
40. Marcus Lemon	SS	L-R	5-10	172	Eustis	Sanford, Fla.	Texas
41. Drew Rundle	OF	L-L	6-3	180	Bend	Bend, Ore.	Arizona
42. Jared Mitchell	OF	L-L	6-0	195	Westgate	New Iberia, La.	
43. Torre Langley	C	R-R	5-8	170	Alexander	Winston, Ga.	Georgia Tech
44. Josh Touchston	RHP	R-R	6-3	225	Kingwood	Kingwood, Texas	Houston
45. Andrew Clark	1B/LHP	L-L	6-3	200	New Palestine	Palestine, Ind.	Mississippi
46. Josh Ravin	RHP	R-R	6-4	190	Chatsworth	Chatsworth, Calif.	
47. Bryan Morgado	LHP	L-L	6-1	205	Florida Christian	Miami	Tennessee
48. Andy Oliver	LHP	L-L	6-3	185	Vermillion	Vermillion, Ohio	
49. Jacob Brigham	RHP	B-R	6-2	185	Central Fla. Christian	Ocoee, Fla.	Central Florida
50. Taylor Hammack	LHP	L-L	6-3	215	Angleton	Angleton, Texas	

#	Name	Pos	B-T	Ht	Wt	School	Hometown	College
51.	Toby Gerhart	OF	R-R	6-1	218	Norco	Norco, Calif.	
52.	Robbie Alcombrack	C	R-R	6-0	200	Bear River	Grass Valley, Calif.	Arizona State
53.	Graham Stoneburner	RHP/SS	R-R	6-0	175	Mills Godwin	Richmond, Va.	Clemson
54.	Chad Arnold	OF/RHP	R-R	6-4	180	Southridge	Kennewick, Wash.	Washington State
55.	Norm Wittkamp	RHP	R-R	6-1	210	Clear Creek	League City, Texas	Houston
56.	Jonathan Piggott	OF	R-R	6-2	180	Seabreeze	Ormond Beach, Fla.	Florida
57.	Drew Poulk	OF	R-R	6-3	185	West Carteret	Morehead City, N.C.	North Carolina
58.	Michael Demperio	SS	R-R	5-11	165	Lovett	Atlanta	
59.	Brandon Holden	RHP	R-R	6-4	170	Stoneman Douglas	Coral Springs, Fla.	Florida
60.	James Gillheeney	LHP	L-L	6-2	185	Bishop Hendricken	Johnston, R.I.	North Carolina State
61.	Nick Fuller	RHP	R-R	6-1	175	Kell	Marietta, Ga.	South Carolina
62.	Ryan Jenkins	RHP	R-R	6-5	215	Cypress Falls	Houston	Baylor
63.	Ross Smith	OF	R-R	6-2	185	Dodge County	Eastman, Ga.	Auburn
64.	Steve Englund	SS	R-R	6-3	195	Bellevue	Bellevue, Wash.	Washington State
65.	Cedric Hunter	OF	L-L	5-10	170	Martin Luther King	Decatur, Ga.	
66.	Jason Taylor	SS/OF	R-R	6-1	210	Kellam	Virginia Beach, Va.	Clemson
67.	Dustin Dickerson	3B	L-R	6-4	205	Midway	Hewitt, Texas	Baylor
68.	Brandon May	3B	R-R	6-0	180	Lassiter	Marietta, Ga.	Alabama
69.	Austin Rauch	C/RHP	B-R	6-3	205	El Capitan	El Cajon, Calif.	San Diego State
70.	Tommy Pham	SS/RHP	R-R	6-2	185	Durango	Las Vegas	
71.	Kyler Burke	OF/LHP	L-L	6-2	200	Ooltewah	Chattanooga, Tenn.	Vanderbilt
72.	Brent Brewer	OF	R-R	6-2	180	Sandy Creek	Fairburn, Ga.	
73.	Kyle Snyder	RHP	R-R	6-1	170	Wellington	Wellington, Fla.	Miami
74.	Michael Morrison	RHP	R-R	6-1	180	Cypress	Cypress, Calif.	Cal State Fullerton
75.	Jonathan Edwards	OF/RHP	R-R	6-5	225	Keller	Keller, Texas	
76.	Austin Evans	RHP	R-R	6-3	185	Chamberlain	Tampa	Alabama
77.	Josh Prince	SS	R-R	6-1	175	Barbe	Lake Charles, La.	Texas
78.	Cam Nobles	LHP	L-L	6-1	175	Jackson	Jackson, Wash.	Washington
79.	Wade Kapteyn	RHP	R-R	6-5	205	Illiana Christian	Lansing, Ill.	Evansville
80.	Lars Anderson	1B	L-L	6-5	205	Jesuit	Fair Oaks, Calif.	
81.	Charles Brewer	RHP	R-R	6-4	180	Chaparral	Paradise Valley, Ariz.	UCLA
82.	Aaron Senne	LHP/OF	L-L	6-2	180	Mayo	Rochester, Minn.	
83.	Neal Davis	LHP	L-L	6-5	195	Catonsville	Baltimore	Virginia
84.	Travis Tartamella	C	R-R	6-0	187	Los Osos	Alta Loma, Calif.	Pepperdine
85.	Justin Reed	C/OF	L-R	5-11	190	Hillcrest Christian	Jackson, Miss.	Mississippi
86.	Kendal Volz	RHP/3B	R-R	6-4	220	Smithson Valley	Bulverde, Texas	Baylor
87.	Erik Castro	C	L-R	6-3	190	Fallbrook	Fallbrook, Calif.	Arizona
88.	Chase Anderson	RHP	R-R	6-5	235	Mandarin	Jacksonville	
89.	Mikie Minor	LHP	R-L	6-2	175	Forrest	Lewisburg, Tenn.	Vanderbilt
90.	Chad Rodgers	LHP	L-L	6-3	180	Walsh Jesuit	Stow, Ohio	
91.	Addison Johnson	OF	L-L	5-7	175	North Forsyth	Pfafftown, N.C.	Clemson
92.	Kent Gerst	OF	L-R	5-10	170	Fort Zumwalt West	O'Fallon, Mo.	Missouri State
93.	Tony Sedlmeyer	RHP	R-R	6-1	195	Snider	Fort Wayne, Ind.	Louisiana State
94.	Gavin Brooks	LHP	L-L	6-3	200	Rancho Buena Vista	Vista, Calif.	UCLA
95.	Kris Davis	OF	R-R	6-0	180	Deer Valley	Glendale, Ariz.	Cal State Fullerton
96.	Brandt Walker	RHP	R-R	6-2	171	St. Stephen's	Austin, Texas	Stanford
97.	Gabby Saade	SS	R-R	5-9	175	Gulliver Prep	Miami	Duke
98.	Ryan Kalish	OF/LHP	L-L	6-1	200	Red Bank Catholic	Shrewsbury, N.J.	Virginia
99.	Alan Oaks	RHP/OF	R-R	6-3	215	Divine Child	White Lake, Mich.	Michigan
100.	Sam Dyson	RHP	R-R	6-1	185	Tampa Jesuit	Tampa	South Carolina

TOP 20 PROSPECTS
FROM EVERY MINOR LEAGUE

A s a complement to our organizational prospect rankings, Baseball America also ranks prospects in every minor league after each season. Like the organizational lists, they place more weight on potential than present performance and should not be regarded as minor league all-star teams.

The league lists do differ from the organizational lists, which are taken more from a scouting perspective. The league lists are based on conversations with league managers as well as scouts. They are not strictly polls, though we do try to talk with every manager. Some players on these lists, such as Ryan Howard and Felix Hernandez, were not eligible for our organization prospect lists because they are no longer rookie-eligible. Such players are indicated with an asterisk (*). Players who have been traded from the organizations they are listed with are indicated with a pound sign (#).

Remember that managers and scouts tend to look at players differently. Managers give more weight to what a player does on the field, while scouts look at what a player might eventually do. We think both perspectives are useful, so we give you both even though they don't always match up with each other.

For a player to qualify for a league prospect list, he much have spent at least one-third of the season in a league. Position players must have one plate appearance per league game. Pitchers must pitch ⅓ inning per league game. Relievers must make at least 20 appearances in a full-season league or 10 appearances in a short-season league.

TRIPLE-A

INTERNATIONAL LEAGUE
1. Delmon Young, of, Durham (Devil Rays)
2. Francisco Liriano, lhp, Rochester (Twins)
3. *Zach Duke, lhp, Indianapolis (Pirates)
4. *Ryan Howard, 1b, Scranton/W-B (Phillies)
5. #Andy Marte, 3b, Richmond (Braves)
6. *Edwin Encarnacion, 3b, Louisville (Reds)
7. *Kyle Davies, rhp, Richmond (Braves)
8. *Brandon McCarthy, rhp, Charlotte (White Sox)
9. Brian Anderson, of, Charlotte (White Sox)
10. *Aaron Hill, ss, Syracuse (Blue Jays)
11. *Jonny Gomes, of, Durham (Devil Rays)
12. *Scott Baker, rhp, Rochester (Twins)
13. *Ryan Doumit, c, Indianapolis (Pirates)
14. Anthony Lerew, rhp, Richmond (Braves)
15. *Kelly Johnson, of, Richmond (Braves)
16. Bryan Bullington, rhp, Indianapolis (Pirates)
17. Dustin Pedroia, 2b, Pawtucket (Red Sox)
18. Kelly Shoppach, c, Pawtucket (Red Sox)
19. *Curtis Granderson, of, Toledo (Tigers)
20. Ryan Garko, c/1b, Buffalo (Indians)

PACIFIC COAST LEAGUE
1. *Felix Hernandez, rhp, Tacoma (Mariners)
2. *Rickie Weeks, 2b, Nashville (Brewers)
3. Prince Fielder, 1b, Nashville (Brewers)
4. Conor Jackson, 1b, Tucson (Diamondbacks)
5. Matt Cain, rhp, Fresno (Giants)
6. *Casey Kotchman, 1b, Salt Lake (Angels)
7. Carlos Quentin, of, Tucson (Diamondbacks)
8. *Dan Johnson, 1b, Sacramento (Athletics)
9. Ezequiel Astacio, rhp, Round Rock (Astros)
10. Jeff Mathis, c, Salt Lake (Angels)
11. Anthony Reyes, rhp, Memphis (Cardinals)
12. *Yuniesky Betancourt, ss, Tacoma (Mariners)
13. Ben Johnson, of, Portland (Padres)
14. Rich Hill, lhp, Iowa (Cubs)
15. Fernando Nieve, rhp, Round Rock (Astros)
16. Ronny Cedeno, ss, Iowa (Cubs)
17. Joe Saunders, lhp, Salt Lake (Angels)
18. Josh Willingham, c, Albuquerque (Marlins)
19. Josh Barfield, 2b, Portland (Padres)
20. Justin Huber, 1b, Omaha (Royals)

DOUBLE-A

EASTERN LEAGUE
1. Francisco Liriano, lhp, New Britain (Twins)
2. Lastings Milledge, of, Binghamton (Mets)
3. #Hanley Ramirez, ss, Portland (Red Sox)
4. Jon Lester, lhp, Portland (Red Sox)
5. Ryan Zimmerman, 3b, Harrisburg (Nationals)
6. Nick Markakis, of, Bowie (Orioles)
7. Jonathan Papelbon, rhp, Portland (Red Sox)
8. Jeremy Sowers, lhp, Akron (Indians)
9. #Anibal Sanchez, rhp, Portland (Red Sox)
10. Joel Zumaya, rhp, Erie (Tigers)
11. #Yusmeiro Petit, rhp, Binghamton (Mets)
12. Dustin Pedroia, 2b, Portland (Red Sox)
13. Hayden Penn, rhp, Bowie (Orioles)
14. Denard Span, of, New Britain (Twins)
15. Merkin Valdez, rhp, Norwich (Giants)
16. Matt Moses, 3b, New Britain (Twins)
17. Eric Duncan, 3b, Trenton (Yankees)
18. Michael Bourn, of, Reading (Phillies)
19. Paul Maholm, lhp, Altoona (Pirates)
20. Franklin Gutierrez, of, Akron (Indians)

SOUTHERN LEAGUE
1. Delmon Young, of, Montgomery (Devil Rays)
2. Jeremy Hermida, of, Carolina (Marlins)
3. *Jeff Francoeur, of, Mississippi (Braves)
4. Chris Young, of, Birmingham (White Sox)
5. Chad Billingsley, rhp, Jacksonville (Dodgers)
6. Joel Guzman, ss, Jacksonville (Dodgers)
7. Andy LaRoche, 3b, Jacksonville (Dodgers)
8. Felix Pie, of, West Tenn (Cubs)
9. *Brian McCann, c, Mississippi (Braves)
10. Russell Martin, c, Jacksonville (Dodgers)
11. Scott Olsen, lhp, Carolina (Marlins)
12. *Matt Murton, of, West Tenn (Cubs)

13. Bobby Jenks, rhp, Birmingham (White Sox)
14. Jonathan Broxton, rhp, Jacksonville (Dodgers)
15. Rich Hill, lhp, West Tenn (Cubs)
16. Dustin Nippert, rhp, Tennessee (Diamondbacks)
17. #Ricky Nolasco, rhp, West Tenn (Cubs)
18. #Renyel Pinto, lhp, West Tenn (Cubs)
19. Chuck James, lhp, Mississippi (Braves)
20. Elijah Dukes, of, Montgomery (Devil Rays)

TEXAS LEAGUE
1. Howie Kendrick, 2b, Arkansas (Angels)
2. Erick Aybar, ss, Arkansas (Angels)
3. Daric Barton, 1b, Midland (Athletics)
4. Thomas Diamond, rhp, Frisco (Rangers)
5. Edison Volquez, rhp, Frisco (Rangers)
6. Andre Ethier, of, Midland (Athletics)
7. Kendry Morales, 1b, Arkansas (Angels)
8. *Yuniesky Betancourt, ss, San Antonio (Mariners)
9. Jason Hirsh, rhp, Corpus Christi (Astros)
10. Justin Huber, 1b, Wichita (Royals)
11. John Danks, lhp, Frisco (Rangers)
12. Joaquin Arias, ss, Frisco (Rangers)
13. Fernando Nieve, rhp, Corpus Christi (Astros)
14. Adam Jones, ss, San Antonio (Mariners)
15. Joe Saunders, lhp, Arkansas (Angels)
16. Steven Shell, rhp, Arkansas (Angels)
17. #Omar Quintanilla, ss, Midland (Athletics)
18. Ubaldo Jimenez, rhp, Tulsa (Rockies)
19. Josh Anderson, of, Corpus Christi (Astros)
20. Kevin Melillo, 2b, Midland (Athletics)

HIGH CLASS A

CALIFORNIA LEAGUE
1. Brandon Wood, ss, Rancho Cucamonga (Angels)
2. Stephen Drew, ss, Lancaster (Diamondbacks)
3. Howie Kendrick, 2b, Rancho Cucamonga (Angels)
4. Ian Stewart, 3b, Modesto (Rockies)
5. Billy Butler, 3b/of, High Desert (Royals)
6. Daric Barton, 1b, Stockton (Athletics)
7. Edison Volquez, rhp, Bakersfield (Rangers)
8. Thomas Diamond, rhp, Bakersfield (Rangers)
9. Adam Jones, ss, Inland Empire (Mariners)
10. Eddy Martinez-Esteve, of, San Jose (Giants)
11. John Danks, lhp, Bakersfield (Rangers)
12. Asdrubal Cabrera, ss, Inland Empire (Mariners)
13. Chris Iannetta, c, Modesto (Rockies)
14. Miguel Montero, c, Lancaster (Diamondbacks)
15. Ubaldo Jimenez, rhp, Modesto (Rockies)
16. Nate Schierholtz, of, San Jose (Giants)
17. George Kottaras, c, Lake Elsinore (Padres)
18. Jim Miller, rhp, Modesto (Rockes)
19. Juan Morillo, rhp, Modesto (Rockies)
20. Chris Lubanski, of, High Desert (Royals)

CAROLINA LEAGUE
1. Jarrod Saltalamacchia, c, Myrtle Beach (Braves)
2. Nick Markakis, of, Frederick (Orioles)
3. #Anibal Sanchez, rhp, Wilmington (Red Sox)
4. Adam Miller, rhp, Kinston (Indians)
5. #Gio Gonzalez, lhp, Winston-Salem (White Sox)
6. Jeremy Sowers, lhp, Kinston (Indians)
7. #Armando Galarraga, rhp, Potomac (Nationals)
8. Jeff Fiorentino, of, Frederick (Orioles)
9. Lance Broadway, rhp, Winston-Salem (White Sox)
10. Adam Loewen, lhp, Frederick (Orioles)
11. Robert Valido, ss, Winston-Salem (White Sox)
12. Tony Sipp, lhp, Kinston (Indians)
13. Ray Liotta, lhp, Winston-Salem (White Sox)
14. J.J. Johnson, rhp, Frederick (Orioles)
15. Kory Casto, 3b, Potomac (Nationals)
16. Brad Snyder, of, Kinston (Indians)

17. Frank Diaz, of, Potomac (Nationals)
18. Hunter Pence, of, Salem (Astros)
19. Stephen Head, 1b, Kinston (Indians)
20. Josh Burrus, of, Myrtle Beach (Braves)

FLORIDA STATE LEAGUE
1. Andy LaRoche, 3b, Vero Beach (Dodgers)
2. Justin Verlander, rhp, Lakeland (Tigers)
3. Lastings Milledge, of, St. Lucie (Mets)
4. *Jason Vargas, lhp, Jupiter (Marlins)
5. Matt Kemp, of, Vero Beach (Dodgers)
6. Matt Moses, 3b, Fort Myers (Twins)
7. Denard Span, of, Fort Myers (Twins)
8. Justin Orenduff, rhp, Vero Beach (Dodgers)
9. David Purcey, lhp, Dunedin (Blue Jays)
10. Jordan Tata, rhp, Lakeland (Tigers)
11. Etanislao Abreu, 2b, Vero Beach (Dodgers)
12. Chin-Lung Hu, ss, Vero Beach (Dodgers)
13. Adam Lind, of, Dunedin (Blue Jays)
14. Brent Clevlen, of, Lakeland (Tigers)
15. Scott Moore, 3b, Daytona (Cubs)
16. Adam Harben, rhp, Fort Myers (Twins)
17. Chuck Tiffany, lhp, Vero Beach (Dodgers)
18. Brian Dopirak, 1b, Daytona (Cubs)
19. Tim Moss, 2b, Clearwater (Phillies)
20. Philip Humber, rhp, St. Lucie (Mets)

LOW CLASS A

MIDWEST LEAGUE
1. Carlos Gonzales, of, South Bend (Diamondbacks)
2. Homer Bailey, rhp, Dayton (Reds)
3. Eric Hurley, rhp, Clinton (Rangers)
4. Javier Herrera, of, Kane County (Athletics)
5. Cliff Pennington, ss, Kane County (Athletics)
6. Travis Buck, of, Kane County (Athletics)
7. Ryan Harvey, of, Peoria (Cubs)
8. Anthony Swarzak, rhp, Beloit (Twins)
9. Rafael Rodriguez, rhp, Cedar Rapids (Angels)
10. Matt Garza, rhp, Beloit (Twins)
11. Jay Rainville, rhp, Beloit (Twins)
12. Trevor Plouffe, ss, Beloit (Twins)
13. Luis Cota, rhp, Burlington (Royals)
14. David Winfree, 3b, Beloit (Twins)
15. Sean Gallagher, rhp, Peoria (Cubs)
16. Eric Patterson, 2b, Peoria (Cubs)
17. Reid Brignac, ss, Southwest Michigan (Devil Rays)
18. Matt Tuiasosopo, ss, Wisconsin (Mariners)
19. Asdrubal Cabrera, if, Wisconsin (Mariners)
20. Wilkin Ramirez, 3b, West Michigan (Tigers)

SOUTH ATLANTIC LEAGUE
1. Scott Elbert, lhp, Columbus (Dodgers)
2. Neil Walker, c, Hickory (Pirates)
3. Marcus Sanders, ss, Augusta (Giants)
4. Troy Patton, lhp, Lexington (Astros)
5. Ryan Braun, 3b, West Virginia (Brewers)
6. Philip Hughes, rhp, Charleston (Yankees)
7. Blake DeWitt, 3b, Columbus (Dodgers)
8. Matt Harrison, lhp, Rome (Braves)
9. Yunel Escobar, ss, Rome (Braves)
10. Brandon Jones, of, Rome (Braves)
11. Jimmy Barthmaier, rhp, Lexington (Astros)
12. #Gio Gonzalez, lhp, Kannapolis (White Sox)
13. Mark Rogers, rhp, West Virginia (Brewers)
14. Greg Golson, of, Lakewood (Phillies)
15. Hunter Pence, of, Lexington (Astros)
16. Collin Balester, rhp, Savannah (Nationals)
17. J.T. Restko, of, Greensboro (Marlins)
18. #Gaby Hernandez, rhp, Hagerstown (Mets)
19. Ian Desmond, ss, Savannah (Nationals)

20. Chris Nelson, ss, Asheville (Rockies)

SHORT-SEASON

NEW YORK-PENN LEAGUE

1. Nolan Reimold, of, Aberdeen (Orioles)
2. Chris Volstad, rhp, Jamestown (Marlins)
3. Wade Davis, rhp, Hudson Valley (Devil Rays)
4. Eduardo Nunez, ss, Staten Island (Yankees)
5. Radhames Liz, rhp, Aberdeen (Orioles)
6. Jacoby Ellsbury, of, Lowell (Red Sox)
7. Jed Lowrie, ss/2b, Lowell (Red Sox)
8. Garrett Olson, lhp, Aberdeen (Orioles)
9. Jacob McGee, lhp, Hudson Valley (Devil Rays)
10. Tyler Greene, ss, New Jersey (Cardinals)
11. Gaby Sanchez, 3b/1b, Jamestown (Marlins)
12. Luis Soto, of, Lowell (Red Sox)
13. Clay Buchholz, rhp, Lowell (Red Sox)
14. Michael Hollimon, ss, Oneonta (Tigers)
15. Welinson Baez, ss, Batavia (Phillies)
16. Jensen Lewis, rhp, Mahoning Valley (Indians)
17. Ryan Patterson, of, Auburn (Blue Jays)
18. Kevin Whelan, rhp, Oneonta (Tigers)
19. Nick Webber, rhp, New Jersey (Yankees)
20. Bobby Parnell, rhp, Brooklyn (Mets)

NORTHWEST LEAGUE

1. Shane Lindsay, rhp, Tri-City (Rockies)
2. Donald Veal, lhp, Boise (Cubs)
3. Taylor Teagarden, c, Spokane (Rangers)
4. Nick Hundley, c, Eugene (Padres)
5. Pablo Sandoval, 3b, Salem-Keizer (Giants)
6. Luis Valbuena, 2b, Everett (Mariners)
7. Dan Griffin, rhp, Salem-Keizer (Giants)
8. John Mayberry Jr, of, Spokane (Rangers)
9. Ben Copeland, of, Salem-Keizer (Giants)
10. Chase Headley, 3b, Eugene (Padres)
11. Jimmy Shull, rhp, Vancouver (Athletics)
12. Michael Mooney, of, Salem-Keizer (Giants)
13. Michael Saunders, of, Everett (Mariners)
14. Steve Murphy, of, Spokane (Rangers)
15. Edgar Guaramato, rhp, Everett (Mariners)
16. Zach Simons, rhp, Tri-City (Rockies)
17. Stephen Kahn, rhp, Everett (Mariners)
18. Jason Ray, rhp, Vancouver (Athletics)
19. Justin Sellers, ss, Vancouver (Athletics)
20. Mark Reed, c, Boise (Cubs)

ROOKIE ADVANCED

APPALACHIAN LEAGUE

1. Brandon Snyder, c/3b, Bluefield (Orioles)
2. Colby Rasmus, of, Johnson City (Cardinals)
3. Eric Campbell, 3b, Danville (Braves)
4. Brandon Erbe, rhp, Bluefield (Orioles)
5. Max Ramirez, c, Danville (Braves)
6. Jesse Litsch, rhp, Pulaski (Blue Jays)
7. Juan Portes, 2b/of, Elizabethton (Twins)
8. Josh Flores, of, Greeneville (Astros)
9. Aaron Cunningham, of, Bristol (White Sox)
10. Bryan Anderson, c, Johnson City (Cardinals)
11. Matt Walker, rhp, Princeton (Devil Rays)
12. John Drennen, of, Burlington (Indians)
13. Jairo Cuevas, rhp, Danville (Braves)
14. Eli Iorg, of, Greeneville (Astros)
15. John Matulia, of, Princeton (Devil Rays)
16. Koby Clemens, 3b, Greeneville (Astros)
17. Alexander Smit, lhp, Elizabethton (Twins)
18. Ryan Mullins, lhp, Elizabethton (Twins)
19. Ryan Mitchell, rhp, Greeneville (Astros)

20. Tyler Herron, rhp, Johnson City (Cardinals)

PIONEER LEAGUE

1. Jay Bruce, of, Billings (Reds)
2. Charlie Fermaint, of, Helena (Brewers)
3. Hainley Statia, ss, Orem (Angels)
4. Angel Salome, c, Helena (Brewers)
5. Francisco Hernandez, c, Great Falls (White Sox)
6. Stephen Marek, rhp, Orem (Angels)
7. Dexter Fowler, of, Casper (Rockies)
8. Chaz Roe, rhp, Casper (Rockies)
9. Jose Arredondo, rhp, Orem (Angels)
10. Will Inman, rhp, Helena (Brewers)
11. Greg Smith, lhp, Missoula (Diamondbacks)
12. Bobby Mosebach, rhp, Orem (Angels)
13. Juan Rivera, ss, Ogden (Dodgers)
14. Mark Trumbo, 1b, Orem (Angels)
15. Chris McConnell, ss, Idaho Falls (Royals)
16. Brandon Roberts, of, Billings (Reds)
17. Mat Gamel, 3b, Helena (Brewers)
18. Corey Wimberly, inf, Casper (Rockies)
19. Brandon Allen, 1b, Great Falls (White Sox)
20. Ivan DeJesus Jr., ss, Ogden (Dodgers)

ROOKIE

ARIZONA LEAGUE

1. Mark Pawelek, lhp, Cubs
2. Nick Adenhart, rhp, Angels
3. Craig Italiano, rhp, Athletics
4. Jeff Bianchi, ss, Royals
5. Johnny Whittleman, 3b, Rangers
6. Jared Lansford, rhp, Athletics
7. Waldis Joaquin, rhp, Giants
8. Lorenzo Cain, of, Brewers
9. Joe Dickerson, of, Royals
10. Shairon Martis, rhp, Giants
11. Sharlon Schoop, ss, Giants
12. Manuel Pina, c, Rangers
13. P.J. Phillips, ss, Angels
14. Kyle Blanks, 1b, Padres
15. Ramon Alvarado, of, Athletics
16. Tommy Mendoza, rhp, Angels
17. Sammy Baez, ss, Cubs
18. Brent Fisher, lhp, Royals
19. Ernesto Frieri, rhp, Padres
20. Gustavo Espinoza, lhp, Angels

GULF COAST LEAGUE

1. Andrew McCutchen, of, Pirates
2. Jay Bruce, of, Reds
3. Chris Volstad, rhp, Marlins
4. Elvis Andrus, ss, Braves
5. Travis Wood, lhp, Reds
6. Beau Jones, lhp, Braves
7. Jose Tabata, of, Yankees
8. Sean West, lhp, Marlins
9. Ryan Tucker, rhp, Marlins
10. C.J. Henry, ss, Yankees
11. Austin Jackson, of, Yankees
12. Paul Kelly, ss, Twins
13. Aaron Thompson, lhp, Marlins
14. Ivan DeJesus Jr., ss, Dodgers
15. Jon Egan, c, Red Sox
16. Jordan Schafer, of, Braves
17. Drew Thompson, 2b, Twins
18. Jeff Lyman, rhp, Braves
19. Miguel Sanfler, lhp, Dodgers
20. Emmanuel Garcia, ss, Mets

INDEX

Diaz, Frank (Nationals) 486
Diaz, Javis (Padres) 395
Diaz, Robinzon (Blue Jays) 474
Dickerson, Chris (Reds) 121
Dickerson, Joe (Royals) 217
Dillard, Tim (Brewers) 264
DiNardo, Lenny (Red Sox) 74
Dittler, Jake (Indians) 139
Dlugach, Brent (Tigers) 172
Donachie, Adam (Royals) 215
Dopirak, Brian (Cubs) 85
Douglass, Chance (Astros) 200
Doyne, Cory (Cardinals) 380
Drennen, John (Indians) 135
Drew, Stephen (Diamondbacks) 18
Duarte, Jose (Royals) 217
Duffy, Chris (Pirates) 357
Dukes, Elijah (Devil Rays) 436
Dumatrait, Philip (Reds) 119
Duncan, Chris (Cardinals) 375
Duncan, Eric (Yankees) 307
Dunlap, Cory (Dodgers) 250
Durant, Michael (Phillies) 344
Durbin, J.D. (Twins) 279
Durkin, Matt (Mets) 296

E

Edlich, Kyle (Twins) 284
Egan, Jon (Red Sox) 76
Einertson, Mitch (Astros) 201
Elbert, Scott (Dodgers) 244
Ellsbury, Jacoby (Red Sox) 68
Endl, Bradley (Braves) 42
Enriquez, Andre (Nationals) 493
Erbe, Brandon (Orioles) 53
Escobar, Alcides (Brewers) 260
Escobar, Yunel (Braves) 35
Espinoza, Gustavo (Angels) 237
Estrada, Paul (Astros) 203
Ethier, Andre (Athletics) 323
Eveland, Dana (Brewers) 260
Everts, Clint (Nationals) 483

F

Fahey, Brandon (Orioles) 59
Feierabend, Ryan (Mariners) 424
Feldkamp, Derek (Devil Rays) 445
Feldman, Scott (Rangers) 456
Fermaint, Charlie (Brewers) 262
Ferris, Mike (Cardinals) 381
Fielder, Prince (Brewers) 258
Fields, Josh (White Sox) 100
Figueroa, Paco (Orioles) 60
Finch, Brian (Orioles) 55
Finigan, P.J. (Tigers) 170
Fiorentino, Jeff (Orioles) 54
Fisher, Brent (Royals) 218
Fleisher, Mark (Orioles) 61
Flores, Jesus (Mets) 294
Flores, Josh (Astros) 198
Fontenot, Mike (Cubs) 93
Fowler, Dexter (Rockies) 150
Fowler, Eric (Blue Jays) 475
Francia, Juan (Tigers) 168
Frandsen, Kevin (Giants) 405
Frazier, Jeff (Tigers) 166
Frieri, Ernesto (Padres) 392
Fruto, Emiliano (Mariners) 421

G

Gaetti, Joe (Rockies) 157
Galarraga, Armando (Rangers) 453
Gallagher, Sean (Cubs) 87
Gallardo, Yovani (Brewers) 259
Galvez, Gary (Red Sox) 76
Gamel, Mat (Brewers) 268
Garcia, Christian (Yankees) 309
Garcia, Edgar (Phillies) 342
Garcia, Emmanuel (Mets) 296
Garcia, Harvey (Marlins) 188
Garcia, Jairo (Athletics) 325
Garcia, Jose (Marlins) 187
Gardner, Brett (Yankees) 310
Gardner, Richie (Reds) 120
Garko, Ryan (Indians) 132
Garza, Matt (Twins) 277
Geer, Josh (Padres) 393
German, Esteban (Royals) 218
Germano, Justin (Reds) 122
Getz, Chris (White Sox) 104
Giarratano, Tony (Tigers) 165
Gimenez, Hector (Astros) 202
Godwin, Tyrell (Nationals) 491
Golson, Greg (Phillies) 339
Gomez, Carlos (Mets) 291
Gonzales, Alberto (Diamondbacks) 27
Gonzales, Carlos (Diamondbacks) 19
Gonzalez, Enrique (Diamondbacks) 23
Gonzalez, Gio (Phillies) 339
Gonzalez, Luis (Rockies) 156
Gonzalez, Rafael (Reds) 116
Gordon, Alex (Royals) 210
Gorneault, Nick (Angels) 233
Gorzelanny, Tom (Pirates) 355
Gothreaux, Jared (Astros) 203
Green, Matt (Diamondbacks) 22
Green, Nick (Angels) 237
Greene, Tyler (Cardinals) 371
Griffin, Dan (Giants) 408
Griffin, John-Ford (Blue Jays) 474
Guerra, Deolis (Mets) 293
Guillen, Rudy (Yankees) 316
Gutierrez, Franklin (Indians) 132
Gutierrez, Juan (Astros) 197
Gutierrez, Tonys (Reds) 124
Guzman, Angel (Cubs) 83
Guzman, Francisco (Nationals) 490
Guzman, Freddy (Padres) 390
Guzman, Javier (Pirates) 362
Guzman, Joel (Dodgers) 243

H

Haberer, Eric (Cardinals) 378
Haeger, Charles (White Sox) 103
Haehnel, Dave (Orioles) 56
Haerther, Cody (Cardinals) 373
Haigwood, Daniel (Phillies) 340
Hall, Mickey (Red Sox) 77
Hamels, Cole (Phillies) 338
Hamilton, Clayton (Pirates) 364
Hammel, Jason (Devil Rays) 435
Hammond, Steve (Brewers) 265
Hansen, Craig (Red Sox) 67
Hanson, Travis (Cardinals) 372
Happ, J.A. (Phillies) 345
Harben, Adam (Twins) 278
Harker, Brett (Phillies) 347

Harman, Brad (Phillies) 341
Harper, Brett (Mets) 293
Harris, Brendan (Nationals) 489
Harrison, Matt (Braves) 38
Hart, Corey (Brewers) 260
Harvey, Kris (Marlins) 184
Harvey, Ryan (Cubs) 85
Hattig, John (Blue Jays) 474
Hawes, Adam (Twins) 284
Hawksworth, Blake (Cardinals) 379
Head, Stephen (Indians) 134
Headley, Chase (Padres) 388
Heether, Adam (Brewers) 267
Hellickson, Jeremy (Devil Rays) 441
Hendrickson, Ben (Brewers) 265
Henn, Sean (Yankees) 312
Henry, C.J. (Yankees) 307
Henry, Sean (Mets) 300
Hensley, Clay (Padres) 388
Hermida, Jeremy (Marlins) 178
Hernandez, Anderson (Mets) 292
Hernandez, Francisco (White Sox) 102
Hernandez, Gaby (Marlins) 181
Hernandez, Luis (Braves) 42
Hernandez, Yoel (Phillies) 349
Herrera, Javier (Athletics) 323
Herron, Tyler (Cardinals) 374
Hill, Rich (Cubs) 84
Hill, Shawn (Nationals) 488
Hinckley, Mike (Nationals) 484
Hines, Carlos (Devil Rays) 443
Hirsh, Jason (Astros) 194
Hoffmann, Jamie (Dodgers) 252
Holliman, Mark (Cubs) 92
Holliman, Michael (Tigers) 170
Holt, J.C. (Braves) 44
Honel, Kris (White Sox) 109
Horne, Alan (Yankees) 312
Horwitz, Brian (Giants) 412
Houser, James (Devil Rays) 442
Howard, Kevin (Yankees) 313
Hoyman, Justin (Indians) 139
Hu, Chin-Lung (Dodgers) 246
Huber, Justin (Royals) 211
Hudgins, John (Rangers) 457
Hughes, Dusty (Royals) 220
Hughes, Philip (Yankees) 306
Hughes, Travis (Nationals) 487
Humber, Philip (Mets) 291
Hundley, Nick (Padres) 389
Hurley, Eric (Rangers) 452

I

Iannetta, Chris (Rockies) 148
Inman, Will (Brewers) 262
Iorg, Eli (Astros) 196
Iribarren, Hernan (Brewers) 264
Ishikawa, Travis (Giants) 403
Italiano, Craig (Athletics) 325
Ivany, Devin (Nationals) 489

J

Jackson, Austin (Yankees) 308
Jackson, Conor (Diamondbacks) 19
Jackson, Zach (Brewers) 262
Jacobs, Mike (Marlins) 182
James, Chuck (Braves) 36
Janish, Paul (Reds) 119

Janssen, Casey (Blue Jays)	468	Lerew, Anthony (Braves)	35	McCann, Brad (Marlins)	186
Jaramillo, Jason (Phillies)	342	Lester, Jon (Red Sox)	67	McConnell, Chris (Royals)	213
Jaso, John (Devil Rays)	440	Lewis, Fred (Giants)	405	McCormick, Mark (Cardinals)	372
Jenks, Bobby (White Sox)	98	Lewis, Jensen (Indians)	137	McCutchen, Andrew (Pirates)	355
Jimenez, Cesar (Mariners)	424	Lewis, Scott (Indians)	140	McGee, Jacob (Devil Rays)	440
Jimenez, Fabian (Padres)	397	Lillibridge, Brent (Pirates)	362	McGowan, Dustin (Blue Jays)	466
Jimenez, Ubaldo (Rockies)	148	Lind, Adam (Blue Jays)	467	McLemore, Mark (Astros)	204
Joaquin, Waldis (Giants)	409	Lindsay, Shane (Rockies)	151	McLouth, Nate (Pirates)	356
Johjima, Kenji (Mariners)	419	Lindstrom, Matt (Mets)	299	Medders, Brandon (Diamondbacks)	25
Johnson, Ben (Padres)	387	Liotta, Ray (White Sox)	101	Medlock, Calvin (Reds)	124
Johnson, Blake (Dodgers)	248	Liriano, Francisco (Twins)	274	Meek, Evan (Padres)	396
Johnson, Elliot (Devil Rays)	441	Lisson, Mario (Royals)	219	Melillo, Kevin (Athletics)	324
Johnson, Grant (Cubs)	89	Litsch, Jesse (Blue Jays)	475	Mendoza, Tommy (Angels)	230
Johnson, J.J. (Orioles)	53	Livingston, Bobby (Mariners)	425	Meredtih, Cla (Red Sox)	73
Johnson, Josh (Marlins)	180	Liz, Radhames (Orioles)	54	Metcalf, Travis (Rangers)	457
Johnson, Rob (Mariners)	422	Lo, Ching-Lung (Rockies)	154	Meyer, Dan (Athletics)	330
Johnson, Tripper (Orioles)	61	Loewen, Adam (Orioles)	51	Meyer, Drew (Rangers)	460
Johnson, Tyler (Cardinals)	375	Lofgren Chuck (Indians)	134	Michael, Mark (Cardinals)	379
Johnston, Andrew (Rockies)	154	Loney, James (Dodgers)	246	Mijares, Jose (Twins)	280
Johnston, Dylan (Cubs)	92	Lopez, Andrew (Devil Rays)	442	Milledge, Lastings (Mets)	290
Johnston, Mike (Pirates)	360	Lopez, Pedro (White Sox)	105	Miller, Adam (Indians)	130
Jones, Adam (Mariners)	419	Lowrance, Marvin (Nationals)	493	Miller, Greg (Dodgers)	249
Jones, Beau (Braves)	37	Lowrie, Jed (Red Sox)	69	Miller, Jim (Rockies)	152
Jones, Brandon (Braves)	37	Lubanski, Chris (Royals)	212	Miller, Matt (Rockies)	157
Jones, Daryl (Cardinals)	374	Lucena, Juan (Cardinals)	376	Milons, Jereme (Diamondbacks)	27
Jones, Justin (Twins)	282	Lumsden, Tyler (White Sox)	105	Misch, Pat (Giants)	413
Joyce, Matt (Tigers)	172	Lyman, Jeff (Braves)	44	Mitchell, Ryan (Astros)	201
Jurries, James (Braves)	43			Mitchinson, Scott (Phillies)	349
Jurrjens, Jair (Tigers)	168			Mock, Garrett (Diamondbacks)	21

M

		Macias, Drew (Padres)	395	Molina, Gustavo (White Sox)	108
		MacLane, Evan (Mets)	301	Montanez, Luis (Cubs)	93

K

		Macri, Matt (Rockies)	150	Montero, Miguel (Diamondbacks)	20
Kaaihue, Kila (Royals)	218	Madsen, Mike (Athletics)	332	Moore, Scott (Cubs)	87
Kahn, Stephen (Mariners)	424	Mahar, Kevin (Rangers)	458	Morales, Franklin (Rockies)	147
Karstens, Jeff (Yankees)	317	Maholm, Paul (Pirates)	355	Morales, Kendry (Angels)	229
Keefer, Ryan (Orioles)	58	Maier, Mitch (Royals)	213	Moran, Javon (Reds)	123
Kelly, Donald (Tigers)	169	Maine, John (Orioles)	56	Morillo, Juan (Rockies)	148
Kelly, Paul (Twins)	278	Maiques, Kenny (Cardinals)	381	Morlan, Eduardo (Twins)	280
Kemp, Blake (Dodgers)	245	Majewski, Val (Orioles)	54	Morton, Colt (Padres)	396
Kendrick, Howie (Angels)	227	Malone, Chris (Dodgers)	253	Moses, Matt (Twins)	275
Kendrick, Kyle (Phillies)	348	Maloney, Matt (Phillies)	346	Moss, Brandon (Red Sox)	71
Kennelly, Tim (Phillies)	347	Manriquez, Salomon (Nationals)	492	Moss, Steve (Brewers)	267
Keppinger, Jeff (Mets)	295	Manzella, Tommy (Astros)	204	Moss, Tim (Phillies)	342
Killian, Billy (Padres)	395	Marceaux, Jacob (Marlins)	188	Mount, Ryan (Angels)	236
Kinsler, Ian (Rangers)	452	Marcum, Shaun (Blue Jays)	470	Mujica, Edward (Indians)	138
Kirkland, Kody (Tigers)	166	Marek, Stephen (Angels)	233	Mulhern, Ryan (Indians)	140
Kniginyzky, Matt (Royals)	221	Markakis, Nick (Orioles)	50	Munoz, Arnie (White Sox)	108
Knoedler, Justin (Giants)	412	Marmol, Carlos (Cubs)	86	Munter, Scott (Giants)	408
Knott, Jon (Padres)	394	Maroul, David (Giants)	413	Murillo, Agustin (Diamondbacks)	28
Komine, Shane (Athletics)	325	Marquez, Jeff (Yankees)	309	Murphy, David (Red Sox)	70
Koshansky, Joe (Rockies)	153	Marshall, Sean (Cubs)	84	Murphy, Donnie (Royals)	214
Kottaras, George (Padres)	387	Marson, Louis (Phillies)	346	Murphy, Steve (Rangers)	460
Kouzmanoff, Kevin (Indians)	139	Marte, Andy (Red Sox)	66	Murphy, Tommy (Angels)	234
Kroeger, Josh (Diamondbacks)	27	Martin, J.D. (Indians)	137		
Krosschell, Ben (Padres)	391	Martin, Russell (Dodgers)	243		
Krynzel, Dave (Brewers)	266	Martinez, Edgar (Red Sox)	71		
Kubel, Jason (Twins)	275	Martinez, Fernando (Mets)	291	## N	
Kuo, Hong-Chih (Dodgers)	247	Martinez, Jose (Cardinals)	381		
		Martinez-Esteve, Eddy (Giants)	403	Nageotte, Clint (Mariners)	422
		Martis, Shairon (Giants)	413	Nanita, Ricardo (White Sox)	108

L

		Mason, Chris (Devil Rays)	438	Napoli, Mike (Angels)	230
LaHair, Bryan (Mariners)	429	Mateo, Juan (Cubs)	376	Navarro, Oswaldo (Mariners)	428
Lahey, Tim (Twins)	284	Mathieson, Scott (Phillies)	340	Neighborgall, Jason (Diamondbacks)	29
Lambert, Chris (Cardinals)	371	Mathis, Jeff (Angels)	227	Nelson, Brad (Brewers)	263
Lambin, Chase (Mets)	298	Mattheus, Ryan (Rockies)	156	Nelson, Chris (Rockies)	149
Lansford, Jared (Athletics)	326	Matulia, John (Devil Rays)	444	Nickeas, Mike (Rangers)	459
Lara, Christian (Red Sox)	72	Maxwell, Justin (Nationals)	486	Nicolas, Cesar (Diamondbacks)	26
Larish, Jeff (Tigers)	165	Mayberry, John Jr. (Rangers)	454	Nicoll, Chris (Royals)	217
LaRoche, Andy (Dodgers)	243	Maybin, Cameron (Tigers)	163	Niemann, Jeff (Devil Rays)	435
Layden, Tim (Cubs)	92	Mazzaro, Vince (Athletics)	326	Niese, Jon (Mets)	293
League, Brandon (Blue Jays)	468	McAnulty, Paul (Padres)	389	Nieve, Fernando (Astros)	195
Leandro, Francisco (Devil Rays)	445	McBride, Macay (Braves)	39	Nippert, Dustin (Diamondbacks)	20
LeCure, Sam (Reds)	122			Nolasco, Ricky (Marlins)	181
				Nunez, Eduardo (Yankees)	308

O

Olsen, Scott (Marlins)	179
Olson, Garrett (Orioles)	52
Orenduff, Justin (Dodgers)	246
Ortmeier, Dan (Giants)	406
Orvella, Chad (Devil Rays)	437
Outman, Josh (Phillies)	346
Owens, Henry (Mets)	300
Owens, Jerry (White Sox)	100
Owings, Jon Mark (Braves)	44
Owings, Micah (Diamondbacks)	21

P

Palmisano, Lou (Brewers)	266
Papaelbon, Jonathan (Red Sox)	67
Parisi, Mike (Cardinals)	380
Parnell, Bobby (Mets)	295
Parr, James (Braves)	39
Parra, Manny (Brewers)	263
Pascual, Rolando (Brewers)	264
Patterson, Eric (Cubs)	85
Patterson, Garrett (Yankees)	315
Patterson, Ryan (Blue Jays)	471
Patton, Troy (Astros)	195
Paul, Xavier (Dodgers)	251
Pauley, David (Red Sox)	71
Paulino, Felipe (Astros)	196
Paulino, Ronny (Pirates)	359
Pauly, Thomas (Reds)	120
Pawelek, Mark (Cubs)	83
Pedroia, Dustin (Red Sox)	68
Pelfrey, Mike (Mets)	494
Pelland, Tyler (Reds)	117
Pellot, Hector (Mets)	296
Pena, Brayan (Braves)	40
Pena, Tony (Diamondbacks)	23
Pence, Hunter (Astros)	196
Penn, Hayden (Orioles)	51
Pennington, Cliff (Athletics)	323
Perez, Fernando (Devil Rays)	439
Perez, Juan (Mets)	297
Perez, Miguel (Reds)	116
Perez, Rafael (Indians)	135
Perkins, Glen (Twins)	275
Perkins, Vince (Blue Jays)	470
Perrin, Devin (Nationals)	492
Pesco, Nick (Indians)	136
Peterson, Matt (Pirates)	363
Petit, Gregorio (Athletics)	328
Petit, Yusmeiro (Marlins)	180
Petrick, Billy (Cubs)	89
Pettway, Brian (Blue Jays)	473
Phelps, Michael (Cubs)	90
Phillips, Andy (Yankees)	316
Phillips, P.J. (Angels)	232
Pickney, Andrew (Red Sox)	77
Pie, Felix (Cubs)	82
Pimentel, Julio (Dodgers)	248
Pina, Manuel (Rangers)	461
Pinto, Renyel (Marlins)	183
Plasencia, Francisco (Nationals)	491
Plouffe, Trevor (Twins)	277
Pomeranz, Stuart (Cardinals)	373
Pope, Kieron (Orioles)	57
Pope, Van (Braves)	40
Portes, Juan (Twins)	281
Poveda, Omar (Rangers)	461
Powell, Landon (Athletics)	329
Prado, Martin (Braves)	40
Prasch, Eddie (Pirates)	365
Pridie, Jason (Twins)	283

Purcey, David (Blue Jays)	467
Putnam, Danny (Athletics)	327

Q

Quarles, Jason (Pirates)	363
Quentin, Carlos (Diamondbacks)	19
Quintanilla, Omar (Rockies)	150
Quiroz, Guillermo (Blue Jays)	470

R

Raab, Kellen (Diamondbacks)	28
Raburn, Ryan (Tigers)	169
Raglani, Anthony (Dodgers)	253
Raglione, Paul (Royals)	221
Ragsdale, Corey (Mets)	300
Rainville, Jay (Twins)	277
Rakers, Aaron (Orioles)	58
Ramirez, Elizardo (Reds)	125
Ramirez, Hanley (Marlins)	179
Ramirez, Ismael (Blue Jays)	473
Ramirez, Maximiliano (Braves)	41
Ramirez, Wilkin (Tigers)	164
Ramos, Cesar (Padres)	390
Rasmus, Colby (Cardinals)	371
Rasner, Darrell (Nationals)	488
Ray, Chris (Orioles)	52
Ray, Jason (Athletics)	330
Ray, Robert (Blue Jays)	476
Redmond, Todd (Pirates)	361
Reed, Eric (Marlins)	185
Reed, Mark (Cubs)	89
Reese, Kevin (Yankees)	316
Reimold, Nolan (Orioles)	51
Reina, Jesus (Giants)	411
Reineke, Chad (Astros)	202
Resop, Chris (Marlins)	186
Restko, J.T. (Marlins)	186
Reyes, Anthony (Cardinals)	370
Rheinecker, John (Athletics)	332
Richard, Clayton (White Sox)	107
Riggans, Shawn (Devil Rays)	438
Rivas, Arturo (Orioles)	60
Rivera, Juan (Dodgers)	249
Rivera, Rene (Mariners)	426
Rleal, Sendy (Orioles)	55
Roberson, Chris (Phillies)	343
Roberts, Brandon (Reds)	121
Roberts, Kevin (Brewers)	269
Roberts, Ryan (Blue Jays)	476
Robertson, Connor (Athletics)	331
Robinson, Chris (Tigers)	171
Robnett, Richie (Athletics)	327
Rodriguez, Rafael (Angels)	234
Rodriguez, Sean (Angels)	235
Rodriguez, Yuber (Blue Jays)	475
Roe, Chaz (Rockies)	147
Rogers, Mark (Brewers)	259
Rogowski, Casey (White Sox)	102
Romero, Alex (Twins)	282
Romero, Davis (Blue Jays)	476
Romero, Ricky (Blue Jays)	467
Rosales, Adam (Reds)	120
Rosales, Leo (Padres)	394
Rosario, Francisco (Blue Jays)	469
Rottino, Vinny (Brewers)	269
Rozier, Mike (Red Sox)	75
Ruiz, Carlos (Phillies)	345
Rupe, Josh (Rangers)	455
Russell, Adam (White Sox)	107
Ryan, Brendan (Cardinals)	374

Ryu, Jae-Kuk (Cubs)	87

S

Salas, Juan (Devil Rays)	444
Salas, Marino (Orioles)	59
Salazar, Jeff (Rockies)	152
Salome, Angel (Brewers)	266
Saltalamacchia, Jarrod (Braves)	34
Sammons, Clint (Braves)	43
Sanchez, Angel (Royals)	216
Sanchez, Anibal (Marlins)	179
Sanchez, Henry (Twins)	281
Sanchez, Humberto (Tigers)	164
Sanchez, Jonathan (Giants)	404
Sanders, Marcus (Giants)	403
Sandoval, Pablo (Giants)	408
Santana, Cristian (Rangers)	458
Santangelo, Lou (Astros)	202
Santiesteban, Danny (Twins)	284
Santo, Joel (Padres)	392
Santos, Sergio (Diamondbacks)	22
Sardinha, Bronson (Yankees)	314
Sarfate, Dennis (Brewers)	267
Saunders, Joe (Angels)	230
Saunders, Michael (Mariners)	423
Schafer, Jordan (Braves)	45
Schierholtz, Nate (Giants)	405
Schlact, Michael (Rangers)	455
Schmoll, Steve (Dodgers)	252
Schumaker, Skip (Cardinals)	377
Scott, Luke (Astros)	200
Seddon, Chris (Devil Rays)	443
Sellers, Justin (Athletics)	328
Shafer, David (Reds)	123
Shappi, A.J. (Diamondbacks)	24
Sharpless, Josh (Pirates)	361
Shealy, Ryan (Rockies)	149
Shell, Steven (Angels)	232
Sherrill, George (Mariners)	428
Shields, Jamie (Devil Rays)	438
Shoppach, Kelly (Red Sox)	68
Shull, Jimmy (Athletics)	329
Simon, Alfredo (Giants)	410
Sing, Brandon (Cubs)	88
Sinisi, Vince (Rangers)	457
Sipp, Tony (Indians)	135
Slayden, Jeremy (Phillies)	347
Sleeth, Kyle (Tigers)	170
Slowey, Kevin (Twins)	279
Smit, Alexander (Twins)	285
Smith, Carlton (Indians)	141
Smith, Greg (Diamondbacks)	23
Smith, Matt (Yankees)	313
Smith, Seth (Rockies)	152
Snelling, Chris (Mariners)	419
Snyder, Brad (Indians)	131
Snyder, Brandon (Orioles)	52
Soler, Alay (Mets)	292
Sonnanstine, Andy (Devil Rays)	441
Soto, Geovany (Cubs)	88
Soto, Luis (Red Sox)	71
Sowers, Jeremy (Indians)	131
Span, Denard (Twins)	276
Spears, Nate (Orioles)	57
Speier, Ryan (Rockies)	155
Spilborghs, Ryan (Rockies)	153
Spoone, Chorye (Orioles)	59
Stansberry, Craig (Pirates)	359
Starling, Wardell (Pirates)	364
Statia, Hanley (Angels)	232
Stavinoha, Nick (Cardinals)	376
Stavisky, Brian (Athletics)	331

Stephens, Jason (Yankees) 317
Stern, Adam (Red Sox) 75
Stevens, Jake (Braves) 41
Stewart, Chris (White Sox) 105
Stewart, Ian (Rockies) 146
Stokes, Brian (Devil Rays) 444
Stokes, Jason (Marlins) 185
Stone, Wesley (Blue Jays) 477
Sutil, Wladimir (Astros) 205
Suzuki, Kurt (Athletics) 326
Swanson, Matt (Pirates) 363
Swarzak, Anthony (Twins) 276
Sweeney, Ryan (White Sox) 100
Szymanski, B.J. (Reds) 115

T

Tabata, Jose (Yankees) 307
Talbot, Mitch (Astros) 204
Tankersley, Taylor (Marlins) 183
Taschner, Jack (Giants) 409
Tata, Jordan (Tigers) 165
Teagarden, Taylor (Rangers) 454
Theriot, Ryan (Cubs) 91
Thigpen, Curtis (Blue Jays) 469
Thomas, Clete (Tigers) 167
Thompson, Aaron (Marlins) 182
Thompson, Daryl (Nationals) 485
Thompson, Drew (Twins) 281
Thompson, Kevin (Yankees) 314
Thompson, Sean (Padres) 390
Thorman, Scott (Braves) 38
Tiffany, Chuck (Dodgers) 247
Timpner, Clay (Giants) 407
Torra, Matt (Diamondbacks) 21
Torres, Carlos (White Sox) 107
Towles, J.R. (Astros) 198
Townsend, Wade (Devil Rays) 439
Tracey, Sean (White Sox) 102
Trahern, Dallas (Tigers) 167
Trumbo, Mark (Angels) 231
Tucker, Ryan (Marlins) 184

Tuiasosopo, Matt (Mariners) 420
Tulowitzki, Troy (Rockies) 147

U

Uggla, Dan (Marlins) 189
Upton, Justin (Diamondbacks) 494

V

Valbuena, Luis (Mariners) 423
Valdez, Merkin (Giants) 404
Valido, Robert (White Sox) 101
Valiquette, Philippe (Reds) 121
Vallejo, Jose (Rangers) 458
Van Benschoten, John (Pirates) 357
Van Buren, Jermaine (Red Sox) 74
Van Kooten, Jason (Rockies) 156
Vandel, Geoff (Padres) 396
Vaquedano, Jose (Red Sox) 74
Varvaro, Anthony (Mariners) 429
Vasquez, Sendy (Tigers) 171
Vasquez, Virgil (Tigers) 172
Veal, Donald (Cubs) 86
Vechionacci, Marcos (Yankees) 308
Verlander, Justin (Tigers) 162
Victorino, Shane (Phillies) 343
Volquez, Edison (Rangers) 450
Volstad, Chris (Marlins) 181
Votto, Joey (Reds) 117

W

Wainwright, Adam (Cardinals) 372
Waldrop, Kyle (Twins) 278
Walker, Matt (Devil Rays) 437
Walker, Neil (Pirates) 354
Wall, Josh (Dodgers) 249
Ward, Zach (Reds) 119
Watson, Brandon (Nationals) 488
Weaver, Jered (Angels) 228
Webber, Nick (Cardinals) 373
Webster, Anthony (Rangers) 459

Weglarz, Nick (Indians) 140
Wells, Jared (Padres) 389
West, Sean (Marlins) 185
Whelan, Kevin (Tigers) 166
Whitaker, Craig (Giants) 406
White, Steven (Yankees) 311
Whitesell, Josh (Nationals) 487
Whiteside, Eli (Orioles) 60
Whitney, Matt (Indians) 141
Whittleman, Johnny (Rangers) 454
Willingham, Josh (Marlins) 182
Willits, Reggie (Angels) 237
Wilson, Andy (Mets) 298
Wilson, Bobby (Angels) 235
Wilson, Brian (Giants) 406
Wilson, C.J. (Rangers) 455
Wilson, Josh (Cardinals) 379
Wilson, Michael (Mariners) 427
Wimberley, Corey (Rockies) 154
Windsor, Jason (Athletics) 327
Winfree, David (Twins) 280
Wood, Brandon (Angels) 226
Wood, Travis (Reds) 115
Woods, Jake (Angels) 236
Worrell, Mark (Cardinals) 378
Wylie, Mitch (Mets) 299

Y

Yates, Kyle (Blue Jays) 472
Young Chris (White Sox) 99
Young, Delmon (Devil Rays) 434
Young, Delwyn (Dodgers) 248
Young, Walter (Orioles) 58

Z

Zeringue, Jon (Diamondbacks) 24
Zimmermann, Bob (Angels) 236
Zimmerman, Ryan (Nationals) 482
Zobrist, Ben (Astros) 200
Zumaya, Joel (Tigers) 163

Give BA a tryout

The magazine for baseball insiders

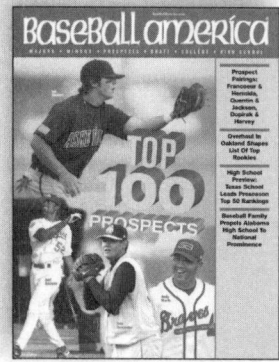

3 TRIAL ISSUES FOR $2

**MAJORS
MINORS
PROSPECTS
DRAFT
COLLEGE
HIGH SCHOOL**

With a trial subscription
you'll discover what
makes our readers
so loyal!